The Family and Local History Handbook 10

In association with

FAMILY HISTORY MONTHLY

ABM Family Tree magazine
Practical Family History

The National Family History Fair

Edited & Compiled by

Robert Blatchford

Assistant Editor

Elizabeth Blatchford

Contents

The Family and Local History Handbook 10   **3**

Start your Family History Research at Familyrelatives.org

ff Births, Deaths & Marriages 1837-2004

ff GRO official index records and images

ff Marriage match search facility

ff Marriage Booster search facility

ff Parish Registers 1538-1837

ff WWI and WWII death records

ff The GRO Overseas records – **FREE**

ff Irish Immigration records – **FREE**

ff USA WWII Army Enlistment – **FREE**

ff USA POW WWII & Korean War – **FREE**

ff USA Casualty WWII records – **FREE**

ff USA Social Security Death Index – **FREE**

Editorial

Welcome to *The Family and Local History Handbook 10*. It is not essential to have read or possess previous issues of the *Handbook* because each one stands alone; although many of our readers have all previous issues. Once again we have tried to provide you, the reader, with a wide and interesting range of articles in all the sections. Our new *Digital Genealogy* section for *The Family and Local History Handbook 9* proved very popular and is again a section in this issue. We hope you find the new articles in all sections of interest and benefit in your endeavours.

This book is intended to be an essential companion to your research whether it is by using the vast array of material in libraries, archives and museums or on the internet. However with regard to the internet, which serves us well, I must raise a cautionary note. There is a vast array of material on the internet. Care must be taken with the use of unverified material found on the internet as it can easily lead us astray The fact that if it is on the internet *'it must be gospel'* will lead many people to include the information provided in their histories. Always remember when dealing with any information from original documents and particularly modern transcriptions it can all be subject to human error. Nothing should be taken for granted and where possible original documention should be checked.

It is essential that our descendants are able to rely upon the accuracy of our researches and by following the advice given above you will create a family history which will become an heirloom.

When I wrote the Editorial for *The Family and Local History Handbook 9* Elizabeth and I were expecting our fourth grandchild. Well, Henry has been with us now since Spring 2005 and is now a very active and inquisitive young man. A brief foray into Henry's family history has produced some surprises and we have shared this with you in the article *'Did you have a pioneering genius in the family?'*

The contribution and help from Elizabeth, my wife, is a great support in producing this book. Her work as Assistant Editor is invaluable however she does leave the design and layout to me. Perhaps I might persuade her to try her hand at that in future issues!

I must not forget our authors whose contribution is an essential ingredient. We were saddened since our last issue by the loss of Jean Cole, Margery Moore and Gabriel Alington.

Please support our advertisers who contribute to the cost of producing the book and if you contact any of them please tell them that you saw their advertisement in *The Family and Local History Handbook 10*.

Suggestions from our readers are always welcome and we receive many which where possible we implement. we hope that you, our readers, enjoy this issue as much as the previous ones. The next issue will be in 2008.

Robert Blatchford

5

Your family is unique

Bring your family tree to life

Packed with expert advice, computer tips, social and military history and much more to help you research your family tree

ON SALE EVERY MONTH

at W.H. Smith, Tescos & all leading newsagents

Save up to 15% by subscribing to Family History Monthly.
Call 0870 734 3030 or email janice.mayne@metropolis.co.uk
www.familyhistorymonthly.com

In association with
**FAMILY
HISTORY**
MONTHLY

Getting Started in Genealogy
Robert Blatchford

This article will have you up and running with your own research and if you have already started then the advice here will help you get the most from your hobby..........

There is no easy route to discovering your ancestors. It involves patience, luck and in some cases perseverance. Do not be put off. It is a great deal of fun. The more you discover the more you will want to know about your ancestors. There is some small cost to this fascinating hobby but the rewards will be great. Where your ancestors have moved around from area to area you will have a ready excuse to holiday in many places both at home and abroad - if some of your ancestors emigrated. There is nothing more satisfying than visiting a town, finding out about the historic events that took place some two hundred years previously and realising that an ancestor of yours may have been a witness or perhaps even took part!

Preparation
You must be systematic and organised. You will collect a lot of information and data. This must be organised and filed for easy reference. In our busy lives it is not always possible to continually work on a hobby and there may be periods when your research has to take a back seat. This may a few days but could stretch into weeks and months. Revision is always useful and may provide new ideas for the future. It is also a record which verifies the value of your research.

What will I need?
A simple filing system using A4 binders with loose leaf pages and subject dividers, an index card file for each of the family names/members and events. Somewhere to keep certificates and other documents. Avoid scraps of paper. Everything has its place. A note book is helpful for recording information as it is gathered for later transfer to your main file. It goes without saying that pens, pencils and the all important rubber are also needed.

How you organise the information is up to you. There are many printed recording aids available or you can create your own. Whatever system you use you must be methodical, identifying the source of the information and the date when it was found.

Do I need a computer?
The easy answer is that it is not a necessity. Many family historians prefer to keep paper records and hand drawn family trees charts. It is cheap and economic. If you would prefer to use a computerised system there are many programs available. However, remember that you do not need to wait until you have a computer or a suitable program to begin your work. If you do not have a computer but intend acquiring one make sure it is a system you want and not one a salesman wants to sell you. The computer is an efficient way of storing, copying, sharing and presenting information, and, along with the usual applications on a computer – word processor programs, email, access to the internet and the ability to scan, edit and print images – there are many programs specifically designed to help you draw up and publish your family tree and history.

Genealogy computer programs are numerous; from shareware to proprietary ones with more features. Windows PC users have a choice between *Brother's Keeper* or the highly recommended *new* British program *Family Historian*. Users of Apple Mac computers can choose between shareware programs such as *Gene* or the highly recommended *Reunion 8*. Available from many software retailers such as S & N Genealogy – www.genealogysupplies.com or My History - www.my-history.co.uk *Heredis,* a new program is available to both Windows PC users and Apple Mac users - www.myheredis.com

Recording data and information
Whilst your record keeping may be methodical it should also be honest. There are always

The Golden Rule
Whatever you do in your research the *golden rule* is to start with yourself and work backwards, generation by generation, ensuring that you have verified your sources. A mistake many people make is to take a name from the past and try to trace his or her ancestors or descendants believing they may be related. This rarely works and is definitely not recommended. In every family there are myths and legends most have some element of truth but as with many stories embellishment has probably occurred in the telling.

The GRO Index
Births, marriages and deaths are listed in separate indexes. Previously known as the St Catherine's Index its official title is now The General Register Office Index. These indexes can be seen at The Family Records Centre, 1 Myddelton Street, London EC1R 1UW. Microfilm copies of these indexes are held by some libraries, record offices, Family History Societies and Family History Centres of The Church of Latter Day Saints. It is also available on the internet at www.ancestry.co.uk and www.1837online.com

skeletons in the cupboard. Do not ignore them. They are part and parcel of the richness of your family history. You will find criminals, marital affairs and illegitimacy - every family has them. They may not be recent but as your research progresses you will eventually find them.

Where should I start?
It is most important to assemble all the information you can about your family from relatives. Gather together all the birth, marriage and death certificates of family members. Where certificates are not available the approximate dates of births, marriages and death should be obtained from family members. Copy certificates of these events can be obtained after consulting The General Register Office Indexes. Compulsory registration began in 1837 and births, marriages and deaths are listed in separate indexes. Birth

The National Archives
The Public Record Office is the national archive of England, Wales and the United Kingdom. In April 2003 the Public Record Office and the Historical Manuscripts Commission will combined to form the National Archives, based at Kew. The National Archives with over 100 miles of records houses one of the most definitive archive collections in the world representing the events and people of the past thousand years. The Public Record Office, Ruskin Avenue, Kew, Richmond, Surrey TW9 4DU Website: www.nationalarchives.gov.uk/

certificate details give sufficient information to help find the marriage of parents, and the marriage certificate usually gives clues for the births of the marrying couple as well as the fathers of each. Microfilm copies of these indexes are held by many libraries, record offices and The Family Records Centre. These Indexes are searchable on the internet at www.1837online.com On this site you will find the entire indexes of Birth, Marriages and Deaths for England and Wales from 1837 to 2002 as well as overseas records - including WW1, WW2, Boer War, Marine and Consular indexes.

Once you have identified the entries in the indexes copy certificates of all registered births, marriages and deaths may obtained from The

General Register Office or the Superintendent Registrar for the area where the registration was made. Certificates may also be ordered online by visiting www.gro.gov.uk/gro There is a fee to pay for copy certificates. A full list of Registrars for England, Wales and Scotland can be found in *The Family and Local History Handbook*.

Interviewing relatives
This sounds extremely formal but it is a source that is invaluable as you set out on your task. Talk to brothers and sisters, cousins, uncles, aunts, parents and grandparents. They will all have information some they will readily tell you but may be reluctant with revealing certain events. Speak to the eldest relatives. Don't make it sound like an interrogation. Ask them about events they have lived through, what they remember about their parents and grandparents. Gently coax the information. Make comprehensive notes. Tell them what you are doing and why. If they are happy use a tape recorder - a pocket memo is ideal. If you have a video camera use that to record discussions. Both of these will become very useful parts of your family history. Listen to the accounts several times to make sure you haven't missed anything. It may also prompt you to ask for more detail on certain events. Don't attempt to carry out the interview in one session. Several sessions are better and it will also help them to forget your recording system.

I was fortunate to find one of my mother's first cousins. George was 92 and in frail health. He told me a lot about my grandfather and my great grandfather, identifying him in some old photographs, his employment, his wife, his personality and about the other members of the family. But George was very reluctant to discuss a *family disagreement* that took place and never revealed anything about it before he died.

No matter how small the detail you learn about remember it is always worth noting. Once your relative has passed on it will be too late. Your elderly relative may be happier jotting down his or her memories in a note book. This is what my wife has done with her own mother.

to start with yourself, moving to your two parents and four grandparents then choosing a branch to follow. Most men research their surname whilst many women, if they are the last of the line to hold their father's surname, research his family. However at some point you may reach a *brickwall. This is the time to pick up another branch of the family until a chance discovery lets you return to your first line of research. This has happened to me on several occasions.

Family History Classes
I always recommend that people join a family history class. Most areas in the country have short classes which give a good grounding in the essentials of family history research together with information written for magazines such as this one.

Should I join a Family History Society
The short answer is *yes*. I always recommend joining a family history society. In fact usually several unless you are positive that your family has lived for many generations in one place. Is there a family history society in your area? A full list of Family History Societies can be found

---

Birth certificate details give sufficient information to help find the marriage of parents, and the marriage certificate usually gives clues for the births of the marrying couple as well as the fathers of each. Access is only to the quarterly indexes and no information is available except in the form of a certificate. There are separate indexes for the births, marriages and deaths of British Subjects returned by Consuls abroad (from 1809), in the Army (from 1761), and at sea (from 1837). Copy certificates for Births, Marriages, Deaths Certificates of all registered births, marriages and deaths since 1837 are obtainable by post from The General Register Office, Smedley Hydro, Southport, Merseyside PR8 2HH or the Superintendent Registrar for the area where the event was registered.

A birth certificate gives date and place where the event occurred, the child's forename(s), as well as the name and occupation of the father, the name and maiden surname of the mother with her usual residence if the birth took place elsewhere, and the name and address of the informant for the registration.

Surnames
Surnames are usually derived from one of four basic roots:
  A Place - *Manchester, Dent, London, Durham*
  An Occupation - *Taylor, Baker, Butcher, Smith*
  From Patronymic (Relationship) - *Nelson* - son of Nell, *Robertson , Robson, McCarthy, Macpherson, Probert*
  or a Nickname - *Redhead, Whitehead*.
The less common the surname, the easier searches can be, and some idea of the number of people bearing a certain surname and their distribution can be obtained by looking at local telephone directories.

Setting your sights
A fairly early decision needs to be made on where to concentrate your researches. You could aim to research your total ancestry. The implications for this are enormous. The data collected will soon overwhelm you. It is better

in *The Family and Local History Handbook.*

The annual subscriptions are modest. Join the local family history society even if you do not research in their area. There are many benefits.

FreeBMD project
FreeBMD stands for Free Births, Marriages, and Deaths. The FreeBMD Project's objective is to provide free Internet access to the Civil Registration index information for England and Wales. The Civil Registration system for recording births, marriages, and deaths in England and Wales has been in place since 1837 and is one of the most significant single resources for genealogical research back to Victorian times. The FreeBMD project only contains index information for the period 1837-1902. The FreeBMD Database currently has over 200,000 records
www.freebmd.org.uk

Census Returns

A Census has been taken every 10 years since 1801 except in 1941 during the Second World War. The census returns for 1801, 1811, 1821, 1831 were not preserved.

However there are some areas where returns for these years have been found.

The first census that is useful to researchers is the one taken in 1841.

The Census returns were taken on:

1841 7th June 1841: 1851 30th March 1851: 1861 7th April 1861: 1871 2nd April 1871: 1881 3rd April 1881: 1891 5th April 1891: 1901 31st March 1901

These census returns can be consulted. They were subject to public closure for 100 years because of the sensitive personal information they contained.

The 1901 Census is now searchable on the internet, for payment, at http://www.census.pro.gov.uk/ There is a comprehensive name index search giving access to over 32 million individuals.

- The annual subscriptions are modest.
- Societies usually have books and information about your area
- They will have Members' Interests lists of surnames being researched
- Many societies regularly publish a journal or newsletter
- They will have meetings with guest speakers, covering items of interest and hints on how to do your own research
- Societies also often hold indexes of monumental inscriptions from churchyards and burial grounds as well as census and parish register indexes.

Research Etiquette

Once you have had your own research interests published with your society you may be contacted by other members researching the same name. They may have a great deal of information for you or they may have come across something they might consider useful to you. Please remember it is etiquette to express thanks as soon as possible even if the information is of no use. If you write to anyone seeking information then *always* as a courtesy

Scotland

Civil Registration for Births, Marriages and Deaths began in 1855 although the registration of baptisms and proclamation of marriages began in 1551. These records are held by the Registrar General at New Register House, Edinburgh EH1 3YT Microfiche copies of the register pages are then made available in the New Register House search rooms. By the end of 2003 the microfiche copies will have been replaced by digital images. To find out more see the GROS web site at http://www.gro-scotland.gov.uk. Pay-per-view search web site is http://www.scotlandspeople.gov.uk

include a stamped self addressed envelope. It is surprising how such a small gesture oils the wheels for further help.

Many people find interesting or famous people in their family history - such as murderers, executioners, politicians, actors, or explorers - but a great many of us do not. Please tell the story about these *famous* ancestors to interested parties but refrain from *boring* everyone with the minutiae of your history and boasting about how far you have *got back*. Our individual family histories are really only interesting to our own families.

A **marriage certificate** gives the names and usually the ages of the marrying couple, their addresses and occupations, the names and occupations of their fathers, the date and place of marriage, and the names of the witnesses.

A **death certificate** records name(s), date, place, age, cause of death, occupation of the deceased, residence if different from the place of death, and the name and address of the informant for registration. It does not show place of birth or parentage. After 1968 more details had to be recorded on the certificate.

Should I use the Internet?

There is a great deal of very useful information available on the internet. If you have not already registered with an Internet Provider you will need to register and will pay telephone charges or a subscription fee. For more advice on using the intternet see the **Digital Genealogy Section**

Where else can I look?

The list is endless. There are Indexes to search. These are usually published by Family History societies, or individuals, and will include information about burials, servicemen, censuses, parish registers and monumental inscriptions as well as indexes for wills. You may like to know about the social history of the area. A family history society may have some but usually a great deal of our social history is uncovered and recorded by a Local History Society. There are records for occupations in all walks of life, Trade and Commercial Directories, electoral registers, newspapers, military service records, diaries and all the family memorabilia collected over the years.

You are about to embark upon a fascinating hobby that will show you your family's past both the pleasing and the not so pleasing. If may become an obsession but will be worthwhile record for you to leave to future generations.

The International Genealogical Index (I.G.I.)
The Church of Jesus Christ of Latter Day Saints has produced the marvellous International Genealogical Index (known as the I.G.I.). The Index is unique source of information on family histories gathered world-wide. For many researchers it is the first location they check for leads in their quest for information on ancestors. It is an index to millions of records of births, deaths and marriages recorded in church records in many countries from medieval times prior to civil registration.

The I.G.I. is on the internet www.familysearch.org where it is also possible to search Ancestral File, Censuses - British 1881; United States 1880; Canada 1881, Pedigree Resource File, US Social security death Index, and the Vital Records Index

Trade, Street and Local Directories
These directories first appeared in the 17th century and are important sources for local and genealogical studies. They include lists of names, addresses and occupations of the inhabitants of the counties and towns they describe, and successive editions reflect the changes in the localities over a period of time. Many of these directories are now being reproduced for sale on CD. The University of Leicester has created a digital library of eighteenth, nineteenth and early twentieth century local and trade directories from England and Wales. High quality digital reproductions of a large selection of these comparatively rare books, previously only found in libraries and record offices, will be freely available online to anyone with an Internet connection. There is also a powerful search engine available so that names, occupations, addresses and other key words or phrases can be located to their exact places on pages within the text. www.historicaldirectories.org

Ireland
The General Register Office (Oifig An Ard-Chláraitheora), Joyce House, 8/11 Lombard Street, Dublin 2, Ireland is the main civil repository for records relating to Births, Deaths and Marriages in the Republic of Ireland. The records of marriages other than Roman Catholic marriages began in 1845 with the registration of Births, Deaths and Roman Catholic Marriages began in 1864. http://www.groireland.ie

Census Returns
A Census has been taken every 10 years since 1801 except in 1941 during the Second World War. Most of the census returns for 1801, 1811, 1821, 1831 were not preserved. However there are some areas where returns for these years have been found - (see *Pre -1841 Censuses* by *Colin Chapman*) The first nationwide census returns useful to researchers are those for 1841. The Census returns were taken on:

1841	7th June 1841	1851	30th March 1851	1861	7th April 1861
1871	2nd April 1871	1881	3rd April 1881	1891	5th April 1891
1901	31st March 1901	1911	2nd April 1911 (Available for consultation 2012)		

These census returns may be consulted. They were subject to public closure for 100 years.

The National Family History Fair

Gateshead International Stadium
Saturday 8th September 2007

10.00a.m. - 4.30.p.m.

Admission £3.00
Accompanied Children under 15 Free

Meet the national experts!

The largest family history event in the British Isles.

**Free help & advice. Internet Demonstrations.
Family History Talks.**

**Easy Access by Road, Rail, Metro & Air.
Free Parking. Café**

www.nationalfamilyhistoryfair.com

2008 - Saturday 13th September 2008

County & Country Codes (Pre 1974 counties)

England	**ENG**	Caernarvonshire	CAE	Carlow	CAR	British Columbia	BC
All Counties	ALL	Cardiganshire	CGN	Cavan	CAV	Manitoba	MB
Bedfordshire	BDF	Carmarthenshire	CMN	Clare	CLA	New Brunswick	NB
Berkshire	BRK	Denbighshire	DEN	Cork	COR	Newfoundland	NF
Buckinghamshire	BKM	Flintshire	FLN	Donegal	DON	North West Terr	NT
Cambridgeshire	CAM	Glamorgan	GLA	Down	DOW	Nova Scotia	NS
Cheshire	CHS	Merionethshire	MER	Dublin	DUB	Ontario	ON
Cornwall	CON	Monmouthshire	MON	Fermanagh	FER	Prince Edward Is	PE
Cumberland	CUL	Montgomeryshire	MGY	Galway	GAL	Quebec	QC
Derbyshire	DBY	Pembrokeshire	PEM	Kerry	KER	Saskatchewan	SK
Devonshire	DEV	Radnorshire	RAD	Kildare	KID	Yukon Territoty	YT
Dorsetshire	DOR			Kilkenny	KIK		
Durham	DUR	**Scotland**	**SCT**	Leitrim	LET	**Europe**	
Essex	ESS	Aberdeenshire	ABD	Leix(Queens)	LEX	Austria	AUT
Gloucestershire	GLS	Angus	ANS	Limerick	LIM	Belarus	BLR
Hampshire	HAM	Argyllshire	ARL	Londonderry	LDY	Belgium	BEL
Herefordshire	HEF	Ayrshire	AYR	Longford	LOG	Croatia (Hrvatska)	HRV
Hertfordshire	HRT	Banffshire	BAN	Louth	LOU	Czech Republic	GZE
Huntingdonshire	HUN	Berwickshire	BEW	Mayo	MAY	Denmark	DNK
Isle of Wight	IOW	Bute	BUT	Meath	MEA	Estonia	EST
Kent	KEN	Caithness-shire	CAI	Monaghan	MOG	Finland	FIN
Lancashire	LAN	Clackmannanshire	CLK	Offaly(Kings)	OFF	France	FRA
Leicestershire	LEI	Dumfriesshire	DFS	Roscommon	ROS	Germany (1991)	DEU
Lincolnshire	LIN	Dunbartonshire	DNB	Sligo	SLI	Greece	GRC
London (city)	LND	East Lothian	ELN	Tipperary	TIP	Hungary	HUN
Middlesex	MDX	Fifeshire	FIF	Tyrone	TYR	Italy	ITA
Norfolk	NFK	Forfarshire	ANS	Waterford	WAT	Latvia	LVA
Northamptonshire	NTH	Inverness-shire	INV	Westmeath	WES	Liechtenstein	LIE
Northumberland	NBL	Kincardineshire	KCD	Wexford	WEX	Lithuania	LTU
Nottinghamshire	NTT	Kinross-shire	KRS	Wicklow	WIC	Luxembourg	LUX
Oxfordshire	OXF	Kirkcudbrightshire	KKD			Netherlands	NLD
Rutland	RUT	Lanarkshire	LKS	**Channel Islands**	**CHI**	Norway	NOR
Shropshire	SAL	Midlothian	MLN	Alderney	ALD	Poland	POL
Somerset	SOM	Moray	MOR	Guernsey	GSY	Romania	ROU
Staffordshire	STS	Nairnshire	NAI	Jersey	JSY	Russian Federation	RUS
Suffolk	SFK	Orkney Isles	OKI	Sark	SRK	Slovakia	SVK
Surrey	SRY	Peebles-shire	PEE			Slovinia	SVN
Sussex	SSX	Perthshire	PER	**Isle of Man**	**IOM**	Spain (Espagne)	ESP
Warwickshire	WAR	Renfrewshire	RFW			Sweden	SWE
Westmorland	WES	Ross & Cromarty	ROC	**Australia**	**AUS**	Switzerland	CHE
Wiltshire	WIL	Roxburghshire	ROX	Capital Territory	CT	Ukraine	UKR
Worcestershire	WOR	Selkirkshire	SEL	New South Wales	NS	United Kingdom	GBR
Yorkshire	YKS	Shetland Isles	SHI	Northern Territory	NT	USSR	SUN
YKS E Riding	ERY	Stirlingshire	STI	Queensland	QL	Yugoslavia	YUG
YKS N Riding	NRY	Sutherland	SUT	South Australia	SA		
YKS W Riding	WRY	West Lothian	WLN	Tasmania	TA	**New Zealand**	NZL
		Wigtownshire	WIG	Victoria	VI	**Papua New Guinea**	PNG
Wales	**WLS**			Western Australia	WA	**South Africa**	ZAF
Anglesey	AGY	**Ireland (Eire)**	**IRL**			**United States**	USA
Brecknockshire	BRE	Antrim	ANT	**Canada**	**CAN**		
		Armagh	ARM	Alberta	AB		

These codes are used to avoid confusion in the use of abbreviations for countries and counties. Those for the British Isles were created by Dr Colin Chapman. A full list of International Codes can be found at **www.unicode.org/onlinedat/countries.html** The codes are internationally recognised and should always be used.

Lochin Publishing, 19 Woodmancote, Dursley, Gloucestershire GL11 4AF

Marjorie Moore FSG

The genealogical world has recently lost two stalwarts. In October 2005 Jean Cole FSG a regular contibutor to this Handbook passed away after a long illness. Marjorie offered to provide us with an obituary for Jean but little did I realise that within a few days of receiving it we would learn of Marjorie's tragic death in February 2006, whilst on holiday in South Africa with her husband Richard. A very popular genealogist Marjorie would be seen at many family history fairs especially The Society of Genealogists Fair each year. Her extensive knowledge and her contibution to genealogy and to the Society of Genealogists were recognised when she was awarded a fellowship.

Marjorie and Richard's advice table at family history fairs was an invaluable resource for researchers. Some exhibitors were privileged to share her home made fruit cake which was delicious. We will all miss her infectious personality and particularly her advice and knowledge which she readily gave. The world of genealogy will be a poorer place without Marjorie.

Robert Blatchford

Family History Around The House

Doreen Hopwood

Although these items may not have any financial value, in terms of genealogical and human interest they are priceless!

We tend to consider such items as birth, marriage and death certificates as the main sources of information to take our research back a further generation, but there are many other resources to be found around the house which can aid the research process. Whilst some of these items may only provide clues or highlight new areas of research, others will enable you to place your ancestors in their contemporary society, adding a very personal touch to the records they left behind.

Items are usually associated with life-events, such as birth/baptism education, work, marriage and death/burial, and come in a whole range of shapes, sizes and formats – from "official" documents and photographs to medals, family bibles and sports trophies. They add the personal dimension which cannot be gleaned from official certificates and provide us with an insight into the interests, abilities and achievements of our ancestors which, in turn, may link to our own interests and characteristics. Here are just a few examples:

Family Bibles
Most researchers consider a family bible to be the 'jewel in the crown' of genealogical sources to be found at home, as these usually contain the names and dates of life-events relating to family members. If you are lucky enough to possess a family bible, you may find that mourning cards or newspaper cuttings have been placed between the pages, so examine it carefully for any such 'finds'. The names, dates and type of event are generally written inside the fly leaves of a bible and may include the day of the week and the time of birth. The latter is only shown on English/Welsh birth certificates relating to multiple births and

"PERSEVERANCE"
Band of Hope
York St., Hulme.

Awarded to

Emily Knowles

for

Regular + Early
Attendance

Nov 16 d 1922

stillbirths, (which were not registered until 1927) but could be entered in the family bible. Look at the date of publication of the bible, and if it's later than the date of the first family event, then it was written retrospectively, possibly transcribed from an earlier bible - or from memory. If events don't appear chronologically, or are all in the same handwriting (or in ballpoint pen!) then they were written up at a later date, thus opening up opportunities for transcription errors.

Birth and baptism
A certificate of baptism, or an entry on a cradle roll (or similar) may provide a date of birth as well as the baptism date and also the names of the godparents and details of the parents' marriage. These are usually pre-printed forms and come in a number of formats, which are given by the minister performing the christening ceremony to the parents, and sometimes to the godparents (or sponsors) as well. Christening gifts, such as silver mugs, cups, teething-rings and bracelets may be engraved with the baby's full names, date of birth and/or baptism. You may even be fortunate enough to find a decorated pottery christening mug providing the above details. These were popular until the mid-1800s.

Baby-books and special albums became popular from the 1940s and reflect the prevailing customs (and fashions) of the time. My own baby-book captures the post-war mood, and woolly vests, pram rugs and matinee jackets feature high in the list of gifts which my parents received when I was born. These books were generally designed to cover the first five years of life and so as well as recording the time, day and exact place of birth, it may chart the height and weight of the child over this period, and even include the nursery or school details. The lists of names of persons who sent presents and/or congratulatory messages can help to identify family relationships – and also work out their marital status (widowed or divorced relatives or "maiden" aunts) at that time. It can also distinguish between genuine aunts and uncles and the 'honorary' ones who were friends or neighbours of the family.

Education
School photographs often show the class name, year and school, so it may be possible to locate surviving school records from the information. These may be deposited at the local or county

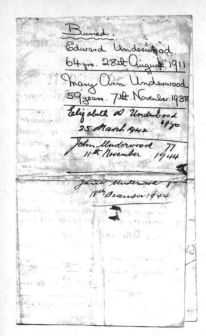

record office, at the relevant Local Education Authority, or could be still at the school. However, there is a hundred year closure on these records and access to them is only by permission from the Education Authority. School reports and educational certificates (school leaver's certificate, 'O' and 'A' level certificates etc.) record the academic prowess of an ancestor, but it is probably only the good reports that have been retained! Prizes – usually books of an edifying nature – were awarded as both day and Sunday school prizes, for good work, good behaviour or for punctual attendance. The bookplates were usually endorsed with the name of the recipient, the institution and the date of presentation together with the reason for the reward, so they can also lead you to educational or parish records. School programmes may contain an article by your ancestor or include a brief history of the school. Degree certificates and graduation ceremony programmes should enable you to contact the relevant authority for records of an ancestor, and lists of graduates of Oxford and Cambridge Universities up to 1900 have been published.

Work

It's important to remember that the school leaving age at the beginning of the twentieth century was thirteen, and pupils were issued with a certificate to confirm that they were old enough to start work and had reached a certain educational standard. Printed on blue/grey paper, they contain similar information to a full copy birth certificate, but include the name of the school the person had attended. If an apprenticeship was served, any indenture papers will contain information about them, the person to whom he was apprenticed, the nature of the trade and terms of the apprenticeship. Trade Union membership cards can also lead to other avenues of research as can membership certificates of professional bodies and associations. Watches and clocks have always been popular as long-service or retirement gifts,

and may be engraved with the following type of statement:

"Presented to James Jones by the Directors of the Whitehead Machinery Company to commemorate 50 years loyal service. 7th December 1920".

This will help you to work out when he was born, and also find out if there are any surviving company records. Former employees of large organisations may be able to locate personnel or pension records, and many of these employers produced their own magazines which included "Hatches, Matches and Despatches". You may also find copies still with the company or deposited at local record offices/libraries and general information about company/business records can be found at the National Archives website at www.nationalarchives.gov.uk. Ancestors who ran their own company or business may have deposited their records with their solicitor who, in turn, may have placed these in the local or county record office.

Military service

Medals – those issued (except for WWII) have the name, number, rank and regiment engraved around the rim. This information will enable you to search for military records – at The National Archives for records prior to 1920 and postal applications can be made to The Army Personnel Centre, Disclosure 1, Mailpoint 520, Kentigern House, 65 Brown Street, Glasgow G2 8EX, for later Army records. The latter are provided free to servicemen/women or his/her surviving spouse, but there is a fee payable to all other applicants. Information about obtaining service records for former members of the Royal Air Force and the Navy can be found at www.mod.uk. Actual Army badges, shoulder flashes and other insignia, or those which can be identified on photographs, can enable you to determine the regiment. The regimental museum may be able to provide further information, as can membership of Old Comrades' Associations. The next of kin of servicemen who died during the First World War were given a $4^{3}/_{4}$ inch circular bronze plague embossed with a figure of Britannia and engraved with the name of the serviceman. Known as "Dead Man's Pennies", and accompanied by a covering letter bearing a facsimile of King George V's signature, these often took pride of place on family mantelpieces.

Coming of Age, Betrothal and Marriage

Announcements may have been placed in local newspapers and the cuttings found in drawers, lofts or amongst photograph albums. During the first half of the twentieth century, gold and

silver lockets were popular gifts as twenty-first birthday presents for girls, whilst their male counterparts often received a cigarette case, a tankard or a watch – all of which may be engraved with the name of the recipient and the date. Engagement, birthday and wedding cards may have been kept, and the name of the sender could reveal relatives of whom you are unaware. A newscutting of a wedding report may list the guests and their gifts, whilst wedding photographs can act as a great "aide-memoire" with older family members who will probably be able to describe the relatives in the group photographs in great detail.

Death and Burial
The sending of black-edged mourning cards giving the name of the deceased and the dates of death and burial has been practised since Victorian times. These generally include the place of burial or cremation – information often leading to other sources, such as death certificates and wills. Once you know the date and place of burial/cremation, you can contact the relevant cemetery/crematorium to locate the resting place, or the Church if in a church burial ground. Addresses of cemeteries and crematoria can be found in this handbook, or you can try the website of the Council where the cemetery is situated (usually under "environmental services"). Mourning jewellery, such as brooches, lockets and rings made of jet and incorporating a lock of hair of the deceased may also be engraved, and receipts for the funeral could be found amongst family papers.

If there is a family grave, the grave papers give details not only of the location of the grave, but each time the grave was re-opened for the interment of another family member, the name of the deceased and date of burial was also added.

A newspaper obituary or death announcement may also be found among papers in the family home, which will also detail the funeral arrangements. A copy of the probated will or letters of administration will provide an 'insight' into the relationship between family members – by who is (and who is not) mentioned in the will. They can also reveal the surnames of married daughters (or other female relatives) and possibly addresses. However, remember that names/addresses are the ones they had at the time the will was drafted, which may have been several years before the death of the person. Messages of sympathy may also have been kept, again helping you to ascertain family relationships.

From the cradle to the grave there are documents which chart our life's progress, including insurance policy certificates, house deeds and leasehold papers, and, for older generations, there may be ration books and identity cards from the Second World War. Vaccination certificates and other health related material, such as National Health Service cards, baby welfare clinic attendance cards can all help to build up a picture of the period in which the person lived.

society at least! Photographs of young people in uniformed organisations, such as brownies, cubs, guides, Church Army/Boys or Girls Brigade etc. may enable you to locate where they attended these activities, and the local/area headquarters may have an archive or a history of the organisation. Membership cards or programmes for club and society events will indicate the hobbies and interests held by an ancestor, and these may be accompanied by prize-winners certificates or a newspaper report of a local horticultural show. Theatre tickets and programmes may denote not only that an ancestor was an avid theatre-goer, but that he/she may have been involved in local amateur dramatics, so look for familiar names in any of the programmes. Whilst I knew that my grandfather's brothers were "on the stage", I was taken by surprise to find them playing the Brokers Men in "Babes in the Wood" alongside famous Musical Hall artistes in the early 1900s. From this information I was able to trace their appearances (on the seaside piers in the summer and in pantomime over Christmas) over several years and a distant cousin provided me with several stage photographs of the duo. Sporting prowess may be measured in the numbers of cups, trophies, medals and certificates won by an ancestor, and these too are usually engraved with the name, date and achievement.

Items of personal memorabilia may not take us further back with our research, but they can give us a glimpse into our ancestor's social world. This is a good point at which to stress the importance of noting why an item has been kept and the personal story behind it for future generations. They are unlikely to realise that a large silk rose is what remains of the hat worn by a great-grandma on her wedding day, or that the rather well worn, scuffed baby shoe was one of a pair that great-grandad wore when he took his first steps. For any items you intend to retain as future family heirlooms, place an explanatory note alongside it – including (of course!) the date.

Leisure and sporting pursuits

Most of have belonged to at least one club, society or other organisation during our lifetime – and many of us are still likely to be members of one or more – probably a family history

Items we think of as ephemeral and even mundane can also provide us with some social history around our ancestors. Things like household receipts, bills and even Christmas lists fall into this category. Again, these won't take your research further back, but it will enable you to see how much the cost of living and tastes have changed over the last hundred years or so. The names to be found in old address and birthday books may relate to persons who have long since died, but there may still be family members living at the same address who may be able to help you fill in the gaps in your family history. Unfortunately, birthday books provide the date of birth, but not the actual year of birth, however this information can still help you to narrow down a search of the General Register Office Index to specific quarters of any year. Old Christmas card lists will

provide you with the addresses of family homes and these can be checked against electoral registers to ascertain how long the family lived there. Old postcards letters/envelopes will also facilitate this type of search and have the added bonus of a date and/or postmark. In this modern age of e-mail and text messages the survival of correspondence between family members is less likely than previously when letter writing was the only way of communicating with family and friends who did not live close by. One of the problems associated with letters is that we generally only have one set of correspondence – those received by our ancestor, often in response to letters written to the sender. Again, these can provide us with an insight about how our ancestors felt about local, national and global events.

You may be fortunate enough to find a scrapbook of cuttings from local (or national) newspapers, and these could cover a whole range of events relating to individuals, families and communities in which your ancestor lived. Annoyingly, the date and name of the newspaper from which the cutting was taken is not always noted, but glean as much information as you can from the text before searching newspaper archives in local, county or national repositories. Details of newspapers held at the British Library (at Colindale) can be found at www.bl.gov.uk. This snippet, showing my father came from a newspaper dated 6 June 1943, but, despite concerted efforts, I still haven't been able to identify which one.

Don't confine your search family history "clues" to paper sources. Items such as family portraits, photos/paintings of family homes, diaries, tools of a particular trade and uniforms and badges can all help to provide avenues for further research and/or "put the flesh on the bones" of our ancestors. Samplers were often worked by young girls in order to demonstrate their prowess with a

needle, and these usually comprise of a moral text with the name, date and age of the needle worker.

The scope of material to be found around the home can help us build up a picture of the lives of our ancestors and give us a greater understanding of what was important to them.

A Day With the Naval Commandos

THEIR JOB IS 'LANDINGS'

By A Special Correspondent

I HAVE just spent a day with some Naval Commandos, the men whose job it will be to put the Army back on the beaches of the Continent. These men serve in the landing craft which range in size from the little "beetle" tank landing craft down to the fine "tank boats" which will rush the infantry into battle with the enemy.

For many months they have been training on shore and at sea, learning to land their fighting cargoes in a matter of seconds on beaches where a couple of years ago it would have been thought impossible to make the attempt at all.

As I walked along the quayside on this peaceful sunny morning I saw seamen with the distinctive badge of "Combined Operations" on their sleeves working quietly at the finishing touches of their craft. They were attending the guns, oiling winches, and testing gear with that indefinable air of men who know there is a test ahead and are ready for it.

Down below in the engine rooms stokers were making adjustments to their engines, reminding me of mechanics fussing over their car engines before the start of a Grand Prix race in the days of peace.

NEARLY all the officers in these craft belong to the Royal Naval Volunteer Reserve. They feel they are opening up a new branch of the Navy and that at the end of the war they will be able to head over to the regular officers a new branch of the Service well established with a technique of its own.

"For don't forget that 20 or 30 years ago no one would have thought ships this shape would have been any use at all," said one officer. "Beaching is a skilled art and has to be learnt. If it is not done properly the ships will just become stranded wrecks and then they are as good as lost."

I spoke to many of the officers and they all have this pride in their new Service. They are looking forward to making tradition.

A GREAT many of them have seen action already.

THIS Commando man is typical of the fine body of fighting men ready to form the invasion spearhead.

had been in light coastal forces, the small craft which raid enemy convoys from Holland round to Ushant.

There was Sub-Lieutenant W. J. Smith, R.N.V.R., from Ramsgate. He had won a Distinguished Service Medal as a gunner in a motor gunboat. When all the guns but his had been put out of action he continued to engage a superior force of E-boats and succeeded in driving them off.

AMONG the ratings I found Able Seaman Eric Stubbs, of Doncaster. Although he is not 20 he was at Dieppe, and Wilfred Dickinson, of Preston, Lancashire, who was an electrician in peacetime, but has had been in the cruiser H.M.S. Ajax when she was in the Mediterranean.

And so you could go on from one man to the next, each with a story to tell of action against the enemy.

Since the early days when they began to come off the production lines these craft have been considerably improved. It is not possible to describe the technical improvements in living quarters for the men and the officers have been made much more comfortable.

One day soon these landing craft will be in the news and I am confident after meeting

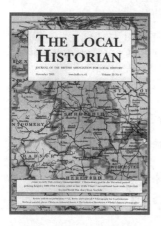

As Poor as a Stockinger
Anne Harvey

Though not on the same far-reaching scale as the woollen or cotton industries, nevertheless the knitting industry played a large part in the prosperity of industrialised Britain in the 19th century. In fact, the knitting industry, through specialising in hosiery, managed to keep going until well into the 20th century, rather longer that its close textile cousins.

Knitting differs from weaving on two counts. First, it is a series of interlocking loops of thread; secondly only one continuous thread is used. The elasticity of the resulting fabric shapes itself to the body and, because of the air trapped between the loops, is warmer for the wearer.

In a similar way to the weaving of cloth, engravings and artefacts from the Middle East and Europe show that the process of hand-knitting is an ancient one but it was the popularity of knitted caps in the 15th century that led to the domestic hand-knitting industry. How this domestic industry came to be centred mainly in the East Midlands rather than anywhere else is not known although it may have had something to do with the quality of wool produced in the area. This was the long-fibred type, called 'staple' and ideal for the weaving of cloth known as worsted. Unlike other areas dedicated to the production of woollen cloth, the East Midlands' farmers never took up weaving, choosing instead to sell their long-fibred yarn to the weavers of East Anglia and the West Riding of Yorkshire.

It was reputedly the women of the East Midlands who took to hand-knitting as a way of increasing the family's income in what was a predominantly rural area. This coincided with increased skill in reproducing the fine quality hose demanded by the Tudor courts (1485-1603) and originally imported from Europe. Paintings of this time show stockings with flamboyant designs – and that was just for the men! (It was a matter of pride to show off a shapely pair of legs beneath an elaborate doublet and balloon-shaped short trunks.) Such designs would be embroidered on after the knitting.

Decreasing or increasing the number of stitches could alter the shape of the hose. This process left a small hole, known as the 'fully fashioned' mark and signified highly-skilled quality knitting. The term 'fully fashioned' was used well into the 20th century, usually applied to women's stockings.

By the reign of Elizabeth I, there were pockets of hand-knitters in several parts of the country but predominantly in the East Midlands. In Calverton, Nottinghamshire, a local clergyman, William Lee, is said to have watched his wife hand-knitting stockings, supposedly to supplement his meagre income, and decided to replicate her actions with a mechanical device. Whatever his reason for inventing the first stocking frame, his first attempt was turned down for a patent in 1589.

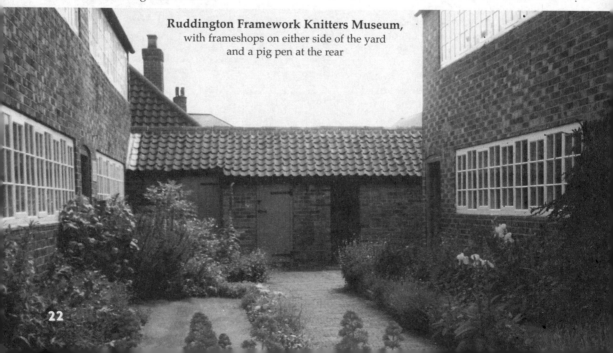

Ruddington Framework Knitters Museum,
with frameshops on either side of the yard
and a pig pen at the rear

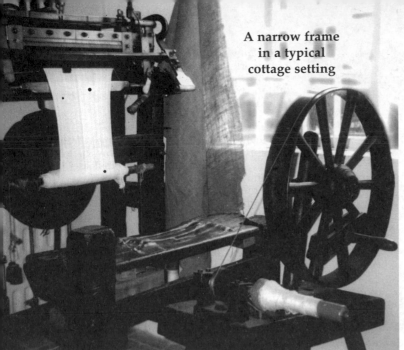

A narrow frame in a typical cottage setting

Many hosiery merchants were wary of the restrictions imposed upon them by such guilds and this was one of the factors that led to the movement of framework knitting away from London. With James Lee in Nottinghamshire building on the work begun by his brother, the East Midlands, with its lower cost of living, was an attractive alternative. By the late 18th century, there were more framework knitters in the East Midlands than in London. Many modifications had improved not only the quality of the cloth but had resulted in increased productivity and versatility.

An earlier modification was the invention of the thread carrier at the end of the 17th century, instead of the knitter having to physically lay the thread across the needles. This meant that wider pieces of cloth could be produced so that several pairs of stockings could be cut from the same piece of cloth. Alternatively, other garments, particularly undergarments, could be cut from the one piece of cloth. These 'cut-ups', as they became known, were later to lead to dissension in the trade.

The knitting machine was an upright wooden frame with a built-in seat for the knitter from which he could operate the treadles. The working parts were made from metal with rows of fixed and hooked needles holding one completed row while the knitter worked on a new row. To do this, he would have to combine complicated hand and foot movements. The intricate work demanded good co-ordination and eyesight.

It the late 17th / 18th century, knitting was very much a family business with the children of the household winding yarn from hanks obtained from the master hosier onto bobbins while the women seamed and embroidered. The latter especially brought in a good income and skilled embroiderers were much in demand. All these activities would be carried out in tandem with farming.

Early experiments with cotton yarn showed that it was unsuitable for framework knitting. However, with the help of Richard Arkwright's water-powered spinning frame in adjoining Derbyshire, which strengthened and standardised the cotton yarn, Nottinghamshire became the centre for the knitting of cotton. In

Life for Elizabeth I had been difficult since her accession with the over-riding need to ensure that Britain remained a Protestant country and the constant threat from the Roman Catholic Mary, Queen of Scots. At a time when the cost of keeping the poor on relief was rising, the last thing she needed, her advisors said, was a potential threat to the hand-knitting industry by William Lee's prototype knitting frame. It was, in any case, incapable of producing the high quality hose demanded by the wealthy. Undeterred, Lee took his stocking frame to France where the development of such devices was encouraged and, together with this brother James, set up in business, absorbing the more sophisticated techniques of the French.

After William died in 1612 and because of a declining political situation in France, James came back to Britain, selling his old frames in London, and returning to Nottinghamshire to continue working on developments to the stocking frame.

For many years, London remained the centre of the framework knitting industry with more than 400 frames in the mid 17th century. In 1657, the Worshipful Company of Framework Knitters was incorporated in London. The working parts of a knitting frame form part of the crest of the Worshipful Company of Framework Knitters. This, and a silver goblet of 1656, owned by the Company, is thought to show the working parts of one of the earliest knitting frames. In common with other craftsmen's guilds, the aim was to restrict foreign imports and to ensure maintenance of high standards.

An example of a framework shop interior

hosier. Inevitably, this led to exploitation of the framework knitters. Many men, attracted by initially high wages, became framework knitters, which led eventually to an over-supply of labour.

In addition, most framework knitters did not own their own frames but rented them from the owner. Although frames were reasonably cheap to make, normally the capital needed was beyond the resources of the ordinary knitter. Tradesmen, attracted by the promise of profit, could afford to buy them and rent them out thus ensuring a regular extra income and one which provided a good return for money. This, in turn, led to most of the knitters' wages being paid in over-priced goods, a practice known as 'truck'. Officially, this practice was illegal from 1831 but it was practically impossible to eradicate.

With wider frames becoming more common after the late 18th century, framework knitters were able to produce cloth faster and at cheaper rate, resulting in framework knitters being paid less. The resultant fabric could be cut into various garments and these 'cut-ups' caused great resentment among the more skilled 'fully fashioned' framework knitters who found that their wages were reduced as a result. The production of 'cut-ups coincided with a change in men's fashions from hose, worn in the 18th century, to trousers in the early 19th century, leading to a slump in the knitting industry.

These factors led to the formulation of secret societies known as Luddites, so-called after 'Captain' or 'General' Ned Ludd from Nottingham, with the express purpose of breaking the machines that they saw as a threat to their livelihood. Framework knitters of Nottinghamshire were the first to smash machines, in particular the wider frames producing 'cut-ups'. The unrest later spread to the Yorkshire woollen industry and the Lancashire cotton industry. In all, more than 1000 stocking frames were smashed when the Luddites were at their most active in the early 19th century. After the French Revolution in the late 18th century, the authorities were fearful of an uprising in Britain. This led to stringent punishments, including hanging, for those caught breaking machines.

The machine-breaking activities had little effect on the knitting industry and wages remained low. In addition to paying rent for his frame, the knitter was also to pay for needles, candles and oil out of his earnings. Very often, if his frame needed repairing, it was easier to do it himself rather than wait for the owner to arrange for its repair. If his wife or children should fall sick or die, he would be forced to pay someone else for the tasks normally performed by his own

Nottinghamshire, too, frames had been adapted so that they could produce the lace for which the county became noted. In Derbyshire, the fast-flowing River Derwent proved a more suitable source of power for the development of the silk knitting industry. Meanwhile, Leicester concentrated on the cheaper end of the market, with the production of woollen stockings.

Another step forward was Jedediah Strutt's rib frame in the mid 18th century. The early stocking frames could produce only a row of plain knitting and a row of purl, to produce the stitch known as stocking stitch. A rib stitch, which was one stitch of plain, one stitch of purl, produced a rib pattern which had more elasticity. To achieve this, the framework knitter had to physically reverse each stitch, a time consuming process. Jedediah Strutt's stocking frame could perform the rib stitch without manual intervention.

Most framework knitting was carried out in towns and villages close to roads so that goods could be transported to larger towns and cities, such as Birmingham, and sold on. This was usually done by agents called 'bag hosiers', who acted as middlemen between the framework knitter and the master hosier. One difficulty with this practice was that the framework knitter rarely knew the 'going rate' for either his finished work or the yarn supplied by the bag family. Likewise, if he should fall ill, the frame rent still had to be paid. After the introduction of the Poor Law in 1834, there was also the spectre of the workhouse. It was from this time that the expression 'as poor as a stockinger' came into being; indeed many framework knitters were forced to claim parish relief for their families as can be seen by various poor relief records. So common were such entries that the occupation of framework knitting was shortened to FWK for convenience.

In 1843, following a petition signed by some 25,000 framework knitters, a Royal Commission was set up specifically to look at the plight of framework knitters. The resulting report claimed that, in the previous 30 years, wages had fallen by some 40% while frame rents and other costs had continued to rise. Although the Commission recommended that changes be made, in particular to the way the trade was organised, the government of the day had little incentive to force through the recommendations.

Frame rents continued to be a cause of dissension but the frame owners were reluctant to lose a valuable source of income. One way of ensuring this was for master hosiers to group stocking frames together in workshops, called frameshops, and charge the knitter for the privilege. These frameshops were situated on the ground floor with elongated windows to gain as much light as possible. The frames were packed in tightly with knitters sitting back to back and with little room to manoeuvre. Tight control was maintained with the master hosier making the knitter pay a standing charge for the space in his workshop, a variation on frame rents.

Because of the complex hand and foot movements of a knitting frame, mechanising the process proved difficult and did not happen until the mid 19th century. In fact, hand frames continued to be used well into the 20th century. In Europe, a circular knitting frame had been introduced but was initially frowned on in England by frame owners reluctance to lose the income from frame rents.

However, the abolition of frame rents in 1874 by an Act of Parliament and with various other Acts making education compulsory, effectively removing cheap child labour, meant that the knitting industry was reluctantly brought into a factory system.

In the late 19th century, the continued demand for 'cut-up' goods meant that knitting became a less skilled job and the increased mechanisation of the process saw women taking over the machine minding jobs. This was particularly so with the gradual introduction of circular knitting frames which were quicker and needed less man power than the old hand frames. Fortunately, many former framework knitters were absorbed into engineering factories which were springing up.

In common with it fellow textile industries, demand for knitted goods was higher during WWI (1914-1918). The period following WWI saw a change in fashion with shorter skirts for women and a greater need for stockings. Knitted outer-wear, such as jumpers and cardigans, also became more popular. All of these changes impacted on the knitting industry. The advent of WWII (1939-1945) saw women as well as men in uniform with a subsequent demand for knitted goods.

It was the introduction of synthetic materials in the 1940s, in particular 'nylon' stockings, introduced to the women of Britain by American servicemen, that spelled the end of the knitting industry. Fortunately, the legacy of framework knitting, spanning some 250 years, is still evident in the small pockets of hosiery and knitwear factories in the East Midlands.

For those who have discovered framework knitting ancestors, either on census entries or parish records, there is a detailed website which explains the various processes (www.knittingtogether.org.uk). In Ruddington, Nottinghamshire, there is an excellent framework knitting museum with frameshops clustered around knitters' cottages (Tel: 0115 984 6914). Also in Nottinghamshire in Calverton village, the birthplace of the knitting frame, there is a folk museum, complete with the elongated windows so typical of a framework knitter's cottage and a display on the history of framework knitting. Opening times - www.welcome.to/calverton. On the outskirts of Leicester, Wigston Framework Knitters' Museum is a master hosier's house and frameshop which is unique in that it was still in use up to the 1950s (Enquiries Tel: 0116 288 3396).

Journey's End: Coroners Records

Jean Cole FSG

Most family historians, sooner or later, will come across a death certificate with the information that a coroner's inquest was held into the cause of death. When this occurs it is always worth trying to track down that particular coroner's inquest or, failing that, a local newspaper report. Here, it has to be pointed out that coroners' inquisitions are subject to a 75 year closure ruling. However, if anyone wishes to see a particular report which falls within the 75 year period, an application in writing by the next of kin can be made to the coroner concerned for permission to present to the record office holding the records, to see that particular record. Again, it has to be stressed that many coroners, throughout the years, destroyed these invaluable records so that in many cases, local newspapers are the only source remaining. *The Star* newspaper 14th April 1794 revealed this tragic case: *Last Saturday, one of the Keepers of Swift's, a Lunatic Hospital, was killed by a maniac under his care – he cried for help but the ferocity of the madman was irresistible and he dispatched him in a few minutes.* Records of this hospital, may, no doubt, reveal much more information.

My interest in this somewhat morbid subject was fired by family stories that various sudden deaths had occurred and that, when questioned, most family members always seemed to change the subject. I had always known that my maternal grandfather had been

killed on a railway line in 1907 when my mother was just ten years of age but that was as far as she wished to discuss the matter. It was only just before her death, that she finally said she and her sister, through the patronage of a local family, had been placed in King Edward's School for Destitute Girls. In my paternal family, as a child, I 'happened' to overhear rumours of an accidental killing. As is always the way when family members declined to reveal details, I determined to discover the truth about this sudden death which had caused such an upheaval amongst the family, changing some of their lives and those of their descendants for ever. Suffice it to say that, although I was unable to find coroners' inquests for both these cases, various local newspaper reports were extremely detailed although harrowing in the extreme. What we need to remember, then, is that these are not just records of sudden and, at times, extremely dramatic deaths, but are the stories of our families 'warts and all' and that repercussions from such events often had an effect on various family members and, in some cases, shaped their destinies and those of future generations.

Coroners were officers of the realm and were mentioned in a charter of 925 but it was not until 1194 that county coroners were established in England. From this time many boroughs and liberties obtained the right to have their own coroners. It was stated that it was a coroner's duty… *to inquire into the cause of unnatural death upon the view of the body.* Coroners were unpaid officers until 1487 when they were allowed to receive fees, but only then for holding inquests resulting from murder or manslaughter. It was an offence, at that time, to receive money for holding inquests into other types of deaths. From June 1752 coroners were paid £1 for every inquest held outside gaols in any place in England which contributed to the county rates and 9d for every mile they travelled from their dwelling place to the inquest. Fees were paid from county rates by order of JP's at Quarter Sessions. Up to the Local Government Act of 1888 a coroner was elected by freeholders of a county but after this his appointment was made by a county council.

Before 1846 a 'deodand' meaning 'given to God' was often demanded. A deodand from early times, was an object deemed to have been the cause, by its movement, or, of being placed in such a position, to be

the cause of death by accident or misadventure, the money being given to the church, the Monarch, the Lord of the Manor or immediate dependants of the victim. Young Thomas Andrews was mortally injured on 2nd June 1800 when the hind wheel of a waggon accidentally fell on his head and fractured his skull. The wheel was valued at 1s which was paid by the owner of the wheel to the Lord of the Manor on whose property the accident had occurred. With the arrival of the railways, the 'deodand' was abolished in 1846 as railway companies would have soon become bankrupt if they had been obliged to pay the cost of an engine, carriage or wagon which had 'moved towards an accidental death'.

Suspicious deaths in the past were not always pursued as they are today because of lack of evidence and verdicts often varied from 'cause unknown' by 'persons or persons' unknown, 'by misfortune or accident' and 'Visitation of God', a popular verdict. It was seen many who caused deaths by accident or by deliberate intention often escaped retribution. For those who were apprehended and who were transported or paid the ultimate penalty for murder or manslaughter some must have been accused unjustly. Records should be consulted in Quarter Sessions and Calendars of Prisoners (county record offices) and/or Assize Records (The National Archives).

One who committed suicide committed the crime of *'felony and murder against himself'* and was not permitted a Christian burial. Suicide continued to be a crime in English law until 1961. If a person aided and abetted anyone to commit suicide, that person, too, was guilty of murder. In the early days, a burial of a suicide would take place at the crossroads with a stake thrust through the heart, but later a law was passed whereby a suicide was permitted to be buried in unconsecrated ground in a churchyard (4 Geo. IV – An Act to alter and amend the law relating to the interment of the remains of any person found *'felo de se'*) One of the first cases I transcribed in the Marlborough Coroner's Inquisitions was that of *Thomas Tarrant, barber of Marlborough, who, on the 4th September 1773 died by taking a fatal dose of poison.* This act made him a felon and the wording of the coroner was grim to read…*not having the fear of God before his eyes, but being seduced and moved by the Instigation of the Devil at a public house on a Saturday the 4th September did voluntarily and feloniously and of his Malice aforethought with a potion of arsenic or some other such drug did poison himself and as a felon of himself, killed himself.* He was buried in the King's Highway near Marlborough Common and here, I have to confess whenever I pass the Common I spare a thought for poor Thomas! As time passed, it seemed most juries went out of their way, particularly in small boroughs and

towns where many parishioners knew one another, to try and prove insanity, temporary insanity or lunacy, so that the deceased was given the benefit of the doubt and was afforded a Christian burial.

Dr Hunnisett transcribed the *'Wiltshire Coroners' Bills 1752 to 1796'* (Wiltshire Record Society 36). With the permission of the Wiltshire county archivist I decided to embark on the transcriptions of the surviving Wiltshire Coroner's records up to 1901 which was completed some time ago. They proved to be of great interest, depressing, but fascinating! The name of the deceased was given often with details of their life and times, together with depositions of witnesses, some of whom may well have been our ancestors?

I decided to widen and vary my research into coroners' records for lecture purposes. The areas included Bath, the Dorset seacoast, rural Dorset, the Forest of Dean with its coal mines, Stroud, Gloucestershire for its mills, manufactories and Stroudwater Canal. The Berkeley coroner, William Joyner, included some districts of Bristol and Bath in his jurisdiction and recorded in his journal…*he lamented the number of accidents that happened through excessive drinking, particularly among the lower class* going on to state… *they will dispense with more necessary Articles of Life in order to Satiate themselves with an imaginary pleasure which never fails to plunge them in misery and ruin.* A true statement as so many deaths occurred through 'demon drink', often described as 'disguised in liquor'. One of Joyner's cases appeared in the Bristol, Bath and Gloucester newspapers when Elizabeth Fitkin, a 20 year old single woman drowned in the River Frome on 25th May 1790. It was said that Joyner's discourse and summing up moved the whole Court to tears when he emphasised the need for a Magdalen Hospital in Bristol. Elizabeth had led a 'disorderly and loose' life, becoming pregnant whilst suffering from a malignant disease so that she ended up without food or anywhere to live. Even her parents had refused her their house and despairing, she 'cast herself in the waters to die'.

The National Archives' Coroners' records include various from the Crown Duchies and Palatinates; a large box of Middlesex inquests and some, which I considered of great interest, belonged to the High Court of the Admiralty. These involved deaths, mainly of convicts and various navy personnel at Portsmouth Harbour and Spithead during the early 19th century. It was obvious when I looked at these particular records that they had hardly ever been disturbed from their boxes since being deposited in TNA!

Who can be discovered in the records of coroners? Rich and poor, men and women, boys and girls, babies, all meeting with sudden, natural and unnatural deaths with various verdicts provided. Verdicts included insanity, run over by coaches, falling from a stagecoach, wagon, horses, falling down in the street, drunkenness - the list was endless. In Bath, the River Avon held a fatal fascination for many who wished to end their lives, or who, against all wisdom and advice, decided to go for a swim during a hot summer day. Many bathed in the river, washed down their horses and carts therefore it was inevitable that accidents occurred. Jerry builders were evident, too, in some records when houses fell down killing occupants and passers by. The Stroud valley with its mills, manufactures and the canal had more than its fair share of accidental deaths and the situation would have been the same all over England in industrial areas and mining areas. Coroners records, I discovered, provided a good indication of social and local history of the times as well as population movement. Witnesses were often neighbours, family, friends, travelling companions, passers by. Contrary to popular opinion, there was a constant movement of people around the country. Marlborough was a staging post on the Great Bath Road and many strangers travelled through the Borough to and from London to the West Country and other places, so it was bound to happen that some travellers died along the way.

During my research I was told by an archivist that one school log book contained an entry concerning a 'half timer' (a child who worked part time in a manufactory and also attended school part time) who was so tired whilst walking to work that he had fallen asleep on his feet and had tumbled into the river and drowned.

One inquest questioned conditions at Hawkesbury, Glos. Poor House:
11th November 1839. Gabriel Viner aged about 90 years. Said to have died in consequence of cruelty and neglect. Visitation of God. The Master of the House deserved censure.

Colliery, mine and industrial deaths were frequent:
Forest of Dean inquests:
14th July 1868 held at the Jovial Colliers, Lydbrook. James Collins, Junior, 12 years. Burnt by explosion of gunpowder in colliery through his neglect. Witnesses: James Collins, senior, of the Boarts, Lydbrook, father, George Lane, collier.
31st July 1868. Fanny May, 9 years, daughter of John May, labourer of Ruspridge. Killed 29th July. Verdict: Fracture of skull by being drawn between the rolls of a clay machine. Witnesses: Harriet May, wife of John May, John Harris, carpenter and John May.

The weather, too, played its part resulting in coroners' inquests.
19th November 1796. William Hunme, late of Moorfields, London, tea caddy maker, aged 16 yrs. Died in an outhouse of Mrs Williams of Alveston, Glos, on the evening 16th instant. Died through the Inclemency of the weather and the want of the common necessaries of life.

Chimney sweepers often met with needless deaths –
15th December 1797, Great Badminton, Glos. William Strawbury, killed by falling from the top of one of the chimneys (35 ft high) belonging to his Grace, the Duke of Beaufort. Instant death – Accidental death.
20th March 1802. John Crookshanks on 19th March. Cast himself into the sea whilst of unsound mind whereby he drowned. Verdict – Insanity. (Lyme Regis, Dorset)
12th February 1806. John Ford of Longfleet, Dorset, thatcher, came to his death by falling off a ladder whilst at work on the roof of a barn belonging to William Meades. Accidental death and misfortune. (Cogdean Hundred, Dorset)

The High Court of the Admiralty revealed innumerable deaths of convicts on HMS Racoon in Portsmouth Harbour –most verdicts included 'Visitation of God'. It is all too easy to see that conditions on board convict ships must have been horrendous. (HCA1/106)
6th January 1826. Joseph Stammers, convict. Visitation of God. Inflammation of the bowels.
19th January 1826. John Moun, convict. Visitation of God. Constipation of the bowels.
4th March 1826. John Place, convict. Visitation of God. Scrofula.
13th March 1826. Ferdinand Smith, convict.

Visitation of God. Erysipilis.

20th April 1826. Jno Frankling, convict. Visitation of God. Pulmonary consumption 20th January to 20th April 1826.

Finally, a sudden death which occurred on Market day in Devizes, Wiltshire, and one always held up to children to tell the truth and that continued long after the event. Thursday, 25th January 1753 - Ruth Pierce of Potterne had struck a deal with three other women to buy a sack of wheat. One of the women discovered one share was missing and demanded it from Ruth who declared that she had paid her share and added *'May God strike me down dead if I've told a lie'* with that she dropped down dead with the money clutched in her hand

It was thought appropriate by the Devizes borough fathers in 1760 that a monument should be erected in the Market Place as a timely warning to passers by. The Monument is still there.

Further Reading

Cole Jean. *Coroners' Records of a Borough: Marlborough 1773-1835* (Wiltshire FHS)

Cole Jean. *Malmeshury Coroners' Records 1830-1854* (Wiltshire FHS)

Cole Jean. *Salisbury City Coroners' Inquests 1876-1901*. 3 Vols. (Wiltshire FHS)

Gibson Guide. *Coroners' Records of England* (FFHS)

Gibson Guide. *Local Newspapers 1750-1920*: England and Wales, Channel Islands, Isle of Man: A Select Location List. (2nd edition FFHS)

Historical Association. *Short Guides to Records* (2nd Series No. 46) Coroners Inquest Records

Jowitt's Dictionary of Law.

Neal W. *With Disastrous Consequences*: London Disasters *1830-1917* (Hisarlik Press 1992)

Jean Audrey Cole FSG 31 August 1926 – 28 October 2005
Marjorie Moore FSG

Jean Audrey Cole the only child of Elton John and Florence Phillips was born in Swindon and lived there all her life. She had been researching her family history for a number of years when in September 1977 she enrolled in an evening class which is where we met, I was the newly appointed Swindon Branch Secretary of Bristol and Avon FHS, I was "sitting in" on the class with a view to recruiting new members. Jean and I became firm friends she travelled with me to meetings in Bristol and Wiltshire and became involved in many aspects of family history in the county going out in all winds and weathers with insect repellent, note books and other equipment to copy monumental inscriptions but it was as a prolific writer, transcriber and indexer where she shone. She had a vivid imagination, which combined, with her wonderful sense of humour and enquiring mind produced a constant supply of articles and books for Wiltshire FHS, and for other journals and magazines. She published many genealogical works (some in conjunction with others) all aimed at helping genealogists. In the 1980s Jean taught family history to night school classes at various venues in Wiltshire where her enthusiasm persuaded many people to become obsessed with research and join Wiltshire FHS.

Whilst she was acknowledged as Family History's "Agony Aunt" to the World through her Questions and Answers column in Family Tree Magazine where she answered more than 2,000 readers questions, to Wiltshire Family History Society and especially Swindon Branch she was ever present on alternate Thursdays as a speaker, meeting reporter and adviser where her quick wit endeared her to everyone. She used to joke about the time when she was in her local supermarket a lady approached and said I have a question for you "do you pickle onions in white or brown vinegar?"

She was made an Honorary member of Wroughton History Group near Swindon where for twenty years she was an invaluable member helping them uncover masses of information about the area, she was instrumental by her inspiration in persuading many of them to also become family historians.

Jean was a regular broadcaster on local radio and she lectured extensively in UK where she was a popular speaker and was also a Keynote speaker in Canada.

In June 2005 Jean was elected a Fellow of the Society of Genealogists for her services to genealogy and was thrilled with the honour and although only a few weeks after her second operation thoroughly enjoyed her day in London when she received her certificate.

Sadly in December 2004 Jean was diagnosed as having cancer and endured three major operations in 2005 and died two weeks after she was informed that her illness was terminal. Even at the very end her sense of humour did not desert her, the family history World has lost a wonderful person and excellent ambassador for genealogy.

Jean was an excellent cook and homemaker, loving wife and Mother; she leaves behind her beloved husband Reg to whom she was married for 52 years and son Peter. Everyone who knew her will remember her with enduring affection.

Newlands Mill Disaster - Bradford 1882
Robert Blatchford

A Coroner's Inquest will have followed the mill disaster in Bradord in 1882. It is a prime example of why and when a Coroner will hold an Inquest.

On Wednesday, 27th December, 1882 workers returned to Newlands Mill in West Bowling, Bradford after their Christmas break. The following day, shortly after 8am, workers were at their morning breakfast break when the mill's massive chimney collapsed. 54 people were killed and many more injured. Had the chimney fallen earlier, during the early morning shift, many more people would have been killed.

Many workers had gone home for the break but those who breakfasted at their looms were caught up in the disaster. Whole families were lost and many of the survivors were seriously injured.

Newlands Mill was part of the vast Ripley Mills complex which spanned Parma Street and Upper Castle Street. Over 2,000 people worked in the mills and many were children. The Newlands Mill chimney was 255 feet high and weighed 4,000 tons. It stood behind the boiler house which provided the steam power to drive the spinning frames and looms.

There had been extensive coal and iron mining on the site of the mill complex and a warren of tunnels and excavations ran under the buildings. Despite some opposition at the time the tall chimney was built directly over the old pit shaft which had been filled in with wood and other debris.

The chimney suffered continually from structural problems and by 1882 cracks, and even a bulge, had appeared and masonry was beginning to fall from the structure. Some repair work had been undertaken during the Christmas break.

Although largely forgotten for 120 years a commemorative stone has now been unveiled in memory of those killed in the disaster. This is part of a general scheme to improve the environment and provide landscaping in the St Stephen's Road area. The people who lost their lives on that day

The Illustrated London News January 1883 depicted the rescue attempts in Bradford

were:

Grace Ellen FAWTHROP Age 15
Sarah Jane HENDERSON Age 13, Broadbent Street
Emma PEARSON Age 12, 9 Emma Gate, Ashley St.
Margaret FIRTH Age 21, 21 Calcutta Street
Harriet HALL Age 18, Cotewall Road
Clara Ellen PEARSON 9 Emma Gate, Ashley Street
Sarah Jane CROWTHER Age 11, 115 Cotewall Road
Ruth FIRTH Age 14, 21 Calcutta Street
Elizabeth OLDRID Age 21, 47 Glover Street
Bridgit RYAN Age 15, 103 George Street
Mary RYAN Age 45, 103 George Street
Lavina COOPER Age 19, Sloane Street
Lydia LIGHTOWLER Age 12, 17 Rydal Street
Lilly BURLEY Age 14, 75 Tudor Street
Margaret Ann TRAVERS Age 21, 60 Caledonia St.
Sarah Jane BURLEY Age 17, 75 Tudor Street

Martha Ann RODGER Age 16, 35 Quill Street
Honora M'EVAN Age 14, 12 Airedale Street
James Henry HANCOCK 322 Bowling Old Lane
Jane EGERS Age 19, Broadbent Street
Mary BROWN Age 16, 75 Granby Street
Dan DELANEY Age 15, 38 Calcutta Street
Annie Catherine HIGGINS Age 23, Granby Street
Mary LODGE Age 31
Selina WOODHEAD Age 32, Emsley Street
Hannah Eliza NAREY Age 13, 98, Tennant
Street.Susan WOODHEAD Age 8, 6 Emsley Street
Charles SMITH Age 50, 30 Little Cross Street
Arthur SMITH Age 12, 30 Little Cross Street
John William RAMSBOTTOM Age 14, Cotewall St.
Mary Ellen WILSON Age 28, Hardy Street
Charlotte Haslam LOASBY Age 15, 19 Townhill St.
George BOLDY Age 6, 77 Ripley Terrace
Edgar NORTH Age 12, 368 Bowling Old Lane
Emily SUNDERLAND Age 17, 44 Bengal Street
Ellen LUMB Age 21, Tichbourne Road
Joseph Ellis BOLDY Age 14, 77 Ripley Terrace
Martha MATHERS Age 17, 81 Grafton Street
John POLLARD 33 Paisley Street
Sarah HOLT 23 Clayton Lane
Sarah Margaret WHELAN, 18 Duncan Street
Mary Hannah CLIFFORD 312 Bowling Old Lane
Ruth Ann DENBY Age 20, Baird Street
Mary HENDERSON Age 15, 45 Broadbent Street
Amy GOODYEAR Age 14, 4 Moulson Street
Emily MITCHELL Age 13, 167 Bowling Old Lane
Walter HICKS Age 14, 161 Lower Round Street
Hartley BALMER Age 13, 336 Bowling Old Lane
William SHACKLETON Age 21, 27 Tudor Street
Annie AKROYD 16 Calcutta Street
Arthur WEBSTER 19 Old Ashfield
Martha SANT 25 Tennant Street
Nancy SAGAR Age 21, 47 Grafton Street
Urina HICKS Age 15, 161 Lower Round Street.

Further Reading:
West Yorkshire Archives - Bradford - *Report by the Yorkshire Boiler Insurance & Steam Users' Company* on the cause of the disaster WYB90/2/6 25 March 1883
Milligan & Ripley Family Records

The Arrest, Trial & Execution of Lord Howe
The Bow Street Runners in the Black Country
David Cox

Stourbridge in 1812 was a burgeoning small town on the south-western edge of the Black Country, with a population of around 4,000. It was already experiencing rapid growth and urbanisation, mainly due to the presence of glassmaking, coal and fireclay mining in the surrounding area. However, it was still predominantly agriculture that supported the local economy and society. The weekly Saturday market (known by 1812 as the 'Old Market', thus suggesting its long tradition) drew a large number of prosperous farmers to its proceedings, and both contemporary and later evidence suggests that a considerable amount of financial transactions took place between such individuals and others within the town.

It was on such a Saturday market day – 18 December 1812 – that Benjamin Robins, a well-respected gentleman farmer who lived at Dunsley Hall near Kinver, carried out his particular business in the bustling town. Mr Robins, perhaps mindful of the cost of the forthcoming seasonal festivities that he was no doubt looking forward to sharing with his family, was carrying on his person two ten pound notes from Messrs Hill, the Old Bank, Stourbridge; a pound note from a Dudley bank, and eight shillings in silver. He left the town at around 4.30 p.m., so that he should get home before the snow that had been falling throughout the day made travelling too difficult.

He set off on the relatively short journey along the unpaved but direct route to Dunsley via the Stourbridge-Bridgnorth road. At around 5.00 p.m. he heard a man's voice behind him requesting him to stop. Being somewhat short-sighted, in the failing light Mr Robins at first mistook the well-dressed man to be one of his brothers, Jeremiah. He consequently waited for the figure to catch up with him, to discover that the man was in fact a stranger who asked directions for the Kidderminster road. Mr Robins told him that they were not far from the required road (now the A449), and asked the stranger to accompany him as they were both going in the same direction.

This proved to be a fateful act of kindness: a contemporary account of what happened next is given in the *Staffordshire Advertiser* of Saturday 26th December 1812 (punctuation is original):

> *On Friday evening, about five o'clock, as Mr B. Robins of Dunsley, was returning from Stourbridge Market; he was overtaken by a man who walked and conversed with him for some distance; but when within less than ? mile of Mr Robins' house, the villain drew behind Mr Robins and discharged a pistol at him, the ball, it is supposed, struck Mr Robins on the backbone, which caused it to take a direction round his ribs to near the belly; the place it entered, to where it was found, was from 14 to 16 inches. The villain, as soon as he had fired, demanded Mr Robins' money, who said, "Why did you shoot me first? If you had asked me for it before, you should have had it." Mr Robins then gave him two £10 notes, a £1 note, and 8s. in silver...*

Dunsley Hall, home of Mr Benjamin Robins

The robber also demanded Mr Robins' silver watch, threatening to shoot him again with a companion pistol, before he ran off. Mr Robins managed to stagger back to his home, where the alarm was immediately raised, and two surgeons sent for to attend his injuries. He managed to give a fairly detailed description of his attacker, and a handbill offering a reward of one hundred pounds above and beyond any statutory government-funded reward was hastily printed and also published in the local newspaper. Despite clinging to life for ten days, Mr Robins unfortunately succumbed to his wounds on the morning of 28 December, dying at the age of fifty-seven.

As the incident took place almost thirty years before Staffordshire gained a County Police force, responsibility for the investigation of the crime fell on the local justices of the peace; in this case the magistrates who sat at nearby Stourbridge, and who would almost undoubtedly have known Mr Robins personally. By the early nineteenth century magistrates were responsible for a wide range of public order duties and regulations, including the overseeing of criminal investigations (although it was extremely rare for the magistrates to involve themselves in the investigative process). Consequently the local parish constable, Mr Jones, was immediately given the task of investigating the unprovoked attack. He was certainly prompt in arresting two local men on the day of the attack, but this seems to have been more a case of rounding up the 'usual suspects' than a stroke of detective genius; both men were quickly released without charge.

The period during which the attack had taken place was a particularly unsettled one; mainland Europe had recently witnessed a cataclysmic revolution and Britain was subsequently in the middle of the Peninsular Wars, with the concomitant problems resulting from a long-term international conflict. The pages of many of the national newspapers of the time were taken up with lists of deserters who had either broken ranks abroad, or, perhaps of more immediate concern to the propertied and relatively well-heeled section of the populace who could afford to read of such events, those who had absconded from their barracks in England. The Luddite disorders were in full swing, and staple food prices were rapidly rising beyond the pockets of those most in need, leading to increased tensions in many areas.

During the early years of the first decade of the nineteenth century there had been sporadic riots throughout many parts of England, and Stourbridge was no exception. Indeed, Stourbridge had been the scene of riots in September 1766 as a result of the high cost of bread, butter and other staple foods. In 1812 threatening letters were sent to those perceived to be profiteering from the scarcity of staple crops, and one such letters had in fact been received by Thomas Biggs, one of the Stourbridge magistrates:

> Mr Bigges,
> Sir
> We right to let you no if you do not a medetley see that the bread is made cheper you may and all your nebern [neighbouring] farmers expect all your houses rickes barns all fiered and bournd down to the ground. You are a gestes [justice] and see all your felley cretyrs starved to death. Pray see for som alterreshon in a mounth or you shall see what shall be the matter.

The attack on Robins undoubtedly unnerved many such members of the upper echelons of local society. As magistrates and farmers, the worthy justices of the peace at Stourbridge therefore had vested interests in ensuring that the perpetrator of the attack upon one of their fellow 'gentlemen farmers' was brought swiftly to justice. The worried Stourbridge magistrates, also conscious of the striking similarities of the attack on Mr Robins to the murder of another gentleman farmer, Mr Edward Wiggan, at Eardington, near Bridgnorth, on 25 November 1812, consequently decided that their local constable, no matter how eager, was not up to

Gibbet Lane, scene of the murderous attack on Benjamin Robins

the job, and therefore decided to bring in the 'professionals'. They wrote a letter to London, requesting the services of one or more Bow Street 'Runners'. What Parish Constable Jones thought of this is unfortunately lost to posterity: perhaps he was relieved not to have had to chase an armed and ruthless individual, but on the other hand he may not have been happy at the possibility of missing out on a share of the considerable rewards on offer for the apprehension of Mr Robins' murderer. At this time there was no bar on official servants of the law sharing any proffered reward.

At the time of the murder of Mr Robins, there was considerable opposition to the creation of a state-controlled professional police force. In December 1811 the Earl of Dudley referred to calls for the creation of such a police force, following a series of particularly grisly murders in the infamous Ratcliffe Highway, London. He wrote:

> They have an admirable police at Paris, but they pay for it dear enough. I had rather half a dozen peoples' throats be cut in Ratcliffe Highway every three or four years than be subject to domiciliary visits, spies, and all the rest of Fouché's contrivances.[1]

There was at the time no such force extant in England or Wales, though a paid full-time police force had existed in Dublin intermittently since 1786, and recent work has shed light upon the creation of pre-1829 police forces in several towns and cities in Scotland. Law enforcement was carried out by parish constables and watchmen at a strictly local level. What could perhaps be considered the only 'national' law-enforcement officers (in the respect that they were used throughout Great Britain) was the force based at Bow Street Public Office, where Henry Fielding, novelist and Chief Magistrate of Westminster, had created an embryonic police force of former parish constables

between 1749 and 1753. By 1792 this force included eight senior or Principal Officers, popularly known as Bow Street 'Runners', who operated solely as detectives.

The two Officers despatched to Stourbridge were amongst the most well-known and respected of the eight Officers employed by Bow Street Office at the time of the murder. Harry Adkins had been a witness to the assassination of Prime Minister Spencer Perceval earlier in 1812, and eventually became Governor of Warwick Gaol, whilst Samuel Taunton continued as an Officer until 1835. Adkins, in his evidence to a Parliamentary Select Committee in 1816, stated that he had been employed at Bow Street since 1801.

Adkins and Taunton arrived in Stourbridge immediately after Christmas. Suspicion had by then fallen on a thirty-two-year-old journeyman carpenter living at Ombersley, William Howe, who had been seen by several witnesses in the vicinity at the time of the attack. Howe by all accounts was a bit of a 'dandy', with a preference for fancy clothes – he was apparently nicknamed 'Lord Howe' by his colleagues for his 'airs and graces'.

An exhaustive investigation by the two diligent officers followed, involving travelling over 400 miles in pursuit of the suspect. Howe was found to have left his employ at Ombersley on 15 December 1812, and not returned until 22 December – he had then arranged for boxes containing his clothes and tools to be sent "in the name of John Wood, to be left at the Castle And Falcon, Aldersgate Street, London, till called for". The Bow Street Officers, through a combination of diligence and good fortune, traced these boxes (which contained a pistol and bullets), and lay in wait for Howe, who was subsequently arrested on 13 January 1813. He denied having been in Stourbridge, and refuted the charge that he had been involved in the attack upon Mr Robins. He was brought back to Stourbridge by Adkins and Taunton and was

100 POUNDS

REWARD

ROBBERY

AND ATTEMPT TO

MURDER

Whereas on Friday evening the 18th December, Instant, a little after 5 o'clock, as Mr. Benjamin Robins, of *Dunsley*, in the Parish of *Kinfare*, in the County of Stafford, Farmer, was returning home from Stourbridge Market, he was accosted by a man near the end of Mr. HILLS Park, who walked, and conversed, with him as they passed along the public road till they came upon Dunsley Hill, where the Man drew behind and immediately shot Mr. Robins, in the back, and afterwards robbed him of two Ten Pound Notes of Messrs. Hill & Co. Stourbridge Old Bank, One Pound Note, of one of the Dudley Banks, Eight Shillings, and a Silver Watch. The Man who committed the above atrocious Acts, is about five Feet six or seven Inches high, appeared rather clean and well Dressed, having on a good Hat and a long dark coloured Coat, down to the calves of his Legs; his Legs a little bowed, and he seemed to walk wide - He was seen loitering about the Heath Gap, in the parish of Oldswinford, Worcestershire, some short time before the Robbery, and afterwards a Person answering to the above Description, was also seen returning along the same Road towards Oldswinford and Stourbridge.

Any Person, whether Accessory or not, who will give Information and Apprehend the above described offender, shall upon his Conviction receive a Reward of

100 POUNDS

to be paid by Mr. ROBINS over and above what is allowed by Act of Parliament.

It is supposed that the above Offender called at some Public House in or near Oldswinford. Any information, however minute or circumstantial respecting him, will be gratefully received by Mr. ROBINS or Mr. Hunt, Solicitors in Stourbridge.

Handbill offering £100 reward for information leading to capture of Mr Robins' attacker

interviewed by Stourbridge magistrates on 19 January. He was transferred to Stafford Gaol on 26 January, where he awaited trial at the Lent Assizes in March 1813.

The inhabitants of Stourbridge seemed to have made up their mind of his culpability before Howe went to trial: the Staffordshire Advertiser of 6 February 1813 reported that "A numerous meeting of persons resident in Stourbridge and the neighbourhood was held in Stourbridge last week, when £50 was collected for Adkins and Taunton, the Bow Street Officers, as a reward for their vigilance in apprehending Howe".

Whilst in gaol, Howe made a desperate attempt to hide further evidence of his misdeeds – he asked another prisoner to pass a letter to Howe's wife via an intermediary, Elizabeth Barlow. This illustrates that Howe was by no means a criminal genius, as unfortunately for Howe, his wife (whom he had only recently married – perhaps bigamously) was completely illiterate, and had to have the letter read out loud to her by a Mary Hodgson, one of the other residents at Mrs Vickers' lodging house, where Elizabeth Barlow was residing. The letter gave details of where a pistol, bullets and a bullet mould had been hidden in a hayrick near Oldswinford – this being either the murder weapon or its companion piece. Mr Vickers, the landlady's husband, read the letter after it had been given to him by Mary Hodgson, and immediately left for Stourbridge, where he informed Mr William Robins, a nephew of the victim. It is not recorded whether or not Vickers subsequently received a share of any reward. The letter had been given back to Mrs Howe, who apparently had sense enough to burn it to prevent its use as further evidence.

The pistol and bullets were duly found and later produced as evidence at Howe's trial. The trial took place at 8 a.m. on 16 March 16 1813, under the jurisdiction of Justice Bayley, and lasted until 4.30 p.m. Over thirty witnesses for the prosecution were called, and a compelling

case was built up by Mr Jervis, the prosecuting counsel. The prisoner objected to one juror who was from the Stourbridge area (and who was subsequently replaced), but otherwise said nothing in his defence (at this time, the accused was not allowed to give evidence on oath). The jury took just seven minutes to find Howe guilty, and Justice Bayley sentenced him to death by hanging and subsequent dissection of his body for anatomical research. Howe apparently received the verdict impassively and "appeared indifferent about his fate."

Following the dictate of the 1752 Murder Act, the sentence had to be carried out within forty-eight hours of the verdict – there was no appeal procedure, and in this case, little chance of a Royal Pardon. (Incidentally Howe was probably hung by Thomas Johnson, who was in 1816 himself found guilty of receiving stolen goods and sentenced to fourteen years' transportation). He apparently confessed to the murder at the gallows, declaring the "badness of his heart", and went to his end "with firmness and composure".

It appears that the Stourbridge magistrates (possibly with the backing of Robins' family) were dissatisfied with the fate of Howe's body and successfully campaigned for the very unusual step of his body to be hung in chains (gibbeted) at the scene of the murder. This request was sanctioned by the Home Secretary, doubtless in an attempt to dissuade other would-be evil-doers. Anatomical dissection was the normal means of disposing of the body of a hanged person; a Christian burial was not permitted in the hope that the fear of not being allowed to rest in consecrated ground would also act as an added deterrent to those considering a serious criminal act.

The choice of gibbeting as a 'further terror' was not new to the eighteenth or nineteenth centuries; 'according to the Rev. J. Charles Cox, the gibbeting or hanging in chains of bodies of executed offenders "was a coarse custom very generally prevalent in medieval England"'.[2] The reasons why this mediaeval 'custom' was still present in nineteenth century England are still the subject of discussion, but many historians hold the view that:

> Its purpose – like that of public executions – was to increase the deterrent effect of capital punishment; to achieve it, the process of executing the capital sentence was as it were, prolonged beyond the death of the delinquent.[3]

To this end, several measures were often taken to prevent the removal of the body from the gibbet, which was often a considerable structure; records show that Howe's gibbet cost £22. 0s. 0d. with the irons costing another £7

19s. 6d. The gibbet was often of a considerable height (in Howe's case, it was apparently in excess of twenty feet high), and often studded with thousands of nails in order to prevent anyone from either cutting it down or climbing it to remove the body from the iron cage. It was remarked by a contemporary commentator that 'the lower classes […] have a great horror of the hanging in chains, and the shame of it is terrible for the relatives of the condemned'.[4] Conversely, for the family of the victim(s), the gibbet could present a 'comforting sight to the relations and friends of the deceased'.[5] It is interesting to note that the gibbet was constructed as near to the site of the murder as possible, but still out of sight of the Robins' family home, suggesting some sensitivity as to its siting.

Howe's body was therefore transported back to the scene of the crime at Fir Tree Hill, Dunsley, where a large iron and wood gibbet had been hastily constructed. The body was fixed to the gibbet by means of iron hooks being drilled into the bones of the cadaver. Howe was one of the last men in England to be gibbeted – the last being James Cook in Leicestershire in 1832 – and various contemporaneous accounts tell of vast crowds flocking to see the body, which was exhibited for a period of over twelve months. Estimates of the spectators vary from 20,000 to 100,000, but the macabre sight was certainly witnessed by huge numbers of visitors – day-long parties took place at the location of the gibbet. The name of the lane where the murder and subsequent gibbeting occurred was later changed to Gibbet Lane, being marked as such on the 1882 OS County Series map. As a gruesome postscript, accounts state that Mr Downing, the surgeon who had attended Mr Robins' wounds, returned to the gibbet over a year after the event and removed the bones, reconstructing the skeleton in his hall as a rather sick practical joke on his visitors. It was also reported that the decayed and dried flesh was left under a bush by Mr Downing, and was discovered by a pack of hunting dogs, but this is probably a lurid fictional addition to an already unpleasant tale.

No sign of the twenty-foot high gibbet survives – it was allegedly made into stile posts for nearby Prestwood Hall. Gibbet Lane has turned into a rutted and little-used byway, but Dunsley Hall still survives as a well-maintained private residence. Benjamin Robins' grave is situated at the eastern end of Enville churchyard, from where one can look toward the area where his murder occurred. No allusion is made as to the reason for his unfortunate demise.

(This article is one of a number to be found in *Foul Deeds and Suspicious Deaths around the Black Country* by David J. Cox and Michael Pearson,(Wharncliffe Books), available from all good bookshops.)

[1] Letter written to his sister, quoted in Emsley, Clive, *The English police: A Political and Social History* 2nd edn (London: Longman, 1996), p22. Joseph Fouché was Napoleon's Minister of Police in Paris, and had created a feared and loathed force.

[2] Radzinowicz,L., *A History of English Criminal Law and its Administration*, 5 Volumes (London: Stevens & Sons 1948) voilume 11, p. 213

[3] ibid., p.215

[4] ibid.

[5] ibid., p.217, quoting Sir william Blackstone

The Northern General Hospital History Project

The Northern General Hospital, Sheffield began life over 120 years ago and has a fascinating history having started life as the Fir Vale Workhouse in the days prior to free medical care for all. The Workhouse also included the Smilter Lane/Herries Rd. Children's Homes.

Over the years many changes have taken place. Even as late as 1967 when the two hospitals that had originated from the Workhouse, the Fir Vale Infirmary and the City General Hospital were renamed the Northern General Hospital, many of the older generation were still afraid of entering its doors. Looking back to the days of the workhouse and all that it entailed it is easy to understand why these fears remained so strongly and so long in people's memories.

On the 31st March 1967, the Sheffield Star carried an article about the change of name and ended with these words –

'The change of name will finally kill the workhouse stigma of Fir Vale that has haunted so many old folk on the brink of needing permanent hospital care.'

The stigma may have gone now but there are still people alive today who have personal memories, photos and memorabilia of the Workhouse, Fir Vale Infirmary, City General Hospital or the Children's Homes or who have heard from parents and relatives of how things were in days gone by.

The projects aims are to –
- Collect and preserve memories, stories, photos and items of memorabilia so they are not lost to future generations.
- Display items of interest in display cases at various safe locations around the hospital.
- From time to time hold exhibitions to stimulate interest and knowledge in the hospital's history.

The project would like to hear from anyone who has memories, memorabilia, stories or photographs of the hospital, or any of the old Sheffield Hospitals. Perhaps you or members of your family worked there. If you or anyone else you know can help expand our collection then please contact the project.

Items of interest can be left at the Clock Tower Reception Mon – Fri 10am - 4pm or posted to - Northern General Hospital History Project, c/o Clock Tower Reception, Northern General Hospital, Herries Rd, Sheffield S5 7AU
Tel: 0114 2715879
Email: ngh.archives@blueyonder.co.uk

Faversham Bricks
Arthur Percival

When Parliament authorised the use of steam locomotives on public railways in 1824, the scene was set for railway mania. The Stockton & Darlington opened in 1825, the Canterbury & Whitstable in 1830. London came later on the scene, probably because of the difficulty of forming routes to the centre through heavily built-up areas. Its first venture was the London & Greenwich, opened in stages between 1836 and 1838.

Greenwich, with its Park, its views over London, and its rowdy Fair, was a good destination to choose. The big problem was that to reach it the railway had to traverse the spider's web of narrow streets and lanes, many unsavoury, which had developed in Bermondsey and Deptford. To build a railway at ground level, with level crossing after level crossing, would have been suicidal. The only alternative was to 'fly' the railway over this intricate fretwork.

It could have been done, perhaps, with a combination of embankments and bridges, but the line engineer had a better idea. He would simply build one long viaduct all the way from London Bridge to Deptford. So, starting on 4 April 1834, this massive structure began to take shape. There were 878 arches in all, and there still are - as you may know, if you travel over them daily as you commute to Cannon Street. Four hundred men were laying 100,000 bricks a day, and every one came by sailing barge from Faversham, landing at Deptford Creek. Never before had so many bricks been used on one job.

This must have made the name of the local product, for as the 19th century went on more and more brickfields opened in Faversham, till it was virtually encircled by them on east, north and west. Even between Preston Street, London Road, St Ann's Road and Cross Lane, on the town centre's doorstep, was one vast brickfield - Kingsfield. The exponential growth of

Victorian London could never have taken place without Faversham brick.

The secret was not just in the brickearth, though this was of high enough quality. It was in the process. For facing bricks the fashion was for yellow; and someone had discovered a century earlier than if you mixed chalk, also readily available, with the brickearth, the end-product came out yellow, instead of the natural red.

Even more important, someone had discovered at about the same time that if you mixed coal-ash with the brickearth and chalk, you ended up with a brick which was self-firing. No need for kilns. You simply stacked the 'green' bricks in huge 'clamps' (the same word as 'clumps', really), lay kindling below, and lit it. The ash still had enough energy left in it to burn, and bake the bricks. These were the famous 'London' stocks - in fact mostly made in Faversham and the Sittingbourne area.

The process was also energy-frugal. The sailing barges which delivered the bricks to quays and wharves in London returned laden with domestic refuse, bought from the 'vestries' (local authorities) for a farthing a ton. Discharged in Faversham, this cargo was sifted for ash and the residue used to strengthen sea defences. Hence 150 years later these became pot-hunters' paradises, until their digging and 'treasure'-hunting became a nuisance.

A re-cycling dream and example to us all today, then? Not quite. The sifting - filthy work - was done mainly by women and children for miserable pay. The bricks were all made by hand - which ensured that they looked better than the bland machine-moulded products which superseded them in the 20th century - but the labour was literally sweated. Making was only possible from April to September and you had to look for another job for the rest of the year - if you could find one. You were paid piecework and only if you were very strong could you earn a reasonable wage - if you could make 50,000 bricks a week (and not many could), you would have handled several tons of brickearth. It was very hot work and a fair bit of your money needed to be spent on beer at the pubs strategically sited close to the brickfields. And the brickfield-owners operated a cartel to ensure that wages did not vary from field to field.

The local industry began to decline when the fletton brick came into production. Fletton is a village near Peterborough and in 1881 it was discovered that the lower Oxford clay, found

underneath a layer of ordinary brickearth there, was oil-bearing. This meant that a brick could be made largely self-firing without having to have ash added to it. The fletton, pink and machine-made, became ubiquitous in London and elsewhere in the home counties. One by one, most of the Faversham brickfields closed in the early 20th century - some had exhausted their brickearth, anyway.

Just one survived - Cremer and Whiting's, between the railway and Bysing Wood Road - and this eventually turned over to the production of specialist red bricks. It remains busy today, with several years' reserves of brickearth. Bricks are still moulded by hand, but some other processes are mechanised, and kilns fired by propane gas are used for firing.

Appropriately, in an historic town, much of its output consists of high-quality facing bricks supplied to architects' specifications for prestigious conservation projects. The rest of its trade is mainly in 'specials', bricks of unusual shapes and sizes required for applications such as copings and quoins.

Local brickmaking skills have left their mark on the town itself, happily. As long as supplies of oak were plentiful, the timber-framed house remained supreme. When they dwindled, and particularly after the Great Fire of London in 1666, brick came to be the only acceptable material.

The Catholic Church Presbytery in Tanners Street is a 'Queen Anne' style building put up well into the reign of George II and sports superb bright red brickwork of the period. Further down the Street are three dourer houses, in a plummier shade of red, put up by the Board of Ordnance in the early 1760s. Between them, the Gospel Mission Hall (1889) - yellow stock brick with red dressings - is both characteristic of its period and a legacy of the

local industry, since the money for it was mostly raised by brickfield workers who wanted to worship in their own independent way.

For those who care to look, rather than just see, all the other ancient town centre streets are rich 'galleries' of varied brickwork. Here and there are to be spotted medieval houses modernised in Georgian times with suave fronts of mathematical tiles - ones hung vertically on laths and designed to look like bricks. Look out for once-fashionable 'white' bricks at Cooksditch and Ospringe Place.

For fine examples of the yellow stock, the Victorian streets are the best places to go. Admire how even on the humblest properties arches are beautifully shaped, and corners elegantly turned. Bricks and brickwork of this standard are seldom found today, even in plush 'executive' homes.

The pointing is often a study in itself. On older houses it will consist of bright white lime mortar, not dirty yellow 'cement'. It may be tinted to match its brickwork: using a range of brick and pointing tints, the brickie had a huge palette from which to draw, and knew how to make the most of it. Here and there, and best seen in oblique sunlight, are even ancient brick graffiti - not the crude vulgarities of the 21st century, but relics far more tasteful.

Sources and further reading
(*on sale at the Fleur de Lis Heritage Centre)
John Freeman, Special Report in
        SE London and Kentish Mercury, 1988
Edward Dobson, The Manufacture of Bricks and Tiles
        Weale, 1850
Syd Twist, Stock Bricks of Swale,
        Sittingbourne Society, 1984
John Woodforde, Bricks to Build a House,
        Routledge & Kegan Paul, 1976
Faversham Society Archives

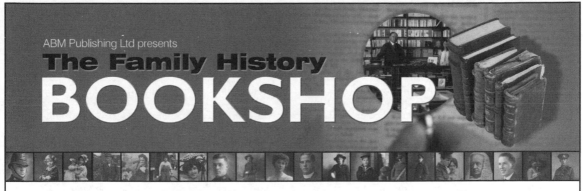

Where did Grandma come from, Daddy?

(Researches around the Cumbrian end of Hadrian's Wall)

Elsie Forster

"Your grandmother came from Low Row." I recall this being said when I was quite small, so I had some curiosity about the family then, but like everyone else did not ask enough questions when there were people around who could give me the answers.

Low Row is in Cumberland, very near the border with Northumberland, north of the A69 from Haltwhistle.

I remember Dad receiving grandmother's copy of the Cumberland News every week after she'd read it – no letter enclosed, but he knew all was well if this arrived. He went to see her occasionally in Haltwhistle, where she spent her last years, but I don't remember ever seeing her; perhaps she was too old to cope with young children. She died at the age of 79 when I was ten years old. Many years later I retired and after an older half-sister had died I thought that I should write down what I knew of the family for the benefit of the younger members.

I would like to tell you about my researches in Cumberland, as it was called when my ancestors lived there, and will concentrate on how I set about finding out about my grandmother and her male ancestry, although I have also obtained the records of the women who married into the family and a great deal about their ancestry.

I started by searching the records of births marriages and deaths or 'bmd', known as the St. Catherine's Index, which is available on microfiche in many local libraries. Then I bought the various certificates from the Registrars' offices in the appropriate area.

The birth certificate of my grandmother, Mary Jane Nichol, showed that she was born in 1868, not in Low Row as Dad had thought but at Whitehills in the parish of Walton. Her parents were William Nichol, Farmer, and his wife Mabel, formerly Smith.

Once I knew the names of her parents it was fairly easy, if time consuming, to find from St. Catherine's Index, that they were married in Brampton in 1864 and I obtained their marriage certificate. The marriage certificate showed 'of full age,' meaning that they were 21 or over – *it was not uncommon, as I found out, for this to be shown on marriage certificates instead of the exact age in the nineteenth century.* William was shown as a farmer, as was his father, also called William, and his address as High Greenhill in the parish of Stapleton, north of Lanercost Priory. Mabel's father, Thomas Smith, was also a farmer, and her address was given as Brampton - *not very helpful!*

It was then sleeves up and eyes down looking for the birth of my great grandparents and I found that Mabel Smith was born in 1843 at her father's farm at Common House, Waterhead north of Gilsland. However, search as I might for William Nichol in the St. Catherine's Index, working back then forward from the year 1843, I could not find him. This was when I discovered that either the Index is not complete or that people did not always register the births of children in the early days. I asked the Carlisle Registrars to do a search but they could not find him either. *Registration commenced in July 1837 but there were no penalties for failing to register.*

Using my newly acquired computer, I obtained lots of information from the IGI, on the site www.familysearch.org which can be searched for births/baptisms and marriages but not for deaths. I found William's baptism was in 1840 in Warwick near Carlisle.

Later, I used the site www.freepages.genealogy.rootsweb.com/~hugh wallis in conjunction with the IGI; this enabled me to search a particular parish register for a particular surname. Information about different areas and records was obtained from the excellent www.genuki.org.uk and another useful site is www.freeukgen.rootsweb.com

I heeded everyone's warnings about needing to check everything in the original sources. *Mistakes can be made and there is sometimes extra information in parish registers and other original sources which is not recorded in the IGI.* So – I needed to go to Carlisle.

Fortunately, I have a supportive family, and several family holidays have been arranged in

Continued page 44 ....

High Flatt Farm
Parish of Scaleby

SPECIAL TRIAL OFFER
3 issues for only £1

Your FamilyTree
THE BEST MAGAZINE FOR GENEALOGY

Every month *Your Family Tree* is packed with...

■ Features on how to find and use old records

■ **Surname histories and region research guides**

■ Fascinating real life case studies

■ **Expert answers to your questions**

■ The best websites for genealogical research

■ **How to record and share your family tree**

And that's not all! Accept our invitation to try this magazine and you'll enjoy...

■ 3 issues for just £1 – that's over 90% off the shop price
■ Each magazine delivered direct to your door
■ Continue your subscription – get 32% off the shop price

Every month you'll get a free CD to help you

Subscribe online...
www.myfavouritemagazines.co.uk/YFT/2010
Please use full web address to enjoy this special trial offer

Alternatively call **0870 837 4722** quoting code **2010**
(Lines open Mon-Fri 8am-9.30pm, Sat 8am-4pm)

High Greenhills, Parish of Stapleton

Cumbria when I have visited the Cumberland Archives in Carlisle Castle and we have explored the different areas in the north of Cumberland where the family lived. In the Archives I was able to consult parish registers, bishops' transcripts, census records (most of these are on film) and the index of some marriage bonds. *Marriage bonds were drawn up if the parties applied for a marriage licence, rather than having Banns called. Unfortunately the Cumbrian marriage bonds were destroyed around 1900, but the index is held for marriages up to 1825.*

There are undoubtedly other resources available which I have not yet investigated due to lack of time. For example, I understand that copies of wills are held in the Cumbrian Archives, although I have already got copies of some by consulting the index held in my local Northumberland & Durham Family History Society and obtaining the copies from York. *Wills, like that of my great-great-grandfather, can give a great deal of information about the family and their circumstances which is otherwise hard to come by.*

In between visits I made further references to the websites already mentioned and, latterly, to www.freeukgen.rootsweb.com which, although not yet complete, gives free access to some bmd's, census and parish register records. More census records are available for a modest charge on www.Ancestry.com and the 1901 Census can also be searched for a charge on www.1901census.nationalarchives.gov.uk

I have looked up various Directories, either copies of the books or, more recently, on line www.historicaldirectories.org - *allow a lot of time for finding what you want!* Some of these should be treated with caution (e.g. the 1873 Post Office Directory shows my great-great-great-grandmother Sarah Nichol as Beer Seller at Newby although she was staying with her son William by 1861 and died at High Greenhill in 1863.)

By looking up the baptisms of my grandmother and her siblings in the parish registers and

looking up census records, I was able to establish that the first child of William Nichol and Mabel Smith was born in 1864 (rather early!) in Brampton, then that the family lived at Whitehills in the parish of Walton where the next five children were born between 1865 and 1872. They moved into their farm at Lees Hill (north of Brampton) where the next six children were born between 1874 and 1886. *Yes, that's twelve children altogether!*

I know from the death certificates that great-grandfather William died at Lees Hill in 1910 and his widow Mabel died there in 1917. Their youngest son George had taken over the farm by that time.

Great-grandfather William's parents were William Nichol and Margaret Palmer. They married in Irthington in 1836. The marriage entry in the Parish Register shows that William was bachelor 'of this parish' and Margaret was a spinster of the nearby parish of Scaleby. *The 1829 Parsons & Wright Gazetteer shows Margaret's father, Matthew Palmer, farming at Hall Flatt, Scaleby.* Again I traced their children and their moves by consulting parish registers and census records. They were farming in the parish of Irthington from 1836 when their first child was born (again rather early!), their second child was also born there but they had moved to the parish of Warwick (near Carlisle, not the more famous one) by the time my great- grandfather William was baptized in 1840. *Although I have not traced his birth certificate, the 1841 Census shows him as aged 9 months, meaning he was born about August 1840, which is probably more reliable than the varying accounts of his age in later records.* The next three children were also baptized in Warwick, taking us to 1846, and the next two in the parish of Irthington, when the family was living at Watch Cross. By 1857, when their youngest child was born (9 in all) they were at the farm shown on modern maps as High Green Hill. They remained there until after the death of William senior in 1883. He died a prosperous man and the will shows that he had helped at least some of his children to buy their own properties.

William's widow Margaret died in 1890 at the age of 77, at the home of her widowed daughter Jane in Cumwhitton.

My great-great grandfather William's parents were Thomas Nichol and Sarah Wannop. Their marriage was in 1802 in the parish of Irthington, when they were both said to be 'of Newby' and Thomas was a husbandman.

Sarah had been baptized in Irthington in 1778. It was fairly easy to find her family as it had been in the parish for some time, but, as there were other Thomas Nichols of about the same age, it

was more difficult to track him down. It is only lately that I was finally convinced that Thomas Nichol was born in 1772 in the parish of Kirkandrews on Esk, chapelry of Nichol Forest, and was the son of William Nichol and Mary Little. Although this had been my 'best guess' by a process of elimination and looking at naming patterns, final confirmation came by chance when I consulted the index of marriage bonds held in Carlisle Archives, looking for someone else. I had not looked there for Thomas as his marriage to Sarah in May 1802 was by Banns, not by Licence – but, luckily, I noticed the following:
'14 Feb 1801 Nichol, Thomas of Cat-Lowdy, parish of Kirkandrews upon Esk, Yeoman.
Wannop, Sarah of Newby, parish of Irthington.
Jordan, John, Carlisle, Flaxdresser.'
John Jordan would be the bondsman, who may have had to pay some money over if Thomas failed to honour his pledge to marry Sarah at that time. I take Thomas's description as Yeoman with a pinch of salt as his father was shown as a labourer and he himself worked up to being a farmer at a much later date.

Once a marriage licence was granted the couple could marry at any time in the following three months but this obviously did not happen in this case. It's impossible to know why – perhaps a change of mind – or was Sarah pregnant, *like almost all of my Cumbrian ancestresses when they married,* but lost the baby and the wedding was therefore deferred to a more convenient time in the following year? I don't think we'll ever know.

Again consulting the Parish Registers, I found that the first two children of Thomas Nichol and Sarah Wannop were baptized in Wetheral, when the family was living at Warwick Bridge, and the other six children were baptized in Irthington, when the family had returned to Newby. Thomas's occupation was initially given as labourer, but he was a husbandman by the time William was born in 1809, then a farmer by the

time Jane was born in 1813. Sadly, two of the children died at the ages of 9 and 4 a few months apart in 1814. Two of the younger children were probably twins as they were baptized on the same day, although this does not always follow.

Thomas himself died at the age of about 52 (the age given in the parish register was 47) and Sarah appears to have kept on farming in Newby and later selling beer, dying at her son William's farm in 1863, when her age was given as 86. *My husband comments 'It's a pity she didn't leave us a recipe of her brew.'*

Searching for the birth records of Thomas Nichol and any other siblings, I found that the Nichol Forest Register for the period was virtually illegible *(or is it my eyes?)* and after noting the baptism of Anne in 1771, when the address was given as Hathwaitegap, I consulted the Bishops' Transcripts which showed that Thomas was baptized in 1772 and the address was given as Hathwaitegate. *On modern maps Haithwaite is almost on the north-west border of Cumberland with Scotland and Canonbie in Scotland is the nearest town.* Four more children were born up to 1781, when the address was given as Catlowdy. Later, Thomas and his two brothers travelled further south in Cumberland, married and made their lives there.

William Nichol and Mary Little were both said to be 'of this Chapelry' (i.e. Nichol Forest) when they married in 1770, but unfortunately we have no idea of their ages – and William would not necessarily have been born locally. *I sighed when I saw from the Bishops' Transcripts that there was at least one other William Nichol having children at the same time as 'my' William Nichol.* There was a William, son of Thomas Nichol and Mary Millican, baptized in Kirk Andrews on Esk in 1742, but another was baptized in the same year in nearby Canonbie, the son of William Nichol and Euphemia Elliott and another baptized in Bewcastle in 1745, the son of Adam (although it

Whitehill, Parish of Walton

is unusual that we have no other children named Adam in the following generations) – and there are many other possibilities further afield.

At the moment I feel that I have reached the proverbial brick wall on the Nichols. Through the www.genforum.genealogy.com site I have had contact with and eventually met two distant Nichol cousins, one of whom has done a great deal more research than I have, and he has a theory about the Nichols coming from Scotland, which I have always thought a possibility, although I remain to be convinced about the rest of his theory. Whatever the facts are, it has been pleasant to meet these two gentlemen and to compare notes - and I have a much better idea about the descendants of the Nichols from them, as I had not done much work on this.

When I hit a brick wall, I leave that line alone for a while in the hopes of finding more information later. I am, however, bearing in mind that we are getting close to the times when 'the debatable lands', a twelve mile stretch on the border between England and Scotland, were the refuge of the lawless and when the border reivers were at large. Neither England nor Scotland could apply the rule of law there until long after James VI of Scotland became James I of England in 1603 - and the Act of Union was not until 1707.

Then there was Cromwell and his effect on Parish Records ….

Did you have a pioneering genius in the family?
Robert Blatchford

How many of us have an ancestor who has changed things nationally or internationally? When we begin our family history research we do not know what we are going to find. When first born we are unaware of our ancestry and only if research has already been carried out, or there is a family 'legend' will we know of this ancestor. Often there are skeletons in the cupboard which are will add interest to an otherwise ordinary tale.

To discover the ancestor who has changed things nationally and influenced many people during his or her lifetime is a wonderful inheritance and worth much more than material riches.

Changes are not always political in the way that the introduction of the national health service under a Labour government or leading the country during the time of war with Sir Winston Churchill may be. However, Singer with his sewing machine, Hoover with his vacuum cleaner, Ford with his motor car and in the field of medicine examples such as Fleming with the discovery of penicillin are all instances where fundamental changes have been made both nationally and internationally.

Important though these examples are there have been fundamental changes in other areas of our lives which may be regarded as being important. In this instance I am talking about our national game – the beautiful game – football.

Don't stop reading because I have reached a topic in which you have no interest. Researching you family history may uncover a topic about which you want to know more. There are many many thousands of people in this country, the United Kingdom, and throughout the world who are avid football fans. As for myself I have always had a passing interest in the sport but cannot claim to be a devotee with an encyclopaedic knowledge. However speak to any devotee of the sport and discuss the 'Napoleon' or 'Emperor' of football and he will be instantly named. Herbert Chapman is synonymous with the game of football.

© Robert Blatchford Collection

Why have I suddenly acquired an interest in the subject of football history? Well, in March 2005 my third grandson, Henry, was born to my son and his wife. Henry is the great great grandson of the man who fundamentally changed the face of the sport of football.

I had briefly heard Herbert Chapman spoken of within the families but did not really know his significance to the development of the game.

My curiosity aroused I began my researches by 'googling' his name on the internet search engine. I received over 10,000 hits. Investigating further I discovered pages obviously written by football devotees.

Why was Herbert Chapman so highly thought of in football circles? From the time he entered football management he had a major impact.

Herbert Chapman 1910 - Northampton
© Mrs Hilary Thomas

There have been hundreds of words written about Herbert and pick up any book and invariably mention will be made of him.

Go to the website www.j31.co.uk/chapman.html and Herbert Chapman is described as Britain's most influential football manager ever! In a top ten of football managers Herbert Chapman is number one. Quite significant that he still occupies the number one position over 70 years after his death. In case you are interested the remainder of the top ten are 2. Jock Stein, 3. Matt Busby, 4. Bob Paisley, 5. Bill Shankly, 6. Alf Ramsey, 7. Bill Nicholson, 8. Brian Clough, 9. Alex Ferguson,

and at 10. Tom Watson. I am sure that someone will dispute this listing but the majority will agree that Herbert Chapman is number one. Alex Murphy for his major article in *The Times* 10th January 2004, headlined it with 'Revealed: a ruthless, pioneering genius who ranks as the best British manager … ever!'

Alex Murphy told us to:
'Forget Fergie, Jock and the rest, Chapman was No 1, SEVENTY years ago today, the greatest pioneer in the history of British football management was buried in Hendon Churchyard, northwest London. The funeral of Herbert Chapman, who led Huddersfield Town and then Arsenal to the pinnacle of the English game, was attended by hundreds of mourners and generous obituaries appeared in every national newspaper.'

For a newspaper to carry such a full and forceful article seventy years after Herbert's death shows the esteeem in which he was held.

So who was Herbert Chapman and what were his origins?

Herbert Chapman was born in Kiveton on 19th January 1878 at 17 Kiveton Wales, Kiveton Park a small mining town some ten miles from Sheffield which expanded when the mining of coal commenced in 1864. However when the coal mine closed in 1994 it only employed 1000. Herbert was the son of John and Emma Chapman and was one of seven children, six boys and a girl. John was a coalminer with no education working long hours in harsh conditions in the local pit. In those days the sons of miners were destined to follow their fathers into mining. However the Education Act of 1870 made school attendance compulsory to the age of twelve. Apart from gaining basic skills in the three 'Rs' sport became an outlet for boys. Playing football in the winter and cricket in the summer the enthusiastic Herbert soon became captain of the school football team playing alongside his brothers. Apart from his

© Mrs Hilary Thomas

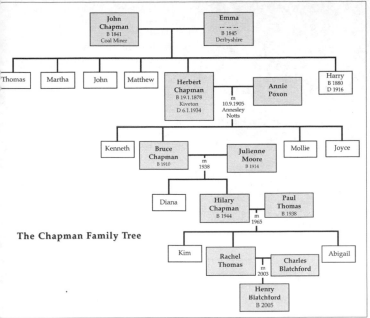

```
                John                      Emma
              Chapman                   ... ... ...
               B 1841                    B 1845
            Coal Miner                 Derbyshire
```

| Thomas | Martha | John | Matthew | Herbert Chapman B 19.1.1878 Kiveton D 6.1.1934 | m 10.9.1905 Annesley Notts | Annie Poxon | | Harry B 1880 D 1916 |

| Kenneth | Bruce Chapman B 1910 | m 1938 | Julienne Moore B 1914 | Mollie | Joyce |

| Diana | Hilary Chapman B 1944 | m 1965 | Paul Thomas B 1938 |

| Kim | Rachel Thomas | m 2003 | Charles Blatchford | Abigail |

Henry Blatchford B 2005

The Chapman Family Tree

participation in sport Herbert was an exceptionally bright child. On leaving school he began an apprenticeship at the local colliery. However with the introduction of new technical courses Herbert studied for a certificate in colliery management and subsequently attended Sheffield Technical College completing a course in Mining Engineering. Herbert continued to use his qualifications and worked in various industrial jobs throughout his life. It was not until he was forty six that he moved from an engineering career. Throughout his early working years Herbert, starting in the Sheffield area played, as an amateur footballer for local clubs in Lancashire and Yorkshire. Sheffield however was a hot bed of football with its own Football Association and this had fed Herbert's early appetite. He was only a moderate player and was not as good as his brother Harry. By 1907 he had turned to football management using the skills and theories on how to run a football club and win matches he had developed with his playing career. Herbert joined Northampton Town taking them from the bottom of the Southern League to second by 1911. He returned to Yorkshire in 1912 to manage Leeds City who were in the Second Division.

Working with the team Herbert hoped to lead them to promotion. His management style where he pioneered regular team talks and planned tactics in consultation with the players achieved success but not promotion. However gate receipts increased and the club showed a profit. Leeds City was managed by Herbert up to the start of The First World War. However 1915 saw the club slump to 15th position in the league. Football matches continued to be played through the uneasy conditions of wartime.

Herbert worked at a local munitions factory. He left Leeds City in the summer of 1916 when he took over as Manager in Chief at the Barnbow Munitions Factory, Leeds. The Barnbow factory started filling shells in December 1915 and became one of the largest in the UK, employing some 16,000 workers at the height of its production. On 5th December 1916 an explosion occurred and 35 women workers were killed. By the end of the war the factory had produced more shells than any other of its size quadrupling the output of ammunition boxes at a 25% reduction in production costs.

An allegation was made in 1919 by the Football League of illegal payments to Leeds City players between 1916 and 1918. All the club officials including their ex-manager Herbert Chapman were suspended. The club refused to open its books and Leeds City were expelled from the league. (Leeds City was eventually reborn as Leeds United) Herbert turned his back on football management feeling that he had been dealt harshly by the Football Association Commission. For the next few years Herbert continued to work in various industrial jobs including a spell as the manager of an Oil and Coke company in Selby. When his appeal was upheld Herbert moved back into football management.

Ken & Bruce Chapman
© Mrs Hilary Thomas

49

© Mrs Hilary Thomas

shook British football out of an age-old slough and was a tireless innovator decades ahead of his time - a champion of such ground-breaking concepts as floodlights, numbered shirts, clocks inside grounds, white footballs, team meetings, physiotherapy and synthetic pitches, to name just a few. Most progressive of all, at a time when sides were selected by self-appointed boardroom cabals, Chapman insisted on total control of team affairs.'

He joined Huddersfield Town in 1920 and herbert led the club in an astonishing sequence of success. Huddersfield Town won the Division One title in 1924 and 1925 having previously won the FA Cup Final in 1922. Having led the club to their first two Championships but before Huddersfield began their third momentous season – when they won the League Championship for the third time (the first league hat trick in history) – Herbert joined Arsenal Football Club.

Herbert was offered a salary of £2000 a year which was the highest in the game. Arsenal had narrowly avoided relation the previous year but by the end of the first season they were runners up to Huddersfield!

Arsenal's first major success was winning the FA Cup Final in 1930 when they beat Huddersfield Town 2 – 0 and were subsequently League Champions in 1931, 1933, 1934, and 1935.

Alex Murphy highlighted Herbert's achievements in his 2004 article:
'Yet you cannot put a value on Chapman's worth simply by weighing the silverware he won. He stands out as the pioneer who

One of Herbert's achievements was persuading London Transport to change the name of the Underground Station from Gillespie Road to Arsenal in 1932. This was no small feat as London Transport would have to change not only the station name but also the directional signs and reprint thousands of tickets and maps! He knew that such a name change for the station would be a crowd pulling benefit for the club.

Away from football and work Herbert was a devoted family man. He had nursed and cared for his brother Harry in his final illness from tubercolisis at Herbert's Leeds home in 1916. Herbert was a regular church attender St Mary's church, Hendon with his family. He was a sidesman and a good friend of the vicar.

While scouting for new signings for Arsenal at Bury on a cold wet New Year's Eve Herbert caught a chill but went on to watch Sheffield United at Sheffield the next day. Sheffield United were playing Arsenal the following Saturday and Herbert felt that it would be a psychological advantage for him to be seen at the match. He returned home his high temperature having worsened. The Arsenal club doctor advised Herbert to rest. The Arsenal reserves were playing the next day at Guildford and Herbert felt that it was too good an opportunity to miss. On his return to Hendon he accepted he was unwell and took to his bed. However it was too late pneumonia had set in and on Saturday 6th January 1934 Herbert died two weeks short of his fifty sixth birthday. Most of his contemporaries would probably have worked down the pit, or maybe in the steel industry. Instead, Herbert became the most successful British football manager of all time. Following a large funeral

---

Sporting Ancestry?

Have you got a sporting ancestor? Football particularly has a a tremendous amount of information. What with records and archives held by football clubs, fanzines (supporters' clubs magazines), programmes, annuals and national and local newspaper reports there is bound to be a mention of your ancestor if he played for a team. Football is regarded as the national game but mention must be made of the other sports - cricket, rugby union, rugby league and a host of other interests. Apart from using the internet with a name or team search local clubs, local studies libraries may also hold information. Many libraries have name indexes for local newspapers often going back a hundred years. If you think there is a sporting connection this may be another avenue of research to discover information about your ancestors.

Herbert was buried in Hendon Churchyard.

Although I did not meet Herbert I have heard him speak. How? Amongst the resources available on the internet there is a vast archive of films and newsreels at www.britishpathe.com. On this website you can preview items from the entire 3500 hour British Pathe Film Archive which covers news, sport, social history and entertainment from 1896 to 1970. Just type in what you are looking for in the field - Search the Pathe Database: - and within minutes you could own a little piece of history!

I typed in 'Herbert Chapman' in the search field and had many hits including two newsreels that were of particular interest. The first from 18th April 1932 was "The North v South Cup Final. Meet Mr Herbert Chapman & his famous 'happy family' Team, Arsenal – the hope of the South...." On this short film Herbert Chapman is asked to introduce the team. His response is that he is so husky he can hardly speak so asks his deputy Tom Whittaker to introduce the team. The second newsreel was even more momentous. We saw the funeral scenes in 2005 when George Best died. However in 1934 similar scenes were seen in Hendon, London. This news report was titled "Hendon A GREAT SPORTSMAN PASSES - and all will join in Mr George Allison's farewell tribute to Mr Herbert Chapman - football genius and great gentleman!" George Allison is seated at his desk speaking to the camera and he talks about the great loss to football and what a great person Herbert Chapman was. As he speaks there are images of the funeral showing the procession of many cars and the coffin covered with flowers passing through crowded streets. When the cortege exits the church the coffin is followed by members of Herbert's family, Arsenal players and other mourners.

I must leave the ending of this article to Alex Murphy, *The Times* 10th January 2004, when he wrote:
    "Chapman was always keen to promote the greater glory of Arsenal Football Club - he bullied London Transport into changing the name of Highbury's nearest Tube station from Gillespie Road to Arsenal. But for all his success and his towering profile in 1930s Britain, he died in relative penury. The Sunday (*Express*) newspaper for which Chapman wrote a column headlined its valedictory "Fortune made for his club but died a poor man.

Yet this humble man's legacy to the British game was so rich, it outstrips the contribution made by any other manager in the sport's history. He had the one eyed will to win of Don Revie, the passion for the game of a Bobby Robson and the footballing intellect of an Arsene Wenger."

I wish I had had the opportunity to meet Herbert but he has surely left a marvellous legacy and family history for his great great grandson Henry Blatchford!

Further Reading:
Herbert Chapman, Football Emperor: A Study in the Origins of Modern Soccer Stephen Studd ISBN: 028563416X Published by Souvenir Press Ltd
Herbert Chapman on Football -
The Times, Saturday 10th January 2004, Page 39 – Alex Murphy – Times Newspapers Ltd
The Barnbow Canaries Anne Batchelor The Family and Local History Handbook 8 Page 108 – Published 2004 ISBN 0 9530297 7 8 Robert Blatchford Publishing Ltd

Websites:
National Football Museum - www.nationalfootballmuseum.com
www.chrishobbs.com/herbertchapman.htm
www.mightyleeds.co.uk/managers/chapman1.htm
www.j31.co.uk/chapman.html
en.wikipedia.org/wiki/Herbert_Chapman
Arsenal Football Club - www.arsenal.com

DEATH OF MR HERBERT CHAPMAN
A GREAT MANAGER

Association football is not so rich in personalities that it can afford to lose such a man as Mr Herbert Chapman, the Arsenal manager, who died suddenly at his home at Hendon on Saturday after a short illness. He was only 55 years of age and, much as he had accomplished, he had such vitality and determination that there seemed even more for him to do in the future. The full effect of his influence on the game cannot be gauged yet, and it also remains to be seen whether or not there will be disciples who will carry on his work of popularizing football, making it attractive to the shilling-paying public.

Chapman, who played professional football himself in his early days, loved the game and understood it as well as any man, but his main interest was in making the game pay, and giving the public what it wanted. His enormous transfer deals when he came to Arsenal – roughly £20,000 was paid out for Jack and James – his schemes of playing football by floodlight, of numbering the players, of building new and comfortable stands, all were shaped to the same end – that of getting the public through the turnstiles and giving it the football and the amenities which would make it come again. Even Chapman could not always get his own way and the game is still played by daylight and players still go unnumbered, but his spectacular career has been amazingly successful, so successful indeed that a novelist would reject it as too far-fetched.

Herbert Chapman began his football career with Swindon in 1896 and he afterwards played for Sheppey United, Tottenham Hotspur, and Northampton-Town, of which club he eventually became player-manager. He was not a brilliant footballer but he was a sound one and his understanding of football tactics and strategy made him a useful member of any side. In 1908-09 Northampton, under his management, finished at the top of the Southern League, but it was not until the 1919-20 season, when Leeds City was disbanded and Chapman went to Huddersfield Town, that he became one of the leading personalities in the game. In that year, Huddersfield were in the middle of a crisis, and it seemed a wild impossibility that in the season of 1921-22 they would win the F.A. Cup and that the next three seasons would see them champions of the League.

And yet it was so. and in 1925-26, Chapman proceeded to Arsenal to conquer new worlds and prove that showmanship can have its uses in football as in any other entertainment the public pays to see. Arsenal had always been a struggling club, but in two or three seasons he made them a great power in the football world, a club feared and envied throughout the land. In his first year they became runners-up in the Championship, in 1926-27 they were F.A.Cup finalists, and in 1929-30 they won the Cup. In 1930-31 they were League Champions, with a record number of points, in 1931-31, Cup finalists, and League runners-up, last year, League champions, and the day he died saw them, with more than half the season over, secure at the top of the table, three points ahead of their nearest rivals. This record is brilliant enough in all conscience, and taken in conjunction with Huddersfield's success under his management it is phenomenal.

His sides won matches not because Chapman was watching them from the Stand, but because he knew how to choose the players who would win the matches for him, and just as important, he knew how to get the best out of them once he had got them. A lot of nonsense has been talked of his 'black-board' lectures on tactics, but he did his sides the inestimable service of making them think about the game and the results of his teaching were obvious on the field of play. He was an autocrat –he had to be to accomplish so much – and he lived for his work and expected others to do the same, but for all that he had an innate Yorkshire geniality which showed itself at unexpected moments. He leaves a widow, a daughter and two sons, one of whom has played Rugby football for Middlesex and in an England trial match.

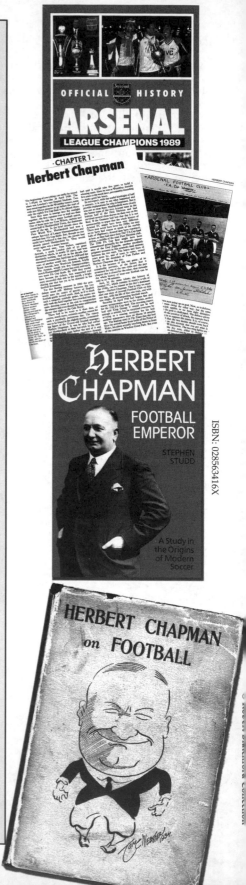

OFFICIAL HISTORY

ARSENAL
LEAGUE CHAMPIONS 1989

· CHAPTER 1 ·
Herbert Chapman

ARSENAL FOOTBALL CLUB
F.A. Cup Winners

HERBERT CHAPMAN
FOOTBALL EMPEROR

STEPHEN STUDD

ISBN: 028563416X

A Study in the Origins of Modern Soccer

HERBERT CHAPMAN
on FOOTBALL

Family History at the FRC
- Sources for Researchers

This is an introduction to the most important records for family historians held by the Family Records Centre. More detailed information about each of these resources is available both at the FRC and on our website at: www.familyrecords.gov.uk/frc.

Births, Marriages and Deaths from 1 July 1837

Civil registration of births, marriages and deaths in England and Wales began on 1 July 1837. The General Register Office (GRO) was established to oversee the registration process and to compile national indexes. The FRC holds a complete set of the GRO's indexes, which are on open shelves in the search room on the ground floor. Microfiche copies of the indexes (1837-1992) are also available. Indexes for recent events are normally available by the end of the year following the one in which the events were registered. Please check on availability before you visit the FRC.

The indexes are arranged in quarters from 1837 to 1983, and annually since 1984. The quarters are usually referred to by the last month in the quarter - i.e. MAR, JUN, SEP & DEC. A birth or death that occurred in one quarter may have been registered in the following quarter. Marriages are registered in the quarter in which they took place. Each index entry records the name of the person, the district in which the event was registered and the reference numbers required to order a copy of the relevant certificate.

The following changes in the indexes should be noted:
Births - From SEP 1911 the maiden name of the mother is shown
Marriages - From MAR 1912 the surname of the spouse is shown
Deaths - From MAR 1866 to MAR 1969 the age at death is shown From JUN 1969 the date of birth is shown

Indexes to Overseas Births, Marriages and Deaths of British citizens

The FRC holds two collections of records relating to the registration of births, marriages and deaths of British citizens living or working overseas. These records are not comprehensive and records of British people who emigrated permanently to other countries (eg Australia, Canada or New Zealand) will generally *not* be found here.

Indexes to the GRO's collections of overseas records will be found in the Overseas section on the ground floor. They include indexes to:

Consular Registers (1849-1965)
Marine Registers (1837-1965)
Regimental Registers (1761-1924)
Army Chaplains' Returns (1796-1880)
Armed Services Returns (1881-1965)
War Deaths (Boer War, First World War & Second World War)

UK High Commission Registers (1940-1981)
General Registers of Births, Marriages & Deaths Abroad (since 1966)

The National Archives has a separate collection of miscellaneous overseas records covering the period 1627-1969, which can be seen on microfilm on the first floor of the FRC.

Most of the records in this collection relate to births, baptisms, marriages, deaths and burials of some British subjects abroad, and inhabitants of countries under British jurisdiction. The events recorded took place in foreign countries, ie not Empire or Commonwealth countries, or on British and foreign ships. They also include some material relating to the Channel Islands and Lundy Island (Devon); marriages on board HM ships, 1842 to 1879; and events registered by British consuls prior to the Consular Marriages Act of 1859.

War deaths include some notifications of deaths of members of the services, prisoners of war, civilians, internees and deaths through aircraft lost in flight during the Second World War; deaths from enemy action in the Far East, 1941-1945; and an incomplete collection of certificates of British military deaths in France and Belgium 1914-1921, issued by the registration authorities of those countries.

There are also some returns of births, marriages and deaths from British Protectorates in Africa and Asia, 1895-1965.

Census Returns, 1841-1901

The FRC holds microform copies of the census returns for England, Wales, the Isle of Man and the Channel Islands. The Census was taken every ten years, with full lists of names from 1841. Census returns are closed for 100 years, so we hold the returns from 1841 to 1901. These can be seen in the reading rooms on the first floor.

Census returns list, house-by-house, details of everyone who slept there on census night. The returns are arranged by address within the same registration districts used in the GRO's birth, marriage and death indexes.

The returns for most census years have now been fully indexed by name, and linked to digitised images. Working back from 1901, they are progressively being made available at www.nationalarchives.gov.uk/census, which can be accessed in the Online Resources Area. There is a small charge for some of these services. The 1881 census index, without the images, is also available on the FRC's Family History Database PCs, online at www.familysearch.org and on microfiche. There are some additional surname indexes for all census years except 1901, but they are not comprehensive and only cover specific areas. About two thirds of the returns for 1851 have been indexed. A number of these indexes are available on the Family History Database PCs but there are many more on CD, microfiche or in printed booklets.

The FRC also holds a series of place name indexes that help to identify the correct microfilm or fiche. There are street indexes for most large towns and cities with populations over 40,000 and a separate index to London streets and their localities for identifying registration districts within London.

The census returns, except those for 1841, record the name, age, address, place of birth, relationship to head of household, marital status and occupation of each individual. The 1841 returns record first name and surname only, age (rounded down to the nearest multiple of 5 for those aged 15 or above), address and occupation. They indicate whether the individual was born in the same county where they were at the time of the census, but do not give the exact place of birth. They also indicate whether the person was born in Scotland (S), Ireland (I) or foreign parts (F).

Probate Records (Wills and Administrations)
Prior to 1858 there were over 300 probate courts in existence, mostly ecclesiastical. The court of probate was determined by where someone died, the property they held and where they held it. Wills of people leaving goods in more than one diocese, or with personal estate to the value of £5 (£10 in London) could be proved in one of two Archbishops' courts, commonly known as the Prerogative Court of Canterbury (PCC) and the Prerogative Court of York (PCY). The FRC holds microfilm copies of PCC wills and administrations, and associated indexes, covering the period 1383-1858. The National Archives DocumentsOnline website www.documentsonline.nationalarchives.gov.uk provides online access to the whole collection of PCC wills.

Wills that were proved in local courts are generally held in local and county record offices. The whereabouts of the records can be identified in the Gibson Guide *Probate Jurisdictions: Where To Look For Wills* (5th Edition, FFHS 2002) available in the Reference Area on the first floor. The problem of identifying the court can sometimes be complex and it may be necessary to search the records of several courts.

Most wills registered during the English Civil War and the Commonwealth (1642-1660) are among the records of the PCC. In addition to these, a small number were registered in local courts after the Restoration. We have microfilm copies of original wills proved 1643-1646, some of which were not included in the main PCC wills series, and therefore are not included in DocumentsOnline. They are not indexed.

The Court of Probate Act 1857 established a single authority that took over probate jurisdiction from the other courts on 12 January 1858. The FRC holds microfiche copies of the indexes covering the period 1858 to 1943. The remaining indexes and the records themselves, from 1858 to present day, are held by the Principal Registry of the Family Division, First Avenue House, 42-49 High Holborn, London, WC1V 6NP.

Death Duty Registers
The Death Duty registers cover the period 1796-1903. They relate to the payment of taxes on legacies and the residues of personal estates worth more than £20 in 1796, increased to £100 by 1853. Legacy duty was imposed in 1796 and succession duty was added in 1853. Both were replaced by estate duty in 1894.

The indexes can be used to identify the court where a will was proved or an administration granted prior to 1858. The registers themselves contain useful information and may provide details about the distribution of the estate that is generally not available elsewhere.

The FRC holds microfilm copies of the indexes 1796-1903, and the registers 1796-1857. The later registers may only be seen at The National Archives in Kew and three working days' notice is required to view them.

Nonconformist Registers
During the latter half of the seventeenth century and throughout the eighteenth century an increasing number of people left the established Church of England and chose to worship and record events in churches of their own faith. These non-Anglican denominations were collectively

known as nonconformists. They include Methodists, Baptists, Presbyterians, Unitarians, Quakers and a number of foreign congregations.

The FRC holds microfilm copies of many nonconformist registers covering the period 1567-1858. These registers were handed in to the General Register Office in 1837 and 1858, and are now held by The National Archives. The collection includes a small number of Roman Catholic registers (including some marriages) mainly relating to Yorkshire, 1663-1840. There are also some Church of England registers not belonging to actual parishes, such as the burial registers for Greenwich and Chelsea Hospitals, and baptisms at the British Lying-in Hospital.

Before the start of civil registration on 1 July 1837, only Church of England registers were recognized as legally valid by the courts and armed forces. In 1742 the Presbyterian, Independent and Baptist churches set up a birth registry in London at the library of Presbyterian minister Dr Williams. This was followed in 1818 by the Wesleyan Methodist Metropolitan Registry of Births, also in London. The Registries were kept open until 31 December 1837 to allow parents time to register births retrospectively. The FRC holds microfilm copies of the records of both birth registries.

Until 1753 the law relating to marriages was complex and confusing, and there were many clandestine or irregular marriages. These might be valid in law, but were not performed according the rites of the Church of England, and there was considerable scope for abuse and fraud. Many of these irregular marriages were performed in the area around the Fleet Prison in London, and a collection of the surviving registers for this and other similar marriage venues in London is held at the FRC. Collectively they are known as the Fleet Registers, and contain not only marriages but also a number of baptisms. There are very few indexes to this collection. Lord Hardwicke's Marriage Act of 1753 meant that from then only marriages in the Church of England were valid in law. Only Quakers and Jews were exempt from this legislation, so there are very few non-Anglican marriages between then and 1837.

Adoptions in England and Wales from 1 January 1927

The FRC holds a series of indexes to legal adoptions in England and Wales. Registration of adoptions began on 1 January 1927. The Children's Act (1975) gave an adopted person over the age of 18 the right to obtain a copy of their original birth record. The indexes held by the FRC contain the adopted name of the child and the date of adoption only.

A contact register is held by the General Register Office in Southport. The register is divided into two parts: the first containing the names of adopted persons and the second, the names of their natural relatives. The National Organisation for Counselling and Adoptees and their Parents (NORCAP) can offer help and advice.

Indexes to Divorce Records
The Court for Divorce and Matrimonial Causes was established on 11 January 1858. It took over jurisdiction in all matrimonial matters, except the granting of marriage licences, from the church courts in England and Wales. Jurisdiction was later transferred to the Probate, Divorce and Admiralty Division of the High Court.

The FRC holds microfilm copies of the indexes to divorce and matrimonial cause files from 1858 to 1958 in series J78.

The actual divorce files, which cover the period 1858 to 1972, have not been microfilmed and must be seen at The National Archives in Kew. The files contain copies of decrees nisi and absolute, formal papers in the case, and usually a copy of the original marriage certificate. From 1938 only a few files for each year were selected for permanent preservation to illustrate the changing nature of divorce. The names of the petitioners are included in the J77 Series list from 1938 onwards, which can be viewed in the Reference Area.

Copies of all decrees from 1858 may also be obtained, for a fee, from the Principal Registry of the Family Division, First Avenue House, 42-49 High Holborn, London, WC1V 6NP.

International Genealogical Index (IGI)
The IGI, compiled by the Church of Jesus Christ of Latter Day Saints (Mormons), is an incomplete index to records of births, baptisms and marriages

extracted from various sources. The majority of the entries on the IGI are taken from Anglican parish registers, mainly dating from the mid-nineteenth century and earlier, but the IGI also covers nonconformist registers and some civil records. The earliest parish register entries date from 1538 when Thomas Cromwell directed the clergy to keep a record of baptisms, marriages and burials, but you may find some earlier entries on the IGI submitted from other sources. There are very few entries after 1870.

For those interested in the origins of surnames the IGI can also be used to identify the distribution of a particular name from the sixteenth to the nineteenth centuries.

The IGI is available as part of the *FamilySearch* program at the FRC on the Family History Database PCs and also on microfiche. The most up-to-date version, however, is online, as part of the *FamilySearch* website at www.familysearch.org

National Burial Index (NBI)
The NBI, produced by the Federation of Family History Societies, contains over 5 million entries extracted from over 4,000 parish, nonconformist and cemetery burial records covering the years 1538 to 2000. However, it is not comprehensive and mainly covers the period from 1800 to 1840 with very few entries from the twentieth century. Coverage also varies greatly from county to county.

The index includes the name of the deceased, date of burial, age, place and county (pre 1974) of burial,

and the name of the family history society or organisation that transcribed the record. The index is available at the FRC on the Family History Database PCs.

British Isles Vital Records Index (BIVRI)
The BIVRI, like the IGI, has been compiled by the Church of Jesus Christ of Latter Day Saints, and contains over 12 million entries of births, christenings and marriages in England, Wales, Scotland, the Isle of Man and the Channel Islands. It mainly covers 1538-1888 and complements the IGI, with very few entries appearing in both indexes. Coverage is not comprehensive and can vary from county to county. The index can be found at the FRC on the Family History Database PCs, but the whole index is not available online.

Trade Directories
Two large collections of trade directories are available at the FRC: on the Family History Database PCs, and online at www.historicaldirectories.org . These are useful for identifying place names, street names, and addresses of individuals, either commercial or residential. There is further small collection of directories on microfiche.

Miscellaneous CD-ROMs
The FRC provides access to a number of miscellaneous family history sources on CD-ROM. These include:

UK InfoDisk
Genealogical Research Directory (GRD) 1990 – 1999
Pallots Marriage Index 1780 – 1837
Who's Who 1897 – 1996
Soldiers Died in the Great War 1914 – 1919

…as well as several CDs relating to emigration (mainly to the USA). A full list of available CDs can be found in the first floor reading rooms.

Further Information
The FRC produces a range of Factsheets and 'How to…' leaflets on most of the topics described above. They can be found in the first floor reading rooms, or downloaded form the FRC website www.familyrecords.gov.uk/frc. The site also contains details of our opening hours, onsite facilities, online exhibitions and our events programme.

Electoral Rolls

Alan Stewart

A helpful, but often overlooked, resource for family historians is the electoral roll. This can be particularly useful for tracking down ancestors in the United Kingdom prior to the 1841 census and after that for 1901. Even in the intervening period in the 19th century, however, finding your ancestors in poll books or electoral registers will help you to find out something about their financial status, as the franchise was related to property qualifications.

The earliest type of electoral roll was the poll book, which lists those who voted in an election and for whom. Poll books were published from around the end of the 17th century until the secret ballot was introduced in 1872.

The Representation of the People Act (RPA) of 1832 (known as the 'Great Reform Act') introduced registers of electors, still compiled today, which list all those who are entitled to vote in parliamentary elections. In addition, there were various burgess and citizens' rolls, or registers of town or county council electors, listing those able to vote in local elections. It has from time to time been the case that more people were allowed to vote in local than in parliamentary elections. Women, for example, were first able to vote in local municipal elections in England and Wales in 1869, nearly 50 years before they received the parliamentary franchise. (It was not until 1928 that everyone aged 21 and over received the vote in the UK, with no women able to vote in parliamentary elections until 1918.)

Today, citizens of the 24 other countries in the European Union are not allowed to vote in the United Kingdom in general elections. They are, however, entitled to vote in elections for local authorities, the Scottish Parliament or the Welsh Assembly, and the European Parliament.

Who was allowed to vote?

You can see how the parliamentary franchise was widened in England and Wales during the 19th and 20th centuries in the following table. Where the situation was different in Scotland and Ireland, this is described below. Boroughs (towns) and counties had different rules until 1884, with the boroughs of Berwick, Bristol, Exeter, Haverfordwest, Lichfield and Nottingham being treated as counties.

Before the Great Reform Act of 1832, nearly half a million men in Britain and Ireland had been entitled to vote, out of a total population of over 24 million. The Act put around 300,000 more people on to the electoral register.

As well as extending the franchise, the 1832 Act abolished the 'rotten' or 'pocket' boroughs, which had been important towns centuries earlier. Despite dwindling in size, places such as

Winchelsea in Sussex, Dunwich in Suffolk (most of which had fallen into the sea), Gatton in Surrey (with six voters) and Old Sarum in Wiltshire (seven) still returned one or two members to Parliament. Other much larger towns, however, such as Birmingham, Manchester, Leeds, Sheffield, Brighton and Cheltenham had no representation other than as part of their counties.

Parliamentary franchise qualifications in England and Wales since 1429

From Date	Electors in a Borough	Electors in a County	From Age	Sex
1429-1832 *	Varied according to local custom. **	Owner of property worth 40 shillings or more.	21	Male
1832	Occupiers (owners or tenants) of property with a rental value of £10 a year.	As above, plus holders of 60-year leases on property worth £10 a year, and tenants or holders of 20-year leases worth £50 a year.	21	Male
1867	All householders, and lodgers in property worth £10 a year, who had been resident for a year.	Owners of property worth £5 a year, and occupiers of property worth £12 a year.	21	Male
1884	(As above)	(Same as borough)	21	Male
1918	Most men. Women aged 30 and over who were householders or married to one.	(Same as borough)	21 / 30	Male / Female
1928	Almost everyone.	(Same as borough)	21	Male and female
1969	Almost everyone.	(Same as borough)	18	Male and female

* Wales included from 1536, Cheshire from 1553, and Durham from 1675.
** In some boroughs, only the corporation or owners of certain plots of land, had the right to vote. In others, it was freemen or ratepayers ('scot and lot' boroughs). In some 'potwalloper' boroughs, all householders who could boil a pot on a fireplace were entitled to vote.

Another RPA was enacted in 1867, by which time the population of Britain and Ireland had grown to around 30 million, with an electorate of over a million. As a result of the second Act, a further million men were enfranchised, while a third RPA in 1884 added another 2.5 million men to the register, principally in the counties. By this time, more than five million men were entitled to vote, out of a total population of about 35 million.

By 1903, the electorate stood at around seven million, out of a total British and Irish population of 41.5 million according to the 1901 census. In 1918, about six million women were enfranchised, as well as a further three million men. By this time the population of Britain had grown to over 42 million. Nearly seven million more women were added to the register in 1928.

You won't find women in poll books, as the last general election for which these books were published was that held in 1868. Women don't appear in registers of electors until after the passing of the Municipal Corporations Amendment Act of 1869.

Theoretically, this allowed women to vote in local municipal elections, subject to the same property qualifications as men. As a woman's property became her husband's as soon as she married, however, in reality few women were able to vote.

This situation led to the Married Women's Property Act (MWPA) of 1870, which allowed women to keep the earnings and property they acquired during their marriage. A further MWPA in 1882 allowed women to keep property they already owned at the time of their marriage.

The Local Government Act of 1888 introduced elected county councils, and extended the franchise to allow women to vote in county council elections. In 1894, elected parish, rural district and urban district councils came into being. Women were able not only to vote for them, but also to stand for election to those councils, and also to county councils from 1907.

What do the records contain?
In a poll book, you're likely to find some of the following information:
Names of the freeholders entitled to vote;
Where their freeholds lay;
Place of residence;
Trade, profession, etc.;
Who they voted for.

A book published in Norwich lists the 'Poll for Knights of the Shire for the County of Norfolk, Taken March 23, 1768', where the candidates were Sir Armine Woodhouse and Thomas de Grey (Tories) and Sir Edward Astley and Wenman Coke (Whigs).

A typical entry in this poll book shows that John Utton was a freeholder with land in the Parish of Garboldisham in Guiltcross Hundred, Norfolk, who lived in Great Finborough, Suffolk and voted Tory.

A register of electors typically contains information on electors under the following headings:
• Christian name and surname of the voter;
• Place of residence;
• Nature of qualification;
• Street, lane, etc. in the parish where the property is situated, or name of the property, or name of the tenant.

As is the case with poll books, the place of

residence is not necessarily in the district for which the electoral register was compiled. For example, the address of John Philip Bevan, one of the voters listed in the 1832 register for Wootton, Bedfordshire is given as '30 Sackville Street, London'.

The final column for this entry reads 'William Burton, tenant', although William Burton was not an elector. This demonstrates that you may still find an ancestor in the register of electors, even though he didn't meet the property qualifications in force at the time.

If you can find an ancestor in the Absent Voters' Lists of servicemen compiled during the First World War, you'll also find his number, rank and regiment or ship. These lists were produced as a result of the 1918 RPA, and list all those serving in the forces at that time.

Although the minimum voting age would not be reduced to 18 for another 50 years, an exception was made for the 1918 general election, at which men aged 19 or 20 were allowed to vote. From 1945 to 1948, service registers were compiled in addition to those for civilians.

Where will you find electoral rolls?
Poll books and registers of electors can generally be found locally in some of the following places: county record offices, reference libraries, museums, and the libraries of archaeological societies and universities. Since 1947, the British Library has received complete sets of electoral registers for England, Scotland, Wales and Northern Ireland.

MEMBER OF PARLIAMENT. "I shall tell my constituents the truth." FRIEND. "Are things *quite* as bad as that?"

In addition, the library has around 20,000 earlier registers of electors, including 28 pre-partition Irish registers for 1885/86, five Dublin registers for 1937, 13 Isle of Man registers for 1961 and 1979, and registers for 10 Jersey parishes (mainly for 1979/80). The British Library also holds over 180 English, Scottish, Welsh and Irish non-parliamentary registers (burgess rolls, etc.) and about 700 poll books (mainly English).

The Society of Genealogists, the Guildhall Library and the Institute of Historical Research at the University of London (all in London) also hold a number of electoral rolls, as do the Bodleian Library in Oxford and the University Library in Cambridge. The National Library of Wales in Aberystwyth has electoral rolls for Wales and the counties of the Welsh Marches.

The Familia website (**www.familia.org.uk**) includes information on the poll books and electoral registers held in public libraries in England, Scotland, Wales, Northern Ireland, the Irish Republic, the Isle of Man and the Channel Islands.

Up to 2002, registers of electors were open to view by members of the public, and were available for sale to companies, other organisations and individuals. In that year, however, the law was changed so that new registers would be published in two forms: full and edited registers.

The full register continues to list all those entitled to vote, but can only be inspected under supervision. The edited version of the register, however, omits those electors who have chosen not to appear in it. This is the version that is now available for sale and used to provide the information on the CDs and websites mentioned below.

The Federation of Family History Societies has published two booklets by Jeremy Gibson and Colin Rogers that will help you to find British electoral rolls:

Poll Books c1690-1872: A Directory to Holdings in Great Britain (3rd edition, 1994, ISBN 1 872094 85 6); *Electoral Registers since 1832; and Burgess Rolls* (2nd edition, 1990, ISBN 1 872094 10 4).

The British Library's holdings are listed in *Parliamentary Constituencies and their Registers since 1832* by Richard HA Cheffins (British Library, 1998, ISBN 0 7123 0844 X). The publication also lists the library's collection of burgess rolls and poll books.

Scotland
Scotland had its own parliament until 1707, when it was united with England as Great Britain. The situation before 1832 had been even less democratic in Scotland than in England and

NEWLY-APPOINTED COUNCILLOR (*at civic function, imperfectly acquainted with use of microphone*). "Hallo there! More champagne at this end, please."

Wales. The qualification for the county franchise had been 40 shillings a year in the 13th century, but an allowance for inflation had been built in, so that by the early 19th century, the qualifying amount had reached about £70 a year.

Of the Scottish burghs, Edinburgh returned a Member of Parliament (MP) of its own, who was elected by its corporation. Fourteen other MPs represented groups of burghs, with the corporation of each burgh in a group electing a single representative, who in turn elected the group's MP. There were fewer than 5,000 voters out of a total Scottish population of 2.3 million at the 1831 census.

The effect of the 1832 Representation of the People (Scotland) Act was similar to that of the RPA in England and Wales. The 1867 RPA had a Scottish equivalent in the following year, but in Scotland, occupiers of property in the counties were able to vote only when their rental was £14 a year or above (compared to £12 in England and Wales).

Otherwise, the extension of the parliamentary franchise in Scotland was similar to that in England and Wales. In Scotland, women first received the franchise for local burgh elections through the Householders of Scotland Act 1881, while they were able to vote in county elections from 1889 (1888 in England and Wales). In 1903, Scotland contained about 700,000 voters out of a population of just under 4.5 million according to the 1901 census.

Scotland had no poll books before 1832, but there

are printed books that list the c.3,000 Scottish voters county-by-county for the years 1788, 1790, 1811 and 1812. The Scottish Room at the Central Library and the National Library of Scotland (NLS), both in Edinburgh, hold all of these books, while the National Archives of Scotland (NAS), also in Edinburgh, and the Society of Genealogists, in London, hold that for 1788. The Institute of Historical Research at the University of London has a copy of the 1790 book.

Scottish poll books after 1832 are mostly in the NAS, while most of the Scottish registers of electors are held by the NLS. The NAS also has some registers of electors, as do local archives in Aberdeen, Dumfries, Dundee and Glasgow.

Ireland
Ireland had its own parliament from 1692 until 1801, when it became part of the new United Kingdom of Great Britain and Ireland. Only Protestants were allowed to vote between 1727 and 1793, after which Roman Catholics were enfranchised too.

The 1832 Reform Act had a similar effect to that in England and Wales, but with the county franchise being extended to £10 freeholders, copyholders and leaseholders for life or 60 years, as well as leaseholders with 14-year leases worth £20 a year. The later extensions of the franchise were similar to those for England and Wales. Like Scotland, by 1903, Ireland contained about 700,000 voters out of a population that had shrunk to just under 4.5 million (according to the 1901 census). The electorate in Ireland grew to just under two million as a result of the 1918 RPA.

There is a database index of lists of Irish freeholders, freemen and voters by county, city and borough (1234-1978) at the US-based ProGenealogists' website (**ireland.progenealogists.com/freeholdersdata.asp**). Searching this database gives you the location of the records (which include poll books and registers of electors), rather than their contents. Most of the records for the counties of Northern Ireland are held by the Public Record Office of Northern Ireland (in Belfast), and those for the counties of the Irish Republic are mainly in either the National Archives of Ireland or the National Library of Ireland (both in Dublin), with a few in local archives.

Electoral Rolls Online and on CD
Various poll books are available online, such as those for Barnsley 1835, Bedfordshire 1722 and 1784, Dorset 1807, Halifax 1835 and various other years, Liverpool 1832, Nottingham 1754, Wakefield 1865 and Westminster 1749. You can find many poll books, voters' lists, etc. through the UK section of the Census Finder website (**www.censusfinder.com/united_kingdom.htm**). In addition, you can use a search engine,

specifying the name of the area and 'poll book', etc.

The Public Record Office of Northern Ireland (PRONI) has put a searchable database of pre-1840 freeholders' records online at **www.proni.gov.uk/freeholders**. The records have been taken from freeholders' lists and registers for the Northern Ireland counties of Antrim, Armagh, (London)Derry, Down, Fermanagh and Tyrone, voters' lists for the cities of Belfast and (London)Derry, and poll books for Belfast, Armagh and Fermanagh, as well as Counties Cavan and Donegal in the Irish Republic.

Several poll books are available on CD from Archive CD Books (**www.rod-neep.co.uk**), including those for Bristol 1830, Newcastle 1777-80, Norfolk 1768 and Westmorland 1820. S&N Genealogy Supplies (**www.genealogysupplies.com**) sells poll books includes those for London and Westminster 1774, 1818 and 1841, Northumberland 1826, Suffolk 1710 and 1790, and Yorkshire 1741. In addition, the poll book for Norfolk 1817 is available from Stepping Stones (**www.steppingstones.co.uk**). Various family history societies have also published poll books on CD.

You can search the edited versions of the current register of electors for the entire UK on a pay-per-view basis at 192.com (**www.192.com**) and Tracesmart (**www.tracesmart.co.uk**).

St Andrews
Sadberge
County Durham

Researching Church of England Ministers
Peter Towey

In my researches into my own family tree, I found that I had several ancestors who were clergymen in the Church of England (also called the Anglican Church). In finding out more about them I realised just how much information there is available. Clergymen are one of the best-recorded professionals in England and Wales over the past 450 years or so.

Probably most English families have Anglican ministers in their family tree at some time in the last five centuries and they can lead you to unsuspected ancestry in the gentry or in some other part of the Country.

Since the Reformation, the Church has needed a constant source of educated clergymen to staff its parishes, provide chaplains to the army & navy, prisons, charities, colonies and noblemen, and even missionaries. Each of these men, because until very recently an Anglican clergyman had to be a man, had to be educated and ordained. Over the centuries vast amounts of paper records have been created and they are now at the service of every family historian. Also, unlike in the Roman Catholic Church, Anglican clergy were allowed, and even encouraged, to marry.

A career open to all.
Traditionally, the Church was considered an appropriate career for one of the younger sons of an aristocratic or gentry family; the eldest son inherited the estates and title if there was one, and other sons had to make their own way in the world. They tended to join the army, the navy or the church, depending on their personal inclinations. However, there were also many cases of the clever sons of farmers, craftsmen, shopkeepers or even labourers, who

caught the eye of the local clergyman or squire, won a scholarship to a university and found a career in the Church. There is a noticeable tendency for clergymen to marry daughters of other clergymen and for their sons to become clergymen too. This could well be because they felt the call to join the clergy but it probably helped that they knew how the Church system worked and had a clear idea of what the benefits of such a life were.

Rector, Vicar or Curate?
Like most professions the Church of England has its own jargon. Most of the terms it uses have specific meanings in the Church but they are not always clear to those outside. There are terms like clergyman, minister, parson and priest that can be used indiscriminately for ordained priests. Other terms in use have more specific meanings:
    Rector: a clergyman who has the right to all the tithes in his living;
    Vicar: a clergyman who only has the right to some of the tithes;
    Curate: an ordained clergyman without a living but who is an assistant to a vicar or rector or acts the minister for an absentee;
    Perpetual Curate: a clergyman who has been instituted to a living but is not entitled to tithes and is paid by the diocese. He has security of tenure unlike a curate.

Originally clergymen were distinguished from ordinary people in writing by having "clerk" placed after their name as in "John Smith, clerk,". This remained the usual method until the 17th, and 18th centuries when it gradually became common to call them eg "the Rev. John Smith"; "Rev." being short for Reverend. Nowadays this is the only usage but applies to all clergy not just Anglican , or even Christian, clergy.

There are many more specialist terms relating to aspects of the Church's role, some of which are explained below.

Researching Clergymen
If you have an Anglican clergyman in your family anywhere in the World in the last 150 years, the best source to use to obtain more details is Crockford's Clerical Directory which has been published since 1858. The entry will tell you what university or theological college they went to, when and by which bishop they were ordained and what livings (ie jobs) they had held with the dates. It does not give ages or places of birth or dates of death but those can often be supplied from other sources. Their entry would cease to appear in Crockford's when they died, so when you find the first edition in which he does not appear, you can be sure that he had died in the previous year. If he was educated at Oxford or Cambridge you can find his entry in the published lists of Old Boys ("Alumni") of those universities and that will tell you how old he was when he matriculated (i.e. qualified to enter the university) and his father's name and parish.

Before 1858, a similar publication called "The Clergy List" had been published since 1841. It was not as detailed as Crockford's at that period but also covers all ordained Anglican clergymen. Before 1841, though, there was no single source for Anglican clergymen. If they had attended Oxford or Cambridge universities, as I think many did, the published lists of Alumni are still the best sources but, if they were educated privately or abroad, you will not find them so easily. The Alumni lists are in most large reference libraries.

Before 1841
The main source for clergymen before 1841, other than the universities' Alumni lists, must be the parish records. Where a clergyman lived in and served his parish, he will appear in the parish registers and the administrative records, almost daily. You will find his signature there and possibly his comments about his parishioners. You should be able to find when he first took over in the parish and when he died or otherwise left and then you can look in the local Bishop's Registers to find the record of his and his successor's institutions. These will usually tell you where he had come from, if he had held a previous living, and whether he had died or moved elsewhere. The most useful source should be a reply to the bishop's questions sent to each parish regularly prior to his triennial "visitation" of the parishes in his diocese. The parish would be asked questions about the minister's education, how he conducts himself and whether he does his job properly. Where the churchwardens had fallen out with their minister, some of the replies could be revealing (but who should you believe?). These records will be among the bishop's records in the diocesan archives which are usually in the County Record Office.

Problems with curates
A major problem for research before 1841 is how to find out about curates. These were assistant clergymen who did not have a permanent living. Sometimes they assisted the incumbent minister who was also resident in the parish. In that case they may well be single young men and have a room in the vicarage or rent accommodation in the parish. They would be appointed by the minister and be paid a wage. Unlike the minister, they could be sacked without notice. Where the instituted minister held several livings, or just did not want to live in the parish, he could appoint a curate to live in the vicarage and effectively act as the minister. He, too, would be paid by the minister. Many such curates married and had families but might find their living removed if the minister died, wanted to take over himself, or just fell out with them. In such cases, it was difficult to find another parish at short notice and, while the bishop would often try to help, it could be a difficult time.

Appointment to a parish: the Advowson.
Curates could aspire to become a vicar or rector though it often depended on whether they knew the right people. The right to appoint ("institute") the minister to most Anglican parishes, the "advowson", was often held by a local gentry family, a bishop, a university or even another minister; those with that right were known as the "patron" of the living. These advowsons were real property and could be bought or sold and left by will. Books were published listing all the parishes in England and Wales and who the patron was. They also listed how much the tithes were worth so were helpful to clergymen who were looking for a living. If you wanted a living you could write to the patron explaining why you were a deserving case. Where such letters survive, they

can be very helpful in filling out the details of your ancestor's life. Often however, where the patron was an individual, there were relatives with a better claim.

Ordination papers.
If you could find when and by which bishop your ancestor was ordained ie admitted to holy orders, you should find in the bishop's ordination papers a copy of his baptism certificate and details of where he was educated. The records should be in the diocesan archives. With his baptism, you are back another generation to his parents. The difficulty here, especially before 1841, and if he did not attend Oxford or Cambridge Universities, is discovering who ordained him and when. This is a particular problem if he never rose above being a curate and if he moved about a lot from temporary living to living.

When, working back through your ancestry, you first find a clergyman ancestor, it is often in the record of the baptism or marriage of a child. If the clergyman was a curate then, you may be able to trace them backwards and forwards through the parish records and find when they first arrived in the parish and when they left. There may be helpful correspondence in the bishop's visitation records, in the diocesan archives, or in the patron's archives, wherever they may be. You may also find that the curate left a will which might be helpful. It might also be worth looking for the will of the vicar or rector of the parish, ie his employer, in case he was mentioned.

The Clergy of the Church of England Database 1540-1835
A very useful new source is now becoming available online: the Clergy of the Church of England database (CCEd). It will in due course include every ordained Anglican clergyman from 1540 to 1837, including where and by which bishop they were ordained, every living they held and when and where they died. When it is complete there will be no more problems with "lost" curates! The database is now at www.theclergydatabase.org.uk So far it covers seven dioceses but additional material is being added monthly and it is intended to cover all dioceses in England & Wales 1540-1835 in a year or two. Besides searchable databases of individuals and parishes there are (or will be) useful background and historical articles. And it is all free.

The Seventeenth Century
If you are lucky enough to be able to trace your ancestry back to the 17th century, there are very helpful published records of those clergymen who were persecuted and thrown out of their livings in the Civil War; both Royalist-leaning

clergy in the Commonwealth period in the 1640s and 1650s, and Puritans after the Restoration in 1660. "Walker Revised" is a biographical dictionary of Anglican clergy persecuted 1642-60 and "Calamy Revised" is a similar dictionary of those ejected after 1660. Both are available in most large reference libraries.

Many Anglican clergymen ejected in 1660 or later, formed non-conformist congregations in or near where they had been the vicar and so you may find that a non-conformist minister had previously been an Anglican and , if he was your ancestor, benefit from these sources. Similarly when Methodism was being founded in the 18th and early 19th centuries, many of the Methodist ministers were already ordained Anglican clergymen and you will be able to find their details in Anglican records.

Anglican Churches in Scotland, Wales & Ireland.
The Anglican Church in Scotland was rarely very large and is usually called the Episcopal Church of Scotland. It was only an established church for a short period in the late 17th century. Ireland and Wales both had established Anglican churches organised on the same lines as in England from the 16th century. The church in Ireland (north & south) was disestablished in 1869 and in Wales in 1920.

Diaries and Sermons
If you are really lucky you will find that your ancestor kept a diary or published his sermons. The Victorians relished a good meaty book of sermons and vast numbers were published then and earlier. A clergyman listed in Crockford's will have his published works listed there and

SHE. "They say the Vicar talks in his sleep."
HE. "Very likely. He talks in mine."

you can then see if you can find a copy in a second hand bookshop or the library. Diaries are even more personal and a surprising number written by clergymen have been published in recent years. Even if your ancestor had not written one, perhaps a clergyman living nearby or in a similar area has and you could learn a lot about your ancestor's way of life from it. Second hand bookshops and libraries are the places to look.

Useful Addresses;
Lambeth Palace Library, London, SE1 7JU. Holds complete runs of the Clergy List from 1841 and Crockford's from 1858 and will provide entries of individual clergymen by post. Please write but only for one or two at a time.

The Representative Church Body Library, Braemor Park, Churchtown, Dublin 14, Republic of Ireland. E-mail: library@ireland.anglican.org Holds substantial records, published and in manuscript, of Anglican clergymen in Ireland.

Diocesan Record Offices usually hold the records of the bishop and are usually combined with the relevant County Record Office. If you are unsure where the records are, contact your local Record Office and ask.

Theological Colleges were set up in the 19th century to train Anglican priests. Most have closed or are now more general colleges. Their records could be in the college still or be in local record offices. Lambeth Palace Library has very few such records. The records of St Bees, one of the more important colleges, are in Cumbria Record Office.
Websites:
Lambeth Palace Library, www.lambethpalacelibrary.org See the very

useful detailed article, "Biographical sources for Anglican clergy" on the website.

Mundus. A searchable database of missionaries working for organisations based in the UK. www.mundus.ac.uk Includes Anglican missionary organisations like the Society for the Propagation of the Gospel, but many, many more. A really useful site.

Further Reading:
"Alumni Cantabrigiensis: A biographical list of all known students, graduates and holders of office of the university of Cambridge, from the earliest times to 1900", Cambridge 1922-54. Available as a searchable database or as a CD from Ancestry.com.

"Alumni Oxoniensis. The members of the University of Oxford", two series 1500-1714 & 1715-1886, Oxford, 1891-2 & 1888. Available on two CD-ROMs from Archive CD Books.

"The Curate's Lot. The story of the unbeneficed English clergy", by A Tindall Hart, James Baker, 1970,

"A Country Parson. James Woodforde's Diary, 1759-1802", Century Publishing, London, 1985, ISBN0-7126-0730-7. There are many other editions of Parson Woodforde's diary. He was curate of various parishes in Somerset to 1774 and then rector of Weston Longueville, Norfolk.

"Victorian Village. The diaries of the Reverend John Coker Egerton of Burwash [Sussex] 1857-1888", edited by Roger Wells, Alan Sutton, 1992. ISBN 07509 0287 6 (paperback).

"Sources for Church of Ireland Clergy" by Raymond Refaussé, Genealogists' Magazine, Journal of the Society of Genealogists, Vol. 27, No. 6, June 2002.

Peter Towey is a Plymouth-based professional genealogist and author, specialising in Devon & Cornwall and German ancestry. He is currently writing a book on researching Anglican clergymen to be published by the Society of Genealogists later this year.

The House of Hanover and their Jewish Subjects

Doreen Berger

The fifteenth of May in the year 1800 was King George the Third's lucky day.

That morning he attended the field exercises of the Grenadier Battalions of the Guards. Volleys were fired. During one of these a ball cartridge was shot from the musket of one of the soldiers and struck Mr. Ongley, a Clerk for the Allotment Department of the Navy Office, who was standing only twenty three feet from the King.

That evening the theatre at Drury Lane was exceptionally crowded. Their Majesties had announced their intention of attending. The princesses came into their box first, followed by the Queen and then the King.

The audience had risen to receive and greet the royal family and clapped their hands and cheered enthusiastically. Just as His Majesty entered and was advancing to bow to the audience, an assassin, who had placed himself about the middle of the front row of the pit, raised his arm and fired a pistol which was levelled at the royal box.

The flash and the report caused an instant alarm through the house. When the audience saw His Majesty was unharmed, an outburst of joy broke out with loud exclamations of "Seize the villain! Shut all the doors."

David Moses Dyte had struck the arm of the assassin, Hadfield, while he was in the act of pulling the trigger.

By this time the curtain was drawn up and the stage was crowded by persons of all descriptions from behind the scenes. One gentleman who was standing next to the assassin immediately seized hold of him, and after a struggle, he was conveyed into the orchestra, where the pistol was wrenched from him. This pistol was given to one of the stage performers, who held it up for public view.

His Majesty had had two very fortunate escapes in one day.

The King was duly grateful and Mr. Dyte was asked what reward he wanted. He asked for and was given the patent of selling opera tickets, which was a monopoly at the royal disposal.

David Moses Dyte was appointed Purveyor of Pens and Quills to the Royal Household in 1820 and traded at 5 Bevis Marks in the City of London. The fifteenth of May was his lucky day as well.

The Great Synagogue in Duke's Place was one of the most important synagogues in London. The wardens of the Synagogue were both delighted and apprehensive to receive the following notice from one of their most important and esteemed members:

No: 27, Finsbury Square,
March 30 1809.
To the Gentlemen Parnassim of the Great Synagogue, Messrs. Samuel Joseph, Asher Goldsmid and Joseph Cohen.

Gentlemen:
Their Royal Highnesses the Dukes of Cambridge and Cumberland having signified to me their intention of visiting the Synagogue on Friday evening, the 14th of April next, pray give me leave to ask if it will be agreeable to you, gentlemen, to receive them on that day, which will oblige him who has the honour to subscribe himself,
Your most obedient and humble servant,
Abraham Goldsmid

Of course, there was no question of a refusal. New crimson curtains were especially presented for this wonderful occasion by Nathan Mayer Rothschild, the young financier. A special order of service was compiled, with verses composed for the great day. Copies of the order of service were even printed in silk. The royal brothers duly arrived at the half past six, accompanied by another of their brothers, the Duke of Sussex, in the carriage of their great friend, Abraham Goldsmid. Flowers were strewn in their path as they walked from their carriage by children of members of the Synagogue. One of these children later grew up to be Secretary to the congregation and would often tell the story of the part he played that evening. The princes entered at the end of the usual afternoon service and were greeted by a choir chanting the following verses:

Open wide the gates for the princely train
The Heav'n-blessed offspring of our King
Whilst our voices raise the emphatic strain
And God's service devout we sing.

There was a choral rendering of the usual

Prayer for the Royal Family, always loyally given at the end of services in all the metropolitan synagogues. This was followed by an ode written for the occasion:

Raise, raise the voice; let congregations sing
With elevated shout, long live the King.

The pulpit in the centre of the synagogue was covered with crimson and gold. The princes were shown to Egyptian chairs between the pulpit and the ark on a specially constructed platform. The Great Synagogue was illuminated with beautiful chandeliers.

The Chief Rabbi, Dr. Hirschell, wore a robe of white satin, given to him for this event by Mr. Abraham Goldsmid. When the Ark was opened to take out the Five Books of Moses the Princes were taken by Mr. Goldsmid to see the interior. The galleries were crowded with attractive women, as the Jewish custom was for women to sit separately from the men. After the service, the princes were invited to Mr. Goldsmid's mansion for an entertainment and grand concert. They drove to the mansion of Mr. Goldsmid at Roehampton, where a sumptuous entertainment was provided, which was followed by a grand concert. The occasion was never forgotten by those who were fortunate enough to be present and is always referred to by historians as a never to be forgotten day.

Doreen Berger is author of two important reference books: The Jewish Victorian: Genealogical Information from the Jewish Newspapers 1861-70 and 1871-80. Available from Robert Boyd Publications, 260 Colwell Drive, Witney, Oxfordshire OX8 7LW. Email: BOYDPUBS @ aol.com. These books contain all the anecdotes from the Anglo-Jewish newspapers of the period, including births, marriages and deaths.

If you have a Jewish ancestor and wish to find out more about your heritage please contact The Jewish Genealogical Society of Great Britain

Ancestors in the Kitchen 1760-1820
Prudence Bebb

If your three greats grandmother wanted to make a Yorkshire Goose Pie, she would take 'a large fat goose', split it down the back and bone it. She then boned a turkey and laid it inside the goose. After cleaning and stewing a hare, she pounded it with butter and pepper using a pestle and mortar; the result was spread inside the turkey. She made rich thick pastry to line a dish, placed the stuffed goose inside, added six woodcocks and, for good measure, a duck at each end. Then she covered it with a pastry lid and decorated that with vine leaves cut from extra pastry. The pie would be baked for four hours in a bread oven before gravy, made from the hare and beaten with half a pound of butter, was poured into it through a pie funnel. The word 'obesity'was not generally used.

If your Georgian ancestress belonged to 'the middling sort'(neither rich nor poor) she would supervise the kitchen but she would have domestic help below stairs. In the dining room she might sometimes carve the meat but not all ladies could carve well. Mrs Raffald wrote: 'Some people haggle meat so much, as not to be able to help half a dozen persons decently from a large tongue, or a sirloin of beef; and the dish goes away with the appearance of having been gnawed by dogs.'

Our unfortunate great-great-great-grandmothers had no food processors nor any electrical contrivances to ease their labour. Consequently some recipes (or receipts as they were called) seem rather daunting. In The

Experienced English Housekeeper, Elizabeth Raffald gives instructions to make a Rice Cake:'Take fifteen eggs, leave out half of the whites, beat them exceeding well near an hour with a whisk, then beat the yolks half an hour, put to your yolks ten ounces of loaf sugar sifted fine, beat it well in, then put in half a pound of rice flour, a little orange-water or brandy, the rinds of two lemons grated, then put in your whites, beat them all well together for a quarter of an hour, then put them in a hoop and set them in a quick oven for half an hour.' If your arm didn't feel like dropping off after that, you'd be lucky. Happily in many kitchens there would be a cook and a kitchen maid to assist the mistress and the 'young ladies', that is her daughters. In many homes family members, like Jane Austen, had to take a share of cooking but those who could afford enough staff would hardly enter the kitchen. Mrs Bennett was very offended when Mr Collins asked which of his fair cousins had cooked the dinner. 'Fifteen eggs' sounds rather a lot for the rice cake. Actually those hens that clucked in Georgian farmyards were smaller than ours and their eggs were similarly smaller; instead of large brown eggs, they produced small white ones. A Georgian egg cup looks miniature beside a modern one.

There was no rushing to Tesco for kiwi and mango; the fruits of summer and autumn had to be preserved for winter use. If there was a garret at the top of the house, apples would be stored there in rows with a space between each

fruit so that one bad apple did not make others go mouldy. Our ancestors made jams and jellies with fruit from their gardens and garths. To keep strawberry jam or redcurrant jelly through the winter, a piece of paper was dipped in brandy and then tied tightly round the top of the jar. No wonder jams were called 'preserves!' Those not needed before January or February were buried in the garden; in a severe winter, like 1813-14 there was a problem digging through the hard frozen ground to unearth them. Our Georgian ancestors had a low opinion of vegetables and would be astonished at the idea of having five portions a day of vegetables and fruit. Cabbage was their greatest abhorrence; they called leafy greens 'worts' and no lady would put them on her table. It is no wonder that they often had recourse to rhubarb pills, a remedy that even the Duke of Wellington took. Their main use for vegetables was to add colour to the table; a 'pretty dish' of peas was often placed at the corner of the table and might be balanced by another diagonally opposite to it.

One vegetable did gain their respect - asparagus, once called Sparrowgrass. Special small dishes were sold to enable each diner to have their own portion of the favoured asparagus. The little dish had sides but no ends so the asparagus spears lay neatly in the slightly fan-shaped container. Each person's dish could be placed beside another until a complete fan had been made if the hostess decided to use them to decorate the table centre.

Then, as now, people worked harder when they had guests staying. In a letter to her sister, Jane Austen wrote with relief, 'When you receive this, our guests will all be gone or going; and I shall be left to the comfortable disposal of my time, to ease my mind from the torments of rice puddings and apple dumplings...'We do not know what type of rice puddings Jane produced but, if she wanted plain ones suitable for children, she would soak the rice then leave it tied in a cloth to swell. Afterwards it was boiled with water and eaten with butter and sugar or milk. However, this boring nursery food might not have satisfied her guests. She may have made 'A Rich Rice Pudding.' After boiling the rice in water, this was augmented with four eggs, a quarter pint of cream, two

ounces of melted butter, four ounces of shredded suet, 12 ozs. of currants with brandy, peach-water, nutmeg and lemon peel. This rich mixture was put in a dish with pastry round the sides and bakes in the oven.

A Georgian kitchen was a place of warmth and appetizing smells; but it was not always very light. The kitchen was often in a basement with a little yard outside topped by railings to prevent anyone falling down into the paved area. Shafts of sunlight, managing to enter at the top of the kitchen window, and firelight flickering from the range, played on the copper utensils arranged on the dresser. In affluent households there would be a complete 'batterie de cuisine' which comprised gleaming copper jelly moulds, saucepans of every size and various fish kettles. A fish kettle was a copper vessel made in the shape of the creature which was to be cooked in it whether turbot, cod, plaice or other sort. In the cupboards at the bottom of the dresser were pastry cutters, rolling pins, sugar sifters, butter pats, colanders and all the impedimenta of good cooking. People, who had to be careful of their money, were recommended to buy two days' supply of fish as the extra amount made it cheaper. In refridgerless days this was rather risky advice but anyway meat was preferred to fish.

If a lady was carving, she would use a smaller carving knife and was adjured not to carve when a joint was placed some little distance from her 'as it gives an awkward appearance.' Very awkward if her silk or muslin gown was filled out at the back with a 'bum roll'. This was a pad attached at the waist; its name was patriotically changed to a Nelson in the year of Trafalgar. She would be bending forwards at a right angle, if the meat dish was too far away and this would certainly exaggerate the effect of her bum roll.

The main meat dish was in the centre of the table for artistic arrangement was very important.
Dinner came in two courses. The first was composed of a variety of fricasses, pies and roast meats but no one would eat everything. We can get a false impression of the stomachic capacity of our ancestors when we read a dinner menu; it looks as if there were at least twenty dishes to consume (more at a formal dinner) but in reality there were only two courses and it was considered polite to eat from the dish nearest to you. This was frustrating if you would have liked the Fricasse of Rabbits at the other end of the table and you felt obliged to eat the Neat's Tongue beside you. One could ask for something to be passed but it was definitely not 'the done thing'.. The first course usually contained two 'Removes', which might

be a tureen of soup and a large fish. When these had been consumed they left messy dishes which were removed to preserve the tasteful appearance of the table.

The second course comprised some more savoury dishes but included sweet ones as well. Tarts, jellies and creams made an appearance. Our ancestors loved syllabub and, of course, the gentlemen loved port afterwards. The ladies left the table to enjoy tea and gossip in the drawing room - a wise custom as the gentlemen's potations meant that they had to use the chamber pot which was discreetly kept in the sideboard cupboard.

Did everybody enjoy such a large dinner? Of course not. Many homes were simple cottages where the breadwinner earned just over £1 a week for agricultural labour. Bread, cheese and onions were the staple diet in the daytime and a cooking pot over the fire provided a potato stew at night with bacon added to it when there was some. Breakfast of oatmeal, ground at the local mill, and made into porridge, could keep a wage-earner going during his working morning. The variety of dishes on an affluent gentleman's dinner table would have astonished a poor labourer's family.
So would the leisurely consumption of breakfast. Many people had wiggs at this light meal. These got their name because they looked like an old gentleman's wig but they were really rather like sweet bread buns. After a late night, it was difficult to rise early so many ladies (and some gentlemen) did not try. Early rising men might go out riding or shooting before a breakfast of cold meats. Our Georgian ancestors were very fond of 'Catsups', which became 'Catchups' and ended as the Ketchups of today.

Much preserving was done by pickling. This had the advantage of producing colourful contents for the pickle dishes which were used as table decorations as well as being useful. The pickles were delicious when made at home but it was possible to buy pickles, possible but ill-advised. Purveyors of green pickles boiled the ingredients in brass or copper saucepans so that the verdigris would add more green to the colour. Mrs Raffald warned her readers: …'nothing ought to be avoided more than using brass or copper that is not well-tinned; but the best way, and the only caution I can give, is to be very particular in keeping the pickles from anything of that kind.' The best copper pans were lined with tin and I hope your ancestors used those because, if they didn't they may have been poisoned. Mrs Raffald's recipe adjures the cook to pour hot vinegar on the pickles as the safest method of getting a nice emerald colour. When cooled and put into a pot to keep for winter, a pig's bladder would be tied over the top to keep the pickle fresh. When it was wanted on the table, it would be poured into a dish shaped like a leaf.

If our ancestors needed to be careful with their money, they might read the advice in A New System of Domestic Cookery Formed Upon Principles of Economy and adapted to the Use of Private Families by a Lady. The Georgians liked long titles and the lady was Mrs Rundell whose husband was a silversmith in the firm of Rundell, Bridge and Rundell.

Mrs Rundell gave useful tips for thrifty housewives, reminding those who lived in the capital that many London shops gave a 5% discount if paid cash or 'ready money' as it was called. Tradesmen usually had apprentices who acted as errand boys to deliver the goods ordered. Mrs Rundell adjured her readers to keep a careful note of how much they paid the deliveryman. She gave hints about buying sugar which may seem strange today. Sugar was normally distributed in tall solid cones wrapped in dark blue sugar paper. The sugar had to be ground before it could be used so many people used a pestle and mortar to grind it to powder. This, Mrs Rundell said, was wasteful and it was better, after pounding it, to roll a bottle over it like a rolling pin and then sift it.

Our Georgian ancestors were familiar with many of the dishes which we eat, such as 'sponge cake' and muffins, but they worked at jobs which would overcome most modern cooks. They fed oysters to fatten them before using them in recipes. In those days oysters were plentiful and cheap so this is what you had to do: 'Put them into water, and wash them with a birch-besom till quite clean; then lay them bottom-downwards into a pan, sprinkle with flour or oatmeal and salt and cover with water. Do the same every day, and they will fatten. The water should be pretty salt'. If you used much tea or brandy in your kitchen, that would be expensive unless you knew all the right smugglers!

Fresh Fields and Pastures New
British Immigrants in South Africa
Rosemary Dixon-Smith

The second decade of the 19th century marked the beginning of the great era of British emigration to South Africa. Emigration from Britain to countries overseas was not solely a phenomenon of that century but it did reach its peak then and for most family historians researching South African ancestry this period is of particular significance.

There had been some arrivals during the First British Occupation of the Cape (1795-1803) – troops to defend the frontier and government officials to do the paper-work, as well as missionaries endeavouring to bring light to the Dark Continent – but these were not immigrants in the strict sense of the word and for many their sojourn in South Africa was relatively brief. Never more than a temporary military regime, this phase gave way to the short-lived Batavian Republic in 1803, followed in 1806 by the Second British Occupation. This time the British Government was there to stay. The Cape was formally ceded to Britain in 1814, and in 1820 about a thousand British families were sent out to settle, precariously, on the eastern frontier of the Colony.

This was the first major organized scheme to colonize British territory in South Africa. Others followed, and such groups are well-chronicled. If your ancestor was an 1820 Settler to the Cape, or a Byrne Settler to Natal in 1849-51, more information about him and his family is likely to be available.

Individual arrivals are less easy to trace. If an ancestor emigrated without government aid, paid for his own passage, and established

himself in whatever area of the country took his fancy or was appropriate for his particular occupation, his arrival may not have been a matter for record. Even if it was, failing a reasonably narrow date parameter or the name of the ship, the search is wide open. In such cases, it's often preferable to take deceased estate documentation as a starting point for research, working back from the ancestor's death, if it took place in South Africa, rather than beginning at his point of entry.

Some confusion exists about the terms 'emigrant' and 'immigrant'. One way of remembering the distinction is to think of an emigrant as a person 'exiting from' a country, while an immigrant was literally an 'in-migrant', coming into a country. Thus, each emigrant leaving Britain became an immigrant when he landed at his place of destination.

Early British Arrivals

For ancestors who were among British immigrants at the Cape in the period 1806-1844, the so-called 'Permissions to Remain' or 'Permissions to Leave', while not immigration records per se, are an excellent alternative. Any individual wishing to stay in the Colony had to obtain permission to do so. Usually, two other solid citizens would be named as securities, and the Governor would issue a permit to remain if the applicant undertook to behave in an orderly manner. Similarly, if an individual wished to leave the Colony, application had to be made, and permission would not be granted unless all debts and taxes owing had been paid by the applicant. The registers of these permits are held at Cape Town Archives Repository as part of the

Colonial Secretary's records (CO). While not all-inclusive, the names supplied are tantamount to a roll of British inhabitants of the area, and indications are given as to place of origin, occupation, and date of arrival in and departure from the Colony.

'British Residents at the Cape 1795-1819' by Peter Philip gives details of 4 800 persons taken from the Permissions and other Cape sources such as directories and newspapers. Included is a list of British regiments serving at the Cape from 1795-1819 and British ships of war at the Cape during the same period, with names of their commanders.

Bear in mind that usage of the term 'English' could also refer to those of Scottish, Welsh or Irish origin. Numerous Irishmen served as soldiers in the British Army in South Africa, many choosing to remain permanently after taking their discharge.

Material held at the Cape Town Archives Repository for the period of the First British Occupation includes Ship Arrivals 1795-1800, Reports on Strangers, and Letters of Permission 1795-1801 (BO).

Cape Immigration Schemes
Once British rule was firmly established at the Cape, the need arose to populate the territory, bringing in people with skills which would be useful in the Colony.

In 1817, Benjamin Moodie of Orkney brought 200 Scottish artisans of various trades – coopers, carpenters, masons, smiths, tanners and others - to the Cape. This venture was not entirely successful, a number of the immigrants absconding and preferring to live as outlaws rather than submit to the conditions of their employment. Some did make their permanent home at the Cape, marrying local Dutch girls. References to Moodie's indentured workers occur in the Philip's volume mentioned above.

There were other private schemes at this period. Henry Nourse, a merchant from London who had settled at the Cape, brought out a small group of Irish people as his employees in 1818 and suggested that a government scheme would be beneficial. The authorities had come to that conclusion themselves: by 1819 the Colony's eastern frontier was a headache, while in Britain there was large-scale unemployment and discontent. The panacea would be to provide sponsored immigration, relieving the burden at home, offering the hope of a brighter future to many, and last but not least, acquiring an inexpensive means of defending the frontier districts by installing a buffer strip of colonists.

This was the underlying purpose which led to the arrival of the 1820 Settlers. Their destination was Albany, a district formerly called, with good reason, the Zuurveld, and described by Lord Charles Somerset in rapturous but less than accurate terms as a 'verdant carpet' with fertile soil suitable for cultivation, cattle and pasture. It's said that as many as 90 000 applications were received from people who wished to hasten to this paradise. The statistic may be exaggerated, though it does indicate the level of response and the prevailing conditions in Britain. In the event, approximately 4 000 in 60 parties arrived on 21 ships between 9 April and the end of June 1820. They were doomed to bitter disappointment: crops failed and hostile tribes harried the frontier settlement. Some of the more persistent settlers adapted to the new environment, but many left their allotted land to try other occupations in towns. Despite initial trials, the impact of these British immigrants as a whole on the life and character of the Colony was deep and enduring and leaders in many fields emerged from their ranks.

The literature which has been published on this topic, as well as information online, may make recourse to original records unnecessary, though the latter exist, including those passenger lists which survive. At Cape Town Archives Repository are Permissions Granted to British Settlers 1820-1824 (CO 6056 volume 2) and a list of immigrants in the year 1820 (CO 6137-6138). There are also Letters Received from immigrants 1820-1825 (CO 136,158, 178, 201, 223 and 249).

A rewarding source is the Grahamstown Journal (its editor was Godlonton, himself an 1820 Settler) not only for fascinating nuggets of information about early families but for its Shipping News on the back page. The lists show name and type of vessel, captain's name, port of embarkation and sailing date, port of discharge and arrival date as well as passengers' names. The Grahamstown Journal 1832-1853 can be accessed at The National Archives, Kew (CO 53) and also held at TNA are, for example, the captain's log (ADM1/3543), the second master's log (ADM52/4655) and the muster roll (ADM37/6145) of the HMS Weymouth which carried 11 parties of 1820 Settlers from

Portsmouth to Algoa Bay.

Correspondence from leaders of the parties and others give details of setbacks encountered even before the immigrants set sail. Leaving everything familiar and going to a new and unknown land was a major undertaking and some settlers were indecisive, getting cold feet before departure, or having personal problems which required financial assistance or prevented them from embarking as planned. In December 1819, letters written from Portsmouth by Samuel James, who led the Westbury party, mention that his wife had been 'put to bed' with two children and he requests an extra allowance; later, that he is 'very sorey to be so trubelsome' but his twin sons were now three weeks old and 'are very likely to live' though their mother was unable to suckle them. The daunting prospect of a long voyage with tiny infants was one which faced many an immigrant family. In this case, James's wife and one of the twins died on board the Weymouth before the ship left Portsmouth, the other baby dying soon after they put to sea. Four more children of the party died during the voyage. Samuel James's correspondence is held at TNA Kew (CO 48).

The Settler Handbook, by M D Nash, is an in-depth study of the 1820 Settlers, compiled mainly from documents in the Cape Town Archives Repository and TNA Kew. The lists of parties, ships and individual names contained in the work, as well as the author's recent addenda and corrigenda to it, can be viewed at www.genealogyworld.net

Included in the 1820 scheme were Irish immigrants from the counties Cork, Wicklow and Armagh. Passenger lists are included in Nash's book. John Ingram, a merchant who had brought out a group from Cork in February 1820, returned to Ireland in 1823 to recruit a further large party of contract labourers, who came out to the Cape in the Barossa. This passenger list can be found in Esme Bull's volume mentioned further on in this article.

In 1826, a Select Committee of the House of Commons came into being, with the aim of investigating the concept of bulk emigration, its advantages and disadvantages – the latter highlighted by the 1820 Settler experience. Ten years later, the Colonial Land and Emigration Board was established, and its Commissioners regulated British emigration policies for the next five decades.

The Situation in Natal
By 1828, an overland route had opened up to Natal, and a small settlement had been founded there in 1824. The inhabitants were hunters and traders attempting to set up commerce with the Zulus and it would be about another twenty years before Natal acquired colonial status. During that period, dissatisfaction with the British government, and especially its abolition of slavery, led to an exodus of the Dutch community from the Cape – the Great Trek of the mid-1830s. Later, the republics of the Transvaal and Orange Free State were formed, but some Voortrekkers crossed the Drakensberg and established themselves in Natal, declaring their Republic of Natalia with its headquarters at Pietermaritzburg in 1838. Conflict with the British followed in 1842, the Dutch moved on, and Natal was annexed by Britain.

With a diminished white population in Natal in the wake of the trekkers' departure, the stage was set for further immigration. Economic depression in the Britain of the 'hungry forties' meant that many were looking for fresh fields and pastures new. Into this promising arena stepped Irish entrepreneur Joseph Byrne, who marketed the concept of emigration, and Natal as the ideal destination, to great effect.

Under the auspices of his Natal Emigration and Colonization Company, approximately 2 200 British settlers headed for the eastern shores of South Africa between 1849 and 1851. Details of the scheme were outlined in Byrne's pamphlet: 'Each adult will be provided with an intermediate passage, including provisions on a liberal dietary scale, for the sum of £19, or a steerage passage for £10; and on arrival in Natal have secured to him twenty acres of freehold land.' Passage monies were to be paid in advance, and a passenger had to take with him knife, fork, tablespoon, teaspoon, metal plate, a hook-pot, a mug and bedding. The scale of provisions for each class of passenger was stated.

Of Byrne's 20 ships, 15 sailed from London, three from Liverpool and two from Glasgow. All were sailing vessels, mostly barques or brigs of low tonnage. The smallest were the Wanderer (the first to arrive at Natal, on 12 May 1849) and the Sandwich (carrying only 12 passengers and arriving 27 July 1850); these vessels were 173 and 180 tons respectively. The largest were the former East Indiaman, the Minerva, 987 tons, and the Unicorn, 946 tons. They carried on average 150 settlers with their baggage, agricultural implements and other possessions. Some of the ships had schoolmasters and clergymen on board and under the Passenger Acts of 1849 each ship was obliged to carry a doctor. A number of children, elderly people and the sickly died on the long voyages of three or four months' duration, but most passengers arrived in good health and spirits. Despite Atlantic gales and baffling winds all the ships save two arrived safely at Port Natal, anchored in the roadstead and disembarked their passengers in boats. The two exceptions were the Minerva and the British Tar, both hit by sudden storms and wrecked shortly after arrival - the immigrants survived.

However, this was the beginning, rather than the end, of the Byrne Settlers' vicissitudes. Their story is eloquently told in A F Hattersley's numerous works, and passenger lists with details of each voyage can be found in J Clark's 'Natal Settler-Agent'. The mammoth project undertaken by Shelagh O'Byrne Spencer in her 'British Settlers in Natal: a Biographical Register 1824-1857' is as yet incomplete. Seven volumes arranged alphabetically by surname are currently available, so far up to 'G'. Even if your ancestor's biography has not yet appeared, the index to each section is well worth checking for incidental references to the name occurring elsewhere in the text.

W J Irons's Christian Emigration and Colonization Society piggy-backed on the Byrne scheme, about 400 Wesleyan Methodists being shipped on some of Byrne's vessels, and settling at Verulam on the Natal North Coast. Similarly, Byrne's ship the Lady Bruce carried a group of immigrants from the Duke of Buccleuch's estate in Hampshire. All these settlers are listed in Clark's book mentioned above.

Byrne's enterprise culminated in his financial ruin, but provided the impetus for other Natal initiatives in the 1850s. Among them were those of John Lidgett and Richard Hackett, bringing Wesleyans in the ships Hebrides, Herald, John Bright, Choice and Nile. The Haidee also brought Wesleyans, from Yorkshire, through the efforts of Henry Boast. Other immigrants arrived on the Ballangeich and Justina, arranged by George Murdoch and Richard Pelly. In 1856 Alexander McCorkindale's group of approximately 80 immigrants came out on the Portia. None of these schemes compared with Byrne's in the size of the settler parties involved.

Original lists for Byrne arrivals are held at Pietermaritzburg Archives Repository under the archives of the European Immigration Department (EI). Comprehensive Byrne passenger lists and others referred to above can be accessed at www.genealogyworld.net

Assisted Immigartion
During the 1830s and 1840s the Cape economy was in the doldrums, which placed limitations on governmental purse-strings as far as immigration was concerned. Individual travellers continued to arrive, bearing their own expenses, and private agents in England such as J S Christopher brought out some parties, though not in any great numbers. The serious shortage of labour in the Colony prompted further discussion on immigration sponsored by government in 1844, but logistics proved difficult. Some child immigrants and female groups arrived - single Irish women, in particular, to redress the balance of the large single male population. Thus, in 1849 the Emigration Philanthropic Society of England sent out 20 such women from the workhouses and the Association of Female Emigration embarked a group of 46 Irish women in 1851. The ship Lady Kennaway landed 157 Irish women at East London in November 1857. Cape Archives Repository holds the Lady Kennaway passenger list, which also includes some artisans and their families.

In the same year, the chronic labour problem at the Cape finally led to an Act of Parliament being passed setting aside funds for the recruitment of immigrants, with an agent in Britain to coordinate arrangements. Immigration Boards were established in Cape centres, and colonists were encouraged to apply for family overseas to come to South Africa. This initiative resulted in over 12 000 new settlers and was the largest government-aided immigration scheme set in place at the Cape. Of 32 ships chartered between 1857 and 1862 the smallest was the Aurifera and The Illustrated London News carried a report on her: 'On Monday the emigrants for Table Bay were embarked at Southampton on board the ship Aurifera, 235 tons, comprising 161 British and Irish emigrants, agricultural labourers, domestic servants and various trades; also 74 Germans – the latter chiefly vine-dressers and wine-makers, selected by Mr. Field, the Cape Emigration Commissioner.'

For immigrant ancestors who came to the Cape during this era, the best source is Esme Bull's 'Aided Immigration from Britain to South Africa 1857-1867', giving names of 12 000 passengers. Conditions on board, provisioning of food and fresh water, and the health hazards encountered, make illuminating reading. Sources used include the Archives of the Immigration Board, Cape Town (IBC), and Archives of the Secretary, Immigration Board, Port Elizabeth (PIB), both held at the Cape Town Archives Repository. Some lists appeared in the Cape Government Gazette and in newspapers.

In Natal, despite the fact that the initial flood of arrivals under the Byrne scheme dwindled and the discovery of gold in Australia tempted a few individuals away between 1852 and 1854 (some to return), the Colony retained its British flavour. Immigrants who had already settled invited family members or friends to follow in their footsteps. Government subsidies were offered as an incentive and this system developed with the efforts of agent Dr R J Mann in the 1860s, including the publication of his Guide to the Colony of Natal. The scheme certainly had advantages: the cheap, rather than free, passages provided, meant that respectable settlers weren't accepting charity and could pay back the government loan. Numbers were disappointing, however: from 1857-1862, of the approximately 2 500 people nominated by Natal settlers for passages, just over a thousand accepted the invitation. In 5 years, only 1 342 immigrants arrived in the 'Cinderella Colony'.

Efforts to attract people to Natal continued. The 1865 edition of the Natal Almanac and Yearly Directory published details of 'Public Aid to Immigrants', indicating that assisted passages in the Emigration Commissioners' ships could be obtained on guaranteeing to the Colonial Government the repayment of passage monies at the rate of £10 per statute adult, within twelve months after landing, and giving a pithy final comment on other colonies:

'Now that the tide of emigration from Great Britain is about turning from America in consequence of the long-continued war, and directing itself into other channels, we think that (the scheme) may be again advanced with benefit to the Colony. English people in general, if not the Scotch and Irish, have become convinced that there is no safety for life and property in the North American states; Canada has never been a resort for any large numbers of the poorer emigrating class; and the southern colonies are gradually becoming better known than formerly, and more highly appreciated.'

Assisted immigrants to Natal received grants of 50 acres of land and were conveyed to and settled upon their allotted property. Since the lands were generally at a great distance from the port where the immigrants disembarked, this was an important point. The voyage out from England averaged 65 days by sailing ship and 40 days by steamship. Private individuals who were well-heeled enough to travel first class to Natal

paid 35 guineas for a berth on a sailing ship, and £52 10s on a mail-steamer. Note the difference between these sums and the £10 passage of the aided immigrant scheme.

In 1879, the year of the Anglo-Zulu War, the Natal Land and Immigration Board reported a downturn in the number of incoming immigrants, 'owing doubtless to the disturbed state of South Africa'. Later in the year the number of arrivals rapidly increased to a monthly average of 31 souls, the total for the year being 287. Additionally, applications had been received for 340 more persons, of whom 72 had arrived up to mid-February 1880. J E Methley was sent to England to select about 40 families for agricultural settlement on land near Pietermaritzburg in 1880; this group became known as the Willowfountain settlers. The passenger list of the Nyanza which brought them to Natal can be found at www.genealogyworld.net and further information is available in the European Immigration Department records at Pietermaritzburg Archives Repository.

Walter Peace took over the reins as Natal immigration agent, and a news report of the arrival of the steamer African paints a typical 1880s scenario:

The Natal Mercury 19 May 1880:
'Arrival of the URMS African: Large Number of Immigrants. The URMS African arrived at the outer anchorage from England early on Thursday morning, after a very good voyage. She had on board 60 immigrants - 20 men and 10 women and children. The men are carpenters, blacksmiths, farm labourers, engineers, gardeners and joiners, and the women, housekeepers and domestic servants. We have little doubt that we have to thank Mr. Walter Peace, the acting immigration agent in London, for such a large and respectable class of immigrants as landed at the Point yesterday. Mr. Peace has this year been instrumental in sending out a total we believe of 200 immigrants. Early yesterday Mr. Reid of the Immigration Depot went out in the Union and boarded the African for the purpose of looking after those who were arriving here under the Immigration Act and in a short time the Union landed them safely on to the wharf. Some friends of the immigrants were present, but there were some more who found themselves on a foreign land without those who required their services being there to receive them. For such parties Mr. Reid had made preparations by having tents erected on the Market Square for their reception, and it speaks well for the friendship formed by this large body when we mention that in no instance was a poor stranger allowed to enter the tents; those who had found friends kindly looked after their less fortunate fellow passengers, and in a short time they were all distributed throughout the town in boarding-houses. They spoke highly of the treatment they received while coming out. An infant, aged a little over a year, died on the 18th of April. The names of the passengers will be found in our shipping column'.

By 1887 more than half of the white population of Natal, then totalling about 36 000 and predominantly English-speaking, were living in the two largest towns, Pietermaritzburg and Durban.

Military Arrivals

Throughout the era of British government in South Africa, there was a movement of troops into and out of the country. Some regiments spent years garrisoning forts or fighting in colonial wars such as the Cape Frontier Wars, the Anglo-Zulu War of 1879, and the Anglo-Boer Wars of 1881 and 1899-1902. Many British soldiers elected to remain in the colonies, producing South African families, and for these a search for deceased estate material may be the sensible approach. Tracing military arrivals isn't easy. Passenger lists sometimes identify officers, but the ordinary soldier is seldom named.

Rare exceptions do occur: men recruited in England for the Natal Mounted Police and who came to South Africa on ships such as the Kinfauns Castle in 1880 are individually named and these lists are in the European Immigration Department records at Pietermaritzburg Archives Repository.

Diamonds, Gold and Railways

By 1875, there was a relatively small European-descended population in South Africa of about 328 000. This had grown by 1911 to 1 276 000. A significant factor was the discovery of diamonds and gold, the lure of which led to an increase in the pace of immigration in the 1870s and 1880s. Men flocked to the diggings and mining towns sprang up overnight. At the same time, a network of railways was being developed, opening up new areas and improving communications. By 1896, the railway line between Durban and Johannesburg was completed, and the following year, Cape Town and Bulawayo were linked by rail. Contingents of British railway workers arrived, usually with their wives and families, brought out by the Government, on ships of the Union-Castle and other lines. Some passenger lists for platelayers engaged by Crown Agents for service on the Natal Government Railways, occur in registers of the European Immigration Department.

European Immigration Department Natal

For passenger arrivals at Natal from 1845 to about 1910, original registers are held in the Archives of the European Immigration Department (EI) at Pietermaritzburg Archives Repository. There is a surname index to the registers (not online) and a local South African researcher would be needed to check this, going to the original volumes if an entry is found, and providing a digital photograph or transcript. Alternatively, access the LDS (Mormon) Family Search site and, under the Family History Library Catalogue section, see the list of available films which can be ordered at LDS libraries.

The original Natal passenger registers are a valuable source, but the lists are far from all-inclusive at any period and, with the approach of the 20th century, factors such as increased volume of shipping, inconsistent record-keeping or lack of preservation of records, may militate against finding certain arrivals. A list of the volume numbers and relevant periods covered by the registers can be found at www.genealogyworld.net

Later Cape Sources

The Archives of the Secretary, Cape Town Chamber of Commerce (CC) at Cape Town Archives Repository contain registers of arrivals and departures of ships at Table Bay and Simon's Bay 1822-1917, as well as arrivals and departures at Algoa Bay 1946-1901. These registers give the name of the captain and sometimes the names of first class passengers.

Letters of Naturalization 1826-1902 and Applications for Letters of Naturalization 1865-1911 are held in the Archives of the Colonial Office (CO) at Cape Town Archives Respository, and can be an alternative to passenger lists. The Archives of the Secretary of Public Works (PWD) include Applications for Aided Immigration 1875-1889, Indexes of Applications 1878-1881 and Registers of Applications 1882-1902.

When searching for an ancestor on the South African National Archives index (NAAIRS) at www.national.archives.gov.za/ should a PIO file reference emerge, these documents are in the Archives of the Principal Immigration Officer, Cape Town, covering the period 1904-1967, and are informative. Passengers entering a South African port were required to complete a declaration form giving details such as name, age, birthplace, nationality, occupation, marital status, names of spouse and children, age and birthplace of spouse, reason for entering the country, port of embarkation and name of ship.

Newspaper Shipping Columns
Shipping columns in South African newspapers are not indexed, though the European Immigration index for Natal does include some passengers' names from The Natal Witness. Generally, a newspaper search isn't feasible unless some idea of date and the name of the ship are known, but these are usually precisely what the family historian is seeking. Passenger lists given in the press may be inaccurate, particularly where spelling is concerned. Most do not provide initials, just surnames. Frequently, first and possibly second class passengers are named, while '156 government immigrants' in the steerage are not. However, occasionally a separate list of the assisted immigrants may appear elsewhere in the same edition.

Mailing Lists
It's worth checking the South African Mailing Lists' archives for passenger lists or names of British immigrant ancestors. These topics crop up frequently in postings on the SOUTH-AFRICA, SOUTH-AFRICA IMMIGRANTS BRITISH and SOUTH-AFRICA EASTERN CAPE Mailing Lists. You may find someone else who is researching the same family or ship, which saves time. To access the Mailing List archives, go to http://listsearches.rootsweb.com/cgi-bin/listsearch.pl and enter the name of the Mailing List required. Search by year and keyword. There's no need to be a subscriber to access the archives, but should you want to subscribe and post your own messages, instructions for so doing can be found in the Beginners' Guide at www.genealogyworld.net

British Sources
For researching emigrants at the point of departure from Britain, Passenger Lists Outwards exist only from 1890-1960 (in BT 27 at The National Archives, Kew), previous lists having been destroyed by the Board of Trade in 1900. These give names of passengers leaving UK where the ship's eventual destination was a port outside Europe and the Mediterranean. Many of the registers are in a fragile condition and take time to search. There are no indexes and most lists are not in alphabetical order. The registers are arranged monthly by port of departure and to use them it's necessary to know an approximate date of departure and the port to have any hope of success. Some ports are known by different names, e.g. Queenstown refers to Cork.

Colonial Office Emigration Correspondence 1817-1896 (not only South Africa-related) is held at TNA in CO 384.

The Twentieth Century
Immigration to South Africa continued in the 20th century, after the Anglo-Boer War and particularly in the optimistic years following World War II. The Union-Castle Company Immigrant Service brought 28 000 British immigrants to South Africa between 1947 and 1949. But that's another story.

Useful Websites
www.national.archives.gov.za/
South African National Archives site including NAAIRS index
www.genealogyworld.net
All 1820 and Byrne Settler lists; miscellaneous passenger lists 1845-1890; Natal shipwrecks and maritime history; Guide to the European Immigration Index; Beginners' Guide to South African research
www.sagenealogy.co.za/
Cape passenger lists, wrecks and survivors
http://sa-passenger-list.za.net/
www.1820Settlers.com
www.familysearch.org LDS site; Family History Library Catalogue
www.union-castle-line.com/

Published Sources
Peter Philip, British Residents at the Cape 1795-1819 (David Philip, 1981)
M D Nash, A Settler Handbook (Chameleon Press, Cape Town 1987)
Esme Bull, Aided Immigration from Britain to South Africa 1857-1867 (HSRC Pretoria 1991)
S Spencer, British Settlers in Natal (University of Natal Press) 7 volumes
J Clark, Natal Settler Agent: the Career of John Moreland, Agent for the Byrne emigration scheme of 1849-1851 (A A Balkema 1972)
G B Dickason, Irish Settlers to the Cape: History of the Clanwilliam 1820 Settlers from Cork Harbour (Cape Town 1973)
G B Dickason, Cornish Immigrants to South Africa: The Cousin Jack's contribution to the development of mining and commerce 1820-1920 (Cape Town 1978)
A F Hattersley, The British Settlement of Natal: a study in imperial migration (Cambridge 1950)
A F Hattersley, Portrait of a Colony (Cambridge 1940)
A F Hattersley, More annals of Natal (London 1936)
A F Hattersley, Later annals of Natal (London 1938)

Housing the Working Classes
Doreen Hopwood

When the 1801 census was taken, the population of England and Wales was just over nine million but, by 1901, it had almost quadrupled to more than thirty-six million people. The problems of housing this increasing population were exacerbated by the exodus of people migrating from the countryside to the industrial towns and cities. During the 19th century the ratio for urban to rural populations saw a complete turnaround, from 74% rural/26% urban in 1801 to 28% rural/72% urban in 1891.

The rise of the textile trade – cotton in Lancashire and wool in Yorkshire – caused towns like Preston and Bradford to grow at an alarming rate. Row upon row of "two-up-two-down" terraced cottages spread along the roads leading to the mills where the people worked. Cheaply built and clustered together, the "ginnels" which ran between the rows were little more than open sewers.

Living conditions in the countryside were little better, especially where agricultural workers occupied tied cottages, which were provided by the employers. If they lost their job their home was also lost, and this was another contributory factor in the movement of people from rural areas to the towns.

Industrial towns witnessed the most rapid increase in population where places such as Manchester, Liverpool, Birmingham and Leeds multiplied as a result of natural increase and the influx of people from the neighbouring countryside, and further afield. This put enormous pressure on the limited amount of housing stock which was available at rents the workers could afford. Published in 1842, Edwin Chadwick's *Report on the Sanitary Conditions of the Towns*, followed by *The Condition of the Working Class in Britain* by Friedrich Engels in 1845 gave graphic descriptions of the appalling housing conditions workers had to endure. Large areas circling the business districts had become little more than slums as the wealthy residents moved out to the healthier outlying areas, which later developed into the suburbs. As their homes fell into dilapidation the land

Back to backs or "two-up, one-down" houses followed a similar design in industrial and manufacturing areas. They usually comprised a ground floor living room/scullery and two rooms above them, together with an attic space and cellar. In some towns, the cellars were also used as dwellings, and in the 1840s, it was estimated that over 35,000 people inhabited cellars in Liverpool. A social investigation carried out in Manchester found up to ten people living in one of these cellar rooms, which measured just ten feet square. Back-to-back houses developed from the practice of building one house directly onto the back of another, so that they shared the central wall which divided the properties. They were mirror images of each other, with the 'front' house opening into the street. Access to the back house, which faced into a central court (yard), was gained through an alley off the street. Such courts could contain as many as a dozen dwellings, with communal facilities being shared by the occupants of both the front and back houses. These included the privies (toilets), middens (dustbins) and wash houses, often with just a single water tap.

Badly built, insanitary and overcrowded, disease spread rapidly through the inhabitants of these courts. Chadwick's report brought the question of housing provision for the working classes under the auspices of Public Health. Legislation in 1858 gave local authorities the power to ban the erection of back-to-back houses, but many councils were slow to respond, and this type of housing was still being built in Leeds in the 1930s. In other towns the "tunnel-back" type of terraced house became prevalent and many survive today.

Medical Officers of Health were appointed by councils from the early 1870s, and they often found themselves in a quandary when it came to decisions about insanitary dwellings. They fully appreciated that these properties were one of the principal causes of the high mortality rates and illness. However, they were also aware that if they condemned the houses as unfit for human habitation, the persons they displaced would either become homeless, placed in the workhouse or, as usually happened, further add to the problem of overcrowding. The working class – especially the unskilled – needed to live close to their places of work, and for many, this meant near to the city centres where markets provided plenty of unskilled jobs. In these areas the population density was far higher than in the growing suburbs, and the difference in mortality rates echoed this trend. Under the Artisan's Dwelling Act of 1875, councils were empowered to acquire, demolish and redevelop

which surrounded these properties was leased or sold off to property developers. More interested in profit than the welfare of the people who were to live in these houses, the dwellings were built as quickly and as cheaply as possible. Demand always exceeded supply, so every piece of land was utilised, and by the mid-19th century, the "back-to-back" house was the most prevalent type of working class dwelling being built. Of all the new houses built in Nottingham in the 1840s, 75% were of the back-to-back type. The actual layout varied from place to place, depending upon the terrain and space available, but manufacturing towns, (such as Birmingham), where employment was still based in small workshops, rather than in large factories or mills, a collar of back-to-back houses ringed the city centre. Speculative builders were responsible for erecting hundreds of thousands of such houses, unhindered by any legal or building regulations, often locating them adjacent to works and stables. This non-interference on the part of national and local government led to the severe housing crises of the 20th century.

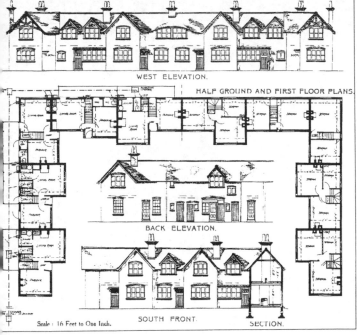

WEST ELEVATION.

HALF GROUND AND FIRST FLOOR PLANS.

BACK ELEVATION.

SOUTH FRONT.

SECTION.

Scale : 16 Feet to One Inch.

some industrialists and manufacturers adopted a paternalistic approach towards their workforce. Titus Salt was one of the pioneers who, when he built Saltaire in the West Riding of Yorkshire, provided schools and churches as well as houses for his employees. Similar estates were later built by Cadbury's at Bournville, at Port Sunlight by the Lever Brothers and by Rowntrees at York, although tenancies of these houses were not always restricted to employees. The houses at Bournville were built in blocks of two or three, rather than rows of terraces, and had private, not shared facilities, for their occupants.

By the beginning of the 20th century even the well built houses of the early 19th century were falling into disrepair as their landlords, whilst happy to collect the rents via their agents, were reluctant to carry out any necessary repairs or improvement to their properties. Local newspapers criticised these property owners, accusing them of "… moral murder… where typhus and premature death are thrown in with the rent".

Town planning began to be taken seriously with the passing of the National Housing and Town Planning Act of 1909 and the idea of building large estates on land adjoining the towns came to the fore.

Just as housing improvements began, the First World War broke out, thus disrupting building work. Lloyd George's election slogan "Homes fit for Heroes" set the tone for house building programmes of the post-war years. The newly formed Ministry of Construction drew up a new standard of housing for workers. This stated that minimum accommodation for a "normal" family should consist of three bedrooms, combined kitchen and living room, parlour with a separate bathroom, larder, scullery, coal store and inside toilet (or one approached under cover). "Normal families" generally meant two parents and their resident children and so most houses were built to cater for such households. Virtually no council provision was made for young couples, the elderly or single persons who were often forced to rent property from private landlords. The rents within the private sector were generally higher coupled with less secure tenancies. The Act made councils chief agents in housing provision with the aid of government subsidies, but subsidies were also given to private builders. Due to the shortages of both labour and materials following the First World War,

slum areas. Enquiries conducted before the Act was passed highlighted the appalling living conditions of the poorer inhabitants in towns. In Birmingham, Councillor Middlemore challenged the owners of these properties: "If he were compelled to stable some of his thorough-bred horses in the houses in question … he would enter a vigorous protest against such accommodation and communicate with the Royal Society for the Prevention of Cruelty to Animals". Analogies comparing housing for animals to those fit for humans were widespread – and it was not unusual to find that pig-stys, stables and barns were described as being the superior homes.

Pressure was now placed upon councils to provide affordable dwellings for the working classes, but many adopted the attitude of *laissez-faire* (or non-interference), hoping that the private sector would step in. However, new building regulations meant that quick profits could not longer be made, and the era of municipal (or council) house building started. This had first been tried as early as 1869 in Liverpool where blocks of flats and cottages were built in dockland. Some councils embarked on renovating existing properties (known as 'slum-patching') combined with new house building programmes. However, the types of housing they offered were only affordable by the skilled working classes, and did not address the problem of the poorer workers who often took in boarders and lodgers in order to meet the cost of their rent.

Despite the lack of attention from councils,

councils tried different methods of building houses – such as iron houses at Dudley, but most proved not to be cost-effective, in terms of building and maintenance costs.

The Wheatley Act of 1924 brought about a new era of council house building, making possible building on a large scale and at rents within the reach of working class tenants. The housing boom of the inter-war years saw the appearance of over 1,000,000 council houses and 2,500,000 privately built houses across the country. Birmingham City Council held a ceremony to celebrate the completion of its 40,000[th] council house in 1933, and at the start of the Second World War in 1939, about a third of the city's inhabitants were living in municipal housing built since 1919. Despite this huge building programme, many Medical Officers of Health were still concerned about overcrowding and the continuing deterioration of older properties.

In the 1930s the need to re-house people who lived in slum clearance areas quickly was paramount, and blocks of flats were deemed to be the remedy, especially as the amount of land available for new housing was decreasing. However this was not seen as an ideal alternative and not popular with the people they were intended for.

Many councils and developers obtained surrounding land for building, and the ideal of the Garden City was widely discussed. However, during this period only Welwyn Garden City became reality. Green field sites were transformed into large estates or satellite towns to serve cities like Manchester, Liverpool and Birmingham. The scale of some of the estates was enormous. With over nine thousand houses, Kingstanding (near Birmingham) became the largest estate in Europe. Despite the much higher living conditions, the creation of these suburban estates was not met with whole-hearted approval. Some occupants felt isolated in their new environment, partly caused by the physical separation of properties because of their gardens and green spaces. Initially the infrastructure was missing – too few schools, community halls and other public buildings and residents complained that goods in the shops on the estate were more expensive than where they had lived previously. Better housing also meant increased rents and whilst many of the people had been able to walk to work from their old homes, travelling expenses also had to be found. This meant that it was only the better-off working class who could afford to move to the new estates, although rent subsidies, introduced after the Second World War helped to relieve this imbalance. People took a pride not only in their own houses, but also in their estate and regular publications such as the

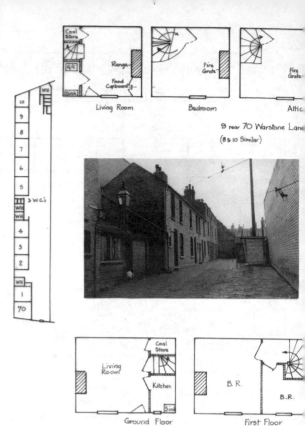

9 rear 70 Warstone Lane
(8 & 10 Similar)

Ground Floor   First Floor
6 rear 70 Warstone Lane
(5 & 7 Similar)

"Weoley Castle Community Journal" ran competitions for the best-kept garden and home-decorating tips.

Slum-clearance programmes involving the movement of large numbers of people from inner cities was well underway by the mid-1930s, with whole areas scheduled for re-development. Housing Departments of large councils found that residents of a street or court applied *en bloc* requesting that they could be allocated neighbouring properties on the new estates. Even though slum-clearance and house-building programmes ran concurrently, the action was still not keeping up with demand, and these fell victim to both bomb damage during the Second World War and the back-log of houses awaiting demolition, coupled with a shortage of manpower and materials. The slogan of the post-war era was "Building a New Britain" and it was estimated that in 1945 Liverpool needed 40,000 new houses to meet its needs. Temporary solutions were sought, such as prefabs and using former military camps, but it was partly the Conservative Party's promise to build 300,000 houses a year that helped them to regain power in the 1951 election. This promise was fulfilled and a contributory factor was the permission granted to local authorities to devote up to half of their subsidies to private builders. This heralded the move away from municipal housing to home ownership, with over 61% of the population falling into this category by 1985.

The "New Jerusalem" ideology focussed on town planning and the development of new towns under the auspices of Development Councils. By the 1960s there were twenty such towns with a total population of one and a half million people. A parliamentary investigation in 1967 confirmed that much of the older housing stock was continuing to deteriorate, and over two million houses were deemed unfit for habitation. A further three and a half million homes were in urgent need of repair and nearly two and a half million still had no indoor sanitation. Wholesale demolition was seen as the only solution and high-rise blocks of flats started to dominate the skylines. Their success was relatively short-lived (as were the buildings themselves) and these multi-storey blocks are now often demolished with a great sense of ceremony.

In many cities today, city-centre housing has come full circle. Streets which were considered to be the worst slums a hundred years ago have now become the sites of the "des-res" as canal-side developments demand high prices. Ironically some of these apartment buildings are built around a central area – not unlike the layouts of the courts they have replaced.

O For the Wings!

Audrey Buxton

As a genealogist I am interested in *all* families, high-born or low, rich or poor. It goes without saying that it is far easier to trace back if they owned land or property (or had dealings with the law), but there is one document sometimes available to us which solves many a puzzle. This document was made not only by the rich: as with marriage licences, it was used by men quite low down in the pecking order as a status symbol, even if they owned no more than a bed and a brass pot. Of course, I am talking about a "will".

Wills and Testaments can be wonderful things, proving a descent which until the moment you find it could only be educated guesswork. In families where children have married and stayed in the parish using traditional Christian names for their own children, a will is invaluable.

In the case of the Wing family of North Luffenham, the name Vincent survived for at least four hundred years. There are many Johns, Williams and Henrys on the "tree" too, but Vincent stands out as unusual together with one other: Tycho. Both these names appear generation on generation and thankfully there are not only many wills; the Wing family archives go much further.

I came across this name some years ago when searching for a marriage, and quickly realised the exceptional achievements of this distinguished family, who appear to have moved into Rutland from Great Ponton, near Grantham in Lincolnshire 'in the time of Henry VII', although their ancestors were said to 'come out of Wales'.

This last piece of information, as yet unsubstantiated by me, came from a printed pedigree held at the Leicestershire, Leicester and Rutland County Record Office in Wigston. Compiled in 1886 by Everard Green, FSA, 'from documents in the possession of William Wing of Market Overton, Esq.' it states that they bore Arms. Again, although these are detailed as a green and silver maunch (sleeve) between two gold wings, the Heralds' Visitations of Rutland of 1618-19 and 1681-82, which give all the proven pedigrees of titled Rutland families and lists those who failed to prove their right to be included, do not mention the Wings at all...

... which goes to show that the printed word can not always be relied upon, not even those written by a Fellow of the Royal Society!

Portrait of Tycho Wing

However, the Pedigree is an invaluable tool, particularly as early North Luffenham records give only the name of the child being baptised, with no mention of who the father is let alone the mother's Christian name.

The first Vincent was christened on 24 March 1587 (actually 1588, as until 1752 the church year ended at Lady Day, 25th March), and was buried there in 1660, aged 73. His first son, also Vincent, was christened on 11th April 1619, but in his case we know exactly when he was born - two days earlier, at 5.48 pm! Why such detail? Because his father was an astrologer. His son became a famous mathematician and astronomer, astrologer, surveyor, and author of seven treatises who even managed to forecast his own early death at 49, having made his will two weeks earlier. He left yet another Vincent to carry the baton who taught himself Latin, Greek, mathematics and astronomy, and went on to publish several books. These include an almanac, published by the Stationers' Company, a London Guild, which sold over 50,000 copies *per annum* - this between 1652 and 1671, at a time when few men could read, mark you.

His descendants continued to bring out updated volumes until 1805, via yet another Vincent; but here we must diverge from the North Luffenham branch and cross over the Great North Road to the hamlet of Pickworth, to where Vincent III's younger brother Moses had moved. Here, the printed pedigree becomes very confusing indeed, with lines squiggling not only downwards but over several pages. But at this point I had another enormous stroke of luck.

Part of the Normanton map by Tycho Wing

Today, it is becoming common amongst the rich to draw up pre-nuptial agreements, but like most things this is nothing new. Moses' son John, who had his country home in Pickworth, had married again following the death of his first wife, Anne Crispe. It was extremely important that her Marriage Portion should go to *her* son, and not to any child of his second wife's. Although evidently it was a complete pain to everybody that the original document had been lost "... *Then to the Right heires of the said John Wing for ever As in and by the said Settlement could the same be produced would more plainely appeare...*"[1]

It is our gain today that the replacement paper survives; a priceless document indeed. Without any doubt John, now Coroner for Rutland, editor of 'The Art of Surveying', editor of the Almanack for 1710, is the son of Moses; and *his* son John, of Pickworth but now also a Citizen of London and a member of the Haberdashers' Guild, is his eldest child and the only survivor of his first marriage to Ann Crispe, daughter of Thomas. (This fact could not have come from any other source known to me; the pedigree has John married to an "Anne, probably Mallory". The pedigree throws up another anomaly too, having John the younger as son of his half-uncle William which is clearly not true.)

John the Younger, now well established in London, married Sarah Hyfield at Great Casterton in 1687. Of their eight children Tycho, born in 1696, is the most famous. Where on earth did his name come from? Astronomy is the clue: he was named for Tycho Brahe, Astronomer Royal to the King of Denmark. Another brilliant man, Rutland's Tycho took on the mantle of his forbears and as well as editing the famous almanack, became Coroner for

Rutland as had his grandfather, taught arts and 'sciences mathematical' at Pickworth where he he may have been buried in April 1750, a month after he had visited his friend, the great William Stukeley, in London. He left a wife - Eleanor, daughter of Conyers Peach of Stoke Dry, and five children, having continued the family's astrological and astronomical tradition, whilst carrying on his main business as a surveyor, of which many references remain. Although several survive, he left no work more beautiful than an illustrated map of Normanton, Rutland, dated 1726 and now held at Lincoln Archives on behalf of Grimsthorpe Estate[2]. A portrait of him, painted by Vanderbank in 1731, hangs in the hall of the Stationers Company.

But were the Wings buried at Pickworth? The old church, said to have been ruined during the Battle of Losecoat Field (1470), was decayed by the end of the sixteenth century, when only the tower and spire were left standing. The latter was removed in 1728 and the tower followed four years later. According to Stukeley the stones were used to repair bridges in Wakerley (Northamptonshire) and Great Casterton. So when the Pickworth parish register records baptisms, burials and marriages just where did these take place? In the open air? A room in a nearby cottage? The new church was not built until 1821 (and not consecrated until 1824), thus there is a great gap. It is unthinkable that these important men had no memorial stones, yet there are no headstones showing above ground, nor stones remaining from the old church at Pickworth except one fourteenth century arch, which stands in the front garden of Clare Cottage, formerly a farmyard. As to the churchyard, what happened to the bones?

I understand that some years ago when British Telecom were installing a new pole, they found two skeletons in the hole they prepared. Were these from the Battle of Losecoat Field, or were they later, churchyard burials? One thing I have discovered is that Tycho's burial did not go unrecognised, although none of the stones in Great Casterton churchyard today bears his name. On page 111 of Thomas Blore's History of Rutland he tells how he visited in 1810 and

Part of the Normanton map by Tycho Wing

years" (his mother), and lastly: "In memory of Tycho Wing, Gentleman of Pickworth who died April ye 16th 1750 aged 54. Also Eleanor his wife, who died Jan. ye 16 1769 aged 63. On the outside of the chancel is a handsome memorial to their third son, another Vincent, who died on 29th July 1776 aged 48 years.

There are so many distinguished members of this prestigious family that it is hard to single out any others from the many who pursued brilliant careers. Some went into the church; a whole line of them became agents to the Duke of Bedford, whilst others took up Law or joined the Army. Without exception they appear to have succeeded at whatever they chose to do.

found several inscriptions: "Ad memoriam Johannis Wing de Pickworth, generosi, nuper Coranotoris pro Comitatu Rutlandiae, qui obit..." This is Tycho's grandfather, the Coroner; already the date of his death was indecipherable. And "Here lyeth the body of Sarah, the relict of Mr. John Wing, who departed this life August the 30th 1746, aged 78

William, who had assisted with the Pedigree which covers over 300 years (so it is not surprising that a few facts became confused) was born at Thornhaugh and succeeded to the estates of his cousin the Rev. John Hinman of Market Overton. An Attorney practising in Stamford, he was a Fellow of Clare College Cambridge, High Sheriff of Rutland in 1866, made a Justice of the Peace in 1868, deputy Chairman of Quarter and Petty Sessions at Oakham Castle from 1881, and a Governor of Archdeacon Johnson's Schools in Oakham and Uppingham. He died on Christmas Day 1887 aged 82 and claimed descent from King Edward I through twenty generations. Beat that if you can!

References
[1] The reference for the Marriage Portion document at Wigston is DE.5109/23 - Lease and Release, North Luffenham RUT 1722

[2.] The Normanton Map reference is: 3 ANC 5/104/1. 'ANC' stands for Ancaster. The Earl of Ancaster owned several properties in Rutland including the village of Empingham, of which Normanton was a hamlet. The map was drawn for Mr. Charles Tryon.

Audrey Buxton, is a Member of the Society of Genealogists and a Committee Member of Rutland Local History Society. Audrey is grateful for the guidance and assistance in her research to the staff at Leicestershire, Leicester and Rutland County Record Office, Long Street, Wigston Magna, particularly Adam Goodwin and the staff at Lincoln Archives, particularly Adrian Wilkinson, and the Grimsthorpe Estate.

The National Archives
John Wood
Customer Relationship Manager

the national archives

The National Archives (TNA) came into being in 2003 when the Public Record Office joined together with the Historical Manuscripts Commission. The National Archives, together with its sister organisation, The Family Records Centre, is the prime resource for all interested in genealogy as well as local, national or international history. TNA attracts nearly 200,000 visitors from around the world annually to its impressive facilities at Kew in Surrey. TNA has one of the largest archival collections in the world, spanning 1000 years of British history from Domesday book onwards and all together has over 9million documents available to all.

The TNA truly has something for everyone interested in family history. The gateway to the TNA is www.nationalarchives.gov.uk (see *Digital Genealogy*) The website portal allows you to plan your visit in advance, search our online catalogue before your visit, order documents in advance, arrange for copies of documents to be made and also pre register for a readers ticket. One of the popular features of the website is that it allows you to download an extensive range of research guides covering nearly 200 topics of interest to genealogists and historians. These replicate the guides available in the reading rooms at TNA.

A few good reasons why
all those interested in family history should visit TNA…over 3 million records of soldiers up to the end World War 1, over a million merchant seamen's records, ships passenger lists, naturalisation records, railway staff records, over a million royal navy service records, RAF (RFC) WRAF, WRENS, Royal Marines, Tithe and Valuation plus over 2 million more maps, divorce, change of name, court records, transportation to the colonies, manorial documents register……….the list of sources available is endless.

Onsite Facilities
The modern Reception area is located within the main entrance to TNA.

The ground floor houses:
- An extensive modern bookshop
- The free Museum featuring the treasures of TNA
- Comprehensive restaurant facilities
- Free cyber café
- Free cloakroom and locker facilities

When you arrive
Admission to TNA is free and, other than for coach parties and large groups, **no** advance booking is required. Researchers need to obtain a readers ticket at Reception to gain admission to the reading rooms. Registering to be a reader couldn't be easier either simply turn up during opening hours with proof of identity and register online or pre register in advance on www.nationalarchives.gov.uk The whole process takes only a few minutes. Suitable means of identification for British visitors are a driving licence, passport, cheque card or credit card. If you have come from abroad then bring your national identity card, driving licence or your passport. If you are still at school or college, aged 14 or over, please bring a letter on headed notepaper, signed by your teacher or tutor, together with some evidence of your age (for example a birth certificate).

There are rules on what you can and cannot take into the reading rooms. For instance, coats and any bags have to be left in the free cloakroom and lockers, pencils only are to be used, and only a notebook, notepad or transparent wallet. portable pc or digital camera can be taken into the reading rooms. Mobile phones and personal audio equipment are not allowed in the reading rooms at all. Full details can be found at www.nationalarchives.gov.uk/visit/whattobring.htm or our contact centre/ information line (see below) can help.

What you can do in the reading rooms
The newly refurbished first floor reading room facilities incorporate an information kiosk, specialist records advice desks and an extensive library and resource centre with browsery area. The main document reading room takes up a large part of the first floor, this is the point where documents that you order are delivered to your own reading room locker. It also has an excellent record copying centre, incorporating state of the art self-scanning facilities so that you can make a permanent copy of that important family history document. You can also use your own digital camera to take photographs of some documents, subject to conditions.

The most popular records, including a large number of military service records have been

made available in the self-service Microfilm Reading Room on the first floor where again there are extensive copying facilities.

Located on the 2nd floor is the Map and Large Document Reading Room. This is where documents too large to be produced elsewhere and where documents prior to 1688 are produced – not forgetting the millions of maps held at TNA.

IT facilities. Throughout the reading rooms are pc terminals where you can browse our catalogue as well as order documents and track your orders. The main document reading room and the ground floor areas are wi-fi enabled, allowing you to browse and use the majority our online facilities from your own PC. Throughout the building staff are on hand to help you make the most of your visit. Dedicated records experts are always hand in the reading rooms to give you expert knowledge as to how best pursue your research.

Opening hours

We are open 6 days a week throughout the year except bank and public holiday weekends and the annual stocktaking - usually in early December. Up to date details of opening times and closure dates are on the website at www.nationalarchives.gov.uk or can be checked with us direct via our contact centre/information line on 020 8876 3444. It is always advisable to call us before visiting for the latest information on opening times, records availability, travel conditions and events.

Please allow plenty of time for your visit to find, order, read and copy your documents. Document ordering times vary so it is best to consult the website or contact us to check the latest information.

Coach parties and groups

Coach parties are welcome to visit TNA. As space is limited for coaches all parties **must** be pre-booked. Bookings are taken up to 18 months in advance. All coach parties receive a dedicated orientation tour for newcomers in their party and are provided with an advance reader ticket registration service. To enquire about available dates and reserve your coach group booking telephone the coach party booking number or use the email facility listed below. **NB:** there is *no* access to the site for coaches that have not pre - booked.

Behind the scenes tours

TNA now offers visitors the chance to see 'behind the scenes' every Saturday that we are open. These free tours provide a terrific opportunity to see the inner workings of Britain's most important archive and will give you a thorough introduction to the collection and workings of TNA. On the tours you can see and touch some of Britain's most significant historical documents, learn how government

Naval Ancestors ?
©The National Archives

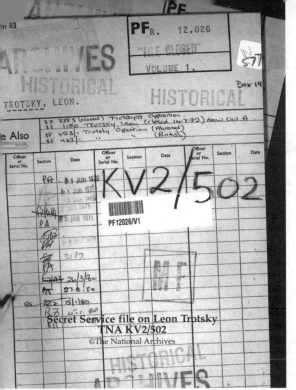

Secret Service file on Leon Trotsky
TNA KV2/502
©The National Archives

documents are selected for preservation and why some are not! As well as visiting our bomb proof, climate controlled storage facilities with over 100 miles of shelving. These immensely popular tours can *only* be booked in advance, you do so by calling the contact center/information line below, or via our website

Transport and Access

TNA is 200 yards level walk from Kew Gardens station, served by the District underground line and the Silverlink Metro rail service. Kew Bridge station is half a mile away. Local bus services such as the 65 and 391 run through Kew (http://origin.tfl.gov.uk/tfl/) and the new R68 bus service runs to the adjacent Kew Retail Park. Road access to the motorway system is good, though traffic in the area can be very heavy. Free parking is available on site. There are easy access facilities for those with disabilities, including a lift to all floors.

Essential contacts and information

The National Archives, Kew, Richmond, Surrey, TW9 4DU, United Kingdom Website and contact forms: www.nationalarchives.gov.uk

Telephone: 020 876 3444
Events: 020 8392 5202
Publications or
bookshop enquiries: 020 8392 5271
Coach party bookings: 020 8392 5393
Coach email (only) :
coaches@nationalarchives.gov.uk

The Enigma of Elizabeth
Joan Dexter

They don't make blankets in Witney any more…
They don't make blankets in Witney any more…

As I snuggle down in my bed of a chilly night, grateful for the cosy warmth of a light-weight goose-feather duvet, I feel guilty nonetheless and repeat to myself, *They don't make blankets in Witney any more*. Yet part of me knows it's foolish to feel remorse at not having a covering of *blankets*! After all, when in my innocence I bought the duvet, I had no reason to make any genealogical connection with Witney. The largest of the market towns in the Oxfordshire Cotswolds, I had never been there, and confess to my shame that I'd not heard of Early's Mill, which I was to learn had been renowned across the world for the traditional manufacture of blankets until its closure in 2002. Although the name Elizabeth Early had featured on my family tree as early as (pun intended!) the mid 1960s, I had been searching for her—not in Oxfordshire—but in Surrey, and failing that, in Kent. It came as quite a shock after about 35 years to discover that her origins could well lie north of the Thames!

Not that I'd searched relentlessly for more than three decades, of course. It's a pick-up-and-put-down situation. Hitting a brick wall for the umpteenth time, I would concentrate research upon somebody else to put flesh on *their* bones instead, always hoping against hope that when I returned to her, something would have crept out of the woodwork. I'd trawled various indexes and surname interest lists, posted queries on the Net and made contact with others researching the Early name, two as far away as Australia, hoping to forge a link. I'd advertised in a premier monthly genealogy magazine. Nothing—until one day at my local Family History Society meeting I idly browsed through a selection of books displayed by the speaker… The one which caught my attention had nothing to do with his talk! Serendipity?

But let us begin the story at the beginning. It concerns a collateral branch of my paternal family, and in order to set the scene we must go back to 1753 or thereabouts, when the brothers Henry and John Dinsdale quitted their home in Bedale in Yorkshire's North Riding, to make the long journey south by stage coach along the Great North Road. Why? Well, London's streets were paved with gold, were they not? Hard-working young men would have more chance to make their fortunes in the capital than in a sleepy little northern market town. Besides,

The Blanket Hall *in the High Street at Witney, Oxfordshire, built in 1721. To ensure the high quality for which Witney was famous, every blanket woven in and around the town had to be taken there to be measured and weighed. On the front of the building is an unusual one-handed clock.*
(Photograph taken by the author, June 2005.)

John had good reason to flee and put the miles between him and his troubles. Having fathered an illegitimate daughter, he left his father and his cousin to pick up the pieces, they signing the Bastardy Bond, thereby agreeing to pay the Churchwardens and Overseers of Bedale 'Forty pounds at Eight pence a week'. That whole unfortunate episode must have been very embarrassing for the family who were well-known and highly respected in the district, John's father (John the innkeeper) having even been one of the town's Overseers himself not long since.

MARRIAGES solemnized in the Parish of *Saint Mary Newington* in the County of *Surrey* in the Year 18*20*

John Durham
Bachelor of *this* Parish

and *Elizabeth Mary Hutchinson*
Spinster a Minor of *this* Parish

were married in this *Church* by *Banns* with Consent of
her Mother this *eighteenth* Day of
July in the Year One-thousand eight hundred and *twenty*
By me *Geo. C. S. Young M. A. Curate*

This Marriage was solemnized between us *{ John Durham Elizabeth Mary Hutchinson }*

In the Presence of *{ Izabella Ann Turner The Mark X of James Woodroff }*

No. 334.

Henry William Dinsdale
Widower of *this* Parish

and *Elizabeth Early*
Spinster of *this* Parish

were married in this *Church* by *Licence* with Consent of
this *eighteenth* Day of
July in the Year One thousand eight hundred and *twenty*
By me *Geo. C. S. Young M. A. Curate*

This Marriage was solemnized between us *{ H. W. Dinsdale Elizabeth Early }*

In the Presence of *{ A Fitch W. Holbrook }*

No. 335.

John Tait
Widower of *this* Parish

and *Frances Matthews*
Widow of *this* Parish

were married in this *Church* by *Banns* with Consent of
this *nineteenth* Day of
July in the Year One thousand eight hundred and *twenty*
By me *Geo. C. S. Young M. A. Curate*

This Marriage was solemnized between us *{ The Mark X of John Tait The Mark X of Frances Matthews }*

In the Presence of *{ W. Williams J. Mason }*

No. 336.

Parish Register marriage of Henry William Dinsdale and Elizabeth Early

It is not with John and his descendants but with Henry and *his* descendants that my tale evolves. Henry settled in the London parish of St Andrew, Holborn, John choosing Lambeth in Surrey, and so it was perhaps through his brother that Henry met Catherine Twycross, the woman who became his wife at the marriage ceremony in her home parish of Battersea, Surrey, in January 1761.

Henry Dinsdale was a haberdasher. In order to trade, he obtained his Freedom of the City later that same year, but not through the auspices of the Worshipful Company of Haberdashers, choosing instead the Worshipful Company of Musicians, whose fees would be less than those of the more eminent Livery Companies. (In the latter half of the eighteenth century, the Musicians' Company had thrown open membership to all comers, becoming essentially a non-musical body, ceasing to take an interest in the Art or Science to which it was dedicated. Between 1743 and 1769, of the 700 Freemen admitted to the Company, only 19 are described as Musicians.)

As the years passed, Henry's business prospered. By 1772, established as a wholesale and retail haberdasher, glover and milliner at No. 28 Holborn, some indication of the quality of his wares and the regard in which they were held can be gleaned from the fact that he received an order from the explorer and naturalist Joseph Banks (later, *Sir* Joseph) in connection with Captain James Cook's second Pacific Voyage in H.M. Ships 'Resolution' and 'Adventure'. (The 18th century was the Great Age of Scientific Discovery and Cook was the greatest leader of exploratory expeditions, particularly in the Pacific Ocean. His third voyage culminated in his death in the Sandwich Islands, since re-named Hawaii, where he was killed—and eaten—in 1799 by the previously friendly natives.) On 22 March 1772, Henry Dinsdale, from 'No. 28 Holborn, The Acorn opposite Leather Lane', made out and signed an invoice, decorated with an acorn in the top left-hand corner, to 'Mr. Banks' for '12 dozen Superior fine Plume feathers @ 3/9 and 117 yards of pink Persian @ 19d, total value £11.10s.3d'. It is believed that these items were for trading purposes with the natives, it being assumed that the Plume feathers would be peacocks' feathers and the Persian would be some kind of fabric, possibly silk.

Henry's business continued to be successful, and by the time he made his will towards the end of 1784 he was able to provide handsomely for his wife and three surviving children, with enough to spare for other relations and friends.

Catherine's will reads as the will of a well-to-do widow, but probate tells a different story, her *'Goods, Chattels and Credits not amounting in value to £600'*. Nearly a decade had elapsed between these dates, and the money she had intended to leave had in those intervening years largely been lavished upon two of her children. Indeed, the will makes clear that much had *already* been handed to her son Henry William Dinsdale and his sister Sarah Vyvyan. Henry William had needed financial assistance to keep afloat the haberdashery business inherited from his father; Sarah's husband Abel Vyvyan had needed financial assistance in his advancement in the service of the Honourable East India Company, and after his premature death in China, Sarah was left a widow with young children to support.

Henry William Dinsdale, the only surviving son of Henry and Catherine, born in 1763 and baptised at St. Andrew, Holborn, holds the distinction of being the first member of my family to be given two Christian names. At the age of 22 he was named in the list of Freemen of the Company of Musicians by patrimony, and less than a year later admitted to the Freedom of the City. He continued the business

The church of St Mary at Cogges, Oxfordshire, with its unusual 14th century 'candle-shaped' square and octagonal tower. (Photograph taken by the author, June 2005.)

of his inheritance, being documented throughout a run of London Directories: from 1802 as a Dutch merchant (i.e. specialising in the importation of goods from the Netherlands) at Queen Street, Cheapside, soon adding linen and cotton yarn to his activities and moving to 59 Bread Street. By 1810 he was a warehouseman selling linen and cotton yarn only, presumably owing to the War when goods from the Continent were almost impossible to get, while trade in linen and cotton yarn was flourishing owing to the difficulty in obtaining any silk. In 1815 he was a wholesale haberdasher and this business continued under the name of W.H.(sic) Dinsdale, glover, hosier and haberdasher until his death in the summer of 1831.

But I am going over my tale. Whilst living in Battersea, Surrey, he had married in 1789 at Cogges in Oxfordshire. I suspect that he travelled for his business in the counties surrounding the capital. (His son, in his turn, *certainly* did.) This would be how Henry William came to meet his bride Elizabeth Luckett. According to the Marriage Licence Bond she was the 19 year old daughter of William Luckett of Cogges.

Concentrating my attentions upon the name *Dinsdale*, it did not occur to me that I might learn more about them if I were to investigate Elizabeth's *Luckett* background, not until the afternoon, years later, when I idly picked up

that book from amongst the display at the Family History Society meeting. In any case, the publication date of the 'Index to the Probate Records of Oxfordshire 1733-1857 and the Oxfordshire Peculiars 1547-1856' was *after* the date when I had obtained the Bond, and so not available to me to have followed up straightaway. To idly while away the minutes until I needed to resume my seat, I looked—as one does—for any surnames of interest. No Dinsdale. That wasn't unexpected. But there were Lucketts a-plenty, 22 in fact, including a couple *at Cogges*, one of these being a William, blanket weaver by trade, and the date could indicate Elizabeth's father. The second Cogges entry was for an Elizabeth, a widow. William's widow perhaps? Curiosity overcame me and I quickly scribbled down the details of the book and the two relevant wills.

Nothing ventured nothing gained: back at home that evening I sent to Oxford's record office and within a short time the postman delivered my purchases. Both wills were easy to read, lengthy and informative, and as I had suspected, those of a man and his widow. Turning first to the detail in William's, he and Elizabeth had three daughters, spinsters Ann and Martha Luckett, and a married daughter Elizabeth about whom William had written, 'Whereas I have at different times advanced and paid to my eldest Daughter Elizabeth the Wife of Henry William Dinsdale of Maiden Lane Cheapside London Gentleman before and

Parish Register copy of the baptism of Henry Earley Dinsdale.

since her Marriage with him the sum of Eight hundred pounds and upwards…' *My Henry William!* Not only had he borrowed from his mother to keep the haberdashery business afloat but also from his father-in-law. My attention was also caught by the name of one of the executors, *John Early*. That Early connection in this context was particularly exciting—for reasons which will become clear in a short while. John's relationship to William's wife Elizabeth was not given, but I set to wondering if they could be brother and sister [they were]. Elizabeth Luckett survived her husband by 14 years, appointing as sole executor her *nephew Edward Early* of Hailey in the parish of Witney, blanket weaver.

Around this time, the Public Record Office at Kew (now The National Archives) began to put online the P.C.C. Will index to 1858, and I was able to download the will of the spinster Ann Luckett and read, 'I give & Bequeath to my sister Elizabeth Dinsdale wife [of] Henry Dinsdale of Bread Street'… and 'my cousin John Early of Witney'… So Elizabeth Luckett must *surely* have been born Elizabeth Early?

Indeed, she was: a clutch of Early wills proved in Oxford included that of John Early of Witney 1706-1796, blanket weaver, in which on 30 July

1794 he had included the words, 'my Daughter Elizabeth Luckett Widow'.

These wills I supplemented with five fascinating out-of-print books purchased via the Internet, books by Richard Early and Alfred Plummer, from which my erstwhile ignorance of the various intermarried blanket making families of Witney was remedied. The Early pedigree I had begun to construct blossomed overnight.

Here I must explain precisely why I had been so excited to learn that my Henry William Dinsdale had an Elizabeth née Early as a mother-in-law. Incredible as it may appear, he also had one as a daughter-in-law! In fact, to complicate matters still further, even more astonishingly it appeared as if he'd had *two* of them for daughters-in-law. What a coil!

Henry William Dinsdale and Elizabeth née Luckett had seven children, but only the second of these, the single son, need concern us here. He was also named Henry William, and so for the sake of clarity I always think of the two of them, father and son, as Henry William the Elder and Henry William the Younger.

Henry William the Younger, born in Holborn on 18 January 1792, followed in his father's footsteps by trading as a traveller, glover, hosier, haberdasher and warehouseman, and becoming a Citizen and Musician. But much of that was in the future. When still a few weeks short of his majority, he fathered a son, born in the parish of St. Saviour, Southwark, Surrey, on 2 November 1812. My solitary reference to the child's mother is at the baptism on 10 March 1813 in the adjoining parish of St. Mary, Lambeth. The baby was named Henry Earley Dinsdale, with his mother's name clearly written in the register as Elizabeth Earley. What is not so clear is whether 'Earley' is her second Christian name or her maiden surname, but from comparison with others on the same page it appears to be the former, and thus the baby legitimate. Henry William is described as a 'Traveller' of 'Kennington', obviously a commercial traveller for his father's haberdashery business. No marriage has surfaced, perhaps due to Henry William's roving occupation; doubtless for the same reason, no burial has been found for Elizabeth.

In due course, Henry William married again. There is no doubt this time as to the circumstances. His bride Elizabeth Early herself applied personally for the Marriage Licence from the Faculty Office of the Archbishop of Canterbury on 17 July 1820, signing her name in exceptionally strong and clear handwriting, and stating that she was 'of the parish of St.

Mary, Newington, Surrey, spinster, of the age of twenty-one years and upwards, and intendeth to marry with Henry William Dinsdale of the same parish, a widower'. The couple married the following day at St. Mary, Newington.

Was he *really* a widower? Did he have one wife *or two*? General opinion, garnered over the years, doubts that a man could marry two women of the same name and that there must only have been one Elizabeth Earl(e)y, whom he married when their child was seven and a half, and that he was described as a widower simply to avoid embarrassment. Perhaps. Certainly he would have been very young to have married before his son was born, but why wait so long afterwards? But if there were two wives, may not they have been related to one another in some way? Men in that strata of society often only had opportunity to marry women known to their own family: perhaps the daughter of one of father's Livery Company associates, or a neighbour or relative. Families tended to perpetuate Christian names and so the two Elizabeths could well have been cousins of some degree. The name Elizabeth Early isn't all that uncommon in the London area. In the I.G.I. for Surrey, I counted 46 female Early entries of whom 7 are Elizabeth. Likewise for Kent, there are 31 of whom 5 are Elizabeth. To those who still find it difficult to believe there could be two women of the same name, I can but state that there is no shadow of doubt about my 7 x great-grandfather Henry Dinsdale marrying firstly Elizabeth Crow and secondly Beatrice Crow. Even more unusual is the pedigree of an American friend whose 4 x and 5 x great grandparents are both named William Merryweather and Isobel née Pearson, this situation having arisen simply due to the families perpetuating the same Christian names, and then in the next generation two first cousins marrying. Truth is ever stranger than fiction.

And so I think it is possible. But I simply do not know. Whereas the burial of the first wife wouldn't solve the problem of her identity, it would at least solve the mystery of 'one wife or two?'. If I could find the burial of the second and learn her age, that might provide a clue. But although she must have died somewhere in the London area, I believe between 20 November 1835 and the beginning of Civil Registration on 1 July 1837—such a small window of time!—I haven't found her. As anyone with ancestors in the London area will know, research there can be a nightmare without the additional minefield of a nomadic lifestyle throughout the surrounding counties. Further evidence of that trekking came two years and two months after their July 1820 marriage when Henry William the Younger and

Elizabeth had a son, born and baptised in Hutton, Essex.

Setting aside for the moment the riddle of 'one wife or two?', I reason there has to be a family connection between the elder Henry William's mother-in-law and his daughter-in-law. Otherwise it beggars belief. The same Christian name and surname cropping up together more than once within so short a period surely cannot be mere co-incidence? I suspect that two sisters of the younger Henry William Dinsdale had marriages 'arranged' by the girls' parents. What more natural than that this is what happened here? But on the other hand, if I assume that the younger Elizabeth Early is related to her namesake of two generations previous, might I be setting about climbing somebody else's family tree? Are the Witney blanket makers a red herring for the wife/wives of Henry William the Younger? Yet still I keep coming across other 'co-incidences'. That will of Ann Luckett, spinster sister of Elizabeth Dinsdale, revealed that although she lived in Witney, she had a 'leasehold house in Newington Butts in the County of Surrey', so another cross-country link. Plummer's book shows the paths of the Early blanket makers and my Dinsdales crossing on occasions: part of a letter headed 'London, 20th Decr. 1814' from 'John Early jun., to his father and Brother' [John and Edward] reads, 'If you come by the light Gloucester I will meet you at Dinsdales in the morn.' An extract from the Order Book of 'John Early, Junr. & Co' shows an order dated '1825 July 27. H.W. Dinsdale' for '3 horse Cloths. full size and dark colours.'

So Elizabeth continues to elude me, continues to keep me awake at night wondering. Did you come from Oxfordshire, Elizabeth? Or Surrey? You're surely not one of those Irish Earlys, are you? No, that would be too fanciful. Speak to me, please! *Who are you?*

Readers may be interested to learn that although it wasn't quite 'Rags to rags in three generations', the haberdashery business begun by Henry Dinsdale from Bedale foundered with the death of Henry William the Younger. *His* son Henry Earl(e)y Dinsdale became a chemist, was imprisoned for debt and involved in a £10,000 jewellery robbery. But that's another story!

If you have enjoyed Joan's article, you may enjoy her book about the long search for her family. **'Blood's Thicker Than Water'** *is available from Mrs J. Dexter, Maplebeck House, Maplebeck, Newark, Notts, NG22 0BS, price £12. 80 incl p&p.*

Pit Voices - *Yorkshire Miners Remember*

Brian Elliott

My interest in oral history began in the 1970s when I used short extracts from conversations with old people so as to illustrate particular points in local history articles and also for use when I was tutoring classes. By the mid-1980s I had started researching my family history so it made sense to tape-record some of the older family members, most of them coming from mining backgrounds. I soon found out that it was easy to get led in the wrong direction but I am so glad that I did carry out the interviews. Eventually, in 2003, a commission by Wharncliffe Books of Barnsley gave me the opportunity to conduct a series of interviews with former coalminers in preparation for the book *Yorkshire Mining Veterans*. This involved completing transcripts from (mostly) digitally-recorded interviews lasting from 30 to 80 minutes. I was also keen to make available extracts from recordings, under the theme of *Pit Voices* on cd. All my original recordings are to be lodged at the National Mining Museum for England, at the former Caphouse Colliery site. Although a relatively small project, *Pit Voices* now includes over 50 recordings, the interviewees ranging in age from 52 to 104.

The virtual destruction of the British coalmining industry in the wake of the 1984-85 miners' strike has underlined the importance of recording mining memories. At the time of writing (September 2005) UK Coal has announced the imminent 'mothballing' of Rossington Colliery, near Doncaster. Following the closure of the Selby complex in 2004 and the more recent end of coal production at Hatfield Main and probably Harworth we are left with just two deep mines in Yorkshire: Maltby, near Rotherham and Kellingley at Pontefract. In my home own of Barnsley, once the epicentre of the old Yorkshire coalfield, a solitary headstock marks the site of Barnsley Main Colliery but there is little else that so obviously reminds younger people of our mining heritage. Big pits that have been a part of communities over several generations have been obliterated from the local landscape. Colliery sites in the Doncaster area, at Bentley, Brodsworth and Hickleton each supported workforces of in exceess of 3,000, well within living memory. Although many of the physical remains of the mining industry have been lost there continues to be a rich, almost untouched source of information available from former miners and their families. But of course the amount of oral information gets less as time progresses. During the short life of this small project one in four of the miners interviewed have died.

The following extracts are taken from edited versions of transcripts taken from my book *Yorkshire Mining Veterans*, published by Wharncliffe Books, 2005.

On a mild November Sunday morning in 2003 I attended the annual service held in Arksey Cemetery, near Doncaster, in remembrance of the Bentley Colliery disaster of 1931 when an explosion in the North East District resulted in the deaths of 45 men. It was the worst Yorkshire disaster since Cadeby Main in 1912 when 88 men and boys were killed and was exceeded in 1936 when the Wharncliffe Woodmoor explosion claimed 58 lives. Always a moving occasion, the ceremony also marked the 25th anniversary of a paddy train accident at Bentley which resulted in 7 fatalities, in 1978. Tommy Henwood (born 1911) was a special guest,

Tommy Henwood (wearing cap) prepares to lay a wreath at Arksey Cemetery in memory of the Bentley Colliery disaster victims

Tommy Henwood (centre) with some of his former mining friends, Bentley Miners' Welfare Park.

laying a wreath in honour of his former work mates who had died 72 years earlier. I subsequently interviewed Tommy in one of his local clubs, Bentley Miners' Welfare. He provided me with a remarkable first-hand account of the immediate aftermath of the explosion when he worked as a volunteer pony driver, taking sandbags to the damaged workings and helping with the grim task of the recovery of bodies. He spoke to me as though the accident had occurred yesterday and with great emotion. Tommy was a colourful local character who enjoyed a game of snooker or dominoes. I always enjoyed meeting him in the club. Sadly, he died in October 2004, probably the last eyewitness of the 1931 disaster. A story that Tommy loved to tell concerned a memorable occasion when he was working naked, alongside his father. Underground temperatures on faces in deep pits such as Bentley could reach 40 C, making working conditions almost unbearable. A deputy instructed Tom to make himself decent as a VIP lady visitor was due any minute. Despite a threatened 'when tha gets home' warning from his father, young Tom refused to put his shorts back on. Along came *Mr* McClusky, the colliery manager (note the emphasis) but once again Tommy declined to dress, insisting that this was the way he worked on a regular basis. After

Stan Potter (right) and his friend Dick Amos tramming a tub on the pit-top at Bullcliffe Wood Colliery c.1980

recovering from shock, the lady mayor, obviously a down-to-earth Yorkshire lass, unpeeled her long gloves and felt his shorts, which were suspended, dripping wet, by his lamp. With a mixture of curiosity and amazement, she wrung them out, sweat pouring onto the ground. Tommy's recollections and stories can not be found in any of the official records but his testimony will now serve as a valuable source for future generations.

I met Stanley Potter (b.1922) for the first time at the revived Yorkshire Miners' Gala, held in Locke Park, Barnsley, on 1 May 2004. The first 13 years of Stan's 45-years in mining included short spells at 13 pits prior to getting married and starting at Bullcliffe Wood Colliery, near West Bretton where he worked until retirement due to occupational ill-health. In 1937, when he was sixteen, the prospect of better pay attracted him to a small drift mine called Guider Bottom near Hoyland Swaine. This was in the days when a collier could employ a young labourer to fill coal into tubs and push or 'tram' them from the working face towards the pit bottom or, in the case of a 'day-hole', to the drift entrance. Stan had had some experience of tramming at Woolley, a relatively modern deep mine, but conditions at small pits were more primitive. In fact the work was more like nineteenth-century mining. Here is Stan's recollections of his first day at Guider:

It [the pay] was five bob a day which I thought was a fortune. I soon found out what tramming was like. First, he [the collier] told me to get some clay out of the bankside near the pit entrance and to keep working it with my hands, like plasticine, spitting on it and getting it going. Then he said, "Here's your candle lad". The colliers had to buy their own candles. We went down and into the pass-by and he uncoupled a tub and started tramming it, to show me what to do. The candle was stuck in the clay and placed on the tub. On the Main Level, about 5 foot high, it was OK but when it came to going up the Low [Gate] it was only a yard high and fairly steep. He pushed it up OK and told me how to drop it off at the end of the rails, leaving a little gap to allow for coal to be thrown into the tub. When the tub was filled he put a locker [temporary break] in the back wheel, lifted it on the rail and pushed it along…it looked easy to do. He then said, "Reight, you take the tub back." Well, it did not work too well for me. I could not push the tub like he did. I tried using my head against it as I had not got enough strength in my arms and had not got his technique…and the tub kept jolting over the sleepers. My clogs hit them [the sleepers] and my back kept hitting the roof. When I got to the end of the gate [underground roadway] my back was streaming with blood, all along the vertebrae. I wore a pair of clogs, a

ramming a tub on a low roadway c.1900. Note the lad's candle, placed on a lip of the tub, near his left-hand.

pair of tramming drawers and was stripped to the waist…and a cloth cap…I earned thirty bob [£1.50] for six days, big money for a kid. Later, when I was in the kitchen getting washed my mother came to wash my back and noticed the torn flesh. She said "Oh Stanley, what a mess. You can't go there again." I told her that I had to as I had told my father that I could do the job. Young pride! I stuck it and got used to keeping my back down and trammed like he did.

Stanley Potter is the only former miner that I have interviewed who worked using candles for light. Before nationalisation (1947) shallow so-called gas-free pits were still allowed to use this form of a light, a throw back to the early years of mining. 'Trammer's scab' was once a well known local term for a common occupational ailment. Stan had a passionate interest in mining history and despite his poor health, allowed me to see him on many occasions. He was thrilled at being part of the *Pit Voices* project, attended a couple of presentations and looked forward to seeing my book in print. Sadly, Stan died in April 2005.

In the course of our lives we may come across a person who is influential to us, someone who we greatly admire and respect. Some of our former teachers and work colleagues may come to mind. For me, it was a retired coalminer, Arthur Clayton, who I met for the first time when I was a student in the late 1960s. Arthur had worked for 52 years, principally underground at Rockingham Colliery, and was a noted local historian, in fact one of the most able that I have ever met. Born in 1901, he was able to recall the dreadful year of 1912 when miners were on strike for a minimum wage and when Cadeby Colliery exploded. He also knew several of the men who were killed in the terrible cage disaster at Wharncliffe Silkstone in 1914. In this extract, recorded when he was 99 years old, Arthur remembered his first day working at Hoyland Silkstone Colliery when he was thirteen:

I went call on a Catholic lad called Joe Brennan. He was a few months older than me. We walked

Stan Potter on a visit to Hay Royd Colliery, near Denby Dale, a small private drift mine still in production.

to the pit for the afternoon shift and he left me. He went up a ladder and disappeared in a cloud of steam…We did not report to anyone but had signed on. I got into this place [the screens] and it wanted John Milton to describe it because it was Miltonic! It was dim and dusty and noisy. There was a big belt, really iron plates, which went round an hexagonal thing and at the end there were some mechanical riddles…bump, bump, pump…you couldn't see for the dust…a boy stood at the bottom of the riddle. He had a rake and would spread it along the belt and there were boys on either side, picking dirt out and throwing it over their shoulders to a place at the back where there was a trap door leading to the wagons. A little Irish man was in charge. When you were dreaming he would shout "I will cut your liver out and put it back and swear I never touched yer".

After a while Arthur managed to escape from the pit-top screens getting a job in the check office, probably, he told me, because his father was a deputy at the same pit. When aged 14 he went underground for the first time, having moved to Rockingham:

I think I was too young to feel frightened. We had a steam winder. You could feel it pulsating and all us boys said that when you got half-way down it felt as though you were coming up. My first job was lamp-carrying, getting four safety lamps from the lamp room on the surface and taking them down the pit, walking a long way…with lots of other boys and men. If some colliers 'lost their lamp' [light was extinguished] I had to swap them. They frequently went out,

Arthur Clayton. Arthur, who died aged 101 in 2002, was honoured with a BEM in 1988 for 'services 'to English Heritage

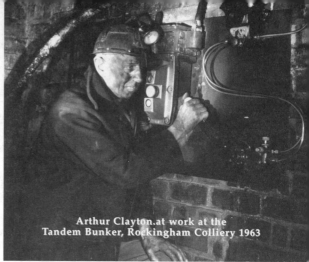

Arthur Clayton.at work at the Tandem Bunker, Rockingham Colliery 1963

just a jerk might do it. Sometimes I fell down and they all went out and sometimes big lads would clout you and take the book off you and write all sorts in it. I did this for a few weeks and then went pony driving. All the new lads had Dan because he ruled himself. He was a small pony and would do anything. There was a bad one called Snap. It used to stand and kick, breaking all its gears. A shaft fitted round the pony, with a chain on this thing that fitted onto the truck and you dropped this long pin through that coupled …on a rare occasions boys were killed when it jerked out and they fell and the trucks ran over them. You would sit behind the pony, like a drayman…keeping your head down…

Pony driving was a common subject recalled by many of the miners. Tommy Hart, aged 100, recalled working with ponies at a small mine called Warren House pit, situated at Upper Haugh, near Rotherham:

There were 36 ponies there. Some were named after First World War battles such as Verdun. They were well looked after. They would walk on their own into the stables and go into their

stalls. It was unbelievable…Sometimes they could be awkward but I never got kicked. I remember riding them. I got on top of the pony and laid down so that my head was below the pony's head [to avoid catching the roof] but you got a clip around the ear [if you were caught].

George Rawson, now aged 92, recalled his pony driving experiences when he was a lad of fourteen, working at Monckton Colliery, near Barnsley:

George Rawson had 48 years mining experience, starting work on the pit-top screen at Wharncliffe Woodmoor 4 & 5 pit at the age of fourteen. Laterly, he worked as a deputy and overman at Redbrook (Dodworth) Colliery, near Barnsley.

I walked out to the stables where *Mr* Silcock was in charge. He was very keen and really did look after the horses…at the end of the shift he would examine them to make sure there were no cuts, bumps or bruises. We put their collar on and their harness or gears which were hung in the pass-by. The chain…about six foot long, was hooked onto the tubs. My pony was called Midget. It was the smallest in the pit but I was only small too, about 5 feet 2 inches. It was well behaved and intelligent but would not stand when you put its gears on. Sometimes ponies would catch their backs on the roof so the deputy would send repair men to dint [lower] the roadway. If we rode ponies we got into

Tommy Hart celebrated his 100th birthday in 2005

trouble. Every so far down the roadways there were manholes where you could go for safety. The stableman might hide there, with a brush and a bucket of whitewash so that when we rode past we were splashed so there was no excuse when we got to the pit bottom. You got a telling-off or even fined.

Several of the miners interviewed progressed to become officials at a young age, the change from working alongside mates and old miners and then being responsible for their safety and deployment was never easy. A typical case was that of Tommy Emms, aged 93, who worked for almost 50 years at one of Doncaster's biggest pits, Yorkshire Main:

By the age of 20 I had already got a lot of mining

Sidney Cutts was a popular and respected deputy at Manvers Main.

Tom Emms, 93-year old, still lives a stone's throw away from the site of Yorkshire Main, at Edlington, near Doncaster, where he spent his entire working life from the age of fourteen.

ground most shifts, often on his hands and knees. He worked out that he had crawled over 3,000 miles in his mining life.

Ted Lunness, 78, has had a highly successful career in the mining industry, starting as a boy trammer and pony driver at Barnburgh. After serving as an official at Kilnhurst he returned to Barnburgh as under-manager and, still in his twenties, was appointed to the new post of substitute-manager, covering for absent managers as and when required. At the age of 30 he became manager of a large colliery soon to undergo modernisation: Cortonwood. Ted recalled with great feeling what it was like to be manager there in 1961, long before mobile telephones, when four of his men suffocated in

experience but I was kept on the haulage until I was 22 and then one of the managers came round and told me that he was looking for officials. I was asked if I would consider being a deputy. I had not done well at school but I was told that I would be taught how to go on. I went to Edlington night school and Doncaster Tech for the examination which I passed. I was 27 or 28. I had a lot of respect when I was a deputy. I always asked the men questions and that's the way I got on – learning their ways and they learning my ways. I had 45 men to look after on a shift. I set the men off, with my book, front rippers, tailgate rippers, men putting packs in, men boring holes, cutter men and so on.

Sidney Cutts, 86, a Manvers Main deputy from his mid-twenties, certainly appreciated the amount of responsibility he had, and also the essential need to have the respect of 'his men':

Some deputies were bullies but I let the men know that I was one of them not the upper crust. I would help a man if he was behind with his work, especially the old ones. I was well liked by the men as I did not believe in pushing them.

Sid told me that he covered a great deal of

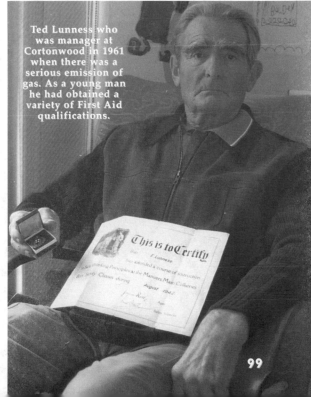

Ted Lunness who was manager at Cortonwood in 1961 when there was a serious emission of gas. As a young man he had obtained a variety of First Aid qualifications.

99

the Silkstone Seam:

It happened on a Monday. I went to work for eight in the morning as usual, and came home about five, had my meal, when the phone rang. It was the under-manager of the Silkstone, Jack Hunter, a wonderful man. He informed me that there had been an emission of gas and all the roadways were full of methane. The rescue teams were sent for but, unfortunately for me, my boss, the group manager, the area deputy production manager and the production manager had gone to a meeting and were not available. I rang Joe Ford, the neighbouring group manager. He, and Fred Steel, the manager at Manvers, came over to assist me. I informed the inspectorate, the police and the press soon got to know. We got the ambulance and rescue men organised as soon as possible. Jack Hunter managed to communicate with some men in the return gate, telling them to turn the compressed air on and to huddle down on the floor. This must have saved their lives…I did not return home until 4 pm the following day. Then my boss rang me at home and instructed me to go back to the pit, to be interviewed by the BBC for the *Six O'Clock News*. I refused as I was exhausted after more than 36 hours at work.

Cadeby miner Eric Crabtree (73) served for 25 years in the mines rescue service until compulsory retirement at 45. He was part of the Cadeby rescue team called to the emergency at Cortonwood in 1961:

We went underground about 12.30 pm, wearing breathing apparatus. There was a lot of gas, even in the airlock at Number 2 shaft on the surface. None of the bodies had come out. The Cortonwood rescue team had done a survey first. We retrieved one body, a big chap found dead on a Panza chain. The seam was only 2 foot 6 inches

high, so it took two hours to get him off. There were some more dead bodies further away but we had used up most of our Proto oxygen. We stayed at the fresh air base on standby until another team took us off. It was 8 am when we came out.

Bernard Goddard (1917-2005) started work as a lad of fourteen on the screens at Grange Colliery, near Rotherham. After a few months he was working underground but quickly developed managerial ambitions:

I wore clogs, short trousers, an old jacket and a scarf. My first job was opening the ventilation doors to allow the tubs on the main and tail haulage roads to proceed. On my third shift I accidentally knocked out my flame lamp and had to use my spare…but the deputy took my spare for a collier to use on the face, leaving me in the dark for several hours, having to listen for the sound of the approaching tubs. When the manager came round everybody stood to attention and I said to myself, rightly or wrongly, that if I was to stop in mining then I would try for the top job…I was determined to push myself.

Bernard overcame several handicaps deliberately placed in his way and, with Grange's manager, John Ernest Longden, as his guide and mentor he gained experience in a variety of underground jobs whilst also studying for mining qualifications. By his early twenties he was an official, telling me that a good deputy was 'a man who knows his job and who does not resort to obscene language to express himself' and was 'someone who led by example.' He soon became an under-manager at Grange, at just 23, the youngest in Yorkshire. His next appointment was even more remarkable. He was successful in his

Eric Crabtree (2nd right) emerges from Cortonwood Colliery with the Cadeby Rescue Team in 1961.

Bernard Goddard a mining veteran with almost 60 year experience, from screens lad to mines inspector, manager and consultant.

experience. I attended many fatal inquests, major explosions, inrushes of water and small fires and was at the first prosecution of the NCB by the Ministry. I carried my gear in the back of the car all the time. Like a bloodhound I was off to the pit [whenever an incident was reported] and was usually the first inspector on the scene.

Frustrated by the lack of further promotion prospects, Bernard took the unusual step of returning to mine management, back in South Yorkshire, as manager of Rockingham Colliery. He subsequently held a variety of senior posts latterly as Director of Mining Environment, based in London and Doncaster. He was chief spokesperson for the NCB when Britain joined the European Iron and Steel Community, visiting many countries. After his retirement from the Coal Board Bernard worked for ten years as a mining consultant. His boyhood ambitions had not only been achieved but exceeded in a remarkable career spanning almost 60 years.

application to be an inspector of mines, having obtained the necessary qualifications, taken an examination and impressed a rigorous interview panel. He was 31 years old, and now Britain's youngest mines inspector, serving the important Northumberland and Durham region:

> I went around all the pits…and did reports every day. I got a reprimand once because I was not taking enough holidays! It was a great

Bernard Goddard at Thorpe Colliery, near Rotherham, in 1958.

Many of the miners talked about strikes. I will never forget my interview with Mick Carter (1943-2004), the former NUM delegate at Cortonwood Colliery who was understandably 'in the news' during the 1984-85 dispute. It was the unexpected closure announcement of his pit that is generally regarded as the spark that ignited the year-long dispute. Despite his ill health Mick was again in demand during the spring of 2004 with newspaper, radio and television reporters keen to record his memories and afterthoughts for 20th anniversary features. Here are Mick's comments about the that historic closure announcement:

Then it happened – at Cortonwood. It could have been Wath or any pit of the 206 and the result would have been the bloody same. It was not a case of being left wing. It was the way it was done. I had been in a meeting with the [Cortonwood] manager on the Thursday. A new face was almost ready to go into production…on 12 March. We were sorting the final manpower list. We were full of hope…I stopped at the pit for half an hour or so and when I was walking up the pit lane Arnie Young, our area agent, came down in his car and honked his horn at me. I walked back and he was stood outside the Union office. That's when he told me. He had just come from a quarterly meeting of the Area, with news that we were shutting on 5 April…on economic grounds. What do you do? You are on an overtime ban, based on any [further] action on closures on economic grounds. Safety factors were involved in previous closures. Geological problems are difficult to argue against. But we knew [and were told] that we had five years left. The new faces had cost millions to develop.

Mick Carter, NUM delegate at Cortonwood during the 1984-85 miners' strike.

There were no lengths that the government would go to get the miners down. We were prisoners in our own village. Phones were tapped. It was obvious. They [the flying pickets] had a feather in their cap if they got to a destination but they were often turned back.

In five years you can prepare and plan for another job but five weeks' notice left us hopeless.

During the strike Mick's home village of Brampton was frequently 'under siege' by the police and the media and he had strong opinions about that dark time in our modern history:

It was only a few years ago that the BBC admitted that they reversed the film footage [at Orgreave] but the damage was done when it went on the news. People have a strong belief in television, even more than newspapers. That was one of the worst crimes of the strike. Nobody could believe me at meetings. We were thugs. It altered public opinion…Orgreave was a solitary lesson.

On the gradual return to work during the winter months and the end of the strike:

Not many went back here. It was disheartening but inevitable. It started as a trickle but became a flood. It was not easy calling the strike off but when you have sacrificed such a lot. We went back with our heads held high but with a dead heart.

Cortonwood closed in November 1985, a few months after the end of the strike and Mick was transferred to Silverwood Colliery. He told me that this was the unhappiest period of his life, having to keep his dignity despite 'silent victimisation'. After Silverwood closed he studied Sociology and Social Policy at York University, graduating in 2000 and, but for his illness, intended to commence a doctorate and a period of teaching.

Copies of *Yorkshire Mining Veterans* (£12, inc. postage) and *Pit Voices* (Vols 1 & 2, £7.99 ea post-free) are is available from the author by contacting him at 12 Ash Dale Road, Warmsworth, Doncaster DN4 9NG. Other mining books by Brian Elliott include *Barnsley Pits & Pitmen; The Miners' Strike Day by Day; Yorkshire Miners* and *Yorkshire's Flying Pickets in the 1984-85 Miners' Strike.*

Putting My Hand on History
Anne Batchelor

Researching my poor old Batchelor "ag.labs." I found myself continually tripping over references to a Daniel Bachiler, lutenist and composer in the royal courts of Elizabeth I and Anne of Denmark. To eliminate such a talented person from my humble farming family, I decided to research his story. All the books I could find about Tudor and Stuart musicians spoke of Daniel Bachiler in very vague terms – "Very little is known of this man", or "This man's life is a complete blank."
Blank my foot! – Let me tell you the story I uncovered.

Once upon a time there was a farmer called Richard Bachiler. He lived with his wife Elizabeth (nee Cardell), and his numerous sons and daughters in Aston Clinton (Bucks). On March 16th 1571/2 they took their newborn son to St Michael and All Angels Church, Aston Clinton, to be christened Daniel. When he was only eight years old he was chosen by his mother's brother, Thomas Cardell, as his apprentice and taken up to London. Uncle Thomas was a lutenist in the court of Queen Elizabeth. I found him described in original taxation records as "one of her Ma(jes)te Lewt Plaiers", and "one of her hyghnes musicians for the luts".

Thomas also appears in the court records as Elizabeth's dancing master. Both Thomas and his young son Francis Cardell were well known as dancing masters as far away as France, where I found them mentioned in French records.

Young Daniel Bachiler lived with his uncle Thomas and Aunt Helen in Kinges Street, Westminster, where I found them mentioned in the Rate Books and church register of St. Margaret's, Westminster. To go from life on a Buckinghamshire farm to the London of Shakespeare and the court of Gloriana herself must have been an amazing magical experience for the young boy. He was taught to play the lute (presumably by his uncle), and obviously had a great talent, being able to compose his own music by the age of about fifteen.

This bright young lad was spotted by the Walsingham family, and the indentures he had originally signed in 1579, binding him to his uncle until the age of twenty-four, were countersigned in 1586 by Sir Francis Walsingham, Principal Secretary of State to the Queen, and her spymaster. Thus, he passed into

the household of the Walsinghams – his first step up the ladder to fame and fortune. "I found this indenture, bearing the signatures of Daniel and his uncle Thomas, at the dusty, much-lamented PRO in Chancery Lane. With a shiver of excitement, I opened up the crackling parchment and saw how neatly young Daniel had signed his name. Someone had obviously impressed upon him the importance of the document he was signing.

I imagined his tongue, sticking out of the side of his mouth as he concentrated on doing his 'best writing'.

The signing of this indenture was a great step up the social ladder for this ex-farm boy. It took him from his uncle's house in Kinges Street to the far grander home of the Walsinghams.

As the person responsible for the music in the household, Daniel composed consort music and is believed to have put together the musical collections in the Walsingham Consort Books. These I hunted down in Hull University. When the Archivist delivered them to my table in their brown cardboard boxes, I felt like a child at Christmas! With trembling hands, I lifted the contents out with as much reverence as if they had been holy relics. These small books – bound in olive pigskin – had all been handled by my

Daniel Bachiler

There seems to have been some special relationship between Daniel, the little lad from the country, and Walsingham's daughter, the Lady Frances. When her young husband, Sir Philip Sidney, died, her father had – with the Queen's special permission- given him a massive state funeral. Riding through the streets of London in the procession is a young boy whose little legs fail to reach the stirrups on Sidney's massive war-horse. He wears a big hat and is led by a footman. Above his head is his name, "Daniell Batchiler" (sic). A far cry from the farm at Aston Clinton!

Some time later, the Lady Frances married again. This time it was a love-match, not an arranged marriage. Her new husband was the dashing darling of Elizabeth's court, the Earl of Essex, Robert Devereux. When the Lady Frances moved into the Devereux family home, she took with her the talented young Daniel. Now aged about seventeen, he appears in 1588 in the Devereux account books receiving £30 per annum – more than a royal lutenist: another step up the ladder for my Daniel.

Combing through original music records, I found a song written by Daniel at this time. It is his only surviving song – "To plead my faith", with words by the Earl of Essex, and music by Daniel. It seems that Elizabeth and Essex had a fiery love/hate relationship, and whenever Essex felt particularly peeved at the Queen's treatment of him, he would complain to her in song, sending some hapless servant to sing his message, and Daniel's song appears to have been one of these.

Daniel. It was a magical moment. In fact, there is a suggestion that, as chief musician, he actually wrote out the contents of each book. Comparing the neat, precise writing in the books with the signature on his indenture, it seemed to me that they were in the same hand. As an ex-teacher, I was quite an expert on recognising the authorship of homework!

Sadly, the one book missing from the Walsingham collection is the lute book. It resides in some American university, I believe. It was amazing, however, to be able to touch something Daniel had undoubtedly held.

I even discovered, in the flute book, in the bottom corner of "Sir Francis Walsingham's Goodnight", a large blot of black ink, bearing a clear thumbprint of whoever wrote the music books. Could it have been Daniel's? The archivist had never noticed it until I pointed it out. Miss Marple rides again!!

Anne with a copy of the Grant of Arms to Daniel Bachiler drawn up by the College of Arms

Then, as now, there was trouble in Ireland, and Essex, who was known for impulsively putting his foot in his mouth on a regular basis, boasted that he was the man to solve the Irish problem. Elizabeth took him at his word and made him Lord Lieutenant of Ireland. Plodding through the wonderful detailed account books of Elizabeth's court, I found her making a payment to my Daniel, in 1599, for carrying letters to the Council and Lord Lieutenant of Ireland – an indication that he could be trusted with what could have been intimate letters of a personal nature, as well as more official state correspondence.

However, the Earl's impulsiveness was to be the death of him. Dashing home to England (against the Queen's express wishes), he burst into her bedroom to see her before she had time to put on her wig and her face. The exasperated Elizabeth turned against him. When his attempted coup failed to give Essex control of the court, he met his end on Tower Green, losing his head on the block. To remove herself to safety, the Lady Frances went with her household to live quietly in the country with her mother, Dame Ursula. Daniel went with her.

In 1603, the remarkable and aged Elizabeth died. At a time when women had little power or influence, she had survived plots and conspiracies to earn the respect and love of her people. Her chosen heir, James, came from

Scotland, bringing with him his wife, Anne of Denmark, and his children. A companion was needed for the young prince Henry and so the Lady Frances was invited to bring her young son Robert to court. With her came her faithful musician, Daniel Bachiler.

The new Queen Anne had a passion for theatre and music, filling her personal court with poets, playwrights, and musicians. As soon as Daniel appeared in court with the Lady Frances, he was appointed a Groom of the Queen's Privy Chamber, a final step on the ladder to fame and fortune. His name appears on court documents receiving an income of £160 per annum – the highest paid of Anne's Grooms.

Now references to Daniel came thick and fast. I found he was granted a coat of arms in 1606. Later he was paid for taking the Queen's lutes and viols for repair by Robert Henlake. Together with William Gomeldon, a fellow Groom, the Queen granted him "a chest of arrows, cast up as a wreck in our manor of Portland." There are regular records of payments for "his liverie and pencion." He was making a good living from his music now. Much of his music has survived in private collections. The son of the great lutenist John Dowland described Daniel in 1610 as "the right perfect musician."

Of Daniel's private life there are fewer records. When he died in 1618/19 he left no widow or children. I have combed the records of London churches but have found no record of a marriage. Several musicians of the time were married in their own homes "swearing before witnesses", and few records survive.

I did find reference to the death of a Cecily Bacheler, wife of Daniel in 1611 at "Twickenham/Hampton", where of course the court was. In the register of St Margaret's Hampton, was an entry, the same year, to the burial of a "maid of the court", (no name given), and a "child of a maid of the court." It is tempting to see this as my Daniel's wife dying in childbirth, but I have no proof.

Daniel's death in 1618/19 at the age of forty seven is recorded in the burial register of St Margaret's Lee (near Lewisham) just across Blackheath Common from the Court at Greenwich. The cause of death is not given but that winter smallpox swept through London and members of the court fell like flies. Other suggested causes of death include a violent mugging as he crossed the notorious Blackheath on his way home from court, or an injury caused

Lady Frances Sidney (neé Walsingham) with her daughter, Elizabeth

The late Viscount de L'Isle with Anne looking at Daniel's portrait in April 1989

in the great fire which destroyed Westminster Hall just thirteen days earlier, when it was recorded – "many are maimed". I am tempted by the mental picture of my lovely musician braving the flames to rescue his precious lute! Who knows?

Daniel left no will, but a legal document does survive describing how his nephew, Samuel, claimed to be his heir. This was contested by his brothers William and John, who were of course next of kin. The brothers won! Daniel did leave a considerable fortune, including property in Suffolk given to him by his grateful Queen. In the burial register of St Margaret, Lee, he is described as "Daniel Bacheler, gentleman". Not bad for a little lad from the country.

So, "this man's life is a complete blank"? I think not.

Researching his story, which had never before been uncovered, was an amazing experience for me – a humble self-taught family historian. Hearing his music, and what went on inside his head, still gives me goose pimples. I've chosen to have my favourite piece played at my funeral!

Coming home from London after a day's research, I sat in my taxi, my head spinning with all the adventures of the day. "Been to London, eh?" said my taxi driver. "Been doing all the big shops?" "No", I told him, "I've been researching the life of a young musician from the Elizabethan court. Today I found his indentures which he signed in 1586 at the age

of fourteen. I have actually touched something HE touched!"

"Wow", said the taxi driver, "You've been putting your hand on history!"

I couldn't have put it better myself!

Wales to Wigan and Back *(Twice)*
Glenys Shepherd

An accurately drawn up family tree is, to a family historian, what an O.S. map is to a geographer-interesting, informative, useful and essential. Although a family tree is all these things it is the photographs, pictures, stories and articles which relate to the tree which add the human interest to the story and bring the tree to life. It can often take many, many years before a family mystery is brought to a conclusion - some never are. In this case, almost a century passed before the mystery was solved.

When I started to investigate my own family history, it opened the floodgates because my husband asked me to do his too. The paternal side of his family -the Shepherds - I am in the early stages of investigating but the maternal side - the Edwards - is opening into a fascinating tale. Over a period of time I did the normal preliminary work of collecting readily available certificates, one or two photographs and a few clues from my sister-in-law, but that was the sum total of information available in the beginning. At the time I started this research, we were working and living in the South of England. My husband Rick had just one elderly aunt and some distant cousins from the Edwards family still living in the Wigan area.

We knew that Rick's grandmother Edwards came from Swansea and that his mother was born in Llanelli, so armed with a few certificates and the information gleaned from them, we decided to spend a few days in the South Wales area. We took photographs of the places where the Edwards and Payne families had lived- (Payne was Grandma Edwards maiden name) - and the house where Rick's mother and more of the family were actually born. From a visit to County Hall in Swansea, we managed to obtain photocopies of old photographs of some of the places where they had lived and worked, (the photocopies being £5 each!). By the end of the holiday we had a fairly accurate picture of the lifestyle of the Edwards and Payne families from the Victorian times.

A few days after we returned home we had a telephone call from Rick's aunt in Wigan. She knew nothing of the workings of a computer but told us that she had received a call from one of her cousins who lived fairly near to her. The cousin had had a phone call from a local vicar (a Family Historian!). He had picked up a message via the internet from a lady in Canada

who was trying to make contact with the Edwards family in Wigan with connections to Swansea. The cousin had responded to the enquiry and rang aunty to tell her that he had made contact with " a relative" in Canada. *Who was she!?* What was the family connection? Back to the roots!

Rice (Rees) Edwards was born in Montgomery in Wales about 1719 and married Ann about 1749. After the marriage they moved to Worcestershire and the next four generations

were born there. Charles (Rick's great grandfather) married Eliza in Worcester, but their seven children were born in Wigan. The last of the seven was Ernest Albert (Rick's grandad) and he married Alma Lavinia Payne in Swansea in November 1919. So from Wales to Wigan via Worcester, then to Wales again. Why did some of the family move to Wales in 1919?

Alma Lavinia Payne was the eighth of nine daughters (no sons!) born to the Payne family in Swansea. When World War One broke out.

Rick's grandad Ernest and one of his brothers were stationed in Swansea. Joseph married Florence Victoria Payne, the youngest of the nine sisters, in November 1917. When the war ended, the "Jobs for the boys" promise did not materialise, so Joseph and Ernest signed up for another year in the army and Ernest married Alma Lavinia in 1919 after his year ended. They moved shortly after this back to Wigan and lived happily to a good old age. Their daughter was Rick's aunt.

However, what about Joseph and Florence? They did not return to Wigan and it was assumed that he had been killed in action. The truth was very different. Their marriage was not a happy one. Joseph wrote a letter to Ernest and Alma in Wigan. He said he could no longer live with Florence and by the time they received the letter he would be thousands of miles away and they would never see him again. They never did. The family were so ashamed at the time that they never showed the letter to anyone - it only

came to light many years later. They never knew what had happened to him except that a daughter, Henrietta, was born to Florence in early 1920, after he had left. Florence later married again.

Joseph travelled to North Africa then India. In India he eventually remarried and had three children - two sons and a daughter. The family of their son Charles eventually settled in Australia; their second son settled in England, and their daughter moved to Australia. It was their daughter i.e. the grand-daughter of Joseph who had disappeared from Swansea in 1919. She now lives in Canada and has spent many years researching her family tree. She made journeys to Wigan but was unable to establish contacts until She appealed on the internet. The circle was completed when the vicar picked up the message and contacted a cousin of the family who then contacted Rick's aunt. There was then a flurry of old photographs being dug out of boxes, copied and forwarded to Canada, and an exchange of family tree information followed by a visit to Wigan. When the original letter was produced about Joseph's flight from Wales the story was complete. The embarrassment which existed around 1919 because of the letter has obviously evaporated now as has the shame of a divorce in the family all those years ago. It has all just taken its place in a family history as something which happened all those years ago.

Perhaps though another story is emerging now from this one.

The maiden name of the mother of Alma Lavinia and the other eight sisters was Henrietta Channon. Whilst we were enjoying our researching holiday in Swansea, we looked in the local telephone directory and found two Channons. A few weeks later I wrote to both of them enclosing a brief explanation of Henrietta Channon. One letter was returned as the lady had died just a short while before, but the second one introduced me to a member of a

Channon family who had just begun to research his family tree. We haven't yet had the time to investigate deeply enough to establish a definite family link, but there is one strong clue. Rick's aunt in Wigan had mentioned two sisters related to Henrietta Channon, who had moved to live in the South West of England area quite a few years ago from Swansea and who would now be very elderly. The Channon family with whom we made the connection via the telephone directory, have given me copies of letters from two elderly aunts who were living in the Somerset area a few years ago. Quite a mystery! Which when I have the time, I will pursue.

Start as you mean to go on
Resolutions for Family Historians
Doreen Hopwood

If your New Year Resolution is to embark upon
the ancestral trail, or if you have already started
to research the history of your family, the
accessibility of records in a wide range of
formats helps to make research easier and
quicker – so long as you follow the golden
rules.

Whilst interest in family history has increased
at a huge rate over the last 20 years it is by no
means new. By 1900, George Marshall's guide
to printed pedigrees was already in its third
edition, and for those of us living outside
London, we no longer have to rely on day trips
to the metropolis to visit major repositories in
order to conduct research. Many national
resources, such as the General Register Office
Index, can now be found in large libraries and
record offices, as well as in London (at the
Family Records Centre) and several other
locations. There is little doubt that the internet
has helped to popularise family history by
bringing information into our homes via the
computer. Whilst we can access records
remotely, rather than having to make personal
visits to record offices and other repositories,
don't assume that you will be able to find
everything on-line. By restricting yourself to
electronic resources, you'll not only be denying
yourself the satisfaction of seeing original

documents bearing your ancestors signatures
(or marks) – albeit on microfilm – but you'll be
missing out on the huge wealth and variety of
material which can help you to place members
of your family within their historical and social
environment.

When you start to research your family's past,
it's easy to become overwhelmed by the vast
range of online resources. These are a great
boon for family historians, but don't assume
that the indexes you find, such as those on
FamilySearch or FreeBMD, include every parish
register entries or civil registration details.
When you find an entry which you think is
"yours", locate and examine the actual
document because what appears in the index
may not be a complete record of the parish
register entry. Some registers of baptism include
the child's date of birth, especially where
several children of the same couple were
baptised together. You may also find that the
vicar has made notes in the margin relating to
the entry.

Surname and other indexes, such as those
covering the Victorian census returns, have all
been transcribed from the original source,
which in many cases is not easy to decipher.
The myth of beautiful copperplate writing is

Register Index that the first entry you find in the right name is yours. Look at least one year either side of the year you think it should be, and include spelling variations in your search. Remember that until the latter part of the nineteenth century many of our ancestors couldn't read or write, and so the name the name was written down as it sounded to the registrar. Obviously, surnames Like Jones and Hall aren't likely to be mis-spelt, but you are more likely to find several entries with the same name as your ancestor, especially in large towns. In these cases, when you contact the relevant local register office for a certificate, provide as much information as you can about the person – such as father's name, his occupation and the mother's name (if possible). If you only request the birth certificate of " Frederick Jones, registered in the March Quarter of 1879", you'll get just that, but if you state that you only want it if he was the son of John Jones, carpenter, then the certificate won't be issued unless the criteria is met, so you won't end up buying unnecessary certificates.

soon dispelled as we attempt to read the information on these returns, especially when the enumerator has scored through the age details and scrawled over the "occupations" column. All records are compiled by humans from records which have been compiled by humans, so "human" errors are bound to occur, especially in indexes containing millions of names, such as census projects. Transcription errors can be frustrating – like the "butter carer" I found in Birmingham in 1901, who, on inspection of the actual census entry was found to be a "button carver"! The key to solving these problems is persistency. Family history often involves a process of elimination, so go through all the possible entries and then weed out the ones that obviously don't meet with your search criteria.

From "Day One" it is important that you keep a methodical record of all your research, and don't rely on your memory and scraps of paper. After a visiting the record office or library (or a session using the internet) write up your findings as soon as you can, and remember to record any negative searches as well. There's nothing more annoying than repeating an exercise simply because you forgot to make a note of the sources you'd looked at. In the same way, make sure that you write down the references (such as page, folio, piece numbers etc on census returns) and the class numbers/name of the repository so that you can easily find them again if you need to re-examine them. If you aren't able to make photocopies of the entries, there are plenty of good pre-printed genealogy forms available.

As well as being methodical, your record-keeping must be honest. There is no harm in "pencilling in" possible family members, but don't add them to your family tree until you have the actual evidence to prove that he/she belongs there. Ages given on census returns and marriage and death certificates are not always accurate, so don't assume that when looking for a birth registration on the General

However, tempting as it may be, never try to research forwards. You are the most important person in your family tree, and effective research can only be carried out by working from the known to the unknown, generation by generation. Whilst you don't need to buy birth, marriage and death certificates for every member of your family, you do need those of your direct ancestors in order to make sure that you are following the correct line. An English or Welsh birth certificate gives you both your parents names (including your mother's maiden name), which leads to the marriage certificate of your parents. This in turn provides their ages and their father's names, enabling you to search for their birth certificates, which then provide your grandparents names, and so on. With so many family histories and trees available online, it is easy to get in touch with other researchers who are investigating your family, but don't try to fit yourself into a family tree which has already been compiled without verifying that it relates to your family.

There is a wealth of information in national, county and local record offices, but if you're just beginning to trace your family's history, don't make these places your first ports of call. Start off by talking to relatives and collect as many birth, death and marriage certificates (or copies of them) as you can from them. By obtaining them in this way you know that you

San. Francisco Cal. Nov 17th 04.
U.S.A.

Dear Mother,
It is just 3 years ago to day that I arrived in London from New-Zealand, that time it was snowing and freezing. to day is an ideal californian day, warm and sunny, more like midsummer, I have no doubt you will be able to recognise this. I will be sending some more by and by, love to all.
yours as ever.

have the right ones, and also you are saving the cost of purchasing them from register offices. Relatives may also have other documents or items which at first may not seem helpful in your research, but you may be surprised at just how much information can be gleaned from old address or birthday books, letters and postcards. The latter usually bears an address and date which can enable you to search the electoral registers. Other items may simply give you an insight into the leisure activities or sporting interests of past relatives. There are plenty of interview forms available which take the form of a questionnaire, and these are particularly helpful if you aren't able to talk to the person face-to-face. However, if you can conduct a personal interview, you'll find the "life-history" approach more rewarding for both yourself and your interview partner. Rather than asking a huge list of questions, which an older person can find daunting (or even intimidating), ask him or her to tell you about an aspect of his or her life (such as childhood, school, work etc.). You'll probably end up with more information, and even get answers to questions you never thought to ask! When talking to relatives, old photographs can serve as a memory jogger, but don't assume that people will "reveal all", and do be sensitive to the feelings of the person you are interviewing. You need to respect the fact that there may be some aspects of your family's past that they're unwilling to talk about. If you're lucky enough to have a collection of family photographs (often without names or dates on them!), this is a good time to fill in the gaps, and it is also a useful exercise to do the same with more recent photographs in your possession. Future generations will thank you for having done it.

Whatever family information has been passed down, unless you have documentary evidence, always check it out before adding it to your research. Most families have (at least) one legend that has been passed down the generations, and these are usually based on events which actually did happen. However, the truth may have become distorted over time, with bits missed off or added on – rather like "Chinese Whispers". By careful and methodical

research you should be able to untangle the facts. If you only make one New Year Resolution concerning family history, let it be that you don't assume anything, however plausible it may be.

For most of us with English or Welsh ancestors we should be able to research back to the start of civil registration in 1837, provided that births were registered, our ancestors got married and that they gave correct information to the census enumerators. Successful research depends upon the survival, accessibility – and legibility – of records, so be realistic in your approach. Where parish registers have not survived, there should be Bishops Transcripts, which are copies sent each year to the Bishop by every vicar in the Diocese, so you need to be aware of alternative sources. Be prepared to think laterally too, because you may sometimes have to go sideways in order to take your research further back. Although civil registration was introduced in 1837, there was no penalty for non-registration of births until 1875 and many children were simply not registered prior to this date. You may find that even though your great-grandmother's birth wasn't registered, that of one of her siblings was. By buying a copy of this birth certificate you will obtain both parent's names (as would appear on your direct ancestors certificate), and so enable you to search for the marriage of your great-grandparents.

Patience is definitely a virtue for the family historian, as is a sense of the past. Don't expect to complete your family tree overnight, or find a direct line back to William the Conqueror. Remember that the number of your direct ancestors doubles with each generation back – two parents, four grandparents etc. – so be realistic in your research targets. It may be easier to concentrate on one particular branch of the family rather than trying to research all of your ancestors at once.

You'll get far more understanding of why your ancestors acted in the ways they did, and what global, national and local factors influenced their lives by looking at the general history of the period. Terminology has changed over time – my nineteenth century "hooker" had a very different occupation than a twenty-first century counterpart. Putting the "flesh on the bones" will add interest to your family's history, helping you to find out about how your ancestors lived, worked and played, rather than just knowing why and when they were born, married and died.

So, whether you are new to family history or an experienced researcher, make sure that you follow the golden rules of research.

Food in Family History:
Or How Parkin from the peasant met the Great Cake from the manor house
Jill Groves

'In England on the whole the food descends less from a courtly tradition than from the manor houses and rectories and homes of well-to-do merchants – latterly from a Jane Austen world. It hands down the impression of the social life of families in which the wives and daughters weren't too grand to go into the kitchen and to keep a close eye on the vegetable garden and dairy.'[1]

Quite often the dowry of an ordinary young woman along with the cart load of goods and occasionally money put out at interest by her parents for any children of the marriage, would include her store of recipes. Some of these were family recipes, passed down from mother to daughter. But since many girls spent their adolescent years as live-in servants, some would be recipes learnt from other households. Some girls became the kitchen maids in great houses or manor houses of local squires and were taught by the cook there how to make cooked cheesecakes, fashionable dishes for great occasions, sponges made light with

whipped egg whites, jams, preserves and distilled 'strong waters'. Some girls became servants in the house of slightly better-off neighbours and learnt older recipes for great cakes and recipes for making cheese. A good dairymaid was her own dowry. So too was a good cook.

Upper class women often kept recipe or receipt books in which they noted down family recipes and others from friends and some from feasts at court. Most ordinary women in the sixteenth to eighteenth centuries could not read and write, so they carried their recipes in their heads, remembering them by day-to-day practice (as those who cook daily from fresh do even now).

As education became more universal so more of the recipes in women's heads were written down in notebooks and in the backs of published recipe books. My mum had a notebook/scrapbook in which she wrote down or stuck in recipes from family, friends and magazines for most of her adult life. However, the important recipe – the one everyone wanted to inherit – her recipe for chocolate jap cake, wasn't written in the cookery notebook. It wasn't written down until her granddaughter's primary school wanted to bring out a book of parents' recipes to raise money for some equipment. Only then, in the early 1990s, was it written down in black-and-white, some thirty years after Mum first made it. My Nana (maternal grandmother – my other grandmother always said she couldn't cook to save her life), another good cook, wrote down recipes in the backs of much used cookery books. She also collected recipes from friends and neighbours on postcards and scraps of paper which she also put into the cookery books. Remember that until the coming of Elizabeth David, Delia Smith and TV chefs cookery books were not as common as they are now. (Neither were they needed as much;, basic cooking was learnt by watching Mum or Gran in the kitchen.) Nana only had a handful of such books, Mum had a couple of shelves full and I have half a bookcase full. Now that cooking is a hobby and not a necessity in the UK, publishers bring out thousands of them!

Most of the recipes Nana had from other people or wrote down from her memory were cake, tarts/pies and sweetmeat recipes, and the occasional very old-fashioned medicinal wine recipe (like something straight out of a seventeenth century receipt book). An example of the latter is:

'Grapefruit Champagne
   Cut up 7 grapefruit in a pan. Pour over 1 gallon of cold water. Let it stand 10 days, then sieve over 4lbs of sugar, and leave another 8 days, stirring every day. Strain into another pan, and remove all scum; let it stand a few more days, removing scum as it rises. Bottle off: Ready for drinking in 3 weeks.'

This recipe is an old-fashioned fruit wine recipe, using natural yeasts found in the atmosphere and on the skin of the grapefruit. These days the recipe would call for equipment to be sterilised (using sterilising tablets), a hot water (not a cold water) infusion and commercial dried wine yeast (all of which is available in chemists or specialist home brew supply shops, if you want to try it). The result is more certain, but it takes all the fun of having a month of work and waiting for it to turn to vinegar because of the yeasts in your kitchen and on the skin of the fruit are the wrong ones.

Nana did not see the need to write down how she cooked a roast dinner complete with her own family recipe for roast potatoes, which no one else does – but which I still use with modern variations. Or the 'dolly mixture'

sweets she made for her grandchildren made with food colouring and home-made marzipan left over from decorating cakes. She also didn't see the need to write down her recipe for slices of potato dipped in batter and deep fried which she served to Granddad with an egg or vegetable as a meat replacement. Nana called them 'potato scallops' as if they were a substitute for real scallops. I have never seen a published recipe for this dish, but something similar was made in Lancashire and known as 'Dads'.[2] Where did Nana learn to make this dish? Did she learn it from her mother Alice, who came from Lowestoft and who died when Nana was nine? Or did it come from Aunt Sue, Nana's maternal aunt, also from Lowestoft, who took in Nana and her younger siblings Len and Ivy.

My mother-in-law also has only a handful of cook books, mostly those that came with the cooker or microwave. She, like many women before her, carries a number of recipes in her head. She doesn't need a recipe to make bread pudding – a cakey (solid, slightly soggy) pudding made with old cake crumbled, dried fruit, spices, eggs and milk. The end result is something very close to the seventeenth century recipe for 'The Lord of Devonshire his Pudding' from Elinor Fettiplace's Receipt Book.[3] Where does it come from – my mother-in-law's mother Augusta May Moxey or her Dart grandmother. My guess is Augusta May. If so, where did she get it from? Her mother Elizabeth Seymour of Swallowfield, Berkshire? Elizabeth Seymour's mother was an Allenor from the Berkshire Hampshire border. The Fettiplace family lived in Berkshire. Could an Allenor or a Seymour girl have been in service with their descendants and learnt the recipe?

My mother had a different way with stale cake. She crumbled it in a bowl, sprinkled cocoa powder on top, bound it together with water or used melted 'cake' chocolate. Then she rolled the mixture into little balls, dusted them with more cocoa powder or drinking chocolate (Mum had a sweet tooth) and put them into little petty four cases. They never lasted long. We three kids could demolish a whole plate before she was finished – if allowed.

Looking through my collection of printed family recipes from the sixteenth to the nineteenth century (not my own family's unfortunately) I can find Spanish/Arab influenced dishes of the fifteenth/sixteenth centuries in the mid-eighteenth century recipe book of a Staffordshire lady[4] and jams and jellies being made in the old-fashioned sixteenth way in the eighteenth century (wetting the sugar, melting and boiling it to soft ball height before adding fruit or juice – a method that deserves reviving since it cuts down on the time that a spitting pan of jam needs to be on the hob, and it can be done for small quantities as well as large).[5] Many of these are manor house recipes moving down the social scale.

Recipes for fatless sponges began to appear in the seventeenth century, when it was realised that beaten egg whites could make a cake rise. Some of the original recipes used ground almonds. Did the idea come from Arab influenced Spanish cooking where almonds are very important or Italy (Italians taught the French to cook, especially cakes and pastries – although the French will never admit it)?

When I travelled to New Zealand in 2005, a museum society treated the party I was travelling with to an excellent buffet lunch. Amongst the things on offer was a Dutch-style apple pie – raisins and spices in with the apple. I didn't find out who baked it but some lady in Christchurch has Dutch ancestry (or a Dutch mother-in-law).

One of my collection of regional recipe books has a recipe entitled 'Young Chickens in a Blanket', which is said to be a Worcestershire recipe from the eighteenth century.[6] The chickens are parboiled, cut into quarters and then finished off in a cream sauce flavoured with lemon, nutmeg and cayenne pepper. It is the addition of *sippets* – fried bread in this recipe – which gives away the medieval origin of this dish. Sippets were the sixteenth century remnants of the trencher bread plates of the Middle Ages. This recipe is also first cousin to a French dish called 'Poulé l'Ancien'. Another

cousin, possibly even a grandparent, is the ancient Lancashire dish 'Hindle Wakes' or 'Hen de la Wakes' as Dorothy Hartley thought it might have been called originally.[7] An old hen stuffed with dried fruit and spices, poached in broth and served cold with a lemon sauce gaze. Did a Worcestershire cook have Huguenot ancestry or an ancestor who was a cook in a medieval great house?

Another recipe from eighteenth century Worcestershire also has much earlier ancestry. 'Quince Marmalet' or quince marmalade. Lady Elinor Fettiplace in the early seventeenth century noted a recipe for quince marmalade – the original solid block type poured into a metal or wooden mould. The original recipe came from Portugal where the name for it is 'Marmalada'. I am not suggesting Portuguese ancestry for the eighteenth Worcestershire cook, because many people, especially in a fruit tree growing area like Worcestershire, would have quince trees in their gardens. And quince marmalade was a very popular dish for the banquets at the ends of sixteenth and seventeenth feasts, nearly as much as its more liquid equivalent at breakfast today. Imported marmalada first began to appear in the records when it came in enough quantities to be worth paying customs dues on in 1495. In those days the marmalada was scented/flavoured with expensive ingredients such as musk, ambergris (from whales – but like musk used in perfumes) and rosewater, common in Arabic and Iberian cuisine but exotic to the English. The first known printed recipe appeared in England in 1562, but there were probably earlier manuscripts versions circulating amongst the ladies of the manor houses. (Portuguese quince

marmalada of the solid variety can still be bought.)

It was the Romans who discovered the 'sugar / fruit-acid / heat bond, which produces pectin' and is the basis of all jams, jellies and marmalades, but only with quince. And since all fruit was held to be: 'generally are noyful to man, and do engender ill humours, and be oft times the cause of putrefied fevers', by North Europeans, it is the Arabs and the Iberians we have to thank for discovering that it was possible to preserve fruit by boiling them in honey causing them to jell.[8]

Family recipes have also evolved and changed as they moved up or down the social scale and as different ingredients became available or new methods devised. Parkin, flapjacks, oatcakes (Scottish version, not the Stafford version) and modern muesli bars have a common ancestor in the Dark Ages, in the Thor or Tharf cakes.

Tharf cakes were an every day type of bannock made of oats, water, salt and perhaps a little lard or butter cooked on a backstone (a stone slab or flat metal sheet heated on the cooking fire on which bread or flat cakes were cooked) or frying pan. Honey was added on feast days and holidays. Gradually other things were added such as ginger in the Middle Ages, wheat flour, sugar, milk, eggs and, last of all, baking powder to turn it into the cake version we know today.

At the same time as the recipes for parkin and tharf cakes changed and as people become more affluent, so the parkin moved up the social scale. Perhaps it didn't appear at afternoon tea in the houses of great aristocrats (too crumbly perhaps to be eaten delicately), but it appeared in many yeoman farmhouses and urban middle class, as well as working class, households. It was easy to make and bake, it could be as rich or as plain as you liked, and it could be kept for weeks in a tin. It didn't have to be baked in an oven – some nineteenth century versions hark back to earlier recipes in calling for the parkin to be baked on a bakestone or griddle.[9]

The great cake, a yeast-raised large cake full of imported dried fruit, and lots of expensive spices, was always a recipe for the rich. The ingredients were expensive and it needed an oven, which many houses didn't possess. In a yeoman farmhouse a great cake might be made for an important feast, but not for everyday eating.[10]

In The Winter's Tale by Shakespeare, Perdita sends her brother to shop for ingredients for a great cake to be baked for a feast:
'Three pound of sugar; five pound of currants; rice... nutmegs, seven; a race or two of ginger – but that I may beg; four pound of prunes, and as many of raisins o' the sun.'[10]

Lady Elinor Fettiplace's seventeenth recipe for a great cake includes currants, cinnamon, ginger, nutmegs, cloves and mace, yeast, ale, milk and butter, with a light seasoning of sugar. The result is more like a fruit loaf. It wasn't until the advent of cast iron ranges in ordinary homes in the mid-nineteenth century that working class people could bake their own versions of the great cake. By then eggs had been added and the ale and yeast replaced by baking powder. The recipe had evolved into a plain fruit or 'farmhouse' cake – a rubbed-in version made light by baking powder, and a richer version made to rise by the creaming together of eggs and butter, baking powder with black treacle for colour, and, of course, the yeasted fruit loaf (plainer than the medieval version, and without the ale in most recipes).

So, if you are lucky enough to have family recipes passed down through the generations, even if it is only Mother's Way of Cooking the Perfect Roast, treat them like family heirlooms. You never know what sort of history lies behind them. If, like my sister, you have inherited your mother's recipe notebook going back to the year dot (well, at least the 1940s) treasure it even more. It's the female side of family history and social history – passed from mother to daughters and daughters-in-law. And practical. It's history that might help you cook for your family.

Notes
1. Jane Grigson, *English Food,* 2nd revised edition, Penguin, 1992.
2. *Food and Drink: Dialect Dictionaries*, North West Sound Archive, Old Steward's Office, Clitheroe Castle, Clitheroe, Lancashire BB7 1AZ.
3. *Elinor Fettiplace's Receipt Book: Elizabethan Country House Cooking* edited by Hilary Spurling, Viking Salamander, 1986.
4. *'Take 6 Eggs': a taste of Staffordshire's past,* Staffordshire County Council Libraries, Arts and Archives – Judith Bridgman, recipe from the 1740.
5. *A Ragoo of Ducks: Household Recipes from York Manuscripts* by 'Cooks and Their Books' class, York Branch of the WEA, 1997 – Mrs Abbs of Yorkshire, eighteenth century.
6. *Herefordshire and Worcestershire Country Recipes,* compiled by Molly Perham, Ravette Books, 1989.
7. *Food in England* by Dorothy Hartley, paperback version, Macmillan and Jane, 1973.
8. *'Banqueting Stuffe'* edited by C. Anne Wilson in Food and Society Series, Edinburgh University Press, 1991.
9. *Traditional Food: East and West of the Pennines* edited by C. Anne Wilson, Food and Society series, Edinburgh University Press, 1991.
10. *The Winter's Tale* by William Shakespeare, in *The Complete Works of Shakespeare*, Avenel Books, New York, 1975.

Fred's story- true or false?
Richard Ratcliffe

One of the most interesting aspects of tracing one's family history is checking out family hearsay stories. Some prove to be surprisingly accurate while others prove otherwise and may have been passed on to cover up a family tragedy or marital breakdown in days goneby when divorce was unobtainable, as well as stories that grew as the years passed.

About 12 months after an abridged version of the story of "*My Great Great Grandmother was Murdered*" appeared in the *Daily Mail Weekend Magazine* in February 2000, I received a letter from Colin Ratcliffe who lived in Middlesex. He had just seen the article which described the murder of my Great, Great Grandmother Ann Tennant at Long Compton in Warwickshire in 1875 (A fuller version of this story appeared in *The Family and Local History Handbook 8*)

In his letter Colin said that his Ratcliffe family also came from Long Compton. His grandfather was called Fred Ratcliffe and that he had a brother called Kent Ratcliffe. He believed that Fred ran away from home to become a boy soldier. Could I confirm that this information was correct? I checked my Ratcliffe Family Tree and quickly located Fred and his older brother Kent who were the sons of James Ratcliffe of

Long Compton, Stonemason, and his wife Hannah, formerly Lane. Fred was my second cousin once removed. My only knowledge of Fred was that he was aged 1 in the 1871 Census of Long Compton and 11 in the 1881 Census of Long Compton and was not living either at home or elsewhere in the Long Compton area in the 1891 Census. I rang Colin to confirm that we were related and then asked him how could I help.

Colin then told me an amazing story. Fred was supposed to have run away from home, joined the Army, fought in the Battle of Omdurman and in the Boer War after which he was discharged and joined the Metropolitan Police Force. He later married and had 5 children and lived in Southwark. One night he came home from duty and found his home burnt out and his wife and 4 of his children had perished in the fire. Later he remarried and had 4 further children who were born between 1921 and 1928. The second of these children was named Fred Orlando Ratcliffe and was Colin's father. Was there any way of proving that Fred's story was true? Colin was unable to provide any further information except that Fred had died in 1959.

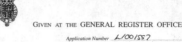

Marriage Certificate

Fred Ratcliffe
and
Minnie Mathilda Storey
12th December 1892

CERTIFIED COPY OF AN ENTRY OF MARRIAGE   GIVEN AT THE GENERAL REGISTER OFFICE

Application Number L100/557

CERTIFIED to be a true copy of an entry in the certified copy of a register of Marriages in the Registration District of _Paddington_

Given at the GENERAL REGISTER OFFICE, under the Seal of the said Office, the ___15th___ day of ___May___ ___2001___

MXA 828885

This certificate is issued in pursuance of section 65 of the Marriage Act 1949. Sub-section 3 of that section provides that any certified copy of an entry purporting to be sealed or stamped with the seal of the General Register Office shall be received as evidence of the marriage to which it relates without any further or other proof of the entry, and no certified copy purporting to have been given in the said Office shall be of any force or effect unless it is sealed or stamped as aforesaid.

CAUTION: THERE ARE OFFENCES RELATING TO FALSIFYING OR ALTERING A CERTIFICATE AND USING OR POSSESSING A FALSE CERTIFICATE. ©CROWN COPYRIGHT

WARNING: A CERTIFICATE IS NOT EVIDENCE OF IDENTITY.

Form MXA Series   Dd 0730 90M 04/01 SPSL(000153)

Proving Fred's Story - My research procedure:

Birth and Death References

I found the Birth and Death references for Fred at the Family Records Centre [FRC].

1871 June Qtr RATCLIFFE, Fred - Chipping Norton R. D. 3a 707

1871 7th March, Fred s/o James RATCLIFFE and Hannah Ratcliffe, formerly LANE, Stonemason, of Long Compton.

1959 March Qtr RATCLIFFE, Fred, 87, Uxbridge 5f 145

1959 21st January at 10 Wescott Waye, Uxbridge, Fred RATCLIFFE aged 87 years, General Labourer died of Cardiac failure and chronic bronchitis.

Both certificates indicated that he was called FRED and not Frederick. This information was to prove vital in my search for Fred's marriages.

Marriages

I then started to look for Fred's marriages. The second marriage was easy to find:

1920 March Qtr RATCLIFFE, Fred [PALMER] Uxbridge 3a 91

1920 January 10th, at Uxbridge Register Office, Fred RATCLIFFE, 38, Widower, General Labourer s/o James Ratcliffe,[deceased], Mason, and Frances Sarah PALMER, 33, Widow d/o John Axten, Market Gardener.

The first marriage took much longer to find. I checked the Marriage Indexes starting in 1889 when Fred would have been 18, and searched to 1905, by which time Fred would have returned from the Boer War. I found only one Fred RATCLIFFE getting married in the London area - 1892 December Qtr Paddington 1a 111. I ordered this even though I had no idea of the name of the spouse- the Marriage Indexes do not show the spouse's surname until 1911 September Qtr. The Marriage Certificate showed that Fred RATCLIFFE, aged 21 , Bricklayer, s/o James Ratcliffe, Mason, married Minnie Matilda

STOREY a 20 year old spinster at St Stephen's Parish Church, Paddington on December 12th, 1892 d/o David Lawson Storey, [deceased], Labourer.

Further research at The Family Record Centre

On my next visit to the FRC, I searched for the Birth of Minnie Matilda Storey in 1872 and for her death along with 4 children in the same Quarterly index - possibly in Southwark R.D. I quickly located the Birth reference:

STOREY, Minnie Matilda - 1872 March Qtr Caxton 3b 469 [which I ordered]. I found no reference for her death or for any children between 1900 and 1920. Just to be certain that I hadn't overlooked a vital reference or had missed an Index, I did a recheck this time looking at all the variants of the surname Ratcliffe - again I drew a blank.

So I made a search of the Birth indexes from 1892 onwards looking for possible clues. I found one promising entry:

1900 June Qtr, RATCLIFFE, George Orlando, Paddington 1a 65, [which I ordered] – purely on the basis that I knew Fred had an uncle John Orlando RATCLIFFE. I carried on the search but only came across the Birth references of the 4 children of Fred's second marriage:

RATCLIFFE Minnie Matilda [Axten] 1921 June Qtr Uxbridge 3a 70

RATCLIFFE Fred Orlando [Axten] 1922 September Qtr Uxbridge 3a 76

RATCLIFFE Rita Maud [Axten] 1925 June Qtr Uxbridge 3a 58

RATCLIFFE James Kent [Axten] 1927 June Qtr Uxbridge 3a 90

When the 2 Birth certificates arrived in the post, alarm bells started ringing! Fred's story was starting to look somewhat shaky!

Minnie Matilda STOREY's certificate showed that she was born in the Union Workhouse at Caxton, Cambridgeshire on January 14th, 1872, d/o Elizabeth Storey, Singlewoman. So she was

REGISTRATION DISTRICT Caxton

1893. BIRTH in the Sub-district of Caxton   in the   Counties of Cambridge & Huntingdon

No.	When and where born	Name, if any	Sex	Name and surname of father	Name, surname and maiden surname of mother	Occupation of father	Signature, description and residence of informant	When registered	Signature of registrar	Name entered after registration
241	Fourteenth November 1893 Great Eversden R.S.D.	Frederick James	Boy	Fred Ratcliffe	Minnie Matilda Ratcliffe formerly Storey	Bricklayer (Journeyman)	M. Ratcliffe Mother Great Eversden	Eighteenth December 1893	D. Smith of Newton Registrar	

CERTIFIED to be a true copy of an entry in the certified copy of a Register of Births in the District above mentioned.

Given at the GENERAL REGISTER OFFICE, under the Seal of the said Office, the ___12th___ day of ___November___ 2002

BXBZ 693796

Birth Certificate

Frederick James Ratcliffe
son of
Fred Ratcliffe
14th November 1893

---

unlikely to be the daughter of David Lawson Storey as stated on her Marriage Certificate.

I immediately checked the 1881 Census and found that Elizabeth was still living in Caxton Workhouse. It was recorded that she was aged 40 and her place of birth was Great Eversden, Cambridgeshire. She had 3 daughters with her in the Workhouse:- Sarah aged 12 born at Great Eversden, Minnie aged 9 and Mary Ann aged 4 both born at Caxton.

The 1881 Census of Great Eversden revealed a Mary STOREY, an unmarried woman of 71 living in Back Lane with 2 grandsons - Samuel George Storey aged 18 and David Lawson Storey aged 14, both Labourers and both born in Great Eversden! Was it possible that these STOREYs were related to Minnie Matilda?

The other Birth certificate was equally interesting.
1900 March 10th at 19 Stanley Street, Paddington - George Orlando s/o Fred RATCLIFFE and Minnie Matilda RATCLIFFE formerly STOREY, Builder's Labourer, Informant M.M.Ratcliffe, Mother, 19 Stanley Street, Padington.

At this time Fred should have been fighting in the Boer war if his story was correct!

More research at The Family Record Centre
On my next visit to the FRC I checked the 1871 Census of Great Eversden.
RG10/1576 Folio 47, Schedule-51 Cart Shed -
Mary STOREY Head U 61 Washerwoman CAM Har[l]ton
Elizabeth STOREY Dau U 26 Washerwoman CAM Gt Eversden
Samuel STOREY G/son 8 Scholar CAM Gt Eversden
David STOREY G/son 4 Scholar CAM Gt Eversden
Sarah STOREY G/child 2 CAM Gt Eversden

Then I checked the 1891 Census of Great Eversden. I found a considerable number of STOREY entries, but found no entry for Minnie Matilda.

The 1901 Census
I then had to wait nearly 6 months for the 1901 Census to become available. Fortunately I visited the FRC in January 2002 when the Census website was working and the first names I looked for were Fred and Minnie Matilda RATCLIFFE.

I located Fred living at 10 Theobald Street, Newington, Southwark in a single room, describing himself as a single man of 28, Bricklayer's Labourer born in Long Compton, Warwickshire.

I found Minnie Matilda at 21 Portman Street, St Marylebone, a single woman of 29 and a domestic servant born in Caxton, Cambridgeshire, but of George Orlando RATCLIFFE their son who would have been 13 months old, there was no sign, nor could I find him on the surname index!

What had happened since the birth of George Orlando? Why were they living apart and passing themselves off as single persons?

Death Indexes
This led me to recheck the Death Indexes after the 1901 Census and this time I noticed the death of a George O Ratcliffe aged 20 in 1920 June Qtr Brentford 3a 205, which I ordered. The certificate showed that George Orlando Ratcliffe, aged 20, a Railway Gateman, ex army, had died of Double Pneumonia on 9th May 1920 and the Informant was H. Bourne, Stepfather!

Back to the Marriage Indexes
So back to the Marriage Indexes to sort out this

CERTIFIED COPY OF AN ENTRY OF DEATH

Given at the GENERAL REGISTER OFFICE

Application Number B365952

Death Certificate

Frederick James Ratcliffe

29th December 1898

REGISTRATION DISTRICT					Kensington			
1899 DEATH in the Sub-district of Kensington Town in the County of London								
Columns:	1	2	3	4	5	6	7	8	9
No.	When and where died	Name and surname	Sex	Age	Occupation	Cause of Death	Signature, description and residence of informant	When registered	Signature of registrar
8	29th December 1898 29 Lonsdale Road	Frederick James Ratcliff	Male	5 years	Son of Fred Ratcliff Labourer 29 Lonsdale Road North Kensington	Found dead suffocation thro' a fire in a room in which the deceased and two other children were locked at a time when they were playing with matches. Accidental.	Certificate received from C. Luxmoore Drew Coroner for London Inquest held 30th December 1898	Second January 1899	C.R. Barnes Registrar

CERTIFIED to be a true copy of an entry in the certified copy of a Register of Deaths in the District above mentioned.

Given at the GENERAL REGISTER OFFICE, under the Seal of the said Office, the .... Fifteenth .... day of December 2004

DAZ 074393

CAUTION: THERE ARE OFFENCES RELATING TO FALSIFYING OR ALTERING A CERTIFICATE AND USING OR POSSESSING A FALSE CERTIFICATE. ©CROWN COPYRIGHT

WARNING: A CERTIFICATE IS NOT EVIDENCE OF IDENTITY.

---

surprising piece of information. I worked backwards from 1920 and in 1912 December Qtr found matching references for Henry Bourne and Minnie Matilda Ratcliffe - Brentford 3a 429. I ordered the Certificate which was to show that Henry Bourne, a bachelor of 37, a railway platelayer, married Minnie Matilda Ratcliffe, a widow of 40 d/o David Lawson Storey [deceased] at Brentford Register Office on November 23rd, 1912. But she wasn't a widow – Fred was still very much alive!

The National Archives
My next move was to visit the National Archives at Kew and look at the microfiche of the 1901 Census of Great Eversden [which were not then available at the FRC] to see if Minnie Matilda's mother Elizabeth was still alive. Yes she was - aged 61 - single and a Laundress but living with her was George RATLIFF, grandson, aged 1 born Paddington! [I should have picked this up earlier through the Advanced Search facility on he 1901 Census website]. But there were still no entries for any other children. I also checked the Divorce Records at Kew but found no entry for Fred and Minnie Matilda.

The Society of Genealogists
Almost as an afterthought, I visited the Society of Genealogists and discovered that they had a printed transcript of the Parish Registers of Great Eversden in their Library. What a find!

In the Baptismal Register 1813-1992, I discovered that Mary STOREY, Single woman had 3 illegitimate children baptised between 1833 and 1856: William [1833], Elizabeth [1845], and John [1856 - but born in 1849].
I found that Minnie Matilda's mother Elizabeth STOREY had 5 other illegitimate children baptised between 1863 and 1877:

Samuel George [1863], Sarah Jane [1865 who died at the age of 3 months], David Lawson [1869 aged 3], a second Sarah Jane [1869], and Mary Ann [1877], in addition to Minnie Matilda [1872].

The Big Breakthrough!
The Baptismal Register of Great Eversden also recorded the baptism of Frederick James s/o Fred and Minnie Matilda RATCLIFFE of Home Road, Battersea, London, Bricklayer on December 24th, 1893.

Back to The Family Record Centre
Having discovered this unexpected entry, I went back to the FRC and found the Birth entry for Frederick James RATCLIFFE [1893 December Qtr Caxton 3b 436]. The Birth certificate recorded his birth in Great Eversden on November 14th, 1893, s/o Fred Ratcliffe, Bricklayer Journeyman, and Minnie Ratcliffe formerly Storey of Great Eversden – not Battersea as shown in the Baptismal Register. The birth was registered on December 18th, 1893 - 6 days before the baptism. I then checked the 1901 Census but found no entry for Frederick James in the Person Search or the Advanced Search.
So I started a search for his death and found a promising entry in 1894 – Frederick James Ratcliff, 0, 1894 Sept Qtr, Sudbury 4a 333],and ordered it without checking all the Death indexes up to the 1901 Census Unfortunately the parents of this Frederick James Ratcliffe were not Fred and Minnie Matilda.

Back to The Family Record Centre - again
On my next visit to the FRC, I extended my search of the Death Indexes from 1894 to 1901, and came across a very interesting reference:
Frederick James RATCLIFF, 5, 1899 March Qtr Kensington 1a 66 and then noticed 2 other entries

Marriage Certificate

Fred Ratcliffe
and
Frances Sarah Palmer
10th January 1920

1920	Marriage solemnized at Register Office in the District of Uxbridge in the County of Middlesex

No.	When Married	Name and Surname	Age	Condition	Rank or Profession	Residence at the time of Marriage	Father's Name and Surname	Rank or Profession of Father
101	Tenth January 1920	Fred Ratcliffe	45 Years	Widower	General Laborer	166 High Street Uxbridge	James Ratcliffe deceased	Mason
		Frances Sarah Palmer	33 Years	Widow		10 Nash Yard Uxbridge	John Axten	Market Gardener

Married in the Register Office according to the Rites and Ceremonies of the by Licence

This Marriage was solemnized between us, Fred Ratcliffe / Frances S. Palmer — In the Presence of us, J. Field / E. E. Clayton — Henry Hugh Hatten Registrar, acting R. Phillips Superintendent Registrar

CERTIFIED to be a true copy of an entry in the certified copy of a register of Marriages in the Registration District of **Uxbridge**
Given at the GENERAL REGISTER OFFICE, under the Seal of the said Office, the **22nd** day of **February 2001**

MXA 779161

This certificate is issued in pursuance of section 65 of the Marriage Act 1949. Sub-section 3 of that section provides that any certified copy of an entry purporting to be sealed or stamped with the seal of the General Register Office shall be received as evidence of the marriage to which it relates without any further or other proof of the entry, and no certified copy purporting to have been given in the said Office shall be of any force or effect unless it is sealed or stamped as aforesaid.

CAUTION: THERE ARE OFFENCES RELATING TO FALSIFYING OR ALTERING A CERTIFICATE AND USING OR POSSESSING A FALSE CERTIFICATE ©CROWN COPYRIGHT

WARNING: A CERTIFICATE IS NOT EVIDENCE OF IDENTITY.

---

in the same quarter with the same reference.
Reta Elizabeth M RATCLIFF – 3 and Dora Mabel
RATCLIFF – 1.
Had I finally found the references of Fred and
Minnie's children who had died in a house fire?
I ordered 3 Death certificates and the Birth
certificates of Reta and Dora. The Certificates
confirmed my worst fears. All three children
were the children of Fred RATCLIFF and the
cause of death was the same on each certificate.
1898 29th December at 29 Lonsdale Road, North
Kensington.

*"Found dead – suffocation- through a fire in a room in
which the deceased and two other children were locked
at a time when they were playing with matches –
Accidental."*

Certificate received from C. Luxmoore Drew,
Coroner for London. Inquest held 30th
December, 1898.

Newspaper Report

I followed this up with a visit to Kensington
Local Studies Library where I located a report
of the tragedy in the *Kensington News* dated
Saturday, December 31st, 1898.

Fatal Fire at Notting Hill
*A disastrous fire, which, while it did not result in
serious destruction of the property, was unfortunately
attended with loss of life of three little children, broke
out last Thursday afternoon at 29 Lonsdale Road,
Notting Hill. The house is one of eight rooms and is
sub-let to no fewer than five families of lodgers. The
front room on the second floor was tenanted by a
bricklayer named Ratcliffe, and it appears that soon
after one o'clock in the afternoon, Mrs Ratcliffe left
the house temporarily, while her three children, a little
boy five years old named Frederick, a little girl of three
named Rita and a baby daughter 18 months old
named Dora remained playing in the room in which
there was a fire. About 20 minutes past one o'clock,
the other inmates of the house detected a smell of fire,*

*and almost simultaneously passers by noticed a blaze
through the windows, and rushed to raise the alarm.
Directly the door was burst open, dense volumes of
smoke poured out of the room, and it was with the
utmost difficulty that an entry was forced into the
place.*

*A period of intense excitement ensued, but without a
moments delay several people dropped upon their
hands and knees and proceeded to search the room,
while messengers were dispatched for the firemen and
pails and cans of water were requisitioned pending
their arrival from Ladbroke Road. One by one the little
ones were brought out. They were in an unconscious
condition, and when removed to a local surgery, the
medical men who were hastily called to the scene
pronounced life to be extinct. In the meantime the
mother had returned, and some heartrending scenes
were witnessed.*

*The firemen from the local stations attacked the
outbreak vigorously with two powerful hydrants, for
the fire was increasing in strength every moment, and
the task was a very difficult one owing to the densely
suffocating smoke which poured from the place. The
flames were overcome in the course of half an hour
when the following official report of the occurrence
was presented to Commander Wells, R.N., by
Superintendent T. Smith:-*

*"Called at half past one p.m. to 29 Lonsdale Road,
Notting Hill, W., to premises tenanted by F. Ratcliffe,
lodger; back room second floor, ditto, E. Wickens,
lodger; front room on ground floor and basement,
ditto, A. Friend, lodger; back room on ground floor,
ditto, T. Dean, lodger; landlord unknown; cause of the
fire unknown – none of the lodgers insured. Damage –
Front room on second floor and the contents damaged
by fire, heat, smoke and water; back room on ditto and
the contents by smoke, water and breakage; rest of
house of eight rooms and the contents slightly by
water and removal. Frederick Ratcliffe, aged five*

years, Rita Ratcliffe, aged three years, and Dora Ratcliffe, aged one year and six months, suffocated.

Gallant attempts to rescue, successful as far as their immediate object was concerned, were made by Mr James BREGAN who lives at 4, Lonsdale Mews; Mr George WILLIAMS and Mr Henry John REDMOND. Each rushed into the room and succeeded in bringing out a child."

What a sad ending to this piece of research.

Ongoing Research

However this is not the end of the story. My research is still ongoing. I have had the Divorce Records of Decrees Nisi searched from 1901-1912 and drawn a blank. These are located at First Avenue House in High Holborn and a fee is payable for a search to be made.

Did they drift apart after an attempted reconciliation following the terrible shock of losing 3 young children in a house fire and later consider themselves free to marry again? Did Fred go to South Africa shortly after George Orlando was conceived and on his return decide to live apart from Minnie Matilda, hence he was living in Newington at the time the 1901 Census was taken? I have found no evidence among Army Records at The National Archives to suggest that he ever served in the army.

My research into Minnie Matilda's family has revealed that she and her second husband Henry BOURNE moved to Mansfield in Nottinghamshire, following the death of George

Orlando Ratcliffe in 1920. They both died there within 6 months of each other in 1959/60 – Minnie was 88 years of age and died of appendicitis. In her will which I located at First Avenue House, she left bequests to 3 nephews and 2 nieces – all children of her half-brother David Lawson STOREY. David predeceased Minnie but from my checks of the Mansfield Electoral Registers held at the Nottinghamshire County Record Office, he and his family were living in Mansfield from the early 1920s with the men working in the Nottinghamshire coalfield. – a rather different way of mining to the local industry of Great Eversden which was coprolite mining.

Of Fred's supposed service in the Metropolitan Police, I have found no evidence – all references that I have found indicate that he was either a builder's labourer, a bricklayer or a general labourer.

My feeling is that he made up quite a lot of the story, especially the death of Minnie Matilda in a house fire, in order to marry Frances in 1920. If that was the case why did he call the first child of his second marriage, Minnie Matilda? Did he think that by 1920, she was dead and therefore he was free to marry again? Neither Colin nor I will ever know the full truth but we are both certain of one thing - he was a good storyteller!

How Events Beyond Our Control Can Change Our Lives

Elizabeth Blatchford

provides an example of how historical events changed the life of one family

One piece of advice which all family historians should heed is to learn about historical events through which our forebears lived – whether local, national or international, and the influence these events may well have had upon their daily lives. The answers to some of the enigmas we come across doing our research may be found when you stop to see what was happening in their environment.
For example: -
'Why did my grandmother have her first child away from the marital home?
'Why did that family move so frequently?'
'Why is grandad's death registered miles from where he was living on the last census return?'
Even families who lead apparently uneventful lives were affected by such things as failed harvests, the spread of industrialisation, disease, epidemics and wars in which innocent people found themselves caught up.

The following article is the result of a delightful encounter I had with a lady whose early life was irrevocably affected by war and its consequences and the bearing this had on her later life. It is the story of one little girl and her family who were living during the turmoil that was Europe immediately before and during World War II.

The account of her life which Johanna Marianne Ludwig (Hansi) gives provides invaluable insights into her own history and answers many of the questions which future generations of her own family may well ask: -
'Why did they move?'
'Where did they come from originally?'
'Why was our family so dispersed?'

Johanna Marianne Ludwig (Hansi) – A Personal Travel Saga.

I was born on 22nd September 1930 at Trautenau (now called Trutnov) – a town in the Sudetenland of Czechoslovakia situated 30 kilometres from the German border. My name at birth was Johanna Marianne Ludwig (known as Hansi) and I was the only daughter of Friedrich and Theresa Ludwig (née Letzel).

Johanna Marianne Ludwig (Hansi)
Early 1939

Generations of my family were born and lived in Trautenau. My grandfather Karl Alois Ludwig who worked in the brewing industry was born in 1873 and died in Trautenau 29th September 1929. His wife, my grandmother Marie Ludwig, (nee Patzak) was also born there on 6th February 1877; and my father Friedrich (Fritz) Ludwig was born in Trautenau on 27th May 1902.

Sadly, when I was only two years old my mother Theresa died when she was expecting her second child and suffering from tuberculosis. Following my mother's death I stayed initially with Theresa's mother (Johanna Letzel). Tiny though I was, I have a memory of sitting under a large kitchen table covered with velour cloth and eating coffee beans which made me sick! Before long I went to stay with my father and his mother Maria Ludwig (known to me as Omi – (grandma)) and his sister, Maria Anna Ludwig. As I was so young I was not aware of some of their activities during this time. Between 1932 and 1937 my father and his sister were helping Jewish people to escape over the German border in winter by skiing over the Riesengebirge (Giant Mountains) into Czechoslovakia and offering

them shelter in the cellar basement of our house, before their onward journey to freedom. I can remember as a child being told not to go near or play in the cellar, a place where we stored apples and vegetables and where these escapees were sheltering. I was aware of people coming, staying, and then moving on from our house.

In 1938 I started school in Trautenau with lessons mainly in German, with Czech as a second language. We were a Catholic family but because we were not regular churchgoers, I well remember, when the priest visited school I was excluded from lessons as were some of the Jewish children.

On 29th September 1938 Hitler, Chamberlain, Daladier and Mussolini signed the Munich Agreement which agreed to the transfer of Sudetenland to Germany.

I did not understand why with no prior warning or preparation my family suddenly left Trautenau and moved to Pocaplech, a small town a few miles south west of Prague. We were now refuges and stayed with some Czech people in a so-called 'safe house'. My father and his friends must have been concerned for their own safety presumably because their activities had become known to the authorities.

My father had met and married his second wife Ritchie (née Bröckl) in Prague in 1939 and aunty Minki had married Walter Kinzel. They hoped to be permitted to go to Canada, to Saskatchewan and to acquire land and start new lives. At the time only family units were being accepted by the Canadian Government.

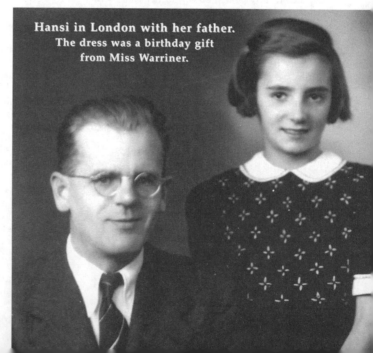

Hansi in London with her father. The dress was a birthday gift from Miss Warriner.

**Johanna Marianne Ludwig (Hansi)
with Grandmother in Trautenau**

Also with us in the safe house were Wenzel
Jaksch, and two other friends and my
grandmother (Omi).

*On the 1st October 1938 the German army moved
into the Sudetenland and in March
1939 the Sudetenland was officially annexed by*

*Germany. A report which appeared in **The
Manchester Guardian** on **17th March 1939**
stated –*

*"A sorrowing Prague, yesterday had its first day
of German rule – a day in which the Czechs
learned of the details of their subjection to
Germany, and in which the Germans began their
measures against the Jews and against those
people who have "opened their mouths too wide."
Prague's streets were jammed with silent
pedestrians wandering about, looking out of the
corners of their eyes at German soldiers carrying
guns, at armoured cars, and at other military
precautions. Some Czechs were seen turning up
their noses at the Germans. Germans were
everywhere. Bridges were occupied by troops and
each bridge-head had a heavy machine-gun
mounted on a tripod and pointing to the sky.
Every twenty yards along the pavement two
machine-guns were mounted facing each other.
Suicides have begun. The fears of the Jews grow.
The funds of the Jewish community have been
seized, stopping Jewish relief work. Hundreds of
people stood outside the British Consulate
shouting; "We want to get away!" According to
an official spokesman of the German Foreign
Office in Berlin last night, the Gestapo will have
rounded up hundreds of 'harmful characters'
within the next few days. So far about fifty to a
hundred men have been put in local gaols. ~ "
There are certain centres of resistance which need
to be cleaned up," said the spokesman. "Also
some people open their mouths too wide. Some of
them neglected to get out in time. They may total
several thousand before we are through." The
head of the Gestapo in Prague is reported to have
been more definite: "We have 10,000 arrests to
carry out."*

**The 'Escape Committee'
April 1939**

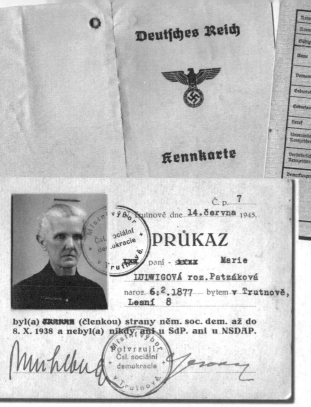

*Already, say Reuter's correspondent, everyone
seems to have an acquaintance who has
disappeared.*

During March 1939 my father, Ritchie, Minki,
Walter Kinzel, Wenzel Jaksch and two others set
off on skis as if they were going on a holiday in
the mountains. They had only their travelling
clothes and small back packs. They made their
way over the frontier and into Poland which
had not then been invaded. In Warsaw they
were met by Miss Doreen Warriner. Miss
Warriner, a Quaker, who lived in London, had
been organising the escape of Jewish people to
Britain and had been corresponding with family
members, particularly Jaksch. She arranged for
the group in Warsaw to get to Sweden where
they arrived on 9th April 1939. In Sweden they
met up with friends who had fled Germany and
Czechoslovakia. Among them was Hanna,
Ritchie's sister (ex wife of Wenzel Jaksch). They
then made their way to the UK, arriving in
London in the summer of 1939. Father and
Ritchie stayed with Miss Warriner at her flat at
24 Belsize Park Gardens, near Hampstead
Heath. I continued to live with Omi in
Pocaplech.

*Following a violent attack on Jewish people in
Germany in November 1938, known as
Kristallnacht, the British Government eased
immigration restrictions and an unspecified
number of children under the age of 17 were
allowed to enter Great Britain from Germany and*

Miss Warriner.

The wedding of
Fritz and Ritchie Ludwig

rescue operations. Jews, Quakers, and Christians of many denominations worked together to bring the children to Britain. Between 1938 and 1939 over 9000 children between the ages of 5 and 17 arrived safely, many left their parents behind and never saw them again.

In late August 1939 Omi received a message to get me and one small suitcase to the railway station in Prague to join a Kindertransport which was leaving. I was briefed that my name was Rebecca and I had not to disclose my true identity to anyone. I was just nine years old. I had taken the place of a Jewish girl of that name who was too unwell to travel and was suffering from scarlet fever. I did not know it, but I was on the very last Kindertransport to leave Prague. With little food or water we took two days to reach Holland, and thence travelled by ship to England. One of my first memories of arrival in England was the white bread which I thought was horrible, and having to be de-loused! I was met and taken to be reunited with my father and Ritchie and we all stayed with Miss Warriner for a while in Hampstead.

Meanwhile Omi was now on her own and made her way back to Trautenau, living throughout the war in poor circumstances and having to sew shirts for the Nazis.

On 3rd September 1939 War was declared. Within a very short time of my arrival in London and the happiness of being back with my father I was evacuated to the countryside with a group of children I did not know. I could not speak English, only German and Czech.

Probably as a result of this I was the last child to be taken in as an evacuee, and had to share a bed with three other children, one of whom was a bed-wetter. I got the blame, again probably because I could not explain, not speaking any English. These were not happy days, and I managed to write home (in German) and was taken back to be with my father. I was enrolled in an English school and learned English quickly.

At this time there were many Czechoslovak refugees living in hostels and camps. The adults were given five shillings per week and the children half a crown. My father was allowed to take up employment and any idea of moving on to Canada was now out of the question due to the torpedoing of shipping crossing the Atlantic. At this time I spent eighteen months in various schools, following my father as he did labouring jobs on farms, for which he got a wage and a tied cottage.

After 1941 my father worked as an internal grinder at an aircraft factory and finally at Battersea Power Station as a plumbers' assistant – mainly on authorised destruction of Bank of England currency notes! At last I experienced a period of permanency when we rented a house in Laurel Gardens, Mill Hill, London. I did well at school, although my English was not good enough for me to attend grammar school; however, I was accepted at Orange Hill Girls School in Burnt Oak.

Back in Trautenau Omi saw the Russians take over the country, then with the help of the Red

Cross, she was able to get to the UK, bringing with her papers of importance to the British Government from the Czechoslovak Government. She arrived on 25th February 1946 and went to live with Auntie Minki and Uncle Walter at Shotley Bridge, County Durham until her death in the early 1950's. She was cremated and her ashes taken in later years to Deisenhofen, near Munich, and placed in the Family Ludwig plot.

In November of 1946 my father and Ritchie left the UK to go to the Munich area of occupied Germany. Father had been asked by the British and American authorities to help set up farming co-operatives on the large estates abandoned by the Nazis. These were co-operatives of five to six farming families formed to establish stable production of food and to look after the environment. By this time, at the age of 15 years, I decided to remain in the UK. I stayed as a paying guest with neighbours in Laurel Gardens so that I could finish School Certificate work. I did quite well and gained seven School Certificates at school in Burnt Oak. My father later took German citizenship enabling him to work as a Civil Servant for the Bavarian State Government at the Bayerisches Staatsministerium für Ernährung, Landwirtschaft und Forsten (The Bavarian State Ministry for Food, Farming and Forests). He had been promoted and appointed Oberamptsrat (national Senior Councillor) before he retired.

After the war in summer of 1947 I asked my Aunt Minki if I could come and stay with them as I did not wish to go to war-torn Germany and in any case by then my German was not good enough for further education there. So I went north to Shotley Bridge, County Durham where I stayed with Aunt and Uncle Walter and Omi once more. I then enrolled in Consett Grammar School, doing sixth form work plus a pre-nursing course.

At 18 years of age I left school to study nursing at Edinburgh Royal Infirmary and after qualifying I went on to study midwifery at Newcastle and Carlisle Hospitals, and then did holiday relief work for district nurses in the Newcastle docks area – returning to Newcastle Midwifery Hospital as a Staff nurse on the labour ward.

On the 26th June 1952 I attained British nationality.

1954 – 1955. Auntie Minki was ill and Uncle Walter was made redundant by the return of the teacher whose place he had taken returning from being called up to the Forces. They had to find jobs and moved to Jardine Hall near

Lockerbie in Dumfriesshire. There Uncle Walter taught mathematics at the independent boys' boarding school at Holt school. Auntie Minki concentrated on producing knitting patterns in Viennese lace, on which subject she published two expert volumes and many instructional pamphlets. I helped them during this move and then sought a new job.

Dumfries and Galloway Royal Infirmary was looking for a Ward Sister and Junior Sister Tutor and I took the latter appointment.

In 1956, while living at Dumfries I met the, then, Flight Lieutenant Hugh Witherow, an officer in the Royal Air Force Regiment and when Hugh returned from a tour of duty with the Aden Protectorate Levies we were married in Lincoln on 20th September 1958. We had a daughter, born there in 1960 (now herself married with three daughters), and in 1962 a son, born in Singapore; he is still single and lives with us.

Since then we have 'followed the Flag' to Singapore, Maldives, Borneo, Cyprus and Malta and also various appointments in the UK. On Hugh's retirement as Squadron Leader in 1982 we settled in Rickmansworth, Hertfordshire.

Peripheral matters —
1. While my father, Uncle Walter, and Auntie Minki had Jewish friends during their time at university in Prague, Vienna and Geneva as students, none of them was Jewish, nor was my stepmother Ritchie: they were all by birth Roman Catholic but never went to church!

2. Untold in this direct, personal account are certain background details and connections of these family names with such significant proceedings as the Ludwigs' action over several years to rescue Jewish refugees; with Social Democrat connections including Willi Brandt and with President Benes's government, perhaps best illustrated by Frau Marie Ludwig's task of conveying papers from Prague to the British authorities shortly after the War. It is also of significance that none of the Ludwigs or Kinzels were ever detained under the Defence 18B Regulations, as was normal for aliens at that time; also that Friedrich Ludwig was particularly selected and asked to take up a senior position in Bavaria.

Sadly Hansi died on the afternoon of 15th September 2005 following a relatively short illness. She was very enthusiastic to share her extraordinary story with us. Her husband, Hugh, has agreed that her story should be published.

Chef to an Earl
Maureen Lavelle

As a Heritage Guide at Croxteth Hall near Liverpool I meet many visitors as they pass through the rooms. Many of them have interesting stories of their own that add to our store of knowledge. Best of all are the people who have been in service at some time in their life. None of them has been as interesting as the man still living on the estate who was the last Chef to the Earl of Sefton.

A lot of my time is spent 'below stairs" in the vast Victorian kitchens that Chef Raymond used during his working life. Although retired now, his comments and observations give a glimpse of another world. His tales of life behind the scenes as he catered for the Earl and his guests can only make us wonder at the way things were.

Raymond Lempereur started to cook at the age of 14 in his homeland of France. By 19 he had survived a world war, witnessed an event that would take him to a War Tribunal and decided to widen his horizons. He left his family and the beautiful girl he had decided to marry and travelled to England.

At 24 he was alone in a strange country, unable to speak the language and cooking for an Earl at his country seat, Croxteth Hall. Within a few years he had brought his new wife (also unable to speak English) to join him.

Their culinary creations here and at the Earl's shooting estate, Abbeystead, over a period of 24 years fed royalty, nobility and Hollywood stars (the Countess was American and had many connections).

Their life below stairs and behind the scenes and the journey Raymond made from Avignon in France, to Croxteth had more interesting twists than many of the films he watched to improve his English. As I listened to his story over many conversations, I felt sure others would be as interested in the details.

It has been said that the ideal combination for every aristocratic household is an English Butler and a French Chef. Little did the young Raymond Lempereur realise that this would one day be his position in life

Raymond was born in May 1925 in Avignon in the south of France. A city once known as the home of The Pope. His mother ran the Laundry. Before her fifth birthday she had died of cancer and Raymond along with his brother and sister

were brought up by their aunt. They moved to a villa outside the town and the extended family included cousins and an uncle. Money was short and life was hard. Grandmother was given coupons to help feed and clothe the youngsters but Raymond often had cardboard in his shoes to cover the holes. Meals could be bread and milk with a drink of coffee. It's not surprising that he contracted polio at a young age leaving him with a weakness for the rest of his life. The only treatment in the 1930's was to spend long periods of time in a sanitorium not seeing his friends or family and missing school.

At the age of 14 he was considered to have finished his education and advised to get a 'seated' job although his ambition had been to be a mechanic. He was found a position in a confectionery. This meant he was on his feet all day and every day but it was the start of a career that meant his family would never again go hungry.

It was 1939, the world went to war and young Raymond had to keep his wits about him. He grew to love his new life, eager to learn all he could about the food he was cooking and the dishes he could create. His lowly position in the kitchens meant he could move around from one Hotel to another as they needed help. He could learn from each kitchen different ways of preparing food. Often he would return to the kitchens during his off duty hours to watch the

Head Chef boning meat or preparing vegetables. The canapés and hors d'oevres he saw being made would be created by himself years later to be served at Croxteth Hall.

As he moved around the town between his home and the Hotel he would often see young men trying to obstruct the occupying germans. Putting sand in fuel tanks or slashing tyres was a risky business. As the Germans had requisitioned parts of the Hotel including a kitchen area Raymond could watch their cooks at work making large pans of sauerkraut with sausages and pieces of pork. Meat, along with other foods was strictly and severely rationed, served only to German officers, so Raymond and his friend would never miss a chance to help themselves straight from the pot as it simmered while the cooks took a break.

The militia were sending all the able young men to work for them and Raymond didn't want to go so had to try and keep one step ahead. Being caught avoiding the 'call-up' meant a concentration camp or being shot as an example to others. Eventually he was traced and made to work in the railway yards. After the war he went back to the kitchens of various hotels. At each new position he was greeted with the words, 'Forget what you've been told, we do things my way here'. Raymond learned many different ways and techniques to prepare food. He kept this store of knowledge ready to use in his own kitchen.

The opportunity to travel across the Channel to England and take up a position in the kitchens of the French Embassy in London seemed too good an opportunity to miss. This would be a fresh start in life even though it meant leaving Elda, his sweetheart.

He had not been at the Embassy long before he realised the Head Chef had a problem, he liked to drink. This was overlooked by his employers until the day of an important visit when he couldn't cook. 'You'll have to take over' Raymond was told. 'I can't' he replied. 'Then what have you been doing these past weeks?' stated his employer leaving the kitchen. . The dinner party for the First Sealord could not be cancelled. He asked his fellow chefs for help. They came from the Belgian and Spanish Embassies and the Savoy Hotel. Each Chef taking a part of the preparation and cooking. The 'Well done' from upstairs boosted his confidence and spurred him to learn more of his craft

In 1949 his reputation was growing among friends and acquaintances. He was offered a short term position working for the film magnate Alexander Korda as a chef on his yacht at £20 a week. This was very good money with good connections and he was very tempted. A phone call from the Countess of Sefton, who luckily spoke fluent French as Raymond had not learned English, changed everything. She had heard of his skills and offered him a position at her home, Croxteth Hall outside Liverpool. Raymond could not leave the home of the French Ambassador, which was considered French territory where he now worked, without a work permit. This was soon arranged by Lady Sefton and he travelled north through a land of bomb sites and destruction.

After the long journey from London an apprehensive Raymond waited by the now empty train, his bags at his feet but no-one came to meet him. . A Liverpool policeman approached him. 'What are you waiting for?' he asked. Raymond tried to explain but his position was made worse by his lack of English. He made a mental note to start learning the language as soon as he could. Trying to explain to a confused policeman didn't work so he reached into his pocket to produce the crested notepaper headed 'Croxteth' In an instant everything changed. The constable hailed a taxi and gave instructions to the driver as a tired Raymond sank into the soft leather seat. He was driven through the streets and out into the countryside eventually turning into the Croxteth Park estate. Through fields and parkland he travelled his eyes widening as he saw the impressive Hall outlined against the evening sky. This was much bigger and grander than he had imagined but it was too late to back out now. The young man needed to show his confidence and intention to be treated with the respect his position deserved. The Chef in large establishments was always highly paid and respected as the reputation of the household would depend on them. To have visitors unhappy with their food would in turn give the 'family' a poor reputation.
Missing the imposing front entrance he was

Croxteh Hall

*Josephine
Countess of Sefton*

taken to the servants' entrance After paying the taxi driver his 'ten bob' (50p) fare, he was ushered in to be met by the Butler. 'The Countess has been asking for you' he said as a swish of evening gown topped by red hair came towards him. 'Good evening' she said and as an afterthought, 'Why are you so late?' Staring at this very glamorous lady Raymond started to explain. She seemed surprised, 'I sent the car for you' she stated as she swept away. He came to know his mistress as a wonderful lady but, rather forgetful at times. When The Queen, along with Princess Elizabeth and Princess Margaret were due to visit she only remembered to tell him the evening before; causing a panic baking session lasting well into the night.

Within days he settled into his rooms behind the large kitchens. Settling into the Hall and Estate was a different thing. It was far bigger than he had imagined, over 1300 acres. A Hall with more than 200 rooms and a family history that could be traced back almost 900 years through 31 generations to a knight who had arrived in Britain with William the Conqueror. They also had more than 18000 acres at Abbeystead in the Trough of Bowland near Lancaster, where the Earl's shooting parties took place. This was a smaller version of Croxteth, well loved by the family and in time Raymond and his family. Raymond was more than impressed as would his family be when they received his letters. He would not see them until a visit home 14 months later.

During his first days the Countess showed him round. He went to the walled garden to meet the Head Gardener who would provide most of the vegetables for the kitchen. On to the Farm and the Manager responsible for eggs, dairy produce and meat. Out into the estate in her car to see the Head Gamekeeper who supervised the rearing of game to provide the Earl and his guests with sport, some of which came to the

kitchen to be served at table later.

After meeting more household staff she took him into Liverpool to visit the various stores used by the Hall. He was introduced to the manager of the prestigious Cooper's, suppliers of groceries, who was informed Raymond had her full permission to order anything he required. A position of considerable responsibility and trust, but also a great privilege.

He settled into his duties gaining the respect and admiration of his employers. He gained particular pleasure from a visit the Earl made down to his kitchen to tell him, 'It's a long time since we had food presented so well at the Hall, keep it up'

Like most aristocratic families they had a ritual almost unchanged for generations. The Earl was Chairman of Chester Racecourse and Steward at Aintree, Newbury, Newmarket and Royal Ascot, so many visitors to the Hall were connected with racing. The biggest racing occasion being The Grand National. These visits tested Raymond's creativity and he gained great pleasure in devising new and interesting ways to prepare and serve dishes for His Lordship and his guests. Some of them, particularly those from Hollywood coming to visit him in his kitchens.

Earl of Sefton

One of the busiest occasions during the year was the Waterloo Cup. Competed for during the annual Hare Coursing meeting it was eagerly awaited. The Earl owned coursing greyhounds and always gave a splendid dinner after the meeting. The grandest event on their calendar. The food was specially prepared and the table set with a white damask tablecloth the gold Waterloo Cup as the centrepiece. The Waterloo Chain made to commemorate the event was draped around the table. An extra link was added each year and a small gold plaque engraved with the winning dog's name. The Earls' dog, 'So Clever' was to win in 1971 causing great celebrations at Croxteth.

One of his first tasks was to master this new language. Although the Countess spoke fluent

French having lived in Paris before her marriage, as did the secretary, Raymond worked hard. The Earl took 10 newspapers and when they had been cleared from 'upstairs' each night Raymond would take them to his room to study. With a dictionary at his side putting words to pictures and the help of the chauffeur he had command of the language within a year, but never lost his French accent. During his off duty time he often went to the cinema in the nearby village to extend his vocabulary and knowledge of English. Westerns were a particular favourite but not much help with the language of a stately home. One afternoon the film was 'Waterloo Bridge' with Robert Taylor and Vivien Leigh. He had already seen this film in Marakesh, dubbed into French which meant he could follow the soundtrack. An enjoyable afternoon with an easy lesson that day. The hardest part was numbers. England was still measuring in imperial units and money was pounds, shillings and pence, all very difficult for a man brought up within a decimal system.

In December 1950, he took time off to return to France to marry his 19 year old sweetheart, Elda. They had seen each other for short periods totalling only 2 months in two and a half years but had got to know each other well through their many letters. After visiting Marseilles and Paris they set sail for England, Raymond having to reassure his apprehensive young bride who was only 19, and thought she would never see her homeland again.

They journeyed to London having a chance to savour 'upstairs' life at The Regency Hotel before travelling on to a cold Liverpool. By this time Raymond had tutored Elda enough to say 'Good Morning' in perfect English. To converse any further took a lot longer, but she too learnt fluent English.

The Earl and Countess were spending Christmas away. This gave the newly weds a chance to spend some time together in between Raymond's duties catering for the staff and he introduced

Elda in kitchen

Elda to the strange new tastes of plum pudding and mince pies.

After a few years Elda joined Raymond in the kitchens and together they perfected a routine for feeding, 'upstairs', and the staff, 'downstairs'. Breakfast, lunch, afternoon tea and dinners of five or six courses were served to the Earl and Countess who always dressed for dinner even if they were alone. Although Raymond created wonderful dishes for 'upstairs' tasting sessions were often confined to what was left uneaten in the silver dishes returned to the kitchens.

The shooting season created extra work in the kitchens as guests were regularly invited. As well as meals at the Hall Raymond would have to provide a lunch to be sent out to the shoot and food for the loaders and chauffeurs. The first day's pheasant or grouse were rushed back to be plucked, prepared and cooked for dinner the same night. Extra birds would sometimes be sent out to a local girl for plucking at 6d (2^1/$_2$p) per bird, she often did as many as 60 birds at a time. The birds had been reared by the estate gamekeepers, who fed them a diet containing currants and sultanas to sweeten their meat.

Raymond had not intended to remain at Croxteth for ever and had plans to return to France particularly as Elda wanted their child to be born in France. Raymond's priority was 'upstairs' and he could not go with his wife when the birth was due so she stayed and their son was born in England. They returned to France for his baptism. Their son grew more English than French as the years went on.

As time went on Raymond was able to make changes to his kitchen bringing it more up to date but he had a bigger task at Abbeystead. Life had remained almost the same at the shooting estate since the family had acquired it in the late 1800's. Rooms were cold and unheated and the kitchen almost non existent. Everything to cater for the Earl and his guests had to be packed into a lorry and taken from Croxteth by the staff. Hampers of food, pots, pans, dishes all had to be transported leaving Croxteth deserted except for a skeleton staff. He prided himself on never forgetting anything but on one occasion the Countess requested parmesan cheese. Realising it had been left behind and knowing the village had only one shop, the Post Office, he had to admit defeat.

Accommodation was as rigid as in Victorian days with male staff on one floor and female staff on another. The old fashioned kitchens had to cater for more than 30 people a day depending how many guests had been invited and a temperamental cooker frustrated

Fire at Croxteth Hall

and causing the loss of many of the Earl's precious belongings.

Raymond stayed until the Earl died in 1972. The widowed Countess asked him to continue working for her in London and Abbeystead. He refused and went on to open his own business in Liverpool. She would send her chauffeur to what she called his 'little shop.' The amazed local shoppers stopped to watch the gleaming Daimler draw up outside. Raymond eventually retired due to ill health but still feels it was 'a privilege to work for Lord Sefton. Hard work but so rewarding and worthwhile. A different world with the kind of life we will never see again. I feel privileged to have been part of it'

Raymond. The corridors were so cold getting food to the dining room while it was still hot meant footmen had to move quickly with their trays. It was here that Raymond and Elda learned to love the English seasons. As the kitchens overlooked wonderful gardens they enjoyed their new hobby of photography, even creating a dark room among the drying teatowels.

Raymond never did make it back to France although he was almost poached by a noble visitor who once 'borrowed' him from Lord Sefton for a short time and tried to entice him to stay at his home in Ireland. Nor did he leave when the Hall caught fire flooding his kitchens

If you would like to know more of Raymond's wartime adventures or his life behind the scenes at Croxteth Park read his story in '*Avignon to Croxteth*' by Maureen Lavelle *ISBN 1 901231 43 7* at bookshops.

Ever wanted to chart your research?
Well now you can.

At The Chartists we've developed a range of template charts including arc, bow tie and circle formats, to allow you to present your research beautifully.

Our aim is to provide only the highest quality chart templates that your research deserves. We achieve this through a unique combination of traditional skills and the most up to date technology.

The Chartists

Display your research *Beautifully*

www.thechartists.co.uk

The Fashions - Expressly designed and prepared for the Englishwoman's Domestic Magazine, May 1861

From Dresses to Drainpipes:
magazines, household manuals and women readers 1859 – 1959
Dr Jane Batchelor

The aim of this article is look at the relationship between women's magazines, household manuals and the nature of women's lives between 1859 – 1959. Looking at these texts aimed primarily at a female audience it is possible to trace a clear shift in tone which I feel is suggestive of the changing nature of women's lives and of domestic life in general during this period.

Dinner, dress and duty: 1859 - 1901
1859 saw the serialisation of Mrs Beeton's *Household Management* in *Englishwoman's Domestic Magazine*, a magazine which Samuel Beeton her husband had edited in the three years before he met her. This manual, first published separately in 1861, was only one of the most popular of several household manuals published in the late nineteenth century to set a high standard for domestic life, and has now gone through more than sixty editions (Briggs, pp. 216 - 217). The introduction to the manual described it as:

The Most Complete and thorough Manual on Cooking and Housekeeping ever offered at the price to the English public.

"At the price": at the beginning of this period commercial printing was beginning to take off for a wider audience as the industrial revolution facilitated cheap mass production of magazines and books (Steinburg, p.350). However it is important to understand that by "At the price" Mrs Beeton meant more available not to everyone but to "all women of middle class" whose "duty" was to cook "plain ordinary dishes" and carry out household tasks

with the assistance of her servant/s, who were expected to show a rigorous attention to detail:

The next work is to wash the dinner things. In this the housemaid should assist the cook; she should do the glass and the plate, leaving the plates and dishes and knives to cook.

The plates and dishes should be washed in a dish-tub… The water should not be so hot for the knives …The silver will require hotter water. (*Household Management* 1861, pp.559 – 560).

The role of the good middle class wife in the home was to supervise the work being done, to ensure that all is ready for when "the master of the house returns", much as Coventry Patmore in his idealised portrait of womanly virtue The Angel in the House (1854) had looked forward to seeing "The gentle wife, who decks his board" (p.170).

Mrs Beeton's book can be seen as both practical and aspirational, a guide to the ideal middle class home. Aspirational is also an adjective which can be given to *Englishwoman's Domestic Magazine*, squarely aimed at women of means hoping to enhance their social status wishing to know how to dress and behave. The 1861 edition contained colour plates of Parisian fashions, for example in May 1861 there is a plate of elaborate woman's bonnets with flowers, ribbons and tassels. Other regular features in the 1861 edition of the magazine were "The Family Secret" a dramatic romantic serial set within a privileged domestic setting where hair was dressed, bell ropes pulled and

PATTERN PAGES

coachmen hired (p. 2, p.7, p.13), glamorous domestic history such as Elizabeth I's life (p.17) and elaborate clothes patterns – a suitable feminine pastime by which middle class women could equal their aristocratic peers. There is also a "Conversazione" section which can be seen as broadly equivalent to a letters page in which the emphasis is on propriety of dress and manners, although there is also some mention of more practical household matters; the June 1861 issue contains advice on the wearing of mourning rings, satin stitch and how to cure warts (p.120).

Trimmings and travel: 1902 - 1939

By the Edwardian period magazines were beginning to reflect a more active role for women, but again for women with means. In *The Lady's Realm* (1903) great attention continued to be paid to London and Paris fashions, for instance there is an elaborate illustration of a woman wearing a wrap described as "A handsome carriage or evening wrap in cream cloth, stitched with cream silk and trimmed with cream fringe, also embroidered in black and gold (p.113) and there is a long article on "hostesses of society" (p.123). At the same time there is a greater emphasis on outdoor pursuits. For instance an article by Baroness von Drachenfels on

Housewife

Eightpence   AUGUST

"Distinguished Automobilists" features photographs of men and women in cars. In her article the Baroness writes enthusiastically about the women drivers whom she knows, clearly equating driving with social importance:

All… lady motorists it would be impossible to mention here; but Lady de Grey, Lady Warwick, Lady Cecil Scott Montagu stand out prominently among those who have shown the way in this most delightful pastime. (*Lady's Realm*, p.120)

A more common form of travel than the expensive automobile was the "easy travel on the railways" (Fussell, p.191) and B. Fane's moral story "Waiting for a train" emphasised how easy. In this comically moral story an extravagant lady in her fashionable "travelling dress" seriously contemplates leaving her husband:

But I could have borne everything if it hadn't been for my *Court* gown. No, never, never, *never* will I go back to him! (Fanes, *Lady's Realm*, p.762).

Missing her train she first curses the porter then calls him "delightful" and returns to her husband and baby (p.764); the episode is thus safely bracketed as female frivolity and the status quo restored. Nevertheless, the very fact that a woman could contemplate doing this stressed the new freedom that was possible with travel. Tellingly in her article "Why do so many women no longer marry" Mrs Nathaniel Fiennes puts the case for women to have increased independence:

Unmarried women now enjoy a freedom and command a respect which were rarely vouchsafed to their maiden aunts… many women quietly refuse eligible offers until they fall in love. I am glad they are so wise and true to themselves. (Lady's Realm, pp. 76 – 77).

In the fashion pages in *Home Chat* (1911) clothes are characterised not just by finery but by practicality, with illustrations of "A Simple Washing Frock" and "A Smart Walking Costume" included (p. 117). Likewise the advice to Ethel a "retiring girl" is to get out more:

… no girl should be allowed to get to the stage when she is content to stay at home and sit in the background…it is a habit that quickly grows on a girl, unless she is encouraged to get out and talk. (*Home Chat*, 1911, p.132).

Freer lives; freer clothes: more fortunate women in the 1920s and 1930s bobbed their hair and wore shorter skirts, inspired by women's magazines such as *Vogue*, *Queen* and *Harper's*

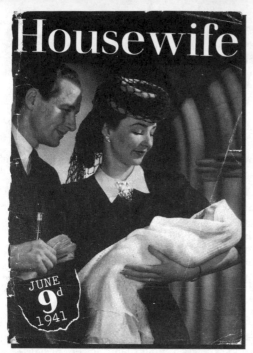

Housewife

JUNE
9d
1941

Bazaar (Horsham, p.91).

Make do and mend: 1940s

In the 1920s and 30s some women had enjoyed new freedoms, but it was the much greater social shift of the Second World War that made a difference to women's lives and to the nature of publications aimed at women. Gone was the privileged woman with domestic help; women of all classes were taking on extra responsibilities to assist with the wartime effort, and women's magazines acted as sources of practical information and advice in a changing world (ipc website). In the post war period magazines and manuals reflected the more active role which women had been taking. In the 1948 edition of *Housewife* the influence of post war frugality could be clearly felt. The magazine opens with a "Housewife diary" in which editor discusses the value of using parachute silk to make clothes and her bargain purchase of a perforated zinc bookcase (pp. 23 – 24). The magazine also contains articles on improving the appearance of your walls, reviving your carpets and making the most of tough meat, all practical everyday tasks. In the 1949 edition of *Housewife* there is a description of the life of a school secretary by Gertrude Bonney that provides an interesting insight into school life. Bonney's article is subtitled "An Ideal Job for a Married Woman with time to spare", a subtitle which emphasises the social acceptability of the job she is doing but also suggests that, for this very reason, other women could take on the same role. Indeed, Bonney is most enthusiastic about her working life:

I never realised before the life that goes on in a school, and I look forward to returning each Monday to a world in which everything is so

young and full of promise .. If there is a school near you and your children are off your hands, don't hesitate to take the post… You will enjoy every minute of it! (p. 117).

Sweet and neat: 1950s

The Practical Handywoman (*c.* 1950) contained advice not only on sewing and mending but on fixing pipes by wrapping them with rags or brown paper. Similarly, women's magazines in the 1950s continued to focus on the day to day living of the ordinary woman. In *Home Chat* (March 1958) a recipe on sheep head's broth "ideal for invalids or children," emphasising the value placed on women as carers in the home (p. 23). The April 1958 issue of *Home Chat* has articles on how to win a "lovely" coffee table by creating a fruit recipe , how a woman can do her nails to get the "new look" and a "helpful home-making" feature on dyeing a carpet to look better (p.7, p.21, p. 26). Perfect people, perfect wives; household manuals such as *Modern Homes Illustrated* (*c.* 1950) outlined the dream:

The nineteenth century housewife spent all her time either in doing her housework and bringing up her children, or in instructing large numbers of servants to do it for her. … Now it is different. Modern mothers wish to give less of their time and energy to housework, so that they may have more to spare for the eager minds of their children. (p. 247).

"More to spare for the eager minds of their children"; women were still encouraged to think of others first, as Mrs Jim reminded a reader:

It's good to for a woman to be able to sit back and let her husband make the important decisions…If you have an idea you believe to be right with regard to household management.. put it up to him as a suggestion. (Home Chat April 1958, p.36).

Yet even if fifties women were still encouraged to think of themselves in terms of others' needs in reading these magazines there is still a sense that "Now it is different". In *Home Chat* (March 8th 1958) there is an article on jobs for women involving travel (p. 33), in *Home Chat* (March 29th 1958) the prize awarded in a crossword puzzle is a maroon hold all (p.31), in *Home Chat* (April 1958) a woman wants a "snappy" outfit to go on a cruise (p13). Horizons were broadening for the ordinary woman and the women's magazines increasingly reflected the opportunities for everyone to "get out" and enjoy their lives.

In conclusion, women's magazines and household manuals are often dismissed as trivial, but in fact they can be viewed as providing an interesting insight into everyday family life and social attitudes. The

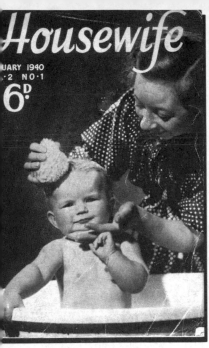

Housewife

JANUARY 1940
Vol 2 NO 1
6ᴰ

popularisation of magazines in this period can be seen as reflecting a more fluid society in which there was more room, on paper at least, for women's voices to be heard and for their experiences to be valued. As Helen Macdonald put it in her article in *Home Chat* (1911):

Men think it is the big things of life that count. Women know it is the small. (p.169).

Bibliography

Beeton, Isabella, *Everyday Cookery* (London, Ward, Lock & Co Limited, first published as a separate volume 1861, previously published *Englishwoman's Domestic Magazine*)

Briggs, A *Victorian Things* (Penguin, London, 1990, first published Batsford 1988)

Englishwoman's Domestic Magazine Vol III – IV (London, 1861)

Fussell, G.E. and K.R, *The English Countrywoman: From Tudor times to the Victorian Age*

Home Chat (Spring Fashion Number) April 1911

Home Chat (March 8th 1958)

Home Chat (March 29th 1958)

Home Chat (April 19th 1958)

Horsham, M, *'20s & '30s Style* (Quintet, Apple Press, London,1989)

Housewife (April 1948)

Housewife (April 1949)

Lady's Realm Vol XIV, May to October 1903 (London, Hutchinson)

Lehnert, G *Fashion A Concise History* (Laurence King, London 1999)

Patmore, C, *The Angel in The House* (Cassell & Company, London 1887 (first published 1854)

Steinburg, S H, *Five Hundred Years of Printing* (Penguin, London, 1961, first published 1955)

The Practical Handywoman: A book of basic principles for the self-reliant woman dealing with the problems of home-making and housekeeping, various authors (Odhams Press Limited, Long Acre, London [n.d.]).

Yerbury, F.R., ed., *Modern Homes Illustrated* (Odhams Press Limited, Long Acre, London [n.d.])

Website

www.ipcmedia.com/about/companyhistory – traces the history of many well known magazines published by this company.

The Trial of John Ystumllyn

Anthony Adolph

It is 1748. The scene is the edge of an African jungle teaming with brightly coloured plants and alive with the cries of exotic birds and the almost deafening buzz of insects. An African woman is watching while her eight year-old son creeps slowly towards a stream, his assegai poised to spear a water bird.

Suddenly, tall men emerge through the tangle of vines and shrubs, their faces flushed salmon pink, their bodies covered in bright-coloured, alien-looking clothing. Thunderous booms and an acrid smell of burning erupt from the end of the sticks they hold. The woman turns to flee, but the boy cannot. He stares wide-eyed at the devils, paralysed with terror. He feels hard, hot hands closing round his bare arms sees the trees spin as he is hoisted up. The screams of his bereft mother echo through the jungle as he is borne away towards the menacing roar of the ocean.

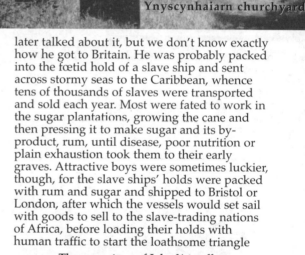

Ynyscynhaiarn churchyard

Two hundred and fifty-four years later, I crouch in front of a grave in the wind-swept churchyard of Ynyscynhaiarn, with a Channel 4 crew filming over my shoulder, reading the words incised on a yellow slate stone. Above, a brisk wind chivvies swallows and ravens across the cloud-dappled sky, sending shadows hurtling across the sheep, cattle and foxglove-speckled hedgerows of a broad, glacially-scoured Carnarvonshire valley.

> Here lieth the Body of John Ystymllyn who Died July the 27th 1791 AGED 46 years

> Yn India gynna'm ganwyd, - a nghamrau
> Ynghymru'm bedyddiwyd;
> Wele'r fan dan lechan lwyd,
> Du-oeraidd y'm daiarwyd.

This means:

> India was the land of my birth,
> but I was christened in Wales;
> This spot, marked by a grey slate,
> is my cold, dark resting place.

The locals were certainly proud that, 'someone from another continent had lived here'. The fact that they mistook Africa for India, and got the year of death wrong, seemed like minor points. 'We're looking for the grave of the black man', explain two women in anoraks. They react with astonishment when we explain that we are making a short film about John's life. Yet they too have a professional interest in him – they are tour guides and are planning to bring visitors to see their local celebrity's last resting-place.

We know how John was captured, because he

later talked about it, but we don't know exactly how he got to Britain. He was probably packed into the fœtid hold of a slave ship and sent across stormy seas to the Caribbean, whence tens of thousands of slaves were transported and sold each year. Most were fated to work in the sugar plantations, growing the cane and then pressing it to make sugar and its by-product, rum, until disease, poor nutrition or plain exhaustion took them to their early graves. Attractive boys were sometimes luckier, though, for the slave ships' holds were packed with rum and sugar and shipped to Bristol or London, after which the vessels would set sail with goods to sell to the slave-trading nations of Africa, before loading their holds with human traffic to start the loathsome triangle

The gravestone of John Ystumllyn

once again. On the journey from the Caribbean to England, senior officers often took a couple of attractive young slaves with them who, despite their personal misery, were supposed to mitigate their owners' hardships on the voyage. Having done their work, these young people were usually sold off as household servants to British families.

John's purchaser was Miss Wynn. She gave him to her brother Ellis Wynn Esq., a descendant of Sir Hywel of the Axe, who beheaded the King of France's horse during the Hundred Years' War. From the London quays, alive with the street vendors' cries and stench of fish and offal, Wynn would have taken John along the deeply-rutted roads through England, then up the winding passes below the looming peaks of Snowdonia and down again through the range's south-western foothills. Here, the bewildered John would have seen the white crests of waves surging angrily against the Carnarvonshire coastline and the grey slate rooftops of the town of Criccieth. Turning off the main road, the coach would have lurched down a narrow track-way, the boughs of ash and blossom-laden hawthorn scraping against the sides of the carriage, until at last the boy set eyes on the Wynn's house: Ystumllyn.

We know from a near-contemporary pamphlet that, when he arrived, he 'could only utter howling noises like an animal'. We don't know what John made of the chatter of excited Welsh voices as the Wynns crowded about to poke and prod their new toy. He was kept locked up at first but, as time passed, the Miss Wynns taught him to speak Welsh and English, whilst from the estate-workers he learned to carve spoons and model boats from pieces of local oak and ash.

'Civilisation'
Now he was 'civilised', it was time to baptise him. This was considered necessary to save him from the eternal fires of Hell, though many slave-owners were reluctant to allow their chattels to become Christian, for they believed this would confer freedom on them. Actually, they were wrong: slavery did not exist in British law, so any slave setting foot on British soil automatically became free. However, until this point was clarified by the Somerset Judgement of 1772, few knew this and those who did largely kept quiet, keeping black people prisoner through a conspiracy of silence. The Wynns, therefore, showed themselves to be of generous spirit by taking their black boy to Ynyscynhaiarn chapel, whose register states records:

1756: John Ystymllyn (a Black), Servt. to Ellis Wynne of Ystymllyn Esqr., Novr. 16th

They chose 'John' themselves, and 'Ystumllyn' was in line with normal practise, identifying him in terms of where he lived. His past identity – whatever that was – was swept away, but even his new names were too much for most local people, so he was usually called simply 'Jack Black'.

Ystumllyn was – and is – a compact country house built of great dark blue ashlar blocks of stone, from whose crevices sprout tufts of pink valerian. From the house's mass spread out an organic network of garden walls and outbuildings, one of which once housed John. When rain cascaded down from the low clouds that slunk around the base of the Snowdonian mountains, John would have sat by the open door of his hut, carving, transplanting seedlings or plaiting twine. When the sun shone, he would be out planting seeds, weeding the flowerbeds and tending the flowers in the gardens around Ystumllyn. The pale-faced strangers with their bewildering languages, and the ash woods and sheep-spotted fields around Ynyscynhaiarn and Ystumllyn, were now the most familiar things in his life. The gardens, where John could create his own order, were where he could be truly happy.

Every lunchtime, Margaret Gruffyd, the young maid from Hendre Mur, would leave John's bread, cheese and beer by the garden gate. At first she would turn and run, scared of the black-faced demon – yet horror was tinged with fascination. 'It is hard to fathom the attraction which this dark boy had for the young ladies of the district', wrote his pamphleteer biographer. Edward Long, a racist from John's century, pulled less punches: 'the lower classes of women in England', he complained, 'are remarkably fond of the blacks, for reasons too brutal to mention'. Put less coarsely,

Ystumllyn manor house and outbuildings

many white women found black men irresistibly attractive, and still do – a quarter of all black British men today have white partners. John was certainly popular with the local girls, but his relationship with Margaret transcended sex. Soon the solitary black boy was carving traditional Carnarvonshire love-spoons for his shy white lover.

Sadly, Margaret was sent away to work for an aunt at Dolgellau. John crept away from his flowerbeds one evening to join her, and they were married there in 1768, with the vicar's son as best man and general approval all round. The Wynns, however, were furious at John's one act of self-assertion, and sacked him.

Married life
John now faced the plight of many black men who left their original owners or bosses: he was not a fresh-faced novelty any more, but was seen instead as a potential threat to white people's jobs, wives and to law-and-order in general. Denied any parish relief by their skin colour, many were forced to turn to crime. John, however, was lucky to be the only black man in North Wales, and thus escaped most of the troubles that befell his compatriots in urban England. He was given the job of estate steward at Ynysgain Fawr, but before long the Wynns relented, giving him another job on their estate and allowing him and Margaret an old thatched cottage called Y Nhyra Isa. Here, they had

A rather badly-drawn likeness of John Ystumllyn made in 1754. I very much doubt that his head really was so strangely shaped!

seven children. In proper Welsh fashion, they received their father's name as a patronymic, so were surnamed Jones.

Perhaps John stood sometimes on the hillock behind Ynyscnhaiarn, gazing out at the frothy waves of the Irish sea, watching a distant sail and wondering if one day a ship would come to bear him home to Africa. But he was settled now, with a wife and family: the idea of actually leaving must have been inconceivable.

In many ways, John was lucky. He was not branded, or forced to wear a collar engraved with his master's coat of arms. Nor was he sent back to the plantations, as so many were, once he had lost his boyish looks. But his colour always marked him out as different. He once appeared unexpectedly in front of a man who, thinking John was a devil, reportedly nearly had a heart attack. Another time two girls asked him if he had blood as black as his face. On that occasion, John's temper snapped. 'You silly fool!', he exploded. 'If you kill a black hen and a white hen, you'll see that both have red blood!' In the 1780's, a man blackened his face and impersonated him, mischievously ordering some garden seed in his name, whilst another made-up impersonator fooled Margaret's elderly aunt into handing over some cheese and butter meant for John.

Only Margaret truly accepted John for himself. When his two year-old son Richard spotted John coming through the crowded market place, Margaret was delighted at the child's ability to recognise his father's face at a distance. She had completely forgotten how much John's black skin made him stand out in the crowd.

John had a great reputation for honesty and, in his later years, for piety, regretting even having played his fiddle on the Sabbath in his youth. The incidents when people impersonated him for dishonest ends – and maybe also the ease with which other were fooled simply by a blackening their faces – sent him into a terrible depression, during which he contracted jaundice and died. He was buried, very unusually, on a Sunday, an act possibility reflecting the locals' nervousness of leaving his black body unburied for any length of time at all. The burial register reads:

1786: John Ystymllyn of Ynnhyrran [Y Nhyra Isa]; *Gardener, July 2d.*

Margaret survived him by 40 years, proud of her ability to sew and knit without needing glasses right up to then end.

John's legacy

In the 18th century, racists lay awake at night fretting over 'miscegenation'. 'In the course of a few generations more', wrote Edward Long,

the English blood will become so contaminated with this mixture, and from the chances, and ups and downs of life, this alloy may spread extensively, as even to reach the middle, and then the higher orders of the people, till the whole nation resembles the Portuguese and Moriscos in complexion of skin and baseness of mind. This is a venomous and dangerous ulcer, that threatens to disperse its malignancy far and wide, until every family catches infection from it.

He needn't have worried. Three of John and Margaret's children married – Ann to James Martin, a musical instrument seller of Liverpool; Lowri to Robert Jones, a butler at Madryn and Richard to Jonet Isaac. Recalling his African past, Richard became huntsman to Lord Newburgh, cutting a handsome figure with his brown skin and dark velvet top hat, velvet jacket and a high white collar. His children were identified in the Carnarvon registers as children of 'Richard Jones (Black)', but in true Welsh custom they were later surnamed 'son of [ap] Richard', ie, Richards, or Pritchard. And after that, the black genes of John Ystumllyn melted away into the local population.

When I asked around for descendants of John's, I got a mixed reaction. 'John Ystumllyn is dear to my heart!', exclaimed one, but another said having a black ancestor was 'a bit like being descended from a criminal'. I was told there were local people with 'a touch of the tar brush', easily spotted in summer because they went browner than the rest – but I didn't see any. I met a woman with slightly dark skin and decidedly frizzy black hair. She said wouldn't mind being descended from John, but did not know if she was. That was the closest I got in the limited time available.

John Ystumllyn is a local celebrity now. While I was in Criccieth, the local children were studying him for a school project. His portrait is the proud possession of the Armstrong-Jones family, local landowners, and the family of Princess Margaret's ex-husband Lord Snowdon. A copy of John's portrait hangs on the wall of a pub in Carnarvon. The pub is called *The Black Boy.*

In association with Family History Monthly

How many ancestors do I have?
Dr Andrew Gritt

Director, Institute of Local and Family History University of Central Lancashire

Each and every one of us has a unique set of ancestors shared only with our siblings. Each child has two parents and so it might seem a very simple question to ask 'how many ancestors do I have? Of course, this is an unanswerable question: we are all the product of an unbroken chain of human reproductive activity that goes into the dim recesses of time and way beyond documented history. But even if we narrow the chronology to the era of documented history, can we offer a reasonable answer to the question?

There is a simple mathematical formula that is often used to demonstrate the scale of our ancestry. Biologically, each individual has two parents, so we can simply double the number of people in each generation as in the *Generation Table*.

Although this table is based on simple maths, and the known biological fact that each individual has two parents, it contains a very obvious flaw: we only need to add two more generations (to the time of the Black Death in the mid-fourteenth century) before each individual has more direct ancestors than the entire population of the British Isles. Continuing this sequence back still further, by the time we get back to the time of the Roman Invasion of Britain in the first century AD, we have more direct ancestors than the entire population of the world at that time: a staggering 36,893,488,147,419,100,000. Even if this figure was correct, none of us could ever hope to actually trace the identity of these individuals, but the flawed logic needs some consideration.

Throughout documented history the population of the British Isles has fluctuated, with periods of growth followed by periods of decline, a pattern that was only finally broken in England in the mid-eighteenth century. At no point before the mid-eighteenth century did the population exceed 5 millions. Nevertheless, it is apparent that as the human population began with very small numbers, even on a global scale, we cannot simply double the number of ancestors in every generation. Indeed, we would not need to delve too far back into our ancestries to discover that almost all the present day

Generation	Year	Number of ancestors
1	2000	2
2	1970	4
3	1940	8
4	1910	16
5	1880	32
6	1850	64
7	1820	128
8	1790	256
9	1760	521
10	1730	1024
11	1700	2048
12	1670	4096
13	1640	8192
14	1610	16384
15	1580	32768
16	1550	65536
17	1520	131072
18	1490	262144
19	1460	524288
20	1430	1048576
21	1400	2097157

population of the British Isles, as well as a significant proportion of the New World population, was related.

So how many ancestors do we have? Although genetic knowledge may one day be able to answer this question, we are still a long way from resolving this issue through scientific investigation. Nevertheless, despite the mathematical simplicity of the table above, the flawed logic renders it indisputable that every single one of us must have converging lines of ascent. In other words, as individuals, we all have ancestors to whom we are related through more than one line.

There are numerous constraints on the number of ancestors we all have, derived from known historical facts. As many academic studies have shown, the English population in the past was only geographically mobile within a small area, often restricted to about 10-15 miles of the birthplace. The best evidence for the persistence of this restricted mobility comes in the form of surname distribution maps. Even today many surnames are uniquely found within the area of their origin several centuries ago. A recent study of marriage horizons even shows that as the eighteenth-century progressed, people were choosing marriage partners from an increasingly restricted geographical area.

Nevertheless, within recent generations the genetic mix of the British Isles has expanded, partly as a result of immigration from overseas and partly as a result of increased levels of long-distance internal migration. To take a personal example, over the last 5 generations I have direct ancestors born in Cornwall, Dorset, Hampshire, Ireland, Lancashire, London, Norfolk, Nottinghamshire, Scotland, Surrey and Yorkshire – this spread may be untypical, but my ancestors of 150 years ago would not have been able to claim the same level of genetic variation. Migration in the nineteenth and twentieth centuries has brought together genetic lines from diverse parts of the country, but the relative absence of long-distance migration before the nineteenth century means that the vast majority of the British population chose marriage partners from a limited geographical area. The mechanism for people from different parts of the country to be related simply did not exist on a large scale.

We can go some way towards measuring long-distance migration using the printed returns of the 1901 census. The population was more mobile by this stage than it had been previously – mass transport and economic change in agriculture as well as industry saw to that – but even by the

end of Victoria's reign long-distance migration was relatively rare. This is demonstrated in the table below which shows that in almost all English counties more than one half of the population had been born there. Moreover, the counties losing population were often the smallest (where a short-distance move might involve crossing a county boundary) or they were economically backward. Also, most migration took place over short distances: of those leaving Rutland, for instance, more than half were resident in either Leicestershire, Lincolnshire, Northampton or Nottinghamshire.

The history of migration in the British Isles demonstrates that it is historically inaccurate to simply double the number of ancestors in each generation. Indeed, the majority of us must be descended from a relatively small number of restricted gene pools, which are themselves geographically limited in extent.

There is a further constraint on the possibility of us being descended from the total sum of the population in the medieval and early modern periods. First, not everybody who was alive in 1340 will have living descendents: the Black Death claimed the lives of about one third of the population of England – and many of those who died will have been either childless, or were children themselves. The Black Death was responsible for the eradication of a number of surnames and genetic lines. The Black Death was only the best known and most deadly of a long series of mortality crises to affect England between the mid-fourteenth and the mid-eighteenth centuries, and this situation continued for another century in Scotland and Ireland. Local mortality crises caused by famine or disease were a normal occurrence and could claim the lives of a significant proportion of the local population. Second, many individuals failed to pass on their genes not because they

Birthplace of the people: 1901 census			
Birthplace	% born in the county of residence	Birthplace	% born in the county of residence
BEDFORDSHIRE	56		
BERKSHIRE	59		
BUCKINGHAMSHIRE	51		
CAMBRIDGESHIRE	52	MONMOUTHSHIRE	69
CHESHIRE	68	NORFOLK	67
CORNWALL	66	NORTHAMPTONSHIRE	69
CUMBERLAND	65	NORTHUMBERLAND	77
DERBYSHIRE	67	NOTTINGHAMSHIRE	75
DEVONSHIRE	71	OXFORDSHIRE	53
DORSETSHIRE	52	RUTLANDSHIRE	36
DURHAM	83	SHROPSHIRE	49
ESSEX	75	SOMERSETSHIRE	54
GLOUCESTERSHIRE	70	STAFFORDSHIRE	74
HAMPSHIRE	73	SUFFOLK	62
HEREFORDSHIRE	46	SURREY (Extra-metropolitan)	63
HERTFORDSHIRE	53		
HUNTINGDONSHIRE	44	SUSSEX	72
KENT (Extra-metropolitan)	67	WARWICKSHIRE	75
LANCASHIRE	91	WESTMORLAND	50
LEICESTERSHIRE	78	WILTSHIRE	52
LINCOLNSHIRE	63	WORCESTERSHIRE	62
MIDDLESEX (Extra-metropolitan)	64	YORKSHIRE	85

failed to live into adulthood or because of high rates of infant mortality, but because they never procreated. It has been suggested that up to one quarter of the population in the seventeenth century never married, and with illegitimacy rates also being low in this period a significant number of the seventeenth-century English population have no living descendants.

The fact that many people failed to pass their genes on to descendents does not invalidate the mathematical progression referred to in table one, but it does indicate a much narrower genetic background for each of us than we might expect. As well as being mathematically impossible for us to simply double the number of ancestors in each generation, it is also historically inaccurate.

We will probably never know just how many direct ancestors we have, but it is possible to provide a model of the minimum number of ancestors each of us might have. The Book of Common Prayer did render illegal many potential matches in the 'table of kindred and affinity'. However, this is even more complex than this table suggests. On marriage a husband and wife became one legal entity – so a man's sister in law was, in the eyes of the law, his *sister*. Consequently, under ecclesiastical law, a man

was not allowed to marry his dead brother's widow, or his deceased wife's sister on the grounds of incest. This ecclesiastical position was based on Leviticus ch. 20 where, it states *'And if a man shall take his brother's wife, it is an unclean thing: he hath uncovered his brother's nakedness; they shall be childless'*. Henry VIII used this text as the basis for his case to get his marriage with Catherine of Aragon annulled as she was the widow of his deceased brother, Arthur. This law was not changed until the passing of the Deceased Wife's Sister's Marriage Act in 1907 although even at this date the union was only recognised as a civil contract.

The Book of Common Prayer, and subsequent legislation governing England's marriage laws, has always allowed first cousins to marry. Although this is considered genetically unwise, and with a *potential* for spontaneous genetic mutations, the marriage of first cousins is not illegal. However, even avoiding first-cousin marriages, it is possible to substantially reduce the number of direct ancestors as the following diagram shows

In each generation we have four married couples with the marriage partners also representing four pairs of siblings. Each marriage produces one son and one daughter and the lines of ascent and the marriage partners are shown in the diagram above. In order for two individuals to be first cousins, they must share one set of grandparents. In the third generation, we can see that Quentin Smith's grandparents were Arthur Smith, Brenda Jones, Charles Brown and Deborah Green whereas the grandparents of his wife, Rosie Black, were Edward Black, Felicity White, George Edwards and Hannah Williams. Their son was Andrew Smith who married Brenda Brown. Andrew's grandparents were Ian Smith, Jenny Brown, Michael Black and Natalie Edwards whereas his wife's grandparents were Kevin Brown, Laura Smith, Owen Edwards and Pauline Black. After the fourth generation the pattern of marriages can simply repeat, so that with only eight individuals in each generation it is possible for first cousins never to marry. Of course, the genetic pool here is very limited, being restricted to 8 genetic lines (from generation one) and only four surnames, so that each marriage partner shares identical great grandparents. In reality this would inevitably lead to severe genetic abnormalities, but as a marriage pattern it is entirely legal.

Returning to the theoretical number of ancestors in table 1, we saw that there were over 2 million individual ancestors by the year 1400. However, in the 21 generations between the present day and 1400 we would only actually need 168 ancestors if marriages

A Table of Kindred and Affinity
Wherein Whosoever Are Related Are Forbidden by the Church of England to Marry Together.

A Man may not marry his	*A Woman may not marry her*
mother	father
daughter	son
adopted daughter	adopted son
father's mother	father's father
mother's mother	mother's father
son's daughter	son's son
daughter's daughter	daughter's son
sister	brother
wife's mother	husband's father
wife's daughter	husband's son
father's wife	mother's husband
son's wife	daughter's husband
father's father's wife	father's mother's husband
mother's father's wife	mother's mother's husband
wife's father's mother	husband's father's father
wife's mother's mother	husband's mother's father
wife's daughter's daughter	husband's son's son
wife's son's daughter	husband's daughter's son
son's son's wife	son's daughter's husband
daughter's son's wife	daughter's daughter's husband
father's sister	father's brother
mother's sister	mother's brother
brother's daughter	brother's son
sister's daughter	sister's son

In this Table the term 'brother' includes a brother of the half-blood, and the term 'sister' includes a sister of the half-blood.

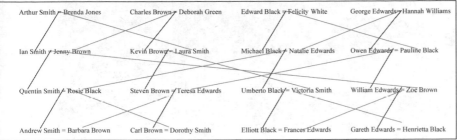

Although some of this argument is purely theoretical, we have arrived at a solution to the impossible maths with which we began. In reality, the marriage of related individuals would not correspond to the neat models proposed above. However, it does not require many marriages of related individuals to substantially reduce the number of ancestors we have. Two unrelated individuals would have eight grandparents between them whereas first cousins only have six. Therefore, if we are descended from the marriage of two first cousins then the number of ancestors in every generation before *their* parents is reduced by one quarter. Using the same logic, if we are descended from the marriage of second cousins then the number of ancestors is reduced by one eighth in each generation before *their* grandparents. Over many centuries, and with limited population movement for most of English history, it is apparent that these factors **must** affect every one of us, and considerably lowers the number of direct ancestors we have.

followed the pattern outlined above. The historical reality is clearly somewhere between these two extremes. Historical knowledge as well as logic dictates that it must be nearer the lower theoretical figure than the highest theoretical figure. And this must certainly be the case for remote, isolated communities as well as groups for whom the potential range of marriage partners was restricted such as the aristocracy.

Although there are many families where first-cousin marriage took place, there must be many others where people married second, third or

Size of marriage cohort	Relationship between marriage partners	Common ancestors	Time lag (years)
4	1st cousins	Grandparents	60
8	2nd cousins	Great grandparents	90
16	3rd cousins	2x Great grandparents	120
32	4th cousins	3x Great grandparents	150
64	5th cousins	4x Great grandparents	180
128	6th cousins	5x Great grandparents	210
256	7th cousins	6x Great grandparents	240
512	8th cousins	7x Great grandparents	270
1024	9th cousins	8x Great grandparents	300

fourth cousins (or even more distant relatives). Many of the marriage partners would not have known that they were related as people may not have known of a common ancestor even as recently as five or more generations previously. Same-name marriages are perhaps an indication of inter-breeding, especially for rare surnames, as would repeated combinations of marriage partners with the same surnames. However, only detailed research would uncover the true extent of such marriages.

As the majority of English families did not migrate very far, even over an extended time period of several generations, then the majority of married couples belonged to a marriage cohort within their own locality. However, as the following table demonstrates, a marriage cohort of just 512 individuals, which might represent that available in an area of several rural parishes before the industrial revolution, would provide enough genetic variation so that no individual would need to marry a relative closer than their 8th cousin. This represents common ancestors for these marriage partners almost three centuries earlier (assuming 30 years per generation). Such a marriage cohort is not likely to lead to genetic mutation but it does significantly reduce the number of direct ancestors each of us has.

Down at Heel in Nineteenth Century Beverley: Life in the Workhouse.

Martin Limon

In an age of the Welfare State people often take it for granted that the government will provide support for them in times of sickness, unemployment or old age. More than 50 years ago however the calamities of life had to be faced with much more uncertainty and for all categories of poor people there lurked the spectre of the workhouse...........

Until recent times the people of Beverley, as in other places, were generally expected make their own provision for times of sickness or for when they became too old to work. There were also other categories of people who, for no fault of their own, could not help themselves: orphans, the insane, deserted wives and the crippled. Unable to survive without support they might be look for help to family, to friends, or to charity.

In the Middle Ages the Church, traditionally, was the major source of charity; Matthew, chapter 25, told the god-fearing to feed the hungry, clothe the naked and take in the stranger. To this end the medieval Church built *hospitals*; historically these were institutions to care for the poor and infirm. Beverley, by the mid 15th century had four church-run hospitals and this tradition of charity was carried on by private individuals in later times. Beverley became the home to several privately funded hospitals and almshouses. Ann Routh's hospital for widows, for example, was established in Keldgate in 1746 and housed 32 inmates while Sir Michael Warton's Hospital in Minster Moorgate had

six poor widows who were allowed three shillings (15p) weekly with gowns and coals annually.

Private charity could not hope to deal with all paupers and by the 17th century parishes were made responsible for the problem. They could either provide *outdoor relief* through cash allowances, fuel, clothing and food to paupers living at home or *indoor relief* to the poor residing in a purpose-built workhouse. To lessen the cost of providing such a workhouse three Beverley parishes (St Martin, St Mary and St Nicolas) joined together to build one in Minster Moorgate in 1727. By the late 18th century this housed thirty or so paupers, mostly adult women and children, but the vast majority of those who obtained help did so through outdoor relief. The cost of poor relief was met by a tax on property values levied on the ratepayers of the parishes.

During the early nineteenth century national concern about the growing numbers of paupers and the increasing cost of poor relief led Parliament to pass the 1834 Poor Law. This combined parishes into *unions* and made indoor relief in a well-regulated workhouse the preferred way of dealing with all classes of paupers. To discourage all but the most desperate from applying the Poor Law Commission in London hoped that life in each workhouse would be made deliberately hard. In the East Riding several new *union workhouses*

The Workhouse
Beverley

MINSTER COURT

were built including ones at Skirlaugh (1839), Driffield (1868) and at Beverley (1861). The new Beverley workhouse replaced that the one in Minster Moorgate, by now considered inadequate to cope with the needs of the 36 parishes in the *Beverley Poor Law Union.* The red-brick Tudor style building for 189 inmates, built close to the Westwood, was designed by John and William Atkinson of York and built at a cost of over £5,000 (twice the estimate).

The aim of most Poor Law Guardians was to keep expenditure in check and so there were few luxuries. The food supplied, for example, was of the most basic kind like bread and gruel with occasional meat and potatoes. The story of the orphan, Oliver Twist, asking for more in the novel by Charles Dickens has a basis in fact!

After breakfast the children were sent to nearby schools while adults were expected to perform tasks such as breaking up cobbles, street sweeping and oakum picking (separating out the fibres of old ropes). Workhouse females performed the tasks involved in the day-today running of a large institution: preparing food, cooking, cleaning and washing.

In one case, at least, the harsh workhouse regime at Beverley seems to have detered an application with fatal consequences. On the 25th January 1865 the East Riding coroner recorded a verdict of death by starvation on a widow called Eliza Smith (aged 60) of Woodmansey. The neighbour who found her told the inquest that Mrs

Smith had no food in the house only "some old bones which had been picked at and an apple or two." The daughter of the deceased told the coroner that in the previous year her mother had applied to the Beverley Guardians for relief during the winter but had been refused unless she came into the workhouse. The inquest was told that the widow had refused the offer saying she would rather starve. The coroner suggested that the Beverley Guardians had been "harsh" in not allowing the woman a "few shillings in the winter after she strove to maintain herself in the summer."

The Guardians' minute books of their monthly meetings show in stark detail the circumstances that drove Beverley's poor to apply for admittance to the workhouse. On the 31st March 1866 Ann McDougle appeared before the Guardians to say that her husband was refusing to maintain her (despite earning 30 shillings a week at a local foundry) and that she was destitute. The same day another woman, Ann Coates, told the Guardians that her husband (a joiner earning 24 shillings a week) had locked her out of the house and was refusing to maintain her. In both cases the women were admitted to the workhouse while the Guardians sought redress against their husbands by asking the Justices to issue warrants for their arrest "for refusing to maintain their wives."

In the interests of economy, and because much of the work could be done by the inmates themselves, the number of

workhouse staff was small. An advertisement for a new Master and Matron (March 1867) show that the Guardians wished to appoint a "husband and wife, without family, between the ages of 25 and 50 years" for salaries of £55 and £25 respectively. The people appointed were James and Elizabeth Shives but they were soon judged to be incompetent and were asked to resign. At times these paid officials found it difficult to keep the inmates in order. Records show that in September 1866 Jane Wilson complained to the Board of Guardians that two other paupers, Ruth Blakeston and Mary Leighton, had struck her. In December 1868 the Workhouse Master complained about a 15 year old boy who "is very bad to manage and likely to corrupt the younger boys and influence them in disobedience."

When we look at the census records of the Beverley Workhouse it becomes clear that this institution combined the functions of an orphanage, old peoples' home, home for unmarried mothers, hospital and mental asylum in one building. The 1881 census, for example shows that that there were 156 residents including five described as "imbeciles from birth." The oldest resident was William Wilson (aged eighty two) a former waterman of Beverley. At the other end of the age scale was Ellen Adams (aged two) whose mother, Mary Adams of North Newbald, was also resident in the workhouse.

The duty of the Beverley Board of Guardians, as they saw it, was to supervise the running of the workhouse and, for the benefit of the ratepayers, to ensure that the system was run as economically as possible. Despite the intention to abolish outdoor relief this continued as before. In fact, the numbers who were given help in the form of money, food and clothes outside the workhouse always exceeded the numbers within it.

Although the Guardians were reluctant to spend public money unnecessarily, expensive improvements to the workhouse, usually prompted by critical inspection reports, were sometimes unavoidable. In 1893 a new infirmary with 60 beds was built while in 1895 a porters lodge and archway over the road at the entrance to the workhouse were added. These changes, costing £8,000, provide a link between the original, workhouse, use of the site (lasting until the 1930s) and its new role as a hospital beginning at the outbreak of the Second World War in 1939 and continuing to the present day.

St George's Square
Liverpool

Dear Old Liverpool Town
Joseph O'Neill

Every visitor seeing St George's Hall and Liverpool's other magnificent public buildings is beguiled by the Victorians' genius for investing their creations with a sense of permanence. Surely these colossal structures have always been here in this great city?

In fact, the place of the 'muddy pool' has played a key role in national life for less than two centuries. Too insignificant to warrant a mention in the Domesday Book, Liverpool was no more than a small hamlet on the banks of the Mersey. It was only in 1207 that she became a port. At the same time she held her first market and fair, attracting craftsmen and merchants from all over Lancashire.

King John's decision to elevate Liverpool to the status of a port is, like so much in her history, the result of her location. England had recently laid claim to Ireland and Liverpool was the means of supplying government forces. The link with Ireland has proved a key factor shaping the character and life of the city.

In 1540 a visitor remarked on another link that was to feature large in Liverpool's history. He observed *'Irish merchants come much hither'* and said *'there is much Irish yarn that Manchester men buy there'*.

Yet the scale of this trade was tiny. As late as 1662 Liverpool did not feature in a list of the

country's largest forty towns, and was dwarfed by Lynn, Ludlow and Ely.

It was the slave trade of the 18th century that gave Liverpool her first growth spurt. In 1746, when Britain stood on the threshold of the industrial age, Liverpool was the country's fifth town with a population of about 35,000 and had only recently surpassed Chester as the major port on the northwest coast.

Throughout the eighteenth century visitors marvelled at the city's spectacular growth. By mid-century it was the equal of Bristol in terms of the volume of its trade. But unlike Bristol it engaged extensively in the highly lucrative slave trade.

The port was the basis of Britain's triangular trade, the structure on which the country's economic wealth rested. Manchester cotton good were shipped to Africa and exchanged for consignments of slaves. This human cargo was ferried across the Atlantic to the West Indies and to meet America's insatiable demand for labour and exchanged for cotton and sugar that provided the return cargo.

From 1709, when Liverpool began its involvement in slaves, the unfortunate human cargo were herded together into the Goree Piazzas. By the middle of the century there were between fifty and sixty Liverpool vessels

regularly engaged in the trade.

Even when the trade was suppressed in 1806, Liverpool's links with the Americas were barely weakened. The city's prosperity remained tied to Atlantic trade and as this increased so did the city's population, which reached 80,000 by 1800. The city's growth and prosperity was due in large part to the prescience of the city fathers. They realised that the city's potential was severely restricted by its lack of an enclosed harbour. They ensured that an Act of 1709 allowed for the building of a wet dock – the first in the country outside London – which was steadily enlarged until by 1747 it was capable of holding one hundred vessels.

At the same time as they built the dock, the corporation also secured by Act of Parliament the right to improve the city's supply of drinking water. Simultaneously they developed navigable sections of the Mersey, Weaver and Dove, which became vital trade arteries, carrying goods for sale in the interior and commodities from northern England for export.

Perceptive commentators, remarking on the city's growing prosperity, invariably mentioned the role of the city's enlightened corporation. The town's ruling body was, in fact, a closed oligarchy and totally undemocratic. It recruited solely by co-option from a narrow group of leading families. Wealth alone was no guarantee of admission to this select inner circle. Dissenters and, of course, Roman Catholics, were exclude from positions of influence, including all the better-paid official posts.

Yet the corporation was as honest as it was wise and farsighted in discharging its responsibilities. In 1748 it secured an Act for the public provision of cleaning and lighting the streets – the first obtained by any town outside London.

The result was a thriving community that made a strong impact on all who saw it. One visitor at the end of the 18th century found a fine large town, its prosperity obvious as it was 'mostly newly built, of brick and stone after the London fashion', with 'handsome paved streets' thronged ' with well dressed and fashionable persons.' Even then the city fathers had the Liverpool penchant for imposing public buildings, having recently built 'a very pretty exchange. It stands on eight pillars, over which is a very handsome Town Hall.'

If the City Corporation was undemocratic, a freak of electoral chance gave the city's shipwrights both the vote in parliamentary elections and a significant role in choosing Liverpool's two MPs. Liverpool's shipwrights were the first group of highly organised skilled workers outside London. The city was later to become famous for the strength and militancy of its trade unions. The shipwrights were cited before the Parliamentary Committee considering the repeal of the Combination Acts in 1824 as an outstanding example of 'trade union tyranny.' Almost a century later, when the city's police joined striking workers, Winston Churchill sent a gunboat to the Mersey estuary in anticipation of a red rising.

As the cotton industry grew into Britain's biggest earner, Liverpool flourished not only as a port but also as a centre of manufacture based on sugar refining, shipbuilding, iron, glass and soap production. The opening of the famous Liverpool to Manchester Railway in 1830 was to prove the greatest single boost to the city's development during the nineteenth century.

The Railway was a spectacular success in reducing costs and increasing the volume and speed of goods traffic. It also boosted the number of passengers using Liverpool, helping to make the city the world's foremost emigration port, the gateway to the new world.

But the railway had an impact far beyond Liverpool. Its success ensured that henceforward railways would be based on locomotives operated by railway companies and not, as many thought, track-ways open to private vehicles. Furthermore, it sparked the first wave of 'railway mania,' massive investment in the new transport.

The railway was only one of the things boosting the city's population, which reached 376,000 in 1851. It was also swelled by an influx of starving Irish fleeing the Famine.

Though all burgeoning industrial towns shared her problems, Liverpool was notorious for the squalor of her slums, a third of the working population living in cellars. Mortality among the poor was high and life expectancy in the worst areas was only twenty years. To add to the hazards of squalor there were also the dangers of the pestilence that regularly took its toll on the city's population.

At a time when Liverpool's slums were among the worst in the country, the city fathers embarked on a massive public building scheme, which was to last until the turn of the century. Most of the city's imposing structures were build during this period. Many of these magnificent buildings survive to ensure that Liverpool's city centre boasts some of the country's finest creations of Victorian architecture.

People from all over the world passed through the city as it became the world's major port of emigration. This is certainly one of the major reasons why many Americans, are so interested in a city which was for their

ancestors the last sight of land as they left home. Such was the diversity of the city's population that many claim Liverpool as Britain's first truly cosmopolitan city with the country's first large Chinese community and a significant Jewish population.

But it was the Irish who had the greatest impact on the city. As late as the 1930s Liverpool's politics reflected the Irish divide between Orange and Green, unionism and nationalism. By that time Liverpool, like all Britain's old industrial areas, was in the grip of a depression. Shrinking world trade and reduced demand for shipping hit the city hard. One in three workers lost their jobs.

As war lifted the blight of unemployment, the port became a major target for the Luftwaffe. Liverpool was bombed so often that in 1941 the rumour the city had surrendered was reported in many Lancashire towns and cities. Churchill believed Liverpool had a key role in the country's survival. Without vital imports from America, Britain's lifeline would be severed and the war lost. The Prime Minister was a frequent visitor to the secret control room under the streets of the city, where the battle of the Atlantic was plotted.

Liverpool enjoyed the post-war prosperity boom, which corresponded with its rise to prominence in popular culture. The city became synonymous with all that was best in pop music, football and entertainment.
In 1980s, however, decline set in. Since then the city's ability to reinvent herself as a major tourist attraction has been crowned with the award of European City of Culture for 2008.

North Americans in particular have a positive image of the city. Many of their ancestors passed through the port in the 19th century on their way to the new world. They associate the city not with economic depression but with what is most vibrant in popular culture.

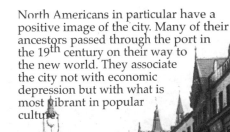

Lord Street, Liverpool

This is hardly surprising. Liverpool was the home of William Ewart Gladstone, four times Prime Minister, the social reformer, Charles Booth and the great Cunard shipping line. But its real glory is its entertainers — Tommy Handley, Ken Dodd, Cilla Black and most of all the Beatles.

The City is rightly proud of its rich heritage and has done as much as anywhere to make it attractive and accessible to those interested in family and local history.

There is no better place to start your search than at the famous Albert Dock. When it and the adjoining warehouses were built in the nineteenth century, they were declared the wonder of the maritime world. Their redevelopment in the 1980s is a model for the rejuvenation of traditional industrial areas. The planners have wisely exploited the site's historical importance. The Merseyside Maritime Museum, (Albert Dock, Liverpool, L34AQ [t] 0151 478 4499) fully reflects the international importance of Liverpool. Its Maritime Archive and Library contain one of the finest collections of merchant shipping records in the UK. It is particularly strong on the role of slavery and emigration in Liverpool's history.
Nearby you'll find The Museum of Liverpool Life, (Pier Head, Liverpool, L3 IP2 [t] 0151 478 4080) which celebrates Liverpool, its culture, its achievements and its contribution to national life.

In the city centre you will find the magnificent Liverpool City Public Library or Central Library, (William Brown Street, Liverpool, L3 8EW [t] 0151 223 5829 and the Local and Family History Service [t] 0151 233 5817). The library is one of the largest public libraries in Britain and is open to all members of the public for reference purposes. The Local and Family History Service holds materials relating to

the history of the city back to the 13th century, including those relating to the Council, schools, churches, businesses and societies. It has an extensive range of old newspapers, street and trade directories, electoral rolls, both Roman Catholic and Anglican parish registers and workhouse papers. One of its most interesting holdings is the photographic archive of the City Engineers' Department.

Liverpool has many academic institutions, which are a boon to the family historian. University of Liverpool Library, the Sydney Jones Library, (Chatham Street, Liverpool, L69 3DA [t] 0151 794 2673 [w] www.liv.ac.uk/library/libhomep.html) is certainly worth a visit. In addition to its unique Gypsy collection, it holds personal and literary papers of individuals, societies and businesses with local connections, including Cunard's archives. It also has the papers of a number of child welfare organisations, such as Barnardo's. It's also possible to plan your research from home by using its on-line catalogue.

The facilities which the Mormons make available to family historians should never be overlooked. This is another area in which Liverpool is well-served. The Mormon Library is on Mill Lane, (West Derby, Merseyside, Liverpool L13 OBW [t] 0151 252 0614.) It has one of the most extensive genealogical collections in the city, covering births, marriages and deaths. Also useful is the St. Helen's Local History and Archives Library, (Victoria Square, St. Helens, Merseyside WA10 1DY [t] 01744 456952.) The library has an extensive holding of birth, marriage and death records, up to 1912 on film and up to 1940 on microfiche.

It's hardly surprising that in a city so influenced by Ireland there is ample provision for those

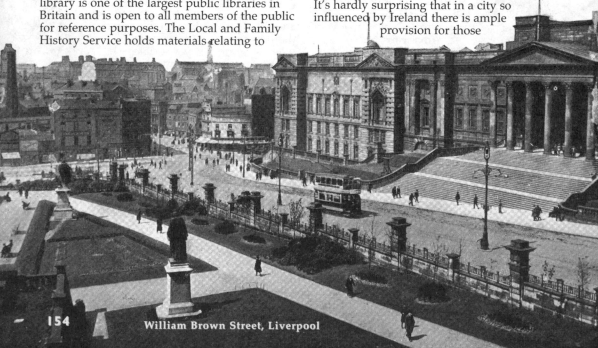

William Brown Street, Liverpool

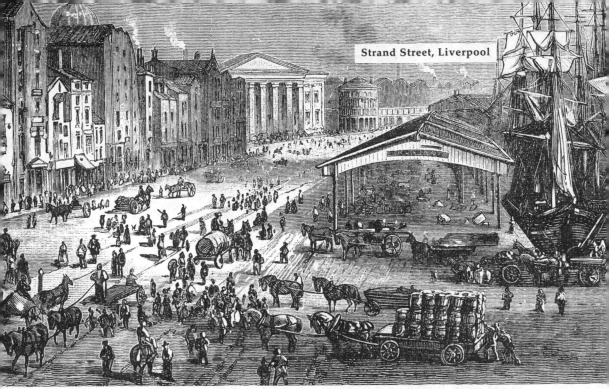

Strand Street, Liverpool

with Irish ancestry. Before you travel, see *Tracing Your Irish Ancestors in Liverpool* ([w] http://freepages.genealogy.rootsweb.com/~hibernia/) which is a splendid site not only for those with Irish ancestry but for anyone interested in genealogy. A brand new resource in this area is St. Anthony's Church and Visitor Centre (Newham Street and Scotland Road, Liverpool L5 5BD [t] 0151 207 0177.) The church is the last resting place of 2,303 of those Irish paupers who fled from Ireland during the Famine, only to die in Liverpool. The new Heritage Centre both commemorates the victims of the Famine and provides facilities for all those wishing to trace the individual stories of those who died. Displays put the tragedy within its historical context and help us to grasp its enormity.

Equally fascinating for both those specifically interested in visual history and those who want to get a feel for a period is the South Liverpool Photographic Society on www.slps.co.uk You can contact the society on [t] 0151 546 4659. The society has an extensive photographic record of Liverpool life.

If you are interested in preserving precious family documents, then you can find out how to do it by visiting the Conservation Centre, (Whitechapel, Liverpool, L16HZ [t] 0151 478 4999.) It is the first national conservation centre in the UK and the only one open to the public. It deals with all aspects of conserving furnishings, paintings as well as documents. Finally, BBC Radio Merseyside has an excellent local history site on http:www.bbc.co.uk/liverpool/localhistory/index It covers a range of areas which are of interest to the genealogist – family history trails, memories of places, heritage journeys and the work of the Liverpool Women's History Group.

Relatively speaking:
How to determine family relationships
Doreen Hopwood

As family historians, we're intent on finding out as much as we can about our ancestors, collecting more and more names to add to our family's tree. However, we may be so busy researching the past that we don't realise just how many living relatives we have - once we take more distant family members into consideration.

In earlier times, people used to talk of "kith and kin" in describing relationships (which, roughly speaking, means 'native land people'), and this term was used for both relatives and acquaintances. Similarly, in the medieval period, families and households were virtually synonymous, and the word "family" is derived from the Latin *famulus* (servant), which developed into *familia* ('household').

At this time it was usual for families to share their homes with members of their wider kin, servants and apprentices. The idea of a private family life where only a married couple and their children live together is a much more recent phenomenon, and is generally described as a nuclear (or simple) family. The extended (or complex) family was common until the early twentieth century when households could have included step-relatives, in-laws, visitors, boarders and lodgers. Families are not rigid entities, but are constantly changing as their members marry, have children and eventually die. Marriage forms a completely "new" family, and brings more relatives into the equation. The husband in the new marriage may also be a brother, son, uncle, nephew, or even a father if he had been married before, and his bride could be a sister, daughter, niece, or a mother. Anthropologists refer to the family into which we are born as the "family of orientation", and the one formed upon marriage as the "family of procreation". Although there is no formal or legal relationship between the parents of the bride and those of the groom, they are generally considered as part of the wider family group, and most of us have had "honorary" aunties and uncles who were family friends or neighbours during our childhoods.

In association with Family History Monthly

Related by Blood	
Uncle/aunt	The brother or sister of your mother or father.
Sibling	Your brother or sister.
Half-sibling	The son or daughter of one of your parents from a previous marriage or relationship. You share one biological parent with a half-sibling.
Cousin	First cousins are the children of your aunts and uncles.
Nephew/niece	The son or daughter of your brother or sister.
Grandfather	The father of your mother or father.
Grandmother	The mother of your mother or father.
Great-grandfather	The father of one of your grandparents.
Great-grandmother	The mother of one of your grandparents.
Great-aunt/uncle	The aunt or uncle of your mother or father.
Maternal	Related through your mother (i.e. your mother's mother).
Paternal	Related through your father (i.e. your father's father).
Related by marriage	
Father-in-law, mother-in-law	The father or mother of you spouse.
Stepson, step-daughter	The child of your spouse's former marriage or relationship.
Step-mother, step-father	The second or subsequent spouse of your mother or father.

Wherever there is a biological link between individuals, the relationship is described as one of "blood" (or consanguinal), and this includes all our ancestors, descendants and siblings. Affinal relationships are formed by marriage, law or custom, so this group incorporates in-laws and step-relatives – individuals with whom there are no biological ties.

Each of us has two biological parents, four grandparents, eight great-grandparents, and so on with the number doubling for each generation we go back. If we work on the assumption that each period of 100 years represents three generations, then we should all have had about thirty three million direct ancestors alive in the year 1100AD. The sums don't add up however, as the total population of England and Wales was only recorded as a million and a quarter in the Great Domesday Survey of 1085/6. The answer to this mathematical conundrum is the intermarriage of second, and more distant, cousins who would have had at least one great-grandparent who appeared in the family trees of both bride and groom. When Henry VIII broke away from the Catholic faith and declared himself Head of the Church of England, it was decided that rulings were needed to prevent people who were related to each other from marrying. A list of some 60 relationships, known as the "Prohibited Degrees", was drawn up in 1563, and was upheld by both civil and canon (church) law. They were printed in the Book of Common Prayer and have been amended several times in the twentieth century to take into account issues such as adoption, divorce and surrogacy.

Whilst it is not imperative for us to recognise our relationships to distant relatives, for the nobility it is of vital importance as there is a very strict procedure for the inheritance of titles. These pass from eldest son to eldest son, and great lengths are taken to ensure that a title doesn't become extinct. In the absence of closer family, the title of one aristocratic family was passed to a sixteenth cousin. Known as "primogeniture", this was the way in which land and property were handed down through the male line. In some areas "partible inheritance" was common, under which all of the sons (and in some areas, daughters too) received equal shares. Pedigrees of the nobility have been published by Burke, Debrett and Cockayne, and Heraldic Visitations were a means by which their pedigrees were verified.

Complicated relationships arise where family members are related in more than one way. The pedigree of Queen Victoria indicates that she was related by blood and by marriage to many of the Royal Houses of Europe. Following the marriages of her children, the links were further strengthened as she became mother-in-law to many rulers and princes.

The terminology of cousin relationships is complex, but by using the chart shown here, it is straightforward to work out the relationship between two individuals who have an ancestor-in-common. Cousins share at least one set of grandparents, and those of the same generation as us can be described as:

First Cousins
The individuals with whom you share two grandparents – the children of your aunts and uncles.

Second Cousins
The individuals with whom you share great-grandparents.

Third Cousins
The individuals with whom you share great-great-grandparents.

and so on.

A further number is added for each generation you go back, in the same way as another "great" is added before grandfather or grandmother to denote each generation. First cousins may also be referred to as "Cousins German", and "double cousinships" occur when siblings from one family marry siblings from another family and have the same four grandparents.

The term "removed" is added to indicate that the cousins are of different generations, and the number refers to the difference in generations between them. In this way, your "first" cousin once-removed is the child of your first cousin, or the child of one of your mother's or your father's first cousins, because he or she is "one generation removed from you".

"Twice-removed" denotes a two generation difference and so on. In reality, we refer to all of these people simply as "cousins" because, in conversation, would you want to be introduced as "my fourth cousin, twice removed"?

The terminology used to describe family relationships has changed over time, and some words which have precise meaning today were often interchangeable or used more loosely in the past. During the nineteenth century, the main reason for the break-up of a family was death. The subsequent re-marriage of the surviving spouse, especially if this marriage was to another person who had been widowed, may bring two sets of children into the new family. These became step-siblings, and any children born to the newly-weds, in turn, became their half-siblings. 'Step' and 'in-law' were often used to denote the same relationship, and, on the Victorian census returns, step- sons/daughters are often referred to as sons- or daughters-in-law. My own great-grandmother married a widower whose son who subsequently married my great-grandmother's younger sister. On their wedding day she must have been surprised to find that she had become the mother-in-law of her own sister! Fortunately, most relationships aren't so complicated, and here are some of the terms which describe them:

	1	2	3	4	5	6	7	8	9	10
1	Common Ancestor	Son or Daughter	Grandson or Daughter	Great Grandson or Daughter	2nd Great Grandson or Daughter	3rd Great Grandson or Daughter	4th Great Grandson or Daughter	5th Great Grandson or Daughter	6th Great Grandson or Daughter	7th Great Grandson or Daughter
2	Son or Daughter	Brother or Sister	Niece or Nephew	Grand Niece or Nephew	Great Grand Niece or Nephew	2nd Great Grand Niece or Nephew	3rd Great Grand Niece or Nephew	4th Great Grand Niece or Nephew	5th Great Grand Niece or Nephew	6th Great Grand Niece or Nephew
3	Grandson or Daughter	Niece or Nephew	First Cousin	First Cousin Once Removed	First Cousin Twice Removed	First Cousin Three Times Removed	First Cousin Four Times Removed	First Cousin Five Times Removed	First Cousin Six Times Removed	First Cousin Seven Times Removed
4	Great Grandson or Daughter	Grand Niece or Nephew	First Cousin Once Removed	Second Cousin	Second Cousin Once Removed	Second Cousin Twice Removed	Second Cousin Three Times Removed	Second Cousin Four Times Removed	Second Cousin Five Times Removed	Second Cousin Six Times Removed
5	2nd Great Grandson or Daughter	Great Grand Niece or Nephew	First Cousin Twice Removed	Second Cousin Once Removed	Third Cousin	Third Cousin Once Removed	Third Cousin Twice Removed	Third Cousin Three Times Removed	Third Cousin Four Times Removed	Second Cousin Five Times Removed
6	3rd Great Grandson or Daughter	2nd Great Grand Niece or Nephew	First Cousin Three Times Removed	Second Cousin Twice Removed	Third Cousin Once Removed	Fourth Cousin	Fourth Cousin Once Removed	Fourth Cousin Twice Removed	Fourth Cousin Three Times Removed	Fourth Cousin Four Times Removed
7	4th Great Grandson or Daughter	3rd Great Grand Niece or Nephew	First Cousin Four Times Removed	Second Cousin Three Times Removed	Third Cousin Twice Removed	Fourth Cousin Once Removed	Fifth Cousin	Fifth Cousin Once Removed	Fifth Cousin Twice Removed	Fifth Cousin Three Times Removed
8	5th Great Grandson or Daughter	4th Great Grand Niece or Nephew	First Cousin Five Times Removed	Second Cousin Four Times Removed	Third Cousin Three Times Removed	Fourth Cousin Twice Removed	Fifth Cousin Once Removed	Sixth Cousin	Sixth Cousin Once Removed	Sixth Cousin Twice Removed
9	6th Great Grandson or Daughter	5th Great Grand Niece or Nephew	First Cousin Six Times Removed	Second Cousin Five Times Removed	Third Cousin Four Times Removed	Fourth Cousin Three Times Removed	Fifth Cousin Twice Removed	Sixth Cousin Once Removed	Seventh Cousin	Seventh Cousin Once Removed
10	7th Great Grandson or Daughter	6th Great Grand Niece or Nephew	First Cousin Seven Times Removed	Second Cousin Six Times Removed	Third Cousin Five Times Removed	Fourth Cousin Four Times Removed	Fifth Cousin Three Times Removed	Sixth Cousin Twice Removed	Seventh Cousin Once Removed	Eighth Cousin

When the good guys go bad
Paul Williams
looks at a few cases where police officers committed murder

Regretfully, murder is a common event and has been throughout time. Regardless of whatever deterrents are in force, someone somewhere will commit murder and this country is no exception to that rule. Just pick up the daily paper and there are bound to be one or more recorded somewhere. And don't forget the many cases that don't reach the papers as space for world events dictates whether they will be included or not.

The majority of murders are committed by people who know each other. The remainder are therefore committed by complete strangers to the victim but thankfully, in both scenarios, the murderer is detected and punished in some way. Knowing this therefore I find it surprising that occasionally a police officer goes astray and changes from hunter to hunted.

3 accused of police murder

From Our Correspondent

Glasgow, Dec. 31

Three men arrested after Tuesday's shooting in Glasgow, when a policeman died, were ~med when they appeared · Sheriff Court to·

One such case occurred on 30 December 1969. Harold Charles John Wilson, 31 years of age, had been a police officer for nine years. He quit the police force when he felt he could go no further in his career and shared a partnership in a greengrocery business. Finding it hard to make ends meet with his new job, he turned to crime. Accompanied by John Sim (22) - also an ex-policeman - and Ian Donaldson (31), they carried out two armed bank robberies.

The first robbery was on Wednesday 16 July 1969 at the British Linen Bank in Williamwood, Renfrewshire, when they shared just over £20,000. With his share of the proceeds, Wilson bought out his business partner and ran the shop with his wife. The second raid was at the Clyesdale Bank in Bridge Street, Linwood, Renfrewshire, at 3.15 pm on Tuesday 30 December 1969 and from that they netted £14,000.

It was at 4.30 pm on that latter date that Inspector Andrew Hislop and Constable John Sellars, who were just leaving Police Headquarters in a Panda car, heard of the raid over their car radio. At that very moment the officers saw three men jump from a vehicle and grabbing some suitcases and a metal box from the boot, hurriedly make their way into the ground floor flat in Allison Street, Glasgow, which was later found to belong to Wilson.

Policeman's intuition told Inspector Hislop that the men were up to no good. He recognised one as an ex-policeman yet even so he knew something was wrong. The officers stopped their car, walked over towards the flat and looked in one of the windows. Still suspicious, Inspector Hislop told PC Sellars to keep watch whilst he went back to the station for assistance. As the Constable kept watch Wilson, the ex-policeman, left the flat. Seeing Sellars he asked what he was doing. When the officer merely told him that he was waiting for his Inspector, Wilson went into a nearby dairy shop. As Wilson came out of the shop Inspector Hislop returned with Constables Edward Barnett, John Campbell and Angus McKenzie. The Inspector told Wilson what he had seen and that he wanted to search the flat. Wilson replied that he had nothing to hide and agreed to the search. The five officers entered the flat and noticed the same suitcases which they had seen taken from the car on the living room floor. The cases were opened and inside were bags of coins. Wilson offered to fetch the rest of the money but when he returned, after a few seconds, had armed himself with a gun. He fired four shots. The first hit Inspector Hislop in the left side of his face. The second hit Barnett in the head as he came out of the kitchen.

When Wilson realised that he had failed to kill Barnett he shot him again. The unfortunate officer died four days later. The last two bullets killed Constable McKenzie almost immediately. Hearing the shooting, suspect Ian Donaldson fled from the building.

Constable Sellars had been searching the bathroom when the shooting started. He hurriedly locked the door and radioed for assistance. When his call for help was heard by Wilson, the latter tried in vain to get into the bathroom, calling to Sim for assistance. Failing to get in Wilson then noticed

P-c dies : 3 face murder charge

After the death of a second policeman involved in the Glasgow shooting on Tuesday, three men on remand at Barlinnie prison were charged yesterday with his murder.

Acting Detective - constable Edward Barnett died early yes-·rday in Victoria Infirmary. ·asgow, where he had been un-·us with head wounds. ·ID. said last ·

Inspector Hislop moving on the floor. Calmly, he walked over to him holding the gun to the officer's head he pulled the trigger, but nothing happened. The gun had jammed. Constable Campbell, who had been searching the living room, witnessed Wilson with his gun at the Inspector's head and saw Wilson's dilemma. Taking advantage of the situation Campbell jumped on the gunman and after a tremendous struggle succeeded in grabbing the weapon from him. Covering both men Campbell then awaited the arrival of further colleagues. The whole incident had taken just minutes.

The third man, Donaldson, who had fled the scene of the killings was arrested soon afterwards back at his home in Paisley.

At the Edinburgh High Court on 13 February 1970 Wilson was sentenced to life imprisonment with a recommendation that he serve a minimum of 25 years. He also received 12 years imprisonment, to run concurrently, for the robberies. Sim and Donaldson each received 12 years imprisonment.

In the mid 1950's the body of a dead female was found lying on Prospecthill Road near Aitkenhead Road, Glasgow. The taxi driver who found her assumed she had been the victim of a hit and run driver. The first officer on the scene similarly thought the same on arrival but soon became suspicious when he found no broken glass near where the accident had happened.

Examination of the body showed the jaw had been broken and there were injuries to body and face but no broken legs. This led to the belief that the body had been dumped in the road after having been killed.

The victim was 40 year old Catherine McCluskey, an unmarried mother who lived in a slum tenement in South Glasgow. Enquiries revealed she had many acquaintances including a Glasgow policeman, one James Ronald Robertson. Robertson was a family man with two children. However, two nights before the body was found a PC Moffat had been on duty with Robertson. Robertson told him he was going off to see a 'blonde lady friend'. He returned later and related how their meeting had gone off well.

On the night of the murder Robertson again told Moffat he was off to see his lady friend. This time however he returned about two hours later with his collar soaked in sweat, scuffed shoes, dusty trousers and acting quite agitated.

Robertson was arrested whilst out on his beat. Examination of his home revealed car registration books and car keys. The Austin car which he had used to go to and from work was also discovered to have been stolen and false number plates fitted. Robertson readily admitted theft of the car and as if to clear his conscience also confessed to the events leading up to the murder. He said he had accidentally knocked her down when reversing the car. He had tried to pull her from under the car but her clothing had become caught and he had to drive backwards and forwards to release her. If he had tried to drag her out there would be blood on his trousers but on examination there was none. He said he had cradled the body in his arms in which cases blood would have been on his uniform. Again examination found none.

The Austin car was examined and under it were found traces of human blood and hair. The prop shaft was also completely enclosed so it was impossible for McClusky's clothes to have been caught in it.

At his Trial the jury disbelieved his story and he was found guilty of murder. He was hanged at Barlinnie Prison on 16 December 1950. Why Robertson killer McClusky will never be known but it was suggested by the prosecution she may have had some hold over him and may perhaps have been blackmailing him.

The first case I can find of a policeman committing a murder was that of PC George

Samuel Cooke in 1893. On 8 June of that year a female body was found by a shepherd on a common that was adjacent to Wormwood Scrubs prison, London. She had been battered to death and was covered in blood. There was however no evidence of any sexual assault. The victim was identified as Maud Smith.

2 December Police went to Rillington Place and found the bodies of Beryl Evans and year old daughter Geraldine dumped in an outside washhouse. Both had been strangled. Evans confessed to the murders but later tried to implicate John Christie by saying the latter had performed an illegal abortion on Beryl. However, no evidence was found of an abortion having been performed. Evans was charged only with Geraldine's murder. At his Old Bailey trial in 1950 Christie was called as a witness for the prosecution and denied any responsibility in the murders. Evans was found guilty of murder and sentenced to death. When sentence of death was passed Christie was heard to be sobbing loudly. Evans later appealed but on 20 February this was turned down and execution took place on 9th March 1950.

10 Rillington Place, the scene of the murders

When news of the discovery reached the prison a warder told police how he had seen, the previous evening, a policeman walking across the common with a young girl. As PC Cooke's beat took him passed the prison he was interviewed but denied knowing the girl. It was soon discovered however that he had been having an affair with her and when his lodgings were searched a blood stained uniform was found and in the garden was discovered a bloodstained truncheon. At his Trial Cooke was found guilty and sentenced to death. He was hanged on 25 July 1893 by James Billington.

Perhaps the most publicised British policeman of all time to have murdered was John Reginald Halliday Christie. Christie was a War Reserve Policeman and it is known that he murdered at least 6 women.

In 1949 Christie was living at 10 Rillington Place in London's Notting Hill area. He and his wife occupied the ground-floor flat whilst in the top floor flat was Timothy John Evans, semi-illiterate van driver, together with his wife and baby daughter.

On 30th November 1949 Evans walked into Merthyr Tydfil Police Station in Wales – he'd been visiting an Aunt - and told them that on 8 November he had returned to his London home after work and found his wife dead, and added that he had put her body down a drain. On

Christie moved from his ground floor flat on 13 March 1953. He sub-let (without authority) his rooms to a Mr and Mrs Reilly but the following day Charles Brown, the landlord, visited the premises and threw them both out. Brown arranged with a Mr Beresford Brown, a Jamaican who lodged in a flat upstairs, to clear out Christie's old rooms. Whilst inspecting the fabric he tapped a kitchen wall and heard a hollow sound. Tearing off some of the tatty wallpaper he found they had been covering a coal-cupboard door. With the aid of a torch he peered through a gap and saw the back of a body.

In the presence of Detective Chief Inspector Griffin, senior police officers and Dr Camps, the Home Office pathologist, the cupboard was opened and three bodies found inside. The first out was that of 26 year old Hectorina MacLennan; next was Kathleen Maloney, 26, and the last 25 year old

War Reserve Constable John Christie

Christie with his wife Ethel

Rita Nelson who was 6 months pregnant. All three had been gassed and strangled.

Later that evening the decomposing body of Mrs Christie was found under the floorboards in the front room. She too had been strangled by a ligature but not gassed.

The garden was also dug up and a mass of bones unearthed which when put together formed two skeletons. They were Ruth Fuerst (21) and Muriel Eady (31).

Since leaving his flat Christie had gone from being a well groomed clean man to penniless and dirty and living in a doss house. He was

Paul Williams worked for the Metropolitan Police in London for 26 years during which time he not only spent several years in their Criminal Record Office but was for over 8 years responsible for their Force Museums. One of these Museums was the world famous Black Museum which holds crime exhibits from notorious criminal cases. Whilst there he lectured, with the Curator, to police officers, members of the Judiciary and eminent people including members of the British and foreign Royal families. Amongst the many interesting visitors he met were Albert Pierrepoint, the last British Hangman and Professor Sir Bernard Spilsby, the pathologist.

As well as running Murder Files, Paul Williams, who is a Winston Churchill Fellow, writes articles for books, magazines and CD-Roms. He provides storylines for TV documentaries and dramas and has been a narrator in front of the camera for a murder reconstruction.

found by police on 31 March leaning on the embankment wall by Putney Bridge. He was taken arrested and later charged with the murder of his wife. On 15 April he was also charged with the murder of the three women found in the cupboard. Five days later he admitted killing Beryl Evans but not baby Geraldine. Two months later he made a statement saying he was responsible for killing Miss Fuerst and Miss Eady.

At the Old Bailey Christie pleaded not guilty to the murder of his wife, but after a four day trial, the jury took just 85 minutes to find him guilty. Sentenced to death he was executed in Pentonville Prison on 15 July by Albert Pierrepoint. After the hanging Pierrepoint recorded in his hanging records '15 July 1953, John Reginald Halliday Christie, age 55, height 5' 8½", weight 149lbs, drop 7'4", Pentonville' with his initials and those of his assistant on the day H. Smith.

Timothy Evans, as you will recall above, was hanged for the murder of his daughter. At his trial he said that Christie had murdered his wife and daughter. In view of the murders performed by Christie, could he (Christie) have murdered Beryl Evans? Had Evans been wronged and hanged by mistake? There was great public disquiet over this issue and in the end the Home Secretary ordered Mr John Scott Henderson to re-examine the evidence of both cases. During the course of this Christie was asked again whether he had killed Mrs Evans or the child. His reply: 'Well, I'm not sure.' In the end Henderson found against a miscarriage of justice because the case against Evans was an overwhelming one; he was satisfied Evans was responsible for the murders of both his wife and daughter, and that Christie's statements that he was responsible for the death of Mrs Evans were not only unreliable but untrue.

After this there were many campaigns and in 1965, under a newly elected Labour government, the death penalty was abolished for a 5 year period and in October 1966 Evans was granted a posthumous free pardon.

Above are just a few cases of murders committed by policemen. There are others and a few have taken place in quite recent years. However, we must bear in mind the families of both victim and accused, who I feel often suffer more through the publicity than the accused.

Murderfiles.com has information on thousands of murders. If you are looking for details of a particular case try www.murderfiles.com first. They may be able to help.

Typical Weavers' Cottages

The Woollen Industry
Anne Harvey

Now that the woollen industry is a mere shadow of its former giant self, it seems hard to believe that it was once an important factor in the prosperity of Britain during the Industrial Revolution. Or that, in earlier times, the production of wool itself was such a major contribution to the national economy that even taxes could be paid in sacks of wool. Its importance is reflected in the fact that the Lord Chancellor's seat in Parliament is a bag of wool known as the Woolsack.

Ancient drawings and engravings show that the production of cloth is a skill that has always been around though most probably on a fairly localised level. In the early middle ages, for instance, when serfs still toiled for the lord of the manor, most households would keep a sheep. Every bit of wool would be used, such as the seasonal moulting and scraps left on bushes or trees. Collecting these was known as 'wool-gathering'. The phrase has passed into everyday language to signify a tendency to daydream while carrying out a boring task.

It was the monastic orders that first started keeping flocks of sheep in order to sell their fleeces, called the 'clip', to fund their ambitious building projects. The Cistercian order of Kirkstall Abbey in Leeds had a flock of 11,000 sheep at one time, herded on land known as 'granges' in the areas surrounding Leeds. British wool gained such a quality reputation that it became the major export in the Middle Ages.

'Clips' were sometimes sold in advance to merchants who, attracted by the high quality of the wool, came from far and wide. This trading practice, although frowned on by the mother abbeys, was widely practised and on such a scale that vast fortunes were made. It was no wonder that Henry VIII, in the 16th century, cast avaricious eyes on the monasteries and dissolved them.

The weaving of cloth, however, was still very much on a domestic level, producing just enough cloth to clothe the family. This was of a poor quality and dyed with readily available vegetable dyes. After the Black Death in 1348/49, when a third of the population died and the lords of manors were forced to pay wages to the remaining labour force, the new money-based economy paved the way for the production and sale of woollen cloth on the open market.

It was in order to regulate such production and set certain standards that guilds were set up in areas where cloth-making was prevalent. Although fulfilling the useful role of supporting tradesmen and regulating apprenticeships, guilds were often severely restrictive. To many it was akin to being bound in service to the lord of the manor, although the guilds were also supportive of members who fell on hard times.

through eye-like teeth and joined up to existing threads on the loom.

In the early days of weaving, the loom was primitive with weights to hold the warp firm and was a job for the women of the household. With the introduction of the more sturdy treadle-operated horizontal loom, weaving was carried out by men, especially as, initially, the weaver had to physically throw the shuttle, containing the weft, through the warp and to manhandle the reed combs backwards and forwards.

The immigration of skilled Flemish weavers in the Middle Ages, many of whom settled in East Anglia, also contributed to the improvement in standards of quality.

The production of cloth was very much a domestic affair with the whole family being involved. Even at an early age, the children would be set to picking burrs and other vegetable matter from the raw wool by hand. The raw wool would then be straightened, again by children, by drawing it through two hand-held cards lined with the thistle-like heads of teasels, a process known as 'carding'. From there, the women of the household took over, spinning the longer lengths of wool to make it finer and stronger. Originally, this involved twisting the fibres between their fingers and spinning and winding it on a distaff spindle, a more or less continuous task but with the advantage of being able to be carried out anywhere and at any time. Later, this process was replicated by the hand-operated spinning wheel, involving the two separate actions spinning and winding, with the woman twisting the fibre as she fed it on to the distaff. Later still, these processes were carried out in tandem with the treadle-operated Saxony spinning wheel.

Families took up the production of cloth to supplement the income from farming which, with fluctuations in weather and problems with pests and diseases, was never a reliable source of income. This was particularly so in the West Riding of Yorkshire where the Pennines proved inhospitable places to farm but the abundant rain provided soft water for the cleaning of wool and the lower hillsides were excellent grazing for sheep.

Prior to weaving, the lengthways fibres, known as warp, had to be sized to avoid breakages and make them more malleable. The strengthened fibres were then wound on a large drum, passed

Wider pieces of woven cloth, called broadcloth, were more labour-intensive as they needed two weavers to pass the shuttle between them. However, in 1733, John Kay invented a device whereby a pull on a central leaver sent the shuttle flying through the warp. Originally used for the cotton industry, the 'flying-shuttle' device quickly became popular in the woollen industry. This, and the later development of shuttle boxes, speeded up the weaving process and often left the weaver waiting for yarn. James Hargreaves, himself a weaver, came up with the answer, the spinning jenny, which could spin several threads at once, then wind them on to bobbins.

In pre-mechanised days, weaving was a time-consuming business and continued whenever there was light to work by. The looms were always situated on the upper floors of the house to catch as much light as possible. The windows were close together to avoid paying window tax, which accounts for the narrow – and allowable – stone mullions that mark surviving weavers' cottages. In 1818, the tax for 1-6 windows was 2s 6d ($12^1/_2$p). To escape paying window tax, many people blocked up windows but painted them to look like windows. These were known colloquially as 'Pitt's Pictures' after the Prime Minister of the day. In 1825, anyone with fewer than 8 windows was exempt from paying tax and in 1851, the tax was abolished.

The loose weave of the finished cloth had to be 'fulled' to matt the fibres together and make the cloth warmer. In the early middle ages, men used to stamp on the cloth as it lay in a trough of stale urine, to which Fuller's Earth (a soft absorbent clay) was added. It is from this process that the surnames 'Walker' and, in the West Country where the fulling process was known as

Typical cottage-type spinning wheel

tucking, 'Tucker' originated. Fulling was one of the first processes of the woollen industry to be mechanised. At the fulling mill, usually built by the lord of the manor, the coarse cloth would be pulverised by giant hammers to obtain a smooth matt grain. Stale urine (for the ammonia) was still used to clean any oily residue and a bucket was always close by!

The pieces of cloth were then stretched out on tenter frames in adjoining fields to be pulled into shape and bleached by the sun. Coating the cloth in stale milk, which contains lactic acid, accelerated bleaching. The phrase 'on tenterhooks', describing someone in a state of tension, stems from this process.

The resultant pieces of cloth, grey in colour but called 'white' to differentiate them from 'coloured cloth', were then taken to a local cloth market in a neighbouring town. Transport would initially be by packhorse then, as road surfaces improved, by wagon. Middlemen, called 'chapmen' were often involved to save the weaver precious time away from his loom.

The 17th century was probably the most productive time for the domestic woollen industry when, for the first time, finished woollen cloth overtook the sale of wool as the country's major export. It was to safeguard the woollen industry that the Flannel Act of 1666/67 was introduced. This meant that everyone had to be buried in wool and an affidavit signed by the next of kin to say that this had been done.

Although the idea of the farmer-weaver being totally self-sufficient is a pleasant one, more often than not a merchant would supply the raw wool on credit and either pay on receipt of the finished piece or the weaver might be employed by the merchant, albeit in his own home. In a similar manner, carding and spinning was given to 'out-workers'. So, while the farmer-weaver might find struggle to keep his family, it was the merchant who stood more chance of becoming rich.

It was the merchants, too, who funded the dyeing and finishing of woollen cloth. From the early Middle Ages, dyeing of cloth had been a specialist trade, providing the richer colours demanded by the upper classes. Once dyed, the cloth was combed by using teasels to raise an even nap. Ironically, teasels are still used today for producing the fine nap of certain fabrics, such as that used for Guardsmen's uniforms. Professional croppers then cropped the cloth to a standard size with outsize shears. It was they who were the first to become machine-breakers in the early 19th century, when they destroyed the new shearing machines.

The early 1800s were troubled times for the woollen industry. As soldiers who had been involved in the Napoleonic Wars (1793-1815) came home, it was to a national depression and widespread unemployment. It was also an era of change as new machinery, originally developed for use in the cotton industry, was adapted for the woollen industry. An example of this was Richard Arkwright's spinning frame, driven by water, which, unlike the spinning jenny, combined the twisting, spinning and winding actions of the old spinning wheel.

Given the costs of such machinery, merchants quickly found that it was cheaper to group machinery under one roof and have the workers come to a 'manufactory' (from whence comes the word factory). This was a purpose-built mill, initially water-driven, later powered by steam engines.

Many enterprising mill owners were at that time building cottages for their workers. Others were bringing handloom weavers under one roof, presumably to make sure the weavers were kept at work and that they were not siphoning off the raw materials to use for their own profit. Many former domestic workers must have struggled with the harsh rules and regulations of the new factory system.

Children played a major part in the production of woollen cloth, whether in the home or at the mill, and were seen as a source of cheap labour. In the early days of the factory system, even children as young as six worked long hours and were often beaten if they should fall asleep. One old mill-worker, born in Mossley, Lancashire, which had both woollen and cotton mills, remembered that he worked from 6am to 8 pm Monday to Friday and until 4 pm on Saturday. He never did attend school and found the hours long and dreary especially in wintertime when they worked by candlelight. (*The Story of Mossley*, Alfred Holt 1974 and 2000, published by the Mossley Civic Society)

Various Factories Acts regulated how many hours children under 13 could work and also

Hand-held 'cards' for straightening wool fibres

that they should receive schooling for two hours a day six days a week. This changed with the 1870 Education Act when elementary education for 5-10 year olds was introduced. It wasn't until 1880 that school attendance became compulsory for children up to the age of ten. Even then, children spent half the day in school, the other half working in the mill. It would be hard to say which was worse for a young child, attending school in the morning after working till late the previous day, or attending school in the afternoon, having worked since early in the morning at the mill.

The late 18th and early 19th century saw the introduction of many more mechanised processes in the woollen industry. One such was a scribbling machine, which straightened the fibres prior to carding and spinning. Introduced first in the domestic woollen industry, the new scribbling machines were seen as a threat to livelihoods. Another invention, the shearing machine, which cropped the cloth, sparked off many machine-breaking activities. The machine-breakers were called Luddites after earlier attacks in Nottinghamshire claimed to have been carried out by followers of 'Captain' or 'General' Ludd. In one notorious case, the activities of the Luddites led to the murder of a woollen merchant in Meltham, near Huddersfield, a crime for which some of the Luddites were hanged.

By nature of its complex operation, the loom was the last process of the woollen industry to be mechanised. It was to be the mid 1800s before all the processes for the woollen industry were fully mechanised and housed in factories. A contributory factor to the industrialisation of the industry was the dying off of the older handloom weavers.

With the introduction of steam engines for the driving of machinery, mills could be built anywhere. Most were built in towns and cities for the ease of transporting supplies and finished goods. Attracted by the high wages, people flocked to work there, living mostly in inadequate and unsanitary housing. It was a boom time for the mill owners, most of whom were former cloth merchants, and six and seven-storey mills became the norm. The growth of the chemical industry meant that all the processes for the production of woollen cloth could be located on the same premises. Demand for quality woollen cloth was high and much of it was exported, contributing to the national wealth, much as the sale of raw wool had done centuries before.

Towards the end of the 19th century, much of the woollen industry was based in West Yorkshire, though there still remained pockets of woollen production in East Anglia and the West Country. During World War I (1914-1918), the woollen industry was working flat-out to produce the cloth for army uniforms and blankets. During the 1920s, cheap imports and the imposition of tariffs on exports led to another slump. The foresight and enterprise that had seen the rise of the mechanised woollen industry gave way to complacency and many mills, by then formed into companies, could no longer compete on the world market. During World War II (1939-1945), the industry was given a reprieve as, once again, the demand for cloth for uniforms became a priority.

But it was not to last and, one by one, the mills ceased production and its workers found other employment. Now the mills and factories, where they survive, are used either for light industrial units or stand as a monument to Britain's once great woollen industry.

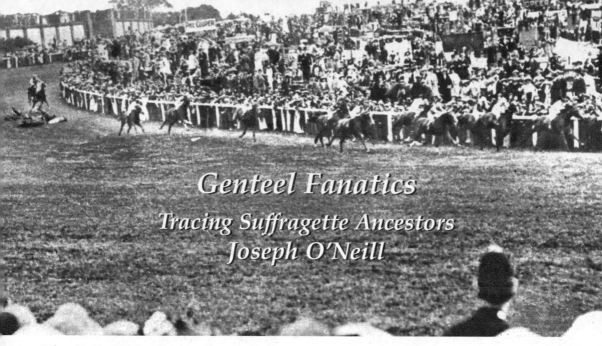

Genteel Fanatics
Tracing Suffragette Ancestors
Joseph O'Neill

When Emily Wilding Davison bent under the barrier and ran onto the Epsom course on 4 June 1913, she claimed a unique place in the history of women's suffrage. The leading horses rounded Tattenham Corner and the eyes of the spectators followed them. Few saw her, hands above her head as she clawed at the reins of the king's horse, Anmer.

Horse and jockey somersaulted, thudding down on Emily. Dazed, Anmer rose and bolted, dragging the jockey, his foot snared in the stirrup, face down. The woman lay motionless. Four days later she died at Epsom Cottage Hospital. She was the cause's only martyr.

In these days of political apathy it is hard to imagine a time when anyone was prepared to die for the vote. Yet Emily Davison and the women who made front page news in the decade before the Great War were not maverick fanatics. They were the culmination of a century long campaign. Nor did they see the vote as an end in itself. For them it was the means by which they would end women's second class status in British society.

The coveture system epitomized women's subordinate position. Once married, a woman, had no rights to her property, children or wages. Charles James Fox expressed the predominant male attitude in the first parliamentary debate on female suffrage in 1792. He won a rousing cheer when he described women as 'children of a larger growth'.

Yet even in 1792 some men disagreed with Fox. Among them were many active in the Victorian campaigns for the abolition of slavery and the property rights of married women. Many of these were Quakers or involved in other radical movements.

The first Englishwoman to publicly demand the vote was Mary Wolstencroft in her book *Vindication of the Rights of Women* of 1792. William Thompson's book of 1825 made a similar plea in his verbose *An Appeal of one Half of the Human Race, Women, against the Pretences of the Other Half, Men, to Retain Them in Political and Thence in Civil and Domestic Slavery.* Both were regarded as part of the crackpot fringe of politics.

Even the Chartists, in their demand for universal male suffrage, rejected the same plea on behalf of women. However, one Chartist society, the Sheffield Ladies' Association, survived the movement's demise and evolved into the Sheffield Association for Female Franchise. It was the first of hundreds of associations to wage the battle for female suffrage.

The first group of women to petition parliament on the matter were members of the Kensington Society, a women's debating group which included many seasoned campaigners. They organised a collected 1499 signatures for their parliamentary petition – one of the most important early sources for family historians.

The major parliamentary skirmishes in this struggle arose every time the extension of male suffrage came up for debate. One of female suffrage's most influential supporters was the philosopher and MP, John Stuart Mill, who promoted the women's cause at every opportunity. He introduced an amendment to the 1867 Reform Bill, designed to extend the vote to women. He won the support of 73 MPs and thus increased the prominence of the suffrage movement.

The following year women's suffrage societies in London, Bristol and Manchester sought to exploit an inconsistency in the wording of the 1867 Act in order to register for the vote. Almost four thousand women in the Manchester area succeeded and some overseers accepted them without question. Others, however, rejected them with the result that a test case was required, that of Miss Mary Abbott. Nor surprisingly, the outcome went against the suffrage societies – despite which thirteen women whose names remained on the roll actually voted — the last to do so before 1918.

Among those outraged at the audacity of the campaigners were many women, including the Queen. Victoria was outspoken in her condemnation of "this mad, wicked folly of women's rights."

She was particularly scathing in her criticism of Lydia Becker. The leader of the movement from 1870 until her death in 1890, Becker set up a committee in Manchester to organize a petition in support of Mill's amendment to the 1867 Act. She edited the *Woman's Suffrage Journal*, the

mouthpiece of the movement for over two decades.

Becker believed in the power of meetings, letters and above all, petitions. In 1877 she presented 9,563 petitions to Parliament. She was the moving force behind what was to become an annual event – the presentation of a Private Members' Bill to extend the franchise to women.

Though all these Bills failed for lack of government support, 1888 saw a major breakthrough. Women householders won the right to vote in elections for the newly formed county councils. At the same time the Corrupt Practices Act made it illegal for parliamentary candidates to pay election helpers. This resulted in an increase in the number of voluntary canvassers, particularly women, organized into the Conservative Primrose League and the Women's Liberal Federation.

Yet as the twentieth century dawned the female franchise seemed as far away as ever. It was at this stage in 1903 that Mrs Emmeline Pankhurst founded the Women's Social and Political Union. The campaign now took on an entirely different form.

The WSPU started life at 62, Nelson Street, Manchester. From the outset it repudiated gradualism. Its aim was 'immediate enfranchisement' by 'political action'. From the start there was a bustling, active spirit about the Union that attracted young women who were tired of the old ways. However, it also attracted vigorous opposition, often hooligans who delighted in pelting its members with rubbish and verbal abuse.

The Union grew in size and influence. By 1910 its headquarters in Charring Cross Road comprised thirty-seven rooms and a bookshop. In four years its income increased by a factor of twelve to £36,000. Its weekly meetings were so popular that it was necessary to hire Queen's Hall.

Within a few years the movement's leading lights were household names. Emmeline Pethick-Lawrence was the treasurer and her husband, Frederick, editor of its newspaper, *Votes for Women*. Annie Kenny, a cotton worker, and Theresa Billington, rubbed shoulders with Lady Constance Lytton, daughter of the former Viceroy of India and Charlotte Despard, the brother of Lord French, commander of the British Expeditionary Force in the Great War.

But most prominent of all were Emmeline's daughters. Sylvia Pankhurst worked to organize the poor women of London and her sister Christabel was the force behind nearly all the violence that kept the Union in the public eye for so many years. It was this militancy that made it so attractive to a generation of young women who found in the suffrage movement a vehicle for their idealism and selfless devotion.

The militancy began during the 1905 General Election. On 13 October Christabel and Annie Kenny attended the meeting at the Free Trade Hall, Manchester, where Sir Edward Grey was to speak. Security men threw them out when they heckled Grey for refusing to back women's suffrage. But this was not enough for Christabel who had earlier in the evening assured friends, "I shall sleep in prison tonight." A confrontation with a constable ensured she got her wish. Thus Christabel and Annie became the first Suffragettes — as the *Daily Mail* dubbed them — to suffer imprisonment. During the course of the campaign almost 1,100 others would suffer a similar fate.

Suddenly women's suffrage was good newsprint. What's more their actions fired the imagination of many women who were happy to suffer for the cause. By 1911 hundreds of women had been to jail and a section of Holloway was so full of suffragettes that one, Ethel Smyth, the composer, formed them into a choir.

Even the most audacious protest soon loses its news value. It was Christabel's genius that each time popular interest began to lag she increased the stakes. When Miss Marion Dunlop refused prison food on 1 July 1909 she made suffrage a matter of life and death. But the prison governor was not about to provide the movement with its first martyr. When all efforts to encourage her to eat failed, and her condition began to deteriorate, he released her.

The government however was not prepared to allow suffragettes' effective immunity to imprisonment by resorting to hunger strike. Instead they adopted a policy of force-feeding,

as used in lunatic asylums. This was an extremely hazardous procedure — on several occasions liquid food entered a prisoner's lung, resulting in hospitalisation. Once more the suffragettes won a propaganda victory and force feeding gave rise to some of the most graphic posters of the whole suffragette campaign.

The government came to realise that the governor's reaction to the first hunger-striker was the wisest response. Now they too released starving women, re-arresting them when they recovered. This was the famous Cat and Mouse Act.

Christabel's next ploy was mass lobbying of Parliament at which hundreds of women descended on the Commons. Many chained themselves to railings to avoid arrest. Others climbed on statues inside the grounds of the House and scrawled slogans on the venerable walls.

Not all women were happy with these tactics. Nor were they happy with the suffragette policy of targeting Liberal candidates. Led by Mrs Despard, a group left the WSPU to form the Women's Freedom League, which provided a forum for those disturbed by the both Christable's tactics and her dictatorial leadership style.

Undeterred Christabel's ingenuity continued to flourish. On 1 March 1910 the suffragettes began their great window breaking spree — starting with the most prestigious shops in Oxford Street, Regent Street and around Piccadilly Circus. They smashed hundreds of panes of glass while another group, Mrs Pankurst at its head, bombarded 10 Downing Street. Police arrested 219 Suffragettes.

 The Prime Minister, Asquith, was incensed. Police swooped on the Union's headquarters at Clement's Inn, arresting the leaders, with the exception of Christabel Pankhurst, who fled to France, where she remained until the outbreak of war in 1914.

Asquith found the Women's Freedom League only slightly less objectionable. Its members eschewed violence, though they refused to pay taxes on the grounds that they had no vote and tried to undermine the 1911 census by avoiding the enumerators. They staged marches and demonstrations, including one from Edinburgh to London. They were also competent organisers and propagandists who built up the League until it had sixty-four branches.

Unable to compete with the Union's monopoly of media coverage, the more traditional suffragist movement, rejecting illegal action, nevertheless prospered. In 1897 the National

THE
MODERN INQUISITION
TREATMENT of POLITICAL
PRISONERS UNDER A
LIBERAL
GOVERNMENT

ELECTORS!
Put a stop to this Torture
by voting against
THE PRIME MINISTER

Union of Women's Suffrage Societies (NUWSS) became an umbrella organisation for nearly five hundred branches grouped into nineteen federations. The NUWSS raised money from personal donations and by selling teas, cigarettes, ribbons and playing cards imprinted with the phrase, "Votes for Women".

The National Union worked on democratic principles, with committees, chairmen, secretaries and other officials elected annually by the membership — all of which was seen as a vital part of the political education of women. By 1914 it had 50,000 members and collected £50,000 annually. It made its greatest impact, however, in a joint venture with the WSPU. On 13 June 1908, in fine summer weather, 13,000 women wended their way from the Embankment, up St. James's Street, and down Piccadilly and Knightsbridge to the Albert Hall. Of course, they had to contend with their share of abuse.

Through its newspaper, *The Common Cause*, the National Union sought to stress its commitment to democratic methods.

But even the moderates' patience was strained

by the events of 1910 and 1911. In July 1910 a Bill to give women the vote came before the House. After two days of debate the Bill passed by a majority of one hundred — the largest majority the Government ever achieved. Amazingly, the Bill fell at Second Reading, mainly because of Asquith's opposition.

Acute disappointment led to a resurgence of suffragette militancy. The WSPU immediately organised the window smashing of March 1912 and from then until the outbreak of war in 1914, destruction and imprisonments continued.

Britain's declaration of war on 4 August 1914 brought a dramatic change of suffragette tactics. Mrs Pankhurst and Christabel announced the immediate cessation of their campaign and threw their weight behind the war effort. Soon the *Suffragette* had a new slogan: *It is a thousand times more the duty of the militant suffragettes to fight the Kaiser for the sake of liberty than it was to fight the anti-suffrage governments*. Mrs Pankhurst demanded that women be allowed to work in munitions factories. The NUWSS called a similar truce. Each of its five hundred branches gave itself over to war work.

Much to the delight of the popular press, former arsonists became window cleaners, postmen, tram drivers, shipbuilders and metalworkers. Over one hundred thousand women joined the Women's Land Army and took the place of the farm labourers who had joined up. By supplementing the depleted agricultural work force they played a major role in ensuring that the German blockade did not lead to starvation.

The most attractive and romantic of war work – most favoured by the daughters of the aristocracy – was the Voluntary Aid Detachment, whose members nursed soldiers behind the front lines. Others went into the Women's Army Auxiliary Corps, the Women's Royal Air Force and the Women's Royal Naval Services, all of which involved women in clerical and administrative tasks which released men to fight.

Most important of all, however, was work in the munitions factories. By the end of the war 900,000 women made up 60% of the workforce. Many gave their lives — most notably the sixty-nine killed when the Silvertown factory in the East End blew up. Others suffered in less dramatic ways — the canaries, whose skin glowed like sulphur due to the effects of toxic jaundice from the chemicals they handled. Others working with TNT wore their gas masks during their entire eleven hour shifts.

Women working outside the home was not new. What was was its extent, the numbers of middle-class women involved and, most of all, the publicity it received. It was this coverage that made the Pankhursts' tactic such a resounding success. Even the most dogged opponents of women's suffrage relented. Lord Northcliffe, owner of the *Daily Mail,* was a notable early convert. The traditionally reactionary *Observer* was disarmingly candid. Speaking of votes for women, its leader wrote, "In the past we have opposed the claim. We were wrong." Even Asquith, the *bete noire* of the suffragettes, changed his view before Lloyd George – a long-standing supporter of the women's cause – replaced him at 10, Downing Street.

Peace brought women the expected reward. The Representation of the People Act, 1918 gave women householders, the wives of householders, and women with degrees over thirty the right to vote in Parliamentary elections. Eight and a half million women went to the polls.

However, it was not until 1928 that women won the right to vote on the same basis as men. Significantly, it was on that day in 1928 when the Bill passed the House of Lords that Mrs Pankhurst breathed her last.

FURTHER RESEARCH
The Women's Suffrage Movement, by Elizabeth Crawford provides a comprehensive coverage of the women's suffrage campaign, including over 800 entries on societies and more than 400 biographical entries. Most of the society entries include names and addresses of their secretaries. Annual reports of the societies contain subscription lists and you may be able to find your ancestor there. The Women's Library Old Castle Street, London E1 7NT, [t.:] 44 (0)20 7320 222 (http://www.thewomenslibrary.ac.uk/) holds a good collection of this material.

The National Archives hold numerous documents relating to the militant campaign, many of them giving names and full addresses of suffragettes. Around 1085 women served prison sentences for the cause and these cases are documented in the records of the National Archives (Ruskin Avenue, Kew, Richmond, Surrey TW9 4DU [t] 020 8876 35555 [w] www.nationalarchives.gov.uk) Calendars of Prisoners, which include ages and occupations, are in classes HO, PCOM, ADM, T, KB and WO.

You will find the relevant prison registers including names, birthplaces, ages, details of crime and punishment, physical description and even photographs in the County Record Office. The Suffolk Record Office is on Gatacre Road, Ipswich IPI 2LQ. Many more militants were arrested during demonstrations and rallies and their cases too will be found in police records and local newspaper reports. Your local library will tell you where you can see these newspapers.

THE
City of York & District
Family History Society

The City of York & District Family History Society, Founded 1975,
covers the modern Archdeaconry of York, a large area of Yorkshire,
which stretches from Coxwold, Hovingham and Sherburn in Harfordlythe in the North
to Ledsham, Birkin, Selby and Drax in the South,
and from Bramham, Bilton and Sherburn in Elmet in the West
to Huggate and Bubwith in the East

check our website for full details:

www.yorkfamilyhistory.org.uk

**Wherever you are, if you have ancestors from our area, or even
if you live locally and are researching elsewhere, come and join us!**

We meet on the **first Wednesday of each month**, excluding August, at:
The Folk Hall, New Earswick, York
at 7pm for 7.30pm

*The Society's **Research Room** is located
at The Study Centre
The Raylor Centre, James Street, York YO10 3DW*

Phone: 01904 412204

email: yorkfamilyhistory@btopenworld.com

Our own
YORK FAMILY HISTORY FAIR
Held every year on a Saturday in March

For details of this and other Society activities
please see our web-site: www.yorkfamilyhistory.org.uk
or contact the Secretary, enclosing s.a.e.
Mrs Mary Varley, Ascot House, Cherry Tree Avenue, Newton on Ouse
York YO30 3BN
email: secretary@yorkfamilyhistory.org.uk

Registered Charity No. 1085228

Smedley Hydro, Southport
Reproduced with the permission of Martin Perry, Southport Civic Society

General Register Office - Certificate Services

The General Register Office is part of the Office for National Statistics and is the central source of certified copies of register entries (certificates) in England and Wales. Since 1837 each entry made in a register of births, marriages or deaths in England and Wales has been copied to the centrally held national record maintained by General Register Office. Certificate Services is the name given to the arm of the General Register Office (GRO) that deals with applications for copies from this record of births, marriages and deaths and is based in Southport, Merseyside.

Many customers who apply to Certificate Services for a certificate do so for legal or administrative purposes such as applying for a passport or pension, but increasingly a large proportion of applications are from family historians and professional genealogists. GRO also has separate sections that deal with adoption certificates and certain overseas records.

Family Records Centre. Many of you will be familiar with the "public face" of Certificate Services, the Family Records Centre (FRC) at 1 Myddelton Street London EC1R 1UW. The FRC is run in partnership with The National Archives *formally The Public Record Office* and aims to provide a one-stop shop for family history research. The Family Record Centre provides access to:
Paper indexes of births, marriages and deaths registered in England and Wales from 1st July 1837.
Indexes of legal adoptions (England & Wales from 1927).
Indexes of births, marriages and deaths of some British citizen's abroad and those relating to British Armed Forces, posted overseas from the late 18th century. These include: Consular and High Commission returns since 1849; Marine

births and deaths since 1837; aircraft births, deaths and missing persons from 1947; Army returns from 1881; Regimental registers 1761-1924; (these cover the UK, Ireland and abroad (including India) Army Chaplains returns 1796-1880; deaths in World Wars I and II and the Boer War; Ionic Islands and Indian State deaths. A CD-ROM index of births which have taken place in Northern Ireland from 1922-1993.

How to go about finding a register entry
It is not possible for applicants to search through copies of the actual register entries themselves. However the indexes may be searched to identify the entry you seek. The indexes are arranged by year and then alphabetically by surname. Before 1983 the indexes are also split into the quarter of the year in which the event was registered e.g. events registered in January, February or March are indexed in the March quarter for the relevant year.

To apply for a certificate of the entry you can choose which method best suits you:
Application in person via the FRC
The Family Records Centre is open to the public at the following times: Monday, Wednesday, Thursday, Friday:9am-5pm Tuesday: 10am-7pm Saturday: 9.30am-5pm

Once you have searched the indexes and identified an entry you simply complete an application form, including the GRO Reference Number listed in the index and take it to the cashiers for payment. The fee for each certificate is £7.00.

Smedley Hydro
All applications made at the FRC are transported overnight to Certificate Services at Smedley Hydro, Southport, Merseyside. Many people have asked about the unusual name of

the office where their certificates are produced. Smedley Hydro was built in early Victorian times and known as the Birkdale College for the education of young gentlemen. It then became a Hydropathic Hotel whose electro-chemical baths were extremely popular "in restoring the work-weary, the enfeebled and those of a naturally delicate organisation". With the outbreak of the Second World War the building was requisitioned by His Majesty's government for the purpose of National Registration and there are now 1000 people working at the Southport Office with over 500 of them employed within Certificate Services.

Production Process
Once your application is received at Smedley Hydro the race then begins to have the applications sorted ready for the staff to retrieve the relevant microfilm, load the film onto a reader, find the entry, scan the image and produce the certificate ready for either posting out on the fourth working day or returning to the FRC for collection on the fourth working day. This is no mean feat when you consider that around ten thousand applications are received via the FRC every week.

Application direct to GRO Southport
If it is not convenient for you to go to central London and visit the FRC, you can apply directly to GRO Southport for your certificates. It would, of course, help us to have the index reference for the entry you want, so you may wish to look this up at one of the many centres around the country which hold copies of the national GRO index on microfiche. There are over 100 such locations including libraries, County Records Offices and Family History Centres within the UK and overseas. To find out the nearest one to you telephone Certificate Services on 0845603 7788.

Alternatively you may wish to view the indexes on line. Recent changes to the conditions of sale of the GRO Indexes now mean that some organisations have made Index information available on the Internet.

Please note that it is not possible for members of the public to search the indexes at our Southport office itself. Personal callers are welcome to leave certificate applications between the hours of 9am – 5pm, Monday – Friday at GRO, Smedley Hydro, Trafalgar Rd, Birkdale, Southport.

Most applicants to GRO Southport prefer to apply by one of the following methods:

By telephone:
Our call centre may be reached by dialling 0845 603 7788. You will hear a menu selection before being transferred to an operator who can take the details of the GRO reference number(s) you want and then arrange for your certificate(s) to be posted out to you within 5 working days. The fee for this service is £8.50, and payment can be made by Visa, Master or Switch. Please note we do not accept Electron or American Express Cards. The Call Centre is available 6 days a week (Monday – Friday 8am-8pm and Saturday 9am – 4pm) .

Our Call Centre has a variety of enquires relating to certificate services and each week deals with over four and a half thousand telephone calls.

By fax or post:
You may wish to fax your certificate application to 01704 550013. Alternatively you can post in your application enclosing a cheque or postal order payable to **ONS** to :
The General Register Office
PO Box 2, Southport, Merseyside PR8 2JD

On Line:
This is a secure website that can be used to place orders using the GRO Index reference number and for certificates in the twentieth century where the exact details are known. For further information visit our website at: www.gro.gov.uk

How to contact our office by email
As the e-revolution continues, certificate services increasingly deals with a large number of enquiries from people who have visited our website. If you wish to contact us by email, our address is certificate.services@ons.gsi.gov.uk

What if you do not know the GRO reference number of the entry you want?
If you do not wish to conduct you own search of the indexes we are happy to do this for you. For a fee of £11.50 we will undertake a search of the indexes for the year in which you tell us the event concerned occurred, and if necessary a year either side as well if it cannot be found in that year. Due to the additional searches involved this service takes a little longer. Once the application is received the certificate is posted out within 15 working days. Should we be unable to find the entry, we will refund your fee minus a search fee of £4.50

To assist us in the search you will need to provide as much information as possible about the person on the certificate you are trying to obtain. For a birth – full name, date of birth, place of birth and if known the parents names including the mothers maiden name. For a marriage, you will need to supply the names of both the bride and groom, date of marriage, place of marriage and if known, the fathers name for both bride and groom. For a death you will need to supply a full name, date of death, place of death and if a female their marital status. The occupation of the deceased is also helpful.

Application to a local Register Office

If you know exactly where the birth, marriage or death that you are looking for took place you may also apply to the local Register Office covering that area. The Superintendent Registrar will be able to provide you with a certificate from his or her records. Please note that the GRO reference number does not refer to these local records, and will unfortunately be of no use to them in finding the entry for you. You will be asked to provide details similar to those listed in the paragraphs above so that they can locate the entry for you.

Other services provided by GRO:
Commemorative Certificates. Something that people may be unaware of is our Commemorative Certificate Section. For a cost of £30 they can provide a commemorative marriage certificate to mark silver, ruby, gold or diamond anniversaries. These certificates are colour printed on high quality paper and come mounted in frame within a presentation box, they do make an unusual and attractive gift. For further information call 0151 471 4256.

Certificate Services welcomes Feedback: We welcome feedback and customer input on the level and quality of service currently being provided. If you have any comments about our services please write to - Public Relations Unit Manager, PO Box 2, Southport, Merseyside, PR8 2JD or email certificate.services@ons.gsi.gov.uk

Overseas Records

The Overseas Section of the General Register Office holds records of births, marriages and deaths of British nationals and members of the British Armed Forces, where the event has taken place abroad and is registered with the British authorities concerned e.g. British Consuls, High Commissions, HM Forces, the Civil Aviation Authority and the Register of Shipping and Seamen. However, it should be noted that the majority of the registrations held are non-compulsory therefore it is possible that the record you are looking for may not be held at the General Register Office.

Furthermore you should be aware that there are certain countries where there is no provision for any form of British Consul or High Commission registration to be made, for example

Australia	Falkland Islands
Zimbabwe	New Zealand
Canada	South Africa

In which case you may have to apply to the relevant authority in the country concerned to try to obtain a locally issued certificate.

Although the records held at the General Register Office (GRO) do not cover every event which takes place involving a British national, we do hold the oldest records held by the GRO as we have the British Army 'Regimental Records' which date back to 1761. We also hold the death records of the men who fell during both World Wars as well as the Boer War.

The types of registrations held and relevant dates are as follows:
Regimental births/baptisms 1761-1924
Regimental marriages 1786-1924 (the regiment is needed for any search to be undertaken).
Ionian Islands births/baptisms, marriages and some burial records relating to the British civil and military population on the Islands of Corfu 1818-1864.
Marine births and deaths since 1837.
Consul births, marriages and deaths since 1849.
War Deaths:
• Boer War 1899-1902
• First World War 1914-1921
• Second World War 1939-1948
Entries held at GRO do not show place of burial or next of kin. Certificates only record Unit/Regiment, service number, name, age at death, country of birth, place (normally theatre of war) and cause of death (normally 'killed in action' or 'died of wounds'.
Army births, marriages and deaths from 1880-1956.
High Commission births, marriages and deaths from date of Independence (e.g. India 1949).
Air births and deaths (events on British aircraft) since 1947.
Deposited Foreign marriage certificates since 1947.
Armed Forces births, marriages and deaths since 1957.
Hovercraft births and deaths (on British hovercraft) since 1972.
Offshore Installation deaths (on British gas and oilrigs) since 1972.

Although the indexes to overseas events are on view to the public at the Family Records Centre and are also available on microfiche the actual volumes holding the entries are housed at the General Register Office in Southport and any search made at the GRO carries a fee.

Certificates of Overseas events can be applied for in person at the Family Records Centre, or by post, fax or telephone to the General Register Office. Certificates can also be applied for online at www.gro.gov.uk Certificates are usually produced within 5 working days. For further information visit us at www.gro.gov.uk .

Adoptions

Adoptions policy in England and Wales is governed by the Looked After Children's Branch of the Department for Education and Skills. The General Register Office administers four statutory functions which have come into being since 1926 and are governed by the Adoption and Children Act 2002.

The Adopted Children Register is a record of all adoptions granted by courts in England and Wales since 1927. When an adoption has been granted, the court issues an order, which is the authority for an entry to be made in the Adopted Children Register. The entire process, which includes instructing the registrar who holds the original birth entry, may take up to six weeks. Once this process is complete adoptive parent(s) will receive a free short adoption certificate.

An adoption certificate is a replacement birth certificate but in an adopted person's new name. It is expected to be used by an adopted person for all legal and administrative purposes in place of the original birth certificate. Replacement certificates can be purchased on-line at www.gro.gov.uk or by telephone on +44(0) 0845 603 7788. Lines are open (excluding bank holidays) Monday - Friday 8am - 8pm and Saturday 9am - 4pm.

The Adopted Children Register also contains some registrations of overseas adoptions.

Adoptions which have taken place overseas may be registered at the General Register Office when the adoptive parents were habitually resident in England or Wales at the time of the adoption; or the child was born in England or Wales. The country in which the adoption occurred is recognised from list of designated and convention countries approved by the Department of Education and Skills. A Registrable Foreign Adoption application may be made by, the adoptive parents(s), any other person who has appropriate parental responsibility for the adopted child or the adopted person when aged 18 or over.

Information on access to birth details for an adopted person.

If you were adopted through a court in England or Wales and are aged 18 years or over the law allows you to gain access to your birth details. These details will enable you to purchase a certified copy of your original birth entry:

If you were adopted before 12 November 1975 you are required to attend an informal meeting to receive information from an approved adoption advisor. This can be an advisor at either your local Social Services, at the General Register Office in Southport, a registered Intermediary Agency or, under certain circumstances, at the agency that handled your adoption. The adoption advisor will be able to able to offer practical advice and guidance as well as discussing any concerns or issues important to you.

If you were adopted on or after 12 November 1975 you have the choice whether you would like to see an approved adoption advisor or have the information sent to you direct. You may find it helpful to see an adoption advisor as they will be able to offer practical advice and guidance as well as discussing any concerns or issues important to you.

If you were adopted in England or Wales and now live outside the UK you can also apply to access your birth records. If you are required to attend an informal meeting to receive your information from an adoption advisor. It is possible for this to take place in the country where you are currently residing, as long as a suitable body or organisation is available. The General Register office maintains a list of approved overseas Adoption organisations that may be able to provide this service.

If you were adopted after 30th December 2005, once you have reached aged 18 years or over you can gain access to your birth details through the agency or social services that dealt with your adoption. If the name of the agency or social services is not known, the adopted person may contact the General Register Office for this information.

Information on access to adoption records for birth relatives

From 30th December 2005, a birth relative wishing to make contact with an adopted person can apply to a registered Intermediary Agency, whose role is to help facilitate contact between birth relatives and adopted people. The Intermediary Agency can apply to the General Register Office for the name of the organisation involved in the adoption or if that is not available the name of the court granting the adoption. They can also apply post-adoptive information which will enable an application to be made for an adoption certificate and information from the Adoption Contact Register.

Intermediary Agencies

Registered Intermediary Agencies may accept approaches from adopted people and birth relatives, aged 18 years or over, to help convey their wishes for communication and contact. A list of registered intermediary agencies can be found at *Commission for Social Care Inspection* (CSCI) which covers England and *Care Standard Inspectorate for Wales* (CSIW). When visiting the CSIW website please note that your search results will appear at the bottom of the Services and Inspection reports page. Alternatively you can contact the General Register Office, please telephone 0151 471 4830.

Adoption Contact Register

The Adoption Contact Register was created in 1991 to put adopted people and their birth relatives in touch with each other if that is what they both wish. The Contact Register cannot help an adopted person to learn of the whereabouts of a birth relative or to know their birth relatives wishes unless the relative has also entered their details on the Contact Register.

The Contact Register is in two parts and to be eligible for registration applicants need to be 18 years or over. Part 1allows for an adopted person to register their details for a fee of £15 and record their wishes for contact, non contact or specific contact with any birth relative(s). Part 2 allows for a birth relative to register their details for a fee of £30 and record their wishes for contact or non contact only.

If a wish for contact is registered and a link is made both parties will be notified, but only the adopted person will be provided with the current name and address.

Adoption services

For further information about adoption services and to obtain application forms please visit the General Register Office website www.gro.gov.uk or telephone 0151 471 4830.

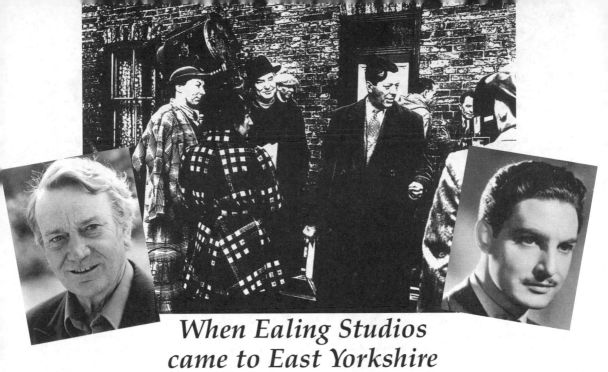

When Ealing Studios came to East Yorkshire
Martin Limon

The varied and often spectacular landscapes of Yorkshire have long been a favourite of film and television producers seeking to find realistic locations for their work. The BBC drama series 'All Creatures Great and Small', the Ken Loach movie 'Kes' and the Yorkshire Television series 'Heartbeat' are just some of the productions where the scenic beauty of the county has added its own particular magic to the story-line. An earlier pioneer of the Yorkshire location was London-based Ealing Studios. In the late 1940s and early 1950s Ealing were in the forefront of Britain's film industry with classic comedies such as Kind Hearts and Coronets, Passport to Pimlico and the Lavender Hill Mob. In early 1954 the Ealing production team, led by Sir Michael Balcon, had a new project in hand called Lease of Life. The story concerned a Yorkshire vicar given twelve months to live and the effect this had on his faith and his family. During March and April 1954 the making of the film was to bring the famous actor Robert Donat and an Ealing production team to the beautiful East Yorkshire village of Lund and the Gothic splendours of Beverley Minster……

Although Ealing Studios were best known for their comedy output they also had a flair for serious drama that reflected the British way of life. The film *Lease of Life*, based on a story by Frank Baker, concerned an impoverished, middle-aged country clergyman called William Thorne, the vicar of the village of *Hinton St John*, who discovered that he only had a year to live. In the story Thorne was invited to give a sermon on School Founders Day at the local cathedral of *Gilchester* and, inspired by thoughts of his imminent demise, he decided to throw caution to the wind and to deliver a highly controversial sermon to the congregation.

In late 1953 and early 1954 the production team of the new film (provisionally called *The West Window*) were searching for locations for the fictional town of Gilchester and the village of Hinton St John. They were looking for a cathedral-type church which would not be confused with Canterbury or York. One of the Ealing staff was the son of the then Archbishop of Canterbury, Geoffrey Fisher. Taking a keen interest in the project, the Archbishop suggested that Beverley Minster would be a suitable location for *Gilchester Cathedral*. Meanwhile the nearby Wolds village of Lund became the setting for Thorne's own parish of Hinton St John. The real vicar of Lund, the Reverend Lancelot Foster, recorded how, on the 21st January 1954, men from Ealing Studios arrived to take photographs of the church and the vicarage. When Foster asked if they had permission to take photographs he was told that approval had been given by *higher authorities!* Ever mindful of good public relations the producers invited the vicar's wife to Ealing in March 1954 to see the replicas of her kitchen, hall and lounge that they had built in the studio.

A significant number of the best names in Britain's film industry at that time were involved in the making of *Lease of Life*. The director, Charles Frend, had worked with Alfred Hitchcock and his previous films included *Scott of the Antarctic* (1948) and *The*

Lund

Cruel Sea (1953). Frend's love of the English countryside was reflected in the masterly skills of the film's cinematographer, Douglas Slocombe, who made excellent use of Eastmancolour photography to capture the scenic beauty of the East Yorkshire Wolds. Slocombe's career spanned over forty years and his cinematography was later rewarded with Oscar-nominations, BAFTA's and a Lifetime Achievement Award in 1995.

The story and the setting for *Lease of Life* called for a bleak wintry outlook and so the location shooting at Lund began on the 21st March 1954. Film stars, production staff and technicians with cameras, arc lights and miles of electric cable descended on the sleepy community and the village hall became their canteen. The producers had already been recruiting local talent in Beverley and surrounding villages for smaller parts and to be 'extras'. On March 20th Robert Newton, an assistant producer at Ealing, had been in Beverley to watch the St Nicholas Players in a J.M. Barrie play called *Half an Hour*. Although it is not recorded if any of the amateurs were given roles in the forthcoming film, we do know that ladies from Lockington, Lund, Walkington and Dalton Holme did play parts.

The filming provided both momentary fame and paid employment to Lund residents who became *'extras'*. We are told that Farmer Walker received thirty shillings (£1.50) for going to church and that his son got two guineas (£2.20) for riding a bike down the main street. David Freear, Lund resident and retired postman, was required by the director to sit reading a newspaper but to look astonished as well!

Newspaper accounts from the time also give us a fascinating insight into how village life has changed in the intervening fifty years. Some of the filming took place at the village green where blacksmith Alfred Teal "continued

working at his forge despite the fact that spotlights were focused just outside." Mr Teal told a reporter that he had never seen a film in his life and was unsure whether he would make the trip into Beverley to see this one when it was released! The director also made use of Mr Wharram's tailor's shop, which became a tobacconists for the purpose of the film. Today, the village of Lund has neither blacksmith nor shop.

The location shooting brought a host of actors and actresses to Lund and Beverley, many of them household names. In the lead role of the Reverend William Thorne was the outstanding theatre and film actor Robert Donat, star of Alfred Hitchcock's *The 39 Steps* (1935) and *Goodbye Mr Chips* (1939). *Lease of Life* was Donat's penultimate film appearance and the sad irony of his performance was that he was a dying man playing a dying man. Donat suffered from asthma and such was the fragile nature of his health that oxygen cylinders were kept close by when he was acting. In some scenes from *Lease of Life* Donat's breathless delivery of his lines is a clear indication of the health problems that were to end his life, prematurely, four years later. Despite these difficulties Donat gave one of his greatest performances as the dying vicar and was nominated *best actor* for this role at the 8th British Film Academy Awards.

Playing the part of Thorne's wife Vera was Kay Walsh who starred in over 60 films between 1934 and 1981. This accomplished actress gave audiences a fine performance as a poverty-stricken spouse trapped in a remote country parish and obsessed by the need to get her musically-gifted daughter through music college. This latter role (that of Susan Thorne) went to the young Scottish actress Adrienne Corri who was later to feature in Stanley Kubrick's controversial film *Clockwork Orange*. Acting the part of Susan's piano teacher, Martin

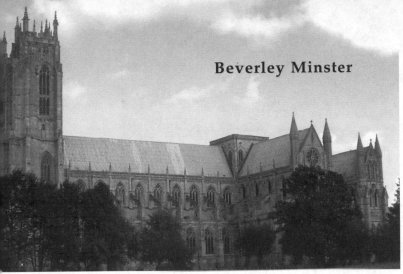

Beverley Minster

Blake, was a gifted young British actor called Denholm Elliott. His film career had begun in 1949 and in the 1950s he tended to play pleasant but ineffectual characters. Denholm Elliott went on to act in over 100 films and his later career included the part of Marcus Brody in *Raiders of the Lost Ark* (1981) and *Indiana Jones and the Last Crusade* (1989). Sadly, Elliott's still

thriving career was cut short in 1992 when he died of complications brought on by AIDS.

Apart from the usual difficulties of location filming far from the studio the work at Lund was also put at risk by an industrial dispute in London. Film-laboratory technicians there went on strike with the result that the Lund cameramen could not see *rushes* of their work and check whether they needed to be re-shot. To make sure, some scenes were filmed six times because as the director, Charles Freer, told local reporters it would be impossible to return to Lund to do them again.

At the beginning of April the Ealing unit moved to Beverley for scenes in the market place and at '*Gilchester Cathedral*'. The Minster became an outsize studio with craftsmen installing an altar and a bigger pulpit for the filming of Thorne's sermon. Since these scenes represented a School Founder's Day service, pupils were drafted in from Beverley Grammar School to provide the schoolboy congregation. The arrival of such a celebrated group of people was, of course, a major social event in 1950s Beverley and the stars and the production team were invited to a civic reception at the Hall in Lairgate (3rd April 1954).

The film Lease of Life received its London premiere in October 1954 but local people had to wait January 1955 before it received its first screening in Beverley (at the Playhouse). Opinions about the film itself remain mixed. It is perhaps an indication of the film's minority appeal, or perhaps its somber story-line, that it is seen so rarely today. Compared to Ealing's more lighter film offerings *Lease of Life* has failed to stand the test of time, even though some of its themes are as relevent today as they were in the 1950s (eg. the decline in church attendance and tabloid journalism). Furthermore, as well as giving us a commanding performance by the actor Robert Donat in one of his last films, the colour cinematography of Douglas Slocombe perfectly captures the atmospheric charm of the Yorkshire Wolds some fifty years ago.

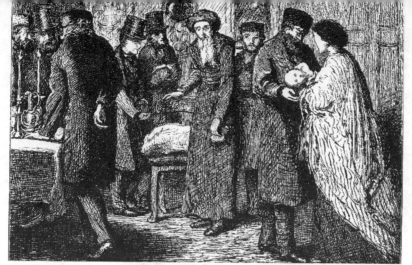

Anglo-Jewry-
its Origins & Its Place in British Society
Judith Joseph

All written material speaks at a variety of levels. Initially, the subject matter may appear obvious. Then come the questions: why was the material produced in a particular manner? Why were names spelled in one of a variety of ways? Why was the material produced at all? When searching for family members there comes an additional question as to why are some people more likely to appear in documents of local interest, ledgers relating to land, rents and rates, or even penalties? Why do some people not appear at all, even when we know they must have lived in that place at that time? For most people born in England, where there are extant records, a person should be found at least once, if only in the parish register as having died, let alone when baptised or married. It is possible that those living under the patronage of the local landowner may appear in the inventory of an estate. There may have been a religious restriction on a person being noted in the Parish registers, particularly where a person belonged to a non-conformist religious group, eg The Society of Friends, Quakers; or possibly where,

from 1656, the person may have been Jewish.

There is also an aspect of political and social manipulation of fact which plays a part in who is recorded and who is denied record, ignored, written out of the script. While it is well-known that there were residents in Britain from Africa and Asia via various slave routes during the 16th - 19th centuries, little is heard of this group as being numbered among the general population of even the larger seaports of the British Isles. With Parish records and literature denying the existence of those who were not of the Establishment which, after the Reformation meant the Church of England, even Catholics were frequently not mentioned or given only passing notice. In literature, 'John Halifax - Gentleman' by Mrs Craik, reflects the life of a Quaker in late 18th and early 19th centuries England - people who were not readily accorded the certainty of safety within the Law when attacked. In the case of Mr Halifax, his home was set ablaze and the peacekeepers turned their faces away. Such was the contemporary condition for non-conformists. For Jews, while they gained some status, literature was divided: Shakespeare wrote in an age where patronage or the State itself dictated the political content of a text - thus distorting not only contemporary history but the nature of the existence of different

---

CERTIFICATE TO BE DELIVERED UP AT THE FUNERAL.

Pursuant to the Registration Act 6 & 7 Will. IV., c. 86.

I *Luther Perkins* Registrar of Births and Deaths in the Sub-District of *W. Bromwich N.E.* in the County of *Stafford*. do hereby Certify, that the death of *John Nathan* [aged *3 days*] was duly Registered by me, on the *30th* day of *Nov*. 187*4*.

Witness my hand, this *30th* day of *November* 187*4*.

Luther Perkins. Registrar.

London : Printed for H.M. Stationery Office by Ford and Tilt.

[See back.

N.B.—The Undertaker, or person in charge of the Funeral, must deliver this Certificate to the MINISTER or officiating ... at the burial of the dead body—AND TO NO OTHER PERSON.—(See Reg. Act, Sec. 27.)

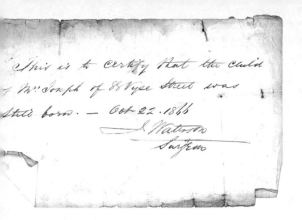

"This is to certify that the child of Mr Joseph of 88 Vyse Street was still born. — Oct 22.1866 J. Watson Surgeon"

groups as seen from the perspective of the Establishment. George Eliot in her 'Daniel Deronda' throws an earnestly friendly light upon Jews, while William Thackeray shows hostility in his portrayal of Becky Sharp in his book of the same name. These are not saints or sinners, merely people who lived under a covert system of restriction.

As Commercial directories became more comprehensive in the 19th century, names of Jewish people were recorded, as members of the general population of a particular locale, rather than as Jews. Synagogues became numbered among places of worship, but such references are easily overlooked. Cartoons most frequently ridiculed or lampooned Jews, distancing the host population from these alien incomers. Jews were not seen as other than different, usually gross or ill-favoured. There is a serious political function in this portrayal, that of denying the stranger a place at the fireside, highlighting differences rather than finding commonalities of purpose. The black and asian immigrant or freed man or woman, was not only exotic but had, generally, come from a position of subjugation. They were not only of a different colour, but were part of a shameful time. They were ignored completely. Contrary to the black and asian experience, the Jews who came to England had no recent history on the island, had not been colonised or enslaved. However, from 1066-1290, the Jews living in England had suffered privation and denigration without remission by the time they were ignobly thrust out of England in 1290. Those Jews who were merchants in the Caribbean were, in the 17th and 18th Centuries, from Holland and Portugal, earlier refugees from the Inquisition in Spain of 1492. Many of that group who came to England in 1656, were therefore from the merchant class who would have been involved in the slave trade at some point. In the late 17th Century, most of the Jews newly arrived from Holland or Portugal were from Europe, from Germany, Poland or Russia. They were frequently impoverished, being refugees from oppression as much as economic migrants. The admixture of the impoverished Jew from Europe, those who were among the influential

merchant class and the Jews of Holland Portugal with their Caribbean and trading background, presented a dichotomy among the administrators and rulers of England.

From the above it may be seen that research requires a knowledge of not only whether an ancestor may be found in the records, as much as why they may not be readily visible. An understanding of society with its changing face is fundamental to any research. A further understanding is required as why a family may move several times a year, even within the same small area , reflecting whether they were upwardly or downwardly economically mobile.

Having briefly glanced at how and why groups tend to be included or excluded in public and literary record, it will become easier to appreciate the following equally brief history of the Jews in England since 1656 and the nature of their being recorded.

When looking at European Jewish genealogy the researcher has to think in historical terms as to where in Europe Jewish people lived, let alone how their surnames came about. In many countries everybody had to have a pass to move from one village to another, or from a village to a town, for any purpose at all. All movement was regulated. In England there was relative ease of movement, though not totally so, especially for those who lacked the means to support themselves without becoming a burden on the local authority of whichever place they were visiting. Freedom of movement was for the wealthy or those with family or friends in other places. In Europe even the wealthy required a travel pass, though for the most part this appears to have been less rigorously applied.

For the Jew in Europe, not only were his movements heavily monitored, but where he could live was dictated by Central Government as much as by local government. There were whole regions where no Jew was permitted to live, and only rarely to visit. Where a closed society exists, there may be little need for specific surnames, everyone being known to everyone else, or even connected by marriage. As surnames became mandatory throughout Continental and Eastern Europe, by the early 1800s, Jews were also to have surnames, if they did not already have one. However, where a member of the Christian host population might choose a name for himself, the Jew was given a surname, usually one which was derisory or unpleasant. '*Katzenellenbogen*' was one such meaning 'Cat's Elbow'. '*Wasserzug*', '*Brenhotz*', '*Zuckerladen*', '*Apfelflaum*', 'Black', 'White, 'Pink', 'Green', 'Blue, 'Brown'; Water-train, To burn, Sugar-load, Appledown; These were nonsense names. As to the names of colours, these were derisory, indicating the people weren't worth

Therefore, when searching for any Jewish ancestry, it is as well to seek advice on how the name may have altered, whether it may have altered, when it may have altered, from where the family may have originated,

more individuality than to be given a token identity. When Jewish people could change their names, the names chosen sometimes related to those of a patriach either in the family or of the Jewish people, eg *Abrahams, Isaacs; Jacobs*. Where it was permitted, names of the trade with which the family were associated might be chosen, eg *Schumacher* (shoemaker), or the sign outside the house by which the family were known, eg *Rothschild*, red shield. Also, the places from which people came were used, eg Hollander, for someone coming from Holland; Berliner, Orel, Moscow, Deutsche, (Berlin, Germany; Orel in northern Russia; Deutsche as from Germany). Down the years as the Jews in England became more aculturated and settled, their names became anglicised. At the beginning of the Great War (1914 - 1919 in Western Europe, 1914 - 1921 in Eastern Europe), many people with German or foreign-sounding names assumed more English sounding names.

and so on. There is no one answer; there are as many answers as there are people being researched. While European Governments decreed unpleasant names by which Jewish people should be known, the bearers of the names were not perturbed. In time, descendants of the original bearers became, in many instances, successful in their chosen fields. Many from the original *Katzenellenbogen* families taking parts of the name as their chosen surname down the generations, eg Katz or Nelson, or Ellenbogen, went into the fields of Medicine and Law, becoming highly respected for their knowledge and expertise. It is not the name which decides how a person fares, but how that person lives his life.

There has been a recorded presence of Jewish people in the British Isles since 1066 including, to a very minor extent, during the years between Expulsion (1290) and Re-Settlement (1656). The earlier records are among the Rolls of Medieval England, showing how Jewry of the day was almost solely concerned with filling the King's coffers. Christian ruling had it that ursury was not to be charged, therefore no good Christian could become a moneylender. A Jew, however, was under no such proscription and the King thereby ensured his chests were full by directing the Jews in England to raise taxes on his behalf. This was not only to be through ursury on loans which were mainly to the wealthy and privileged, but also through directing each Jewish community to pay an additional tax on their own community. When funds were not forthcoming, hostages might be taken, leading members of a community would be taken into custody redeemable through the payment of a levy or fine. Richard Lionhart brought 'his' Jews to England. They were under his care and protection, known as Court Jews, were specifically to raise funds for his use. His knights and nobles were unsympathetic to this method of the king's raising monies and, at the coronation of the King in 1190, those Jews who had gone to London to pay homage to the king on his coronation were treated as insurgents and

184.

archives containing births, marriages and deaths, which are readily accessible, from the Spanish and Portugese Jews' Community's Archivist, the Jewish Genealogical Society of Great Britain and various other libraries and resources. When considering Jewish archives it must be understood that nearly all those born into a Jewish family will have two sets of forenames, those used for synagogual and religious purposes and those for daily use. Hebrew names will give the name of the person as being the son/daughter of a particular father. The name of the mother is not used for this purpose.

Sephardic naming customs are different to those of Ashkenazim. In Sephardic families boys may be named for living grandfathers, in Ashkenazic families the new child might be named for a deceased relative. Therefore it is important to understand which custom is being followed. In this way it may well be possible to trace a family down the generations getting a time-line on when each generation lived and died.

Obviously there are always exceptions. Equally, where the original European surname has been anglicised, knowing the Hebrew names will become even more important when searching for forebears with similar surnames. Today the continuation of sequential use of names is out of fashion, which makes it all the more important that records are kept by families for the ease of future generations of researchers.

With the Sephardim arriving earlier and in generally better economic condition than the Ashkenazim, their communities became established in different cities more swiftly and at a more affluent level. That is not to say that all were wealthy. As with any migrant group, there is a small top-layer of wealth with a greater subsidary layer of not only lesser wealth but of poverty. By the time the Ashkenazim were established, Guardians of the Poor with responsibility to ensure that no Jewish person became a burden on the State, had been active for a good hundred years or more. As the centuries progressed, the Ashkenazim promoted the well-being of the young, in their orphanages, as early as 1796, with a more formal constitution in 1823. As each wave of immigrants arrived into England care was taken to see that they were provided with at least one meal and a lodging prior to travelling from the port of entry to, possibly, Liverpool, their port of emigration to the United States of America, the main goal of many. By 1880, with Europe on the move, great numbers of citizens from all countries wished to flee poverty and repression, seeing the new country of America

many were killed. This history is well-recorded, school children are told of it. Shortly after that time, there is a great gap, which scholars are only now unravelling. Where most modern Anglo-Jewish History starts and, with it, the genealogies of those who came to England and either aculturated or assimilated, is from 1656, known as 'the Re-Settlement'. Oliver Cromwell was convinced that having Jewry in England would not only benefit England's economy, but would bring about the coming of the Second Messiah. Again, his thinking was not popular, but while the relevant page in the Statute book is missing, having been removed at some time, there has been no repeal of the 1290 Act of Expulsion.

Many of those Jews who came to England in the first decade or two following Re-Settlement were of Sephardi origin. European Jewry at the time comprised two groups, Sephardim and Ashkenazim. Sephardim were those who came from Holland having fled Spain and Portugal in 1492 at the time of the Spanish Inquisitions. This group were merchants, traders, and much concerned with the new lands of the spice islands and the Caribbean, and the Americas. The second group, the Ashkenazim, were mainly from Russia, Poland, Germany, some were merchants, others more impoverished, all fleeing persecution and economic deprivation. The leading Jewish figures of the late 17C in England, mainly in London, were Sephardim. There had been commercial transactions between businesses in England and those in Holland, with a mutual interest in the West Indies. From this grouping came the first Jews wishing to re-establish themselves in England. They came to the City of London, with its Port from which international trade, the lifeblood of England, was ever expanding England's interests around the world.

The group built a synagogue known as Bevis Marks, which stands as it did then, lit by candles in its main parts. The customs and rites of Sephardic Jewry remain as they have been for 350 years. The names of the era ring down the ages, their descendants having become fully integrated with England and her ways. Many have assimilated or aculturated, the links are forged close. This particular grouping has

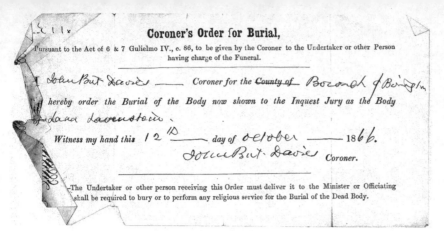

for many. Admittedly, a good percentage of those arriving in London did wish to continue their journey to South Africa, rather than America. Being without funds or friends, this new Shelter would be able to house arrivals for a night or more, even up to three weeks, until a relevant passage could be arranged. In other cities the local communities, themselves fairly impoverished, saw that boats were met, people taken care of, if only on a very modest scale, put on to trains or carts, to go to larger cities where the Jewish Communities were better able financially to fund the arrival and needs of the impoverished co-religionist. There was also the worry of White Slavers. It is nothing new that women are trafficked. But in the 1880s the Jewish community were aware they needed to ensure that not only were people not trafficked, but they were not a burden on the State.

With that sorry history, comes the benefit for later generations. While English records show who lived in which Parish, there is frequently no link between one generation and the next. Being on a Parish register meant even to the non-Christian, that in times of hardship, their children would receive money each week, sufficient to buy some bread or, with several children, to pay the rent of their home, often one room. However, where communities are close-knit, families living side by side and coming from the same foreign places, let alone with a second set of names, research may be assisted. The family would be known by an English name, and in the Jewish community that English name would be connected to a Hebrew name. The earlier larger synagogues in London, having the right to register civil marriages, kept not only records of the religious marriage, but also of the civil marriage. From 1858 these religious marriages were regularised by an authorisation of the Chief Rabbi of England. Authorisation Certificates show the groom's name in English and Hebrew, and where he was from; sometimes only the country is shown, other times a city or region may be written. The certificate will also show the bride's name, her Hebrew name, whether she has brothers and if they will be at the wedding, sometimes their Hebrew names are given, if only the first part, their own Hebrew forename.

By 1861 the Census was well-established which would give an additional item of information and where applicable, whether a foreign-born

as the redeemer of all fortunes. Unfortunately, many who travelled arrived ill, undernourished and, being without funds, family or friends, were turned back to Europe. America did not want to take in the tubercular, or the ineffectual of any kind. These would be a drain upon the economy. For the Jewish people who travelled across Europe, sometimes walking a thousand miles in short stages, or taking illegal passage, their plight was worst of all. If the average peasant was feeling oppressed, the average Jew was without hope. They were beyond oppression. To ameliorate this shortcoming, between those who wished to emigrate and their diminished condition of health, let alone of wealth, there were transit camps set up in Hamburg, en route to the main Port of Embarkation, where poor Jews could come, be registered, be fed and cared for until healthy and well, able to travel and to work once through Immigration in New York. There were other ports of entry, but New York was the biggest and best known, with the advent of Ellis Island becoming the definitive port of entry for many immigrants. Significant numbers disembarked elsewhere, eg Boston. While many did emigrate in this way, others preferred to take an alternative route of arriving at Hull, crossing England to Liverpool taking a ship from there to USA. Other emigrants arrived from the Baltic port of Riga, Latvia, for instance, to Grimsby or other ports on the North East Coast of Britain. In some cases their arrival was by default. They'd thought their money had bought a passage to the USA, but not knowing English or being able to read the English alphabet, found they were stranded in England. Most of this group were from Hamburg arriving at Tilbury, rather than Hull or Grimsby. Nothing changes, much is the same today for more recently-arrived immigrants wishing for a better life.

England didn't have to contend with the massive bulk of immigrants as the USA, pleading to be allowed to stay. However, there was a sufficient flow to cause a Poor Jews Temporary Shelter to be organised in 1889, in London whose Port was also a point of arrival

person had naturalised. Once that was known, then a naturalisation certificate may be applied for. Variant spellings must always be looked at, to ensure that all avenues to searches are covered.

Primarily, today, working backwards as with any other search, it is still helpful to look at both civil and religious marriages. The religious marriage certificate may yield yet more concrete evidence ratifying previously known or conjectured information. Surnames are only as good as the day they were used. It is possible to have several names by which a person is known. Then it becomes an art form to pull all the pieces of information together to ensure that the differently-named people are, indeed, one and the same.

Having looked at how Anglo-Jewry came into being, it is important to know how and why certain trades were carried on while others were not. Bearing in mind that ursury was officially prohibited to the Christian host community, when Jewry re-settled in England from 1656, Jews did indeed become pawnbrokers and moneylenders. It should be understood that the Guilds did not permit those outside the Christian faith to number among their members. Not only were Jews discriminated against, but those who were of the Independent or Dissenting Churches, including the Catholics and Quakers. Until the middle of the 19th century life was made difficult for Catholics in various ways, including that of obtaining a University Degree. Quakers and Jews had only one advantage over any other grouping which was the Hardwicke Marriage Act of 1753 enabling them to marry outside a Church, which was only permitted to the general population within the last ten years.

Jews were permitted to be pedlars, ragmen, glaziers, tailors - all the more menial and labour-intensive jobs. While there were Jewish merchants, it wasn't until the mid-19th century that Jews could enter into the professions, but not everywhere and not to full qualification, especially where a university degree was required. Even to become a skilled craftsman with rights to applying for membership of a Guild, a Jew would have to had leave London and go to centres where the Establishment ruling of being a member of the Church of England was not enforced. Birmingham was one such centre of excellence for the gold and silver trade in its Jewellery Quarter. In the mid-19th century entrepreneurial businesses were frequently started by Jews eg in Birmingham, steel nibs were brought into being superceding the use and manufacture of quill pens. In the 20th Century Birmingham Jewry played a leading part in the birth of the cinema industry, with Oscar Deutsch bringing into being a chain of Cinemas, taking as an acronym their name

ODEON: Oscar Deutch Entertains Our Nation. In every which way the Jews who came to England have given to England of their enterprise, energy and stamina. In times of War Jews were among the first to go to the Colours, often under age, making little of their flat feet or poor eyesight. The Masthead of the London Jewish Chronicle during The Great War was: 'England has been everything to the Jews, the Jews will now be everything to England.' When looking for forebears who might have been Jewish, look to the War records of the First and Second World Wars; look to military citations and medals. In WW1 eight VC's were awarded and as was many a mention in despatches; In WW2 there were few who didn't volunteer for service, many of whom were under age, among them one of my own uncles, while another uncle became a Chaplain with the Air Force. Look to the Medical Schools' record books, and the Universities books of Alumni. Law, Accountancy, Pharmacy, Dentistry, were but some of the professions where the children of Jewish immigrants gained qualification and worked towards bettering the quality of life within the British Isles. For more than a century, Jews have played an important role in the governance of the British Isles, from within the Houses of Parliament. It may fairly be stated that where there is no proscription on any person entering into a field of endeavour,

should a Jewish person wish so to do, he or she now may. As with all people, there are those who do a disservice to their people and their country, but for the most part, we can be found in the annals of trades, professions, music halls, theatre, hospitals, even occasionally among the aristocracy. Our record of philanthropy is second to none, and, overall, we are fighters for the rights of man to be free, without discrimination.

Archives are a priority. Society is on the move, its given behaviour patterns of a millennium are altering: today there are surrogate mothers andunidentified sperm donors, which cause records to become difficult to keep. New guidelines are required. Ethics regarding conception, biological parenting, confidentiality of sperm donor, require much discussion leading to laws being brought into being which will ensure the safety of the child and of the future. DNA testing is a wonderful tool, but it does underline the fundamental difference between the world up to 1960 and that post-1960. Where the majority of babies most certainly came from standard procreational practices before 1960, from then a hazard line has been inculcated into the system of record-keeping. Previously, adoptions had proved to be the worrying factor, trying to trace a parent or child. Now, that factor has been multiplied exponentially. To the Jewish genealogist any union which is not of standard procreational variety, and is not recorded as fully as possible, could lead to a disastrous situation: The child of a standard union, where the mother and the father are known, are either married to each other, or are free to be married to each other, the child of that union is generally without any religious restriction as to its position in Jewish law and who it may or may not marry. However, there are Judaic laws prohibiting certain unions ie where a woman is not divorced but carries the child of a man not her husband, that child has a different status from the child of a standard union. Unfortunately, the religious status of a child from a proscribed union does not remain solely a difficulty for that child, but descends the generations tenfold. This is a strict and awesome proscription, intended to regularise and keep ethical and pure the sanctity of marriage and the procreation of children. Where a Jewish woman has a child with a non-Jewish man, in Jewish law, the child is Jewish. Where a Jewish man has a child with a non-Jewish woman, that child is not Jewish. In this way the matrilineal link has been followed for nearly a millenium, as it is usually the mother who is without a doubt known, whereas the father might not be known. Indeed, there are names of fathers on birth certificates where it is impossible for them to have fathered that particular child - perhaps the named father only met the mother when she was already pregnant, but chose to give the child a name to prevent the child from being stigmatised. Even in the general population, children from informal unions carried a lifetime's stigma, frequently blighting their very existence, as to what job they could do, or even whom they could marry. In England those of rank and wealth have been able to arrange matters so that an illegitimate child lived as well as others of like rank but formally recognised, ie legitimate. The average person did not share this ease of living. In Jewish law there is no concept of bastardy, only of the concept of the fitness of the union. A child may not have a known father but is still a Jewish child without religious restriction as to education, occupation or marriage.

While the civil marriage certificate gave a woman status and protection in law, so a birth certificate ensured a child passage through life. Death certificates are a little less certain as those informing of the death may not know the earlier life of the deceased and so may put a muddle of wrong names to the deceased, a mistaken place and date of birth.

Many Jewish communities in the British Isles retain their own marriage and death records. Some communities are now so diminished that their records are lodged for safe-keeping with their

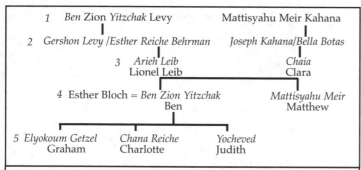

Where "Levy" is seen here, in any synagogual service, at time of marriage, birth of a child, or at death, the name would have had "HaLevi" added, as this family descends from Moses, his descendants being the attendants/administrators of the Temple.

Where "Kahana" is seen, this becomes "Cohen" in England/Western World, and would have had similar treatment to "Levi", being from priestly descent, from Aaron, Moses' elder brother from whom the priests descend.

"Bloch" denotes variously, 'wanderer' or 'Italian'.
"Yocheved" becoming "Judith" arises through a father's kindness in not saddling his daughter with an awkward name for daily use.

City Archives or the Chief Rabbi's Office in London. One or two have archived/catalogued their cemeteries, with photographs and transcriptions of the tombstones. Bear in mind, headstones are frequently illegible where of poor-quality stone, or stone likely to deteriorate in a heavily polluted atmosphere as well as from general weathering. It should be remembered that until approximately the 1960s England had fogs and smogs, engendered or made worse by emissions from homes and factories, and even from trains as they crossed the country.

By the 19th century newspapers and journals became another source for researchers. With for example Aris's, *The Gentleman's Magazine, The Voice of Jacob* - later to be subsumed into the *London Jewish Chronicle*, social information was recorded and became widely accessible. Today The Newspaper Library at Colindale, London NW9, houses most newspapers and journals from the earliest days.

Genealogists, historians, archivists will all err in favour of recorded history as the way to the future. To know and understand the past ought in priciple to direct mankind to bettering their future. To simply know who begat whom is hardly going to impart much knowledge of how lives were lived, why people stayed put and while others were on the move. Through our researches, the more we know of the past ought to give us a valuable tool to promoting a richer and more certain future.

Resources:
Chief Rabbi's Office for Marriage Authorisations

& Cemetery Records - Adler House, 745 High Street, North Finchley, London N12
The Spanish & Portugese Jews' Congregation - Archivist - 2 Ashworth Road, London W9 1JY
JGSGB (Jewish Genealogical Society of Great Britain) P O Box 13288 London N3 3WD or www.jgsgb.org.uk
Dr Anthony Joseph - authority on Anglo-Jewish Pedigrees/Genealogist - 3 Edgbaston Road, Smethwick, West Midlands B66 4LA [to whom also appreciation for scrutinising this article for any glaring errors and for including additional details]
International Jewish Genealogical Resources UK (IJGRUK) [Mrs Judith Joseph -genealogist & Hon. Archivist of the Birmingham Hebrew Congregation] 25 Westbourne Road Edgbaston Birmingham B15 3TX
JHSE - Jewish Historical Society of England 33 Seymour Place London W1
For any enquiries include 2 self addressed envelopes with two stamps. Fees will be payable for most searches, although initial enquiries are gratis.

A family with both Hebrew & English Names

Ben Zion Yitzchak Levy / Zipa Marks		Mattisyahu Meir Kahana			Aaron		Avrom		
1				R. Shmariyahu Yitzchak Bloch/Rachel Rokeach		R. Meir Zvi Jung/Ernestine Esther Silberman			
Gershon Levy /Esther Reiche Behrman	Joseph Kahana/Bella Botashana								
2									
Arieh Leib	Moses Chaim	Aaron	Chaia Chaim Pesach Feige Liba Golda David		Elyokoum Ephraim Chana Malka Esther		Leah Eliyahu Yitzchak Moses Gabriel Berthe		
Lionel Leib	Moss	Arnold Clara	Fanny		Getzel Ze'ev Annie Millie		Lolla Leo Julius Max		
					George Getzel Harry				
3	Ben Zion Yitzchak Bella Mattisyahu Meir			Esther Shabbtai Moshe Avrom Romeo Shmariyahu Yitzchak Meir Zvi		Jehudit Eliezer Yehoshua			
	Ben	Matthew		Sebastian Morton	Sidney Isaac	Maurice	Judith Leonard Joshua		
4	Elyokoum Getzel	Chana Reiche	Jocheved						
	Graham	Charlotte	Judith						

From this table it can be seen that within four generations a family arriving in England from Europe may well have altered their names and naming customs for daily use, if not for relgious requirements.   Note, some names didn't change as the environment in which those named were living didn't require any changes.

In the header family line, BZY/G/AL/BZI skip to EG from the 2nd line, maternal grandfather. Paternal grandfather was living at the time of 4th generation's birth
MM of the header family line has no Joseph in the third line, where it might have been anticipated, as Joseph was alive, which gave the child his gt grandfather's name
In the header family line SY waits for No.3 grandson to be born before his name is used once ore. MZ of the header family line also waits for a further gt grandchild.
However, in this instance, SY dies AFTER MZ which makes for an anomaly, as to why the later deceased's name is given before the earlier deceased's. Simply, SY died just before the gt grandchild was born, while MZ had been deceased some years. It is customary to give the more recently deceased's name in precedence to that of the longer deceased.

In point of fact all the 5th generation have Hebrew names, but not all use them at any time as not all that generation married Jewish spouses, and so had little cause for the Hebrew names.

Where "Levy" is seen here, in any synagogual service, at time of marriage, birth of a child, or at death, the name would have had "HaLevi" added, as this family descends from Moses, his descendants being the attendants/administrators of the Temple.

Where "Kahana" is seen, this becomes "Cohen" in England/Western World, and would have had similar treatment to "Levi", being from priestly descent, from Aaron, Moses' elder brother from whom the priests descend.

"Bloch" denotes variously, 'wanderer' or 'Italian'.   "Judith" arises through a father's kindness in not saddling his daughter with an awkward name for daily use.

The 16th Century Land Grab
and its effect on Landlords and Tenants
Jill Groves

According to Charles Foster in his recent magnum opus *Capital and Innovation – how Britain became the first industrial nation: a study of the Warrington, Knutsford, Northwich and Frodsham area 1500-1780*, there was a small change in land law in the sixteenth century which led to 'the creation of 'customary' tenants, whose rents were fixed and who could not be ejected'.

Then the law of unintended consequences kicked in when the market rental value of land inflated later in the sixteenth century. This put a lot of capital in the form of land into the hands of tenants. One result was that at the beginning of the century the monarchy was getting market rents for its lands, but by the end it was only getting 5%-10%. Even when the Crown took over monastic land in the 1540s and sold it, about 90% was held by 'customary' tenants. 'This wealth was a windfall for the tenants but a loss to the Crown, the Church and the old landed gentry on whose lands the tenants lived', says Charles Foster.

This article looks at what two land owning families, the Tattons of Wythenshawe, and the Booths of Dunham Massey, did in the eighteenth century to redress the balance without stamping on the entrepreneurs too hard. They chose entirely different ways – one of which involved the desperate need of the Royal Navy (and many others) for good timber.

Why did these two landowners want to change the status quo at the beginning of the eighteenth century? Because, for different reasons, their estates were heavily in debt. The Tattons had had a disastrous civil war, backing the wrong side and paying heavy fines, followed by the early deaths of heads of the family. In the 1670s and the 1700s they made tenants surrender leases and released them back on customary leases, the entry fines of which were c. six times the rent, and were used to service the interest on the mortgages. The tenants were still winning handsomely on the value of land. But by the 1720s, the Tattons had changed tack. The tenants were still winning, but only just. The Tattons were financially on the up, buying land like it was going out of fashion, and making very good marriages – notably with the Egertons of Tatton, near Knutsford, which led to the Tatton family inheriting that estate, and doubled the family's landholding, the heir later taking the name

In association with Family History Monthly

Egerton, before the two estates separated again in the nineteenth century.

George Booth, earl of Warrington, inherited a bankrupt estate, encumbered with jointures, etc., for younger brothers and older sisters, at the age of nineteen in 1696. By the time he died in 1758, he had turned the estate around, and made a good marriage for his only, beloved child Mary, with the heir of the Earl of Stamford. He did this at the cost of his own personal happiness (making a disastrous marriage for money, but not as much as he was led to believe). Tree planting comes into George Booth's success.

Tatton of Wythenshawe, Cheshire
By 1600 the Tatton family of Wythenshawe Hall held two adjacent manors in North-east Cheshire a handful of miles west of Stockport, Northenden (centred on the village of Northenden and just south of the River Mersey) and Etchells (a series of scattered hamlets – Gatley, Heath Houses, Shadow Moss, Woodhouse Lane, Poundswick, Brownley Green, Sharston, Cross Acres – between the River Mersey and what is now Manchester International Airport). The Tattons themselves had benefited from the sixteenth century land grab when they acquired the manor of Etchells in the 1550s.

Leases and estate schedules and rentals dating from the early seventeenth century for tenants of the Tatton family in Northenden and Etchells detail rents, boons and services (such as ploughing two days on the lord's demesne or supplying a capon for the lord's table), heriots (the best good, best beast or money paid on the death of a tenant), the entry fine at the beginning of the lease and the yearly value of the tenement or small farm.

The customary leases on both the Wythenshawe and Dunham Massey estates were three-life leases. These were common in the North-west and in other parts of the country. The leases ran – in theory – for the length of the lives of three people named in the lease indenture or ninety-nine years (whichever was the shorter). In practice, 'lives' were often added to the lease once one or two 'lives' had died, at a price of course. The Tattons had their tenants with two lives or less in the lease surrender their leases en masse – in 1673 and 1700 – shortly after the estate had been remortgaged.

The value of a tenement to the owner of the estate was the rent, boons and services, heriot, and entry fine. The value to a tenant was just the yearly value, which was the rack rent or commercial rent that could be charged – and many tenants did rent out part of their farms to others, and in turn rented land from others as a way of consolidating their holdings without going to the bother of having the lease changed, or, later, buying and selling land. This may seem that the landlord had many more ways of increasing his income from a tenement, but rents and boons and services (combined in the early eighteenth century) were set at sixteenth century levels and the heriot likewise. Only the entry fine could be increased. So even taking twenty-five years (the average length of a lease), boons and services, heriots and entry fines, the landlord's income on a 21 acre farm (a good sized farm in this part of North-east Cheshire) in 1700 was only just under £192, whereas the value to the tenant for the same period (if the whole farm had been rented out at a commercial rate) was just under £519, three times what was due to the landlord. Entry fines for large farms of 20 acres and over in 1700 valued farms at approximately £7 an acre. (Landlords could add to the £192 by treating the £150 in 1700, a large sum of money for anyone to find, as a loan to the tenant and add interest on top.) Smaller farms were valued t £4 for entry fines. Having said this, there were exceptions. The largest farm on the Wythenshawe estate, outside the demesne lands attached to Wythenshawe Hall in Northenden and Peele Hall in Etchells, Highgreave Farm in the hamlet of Heath Houses (between Cheadle, Gatley and Styal, a long strip either side of Styal Road from Gatley to the outskirts of Manchester International Airport) was nearly 40 acres in size and yet the entry fine paid was only £180 in the late seventeenth century when it should have been at least £280. It also had highly valued land at £43 a year, when the norm was £1 an acre. So the tenants, the Ryle family until 1735 [check], had a farm worth nearly £1,100 over twenty-five years. In 1735, the entry fine had risen to £240, but even so the tenants were winning by three times.

In 1700 the Tatton family under William Tatton

changed tact. A large mortgage of £10,000 (£8m in today's money) had been taken out with Sir Nicholas Curzon and his heirs. The yearly interest on such a loan would be between £1,000 and £800. The Tattons needed a means of servicing the interest at least. They did it by gradually selling the larger farms to the tenants. The entry fine on new leases between 1700 and 1710 were increased from an average of six times the rent to an average of thirty times the rent and the lease indentures have the words 'granted for ever' included and there are no named lives. The entry fines were treated as loans to the tenants and charged interest. The tiny rents and boons and services were converted to yearly chief rents and were now purely cash. It did mean that the Tattons lost most of their direct control over their larger farms – for a period. Not that, with the customary lease system, they had ever had that much control anyway over what tenants grew and where or what they built, so long as it wasn't on the mosses or was kept in good repair. That was left to the Courts Leet and Courts Baron of Northenden and Etchells, and whilst that was nominally under the control of the lord of the manor and his steward, most of what went on there was largely a matter of common agreement amongst the tenants. By 1700 the four yearly courts (two courts leet at Easter and Michaelmas at the end of September, and two courts baron at Midsummer and Martlemas in early November) dealt with the same things – use and abuse of the common

pastures, etc., minor criminal offences, defaulting debtors and noting who had died and who were the new tenants – with the exception of the Michaelmas Court Leet when the township officers were elected for the year.

There were considerable trade-offs for both the Tattons and their larger tenant farmers in the new regime. The Tattons got money, and quite a lot of it, whether the tenant had the entry fine as a loan with them or with someone else. They had no responsibility towards the tenants. The tenants got the freedom to mortgage their farms for the first time (a mixed blessing for some), which meant they could pay the entry fine and invest in improving their farms, if they wished. They could also sell and buy land. The greatest part of consolidation of landholding by buying and selling in Northenden and Etchells took place in the early to mid-eighteenth centuries, all without benefit of Parliamentary enclosure. Previously it had been done by exchange renting and other informal means. Now the large open fields around Northenden and in Etchells were divided into closes or enclosed fields. (In the North-west open fields were usually divided into smaller divisions called shuts or furlongs, which meant that one open field could grow many different types of crop. Tenants with strips of land – or lounts as they were called – in one particular furlong or shut could decide amongst themselves what to grow. The difference now was that these shuts and furlongs were enclosed with hedges instead of the earth banks of butts and headlands where ploughs had turned for centuries.) The 'granted for ever' tenants could grow what they liked where they liked – even the potato not beloved of the Tattons. The more progressive and ambitious of these farmers would do just that. The lazy and the just unfortunate would have to sell their farms.

Amongst the most unfortunate were the Shelmerdines of Chamber Hall. In 1700 Matthew and Mary Shelmerdine bought the 17.5 acres from the Tattons for £90. Their son, also Matthew, mortgaged Chamber Hall farm with Ralph Henshaw. Unfortunately, Matthew

Shelmerdine died as a relatively young man in 1732 and his widow Anne eventually had to sell the farm to repay Mr Henshaw. The Reverend Twyford of Didsbury (across the Mersey from Northenden) and a charity in Didsbury bought it, but they could not really make it pay. So, in 1751, the farm was sold to the Tattons. By this time the Tatton family were on the rise and rise. William Tatton (son of the above-mentioned William Tatton) had made a good second marriage to Harriet Egerton of Tatton, near Knutsford, Cheshire, sister of Samuel Egerton. When Samuel Egerton died in 1740s [check], his estates were left to his Tatton nephews on the condition that they changed their surnames to Egerton, which they did. It was the Tatton-Egertons who continued their uncle's work of rebuilding Tatton Hall and the emparkment of the surrounding land as leases fell-in. In addition, as land became available to buy, the Tatton-Egertons bought – in neighbouring Baguley, acquiring most of it by the end of the eighteenth century from Viscount Allen and his heirs, and on the border of Cheshire and Derbyshire (in the old Cheshire 'panhandle'). So when Chamber Hall, which was next door to Peel Hall, the old manor house and demesne land of Etchells and the only large farm in Etchells to be kept in Tatton hands directly, came up for sale the Tatton-Egertons eagerly bought. At first the farm was the same size as it had been in 1700 and rented by Thomas Walker for an annual rent of £26. However, when Henry Meers/Meyers became the tenant in 1756 the farm was enlarged with fields from Peel Hall and the rent was upped to £80 a year. For the next 200 plus years the farm continued in the Etchells/Wythenshawe estate. Only in the 1990s was the farmhouse and farm land sold by Manchester City Council (having bought the whole estate from the Tattons in 1926). This was not the only large farm to return to the Tatton-Egertons.

The Tattons dealt differently with the smaller farms and tiny smallholdings. These were not sold off to the tenants but as the leases fell-in they were converted to commercial rents. Some of the larger farms which remained in the hands of the Tattons, such as the 15 acre Moorside farm, Northenden, tenanted by the lawyer John Worthington of Sharston Hall until his death in 1763 for £30 a year, were divided into seven smallholdings on short-term leases at commercial rents of an average of £2 5s per acre. On the face of it, this might seem to be folly when the 70 acre (the demesne had been 106 acres in 1648) at Peel Hall paid a commercial rent of £125 to £170 a year and an entry fine of about £160. However, the smallholdings paid higher commercial rents per acre. Why? Because these smallholdings were evolving into market gardens, producing fruit and vegatables to feed the growing town of Manchester and its markets, or the smaller ones of Altrincham and Stockport. Even a half acre croft rented by a labourer could produce enough to feed his family and send the surplus to market. William Tatton got £14 an annum more from the seven smallholders than from letting the land as a whole to Mr John Worthington.

The Accounts show that between 1750 and 1766 the Wythenshawe estates increased the number of tenants paying commercial rents from eighteen to thirty-four and the rents paid from £501 1s to £747 15s. Part of this was due to land buying around Northenden and Etchells. As well as Chamber Hall farm, William Tatton bought Shadow Moss farm (near Manchester International Airport), Twyford's farm, Alvanley Hey farm, the cottages at Heyhead, Shadow Moss (under a terminal at MIA), Wellbrow House and various other small fields. Every time William Tatton bought he raised the rent.

All this (plus the fortunate marriage) meant that the Tattons were winning in the mid-eighteenth century as they hadn't since the mid-sixteenth when they first bought Etchells.

George Booth and the Dunham Massey estates
When George Booth inherited his title of Earl of Warrington and estate in Cheshire, Lancashire and Leicestershire, from his father Henry at the young age of nineteen, the estates were nearly bankrupt. This was the result of a combination of family involvement in national politics, a couple of spells of imprisonment in the Tower of London, and broken promises about pensions and compensation made by at least monarchs. George's father and grandfather, another George, had taken part in the English Civil Wars (1642-1660) (on the side that eventually lost), the Monmouth Rebellion (1685 – on the losing side) and the Glorious Revolution of 1688 (on the winning side). This meant that close management of the estates was in the hands of farm stewards like John Edmonds, William Andrews and bailiffs like William Tipping. George Booth suspected these servants of his father's of being lax. They weren't, and they were very loyal to the Booth family, but perhaps, without close supervision by their employer, they were inclined to let customary leases run until there was only one life left (even none), instead of 'suggesting' tenants add lives (at vast expense) at the first death (which seems to have been the practice of the Tattons of Wythenshawe). The tenants on the Dunham Massey estate, like those of the Tattons, were winning handsomely on the value of the lands they rented for tiny amounts. Unfortunately, the Dunham Massey estate

rentals of 1701, 1704 and 1709-1760 which is being used for this short study don't give entry fines, but it is clear from them, nevertheless, that George Booth did not adopt the Tattons' regime of selling large farms to the tenants and converting smallholdings and tiny crofts to commercial rents. However, he did charge c.£24 to add an extra life – a high rate.

George Booth, earl of Warrington, let his tenants add-in lives or lengthen the tenancy as they wished. But he kept a close eye on the leases and if any tenant had argued with the sometimes irascible earl then their lease was not renewed. This may make George Booth sound an unfair man, but he often had good reason not to renew a lease if a tenant had been told to pull his socks up and farm properly, even if the reasons were stated in terms such as 'because of his ill-carriage towards me and my family'.

George Booth needed money in a hurry to pay legacies to his younger siblings (who were resorting to the court of Equities to get them) and to put his near bankrupt estates on a sound financial footing. For some reason, a financial saviour like Sir Nicholas Curzon was not available to the young earl. So he needed to marry money. Normally, he would have done this by marriage to another aristocrat. But few of them would look at a penniless young earl. So it had to be the daughter of a very wealthy London merchant, Mary Oldbury, and quickly. This was partly because George needed money in a hurry because he was young, impatient. Mary Oldbury was young – too young – and came with a large fortune, but not as large as George first thought he was going to get. And it took George some time to get the money out of her guardian. This would not have been so bad, if Mary had been trained to run a household, but her mother had died when she was very young and her father had indulged her and her sister and allowed them to go their own ways. Within a few years the marriage failed and she and George ended up hating each other, living in separate parts of the house. Inviting both to a dinner party was not a good idea, as their neighbours soon found out. The atmosphere would be sour and frosty on her side, bad-tempered and monosyllabic on his. As a result of this marriage, George Booth wrote a polemic on divorce – advocating divorce on the grounds of incompatibility and irretrievable breakdown, two hundred and eighty odd years before it was available. However, the only child of the marriage, Mary, was adored by her father, who set himself the task of getting the estate on its feet for Mary and training her in how to run the estate.

One of the features of the Dunham Massey estate rentals of 1704 and 1709-1760 is the requirement of tenants to plant trees. In 1704 George Booth's Cheshire estates in the Greater Altrincham/Sale areas, the Wilmslow area and the 'panhandle' of Cheshire 1018 trees were planted per year, whilst on the Booth estates in Lancashire around Ashton-under-Lyne (in what is now Tameside in Greater Manchester) and Warrington 665 trees were planted annually. By the time of the 1709-1760 rental this had risen to 1525 in Cheshire. (There are no numbers given for Lancashire in the 1709-1760 rental.) The total planted in fifteen years – the average length of time of a planting programme for a tenant – from 1704 onwards was 1075 in Cheshire and 7341 in Lancashire. The total planted in fifteen years from 1709 onwards in Cheshire was 13691 – an increase of 27%. The varieties of tree to be planted were oak, elm, ash and, from 1709 onwards, black poplar. Three varieties could be used in both house building and shipbuilding. The fourth, poplar, was used as a quick growing substitute for oak in house building. And every bit of every tree could be utilised for building, floor boards, furniture, carts, waggons, machinery, brushwood hurdles, charcoal, besoms, domestic fuel and, finally, the bark would be sold to tanners to tan skins.

This planting by the tenants was in addition to the famous planting of elms in the park at Dunham Massey. When people complained of his extravagant planting of trees, George Booth replied that he was planting for his daughter and his Grey grandson. With his ever astute financial eye, the earl of Warrington declared that the trees would be worth a great deal more money in years to come. There was indeed a 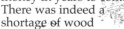 shortage of wood

in the early eighteenth century for house- and shipbuilding, which continued for most of that century. The Tatton family and Dr Peter Mainwaring, lord of the manor of Sale in 1784 agreed to sell trees from three small farms (fir, alder, walnut and willow as well as the usual oak, poplar and ash) to James Greatrex of Baguley, timber merchant, and Amos Banister of Stretford, wheelwright for £290 (nearly £? million in today's money). With such handsome profits, they must have wished they had instituted a tree planting programme amongst their tenants on the lines of that of the earl of Warrington.

When George Booth talked of his descendants reaping the rewards of his planting, it is possible that some of those trees would have started to pay for themselves within five years if some were first coppiced or pollarded for small branches for hurdles and fuel. Others would have been thinned out after ten or fifteen years. Two-thirds of the trees planted were the slower growing oak and elm, one-third the faster growing ash and black poplar. So whilst George Booth looked to the long-term future, he was expecting the trees to show a profit within the medium term.

Trees were not the only means by which George Booth brought the estates back into profit. A frugal lifestyle for an aristocrat (which annoyed his extravagant wife who liked shopping and parties), the albeit erratic payment of annual pensions by the government, inheriting the estate of his brother Langham Booth and close management of the estates, also helped. Much of the Warrington estate was sold off – a very sensible move at a time when that town was increasing in population and in wealth, which would have brought in quite a bit of money if sold at commercial rates. Some of the moss around Carrington was enclosed and drained, so the rents increased.

Conclusions
The end result for both the Tatton-Egertons and Mary Grey, Countess of Stamford, daughter of George Booth, was two enlarged estates in profit. The Tatton-Egertons did split in two, the Egerton branch taking over the Tatton estate near Knutsford and the Tatton branch taking over the Wythenshawe estate and ther other Cheshire and Lancashire lands. The Greys kept the Dunham Massey estate in Cheshire, Lancashire and Leicestershire together and began to take part in national politics again. Despite her marriage to Henry Grey, earl of Stamford, Countess Mary was very much hands-on when it came to the management of the Dunham Massey estate, as her father had been. She continued his work.

If the Tattons had not sold farms to their tenants, if George Booth hadn't taken up tree-planting and careful estate management, then both estates would probably have been bankrupted and sold off whole by the mid-eighteenth century, or sold off piecemeal, as happened to the nearby manors of Sale and Ashton-on-Mersey which disappeared by the mid-eighteenth century. As it is both estates survived into the twentieth century, Wythenshawe to 1926 (when it was sold for housing to Manchester City Council) and the Dunham Massey estate to 1973 (when it was sold to the National Trust).

Sources
Capital and Innovation – how Britain became the first industrial nation: a study of the Warrington, Knutsford, Northwich and Frodsham area 1500-1780 by Charles F. Foster, Arley Hall Press, 2004.
The Protector of Dunham Massey: Dunham Massey estate in the 18th Century. A study of the management carried out by George Booth, 2nd Earl of Warrington by Joyce Littler, Joyce Littler Publications, 1993.
The Booths of Dunham Massey by David Eastwood, Churnet Valley Publications.
Wythenshawe: A History of the Townships of Northenden, Northen Etchells and Baguley. Volume 1: to 1926 edited by W.H. Shercliff, E.J. Morten, 1973.
1701,1704, 1709-1760 Rentals of Dunham Massey estate, transcribed by Joyce Littler.
Tatton Family Muniments, Rentals for 1648, 1670, 1699, 1656 Schedule for Northenden, leases for Northenden and Etchells 1636-1750, Accounts Book, 1750-1766.

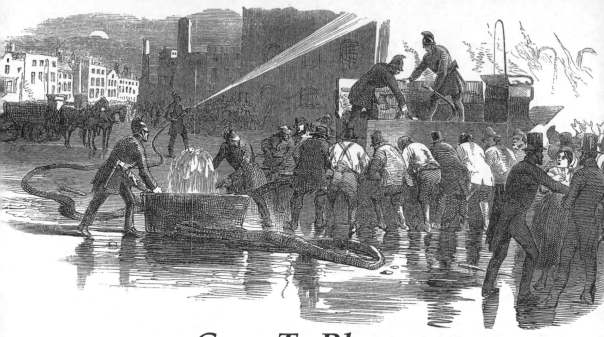

Gone To Blazes:
East Yorkshire Fire Fighting Through The Ages
Martin Limon

In the 21ˢᵗ century we often take for granted that, in an emergency, we can rely on professionally trained and well-equipped public services to come to our aid. The Humberside Fire and Rescue Service covering over a thousand square miles of East Yorkshire and Northern Lincolnshire responds to over 20,000 incidents every year ranging from chip-pan fires in the home to major incidents like Beverley's Bartoline inferno of May2003. The skilled personnel and specialised equipment of a modern fire service is however a far cry from the more primitive arrangements that existed in the past........

For many centuries the towns and villages of the East Riding had no organised way of fighting fires and relied on basic equipment such as leather buckets, hooks and grappling irons. If a fire took hold in the timber and thatch dwellings of the past often the only way of stopping it spreading was to create *fire-breaks* by pulling down houses using a crook and chain. Following the *Great Fire of London* of 1666 when huge areas of the capital were laid waste it seems that the authorities in Beverley began to take the risk more seriously and ordered the purchase of buckets and fire hooks. Before the advent of professional firefighters volunteers had to be summoned to deal with blazes by the ringing of church bells. To encourage this aspect of citizenship Beverley Corporation, in 1681, gave rewards to those people who attended a fire. They also sought to deter, through fines, a lack of care by Beverley tradesmen using candles

near combustible materials. In January 1738 they ordered that any person *"dressing flax by candlelight or carrying a lighted candle where flax is"* should be fined 10 shillings (50p). This was a large sum by eighteenth century standards and reflected the Corporation's concern that *"there had been several fires of late in the town from this cause."*

The fire hazards of carrying on a trade were also evident in East Riding villages. In May 1711 Mathew Borman of Leven suffered a fire that began in his blacksmith's shop and spread next door to the carpenter's shop of Thomas Newton.

In an age of open fires and lighted candles there was also a high risk of domestic fires being started by accident. Records show how a careless servant of Marmaduke Ward of Aike (near Beverley) had, in 1748, caused a fire by sweeping ashes from a fire onto straw laid on the floor of his master's house. To deter such carelessness an act of 1774 warned servants that if their actions led to the destruction of a house they faced a fine of £100 or 18 months imprisonment with hard labour.

From the eighteenth century there was limited improvements in the technology of fighting fires through the introduction of fire engines. Beverley's first engine, it seems, arrived in 1725 thanks to the generosity of a local resident called Fotherby. Beverley Corporation thanked him for his gift and went

on to order the employment of twelve people to work the engine on a casual basis and to be *"ready and diligent upon all occasions when a fire shall happen."* In 1831 it became necessary to buy a new engine and so one was ordered from *Simpkin and Loft* of London that was capable of *"ejecting two bodies of water in different directions with great force."* In order to pay for the engine a subscription was organised with an appeal for funds being made to residents of the town and to fire-insurance companies like *Norwich* and the *Phoenix* (who each subscribed £10). Fire insurance was a lucrative business and, to encourage those who could afford it, insurance companies provided customers with 'Fire Marks' to fix to the walls of their houses to indicate that they had cover. One of these can still be seen on Tymperon House in Beverley's Walkergate.

Throughout much of the nineteenth century fighting fires continued to rely a great deal on voluntary effort and in an age of limited-speed, horse-drawn fire appliances this had to be local. Some communities made more effort than others. Beverley had a volunteer brigade by 1885 while the Cottingham Fire Brigade, composed of sixteen volunteers, was formed around 1887. It operated from a station house in Northgate using an engine provided by the Cottingham Local Board and horses loaned by local residents. In the brigade's first annual report (March 1888) the Captain of the Volunteers, Charles Naylor, recorded how the Cottingham engine had only attended four fires but had been out *"twenty times on drills and practices"*. Naylor, who by day was the station-master of Cottingham Railway Station, asserted that his men had been *"thoroughly well drilled during the summer evenings"* to encourage them to be smart at their work.

By the late 19th century local authorities had the power to meet the expenditure of maintaining a fire brigade from out of local taxation and many used this opportunity. Sometimes authorities would join together to minimise the costs involved. In 1912, for example, Driffield's Urban District Council and Rural District Council established a joint brigade and purchased one of the newly developed motor fire engines. Since they were paying the costs involved, the joint committe laid down charges for fighting fires outside their own area. For the use of their new fire engine they charged non-residents 5 guineas (£5.25) for the first hour!

As Chief Officer of the joint Fire Brigade they chose John Alton and decided to pay him a retaining fee of £15 per year while the other eight retained firemen would each get one pound. Within a year of taking up his post it seems that Alton was at odds with the Chairman of the Fire Brigade Committee, Councillor Ullyott, and his resignation was called for. However, Alton stood his ground and wrote to the Committee claiming that he broken none of the rules of the brigade or done anything to warrant his resignation. It seems the Committee agreed with him for his position as Chief Officer was confirmed by four votes to two! A clash of personalities between Alton and Ullyott is indicated by the fact that Alton was soon looking elsewhere for employment and in February 1914 was appointed as Engineer of the Western Australian Fire Board.

Back in Beverley the volunteer fire brigade continued until 1924 (with financial support from Beverley Corporation) when a new professional force of nine firemen was established. In the same year the corporation bought a motor fire engine and a fire station was constructed using unused police cells at Beverley's Guildhall. The brigade was to fight all fires in the borough and also served Beverley Rural District Council.

Further changes were to follow during the years of the Second World War when all of the East Riding's independent brigades became part of the National Fire Service under the control of the Home Office. After the war the need for efficiency and professionalism led to the formation of the East Riding Fire Brigade. To serve Beverley and places nearby a fire station was established at a former drill hall in Albert Terrace in Beverley. This *Old Fire Station* was, in turn, replaced by purpose-built premises in New Walkergate which opened in 1983.

The Beverley Fire Station is today complemented by others scattered across the huge operational area of Humberside Fire and Rescue including those at Driffield, Bridlington, Sledmere, Market Weighton and Pocklington and these are largely staffed by retained firefighters. Following national trends an important part of the strategy of today's fire service is *Community Fire Safety* with the aim being to reduce the number of fires and fire casualties. To this end Humberside Fire and Rescue seeks to change attitudes to fire prevention and detection by householders and encourage them to make an escape plan should a fire break out.

Females can be murderous too
Murder cases where the villain was female
Paul Williams

Isn't it strange that whenever anyone points out a murder in their family tree the viewer always says words to the effect of "What happened? Who did it? Was he hanged?" People always seem to assume it was a 'he' that did the heinous crime and not a 'she'!

Sorry ladies, but I am afraid that looking through some of my Murder File records it is obvious that women can be just as cool, calm and calculating as the men! Since 1868, when executions ceased to be public affairs, to 1965 when capital punishment was abolished, 38 women were hanged for murder.

Some murders by females tend to be remembered more than others and Ruth Ellis is probably the best example of this. It was the public outcry over her execution on 13 July 1955 inside North London's Holloway Women's Prison that was to lead later to the abolition of

The Magdala Tavern

Ruth Ellis

hanging. Ruth was the last woman to hang in Britain. Ruth had led quite a complex life. In 1944 she had a child by a French-Canadian serviceman. In 1950 she married a dentist called George Ellis. The marriage didn't last long and on departing she became a call-girl and club-manageress. She then met David Blakely, a 24 year old racing driver. In 1953 there followed an abortion after which Blakely offered to marry her. This she declined but they did live together. Ruth however was still seeing other lovers and it was a quarrelsome partnership. It was shortly after a miscarriage that on 10 April 1955, after Blakely had tried to extricate himself from her and attempted to conceal his whereabouts, she traced him to the Magdala Tavern in North London. She waited outside until he left and was walking to his car parked virtually outside. As he reached the side of the car Ellis walked towards him and fired a Smith and Wesson at him. She was arrested almost immediately, gun still in her hand, by an off duty policeman.

It was Ruth's own words that had led to her death sentence. When asked at the Trial what her intention had been when she fired the revolver she replied *"I intended to kill him"*. The murder was obviously premeditated and not a spur of the moment decision and the jury took just 14 minutes to find her guilty of murder. The day before she hanged Ruth wrote a statement in which she implicated another person who had given her the gun and driven her to the public house. This was not given to police until 25 years later but after investigation and denial by the person mentioned no further action was taken.

Ruth Ellis was hanged by Albert Pierrepoint who recorded in his hanging notes that Ruth was 28 year of age, 5ft 2inches, weighed 103lbs, and required a drop of 8ft 4 inches.

It is probably fair to say that if Britain still had the death penalty today and the case had taken place today Ruth would probably have got off with a prison sentence. The murder has been described as a crime of passion but unlike the French we don't have this as a defence in this Country. However she had just prior to the murder had a miscarriage and the defence could justifiably have argued that Ruth's mind was still unstable following this.

Pierrepoint resigned from his role as public executioner after this case but not because of it as the media suggested. He had resigned because he had received a letter to go to Manchester's Strangeways Prison to hang a man named as Thomas Bancroft. Bancroft was, fortunately for him, to be reprieved. The Under-Sheriffs then sent Pierrepoint £1 to cover expenses! He should have been paid £15 and after a protest to the Prison Commissioners, the fee was raised by the Under-Sheriff to £5 which he returned in disgust, sending also his resignation.

All murder is horrendous but some cases do tend to stick in the mind more than others. One

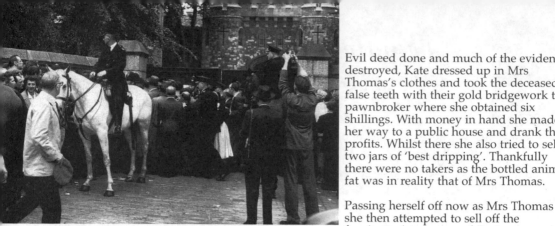

such case involved an Irish woman called Kate Webster who, although killing just one person, is remembered more for her deeds after the murder. Born in 1849 Kate was raised by her poor but respected parents. However, from an early age she was often caught stealing lace and jewellery and brought back to her parents by a constable. Every time she begged forgiveness and sobbing loudly vowed never to do it again. That is until the next time!

As a teenager she stole some money, sailed to Liverpool and immediately started pick-pocketing. In fact for several years this was her sole means of making a living. At age 18 however she was caught with her hand in someone else's pocket and sentenced to 4 years imprisonment. On her release she moved to Kingston-upon-Thames where she gave birth to a son. It appeared that she genuinely loved the child but alas not enough to stop committing crimes. She took to thieving from lodging houses, removing anything sellable at the pawnbrokers before moving on to another unsuspecting lodging house keeper. Many arrests and short prison sentences followed including an 18 month sentence in 1875. On release she moved to nearby Richmond with her son. She obtained employment as a maid to a wealthy lady called Mrs Julia Thomas. It was not long however before Kate was back thieving resulting in Mrs Thomas giving her notice before the latter went off to Church with Kate Webster telling her in no uncertain terms exactly what she thought of her.

On her return from Church Mrs Thomas went back up to her room and removed her hat. As she did so Kate Webster burst in wielding an axe in her hand. There was a violent struggle which took them into the hallway and onto the landing of the staircase. Here, Mrs Thomas lost her balance and fell down the stairs. Kate ran down after her and with the axe killed her. She dragged Mrs Thomas into the kitchen where she cut her up and boiled the remains. Later she wrapped these in brown paper and packed them into cloth bags. The following day she fed the remains onto a kitchen fire.

Evil deed done and much of the evidence destroyed, Kate dressed up in Mrs Thomas's clothes and took the deceased false teeth with their gold bridgework to a pawnbroker where she obtained six shillings. With money in hand she made her way to a public house and drank the profits. Whilst there she also tried to sell two jars of 'best dripping'. Thankfully there were no takers as the bottled animal fat was in reality that of Mrs Thomas.

Passing herself off now as Mrs Thomas she then attempted to sell off the furniture. A man named Porter suggested a John Church, a used furniture dealer may be interested. Kate said she would see him but in the meantime she made her way, with Porter, to various public houses. At one she excused herself for a few minutes saying she had to deliver a large black bag to a friend on the other side of Hammersmith Bridge. Dragging the bag she departed and returned later without the bag.

Porter then escorted Kate back to her Richmond house where she asked him to help her deliver a large wooden box. Making their way to Richmond Bridge she told Porter to leave it with her in the middle of the bridge and to return home. She would catch up with him later, after she had delivered the box. A short time later there was a large splash and Kate Webster returned back to Mrs Thomas's house where she (Kate) continued to live as Mrs Thomas.

The next day, fishermen, found a cord bound box on the riverbank. On opening it, much to their shock, they found the cooked human remains. Police were called but they were unaware at that time of the fate of Mrs Thomas. That came later when a neighbour, suspicious of furniture being removed from Mrs Thomas's house, called the police. As they arrived Kate slipped out the back and made her way back to Killane, Ireland.

Kate Webster attacks Mrs Thomas with an axe

Kate Webster was arrested by the Royal Irish Constabulary still wearing the dress and rings of Mrs Thomas. Returned to England she was taken to Richmond Police Station where she was confronted by Church, the furniture dealer. Immediately she said Church was the murderer and Church found himself under arrest and charged with Webster for the murder of Mrs Thomas! Enquiries followed and then it was found that Church had been no where near the Thomas house on the day of the murder.

All the way through the 7 day trial, Kate continually proclaimed her innocence but the Court found her guilty. She immediately said she was pregnant which would have meant she could not be hanged. This lie was soon disproved by the Court Matrons. The day before her execution she admitted her guilt to the governor of Wandsworth Prison and the prison chaplain and went to the gallows on 29 July 1879 still defiant and remorseless.

In recent years several murders have been committed following 'road rage'. On 1 December 1996, Tracie Andrews (28), drenched in blood, banged on the door of Keepers Cottage in Coopers Hill near Alvechurch and told the occupier, an ex-policewoman, how she and her partner, Lee Harvey (25) , had been the subject of a 'road rage' and that Harvey had been stabbed. Naturally police were called and Harvey found dead with 40 stab wounds, 30 of which were in the neck, the rest to the face, back of head, chest, body and back.

Tracie Andrews

The following day Tracie Andrews made an emotive nationwide TV appeal in which she described how her lover had been murdered by a fat man with 'starey eye'. She said how the man had 'ruined my life and he has ruined the life of Lee's parents. She added how the killing was 'the most stupid, vile thing that could come out of a car chase'.

Police however were already starting to have doubts as to what actually happened. Andrews had taken over 15 minutes from the time of the attack to calling at the cottage and forensic evidence was starting to blow a hole in her statement. Six days after the attack she was arrested and charged with the murder on 20 December.

Andrews and Harvey had met in 1993 in a Birmingham nightclub. A year later she moved into his flat in Alvechurch. Both had children from previous marriages. Their two years together during which they had become engaged, can only be described as turbulent for most to the time. Neighbours told of arguments sometimes several times each week. On some occasions police had been called and a former boyfriend of Andrews is said to have warned Harvey as to her violent personality. He added that he had been attacked by her several times and she had even pulled a knife on him.

At the Trial in Birmingham Crown Court, the Court heard how they had argued the day of the murder. In the evening they had been to the Marlbrook public house where they stayed for about 2 hours, having four drinks each. Leaving at about 10pm they drove home. During the journey Andrews had given him a black hat, similar to those commonly worn by young urban blacks. This had greatly annoyed Harvey as he was very sensitive about his dark skin. As a result of his anger he had missed the turning to Coopers Hill and was forced to reverse to turn into it. This manoeuvre was witnessed by two people both of whom later told police there was no other vehicle pursuing them. The car stopped near Keepers Cottage where, according to the prosecuting QC, they had their final confrontation. There, Andrews had stabbed Harvey, cutting his carotid artery and jugular vein. Harvey had probably died within a minute. Then, Andrews had made up her story of how they had been pursued, the attacker with the 'starey eyes', having stabbed Harvey then also attacking her, knocking her down. When she got to her feet she saw Harvey lying in the road.

Forensic evidence however suggested otherwise. A bloodstain was found inside one of Andrew's snakeskin-style boots. The prosecution said she had hidden the imitation Swiss army penknife in the boot and disposed of it whilst in the toilet of the Alexandra Hospital, Redditch. A nurse told of the unusual length of time Andrews had spent in the toilet whilst awaiting treatment. On the sweater Andrews had worn were some bloodstains which suggested that as she stabbed Harvey she had become covered in his arterial blood. Andrews refuted this saying the blood was as a result of her cuddling Harvey as he lay on the ground. David Loxley, Forensic scientist, said however that the distribution of the blood on the sweater indicated the person was facing the severed vessel. Blood was also found on the ground at the rear of the car – Andrews had stated Harvey was attacked at the front.

Nearly 100 strands of Andrew's hair were also found close to Harvey's body, suggesting she pulled them out as he attempted to defend himself. Andrews could also not explain the lengthy delay in reporting the murder nor the cut on her finger, consistent with a penknife blade.

Forensic evidence was more than sufficient to lead to Andrews being found guilty of murder and receiving a life sentence. In October 1998 she appealed against conviction on the grounds there had been a miscarriage of justice because of the adverse pre-trial publicity. The Appeal was dismissed.

The cases mentioned above are just a few of many held in Murder File records. Perhaps you have a distant relative (male or female) in your family tree who died at the hands of the official hangman, was a victim of murder or indeed was the perpetrator of a murder. If so and you want to know more about the case, why not contact www.murderfiles.com

Paul Williams worked for the Metropolitan Police in London for 26 years during which time he not only spent several years in their Criminal Record Office and for over 8 years was responsible for their Force Museums. One of these Museums was the world famous Black Museum which holds crime exhibits from notorious criminal cases. Whilst there he lectured, with the Curator, to police officers, members of the Judiciary and eminent people including members of the British and foreign Royal families. Amongst the many interesting visitors he met were Albert Pierrepoint, the last British Hangman and Professor Sir Bernard Spilsby, the pathologist.

As well as running Murder Files, Paul Williams, who is a Winston Churchill Fellow, writes articles for books, magazines and CD-Roms. He provides storylines for TV documentaries and dramas and has been a narrator in front of the camera for a murder reconstruction.

Fruit of the Loom
Joseph O'Neill

When family and local history touch, our ancestors' lives are cast in bold relief. We see them grappling with forces outside their control, shaping and reacting to the changes which formed their community. But when we discover they were caught up in the events that have shaped the world, the details of their lives acquire an altogether greater significance. In their experiences we now see the human impact of history as it stamped itself on every facet of life.

In many ways Manchester's history is a microcosm of the British experience. The difference is that many of the developments that shaped the country happened first in Manchester – and in a more extreme form. Manchester has always wanted to be first – the first industrial city, the first modern artificial waterway, the first purpose built passenger railway, the first electronic computer.

That's why your Manchester ancestors, whenever they lived in the city, were probably caught up in great social, political or economic developments.

The original settlement was in the area where the rivers Irk, Irwell and Mersey meet. The Romans, however, were the first to make their mark. In 79 they built a fort at the confluence of the Irwell and Medlock in what is now the Castlefields area of the city. This was a major stronghold in the area and some suggest that it is from the Roman words for 'mother' and 'fort' that we get the name Manchester.

A millennium later the Domesday Book mentions the city and its parish church but gives no indication of its future importance. It is merely one of many small settlements in sparsely populated Lancashire.

An intimation of the city's future industrial prominence came in 1322 when evidence of a textile industry in the area was first recorded. This development, commemorated in the names of several pubs, is associated with an influx of Flemish weavers.

Manchester remained an important textile centre throughout the seventeenth century when it manufactured linen goods and 'Manchester cottons', which were in fact a mixture of various textile yarns. The town continued to grow and in the first half of the eighteenth century was known as 'the first village in England.' Even then, however, there was nothing to suggest it might supersede Yorkshire or East Anglia as the leading producer of textiles.

In the 1760s, on the eve of its transformation, Manchester was a squat and busy town. Among its few ancient buildings were its parish church and the Grammar School, founded in 1519.

Soon it became both the engine and the product of the industrial revolution. It was the wonder of the world, the prototype for a new method of production that transformed the way people worked and lived.

The event that sparked this transformed began in 1761 when the Duke of Bridgewater started his canal to transport cheap coal from his pits in Worsley to Manchester. Entrepreneurs and inventors were combining to transform the domestic system of cotton production into the new factory system, made necessary by the invention of powered machinery, such as the water-frame. At first water power was used but the development of the steam engine meant that Manchester, with its large supply of cheap fuel and labour, its ideal location and damp climate was the natural centre of the cotton industry.

The mills acted as a magnet for the droves of agricultural labourers dispossessed by enclosure and the revolution in farming methods. In 1788, the year before the construction of the first steam engine used in a cotton mill, the town's population was almost 50,000. Twenty years later it had doubled to almost 100,000.

Now merchants transported the raw cotton from the nearby port of Liverpool and made the cloth on their new powered machinery housed in the revolutionary 'manufactories'. By the end of the 18th century Manchester was the focus of the cotton industry, which was rapidly becoming 'King Cotton', Britain's most profitable export.

Just as industry spawned warehouses and palatial homes for the mill owners, it also gave rise to cheap housing for the workers, most of which stood in the shadows of the factories. Some of these were later to become infamous as the worst slums in Western Europe. When social commentators like Marx and Engels talked about the degradation and suffering wrought by capitalism, it was primarily Manchester's 'Little Ireland' they had in mind. This area and the town's ironically named 'Angel Meadow' fascinated students of this terrifying new phenomenon, the industrial city. Both feature prominently in Engels' *The Condition of the Working Classes in England.*

The city was on the front page of every newspaper in 1819 when the local yeomanry massacred eleven of those attending a reform meeting in St. Peter's Fields, near the site of the city's Central Library. The struggle of the new working class for political representation was nowhere more bitter. Yet they had allies in the new middle class, who in 1820 established the *Manchester Guardian,* which soon became a national vehicle for advanced liberal ideas.

The city became synonymous with the ideas that were challenging the old social structure and a political system dominated by the landed aristocracy. The Anti-Corn Law movement, which aimed to expose agriculture to foreign competition, was at the centre of political controversy in the 1830s and 1840s. Appropriately it was founded in Manchester which remained the centre of its activities.

The city also gave its name to a school of economic thought that would eventually open up the world to British commerce. Central to the thinking of this Manchester School was the free trade ideal. Its role in the city's development is commemorated in the Free Trade Hall on Peter's Street. The interior is now a luxurious modern hotel, one of the many that has sprung up in recent years. But the façade remains, a reminder of the city's role in producing ideas that have transformed the world.

It was not only in social and political thinking that the city was in the vanguard of new developments. The city was at the forefront of applied scientific ideas. In 1821 Charles Macintosh's Manchester factory produced the first rubberised cloth. The obscure work of a Manchester scientist was to prove of infinitely greater significance. Before the Manchester Literary and Philosophical Society in 1803 John Dalton propounded the first atomic theory and the first table of atomic weights and elements.

Manchester and Liverpool businessmen were quick to grasp the advantages of the new transport of the 1820s, the railways. The result was the Liverpool to Manchester railway, opened in September 1830. By further slashing the cost of coal and raw cotton, the railway gave the burgeoning cotton industry another boost.

Manchester's elite craved monuments to their success. In 1846 one of the city's foremost textile entrepreneurs, John Owens, left a large bequest to establish Owens' College, which developed into Manchester University. It was there, in 1948, that the world's first electronic computer was built.

In 1867 the city fathers invited submissions for a new town hall. No expense was spared and the winning entry, that of Waterhouse, allied the most advanced building technology – a metal frame and fireproof concrete ceilings – with elaborate Gothic design to create one of the marvels of Victorian architecture.

But it was the expanding prospect of work, not lavish municipal buildings, that maintained the increase in the city's population. By 1851 the population was almost 500,000, many living in cellars and conditions so insanitary that only forty per cent of children survived to the age of five.

At the other extreme, the city's affluent were spreading out along the ribbon development to the south of the city. By Oxford Road, where Marx and Engels had strolled while planning the overthrow of capitalism, Victoria Park sprang up. Within this walled enclave the cotton magnates lived in grandeur, devising schemes to develop the city's industrial power.

One such scheme was the construction of the Manchester Ship Canal, linking the city to Liverpool and creating a great inland dock. The building of the canal was one of the century's greatest engineering feats, involving the labour of thousands of navvies drawn from every corner of Britain.

While some of Manchester's permanent residents arrived from the adjacent countryside, others, like many of those who built the Canal, came from Ireland and Eastern Europe. The latter strengthened the city's vibrant Jewish community, the size of which is surpassed only by London and Leeds. Among their contributions to the city is a splendid synagogue, built in the Spanish style. Later Italians, Ukrainians, Asians and Chinese joined them in large numbers, making Manchester one of Britain's most cosmopolitan cities. Two of the city's great attractions are its famous Chinese quarter and the Rusholme's 'Curry Mile', which boast some of the finest restaurants in the country.

Cotton was not the only magnet drawing people to the city. Engineering and manufacturing were also key elements of the city's economic life. Amongst other things the city became a focus of the aircraft industry. Appropriately, Allcock and Brown, the first to fly non-stop across the Atlantic, were Mancunians. They achieved this feat in 1919, the year in which another of the city's famous sons, Rutherford first split the atom.

It was at this time that Trafford Park, in adjacent Stretford, became the biggest industrial complex in the western world and the target of the Luftwaffe, especially during the winter of 1940 when the city suffered substantial damage.

In the post-war boom years Manchester became the destination for Irish and Commonwealth immigrants. The former added to the city's large and well-established Irish community.

Manchester's enduring association with the struggle for Irish independence was confirmed in 1867 when the Fenian leaders, Kelly and Deasy, were rescued from a prison van. Subsequently, three of those involved were executed at Salford prison in what was to prove Britain's last public multiple execution.

Many of the new migrants found work in the slum-clearance and re-housing programmes of the late 1960s and early 1970s, which swept away almost all of the old city. St. John's Street, off Deansgate, is the best example of the city's Georgian past.

The city's reputation as a centre of sporting and cultural excellence flourished in the post-war years. Famous for Granada Television and its two leading soccer teams, Manchester is the home of the Halle Orchestra and major developments in popular music associated with such groups as Oasis and Guns and Roses. Its status as one of Britain's leading sporting centres was confirmed in 2002 when the city hosted the Commonwealth games.

By then a large section of the city centre's 1960s development had been destroyed by the IRA bomb of 1996, the largest mainland explosion of the Troubles. The resulting redevelopment produced a cleaner, lighter and more exciting area, the centre of the city's vibrant nightlife.

Fortunately for the family historian, Manchester has the research facilities its rich past deserves. Don't neglect the many splendid histories of the city. You can do no better than begin with one of the more recent accounts, such as Alan Kidd's *Manchester* (November 2002, Carnegie Publishing, ISBN: 0748615512, £17.74), Cliff Hayes' *Exploring the Changing Face of Manchester*, (September 2001, Breedon Books, ISBN: 1859832377, £14.99), Stuart Hylton's *A History of Manchester*, (October 10, 2003, Phillimore & Co Ltd, ISBN: 1860772404, £18.99) or the Manchester Evening News, *Memories of Manchester*, (1998, True North Ltd., ISBN: 190046327X, £10.95.)

The starting point for family history research is the Archives and Local Studies section of Manchester Central Library. It will save time if you first look at the excellent website listing its full holding of registers. You'll find it at http://www.manchester.gov.uk/libraries/arls/registers/index.htm It includes details of the many invaluable sources available there, which include copies of church and cemetery registers, the IGI on microfiche, copies of census returns, local newspapers, indentures, deeds, rate books, school records, maps, directories and electoral registers.

The address is Manchester Archives and Local Studies, Central Library, St Peter's Square, Manchester M2 5PD T: : 0161-234-1979/80 [F] : 0161-234-1927 [E] archives@libraries.manchester.gov.uk [w] lsu@libraries.manchester.gov.uk

The Council's Registrar's Office, which provides help with birth, marriage and death certificates is at Heron House, 47 Lloyd Street, Manchester, M2 5LE.Telephone 0161 234 7878 or email register-office@manchester.gov.uk

For cemetery records not held by Manchester Archives and Local Studies you will need to contact the appropriate cemetery. For later records for Gorton, Philips Park and Manchester General (and for indexes to the earlier records for the first two), and also for Blackley Cemetery and Crematorium, contact the Registrar at Blackley Cemetery and Crematorium, Victoria Avenue, Higher Blackley, Manchester, M9 8JP.

For records of Southern Cemetery, contact Southern Cemetery, Barlow Moor Road, Chorlton, Manchester, M21 2GL. For St Joseph's Roman Catholic Cemetery in Moston, write to the cemetery, at Moston Lane, Moston, Manchester, M10.

If you have Roman Catholic ancestors you will almost certainly need to visit the Lancashire Records Office, the official depository for registers. If you wish to view the National Index of Births, Marriages and Deaths or need to research 20th century coroners' records, you will have to visit the Greater Manchester County Records Office, which also holds 20th

century coroners' records, indexes 1918-1998 and inquests 1959-1998. It also holds copies of the National Index of Births, Marriages and Deaths from the General Register Office. The address is 56 Marshall Street, New Cross, Manchester M4 5FU, England [t] 161 832 5284 [Fax] 161 839 3808 W: /www.gmcro.co.uk/ E: archives@gmcro.co.uk

Pre-1858 wills and Bishops' Transcripts are held in the Lancashire Record Office in Preston and you can get certificates of birth, marriage and death from the Council's Registrar's Office. The address is Lancashire Record Office, Bow Lane, Preston, Lancashire, PR1 2RE, United Kingdom. T: 01772 533039 F: 01772 533050 E: *Record.Office@ed.lancscc.gov.uk* W: www.archives.lancashire.gov.uk

You will certainly save yourself a great deal of unnecessary labour by joining a family history group such as the splendid Manchester and Lancashire Family History Society. Among its many excellent features is its Irish Ancestry Branch. The contact details are the Manchester and Lancashire Family History Society, Clayton House, 59, Piccadilly, Manchester M1 2AQ W: www.mlfhs.demon.co.uk E: office@mlfhs.demon.co.uk T: 0161-236 9750.

If you are searching for someone who may still be alive you might like to try contacting Virtual Manchester. They have a bulletin board, *Looking For*, which can be used to trace family. The website is www.manchester.com/

To get a feel for the city's rich industrial heritage, visit some of the superb museums. Manchester Museum of Science and Industry has many splendid exhibitions on the working life. The Fibres, Fabrics and Fashion Gallery currently has one on the city's cotton mills. The address is Liverpool Road, Castlefield, M3 4FP. T: 0161 606 0156 W: http://www.msim.org.uk/

The Lancashire and Yorkshire Railway Society has a web site for those interested in railway history, including the city's role in its development. The site is www.netcomuk.co.uk/~fmetcalf/index.html For those interested in the canals of Greater Manchester, which played such a vital role in the city's industrial development, should visit www.canalarchive.org.uk.

The Mormon Family History Centre, Altrincham Rd, Wythenshawe, Manchester. T: 161 902 927 W: www.salecommunityweb.co.uk/mormonfhc.ht m has the full range of research facilities associated with the Church of Latter Day Saints.

Evocative Smells

Maureen Lavelle

It can happen to anyone going about their normal daily lives, a slight smell is located by the nostril and the brain clicks into action. You are transported to another time, another place. It happens to me when I detect that standby of many men of a certain age - Brylcreem. My father was a builder during his working week but on a Sunday he and his friends would dress in their Sunday best (everyone had those special clothes worn on high days and holidays) and take a drink at the local pub while 'the wife' cooked Sunday dinner. That slightly scented grease takes me to a warm kitchen in the 1950's with my mother busy among her steaming pans and the radio playing the familiar tunes of Family Favourites to reunite servicemen and their loved ones across the airwaves. If he was late returning I'd walk along the road to meet him. The smell of beer and cigarette smoke getting stronger as I got nearer, if the door opened and a man came out there would be a strong blast of the polluted air. So different from the slightly heady smell of incense found in the Church earlier in the day or the salt fish that had cooked slowly in the pan for Sunday breakfast, after soaking in water overnight.

It's the same when those large machines come to relay the road. I'm back sitting on the edge of the pavement outside my house with a group of friends poking a finger into the 'bubbles' of tar that have landed on the flags but not yet 'set'. Then trying to clean my fingers on my dress but just transferring the black sticky substance to clothes which in turn meant a telling off as it couldn't be washed away.

Nowadays we are very conscious of 'personal body odour' but it was possible to pick out the people who lived over the local fish & chip shop, the smell of grease and fat would cling to their clothing and hair.

To visit a patient in hospital would invoke fear just walking through the doors, so strong was the smell of antiseptic in the nostrils. A dread of the unknown could be seen on the faces of those passing through and relief that they didn't have to join those staying for treatment. Nurses may be called 'Angels of Mercy' but woe betide anyone who did not follow their instructions, 'Only 2 visitors and NO sitting on the bed', in a voice that had to be obeyed, such was the respect they commanded, particularly the Ward Sister. Equally strong but bringing a smile to the face of all who breathe it is the delicate smell of a newborn baby welcomed home from another part of the same hospital.

Open a small packet of colouring crayons with their shiny coating and the faint waxy odour can transport you back to that low table and chair in a large busy classroom. Small fingers held the sticks, trying so hard to concentrate on that first picture which when successfully completed you could take home in triumph to show how hard you worked at your lessons.

The walk home from school would take you past houses with their front doors left open (there wasn't the need for the security we have today), to allow floors and steps to dry after scrubbing , their wetness giving off the fresh smell of 'Aunt Sally' the cleaning liquid used by most housewives. Tantalising smells gave a clue

In association with Family History Monthly

of what was cooking for tea. Pans of soup or stew that had been cooking slowly during the day as the scrubbing was done. Maybe the tang of a ginger cake or chocolate pudding to follow if you cleaned your plate!.

The streets could be full of that equally strong 'scent' of manure left by the horse that pulled the coal cart. It would be eagerly collected in a bucket for granpa's allotment. That was a place of very different smells, the freshness after rain on the rows of vegetables or the wood smoke when he tended a small open fire to burn diseased plant material or damp wood and any rubbish.

His shed or 'lean to' had another smell, pipe tobacco. It was a completely different odour to cigarettes, you could almost taste it. Many a man spent all day with his pipe in the corner of his mouth. An elderly neighbour would light it on waking and not put it out until he went to sleep at night. His house held many other interesting smells like the strange yellow liquid he would slice his boiled eggs into, the hot spicy sauce was unknown to me but if I smell curry now I am back in that small room by the pan on the kitchen range listening to his tales of life at sea.

Outdoor smells can waft along on the air, the hint of newly mown grass welcoming part-time sportsmen to the cricket pitch, informing them it's ready for the village team to meet its rivals. A steam room brings back the damp clinging wetness of fog breathed through a scarf that had been wrapped across the mouth and held together at the back with a safety pin by a doting mum to 'stop you breathing it in' on the way to school. It was a different dampness to that found on a crowded bus, passengers would sit or stand in coats wet with rain from waiting patiently in a queue. As they huddled together the steam would start to rise from their clothing giving a steamy soggy smell not as clean as the steam of washing day. That day gave soap suds and starch followed by the warm cosy smell of the iron hitting damp material and a tinge of burn if not removed in time. There was

even a 'sizzle' as grandma spat on the iron heated by a fire, to test its temperature.

Familiar smells of remedies used for generations to treat illness and bring comfort. The recoil reaction to eucalyptus to ease a blocked nose often went with the sharp crack of stiff paper as you moved. Brown paper, saved from a parcel, was placed between skin and cotton vest to stop the goose grease, which had been thickly applied to the chest, from getting onto clothing. The grease was thought to help with chesty coughs. A practise passed down through families in the days before free medical treatment. These remedies have now passed into history, like putting margarine on burns and hot poultice on boils. The poultice would smell as it softened over hot water before it was ready to use, a bit like the putty used to fit the glass in window panes. Another one is cod liver oil, now taken by capsule, it was given to all children on a spoon to make them healthier but disliked and often followed by a further spoon of malt to mask the taste.

In the days before central heating a coal fire was the only source of heat in most houses. The delicious smell of toast made by piercing a piece of bread with a long toasting fork and holding it against the fire embers led to a treat. Quickly smothered in butter it has a taste no modern toaster can match. Together with a cup of hot sweet tea it solved many a problem. The atmosphere in a room lit only by a coal fire was magic, creating 'pictures' in the flames and shadows to dance along the walls of the room. To be in a room alone would give a child an eerie feeling, fearful of turning round to see 'monsters' lurking on the walls.

Coal bricks from the local chandlers shop topped with used tea leaves 'backed up' the fire and kept it burning longer. To be sent to buy one meant a trip to the shop where they were stacked high waiting to be sold, then a quick walk home with the brick wrapped in newspaper. As they burnt slowly they were more economical.

Fresh flowers are readily available today and their perfume gives

209

On a warm day children would sit on the pavement outside the Baker's shop to enjoy the wonderful hot air that escaped from doorways and vents as the bread cooked. To be sent for a 'new' loaf meant running home as quickly as possible to taste a slice while it was still warm as the butter started to melt into it. The cold smell of raw meat can take me back to the Butcher's shop with its floor covered in sawdust as I tried not to look at the rabbits hanging against the wall waiting to be sold and turned into pies. Another place with a smell all its own was the Pet Shop. The open sacks of seed, grain and small pens with puppies or rabbits rummaging through straw held delights for the shopper or passing watcher.

Waking on 6th November you can always smell gunpowder on the air, the remnants of the fireworks from the night before, if it's cloudy and still it can hang around for days reminding everyone of baked potatoes and stinging eyes caused by rockets and Catherine wheels.

Smells can be comforting, warning or disturbing, alerting the brain to what is about to happen. The sense of a perfume or 'known smell' on a regular basis when no-one is present, some say it's a spirit or 'Guardian Angel' some say it's imagination working overtime but if it gives comfort who are we to take that away. The power of the senses is very strong, especially the sense of smell.

pleasure to everyone but they often meant illness as they were only seen in hospitals or churches. Carnations for weddings, still used for buttonholes. The beautiful and strong smell of fresh blooms, particularly moss or chrysanthemums, usually meant a funeral, the only time more than a 'bunch' was in one place. The wreaths set on the ground outside the home of the deceased alerting neighbours and anyone passing to pause and pay their respects.

As you got older you would be allowed those teenage outings to a visiting fairground without a supervising adult. When darkness fell it became a magical place full of flashing lights and loud music played on bumpy colourful rides. You'd smell the thick black grease used to lubricate the machinery from a distance as the rides whirled round. Then the hot smell of fried onions would then entice eager customers to a stall selling hot dogs with mustard or another giving off the sweet sugary odour of candy floss as it was caught on a stick twirled around by the stall holder.

Walking past a line of shops meant a bombardment of scents. The medicinal qualities of the chemist or if it was a bigger shop one section would smell of perfume or 'scent', the answer to many a maiden's dreams. Equally it meant potions and mixtures to restore good health. The big store in the town centre had an enticing selection of smells the strongest of which was coffee. Passing the doors you took a deep breath to savour the aroma.

All Saints Parish, Wilden
- a hidden treasure
Pam Craven

From the outside the plain brick exterior of Wilden church excites little interest. Many local residents tell of driving to work past the church for 25 years without knowing of the amazing interior and the story behind its treasures. However, on a cold, wet February day in 2005 all this changed when over a thousand people stood waiting in the rain, queuing to view the Burne-Jones windows and Arts and Crafts furnishings of All Saints church. This amazing scene was a result of several articles published in national newspapers, and awakened the nation's interest in this hitherto unknown treasure. A similar scene had taken place on another drab February day almost a hundred years earlier. In 1908 an estimated 3,000 people converged on Wilden church for the funeral of Alfred Baldwin.

The story of Wilden Church and its associations with the Baldwin family really begins in the landscape around the church. Nowadays horses graze in the opposite fields which border a series of 'industrial units', but in the 1880's the fields were clouded by smoke from the ironworks around which the hamlet of Wilden had grown.. From the fifteenth century, the river Stour at this point had been the scene of industrial activity. The earliest Wilden forge and was recorded in 1669 at which time it was owned by the Foley family, being one of a number of varying types of mills powered by the waters of the River Stour. A record of 1692 stated that Wilden Forge used more river pig iron than others.

In 1812 the forge was sold 'to pay for Baron Foley's debts'. The new owner was Mr. Lewty, who renamed the forge as 'The Wilden Iron and Tin Plate Company and installed a beam engine and steam power. He employed around 50 people but in 1840 was forced to relinquish the company due to bankruptcy.
The company was then bought by a family originally from Broseley, Shropshire The family

name was Baldwin, and the family was to make a huge impact on Wilden and Stourport-on-Severn. The family managed already owned several local enterprises such as an Iron Foundry and the Anglo American Tin Stamping Company, (both in Stourport) and owned various companies across the Midlands including carpet manufacturing works at Bridgnorth and Tinplate works at Wolverhampton).

In 1840 Alfred Enoch Baldwin with his nephews, Pearce and William changed the company name and began trading as "E. P. & W. Baldwin of Wilden". From this time, the Wilden works was regarded as the family's prime interest. The year 1840 also saw the death of George Pearce Baldwin from scarlet fever. His untimely death meant that he never knew his 12th child, Alfred, who was born in the spring of 1841. Alfred was brought up by his mother, Sarah and when he was old enough joined the family firm.

At the age of 21, Alfred started work under his brothers, half-brothers, uncle and cousins. In 1864 two half brothers died and the control of Wilden passed in to the hands of two elder brothers.

In 1866 Alfred married Louisa MacDonald, and together the couple set up their first home in Lower Park, Bewdley. On an August morning in 1867 as he set off for work at Wilden, Alfred had not realised that their child's birth was imminent. By the time he arrived home, Louisa had given birth to their only child, a son who they named Stanley. The servants had already carried the baby to the highest point in the house as a sign that the child would 'rise in the world'. This prophecy was duly fulfilled. In 1888, Alfred's 21year old son Stanley joined the company as a partner, where he spent 20 years in the business before going into politics, ultimately becoming Prime Minister (1923,

1924-29 and 1935-37).

Meanwhile, 'back at the shop', Alfred's brothers through mismanagement brought the Wilden iron works close to bankruptcy.

In September of 1870 at the age of 29 Alfred took control, dissolved the partnership, bought out his two brothers and by business acumen and hard work put the company back into profit.
After taking sole charge, Alfred changed the company name to Baldwins Ltd. Alfred and the family moved from Bewdley to Wilden so that he could be near his employees to whom he became a father figure and benefactor. Wilden House lay just across the lane from the forge and Alfred described this as 'living over the shop'. When the wind was from the west the smoke blew into the windows of the house. Most of the employees lived in company houses, many of which still exist to this day. Alfred provided medical facilities and ensured that no worker was ever given the sack. When the church commissioners gave a site for a church and a portion of land for burial, Alfred offered to erect a suitable church.

On May 3rd 1879, Alfred Baldwin laid the Foundation Stone for Wilden Church, which he had generously provided for the community. The church was built by J. Cook of Hartlebury, having been designed by W. F. Hopkins. It is described as 'brick built with lancet windows'. The total cost of the building was £3,000 which included 'fittings of stained pitch pine, an organ, boundary wall and other requisites'. The first windows were of plain glass.

In his diary, Alfred Baldwin recalls that "Mr. Stanley Baldwin arrived at Wilden House on 20th April, 1880 to stay for the consecration" On the 30th April 1880 Alfred Baldwin was hoping that all would be ready on time.

On Sunday 4th May, 1880 Alfred met Bishop Philpott at the Church at 11 am and the service proceeded without a hitch. Mr Haviland read the 1st Lesson, Mr. Boyle the 2nd and the Bishop preached the Sermon and also conducted Holy Communion. There were 49 communicants, and the service lasted until 2 pm. At 7.30 pm the Church was packed for Evensong, and the offertories were good. At the end of the day Alfred Baldwin records in his diary,
"To bed, very tired, the work is done, thanks be to God, and may His blessings be on me and mine, and the whole Church".

Wilden was made a parish in 1904 and a vicarage was built in 1905 as a gift from Stanley Baldwin. Alfred also provided the village hall and the school and playing fields where the Baldwin Works' cricket team played were also provided. In 1892 Alfred became MP for West Worcestershire. He had also become Chairman of the Great Western Railway and these appointments involved frequent trips to London. It was on one of these occasions that Alfred died suddenly on 13 February 1908. He had gone to London with Louisa to attend the half yearly meeting of the Great Western Railway Company at Paddington. Louisa wrote *'In the mercy of God he was saved pain, illness, apprehension of death and the sorrow of parting'.*Stanley brought Alfred's body back to Wilden where it lay, surrounded by his workmen, in the Church that Alfred had built. On the night before the funeral Stanley and his cousins kept vigil by the coffin. An estimated 3,000 people attended the funeral. Some came by train and as the train slackened speed over the embankment into Stourport Station it could be seen that "crowds were already assembled within and without the churchyard and people in mourning were streaming through the fields from Stourport."

The above narrative describes with simple logic how the church came to be installed, but not why a church in an industrial hotspot, built by a politician should be blessed with an abundance of Arts and Crafts treasures.

I have already stated that Alfred Baldwin had married the daughter of a Methodist minister, Louisa MacDonald. That wedding took place on August 9th 1866 in the parish church, Wolverhampton and was a double wedding at

FUNERAL OF MR ALFRED BALDWIN

TO THE GLORY OF GOD AND IN LOVING MEMORY OF ENOCH BALDWIN WHO DEPARTED THIS LIFE JVNE 11TH 1905 AGED 82 YEARS

which Louisa's sister, Agnes married Edward Poynter. Edward Poynter was a classical Victorian artist, who was at one time President of the Royal Academy and therefore in his time an important figure..

Two more of Louisa's sisters made influential marriages. Alice married John Lockwood Kipling and their son Rudyard found fame as an author, (The Jungle Book, Kim etc.), and Georgiana had married the pre-Raphaelite painter, Edward Burne-Jones in 1860. All the MacDonald sisters were portrayed by Burne-Jones as models, but Agnes having 'the most symmetrical face' was reported to have been the best model.

Edward Coley Burne-Jones was born in Birmingham in 1833. As a young man he attended to Exeter College, Oxford where he studied theology with the intention of becoming a clergyman. Here he met William Morris who was also a student and also Harry MacDonald, the brother of his future wife. Soon Burne-Jones became

interested in literature and book illustration and he abandoned theology. After meeting Dante Gabriel Rossetti he left Oxford and moved to London to study art. William Morris soon followed. Burne-Jones' style was influenced by Rossetti, his subject matter came from legends and fairy tales and combined romantic idylls with heroic symbolism, whilst retaining an interest in religion.

Edward and Georgiana's first home was at Great Russell Street, London and they were regular guests of William and Jane Morris at Red House, which Burne-Jones helped to decorate. Edward also designed stained glass for several manufacturers before becoming the principal designer for Morris' firm, especially after its reconstitution in 1875.

It has already been noted that the first windows set in Wilden church were of plain glass, but between 1900 and 1927 these were replaced by the Burne-Jones windows that are seen today. As brother-in-law to Louisa and Alfred Baldwin it seemed appropriate that Edward's designs should be chosen for the windows of All Saints.

All Saints has 14 window spaces all of which are fitted with a Burne-Jones window. We believe the only other church in Great.Britain to have a complete set of Burne-Jones windows is All Hallows in Liverpool although Brampton, St. Michael's in Cumbria also possesses an impressive number of Burne-Jones windows.

The windows all have "BJ" catalogue numbers to confirm their authenticity as Burne-Jones designs and were produced by the Morris Company. Visitors will realise that as the windows were installed between 1900 and 1927, they were produced after the death of Burne-Jones and this is not at all unusual. The designs were still available and it is not unusual to find similar designs in other churches.

The 'Minstrel Angel' design can be seen a few miles away in Ribbesford church, although the colourings are different. The Burne-Jones window at Ribbesford was commissioned jointly by Edward Burne-Jones and Alfred Baldwin in memory of their mother-in-law, Hannah MacDonald who was the mother of the MacDonald sisters and therefore also grandmother to both Stanley Baldwin and Rudyard Kipling. Hannah is buried in Ribbesford, and this was also the church in which Rudyard married.

The 'Good Shepherd' is known to appear in Bath and the Gordon Chapel, Fochabers against a different foliage background.

The altar window of 1902, was placed in recognition of Louisa and Alfred's happy married life, and was the couple's gift. The lower right panel is reported to show Stanley

Baldwin setting out on his life's journey led by his guardian angel. (This latter claim went unchallenged until a few weeks ago when I was explaining this association to a group of visitors when one produced a postcard showing the identical panel with a different border. I was informed that the picture depicted Margaret Burne-Jones, daughter of Edward and Georgiana, as shown in a window at Rottingdean church, 'starting out on her life's journey led by her guardian angel!')

Other windows have Baldwin dedications. Agnes (MacDonald) Poynter is fittingly remembered in the window depicting St. Agnes. Enoch Baldwin is also shown by the biblical figure Enoch, (a figure which is also seen in the Burne-Jones windows of Brampton church). In Wilden's 'Enoch' window, dedicated to Alfred's nephew Enoch Baldwin, Enoch is shown holding the 'Hand of God' which is stretched out from a piece of rolled back sky. The 'Hand of God' is also seen in a depiction of 'Faith, Hope and Charity' in an Oxford chapel, in which God's hand stretches forth to grasp the hand of Hope.

A nephew of Alfred, and therefore a cousin of Stanley is remembered in the window panels 'Fortitude and Triumph'. The accompanying inscription is dedicated to Arthur who 'departed this life suddenly at the age of 37 years'. Arthur had worked at the family ironworks at Wilden and unfortunately suffered a fatal heart attack while cycling to his family home, (which is now better known as Stourport's Manor Hotel). Outside in Wilden churchyard, his grave is shared by his wife Lucilla, who was also his first cousin, so that her epitaph refers to 'Lucilla Baldwin Baldwin'. An earlier tragedy which struck the couple was the loss of their baby daughter, Phyllis at eight months old. On this occasion the couple presented an illuminated prayer book to the church. The book has an embroidered cover

and gold tooled edges and is to be seen on the altar on Open Days.

Also displayed on Open Days is the silver communion plate given to the church by Alfred's wife, Louisa. The vessels are set with Louisa's personal jewels. One of Alfred's grandson's was later to describe how on their honeymoon in Scotland, Alfred bought Louisa a tartan shawl and a 'Scottish silver brooch' with which to fasten it. It is possible that this is the thistle-shaped brooch with amethyst which is on the wine jug.

Louisa's mother, Hannah, and Edith, (the MacDonald sister who remained unmarried), lived nearby in Bewdley, until Hannah's death in 1875. Hannah is buried in Ribbesford churchyard and Alfred Baldwin and Edward Burne-Jones commissioned a window in Ribbesford church to their mother-in-law's memory. Naturally this was one of Edward's designs. After her mother's death, Edith came to live in Wilden House with Alfred and Louisa where she eventually outlived the couple. Edith was a fine needlewoman and was largely responsible for the working of an altar frontispiece in intricate gold thread. It was the design of William Morris and Edith had help from her sisters and other ladies of the village. Edith was the last resident of Wilden House which in 1939 was demolished as part of a road widening scheme.

In 1945 Baldwins Ltd. merged with the firm of Richard Thomas and finally closed in 1956. So what of Wilden's industrial heritage? In Stourport many of the family houses and work foundations are still standing although are now office blocks or guest houses, (Anglo House, Oakleigh and Stourport Manor Hotel).

Apart from the demolition of Wilden House, the village is little changed. Many of the workers' houses remain and the river Stour, the

GLORY TO GOD   IN THE HIGHEST   ERECTED AD 1902

canal and the dismantled railway line hint at the one-time busy industrial traffic. However, Wilden Lane which dissects the village is a busy commuter route between Kidderminster and Stourport. Small wonder that few passers-by on their way to work paused to wonder what lay behind the brick exterior of Wilden Church until that incredible February day. Now the church is sharing its secrets and visitors are witnessing the legacy left by a caring businessman and his artistic relatives.

The Open Day served to highlight a vast interest in historical heritage that could be employed to benefit the rural community. A chance remark made by a neighbouring parishioner to the effect that 'we can't hold an Open Day like that as we don't have special windows', brought the realisation that even if all churches don't have Burne-Jones windows, all have unique or interesting features in some form. These may be architectural features, important tombs, or treasured furnishings. Each church is also the most consistent link with the historical past and the social origin of each community. Even the newest of churches will display several generations of historical activity shaped by the environment. But how to present them to the public? A meeting was called to discuss the project and lo, the 'Wilden to Witley' country church trail was born!

The Trail leads visitors around 12 churches through some of the most spectacular Worcestershire countryside. Starting at Wilden the Trail visits Stourport, St. Michaels, Ribbesford, Areley Kings, Astley, Shrawley, Holt, Great Witley, Abberley, St. Mary's, Abberley, St. Michael's, Rock and finally Heightington, (although a starting point can be made any where on the route). Covering 800 years of history, the churches offer a great diversity of attractions; architectural features range from the simplicity of Norman building (Abberley and Rock), to modern 20th century form (Stourport, St. Michael's). The Baroque decoration of Great Witley provides a contrast with the pre-Raphaelite styles seen in Wilden Church. The painted medieval painted tombs of Astley are very different from the monumental iron tombs of Stourport, St

Michaels, cast at the Baldwin's own works. Box pews at Shrawley and stocks in Rock are just some of the other unusual features to be found in the 12 churches. Carved monsters on the Norman font at Holt contrast with folk tale carvings on the Ribbesford pulpit, (including a pig playing the bagpipes). Painting styles range from the simplicity of the medieval wall painting at Heightington to the elaborate Baroque paintings at Great Witley which are said to include the first representation of a Downs Syndrome child and angels with TB scars.

It is hoped that the enthusiasm and belief which has gone into the Trail venture will provide a permanent opportunity to explore some of Worcestershire's hitherto unrecognised treasures and prove an accessible link to local social history.

Further Reading
Baldwin, A. W. 1955 *My Father: The True Story.* George Allen & Unwin Ltd.,London.
Barringer, T. 1998 *The Pre-Raphaelites: Reading the Image.* The Everyman Library, Calmann & King Ltd., London.
Bradford, A. 2000 *Stourport-on-Severn: A History of the town and local villages.* Hunt End books, Redditch
Flanders, J. 2001 *A Circle of Sisters; Alice Kipling, Georgiana Burne-Jones, Agnes Poynter and Louisa Baldwin.* Viking, London
Marsh, J. 1996 *The Pre-Raphaelites; Their lives in letters and diaries.* Collins & Brown, London

The Patent Impulsoria

It's Patently Clear!
Tracing inventors and inventions
Doreen Hopwood

Many of us have heard the claim that great-great-uncle so-and-so was an inventor who invented *"something of great importance"* but he was robbed of the idea because he didn't apply to patent it. The records relating to patents can tell us much about the inventor, the invention and the social and economic history of the period. The applications for patents reflect the needs of the time and in 1887 alone, United Kingdom (UK) patents were granted for inventions as diverse as fire-engines and a machine for connecting a lady's muff to a boa.

Today double glazing is used for insulation purposes, but, long before these properties were recognised, it was acting as a means of protection for the stained glass windows in Henry VIII's Hampton Court Palace. Many other "modern" innovations aren't really new – some Victorian infants were learning to walk with the aid of baby walkers.

Inventors come from all walks of life and from both sexes. The earliest recorded patent dates back to 1449 when John of Utynam was granted Letters Patent for coloured glass (for windows at Eton College), and the first female patentee was recorded as early as 1637. Whilst many patents applications relate to major industrial processes, just as many are in respect of domestic items, and (as expected), most of the patents granted to women were for items associated with the home, family or for medical and nursing purposes. However, there were exceptions; the windscreen wiper was invented

by Mary Anderson after she experienced a New York tram journey in a blizzard. In 1895, Octavia Hill was granted a patent for the Foundation of the *National Trust for Places of Historic Interest or Natural Beauty*.

A patent is described by the Patent Office as *"an intellectual property right, granted by a country's government for a limited period"*. This used to be a term of fourteen years, which was the equivalent of two generations of apprentices, but now a UK patent has a life of 20 years, provided that the relevant renewal fees have been paid. In practice, the granting of a patent prevents the invention being used by other people and also permits the patentee (the person to whom the patent is granted) to sell or bequeath the patent.

There are strict regulations concerning the granting of patents and these are detailed in full at the Patent Office's website at www.patents.gov.uk. In order to be considered patentable the process must be:
Entirely new and not already in the public domain anywhere in the world.
Innovative – not merely a modification
Capable of an industrial application – making a significant contribution to any form of industry.

There are equally clear guidelines about inventions which cannot be patented. These include food or medicines made from known ingredients, schemes, methods or rules relating to the performing of a mental act, such as mathematical or scientific theories or anything

POOR MAN'S TALE OF A PATENT.

I AM not used to writing for print. What a working-man that never labours less (some Mondays, and Christmas Time and Easter Time, excepted) than twelve or fourteen hours a day, is ? But I have been asked to set down, plain, what I have got to say ; and I take pen-and-ink, and do it to the best of my power, hoping defects will find excuse.

I was born, nigh London, but have worked at a shop at Birmingham (what you would call Manufactories, we call Shops), almost ever don't think that's the way to set them right. If I did think so, I should be a Chartist. But I don't think so, and I am not a Chartist. I read the paper, and hear discussion, at what we call "a parlor" in Birmingham, and I know many good men and workmen who are Chartists. Note. Not Physical force.

It won't be took as boastful in me, if I make the remark (for I can't put down what I have got to say, without putting that down before going any further), that I have always been of an ingenious turn. I once got twenty pound by a screw, and it's in use now.

that is a "mere form of words". This latter category includes literary works and computer programs. Inventions which are considered as being injurious to morality, frivolous or contrary to the law cannot be patented. The first application to patent a water closet was refused on the grounds of impropriety.

By the early 17th century, the system of issuing Letters Patent [open letters] under the Great Seal of the Sovereign was seen as means by which the Crown granted monopolies in order to replenish the royal coffers. The Statute of Monopolies of 1624 effectively set out the considerations to be made before the granting of a patent. However, until the establishment of the Patent Office in 1852 the process was lengthy, cumbersome and very expensive, and there were separate systems for Scotland and Ireland until the passing of the Patent Law Amendment Act in 1853. In *A Poor Mans Tale of a Patent*, published in 1850 (in *Household Words*), Charles Dickens described the thirty-five stages each application passed through, requiring payments of almost £100 and Queen Victoria's signature. The Chief Officer of the Patent Office was given the title of Superintendent of Specifications and Indexes.

In order to start your search for an inventor and invention the Patent Office website (www.patents.gov.uk) provides addresses and contact details of the thirteen libraries within the PATLIB UK as well as an outline of their holdings. Whilst you need to have some idea of the name of the patentee and when and for what purpose the patent was granted, you can start with as little information as *William Tongue, fire extinguisher, 1850-1870*.

You can use this information to search the surname index of patentees, which covers the years 1617 to 1980 and is arranged alphabetically. If you are unable to view the index on microfiche then there are also surname indexes which are annual compilations in book form – but be prepared for a lengthy trawl if you do not have a date! These indexes provide details of the patentee, date and number of the application, together with its subject. Once the patent number has been found you will be able to examine the Abridgement of Specifications, which provides a summary of the invention, and may be accompanied by a drawing or drawings of the invention. A patent (No. 2341) was granted to William Tongue for his Self Acting Engine for Extinguishing Fires on 19th September 1861.

The Abridgement Class volumes, arranged by subject, can be consulted if you know that *"Great-uncle Thomas invented a new type of vacuum cleaner"*. This will enable the Abridgement of Specifications to be searched, and thus determine the Patent number. Copies of the patent can usually be purchased (by personal visit) from any of the PATLIB UK libraries, or by post from the Patent Office, Concept House, Cardiff Road, Newport, South Wales NP10 8QQ (from 1853 for the British Isles). There are no surviving records for Ireland prior to this date, and the records for Scotland (up to 1852) are held at The Record Office for Scotland in Edinburgh.

Some early patents are deposited at the National Archives and information about these can be found on the website at www.nationalarchives.gov.uk. Until 1711, most patents consisted of only a brief description of the invention, but by the mid-18th century, most were accompanied by drawings. Unfortunately, many of these are too large or too fragile to be copied. The 1846 specification submitted in respect of a sewing machine by Elias Howe

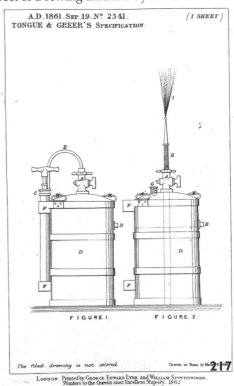

A.D.1861. SEP.19. No. 2341.   (1 SHEET)
TONGUE & GREER'S SPECIFICATION.

FIGURE.I.   FIGURE.2.

The filed drawing is not colored   Drawn on Stone by Malby

LONDON: Printed by GEORGE EDWARD EYRE and WILLIAM SPOTTISWOODE.
Printers to the Queens most Excellent Majesty. 1862

Junior included three huge sheets of diagrams detailing all of the components of his invention. This was the machine from which Isaac Singer's famous model was developed and patented in 1851.

The *"Old Series"* of patents – those granted between 1617 and 1852 – were numbered retrospectively after the Patent Office was established and form a continuous run starting at 1/1617 and finishing at 14359/1852. When applying for a patent granted between 1853 and 1915 it is imperative that you identify the

correct year, as a new numbering system, starting at number one, commenced at the beginning of the year. From 1916 the numbers run consecutively.

Patents have their own legalistic terminology (known as *patentese*), although this can usually be understood, providing you bear in mind that a spade isn't likely to be called a spade – it is more likely to be described as an "implement for digging holes". The documents tend to follow a similar format, containing the following information:
  The date of filing (making) the formal application.
  The unique number allocated at the time of application.
  A description of the invention.
  The name(s) and address(es) of the applicant(s).
  The date on which the patent was sealed – granted following the payment of a fee.
  A provisional specification (after 1852) protected the invention until work was completed. Not all inventions went beyond the provisional stage.
  The specification, which may be several pages long, provides the technical information about the invention, and has to be logged within six months of any provisional specification. It also includes statements to provide protection for the invention until the full application has been filed and to indicate that it is an improvement or innovation.
  Drawings (may be attached).
  The signature and date of completion of the specification.
  The name and address of one or more witnesses.

CORDINGLY'S FLOATING BATH.

A SIMPLE and ingenious novelty is now preparing for the convenience and comfort of those who may wish to enjoy a private bath in mid-day, on the Serpentine, or elsewhere. It is a boat, as represented in the Engraving, easily managed by one man. The bathing-place is situate at the stern, and is about four feet six inches wide, by six feet long, and from two feet six inches to five feet deep; the depth being regulated by the man, who, by working the windlass, can hoist or lower the bottom of the bath with great facility, as, being constructed principally of wood, the parts which slide into each other, like the tubes of a telescope, are so nearly buoyant as to be adjusted with little or no effort. Adjoining the Bath is a small but convenient place for preparation; the whole being enclosed with curtains. We understand it to be the invention of a working shipwright, who has registered it for three years, and intends it for sea, river, or lake bathing, as, from its lightness, it can be used for rowing; and the Bath being made to hoist up even with the bottom, the boat can be allowed to take the ground at any time without in jury. We think such a convenience would be a delightful adjunct to many parks and pleasure-grounds, with a river or lake.

Since 1854, the Patent Office has published its own journal under various titles – the Illustrated Official Journal (Patents) until 1930, and currently the Official Journal (Patents). Copies can be found in all of the PATLIB UK libraries, as well as in other large reference or business libraries. National and local newspapers often included descriptions of newly-granted patents, and these may include a photograph and a brief biography of the inventor and his/her invention. The London Gazette included some patents until the late 1940s, and these are included in the "State Intelligence: Patents and Designs Acts" section. Copies are deposited in major libraries and record offices and it also available on the internet at www.gazettes-online.co.uk.

Town and county directories include numerous advertisements, and these sometimes refer to patented goods – such as "L'Extincteur": Dicks patent portable self acting fire extinguisher", which was patented in October 1866. As well as finding copies in book form at local and county record offices, many 18th and 19th century directories can be accessed at www.historicaldirectories.org.uk. Some record offices and major libraries may have a name index to local patentees, and the one held at Birmingham Central Library indicates that virtually all of the patents granted in respect of button manufacture were to Birmingham inventors between 1840 and 1865.

Prior to the passing of the Married Women's Property Act in 1882, patents were generally only granted to widows or spinsters. However, some married women did become patentees in their own right, but any financial proceeds from their inventions had to be made to their husbands.

Although finding a patent granted to an ancestor won't help you to get further back with your research, it will certainly add to your knowledge of his/her life and times.

YORKSHIRE
FAMILY HISTORY FAIR
KNAVESMIRE EXHIBITION CENTRE
YORK RACECOURSE

SATURDAY 30TH JUNE 2007
10.00.a.m. to 4.30.p.m.

Many Stalls including:
Society of Genealogists, Federation Publications
The Family & Local History Handbook
Family Tree Magazine, Local Archives,
Family History Societies from all over Great Britain
Maps, Postcards, Printouts,
New & Second-hand Microfiche Readers
Genealogy Computer Programs
Advice Table

248 Tables in 2006

FREE CAR PARKING
ADMISSION £3.00

Further Details from:
Mr A Sampson
1 Oxgang Close, Redcar TS10 4ND
Tel: 01642 486615

NOTE FOR YOUR DIARY:

YEAR 2008 - YORKSHIRE FAMILY HISTORY FAIR
SATURDAY 28TH JUNE 2008

YEAR 2009 - YORKSHIRE FAMILY HISTORY FAIR
SATURDAY 27TH JUNE 2009

YEAR 2010 - YORKSHIRE FAMILY HISTORY FAIR
SATURDAY 26TH JUNE 2010

In association with Family History Monthly

Rate and Poll Books
Joseph O'Neill

Once the family historian has constructed the trunk and major branches of his family tree, he will want to flesh out the details of his ancestors' lives. Records which provide us with insight into their social standing and political activity help create a rounded picture of their community life. Particularly for the pre-1837 period, few sources are more valuable than rate and poll records.

A local tax based on the value of property is known as a rate. At various times over the last seven centuries rates have been levied for a range of purposes, from maintaining bridges to paying for the upkeep of local drainage systems. Some of these lists of occasional taxpayers have survived.

Nation-wide, compulsory registration of ratepayers, however, began in the early 17th century. The 1601 Relief of the Poor Act provided for registration of all property in order to determine the individual's contribution to the cost of providing for the poor. Once the administrative framework was established, the system was extended to raise money for other purposes, particularly the maintenance of local roads and gaols.

The parish was the normal administrative unit for the collection of the rates. Consequently, the records are usually held as part of the church records or in the County Record Office. Unfortunately, rate books – perhaps because there were so many of them – were not regarded as very important and hence many have been lost. Complete coverage of a parish for the 17th and 18th centuries is rare.

Earlier books, for the period before compulsory registration, are rarer still. Those that survive relate to the cities of London and Westminster, Southwark and the town centre parishes of the older boroughs. The survival of so many books from 1744 is partly due to an Act of that year which gave residents the right of inspection.

It is sometimes possible to fill the gaps in the Poor Rate books by referring to other rate books, such as those for scavengers' wages and sewer maintenance. Many of these post-1700 London books survive. Their great advantage is that they sometimes name the owners as well as the occupiers of the property. However, few pre-1700 books survive and as neither tax was levied every year, their coverage is patchy.

There are other problems with the early rate books. It was only in the late 18th century that a standard printed rate book came into use. Prior to that the information was recorded on a variety of sheets, which were usually wrapped together with old parchment deeds. Later many compilers favoured school exercise books.

changes in both numbering and street names and guard against the possibility of confusion by noting three names on each side of the house you are tracing.

If, however, your aim is to trace where an ancestor lived, then it is advisable to start with the first record of the ancestor's name and work forwards. By copying the three names on either side you will ensure that you are not thrown off track by name and numbering changes.

The numbering of London houses was authorised by a series of Acts dating from 1767 which provided for the improvement of public thoroughfares. Renumbering was a frequent occurrence in the next sixty years. The first general Act authorising numbering in the provinces was the Towns Improvement Act of 1847.

These idiosyncrasies are, however, often a delight. Occasionally the occupation of the ratepayer is noted or a brief description of the property included. Unexpectedly the researcher discovers that an ancestor's dwelling consisted of a 'house, two barns and large garden.' Even more interesting are the collector's marginal notes, telling us that the occupant is 'poor' or the premises consisted of 'a tannery.'

What is the value of these sources to the family historian? They are basically a list of householders or owners – sometimes both – together with the value of the property each occupied and the taxation due. From this information it is possible to make a number of inferences.

They allow us to confirm that an ancestor lived in a particular place at a specific time. From the amount of property he owned we can deduce his economic standing and perhaps his occupation. From this it is a short step to infer his role and status in the community.

We can also infer from the date when a building was first occupied and when it was built. We now know the date prior to which he lived elsewhere and this helps focus our search to locate his previous home. We can also work out when particular street names came into use.

Normally houses are listed street by street or road by road. This makes it easy to see who our ancestor's neighbours were. This information is frequently helpful as 17th and 18th century neighbours were more often related than is the case today.

The rate books can also be used to trace the occupants of a particular house over a number of years. The best way to do this is by working backwards, using street directories for the twentieth century. Beware of the possible

Rate books, like every source, have their own particular difficulties, which are most troublesome when houses are not numbered. In such cases you should always note the value of the property as a great change in the assessment suggests either that you may have been wrongly identified or that major building has taken place on the site.

Corner houses can also cause problems as they may be listed as part of one street in one assessment and part of another in a subsequent assessment. The splitting or combining of buildings between assessments may also lead to confusion as does the fact that compilers sometimes changed the order in which they listed dwellings, sometimes starting from one end of the street when previous records started from the other.

Another fascinating source, which may often supplement rate records, is the poll book.

Poll books detail how those entitled to vote in parliamentary elections exercised their right. This invaluable source came about because of the notorious partiality of returning officers in the general election of 1695.

The 1696 law required returning officers to make available to the public a copy of the poll and this continued until the 1868 general election, the last for which poll books were produced. The introduction of the secret ballot in 1872, meant that voting in parliamentary elections was no longer a public act, details of which were available to all.

From medieval times England was divided into parliamentary constituencies. Until the reform Act of 1832 each English county was a constituency entitled to return two MPs. Yorkshire was the exception, electing four. Welsh counties had one MP each, and most Welsh boroughs shared a representative with a neighbouring borough.

English boroughs generally elected two Members. Most of these were in the south of England until 1832 when the new concentrations of population in the industrial towns of the north and midlands gained fairer representation.

Local printers generally took on the task of producing the books and presenting the information, as they thought best. The result is that the format varies from area to area and over time. Some are a mine of information, providing the names, addresses, occupations and votes of all those who cast a vote and also the names of freemen who did not vote.

Others give no addresses but group voters according to their occupations. Poll books for county areas customarily listed voters in alphabetical order of parishes and provided the names, residences, place and nature of freehold and the occupier. Even more useful for those interested in the context of their ancestors' lives, some give details of the election campaign, including the candidates' speeches, street ballads, advertisements and even samples of the abuse hurled at opponents. Better still, those copies used by election agents are often annotated, providing snippets of information about our ancestors.

Fortunately, thousands of poll books survive. Most are in the county record offices for the area. Most of the more extensive sets are for the old towns and cities, such as Colchester, Coventry, Lincoln and Rochester. In areas where the electorate was tiny, the poll appeared in the local newspapers. Occasionally, where there are no surviving poll books, the original

manuscripts are sometimes to be found in the county record office.

Poll books are extremely rare for the period prior to 1696, when the sheriff became responsible for keeping a record of the poll in county elections. An Act of 1711 required the books to be deposited with the Clerk of the Peace and consequently most of the surviving books are from after this date.

If the ancestor you are tracing was a parliamentary candidate, the poll book can tell us a great deal about him. It is possible to discover not only what he said to the electorate but the social and economic status of those who supported him. By studying poll books over a long period it is possible to uncover patterns of political allegiance and to examine the extent to which they overlapped with family ties.

It is important to remember that prior to the Reform Bill of 1832 the franchise was restricted to property owners and only a minority of men had the right to vote. Fortunately, this is not necessarily a major problem for all parts of the country. In many constituencies, especially the 'potwalloper' boroughs where all householders had the vote, most adult males enjoyed the franchise, including labourers and artisans.

For these it tells us about their political allegiance, their occupation and their address.

Poll books are the precursors of electoral registers. Only those included in the register were entitled to vote, so registration was far more comprehensive than for the poll book and there are electoral registers for national elections for every year since 1832 (except for 1916-17 and 1944-5). However, the register has no information about who actually voted or how they cast their vote.

Nor are the registers a complete record of all adults. The franchise was extended on a number of occasions during the previous two centuries, most significantly in 1832, 1867 and 1884. On the latter occasion the result was to enfranchise the majority of male householders over the age of twenty-one. However, historians estimate that as late as 1911 only about 60% of adult males had the vote.

The major change was in 1918 when all men over the age of twenty-one – provided they were normally resident in the community – got the vote. This was also the year when women first got the vote in national elections, though it was limited to those over 30

Electoral registers are also useful for tracing families after the 1901 census. Once you have located the family at a specific address you can use the registers to determine how long they lived there and roughly when they moved. You should bear in mind, however, that the information in the register was compiled about six months prior to its issue. Between those two dates many of those listed died or moved away.

Despite their limitations, these sources help locate our ancestors within the web of social and political relationships, which made up a large part of their public lives.

who were householders or married to householders. It was not until 1928 that they got the vote on the same basis as men.

Until 1918 electoral registers contained names, addresses and the qualification to vote of every elector in the constituency. Remember, however, that many 19th century registers were in two sections: one for property owners and one for occupiers, so it is necessary to check both. It is also helpful to keep in mind the way in which the organisation of registers changed during the 19th century: in the early period they listed electors in alphabetical order but as they grew in numbers this arrangement proved unwieldy. Most registers then listed voters by wards and then streets and finally by house number. This became standard practice after 1918 when the extension of the franchise swelled the electorate. In effect it is extremely difficult to locate an individual in a post-1918 register without the address.

This is particularly the case with the Service Voters' registers which were compiled in 1945 to permit service men and women to vote in the General Election in their home constituency. Some of these registers survive in the local record offices or the local authority archives. They include the person's name, address, unit and number. Unfortunately, they are not indexed by name, so you will need a home address to track down a serviceman and find the unit in which he served.

Despite these limitations, the registers are useful for tracking down relatives when you know the general area in which they lived – though this may prove a major task when searching post-1918 registers which are very large and organised according to electoral wards.

Further Reading
As a general introduction to the subject it is still hard to beat *The History of the Local Rates in England* by E. Cannon. Most rate books, poll books and registers are in your local County Record Office. You can find details of your all CROs at *www.ukonline.gov.uk* But you should not assume that they hold all the relevant sources. There are also some important regional archives, such as the National Library of Wales at *www.llgc.org.uk* the National Archives at *www.nationalarchives.gov.uk* and the National Library of Scotland at *www.nas.gov.uk*.
The West Country Studies Library is in Castle Street, Exeter EX4 3PQ, T: 01392 384216 W: www.devon-ccgov.uk/library/locstudy It is invaluable for anyone researching ancestors from Cornwall, Devon, Somerset or Dorset. The Guildhall Library (details below) is extremely important for all with London ancestors and also has much of interest to other researchers, including a large holding of rate books.

Poll books and registers
If you think an ancestor was an MP, you will find details of the election in Judd IV, GP, *Members of Parliament 1734 – 1852* or McCalmont, FH, *The Parliamentary Poll Book of all Elections 1832 –1906*. The location of most electoral registers, organised by county, is listed in Gibson J.& Rogers C, *Electoral registers since 1832 and burgess rolls* (FFHS). Gibson J. & Rogers C, *Poll Books* (FFHS) has maps of England and Wales showing borough and county constituencies both before and after 1832. You can check out the major holdings of poll books and registers at the major repositories online: **Guildhall Library**, Aldermanbury, London EC2P 2EJ at *www.ihrinfo.ac.uk/gh www.ihr.sas.ac.uk/ihr/ghmnu www.collage.nhil.com*
The Society of Genealogists, 14, Charterhouse Buildings, Goswell road, London EC1M 7BA at www.sog.org.uk/ You will find details of the British Library's collection in Cheffins, RHA, *Parliamentary constituencies and their registers since 1832* (The British Library)

Workhouse People
Ray Whitehand

When ever the word Workhouse appears in research, it always conjures up an image of destitution and hardship; of paupers and beggars, and of the most base of society. For this reason, when the topic is brought up in research circles, a common response often heard is "Oh no, my ancestor was too well off to have been found in that place". Don't you believe it! You can find reference to just about anyone within Workhouse records, whether it is the weekly or monthly minute books of the House of Industry, or the Overseers accounts of the parish workhouses which predated them.

Gentry:
In the first instance with all these establishments, whether Parish Workhouse, House of Industry, or Union buildings, it was the local **'landed gentry and business persons'** who were responsible for the very **creation** of the workhouse. Premises had to be acquired, either by benevolence or purchase, from those affluent landowners. So it is to that sector we begin the story.

Was your ancestor the wealthy James Vernon, land owner of Great Wratting. He was one of the most benevolent of them all. In his Will he not only left a messuage called Weathercock Farm, to be used as a workhouse for the three villages of Great Wratting, Great Thurlow & Barnardson, he also left other lands and properties to be rented out to provide the income for the workhouse master etc. Equally when the parish of Barkig debated the need for a workhouse in the village, it was a property left to the parish by the late Lord of the Manor,

Sir Francis Theobald, which was converted into a Workhouse for the benefit of the poor.

Such generosity benefited the whole community, in as much, while it obviously provided aid to the poor, it also benefited the rate payers, as funding such projects ultimately fell on the shoulders or rather in the pockets of the parishioners. Those who did not own properties often made monetary gifts or loans. In the instance of the aforementioned Barking parish. The cost of converting the building amounted to £231.8.8 ?d. This was partly funded by loans from individuals including £8.14.0d by Mr John Chenery, £100 from Mrs Ruffols, and £60 from Mr Parker. All of which contributed to bring the final amount required from the parish rate to just £62.14.8^{1}/2d.

With the advent of the Houses of Industry, a more organised approach was called for. Larger more imposing buildings were now the order of the day. This meant land had to be purchased, buildings planned and constructed. Funding such projects took an enormous amount of effort, private moneys being gratefully accepted. We learn from the Samford Incorporation weekly minute books for 1766 of Mr James Lynn, who loaned the sum of £400, **until proper security had been obtained.** Thereupon he would receive interest on his loan at a rate of £4 10s per cent per annum. At the same meeting it was agreed three pieces of land were to be purchased from the estate of Mr Edmund Jennings for the building of the new House of Industry.

Elsewhere, funds for the building of the Wangford House of Industry at Shipmeadow included £500 from Nathaniel Colby of Great Yarmouth, with other benevolents including Mr Richard Chase of St John who lent £200; Mr Isaac Whayman of Sudbourne who lent £100; and Mr Aldous Arnold of Lowestoft who lent £100.

Workhouse designers:
Before they could be built these buildings had to be designed. This involved people like Thomas Fulcher of Ipswich, who designed the Houses of Industry at both Bulcamp in 1764 and Onehouse in 1779-80. For Bulcamp he received 15 guineas plus the cost of his journeys and attendances. These men had to present their work to the stearing committees for approval. The *SHIPMEADOW MINUTE BOOK 1764-1768* gives detail of the debate relating to the standard of a set of plans presented by a Mr Bame. While his efforts were acknowledged as the most acceptable, there was a question over the accuracy of his plans. The person in charge of the construction, Mr Redgrave was *'desired to draw out a perfect plan upon the outlines of the plan produced by Mr Bame'*, and present them at the next Directors meeting.

Construction workers
Whether small parish workhouses or enormous House of Industry, local builders were sought to carry out the construction work. At Wingfield in 1757, local builder Thomas Card of Stradbroke provided a quotation for converting a cottage into the Workhouse. Totalling £31.3.11d it itemised such as *'for pouling* [pulling] *down the old stayrs* [stairs] *and putting up the new, and finding all materials £0-14-0d*, and *'for 1,500 plain tiles and 20 roof tiles £2-8-4d*

On the larger House of Industry buildings a surveyor was employed to oversee the construction of the premises. We learn from the first quarterly minute book that in July 1766 John Redgrave was elected as Surveyor and Inspector of the building of the new Workhouse at Bulcamp; while the weekly minute books of the Samford Incorporation give detail relating to 'site foreman' Robert Harland Esq. such as when he was instructed to inform Mr Chandler of the Scantlings to supply timbers etc for the building of the workhouse, and to *procure some*

skilful workman to carry out the work. Standards of workmanship were vigorously monitored. If any work was found to be substandard retribution was implemented. Thomas Hunt, builder of Oulton was informed the lump and paving bricks he had supplied the House of Industry at Bulcamp with, were *'not as good as the original sample, and therefore not acceptable'*. A subsequent inventory of the stock detailed the bricks supplied as 1600 good bricks; 1050 bad and soft ones, 200 soft lumps, 2000 well burnt and 1500 good stock bricks. A letter was sent out informing him payment would not be made for the 1050 bad bricks or the 200 lumps but that they would be returned. For a small business man this could have been drastic, even putting him out of business, and at the mercy of the workhouse himself. A second instance reported at the same weekly meeting involved the aforementioned site manager Mr Redgrave, who reported the washing copper delivered by Mr Preston was some thirty gallons over size. This resulted in Mr Preston losing the 'contract' to supply, instead it was given to a Mr Aldridge of Harleston. One mans loss another mans gain.

Management:
The early Parish Workhouses were controlled by **parish overseers and churchwardens**. These would have been such as local businessmen or dignitaries. They would hold the post for a period of either 6 months or a year. Part of their responsibility was the day-to-day management of the workhouse. Their account books not only give detail of the parishes affairs, but by definition can show the degree of literacy or numeracy of the residing Overseer. If your ancestor filled this position, then you can gain a very good picture of his office skills.

The *'Directors and Acting Guardians'* who ran those Houses of Industry were identified as *'Gentlemen, Clergy and Principal Inhabitants'*. These would invariably be identified in the Minute books, as in Blything's opening minute book, where in excess of 200 persons from the parishes which encompassed the Incorporation are identified. From this gathering the initial Quarterly committee was selected. They would sit 4 times a year to debate and sanction all aspects of the management of the poor. From within this group a **second committee** was formed, whose responsibility it was to run the Workhouse itself. This committee would sit every week. The judgements and decisions of these two committees, together with the names of those attending each meeting were recorded in Quarterly or Weekly Committee books. Again an informative picture of those involved can be gauged from the various references, whether by instance or inference. Such as Mr Marriott, one of the Director's of Stow House of Industry, who it would appear may have been forgetful, as on 2 November 1807 a letter was dispatched to him: '*Sir lest it escape your memory I beg to remind Mr Marriott of his being Director at Stow House of Industry for the month of November 1807. I am Sir Your Most Onorable [sic] servant James Claxton, clerk*.

Staffing:

This was one of the key issues in running a good workhouse. Numbers were kept to a minimum to ensure the smallest of burdens on the local ratepayer, while ensuring sufficient to maintain the disciplined reguime, which was demanded.

By very definition, the parish workhouse did not require either the number or range of staff the later establishments did. The role of the **Workhouse master or governor** here would have been a hands on position in all bar the largest of organizations. For this reason the Overseers tended to employ people with a range of skills. The typical character targeted was one of good local standing. As Religion played a big part in the ethos of the workhouse, as indeed it did in the everyday world of the 17th and 18th century, a person of C of E faith was essential. Experience within the Workhouse was important. Adverts would invariably state a minimum age for potential candidates, While St Margaret's Ipswich required someone not under the age of 45, the overseers of Woodbridge narrowed the eligible down to between 30 and 50, while at Wilby in 1803 a woman aged between 40 and 50 was sought. Positions would customarily be offered for a specific period of time, as at Framsden in 1817

when the position was advertised for a person 'desirous of taking the poor of the workhouse' for a period of three years. Another key attribute was the knowledge of the particular work undertook in the establishment. At Haverhill the overseers stipulated the applicants need to be qualified in the 'sack industry', while when the same post at Hadleigh became vacant, one of the criteria required was a knowledge of the spinning trade.

As in all walks of life there were **good and bad masters**. Temptation was always only a hands reach away. On 29 June 1781 at Loes and Wilford, the Governor of the House of Industry, Mr Thomas Tibbs was charged with *imbezzling and misapplying the monies goods and chattels belonging to the Corporation* and also of disobeying the orders of the Directors and Guardians. This resulted in not only a loss of employment, he was duly charged with '*imbezzling and misapplying of the monies goods and chattells of the said Corporation according to the Act of Parliament for such hundreds*. The same committee ordered John Elliott the Schoolmaster and House Clerk to take charge of the house while a new Governor was sought.

Professionals

Some of the key staff were the medical personnel, surgeons, apothecaries and nurses. As with most of the employment in the workhouse, conditions and responsibilities were laid down by the Quarterly committee. At Shipmeadow when two newly appointed surgeons Mr Wolfram Lewis of Bungay and Mr J Chambers of Beccles were taken on in 1768, rules designated that at least one of them was to attend the house twice a week, and at any other time as required or deemed necessary. However, while it was their responsibility to ensure a female midwife was available to attend to every woman in labour in the house, they themselves only need attend if requested to by either patient or nurse. For this they would receive a salary of £80 for the forthcoming 12 months.

Conditions in the workhouse were often grim, the threat of an infectious outbreak was potentially deadly. When an infestations of small pox hit the Melton House of Industry in January 1781 the surgeon Mr Salmon was ordered to inoculate all of the inmates 'who desired it'. It would appear Directors would recognise a good employee. Susan Plumb, a nurse at Shipmeadow in the 1785 was given a gratuity of one guinea '**for the great fatigue and trouble she has had in nursing for the small pox at the pest house, which she has executed with great diligence and attention**'.

A few of the Parish Workhouses employed a Schoolmaster or Teacher though often only once or twice a week. However with the advent of the House of Industry, this post became a full time position in the workhouse. In March 1781 the Loes & Wilford committee appointed John Elliot of Ufford as School Master & House Clerk. His remit was to teach the children to read and write and to keep the weekly accounts of the whole workhouse. On top of his salary he received board, washing and lodging in the House. He was also allowed to dine with the Governor and have his own bedroom.

At Samford in June 1764 John Shave of Ipswich in the County of Suffolk bookseller was elected treasurer of the Incorporation with a salary of £5 per annum; while at the same meeting John Kirby, an Attorney of Law was selected as clerk with a payment of £10 per annum

As spinning and weaving was such an important aspect of the work in the house, another key job was that of a Woolcomber. William Barber of Nayland, assumed this role at the Loes & Wilford H of I. having been recommended by John Roche, a manufactorer of Norwich. Part of his role was to acquire sufficient wool for distribution to the workhouse. For this he was paid £9 per annum plus house board, washing and lodgings for his trouble and care. Again if William was your ancestor, there is a wealth of information on his dealings.

Wages
Details of salaries and remunerations for the staff can be found in the Overseers account, Wages for the housemaster were comparable with those of other 'professional' occupations. When the above Thomas Tibbs, yeoman of Ipswich accepted the position of Governor to the Loes and Wilford workhouse in February 1768 he received a salary of £35 per annum. In June 1775 this rose to £50 per annum. By comparison in June 1768 the surgeon Samuel Salmon received a salary of £40 per annum, while George Jones Palmer, chaplain, received £35 per annum. However a schoolmaster in 1780 could expect just £16 per year.

Tradesmens
Throughout the whole period of the workhouse, be it Parish, House of Industry or Union, there would have been regular work for local trademen. We have already discussed the involvement of builders in the construction of the premises. Once the buildings were up and running there would still have been regular amounts of work for them. Improvement and repairs would have provided virtually constant employment for a reliable builder. Instances of the persons who carried out such work are

scattered throughout accounts and minute books. As an instance, within two years of it opening, the Wangford House of Industry's governor reported 75 squares of glass in the windows on the south side of House; 26 on the north side; 42 on the east front; 40 on the west front and 17 in the cellar in the 'Capitol House' were broken. A second report two weeks later reported a further 39 squares on south side, 36 on east court; 21 on west court, 16 on north side, 7 in weaving shop; and 4 in cellars. This would suggest a regular income for the chosen glazier.

Once the establishments were inhabited, provisions would have been required for both the inmates and the staff. Tradesmen such as butchers, grocers, cheesemen drapers, and tailors etc were sought to provide those daily necessities. These could be a lucrative form of business. Prior to the opening of Shipmeadow, Mr John Girling, of All Saints initially tendered to supply the house with cheese and butter until the following Christmas, including *true made four meal cheese and meal of milk as comes from the cow at 39s 6d per weigh*; and *ffirkins of butter fresh put up that will stand a long time if required* at 26s 9d. however following the acceptance of his proposals, Mr Girling supplied on average 8 to 10 whey of cheese a week to the Incorporation. Although he received at least one rebuke for providing cheeses of sub standard, he continued to supply the house until his death in the late 1780s.

An example of the involvement of the local community is clearly demonstrated in a Governor's weekly bill. The following shopping list was obtained by the Governor of Wangford House of Industry in the summer of 1782:
William Hunter, drapery; £25-15-1^1/2d
Robert Moore, grocery, £12-10-0d
John Price, tiles, £6-3-6d
John Plowman, leather, £ 6- 2-7^1/2d
Thomas Baldwin, bricklayer, £6-14-4?d
William Cattermole, shoes, £7-6-5d
Owen Holmes, grocery, £ 6-17-10d
William Barber, coffins, £3-12-2d
Robert Boyden, malt, £14-10-0d
Gooch and Cotton, lime, £1-4-6d; tiles, ^{3}/4d;
flour, £27-0-0d; coals, £10-1-0d
Thomas Hunt, hosiery, £8-18-0d
John Boby, for a warp, £1-9-1d
James Howton, burial fee £1-10-0d
James Gooch, blacksmith, 14/11d
James Cuddon, wheel mending, 18/3d
John Kinsgbury, oatmeal, £1-13-4d
John Robbitt, whitesmith, £1-4-7^1/2d
Frances Balls, cheese, £16-16-0d
Frances Doughton, paint, 1/9?d
John Wilson , corn grinding, £2-12-6d

Another area where outdoor business was required was in the provision of equipment and material for the employment of the inmates. According to the 1767-1780 minute book for Bulcamp, notices were sent to several tailors for anyone interested in making up clothing for the poor of the house to attend an interview later that month. The Wangford weekly committee sent out an order on 3 August 1767 that Mr Deeks was to send enough leather into the house to employ one man for a month making shoes. It was further noted that Matthew Spilling and Rhoda his wife should be employed in **cutting out shirts, shifts, caps, mobs, aprons mantles hankerchiefs, under petticoats and upper ones** for the poor, with the work of making the garments put out to tender amongst the local tailors.

Workhouse production:
The production side of the workhouse meant contacts with business men of the outside world was essential. On 5 May 1767 a Mr Mark Butcher propositioned the committee to buy all the yarn spun in the house, at the agreed regulation rate for spinners at 10s for every twenty one skains or seven pence a clew for spinning, while at Wangford, the Governor reported that on 23 June 1767 he recieved from Mr John Spilling of Earsham for the spinning of 170 clew of tow yarn at 6d per clew which equated to £4.5.0d.

A good instance of how the dealings and decisions of the workhouse reguime affected individuals in the locality is demonstrated in the story of one James OAKES, a yarn merchant who supplied the House of Industry at Melton with materials and cloth. Described as a man of some consequence of Bury St Edmunds, he originally enjoyed a period of some benefit as a direct result of his dealings with the workhouse. However during the depression of the 1780s when the profits from spinning slumped dramatically he suffered a drastic turn of fortune, when the Directors and Guardians of the House decided to dispense with his services. Instead they employed local paupers and inmates from the workhouse. The idea was for the yarn spun in the house to be delivered

to Norwich by a Melton carrier. When this scheme failed, largely due to the inexperience of the Directors and Guardians in the cloth trade, it only served to highlight the value of knowledge in a given trade. But whether James Oakes gained any solice from the demise, the history books don't tell us.

Another area where local businesses were directly involved was the taking on of apprenticeships of the inmates with local businesses. Again workhouse minute books, or accounts can highlight the involvement of local businesses in the scheme. For instance the Shipmeadow records record that Mr William Felmingham of South Elmham St James, agreed to take on 12 year old Ann Smith until she reached the age of 18, 'according to the Act of Parliament governing such matters'. Many inmates would partake as 'outworkers' with local farmers. Here they would spend the day working on the farm, only to return to the workhouse for board and lodgings.

So even if your ancestors were amongst the fortunate ones not to have found themselves at the door of the workhouse, you could very well find instances of how their lives were affected and possibly enriched by this most demised of institutions. While it was always deemed the last place on earth, it provided an income and livelihood for many who lived during the 300 plus years of the existence of THE WORKHOUSE.

Sources:
Samford Union Committee book 1766-1769, ADA7/AB1/1.
Shipmeadow Minute Books 1764-1790;
S.R.O.(L)36/AB1/#
Stow documents: . I.R.O. FB23/G8/1.
Bulcamp minute books 1767-1790 ADA1/AB3/#
The Oakes Diaries: Business, Politics and the Family in Bury St. Edmunds, 1778-1827: Volume I: Introduction; James Oakes' Diaries 1778-1800 edited by Jane Fiske. The Boydell Press for Suffolk Records Society, 1990.
A History of Suffolk: by Dymond and Northeast. Published by Phillimore & Co 1985.

Where do you go next?
Why not try the Society of Genealogists?
Else Churchill - Genealogy Officer Society of Genealogists

The Society of Genealogists is a remarkable library of printed source materials and unique manuscript collections. Now comprising four floors, the library holds all the sources that one would expect to help family historians begin their research and there is indeed a lot for anyone who is researching in the period from 1837. With access to online indexes, often free, along with guides and text books the library holds everything one needs to get started.

However, most people approach the Society having already undertaken some research and are generally wondering what to do next after having reached the early 1800s. The Society is very much seen as a place to come if you are researching before 1837 and possibly have reached an impasse.

Where did your ancestors live?
The Middle Library (on the first floor) holds thousands of indexed transcripts of parish registers from all the counties in the UK. The library has also been keen to collect fiche or film copies of original PRs or BTs so that we hold most registers that are available. We hold the largest collection of copies of monumental inscriptions from churches, churchyards and cemeteries all around the UK (and overseas), which often supplement burial register information. There are a huge number of other sources for places noted in the Society of Genealogists' library online catalogue that give the names of the inhabitants. The strength of course is our diversity bringing together this material from counties all around the UK and further afield.

Lists of Names
The Society has always gone out of its way to collect lists of people living in a particular place at a particular time. Even if a list doesn't give as much information as the census itself it can at least prove that your ancestor was what we genealogists call "flourishing". The most extensive collection of lists of this type held in the library are the Trade Directories and Poll Books (listing those who voted) – largely from the eighteenth and early nineteenth centuries.

Lost in London?
We have regular requests for help from family historians who have found an ancestor in London, say in the late 1700s, but have no idea of where they may have come from. Most families will have some connection with London, nearly all surnames are to be found there and it is said that by the middle of the 1700s London made up about one fifth of the population of England. There are many sources in the library for London.

Pallot's Marriage Index - the most comprehensive finding aids for marriages in this area from 1800-1837 can be used free of charge via access to the Ancestry.co.uk website at the Society's Library. Don't forget that many Londoners obtained marriage licences from the Archbishop of Canterbury's courts of the Vicar General and Faculty Office. These are indexed and can be viewed on Britishorigins.com and the films of the original allegations are held in the Lower Library at the SoG. Percival Boyd's Marriage index (also on Britishorigins.com) has a good coverage of London before 1754.

Several useful SoG databases of Londoners can be found at the Library via the Britishorigins website. These include various City of London Livery Company Apprentice Registers, which have hundreds of thousands of references from the earliest entries to the mid nineteenth century. You might find Cliff Webb's book *My Ancestors were Londoners* useful for ideas. Boyd's Inhabitants of London is a remarkable collection of notes on some 60,000 families in the City mostly for the seventeenth and eighteenth centuries but with some earlier and a very few later entries. The index and images of the notes can be found on line. Many of the sources used by Boyd are described in the Society's publication *My Ancestors were Freemen of the City of London* by Vivienne E Aldous. Boyd's London Burials Index includes approximately a quarter of a million entries for adult males from many registers in London before 1837 is the Britishorigins website.

What did your ancestors do?

The Society of Genealogists has always collected printed sources relating to our ancestors' occupations. There is an area in the Upper library specially designated for professions, trades and occupations and the Library has some unique unpublished materials as well as printed lists. Along with many sources relating to professions on these shelves there are also directories of civil servants, parliamentarians, accountants, architects and artists. There is a lot on sportsmen and women and of course on craftsmen who made things such as clockmakers, scientific instrument makers or furniture makers. A recent publication from the Society is *My Ancestor was a Lawyer* by Brian Brooks and Mark Herber.

The Trinity House Petitions relate to families of mariners who fell on hard times after the death of the seaman from1787- 1854 with a few miscellaneous petitions and pensions to 1899. The index is reproduced on Britishorigins and the films of the petitions are in the Lower Library. The records of the Teachers Registration Council (1902-1948) were passed on to the Society of Genealogists from the Department of Education in the 1990s.

The religions shelves bring together sources not only for Anglican clergy but other denominations and nonconformists, especially Quakers and Huguenots, Baptists, Methodists and Jews. Peter

Towey's new work *My Ancestor was an Anglican Clergyman* may be of interest.

If you have had problems tracking down a will before 1858 then the Society of Genealogists is a good place to start looking for it. If there is an index or finding aid telling you whether the will exists then the SoG will have it. Will abstracts and other evidences of death made for the purposes of the Bank of England from 1717-1845. are indexed via British Origins. It's interesting how many of these BoE abstracts suggest a will from the PCC was presented to the Bank as evidence but which can't be found in the probate films at TNA/FRC so it's fortuitous that this is another collection rescued by the SoG that would otherwise have been destroyed.

The Society holds all published school registers and alumni records of universities that it can find. One might consider apprenticeship as a form of education. One of its first projects was to index the Inland Revenue (IR1) records of the tax levied on eighteenth century apprenticeships. *The Apprentices of Great Britain* volumes covering the period 1710-1774 are in the Upper Library and reproduced on the British Origins site.

Your ancestor may have been the litigious argumentative sort. An invaluable index to many Chancery, Exchequer and other records, known as the Bernau Index is held at the Society. This largely deals with cases before about 1750. The Society publishes a guide *How to use the Bernau Index* by Hilary Sharp that explains what records are indexed and how to follow up a reference at TNA

What's Been Done Before?

The Society has always encouraged genealogists to write up their family history and deposit copies in the library.

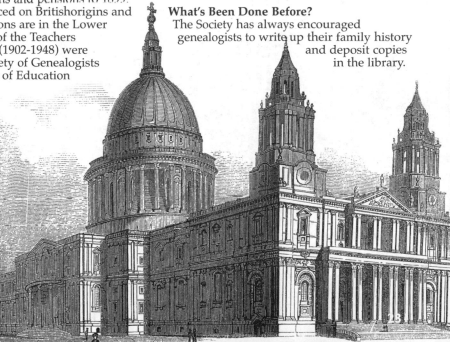

There are literally thousands of bound family histories on the Family History Shelves that will never be found elsewhere. The Library also provides a home for research should no other family member be interested. The Special Collections and the Document Collection of miscellaneous, manuscript, genealogical research notes are a tremendous resource, containing much that is unique.

Getting the best from the Society of Genealogists
Visitors are always amazed by the size of the Society's Library and it takes a while getting to know our little idiosyncrasies and hiding places. There are regular free tours of the Library on alternate Saturday mornings, the Librarian gives regular free onsite lectures on using the library and the catalogue and we run a ten week course on getting the best from the library each Autumn. We try our hardest to welcome and look after beginners and new visitors knowing that there will be much that could help them take their family history back into the eighteenth century and beyond. The volunteers offer help at the information desks on each floor and one-to-one advice sessions can be booked on tour Saturdays.

Anyone using the library must check the online computer catalogue. It's designed for family historians to tell you what we have, what it looks like and where it is. It lists what the Library holds for places, surnames, general searches for county wide sources, occupations, religions, indexes, finding aids and much, much more. The catalogue can be accessed from all floors and via a link from our website www.sog.org.uk. The catalogue is the gateway to the remarkable library of the Society of Genealogists. Open the door and come inside.

The Society of Genealogists can be found at 14 Charterhouse buildings, Goswell Road, London EC1M 7BA tel. 020 7251 8799 www.sog.org.uk

Non members are welcome but as the library has no public finding will have to pay a day search fee ranging from £4 per hour to £18 for a whole day. Hence it may be cheaper to become a member. There is a joining fee of £10 (payable once only) and an annual subscription of £43 (£41.50 if paid by direct debit). Overseas subscription is just £25 per year. Members have free access to the library, discounts on publications, events and some free access to SoG data published on Britishorigins.com. The library is open Tuesday to Saturdays, usually from 10-6pm but stays open until 8pm on Thursdays.

WHERE CAN YOU

- Access over 100,000 items on local & family history?
- Use the largest collection of parish register & census index copies in Britain?
- Get immediate, valuable advice from experienced genealogists?
- Attend informative lectures presented by experts?
- Browse our great range of publications?
- Surf a growing range of online records?

YOU WILL GET ALL THESE AND MORE FROM

THE SOCIETY OF GENEALOGISTS
the one-stop resource for everyone in family & local history

Take advantage of our unique, refurbished **LIBRARY** with over 9,000 Parish Register copies and wide-ranging material on Civil Registration, Censuses, County Records, Poll Books, Heraldry & Family Histories - on microfilm, fiche and PC.

Visit our online sales ordering system at www.sog.org.uk for details of society **PUBLICATIONS** – over 150 titles containing valuable information on where to find source material. Titles include My Ancestor was a Lawyer, My Ancestors were Watermen and My Ancestor was an Anglican Clergyman.

Join the Society – **MEMBERSHIP** gives you:

- FREE access to the library & borrowing rights
- A 10% discount on all Society publications and a 20% discount on lectures & courses
- FREE copies of the highly respected Genealogists' Magazine
- FREE access to an increasing range of online records

all for **just £43 a year!** *

For an **INFORMATION PACK**, simply email the Membership Team on:
membership@sog.org.uk   OR   Tel: 020 7553 3291

MAKE THE MOST OF YOUR RESEARCH WITH:
Society of Genealogists, 14 Charterhouse Buildings, Goswell Road, London EC1M 7BA
Tel: 020 7251 8799   Fax: 020 7250 1800   Web: www.sog.org.uk

* Initial Joining Fee £10.00

Registered Charity No. 233701. Company limited by guarantee. Registered No. 115703. Registered office, 14 Charterhouse Buildings, London, EC1M 7BA

General Register Office for Scotland
The Registration of Births, Marriages and Deaths in Scotland

Registration of baptisms and proclamations of marriage was first enacted in Scotland by a Council of the Scottish clergy in 1551. The earliest recorded event - a baptism of 27 December 1553 - can be found in the register of baptisms and banns for Errol in Perthshire. Following the Reformation registration of births, deaths and marriages became the responsibility of the ministers and session clerks of the Church of Scotland. Standards of record-keeping varied greatly from parish to parish, however, and even from year to year. This together with evidence of the deterioration and loss of register volumes through neglect led to calls for the introduction of a compulsory and comprehensive civil registration system for Scotland. This came into being on 1 January 1855 with the establishment of the General Register Office for Scotland headed by the Registrar General and the setting up of 1027 registration districts. In 2006 registration districts numbered 156.

Records in the custody of the Registrar General

The main series of vital events records of interest to genealogists are held by the Registrar General at New Register House in Edinburgh. They are as follows:

Old Parish Registers (1553-1854): the 3500 surviving register volumes (the OPRs) compiled by the Church of Scotland session clerks were transferred to the custody of the Registrar General after 1855. They record the births and baptisms; proclamations of banns and marriages; and deaths and burials in some 900 Scottish parishes. They are far from complete, however, and most entries contain relatively little information. Microfilm copies of these records are available world-wide and there are computerised and microfiche indexes to baptisms and marriages. A project to index the death and burial entries got under way in 1997 and is still on-going.

Register of neglected entries (1801-1854): this register, compiled by the Registrar General, consists of births, deaths and marriages proved to have occurred in Scotland between 1801 and 1854 but which had not been recorded in the OPRs. These entries are included in the all-Scotland computerised indexes.

Statutory registers of births, deaths and marriages (from 1855): these registers are compiled by district registrars. They are despatched by the district examiners to New Register House at the end of each calendar year.

Adopted children register (from 1930): persons adopted under orders made by the Scottish courts. The earliest entry is for a birth in October 1909.

Register of divorces (from 1984): records the names of the parties, the date and place of marriage, the date and place of divorce and details of any order made by the court regarding financial provision or custody of children. Prior to May 1984 a divorce would be recorded in the RCE (formerly the Register of Corrected Entries, now the Register of Corrections Etc), and a cross-reference would be added to the marriage entry.

Births, deaths and marriages occurring outside Scotland (The Minor Records): these relate to persons who are or were usually resident in Scotland.

Marine Register of Births and Deaths (from 1855)
Air Register (from 1948)
Service Records (from 1881)
War Registers - Boer War (1899-1902), two World Wars
Consular returns (from 1914)
High Commissioners' returns (from 1964)
Foreign Marriages (from 1947)
Register of births, deaths and marriages in foreign countries (1860-1965)

Census records (from 1841): these are the enumerators' manuscript books of the decennial census of the population of Scotland. They record the name, age, marital state, occupation and birthplace of every member of a household present on census night. Census records are closed for 100 years and only the schedules for the 1841 to 1901 census are open to the public.

To discover more details about the history of these records please see GROS's publication *"Jock Tamson's Bairns: a history of the records of the General Register Office for Scotland"* by Cecil Sinclair, ISBN 1 874451 591, 52 pages, cost £2.00. See www.gros-scotland.gov.uk for details of how to order.

Searching at New Register House

New Register House was opened in 1861 as a purpose-built repository for Scotland's civil

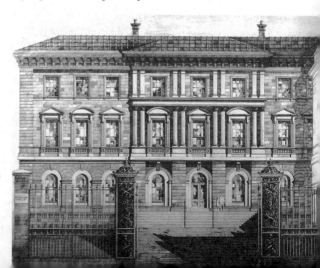

registration records. Information about services and opening hours is available on the family records pages of GROS's website www.gro-scotland.gov.uk.

Indexes to the statutory records (including overseas events), OPR baptism and marriage entries, and the 1871, 1881, 1891 and 1901 census records are available on computer with most entries linked to digital images created as part of the DIGROS (Digitally Imaging the Genealogical Records of Scotland's people) project. For records not yet in digital form, there is self-service access to statutory register pages on microfiche and OPR and Census records on roll microfilm. It is also possible to order official extracts of any entry.

Online Access to the New Register House Indexes

The all-Scotland computerised indexes and images can also be accessed from local registration offices which have links to the New Register House system. Some offices provide search room facilities. The indexes and images to birth records over 100 years old, marriage records over 75 years old and death records over 50 years old are available for searching on the pay-per-view website ScotlandsPeople www.scotlandspeople.gov.uk.

Scottish Family History Service **project**
GROS is working with the National Archives of Scotland and the Court of the Lord Lyon to create a joint family history centre - to be called the ScotlandsPeople Centre - based in General Register House and New Register House. Further information about this project is available on the Scottish Family History Service Project information website at www.scotlandspeoplehub.gov.uk.

Maiden Names in Scotland
David W Webster FSA Scot

More and more Scottish statutory records are becoming available on-line. At present births are available from 1855 – 1904, marriages from 1855 – 1929, and deaths from 1855 – 1954, i.e. closure periods respectively of 100, 75 and 50 years. In all cases it is both indexes and digitised images that are available. In January 2006 the data for an additional year will be added to each record series.

At present indexes and digitised images for the 1901, 1891 1871 and 1861 censuses are available, together with an index and transcripts of the 1881 census. By the time that you read this article the 1841 will also be on line, and maybe the 1851.

The purpose of this article is to explain how maiden names are treated in these records; both in terms of the information in the full register entries and the indexes that have been created from them.

Unless this aspect is fully understood, it is easy to miss a record of interest.

Women in Scotland have always retained their maiden names during the whole of their life, even after marriage. When Jean Smith marries John Brown she might well follow general convention and be known as Mrs Brown, but in the eyes of Scots law she is Jean Brown maiden surname Smith.

Should she divorce or her first husband die, and she then remarries Alexander McDonald, then, formally she is known as Mrs McDonald, formerly Brown maiden

surname Smith, and if she married for a third time to James Clark, then she would correctly be known as Jean Clark, formerly McDonald, previously Brown, maiden name Smith, although it isn't always that such a marital history is fully described in this detailed manner! It's not unknown, however, to find this on register entries, in which case it can be a real bonus.

In everyday life it wasn't uncommon for her still to be known to her friends and family as Jean Smith, who happened to have married John Brown.

On her gravestone it was common practice for her to be shown as Jean Smith wife of John Brown, or if John had predeceased her, then the gravestone might show John Brown and wife Jean Smith.

Scottish statutory registration, i.e. state sponsored civil registration, started in 1855, and the register entries have always contained more information than the English and Welsh equivalents. Although a later start than in England and Wales where civil registration began in 1837, statutory registration of births, deaths and marriages was compulsory from the start in Scotland, whereas it didn't become compulsory in England until 1875.

One of the differences in the information in Scotland is the consistent use of a married woman's maiden name. On a birth register entry, where the parents are married, regularly or irregularly, the child's parents will be shown as John Brown and Jean Brown MS

Smith. "Irregular" in this context does not mean illegal, only not in conformance with the requirements of the various churches. Up to 1936 there were three forms of irregular marriage, one of which - "by habit and repute" - survives to the present day. Only in 1936 did a marriage become possible by the registrar in his office.

In the birth indexes for 1855, and then from 1929 onward, the mother's maiden name is also shown. This can make tracing forward straightforward. As records for other years are being checked this information is being added, but it will be many years before the process is complete for the whole period of 1856 to 1928

Up to 1900 somewhere between 8 and 10 per cent of births registered were illegitimate. In these cases there will always be an index entry under the mother's maiden name. Note that a substantial proportion of these births were later legitimated by the subsequent marriage of the parents, a fundamental difference in Scots law compared to England.

On marriage register entries, the names of both the father and mother of the bride and groom are shown, the mothers' names in the format Ann Smith MS Clark. In the indexes it is possible to carry out a cross check search for the marriage using both the surname of the bride and that of the groom. The only point to be careful of is the surname that a widow used, as she might have reverted to her maiden name instead of using her previously married name. It wasn't always the case that a previous surname would be used. In other words the Jane Brown maiden name Smith marrying Alexander McDonald could appear on the new marriage register entry as Jane Brown, Jane Smith, or Jane Smith formerly Brown.

In the situation where the previous married name only is used then there will be entries in the index under both that surname and the maiden name. In the period starting from 1856 until the system had settled down at the end of the 1850s, start of the 1860s, be prepared to find exceptions.

Where the maiden name only is used, there can only be an index entry for that name.

Where both names were used, there also should be index entries under both surnames, or more if a third or subsequent marriage was involved.

The information on death register entries in Scotland makes them well worth tracking down since, always assuming that the informant provides the information then there is the name of the spouse or spouse(s), the names of the parents including the mother's maiden name and any other names by which she was known.

When statutory recording started in Scotland in 1855, ambitions were very high, which is why it can be a great advantage to find an 1855 record due to the "extra" information.

This "extra" information, along with some other information was dropped in 1856, with just a small amount being restored over the next decade.

In the case of death register entries, an 1855 record shows the name of the spouse, including the maiden name in the case of a married male death.

For 1856 to 1860, however, only the marital status of the deceased is shown, i.e. no name of the spouse, but there will sometimes be the occupation of the spouse for a female death. The 1855 information showing the name of the spouse was restored in 1861.

Sometimes this means that it's not possible to be certain that the record is the correct one, but occupation, informant's name and relationship, never mind address, will often help.

That written, I've seen the full name of the spouse on a register entry in the period 1856 - 1860, and the information missing on a record from the early 1860s.

It's important to appreciate that registrars were ordinary human beings, with all the foibles that you can imagine, and maybe some of them didn't agree with the instructions from Edinburgh in 1856 - 1860, or some, in the early 1860s, hadn't read their memos from the Registrar General.

However, the complications don't stop there, - if only it were so easy!, - as it's the indexes that we first search, not the register entries, and for the first few years of statutory recording the situation regarding the treatment of maiden names was complicated.

So, for married females' deaths, the treatment of the maiden surnname varies as follows:

For **1855** the death is indexed under both the married surname and the maiden surname.

From **1856** to **1858** the only entry is under the name reported, i.e. normally the married surname for a married female, but if a widow had reverted to her **maiden** surname, then that may have been the surname used.

From **1859** onwards there **should** be entries under both the maiden and married surname, or surnames if married more than twice and that information has been reported.

There are several important points here. First, as always, the information in a death register entry and the related index is 100% dependent on the informant.

Secondly, the female death cross check search will not produce a result in 1856 - 1858; and, when you are searching on the married surname and don't get a match, don't give up before you repeat the search for the maiden surname alone.

Again, indexers sometimes made mistakes so don't be surprised if there turn out to be occasional exceptions to these "rules".

In later registers and indexes remember that the information given and then indexed depends on the informant, and it's far from uncommon to find an informant who didn't know the maiden name of the wife of the deceased, or who didn't know that the deceased had been married more than once, - in the latter case, even very close family informants sometimes didn't know, or didn't report this information (did every registrar make it obvious that the register entry required not only the name of the current spouse but also any previous spouse[s]?).

If the information isn't there in the register entries, it can't appear in the indexes.

From 1974 onwards, both the male and female death indexes also show the maiden name of the deceased's mother, - again of tremendous value when tracing forward.

The situation in terms of censuses, however, is different. Generally a wife is shown by her married surname, unless she is a widow, in which case she may have reverted to her maiden name, or a previous surname. That's not to say that you will not come across census entries where a wife is shown with her maiden name, - this can often be shown via a check in the marriage records not to mean that they weren't married.

Occurrences of this practice, in my experience, have occurred more in the southwest of Scotland than elsewhere. This tends to suggest that rather than being random, - e.g. a particular couple or a particular enumerator believing in showing the wife's maiden name, - that it is a geographical effect. That written I've just come across one enumeration district in Glasgow in 1871 where the wives' maiden names are consistently shown.

It should be mentioned that Scottish law allows a person to use whatever name they like as long as there is no fraudulent or criminal intent.

For the small number of Scots who left testaments, i.e. wills, that underwent the process of confirmation, i.e. probate, a married woman will always be referred to by her maiden name, most often in the format "Jean Smith, married to, or relict of John Brown". "Relict" is the Scots legal term that means either widow or widower.

Help up the Family Tree
Rosemary Bigwood

The family historian of today is spoilt for choice. There is a continuing stream of new genealogical information which is appearing online – digitised documents, indexes, guides to sources, shared research findings on websites and catalogues of holdings of archives, libraries and collections. Some claim that all this makes it quick and easy to trace your family history but those who are really curious and committed may find that they are faced with some problems and others, who are perhaps inexperienced, may require assistance.

The need for help
Before the opening of local history centres and the development of websites, professional researchers were commonly called upon to trace a complete family tree and some people still ask for this to be done – the completed work designed as a special present for a relative. Now more and more family historians have the satisfaction and interest of doing a great deal of the work themselves but at some point many come up against a brick wall. Unwilling to face the end of the quest, the advice of a professional is often sought to see if there are less known sources which may provide a break-through.

A frequent cause of frustration is in finding a reference to a series of documents in a catalogue or archive repertory which might be of interest but which are housed far away from where you live. Another difficulty is experienced when you download a digitised document relating to a distant ancestor – a will, for example – and find that you cannot read it. In such cases, the services of a local or experienced researcher are necessary.

Choosing a researcher
There is no shortage of advertisements published by those offering their services in carrying out research. Genealogical publications such as *Family Tree Magazine, Ancestors, The Scots Magazine* and family history society magazines all include advertisements of individuals or larger concerns offering fast, efficient, enthusiastic, friendly or professional help. Local societies often keep lists of local researchers and main archives such as the National Archives, the National Archives of Scotland and the General Register Office for Scotland advertise the names of private researchers – but do not take responsibility for the quality of work done.

Unfortunately, there is no guarantee of the standard of work produced by those who advertise and there are, as in all trades, many cowboys! To raise the standards of research, several associations have been set up whose members are examined for competence and all of whom comply with a code of practice. The two associations in Britain are:

AGRA – the Association of Genealogists and Researchers in Archives (www.agra.org.uk)
ASGRA –the Association of Scottish Genealogists and Researchers in Archives (www.asgra.co.uk)

Study the details given of the field of interest and claimed capabilities of a researcher given in any advertisement. Some may carry out research in particular geographical areas (particularly important in England where local archives are involved), some may have specialist interests – in army or navy records, for instance - and others may be especially concerned with seventeenth and eighteenth century family history.

If you want older records researched, make sure that the researcher you choose can read older handwriting and a knowledge of Latin, particularly in Scotland where many pre-1700 records are in Latin, may also be needed.

Costs of research
Charges made by researchers vary widely but bear in mind that the cheapest is not always the best. Some researchers charge for travel expenses or for entrance to certain institutions. A day's ticket to New Register House, for example, currently costs £17. This has to be paid by the researcher for access to the records and the fees are reflected in the charges made to you. Some searchers ask for a registration fee or a deposit which is put towards the final cost, some request that all fees should be paid in advance, while others make no charge till the work is done. Charges are sometimes made for initial consultations. Costs may be estimated on an hourly basis or on a daily basis. Many researchers charge fixed amounts - £60 or £100 or more – but there is no guarantee as to how much you will receive for this.

Budgeting is important as research is an open-ended pursuit. Make sure that you know what you are going to have to pay and on what basis. It often works well if you agree a budget of research hours (or days) and ask for a report at the end of that time. If there is more to be found, then you can embark on another instalment. Remember that unless you want only one particular document consulted or one or two facts confirmed, it is rarely practical to ask a researcher to do just one hour's work.

Sometimes you may feel that you are not getting your money's worth as results reported may mostly be negative – but this can be as important as positive findings and take as much time. Difficult handwriting, lack of indexes and long legal documents contribute to length of time taken in a search. Remember that a good researcher is a professional and bear in mind how much you pay to get a leaking pipe mended or your car repaired!

Briefing the researcher
Think carefully what research you want carried out and instruct the researcher accordingly. Do you want to know everything about your ancestry, as far back as possible? Do you want both the paternal and maternal lines followed out? Do you want just the "skeleton" of the family or are you interested in knowing something about the social background of the family? On the other hand, do you only want details extracted from one particular document or source?

It is very important to put down clearly what you already know about the family as this information will provide the starting point for research. You should indicate whether these details have been confirmed beyond doubt or whether they based on hearsay. Make sure that you have included all salient details and refer to any documents you already hold. It is infuriating for a researcher (and frustrating for the recipient) to find that time and money has been spent in carrying out searches which result in information already known to the client. On the other hand, the receipt of a huge packet of papers accompanied by a letter saying that the client has just put in all he or she could find is usually greeted with dismay by a researcher who may make charges for the time taken to digest this mass of material.

Find out when the work is likely to be completed and make it clear from the outset if you want the results in a hurry. Many researchers have a lot of work on hand and may not be able to fit in your research immediately.

What a researcher should provide
The style of writing a report depends on the researcher. Often this may be presented in note form, accompanied by transcriptions, abstracts or copies of documents. Other researchers adopt a more narrative style. Whatever the method of presentation, the reasoning leading to the connecting of generations and the interpretation of events should be clear and logical and any doubts (which are often unavoidable) about the relevance of findings must be stated. References to documents and books consulted should be included. If you have preference about the style of the report, discuss this before the work starts.

Finding a researcher whose work you trust may be a matter of trial and error. If you first have a small piece of work carried out, you can often judge as to the quality of what has been done and then make further requests. Having all your research done for you can be expensive but assistance in a limited piece of work – the transcription of a document or check on a limited range of sources – may not break the bank and may provide some valuable footholds in climbing further up the family tree.

Scottish Irregular Marriages

David W Webster FSA Scot

Before 1834 (after the reformation obviously) only Church of Scotland ministers were permitted to perform "regular" marriage ceremonies. This right was extended in 1834 to ministers and priests of other denominations. From 1878 notice to the registrar was available as a legal preliminary to marriage as an alternative to banns and since 1939 Civil Marriage has been available in Scotland. The present marriage laws date from 1977.

Before 1 July 1940 there were 3 forms of "irregular" marriage in Scotland of which one only survives. It has to be noted that these were perfectly legal ways of getting married and the couple acquired the same rights as any other married couple though they might have to prove they were married.

The 3 forms of marriage were
1. declaration of present consent
   (*per verba et praesenti*)
2. marriage by cohabitation with habit and repute
3. a promise of marriage followed by sexual intercourse on the faith of that promise.
   (*per verba de futura subsequenta copula*)
Of these only the second is the survivor to the present day.

For declaration of present consent all that was required was that the parties agreed from that time onwards to be husband and wife (not the same thing as agreeing to marry at some future date which is merely a betrothal). There was no need for witnesses for the marriage to be legal. However if the couple wished to register the marriage they had to apply to the Sheriff for a warrant to register the marriage. In those days, the person granting the warrant would be known as the Sheriff Substitute but his function was the same as the present day Sheriff. For that you would need to prove the consent i.e. to have witnesses. Once the warrant was granted you could go off to the registrar to register the marriage. Hence the narration on the marriage certificate.

Marriage by cohabitation with habit and repute is still available and for that the parties have to live together as husband and wife for some considerable time and, this is the rub, they must have the repute i.e. they must present themselves to the world at large and be believed to be a married couple, rather than people who are simply living together as cohabitants. The cohabitation has to be in Scotland and the parties must be free to marry.

If the cohabitation, the length of time and the repute were proved it is then presumed that at

some point the parties have tacitly consented to become husband and wife. This presumption can be overturned if there is proof of lack of consent. In the old cases there are some wonderful class ridden comments such as "A man will not be presumed to marry his housekeeper".

This form of marriage is still used, largely to try to get Bereavement Benefits from the Department of Work and Pensions (DWP). Where people usually fall down is on the repute. Nowadays most people who are co-habiting without marriage are quite open about this.

If one party needs to have a declarator of marriage in these circumstances, usually because the other has died and they want to inherit, they have to take the case to the Court of Session. The Sheriff Court won't do for this. However bodies such as the DWP or the tribunals which hear Social Security cases can accept that a couple were married in this way without a court order having been granted.

By habit and repute has been defined by one legal commentator as ....

When a single man and woman cohabit together openly and constantly, as if they were husband and wife, and conduct themselves towards each other, for such a length of time, in the society and neighbourhood of which they are members, so as to produce a general belief that they are truly married persons, their lawful union in matrimony is held to be established by complete and harmonious proof of these facts, without any more direct and positive evidence.

Or, as expressed more poetically by Lord Neave:

*A third way of tying the tether,
Which sometimes may happen to suit,
Is living a good while together,
And getting the married repute.*

The third form of irregular marriage required that there was a promise of marriage followed by sexual intercourse on the faith of that promise. Both the promise and the intercourse had to be in Scotland. I don't think this ever really caught on as a way of getting married and certainly by the time it was abolished was largely irrelevant. There is a marvellous quote by a judge, which shows so much about class/gender prejudices and attitudes that I just have to share it. The quote is from Lord Sands in the case of **N v C** in 1933 and runs thus:

"According to the theory of the law, when two persons who are engaged to be married indulge in sexual intercourse, presumably they there and then exchange matrimonial consent and become married persons. But, according to the view in those sections of the community in which antenuptial fornication is most apt to occur, they do nothing of the kind. They yield to desire and indulge in immoral intercourse, robbed doubtless of some of its dangers by the prospect of future marriage....Parents, employers and clergymen in rural Scotland have often had occasion to deal sorrowfully with a girl whose betrothed had got her in the family way. I much doubt if it has ever happened that the girl advanced the plea in excuse that she was a married woman... Marriage by promise subsequente copula is a plant nourished by the law which has never taken root in the understanding or the conscience of the common people."

These two quotes above are taken from Lean Leneman's recently published ***Promises, Promises; Marriage Litigation in Scotland 1698 - 1830***, NMS Enterprises Ltd., National Museums of Scotland, ISBN 1-901663-52-3; not inexpensive at £20, but utterly fascinating, as the above 3 types of irregular marriage open up all sorts of possibilities for legal actions based on "But Ah didnae say that", or "... mean that ", or "But I had drink taken at the time", etc., etc...........

But please, please, don't even begin to consider the purchase of this book unless 241 pages of

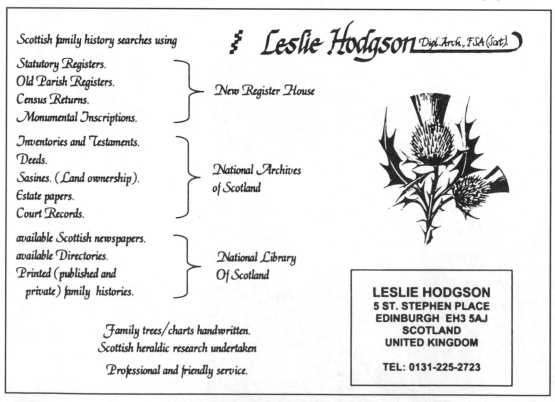

the legal niceties and intricacies involved sounds like interesting bedtime reading!!! (I'm currently at p93!) On the other hand you will get a quite fascinating insight to this aspect of Scottish society.....

I note that there is an earlier work by Leah that I have not previously come across, - *Alienated Affections - The Scottish Experience of Divorce and Separation 1684 - 1830", Edinburgh 1998.*

The possibility for marriage by declaration was not possible in England and Wales after 1753, which is the basis of "Gretna Green" marriages where a couple could cross the border and make an immediate declaration in the presence of witnesses, - traditionally the blacksmith, - "pledging their troth over the anvil". There was no need for an anvil or a blacksmith and there were many who made a business out of this, not just in Gretna, which had the advantage of being on the main road north to Scotland on the West coast, and only a mile or so over the border.

Other such locations were Coldstream, Haddington, Portpatrick (which had a regular ferry service from Northern Ireland), Annan, and Lamberton.

Such marriages became prevalent after the Hardwicke Act of 1753 which banned irregular marriages in England and Wales, with a similar act applying to Ireland. Up until 1856 there was no residence qualification in Scotland, but after a 3 week period was introduced in 1856, the number of such marriages declined.

The following list of the extant records of such marriages is reproduced courtesy of the General Register Office Scotland.

This list of Custodians and Owners of all the known existing records of Scottish Irregular and Runaway Marriages, is based upon an original list compiled in 1927 by Mr G W Shirley of the Ewart Library in Dumfries. The list was extended by Mr George Crighton in a leaflet published by the Society of Genealogists, and after considerable research and communication with all the Custodians, further extended by Ronald Nicholson. Having taken great care to authenticate the accuracy of the information gathered, I feel able to present this list as up to date and fully comprehensive.

Since the publication of the list, the records of some 4,500 Gretna marriages between 1795 and 1895 have been acquired by Achievements of Canterbury. These can be accessed, for a cost, on their web site at http://www.achievements.co.uk/services/gretna/index.php.

Searching the on-line index is free, but the full details of the marriage as given in the register cost £15. Extractions of further entries for a surname can be obtained at the rate of £40 per 12 entries pro rata.

List of Custodians and Owners of all the known existing records of Scottish Irregular and Runaway Marriages Compiled by Ronald Nicholson, 42 Westrigg Road, Carlisle, CA2 6LF 28 April 2000 © *Copyright Ronald Nicholson 2000* N.B. Some Custodians require a fee for search and copy of Register Entries.

1754 – 1826
Place Portpatrick, Stranraer, Stonykirk, Leswalt
"Priests" Dr John McKenzie
Description: Irregular Marriages Extracted from Parish Records by Arthur Brack 247 entries Irish Runaways
Owners & Custodians Mr A Brack 17 Lockharton Gardens, Edinburgh EH14 1AU Copies held by Society of Genealogists, Dumfries & Galloway Family History Society Research Centre

1762 – 1795
Place Haddington
"Priests" J Buchanan Minister
Description: Register of the Episcopalian Chapel of Holy Trinity Church, Haddington.These are regular marriages but are included because they are Runaway Marriages 3 Volumes Thin Quarto 222 entries
Owners & Custodians The National Archives of Scotland HM General Register House Edinburgh Transcript in Northern Notes & Queries Vol 111 (1889) Vol IV (1890)

1782 – 1856
Place Coldstream
"Priests" William DicksonWilliam Armstrong & others
Description: Extracts from the Coldstream Registers by F L Carter 45 entries
Owners & Custodians Berwick upon Tweed Record Office

1783 - 1895
Place Springfield, Gretna Green
"Priests" David Lang Simon Lang William Lang
Description: 4 Bound Volumes 2 Paper Bound Volumes 3 Bound Index 1 Unbound Index
1 Chest containing photos and numerous documents including statements of residence, bills and receipts
Owners & Custodians Institute of Heraldic & Genealogical Studies

1793 – 1797
Place Coldstream
"Priests" Not Known
Description: 1 Volume (633 entries
Owners & Custodians Scottish Borders Council Coldstream Museum. Copy at Berwick upon Tweed Record Office and at Scottish Borders Archives

1797 – 1854
Blue Bell Inn, Annan
"Priests" Isaac Hope
Description: Irregular Marriages extracted from Parish Records by Arthur Brack 405 entries
Owners & Custodians Mr A Brack 17 Lockharton Gardens, Edinburgh EH14 1AU Copies held by Society of Genealogists and Dumfries & Galloway Family History Society Research Centre

1804 - 1816 and **1849 – 1855**
Place Lamberton Toll
"Priests" George Lamb, George Sharpe

Description: Index only 2000 entries approx
Owners & Custodians Northumberland County Records Office

1808 – 1864
Coldstream, Lamberton & Eastern Borders
"Priests" Not known
Description: Extracted from Berwick Newspapers by Northumberland CRO Staff 1996 Entries
Owners & Custodians Norhumberland County Records Office

1811 – 1840
Place Springfield, Gretna Green
"Priests" Robert Elliot and a number of Joseph Pasley entries
Description: 2 Bound Volumes 6 Booklets 3 Unbound Booklets 1 Small Notebook 33 Envelopes & Folders containing parts of notebooks, loose sheets & fragments some dating from 1746
Owners & Custodians Durham University Library Archives & Special Collections

1820 – 1897
Place Lamberton & Area
"Priests" Andrew Lyons & others
Description: Extracts from various Registers by A C A Steven 52 entries
Owners & Custodians Berwick upon Tweed Record Office

1820 – 1840
Place River Tweed, Union Bridge, Paxton, Lamberton, Coldstream, Mordington
"Priests" John Forster, Joseph Atkinson, Edward Gray, Henry Collins, Thomas Dunn, Peter Moodie D P D Muddiless or Mordilee, John Armstrong, A N Pringle
Description: Irregular Border Marriage Certificates 74 Marriage Certificates collected and transcribed by Linda A Bankier MA DAA
Owners & Custodians Berwick upon Tweed Record Office

1825 – 1855
Place Gretna Hall
"Priests" John Linton & others
Description: 1 Bound Volume 1 Contemporary Index 1 Modern Index 36 Files of Duplicate Certificates & Roll of Tables of Correction 1233 Entries Index 1829 - 1855 printed by Scottish Record Society 1949 1130 entries
Owners & Custodians Ewart Library, Dumfries Copies held by Public Library The Lanes Carlisle Tel: 01228 24166 also Gretna Hall Hotel Old Blacksmith Shop, many libraries and Genealogical Societies

1832 – 1835
Place Sark Toll Bar, Gretna
"Priests" George McQueen
Description: 3 Bound Volumes (342 entries)
Owners & Custodians Ewart Library, Dumfries

1834 - 1843 and 1844 – 1849
Place Lamberton Toll
"Priests" Henry Collins
Description: 2 Volumes (2544 entries)
Owners & Custodians Transcription & Index published by Northumberland & Durham Family History Society Also General Register Office, New Register House Edinburgh Copy on microfilm at Northumberland Record Office. Copies at Society of Genealogists and many libraries and Family History Societies

1840 – 1841
Place Lamberton Toll, Mordington & Paxton
"Priests" Unknown
Description: Miscellaneous papers Deposit No AD58/125 from Lord Advocates Office 48 entries Transcribed by Arthur Black
Owners & Custodians National Archive of Scotland HM General Register House
Transcription Published & held by Northumberland & Durham Family History Society

1843 – 1862
Place Queens Head Inn, Springfield, Gretna
"Priests" John Douglas
Description: 4 Bound Volumes (934 entries
Owners & Custodians General Register Office New Register House, Edinburgh Photocopy at Ewart Library, Dumfries, National Archives of Scotland and Register Office,Gretna

1843 – 1865
Place Allisons Toll Bar Gretna
"Priests" John Murray & Daughter
Description: 16 Bound Volumes (6828 entries)
Owners & Custodians Mounseys Solicitors 19 Castle Street Carlisle CA3 8SY Tel: 01228 5251

1896 -1940
Place Blacksmiths Shop, Gretna Green, (Headless Cross)
"Priests" Peter Dickson, Thomas Johnstone, Jessie Graham, Richard Nugent, Richard Rennison & others
Description: 22 Bound Volumes (11 Volumes of Certificates plus 11 Volumes of Registers) 4054 entries
Owners & Custodians Gretna Museum & Tourist Services Ltd The Old Blacksmith Shop Gretna Green Dumfriesshire Tel: 01461 338441

1928 – 1933
Place Gretna Toll Bar
"Priests" Arthur Stephenson
Description: Bound Volume of Certificates and a contemporaryindex (142 entries)
Owners & Custodians Mr J Stephenson 46 Pretoria Road Eastriggs Annan Dumfriesshire DG12 6NU

1937 – 1940
Place Gretna Hall
"Priests" David Ramsay McIntosh, Jessie Graham
Description: 2 Bound Volumes (473 entries)
Owners & Custodians North British Trust Hotels, Gretna Hall Hotel, Gretna Green Tel: 01461 337635

QUEEN'S BRIDGE, BELFAST.

The Public Record Office of Northern Ireland
Valerie Adams

An Agency within the Department of
Culture, Arts and Leisure

www.dcalni.gov.uk

The Public Record Office of Northern Ireland (PRONI) is the only dedicated archive repository in Northern Ireland, providing an integrated archival service for the whole country. It receives not only public records (those created by government departments, courts, local authorities and non-departmental public bodies) but also private records from a wide range of sources - individuals, families, businesses, charities, churches, societies, landed estates, etc. You might think that PRONI only holds archives relating to the six counties of Northern Ireland but in fact there are archives relating to other parts of the island of Ireland and to numerous locations all over the world from Jamaica to India and from South Africa to China. This unique combination of private and public records amounting to over 35Km, makes PRONI the most important resource for anyone researching their family tree or their local area.

On PRONI's website you will find out how to make best use of the records. There is a 'Frequently Asked Questions' section, copies of all our information leaflets and details of our policies on preservation and copying. You will also find on the website the introductions to the major private archives and to the classes of records of the Ministry/Department of Education some of which will be of interest to the family historian if one of your ancestors was in the teaching profession. Also on the website will be news of new developments that are taking place.

Public Records
Because of the fire in the Public Record Office of Ireland in Dublin in 1922 many people are under the impression that there are no surviving public records before that date. In fact, there are many series of records that go back to the early 19th century and even into the 18th century in the case of the Grand Jury Presentment Books that will give the names of those who received money for

the construction and repair of roads, bridges, gaols, etc. The most popular records for the family and local historian relating to the six counties of Northern Ireland are: the valuation records from the 1830s to the present; the tithe applotment books, 1823-37, giving details of landholders and the size of their holdings; copy wills from 1838 - c.1900 and all original wills from 1900 to 2000; registers and inspectors' observation books of c.1,600 national/public elementary/primary schools dating mainly from the 1870s; the grant-aid applications of the Commissioners of National Education which record the history and state of national schools from 1832 to 1889; the Ordnance Survey maps at various scales from 1831 to the present; the minutes, indoor and outdoor relief registers, etc of the Boards of Guardians who administered the workhouse system from 1838 to 1948; the records, including admission registers, of lunatic asylums, some dating back to the mid-19th century (but these are subject to extended closure for 100 years); and the title deeds, leases and wills in the Irish Land Commission and the Land Purchase Commission archive some of which date back into the 18th century.

Guides to the tithe applotment books, the large scale Ordnance Survey town plans, education records and probate records are available in PRONI.

Private Archives
Because so many of the public records for the island of Ireland have not survived it is not surprising then that private archives have assumed a much greater importance for family and local history.

The most valuable are those of the great landed estates (many of which go back into the 17th and 18th centuries), of solicitors' firms which include copies of wills, leases and title deeds, of railway companies, and of churches. Equally important are family and personal papers and the working notes of antiquarians and genealogists who worked in the Public Record Office of Ireland prior to 1922 and who took copious notes from the records some of which date back to the 17th century. Almost all the major estate archives are held in PRONI and you can find descriptions of many of them on the PRONI website. Among the more notable estate archives are: Downshire (Cos Down and Antrim); Antrim (Co Antrim); Abercorn (Co Tyrone); Belmore (Co Fermanagh); Gosford, Brownlow and Caledon (Co Armagh); and Drapers' Company (Co Londonderry). A comprehensive listing of all the estate records in PRONI will be found in the 'Guide to Landed Estates' available in PRONI or at the Local Studies Libraries of each Education and Library Board.

Church records are an invaluable source for the family historian, especially those that pre-date civil registration of births and deaths (births, deaths and all marriages from 1864 and Non - Catholic marriages from 1845). Microfilm copies of almost all pre-1900 church records of the main denominations are available in the Self-Service Microfilm Room in PRONI. On the PRONI website you will find an index of reference numbers to many of these microfilmed church records but fuller details can be found in the 'Guide to Church Records', the most up to date version of which is available in PRONI.

Printed Sources Street directories are often a neglected source of information for the family and local historian. PRONI holds a very comprehensive set of the Belfast and Ulster Street Directories from c.1840 to 1996 and of Thom's Directories from 1845 to 1958. Another useful source are the printed will calendars that give a brief summary of every will proved and of letters of administration taken out in the civil courts from 1858 to 2000; those from 1922 relate to Northern Ireland only.

Improvements to service PRONI's commitment to raising standards of public services is reflected in the major re-furbishment of the Public Search Room and Reading Room - this included air –conditioning, improved lighting, a new document issue desk and new furniture and additional computer terminals. PRONI can now provide modern, spacious and pleasant facilities for customers as well as an improved copying service. Regular consultation with users is vital to help identify where improvements are needed and to get feedback from users on improvements either implemented or planned. The PRONI Users Forum continues to provide the mechanism for doing so.

Forthcoming Developments
One of the largest projects (the 'eCATNI Project') that PRONI has ever embarked on and that will become available in stages from the summer of 2006 is the retrospective conversion of all our catalogues, right down to item level, which will eventually be accessible on the PRONI website.

The project aims to create comprehensive, accurate and up-to-date electronic catalogues that can be accessed at the touch of a button. This will permit remote access to a rich archival heritage, opening up the opportunities for lifelong learning to a new and wider customer base and improving the efficiency and accessibility of PRONI's customer service.

Self-Service Microfilm Room In order to speed up access to the archives, the most popular sources on microfilm for the family and local historian are available in the specially equipped Self-Service Microfilm Room. There you can view microfilms of church records, the 1901 census for Northern Ireland, the copy will books, 1858-c.1900, the tithe applotment books, the civil birth indexes, 1864-1922, and the surviving fragments of the 1831-1851 census returns for some parishes in Cos Antrim, Fermanagh, Londonderry and Cavan.

Finding Aids Besides our extensive catalogues which include virtual transcripts of important runs of estate correspondence, PRONI provides a range of finding aids: guides to different categories of records (eg women's history) and county guides; subject, place and personal name indexes (although the latter is by no means complete it is often a useful starting point if you do not know precisely where your ancestors came from); an extensive leaflet series on different types of records for family and local history and also leaflets on historical topics such as the Great Famine, the Act of Union and the Belfast Blitz.

New Acquisitions of interest to the family historian Among the diverse range of archives either recently deposited or microfilmed and of most interest to the family historian are: baptisms for York Street Congregational Church, 1819 -1945, and marriages for Kilmainham Congregational Church, 1892-1978, both in Dublin, and baptisms, 1871-1928, marriages, 1845-1996 and burials, 1871-1952 for Ahoghill Parish Church, Co Antrim.

On-line records On PRONI's website you can access free of charge two major collections. The freeholders' records relating largely to the six counties of Northern Ireland from the mid 18th to early 19th centuries record the names and places of residence of those who were entitled to vote or who actually voted at elections. This on-line resource of over 5,000 high quality images of the registers which is fully searchable will provide speedier access to a unique resource for family and local history at a period when there is a scarcity of documentary sources. Also available on-line is a searchable index to the names of the half a million people who signed the Ulster Covenant in 1912 and images of the actual signatures. The current digitisation projects that are now almost completed are the indexing and scanning of the wills for Northern Ireland from 1858 to c.1900 and the Ordnance Survey maps for Northern Ireland.

External Relations PRONI staff are available to give talks and lectures about PRONI and the sources we hold to outside organisations, including family and local history societies. These can be delivered either on-site or off-site. Regular monthly series of talks on sources for tracing your family and local history are given in PRONI with occasional ones delivered elsewhere. These are open to everyone, especially if you have never been to PRONI before. PRONI's website will give details of forthcoming talks.

Facilities and Services There is limited carparking within the PRONI site but space has been made available for those with a disability. Free off-street parking is available but you should park responsibly as residents do need to get in and out of their driveways. Restaurant facilities are available on-site where you can purchase snacks, beverages and lunches that can be consumed in our new modernised and expanded restaurant area. It is possible to purchase a late evening meal on Thursdays when the Office is open until 8.45 but you must order this in advance at lunchtime.

Visiting PRONI and Opening Times PRONI is open to the public without appointment and research is free for those pursuing personal and educational research. However, users will need to obtain a reader's ticket at Reception and will require proof of identity to gain admission and to use the computerised document ordering system. No advance booking is required. Group visits are very welcome but must be booked in advance.

Mon - Wed and Fri 9.00 – 16.45 Thurs - 10.00 – 20.45 (*please check in advance*) Last orders for documents -16.15 apart from Thursdays when it is 20.15 PRONI is closed annually for stocktaking during the last week in November and the first week in December and on public holidays (see the PRONI website for details as there are different public holidays in Northern Ireland).

While there are detailed catalogues, guides and leaflets available, staff are always available at the Help Desk in the Public Search Room to give advice or help to researchers.

How to get there
If you are coming by car, there is easy access from the motorways and you should exit at Balmoral. While there is limited on-site carparking you can park in the vicinity of Balmoral Avenue. However, those with a disability will be accommodated on-site. If you are coming by bus, Metro 8 or 9 route from the City Centre will take you to Balmoral Avenue and it is then a short walk from the bus stop. Alternatively, Balmoral railway station on the Lisburn Road is only a short distance from PRONI.

Public Record Office of Northern Ireland
66 Balmoral Avenue, Belfast BT9 6NY
Tel: 028 9025 5905   Fax: 028 9025 5999
E-mail: proni@dcalni.gov.uk
Web: http://www.proni.gov.uk

Reach over 120,000 North American Family Researchers through Family Chronicle!

Family Chronicle is North America's most popular genealogy magazine and is filled with articles from the world's best genealogy writers. Top genealogy software, book and CD publishers, genealogy services companies and professional genealogists advertise regularly in *Family Chronicle*. If you want to break into the huge North American genealogy market, you can do so very affordably with *Family Chronicle*.

Examples of Small Ads (payable in US Dollars)
40 word classified $20
Marketplace – black and white (2½" x 3⅛") $55

Call Victoria Pratt at 416-491-3600 x 114 or *victoria@moorshead.com* for full details on small space advertising programs or Jeannette Cox at 416-491-3699 x 111 or *jeannette@moorshead.com* for details on display advertisements, fax: 416-491-3996 or write
Family Chronicle, PO Box 194 Niagara Falls NY 14304 USA

www.familychronicle.com

In association with Family History Monthly

BRITISH ASSOCIATION FOR LOCAL HISTORY

the national charity promoting local history

 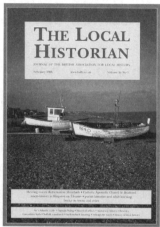 

Local history enriches the lives of both individuals and whole communities, and is an area where amateur and professional meet and work profitably together.

Members receive both
The Local Historian and *Local History News*
four times a year

Send for full details and complimentary back numbers of
The Local Historian and *Local History News* to

PO BOX 6549, Somersal Herbert, Ashbourne DE6 5WH
Tel: 01283 585947

www.balh.co.uk

The Family and Local History *Handbook*
Digital Genealogy Section

in association with

ABM Publishing Ltd

The award-winning genealogical publishers of
Family Tree Magazine and *Practical Family History*

Researching your family history has never been easier.
Check out the magazines' computer sections for websites, software and
CD-ROM reviews. The free cover CDs contain useful resources and back issues
of your favourite magazine.
Our publications will guide you through your voyage of discovery!

For details of how to subscribe to
Family Tree Magazine and
Practical Family History give us a call on
08707 662272
or visit our website at **www.family-tree.co.uk**

Herbert Henry ASQUITH

Nurse Edith CAVELL

Winston Churchill

The Famous Fifty in 1881
Roy Stockdill
finds some celebrated Victorians on the 1881 census CDs

We have become accustomed today to most of the Victorian censuses being widely available on CD-ROM and also on the Internet, making the search for ancestors so much easier. However, when the 1881 census of Britain first appeared on a set of two dozen CDs in 1999, the launch was a major sensation in the genealogical world.

For the first time, family historians had at their eager disposal a census transcription of the entire country, and not only that but one which was instantly searchable by surname. Despite everything that has happened since, and notwithstanding the fact that census transcriptions and indexing have moved on rapidly since then, the 1881 discs are still my favourite genealogical "plaything".

Because they are so simple to search - even though you sometimes have to think laterally to find people who have been mistranscribed - it's relatively easy to spot famous Victorians on the census, and this is a game I've enjoyed ever since the discs first appeared. Here, then, is my A-Z guide to what I've called the Famous Fifty, comprising celebrated Victorians in the world of royalty, politics, art, literature, crime and other arenas...

Frederick George ABBERLINE, the man who led Scotland Yard's hunt for the notorious murderer Jack the Ripper in 1888, was aged 38 in 1881 and a police inspector, living at the police station at 160 Commercial Street, Shoreditch, in London's East End, with his wife Emma, 35. He has been transcribed as Aberline with one "b".

Elizabeth Garrett ANDERSON, feminist, women's medical pioneer and founder of a famous London hospital, was aged 44 and living at 4 Up Berkeley Street, St Marylebone, London, occupation Physician MD Paris LSA London, with her shipowner husband, James G S Anderson, 43, a son and daughter and six servants.

Poet and critic Matthew ARNOLD was 58 in 1881 and his occupation given as Inspector of Schools. He was a visitor at a stately home, the Park Mansion, Aston Clinton, Buckinghamshire, belonging to Lousia de Rothschild, a baronet's widow, along with several other guests and more than 20 servants.

Herbert Henry ASQUITH, a Yorkshireman from Morley, near Leeds, who became prime minister in 1908, was a practising barrister of 28 and living with his wife and two young sons at 12 John Street, Hampstead.

The author of world-famous children's classic *Peter Pan*, James BARRIE was aged 21 in 1881 and a student boarder at 3 Great King Street, Edinburgh.

James BERRY, who succeeded William Marwood as the public hangman, was in 1881 a 29-year-old carrier living with his wife Sarah, their two young sons, and his 58-year-old widowed mother in law at 58 Thorp Street, Bradford, Yorkshire.

Jessie BOOT, who transformed the Boots chemists' firm founded by his father into a nationwide empire, was at 16 Goosegate,

Charles Darwin

Banjamin Disraeli

Edward Elgar

Nottingham, aged 30, with his 54-year-old widowed mother Mary and sister Jane, aged 21.

John BROWN, aged 54, from Crathie, Aberdeen, occupation Queens personal servant - an interesting description for one who was rumoured to fill a somewhat more intimate role in Queen Victoria's life - was at Windsor Castle, Berkshire, along with the rest of the royal household.

Robert BROWNING was at 19 Warwick Crescent, Paddington, aged 68, with his sister Susanne Browning, 66, both giving their occupation as No Profession Poet.

Lewis CARROLL, in his real name of Charles L Dodgson, was aged 49, an MA student and lecturer, at Christ Church College, Oxford.

Nurse Edith CAVELL, who became a national heroine when shot by the Germans in 1915 as a spy, was aged 15 in 1881 and living with her father Frederick and three younger siblings at the Vicarage in Swardeston, Norfolk, where her father was the incumbent.

Britain's future World War II prime minister, Winston CHURCHILL, was a schoolboy of six, living at 29, St James's Place, Westminster, with his parents, Lord and Lady Randolph Churchill.

Charles DARWIN, whose theory of evolution revolutionised scientific thinking, was aged 72 in 1881. His sizeable household at Downe House, Downe, Kent, comprised himself, his wife Emma, also 72, four sons, a daughter, a daughter-in-law, a grandson, a niece, a cousin, two visitors and eight servants.

Benjamin DISRAELI, appears as the Earl of Beaconsfield at 19 Curzon Street, St George Hanover Square, London, in the elegant Mayfair area, his occupation being given as Ex Prime Minister. Disraeli died just 16 days after the census, on April 19 1881.

Sherlock Holmes author Arthur Conan DOYLE was a 21-year-old student of medicine, living with his mother, four younger siblings and a female servant at 15 Lonsdale Terrace, Edinburgh.

Composer Edward ELGAR was aged 23 and a boarder at Chesnut Walk, Claines, Worcestershire, occupation Professor of Violin.

Writer E M (Edward Morgan) FORSTER, author of *A Room With A View* and *Howards End*, was a child of two in 1881, living with his widowed mother Alice, 26, and three female servants at 6 Melcombe Place, St Marylebone, London.

David Lloyd GEORGE, the Welsh Wizard who was actually born in Manchester but brought

LLoyd George

up in North Wales after his father died, was aged 18, a solicitor's articled clerk, and living with his widowed mother, Elizabeth Lloyd (she appears on the census in her maiden name), an elder sister and younger brother, and his uncle, Richard Lloyd, a pastor, at 3 Tanygrisiau Terrace, Criccieth, Caernarvon.

William Schwick GILBERT - the words half of Gilbert and Sullivan - was aged 44, occupation Dramatic Author, living at 24 The Boltons, Kensington, with his wife Lucy, 33.

William Ewart GLADSTONE was on his second term as Prime Minister and must have been at home at 10 Downing Street, Westminster, on census night, for he is shown there, aged 71, with his wife Catherine, 69, an unmarried daughter, Mary, 37, and a number of servants.

W G Grace

W S Gilbert

W E Gladstone

Henry Irving

The Victorian era's most famous sportsman, Dr W. G. GRACE, the mighty, bearded cricketer, was at 61 Stapleton Road in the census district of Bristol St Philip and Jacob Out, Gloucestershire, aged 32, his occupation Surgeon M.R.C.S. L.R.C.P.&S.. With him were his wife Grace, 27, two sons and a daughter, a brother-in-law, two visitors and two servants.

James Keir HARDIE, revered by socialists as the founder of the Independent Labour Party in 1893, was still cutting his political teeth in the trade union movement in 1881. He is found, aged 24 and described as Secretary for Miners Union, as a visitor staying with a fellow union agent Alexander Chapman and his family at Glaisnock Street, Old Cumnock, Ayrshire.

James Keir Hardie

Novelist Thomas HARDY, author of works like *Far From the Madding Crowd* and *Tess of the D'Urbevilles*, was aged 40 and living at 1 Trinity Road, Wandsworth, Surrey, with his 35-year-old wife Emma and one female servant.

From the theatre, the great Henry IRVING (knighted in 1895) is found as a lodger and head of the household, aged 43, described as a Comedian, at 15A Grafton Street, St George Hanover Square.

Thomas Hardy

Jerome Klapka JEROME, author of *Three Men in a Boat*, was a 21-year-old lodger and a Shorthand Writer To Solicitors Etc at 36 Newman Street, St Marylebone, London.

Poet and short story writer Rudyard KIPLING was 15 in 1881 and a boarder-scholar at Kingsley College Priory, Northam, Devon. On the CDs he is mistranscribed as Joseph R Kitsling.

Scottish singer and giant of the music halls Harry LAUDER was aged 10 and

Rudyard Kipling

Harry Lauder

shown as Henry Lauder, living with his parents and five siblings at Browns Buildings, Invereesk, Edinburgh.

Marie LLOYD, the queen of the music halls, was aged 11 in 1881 and in her real name of Matilda Wood was living with her parents John and Matilda Wood and five younger siblings, at 3 Bath Place, St Luke, London.

The Earl of LUCAN, who was blamed by historians for the fiasco of the Charge of the Light Brigade during the Crimean War, was at 12 South Street, Mayfair - ironically, only two doors away from the Lady of the Lamp Florence Nightingale, whose nursing saved many lives in the war.

Marie Lloyd

Karl Marx　　**Florence Nightingale**　　**George Bernard Shaw**　　**Emily Pankhurst**

William MARWOOD, the most famous public hangman of Victorian times, was aged 62 and living at 64 Foundry Street, Horncastle, Lincolnshire, with his 55-year-old wife Ellen. His given occupation is perhaps among the more bizarre on the 1881 census: Executioner Shoe Dealer!

Karl MARX, the founder of Communism, appears on the census CDs, somewhat curiously, as Karl Wass, aged 68, living with his wife Jenny and an unmarried daughter of 26, at 41 Maitland Park Road, St. Pancras, London. His occupation is given as Author Political Economy. Wass was an obvious mistranscription.

The artist designer and socialist reformer William MORRIS was at Kelmscott House, Hammersmith, aged 47, with two daughters and three servants, but his wife was not at home.

Edith NESBIT, author of the popular classic *The Railway Children*, was found in her married name of Edith Bland, authoress, age 22, at 28 Elswick Road, Lewisham, Kent, with her mother and a 10-months-old son, but husband not present.

A near neighbour of Benjamin Disraeli in Mayfair was Florence NIGHTINGALE. She was living at 10 South Street with four servants, then aged 60, and described as Directress of Nightingale Fund For Training Hospital Nurses.

Mrs Emmeline PANKHURST's years as the leader of the suffragettes were still in the future in 1881. She is found aged 22, with her barrister husband, Richard Marsden Pankhurst, who at 44 was twice her age, at 1 Quayton Terrace, 3 Chester Road, Stretford, Lancashire, along with their then six-months-old daughter Christobel Harriet Pankhurst, who was to become as famous as her mother.

Artist and poet Dante Gabriel ROSSETTI was a widower of 52 living at the family home at 16 Cheyne Walk, Chelsea, with two female servants.

At 159 Queens Crescent, St Pancras, was a provision merchant with three shops called John J SAINSBURY, aged 36, living with his wife Mary Ann, 33, and their six children aged from 10 to 11 months. John and Mary Ann were founders of the mighty Sainsbury's supermarket empire.

Writer George Bernard SHAW, aged 24 and described as Author Writer of Fiction, was living with his mother, Lucinda, a teacher of singing, at 37 Fitzroy Street, St Pancras, London.

Painter Walter Richard SICKERT, whose name has been suggested by some crime writers as a possible candidate for Jack the Ripper, has been transcribed to the 1881 CDs as Robert Sickert, aged 19, a merchants clerk, living with his parents, Oswald Sickert, a 53-year-old artist, and Eleanor, 50, and four siblings at 12 Pembroke Gardens, Kensington, London.

Bram STOKER, author of *Dracula*, aged 33, a theatrical manager, was with his wife Florence, a 21-year-old artist, son Irving aged 15 months, and brother George, 26, a surgeon, at 27 Cheyne walk, Chelsea.

Swedish-born Elizabeth STRIDE, known as "Long Liz" who was to become a victim of Jack the Ripper in 1888, was in 1881 the 34-year-old wife of a carpenter, John T Stride, 54, living at 69 Usher Road, Bow, in London's East End.

The musical half of Gilbert and Sullivan, Arthur SULLIVAN was aged 38, unmarried, described as Doctor of Music and living alone at St Margaret, Westminster. No address was given but he appeared to be next door to a Metropolitan Fire Brigade station.

Arthur Sullivan

Ellen Terry

H G Wells

Alfred, Lord Tennyson

Poet Alfred TENNYSON, aged 71, whose occupation was given as Poet Laureate, was with his wife Emily, 67, son Hallam, 28, and nine servants at 9 Upper Belgrave Street, St George Hanover Square.

Actress Ellen TERRY, who starred as Henry Irving's leading lady for over two decades, is found on the census as Ellen Wardell - the real name of her second husband, actor Charles Kelly - living with her children, Edith, aged 11, and Edward, 9, at 33 Longridge Road, Kensington, but the husband was not present.

Queen VICTORIA was at Windsor Castle, aged 61, occupation Queen of Great Britain and Ireland. Also in the household were four of Victoria's grandchildren, the son and three daughters of Prince Alfred, Duke of Edinburgh; a visiting foreign dignitary, ex-Empress Eugenie of France; plus an assortment of lords and ladies-in-waiting, court officials and more than 100 servants.

Albert Victor, Prince of WALES, aged 17 [the Duke of Clarence] was serving as a

midshipman aboard the Royal Navy ship Bacchante, either at sea or in a foreign port.

George, Prince of Wales, 15 [later King George V], was also a midshipman aboard the Bacchante.

Author of science fiction novels H G (Herbert

Albert Victor Duke of Clarence

George V

George) WELLS was aged 14 in 1881 and a boarder-scholar at a grammar school at South Street, Midhurst, Sussex.

Oscar WILDE, aged 24, occupation Literature (Author), was a boarder at 1 Tite Street, Chelsea, head of the household being his artist friend Frank Miles, 28. Also present were a female housekeeper, a 13-year-old male visitor who was probably the housekeeper's son and another male visitor, a 22-year-old printer.

Composer Ralph Vaughan WILLIAMS was aged eight and living with his grandmother, Caroline Wedgwood, 80, widowed mother Margaret Williams, 37, sister Margaret, 10, and seven servants at the Wedgwood home, Leith Hill Place, Wotton, Surrey.

Queen Victoria

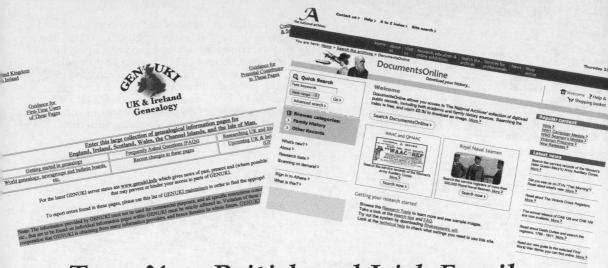

Trace Your British and Irish Family History Using the Internet
Alan Stewart

The number of websites with family history resources continues to grow, as does the amount of information accessible through them. In the last year, several new sets of primary records have become available online: both Ancestry.co.uk and 1837online.com have added the 1861 census of England and Wales to their offerings, Ancestry has also added the 1851 census, while British Origins has added the 1841 and 1871 census returns. In addition, Scotland's People has added the 1861 and 1871 censuses of Scotland to its available records.

A new website, FamilyRelatives, has provided a searchable database of the English and Welsh civil registration indexes covering the period 1866-1920, and it looks as though the Office of National Statistics may make the birth, marriage and death records themselves accessible online in a few years time.

A. General Britain and Ireland
1. Commonwealth War Graves Commission
www.cwgc.org
At this website, you can search free

of charge for information on the 1.7 million Canadian, Australian, New Zealand, South African, Indian and UK servicemen and - women (and 67,000 civilians) who were killed in the First and Second World Wars.

2. Documents Online
www.nationalarchives.gov.uk/documentsonline
One million wills proved at the Prerogative Court of Canterbury (covering the south of England and most of Wales) between 1384 and 1858 are indexed on this site. This index is searchable free of charge, as are those of over five million First World War campaign medals, more than 100,000 Second World War merchant seamen's medals, half a million Royal Naval seamen's service registers (1853-1923), death duty registers (1796-1811), the muster rolls of four French ships captured after the Battle of Trafalgar, and 620 photographs of Victorian prisoners. Viewing an image costs £3.50.

3. FreeCEN *freecen.rootsweb.com*
Volunteers are transcribing and indexing the 1841-1871 and 1891 censuses for England, Scotland and Wales, and these are being made accessible on this website free of charge. Counties with over 50% of the census returns available include (for 1841) Aberdeenshire, Angus, Argyll, Ayrshire, Banffshire, Bute, Caithness, Cornwall, East Lothian, Inverness-shire, Kincardineshire, Kinross-shire, Midlothian, Nairnshire, Renfrewshire, Roxburghshire, West Lothian and Wigtownshire, (for 1851) Banffshire, Bute, Caithness, East Lothian and Nairnshire, (for 1861) Bute, Cornwall, East Lothian and Scottish Shipping, (for 1871) Flintshire, (for 1891)

information on privates and non-commissioned officers (but not commissioned officers) in the British Army who left and received a pension between 1760 and 1854. You can find Royal Navy officers and ratings service records (1802-1919) indexed in the catalogue under series code "ADM 29", and correspondence about prisoners of war (1915-19) under series code "FO 383", in both cases searching with the relevant surname also.

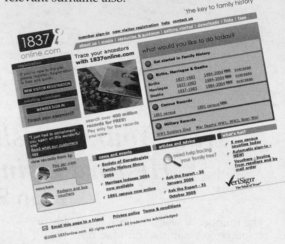

Bedfordshire, Cornwall, Denbighshire, Devon, Flintshire and Warwickshire.

4. GENUKI www.genuki.org.uk

This free "virtual reference library" about the UK and Ireland contains all sorts of useful information for family historians. The information is organised at national, county and parish level, and covers topics such as monumental inscriptions, photographs, descriptions of the countryside, its history, maps, and population figures.

5. LDS FamilySearch www.familysearch.org

The Church of Jesus Christ of Latter-day Saints (the 'Mormons') have made the International Genealogical Index (IGI) of parish register (and some civil registration) entries available on this website free of charge. You can also search the 1881 census there for England, Wales, the Isle of Man, and the Channel Islands (but not Scotland).

6. The National Archives

www.nationalarchives.gov.uk
At the website of The National Archives (TNA), you can search free of charge in a database of those who served on the British side at the Battle of Trafalgar. In addition, you can search in the Manorial Documents Register, which lists the location of documents relating to mediaeval manors in the English counties of Hampshire, Isle of Wight, Middlesex, Norfolk, Surrey and Yorkshire, as well as in Wales.

7. National Archives Catalogue

www.catalogue.nationalarchives.gov.uk
Formerly known as PROCAT, this is a free online index to documents held by the UK National Archives. If you're looking for soldier ancestors, you'll find entries in the index, if you search with a name and series code "WO 97" or "WO 121". These record series contain

B. England and Wales
1. 1837online.com

www.1837online.com/Trace2web
At this website, you can view images of the printed indexes of births, marriages and deaths (covering the period 1837-1983) on a pay-per-view basis. Records from 1984 onwards are held in a fully-computerised database. The site also contains indexes of consular, high commission, and armed forces births, marriages and deaths. Each page in the indexes costs one unit to view, with units costing between £5 for 50 units (which are valid for 90 days) and £120 for 2,400 units (valid for 365 days). Records from the 1861 census are also accessible through 1837online, with searching free of charge, and census images or household transcripts costing 3 units each.

2. 1901 Census

www.1901census.nationalarchives.gov.uk
The UK National Archives has made the 1901 census available at this site, now managed by Genes Reunited, with a full index that can be searched free of charge. It costs 75p to view the image of a page from the census, or 50p for a transcription of one person's details, and a further 50p for a transcription of the rest of the household. For multiples of £5 (with a default amount of £20), you can buy a seven-day credit card session, although £5, £10, and £50 vouchers are valid for six months from the date

of first use.

3. Ancestry.co.uk *www.ancestry.co.uk*
This is the UK website for the American family history company Ancestry.com. The most useful of the many databases accessible through an annual subscription of £69.95 (or £29.95 quarterly) are the English, Welsh, Isle of Man, and Channel Islands censuses for 1851-1901 (all containing digitised images of the records). Ancestry also holds the Pallot marriage index

1780-1837, covering mainly London and Middlesex. Instead of subscribing, you can view up to 20 records at a charge of £6.99 on a pay-per-view basis valid for seven days.

4. BMD Index.co.uk *www.bmdindex.co.uk*
This website provides access to the English and Welsh civil registration indexes on a subscription basis. The site holds images of the printed indexes of births, marriages and deaths from 1837 to 1983, as well as a database of those from 1984 onwards. A three-month subscription

will cost you £5, or you can pay £14.95 for a year. See also 'The Genealogist' below.

5. British Origins *www.britishorigins.com*
Despite now being called British, rather than English, Origins, this subscription-based website provides access to a number of databases including the 1841 and 1871 censuses and various wills indexes, all related to England and Wales. The Society of Genealogists, the UK's oldest genealogical society, has provided some of the databases, including Boyd's Marriage Index, which contains over six million entries for marriages in England and Wales between 1538 and 1840. A 72-hour trial of the site will cost you £5.95, almost as much as the cost of a month's subscription (£7.95). The charge for three months is £12.50 and for a year £22.50.

6. Cornwall On-line Parish Clerks
www.cornwall-opc.org
Since 2001, volunteers have been collecting,

collating and transcribing parish registers, census records, monumental inscriptions, and local histories for each Cornish parish, and making them available online free of charge. This site contains links to seven other similar on-line parish clerk schemes: Cumberland/Westmorland, Devon, Dorset, Kent, Lancashire, Sussex and Wiltshire.

7. FamilyHistoryOnline
www.familyhistoryonline.net
You can view online various indexes compiled by family history societies at this pay-per-view website set up by the Federation of Family History Societies. The indexes include baptisms, marriages, burials, monumental inscriptions and census returns for the majority of English counties and some Welsh ones. Payments from £5 to £50 can be made online, with individual items costing between 3p and 10p each.

8. FamilyRelatives *www.familyrelatives.org*

This pay-per-view website contains an online database of transcriptions of the indexes of births, marriages and deaths in England and Wales from 1866-1920, as well as from 1984-2003. For the periods 1837-1865 and 1921-1983, you can view images of the printed indexes. The charge for using the site is £6 for 60 credits, valid for 90 consecutive days. Searching is free, but it costs two units to view the results of a search in the transcribed database and one unit to view a non-transcribed printed image.

9. FreeBMD *freebmd.rootsweb.com*
For several years, a team of volunteers has been creating a free index of births, marriages and deaths in England and Wales, covering the period 1837-c.1910. The database now contains over 100 million records and is expected to be complete by 2007. You can also view free of charge the images of the original paper indexes used by FreeBMD's volunteers.

10. The Genealogist *www.thegenealogist.co.uk*
Many English census name indexes have been put on to this subscription site by S&N Genealogy, publishers of the British Data Archive census CDs, which

are not indexed. The charge for access to the index for one census (e.g. Durham 1891) is £5 for 90 days or £14.95 for a year (for partial indexes) and £19.95 (for complete indexes).

The site also contains many census transcripts, as well as some directories and parish records. You can buy access to all of The Genealogist's online databases (including those of its sister site, BMD Index) at prices varying from £5 a month to £68.95 a year (and £149.95 a year for professional genealogists).

11. General Register Office
www.gro.gov.uk/gro/content/certificates
Wherever you live in the world, you can place an online order for English and Welsh birth, marriage and death certificates at this official website, and the certificates will be delivered to you by post. If you know the reference number for the certificate, the cost is £7, and if not, £11.50.

12. The National Archivist
www.nationalarchivist.com
You can view the images of a variety of records at this pay-per-view site. These include army lists, births, marriages and deaths at sea (1854-90), death duty registers (1796-1903), and passport applications (1851-62 and 1874-1903). Searching the indexes is free of charge. There is a charge of 1-4 credits for viewing a record, where 35 credits (valid for 45 days) will cost you £7, and 360 credits (valid for 90 days) £50.

13. National Library of Wales *www.llgc.org.uk*
At this free website, you can search indexes of marriage licences (1661-1837) and gaol files of the Court of Great Sessions (1730-1830), covering Wales and some border areas of England. You can also view online images of the St. Asaph 'Notitiae', which are lists of householders compiled in the 1680s in 108 of the parishes of the diocese of St. Asaph in north-eastern Wales. Also at this site are records of the Cardiganshire Constabulary register of criminals (1897-1933), complete

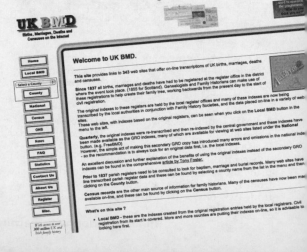

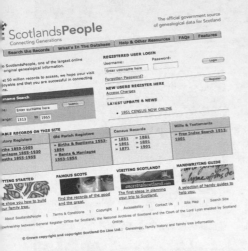

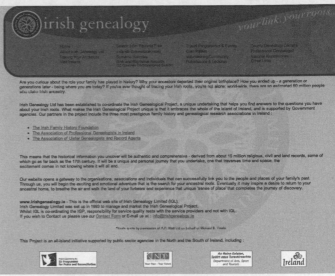

with photographs.

14. UKBMD *www.ukbmd.org.uk*
Around 19 local indexes of births, marriages and deaths in England and Wales can be reached through this site. These are free of charge, apart from the index for Derbyshire County Council, which is available through FamilyHistoryOnline *(see above)*. The indexes have been put online by local registry offices, the first to do so having been Cheshire County Council's in 2000. You can print out an application form and then order a certificate from a local office for £7.

C. Scotland
1. Scotland's People *www.scotlandspeople.gov.uk*
At this official pay-per-view website, you can view and download images of the Scottish civil registration births (1855-1905), marriages (1855-1930) and deaths (1855-1955). In addition, the records of the 1861-1901 censuses are available online. All of these records are indexed, as are the Old Parish Register (OPR) baptisms and marriages/proclamations of banns (1553-1854). The 1841-1851 census records and images of the baptisms and marriages are expected to follow, as are OPR burials. Thirty 'page credits', valid for seven consecutive days, will cost you £6, with unused credits added to your next session. One credit buys a page of up to 25 names from one of the indexes, while the image of one of the records costs five credits. The 520,000 Scottish wills and inventories (1513-1901) that were formerly available at the Scottish Documents website are now available from Scotland's People. Searching the index is free of charge, but downloading the image of a will or inventory costs £5.

2. Scottish Strays Marriage Index
www.mlfhs.org.uk
An index of marriages that took place outside Scotland, where at least one spouse was born in Scotland, has been compiled by the Anglo-Scottish Family History Society (ASFHS). You can search the index free of charge at the website of the Manchester & Lancashire FHS, which is the parent society of the ASFHS.

3. The Statistical Accounts of Scotland
edina.ac.uk/statacc
This site provides free access to digitised copies of these descriptions of life in the 938 parishes of Scotland in the 1790s and 1830s/40s. The fascinating accounts were compiled by the local Church of Scotland ministers, and give a great deal of information about the parishes, but mention few people by name.

D. Ireland
1. Irish Ancestors *scripts.ireland.com/ancestor*
Irish genealogist John Grenham runs this website in conjunction with *The Irish Times*. You can use the site to search for a surname in Griffith's land valuation (carried out from 1848 to 1864), and also for a second surname in the same parish. The site also contains placename and ancestor search facilities. The latter lists resources you can use to search for records of your ancestor, with more information available through a pay-per-view payment of US$8 or a subscription payment of $60 for 30 credits.
2. Irish Genealogy *www.irishgenealogy.ie*
At this website, you can search free of charge in the computer index of nearly three million records held by 11 of the Irish Genealogical Project's 33 county-based family history research centres. In addition, you can order and pay online for research to be carried out at one of the centres, and download a free booklet entitled *Tracing Your Ancestors in Ireland*.

3. Irish Origins *www.irishorigins.com*
You can view Griffith's Valuation at this pay-

per-view site, as well as Irish wills (1484-1858) and various other databases. The wills consist of a mixture of original documents, copies, transcripts, abstracts and extracts. A 72-hour trial of the site costs £3.95, while subscriptions cost £7.95 for a month, £12.50 for three months, and £22.50 for a year.

4. Leitrim-Roscommon Genealogy Website
www.leitrim-roscommon.com
This site contains several databases created by volunteers and accessible free of charge. The databases include the 1901 census, complete for the counties of Leitrim and Roscommon, and partial for Mayo, Wexford and Sligo. Other databases provide details of the townlands (subdivisions of a parish) for Leitrim and Roscommon, and also for the whole of Ireland.

5. Otherdays *www.otherdays.com*
This subscription-based website includes fully-indexed images of Griffith's Valuation, as well as Dublin wills and marriage licences (1270-1857), and a census of County Antrim taken in 1803. There are also many other databases of Irish records, including county and occupational directories, indexes of births, marriages and deaths for certain counties, and burial indexes for some graveyards. Charges range from US$8 for 72 hours to $44 for a year's subscription.

6. Ulster Historical Foundation
www.ancestryireland.co.uk
Member of the Foundation's Ulster Genealogical Historical Guild (which has an annual subscription charge of £30) can carry out online searches of the Foundation's indexes. These cover over half a million records including lists of householders and flax growers. Another 1.2 million records of baptisms/births and marriages in Counties

Antrim and Down have been transcribed and can be searched by anyone free of charge, with access to the transcriptions of ten records costing £10. Deaths are expected to become available online in the future.

Miscellaneous websites
Several other websites (with free access) contain information useful to family historians:
Access to Archives (A2A)
www.nationalarchives.gov.uk/a2a (the catalogue of nearly 400 English archives)
Archives Network Wales
www.archivesnetworkwales.info (the Welsh equivalent of Access to Archives)
Association of Family History Societies of Wales *www.fhswales.info* (with links to seven Welsh family history societies)
British History Online *www.british-history.ac.uk* (includes parts of the *Victoria County History* for more than 30 English counties)
Census Finder
www.censusfinder.com/united_kingdom.htm (over 2,000 links to censuses and other family history resources)
Cheshire County Council Wills Database Online *www.cheshire.gov.uk/Recordoffice/Wills* (index of wills 1492-1940)
Clare County Library
www.clarelibrary.ie/eolas/coclare/genealogy/genealog.htm (1901 census, Griffith's valuation, tithe applotment books, directories, etc.)
Cobh Genealogical Project
www.cork.anglican.org/Parishes_overview.htm (computerising all Church of Ireland (Anglican) registers for County Cork)
Cyndi's List *www.cyndislist.com* (over 240,000 links to family history sites worldwide)
Dumfries and Galloway Historical Indexes
www.dumgal.gov.uk/dumgal/MiniWeb.aspx?id=86&menuid=921&openid=921 (includes a local index to the 1851 census, as well as kirk session minutes)

Durham Records Online
www.durhamrecordsonline.com (database of
transcriptions of census returns and parish
register entries. Free search, but charges for
viewing records)
Families in British India Society *www.fibis.org*
(includes indexes and transcriptions of
baptisms, marriages, burials, embarkation lists,
military records relating to the British in India)
Family History in India
members.ozemail.com.au/~clday (more about the
British in India, including marriage indexes for
Calcutta (1713-1800) and Bengal (1855-96))
Federation of Family History Societies
www.ffhs.org.uk (with links to nearly 90 family
history societies in England, eight in Wales,
three in Ireland, and many around the world)
Friends of Dundee City Archives
www.fdca.org.uk (includes databases of burials
and Methodist baptisms)
Genes Reunited *www.genesreunited.co.uk* (match
your ancestors with names on

its database to contact distant cousins.
Searching is free, but membership costs £9.50 or
£7.50 to renew)
Gloucestershire Genealogical Database
www.gloucestershire.gov.uk/genealogy/genealogy.dll
(includes an index of wills, non-conformist
church records, and gaol registers)
Historical Directories
www.historicaldirectories.org (local and trade
directories for England and Wales from 1750 to
1919)
Irish Ancestral Research Association
www.tiara.ie (American site containing
links to many Irish family history and
cultural websites)
JewishGen UK Database
www.jewishgen.org/databases/UK (database
of Jewish records, including marriages
and burials)
London Signatures
www.cityoflondon.gov.uk/corporation/wills
(wills proved in the Archdeaconry Court
of Middlesex. Free search, but £4 to

download a will)
Lost Generation
www.channel4.com/history/microsites/L/lostgenerati

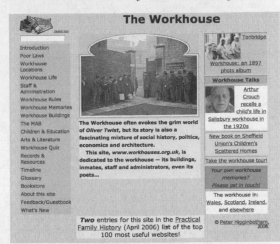

on/index.html (database of soldiers' names from
World War One war memorials)
Moving Here *www.movinghere.org.uk*
(information on Irish, Jewish, South Asian and
West Indian immigration to Britain)
National Archive of Memorial Inscriptions
www.memorialinscriptions.org.uk (database of
memorial inscriptions – in its early stages)
Police, 'Black Sheep' and Other Indexes
www.lightage.demon.co.uk (various useful
indexes)
Proceedings of the Old Bailey
www.oldbaileyonline.org (records of over 100,000
trials at the Central Criminal Court in London)
Scottish Archive Network *www.scan.org.uk* (the
catalogue of 52 Scottish archives)
**Scottish Association of Family History
Societies** *www.safhs.org.uk* (with links to 20
family history societies in Scotland, and many
others worldwide)
Waterford County Library
www.waterfordcountylibrary.ie/index.html (1901
and 1911 censuses, tithe applotment books, etc.)
Welsh Family History Archive
www.jlb2005.plus.com/wales/index.htm (all about
Welsh family history)
Workhouses *www.workhouses.org.uk*
(all

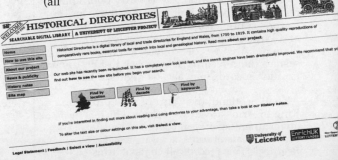

about the workhouses of the British Isles)

Future Digitisation and Other Projects

The UK Government had expected to change the civil registration system for England and Wales through 'regulatory reform orders'. A reform order covering births and deaths was presented to Parliament in July 2004, with a further order for marriages expected to follow. Regulatory Reform Committees of the Houses of Commons and Lords rejected this use of reform orders for such major changes in the law, however, so that the Government will need to pass a completely new Act of Parliament.

In the meantime, the Office of National Statistics (ONS) is proceeding to digitise the existing birth, marriage and death records, and will send the digitised images to India, where a computerised index is to be produced. The ONS expects the indexing to be completed by the beginning of 2008, after which the digitised records will probably be viewable online. Unless the ONS computerised index includes more than forename, surname and registration district, then for the period 1837-1910, this new index will merely duplicate the one that FreeBMD's volunteers have been creating since 1998.

FreeREG *freereg.rootsweb.com* is a sister project of FreeBMD and FreeCEN, and aims to index all parish and non-conformist registers in the UK, starting with those in England and Wales. The index is still being built and not yet open for searching, although initial testing of the search engine began in November 2005.

Ancestry.co.uk has a non-exclusive agreement with the Office of National Statistics to digitise and index the remaining census (1841) for England and Wales, and will be doing so over the coming years. The Scottish censuses for 1841-51 are also expected to become available online over the next few years.

A project is under way in Scotland to digitise the records of the kirk sessions (church courts dealing with the moral transgressions of their congregations), which may take several years to complete. In addition, 19th century poor relief registers are being digitised, with those for the historic counties of Caithness, Ross & Cromarty, and Wigtownshire being tackled first. The National Archives of Scotland's collection of sasines (land records dating back to 1599), and taxation records may also be digitised later.

Also in Scotland, the Court of the Lord Lyon King of Arms *www.lyon-court.com* which is the government agency in charge of registering Scottish coats of arms, is digitising its *"Lyon Register"*. This records all coats of arms

authorised since 1672, and contains genealogical information on well-to-do Scottish families.

The register is expected to be online by 2007, and will form part of the forthcoming Scottish Family History Research Service, which is expected to become operational in 2006. This will provide an integrated service, which will be online through the *Scotland's People* website. Also expected on the *Scotland's People* site in the future are digitised Roman Catholic baptisms, marriages and burials.

The all-Ireland Irish Genealogical Project has transcribed many parish registers and other records and made them available locally through 33 county-based family history research centres. So far, however, only one of those centres has made its records accessible online (the Ulster Historical Foundation with the records for Counties Antrim and Down). Hopefully, other centres will follow its lead.

The Republic of Ireland is already carrying out new civil registrations electronically, as the UK Government had intended to do in England and Wales. In addition, existing records are being digitised, although these will not be accessible via the Internet initially.

The 1901 and 1911 censuses of Ireland are being digitised and indexed by the National Archives of Ireland in conjunction with the National Archives of Canada. The first phase of the 1911 census, covering the City of Dublin, is expected to go online in December 2006. The project is scheduled for completion after a further three years.

Alan Stewart is the author of Gathering the Clans: Tracing Scottish Ancestry on the Internet *(www.phillimore.co.uk)*

© Apple Computer

More About Computers
for Family & Local History
Graham Hadfield

Do you actually need a computer?
This was the first question I asked in the Basic Guide published in the ninth edition of the Family and Local History Handbook. Has the answer**More About Computers for Family & Local History**.

Do you actually need a computer?
This was the first question I asked in the Basic Guide published in the ninth edition of the Family and Local History Handbook. Has the answer changed with the march of time? No it hasn't - a computer is still only a tool and only any good if you have a use for it. This article goes beyond the basics of the last one to explore (mainly) computer hardware in a little more depth and, hopefully, to remove the "mystique". The article will concentrate on PCs but the same principles apply to Apple Macintosh machines as well.

What is a modern computer made of?
At the time this article was written (March 2006) computer magazines were reviewing desktop PCs which came with:
- processors up to 4 Ghz (short for Gigahertz); memory (RAM) of up to 2 GB (Gigabytes);
- a hard drive of up to 300 GB (even two hard drives in some cases);
- 6 to 8 USB (Universal Serial Bus) ports;
- 17, 19 or even 20 inch flat panel TFT (Thin Film Transistor) display screens;
- drives which will read, write and rewrite CDs and DVDs at faster speeds than ever;
- readers for multiple types of memory card;
- networking capability;
- graphics cards with up to 512 MB (Megabytes) of RAM on board;
- TV / radio tuners;
- and various software packages.

All have empty slots which allow their capabilities to be increased by the installation of extra hard drives, RAM and expansion cards.

These machines are priced somewhere between £1,300 and £2,200 - but the price for this specification (or even better) will, of course, be rather less by the time you read this.

Not mentioned above but essential parts of the computer are the keyboard and mouse. It is important that both are comfortable to use. The keyboard should feel solidly built rather than soft. Optical mice are now both more common and affordable and tend to be more accurate that the older ball mice. A mouse with a centre scroll wheel is very useful for scrolling down long web pages and the pages of data CD publications.

So are these features of value to the family and local historian?
Basically, the bigger the numbers the faster the machine. The big numbers come into their own when the machine is doing the work (e.g. editing video files) as opposed to the human being using it (e.g. typing in text).

USB is the method by which most modern day peripheral (external) devices connect to the computer. Some machines still come with the older serial and parallel ports which are useful if you have old devices (e.g. a printer) which you still wish to use. USB is much faster and devices connected to USB ports are "hot swappable" which means that they can be plugged in and removed without the need to turn the computer off. The more USB ports the

better - look for USB 2 which is much faster then the old USB 1.1. Most peripherals which are able to be connected via a USB port are termed "plug and play". This means that, once the driver programs supplied with the device are loaded, the computer will recognise the peripheral as soon as it is connected to a USB port.

Recent years have seen flat panel display screens becoming more common and replacing the older CRT (Cathode Ray Tube) TV style monitors. Some of the earlier flat panel screens could be fuzzy but the modern ones tend to be sharper with less flicker than CRTs. Flat panel displays take up much less desk space whilst providing larger displays because the image reaches right to the corners. A 15 inch TFT screen is equivalent to a 17 inch CRT and a 17 inch TFT to a 19 inch CRT and so on.

Most modern software comes on CDs or DVDs rather than the old floppy disks. This is also true of the growing number of data publications (scanned books and maps plus data transcripts). Some computers still come with floppy disk drives but these are being phased out (if your machine doesn't have one and you need one you can buy an external drive which will attach via a USB port). The ability to write CDs and/or DVDs allows you to share your data with friends and relations and to undertake that most important operation - **back up your files regularly**.

Memory card readers are typically used to transfer photos from digital cameras without having to plug the camera into the computer. The readers usually accept several different types of memory card to cater for the different standards on the market.

Most computers will have graphic display and sound circuitry built into the main component board (the Motherboard). For people who want

to use their machines for video editing, separate graphics and sound cards will be useful - to connect a video camera or recorder requires a special expansion card.

Printers
The basic types of device are still the same as they have been for many years (inkjet and laser). The main developments have been the reduction in price and the capabilities of the devices. One feature that is now becoming more affordable on both inkjet and laser printers is automatic duplex (double sided) printing.

Colour inkjet printers traditionally came with two cartridges, one containing black ink and the other containing cyan, magenta and yellow inks. The disadvantage of the single colour cartridge is that one colour may run out before the others, meaning that ink (and money) is wasted. Printers with separate colour tanks and with five, rather than three, colours are now becoming more common. This, combined with edge to edge printing and advances in printer technology generally, means that some printers can now produce photographs to rival traditional prints. One thing to watch out for is that some inkjet printers are designed for photo rather than general printing, with the result that text printing can be rather slow. If your main requirement is to print text, perhaps with photos embedded, then a decent general inkjet will probably be more useful and will still produce acceptable photographic results.

Laser printers for home use have traditionally been capable of only black and white simplex (single sided) printing. The drop in price has, perhaps, been more dramatic for laser printers than inkjets. For example, a Hewlett Packard Laserjet 6L printer which cost us £310 in November 1997 was replaced by its modern equivalent for £80 in March 2005. As mentioned above, duplex laser printers are now becoming affordable for home use. In addition, colour laser printers are also becoming more common - and for less money than our HP Laserjet 6L!

The above notes apply to printers which handle up to A4/Letter size paper. The range of printers capable of large sheet/banner output is still much smaller and more expensive. This means that family historians requiring a large family tree chart on a single piece of paper are faced with the choice of buying an expensive printer (plus special paper) or going to a company which offers a large print service.

Scanners
Scanners enable family and local historians to digitise paper documents for including in

electronic files and/or publications. The first scanners available for home use in the mid 1990s came with adapter cards that had to be installed inside the PC system unit. These were followed fairly soon by scanners which plugged into a parallel port and had a pass through system to enable a printer to continue to use the same port. Scanners connected via a parallel port tended to be rather slow but this all changed with the advent of USB (and, especially, USB 2).

As with printers, most scanners aimed at home use still only handle documents up to A4/Letter size but A3 scanners are now becoming more affordable. A more common development in recent years has been that a number of scanners on the market come with a transparency adapter. This is basically a small light box which enables scanning of negatives and slides in addition to photographs and other documents.

A limitation for many family and local historians is that the transparency adapter is too small to take older negatives, and certainly much too small for glass negatives. Scanning of these older negatives requires a separately sourced light box which can be used with a scanner which is capable of scanning negatives (some scanners do not have that capability). As with large prints, there are a number of

companies which have the necessary equipment.

Scanners usually come with photo processing software which, apart from allowing modern day photographs to be manipulated, can also be used for digital restoration of damaged originals. This "bundled" software, manipulated through a mouse, tends to be fairly basic and it is not always possible to obtain good results. Companies which offer a restoration service will usually have more sophisticated software and will use a graphics tablet, a peripheral device which allows much more precision than a mouse.

Portable computers.
Laptop computers, sometimes termed notebooks, have two main differences from desktop PCs (apart from the obvious one that they are portable). The first is that, price for price, they have a lower specification and the second is that they tend not to be internally expandable, except for the ability to add extra RAM. They do have ports (usually USB) to allow devices such as printers and scanners to be plugged in and they will run the same software as their desktop "big brothers and sisters", making them ideal for transporting data files when the weight of carrying a laptop is not a problem

Hand held computers, also known as palm tops, are now becoming more common. They are not expandable and can't be linked to peripherals in the same way as desktop and laptop machines. However, they can be plugged into a desktop or laptop via a USB or serial port and often have built in connection capabilities such as infra red. Some come with a slot which will take a memory card (similar to those used by digital cameras) and that can be used to transfer data to and from the main machine. Software is much more restricted but they tend to have word processor and spreadsheet programs and there are a number of family history database programs available for using on them. They can, therefore, be useful for carrying round a copy of data and notes when visiting record offices and taking a laptop is not convenient.

Networking.
Home networking has gained rapid strides in the last couple of years as a result of the increased use of broadband Internet connections and people buying a second computer but keeping the old one so that another family member can share the connection.

Traditional networks are based on having a "hub" or "router" with a number of "ports" on it. Each computer is connected to a port by a special cable. This is both relatively cheap and easy, especially where the computers are physically close to each other and to the point where the broadband connection enters the house.

Some people find it inconvenient to have to run cables, especially over long distances between rooms, and that has led to the growth in popularity of wireless networking. This is basically the same as a wired network but instead of the various computers connecting to the hub or router by cable they connect via a special radio link. Another advantage of wireless networking, if you have a laptop, is that you can use it in a number of locations so long as they are within the range of the hub or router.

One thing to be careful of when setting up a wireless network is in setting up security measures to prevent hackers breaking into the network. Despite the use of technical terms such as "SSID" and "MAC address", this isn't particularly difficult. The hardware is accompanied by instruction leaflets and PC magazines carry step by step articles on how to do it.

More and more record offices, archives and libraries are installing wireless access points which allow visitors with laptops equipped with wireless capabilities to connect to their internal networks.

Software and data
This article has concentrated on hardware because that is where the majority of changes have happened in the last year. However, we must not ignore the fact that the software houses which publish family history programs have, of course, continued to publish upgraded versions of their products and some new products have come onto the market.

A more significant advance, though, is in the amount of data available - both on-line and on CD/DVD. The increase in on-line data has tended, not surprisingly, to congregate around the areas of census, parish register and civil registration data. This has come about as a result of the efforts of both commercial concerns and family history societies.

The past year or so has seen an increased number of small businesses publishing data on CD and DVD. In the main these tend to be scans of out of copyright items such as directories, maps, topographical guides and general historical publications but there are also a number of companies and societies publishing transcribed data in this way.

These factors have to be good for family and local historians because of the increased ease of access to data without the time and expense of travelling.

So what does the future hold?
The "next big thing" for personal computers will be the increased availability of machines based on "64 bit" processors (most current processors are 32 bit). As users all we really need to know, once again, is the bigger the number the faster the machine - though in this case the speed increase will mainly benefit people using programs which manipulate large graphics files.

Prices seem to have "bottomed out" in many areas of the market, the result being that they drop no further but the specification of the machine which the same money buys rises over time.

Perhaps of more significance for family and local historians is that the availability of data in electronic form will continue to expand. Whilst there will be associated costs (e.g. on-line subscriptions and CD purchase prices) these will be less than the costs of travel to distant record repositories - though the coverage is far less than the holdings of record offices. It is still true to say that the person who can trace their family tree merely by using the Internet and other electronically recorded data is extremely rare, even if he or she exists at all. As I stated at the top of this article, the computer is a tool. Like any tool it has to be used properly and its limitations must be recognised.

The Author
Graham Hadfield spent over 30 years in IT before forming JiGraH Resources with wife, Jill, in September 2001. The company provides computer services for family and local historians including printing of large family trees, photo restoration (including from glass negative originals), data rescue and a growing range of old books and maps on CD.

Choosing Genealogy Software
Tony Beardshaw

If you're still using pen and paper to draw your family tree diagrams or you've just inherited a nicely typed family tree with lots of additions hand written over the years then you're probably thinking about how you can easily produce up-to-date diagrams and reports. Using a good family tree program on a computer will not only produce excellent printed results but it will also help you keep track of all your family information and reduce the amount of paper work you need to keep. However before you take the plunge and buy a piece of software, take a little time to consider how much experience you have with computers, what computer is available, what do you want to achieve and who is going to see the results. This article explains the popular features available in modern genealogy software and what to look out for when choosing to buy. Although there are some free programs available they are often free because they are old software and do not have some of the modern features, ease of use and choices of diagram/report printing that are now standard in most commercial software.

How much computer experience do you have?
There are some programs around that are easy to learn and suitable for beginners in computing. They won't necessarily be good at storing lots of details or printing complicated trees, but if all you're after is a series of simple diagrams and reports then they might be just right for you. Two programs; 'The Times Family Tree' and 'Family Tree Maker 2006' will get you started without having to get to grips with too many features and menu options that only serve to confuse.

For the more experienced computer users there are some excellent programs around and although this article is not intended to be a review of any particular piece of software many of the features discussed in the following text are available in such programs as "Family Historian", "Family Tree Maker 2006", "Legacy", "Heritage Family Tree" and "Roots Magic" for the PC and "Reunion" and "Heredis"for the Macintosh. These programs are fully functioning genealogy programs packed full of features that will allow complicated tasks such as merging two family files or dealing with marriages between cousins.

Data Transfer
If you are already using software but it is getting rather old then you may be thinking at this stage that it will be too much trouble to re-key all the information you have gathered over the years into a new program. Most software (even the old ones sold many years ago) will produce an output file in GEDCOM format which has been developed by the LDS church to encourage the sharing and transfer of family tree data. It is a very simple process to move all your information from your old software and into the new, leaving you time to check it all and look for any errors. It is never advisable to type it all in again, because with the best will in the world you will almost certainly introduce some new errors. The specialist genealogy retailers in this book will be able to offer support during this process if you require help.

What computer do you need?
It is not really necessary to have the most up-to-date or a very fast computer for family tree work. Most of the modern programs will work on older versions of windows such as windows 98 and ME. If all you intend to do at the beginning of computerising your family tree is to input data and print diagrams then an older computer will be fine. However you must have a CD drive in your machine to allow loading of programs. If you want to add digital photographs of current family members or you would like to scan old photographs then you will need to start connecting extra equipment to your computer and this is where problems can start with older machines such as those running Windows 95, 98 or ME. Adding components can be frustrating at the best of times and new

© Apple Computer

components linked to older machines sometimes take a lot more time to set up compared to connecting to Windows XP. However don't let this put you off if you only have access to an older PC, other family members (usually children or grandchildren!) can always scan/transfer your pictures and pass the results over to you on CD.

Fans of the modern Apple computers will be aware of the excellent multimedia facilities built into the operating system but unless you have other reasons for buying such a machine an ordinary PC will be perfectly adequate for most genealogists. If you decide to buy a new PC it is not really necessary to purchase an expensive high specification machine for family tree work.

What do you want to achieve?
You may want to record everything you find out about your family as pure facts and figures and then present it just as a family tree diagram or chart. There are various chart layouts which will be discussed later. Alternatively you may wish to add details about their lives and how they lived and then present it as a narrative. Are you going to include siblings in all your tree diagrams? Do you want to record the source of every piece of information so that you may check back in future years? If you share information with other family members then they may well be pleased to know where you found some of your information.

Consider also, long term storage of your data. How future proof is your means of storage. If you have been fortunate enough to have inherited some family tree detail that goes back over 150 years then it is possible that someone at the end of the 19th century started making notes about your family tree (perhaps at the front of a family bible). One thing is certain, the written note has survived and can still be read. Are those floppy discs/CDs going to be useable in 50 years! There are two types of data you are storing; i) data which you wish to publish and what most relatives will be interested in and, ii) references as to where you found the data – sources and repositories. It may be worthwhile at some stage making at least one or two sets of

printouts that contain all the information you have keyed in to your program. A good program will allow you to print out notes in several different ways with or without all those precious source notes.

Who is going to see the results?
The majority of family members may be happy to look over the results of your research and the more interesting it becomes the more likely they are to ask questions. Whilst a printed version of events is probably essential for older family members, consider the needs of the next generation of computer literate youngsters in the family who may be more comfortable clicking and browsing family details as they would browse the internet. At this point, also bear in mind the fact that after all your hard work you probably want people to be able to benefit from it in 50 - 100 years time! Not everything will survive and the least likely is information stored on computers or discs unless family members keep the access to the data up-to-date. Leaving discs in a drawer for 50 years may not be a good idea.

The rest of this article explains some of the main features to look out for when buying a family tree software package.

Ease of data input
It's important that you find inputting the data an easy task. Don't always expect a comprehensive printed manual to come with your program. Most software packages now have a small printed quick start manual and a further comprehensive manual on the installation disc for printing out if you prefer. All the modern programs available to buy, have on-screen help which in most cases is good and in the case of Legacy and Family Historian they are better than average. Family Tree Maker not only has a good book available (at extra cost) to help the novice user around the software but there are also available two DVD tutorials; 'beginners' and 'advanced' at quite reasonable prices. This is a first for genealogy programs and makes learning about the features easier when you see tasks performed on screen.

Researching your tree
Some programs provide links to (and free trials of) online databases and will sometimes, as in the case of *Family Tree Maker*, try to find matches to individuals in your family tree in the attempt to provide you with extra family members you did not know existed. Although the amount of online data for 1837 – 2000 is growing daily the likelihood of finding family members prior to 1837 is limited. However don't let this put you off using the free trials as they can often turn up relatives recorded in the 1841-91 censuses or new information about a known ancestor. Don't sign up too soon to the free trials. Use them once you have got to grips with the software and make

A data input screen in Family Historian

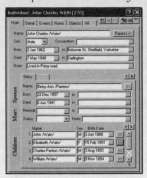

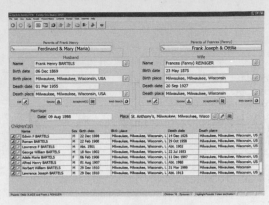

Family View data input screen in Family Tree Maker

sure you take advantage of the free trial period by doing plenty of research.

Charts
As you may be already aware there are various ways in which your family members can be presented in a diagram. Traditionally a family tree would have been drawn on paper with the oldest person at the top and subsequent generations presented in rows below. This is

Ancestor or Pedigree charts in a few programs tend to be drawn from left to right with the root person on the left and the parents, grand-parents, g-grandparents in columns to the right. This is often the way they are displayed on screen and allows easy navigation up and down your tree. See the ancestor chart from Heritage Family Tree for an example. In Family Tree

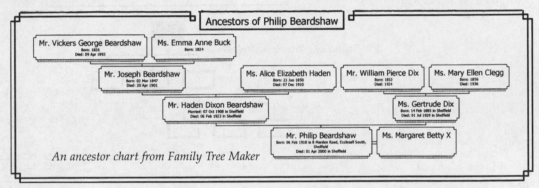

An ancestor chart from Family Tree Maker

sometimes know as a drop line chart and has only been possible in recent years as family tree software has become more powerful and sophisticated. Some of the older and free programs tend to display trees starting on the left and showing newer generations in columns to the right. Some programs will allow you to set out the diagrams as you want them and you may include whatever information you like in the boxes for each person. It is also possible to alter the whole style of the diagram as well as making the boxes for males different from females. In fact you don't even have to have boxes, your diagram can be as plain or as complex as you like. If producing charts is important to you then check out the chart capability of a program to suit your own preferences before purchasing.

Maker the diagram shown is sometimes preferred where the root person is at the bottom of the printout with parents in the row above and grand-parents in the next row up etc.

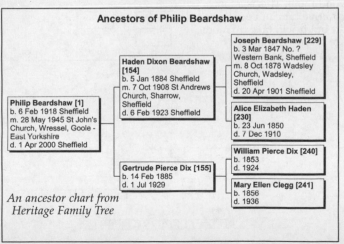

An ancestor chart from Heritage Family Tree

Descendant charts are often used to show all the descendants of a particular ancestor and will include siblings and their own descendants for as many generations as you want to show.

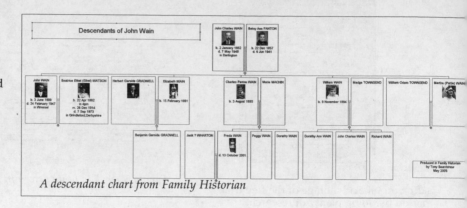

A descendant chart from Family Historian

Hourglass Charts will show all the ancestors of a particular person and their descendants. Not to be confused with a all-in-one chart

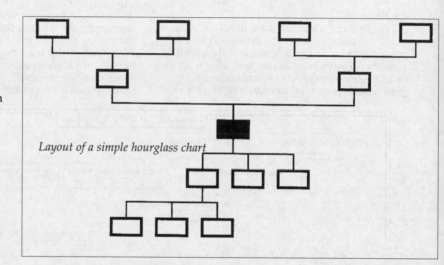

Layout of a simple hourglass chart

Bow-tie Charts are another type of chart sometimes confused with the hourglass chart. This actually shows an individual with their parents either side and grand parents beyond them. This is a more decorative type of pedigree chart but it will take up more space on paper than an ordinary pedigree chart.

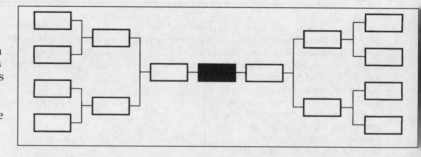

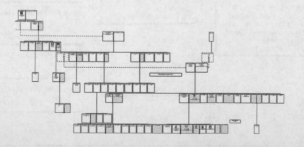

An All-in-one diagram from Family Historian

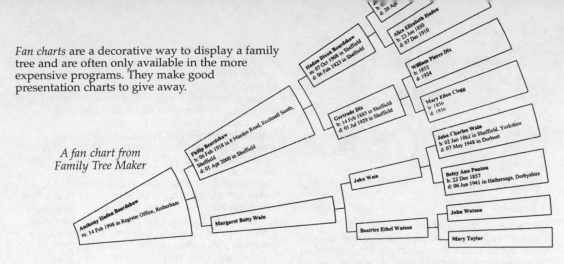

Fan charts are a decorative way to display a family tree and are often only available in the more expensive programs. They make good presentation charts to give away.

A fan chart from Family Tree Maker

All-in-one charts are very useful on occasions where you want to show all the relatives of a particular person. They can become rather complicated and only the best programs seem to be able to cope with the complexities of laying them out in a logical format. There usually has to be a compromise between size and making the chart easy to read and understand.

Reports.

Reports are where the software takes your data and turns it into a narrative to make easy reading for a non-genealogist. These reports can be created for one person, a family or a person and all their descendants. The more expensive software packages will give you greater flexibility in what they contain and how the information is presented. One program in particular, *Family Tree Maker*, will actually allow the user to set out pages of narrative as a book along with diagrams, reports and even contents and title pages. Family Historian also has good narrative reports.

Photographs and other multi-media

If you are lucky enough to have old family photos and you know who the people are, then you will be able to enhance the presentation of your more recent family tree. You will of course need to be able to get these into your computer by scanning. Most programs like *Family Tree Maker*, *Heritage Family Tree* and *Legacy* will link any number of photos to individuals in your tree and you can even adjust the size and crop them in some of the programs. Family Tree Maker will also let you scan directly from the program thus saving a little time if you have not already scanned your pictures using a dedicated scanning program.

One piece of software that particularly stands out from the rest in the way it handles photos is *Family Historian*. This software allows the user to link a group photograph to the file and thereafter different individuals in your family tree can be linked to parts of the photo. On-screen this is particularly useful as it allows the user to look at the close-up of the person or the whole photo. Double clicking on someone's face will automatically bring up their details on screen.

You may also link sound clips and even short movie clips to the more advanced programs but remember these will only be able to be accessed via your computer and the software at present until a more interactive way of presenting the media is offered to non-genealogists.

Web Publishing

Some programs have an integrated web publishing facility, which means they will publish pages of information or diagrams ready to go onto the internet. Most of this information is static at present but expect to see software in the future that will build a site from your whole family tree and be interactive allowing browsers to delve into your family history. If you require web pages now, then look out for the more advanced programs such as Family Historian, Family Tree Maker 2006, Legacy, Family Tree

The Family Historian Mutli-media window

Legends and Roots Magic all of which have capability to produce pages as HTML or PDF files and occasionally JPG.

Sources and repositories

If you have been working at your family tree for a number of years, you are likely to be suffering from paper overload or indexing fatigue and you may also be wondering where some of your facts came from in the first place. For instance you might have two conflicting pieces of information regarding the birth of a family member and you need to go back and review the source of your original data. It is at this point that you realise you can't remember whether it was the local library, The Family Records Centre or if you found it on the internet. Make sure the program you are considering has ample scope for linking sources to your facts so that you don't waste time at a future date trying to find the information again.

Finally – How secure is your data?

It's safe to say that genealogy is an addictive hobby and you're likely to build up a mountain of paper records containing snippets of information about individuals in your tree. There is nothing wrong with this and if it is well indexed then it will last for years and unlike digital information it won't get wiped out overnight if your hard disc fails. There are many advantages of storing information on computer, and there is not enough room here to go through them all except to say that it is important to make a back up of your tree on paper or disc on a regular basis and if it is on disc to periodically try restoring the information to make sure you know how to do it and to verify that the data exists as you expect. If you have a computer with a CD writer then you should consider backing up at least once or twice a year and perhaps more often if you have just keyed a large amount of data.

What products to look out for?

There are several specialist genealogy suppliers advertising in this directory and family history magazines available at newsagents. These suppliers stock a variety of programs and it is worth your while to consider your needs and what the individual programs will do before making a purchase. One or two suppliers provide a comparison table of family tree software so that you may see at a glance what each program is capable of.

The History Portal! *www.nationalarchives.gov.uk*
John Wood
Customer Relationship Manager

The National Archives award winning website tells you all you need to know about The National Archives and hosts millions of online records.

Starting research online
Our 'I'm interested in' link from the homepage gives you great pointers and sets you off in the right direction for your research. From there you can download for free copies of the hundreds of research guides available.

Documents online
The DocumentsOnline section of our website at www.nationalarchives.gov.uk/documentsonline/ is extremely popular for a good reason – hundreds of thousands of popular records have been digitised and made available online for you to download. A simple name search can lead to up to half a million Royal Navy ratings service records, over a million PCC wills, millions of WW1 campaign medals, thousands of WW2 Merchant Seamen's medals and the whole collection is growing!
Searching is free on DocumentsOnline, there is online help and for a fee of £3.50 per document you can download your ancestors record from the comfort of your chair!

Search our collections
The 'search our collections' section of the website – linked form the navigation bar on the homepage - gives you options to search numerous databases for free (as well as link to DocumentsOnline). Included in these links is our famous online catalogue. 'The Catalogue' has an advanced search facility and online help that allows you to search over 9 million record descriptions and then order in advance of your visit to The National Archives. You will also find links to popular searchable databases such as The National Register of Archives and Access to Archives (A2A) medieval taxation records, legal papers and the award winning 'Moving Here' collection of online material looking at immigration to England over the last 200 years.

Census
You can link direct from our website to our licensed partners for online census records from 1841 to 1901 at www.nationalarchives.gov.uk/census/

Plus
Also you can use our website portal - to:
- Keep up with the latest news and record releases
- Subscribe to our free monthly email newsletter jam packed with research information
- Buy books and gifts from The National Archives shop, to be delivered to your door
- Book tickets for the free behind the scenes tour and events at Kew
- Learn online aimed at helping children with their own research whether for homework or just for fun
- Browse 1000 years of history online - see famous images and transcripts of documents such as The Domesday Book or Jack the Ripper's letters
- Use The National Archives online image library

Essential contacts and information The National Archives, Kew, Richmond, Surrey, TW9 4DU, United Kingdom
Website and contact forms: www.nationalarchives.gov.uk
Telephone: 020 876 3444 Publications or bookshop enquiries: 020 8392 5271

www.nationalarchives.gov.uk

The Scotlands People Internet Service

Raymond Evans

General Register Office for Scotland

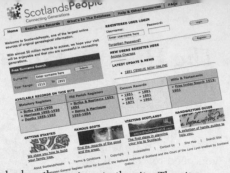

Since September 2002, *ScotlandsPeople* has been giving access to indexes and digitised images of GROS's historical records on the Internet. Records from the National Archives of Scotland (NAS) were added in June 2005. ScotlandsPeople is a fully searchable pay-per-view website provided by a partnership between General Register Office for Scotland, the National Archives of Scotland and the Court of the Lord Lyon and enabled by Scotland On Line.

ScotlandsPeople.gov.uk gives access to a uniquely comprehensive range of Scottish genealogical data including:
• Indexed digital images of the statutory registers of births for Scotland, 1855-1905
• Indexed digital images of the statutory registers of marriages for Scotland, 1855-1930
• Indexed digital images of the statutory registers of deaths for Scotland, 1855-1955
• Indexed digital images of the 1861, 1871, 1891 and 1901 census returns for Scotland
• Indexes to the 1881 census returns for Scotland
• Indexes to the Old Parochial Registers of baptisms and proclamations/marriages for Scotland, 1553-1854
• Indexed digital images of Scottish wills and testaments from 1513 to 1901 (NAS source - free to search)

In addition, the 1841 and 1851 census returns will become available on ScotlandsPeople.gov.uk during 2006;.and the digital images of the Old Parochial Registers of baptisms, proclamations of banns/marriages and deaths at a later date.

The various cut-off dates detailed have been applied to the statutory registers to avoid raising concerns about browsing on the Internet among records relating to living people. An additional year of index data and images is added to the site at the beginning of each year, so 1906 birth data, 1931 marriage data, and 1956 death data will be available from January 2007.

Features
The site includes a number of free features, including a free surname search where the customer can see how many index entries there are relating to particular surnames , features on famous Scots, help with Scottish handwriting, occupations, and unusual words, a place-name search, and news items.

Registration
Customers need to register the first time they access the database. Once registered, customers only need to use their customer name and password when they return to the site. The site uses customer registration forms and order forms so that customers can request particular products, but does not handle credit or debit card details. This information is entered once customers have been directed to the Streamline secure payment gateway of the Royal Bank of Scotland Group, a major UK bank. No credit card or debit card information, is retained by Scotland On Line or GROS at any time.

It costs £6, payable by credit card, to access the index database for GROS data. This gives 30 'page credits' and allows access for a period of 168 hours (starting from the time a credit card payment is authorised), however many times the customer logs on and off in that time. Further credits can be purchased. No charge is made for accessing the index to Scottish wills and testaments but access to the related colour digital images costs £5 per document regardless of length. Customers can access any of the previous records they have downloaded, outside the 168-hour registration period. The site also offers a timeline feature to help customers keep track of the records they have found. Customers can also order hard copies from any of the previously viewed GROS records without having to pay the £6 again.

Searching
Searching is straightforward, with Soundex and wild card search options available. The customer can search across all the records on the database or narrow their search by type of record, time period or geographical area. Each time a search is done, the number of records found is displayed; each record refers to a specific event, ie a particular birth/baptism, marriage or death. When the customer decides to download these records to their PC, they are displayed in pages each containing a maximum of 25 records. In the case of GROS records, each page they choose to download costs 1 credit. The index page will indicate if a digital image of each record is available - if so, it can be accessed at the click of a mouse. To view a digital image of a GROS record costs 5 credits.

If a customer wishes to order an extract of any GROS register entry found in the index, they can do this on-line, again making a credit card payment. The system automatically transfers the request to the General Register Office for Scotland to fulfil the order and mail the extract. A fixed fee of £10 is payable per extract.

You can access the records of ScotlandsPeople at http://www.scotlandspeople.gov.uk

Netting Your Scottish Ancestors

Stuart Raymond

If you have Scottish ancestors, count yourself lucky! Not only are their births, marriages, and deaths, and their relationships, well documented, but many of these documents are thoroughly indexed, and digitised copies of them can be read on your home computer via the internet. It is easy to check civil registers of births, marriages and deaths, the old parish registers, census records, and probate records - the basic information needed to construct Scottish family trees. Indexes to these records on the Scotland's People web-site www.scotlandspeople.gov.uk lead directly to facsimile copies of the original documents. Scottish family historians have no reason to question the accuracy of transcripts on this website: there are none (apart from the 1881 census). And the camera, in this case at least, cannot lie - although there may be the odd occasion when it misses a page or cuts one in half.

The English are entitled to be envious of the riches available to Scottish genealogists on the internet. True, indexes to English civil registers (but not the registers themselves) are available on several different sites from 1837. In terms of the census, the English are almost as far advanced as the Scots. But although there are innumerable transcripts and indexes of parish registers on the web (see my Births, Marriages & Deaths on the Web - 2 Vols. 2nd ed. F.F.H.S., 2005) coverage is extremely patchy and is unlikely to be comprehensive for many years yet. Wills from the Prerogative Court of Canterbury are available on the National Archives website www.documentsonline.nationalarchives.gov.uk - but the majority of wills were proved in diocesan and archdeaconry courts, which are now mostly in county record offices. The Scots are reaping the benefits of centralisation: their old parish registers and wills are held centrally by a single authority. The English equivalents are dispersed amongst hundreds of record offices.

Scottish records differ from those in England. Scotland is a kingdom in its own right, and has its own system of government. Scottish civil registration began in 1855, although it had begun in 1837 in England. The Scottish civil registers are much fuller than their English equivalent. Birth, marriage, and death registers all provide information on the relatives of those who were born, married and died. In 1855, birth registers recorded:
- The child's forename(s) and surname
- The baptismal name (if different)
- The place of birth   • Sex
- The father's name and occupation
- The mother's maiden name
- The date and place of the parents marriage
- The ages and birthplaces of both parents Details of the person recording the birth, including their relationship to the child, and address
- The number and sexes of the child's siblings, both alive and dead
- The place and date of registration, with the registrar's signature

Some of this information was dropped in 1856 - the baptismal name, details of parents ages and birthplaces, and the number of siblings. However, details of parents' ages and birthplaces were restored in 1861. Hence, once an entry for a birth has been located in the register, it should be possible to quickly locate entries for the births of parents and grandparents etc. back to 1855, provided they too were born in Scotland.

Indexes to births, 1855 - 1904 are available on the Scotland's People web-site. An annual index is added each year, but privacy concerns mean that indexes under 100 years old are not available on the internet. Each index entry gives the year of registration, surname, forename(s) and sex, together with the registration district, county, and General Register Office Scotland reference. The latter is needed to identify the page in the register where the particular entry is to be found. Before you view images, you should read the Viewing Images page on the site.

The Scottish marriage registers record, from 1856:
• When, where, and how married
• The names, marital status, addresses, and occupations of both parties
• The ages of both parties
• The names and occupations of both partners parents
• The signatures of witnesses (with addresses) and the officiating minister
• The place and date of registration, and the registrar's signature

In 1855, additional information was also given, including the birth dates and places for both partners. Birth information was re-instated in 1972. Indexes to the marriage registers are available for 1855-1929. The information in Scottish death registers includes:
• Name
• Place and date of death   • Sex   • Age
• The name and occupation of the deceased's father
• The forename and maiden name of the deceased's mother

• The cause of death
• The signature of the informant, and his/her residence
• The place and date of registration, and the signature of the registrar

Between 1855 and 1860 additional information is also given. This includes the burial place, the name of the person who certified the burial, and when the deceased was last seen by the doctor. For 1855 only, additional information includes the place and date of birth, details of children, and the name of the deceased's spouse. The spouse's name was not specifically asked for after 1861, but was nevertheless usually entered.

Indexes to the death registers cover 1855-1954. They indicate dates of birth, which may be helpful in identifying the specific entry if a search finds many hits.

In theory, it should be possible to construct a pedigree simply using the records of civil registration on the Scotland's People website. However, identifying the relevant records is not always straight forward. Even if it is, the civil registers will only provide you with the bare bones of your family tree. The information they provide should always be compared with the information provided by the census. Currently (July 2005) Scotland's People has indexes and images of the original returns for 1871, 1891 and 1901. It also has indexes and transcripts of the 1881 return (which is also available at www.familysearch.com. The 1881 index differs

from that for other census years. It was compiled under the direction of the Latter Day Saints, and offers more flexible searching capabilities. The transcript on the Scotland's People site is due to be replaced by digitised original returns. The 1881 index and transcript may also be viewed at www.familysearch.org

The purpose of the census was to count the entire population; it recorded names, addresses, ages, occupations, and places of birth. From 1851, it also recorded the relationship of each person enumerated to the head of the household in which he/she lived, the marital status of each individual, and whether they were blind, deaf or dumb.

There were other minor variations in the questions asked in different census years, and the 1841 returns in particular, are less detailed than later censuses. The Scottish census questions were identical to those asked in England, except that in 1891 and 1901 everyone was asked whether they spoke Gaelic.

The great advantage that the census has over the civil registers is that it records the members of entire households at specific dates, showing (except in 1841) relationships to the head of the household. It is thus possible to see at a glance how many children each householder had

living at home, the names of spouses, and whether other relatives were present. This information may enable you to go back to the civil registers and search for more birth and marriage entries. The disappearance of individuals between census years may suggest that a search be made in the death registers.

Civil registration and census records only go back to the mid-nineteenth century. If you want to go back further, then you will need to consult the old parish registers and wills. Both of these are also available on the Scotland's People website.

Until 1855, baptisms, marriages, banns, and burials, were recorded in Church of Scotland registers, usually by sessions clerks or schoolteachers rather than clergymen. A few registers survive from the mid-sixteenth century, but most begin later - some not until the nineteenth century. Even when they were kept, many events were not recorded in them: the proliferation of denominations, and the imposition of a stamp duty of three pence on every entry in 1783 (repealed in 1792), meant that Church of Scotland registers were not kept as they should have been. Scotland has no bishops transcripts to fill the gaps. Nevertheless, the old parish registers are the most important source of pre-1855 information on births, marriages and deaths. It is fortunate that most of them were collected by the Registrar General. They are all fully indexed on the Scotland's People website, and it is probable that, by the time you read this, images of the original registers will also be available.

Scottish wills and testaments are also held centrally, and can be read at Scotland's People'. These are amongst the most personal records of your ancestors that you are likely to encounter. Wills provide instructions for the disposal of estates after the death of the testator, and name the executor/executrixes who were to be responsible for distribution of estates. Executors had to be confirmed in their office by a testament testamentar, issued by a Commissary Court (or Sheriffs Court after 1823). If there was no will an administrator was appointed by testament dative. In either case, an inventory of the deceased's goods had to be drawn up, This would exclude heritable property, which was subject to the law of primogeniture until 1804, and could not be bequeathed by will. Probate documents are likely to reveal valuable information about the deceased's relations and friends, about his lifestyle, and about his wealth. The Wills & Testaments Index has over 611,000 entries for the period 1513 to 1901. Each entry lists surname, forename, title, occupation and place of residence. It also indicates the court in which the testament was recorded, and the date.

Scotland's People provides the researcher with much more comprehensive genealogical information than is available on any site for any other country. It has, however, cost a lot of money to establish, part of which has to be recouped by charging fees for its services. Details of these are given on the website.

Scotland's People is not the only website of interest to Scottish genealogists. There are many others, including some which provide identical information for free. Scotland Free Reg http://home.chilitech.net/~nmjeffery/scotland freereg.htm aims to provide free internet searches of registers of baptisms, marriages and burials. It has a long way to go before it is complete, but is worth checking before you visit Scotland's People, especially as it aims to include nonconformist and Roman Catholic registers, which are not covered by Scotland's People'. Its sister site, Free Cen Scotland' home.chilitech.net/~mmjeffery/myweb9/index .htm aims to provide free indexes to Scottish census returns. Many returns for 1841-71 (and especially 1841) have already been indexed, although again there is a long way to go.

A wide variety of other sites provide transcripts and/or indexes of parish

and nonconformist registers, and of census returns. Mostly these cover single parishes or small areas, for example, the Wesleyan Register of Baptisms, Dundee 1785 - 1898 is on the site of the Friends of Dundee City Archives at www.fdca.org.uk/methodists.htm. Many of these sites may be found by consulting the county and parish pages of Genuki Scotland www.genuki.org.uk/big/sct/

There are also two gateways dedicated to census sites:
Scotland Census Records
www.censusfinder.com/scotland.htm
www.scotlandsclans.com/census.htm

The Genuki site also has much general information, together with separate pages for all counties and many parishes, listing local resources, and providing links to numerous other sites. It includes a number of gazetteers to help you locate particular places and pages on topics as diverse as archives and libraries, church history and emigration and immigration. Its aim is to be a virtual reference library of information about British genealogy. Its focus is on sources. It does not include pedigrees or pages dealing with research on particular families; nor does it include links to purely commercial sites.
There are two other major sites which complement Genuki. Scotland Genweb www.scotlandgenweb.org has many county pages with local information (although not parish pages). The Scotland Research pages of UK Genealogy

www.ukgenealogy.co.uk/scotland.htm has similar information. Both provide addresses of societies, libraries and archives, mailing lists, and links to a wide range of other pages. Both sites place greater emphasis on the results of research than Genuki does; they also provide some links to the more important commercial sites.

There are many other pages providing useful advice on Scottish family history. A useful tutorial dealing with a wide variety of sources is provided by the Scotland Genealogy pages at Mother Hubbard's Cupboard www.gaia.edu/genclass/205/gen205.htm

Authoritative guidance is provided by the fact sheets on the National Archives of Scotland's website www.nas.gov.uk/family_history.htm These cover a wide range of subjects, ranging from deeds to emigration, from the poor to taxation records. Also authoritative are the Research Tools - and especially the Knowledge Base - on the Scottish Archive Network www.scan.org.uk/researchtools/index.htm Topics such as liquor licensing records and school admission registers, vehicle registers and passports may seem esoteric to the uninitiated, but all these sources may help to fill in the details of our family histories.

The primary purpose of the Scottish Archive Network www.scan.org.uk is to provide an online catalogue of the archival holdings of record offices throughout Scotland. Fifty-two offices were covered at the time of writing: the website provides a directory (including web-page addresses). Every family historian would be well advised to search the catalogue for both the names being researched, and for the places where ancestors are thought to have lived. Over 20,000 collections of historical records are identified, and a search is quite likely to throw up valuable leads.

The major record office in Scotland is the National Archives of Scotland www.nas.gov.uk. In addition to the archives of Scottish central government, it also holds many church and burgh records. The registers of sasines (sasines are Scottish title deeds) are particularly useful, since they enable you to trace the ownership of every house and piece of land in Scotland since the seventeenth century. Unfortunately it is not online, although the N.A.S. website does include a useful fact sheet.

More helpful advice is provided by the websites of family history societies. The Scottish Association of Family History Societies www.safhs.org.uk is the umbrella organization for Scottish societies, and its site provides links to them. Links can also be found on Genuki's

Family History and Genealogy Societies Scotland page www.genuki.org.uk/Societies/Scotland.html. Most society websites provide basic information about the society, including contents, activities and publications; they also usually include local information of use to researchers in their area, and may also have transcripts and indexes of sources. Fife Family History Society's website (www.fifefhs.org) for example, has numerous records for particular parties, e.g. a calendar of Auchtermuchty deeds 1757-1854, extracts from the burgh records of Crail listing Crail weavers 1694-1845, a list of Dalgety jurors 1851, etc., etc.

Some family history societies also have pages listing the surnames their members are researching. There are also many other surname interests lists on the web. The most important for Scottish genealogists is probably the Online Scottish Names Directory www.list.jaunay.com/sctnames/ which has separate pages for most counties. So does UK Surnames www.county-surnames.co.uk/ These enable you to make contact with other researchers who may be researching the same names as you.

Another means of making contact with other researchers, and of obtaining general advice, is provided by numerous mailing lists. These enable you to send emails to others who may share your interests. Many mailing lists are devoted to specific surnames, but these tend to be dominated by American researchers. More useful are the mailing lists devoted to specific counties. There are also some which deal with specific interests such as the Highland Clearances or Scottish war prisoners.

Rootsweb lists.rootsweb.com hosts an enormous number of mailing lists including many related to Scotland. There are a variety of other sites; a full listing is provided by John Fuller's Genealogy Resources on the Internet: Scotland Mailing Lists www.rootsweb.com/~jfuller/gen_mail_county_unk_sct.htm

This article has only skimmed the surface of the material available to Scottish genealogical researchers on the internet. I have listed thousands of other sites in *Scottish family history on the web* (see below). A more detailed discussion is provided by Alan Stewart's *Gathering the clans: tracing Scottish ancestry on the internet* (Phillimore, 2004).
Stuart Raymond is a well known genealogical author and bibliographer. The second edition of his *Scottish family history on the web* was published by the F.F.H.S. in 2005, and is available from him at P.O.Box 35, Exeter EX1 3YZ Other relevant titles include *Family history on the Web: an internet directory for England and Wales*, the fourth edition of which should be available by the time you read this, and *Irish Family History on the Web*, price £6.60.

Catalogues

The travel brochures

of genealogy

- the Scottish Scene

Rosemary Bigwood

The ways in which we search for ancestors have undergone dramatic changes in the past few years thanks to the internet and it is often claimed that tracing your family history is now both quick and easy. By using websites and other online facilities it is possible to exchange information with others round the world, often discovering unknown relatives or linking up with research done elsewhere. You can find out a great deal about people, places and events on information sites at the click of a key. There is an ever-growing number of indexes to valuable sources such as monumental inscriptions, war dead, immigrants and emigrants (to name only a few) and transcripts of texts such as censuses and extracted listings can be viewed on websites. The National Archives and the National Archives of Scotland (among others) are engaged in digitisation programmes which enable you to consult a range of documents at home. In Scotland we are well served by the ScotlandsPeople website (www.scotlandspeople.gov.uk) giving access to Scottish wills, census returns and statutory registers of birth, marriage and death, with the prospect of parish registers and kirk session records to come. Not all sites are free but the expenditure of a relatively modest sum of money can produce valuable results without the necessity of moving from your computer at home.

A word of caution is, however, necessary. The view that ancestry can now be traced successfully without pain or problems is misleading – and limiting. There are dangers in making use of this wealth of online information. Contributors to website forums, message boards or mailing lists are not always well informed. Reliance on indexes alone is a perfect recipe for disaster and failure to take the time to look at full entries in the records may introduce many cuckoos in the genealogical nest. Transcripts are by no means always accurate – omissions, wrong readings and dubious assumptions are not infrequent - and ease of access to indexes and digitised documents can induce tunnel vision. While enjoying the ability to search testamentary material online, for example, many forget that there is a great deal of other relevant source material which can still only be consulted in paper form such as deeds or edicts. It is most unlikely that all manuscript material will ever be available on a computer.

Searching for catalogues

Family historians are rightly grateful for the enormous opportunities in finding so much information which can be tapped online, particularly those who live far from their forebears' homelands and do not have ready access to the original records. There is, however, an abundance of other material "out there" which may also be interesting, possibly of vital importance, and which is often overlooked. Having explored and exploited the core sources for family history - statutory

registers, census returns, parish registers and testamentary material, it is time to look further afield.

The first questions to be asked in this quest for source material for family history are: "Is there anything else which might be relevant to my family?" "What can I find?" and "Where is it kept?" and in the past, it has been difficult or impossible to discover the answers. The National Archives of Scotland hold a vast range of documents covering every aspect of administration and life from the middle ages. Searching a bulky paper catalogue – even if you can find one outside the archive - is a daunting prospect. In Scotland, more records are centralised than south of the Border but local council archives, libraries, various institutions and specialised collections also hold a great deal of valuable material. The complexities of locating records are often made greater as collections may have been split – some kept in the NAS, more in a local repository, some in private hands. The result has been that the treasure hunt might often end in disappointment and failure to find something of interest.

More and more catalogues are now becoming searchable online. This is one of the most exciting new aspects of research and offers potential which is often overlooked. Catalogues are the travel brochures of genealogy. They provide a view of what you can find in a particular place and information about what you may see there. If you know the name of a particular archive or library which you think may hold relevant material, you can key in the name of the institution through an online search engine such as Google and bring up the website. On the other hand, there are now several very useful sites which list repositories under certain categories and by clicking on a particular entry, you can find a great deal of detailed information about the holding. The following are useful:

ARCHIVES HUB (www.archiveshub.ac.uk) – details of holdings of 140 universities and colleges in the United Kingdom. You can search under various categories, including by person, place or subject. Entering "whaling in Scotland" as the subject, produced a reference to two sites and it was then possible to bring up a detailed description of each deposit. Scope and content of each holding (with dates covered) are indicated, as well as notes on finding aids and references to any related material.

ARCHON (www.nationalarchives.gov.uk/archon) – repertories of 230 repositories and institutions in the United Kingdom and elsewhere in the world which hold substantial collections of manuscripts. If you click on Scotland in the alphabetical list of countries, you can find entries as varied as Arbroath Museum, Atlantic Salmon Trust and Ayrshire Archives. You can then bring up the link address and a general description of the repository. Archon includes references to the collections listed in the National Register of Archives.

FAMILIA (www.familia.org.uk) – a guide to genealogical resources in public libraries in the United Kingdom and Ireland. The entries vary in the amount of detail given but some (not all) individual catalogues can be searched through this site.

SCAN (www.scan.org.uk) – catalogues of 52 Scottish archives, including council and other archives, libraries, museums and health boards. The list includes the National Archives of Scotland and the National Library of Scotland. By clicking on the name of the repository in which you are interested, you will see a summary of the collection which may be a general description or a more detailed one. Dates covered by the various classes of documents are given, as well as an indication of how many metres of shelving are taken up by the records, a note of finding aids (if any), and sometimes a reference to related holdings kept elsewhere. Under the heading of Lothian Health Board archives, you will find an entry for the Royal Infirmary, Edinburgh 1727-2001 and clicking on that brings up more detailed information, showing that among many other records are details of patients there from 1762-1963.

Using catalogues

The level at which the holdings of archives are described in their online catalogues varies widely and much work is still on-going. In some cases, the entries only give very general information on the holdings of the archive or organisation. Others are very detailed, down to item level. Very rarely will a particular document be reproduced online. Much, however, can be achieved at home by looking for interesting references and then narrowing the choice of classes of records which are likely to be useful. For example, if you know that an ancestor worked at New Lanark Mills in the first half of the nineteenth century, on the Archives Hub site you will find details of a large deposit of papers kept by the Glasgow University Archive Service which includes a register of births, deaths and marriages for the years 1818-1853. The entry also notes that the Glasgow City Archives hold plans of mills and villages.

Catalogues should be regarded as a research tool and like all tools, skill is necessary to produce the best work. Coping with the enormous range of material which is listed on websites is not always easy, particularly in the case of large national archives. You may be faced with having to scroll through innumerable entries and the content of many records may be unfamiliar. Terms such as diligence, warrants, decrees or adjudications may mean little and there is no indication as to whether these documents might be useful. Sometimes assistance is given in picking out the types of records which are most likely to be of value in your search. The website for the Perth and Kinross Council Archives suggests sources for family history – sasines, lists of individuals and records of burghs, militia, parochial boards, criminals and estates. The online catalogue for the National Archives of Scotland – OPAC (online public access catalogue – www.nas.gov.uk) – includes descriptive notes on the content and history of various classes of records and you can download useful leaflets from the NAS website which act as guides to their holdings.

When you are searching catalogues, you are unlikely to be rewarded by finding the name of your ancestor (unless famous, notorious or influential) and it is therefore important to think laterally when attempting to find relevant records. What did your ancestors do? Where did they live? When did they live? If your forebear was a tenant farmer, there is little chance of locating an entry in the catalogue under his name but if you can identify the part of the country where he lived and the likely name of the proprietor of the lands which he worked, then you can look for records of that estate and possibly find rentals of the appropriate time. If you are looking for a craftsman ancestor in a royal burgh, then you can search for records of that burgh and see if there are apprentice or craft records or burgh sasines which might refer to him.

Computers are literally minded and will only respond to your search commands. When searching for particular classes of records, think of possible alternatives for the terms used. Keying in "poll tax" and also 'pollable persons" may bring up different entries forming part of the same series of records.

Catalogues play a very important part in the search for sources and in pointing you in the right direction. They provide an introduction to wide vistas of what one can term *a research countryside*" but they cannot tell you everything. They often provide you with an opportunity to select what material is likely to be relevant in tracing your family history and then, if the source seems interesting, you must go and read the documents yourself or employ a researcher to do this for you. There can be no shortcuts. As with a holiday selected from a travel brochure, only a visit to the destination will prove whether your choice was what you really wanted.

military history

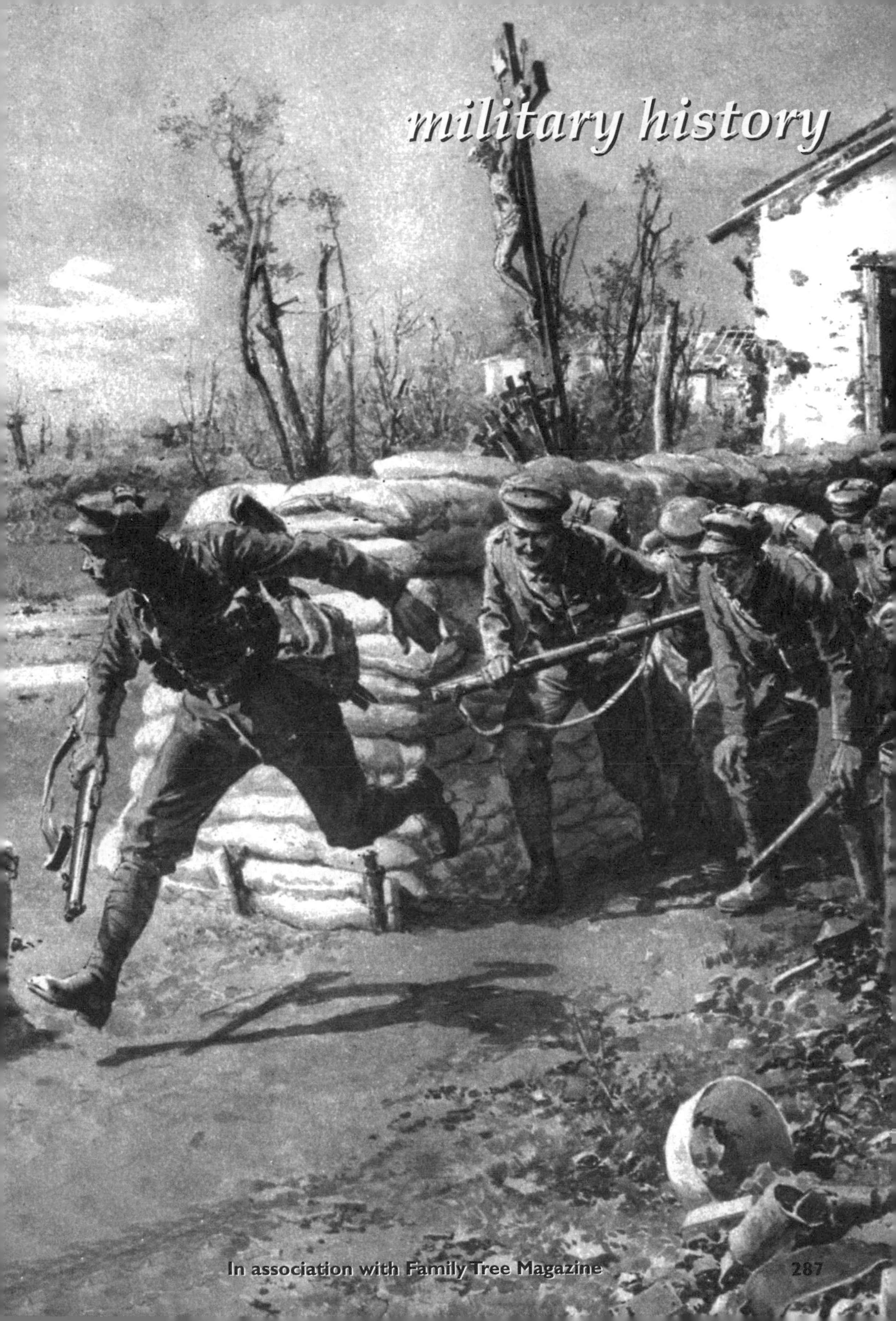

What's new at the
Imperial War Museum
Sarah Paterson - Department of Printed Books

This has been another very period for the Imperial War Museum, with many new online developments that are detailed below. This means that you will be able to gain access to more materials held at the Museum without leaving the comfort of your own home – although visiting in person to see the exhibitions or make use of the research facilities is still recommended!

Some of you may have seen the regional *Their Past Your Future* exhibitions that have been travelling around the country. *The Big Lottery Fund* made this ambitious programme possible. The travelling exhibitions were only one component of this educational venture that commemorated the end of the Second World War by examining the conflict itself and its legacy. Have a look at the website www.theirpast-yourfuture.org.uk for more information.

One of the strands of the project was a major digitisation programme undertaken by the Collections Division of the Imperial War Museum. Many items can now be viewed on **Collections Online** at www.iwmcollections.org.uk

Some departments had already made a start on digitisation, but this was a challenging process for those who were new to it, with issues such as copyright, legibility and storage being prominent. We hope you will like the results though, and once everything has been loaded, it should be possible, for example, to see an image of a Royal Navy Ship and read a short typescript history of it and sometimes, hear short extracts

from an interview with an ex-sailor who served on board.

Another initiative has been **Your History** – which opened at *Imperial War Museum North* in Manchester in the summer of 2005. This is the first part of a larger project aimed partly at making the resources of the Museum available online in the galleries, and possibly ultimately through the internet. Anybody can use the computers at IWMN and you can find out more about objects in the collection and there are many 'frequently asked questions'. As family history is one of the areas that we are most often asked about, there are pages that will enable you to find out more about the wartime service of your relatives, as well as links to other websites, such as the Commonwealth War Graves Commission and The National Archives.

Many of you will be aware of, and may even have contributed to, the United Kingdom *National Inventory of War Memorials*. Their website, with details of about 53,000 war memorials in the United Kingdom, was launched in November 2005 – this is still not complete and work is ongoing. So have a look (www.ukniwm.org.uk) and if you know of a war memorial that doesn't feature on the site, do contact the UKNIWM to see if they are aware of it. They rely very much on the hard work of the volunteers who record information about the different memorials in their local area. Through the website you can also gain access to a microsite run by Channel 4, which has lists of names which feature on some of the memorials – it isn't a comprehensive listing although perhaps

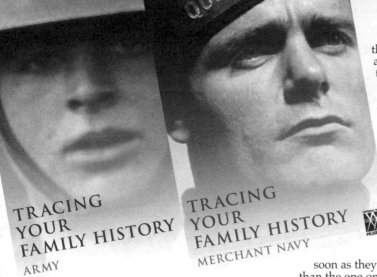

TRACING YOUR FAMILY HISTORY
ARMY

TRACING YOUR FAMILY HISTORY
MERCHANT NAVY

this is an excellent guide for anyone wanting to know about the structure of the Army in the Second World War. It was produced as a Technical Manual for the American Army to enable them to fully understand how their ally operated. It is an absolute mine of information and still recommended reading for new members of staff at the Imperial War Museum.

Every year we reproduce a couple of information sheets for family historians in this book. It sometimes seems as if our leaflets are out of date as soon as they are produced, and none more so than the one on the Royal Navy where there seem to have been vast changes with the location of records and availability of material. As there have been major alterations since this was featured here last year, we are repeating the new edition, and also a leaflet on the Royal Canadian Navy. This was one of five information sheets done in conjunction with the **Commonwealth Navies** exhibition on HMS *Belfast*. The other titles, allowing you to trace Australian, Indian, New Zealand and South African naval personnel can be found on the Museum website at www.iwm.org.uk

If you wish to make an appointment to visit our Reading Room, or have a question you would like to ask (bearing in mind that we cannot embark on detailed research for you), please contact us in one of the following ways:
Telephone (enquiries): (020) 7416 5342
Post: Imperial War Museum, Department of Printed Books, Lambeth Road, London SE1 6HZ
Email: books@iwm.org.uk
Website: www.iwm.org.uk

that might come with time.

The final website plug is for the Museum's **Women's Work Collection**. This is a fascinating treasure trove of material relating to women in the First World War, and it has been digitised by Thomson Gale, and made available as a commercial website called **Women, War and Society, 1914-1918**, with a search mechanism. Although the product is only available on subscription and is geared towards academic libraries (you may find a library near to you has it) it can be viewed free of charge at the Museum. This is an excellent source for information about many long forgotten organisations (how many of you know about Miss Gladys Storey's Fund for Bovril for the troops? Or Lady Smith Dorrien's Hospital Bag Fund?) but also has details about women who were decorated or who died (and being able to search for a name is an extremely useful tool).

New editions of our *Tracing Your Family History* guides are now available. These sell for £5.99, and we have copies for the Army, Royal Navy, Merchant Navy and Royal Air Force. Copies can be purchased through the website at www.iwmshop.org.uk

Other new publications with some relevance for family historians are two facsimile publications of HMS *Belfast* Commissioning Books, which detail where the ship sailed and what she did during the period in question. There are books for 1950-52 (£6.99) and 1961-62 (£7.99). Finally, we republished **Handbook of the British Army, 1943: with supplements on the Royal Air Force and Civil Defence Organizations** (£28.00) –

TRACING YOUR FAMILY HISTORY
ROYAL AIR FORCE

TRACING YOUR FAMILY HISTORY
ROYAL NAVY

Voices of The First World War.
John Holland

These accounts are taken from an album that my Grandfather John William Glew, of the 20th Hussars, had in his possession at the time of his death on 4th July 1959. The water colour picture was painted in the album by my Great Uncle Albert Harrison. The date is unknown.

The Album was passed around a hospital for the wounded to record their own hand written accounts as to how they succumbed to injury on the battlefield of the Great War.

Sgt W. Weston 2 Sherwood Foresters 26th Nov. 1914

My Movements the Day I was wounded 20th Oct. 1914 Our Brigade had taken a Village nearly three miles in front of the Main Line. About 1.a.m. on the 20th Oct. 1914, our Reg't relieved the Durham's Light Infantry, which Reg't had forced our advance through this Village.

I was detailed with a party of men to dig a communication trench when the officer put his glasses on him and he saw a man in civilians with hat on ready for departure. He (the Officer) watched this small window in the roof of this house, and to his surprise a carrier pigeon flew out of the window right over our trenches into the German lines.

My officer said Weston go to Major Gower (who was our C.O) and report there is a spy & about the carrier pigeon, and ask him for a few men and fetch him out.

As soon as I got out of the trenches, a heavy cannonade commenced on the village, (where our supports had us stayed). After a struggle dodging shell & houses falling, I got to our Major at Headquarters, and commenced reporting the matter to him, when a shell came over and blew one of the walls of the house in. (Luckily we never got touched). So we went across the road to another house to tell him, when another shell came and blew an hole clean through the wall. He says *"this is a bit rough"* so we went into the open against the side of a wall when at last, I explained my message to him. Well, he says, you cannot go now whilst this cannonade is on, no doubt the house will soon be blown down, and it will save you a lot of trouble then. You may stop here he said. I said I would like to go back to the trenches, as I might be required, so he told me to please myself, so I left for the trenches, and as there was only one main street I had to go through that.

I got half way through and was near the Church when they concentrated their fire on the Church. (By now the houses were falling and burning. Goods from the shop windows were flying in every direction. It was just like *"Hell upon Earth"*). I could not get any farther than the Church on account of the heavy shelling. So I laid down alongside the Church wall, giving all up wishing the end would come quicker. (Every time a large shell fell on the Church or in the Churchyard, I was lifted off the ground three or four inches often wondering if I was dead.)

I lay there for two solid hours, which I thought were weeks. Dozens of shells had dropped on the Church. Only one shell hit the wall that I was lying against, this shell blew the top off the wall that did not drop on me, as I was close up to the wall. The shells seemed to be falling off a bit from hitting the Church so I chanced my arm (so to speak) and got up, and to my surprise the Church was as flat as a pancake just burning a little here and there.

The gravestone, and Globes were all smashed to atoms. I went along the main street dodging shells and bricks, (By the way the street was one mass of wreckage) and I had to climb over heaps of furniture & bricks to get along. I got as far as the Mill, and I met a L'Cpl. Grundy there. He says *"for God's sake don't go beyond this it is Hell upon Earth"* I said to him it is Hell down there and I pointed and he said *"Good God"* so we both sat down, (making the best of things) aside the Mill. We were just beginning to talk on how we were getting on in the trenches when a nice heap of tiles dropped between us, and he said, *"I am off"*, and he went into the direction of the trenches. I sat there for a few more minutes and was looking around, and I saw a German Column coming on our right flank, which was weakly protected. I took out my note book, and made a report, which I was just finishing, when I was stunned for a second, and I had been lifted off the ground about two feet and as I dropped on the floor it seemed to bring me back to my senses, I found that a large shell had dropped at my back the other side of the wall, there were an hole through the wall and the bricks had been blown through my legs into the middle of the street and an odd brick came rolling down my back. I thought I was dead. I kept pinching myself and rubbed my eyes. (Reader you may laugh but it is quite true, it was the nearest escape I had of being buried alive.)

At last I got up and finished my report, and set off to let Major know about this German column. I went through the Hell of the village again, which was being continually shelled. I found this Major and told him he asked me to show him where they were so we went through this Hell again and as we were going through he says drop and a shell burst about 10 yds in rear of us, it missed us. So we went through the village to an open field so as I could explain to him exactly where the German column was. I stayed with him a little time then I made best my way to the trenches again. I got through that awful village again and I chanced it through the open into the main trenches, it was simply luck that I got through that Hail of Bullets & Shells.

When I got into the trenches my comrades said If I were you I should not have chanced it. I said I had been hanging on long enough. When I arrived in the trenches I asked then what sort of time they had been having and they said "A pretty hot one." I need not have asked for as soon as I looked round I could see dead and wounded which told the tale, and I found my trench had been

blown up, so I had to chum in with someone else for a bit of shelter. I also found that our Officer & two senior Sgt's had been wounded (Lt. Wickes, Sgt's Foy & Spencer) so I was in command. After I had been in the trenches for half an hour I could see that to my left front the enemy was massing for an attack. I hardly knew what to do for the best, we kept up a steady fire, and one by one my men were falling until I had only about 20 left out of 56. On my left the West Yorkshire Reg't had retired, and on my right what few there were left were ordered to move farther to the right to strengthen the right where another attack had commenced. (*Oh it was a sickening sight watching your own comrades fall. If they were wounded they would say have a shot for me. Poor fellows*). I shall never forget the sights. It was a machine gun which did most of the damage in my trench, for the shells we could see leave the gun, and we had time to duck except when they fired rapid, which was very often. One poor chap next but one to me, was kneeling passing ammunition along when this machine gun shot him clean through the neck, and it appeared to me that his brains commenced rolling down his back. Two or three minutes afterwards the fellow next to me (Pte. Hickling) was passing me a bandolier of ammunition when he got shot through the shoulder with this machine gun.

He swore and I bandaged him up, and whilst I was doing so this machine gun could see me, and bullets whizzed by me, and went thud into the earth, there were five in all, and I could have surrounded them with a two inch ring. The enemy did not attack us but went away to the extreme left, I suppose to work round our flank where our guns were. So the men who had been fighting hard all day looked very grave. Now I was troubled about getting the wounded away, and I stood up to see how things were going and I got two bullets from the machine gun into my belt thanks to me being sideways they never entered the flesh. We could not get the wounded away by the

communication trench as where it were shallow the machine gun was ready waiting for any movement to be seen.

So at the finish I said to the wounded, *"you that are wounded in the upper limbs will you chance your arm if I go with you as far as the Village."* Some said they would rather stop there and die happy than be shot down again. Anyway one fellow (the chap that was shot in the shoulder Pte. Hickling) says I will, so I said have you everything you want and he said yes. I said wait a minute, and I gave him my mother's address and I said write and give her my best Love, and tell her I am going on alright, so he put the address in his pocket. I said are you ready, he answered yes and we jumped out of the trench and ran across that open ground just like mad men. God in heaven only knows how we got through that hail of bullets. Well I said goodbye to him whilst we were on the run and I turned back once more through the hail of bullets. I got into the trenches and I found I had got a bullet hole in my left sleeve, but I did not know when I received it. When I got back again I found that they had commenced the attack on the extreme left. The men appealed to me to get some reinforcements, I had expected this a long time, and I should have seen about them myself but I knew there were not any spare men anywhere as they had gone to support the right flank. Just then a shell burst over our heads and a piece of the case caught my water Bottle and cut it clean in two one side and the water ran out, what drop we saved we handed round it was a near shave for me. I had a bit more luck two or three minutes afterwards when we ducked to dodge another shell and a portion of it cut the knee of my trousers about 4 inches just catching my knee cap. Well I said *"chaps I don't like asking any of you to go through that Hell to Bn' Head Quarters, and asked for reinforcements, so if you'll promise me that you'll stick to your Guns I will go myself"* and each man answered *"We'll stick it"*. So I jumped out of the trench and raced across that open piece of ground through the Village, and I met the Adjutant (Lt. Willcose) and I told him what I wanted, and he said "haven't you received the orders to retire yet". I said "No" the orderly was just aside him, and he said "I am just going Sir" I said I would take the message, and off I trotted back towards the trenches, I was just on the verge of dashing across that open piece of ground when I heard Lt. Willcox shouting Weston, Weston, and I returned and he asked me for the message back, he tore it up, and said for God's sake take my cycle and catch Pte Coventry A.Coy's) and tell him to tear the message up, I rode through the village what part I could, and was at the other end of the village asking for "A" Coy's trenches when a shell burst and blew my cycle out of my hand, and almost immediately I was shot through my right arm, Sgt. Mortimer our machine gun Sgt, was just shouting get off the road snipers are only 300 yds away, but it was too late I had got it. I went towards "A" Coy's trenches and a man

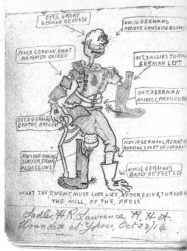

was just going into them so I delivered the message to him and he took it to the O.C. 'A'. Coy.

I then returned to the road my arm feeling numbed, I got a fellow to cut the coat sleeve on my right arm and I placed an emergency bandage on it. I then picked up the cycle, and to my surprise the wheels went round so I jumped across it, and rode into the middle of the village, over bricks, and large holes (of course the tyres were flat). I left the cycle against the Mill and went into my own trenches, and the men wanted to know what I had been up to. I told them a sniper had nipped me. I told them to stick to their trenches as reinforcements were coming, and I wished them luck and then I dashed once more into the hail of bullets through that part of the village for the last time that day, but my troubles were not all over as when I got through the village no one knew where the hospital were [sic], as it had been blown up three times, so I was directed to go to the 1st clearing Hospital which was Armentiers 2 1/2 miles away.

Our dear Major was just saving the Guns as they had broken through, and they were protecting both flanks under major Gower whilst they got the wounded away as quick as possible. All the way to this Hospital we were fired at but thank God I got there safely. But on the way to Hospital I saw many of my comrades and personal chums asleep never to awaken in this world *"Heroes every one"*. God bless them. Oh the sights I can never lose from my sight, men wounded past recovery and dead. One cannot describe the sights. I was sent as soon as they possibly could by ambulance wagons to Hoyzelbruck and from Hoyzelbruck to St. Omer by motor ambulance, from St. Omer by

Britain rules the warves.

A, Harrison.
Dec: 25th 1914

Pte G. Robinson
Royal Scots Fusiliers
I have no story to tell you of deeds and
valour so bold
I've simply done my duty like my fathers in
Days of old
I've been in the thick of the fighting, it
resembles nought but hell
But I fought side by side with my
comrade
till crippled by German Shell
But still I've done my duty though
wounded my pain I Bear
And by name I am simply G. Robinson
By the Royal Scots Fusiliers.

Wounded on the Aisne in the forearm
by Shrapnel, which injured the bone

And by name I am simply G. Robinson
Of the Royal Scots Fusiliers

Private Robinson was wounded on the Aisne in the forearm by Shrapnel, which injured the bone.

5138 Private C.H. Tapp 3rd Battalion Coldstream Guards

On the outbreak of the War I was recalled off the Army Reserve from Canada. I arrived at Windsor after a[n] eventful voyage. I stayed three Days and was then sent to St. Nazaire, France. After a short stay we were sent to join our Batt'n on the River Aisne where I escaped all injury. We were Relieved by the French Infantry and then sent to Ypres, Belgium where I got hit on the second Day of that Battle But I am Pleased to say I am making a[n] Excellent Recovery.

Go Right On And At the End Of The Road
Victory And Honour Will Be Found.

Pte. William Dawn 1st Batt'n, Grenadier Guards Wellington Barracks. London

I was wounded at Ypres on the night of Nov 1st. Had rather a rough journey back to England. Stayed in Hospital at Brighton 5 weeks then I was transferred to Derby , Dec 11th . Am getting on fine, only waiting to be discharged.

Motto: Never put off till to-morrow
What you can do to-day

train to Boulogne where we got into a Hospital ship and arrived at Southampton, we then got out of the ship into a train and finally I arrived at Newcastle-on-Tyne Hospital. I was there two days and I went furlough, whilst on [furlough] my Mother received a beautiful letter from Pte. Hickling saying that I had seen to him and was alright & so on, of course I had to laugh, Mother wrote and told him that I was at home and wounded about an hour after him. Whilst we were coming across on the ship L.Cpl Conduit caught us up and he said Major Gower & Lt. Willcox made four bayonet charges to regain the trenches during that night, but after a great struggle he was forced to retire. Conduit was wounded in the spine and he crept along a ditch 2 miles to Hospital. Next morning the 21st Oct. 1914 at roll call there were only 50 answered their names, but during the day stragglers came making the Bn. to 235 strong. (we went into action that morning 1150 strong). After furlough I reported at the Derby Depot, and was attending two days with my arm and I caught a chill and the Doctor (Dear Major Peak) put me to bed and I was in the bed 11 days and just allowed up for an hour today. I may say that the sisters here are fine, and really look after us too well. They belong to St. John's ambulance except one and she is a Red Cross sister but they are all fine sticks.

Private G Robinson Royal Scots Fusiliers

I have no story to tell you of deeds and valour bold
I've simply done my duty like my fathers in days of old
I've been in the thick of the fighting, it resemble nought but hell
But I fought side by side with my comrades till crippled by German shell
But still I've done my duty though wounded my pain and Bear

The Annuity Meritorious Service Medal
1847-1953
Brian Prescott

"We deem it expedient to afford a greater encouragement to the non-commissioned officers and soldiers of Our Army who may have distinguished themselves or who may have given good, faithful and efficient service."

Thus was the award of the Meritorious Service Medal introduced in a Royal Warrant, ordained by Her Majesty, Queen Victoria, under Her Sign Manual, dated 19 December, 1845.
The Warrant continued:

"It is Our further will and pleasure that a sum not exceeding £2,000 a year be distributed for the purpose of granting annuities as rewards for distinguished or meritorious service to sergeants who are now, or who may be hereafter in the Service, either while serving or after discharge, with or without Pension, in sums not exceeding £20 which may be held during service, and together with pension."

The amount available annually for annuities was increased periodically:
1) By Royal Warrant 4 June 1853 to £2,250 then by annual amounts of £250 to £4,000 per annum by 1861.
2) To £5,000 in 1868 (re-confirmed in Royal Warrant of 10 June, 1884).
3) To £7,500 in 1906 (re-confirmed in London Gazette 19 November, 1920).
This accounts for the large number of Edward VII type MSMs issued that year.

Ian McInnes, author of several books on *Meritorious Service Medals,* is to be congratulated on his painstaking research, conducted over fifteen years, which resulted in this wonderful, definitive Roll of almost 6,000 such men (later raised to 6,250 in the First Supplement), with almost all of the entries accompanied by some biographical details and many by a significant amount of research data. These 6,000 men were awarded their MSMs, except for a few hundred, with annuity, between 1847 and 1953 including a number of Yeomen Warders and Yeomen of the Guard, whose medals were without annuity. The remainder, also awarded the medal without annuity, gained their award under the terms of Army Order 98 of 1953. This states, *"Those men registered before 1 January, 1951, shall be eligible for the award notwithstanding that they have not yet been selected for the award of the annuity."*

As the men who were awarded the Annuity MSM had to be senior N.C.O.s with long service and clean records they are considered by many to have been the cream of the British Army. To have an ancestor or living relative who received the MSM is a reason for pride. It had always been imagined that men recommended for, and subsequently awarded, the MSM and the not

insignificant annuity would, therefore, have had almost unblemished service records. However, once the WO101/7 series in the PRO was examined, this was found to be far from the truth as these startling anomalies show: Troop Sgt. Major WARD, 5th Lancers, had no less than 24 entries on his Defaulters' Sheets, or Colour Sgt. McCarthy, 60th Rifles, who had 22, or to Farrier Quartermaster Sgt. Cowan, 16th Lancers, who had 20. Sgt. Stevens, 18th Foot, who enlisted aged nine, had 18. Even more amazing were the service records of Colour Sgt. Going, 21st Foot, who was given 30 lashes for absenting himself from duty in the trenches before Sebastopol, and Colour Sgt. Stewart of the same Regiment, who was awarded 56 days' imprisonment for desertion. For the same offence Sgt. Major Hotson of the 84th Foot, was imprisoned for even longer, 73 days, and forfeited four years' service. Colour Sgt. Gowrie, 71st Highland Light Infantry, was given 42 days' imprisonment for striking a Private, whilst Sgt. Galway of the 44th Foot lost two years', 188 days' service at one point, and Sgt. Instructor of Musketry Dickarty, 60th Rifles, suffered a Drum Head Court Martial and was reduced to the ranks and sentenced to five years' penal servitude for cowardice, but the latter was remitted. Others who had fairly severe sentences by Courts Martial were Colour Sgt. Ledden, of the 49th Foot, for threatening an NCO whilst drunk, Sgt. Sheward, of the 97th Foot, for sleeping at his post in the Indian Mutiny and QMS Gillies, of the Royal Scots Fusiliers, who was reduced to Corporal from Colour Sgt. One of the strangest offences was that of Colour Sgt. Higgins, 76th Foot, *"attempting to parade with a piece of rag at morning inspection and disrespect towards his Company Officer"*, for which he was sentenced to seven days' imprisonment. Even more bizarre was the seven days' confinement given to Colour Sgt. Thomas, 97th Foot, for *"purchasing a pair of trousers"*, in India in 1857. Lastly, I must mention Sgt. Groves, 3rd Dragoon Guards, reduced to the ranks "for having a female locked in his room."

The format in the books consist of headings for each regiment, which then contain lists of recipients indexed by surname for ease of finding. For each individual, the Army Orders, date of award, amount of annuity, date of birth, date of enlistment, last recorded date when known to be alive or date of death, rank, service number, service in other regiments, and other awards may be included in the listing. Where medals have appeared in the market, or have been noted in private collections, details are shown. It is remarkable to see that one recipient, de Souza, was only five years old when he enlisted in Portugal during

the Peninsular War as a drummer boy. He eventually retired to Chester and his descendants are there still.

In the Supplement there is a list of the original 107 recipients of the 1847 version of this coveted award. A bibliography and eleven appendices give this comprehensive work a completeness that belies its status as a supplement. It is a thorough work in its own right. Ian McInnes again worked hard, with much valuable help from members of The Orders and Medals Research Society and The Orders and Medals Society of America, to produce this promised supplement to a superb, much-acclaimed book. Apart from the names listed in Army Orders are those whose medals have appeared on the market or in private or Regimental collections. This would help the many family historians who try to buy back their ancestor's medals.

The following is a list of such men showing enlistment and award dates plus identifying their first campaign medal and throughout the book there are many similar examples.

Enlistment	Annuity	Years	Name	Regiment	First Campaign
1836	1904	68	MANN	57th Foot	Crimea
1886	1953	67	TARPEY	R. Garr. Rgt	Samana 1891
1842	1907	65	ELLIOTT	1st Foot	Crimea
1876	1939	63	SEGGIE	R. Engineers	South Africa 1879
1845	1907	62	RULE	20th Foot	Crimea
1891	1953	62	WATTS	R.Artillery	Queen's S. Africa
1889	1950	61	GENT	R.A.M.C.	Brit. War Medal
1889	1950	61	STRETCH	R.W. Fus.	Queen's S. Africa
1846	1907	61	RANDOLL	2nd Foot	South Africa 1853
1868	1929	61	JEROME	R.Engineers	Tel-el-Kebir
1894	1953	59	WILLIAMS	R.Engineers	China 1900
1885	1944	59	HAYCOCKS	21st Lancers	Queen's Sudan
1873	1932	59	BOND	21st Foot	South Africa 1879
1870	1928	58	McINNES	A.S.C.	South Africa 1879
1878	1936	58	DUGDALE	R.A.M.C.	Suakin 1885
1890	1946	56	DODGSON	19th Hussars	Queen's S. Africa
1877	1932	55	WATSON	R. Artillery	Tel-el-Kebir
1888	1943	55	McFATSON	R. Artillery	Punjab Frontier
1858	1912	54	BEER	60th/104th	China 1860
1854	1908	54	CARR	7th Foot	Umbeyla
1809	1862	53	McGOWAN	27th/59th	Mil. Gen. Serv. Medal

Men whose medals were awarded under the terms of Army Order 98 of 1953 had been registered for many years, often with service stretching back to Queen Victoria's Reign. One of these men was Acting/Regimental Sgt. Major S. C. Lindsey, late 16th Battalion, London Regiment

A limited number of Victoria Cross recipients were also awarded the MSM. Those listed in this work are shown below:

QMS Wm. GARDNER 42nd Foot VC, 1858 MSM, 1853
Sgt John PEARSON 8th/19th Hussars VC, 1858 MSM, 1867
RSM James CHAMPION 8th Hussars VC, 1858 MSM, 1878
SM Cornelius COUGHLAN 75th Foot VC, 1857 MSM, 1883
SM Patrick MULLANE Royal Artillery VC, 1881 MSM, 1905
QMS Norman A. FINCH Royal Marine Artillery VC, 1918 MSM, 1946
Sgt Bugler J.D.F. SHAUL Highland Light Infantry VC, 1899 MSM, 1946
RSM Donald D. FARMER Queen's Own Cam High VC, 1900 MSM, 1953

and formerly 2nd King's Royal Rifle Corps. He was registered for the MSM and annuity on 10 February, 1936, one day after his discharge, when he had been RSM, Queen's Westminster and Civil Service Rifles, at the end of 22$^{1}/_{2}$ years in uniform.

The effect of the various rules meant, of course, that very, many men on the register did not survive to draw the annuity and to receive the medal. On the other hand, it also meant that many men waited well over 50 years from enlistment to the award of the MSM and annuity.

Under a Royal Warrant, dated 4 December, 1854, a number of men received the MSM for non-combatant services in the Crimea rather than the DCM. For example: Hospital Sgt. John McROBERTS, 2nd Battn, 1st Foot; Sgt. Major G.T.C. BURGUM, 82nd Foot; SM J. GORDON, 92nd Highlanders; RSM C. HICKMAN, 10th Hussars and Col. Sgt S. FRANCIS, 48th Foot. In addition, one man, RQMS James LINFORD, 63rd Foot, was awarded a DCM and annuity for services in the Crimea by a submission, dated 7 February, 1855, but this was exchanged for an MSM on 25 April, 1855. Presumably, it was decided that a non-combatant award was more appropriate.

The rolls in the Army Estimates indicate when a man was still drawing the annuity in 1926, by the notation 'He was alive in 1926.' However, this is not altogether reliable. For example, Lt. Col. Campbell, OBE, O of St. J., DCM, late AIF, formerly Queen's Own Cameron Highlanders, died 18 April, 1924, but is still shown in Army Estimates of 1926. It should be noted the Army Estimates did not initially include the names of men of the Royal Artillery, nor the Royal Engineers, or the Royal Sappers and Miners, who at that time were controlled by the Board of Ordnance.

The number of MSMs to any particular Regiment or Corps has been printed in brackets under each title before the first entry. Naturally, the numbers issued depended upon the size of each Corps or Regiment and the length of time it was in existence between 1847 and 1953. Thus the Royal Artillery, with all its predecessors (Royal Field Arty, R. Garrison Arty. etc.,) takes pole position with 1,125 awards and second in number of MSMs comes the Royal Engineers with 376 awards. 58 awards have been traced to the Grenadier Guards, 100 to the Rifle Brigade, 49 to the Black Watch (Royal Highlanders) but only 25 to the Leinster Regiment (100th and 109th Foot).

At the other end of the scale several units show a single unique award; Royal Garrison Regiment; Ceylon Mounted Rifles; Guernsey Artillery Militia; Royal Malta Fencible Artillery; Royal Pioneer Corps; Intelligence Corps; Royal Military Academy Band

Corps (Sandhurst) and the Army Catering Corps.

A number of Victorian and Edwardian awards were made to Yeomen of the Guard and to Yeomen Warders of the Tower of London, with annuity. It is believed that the vast number of these have been identified. From 1907 awards were made to these men without annuity. All these have been traced. In 1946, successful applications were made on behalf of 21 Yeomen Warders and 52 Yeomen of the Guard including three former Royal Marines and two former members of the Royal Air Force. All these are notated in the rolls and are listed in Appendix Eight together with the correspondence traced. As the records of men from between the wars and for the Second World War are not yet released by the National Archives books like this give family historians the chance to check their military antecedants now.

The Annuity Meritorious Service Medal, 1847-1953 comprises 500 pages and is printed on archive quality paper, is a hard-back and comes in a slip-case. The book is available from Jade Publishing Limited, 5, Leefields Close, Uppermill, Oldham, Lancashire, OL3 6LA discounted from its launch price of £95 to £65. Postage and packing is also reduced at £5. The First Supplement comprises 390 pages of new material and increases the number of men to 6,250. The supplement was published at £75 but is now reduced to £55 with postage at £5. Email: jade.publishing@virgin.net, website: www.jadepublishing.com, or telephone 01457870944.

References:
  Royal Warrant of 19 December, 1845,
  Royal Warrant of 4 June, 1853,
  Royal Warrant of 4 December, 1854,
  Royal Warrant of 10 June, 1884,
  For 1847 to 1911 WO/101/1 to WO/101/7 at the National Archives.
  From 1885 onwards in AO/176 of 1951, AO/82 of 1952, AO/156 of 1953, AO/98 of 1953 at the National Archives.

For the Immediate MSM see AO/183 of June, 1916, AO/352 of 4 October, 1916, AO/45 of 3 January, 1917 and AO/238 of August, 1917.

Also consulted were Army Estimates in Parliamentary Papers 18481926 and the London Gazette of 19 November, 1920, AO/ of 5 February, 1950 and AO/ 250 of November, 1902.

Especially recommended, to those beginning their research into military records, is the excellent My Ancestor was in the British Army - How can I find out more about him? by Michael J. and Christopher T. Watts which lists fully the Army Records held at the National Archives. It was first published in 1992 and has been updated and republished recently.

British Pensioners Abroad by Norman K. Crowder is useful for the Napoleonic period and was published in 1995 by Genealogical Publishing Co. Inc., 1001, North Calvert Street, Baltimore, MD21202, USA. For the same period Barbara Chambers has printed books and microfiches of some regiments and copies can be bought by writing to her at 39, Chatterton, Letchworth Garden City, Hertfordshire, SG6 2JY, or from her web site http://members.aol.com/BJCham2909/homepage.html, or by email at BJCham2809@aol.com.

Finally, a series of books of interest to medal collectors and genealogists has been published by Jade Publishing Limited, who will supply direct. See address details above. The books contain many details of interest to family historians. They are: Gazetted awards to N.C.O.s and Other Ranks of the Aerial Forces 1914-1924, comprising a surname index of about 6,000 men with forename(s), service number, rank, hometown/squadron/theatre of war, medal entitlements, The London Gazette date and page number. In addition, biographical details for many of the men are included especially citations; The Yeomen of the Guard including the Body of Yeoman Warders of H.M. Tower of London, members of the Sovereign's Body Guard (Extraordinary) 1823-1903 contains much biographical information on 477 men who served during that period and there are almost 200 illustrations of the men and their medals. In Adversity - Exploits of Gallantry and Awards made to the R.A.F. Regiment and its Associated Forces, 1921-1995 is of 360 pages in A4 format, hard-back with a dust cover contains lists of awards and articles with much biographical information of the men. For the Napoleonic period are the following: The Beckett Soldiers Index A-C and the second volume covering D-G; Sudden Death, Sudden Glory the story of the 59th Foot from 1793-1830 with biographical details and casualty returns of the officers and men who served in the Peninsular 1808-1809 and 1812-1814, at Walcheren 1809, at Java 1811, at Waterloo in 1815, Bhurtpoor 1825-26 and The Army Long Service and Good Conduct Medal 1830-1848, which details almost 3,000 men.

Ian McInnes books include:
Meritorious Service Medals to Naval Forces (1983); Meritorious Service Medals to Aerial Forces (1984); Ashanti 1895-96 (1987); A Contemptible Little Flying Corps (1991), reprinted 2002; The Meritorious Service Medal - The Immediate Awards 1916-1928 (1992), reprinted 2002; Cotton Town Comrades (1993); The Annuity Meritorious Service Medal 1847-1953 (1995); The Army Long Service and Good Conduct Medal 1830-1848 (1995), The Army Long Service and Good Conduct Medal 1830-1848, First Supplement (1999) and The Annuity Meritorious Service Medal 1847-1953, First Supplement (2000) – all Jade Publishing Ltd THE YEOMEN OF THE GUARD including the Body of Yeoman Warders H. M. Tower of London, members of the Sovereign's Body Guard (Extraordinary) 1823-1903 – Jade Publishing Ltd 2002

Brian Prescott of Jade Publishing Limited is Vice-President, Northern Branch of the Orders and Medals Research Society and a Member of The Manchester and Lancashire Family History Society

In addition, two men were awarded the immediate MSM under the terms of the 4 October, 1916 Army Order, without annuity. These were:
  Private James PITTS Manchester Regt VC, 1900 MSM, 1918
  QMS Robert SCOTT Manchester Regt VC, 1900 MSM, 1919
  They won their Crosses in the same action at Ladysmith in 1900.
A number of MSMs are noted which were awarded in recognition of acts of gallantry. Some of these are to:
  Armourer Sgt Henry ULYETT 13th Foot 1847
  QMS John MURPHY 91st Foot 1848
  Col Sgt James YOUNG Royal S & Miners 1848
  Sgt Luke DUNNE 36th Foot 1848
  Sgt Michael BURKE 60th Rifles 1855
  Sgt Major Lewis PURNELL 54th Foot 1860
  Sgt Thomas DANVERS KRRC 1882
  Col Sgt James SHORT 27th Foot 1882
  Col Sgt H.J. HARROLD 2/Yorks & Lancs 1897
  Sgt John ALLEN KRRC 1897
  SM Wm. FLETCHER Grenadier Gds 1899

18th Century Wiltshire Militia Men

Jean Cole FSG

Some years ago, whilst browsing around the shelves of the local studies room in my home town, I happened across a small book dated 1772 with a remarkably dull title, *Military Orders and Instructions for the Wiltshire Battalion of Militia*. Nevertheless. I picked it out, sat down and began to read. It was intriguing. It stated that the County of Wilts in 1757 had made progress towards the execution of the acts 'for the better ordering of the Militia Forces'. The 1757 Militia Act for Wiltshire stated that it was obliged to provide 800 men drawn from every parish and tything in the county and so the Wiltshire Militia was formed on the 8th November 1758 and became embodied for actual service on 21st June 1759. A further Militia Act of 1761 confirmed this requirement. In 1758 the receivers of land tax for the county, Thomas Phipps and John Turner had the unenviable task of dividing the county into ten areas of parishes, tythings and places which were to supply between them 80 men each. These divisions made up the ten companies of the Militia, each commanded by a notable landowner such as Lord Thomas Bruce who became Colonel of Great Bedwin Company, with other local dignitaries including Thomas Goddard as Captain of Swindon Company with other county aristocracy as officers under their command.

I have to say I really had no particular interest in military matters or the militia but this superb and informative book held so many names of Wiltshire militiamen, the crimes they had committed with resulting punishments, desertions, promotions and demotions, discharges and general information concerning not only this Militia but other county militias and regiments where the 'Wiltshire's' were stationed. Most punishments, to my mind, were harsh and cruel for what seemed, on the whole, to be petty misdemeanours although some were serious enough and warranted more extreme sentences.

I came to the conclusion that it would be in the general interest to transcribe the book as it was particularly apt for those researching Wiltshire ancestry. With the permission of the local Reference librarian, I began the transcription. How fortunate it was that I did so, for after a few years, when I looked again for the book, it had disappeared!

It included militia rules, regulations and punishments with detailed dates and places of the marches of the Wiltshire Militia. For example, the militia travelled through Blandford, Dorchester, Bridport, Axminster, Honiton, Exeter, Newton Bushell, Totnes and Modbury arriving in Plymouth on the 18th November 1761. How many men, I wondered to myself, either became ill or died en route and were buried in some of these towns – how many others became friendly with local girls who may have given birth to illegitimate children nine months later? Would parish registers reveal such information? It certainly helps to have a suspicious and enquiring mind when researching family and local history! Surely, too, the activities of Wiltshire Militiamen during this period would be typical of other county militias?

Various regiments were mentioned, for example, the Essex and Yorkshire Regiments who, at one period, were stationed at the same camps as the 'Wiltshire's'. I discovered William Dyal, aged 21 of Captain Crosbie's Company of Grenadiers in HM's 66th Regiment of Foot under Major General John La Faussile's command, had decided to desert at Plymouth Dock on 27th March 1762. An added bonus included Dyal's description – 5ft 10 ins, brown complexion, dark brown hair, grey eyes, strong built, round and smooth faced, born in Hexham, Northumberland, by trade a blacksmith. Inlisted (sic) Morpeth on 19th January 1757. Dyal deserted with Corporal Thomas Clark. Immediately a warrant had been issued for their capture and return and whoever apprehended the pair would receive five guineas reward. Corporal Clark, 19 years, from the same Regiment, stood 5ft 10ins high, brown complexion, brown hair, grey eyes, straight and well made, a little pock marked, born in Kingston, co. Leicester, by employment, a gentleman's servant. Enlisted Oxford 17th May 1761 with Ensign Humphrys. Unfortunately, we are left wondering whether the pair were ever caught and returned to their Regiment for punishment. One sure thing, punishment would have been severe.

As to be expected wherever the militia made camp the general population complained about the behaviour of the men. On 13th July 1760 Peter Gregory, farmer, of Winchester, Hampshire complained to the militia authorities that soldiers had torn down and destroyed his hedges and spoilt his garden through which there was a path to the town. The authorities acted swiftly and men from the Gloucestershire Regiment were posted to the site to keep watch but Gregory continued to complain stating the 'sentinel' would not take in charge any soldiers so doing as he considered them frivolous complaints. No more was heard of poor old Gregory. Drunkenness and petty thieving were amongst other causes for complaint.

Various epidemics struck the militia including smallpox - 12th May 1760, Serjeant George (Wilton Company), was left behind at Marlborough with a man of each Company that already had the smallpox, to care for the sick men suffering from this disease. Each company was to pay a fortnight's subsistence to Serjeant George for the men who were paid daily and Serjeant George was to ensure they discharged their quarters. In 1761 we also discover smallpox had been rife in Winchester where the Militia been stationed. The Itch (Scabies) caused by a small mite, was a common complaint which was treated by local doctors along the routes of march. It was inevitable, too, that some men succumbed to venereal disease.

The period during which the militia was embodied was the period of the Seven Years' War 1756–1763, the conflict between Britain and France for colonial possession in America and India. In

Europe the war was between Prussia, supported by Britain and Hanover against the alliance of France, Austria, Russia, Sweden and Spain. William Pitt, the elder, masterminded the British involvement and thus Britain's shores were to be guarded by county militias composed of embodied men who were trained and exercised for the defence of the country and who were to make themselves readily available for duty. These men were drawn from English and Welsh counties by ballot, volunteers or militia substitutes, as decreed by the Militia Acts. At the end of the war the Wiltshire Militia met at regular intervals for training and exercise.

It is worth mentioning that, after reading many Acts of Parliament during my research, not only regarding the Militia, but other aspects of history such as the poor law, settlements etc, I found they were not quite so boring as they sounded, in fact, can make absorbing reading. Looking at the 1761 Militia Act 2 Geo 111. c 201 I discovered one or two intriguing clauses which included the fact that any Quaker who refused to take the Oath or provide a Substitute in his place for three years was liable to have his goods and chattels levied by distress and sold. Other clauses were equally informative.

XXXV11 *That no person keeping any House of public entertainment or who shall sell any Ale, Wine, Brandy or other spirituous Liquors by Retail, shall be cupable of being appointed or continuing a Serjeant in the Militia.* XL111 *Exemptions: No officer or man serving in any of His Majesty's other Forces, Castles or Forts; nor any Commission Officer serving or who had served four years in the Militia' nor any person being a member of either of the Universities, clergymen, licensed teacher of any separate congregation, constable, peace officer, articled clerk, apprentice, seaman or seafaring man; nor any person mustered, trained and doing duty in any of HM's Docks; nor any person being free of the Company of Watermen on the River Thames, nor any poor many who has three Children born in Wedlock – shall be compelled to serve personally or provide a Substitute to serve.*

Militia rules were to be rigidly observed but, obviously, men being men, rules were often ignored. On 18th August 1759, Lord Bruce had been extremely concerned about the indolent manner of the private soldiers…*who, under pretence of buying necessaries, go into Winchester and lie about the streets in an indolent manner and in great numbers sleep about the market cross and other parts of town.* On 27th August 1759 Lord Bruce again observed…that *the men appeared in the streets 'with their hair untied, coats unhooked, stockings ungartered, hats slouched, handkerchiefs about their necks, and in all respects in a very slovenly manner.'* Discipline was enforced in an endeavour to pull the Wiltshire militiamen into some sort of disciplined army.

26th November 1761 – *'Rules to be observed in the barracks'* When the weather is dry and weather will permit, the bedding to be aired, at

least once a week. No woman with young children to be allowed in the barracks on any account, nor any ironing on the blankets. The men must not piss against the walls, nor damage the buildings. On 22nd July at Plymouth - complaints from the neighbourhood about the soldiers being out of camp by night, lying in barns with disorderly women and disturbing the neighbouring people. Lord Effingham ordered these practices to cease, but naturally it continued, men, particularly militiamen, still offended against the rules usually resulting in a court martial.

It was sometime later that the Wiltshire and Swindon Record Office staff finally completed the cataloguing of the massive Ailesbury Papers collection which contained original documents concerning the Courts Martial of the Wiltshire militiamen during this period - where and when the courts martial took place, sometimes in buildings, inns, often in tents whilst on the march. The transcription of these particular papers proved to be even more, if this was possible, intriguing than the book. This was militia life in the raw and nothing was left to the imagination but then, some of these men were our ancestors for good or bad, 'warts and all'.

What were the crimes and punishments handed out to men who defaulted? A typical example concerned Philip Bath, Captain Egerton's Company (Wilton Company) 7th July 1761. Regimental Court Martial held at the Quarter Guard Tent (at Plymouth) before Captain Vilett, President, Lts Biggs, Merrewether, Webb and Ensign Durnford. Bath was charged with being drunk on duty under arms. Adjutant Peck - 'that on mounting the piquet last Sunday evening he observed the prisoner awkward in his motions and on going to him found him in liquor so much as not to be able to his duty.' Serjeant George of Captain Egerton's Company – 'the prisoner on being delivered to him to be confined observed that he was very much in liquor and upon his reproving him the prisoner swore and behaved very impertinent.' Serjeant Langridge of the same company made a similar observation and

revealed that some soldiers stated Bath had consumed a whole quart. Bath, however, stated he thought he had been quite capable of doing his duty. The Court considered the evidence and found the prisoner guilty of breaching the Articles of War and ordered him to receive 100 lashes (with a cat o'nine tails). Colonel Bruce confirmed the sentence to take place with immediate effect.

A précis of one or two other cases:

5th August 1759.
John Faulkner, drummer of Salisbury Company, 200 lashes for appearing in the field without his breeches, his offence aggravated by his insolence to the Court – drummed out of the Regiment.

27th August 1759.
Thomas Still, Hindon Company – deserted from the Regiment and apprehended – was a deserter from the English Fusiliers before entering the Militia. Surrendered to an officer of the Duke of Richmond's Regiment – took advantage of HM's proclamation, was acquitted and sent to the Duke of Richmond's Regiment stationed at Winchester.

30th October 1761:
Thomas Dodimead, Warminster Company, found guilty of neglect of duty and of behaving to the prejudice of good order and military discipline by continuously appearing in a very slovenly condition. 100 lashes to be inflicted next morning at troop beating at Salisbury.

14th April 1762:
Corporal White, Devizes Company. Misbehaviour by suffering himself and his party of which John Kingston was one, to be treated with liquor at the expense of some French prisoners of war as they were conducting them on board the 'Royal Oak'. White was reduced to the pay and duty of a private but afterwards deserted and entered himself on board a ship of war at Plymouth.

1st October 1762:
Benjamin Jennings, Swindon Company, for stealing fowls at the White Hart, Bishops Waltham on the march from Gosport. 200 lashes at Winchester. Other men involved who received the same punishment were Thomas Palmer and Joseph Baker.

17th May 1767:
Corporal Matthews of Captain Eyre's Company (Salisbury Company) was reduced to the pay and duty of a private man for being drunk on duty at Devizes.

Finally, a case which concerned one Isaac Sparrowbill, private of Great Bedwin Company on 3rd December 1760 at the Angel Inn, Marlborough – found guilty of absenting himself from quarters without leave – 50 lashes. However, poor Isaac was found guilty of a crime on 9th January 1761 and was ordered to receive 500 lashes at two separate times for making a disturbance in his quarters in the night by forcing himself into the bedchamber of one Anne Dore, a maid servant, and attempting to get into bed to her. Isaac received 300 lashes but was spared the further 200 when it appeared that he had actually gone to Anne Dore's bedroom with her consent and when her master, Mr Merriman, had discovered Isaac in her bed, Anne had charged Isaac 'as taking her by force to save her good character'.

The Wiltshire Militia was eventually disbanded in December 1762 although annual exercises continued from 1763 to 1770 at Devizes, in the eventuality that the militia was needed again to guard Britain's shores. True to form, punishment was severe for those men who failed to turn up for this annual event.

Conclusion: From this brief excursion into the lives of the Wiltshire Militiamen it is easy to see that things have not really changed over the centuries – men will be men but, these days,

such severe and harsh punishments which must have caused physical and mental disabilities, thankfully, have become a thing of the past.

Sources & Reading
Many records concerning the Wiltshire Regiment and militia can be found at the Berkshire, Gloucestershire and Wiltshire Regimental Museum, The Wardrobe, The Close, Salisbury. Many of these have been and are in the process of being indexed.
Cole J. *Wiltshire Militia Courts Martial 1759-1770* (Wiltshire FHS 1997)
Cole J. *Wiltshire Militia Orders 1759-1770* (Wiltshire FHS 1994)
Corbett JS. *England in the Seven Years' War* (reprint Greenhill Books)
Gibson Guide *Militia Lists and Musters 1757-1876* (FFHS)
Thomas G. *Records of the Militia* (PRO Guide 3. 1993)
Watts MJ & CT. *My Ancestor was in the British Army*: how can I find out more about him. (SOG)

Auxiliary Home Hospitals in World War I
David Barnes

The British Red Cross Society had been organised on the assumption that the Territorial Army might be employed on active service to repel invasion. Voluntary Aid Detachments were formed with a view to serving Territorial Army formations fighting in this country and to staff improvised hospitals required by the Army in the field.

One of the duties of the British Red Cross Society had been to ascertain which buildings were suitable as temporary hospitals, what equipment could be rapidly assembled and

how these hospitals could be staffed. County Directors had many promises of houses and equipment to place before the Military Authorities. However after the outbreak of war in August 1914 a very large number of spontaneous offers, from both public bodies and individuals came forward. Whilst some were unsuitable the Red Cross checked the exact nature of each offer. If the building appeared useful it was inspected and its capabilities ascertained. Those found suitable were then considered from the point of view of Equipment, Doctors, Nursing Staff and the

Town Hall Military Hospital
Thirsk North Riding of Yorkshire 1916

extent to which the cost of maintenance could be borne locally.

In total some 5,000 buildings were offered. Some 2,030 Auxiliary Home Hospitals were established in England, Scotland, Wales and Ireland and operated at various periods during the 1914-1918 war. All counties were represented and a number of towns had more than one Auxiliary Hospital.

These Auxiliary Home Hospitals were not under direct military control, but controlled by

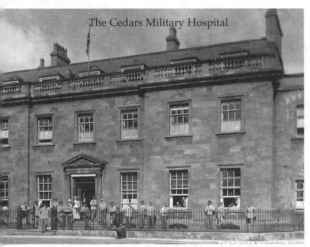

The Cedars Military Hospital

County Directors of the British Red Cross Society, and staffed by members of the British Red Cross Society, St John Ambulance and the Voluntary Aid Detachment. Often these hospitals were established as a result of local effort with the general desire to do something for the sick and wounded

It is beyond the scope of this article to record the names of the individuals and public bodies whose generosity in lending hospital accommodation took various forms.
In some instances the owners of the property entirely funded the running of the Hospitals and patient care. Other owners vacated their homes in full or occupied a small part of it, whilst it was used as a hospital. It should also be remembered that a number of public buildings, such as Town Halls, Elementary Schools etc were loaned by a number of Local Authorities for use as hospitals.

A fully searchable Excel spreadsheet of all 2,030 Auxiliary Home Hospitals operating during the First World War is available. This listing of Auxiliary Home Hospitals does not cover Military Hospitals, Private Hospitals under direct Military control or Civilian Hospitals which set beds aside for wounded servicemen.

To obtain the fully searchable Excel spreadsheet of all 2,030 Auxiliary Home Hospitals operating during the First World War on a CD Rom please contact the author David J Barnes, 148 Parkinson Street, Burnley, Lancashire, BB11 3LL

The CD, which can be used on PC's using Windows, Mac or Linux operating systems, can be searched by the name of Hospital, Town or County and costs £3.00 from the author Cheques should be made payable to 'D J Barnes' or payment can be made via Paypal to djbarnes@hotmail.com

Stanford Road War Hospital, Norbury Ward 8

Bayeux War Cemetery

Unknown WW2 British & Commonwealth Airmen's Graves
cared for by the Commonwealth War Graves Commission
David Barnes

There is no detailed listing of Unknown World War IIAllied Airmen's Graves recorded and they are not included on the CWGC 'Debt of Honour' Database. The CWGC in their old printed Cemetery Registers recorded only the number of 'Unknown' graves in the Cemetery Description - there was no formal recording of Rank or date and in some cases even an approximate date of death. Information recorded on the individual headstones with some having a Rank or indication of Officer and on occasions a date of death is given. Having gone through the numerical data supplied by the CWGC there are 2,536 Unknown Allied 'Air' Graves listed by country which are cared for by the CWGC.

Algeria 6: Australia 1; Austria 6; Azores 1; Bangladesh 1; Belgium 88; Canada 3; Cyprus 1; Czech Republic 1; Denmark 94; Egypt 74; France 323; Germany 888; Greece 45; Hungary 1; India 6; Indonesia 74; Ireland, Republic of 3; Italy 103; Lebonese Republic 5; Libya 98; Madagascar 1; Malaysia 1; Morocco 1; Myanmar 57; Netherlands 480; New Caledonia 4; Norway 19; Papua New Guinea 1; Poland 8; Singapore 6; Spain 4; Sweden 5; Syria 1; Thailand 3; Tunisia 30; Turkey 1; British 83; Yugoslavia 9 Total: 2536

Broken down by Cemetery / Graveyard etc – the analyis is as follows:
British in Nationality column usually indicates RAF / RAFVR etc Australian in Nationality column usually indicates RAAF Canadian in Nationality column usually indicates RCAF etc

British Cemeteries
Aberdeenshire
Dyce Old Churchyard - British 1
Anglesey
Holyhead (Maeshyfryd) Burial Board Cemetery British 2
Ayrshire
Dunure Cemetery - British 1
Banffshire
Banff Cemetery, Banffshire British 1
Caithness-shire
Wick Cemetery   British 1
Cambridgeshire
Cambridge City Cemetery - British 3
Carmarthemshire
Pembrey (St Illtyd) Churchyard - British 1
Cheshire
Chester (Blacon) Cemetery - British 1
Cornwall
Illogan (St Illogan) Churchyard - British 7
St Columb Major Cemetery - British 1
County Fermanagh
Irvinestown Church of Ireland Churchyard - British 2

County Londonderry
Drumachose (Christ Church) Church of Ireland
Churchyard - British 1
Cumberland
Haverigg (St Luke) Churchyard, Millom British 1
Silloth (Causewayhead) Cemetery, Holme Low - British 2
Devon
Ford Park Cemetery (formerly Plymouth Old Cemetery)
(PennyComequick)British 1
Dorset
Warmwell (Holy Trinity) Church British 2
Dumfriesshire
Troqueer New Burial Ground, Dumfries British 1
Glamorganshire
Llantwit Major Cemetery - British 1
Port Talbot (Goytre) Cemetery - British 1
Gloucestershire
Cirencester Cemetery - Polish 1
Hampshire
Bournemouth North Cemetery - British 1
Inverness-shire
Kilmuir Burial Ground,North Uist British 1

Kent
Isle of Grain (St James) Churchyard - British 1
Leysdown (St Clement) Churchyard - British 1
Margate Cemetery - British 1
Orpington (St Mary Cray) Cemetery - British 2
Whitstable Cemetery - British 1
Leicestershire
Quorn Baptist Churchyard - British 1
Lincolnshire
Coningsby Cemetery - British 1
Lincoln (Newport) Cemetery - British 2
Manby (St Mary) Churchyard - British 2
Market Rasen Cemetery - British 1
Sutton Bridge (St Matthew) Churchyard - British 1
Merionethshire
Tywyn Cemetery - British 1
Norfolk
Bacton (St Andrew) Churchyard - British 1
Great Bircham (St Mary) Churchyard - British 1
Great Yarmouth (Caister) Cemetery - British 2
Sheringham Cemetery - British 1
Wells-next-the-Sea Cemetery - British 1
Pembrokeshire
Manorbier (St James) New Churchyard - British 2
Pembroke Dock (Llanion) Cemetery - British 1
Shetland
Lerwick New Cemetery - British 1
Suffolk
Beck Row (St John) Churchyard - British 5
Surrey
Brookwood Military Cemetery - Canadian 2: British 3
Sussex
Littlehampton Cemetery - British 2
Northiam Cemetery - British 1
Tangmere (St Andrew) Churchyard - British 1
West Thorney (St Nicholas) Churchyard - British 1
Wigtownshire
Kirkinner Cemetery - British 1
Stoneykirk Cemetery - British 1
Yorkshire (East)
Brandesburton (St Mary) Churchyard - British 4
Yorkshire (North)
Harrogate (Stonefall) Cemetery - British 1
Selby Cemetery - British 1
Yorkshire (South)
Finningley(Holy Trinity & St Oswald) Churchyard
Extension - British 1

Cemeteries in Other Countries
Algeria
Bone War Cemetery, Annaba - British 1
Dely Ibrahim War Cemetery - British 1
La Reunion War Cemetery - British 1
Le Petit Lac Cemetery - British 3
Australia
Brisbane (Lutwyche) Cemetery - Australian 1
Austria
Klagenfurt War Cemetery - British 6
Azores
Lajes War Cemetery - British 1
Bangladesh
Chittagong War Cemetery - Indian 1
Belgium

Adegen Canadian War Cemetery - Australian 1:
Canadian 1: British7:
Adinkerke Military Cemetery - Czechoslovakian 1
Blankenberge Town Cemetery - British 7
Braine-L'Alleud Communal Cemetery - British 1
Bredenee Churchyard - British 2
Brussels Town Cemetery - British 1
Cement House Cemetery - Australian 1: British 2
Coxyde Military Cemetery - British 2
De Panne Communal Cemetery - British 1
Estaimbourg Churchyard - British 1
Froyennes Communal Cemetery - British 1
Gembloux Communal Cemetery - British 1
Heverlee War Cemetery - British 15
Hotton War Cemetery - British 13
Leopoldsburg War Cemetery - British 3
Leuven Communal Cemetery - British 2
Lombardsijde Churchyard - British 1
Middelkerke Communal Cemetery - British 2
Nieuwmunster Churchyard - British 1
Oostduinkerke Communal Cemetery - British 1
Oostende New Communal Cemetery - British 8: Polish 1
Ramegnies-Chin Churchyard - British 1
Rekem Communal Cemetery - British 1
Schoonselhof Cemetery - British 3
Slijpe Churchyard - British 1
Wenduine Communal Cemetery - British 2
Westende Communal Cemetery - British 1
Wevelgem Communal Cemetery - Canadian 1: British 1
Canada
Dutton (Fairview) Cemetery - Canadian 1
Meadow Island Cemetery, Bella Bella- Canadian 1
Quebec City (Mount Hermon) Cemetery - Canadian 1
Nicosia War Cemetery - British 1
Czech Republic
Prague War Cemetery - British 1
Denmark
Aabebraa Cemetery - British 3
Bostrup Churchyard - British 1
Copenhagen (Bispebjerg) Cemetery - British 8
Dannemare General Cemetery - British 1
Draaby Old Churchyard - British 1
Esbjerg (Fourfelt) Cemetery - Canadian 1
Esbjerg (Fourfelt) Cemetery - British 24
Fjaltring Churchyard - Canadian 1
Fredericia Northern Churchyard - British 1
Frederikshavn Cemetery - British 5
Furreby Churchyard - Australian 1
Gedser New Cemetery - British 1
Hvidbjerg on Aa Churchyard - Canadian 1: British 2
Hviding Churchyard - British 2
Hyllested New Churchyard - British 1
Kappel Churchyard - British 2
Kirkeby Churchyard - Australian 1
Kirkeby Churchyard - British 6
Korsor Cemetery - British 1
Lemvig Cemetery - British 5
Magleby Churchyard, Zealand Australian 1
Norre Havrvig Churchyard - British 1
Norre Vorupor Cemetery - British 1
Nyborg New Cemetery - British 2
Odby Churchyard - British 1
Odder Sogns Churchyard - British 1

Bayeux War Cemetery

303

Odense (Assistens) Cemetery - British 2
Oksby Churchyard - British 1
Rindby Cemetery - British 1
Sonderho Cemetery - British 1
Sondre Nissum Churchyard - British 1
Stubbekobing General Cemetery - British 1
Svino Churchyard - Australian 1: British 7
Tranebjaerg Churchyard - British 2
Vestre Vedsted Churchyard - British 1

Egypt
Alexandria (Chatby)
Military and War Memorial Cemetery - British 1
Alexandria (Hadra) War Memorial Cemetery - British 2
El Alamein Cemetery - South Africa 2: British 46
Halfaya Sollum War Cemetery - Australian 1: South
Africa 1: British 21

France
Abbeville Communal Cemetery - British 24: Australian 1:
Canadian 3
Albert Communal Cemetery Extension - British 1
Ars-en-Re Communal Cemetery - British 1
Banneville-la-Campagne War Cemetery - British 2
Baudre Churchyard - British 3
Bayeux War Cemetery - British 16
Besancon (St Claude) Communal Cemetery - British 2
Biarritz (Du Sabaou) Communal Cemetery - British 1
Biguglia War Cemetery - British 1
Boulogne Eastern Cemetery - British 14
Boves West Communal Cemetery Extension - British 1
Brest (Kerfautras) Cemetery - British 3
Bretigny-sur-Orge Communal Cemetery - British 2
Bretteville-sur-Laize CanadaWar Cemetery - Canadian 2
Bretteville-sur-Laize Canadian War Cemetery - British 3
Brignogan-Plage Communal Cemetery - British 1
Brouay War Cemetery - British 1
Calais Canadian War Cemetery, Leubringhen British 1
Calais Canadian War Cemetery, Leubringhen British 3
Camaret-sur-Mer Communal Cemetery - British 1
Cayeux-sur-Mer Communal Cemetery - British 7
Chatelaillon-Plage Communal Cemetery - British 1
Choloy War Cemetery - Australian 1: Canadian 1
British 13
Clincy Northern Cemetery - British 2
Couvron-et-Aumencourt Communal Cemetery - British 1
Criel-sur-Mer Communal Cemetery - British 1
Crozon Communal Cemetery - British 1
Dieppe Canadian War Cemetery, Hautot-sur-Mer
Australian 1: Canadian 1: British 12
Dinard English Cemetery - British 1
Dreux Communal Cemetery - British 2
Dunkirk Town Cemetery - British 15
Eringhem Churchyard - British 1
Escoublac-la-Baule War Cemetery - British 6
Etaples Military Cemetery - British 8
Etretat Churchyard Extension - British 1

Evreux Communal Cemetery - Canadian 1: British 1
Fecamp (Le Val aux Clercs) Communal
Cemetery - British 2
Fontenay-Le-Pesnel War Cemetery, Tessel British 1
Grandcourt War Cemetery - British 1
Guidel Communal Cemetery - British 8
Hellemmes-Lille Communal Cemetery - British 1
Hermanville War Cemetery - British 1
Hesdin Communal Cemetery - British 1
Janval Cemetery, Dieppe British 2
La Bernerie-en-Retz Communal Cemetery - British 3
La Delivrande War Cemetery, Douvres British 2
La Tremblade Communal Cemetery - British 1
Le Crotoy Communal Cemetery - Polish 1
Le Mans West Cemetery - British 3
Le Paradis War Cemetery, Lestrem British 1
Le Treport Military Cemetery - British 1
Le-Bois-Plage-en-Re Communal Cemetery - British 1
L'Epine Communal Cemetery - British 1
Les Baraques Military Cemetery, Sangate British 1
Les Sables-D'Olonne (La Foire-aux-Chats)New
Communal Cemetery - British 1
Liesse Communal Cemetery - British 3
Lisieux Communal Cemetery - British 1
London Cemetery and Extension, Longueval British 9
Lorient (Kerentrech) Communal Cemetery - British 4
Marissel French National Cemetery - British 3
Marquise Communal Cemetery - British 4
Mazargues War Cemetery, Marseilles British 1
Mers-les-Bains Communal Cemetery - British 2
Merville-Franceville-Plage Churchyard - British 5
Nantes (Pont-du-Cens) Communal Cemetery - British 1
Noirmoutier-en-L'ile (L'Herbaudiere) Communal
Cemetery - British 1
Noirmoutier-en-L'ile Communal Cemetery - British 1
Novion-Porcien Communal Cemetery - British 2
Olonne-sur-Mer Communal Cemetery - British 2
Oye-Plage Communal Cemetery - British 2
Peronne Communal Cemetery Extension - British 1
Pihen-les-Guines Cemetery - Canadian 2
Pihen-les-Guines Cemetery - British 6
Pihen-les-Guines Communal Cemetery - British 5
Plouguerneau Communal Cemetery - British 4
Poix-du-Nord Communal Cemetery Extension - British 1
Pontoise Communal Cemetery - British 1
Pornic War Cemetery - British 16
Prefailles Communal Cemetery - British 1
Quiberon Communal Cemetery - Australian 1
Quiberville Churchyard - British 1
Rancourt Military Cemetery - British 3
Remilly-et-Aillicourt Communal Cemetery - British 1
Ryes War Cemetery, Bazenville British 1
Sassy Churchyard - British 1
Sedan-Torcy French National Cemetery - British 5
Sessenheim Communal Cemetery - British 1

Menin Gate
Ypres, Belgium

St Brieuc Western Communal Cemetery - British 1
St Charles de Percy War Cemetery - Canadian 1
St Georges D'Oleron Communal Cemetery - British 1
St Gilles-sur-Vie Communal Cemetery - British 1
St Hilaire-de-Riez Communal Cemetery - British 1
St Martin-de-Re Communal Cemetery - British 1
St Pierre Cemetery, Amiens British 1
St Sever Cemetery Extension, Rouen British 2
St Valery-en-Caux Franco-British Cemetery - British 5
Ste Marie Cemetery, Le Havre Canadian 1
Ste Marie Cemetery, Le Havre British 9
Terlincthun British Cemetery, Wimille British 1
Tourgeville Military Cemetery - British 1
Verneuil-sur-Avre Communal Cemetery - British 3
Villerville Communal Cemetery - British 1
Void Communal Cemetery - British 1
Yves Communal Cemetery - British 1

Germany
Becklinghen War Cemetery - British 47
Becklinghen War Cemetery - Polish 2
Berlin 1939-1945 War Cemetery - Australian 2:
        Canadian 7: New Zealand 1:British 339
Durnbach War Cemetery - Australian 1: Canadian 1:
        British 68: Polish 1
Hamburg Cemetery - Australian 2: Canadian 2: British 39
Hanover War Cemetery - Australian 2: Canadian 2:
British 46
Kiel War Cemetery - Australian 3: Canadian 1: British 58
Reichswald Forest War Cemetery - Australian 1:
        Canadian 1: British 68: Polish 1
Retzow Cemetery - British 6
Rheinberg War Cemetery - Canadian 1: British 111
Sage War Cemetery - Canadian 3: New Zealand 1
        British 71

Greece
Phaleron War Cemetery - Australian 1: Canadian 1: South
African 1: British 18: British 3
Suda Bay War Cemetery - British 21

Hungary
Budapest War Cemetery - British 1

India
Gauhati War Cemetery - British 1
Imphal War Cemetery - British 5

Indonesia
Ambon War Cemetery - Australian 4
Ambon War Cemetery - British 3
Ambon War Cemetery - Dutch 15
Jakarta (Ancol) Netherlands Field of Honour British 26
Jakarta War Cemetery - Australian 1
Jakarta War Cemetery - British 25

Ireland
Grangegorman Military Cemetery - British 1
Malin CofI Churchyard - British 1

Milltown Malbay CofI Churchyard - British 1
Italy
Ancona War Cemetery - South African 1: British 4
Arezzo War Cemetery - British 1
Assisi War Cemetery - British 1
Bari War Cemetery - British 2
Beach Head War Cemetery, Anzio British 2
Bolsena War Cemetery - Canadian 1
Bolsena War Cemetery - British 2
Cagliari (St Michele) Communal Cemetery - Canadian 1:
        British 9
Cassino War Cemetery - British 1
Catania War Cemetery, Sicily Australian 1:
        South African 1: British 25
Coriano Ridge War Cemetery - Australian 1: British 2
Florence War Cemetery - British 1
Forli War Cemetery - British 2
Milan War Cemetery - British 3
Moro River Canadian War Cemetery - British 7
Naples War Cemetery - British 2
Padua War Cemetery - Canadian 1: British 6
Ravenna War Cemetery - British 5
Rome War Cemetery - British 2
Salerno War Cemetery - British 4
Sangro River War Cemetery - British 1
Staglieno Cemetery, Genoa British 5
Syracuse War Cemetery, Sicily British 3
Udine War Cemetery - South African 1: British 5
Lebanon
Beirut War Cemetery - British 5
Libya
Benghazi War Cemetery - Australian 1: British 32
Knightsbridge War Cemetery, Acroma Australian 1: South
African 5: British 33
Tobruk War Cemetery - British 10
Tripoli War Cemetery - British 16
Madagascar
Diego Suarez War Cemetery - British 1
Malaysia
Labuan War Cemetery - Australian 1
Morocco
Tangier (St Andrew) Churchyard - British 1
Myanmar
Rangoon War Cemetery - Australian 3: British 16
Taukkyan War Cemetery - British 38
Netherlands
Ambt-Delden General Cemetery - British 2
Ameland (Nes) General Cemetery - British 6
Ameland (Nes) General Cemetery - Polish 2
Amerongen (Holleweg) General Cemetery - British 1
Amersfoort (Oud Leusden) General Cemetery -
Australian 1: Canadian 1: British 10
Amsterdam New Eastern Cemetery - Australian 2:

Rhodes War Cemetery

Poix-Du-Nord Communal Cemetery

Isle of Grain St James Churchyard Kent

Canadian 1: British 41: Polish 2
Andijk Western General Cemetery - British 1
Arnhem Oosterbeek War Cemetery - British 1: Dutch 6
Baarderadeel (Schillaard) General Cemetery - British 1
Barradeel (Pietersbierum) Protestant Churchyard -
    Canadian 1: British 2
Bergen General Cemetery - New Zealand 1: British 39
Bergen General Cemetery - Polish 1
Bergen-op-Zoom Canadian War Cemetery - Canadian 1:
    British 12
Bergen-op-Zoom War Cemetery - British 53
Beverwijk (Wijk-aan-Zee) Protestant
    Churchyard - British 1
Castricum Protestant Churchyard - British 1
Delfzijl General Cemetery - British 2
Eindhoven (Woensel) General Cemetery - Canadian 1:
    British 6: Polish 1
Enkhuizen General Cemetery - British 2
Enschede Eastern General Cemetery - British 2
Ferwerderadeel (Blija) Protestant Churchyard - British 1
Flushing (Vlissingen) Northern Cemetery - British 18
Franeker General Cemetery - Canadian 1
Gaasterland (Nijemirdum) General Cemeery British 2
Goedereede General Cemetery - Canadian 1
Groesbeek Canadian War Cemetery - Canadian 3:
    British 3
Harderwijk General Cemetery - British 3
Harlingen General Cemetery - Canadian 1: British 20:
Polish 1
Heerde (Wapenvelde) General Cemetery - British 1
Heerlen General Cemetery - British 1
Hemelumer Oldeferd (Scharl) General Cemetery -
Australian 1: British 1
Het Bildt (St Jacobiparochie) General Cemetery - British 3
Heteren General Cemetery - British 2
Hindeloopen Protestant Churchyard - Canadian 2: British 3
Holten Canadian War Cemetery - British 2
Hook of Holland General Cemetery - Canadian 1: British 4
Jonkerbos War Cemetery - Canadian 1: British 14
Kampen General Cemetery - Australian 1
Kampen General Cemetery - New Zealand 1: British 3
Leeuwarden Northern General Cemetery - British 6
Lemsterland (Lemmer) General Cemetery - Canadian 1:
British 7
Mook War Cemetery - British 1
Nederweert War Cemetery - British 1
Nieuw-Helvoet General Cemetery - British 1
Noordwijk General Cemetery - Australian 1: Canadian 1:
British 15: Polish 1
Oldebroek General Cemetery - British 2
Oostvoorne Protestant Cemetery - British 1
Ouddorp General Cemetery - British 6
Overloon War Cemetery - British 3
Rockanje (Zeeweg) General Cemetery - British 2
Rotterdam (Crooswijk) General Cemetery - Canadian 1:
    British 3
Ruinerwold General Cemetery - British 2
s Gravenzande General Cemetery - British 1
Schellinkhout Protestant Churchyard - British 1
Schiermonnikoog (Vredenhof) Cemetery - British 13:
    Polish 1

Schipluiden General Cemetery - British 1
Sittard War Cemetery - British 3
Terschelling (West-Terschelling) Gen Cemetery -
Australian 1: British 16
Texel (Den Burg) Cemetery - New Zealand 1: British 31
The Hague (Westduin) General Cemetery - Australian 2:
    Canadian 2: British 11
Uithuizermeeden General Cemetery - British 1
Ulrum General Cemetery, De Marne British 3
Veghel Roman Catholic Churchyard - Polish 1
Velsen (Driehuis-westerveld) Private Cemetery - British 2
Venray War Cemetery - British 12
Vlieland General Cemetery - Canadian 1
Vlieland General Cemetery - British 8
Weers. Weerselo Roman Catholic Cemetery - British 5
Westdongeradeel (Wierum) Protestant
    Churchyard - British 1
Westenieland General Cemetery, De Marne British 1
Wieringermeer (Middenmeer) General
    Cemetery - British 2
Wonseradeel (Makkum) Protestant Churchyard - British 3
Zelhem General Cemetery - British 1
Zoelen General Cemetery - British 1
New Caledonia
Bourail New Zealand War Cemetery - New Zealand 4
Norway
Andalsnes Church Cemetery - British 1
Egersund (or Ekersund) Churchyard - British 1
Haugesund (Rossebo) Var Frelsers Cemetery - British 1
Kristiansand Civil Cemetery - British 1
Nesbyen Churchyard - British 1
Sola Churchyard - British 2
Trondheim (Stavne) Cemetery - Canadian 1: British 11
Papua New Guinea
Port Moresby (Bomana) War Cemetery - Australian 1
Poland
Malbork Commonwealth War Cemetery - British 1
Poznan Old Garrison Cemetery - British 7
Singapore
Kranji War Cemetery - British 6
Spain
Bilbao British Cemetery - British 4
Sweden
Falkenberg Forest Cemetery - British 1
Kviberg Cemetery - Canadian 1
Kviberg Cemetery - British 1
Ockero Churchyard - British 2
Syria
Damascus Commonwealth War Cemetery - British 1
Thailand
Kanchanaburi War Cemetery - British 3
Tunisia
Enfidaville War Cemetery - Canadian 7: British 8
Massicault War Cemetery - British 3
Medjez-el-Bab War Cemetery - British 9
Sfax War Cemetery - British 2
Tabarka Ras Rajel War Cemetery - British 1
Turkey
Haidar Pasha Cemetery - British 1
Yugoslavia
Belgrade War Cemetery - Australia 1: British 8
Total: 2536

I would be interested in logging full details of these, so if anyone has any notes on Unknown 'Air' Graves - or if you are visiting any of the above cemeteries, please let me know.

Whilst it is true that all 'Missing' or 'Unknown Airmen are recorded on other CWGC Memorials, it may be possible with cross referencing to aircraft crashes, dates, locations etc to suggest identities can be put forward for some of these 'Unknown' Airmen. The recent case of the RAF Photo Reconnaissance 'Ace' Wing Commander Adrian Warburton DSO and Bar, DFC and Bar proved that this type of research can lead to correct identification of a Grave. If anyone can supply info on any of details recorded on the 'Unknown' Airmen's headstones, please let me know so this listing can be periodically updated. Please record Country, Cemetery, Grave Details - Badge Officer / Airman Date of Death Any other comment Location in Cemetery Graves lost / destroyed
It is appreciated that the Graves of some servicemen buried in a war zone were subsquently lost due to 'action of war, i.e.

bombardments, bombing etc there are other graves that have been lost .. or deliberately erased. Whilst the names of 'Missing' servicemen are recorded on various Memorials, it would be nice to record the original resting place, even if the body was subsequently moved or lost

Help is also sought about the airmen missing during the two raids over Konigsberg, East Prussia. The raids took place on 26/27th and 29/30th August 1944 from which 20 Lancasters failed to return. It is believed ten aircraft came down over Konigsberg, with 71 aircrew, 56 of these man are classified as 'Killed in Action – No Known Grave and 15 men who were made Prisoners of War. There is an eleventh aircraft which crashed 30 miles North-North-West Konigsberg from which one RCAF member escaped to become a Prisoner of War, the other 6 aircrew were listed as 'Killed in Action – No Known Grave.

A typical example is the following; *Bomber Command* Raid on Königsberg, Germany (by 189 Lancasters - 15 lost)

630 Squadron, RAF (East Kirkby, Lincolnshire - 5 Group)

Lancaster III ND982, Coded LE-Y - took off from R.A.F. East Kirby at 20:15 hours on nighr of 29 August 1944 and was shot down some 25km South-East of the target area, crashing at Gr Haferbeck(?), 6km east of Underwangen, at 0148.

According to German documents the seven crew were buried in the local cemetery at Underwangen on 3 September.

However, restrictions imposed by the Russian authorities prevented a visit to the area by post-war search teams and the crew are therefore commemorated on the Runnymede Memorial.

Flying Officer D G Twidle RNZAF - Pilot
Sgt C W Garner - Flight Engineer
Sgt J A Akers - Navigator
Sgt S Stanton - Air Bomber
F/Sgt L Prior - Wireless Operator
Sgt E J Walton - Mid-Upper Gunner
Sgt H W Wickenden - Rear Gunner

Presumably with German thoroughness, the bodies of the crews would have been recovered where possible and details of the aircraft logged. However, following the Russian invasion of East Prussia in early 1945, East Prussia was annexed to the then Soviet Union (now Russia) and a very thorough form of ethnic cleansing was carried out, to the extent that no German remained. Anything pertaining to be German was destroyed, including cemeteries. It is believed that the graves of the Allied airmen were also destroyed at this time. Post war, due to the sensibilities at the time it is presumed that these airmen were officially forgotten about and their names listed on the Runnymede Memorial. Some relatives of the missing and members of the Bomber Command Association are campaigning for either the graves to be traced and individually marked by the CWGC or for an official memorial to be erected on Russian soil, recording their names. The Russian Government are actively co-operating with the project although the Ministry of Defence are refusing to release the relevant files which we believe will hold details from the International Red Cross about the recovery and burial positions of the missing airmen, which would have been forwarded. Can anyone suggest any archives or reports that we could find out which and where the airmen are buried?

David J Barnes, 148 Parkinson Street, Burnley, Lancashire BB11 3LL Email: rafcasualty@hotmail.com

Reality behind a Myth
The Life of a Spithead Mutineer 1797
Len Barnett

As a freelance maritime researcher it is not often that I am called on to investigate known characters. So, when I was approached to look into Valentine Joyce, I was delighted: having recently read James Dugan's stirring book *The Great Mutiny*. This seaman seemed more than slightly intriguing. In this work he had been portrayed as a Belfast tobacco seller that had been gaoled for sedition and consequently conscripted into the monarch's navy as a quota man. As one of this stunningly effective mass mutiny's *principle* lower deck delegates, he seemed to be a young Irish firebrand republican. While reading Mr. Dugan's book there had been a few points that jarred, but I was sure that these could well be resolved with a little research

Even with the inherent problems of researching lowly ratings in naval service at this time, knowing that Val (as he was to be known throughout the fleet) was on the *Royal George* in April 1797, I immediately sought out this man-o-war's muster lists and pay books at The National Archives, Public Records Office, Kew. These brought surprises. He was not shown as born in Belfast, but Jersey. This partly explained one of the Dugan issues, as his mother and

sister were said to have lived in Portsmouth. As he was a quota man I did not expect to have to travel very far back from spring 1797, as the relevant legislation was not enacted until 1795 and 1796. However, Joyce proved to have had significantly more time in His Majesty's Navy and therefore for this reason alone, could not have been a quota man. So, I then continued forward from the end of the mutiny in the May of 1797, knowing that all had received Royal pardons (in order that there were no hangings, as in previous cases such as that of *Culloden*). I was fascinated to find that he had carried on in his rate of quartermaster's mate (another point that had grated in Dugan's book) on the *Royal George* until May 1798 when he had apparently disappeared after becoming ill.

My client did not wish to take the research any further, but I have recently resurrected this through my own curiosity. In conversation with other interested parties, I have kindly been given some further good avenues. One of these led to his date of baptism: something that is missing from *every* other source that I have seen. Another was a doctoral thesis - David London's *Mutiny in the Public Eye* (University of London: King's College, 2001). This gave one especially important detail that I had lacked: brief circumstances around Valentine Joyce's death. (His demise can also be found in the modern edition of the Oxford *Dictionary of National Biography*.) There was also a secondary point that indicated further earlier naval service. Again working backwards in original naval administrative and operational records, consulting reliable published sources and newspaper reports (some other than those mentioned by Dr. London), it has been possible to build up a picture of this man that is *very* different from what has been *conventionally* understood. So, before giving a short account of his life, it is worth stressing that seemingly good published works sometimes can be *far* from accurate. And, although documentary sources are not always entirely trustworthy, as can be seen below, generally they are more reliable. Incidentally, I also found a few *slight* problems relating to Val's naval career in Dr. London's thesis.

According to G.R. Balleine's *A Biographical Dictionary of Jersey* Valentine Joyce had been born in Elizabeth Castle on this same island and had been baptised there on 13th August 1769. He had the same Christian name as his father, who was said to have been in the Corps of Invalids serving at the castle and his mother was shown as Elizabeth Lamb. The relevant muster lists show that Joyce senior was then a corporal in the 41st Regiment of Foot (Invalids).

A letter written by the man himself to *The Portsmouth Gazette and Weekly Advertiser* during the mutiny (not published until months after) stated that he had been at sea in the King's service since at least 1780. Whether even then this was his first sea time is (probably) not known.

His first proven presence in the Royal Navy was on 1st December 1788 when he joined the fifth-rate, 36-gun frigate *Perseverance*, at Portsmouth and was rated able seaman. From her pay and muster books it would seem that he had gone through a receiving ship shortly before. (No records for this port's receiving ships for this year survive and he does not show up in the muster books of the then seven guardships.) It then being peacetime it is not unlikely that he had been paid off from another man-o-war and had spent some time at home before 'rejoining'. His age on going on the books of *Perseverance* was stated as 23, but this was erroneous.

Anyway, under the command of Commander Isaac Smith, in February 1789 and in company with four sloops, she sailed for the East Indies. There she remained through an interesting political period in competition with the French in India, until early 1793. Contrary to the order of battle abroad at the beginning of the Revolutionary Wars, as stated in William Clowes' standard multi-volume history of the Royal Navy, *Perseverance* had already begun her transit home from Bombay on 19th January 1793. Having called at Saint Helena, in mid April she convoyed a number of merchantmen including some East Indiamen back to the UK: anchoring on Sunday 9th June at Spithead. On 25th July all petty officers and seamen were turned over to another vessel though, as part of her complement. This was on the order of Admiral Sir Peter Parker, Commander-in-Chief Portsmouth.

The second-rate, 98-gun, ship-of-the-line *Boyne* had also arrived back at Portsmouth in early June. With Captain William Albany Otway in command, she had previously sailed from Hamoaze (Plymouth) in February as part of the escort for eighteen merchantmen (nine being East Indiamen) to the Spanish Canaries (Spain not then being a British enemy). On her way back she had encountered the French 20-gun privateer *Guidelon* and prevailed, bringing her back as a prize. But, Valentine Joyce and the others late of *Perseverance* were not to get their chance of death, glory or prize money onboard *Boyne*. By the time they joined her she was in the dockyard, lashed alongside a hulk. They were a mere work party and in all likelihood little interest was taken in them, as in Joyce's case no age on entry was recorded. Still, he was not to remain in this duty for long.

Per a 'Lords' order' a draft of

was then at sea 'off Ushant' and there is no mention of him leaving in either the captain's or master's logs. But then, that is hardly surprising considering the details noted in sea officers' logs on ships of this size.

At this point he disappeared in naval records. He is not recorded in Haslar's muster books of patients (or even in the establishment's pay list of staff as suggested by a knowledgeable friend). It is

fifty men was required for the first-rate, 100-gun, ship-of-the-line *Royal George*, under the command of Captain William Domett. Mostly able seamen, Val was one of these. Appearing on 14th October 1793 he was then rated quartermaster's mate - an 'inferior' petty officer. His age of entry on pay and muster books is shown as 25. If correct, then this may reflect his date of birth, rather than date of baptism (and does not quite tally with his age as claimed in his letter to the press). The *Royal George* was part of the Channel Fleet that in war was committed to maintaining 'command of the sea' not only in the English Channel, but also the south-western approaches. Depending on wind and weather, this required significant periods off the French Atlantic coast and further out to sea. When not possible though, long periods were also spent back in the English Channel, in Tor Bay or even as far away as Spithead, sheltering.

The *Royal George* was involved in Admiral Lord 'Black Dick' Howe's Glorious First of June 1794; and in Admiral Lord Bridport's fleet action off the Isle of Groix on 23rd June 1795: the latter as flagship. Lord Bridport had been Howe's relief as Commander-in-Chief Channel Fleet. The ship's musters show that Val was onboard for both these battles and he was also lent on a few occasions. Deeper study of operational records *may* shed light on these short periods elsewhere.

Much has been written of Valentine Joyce's diplomatic and skilful leadership during the Spithead Mutiny of spring 1797, so I need not devote any space here, although Dr. London's account has proved that this had little 'revolutionary' fervour and was in reality, a labour dispute. Per their word, the higher authorities of the Royal Navy apparently sought no revenge and Val continued in his rate and ship for another year. He is recorded as having been discharged to the naval hospital at Haslar (on marshy ground across the river from Portsmouth) on 9th May 1798. The *Royal George*

definitely known that Val's family had been living in Portsmouth for some years and since Haslar had such a bad name among 'Jack', it *may* be that he went home instead. That then would have presented a problem. Unless he was careful, at best he would have been regarded as a 'rambler' and at worst as having 'run' (deserted). If he did not go to Haslar, then somehow he managed to extricate himself.

His date of appearance (that is the day that he was on this ship's books for both pay and victuals) on the diminutive, Infernal class, bomb vessel *Vesuvius* was 23rd June 1798. But, both the entries in this vessel's pay books and muster lists are a complete mess and cannot be relied on. Most of the entries show that he was rated as a quartermaster on coming on board, but the first muster states that he was rated able seaman previous to 23rd June. The captain's log for 22nd June contains an intriguing entry, '... Received 2 men from the Hospital' and Haslar's muster has an entry that almost confirms this. On the 21st two landsmen that had been suffering from scurvy were discharged to the very same bomb vessel. However, neither appears on the ship's musters, or pay books. So, it would seem that they were rejected. But, this was a period of change onboard. The individual with the ship's book number immediately prior to Val was Commander Robert Lewis Fitzgerald, the new captain who had only come onboard on June 20th. Holding the ship's book number following Val was Lieutenant Alexander Lighteness, who appeared on July 1st. As for Valentine Joyce himself, he is shown as 'late Royal William late Royal George'. Perhaps he presented himself onboard the guardship *Royal William* (flying the flag of the C-in-C Portsmouth, Admiral Sir Peter Parker), even if he is not shown on her musters or pay books and he was directed to join *Vesuvius* immediately.

No matter the means for getting onboard, once there he improved his status rapidly and substantially. There was a second interesting entry in the captain's log for 22nd June that required *Vesuvius* transfer a petty officer to the guardship. This, therefore, *may* explain Val's rating of quartermaster on the 23rd. But, he was only in this rate for a week (she was then at anchor at Spithead), before being re-rated as a midshipman. This was also a petty officer rate, but one that was regarded as far superior and that was required to be held by candidates seeking to be commissioned.

Vesuvius had previously been patrolling in the English Channel off Cape Havre and she returned there on sailing on 10th August. After September anchored at Spithead and St. Helens, she was re-deployed and October was sent in transit to Gibraltar. Until July 1799, when she returned to Spithead, *Vesuvius* operated in the Western Mediterranean, the Straits of Gibraltar and out on the Atlantic coast at least as far as Portugal. On 27th January 1799 Val was made the bomb vessel's master's mate, which was another superior petty officer rate. But, this was only temporarily, being re-rated midshipman on 14th February. This can be explained as follows. While at Lisbon in early December 1798 Commander Fitzgerald and a handful of men, including the master's mate, were ordered to *Tonnant* (taken at the Nile). A Lieutenant George Miller then came aboard in command, but in an acting capacity. Commander William Moore subsequently joined her at sea, by cutter, on 24th January 1799: with his commission as captain being read onboard three days later. On 14th February *Vesuvius* received a man rated master's mate, 'Per Order Earl St. Vincent' (Admiral John Jervis, C-in-C Mediterranean).

On her return to the UK, she remained at anchor at Spithead until early November. Entries do not quite match, but on the 4th or 5th, during 'stormy gales' she was paid off and the ship's company was discharged into the *Royal William*, on the orders of the port admiral.

Unfortunately for Midshipman Joyce, on 5th November he became one of a draft of four immediately turned over to the eighteen-gun sloop *Brazen*. She had been the French privateer *L'Invincible General Buonaparte* until taken as a British prize in April 1799. Under Commander James Hanson, while on patrol in the Eastern English Channel 'for the protection of the Trade and annoyance of the Enemy', she was lost in the early hours of 26th January 1800, on Ave Rocks, near Newhaven, Sussex. During a gale, she was smashed to pieces below cliffs. Most sources maintain all but one of her company were lost in this terrible accident. At least one contemporaneous press account (reported variously) states that others escaped though. The day before *Brazen* had taken a prize and

seven men had been put onboard to take her into Portsmouth. Valentine Joyce was not among these eight men.

Largely, the records used to construct the above are at Kew. As mentioned throughout, overwhelmingly ships' pay books and muster lists were the tools to construct his naval service. Captains' and masters' logs are more than slightly useful for getting salient operational information (also including weather conditions, changes to sail and stores taken on and discharged). Incidentally, often there is far more detail in masters' logs. There are also other types of administrative and operational records that may add detail. Newspapers can frequently also be of use. Some can be found at the British Library's outstation at Colindale. For earlier centuries there are also others, such as within the Burnley Collection; and 'Early English Newspapers': microfilm copies of which are at the main British Library, Camden, London. From there, all sorts of other secondary sources can be used to get a fuller picture, especially technical detail on warships. For this, the library of the National Maritime Museum, Greenwich can be highly useful.

Finally, in searching the various records there is the potential for genealogical leads. Val is shown on joining *Vesuvius* in 1798 as already having an annual allotment. This would seem to indicate that he made this out in 1795 while on the *Royal George*, but due to missing ledgers the details are now lost. Allotments were designed primarily to aid lower-deck mariners' wives and/or their children; or if single, their mothers. Apart from there being no apparent sign of Valentine Joyce having married within civil records, in the one obituary found no dependants were mentioned. No will was found either. All in all, it is not unlikely that died a single man.

However, he *was* known to have come from a large family. In the surviving 1798 allotment books there was an ordinary seaman on the *Royal George* by the of name Thomas Joyce, born in Portsmouth and whose mother's name was also Elizabeth. And, the information recorded in the battleship's muster books (originally joining her as a volunteer 3rd class on or around 1st November 1797) is entirely consistent with the baptism records for this to have been a younger brother. Incidentally, varied other checks on men with the surname Joyce then in naval service, found purely in passing, show them as also coming from London, Devonshire, Galway and Cork

More detailed historical and genealogical information on naval subjects can be found on my website:
www.barnettresearch.freeserve.co.uk

Beaumont Hamel Memorial Park
and The Memorial to The Royal Tank Regiment

Elizabeth Blatchford

In The Military History Section of *The Family & Local History Handbook 9*, we published an article *'Touring the Western Front'* by Simon Fowler. In this article he refers to a number of the First World War battlefield memorials in France and Belgium, and specifically Beaumont Hamel Memorial Park.

"Beaumont Hamel Memorial Park (Beaumont Hamel) is dedicated to the memory of men of the Newfoundland Regiment who fought and died here on 1st July 1916. In less than thirty minutes, 710 of the 776 men who had left the trenches had been killed, wounded or reported missing; probably the greatest loss of any unit on the day. The site still contains the trenches, shell holes and twisted remains of 'Danger Tree', which were left after the Armistice, although after 85 years they are little more than hollows in the ground. The site is dominated by a giant caribou; the emblem of the Newfoundland Regiment."

We were delighted to receive the following from one of our readers – Mary Witherow writes:

On page 338 of your book you show a picture of the Newfoundland Regiment's Memorial Park at Beaumont Hamel and refer to the magnificent statue of a caribou which dominates the landscape near the entrance. It does not however mention that beyond the trees aligning the southern horizon of the picture is a part of the park donated in perpetuity by the Government of Newfoundland to Scotland for the great, equally dominant, memorial to the 51st Highland Division. This gesture was in recognition of the affinity between the Newfoundlanders and the Scots alongside whom they had fought. It was made when the land in Beaumont Hamel allotted to the Division by the local population, was found, almost at the last moment before the Memorial's emplacement, to be liable to subsidence on account of the coal mines beneath.

My father, George Henry Paulin, who had served in the Army in both The Lothian and Border Horse and the Royal Flying Corps during the War, created the Memorial. He was a graduate of the Edinburgh Art School and later gained fame as a very eminent sculptor, being among other things, the Representative of the Royal Scottish Academy in London from 1926 until 1957.

The memorial he created at Beaumont Hamel was a bronze figure of a Highland soldier standing at rest, about 12 feet high and atop a Scottish granite plinth of rather greater height, itself on the top tier of a three-tier stepped terrace. The plinth is carved with thistles and bears plaques among which one evokes the historic 'Auld Alliance' between Scotland and France. The whole is flanked by two symbolic guardian Scottish lions, also in bronze, one of which bears my Father's signature. The model for the statue is said by the present (Canadian) custodians to be a Canadian Army Warrant Officer. I do not really know why it should be. First, Newfoundland was not incorporated into the Canadian Federation until 1949, well after the Second World War. Second, the work was executed in my Father's Glasgow studio a full three years after the Armistice so any Canadian or even Newfoundland, involvement seems extremely unlikely amid several million Scots from whom to choose! Moreover, the Newfoundland connection did not arise until after the work was completed, when the site Surveyors realised it was too heavy for the originally intended site in the village of Beaumont Hamel itself, because old mine workings subsidence would have jeopardised it. However, whilst that will probably never be conclusively resolved, in my family it is believed that the face is a portrait of my Father's younger brother, Carl,

Photo taken 1921 of George Henry Paulin finishing the clay model of the main 51st Highland Division figure. For some idea of the scale, George H. Paulin was 6'3" tall

television as it has been used at least twice in recent years to introduce the broadcast of the Annual Remembrance Day Service from the Cenotaph and once for the Royal Albert Hall Festival of Remembrance. There is a local legend at Beaumont Hamel that Hitler wanted to transport this statue to Berlin as a war-trophy after the conquest of France, as he often did in conquered countries, but just before implementing the plan, there was intense RAF aerial activity at low-level over the site. The local German garrison feared that they had been rumbled and abandoned the plan as not worth the cost, should they take an air strike in consequence. There is no official record known of this incident, but it is an interesting apocryphal story which I only learned when visiting there about six years ago. There is a further Memorial in Beaumont Hamel itself, in the form of a granite Celtic Cross, to the 8th Battalion, The Argyll and Sutherland Highlanders, which my father also created at about the same time.

More recently, a design and prototype which he had prepared for a Second World War memorial to The Royal Armoured Corps, but which for various internal reasons within the Army at the time was never executed after being selected competitively in 1952, was successfully resurrected from his maquette. This monument was created during 1999, with my agreement, by a brilliant contemporary Sculptress, Mrs Vivi Mallock, as a Memorial to

an Inspector in the Indian Police who had died of a tropical disease in India in 1916! However, there is no-one still alive from that generation to answer this query.

The main Scottish granite plinth for the soldier-figure is beautifully carved with a climbing thistle and it bears inscriptions memorialising the 51st Division and an invocation of the ancient memory of 'The Auld Alliance', between Scotland and France. One of the two guardian lions bears his signature on the left hind-quarter. I also remember him carving a further plaque at home after the Second World War for those of the 51st Highland Division killed in that conflict, which was then affixed in a more modest ceremony on the site in, I think, 1946.

The entire design of The Memorial is my father's work, as is all the statuary and stone carving and was unveiled on 28th in September 1924 by Marshal Foch, the Allied Commander-in-Chief during the Great War. You may have seen this memorial on the

The granite Celtic Cross in memory of the 8th Battalion Argyll and Sutherland Highlanders just outside Beaumont Hamel. They were part of the 51st (Highland Division)

The Royal Tank Regiment and its ancestor, the Machine-Gun Corps. Although the original design is attributed to my father, credit for the final figure must be attributed to Mrs Mallock who did such a magnificent job in bringing another's concept to such perfection. It depicts the five-man crew of a Second World War Comet tank and stands, in bronze, 9 feet high from pavement level, in London at the junction of Whitehall

H.M. The Queen
unveiling the Memorial to
The Royal Armoured Corps in 2000

Place and Whitehall Court, adjacent to the Old War Office Building. It is close to the office where, in 1900, the first known memorandum was written which called for an 'armoured land ship' to be developed for modern warfare – The Tank. The Memorial was unveiled by HM Queen on 13th June 2000, the centenary date of that memorandum. It has had even more TV exposure than the Highlander recently, being used by both major TV networks as a backdrop for many of the out-of-doors Ministry of Defence interviews during the Iraq War of 2003.

In this case, Mrs Mallock sought my permission to vary the original work by using living models for the portraits. I agreed, subject to the crew Commander, the central figure, still representing my late brother who had modelled for it in 1952. This did not solve the 'living model' issue, so we settled on my elder son, who is a 'living image' of his uncle. He was a Captain in the Army in 2000, and was exactly the right age for the role. We have a photograph of him taken immediately after the unveiling, in the pose of the figure, standing in front of it. The likeness is excellent.
Mary Witherow.

We are extremely grateful to Mary Witherow for supplying us with such detailed and personal background, and giving us permission to incorporate her family reminiscences in this publication.

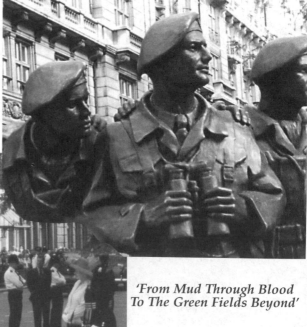

'From Mud Through Blood
To The Green Fields Beyond'

314

"Swing the Light"
Analysis of an old soldier's tale
Fred Feather

Sometimes a glazed look comes over the faces of grandchildren, of which I have eight, when I commence to tell a perfectly good tale of my days serving Her Majesty. *"Oh! No! Not the square dumplings again"* they quaver, as I attempt to tell them once again the perfectly true story of how I inadvertently came to invent the army's most deadly weapon of warfare. In the forces there was a ancient saying *"swing the light."* When activated the raconteur had to finish his story before the lamp in the cabin stopped swinging. Sometimes old soldier stories are one hundred per cent true, and can be demonstrated so to be, thus:

Och aye!
According to the Chelmsford Chronicle for March 1808, Serjeant Lindsey of the Perth Militia, stationed at Dover, on being informed of his succession to the Earldom of Crawford and Lindsey, with an estate of £42000 per annum, left that place in a chaise and four for London, accompanied by his wife, who was at the washtub when the news was announced; and on being told by her husband that she was become a Countess coolly replied "she would nevertheless finish the shirt she was washing" which she accordingly did, and then throwing the tub away, exclaimed " It is now high time to leave off this business."

In my police service I met some splendid examples of the canteen story-teller, but none apparently to match one Georgian soldier and policeman from *"over the border."* . For this story I wish to thank the *Falkirk Herald* of 12th April 1853.

Death of a veteran

"We have to record the death of John FISHER, rag and bone merchant, who expired at his residence in Kirk Wynd on yesterday week, in the 75th year of his age. The deceased, who was a native of Berwick-upon-Tweed, had a singularly romantic and eventful history, and was intimately associated with some of the most memorable events of the present century."

"He was a tall, powerful, fine-looking man, distinguished alike for strength and agility. At an early age he entered the British army, and fought in the Peninsula under Sir John Moore against the troops of the great Napoleon. He was taken captive at the retreat of Corunna, where his leader fell, and conveyed to a French prison, where he was shut up for some time in rather uncomfortable quarters."
"When Napoleon was organising his enormous and ill-fated expedition to Russia, he offered several of the British prisoners of war the alternative of taking service in one of the regiments to take part in the campaign, or remaining in "durance vile". Fisher and several of his comrades accepted liberty on the terms proposed, and were duly enlisted in the Grand Army of France."

He had a share in the early glories and ultimate horrors of the luckless expedition to Moscow, and saw that proud city committed to the flames to prevent it from affording shelter and sustenance to the Gallic invaders. He fought at Smolensk, and crossed the Beresina on that awful day when so many thousands perished, and was one of the wrecks of that magnificent host, who arrived in safety at Paris.

His position was in the rear of the French army on the march into Russia, but in the front during the retreat – a circumstance which may have preserved his life, for the rear of the ill-starred fugitives suffered as much from the Cossacks as from the fierce cold, to which alone the front ranks were exposed. Fisher has often told that himself and two associates were glad to steal a pig, and to eat it raw, during that dreadful march.

At the close of the campaign, Fisher laid down his arms and peremptorily declined to fight against his native country. By and by, he was set at liberty, and having found his way to the headquarters of the British regiment to which he belonged, and having represented all the circumstances he duly received a pardon for going to Moscow.

When he was discharged from our own army he travelled for nine months from town to town in his soldier's undress, and while living in low lodging houses obtained a keen insight into the habits and customs of beggars and vagabonds, which was of great value to him in the profession which he subsequently adopted.

He then made application to be admitted to the Edinburgh police force, and was appointed an officer in the detective establishment where he rapidly rose to the rank of sergeant. During this period of his history he captured no fewer than four noted criminals who were afterwards executed. He was the officer who apprehended the notorious Burke and Hare, along with the wife of the former murderer. Many of his detections were remarkably clever and far-sighted, quite worthy of even McLevy or Vidocq. In many of them he also manifested great moral courage and exercised unusual physical strength. He was wont to relate with great glee, an exploit which he accomplished in the canal tunnel near Falkirk, when he presented a "leadless pistol" without a lock at three vagabonds, who surrendered on his threatening to shoot them. The deceased left the Edinburgh detective force to come to Falkirk in a similar capacity, combined, we understand, with that of a sheriff officer. He held that position till he quarrelled with the then Fiscal, when he retired and opened an ale and spirit shop in the Kirk Wynd. The leading incident, which happened while he was in that trade, was the entrance of his premises by housebreakers, who carried off a barrel of whisky, and three sovereigns in cash.

Fisher next became an auctioneer, but did not continue in that profession for any length of time. He finally became a rag and bone merchant, in which business he continued till his death, and which will now, we believe, be conducted by his widow.

The deceased was well known in Falkirk. He always went about the street with his apron on, and was invariably bare-headed, no matter how wet, cold, or boisterous the weather might be. He was an active, shrewd, intelligent man, and was wont to narrate the events of his life with peculiar zest and graphic descriptive power. He always maintained that he know how long he would live, as a Gypsy woman, who had "spaed the fortune" of himself and two comrades on the march to Moscow, had predicted that two of the number would perish in the campaign, but that the survivor would live to a good old age.

Alpha and Omega – soldiers of the 26th Foot in the rank and uniform that John Fisher would have worn as a private in 1802 and as sergeant-major in 1823 at the start and end of his army career – Artist R.J.Marrion.

Altogether, the life of John Fisher was an interesting, instructive and valuable one."

What a challenge! Was it all true, or was something overheard in a Falkirk pub by a reporter who caught his editor on a "slow news day."

The Search
It did not take long on the internet to find that a John Fisher actually was the arresting officer in the case of the notorious "Burke and Hare."

"Helen and Margaret rushed off to tell their husbands and Burke and Hare immediately had Mary's body taken in a large chest to Surgeon's Square for dissection. James Gray reported the body to Sergeant-Major John Fisher who began an immediate search. Sergeant Fisher and patrolman John Findlay went to Tanner's Close to find evidence of the crime, but they could find no body. Blood was found on a pile of straw, which Helen argued came from a woman during childbirth. A search was also made of 10 Surgeon's Square on November 2, 1828 and, in a corner of the surgery's basement, Patrolman Fisher opened a tea chest and found the body of Mary Docherty. She was identified by the guests at the Halloween party. William Burke, William Hare, Margaret Hare, and Helen McDougal were arrested for her murder."
www.thecrimeweb.com/william_burke_and william.hare From this article we can infer that Fisher had been a soldier, for, to the best of my knowledge, there was no rank of sergeant-major in the Edinburgh Police. Readers are pointed towards a valuable booklet about the early policing of Edinburgh, price £2.50p plus 50p postage, obtainable from Mr J. Thomson, 52, Grove Street, Edinburgh, EH3 8AT

The point in the newspaper story on which I first focused was the death of Sir John Moore at Corunna. A number of Scottish regiments were in the battle order and I wrote to the Royal Scots (1st Foot) the Black Watch (42nd Foot) and the Argylls (92nd Foot) , plus a few other museums who were not wholly military. All replied courteously but could not take the story any further and all urged a visit to the National Archive at Kew. Ignoring the five hours travelling to get there and back I did so.

As Fisher appeared to have an Edinburgh connection I started by obtaining pay lists for 1st, 42nd and 71st regiments of Foot (WO12). Immediately I struck gold for a John Fisher had served for 19 years at the right time, with the 71st Foot, transferring to the 83rd in June 1819. (WO12 8683). I then discovered a splendid short-cut, for in former times when I searched for a soldiers document (WO97),the names were alphabetically sorted after 1881, but before that you needed a regiment. Joy of joys, the pre-1881 documents are now sorted by name and on microfilm. John Fisher of 83rd Foot was on WO97 925 – he had served 19th years 177 days since joining 71st on 25th September 1802 at the age of 19 and, having been born at Woodham in Essex, had remained a private until his discharge with Hepatitis. Which did not at all fit in with the facts the *Falkirk*

The Edinburgh Town Guard

M BOOKS

The story of the capital's first police force

Cover of Mr Thompson's book.

Herald described!

But there were many more John Fishers and I worked through them gradually, until Sergeant Major John Fisher of 26th Foot appeared on the screen. WO97 453 - page 52 recorded that this John Fisher was born in Perth and retired on 7th June 1823.

The 26th Foot or Cameronians

The Cameronians were only vaguely known to me. My late brother-in-law Charles Rae Taylor recalled (when I was about 8) losing his kilt at the Battle of El Alemain. Although he was in the RASC he had been in the 51st Highland Division and attached to the Cameronians. At least I learned that they were a different regiment from the Cameron Highlanders (79th Foot) and made of such proud stuff that they refused to be amalgamated with any other regiment in the 1970's and were voluntarily disbanded. In the library at Kew I found the *"Historical Record of Cameronians"* dated 1867.

In 1802 the 1st battalion of the 26th Foot moved from Plymouth Dock to Stirling Castle, where on 9th October, Fisher joined Captain Fountaine Hogg's company. His entry on the pay-list marked *"paid by Edinburgh District to 8th October."* By 1805 both the regiments battalions were in Ireland and the 1st embarked on the transports *Aurora, Pelican and Marie* en route to Germany. *Maria* sank off the Texel in Holland and *Aurora* foundered on the Goodwin Sands in December 1805. Nearly 500 men and women and children of the battalion were lost. Fisher soon after became Corporal and the losses were made up with a draft from 2nd battalion. 1st battalion had 4 companies in Germany in 1806 then returned to Ireland whilst the 2nd battalion recruited in Scotland. In 1808-9 Fisher became a Sergeant and the 1st battalion were Spain and at the Battle of Corunna. After our defeat the remnants were taken off by boat, and the 26th left 2 sergeants, 3 drummers and 187 privates behind. Many women escaped with them and the shocked survivors were said to be in a diseased state and in tatters. 43 of the lost men later regained the battalion, which returned to Plymouth

Fisher's discharge papers (WO97 as above) record that he was back in action at the Siege of Flushing in the summer of 1809 and then returned to the Iberian Peninsula. In 1812 Sergeant John Fisher was recorded on the 26th Foot's pay lists as being with 1st battalion fighting the French in Portugal and he became

Colour Sergeant on 25th June 1813 in Gibraltar. After the Napoleonic Wars he was promoted Sergeant Major. He was then earning 2/6d per day, which was later raised to 3s-0d per day. In 1822 the sole battalion (the 2nd had been disbanded) was in Edinburgh, Glasgow and Dumfries, being deployed against civil unrest and accompanied by police. The regiment was commanded at this time by Lieutenant General George, the Earl of Dalhousie. Fisher was pensioned out of the regiment on 15th May 1823 in Ireland and "placed on out div 18th June 1823." Voucher 19 was for him to proceed to Dublin. Thus ended his army career.

Conclusions

Few men reached the rank of Sergeant Major in a Scottish Regiment and no other of that name has been found to have obtained that rank and a pension at this time. The story of the regiment fits in well with that of the newspaper article. Fisher was reported in the paper as a native of Berwick on Tweed which, depending upon his parents' lives, is not inconsistent with his army birthplace at Perth. His discharge describes him as a weaver. A police career would be a likely career move for the eminent and respected leader of men he had shown himself to be.

His name did not leave the pay roll during the Napoleonic Wars (1802-1815) and no mention was made of him being captured. Service with the enemy was desertion and a capital offence. Fisher was rapidly promoted. Could the tales of service with the French be an old soldier's story, told in a pub in his later years, and "swallowed" by a newspaper reporter. The rest of his story appears to be checkable.

Epilogue.

If only graves could reveal the secrets of their inmates! In the yard of Saint Paul's Church at Fort Eyrie in Canada, an East Indian veteran has the following on his tombstone. Within a medallion surmounted by a crown, is an elephant, in the circle around the words, "Hindoostan Peninsula LXXVI. Major Rooth, 1849, aged 65. In the United Service Journal it is told of Benjamin Rooth that he was one of those who laid the gallant Sir John Moore in his grave in the ramparts of Corunna, "the sod with their bayonets turning." Five days after his death his Peninsula medal arrived with clasps for Nive, Nivelle, and Corunna." I would wager money that Major Rooth would have known John Fisher

That is just the beginning of my quest. Nothing has yet proved Cameronian Fisher to be the Falkirk veteran, but many circumstantial clues have pointed in that direction. I do hope that this article may bring to light more information about his Edinburgh and Falkirk police and civilian careers.

Gentlemen in Khaki
The Anglo-Boer War 1899-1902
Rosemary Dixon-Smith

For many family historians, the only surviving relic of an Anglo-Boer War ancestor is a man wearing khaki uniform, staring unblinkingly out of a faded photograph. Details about him are often scant, his regiment usually unknown. *'He fought in the Boer War of 1899-1902. How do I find out more about him?'* is the frequently-asked-question. The answer is, with some difficulty.

In the run-up to the war, there were about 10 000 British troops in the Cape and Natal. Before the delivery of the ultimatum, Britain dispatched reinforcements of another 10 000, about 6 000 officers and men being sent out from India. Before the end of the war was in sight, some 500 000 men were in the field. If the ancestor in your photograph was in the British Imperial forces, he could have been in the Regular Army (Cavalry, Artillery, Infantry etc) or a Reservist. He may have been a member of the Militia (reinforcements attached to the Regulars) or among the Yeomanry. Over 120 000 recruits who had no military experience whatsoever joined the British Army during the Anglo-Boer War. If the ancestor served in the British Colonial forces, about 16 000 came from Australia, 6 600 from New Zealand, 6 000 from Canada and over 52 000 from South Africa itself. Statistics vary, but these give some indication of the task ahead when trying to find information about one particular individual.

On 16 October 1899, Rudyard Kipling penned his verses *'The Absent-Minded Beggar'*, which burst upon the British nation through the medium of the press, whipping up a remarkable degree of patriotic fervour. The theme of the poem was the very 'gentleman in khaki' that we're attempting to find, our unknown warrior of the Anglo-Boer War:

'When you've shouted Rule Britannia, when you've sung God Save the Queen,
When you've finished killing Kruger with your mouth,
Will you kindly drop a shilling in my little tambourine
For a gentleman in kharki ordered South?'

Most of us are familiar with the word 'Khaki' – though perhaps not with Kipling's spelling of it – but its origins are less-often considered. Said to stem from the Indian word meaning dust-coloured, opinion is divided as to how this form of apparel emerged. The Indian Corps of Guides in the 1840s may have been the first to dye their clothes as a form of camouflage, using a substance obtained from the mazari palm. Elsewhere, it's suggested that at a dangerous outpost on the Indian frontier, an officer dipped dazzling-white uniforms into coffee to make them inconspicuous while on patrol. This proved serviceable and was followed up by a request for an issue of properly-dyed uniforms in the colour, an idea which was gradually adopted by the British Army for its colonial campaigns. All troops serving in the re-conquest of the Sudan in 1897-1898 wore full khaki uniform.

The *Natal Mercury Pictorial of 1915* gives the following intriguing version:
'Khaki was discovered by a happy accident. British troops in India wore a cotton uniform which when it was new was khaki in colour, but after a visit to the laundry was indescribable. A Manchester businessman, discussing this defect, casually remarked that a fortune awaited the man who could find a khaki dye that neither sun, soap, nor soda would fade. A young officer heard the remark, hired a skilled native dyer, and began the search. Years passed in fruitless experiment, till one day turning over a heap of rags, relics of their failures, they chanced upon one piece which was still khaki, though the laundry had worked its will. But it had received no special treatment, so far as they knew, except that it had fallen into a metal dish. That was the secret. The metal of the dish and the chemicals in the dye had combined to produce that fadeless khaki colour which makes our soldiers invisible and turned the lieutenant into a millionaire.'

Whatever the truth, khaki became standard overseas service issue in 1896 and its use spread into civilian life as well, men's khaki jackets and trousers being advertised in South African newspapers from about 1899. Because of the universality of the khaki uniform, it's not easy to identify photographs as being specifically of the Anglo-Boer War period, or even to know whether the pictures were taken in South Africa at all, rather than in other parts of the Empire – India, perhaps, or the Far East. Many photographs of this era were 'mock-ups' taken a long way from the veld.

Basically the uniform consisted of tunic and trousers, worn with puttees (a strip of cloth wound round the leg from ankle to knee), and a khaki-covered helmet as protection against the sun. There were some changes – the original uniform fabric, a firm coarse cotton known as drill, was replaced by serge, and the style of the helmet underwent some modification. Sometimes a flap of material attached to the back of the helmet shaded the neck – or the helmet was simply reversed so that the longer part of the brim served that purpose. There was a regulation pith hat as well. The felt slouch or *'smasher'* hat with the brim turned up on one side, as worn by colonial volunteers, was found to be more practical than the helmet, and this headgear also became popular among Imperial troops, so if the man in your photograph is wearing the slouch hat it may not necessarily mean that he was in a colonial unit.

There were minor variations in dress according to regiment. The Canadians had their own

He is out on active service, Wiping something off a slate.—KIPLING.

distinctive hat with a high crown. Imperial cavalry regiments wore chains on the shoulders of their tunics, boots rather than puttees, and leather gauntlets. Certain regiments affected coloured puggarees wound round the helmet. It's not difficult to pick out a member of a Scottish regiment in kilt and sporran (which must have been hot in the tropics, and sometimes a khaki apron was added to this ensemble). Some of these differences may aid in identification of an ancestor's photograph, but in the field there were often highly-individualistic alterations to the regulation uniform.

The soldier's accoutrements can provide clues as to date, regiment and rank. For example, in the Border Mounted Rifles, a Natal permanent volunteer corps, up to 1896 ammunition was carried in a pouch with a brown leather crossbelt. Later, what was derogatively known as the *'Royston Entanglement'* was adopted - a combined rifle sling and bandolier used by NCO's and troopers. Officers and Warrant Officers of the unit wore the Sam-Browne sword belt. Incidentally, the Alexandra Mounted Rifles, which evolved to become the Border Mounted Rifles in 1894, adopted the used of khaki for its field service uniform in 1874. This is the earliest recorded military use of khaki in South Africa, a possible exception being the 2nd Highland Light Infantry (74th Highlanders) who, in the 8th Frontier War 1850-1852, fought in doublets of that colour.

As family historians know to their cost, names, dates and places are notoriously absent from the back of photographs. In Anglo-Boer War groups badges and insignia may not be visible or easily identifiable; it could be worth asking for specialist advice. If you're fortunate enough to own a medal awarded to the ancestor, engraved on the rim will be his name, rank and unit, which is an excellent start. Most men serving in the Anglo-Boer War were eligible for one or both of the two campaign medals – the Queen's South Africa and the King's South Africa. This topic, including the use of the medal rolls for tracing Anglo-Boer War ancestry, was covered in detail in David Barnes's article *"The British Army in the Anglo-Boer War"*, in the 6th edition of *The Family and Local History Handbook*. Several published medal rolls are available: D R Forsyth's *'Defenders of Kimberley Medal Roll'*, and S M Kaplan's *'Medal Roll of the Queen's South Africa Medal with Wepener Bar'*, and *'Medal Roll of the Queen's South Africa Medal with Bar Relief of Mafeking'*.

The Colonial Volunteers

Some of the most interesting departures from standard uniform were seen among the colonial volunteer regiments. It was not unknown for certain of these to take to the field in their shirtsleeves, which deplorable habit occasioned much comment from more conventional echelons. However, the colonials were valuable and courageous troops, well-suited by experience to the conditions which they faced in South Africa. This is particularly true of the colonial mounted regiments – they formed two-fifths of the entire mounted force participating in the war.

Should an ancestor have been among the colonials, there are numerous possibilities as to the regiment in which he may have served. On the outbreak of the war, thousands of troops from the overseas colonies were sent to South Africa from Canada, India, Ceylon, Australia and New Zealand. In South Africa itself, there were permanent regular forces including the Natal Police, Cape Mounted Police and Cape Mounted Rifles. These should not be confused with the permanent volunteer units which had been in place for some years, such as the Natal Carbineers, Durban Light Infantry, Diamond Fields Artillery and Diamond Fields Horse, Border Mounted Rifles, Kaffrarian Rifles, Cape Town Highlanders, the Kimberley Regiment and others.

Also, certain corps were raised at the beginning of the war and specifically for service in that conflict. These 'irregulars' carried an aura of glamour and nonconformity: Brabant's Horse, Thorneycroft's Mounted Infantry, Roberts's Horse, the Imperial Light Horse, the Imperial Light Infantry, Steinaecker's Horse are all names to conjure with. They were the stuff of legend and a typical tale is that of Major C B Childe who led 300 South African Light Horse (like the ILH largely composed of Uitlanders) at the taking of Bastion Hill from the Boers in January 1900. Major Childe is said to have had a premonition on the day before the battle that he would be killed, and asked fellow officers to

ensure that a biblical quotation would be engraved on his tombstone. Taken from the second book of Kings 4.26, it read: 'Is it well with the child? and she answered, it is well'. As he'd foreseen, Childe fell at Bastion Hill and his request was duly honoured.

Some forces came into being further on in the war, among them Kitchener's Fighting Scouts, raised in December 1900, Ashburner's Light Horse, the Bushveld Carbineers, Dennison's Scouts, Driscoll's Scouts – and the Cape Colony Cycle Corps.

The best place to research local armed forces serving in South Africa from 1899-1902 is The National Archives, Kew, which holds nominal rolls (soldiers' names) and enrolment forms (completed by each man) in WO 127 and WO 126. A full list of units, with the relevant record box number at Kew, can be found at www.genealogyworld.net

The start of an on-going project to index attestation papers of colonial soldiers from WO126 can be found at http://hometown.aol.co.uk/kevinasplin.home.html. So far the regiments available are Ashburner's Light Horse, Bechuanaland Rifles, Bethune's Mounted Infantry, Border House,

Border Scouts, Brabant's Horse, Bushmanland Borderers and Canadian Scouts.

If the ancestor died during the war, there are other avenues to follow. The Anglo-Boer War Museum in Bloemfontein is currently compiling a computerized database of casualties, but in the interim offer a look-up service and can be contacted at museum@anglo-boer.co.za or through their website http://www.anglo-boer.co.za/

A roll of Natal Field Force casualties of the first part of the war, from 20 October 1899 – 26 October 1900 can be found at http://surreygenealogist.com/sgdatabase.htm On this site 11, 188 casualties are searchable by surname.

Names of Anglo-Boer War casualties taken from the South African Defence Force Roll of Honour can be accessed at http://www.justdone.co.za/ROH/

Using the NAAIRS Index
The South African National Archives online index (NAAIRS) available at www.national.archives.gov.za/ can help when tracing Anglo-Boer War ancestors. The Gravestones database (GEN) offers memorial inscriptions collected by the Genealogical Society of South Africa (GSSA), some of which refer to casualties of the Anglo-Boer War. A South African cemetery index on CD, now in its third edition, is also produced by GSSA – this compilation has recently helped me to find an Australian trooper buried in a small graveyard in the Orange Free State.

A search of the NAAIRS index may reveal an ancestor's deceased estate file with a Death Notice included, and these are extremely informative. Sometimes there are two Death Notices found in estate files of the Anglo-Boer War period: one filled in briefly at the place of death, by the Adjutant perhaps, and another notice completed more fully later.

To illustrate this application of the online index, an example from my own research: William Dixon Smith, of Northumberland origins, emigrated to Natal in 1880, settling in Alexandra County where he established himself as a wagon-builder and blacksmith. He joined the local permanent volunteer force and at the time of the outbreak of the Anglo-Boer War was Lieutenant Quartermaster of the Border Mounted Rifles. All volunteer units responded promptly to the call for mobilization and William, along with the rest of his contingent, entrained for Ladysmith on 28 September 1899. By January 1900 he was dead, one of many who died of enteric during the Siege of Ladysmith. The Death Notice provided his age at death, his occupation, his birthplace and parents' names, his marital status, the name of his spouse and place of marriage, and the names and ages of his children. Other documents in the deceased estate file included a detailed inventory of his possessions, including the forge and anvil and other tools of his trade as well as household items, giving a picture of his lifestyle in the colony. Muster rolls preserved in Natal Defence Force records made it possible to track William's career in the volunteers from the time of his enrolment.

Correspondence in archival files could give further information about the next-of-kin: widows or mothers claiming the deceased's pay or the five pound 'war gratuity', a seemingly scant return for the supreme sacrifice. A poignant memo mentions a youthful soldier's only piece of movable property – his horse, 'killed for food during the Ladysmith siege'. Other documents in the case of this trooper showed that he had several younger siblings dependant on him. Such details take us beyond mere statistics and bring the human story to light.

Police
In the second half of the 19th century there were a number of semi-military police forces in South Africa. These arose out of the need to maintain law and order over large areas and difficult terrain in the many districts of which the country was comprised.

One of these units was the Natal Mounted Police, which was first raised after the Langalibalele Rebellion in 1874 and saw action

in the Anglo-Zulu War of 1879. This corps continued to serve through the Anglo-Boer War 1899-1902 (at the Siege of Ladysmith) and the Bambata Rebellion of 1906, until finally being incorporated into the South African Mounted Riflemen in 1913. The force numbered just over 300 at the beginning of the Anglo-Boer War. Many of its members were recruited in England in the early years of the corps and it's interesting that some of these men are individually-named on passenger lists, coming out on such ships as the Kinfauns Castle and Roslin Castle in the 1880s. These lists occur in the European Immigration Department registers (source code EI) held at Pietermaritzburg Archives Repository. If an ancestor was in the NMP, the chances of finding out more about him are good. The history of the corps is told in Holt's 'The Mounted Police of Natal'. 16 volumes of original NMP records are preserved at Pietermaritzburg Archives Repository. This treasure trove includes nominal rolls, enlistment registers from 1874-1913, records of service covering that period, and a roll of individuals granted Long Service and Good Conduct Medals 1882-1907. That's not all: a search of the NAAIRS index on the words 'Natal Mounted Police' brings up over 500 files of various types – Colonial Secretary's Office correspondence, Magisterial archives etc – each containing useful material.

Similarly well-documented, the Cape Mounted Police came into existence in 1882. Enrolment records are held in the Cape Town Archives Repository, and searches on the NAAIRS index would be beneficial for anyone in pursuit of a CMP ancestor.

The Cape Mounted Riflemen, a totally separate semi-military entity from the above, started off as the Frontier Armed and Mounted Police (FAMP) circa 1855, with the change in title dating from 1878. Their history is recounted by Basil Williams in his 'Record of the Cape Mounted Riflemen' and again NAAIRS offers a large number of references to files concerning the CMR, held in the Cape Archives Repository. Anglo-Boer War casualty lists for the CMR can be found at www.genealogyworld.net

South African Constabulary

In 1900, the South African Constabulary was established, somewhat optimistically, to keep peace in the melting-pot which was then the Transvaal, Orange River Colony (Orange Free State) and Swaziland. Master-minded, under orders from Roberts, by Baden-Powell, fresh from his successful leadership of the garrison during the Siege of Mafeking, this was a military body disguised as a police force. It was recruited from British men in the Cape and Natal, as well as from further afield – Britain itself, Australia, New Zealand, India and Ceylon. In addition, over 1 200 Canadians were dispatched to swell the ranks of the SAC, and because these men were not recruited or paid by the Canadian government, their records are held mainly in South Africa rather than in their home country.

Baden-Powell, true to form, came up with a comfortable khaki uniform topped by a broad-brimmed American hat known as the 'Boss of the Plains' pattern. Since the term was usually shortened to 'B.P.', Baden-Powell remarked that this 'brought about the mistaken notion that they had something to do with me.' Later, when he established the scouting movement, the uniform echoed that of the SAC, including the now-famous hat.

Many members of the Constabulary, particularly Britons, made South Africa their permanent home. Records of Conduct and Service of the SAC held in the National Archives of South Africa provide remarkably comprehensive information. A typical record sheet offers a detailed physical description of the man, his date and place of birth, marital status, calling (occupation), religion, and name and address of his next-of-kin, as well as a list of promotions or transfers. His Defaulter's Sheet may reveal the odd blot on his career. Should an ancestor's SAC file reference emerge on the NAAIRS index, the contents would take any family historian's knowledge several leaps forward.

The combined use of British and South African archival records, published sources, as well as information available online, can help in the search for a gentleman in khaki who was, in Kipling's words, 'out on active service, wiping something off a slate'.

Useful Published Resources

Steve Watt: *'In Memoriam'* (University of Natal Press Pietermaritzburg 2000 ISBN: 9-780869-809686) provides a Roll of Honour of Imperial Forces in the Anglo-Boer War 1899-1902, 25 000 soldiers, women and civilians in military employ all of whom laid down their lives for the British cause, whether they were from Britain itself, South Africa, Rhodesia, Australia, Canada, or New Zealand. It lists alphabetically the individual's name, regimental number, regiment, type of casualty, place, date of death, where buried, and whether the name is listed on a monument or in a graveyard, with location. Where available, particulars of age and religion of the deceased are given.

Darrell Hall: *'The Hall Handbook of the Anglo-Boer War'*(University of Natal Press 1999 ISBN 0-86980-949-0) gives a useful list of British Regiments and the dates of their period of service in South Africa, with the battles or operations at which they were present. This helps to sketch an outline of the ancestor's activities and time spent in this country. Hall also gives a list of the Colonial Forces with SA arrival and departure dates, and a list of SA units with details such as when and where these were raised and disbanded. Men who were awarded the Victoria Cross during the Anglo-Boer War are listed alphabetically, as are names of graveyards where Imperial Soldiers were buried. There are brief biographies of some of the major personalities associated with the war.

John Stirling: *'The Colonials in South Africa 1899-1902'* (Blackwood, Edinburgh 1907) A mine of information; some individual names, such as those mentioned in dispatches, are included as well as details of each unit's operations during the war.

'Diary of the Siege of Ladysmith' (Ladysmith Historical Society, several volumes) gives first-hand accounts by such people as Major G F Tatham of the Natal Carbineers, Bella Craw, niece of Major Tatham and resident in Ladysmith during the Siege, letters of Lt Col C W Park of the Devonshires, notes on the campaign written by A J Crosby of the Natal Carbineers and the experiences of a Siege Nurse, Kate Driver.

Johan Wasserman & Brian Kearney (ed.): *'A Warrior's Gateway: Durban and the Anglo-Boer War 1899-1902'* (Protea Book House, Pretoria 2002). Excellent photographs.

Basil Williams: *'Record of the Cape Mounted Riflemen'* (Sir Joseph Causton & Sons, London 1909).

G T Hurst: *'Volunteer Regiments of Natal and East Griqualand'* (Knox, Durban 1945)

G F Gibson: *'The Story of the Imperial Light Horse in the South African War 1899-1902'* (G.D. & Co. 1937)

G Tylden: *'The Armed Forces of South Africa'* (Africana Museum, Johannesburg 1954)

H.P. Holt: *'The Mounted Police of Natal'* (Murray, London 1913)

Websites

www.national.archives.gov.za/ South African National Archives and Record Service incorporating NAAIRS index
http://hometown.aol.co.uk/kevinasplin.home.htm l Index to some attestation papers held at The National Archives, Kew
www.genealogyworld.net Guide to Tracing Anglo-Boer War Ancestors; list of local forces whose records are held at The National Archives, Kew; Muster Roll of the Natal Carbineers in Anglo-Boer War; Casualty Roll of the Cape Mounted Riflemen.
www.militarymuseum.co.za/ South African National Military History Museum; recommended article 'Researching Ancestors who were Servicemen'; details of published medal rolls.
http://rapidttp.co.za.milhist/ Anglo-Boer War articles from the South African Military History Society
http://www.lib.sun.ac.za/roh/ There is a facility to add a Dedication to and a Story about any individual listed on this site.
http://surreygenealogist.com/sgdatabase.htm Roll of Natal Field Force Casualties
http://khozi2.nu.ac.za/kafricana.htm The Campbell Collections, Natal, online catalogue and photographs
http://home.global.co.za/~afrilib Africana Library Kimberley, material on Siege of Kimberley
www.talana.co.za/ Talana Museum Dundee
www.pinetreeweb.com/ Baden-Powell, numerous links
www.perthdps.com/military/index.html Australians serving in South Africa 1899-1902 listed alphabetically by state and contingent.
www.naa.gov.au/fsheets/fs67.html Australian participation in the Anglo-Boer War, sources for service records, medal rolls, attestation papers, enrolment forms, returned soldiers' records.
www.awm.gov.au/database/boer.asp Australian War Memorial site with Boer War Nominal Roll Database, searchable by name, unit and keyword.

The Polish Air Force in the West
David Barnes

The early years of the 1920's saw the Polish Air Force being developed into Europe's second largest airforce under the direction of General Wlodzimierz Zagorski and later General Ludomil Rayski was the driving force behind Poland's military aviation industry. By 1929 the PZL (Panstwowe Zaklady Lotnicze) P.1 had flown. This all metal, gull winged aircraft was an advanced fighting machine and production largely went for export to countries like Rumania, Bulgaria, Turkey and Greece. By 1936 15 Polish Squadrons were equipped and then General Ludomil Rayski shifted the production of aircraft towards bomber production at the expense of fighter development and up-grading.

In 1934 work had begun on the PZL P.37 'Los' bomber which began to enter service in 1938. With Aircraft production geared towards export, the relatively small defence budget was no match for the European arms race and by the late 1930s Poland had slipped behind Russia, Britain, France and Germany in terms of the numbers of aircraft available as well as design / technology, armament and speed. Whilst the investment in aircraft was poor, it must be said that the training of Polish Airmen was very good. Young men from all backgrounds were encouraged to learn to fly and Technical Training Schools were set up as will as Officer Training Establishments

This lack of investment in equipment for the Polish Air Force was highlighted during the German Invasion of Poland on 1 September

1939, when the German Luftwaffe had almost 3,800 modern aircraft available, whilst the Poles had 390 obsolete Combat Aircraft, of which 150 were Fighters. Despite being overwhelmingly outnumbered the Polish Air Force and anti-aircraft batteries destroyed around 300 German aircraft and also damaged a similar number.

While most air units quickly retreated into the heartland of Poland, spares and fuel became an increasing problem. Communication between units and the army soon broke down. Pilots and ground-crew fought heroically with limited resources and often became separated for up to three days before rejoining their squadrons. On the 3rd September all units were to withdraw to South-East Poland in order to re-group. All personnel and reservists had been called up and by the 5th September, the Air Force had lost 30% of its aircraft. On the 10th September 200 pilots and technical staff were ordered to Rumania to collect replacement machines, this included 14 Hurricanes and 36 Fairey Battles shipped from Liverpool bound for Gdynia, but re-routed to the Rumanian port of Galti on the Black Sea once hostilities commenced. Unfortunately, Rumania under German pressure rescinded its alliance with Poland and became neutral. The ship carrying its valuable cargo had passed Gibraltar as Rumanian neutrality was announced and unknown to the Poles, the ship was once again re-routed. By 16th September 1939, combat casualties to aircraft and personnel meant that squadrons were being annihilated or simply running out of fuel and spares. On the 17th

September 100 military aircraft and 50 civilian aeroplanes flew into an airfield at Galati, Rumania. The crews suddenly realised that their war was over and that Rumania, Britain and France had not supported them in their hour of need.

In Eastern Poland, the Polish army and air force were engaging both the German and Soviets and continued to fight hard until 6th October. In the aftermath, it appeared significant numbers of military personnel had escaped and started their campaign in exile. Some 900 airforce personnel had made their way to Hungary and approximately 1,000 to the Baltic States of Latvia and Lithunia. Another 1,500 had been captured by the Soviets and sent to the gulags – sadly many did not survive Security at the internment camps was poor and the inmates were very keen to get to France and Britain to continue to fight while in exile. 90,000 Polish military personnel were to be clandestinely removed from the Balkans through an underground network.

Evacuation Routes 1939 -1940
The decision to evacuate was based on the notion that after the fall of Poland, its navy, soldiers and airmen would be needed in the defence of France an Britain. Internment was expected in neutral countries like Romania (who had signed an alliance with Poland before the war) Hungary, Latvia and Lithuania. The evacuation was meticulously planned in terms of logistics in civilian clothing, visas and passports despite growing pressure by Germany upon the Romanians and Hungarians to keep the Poles caged up in 'camps' .

Almost all those interned in transit camps in Hungary and Rumania escaped between the autumn of 1939 and the summer of 1940 and amounted to 15,978 officers and other ranks to Britain with another 1,378 from other countries. Under pressure, the Hungarian and Romanian governments became anti-Polish while the people remained largely supportive and assisted in escapes. Conditions in the camps were very poor and medical support at best totally inadequate. Shortages of quinine meant many interned in camps in the Danube basin in the region of Tulcea suffered from malaria.
On 25 October 1939 the British, Polish and French delegates met at the French Air Ministry, Paris to discuss how to utilise the Polish armed

services personnel now available. General Sikorski had become the new commander in chief and was highly respected by the Polish Air Force. The Poles wanted to re-establish their air force in Britain due to the RAF having superior equipment than the French and they had also been given some training on British made equipment.

It was the French who suggested the service personnel should be divided equally for incorporation into their armed services for a speedier reinforcement. Britain agreed to take 300 pilots and 2,000 technical support staff while the residue would be eventually moved to front-line units in France.

Group Captain A.P. Davidson who had acted as the Air Attaché in Warsaw had a high regard for the quality and training of the PAF and saw an opportunity to borrow navigators to make up a shortfall in the RAF. The British and French Legations in Bucharest were contacted to help General Zajac, the commander of the PAF to help set up a clandestine network for the evacuation of over 90,000 personnel from the Rumanian camps. This was done under the noses of Gestapo agents who now riddled the country, watching all movement and traffic . Most escapees were directed to Constanza, Balic or Efori on the Black Sea then via Syria or Malta and then onto France. Another major route directed escapees to Split in Yugoslavia and then by ship to France. Some were directed to Piraeus in Greece. Some solo escapees went by foot through Yugoslavia through northern Italy and into France.

Those 8,000 members of the PAF arriving in France were disappointed by their reception. It appeared that no arrangements had been made for them, the French authorities treated them with indifference or aversion. The French Headquarters trusted their Maginot Line as a form of defence, they were not interested in experience from the Poles of German tactics during the September 1939 campaign.
For a while there was no action on the Western Front during the 'Phoney War', Polish Airmen stayed in all kinds of camp, they had no uniforms, no money. The plan was to form two fighter Squadrons and Two Reconnaissance Squadrons in France.

On 10th May 1940 the 'Phoney War' became a reality when the German's attacked with a force of around 3,500 aircraft. The French Air Force was unable to counteract efficiently and the situation deteriorated. About 150 Polish Fighter pilots, using French Aircraft, took a very active part in fighting the Luftwaffe, gaining tremendous victories, shooting down over 50 enemy aircraft, whilst suffering painful losses, including 11 fighter pilots and a number of Airmen when Polish airfield at Lyon was bombed. Their activities were brought to a halt when the French Marshal Petain requested an Armistice with the Germans.

Despite the surrender of their French Ally, the Polish Airmen never intended to lay down their arms and started another journey, obeying General Wladyslaw Sikorski's orders, they were taking every possible route to the '*Island of Last Hope*' – England.

Island of Last Hope

The Polish Airmen arriving in England knew little about the Great Britain and its Empire, or it's people. They were unfamiliar with the language and customs. Poles disembarking at Liverpool and Glasgow were immediately impressed by the efficient organisation and friendly nature of their new hosts.

In the dark days after Dunkirk, much work went into reorganising and re-equipping the British Army, which had lost a lot of its equipment. The Royal Navy was a strong force to be reckoned with, but a lot of the defence of Great Britain would have to be carried out by the Royal Air Force which was well equipped, but small in number.

The Polish Navy had been fighting by the side of the Royal Navy since the beginning of the war. The Polish Army was concentrated in Northern Scotland, it was re-armed and entrusted with the defence of long stretches of the Eastern Coast of Scotland.

The Polish Air Force

Before May 1940 around 2,300 Polish Airmen had arrived in England as a result of the French-Anglo-Polish Military Agreement. The majority of these men were posted to R.A.F. Eastchurch in Kent. They were trained in a methodical and systematic manner – learning the English language, learning the customs and the way of life, R.A.F. Regulations, general tactics and the theory of air fighting.

Initially there was no flying and no immediate plans to form operational Polish Units, though there were general, long term plans to form Polish Squadrons at some time in the future.

Following the Fall of France, around 7,000 members of the Polish Air Force arrived in England and began it's reorganisation. After signing further Military Agreements the Polish Air Force remained a separate fighting force, run by Poles, though it was strategically and tactically linked to the Royal Air Force.

The Inspectorate of the Polish Air Force was established for organisational and administrative purposes.

Uniforms of the Polish Air Force were of the same colour and pattern as the Royal Air Force, but they differed in detail.

British ranks were denoted by stripes on the sleeves, miniatures of Polish distinctions were worn on the lapels. 'Poland' Nationality Titles were sewn on the top of the sleeves, with golden eagles on the tunic buttons. On the left side of the tunic, above the breast pocket, traditional Polish metal aircrew badges were worn. Later miniature RAF flying brevets were worn over the right Breast Pocket. Polish Gold Eagle badges were worn on Officers Caps, Silver Polish Eagles were worn by NCO's and Other Ranks.

Payment rates were exactly the same as in the Royal Air Force, Officers were paid by cheque, Other Ranks were paid by cash. All Polish Airmen had the same rights and privileges as the personnel of the Royal Air Force.

Comparison of Royal Air Force and Polish Air Force Ranks WW2			
RAF Rank	**Abbr**	**PAF Rank**	**Abbr**
Other Ranks			
Aircraftman 2nd Class	AC2	Szeregowiec	Szer.
Aircraftman 1st Class	AC1	Starszy Szeregowiec	St. Szer.
Leading Aircraftman	LAC	Kapral	Kpr.
Corporal	Cpl	Plutonowy	Plut.
Sergeant	Sgt	Sierzant	Sierz.
Flight Sergeant	F/Sgt	Starszy Sierzant	St. Sierz.
Warrant Officer	W/O	Chorazy	Chor.
Officers			
Pilot Officer	P/O	Podporucznik	Ppor.
Flying Officer	F/O	Porucznik	Por.
Flight Lieutenant	F/Lt	Kapitan	Kpt
Squadron Leader	S/Ldr	Major	Mjr
Wing Commander	W/C	Podpulkownik	Pplk
Group Captain	G/C	Pulkownik	Plk
Air Commodore	A/C	Brak Odpowiednika	
Air Vice Marshal	AVM	General Brygady	Gen. Bryg.
Air Marshal	AM	General Dywizji	Gen. Dyw
Air Chief Marshal	ACM	General Broni	Gen. Br.
Marshal of the RAF		Marszalek	

After the verification and selection, Polish Airmen were chosen for regular duties and posted to various units. Former members of Polish Fighter and Bomber Squadrons were earmarked for operational units, then the Polish Operational Squadrons were organised. The less experienced personnel, mainly reserve flyers, joined Training and Ferry Units. Bases were established and training programmes were set up.

R.A.F. Fighter Command was compact and skilfully organised, it's Squadrons owed their efficiency to teamwork. At first Polish personnel were not wanted in Fighter Command, the RAF Authorities did not believe that the Poles could keep their fighting spirit, having taken part and been defeated to the campaigns in Poland and France. The RAF Authorities also thought that foreigners, not knowing the English language, were not familiar with aircraft and equipment and not knowing RAF tactics would be an hinderance, rather than a help. It was thought that by attaching foreign Pilots to Fighter Squadrons would mean weakening their strength however foreign aircrew were to be attached to Bomber Command.

Bomber crews operated differently, each aircraft flying separately (at night), so it was felt that Polish aircrew could participate in Bomber Command duties, without disrupting the Squadrons.
Due to the unfolding events of the war, these plans were abandoned as the defence of the United Kingdom became the priority. In defence, the whole burden of the Air Force falls on the fighter pilots and fighter aircraft. The British industry produced enough aircraft but it was not possible to train enough pilots in such a short time. The Polish Air Force had a surplus of fighter pilots and they began to train on British Aircraft, even before the Battle of Britain some Polish fighter pilots were posted to R.A.F. Fighter Squadrons.

The 19 July 1940 was an important day for the Polish Air Force in Britain, Flying Officer Antoni Ostowicz destroyed a German aircraft, gaining the first Polish air victory for Great Britain. Polish Pilots played a most distinguished role in 1940 when the Battle of Britain took place (8 August – 31 October 1940). In the first phase of the Battle of Britain (8-19 August 1940) Polish fighter pilots in British Squadrons destroyed 20 enemy aircraft, this amounted to 4% of all RAF Victories and was one of the deciding factors to increase the Polish Air Force in the West

During the Battle of Britain the Poles shot down 203 Luftwaffe aircraft which stood for 12% of total German losses in this battle. It was very significant that these 'new' fighter pilots often possessed more experience and skill than members of the Royal Air Force, and their air knowledge, gained in the Polish and French Campaigns, was greater.
Therefore the role of foreign airmen, of whom the greatest group were 151 Polish pilots, cannot be overemphasised. Polish Pilots fought both in the British and Polish Squadrons (302 and 303 fighter and 300 and 301 bomber squadrons).

Air Marshall Hugh Dowding, who was in charged of Fighter Command during the Battle of Britain wrote in 1941 the following in his report on the Battle of Britain:
'I must confess that I had been a little doubtful of the effect which their experience in 5their own countries and in France might have had upon the Polish and Czech pilots, but my doubts were laid to rest, because all three squadrons (Polish Squadrons 302 and 303. Czech Squadron 310) swung into the fight with a dash and enthusiasm which is beyond praise. They were inspired by a burning hatred for the Germans, which made them very deadly opponents.
The first Polish Squadron (303) in No.11 Group, during the course of the month shot down more Germans than any British unit in the same period. Other Poles and Czechs were used in small numbers in British Squadrons, and they fought very gallantly, but the language was difficulty, and they were probably most efficiently employed in their own national units.'

Polish Squadrons
300 'Masovian' Bomber Squadron Formed 1 July 1940 at Bramcote, Warwickshire Moved to Swinderby and later operated from Hemswell, Ingham and Faldingworth Operational 14 September 1940 Equipped with Fairey Battle, Armstrong-Whitworth Wellington, Avro Lancaster
302 'City of Poznan' Fighter Squadron Formed 13 July 1940 at Leconfield, North of London Operational 15 August 1940 Moved to Northolm then Isle of Man, Lincolnshire, Yorkshire, then joined 2nd Tactical Air Force Equipped with Hawker Hurricane and Supermarine Spitfire
301 'Pomeranian' Bomber Squadron Formed 26 July 1940 at Bramcote, Warwickshire Operated from Swinderby and Hemswell Equipped with Fairey Battle, Armstrong-Whitworth Wellington, Handley-Page Halifax, Disbanded 7 April 1943, crews absorbed into 300 Squadron Re-formed 7

November 1944 at Brindisi, Italy from 1586 (Special Duties) Flight Equipped with Handley-Page Halifax and Consolidated Liberator

303 'Kosciuszko' Fighter Squadron Formed 22 July 1940 at Northolt, West of London Operational 31 July 1940 Later served in Yorkshire, Merseyside, Lincolnshire, Northern Ireland before joining 2nd Tactical Air Force Equipped with Hawker Hurricane, Supermarine Spitfire, North American Mustang

304 'Silesian' (Prince Jozef Poniatowski) Bomber Squadron Formed 22 August 1940 at Bramcote, Warwickshire Operated with Bomber Command in Lincolnshire, later transferred to Coastal Command Equipped with Fairey Battle, Armstrong-Vickers Wellington

'Wielkopolski' Bomber Squadron Formed 29 August 1940 at Bramcote Operated from Nottinghamshire, Lincolnshire before joining No.2 Group Equipped with Fairey Battle, Armstrong-Whitworth Wellington, North American Mitchell, De Havilland Mosquito

306 'City of Torun' Fighter Squadron Formed 28 August 1940 at Church Fenton Became operational 8 September 1940 Operated from Northolt, Merseyside, Lincolnshire, Yorkshire, before joining 2nd Tactical Air Force Equipped with Hawker Hurricane, Supermarine Spitfire, North American Mustang

307 'City of Lwow' Night Fighter Squadron Formed 5 September 1940 at Kirton-in-Lindsey Moved to the Isle of Man, becoming operational 8 December 1940 Later moved to Merseyside, Devon, then Lincolnshire Equipped with Boulton Paul Defiant, Bristol Beaufighter, De Havilland Mosquito

308 'Krakoski' Fighter Squadron Formed 9 September 1940 at RAF Polish Depot, Squires Gate, Blackpool Moved to Speke 12 September 1940, becoming operational 12 December 1940 Later served at Northolt. Lancashire, Yorkshire before joining 2nd Tactical Air Force Equipped with Hawker Hurricane, Supermarine Spitfire

309 'Ziemia Czerwienska' Army Co-operation Squadron Formed 8 October 1940 at Abbotsinch ro work with the Polish Army in Scotland Moved to Gatwick for Tactical Reconnaissance Missions over France Later served in East Anglia Equipped with Westland Lysander, North American Mustang , Hawker Hurricane

315 'City of Deblinski' Fighter Squadron Formed at Acklington 21 January 1941 Moved to Speke, then Northolt. Served in Lancashire, Yorkshire, Northern Ireland before joining 2nd Tactical Air Force Equipped with Hawker Hurricane, Supermarine Spitfire

316 'City of Warszawski' Fighter Squadron Formed at Pembrey 15 February 1941 Engaged in Defensive duties over South-West England. Moved to Northolt, served in Yorkshire, East Anglia Equipped with Hawker Hurricane, Supermarine Spitfire, North American Mustang

317 'City of Vilno' Fighter Squadron Formed at Acklington 22 February 1941 Served in Devon, Northolt, Northern England before joining 2nd Tactical Air Force Equipped with Hawker Hurricane, Supermarine Spitfire

318 'City of Gdansk' Fighter-Reconnaissance Squadron Formed at Detling 20 March 1943 Left for the Middle East August 1943, then to Italy on April 1944 Co-operated with Polish Army in Middle East and Italy Equipped with Hawker Hurricane, Supermarine Spitfire

Polish Fighting Team (The Skalski Circus) 15 Volunteer Fighter Pilots Operated in 1943 North Africa and Tunisia

663 Artillery Co-operation Squadron Operated in Italy Belonged to 2nd Polish Army Corps

Polish Pilots also flew with Air Transport Auxiliary, Ferry Command / Transport Command

There were also Schools for Polish personnel established in RAF Training Command. These were Elementary Flying Training Schools, Operational Training Units as well as training courses

The Polish Auxiliary Air Force was formed in 1943, this consisted of Polish women from the Soviet Union, Canada and the USA.. In 1944 their strength was 1,400.

Polish pilots protected England, e.g. by destroying 193 German V1 and V2 missiles, and participated in many operations over the continent, escorting the bombers, bombing different targets (e.g. Ruhr, Hamburg, Brema), provided air support to the landing troops during the invasion in June 1944.

In November 1941 a Polish crew in 138 (Special Duties) Squadron, RAF flew to Poland to drop supplies for the Polish Underground Home Army (Armia Krajowa)

In 1944 the Polish 1586 Flight operating bombers from RAF Brindisi in Italy air-dropped in men and equipment for the Poland Home Army, and during the Warsaw Uprising the Polish crews flew 91 times with the supplies for the fighting insurgents.

From 1940 to 1945 the Polish squadrons and the Polish pilots serving in British units achieved 621 confirmed kills, and together with campaigns of 1939 and France achieved 900 confirmed kills and 189 probables.

Group Captain McEvoy, the Officer Commanding RAF Station Northolt wrote the following, titled 'The Polish Fighter Pilot' dated 10 September 1941:

'The Polish Fighter Pilot is imbued with the determination to exterminate Germans. All his energies are absorbed in this purpose.

Their pride is without Vanity… Polish Pride includes such attributes as Courage, Honour, Patriotism (and Esprit de Corps), Self-Respect, Good Manners, Skill, Determination, and at the lower end of the scale, Obstinacy.

High Courage seems inborn in most Poles. Their escapes from Poland give astonishing evidence of their bravery … Implacable in battle they are yet gentle and considerate at other times…

All who met the Poles are impressed by their good manners. They are scrupulously polite to superior officers and to women, but at the same time, natural and friendly and without affectation.

The high qualities of the Polish Fighter pilots may be accounted for their being the pick of the Polish people. In any event, there are no fellows more admirable and lovable than the Polish fighter pilots.'

In a 'Note on Polish Air Crews' dated 28 June 941, written by Group Captain L F Pendred, Officer Commanding R.A.F. Station Swinderby;

'To the Britisher, an English speaking Pole appears to be almost British. He talks about the same thinks, enjoys similar jokes, appreciates the English countryside, is prone to speeding in sports cars, grumbles about food, drinks moderately but makes the most of the party, enjoys his bath and is careful of his personal appearance.

A more intimate study reveals un-British traits which generally stand to his credit. Age for age, he is more grown up, more seriously minded, a deeper thinker. He is more actually aware of what is at stake and operations to him are a grim and awful business necessitating the maximum personal effort in preparations and executions.

He is more careful about money matters, his manner are better particularly towards women and his superior officers. He is always punctual where operations are concerned.

In short my opinion is that the Polish Bomber aircrew as an individual is every bit as fine as his British counterpart.

The foregoing contains little, if any, adverse criticism of Polish aircrews. They are represented as being really first-class material. This is the considered opinion of the writer who is commanding the station on which there have been two Polish Bomber Squadrons for the last 10 months..'

Following the Tehran Conference in November / December 1943 Winston Churchill, President Franklin D Roosevelt and Marshal Joseph Stalin expressed a determination to work together to win the war in Europe and in Asia and establish an "enduring peace." Details of what was discussed were not revealed until after the war.

The western allies assured Stalin they would invade France and ease the pressure on Soviet troops fighting on the eastern front. A date for what was code-named Operation Overlord was set for May 1944 - later delayed until 6 June 1944. Stalin confirmed that the Soviet Union would join the war against Japan following the defeat of Germany, much to the relief of Roosevelt and Churchill.

Turkey's involvement in the war was also discussed, as was the future of Poland and Finland and support for the partisans led by Tito in Yugoslavia.

It was at this meeting that they agreed that Poland would become part of the Soviet Union. Poles fighting in exile for a 'Free Poland' were horrified by this, it was against what they were fighting for. Poland had been under the control of foreign powers for centuries and once they had defeated the Nazi regime, they were looking forward to a 'free' Poland that was totally self governing. Instead they moved from one cruel master to another - a number of Poles had suffered at the hands of the Russians before coming to the West to fight, so they knew what to expect.

The Polish Forces were effectively 'sold down the river' when agreement was made to hand Poland over for purely Political reasons.

In August 1939, Germany and Russia signed a mutual non-aggression treaty. The agreement secretly included their partition of Poland. On September 1, 1939, Poland was invaded by Germany, Great Britain and France declared war on Germany quickly thereafter. On September 17, 1939, Russia invaded Poland, but within a month they were defeated by the Poles. In 1941, Germany attacked Russia and seized all of Poland.

At the end of the war, in 1945, Poland once again takes control of her country but under the dominance of the U.S.S.R. Poland wouldn't be truly free until the fall of the U.S.S.R.

In the Victory Parade in June 1946, a nine mile parade of at least 10,000 men and women, marching twelve abreast, from the armed and civilian services of His Britannic Majesty, King George VI, followed by a fly-past of a variety of aircraft; fighters, bombers, flying boats, transports. The members of this Parade represented more than thirty victorious Allied Nations. Amongst those represented were Americans, Arabs, Australians, Belgians, Brazilians, Canadians, Chinese, Czechs, Dutch, Ethiopians, Fijians, French, Greeks, Indians, Iranians, Labuanese, Luxembourgers, Mexicans, Seychellians, South Africans.

Despite being amongst the most effective fighting forces, the Poles who had fought under British command were deliberately and specifically barred from the Victory Celebration

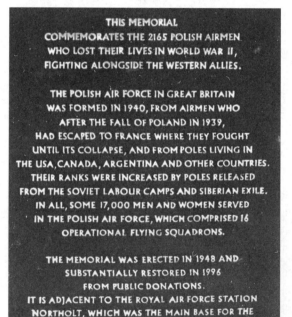

THIS MEMORIAL
COMMEMORATES THE 2165 POLISH AIRMEN
WHO LOST THEIR LIVES IN WORLD WAR II,
FIGHTING ALONGSIDE THE WESTERN ALLIES.

THE POLISH AIR FORCE IN GREAT BRITAIN
WAS FORMED IN 1940, FROM AIRMEN WHO
AFTER THE FALL OF POLAND IN 1939,
HAD ESCAPED TO FRANCE WHERE THEY FOUGHT
UNTIL ITS COLLAPSE, AND FROM POLES LIVING IN
THE USA, CANADA, ARGENTINA AND OTHER COUNTRIES.
THEIR RANKS WERE INCREASED BY POLES RELEASED
FROM THE SOVIET LABOUR CAMPS AND SIBERIAN EXILE.
IN ALL, SOME 17,000 MEN AND WOMEN SERVED
IN THE POLISH AIR FORCE, WHICH COMPRISED 16
OPERATIONAL FLYING SQUADRONS.

THE MEMORIAL WAS ERECTED IN 1948 AND
SUBSTANTIALLY RESTORED IN 1996
FROM PUBLIC DONATIONS.
IT IS ADJACENT TO THE ROYAL AIR FORCE STATION
NORTHOLT, WHICH WAS THE MAIN BASE FOR THE
POLISH FIGHTER SQUADRONS DURING THE
BATTLE OF BRITAIN.

by the British Government, for fear of offending Joseph Stalin.

In all, some 17,000 Polish airmen fought alongside the Royal Air Force during the war. Their motive was simple, they wanted Poland back from the invader. Winston Churchill vowed 'We shall conquer together or we shall die together' to the Polish Prime Minister, General Wladyslaw Sikorski, after the fall of France. The War Secretary, Anthony Eden made a declaration to Polish troops arriving in England in June 1940, "We shall not abandon your sacred cause and shall continue this war until your beloved country be returned to her faithful sons'.

After the War ended, two letters were published in The Daily Telegraph on 24 June and 2 July 1946, a fund was started for a memorial to Polish Airmen.

On All Souls Day, 2 November 1948 an unveiling ceremony took place near Western Avenue, on the North-Eastern edge of Northolt Aerodrome, the monument was dedicated: TO THE MEMORY OF FALLEN POLISH AIRMEN.

The memorial carries the badges of Polish Operational Air Force Units, it also lists the names of 1,241 Polish Airmen who lost their lives in action, whilst taking off from Great Britain. The names of those who lost their lives in non-operational flying had to be omitted owing to the lack of space.

There are also hundreds of Polish Graves throughout Great Britain, with many in the Midlands. A large number of Polish airmen rest in the Polish War Cemetery in Newark, Nottinghamshire.

For thousands of Polish Air Force personnel in Britain the Spring and Summer of 1946 was a very difficult time, The Polish Air Force in the West ceased to exist in March 1946. They wanted desperately to return to their homes and families in Poland, but did not want to go back to a Poland controlled by Communists. A large number had previously been held in Soviet Gulags before escaping to the West, so had experience of Soviet attitudes and conditions. If they decided to stay in Britain, what would they do, they would be without money, jobs or prospects.

In the end less than 20% of the Polish Armed Forces in Britain, around 30,000 people, decided to return to Poland.

In Mid-1946 the British Government set up a Polish Resettlement Corps, which was to offer temporary jobs until they could find permanent work.
Former Polish Air Force personnel found themselves in Settlement Camps a Hucknall, Cammeringham, Castle Coombe, East Wretham, Framlingham, Portreath, Skipton-on-Swale, Melton Mowbray and Dunholme Lodge.

Sadly they was an attitude in Britain in June 1946, highlighted in a nation-wide survey which showed that 56% of Britons polled favoured sending the Poles back to Poland. Anti-Polish graffiti appeared – England for the English/. And *Who do you think will give you a job, while English lads are looking for work?'* This change in British attitude was difficult for the Poles to bear.

Some 8,000 Polish airmen decided to remain in Britain after the end of the Second World War, some 500 joining the post-war Royal Air Force, others as commercial and test pilots and as technical experts for aircraft manufacturers.

In all, some 2,500 Polish Pilots left Britain to live in countries whose governments had agreed to accept Polish Refugee Servicemen and their families. Most went t South America, Australia, New Zealand, Canada, the United States of America, and South Africa (the latter country only accepting about one hundred)

Some 3,000 Polish Airmen were repatriated to Poland, their love for family and Poland being greater than the fear of a future under Soviet rule.

The Soviets looked on any previous contact with the West as treachery. Innocent men and women were frequently tried as traitors or spies.

Thousands of Poles who had fought the Germans, both resistance fighters and members of the returning Polish Armed Forces, were arrested and imprisoned. By 1947, well over 100,000 had been taken into custody by the Soviet and Polish Secret Police and Prisons in Krakow, Poznan and Lublin were overflowing.

Amongst those arrested were Polish Pilots who had flown in Britain, often accused of spying for 'American and British imperialists'. A general amnesty was declared for Polish Political prisoners in 1956.

Any tombstone or obituary noting the deceased as being a member of the Polish Home Army, or having served with the Polish Armed Forces in the West were strictly forbidden.
It was only after Stalin's Death in 1953 did the Communist Controlled Polish Government begin to soften it's attitude towards returnees who had fought with the British

Further Reading
There are a number of books on the subject, the following are very useful and most have further references for those wanting to look into this area more deeply
Destiny can wait; The Polish Air Foce in the Second World War M Lisiwicz 949.Reprinted by Battery Press, Nashville, Ten., USA
For your freedom and ours – the Kosciuszko Squadron Lynne Olson and Stanley Cloud Arrow Books, London 2003
Polish Wings in the West Bohdan Arct Interpress Publisers, Warsaw 1971
The Polish Air Force at War – The Official History – 2 Volumes Jerzy B Cynk Schiffer Military History, Atglen, PA, USA 1998
White Eagles – A Collection of Memories from the Nottinghamshire Polish Air Force Community Phil Barton Nottinghamshire Living History Archive 2002
Data Source
Polish Air Force in the West Second World War OPERATIONAL LOSSES in the European Theatre of War on CD-Rom Excel Spreadsheet of 2270 Polish Air Force in the West Operational Losses in the European Theatre of War covering Aircraft and Aircrew 1940-48. Dual Polish and English ranks listed.

**Czesc ich pamieci
May their memory be honoured**

The 'Auxiliary Patrol'
A forgotten aspect of the Great War at Sea 1914-19
Len Barnett

According to popular understanding in the UK, until relatively recently Britannia 'ruled the waves'. Apart from the ubiquitous merchantmen trading throughout the world, the Royal Navy's battlefleets had 'command of the sea'. Even within the tight constraints of military thinking, this was something of a confidence trick. But, if this claim is actually tested in any particular time frame, overwhelmingly this is to be found wanting: often severely. The Great War 1914-19 is a case in point. Even with the German Imperial Navy assuming a strategic defensive, the RN's claim to 'command' of its operational areas is *highly* debatable. In reality, the majority of the combat was *very* different and mostly not even fought by the regular British navy at all. Taking all those engaged in a miscellany of tasks, the not entirely accurate term 'Auxiliary Patrol' was officially adopted in the spring of 1915, although it had its origins the autumn before.

Historical background
The Royal Navy of 1914 may have looked exceedingly competent when lined up in fleet review, but this masked unpalatable weaknesses. Technologies had changed dramatically, especially from the last quarter of the 19th century onwards. But, unfortunately, not *only* in capital-ship design that the British

were concentrating on. Other aspects of organisation and war fighting were not accorded high priorities.

One of these was mine defence. In spite of obvious lessons from the Russo-Japanese War (1904-05) British tactical thought, both in defence and offence, was ill defined. Apart from a small number of fleet minesweepers, in 1910 a Royal Naval Reserve (Trawler Section) had been formed, but only to sweep naval port areas for the entrance and exit of 'the fleet'; and also (in some not particularly realistic plans) to clear sections of enemy minefields for British battlefleet incursions.

Coastal patrolling had been seen as the prerogative of destroyers and submarines, although even limited peacetime exercising had shown that they were not necessarily suitable in this role. Meanwhile, in spring 1914 motor boat owning civilians, with the support of a few naval officers, had basically pressured the Admiralty into accepting them into the Royal Naval Volunteer Reserve as an entity in their own right. (For an understanding of the RNR and RNVR please see my article 'The Royal Navy's Seagoing Reserves' in the eighth edition of *The Family and Local History Handbook*.)

Tactical thought in relation to trade defence had

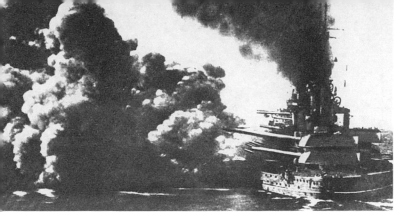

'Auxiliary Patrol'.

Around the UK (and from the summer of 1915 onwards within the Mediterranean and adjacent seas) the units of the AP took on more and more duties: its organisation growing exponentially. Sweeping the War Channel and ports for newly laid mines became a never-ending routine after the Germans deployed specialist minelaying submarines from Flanders (as well as clearing British mines adrift). The patrolling became far more dangerous, as such craft were called on to fend off U-boats attacking merchantmen in coastal waters: the defenders only having relatively light-calibre guns. Without any *effective* anti-submarine weapons, lines of drifters were also used in 'net barrages', in the hope of enemy submarines becoming entangled. Others were used as decoys, or unarmed intelligence gatherers. As tactics changed later in the war, many were routinely employed in convoying merchantmen (as destroyers could hardly ever be spared from their duties protecting the battlefleets), with the attendant increased risks of also being sunk by far heavier armed U-boats. And, again later in the war, those fitted with hydrophones were part of 'hunting' groups, with the aim of detecting and destroying the enemy submarines. Although a few became floating post offices, or even meat boats for the fleet in or around the defended anchorages and ports, for the vast majority in the AP life was gruelling. Provably spending *far* more time at sea than the pukkah warships, as far as they were able they operated in all weathers and conditions: often until total exhaustion of hulls or crews set in. Not insignificant losses through combat and accident were suffered (including some sweepers post war, in clearing the hundreds of thousands of mines laid by both sides and neutrals all through the effected areas).

for generations been less than intellectually rigorous, with some 19th century proposals being positively bizarre. By 1914, in home waters a general 'command of the sea' was supposed somehow to protect merchantmen from enemy men-o-war, while in the oceans, the answer was seen in cruiser patrols.

The acid test of war in August 1914 proved the professionals' pronouncements to be nothing more than drivel. The minesweeping organisation failed within the first few days, after one genuine minelaying raid and two false alarms. Shortly after, the decision was taken to expand the RNR(T) massively. Not only were increasingly large numbers of trawlers required, so were drifters (even although there had been no peacetime experimentation into how to deploy the latter). After not inconsiderable losses through their trial and error employment in the early months, shallow draught paddle-steamers were also pressed into service. While destroyers and submarines were not withdrawn from patrol duties, their use changed more than once within the first four weeks of combat. But, within days it was accepted that the regulars could not manage the task alone and civilian patrol craft were also increasingly taken up for this. Again trawlers and drifters were used, but so too were steam yachts and of course, inshore the motor boats. Not long after, in some waters tugs too were utilised. Later in the war, specialised craft, such as whalers and sloops were also built.

The German Imperial Navy began the war employing a tactic known as *Kleinkrieg*. Translated literally as 'little war', it used torpedo boats, surface minelayers and submarines with the aim of reducing the RN in capital ship strength to the point that main fleet action became a realistic proposition. This failed for a number of reasons and soon arguments for using their *Unterseebooten* (submarines) in *Handelskrieg* (trade war) were being articulated. This resulted in the first declaration of unrestricted U-boat warfare on 18th February 1915. Apart from British retaliation in tightening its own economic blockade on Germany, the up-to-then relatively localised minor naval forces were reorganised as the

They all required crews and these men came from amazingly varied backgrounds. The fishing boats' crews became part of the RNR(T), their peacetime skippers usually retaining command as warrant officer skippers. Many of the yachts also kept their old crews, including their owners and some university students, as part of the RNVR. Originally unit commanders had been specially trained RN officers on the retired or emergency lists, but with the expansion many more bodies were required. After some hesitation merchant service officers were encouraged to volunteer for temporary RNR commissions and within months minesweeping and patrol units were

commanded by these sub-lieutenants RNR. In time, very experienced master mariners, as temporary commanders and captains RNR, were appointed area commanders. Others, without formal qualifications, were commissioned into the RNVR in *many* other roles. Pensioner senior rates of the Royal Navy and Royal Fleet Reserve men were used to stiffen crews. Ratings of the RNR and RNVR were also drafted into these craft. And, at least in the early months, some boys served too. With a serious shortage of signalmen, scouts were in some small craft.

Researching individuals
This can be no more than an introduction into this highly complex subject. So, for this exercise I shall split this section into commissioned officers and ratings: with warrant officers straddling both types of records. Unless otherwise stated, all service records are held at The National Archives, Public Records Office, Kew.

The RN commissioned officers' service sheets should prove no problem to find, with one possible exception. Those on the first two supplementary lists are missing. It should be noted, for *all* varieties of naval officers, their *Navy List* entries are not necessarily accurate. Nevertheless, especially in the case of RNR officers, the *Navy List* should be used, in order at least to find out what list they were on. This should then determine which varieties of records to search for their service sheets. For RNR officers, it is also salient to mention that originally two largely different sets of service records were maintained. Being professional seamen, not only did the Admiralty keep their normal ledger entries, but the office of the Registrar General of Shipping and Seamen also kept an alphabetical card system. While only a small proportion of the latter body of records survive, it can be very worthwhile searching this. Not only is there often more information on individuals' naval service on these cards, their civilian employment was also supposed to be noted: as well as other details, such as particular skills and their home addresses. For commissioned officers in the RNVR, having

negotiated the PRO's card index, I have not encountered many problems finding their service sheets. It should be stressed that *all* these naval service sheets are often in a highly abbreviated form though and can be difficult for non-specialists to fully understand.

As far as I know, the only warrant officers in these roles were RNR skippers. Harking back to when WOs were sea officers (please see my article 'The Royal Navy - historical background and pointers for genealogists' in the ninth edition of *The Family and Local History Handbook* for an explanation of sea officers), they are also to be found in the *Navy List*. Nevertheless, when surviving, these skippers' service records are to be found within those of RNR ratings.

Regarding RN ratings, whether fleet reservists, pensioners or others, their service sheets were kept in precisely the same manner as normal. The surviving RNR ratings' service sheets are those of the RGSS' card system. (My investigations into the possible existence of their 'Admiralty' service sheets have drawn a blank.). As in the commissioned officers' card system, this too is *far* from complete. For instance, records for individuals that subsequently became commissioned officers (or even just midshipmen) are, in my experience, missing. It should also be noted that the RNR ratings' records at Kew are only copies. The originals are held at the Fleet Air Arm Museum, RNAS Yeovilton, Somerset. In relation to RNVR ratings within the AP their service sheets, overwhelmingly, are to be held within those of the peacetime divisions and the motor boat reserve. However, I have seen one case where a signalman's papers are partially also within those of the Royal Naval Division (as late as 1916 when most RND elements were being turned over to the army). These are held separately in yet another card system.

Operational Records
Having found individuals' service sheets, for most researchers the only useable information are lists of 'ship' names and dates. So, initially one must identify these as shore establishments, depot ships and seagoing craft. There are a few

standard published works that can sort these out and are held at the major institutions.

Even then, at this stage, in the case of seagoing vessels only dry and brief technical details are recorded in these books. Between comments in service sheets (for officers at least) and the above publications for shore establishments, as an example, *Defiance* can be understood as being in Devonport, even if 'additional for modified sweep course' still will not make much sense. (Incidentally, the modified sweep was an explosive charge on wire strung between two craft.) Similarly, as an example of a depot ship, the old cruiser *Brilliant* was variously employed around the Orkneys and Shetlands and will at least allow for a location to be learned. But this will do little for an understanding of time subsequently spent in these hazardous waters. Therefore, more research is required.

One result of the first U-boat assault on British and neutral shipping in spring 1915 was that local naval commanders were required to make weekly returns. With these the AP's order of battle was routinely issued as the *Red List*. Again not complete by any means, a good collection is to be found at the National Maritime Museum, Greenwich. Consulting these can give good information. If individuals served from this time onwards, this is the next logical step to take.

Armed with all the above information, the main collection of operational records are there for study, at Kew. This is a *vast* body of documents (ADM 137), collected by the Naval Historical Branch and was subsequently used in writing up the official history. The AP records alone run literally to hundreds of bound volumes (with additional packs collected from other divisions and departments). Prior to spring 1915 documentation is less well organised and the subject index should be consulted under various headings. Some papers are simple enough to locate, such as court of enquiry records for sinkings. But, apart from the obvious, there are also all sorts of bits and pieces, in volumes relating to the activities of the Trade Division and much else. From spring 1915 onwards research becomes more of a routine task. The weekly reports were filed by operational area (which is why the *Red List* should be consulted). Down to individual commanders as to format and the detail reported, often the information gained is not spectacular, quite the reverse in fact. Nevertheless, this alone can give a *slight* idea of the sheer monotony of the AP. There is also another series of volumes that should be studied. These are reports of incidents, whether coastal escort reports (not all being kept), or contacts with the enemy. All this is very time-consuming, but generally there are no short cuts. (It may be that specific actions have been mentioned in the various post First World War books on the subject, overwhelmingly forgotten now. Even then, often the published accounts and the original reports differ *significantly*.) As in the records pre spring 1915, there are also others for the latter part of the war also scattered through other bodies of documentation: naval and mercantile.

For commissioned officers in command there is a relatively good chance of them being mentioned in dispatches, or possibly receiving a decoration (especially if involved in a successful action against an U-boat). Even for MIDs, it can be worthwhile finding the relevant citation(s) in the rather difficult to use microfilmed copies of the original ledgers.

A few words of warning would not go amiss. Apart from commissioned officers that are *sometimes* mentioned by name, all others generally are not. And, most importantly, the operational records were working documents understood by the officers and officials handling them. With the exception of the *Red Lists* there are no neat tables of abbreviations or the like. Therefore, a good knowledge of matters naval, operational and administrative, is really required to get the best out of these documents.

More detailed historical and genealogical information on these subjects can be found on my website -
www.barnettresearch.freeserve.co.uk

In Adversity
Exploits of Gallantry and Awards - RAF Regiment and its Associated Forces, 1921-1995
Brian Prescott

This article, and its companion on the *Annuity Meritorious Service Medal*, is to help family historians to be aware of the wealth of more contemporary military information that there is from the medal collecting fraternity. Most of us want to know what our forebears did in the Victorian era and we are used to delving into the National Archives or turning to the many excellent printed sources extant on the market. Even those who have not yet progressed their researches beyond the First World War are familiar with the 'burnt' and 'unburnt' series of soldiers' documents available for that tragic conflict. However, many are patiently waiting for the release of more recent papers that cover the inter-war years and the Second World War. There is no need to wait. There are some wonderfully informative and published rolls compiled by medal collectors particularly those who are members of the Orders and Medals Research Society (O.M.R.S.). The majority of members collect medals with the emphasis on research. They want to know all they can about 'the man behind the medals' - to the extent that they create a fascinating biography of 'their' man, thus preserving his story for future generations.

In 1997, *In Adversity* was published having been compiled by Squadron Leader Nick Tucker an officer serving with the R.A.F. Regiment. The writing of the book was made possible only by a unique combination of circumstances. First, Nick held two consecutive appointments

within the R.A.F. Regiment Depot between 1990-94 during which time he also carried out the duties of the Director of the RAF Regiment Museum. This length of time in the latter appointment provided a continuity not normally experienced by the incumbent, and provided the opportunity to conduct a number of long-term projects. One of these was the compilation of a register of honours and awards to members of the R.A.F. Regiment and its Associated Forces, continuing initial work undertaken by Group Captain M. K. Batt, MBE, a previous Museum Director. A life-long interest in decorations and medals, membership of the O.M.R.S., a further additional appointment as Liaison Officer to the Associations of the RAF Regiment, and a desire to write, all combined to provide the contacts and impetus to compile the material produced.

The title *"In Adversity"* is intended to have double significance, being a close translation of the RAF Regiment's Latin motto, *"Per Ardua,"* as well as alluding to the circumstances behind the exploits depicted in the book.

The aim of the book was to satisfy the interests of three main groups: those interested in the history and exploits of the R.A.F. Regiment and its Associated Forces; researchers and collectors of decorations and medals, particularly those with

R.A.F. interests; and finally, those with an interest in personal short stories and biographies. This book is not intended to be merely a record of exploits of gallantry, but hopefully will provide a more general overview of operations and tasks conducted by the R.A.F. Regiment and its Associated Forces which will inform future generations of what their forefathers did.

Whilst concentrating on a fairly narrow field within the interests of the O.M.R.S., this book should find appeal to a wider readership due to the depth of data and material not normally available to the average researcher. Perhaps, genealogists will find the lists of names of most interest but, in my view, they should not overlook the wider picture. Each of the stories tells of individual human endeavour, leadership, courage and selfless devotion to duty. Many of the deeds described were performed not by full-time or regular members of the Services, but by men called up for the duration of the Second World War, or on other short-term engagements. In this context they only serve to highlight the professionalism and performance of duty by men who may be, or were, our grandfathers or great grandfathers.

Every account in the book relied upon a minimum of four separate sources of information to compile each individual story. Many required cross-reference to other sources, and some details were only arrived at after a lengthy process of elimination through surviving official records. It required continuous contact with and assistance from official departments, and individual correspondence with survivors of the accounts, comrades or members of their families. At the time Nick Tucker did his research, he had official permission and the relevant passes to access documents not yet in the public domain. Previously unpublished citations are included.

Some readers may be surprised to find that there are no instances of the highest awards for gallantry being made. This situation is symptomatic of the role and primary function of the organisations covered, and not of their conduct or record of service. They were or are organisations whose primary function was or is defence or protection, and awards for gallantry are hard to gain under such circumstances. Consequently, as shown in the accounts, many of the awards were the result of enemy action against airfields, or dangerous situations and accidents which arose without contact with the enemy. However, when given the opportunity to conduct offensive operations, as seen with the Armoured Car Companies, and with the R.A.F. Regiment units which served alongside or in place of the Army in forward areas, as witnessed in Italy, Greece, North West Europe and Burma in the Second World War, and Aden and Malaya in the 1940s and 1950s, the R.A.F. Regiment and its Associated Forces acquitted themselves well.

The first awards covered relate to operations by the Armoured Car Companies in Kurdistan in 1924, and whose sequence of awards ends in the Western Desert in 1942. The Ground Gunners won their first awards during the Battle of Britain and the last award was also won in the Western Desert in 1941. The R.A.F. Regiment's first award was won only 14 days after the official formation of the Corps, by an officer in Sumatra on 14 February, 1942. In this, the largest section, the awards covered continue up to more recent times, although the last Military Cross was won as far back as 1959. The last Military Medal, of the 38 covered by this book, was gained in 1957. The Associated Overseas Forces, which won awards for gallantry, covered a relatively short period during the late 1940s and through the 1950s. However, no awards for gallantry to the R.A.F. Levies (Iraq) have been found during the period, post World War Two, when that force was under R.A.F. Regiment control. Similarly, the awards to the Royal Auxiliary Air Force Regiment and the R.A.F. Regiment Band are also for meritorious service only. The awards relating to the R.A.F. Firemen date back to the antecedents of the current organisation and begin in 1940, and continue up to recent years. Finally, those personnel who were holders of the Victoria Cross, and who subsequently served in the R.A.F. Regiment, have been acknowledged in their own chapter, which is followed by the Appendices listing those principal awards held by officers who have served in the Armoured Car Companies and the R.A.F. Regiment, but which were gained in service prior to that with the Armoured Car Companies or the R.A.F. Regiment. It was felt that this was both necessary and useful to avoid confusion or doubt when officers are referred to as having served in these two organisations, or are identified as having awards, but have not been covered in the main text of this book. The same information, however, is not easily obtainable for the non-commissioned ranks.

Notwithstanding the effort which has gone into compiling the lists of decorations and awards there is a caveat. Whilst it has been possible to confirm the number of awards of the Military Cross, George Medal, Distinguished Service Medal and Military Medal, and some of the categories of foreign awards, the same is not true for appointments to the various orders of chivalry, primarily the Order of the British Empire, or awards of the British Empire Medal. The numbers of awards made in these categories, particularly for World War Two, without citation or identification of the branch or trade of the individual, would require much lengthier research than has been possible for this book. The same situation applies, but on a much greater scale, when identifying Mentions in Despatches and King's or Queen's Commendations for Brave Conduct. Therefore, appointments to the various Orders, primarily the Order of the British Empire, and awards of the British Empire Medal, Mentions in

Despatches and King's or Queen's Commendations for Brave Conduct, especially those for the World War Two period, can only be claimed to be provisional. It must also be pointed out that the Order of the British Empire and the British Empire Medal "for Gallantry," were awarded under this title only between 1957 and 1974, and such awards were denoted by the wearing of crossed silver oak leaves on the ribbon. Nick Tucker has, however, included awards of the Order and its Medal made prior to 1957 *"for Meritorious Service,"*, but made specifically in recognition of acts of gallantry and bravery, even though these did not attract the wording *"for Gallantry,"* or the gallantry emblem.

The sequence and format has been driven by the need to provide some historical chronology as well as individual account or simple statistical data. Each organisation under the title R.A.F. Regiment and its Associated Forces follows the chronological order of its formation or linkage with the R.A.F. Regiment; the latter organisation being central to the overall subject. Within each of the organisational groupings the awards are grouped by theatre of operations and within each of these groups the individual accounts are listed in chronological date order of the action which resulted in the award. This has been done to allow some sequence in subsequent or related accounts. Where more than one award resulted from the same action the whole account, and details of other award winners, is found under the same write-up. Each chapter ends with a surname register of known and/or confirmed awards made to that particular organisation, following the same principle of listing in precedent order.

A great deal of personal satisfaction was gained where the award winners, or their surviving close relatives, had been traced: and it was particularly gratifying to be able to put old comrades in touch with each other. One of the most poignant examples was the location of Mr Harry Green, M.M. and Mr Tom Squire, M.M., (since deceased) both of whom won their awards with No. 2721 Field Squadron, R.A.F. Regiment in Italy during World War Two. They were both discovered to be living in Yorkshire, within a few miles of each other, unaware of each other's existence, and having not met since the end of World War Two. Another remarkable coincidence followed the publication of a notice in a local Sussex newspaper in an effort to trace Mr L.C.E. Harris, M.M. It was seen by a friend of the family just weeks before Mr Harris, then living in Australia, returned for a brief visit to England. Sadly, many of those who are written about in the following pages have died since the events which won them their awards, and some only a short time before their whereabouts became known to the author.

Nick Tucker's book is a tribute to those whose actions made his publication possible, and it is hoped that the record will continue to inform future generations of the deeds and sacrifices of those who served in the R.A.F. Regiment and its Associated Forces.

In Adversity - Exploits of Gallantry and Awards made to the R.A.F. Regiment and its Associated Forces, 1921-1995 - Jade Publishing Limited, 5, Leefields Close, Uppermill, Oldham, Lancashire, OL3 6LA discounted to £30 from its published price of £48. Postage and packing is £5. Email: jade.publishing@virgin.net, website: www.jadepublishing.com, or telephone 01457 870944.

References:
Finally, a series of books of interest to medal collectors and genealogists has been published by and obtainable from Jade Publishing Limited The books contain many details of interest to family historians. They are: Gazetted awards to N.C.O.s and Other Ranks of the Aerial Forces 1914-1924, comprising a surname index of about 6,000 men with forename(s), service number, rank, hometown/squadron/theatre of war, medal entitlements, The London Gazette date and page number. In addition, biographical details for many of the men are included especially citations; The Yeomen of the Guard including the Body of Yeoman Warders of H.M. Tower of London, members of the Sovereign's Body Guard (Extraordinary) 1823-1903 contains much biographical information on 477 men who served during that period and there are almost 200 illustrations of the men and their medals. The Annuity Meritorious Service Medal 1847-1953 and its subsequent First Supplement.; which list about 6,000 men with much biographical information. For the Napoleonic period are the following: The Beckett Soldiers Index A-C and the second volume covering D-G; Sudden Death, Sudden Glory the story of the 59th Foot from 1793-1830 with biographical details and casualty returns of the officers and men who served in the Peninsular 1808-1809 and 1812-1814, at Walcheren 1809, at Java 1811, at Waterloo in 1815, Bhurtpoor 1825-26; The Army Long Service and Good Conduct Medal 1830-1848, which details almost 3,000 men.
Brian Prescott of Jade Publishing Limited is a Member of The Manchester and Lancashire Family History Society and Vice-President, Northern Branch of the Orders and Medals Research Society

Tracing Army Ancestry

Sarah Patterson
Imperial War Museum

Where to Find Army Service Records

The most important piece of information is the unit that an individual served with (it is a sad fact that those who died during the World Wars will be easier to trace than those who survived, and this information is readily obtainable from the **Commonwealth War Graves Commission**). The personal service record should be the starting point, but not all of these records for the First World War survived Second World War bombing. Records are located according to an individual's date of discharge.

The Imperial War Museum only covers the period from the First World War onwards. Military history from 1485 to date is covered by the **National Army Museum, Royal Hospital Road, Chelsea, London SW3 4HT (Tel: 020 7730 0717; Website: www.national-army-museum.ac.uk)**. Pre-1914 service records are held at **The National Archives, Ruskin Avenue, Kew, Richmond, Surrey TW9 4DU (Tel: 020 8392 5200 www.nationalarchives.gov.uk)**. The National Archives (TNA), formerly Public Record Office, also holds all surviving First World War service records for officers who left the Army before 1922. Surviving First World War service records for other ranks who ceased service before 1920 are now held at the TNA where they can be consulted on microfilm (unfortunately large numbers of these were destroyed by bombing in the Second World War). The publication *Army Service Records of the First World War* by William Spencer, 3rd edition, (Richmond, Surrey: PRO, 2001) is essential reading for those interested in First World War records, and *Army Records for Family Historians* by Simon Fowler and William Spencer, 2nd edition, (Richmond, Surrey: PRO, 1998) will also prove helpful.

The records of any First World War soldier who saw service after these cut-off dates or who rejoined the Army are held by the Ministry of Defence. These can be applied for by post from **Army Personnel Centre, Disclosures 4, MP 400, Kentigern House, 65 Brown Street, Glasgow G2 8EX**. Initial contact with the Army Personnel Centre (APC) can be made by telephone (**0845 600 9963**) or e-mail with your postal address (**apc_historical_disclosures@btconnect.com**). Records will be released to proven next of kin for a £30 fee, but there may be a lengthy wait for this service.

The Brigade of Guards form an exception to this as records for other ranks (officers' records are held by TNA/APC) are held by the **Regimental Headquarters Grenadier/Coldstream/Scots/Irish/Welsh Guards, Wellington Barracks, Birdcage Walk, London SW1E 6HQ**. Household Cavalry records are held at TNA - also accessible on microfiche at the **Household Cavalry Museum, Combermere Barracks, Windsor, Berkshire SL4 3DN www.householdcavalry.co.uk**

The careers of Army officers can be traced using the regular official publication the *Army List*, and the Department of Printed Books holds an almost complete set of these from 1914 to date.

Casualty Records

The **Commonwealth War Graves Commission, 2 Marlow Road, Maidenhead, Berkshire SL6 7DX (Tel: 01628 507200)** has details of all service personnel who died between the dates 4 August 1914-31 August 1921 and 3 September 1939-31 December 1947. *The Commonwealth War Graves Commission* (CWGC) may charge a fee for postal enquiries, but the website containing their computerised database, *Debt of Honour* can be consulted at **www.cwgc.org**.

Details of service personnel buried in 'non-World War' graves are available from the **Armed Forces Personnel Administration Agency (JPAC), Joint Casualty and Compassionate Centre, Building 182, RAF Innsworth, Gloucester GL3 1HW**. Please mark your enquiry 'Memorials and Graves'.

Sources held by the Department of Printed Books (DPB) include a complete set of the CWGC's memorial and cemetery registers and the 80 volume *Soldiers Died in the Great War, 1914-19*. This was originally published in 1921 by HMSO but was republished by J.B. Hayward in 1989. It is also now available on a CD-ROM produced by Naval and Military Press. *Officers Died in the Great War, 1914-19* is less detailed and has probably been superseded by *Officers Who Died in the Service of British, Indian and East African Regiments and Corps, 1914-1919* by S.D. and D.B. Jarvis (Reading: Roberts Medals, 1993).

A CD-ROM for Army personnel who died in the Second World War has also been produced by *Naval and Military Press*, and can be consulted in our Reading Room. Rolls of honour for other later conflicts are also held, and in addition the DPB has a large collection of published rolls of honour for localities, schools, institutions, etc. Regimental histories and journals often contain rolls of honour.

The soldiers' own home area should not be forgotten when researching an individual's service - there may be local war memorial records, a local account of war service may have been published, and contemporary local newspapers can prove very helpful. It is also possible that school, church or workplace records may still exist.

Medal Records
Campaign medals are those given to soldiers who are eligible for them because they were in a particular theatre of war within given dates. The First World War Medal Roll which provides a listing of all those who qualified for the 1914 Star, 1914/15 Star, British War Medal, Victory Medal, Territorial Force War Medal and/or the Silver War Badge is held at TNA. If a First World War record was destroyed some basic information about a soldier's service may be found in this.

Gallantry medals are those medals awarded for an especially heroic deed or action. Records for these are held at TNA, but may not be very detailed. Notifications and citations (if published, which was not the case for awards such as the Military Medal and Mentions in Despatches) appeared in the official journal

London Gazette. A complete set of this, and the all important indexes, is held at TNA. **The London Gazette Online Archive** at www.gazettes-online.co.uk provides access to First and Second World War entries. The DPB has some published listings of medal awards for decorations such as the Victoria Cross and Distinguished Conduct Medal. Usually you will need to go either to the official unit war diary (held at TNA) or to a published unit history to see whether you can find out more about the action for which the decoration was awarded.

Regimental Histories
The DPB has an excellent collection of regimental histories. For those unable to visit our Reading Room (open 10am-5pm, Monday to Saturday), *A Bibliography of Regimental Histories of the British Army* compiled by Arthur S. White (London: London Stamp Exchange, 1988) provides details of published histories that may be available through your local library's inter-library loan scheme. Regimental journals and forces newspapers should not be overlooked.

A useful title for locating regimental museums (although these are unlikely to hold information about individuals) is *A Guide to Military Museums: and Other Places of Military Interest* by Terence and Shirley Wise (Knighton, Powys: Terence Wise, 2001).

We can also advise on the addresses of Old Comrades Associations. The internet has made it easier to establish contact with people who may have served in the Forces, or who may be conducting research similar to your own. The British Legion website at www.britishlegion.org.uk is a good place to start. An excellent site for First World War Orders of Battle and Army information is www.1914-1918.net. Other websites of interest include The Western Front Association at www.westernfront.co.uk and Land Forces of Britain, the Empire and Commonwealth at www.regiments.org.

More detailed information can be found in our publication *Tracing your Family History: Army* – this can be purchased from the Imperial War Museum for £5.50. The Museum does not hold any personal service records or official documentation, but can help the enquirer as long as some basic facts are known. The Department of Printed Books welcomes visitors by appointment and is able to provide useful reading material and advice for finding out more about those who served. Other reference departments in the Museum - Art, Documents, Exhibits and Firearms, Film and Photograph Archives, and the Sound Archive - may also be able to assist.

Department of Printed Books, Imperial War Museum, Lambeth Road, London SE1 6HZ
T: (+44) 020 7416 5342 F: (+44) 020 7416 5246
W: www.iwm.org.uk E: books@iwm.org.uk

Tracing Australian Naval Personnel
Sarah E Paterson
Imperial War Museum

The purpose of this article is to provide guidance on tracing Australian Naval personnel and advise on sources for useful background information on their activities. The Imperial War Museum does not hold any official personal service records or documentation, although addresses are provided for finding these in Australia. The Imperial war Museum, Department of Printed Books has a very good library relating to all aspects of Australian history since 1914. Visitors are welcome to visit the Reading Room by prior appointment between 10 am and 5 pm, Monday to Saturday, subject to weekend closures for Bank Holidays.

Royal Australian Navy
A decision was taken to establish an Australian naval force in 1909, and in July 1911 the Royal Australian Navy (RAN) came into existence. It numbered approximately 3,800 members on the outbreak of war in 1914, and by the end of the war this had risen to 5,263. Reserves also supplemented the RAN, and these numbered 127 officers (76 serving at home, with 51 overseas) and 4,155 ratings (2,380 at home, with 1,775 overseas). 196 members of the RAN lost their lives between the outbreak of the First World War and the end of March 1921.

In 1939 on the outbreak of the Second World War, the RAN numbered 5,010. At peak wartime strength on 30 June 1945, the RAN comprised 3,765 officers and 33,211 ratings, a total of 36,976. 2,170 members of the RAN lost their lives in the Second World War.

Women's Royal Australian Naval Service
In 1941, the Women's Royal Australian Naval Service (WRANS) was established. On 30 June 1945, 108 officers and 2,509 ratings were serving.

6 ratings died during the War. The WRANS was disbanded in September 1946.

In 1951 the WRANS was re-established, and on 1 January 1985 it ceased to exist as a separate service, being amalgamated with the RAN.

Royal Australian Naval Nursing Service
The Royal Australian Naval Nursing Service was established in 1942. On 30 June 1945, there were 57 nursing sisters in the service. It was disbanded in 1948, but re-established in 1964. In 1985, the RANNS became fully integrated into the RAN.

Service records
RAN, WRANS and RANNS records for the period 1911 to 1970 are held by the National Archives of Australia. You can apply for these by post from: **Defence Service Records, National Archives of Australia, PO Box 7425, Canberra BC ACT 2610, Australia**. The website address is www.naa.gov.au - you may wish to have a look at their fact sheet 30 on Navy Service Records.

If an individual is trying to obtain their own record, the address to contact is: **Department of Defence, Navy Records, Queanbeyan Annexe, Department of Defence, Canberra ACT 2600, Australia**.

Career details of officers who served in the RAN can be found in the official publication, the *Navy List*. A near complete run of this publication from 1914 can be found at the Imperial War Museum. **The National Archives, Ruskin Avenue, Kew, Richmond, Surrey TW9 4DU** (www.nationalarchives.gov.uk) has a complete set.

Australians in the Dardànelles

Casualty records

If your relative died in either the First or Second World War, you should be able to find where they are buried or commemorated in the Debt of Honour database on the Commonwealth War Graves Commission website at www.cwgc.org You can also contact the Commission by post: **Commonwealth War Graves Commission, 2 Marlow Road, Maidenhead, Berkshire SL6 7DX**.

The Australian War Memorial also has a Roll of Honour database on their website at www.awm.gov.au Many of the records on the website have digital images of the original circulars. If you don't have internet access, the address to write to is: **Australian War Memorial, GPO Box 345, Canberra ACT 2601, Australia**.

World War Two nominal roll

An online nominal roll of members of all branches of the Australian Armed Forces and the Merchant Navy can be found at www.ww2roll.gov.au

Medal records

The postal address to contact for medal claims, although these will only be issued to the original recipient is: **Navy Medals Sections, Directorate of Honours and Awards, T-1-49, Department of Defence, Canberra, ACT 2600, Australia**. Some information about gallantry awards can be found on the website www.itsanhonour.gov.au

Further information

The Australian War Memorial holds Letters of Proceedings, and Reports of Proceedings for RAN ships and shore establishments. In addition, they also hold First World War log books for RAN ships.

Official records relating to ships and naval operations will be held at the National Archives of Australia. The RAN Heritage Centre opens in October 2005; the postal address is **RAN Heritage Centre, Locked Bag 12, Pyrmont, NSW 2009, Australia**. You can view the website at www.navy.gov.au/ranhc

Further Reading

Royal Australian Navy Alun Evans.Time-Life Books Australia, 1988. (Australians at war).ISBN 0-949118-24-9

Of Nautilus and eagles: history of the Royal Australian Navy Peter Firkins. - Melbourne: Hutchinson, 1983. ISBN 0-09-148290-9

The Royal Australian Navy: its origin, development and organization Frances Margaret McGuire. - Melbourne: Oxford University Press, 1948.

First World War

First in, last out: the navy at Gallipoli T.R. Frame & G.J. Swinden. - Kenthurst, New South Wales: Kangaroo Press, [1990] ISBN 0-86417-289-3

The Australian Navy, 1914-1918 Arthur W. Jose. - 7th ed. - Sydney: Angus and Robertson, 1939. (*Official history of Australia in the war of 1914-1918. Volume IX*).[This can be consulted online at the Australian War Memorial website at www.awm.gov.au/histories/ww1/9/index.asp]

Second World War

Royal Australian Navy G. Hermon Gill. - Canberra: Australian War Memorial, 1957-1968. - 2 vols. (Australia in the war of 1939-1945. Series Two : Navy). Volume I : Royal Australian Navy, 1939-1942 Volume II : Royal Australian Navy, 1942-1945

W.R.A.N.S.: The Women's Royal Australian Naval Service M. Curtis-Otter. - Garden Island, New South Wales: Naval Historical Society of Australia, 1975. -

ROYAL AUSTRALIAN NAVY H.M.A.S. [Mk. I-IV] / written and prepared by serving personnel of the R.A.N. - Canberra: Australian War Memorial, 1942-1945. Published for the Royal Australian Navy H.M.A.S. Mk. I, Mk., Mk. III, *The Royal Australian Navy in World War II* / edited by David Stevens. - Sydney: Allen-Unwin, 1996. ISBN 1-86448-035-1

Medical services of the R.A.N. and the R.A.A.F.: with a section on women in the army medical services Allan S. Walker and others. - Canberra: Australian War Memorial, 1961. -(Australia in the war of 1939-1945. Series 5 (medical); vol. 4).

Websites

Australian National Maritime Museum – www.anmm.gov.au

Australian War Memorial – www.awm.gov.au

Royal Australian Navy – www.navy.gov.au

Royal Australian Navy Gun Plot (private site run by Russ Graystone) – www.gunplot.net

Western Australian Maritime Museum – www.museum.wa.gov.au

Tracing Indian Naval Personnel
Sarah E Paterson

The origins of the Indian Navy began with the Honourable East India Company in the seventeenth century. In 1892 the Royal Indian Marine was established. On the outbreak of the First World War it consisted of four troopships, two survey ships and three riverine steamers. It served chiefly in a transporting and patrolling role. Figures are difficult to confirm, but it would appear that about 13,000 men served in the Royal Indian Marine during the war.

When peace returned, the Royal Indian Marine diminished in strength, but in October 1934 the Royal Indian Navy was formed, together with provision for a Royal Indian Naval Reserve (RINR), Royal Indian Fleet Reserve (RIFR) and Royal Indian Naval Volunteer Reserve (RINVR). Naval Headquarters was based at Bombay (although in 1941 this moved to Delhi). The first Indian officer, Engineer Sub-Lieutenant D N Mukerji had been commissioned into the Royal Indian Marine in January 1928, and a third of all officer vacancies (which in peacetime were few) were for Indians. In October 1939, the Royal Indian Navy strength stood at 114 officers and 1,732 men. By the end of the war this had risen to over 25,000 officers and ratings.

On 9 April 1942, the Women's Auxiliary Corps (India) was established. Although originally the women served with the Army, naval and air force wings were established. In February 1944, the naval wing was renamed the Women's Royal Indian Naval Service (WRINS) and acquired a distinctive naval uniform. In December 1945 the decision was made to disband the women's services.

In 1950, following independence in 1947, the Royal Indian Navy split to become the Indian and Pakistan Navies.

Service Records
Service records for British and Eurasian officers, seamen and staff are held in the India Office records section at the British Library. Second World War officer personnel files for the Royal Indian Navy and Royal Indian Naval Volunteer Reserve are not yet open (files remain closed until 85 years after the individual began his service), but information may be supplied on written application. The address to contact is **Asia, Pacific and Africa Collections, The British Library, St Pancras, 96 Euston Road, London NW1 2DB** www.bl.uk/collections/orientalandindian.html. The British Library produce a very helpful **'Military Records Fact Sheet'** which provides full details of how files can be accessed . You can apply for this fact sheet and the form to fill in for Second World War officer records by email (luke.marriage@bl.uk). More information can be found in the 3rd edition of *Baxter's Guide: biographical sources in the India Office Records* by Ian A Baxter (*Families in British India Society* in association with the British Library, [London], 2004) or on the Access to Archives website at www.a2a.org.uk

Careers of Indian naval officers, like those of the Royal Navy, can be traced through the official

publication the *Navy List*. These regularly produced listings contain seniority lists of all officers, cross referred to individual ships. A near complete run of this publication from 1914 can be found at the Imperial War Museum. **The National Archives, Ruskin Avenue, Kew, Richmond, Surrey TW9 4DU** has a complete set. www.nationalarchives.gov.uk

We believe records of Indian personnel are held **The Adjutant General's Branch, Army HQ, West Block No III, R K Puram, New Delhi 110066, India**. It might also be worth contacting the **National Archives of India, Janpath, New Delhi 110001, India**. The website address is http://nationalarchives.nic.in

Casualty Records
The **Commonwealth War Graves Commission, 2 Marlow Road, Maidenhead, Berkshire SL6 7DX** Tel. 01628 634221 www.cwgc.org holds details of the burial place or commemoration site for all those who died in service during the First and Second World Wars. Their website also provides free access to the *Debt of Honour* database.

The **British Association for Cemeteries in South Asia, Honorary Secretary, 76? Chartfield Avenue, London SW15 6HQ** is a charity that has compiled listings of the graves and memorials in the South Asia area, and works to maintain them. Their archive can now be consulted at the British Library. The organisation also produces the magazine *Chowkidar* twice a year.

Further information
The British Library will be the best source of information, but there are other institutions and organisations that may be able to help.

The **Indian Military Historical Society** may be of interest to you. It produces a quarterly journal called *Durbar* – copies of this dating from 1998 can be viewed in our Reading Room. If you are interested in finding out more about this organisation please contact the Secretary/Editor **A N McClenaghan Esq, 33 Tilbrook, Huntingdon, Cambridgeshire PE18 0JP**.

The **British Empire and Commonwealth Museum, Clock Tower Yard, Temple Meads, Bristol BS1 6QH** should also have some information. - www.empiremuseum.co.uk

The different collecting departments of the Imperial War Museum have a variety of items that might be of interest. Although there is more material relating to British officers (because these

men and women came back to Britain) we would be very keen to expand our holdings relating to Indian sailors and officers. You can search the various catalogues using the *Collections Online* database at (http://collections.iwm.org.uk). The books listed below will provide you with more information and you may be able to obtain copies through your local library's inter-library loan scheme. Alternatively, you would be very welcome to make an appointment to consult these in our Reading Room.

Further Reading
Bombay Buccaneers: memories and reminiscences of the Royal Indian Navy / collected and edited by Commander D.J. Hastings. - London: BACSA, 1986 ISBN 0-907799-15-9 (pbk.)
The Royal Indian Navy by Instructor Lieutenant D.J.E. Collins, Indian Navy; edited by Bisheshwar Prasad. - New Delhi: Combined Inter-Services Historical Section (India and Pakistan), 1964 (Official history of the Indian armed forces in the Second World War 1939-45).
The Royal Indian Navy, 1612-1950 by Commander D.J. Hastings, R.I.N.V.R. - Jefferson, North Carolina: McFarland, 1988 ISBN 0-89950-276-8
The Women's Royal Indian Naval Service - [New Delhi: Naval Headquarters and Public Relations Directorate, General Headquarters (India)
The Indian Navy: an illustrated history - New Delhi: Directorate of Naval Operations, Navy Headquarters, 1989
In the Wake: The Birth of the Indian and Pakistani Navies by Commander E.C. Streatfeild-James. - Edinburgh: Charles Skilton ISBN 0-284-98580-5
Under Two Ensigns: the Indian Navy, 1945-1950 Rear Admiral Satyindra Singh. - New Delhi: Oxford and IBH ISBN 81-204-0094-1

Websites
Bharat Rakshak – www.bharat-rakshak.com
Families in British India Society – www.fibis.org
Indiaman [magazine] – www.indiaman.com
Indian Navy – http://indiannavy.nic.in
Ministry of Defence - *We Were There* – www.mod.uk/wewerethere
Moving Here – www.movinghere.org.uk
Pakistan Navy – www.paknavy.gov.pk

The
Genealogical
Services
Directory

In association with
The National Family History Fair

Family History Societies

British Association for Local History PO Box 6549, Somersal Herbert, Ashbourne, Derbyshire DE6 5WH T: 01283 585947 F: 01722 413242 E: amjones-balh@supanet.com (Business Manager) W: www.balh.co.uk
Federation of Family History Societies PO Box 2425, Coventry, CV5 6YX T: 024 7667 7798 E: info@ffhs.org.uk W: www.ffhs.org.uk
Institute of Heraldic & Genealogical Studies 79 - 82 Northgate, Canterbury, Kent CT1 1BA T: 01227 462618 F: 01227 765617 E: ihgs@ihgs.ac.uk W: www.ihgs.ac.uk
Society of Genealogists - Library 14 Charterhouse Buildings, Goswell Road, London, EC1M 7BA T: 020-7251-8799 F: 020-7250-1800 E: library@sog.org.uk - Sales at sales@sog.org.uk W: www.sog.org.uk

England
Bedfordshire
Bedfordshire Family History Society PO Box 214, Bedford, Bedfordshire MK42 9RX E: bfhs@bfhs.org.uk W: www.bfhs.org.uk

Berkshire
Berkshire Family History Society Research Centre, Yeomanry House, 131 Castle Hill, Reading, Berkshire RG1 7TJ T: 0118 966 3585 E: chairman@berksfhs.org.uk W: www.berksfhs.org.uk

Birmingham
Birmingham & Midland Society for Genealogy and Heraldry 5 Sanderling Court, Spennells, Kidderminster, Worcestershire DY10 4TS T: 01562 743912 E: gensec@bmsgh.org W: www.bmsgh.org

Bristol
Bristol & Avon Family History Society 50 Russell Grove, Westbury Park, Bristol, BS6 7UF T: 0117 967 7288 E: secretary@bafhs.org.uk W: www.bafhs.org.uk

Buckinghamshire
Buckinghamshire Family History Society PO Box 403, Aylesbury, Buckinghamshire HP21 7GU E: society@bucksfhs.org.uk W: www.bucksfhs.org.uk
Buckinghamshire Genealogical Society Varneys, Rudds Lane, Haddenham, Buckinghamshire HP17 8JP T: 01844 291631 E: eve@varneys.demon.co.uk W: http://met.open.ac.uk/group/kaq/bgs.htm

Cambridgeshire
Cambridge University H & G S c/o Crossfield House, Dale Road, Stanton, Bury St Edmunds, Suffolk IP31 2DY T: 01359 251050 F: 01359 251050 E: president@one-name.org W: www.cam.ac.uk/societies/cuhags/
Cambridgeshire Family History Society 45 Wachard Road, Cambridge, Cambridgeshire CB3 0HZ E: secretary@cfhs.org.uk W: www.cfhs.org.uk
Fenland Family History Society Rose Hall, Walpole Bank, Walpole St Andrew, Wisbech, Cambridgeshire PE14 7JD W: www.cambridgeshirehistory.com/Societies/ffhs
Huntingdonshire Family History Society 42 Crowhill, Godmanchester, Huntingdon, Cambridgeshire PE29 2NR T: 01480 390476 E: secretary@huntsfhs.org.uk W: www.huntsfhs.org.uk
Peterborough & District Family History Society 111 New Road, Woodston, Peterborough, Cambridgeshire PE2 9HE E: meandmygarden@hotmail.com W: www.peterboroughfhs.org.uk

Cheshire
Family History Society of Cheshire 10 Dunns Lane, Ashton, Chester, Cheshire CH3 8BU T: 01829 759089 E: info@fhsc.org.uk W: www.fhsc.org.uk
North Cheshire Family History Society 2 Denham Drive, Bramhall, Stockport, Cheshire SK7 2AT T: 0161-439-9270 E: r.demercado@ntlworld.com W: www.nchfs.org.uk
South Cheshire Family History Society incorporating S E Cheshire Local Studies Group PO Box 1990, Crewe, Cheshire CW2 6FF W: www.scfhs.org.uk

Cleveland
Cleveland Family History Society 1 Oxgang Close, Redcar, Cleveland TS10 4ND T: 01642 486615 F: 01642 486615 W: www.clevelandfhs.org.uk/
Hemlington Family History Club 34 Eskdale, Hemlington, Middlesbrough, Cleveland TS8 9LU T: 01642 591735 E: bezkay@teesonline.org W: www.teesideonline.org/hfhc

Cornwall
Cornish Forefathers Society Credvill, Quakers Road, Perranwell, Truro, Cornwall TR3 7PJ T: 01326 564238 E: forefathers@ukonline.co.uk W: www.cornish-forefathers.com

Cornwall Family History Society 5 Victoria Square, Truro TR1 2RS T: 01872 264044 E: secretary@cornwallfhs.com W: www.cornwallfhs.com
Fal Worldwide Family History Group 57 Huntersfield, South Tehidy, Camborne, Cornwall TR14 0HW T: 01209-711557 F: 01209-711557 E: cfdell@clara.net W: http://beehive.thisiscornwall.co.uk/falwwfhg

Coventry
Coventry Family History Society 61 Drayton Crescent, Coventry, CV5 7EL T: (024) 7646 4256 E: enquiries@covfhs.org W: www.covfhs.org

Cumberland - see Cumbria Family History Society

Cumbria
Ambleside Oral History Group 1 High Busk, Ambleside, Cumbria LA22 0AW E: history@amblesideonline.co.uk W: www.aoghistory.f9.co.uk
Cumbria Family History Society "Ulpha", 32 Granada Road, Denton, Manchester M34 2LJ E: webmaster@cumbriafhs.com W: www.cumbriafhs.com
Furness Family History Society 64 Cowlarns Road, Hawcoat, Barrow-in-Furness, Cumbria LA14 4HJ T: 01229-830942 E: julia.fairbairn@virgin.net W: www.furnessfhs.co.uk
Shap Local History Society The Hermitage, Shap, Penrith, Cumbria CA10 3LY T: 01931 716671 E: liz@amosshap.demon.co.uk

Derbyshire
Buxton & District U3A - Family History Group Yarrow, 8 Carlisle Grove, Buxton SK17 6XP T: 01298 70959 E: iw.taylor@ic24.net
Chesterfield & District Family History Society 2 highlow Close, Loundsley Green, Chesterfield, Derbyshire S40 4PG T: 01246 231900 E: cadfhs@aol.com W: www.cadfhs.org.uk
Derbyshire Ancestral Research Group 86 High Street, Loscoe, Heanor, Derbyshire DE75 7LF T: 01773-604916
Derbyshire Family History Society Bridge Chapel House, St Mary's Bridge, Sowter Road, Derby, Derbyshire DE1 3AT T: 01332 608101 E: dave@bulld.fsnct.co.uk W: www.dfhs.org.uk

Devon
Devon Family History Society PO Box 9, Exeter, Devon EX2 6YP T: 01392 275917 E: secretary@devonfhs.org.uk W: www.devonfhs.org.uk
Thorverton & District History Society Ferndale, Thorverton, Exeter, Devon EX5 5NG T: 01392 860932

Dorset
Dorset Family History Society Treetops Research Centre, Suite 5 Stanley House, 3 Fleets Lane, Parkstone, Poole, Dorset BH15 3AJ T: 01202 736261 E: contact@dorsetfhs.freeserve.co.uk W: www.dorsetfhs.freeserve.co.uk
Somerset & Dorset Family History Society PO Box 4502, Sherborne, Dorset DT9 6YL T: 01935 389611 E: society@sdfhs.org W: www.sdfhs.org
West Dorset Research Centre 45 West Street, Bridport, Dorset DT6 3QW T: 01308 458061 E: wdhgrc@dorsetmigration.org.uk W: www.dorsetmigration.org.uk

Durham
- see Cleveland Family History Society
Elvet Local & Family History Groups 37 Hallgarth Street, Durham, County Durham DH1 3AT T: 0191-386-4098 F: 0191-386-4098
Newton Aycliffe Family History Society 4 Barnard Close, Woodham Village, Newton Aycliffe DL5 4SP E: jtb2@totalise.com
- see Northumberland & Durham Family History Society

Essex
Essex Society for Family History Research Centre, Essex Record Office, Wharf Road, Chelmsford, Essex CM2 6YT T: 01245 244670 E: secretary@esfh.org.uk W: www.esfh.org.uk
Waltham Forest Family History Society 49 Sky Peals Road, Woodford Green, Essex IG8 9NE

Gloucestershire
Campden & District Family History Group 9 Wolds End, Chipping Campden GL55 6JW T: 01386 840561 E: familyhistory@judithellis.org.uk
Gloucestershire Family History Society 37 Barrington Drive, Hucclecote, Gloucester GL3 3BT T: 01452 524344(Resource Centre) W: www.gfhs.org.uk
Sodbury Vale Family History Group 36 Westcourt Drive, Oldland Common, Bristol, BS30 9RU T: 0117 932 4133 E: sladekf@supanet.com

Hampshire

Hampshire Genealogical Society 3 Elaine Gardens, Lovedean, Waterlooville, Hampshire PO8 9QS E: society@hgs-online.org.uk W: www.hgs-online.org.uk

Herefordshire

Herefordshire FHS 6 Birch Meadow, Gosmore Road, Clehonger, Hereford, Herefordshire HR2 9RH T: 01981-250974 E: prosser_brian@hotmail.com W: www.roortsweb.com/~ukhfhs

Hertfordshire

Codicote Local History Society 34 Harkness Way, Hitchin, Hertfordshire SG4 0QL T: 01462 622953

Hertfordshire Family History Society 4 Newlands Lane, Hitchin, Hertfordshire SG4 9AY T: 01462 620587 E: secretary@hertsfhs.org.uk W: www.hertsfhs.org.uk

Letchworth & District Family History Group 49 Haysmans Close, Letchworth Garden City, Hertfordshire SG6 1UD E: website_editor.ldfhg@which.net W: www.letchworhgardencity.net/LDFHG/Index.html

Royston & District Family History Society Baltana, London Road, Barkway, Royston, Hertfordshire SG8 8EY T: 01763 848228 E: keith-curtis@lineone.net W: www.roystonfhs.org

Welwyn & District Local History Society 40 Hawbush Rise, Welwyn, Hertfordshire AL6 9PP T: 01438 716415 E: p.jiggens-keen@virgin.net W: www.welwynhistory.org

Hull

Hull Central Library Family and Local History Club Central Library, Albion Street, Kingston upon Hull, HU1 3TF T: 01482 616828 F: 01482 616827 E: gareth.watkins@hullcc.gov.uk W: www.hullcc.gov.uk/genealogy/famhist.php

Isle of Wight

Isle of Wight Family History Society 9 Forest Dell, Winford, Sandown, Isle of Wight PO36 0LG E: brendave@dodgson9.freeserve.co.uk W: www.isle-of-wight-fhs.co.uk

Kent

Folkestone & District Family History Society Kingsmill Down, Hastingleigh, Ashford, Kent TN25 5JJ E: alisonfhs@aslan-consultancy.freeserve.co.uk W: www.folkfhs.org.uk

Kent Family History Society Bullockstone Farm, Bullockstone Road, Herne Bay, Kent CT6 7NL E: membership@kfhs.org.uk W: www.kfhs.org.uk

North West Kent Family History Society 58 Clarendon Gardens, Dartford, Kent DA2 6EZ E: secretary@nwkfhs.org.uk W: www.nwkfhs.org.uk

Tunbridge Wells Family History Society 5 College Drive, Tunbridge Wells, Kent TN2 3PN E: s.oxenbury@virgin.net W: www.tunwells-fhs.co.uk

Woolwich & District Family History Society 54 Parkhill Road, Bexley, Kent DA5 1HY E: FrEdnafhs@aol.com

Lancashire

Accrington Uncovered 15 Christ Church Street, Accrington,BB5 2LZ T: 01254 398579 E: jhunt@christchurch92.freeserve.co.uk W: www.accringtonuncovered.co.uk

Bolton & District Family History Society 205 Crompton Way, Bolton, Lancashire BL2 2RU T: 01204 525472 E: bolton@mlfhs.demon.co.uk W: www.mlfhs.demon.co.uk

Lancaster Family History Group 116 Bowerham Road, Lancaster, LA1 4HL E: membership@lfgh.org W: www.lfhg.org

Liverpool & S W Lancashire Family History Society 11 Bushbys Lane, Formby, Liverpool L37 2DX E: secretary@liverpool-genealogy.org.uk W: www.liverpool-genealogy.org.uk

Manchester and Lancashire Family History Society Clayton House, 59 Piccadilly, Manchester, M1 2AQ T: 0161-236-9750 F: 0161-237-3512 E: office@mlfhs.org.uk W: www.mlfhs.org.uk

North Meols Family History Society 6 Millars Pace, Marshside, Southport, Lancashire PR9 9FU E: sally.dean@virgin.net W: www.nmfhssouthport.com

Oldham & District Family History Society Clayton House, 59 Piccadilly, Manchester, M1 2QA T: 0161 236 9750 F: 0161 237 3512 F: office@mlfhs.org.uk W: www.mlfhs.org.uk

Ormskirk & District Family History Society PO Box 213, Aughton, Ormskirk, Lancashire L39 5WT T: 01695-578604 E: secretary@odfhs.org.uk W: www.odfhs.org.uk

Rossendale Family History & Heraldry Society c/o LFHHS, 2 The Straits, Oswaldtwistle, Lancashire BB5 3LU T: 01254 239919 E: rossendale@lfhhs.org.uk W: www.rossendale-fhhs.fsnet.co.uk

Wigan Family History Society 678 Warrington Road, Goose Green, Wigan, Lancashire WN3 6XN W: www.ffhs.org.uk/members/wigan.htm

Lancashire - North

Cumbria Family History Society "Ulpha", 32 Granada Road, Denton, Manchester M34 2LJ E: webmaster@cumbriafhs.com W: www.cumbriafhs.com

Leicestershire

Leicestershire & Rutland Family History Society 37 Cyril Street, Leicester, Leicestershire LE3 2FF T: 01572 787331 E: secretary@lrfhs.org.uk W: www.lrfhs.org.uk

Lincolnshire

Isle of Axholme Family History Society 4 Cheyne Walk, Bawtry, Doncaster, North Lincolnshire DN10 6RS T: 01724 710578 E: secretary@axholme-fhs.org.uk W: www.axholme-fhs.org.uk www.linktop.demon.co.uk/axholme/

Lincolnshire Family History Society Unit 6, 33 Monks Way, Monks Road, Llincoln, Lincolnshire LN2 5LN E: secretary@lincolnshirefhs.org.uk W: www.lincolnshirefhs.org.uk

Liverpool

Liverpool & S W Lancashire Family History Society 11 Bushbys Lane, Formby, Liverpool L37 2DX E: secretary@liverpool-genealogy.org.uk W: www.liverpool-genealogy.org.uk

London

East of London Family History Society 23 Louvaine Avenue, Wickford, Essex SS12 0DP E: ean23@btopenworld.com W: www.eolfhs.org.uk

Hillingdon Family History Society 20 Moreland Drive, Gerrards Cross, Buckinghamshire SL9 8BB T: 01753 885602 E: gillmay@dial.pipex.com W: www.hfhs.co.uk

London, Westminster and Middlesex Family History Society 57 Belvedere Way, Kenton, Harrow, Middlesex HA3 9XQ T: (020) 8204 5470 E: joan.pyemont@virgin.net W: www.lnmfhs.dircon.co.uk

Manchester

Manchester and Lancashire Family History Society Clayton House, 59 Piccadilly, Manchester, M1 2AQ T: 0161-236-9750 F: 0161-237-3512 E: office@mlfhs.org.uk W: www.mlfhs.org.uk

Merseyside

Liverpool & S W Lancashire Family History Society 11 Bushbys Lane, Formby, Liverpool L37 2DX E: secretary@liverpool-genealogy.org.uk W: www.liverpool-genealogy.org.uk

Middlesex

Hillingdon Family History Society 20 Moreland Drive, Gerrards Cross, Buckinghamshire SL9 8BB T: 01753 885602 E: gillmay@dial.pipex.com W: www.hfhs.co.uk

London, Westminster and Middlesex Family History Society 57 Belvedere Way, Kenton, Harrow, Middlesex HA3 9XQ T: (020) 8204 5470 E: joan.pyemont@virgin.net W: www.lnmfhs.dircon.co.uk

West Middlesex Family History Society 32 The Avenue, Bedford Park, Chiswick, London, Middlesex W4 1HT E: secretary@west-middlesex-fhs.org.uk W: www.west-middlesex-fhs.org.uk

Norfolk

Mid - Norfolk Family History Society 47 Greengate, Swanton Morley, Dereham, Norfolk NR20 4LX E: joanallson@hotmail.com W: www.mnfhs.freeuk.com

Norfolk Family History Society Headquarters, Library & Registered Office, Kirby Hall, 70 St Giles Street, Norwich, Norfolk NR2 1LS T: 01603 763718 E: nfhs@paston.co.uk W: www.norfolkfhs.org.uk

Northamptonshire

Northamptonshire Family History Society 22 Godwin Walk, Ryehill Estate, Northampton, Norrthamptonshire NN5 7RW E: secretary@northants-fhs.org W: www.northants-fhs.org

Northumberland

Northumberland & Durham Family History Society 2nd Floor, Bolbec Hall, Westgate Road, Newcastle-on-Tyne, Tyne and Wear NE1 1SE T: 0191-261-2159 E: secretary@ndfhs.org.uk W: www.ndfhs.org.uk

Nottinghamshire

Mansfield & District Family History Society 15 Cranmer Grove, Mansfield, Nottinghamshire NG19 7JR E: betty@flintham.freeserve.co.uk

Nottinghamshire Family History Society 26 Acorn Bank, West Bridgford, Nottingham, Nottinghamshire NG2 7DU E: nfhssec@nottsfhs.org.uk W: www.nottsfhs.org.uk

Oxfordshire
Oxfordshire Family History Society 19 Mavor Close, Woodstock, Oxford OX20 1YL T: 01993 812258 E: secretary@ofhs.org.uk W: www.ofhs.org.uk

Rutland
Leicestershire & Rutland Family History Society 37 Cyril Street, Leicester LE3 2FF T: 01572 787331 E: secretary@lrfhs.org.uk W: www.lrfhs.org.uk

Shropshire
Cleobury Mortimer Historical Society The Old Schoolhouse, Neen Savage, Cleobury Mortimer, Kidderminster DY14 8JU T: 01299 270319 E: paddy@treves.freeserve.co.uk
Shropshire Family History Society Redhillside, Ludlow Road, Church Stretton SY6 6AD T: 01694-722949 E: secretary@sfhs.org.uk W: www.sfhs.org.uk

Somerset
Burnham & Highbridge FHS - Disbanded April 1998 1 Greenwood Close, West Huntspill, Somerset TA9 3SF
Somerset & Dorset Family History Society PO Box 4502, Sherborne DT9 6YL T: 01935 389611 E: society@sdfhs.org W: www.sdfhs.org
Weston-Super-Mare Family History Society 32 Marconi Close, Weston Super Mare, Somerset BS23 3HH T: 01934 627053 E: kes.jack@virgin.co.uk

Staffordshire
Ancestral Rescue Club 19 Mansfield Close, Tamworth, Staffordshire B79 7YE T: 01827 65322 E: ancestra.rescue@ntlworld.com W: www.rootsweb.com/~engarc/index.html
Audley & District Family History Society 20 Hillside Avenue, Endon, Stoke on Trent, Staffordshire ST9 9HH E: famhist@audley.net W: www.acumenbooks.co.uk/audleynet/famhist/index.htm
Birmingham & Midland Society for Genealogy and Heraldry 5 Sanderling Court, Spennells, Kidderminster, Worcestershire DY10 4TS T: 01562 743912 E: gensec@bmsgh.org W: www.bmsgh.org
Burntwood Family History Group 8 Peakes Road, Rugeley, Staffordshire WS15 2LY W: bfhg1986@yahoo.co.uk

Suffolk
Felixstowe Family History Society Drenagh, 7 Victoria Road, Felixstowe, Suffolk IP11 7PT T: 01394-275631 F: 01394-275631 W: www.btinternet.com/~woodsbj/tths
Suffolk Family History Society 2 Flash Cottages, Saxmundham, IP16 4RW W: www.genuki.org.uk/big/eng/SFK/Sfhs/Sfhs.htm

Surrey
East Surrey Family History Society 119 Keevil Drive, London, SW19 6TF E: secretary@eastsurreyfhs.org.uk W: www.eastsurreyfhs.org.uk
Reigate District Family History Group St Mark's Hall, Alma Road, Reigate, Surrey T: 01737 766 135 E: johnsonjackie@hotmail.com W: www.qurl.com/rdfhg
West Surrey Family History Society 21 Sheppard Road, Basingstoke, Hampshire RG21 3HT E: secretary@wsfhs.org W: www.wsfhs.org

Sussex
Eastbourne & District (Family Roots) Family History Society 8 Park Lane, Eastbourne, East Sussex BN21 2UT E: johnandval@tiscali.co.uk W: www.eastbournefhs.org.uk
Hastings & Rother Family History Society 355 Bexhill Road, St Leonards on Sea, East Sussex TN38 8AJ E: enquiries@hrfhs.org.uk W: www.hrfhs.org.uk
Sussex Family History Group 40 Tanbridge Park, Horsham, West Sussex RH12 1SZ E: secretary@sfhg.org.uk W: www.sfhg.org.uk

Tyne & Wear
Northumberland & Durham Family History Society 2nd Floor, Bolbec Hall, Westgate Road, Newcastle-on-Tyne, Tyne and Wear NE1 1SE T: 0191-261-2159 E: secretary@ndfhs.org.uk W: www.ndfhs.org.uk

Waltham Forest
Waltham Forest Family History Society 49 Sky Peals Road, Woodford Green, Essex IG8 9NE

Warwickshire
Birmingham & Midland Society for Genealogy and Heraldry 5 Sanderling Court, Spennells, Kidderminster, Worcestershire DY10 4TS T: 01562 743912 E: gensec@bmsgh.org W: www.bmsgh.org
Coventry Family History Society 61 Drayton Crescent, Coventry, CV5 7EL T: (024) 7646 4256 E: enquiries@covfhs.org W: www.covfhs.org

Nuneaton & North Warwickshire
Nuneaton & North Warwickshire Family History Society PO Box 2282, Nuneaton, Warwickshire CV11 6ZT E: chairman@nnwfhs.org.uk W: www.nnwfhs.org.uk
Rugby Family History Group Springfields, Rocherberie Way, Rugby, Warwickshire CV22 6EG T: 01788 813957 E: j.chard@ntlworld.com W: www.rugbyfhg.co.uk
Warwickshire Family History Society 44 Abbotts Land, Coundon, Coventry, Warwickshire CV1 4AZ E: n.wetton.@virgin.net W: www.wfhs.org.uk

West Midlands
Birmingham & Midland Society for Genealogy and Heraldry 5 Sanderling Court, Spennells, Kidderminster, Worcestershire DY10 4TS T: 01562 743912 E: gensec@bmsgh.org W: www.bmsgh.org
Sandwell Family History Society 9 Leacroft Grove, Hill Top, West Bromwich, West Midlands B71 2QP T: 0121 556 0731 E: a.hale@talk21.com

Wiltshire
Wiltshire Family History Society 42 Stokehill, Hilperton, Trowbridge, Wiltshire BA14 7JT T: 01225 762648 E: society@wiltshirefhs.co.uk W: www.wiltshirefhs.co.uk

Worcestershire
see Birmingham & Midland Society for Genealogy & Heraldry
Malvern Family History Group Apartment 5 Severn Grange, Northwick Road, Bevere, Worcester, Worcestershire WR3 7RE W: www.mfhg.org.uk

Yorkshire
Yorkshire Archaeological Society - Family History Section Claremont, 23 Clarendon Road, Leeds, LS2 9NZ W: www.yorkshireroots.org.uk
Yorkshire Consortium of Family History Societies - London Group 1 Waverley Way, Carlshalton Beeches, Surrey SM5 3LQ

Yorkshire - East
see Hull Central Library Family and Local History Club
East Yorkshire Family History Society 12 Carlton Drive, Aldbrough, East Yorkshire HU11 4SF E: secretary@eyfhs.org.uk W: www.eyfhs.org.uk

Yorkshire - North
Cleveland Family History Society 1 Oxgang Close, Redcar, Cleveland TS10 4ND T: 01642 486615 F: 01642 486615 W: www.clevelandfhs.org.uk/
Harrogate & Dist FHS 18 Aspin Grove, Knaresborough HG5 8HH
Ripon Historical Society & Family History Group 42 Knox Avenue, Harrogate, North Yorkshire HG1 3JB E: RHSinfo@aol.com W: www.yorksgen.co.uk/rh/rh1.htm
Ryedale Family History Group 5 High Street, Hovingham, York YO62 4LA T: 01653 628952 E: info@ryedalefamilyhistory.org W: www.ryedalefamilyhistory.org
Selby Family History Society 8 Broadacres Garth, Carlton, Goole, East Yorkshire DN14 9QD
Upper Dales Family History Group Croft House, Newbiggin in Bishopdale, Nr Leyburn, DL8 3TD T: 01969 663738 E: glenys@bishopdale.demon.co.uk W: www.bishopdale.demon.co.uk
Wharfedale Family History Group 1 West View Court, Yeadon, Leeds LS19 7HX T: 0113 258 5597 E: wfhg@yorksgen.org.uk W: www.wfhg.org.uk http://web.onetel.net.uk/~gdlawson/wfhg1.htm

Yorkshire - South
Barnsley FHS 4 Cranford Gardens, Royston, Barnsley S71 4SP E: secretary@barnsleyfhs.org.uk W: www.barnsleyfhs.co.uk
Doncaster & District Family History Society 5 Breydon Avenue, Cusworth, Doncaster, South Yorkshire DN5 8JZ T: 01302 782685 E: secretary@doncasterfhs.co.uk W: www.doncasterfhs.co.uk
Grenoside & District LHG 4 Stepping Lane, Grenoside, Sheffield S35 8RA T: 0114 257 1929 E: info@grenosidelocalhistory.co.uk W: www.grenosidelocalhistory.co.uk
Rotherham Family History Society 36 Warren Hill, Rawmarsh, Rotherham, South Yorkshire S61 3SX E: brian_allott@msm.com W: www.rotherhamfhs.co.uk
Sheffield & District FHS 5 Old Houses, Piccadilly Rd, Chesterfield S41 0EH E: secretary@sheffieldfhs.org.uk W: www.sheffieldfhs.org.uk

Yorkshire - West
Aire-Worth Ancestors 106 Banks Lane, Riddlesden, Keighley BD20 5PQ
Boothferry Family & Local History Group 17 Airmyn Avenue, Goole DN14 6PF E: howardrj@madasafish.com

Bradford Family History Society 5 Leaventhorpe Avenue, Fairweathergreen, Bradford, West Yorkshire BD8 0ED E: secretary@bradfordfhs.org.uk W: www.bradfordfhs.org.uk

Calderdale Family History Society inc Halifax & District 15 Far View, Illingworth, Halifax HX2 0NU W: www.cfhsweb.co.uk

Huddersfield & District Family History Society 63 Dunbottle Lane, Mirfield WF14 9JJ E: secretary@hdfhs.org.uk W: www.hdfhs.org.uk

Keighley & District Family History Society 2 The Hallows, Shann Park, Keighley BD20 6HY T: 01535 672144 E: secretary@keighleyfamilyhistory.org.uk W: www.keighleyfamilyhistory.org.uk

Morley & District Family History Group 1 New Lane, East Ardsley, Wakefield, West Yorkshire WF3 2DP E: carol@morleyfhg.co.uk W: www.morleyfhg.co.uk

Pontefract & District Family History Society 10 Saddlers Grove, Pontefract WF9 1PE E: pontefractfhs@onetel.com W: www.pontefractfhs.co.uk

Wakefield & District Family History Society 12 Malting Rise, Robin Hood, Wakefield, West Yorkshire WF3 3AY T: 01924 373014 E: secretary@wdfhs.co.uk W: www.wdfhs.co.uk

Wharfedale Family History Group 1 West View Court, Yeadon, Leeds, West Yorkshire LS19 7HX T: 0113 258 5597 E: wfhg@yorksgen.org.uk W: www.wfhg.org.uk

Yorkshire - York
City of York & District Family History Society Ascot House, Cherry Tree Avenue, Newton on Ouse, York, North Yorkshire YO30 3BN E: SecretaryYFHS@mvarley.freeserve.co.uk W: www.yorkfamilyhistory.org.uk

Isle of Man
Isle of Man Family History Society Pear Tree Cottage, Llhergy Cripperty, Union Mills IM4 4NF T: 01624 622188 E: iomfhs@manx.net W: www.isle-of-man.com/interests/genealogy/fhs

Channel Islands
Guernsey
Family History Section of La Société Guernesiaise PO Box 314, Candie, St Peter Port, Guernsey GYl 3TG E: societe@cwgsy.net W: www.societe.org.gg

Jersey
Channel Islands Family History Society P0 Box 507, St Helier, Jersey JE4 5TN E: queenie912001@yahoo.co.uk W: www.channelislandshistory.com

Wales
London Branch of the Welsh Family History Societies 27 Princes Avenue, Carshalton Beeches, Surrey SM5 4NZ E: regandpaddy@btinternet.com

Welsh Association of Family History Societies 3 Cagebrook Avenue, Hunderton, Hereford, Herefordshire HR2 7AS

Brecknockshire - Powys
Cardiganshire
Cardiganshire Family History Society National Library of Wales, Aberystwyth SY25 3BU W: www.cardiganshirefhs.org.uk

Carmarthenshire see **Dyfed**
Ceredigion see **Dyfed**
Clwyd
Clwyd Family History Society The Laurels, Dolydd Road, Cefn Mawr, Wrexham, LL14 3NH T: 01978 822218 E: secretary@clwydfhs.org.uk W: www.clwydfhs.org.uk

Denbighshire - see **Clwyd**
Dyfed
Dyfed Family History Society 12 Elder Grove, Llangunnor, Carmarthenshire SA31 2LG T: 01267 232637 E: secretary@dyfedfhs.org.uk W: www.dyfedfhs.org.uk

Flintshire - see **Clwyd**
Glamorgan
Glamorgan Family History Society 22 Parc y Bryn, Creigiau, Cardiff CF15 9SE E: secretary@glamfhs.org W: www.glamfhs.org

Gwent
Gwent Family History Society 11 Rosser Street, Wainfelin, Pontypool, Gwent NP4 6EA E: secretary@gwentfhs.info W: www.gwentfhs.info

Gwynedd
Gwynedd Family History Society 36 Y Wern, Y Felinheli, Gwynedd LL56 4TX T: 01248 670267 E: Gwynedd.Roots@tesco.net W: www.gwynedd.fsbusiness.co.uk

Monmouthshire - see **Gwent**
Montgomeryshire
Montgomeryshire Genealogical Society Cambrian House, Brimmon Lane, Newtown, Powys SY16 1BY T: 01686 624753 E: sue_powys@hotmail.com W: http://home.freeuk.net/montgensoc
- also see **Powys**

Pembrokeshire see **Dyfed**
Powys
Powys Family History Society Waterloo Cottage, Llandeilo Graban, Builth Wells, Powys LD2 3SJ E: pearson287@btinternet.com W: www.rootsweb.com/~wlspfhs/faq/

Ystradgynlais Family History Society c/o Ystradgynlais Library, Temperance Lane, Ystradgynlais, Powys SA9 1BS T: 01639 843104 E: Caryljones@tiscali.co.uk
 W: www.ystradgynlaisfhs.co.uk

Radnorshire see **Powys**

Scotland
Scottish Genealogy Society 15 Victoria Terrace, Edinburgh, EH1 2JL T: 0131-220-3677 F: 0131-220-3677 E: sales@scotsgenealogy.com W: www.scotsgenealogy.com

Aberdeen
Aberdeen & North East Scotland Family History Society 158 - 164 King Street, Aberdeen, AB24 5BD T: 01224 646323 F: 01224 639096 E: enquiries@anefhs.org.uk W: www.anesfhs.org.uk

Angus
Tay Valley Family History Society & Family History Research Centre Family History Research Centre, 179–181 Princes Street, Dundee, DD4 6DQ T: 01382 461845 F: 01382 455532 E: tvfhs@tayvalleyfhs.org.uk W: www.tayvalleyfhs.org.uk

Argyll
Glasgow & West of Scotland Family History Society Unit 13, 32 Mansfield Street, Partick, Glasgow, G11 5QP T: 0141 339 8303 E: publicity@gwsfhs.org.uk W: www.gwsfhs.org.uk

Islay Family History Society Highfield, High Street, Bowmore, Isle of Islay, Argyll PA43 7JE E: islayfamilyhistory@lineone.net W: www.isle-of-islay.com/genealogy

Ayrshire
Alloway & Southern Ayrshire Family History Society c/o Alloway Public Library, Doonholm Road, Alloway, Ayr, Ayrshire KA7 4QQ E: asafhs@mtcharlesayr.fsnet.co.uk W: www.maybole.org/history/resources/asafhs.htm

East Ayrshire Family History Society c/o Dick Institute, Elmbank Avenue, Kilmarnock, East Ayrshire KA1 3BU E: enquiries@eastayrshirefhs.org.uk W: www.eastayrshirefhs.org.uk

Glasgow & West of Scotland Family History Society Unit 13, 32 Mansfield Street, Partick, Glasgow, G11 5QP T: 0141 339 8303 E: publicity@gwsfhs.org.uk W: www.gwsfhs.org.uk

Largs & North Ayrshire Family History Society Bogriggs Cottage, Carlung, West Kilbride, Ayrshire KA23 9PS T: 01294 823690 E: membership@largsnafhs.org.uk W: www.largsnafhs.org.uk

SW Scotland Local / Family History Maybole Historical Society 18A Shawfarm Place, Prestwick, Ayrshire KA9 1JQ T: 07776 445033 E: maybole@scotsfamilies.co.uk W: www.maybole.org

Troon @ Ayrshire Family History Society c/o M.E.R.C., Troon Public Library, South Beach, Troon, Ayrshire KA10 6EF T: E: info@troonayrshirefhs.org.uk W: www.troonayrshirefhs.org.uk

Berwickshire
Borders Family History Society Glenside Stables, St Boswells, Scottish Borders TD6 0AD E: pmunro@bordersfhs.org.uk W: www.bordersfhs.org.uk

Bute
Glasgow & West of Scotland Family History Society Unit 13, 32 Mansfield Street, Partick, Glasgow, G11 5QP T: 0141 339 8303 E: publicity@gwsfhs.org.uk W: www.gwsfhs.org.uk

Caithness
Caithness Family History Society Mill Cottage, Corsback, Dunnet, Caithness KW1 48XQ E: a.e.lewis@btinternet.com W: www.caithnessfhs.org.uk

Central Scotland
Central Scotland Family History Society 11 Springbank Gardens, Dunblane, Perthshire FK15 9JX T: 01786 823937 E: secretary@csfhs.org.uk W: www.csfhs.org.uk

Clackmannanshire
Central Scotland Family History Society 11 Springbank Gardens, Dunblane, Perthshire FK15 9JX T: 01786 823937 E: secretary@csfhs.org.uk W: www.csfhs.org.uk

Dumfries
Dumfries & Galloway Family History Society Family History Research Centre, 9 Glasgow Street, Dumfries, DG2 9AF T: 01387-248093 E: secretary@dgfhs.org.uk W: www.dgfhs.org.uk

Dumfrieshire
Clan Moffat Whinney Brae, Tundergarth, Lockerbie, Dumfrieshire DG11 2PP E: east@albasw.wanadoo.co.uk

Dunbartonshire
Glasgow & West of Scotland Family History Society Unit 13, 32 Mansfield Street, Partick, Glasgow, G11 5QP T: 0141 339 8303 E: publicity@gwsfhs.org.uk W: www.gwsfhs.org.uk

East Lothian
Lothians Family History Society c/o Lasswade High School Centre, Eskdale Drive, Bonnyrigg, Midlothian EH19 2LA T: 0131 660 1933 F: 0131 663 6634 E: f.t.mitchell@btinternet.com
  W: www.lothiansfhs.org.uk
Edinburgh
Lothians Family History Society c/o Lasswade High School Centre, Eskdale Drive, Bonnyrigg EH19 2LA T: 0131 660 1933 E: f.t.mitchell@btinternet.com W: www.lothiansfhs.org.uk
Fife
Fife Family History Society Glenmoriston, Durie Street, Leven, Fife KY8 4HF T: 01333 425321 E: fife@ffhoc.freeserve.co.uk W: www.fifefhs.pwp.bluyonder.co.uk
Tay Valley Family History Society & Family History Research Centre Family History Research Centre, 179–181 Princes Street, Dundee, DD4 6DQ T: 01382 461845 F: 01382 455532 E: tvfhs@tayvalleyfhs.org.uk W: www.tayvalleyfhs.org.uk
Glasgow
Glasgow & West of Scotland Family History Society Unit 13, 32 Mansfield Street, Partick, Glasgow, G11 5QP T: 0141 339 8303 E: publicity@gwsfhs.org.uk W: www.gwsfhs.org.uk
Highlands
Highland Family History Society c/o Reference Room, Inverness Public Library, Farraline Park, Inverness, IV1 1NH E: jdurham@highlandfhs.org.uk W: www.highlandfhs.org.uk
Invernesshire
Highland Family History Society c/o Reference Room, Inverness Public Library, Farraline Park, Inverness, IV1 1NH E: jdurham@highlandfhs.org.uk W: www.highlandfhs.org.uk
Kinross-shire
Tay Valley Family History Society & Family History Research Centre Family History Research Centre, 179–181 Princes Street, Dundee, DD4 6DQ T: 01382 461845 F: 01382 455532 E: tvfhs@tayvalleyfhs.org.uk W: www.tayvalleyfhs.org.uk
Lanarkshire
Glasgow & West of Scotland Family History Society Unit 13, 32 Mansfield Street, Partick, Glasgow, G11 5QP T: 0141 339 8303 E: publicity@gwsfhs.org.uk W: www.gwsfhs.org.uk
Lanarkshire Family History Society Unit 26a Motherwell Business Centre, Coursington Road, Motherwell, Lanarkshire ML1 1PW W: www.lanarkshirefhs.org.uk

Midlothian
Lothians Family History Society c/o Lasswade High School Centre, Eskdale Drive, Bonnyrigg, Midlothian EH19 2LA T: 0131 660 1933 F: 0131 663 6634 E: f.t.mitchell@btinternet.com
  W: www.lothiansfhs.org.uk
North East Scotland
Aberdeen & North East Scotland Family History Society 158 - 164 King Street, Aberdeen, AB24 5BD T: 01224 646323 F: 01224 639096 E: enquiries@anefhs.org.uk W: www.anesfhs.org.uk
Orkney
Orkney Family History Society Community Room, The Strynd, Kirkwall, Orkney KW15 1HG T: 01856 761582 (Home) E: secretary@orkneyfhs.co.uk W: www.orkneyfhs.co.uk
Peebleshire
Borders Family History Society Glenside Stables, St Boswells, Scottish Borders TD6 0AD E: pmunro@bordersfhs.org.uk W: www.bordersfhs.org.uk
Perthshire
Tay Valley Family History Society & Family History Research Centre Family History Research Centre, 179–181 Princes Street, Dundee, DD4 6DQ T: 01382 461845 F: 01382 455532 E: tvfhs@tayvalleyfhs.org.uk W: www.tayvalleyfhs.org.uk
Renfrewshire
Glasgow & West of Scotland Family History Society Unit 13, 32 Mansfield Street, Partick, Glasgow, G11 5QP T: 0141 339 8303 E: publicity@gwsfhs.org.uk W: www.gwsfhs.org.uk
Renfrewshire Family History Society c/o Museum and Art Galleries, High Street, Paisley, Renfrewshire PA1 2BA E: webmaster.rfhs@ntlworld.com W: www.geocities.com/renfrewshirefhs
Roxburghshire see **Borders Family History Society**
Selkirkshire see **Borders Family History Society**
Shetland
Shetland Family History Society 6 Hillhead, Lerwick, Shetland ZE1 0EJ E: secretary@shetland-fhs.org.uk W: www.shetland-fhs.org.uk
Stirlingshire
Central Scotland Family History Society 11 Springbank Gardens, Dunblane, Perthshire FK15 9JX T: 01786 823937 E: secretary@csfhs.org.uk W: www.csfhs.org.uk
Glasgow & West of Scotland Family History Society Unit 13, 32 Mansfield Street, Partick, Glasgow, G11 5QP T: 0141 339 8303 E: publicity@gwsfhs.org.uk W: www.gwsfhs.org.uk

West Lothian
Lothians Family History Society c/o Lasswade High School Centre, Eskdale Drive, Bonnyrigg, Midlothian EH19 2LA T: 0131 660 1933 E: f.t.mitchell@btinternet.com W: www.lothiansfhs.org.uk

Northern Ireland
Irish Heritage Association A.204 Portview, 310 Newtownards Road, Belfast, BT4 1HE T: (028) 90455325
North of Ireland Family History Society c/o Graduate School of Education, 69 University Street, Belfast, BT7 1HL E: enquire@nifhs.org W: www.nifhs.org
Ulster Historical Foundation Balmoral Buildings, 12 College Square East, Belfast, BT1 6DD T: (028) 9033 2288 F: 028 9023 9885 E: enquiry@uhf.org.uk
andrew@uhf.org.uk W: www.uhf.org.uk
www.ancestryireland.com

Ireland
Genealogical Society of Ireland 11 Desmond Avenue, Dun Laoghaire, Co Dublin T: 353 1 284 2711 E: GenSocIreland@iol.ie W: www.gensocireland.org
Irish Family History Society PO Box 36, Naas, Co Kildare E: ifhs@eircom.net W: http://homepage.eircom.net/~ifhs/
The Huguenot Society of Great Britain and Ireland University College, Gower Street, London, WC1E 6BT E: secretary@huguenotsociety.org.uk W: www.huguenotsociety.org.uk
Irish Ancestry Group Clayton House, 59 Piccadilly, Manchester, M1 2AQ T: 0161-236-9750 F: 0161-237-3512 E: office@mlfhs.org.uk W: www.mlfhs.org.uk
County Cork
Cork Genealogical Society c/o 4 Evergreen Villas, Evergreen Road, Cork City, Co Cork T: 086 8198359 F: E: micaconl@eircon.ie W: http://homepage.eircon.net/~adcolemen
County Dublin
Genealogical Society of Ireland 11 Desmond Avenue, Dun Laoghaire, Co Dublin T: 353 1 284 2711 E: GenSocIreland@iol.ie W: www.gensocireland.org
County kildare
Kildare History and Family Research Centre River Bank, Main Street, Newbridge, County Kildare T: +353 45 433 602 E: kildaregenealogy@iol.ie W: www.irish-roots.net

County Wexford
County Wexford Heritage and Genealogy Society County Wexford Heritage and Genealogy Society, Yola Farmstead, Folk Park, Tagoat, Rosslare, County Wexford T: +353 53 32611 E: wexgen@eircom.net W: www.irish-roots.net
Irish Family History Foundation (Irish Roots) County Wexford Heritage and Genealogy Society, Yola Farmstead, Folk Park, Tagoat, Rosslare, County Wexford T: +353 53 32611 E: wexgen@eircom.net W: www.irish-roots.net
Wexford Family History Society 24 Parklands, Wexford, Co Wexford T: 053-42273 E: murphyh@tinet.ie
County Wicklow
Wicklow County Genealogical Society 1 Summerhill, Wicklow Town, Co Wicklow
Dublin
Ballinteer FHS 29 The View, Woodpark, Ballinteer, Dundrum, Dublin 16 T: 01-298-8082 E: ryanct@eircom.net
Council of Irish Genealogical Organisations 186 Ashcroft, Raheny, Dublin 5,
Flannery Clan / Clann Fhlannabhra 81 Woodford Drive, Clondakin, Dublin, 22 E: oflannery@eircom.net W: www.flanneryclan.ie
Raheny Heritage Society 68 Raheny Park, Raheny, Dublin 5, Dublin T: 01 831 4729 E: joan.sharkey@gmail.com
Irish Genealogical Research Society 18 Stratford Avenue, Rainham, Gillingham, Kent ME8 0EP E: info@igrsoc.org W: www.igrsoc.org

Specialist Family History Societies
1788-1820 Pioneer Association PO Box 57, Croydon, New South Wales 2132 T: (02)-9797-8107
Anglo-French Family History Society 31 Collingwood Walk, Andover, Hampshire SP10 1PU W: www.anglo-french-fhs.org
Anglo-German Family History Society 20 Skylark Rise, Woolwell, Plymouth, Devon PL6 7SN T: 01752 310852 F: 01752 310852 E: jennytowery@blueyonder.co.uk W: www.agfhs.org.uk
Anglo-Italian Family History Society 3 Calais Street, London, SE5 9LP T: 020 7274 7809 E: membership@anglo-italianfhs.org.uk W: www.anglo-italianfhs.org.uk
Anglo-Scottish Family History Society Clayton House, 59 Piccadilly, Manchester, M1 2AQ T: 0161-236-9750 F: 0161-237-3512 E: office@mlfhs.org.uk W: www.mlfhs.org.uk

Australian Society of the Lace Makers of Calais Inc PO Box 946, Batemans Bay, New South Wales 2536 T: 0244-718168 E: carolynb@acr.net.au

Black and West Indian - Every Generation Unit 4-5 1st Floor West, Universal House, 88-94 Wentworth Street, London, E1 7SA T: 020 7247 5565 E: info@everygeneration.co.uk W: www.everygeneration.co.uk

British Ancestors in India Society 2 South Farm Avenue, Harthill, Sheffield, South Yorkshire S26 7WY T: +44 (0) 1909 774416 F: +44 (0) 1909 774416 E: editorial@indiaman.com W: www.indiaman.com

British Association for Cemeteries in S.Asia 76 1/2 Chartfield Avenue, London, SW15 6HQ T: (020) 8788-6953 W: www.bacsa.org.uk

Catholic Family History Society 9 Snows Green Road, Shotley Bridge, Consett, County Durham DH8 0HD E: margaretbowery@aol.com W: www.catholic-history.org.uk/cfhs

Catholic Record Society 12 Melbourne Place, Wolsingham, County Durham DL13 3EH W: www.catholic-history.org/crs

Chapels Heritage Society - CAPEL 2 Sandy Way, Wood Lane, Hawarden, Flintshire CH5 3JJ T: 01244 531255

Descendants of Convicts Group PO Box 12224, A'Beckett Street, Melbourne, Victoria 3000 E: gulliver@cosmos.net.au W: http://home.vicnet.net.au/~dcginc

Genealogical Society of Utah (UK) 185 Penns Lane, Sutton Coldfield, West Midlands B76 1JU T: 0121 384 2028

Heraldry Society PO Box 32, Maidenhead, Berkshire SL6 3FD T: 0118-932-0210 F: 0118 932 0210 E: heraldry-society@cwcom.net

Historical Medical Equipment Society 8 Albion Mews, Apsley, Hertfordshire HP3 9QZ E: hmes@antiageing.freeserve.co.uk

Hugenot & Walloon Research Association Malmaison, Church St, Great Bedwyn, Wiltshire SN8 3PE

Hugenot Society of Great Britain & Ireland Hugenot Library University College, Gower Street, London, WC1E 6BT T: 020 7679 5199 E: s.massil@ucl.ac.uk W: (Library) www.ucl.ac.uk/ucl-info/divisions/library/huguenot.htm (Society) www.hugenotsociety.org.uk

International Police Association - British Section - Genealogy Group Thornholm, Church Lane, South Muskham, Newark, Nottinghamshire NG23 6EQ T: 01636 676997 E: ipagenuk@thornholm.freeserve.co.uk

International Society for British Genealogy and Family History PO Box 350459, Westminster, Colorado 80035-0459 T: 801-272-2178 E: isbgfh@yahoo.com W: www.isbgfh.org

Irish Ancestry Group Clayton House, 59 Piccadilly, Manchester, M1 2AQ T: 0161-236-9750 F: 0161-237-3512 E: office@mlfhs.org.uk W: www.mlfhs.org.uk

Irish Genealogical Research Society 18 Stratford Avenue, Rainham, Gillingham, Kent ME8 0EP E: info@igrsoc.org W: www.igrsoc.org

Jewish Genealogical Society of Great Britain 48 Worcester Crescent, Woodford Green, Essex IG8 0LU T: 020 8504 8013 E: pnking@onetel.net.uk W: www.jgsgb.org.uk

Jewish Genealogical Society (United States) PO Box 6398, New York, New York 10128 E: info@jgsny.org W: www.jgsny.org

Lighthouse Society of Great Britain - Disbanded 2005

London & North Western Railway Society - Staff History Group 34 Falmouth Close, Nuneaton, Warwickshire CV11 6GB T: 024 76 381090 F: 024 76 373577 E: nuneazon2000@aol.com W: www.progsol.co.uk/lnwr

North East England Family History Club 5 Tree Court, Doxford Park, Sunderland, Tyne and Wear SR3 2HR T: 0191-522-8344

Pedigree Users Group 11 Corn Avill Close, Abingdon, Oxfordshire OX14 2ND W: www.pugweb.org.uk

Quaker Family History Society 1 Ormond Crescent, Hampton, Middlesex TW12 2TJ E: info@qfhs.co.uk W: www.qfhs.co.uk

Railway Ancestors Family History Society Lundy, 31 Tennyson Road, Eastleigh, Hampshire SO50 9FS T: (023) 8049 7465E: jim@railwayancestors.fsnet.co.uk W: www.railwayancestors.org.uk

Rolls Royce Family History Society 25 Gisburn Road, Barnoldswick, Colne, Lancashire BB18 5HB T: 01282 815778 E: ken@ranson.org.uk

Romany & Traveller Family History Society 6 St James Walk, South Chailey, East Sussex BN8 4BU W: http://website.lineone.net/~rtfhs

Scottish Association of Family History Societies c/o 9 Glasgow Street, Dumfries, Dumfrieshire DG2 9AF W: www.safhs.org.uk

Society of Brushmakers Descendants Family History Society 13 Ashworth Place, Church Langley, Essex CM17 9PU T: 01279-629392 E: s.b.d@lineone.net W: www.brushmakers.com

Society for Name Studies in Britain & Ireland 22 Peel Park Avenue, Clitheroe BB7 1ET T: 01200-423771 F: 01200-423771

Tennyson Society Central Library, Free School Lane, Lincoln, LN2 1EZ T: 01522-552862 E: linnet@lincolnshire.gov.uk W: www.tennysonsociety.org.uk

The Clans of Ireland Ltd 2 Westbourne Terrace, Quinsboro Road, Bray, County Wicklow Ireland E: theclansofireland@ireland.com

Victorian Military Society PO Box 5837, Newbury, Berkshire RG14 7FJ T: 01635 48628 E: vmsdan@msn.com W: www.vms.org.uk

One Name Societies

Alabaster Society No 1 Manor Farm Cottages, Bradenham, Thetford, Norfolk IP25 7QE T: 01362-821243 E: laraine@alabaster.org.uk W: www.alabaster.org.uk

Alderson Family History Society 13 Spring Grove, Harrogate, North Yorkshire HG1 2HS E: secretary@afhs.org W: www.afhs.org

Alderton Family 16 Woodfield Dr, Gidea Park, Romford RM2 5DH

Allsop Family Group 86 High Street, Loscoc, Heanor DE75 7LF

Armstrong Clan Association Thyme, 7 Riverside Park, Hollows, Canonbie, Dumfriesshire DG14 0UY T: 013873 71876 E: ted.armclan@aol.com W: www.armstrongclan.info

Badham One Name Society Old School House, Old Radnor, Presteigne, Powys LD* 2RH W: www.badham.org

Baldry FHS, 17 Gerrard Road, Islington, London, N1 8AY T: 020 7359 6294 E: ken@art-science.com W: www.baldry.org.uk

Beresford Family Society 2 Malatia, 78 St Augustines Avenue, South Croydon, Surrey CR2 6JH T: (020) 8686 3749 F: (020) 8681 3740 E: secretary@beresfordfamilysociety.org.uk W: www.beresfordfamilysociety.org.uk

Birkbecks of Westmoreland and Others One Name Study 330 Dereham Road, Norwich, Norfolk NR2 4DL E: Seosimhin@btopenworld.com W: www.jgeoghegan.org.uk

Blanchard Family History Society 10 Stainers, Bishop Stortford, Hertfordshire CM23 4GL E: colin@blanshard.org W: www.blanshard.org

Bliss Family History Society Old Well Cottage, Washdyke Lane, Fulbeck, Lincolnshire NG32 3LB T: 01400 279050 E: bliss@one-name.org W: www.blissfhs.de

Braund Society 12 Ranelagh Road, Lake, Sandown, Isle of Wight PO36 8NX E: braundsociety@fewlow.freeserve.co.uk W: www.braundsociety.co.uk

Brooking Family History Society 48 Regent Close, Edgbaston, Birmingham, West Midlands B5 7PL T: 0121 249 1226 E: marylogan@blueyonder.co.uk W: www.brookingsociety.org.uk

Bunting Society 'Firgrove', Horseshoe Lane, Ash Vale, Surrey GU12 5LL T: 01252-325644 F: 01252-325644 E: firgrove@compuserve.com W: http://freespace.virgin.net/teebee.axmeister/BuntingSociety.htm

Caraher Family History Society 142 Rexford Street, Sistersville, VA 26175

Cave Family History Society 45 Wisbech Road, Thorney, Peterborough, Cambridgeshire PE6 0SA T: 01733 270881 E: hugh-cave@cave-fhs.org.uk W: www.cave-fhs.org.uk

Clan Davidson Association Ballynester House, 1A Cardy Road, Greyabbey, Newtownards, Co Down BT22 2LS T: 028 427-38402 E: clan.davidson@virgin.net

Clan Gregor Society Administrative Office, 2 Braehead, Alloa, Clackmannanshire FK10 2EW T: 01259-212076 F: 01259-720274 E: clangregor@sol.co.uk W: www.clangregor.com/macgregor

Cobbing Family History Society 89a Petherton Road, London, N5 2QT T: (020) 7226-2657

Cory Society 3 Bourne Close, Thames Ditton, London, KT7 0EA E: cory@one-name.com W: www.coryfamsoc.com www.corysociety.org.uk

Courtenay Society Powderham Castle, Kenton, Exeter, Devon EX6 8JQ T: 01626-891554 F: 01626-890729 E: courtenay@courtsoc.demon.co.uk W: www.courtenaysociety.org

Dalton Genealogical Society 11 Jordan Close, Leavesden, Watford, Hertfordshire WD25 7AF T: 01923 661139 E: pam-lynam@lineone.net W: http://members.aol.com/daltongene/index.html

East Family History So 45 Windsor Road, Ealing, London, W5 3UP

Entwistle Family History Association 58 Earnsdale Road, Darwin , Lancashire BB3 1HS E: entwistle@one-name.org W: www.entwistlefamily.org.uk

FHS of Martin PO Box 9, Rosanna, Victoria 3084

Geoghegan/McGeoghegan One Name Study 330 Dereham Road, Norwich, Norfolk NR2 4DL E: josi@geoghegan18.fsnet.co.uk W: www.jgeoghegan.org.uk

Goddard Association of Europe 2 Lowergate Road, Huncoat, Accrington, Lancashire BB5 6LN T: 01254-235135 E: johnc.goddard@virgin.net W: www.goddard-association.co.uk

Guild of One Name Studies 14 Charterhouse Buildings, Goswell Road, London, EC1M 7BA T: 01293-411136 E: guild@one-name.org W: www.one-name.org

Hamley, Hambly & Hamlyn Family History Society 59 Eylewood Road, West Norwood, London, SE27 9LZ T: (020) 8670-0683 F: (020) 8670-0683 E: hamley@one-name.org W: www.hhh-fhs.com

Hards Family Society Venusmead, 36 Venus Street, Congresbury, Bristol, BS49 5EZ T: 01934 834780 F: 01934 834780 E: rogerhards-venusmead@breathemail.net W: www.hards.freewire.org.uk

Holdich Family History Society 19 Park Crescent, Elstree, Hertfordshire WD6 3PT T: (020) 8953 7195 E: apogee.dtaylor@btopenworld.com

Holt Ancestry 26a Avondale Road, Bath, Somerset BA1 3EG E: victoria-holt@holtancestry.co.uk W: www.holtancestry.co.uk

Hotham/Owst One Name Study 65 Northolme Road, Hessle, Hull, East Yorkshire HU13 9JB E: jbresearch870@hotmail.com

International Haskell Family Society 36 Hedley Davis Court, Cherry Orchard Lane, Salisbury, Wiltshire SP2 7UE T: 01722 332873 F: 01722 410094 E: pat.haskell@ntlworld.com W: http://kinnexions.com/ancestries/surname/haskell.htm

International Relf Society Chatsworth House, Sutton Road, Somerton, Somerset TA11 6QL T: 01458-274015 E: chris.relf@bucklebury.demon.co.uk

Kay Family Association UK 47 Moorway, Poulton le Flyde, Lancashire FY6 6EX T: 01253 886171 E: patricia.kay@btopenworld.com W: http://homepages.rootsweb.com/~kayefile/kfa_uk.html

Krans-Buckland Family Association P0 Box 1025, North Highlands, California 95660-1025 T: (916)-332-4359 E: jkbfa@worldnet.att.net

Leather Family History Society 134 Holbeck, Great Hollands, Bracknell, Berkshire RG12 8XG T: 01344-425092 E: s.leather@ic.ac.uk

Lin(d)field One Name Group Southview, Maplehurst, Horsham, West Sussex RH13 6QY T: 01403-864389 E: lindfield@one-name.org W: www.lindfield.force9.co.uk/long

Mackman Family History Society Chawton Cottage, 22a Long Ridge Lane, Nether Poppleton, York, North Yorkshire YO26 6LX T: +44-(0)1904-781752 E: mackman@one-name.org

Marsden One Name Study E: john@marsden-ons.co.uk W: www.marsden-ons.co.uk

Mayhew Ancestory Research 28 Windmill Road, West Croydon, Surrey CR0 2XN

Metcalfe Society 57 Westbourne Avenue, Hull, East Yorkshire HU5 3HW T: 01482 342516 E: enquiries@metcalfe.org.uk W: www.metcalfe.org.uk

Morbey Family History Group 23 Cowper Crescent, Bengeo, Hertford, Hertfordshire SG14 3DZ

Morgan Society of England & Wales 11 Arden Drive, Dorridge, Solihull B93 8LP T: 01564 774020 E: morgansociety@tesco.net W: http://freepages.genealogy.rootsweb.com/~morgansociety

Mower Family History Association 615 County Road 123, Bedford, Wyoming 83112 E: jmower@silverstar.com W: www.mowerfamily.org

Moxon Family Research Trust 1 Pine Tree Close, Cowes, Isle of Wight PO31 8DX T: 01983 296921 E: john.moxon@virgin.net W: www.moxon.org.uk

Moxon Society The Coach House, Bretton Park, West Bretton, Wakefield, West Yorkshire WF4 4JX W: www.moxon.org.uk

Offiler Offley Family Society 39 Windmill Fields, Old Harlow, Hertfordshire CM17 0LQ T: 01438-820006 E: offleyfamilyhistory@ntlworld.com W: www.offleysociety.co.uk

Orton Family History Society 25a Longwood Avenue, Bingley, West Yorkshire BD16 2RX E: ortonfhs@redflag.co.uk W: www.redflag.co.uk/ortonfhs.htm

P*rr*tt Family History Society 48 Prospect Drive, Matlock, Derbyshire DE4 3TA E: membership@p-rr-tt.org.uk W: www.p-rr-tt.org.uk

Palgrave Society Crossfield House, Dale Road, Stanton, Bury St Edmunds, Suffolk IP31 2DY T: 01359-251050 F: 01359-251050 E: DerekPalgrave@btinternet.com W: www.ffhs.org.uk/members/palgrave.htm

Penty Family Name Society Kymbelin, 30 Lych Way, Horsell Village, Surrey GU21 4QG T: 01483-764904 E: pentytree@aol.com

Percy-Piercy Family History Society 32 Ravensdale Avenue, North

Plant Family History Group 22 Chapel Croft, Chelford, Macclesfield, Cheshire SK11 9S E: keithandmavisplant@uwclub.net W: www.plant-fhg.org.uk

Polperro Family History Society The Crown House, Clifton on Teme, Worcestershire WR6 6EN E: jeremy.johns@polperro.org W: www.heritagepress.polperro.org/famhist.html

Rix Family Alliance 4 Acklam Close, Hedon, Hull, HU12 8NA W: www.rix-alliance.co.uk

Rose Family Society - disbanded 1st March 2002

Serman, Surman Family History Society 24 Monks Walk, Bridge Street, Evesham, Worcestershire WR11 4SL T: 01386 49967 F: 01386 49967 E: design@johnsermon.demon.co.uk W: www.johnsermon.demon.co.uk

Silverthorne Family Association 1 Cambridge Close, Swindon, Wiltshire SN3 1JQ T: 01793 537103

Society of Cornishes 1 Maple Close, Tavistock, Devon PL19 9LL T: 01822 614613 F: 01822 614613 E: cornish@one-name.org W: www.societyofcornishes.org

Sole Society 49 Kennel Ride, North Ascot, Berkshire SL5 7NJ T: 01344 883700 E: info@sole.org.uk W: www.solesociety.freeserve.co.uk

Spencer Family 1303 Azalea Lane, Dekalb, Illinois 60115

Stendall & Variants PO Box 6417, Sutton in Ashfield, Nottinghamshire NG17 3LE T: 01623 406870 W: www.genealogy-links.co.uk

Stockdill Family History Society 6 First Avenue, Garston, Watford, Hertfordshire WD2 6PZ T: 01923-675292 F: 01923-675292 E: roy@stockdillfhs.org.uk W: www.stockdillfhs.org.uk

Stockton Society The Leas, 28 North Road, Builth Wells, Powys LD2 3BU T: 01982 551667 E: cestrienne@aol.com

Stonehewer to Stanier Society The Shires, 71 Knutsford Road, Row of Trees, Alderley Edge, Cheshire SK9 7SH W: http://freepages.genealogy.rootsweb.com~stanier/

Swinnerton Society 30 Coleridge Walk, London, NW11 6AT T: (020) 8458-3443 E: roger.swynnerton@whichnet

Talbot Research Organisation 142 Albemarle Ave, Elson, Gosport., Hampshire PO12 4HY E: mjh.talbot@tinyworld.cor.uk W: www.kiamara.demon.co.uk/index.html

The Johns Family History Association E: Johns-L@rootsweb.com W: http://freepages.genealogy.rootsweb.com/~johns/njfrg

The UK Family History Society of Martin 63 Higher Coombe Drive, Teignmouth, Devon TQ14 9NL E: membership@fhsofmartin.org.uk W: www.fhsofmartin.org.uk

Toseland Clan Society 40 Moresdale Lane, Seacroft, Leeds, West Yorkshire LS14 5SY F: 0113-225-9954

Tyrrell Family History Society 16 The Crescent, Solihull, West Midlands B91 7PE W: www.tyrrellfhs.org.uk

Watkins Family History Society 20 Buttermere Avenue, The Glebe, Nuneaton, Warwickshire CV11 6EP E: watkinsfhs@alltel.net W: www.iinet.net.au/~davwat/wfhs/

Witheridge Family History Society 16 Haven Close, Dunster, Minehead, Somerset TA24 6RW W: www.witheridgefhs.com

Australia
National
Genealogical Society of Victoria Level B1, 257 Collins Street, Melbourne 3000, Victoria T: +61-03-9670-7033 F: +61-03-9670-4490 E: gsv@gsv.org.au W: www.gsv.org.au

Society of Australian Genealogists Richmond Villa, 120 Kent Street, Observatory Hill, Sydney 2000, New South Wales T: 61-02-92473953 F: 61-02-92414872 E: socgenes@ozemail.com.au

Australian Institute of Genealogical Studies PO Box 339, Blackburn, Victoria 3130 E: info@aigs.org.au W: www.aigs.org.au

ACT
The Heraldry & Genealogy Society of Canberra Inc GPO Box 585, Canberra, ACT 2601 T: 02 6282 9356 (library) F: 02 6282 4865 E: hagsoc@hagsoc.org.au W: www.hagsoc.org.au

Capital Territory
The Heraldry & Genealogy Society of Canberra Inc GPO Box 585, Canberra, ACT 2601 T: 02 6282 9356 (library) F: 02 6282 4865 E: hagsoc@hagsoc.org.au W: www.hagsoc.org.au**New South Wales**

1788-1820 Pioneer Association PO Box 57, Croydon, New South Wales 2132 T: (02)-9797-8107

Australian Society of the Lace Makers of Calais Inc PO Box 946, Batemans Bay, New South Wales 2536 T: 0244-718168 E: carolynb@acr.net.au

Bega Valley Genealogical Society Inc PO Box 19, Pambula, New South Wales 2549

Berrima District Historical & Family History Society Inc PO Box 851, Bowral, New South Wales 2576

Blayney Shire Local & Family History Society Group Inc c/o The Library, 48 Adelaide Street, Blayney, New South Wales 2799 E: blayney.library@cww.octec.org.au

Blue Mountains Family History Society PO Box 97, Springwood, New South Wales NSW 2777 F: 02-4751-2746

Botany Bay Family History Society Inc PO Box 1006, Sutherland, New South Wales 1499 W: http://au.geocities.com/bbfhs/

Broken Hill Family History Group PO Box 779, 75 Pell Street, Broken Hill, New South Wales 2880 T: 08-80-881321

Burwood Drummoyne & District Family History Group c/o Burwood Central Library, 4 Marmaduke Street, Burwood NSW 2134

Cape Banks Family History Society PO Box 67, Maroubra, New South Wales NSW 2035 E: hazelb@compassnet.com.au W: www.capebanks.org.au

Casino & District Family History Group Inc PO Box 586, Casino, NSW 2470 E: hughsie@nor.com W: www.rootsweb.com/~nswcdfhg

Central Coast FHG Inc PO Box 4090, East Gosford, New South Wales 2250 W: www.centralcoastfhs.org.au

Coffs Harbour District Family History Society Inc PO Box 2057, Coffs Harbour, New South Wales 2450

Cowra FHG Inc PO Box 495, Cowra, New South Wales 2794

Deniliquin FH Group Inc PO Box 144, Multi Arts Hall, Cressy Street, Denilquin NSW 2710 T: (03)-5881-3980 F: (03)-5881-1270

Dubbo & District FHS Inc PO Box 868, Dubbo, New South Wales 2830 T: 068-818635 W: au.geocities.com/ddfhs_2000/

Family History Society - Singleton Inc PO Box 422, Singleton, New South Wales 2330

Fellowship of First Fleeters First Fleet House, 105 Cathedral Street, Woolloomooloo, New South Wales 2000 T: (02)-9360-3988

Forbes Family History Group Inc PO Box 574, Forbes, New South Wales 2871 T: 0411-095311-(mobile)

Goulburn District Family History Society Inc PO Box 611, Goulburn, New South Wales 2580

Griffith Genealogical & Historical Society Inc PO Box 270, Griffith, New South Wales 2680

Gwydir Family History Society Inc PO Box EM61, East Moree, New South Wales 2400 T: (02)-67549235-(President)

Hastings Valley Family History Group Inc PO Box 1359, Port Macquarie, New South Wales 2444

Hawkesbury FHG C/o Hawkesbury City Council Library, Dight Street, Windsor, New South Wales 2756

Hill End Family History Group Sarnia, Hill End, New South Wales 2850

Hornsbury Kuring-Gai FHS Inc PO Box 680, Hornsby, New South Wales 2077

Illawarra Family History Group The Secretary, PO Box 1652, South Coast Mail Centre, Wollongong, New South Wales 2521 T: (02)-42622212 W: http://sites.archivenet.gov.au/IFHG

Inverell District FHG Inc PO Box 367, Inverell NSW 2360

Ku-Ring-Gai Historical Society PO Box 109, Gordon, New South Wales 2072 E: khs@kuringgai.net W: www.kuringgai.net/khs

Leeton Family History Society PO Box 475, Centre Point, Pine Avenue, Leeton, New South Wales 2705 T: 02-6955-7199

Lithgow & District Family History Society PO Box 516, Lithgow, New South Wales 2790 W: www.lisp.com.au/~ldfhs/

Little Forest Family History Research Group PO Box 87, 192 Little Forest Road, Milton, New South Wales 2538 T: 02-4455-4780 E: cathyd@shoalhaven.net.au W: www.shoalhaven.net.au/~cathyd/groups.html

Liverpool & District Family History Society PO Box 830, Liverpool, New South Wales 2170

Maitland FH Circle Inc PO Box 247, Maitland, New South Wales 2320 W: www.rootsweb.com/~ausmfhc

Manning Wallamba FHS c/o Greater Taree City Library, Pulteney Street, Taree, New South Wales 2430

Milton Ulladulla Genealogical Society Inc PO Box 619, Ulladulla, New South Wales 2539 T: 02-4455-4206

Moruya & District Historical Society Inc PO Box 259, Moruya, New South Wales 2537 W: www.sci.net.au/userpages/mgrogan/mhs/

Nepean Family History Society PO Box 81, Emu Plains, New South Wales 2750 T: (02)-47-353-798 E: istack@penrithcity.nsw.gov.au W: www.penrithcity.nsw.gov.au/nfhs/nfhshome.htm

New South Wales Association of Family History Societies PO Box 48, Waratah, New South Wales 2298

Newcastle Family History Society PO Box 233, Lambton, New South Wales 2299 W: www.ozemail.com.au/~ahgw/nfhs/

Orange Family History Society PO Box 930, Orange, New South Wales 2800

Port Stephens-Tilligerry & Districts FHS PO Box 32, Tanilba Bay, New South Wales 2319

Richmond River Historical Society Inc PO Box 467, 165 Molesworth Street, Lismore, New South Wales 2480 T: 02-6621-9993

Richmond-Tweed Family History Society PO Box 817, Ballina, New South Wales 2478 E: warmer@nor.com.au

Ryde District Historical Society Inc 770 Victoria Road, Ryde, New South Wales 2112 T: (02)-9807-7137

Scone & Upper Hunter Historical Society Inc PO Box 339, Kingdon Street, Upper Hunter, Scone, New South Wales 2337 T: 02-654-51218

Shoalhaven Family History Society Inc PO Box 591, Nowra, New South Wales 2541 T: 02-44221253 F: 02-44212462 E: wvost@shoal.net.au

Snowy Mountains FH Group PO Box 153, Cooma NSW2630

Society of Australian Genealogists Richmond Villa, 120 Kent Street, Observatory Hill, Sydney 2000, New South Wales T: 61-02-92473953 F: 61-02-92414872 E: socgenes@ozemail.com.au

Tweed Gold Coast FH & HA Inc PO Box 266, Tweed Heads, New South Wales 2485 W: www.geocities.com/twintownsfamilyhistory/

Wagga Wagga & District Family History Society Inc PO Box 307, Wagga Wagga, New South Wales 2650

Wingham FHG PO Box 72, Wingham, New South Wales 2429

Young & District FHG Inc PO Box 586, Young, NSW 2594

Northern Territory

Genealogical Society of the Northern Territory PO Box 37212, Winnellie, Northern Territory 0821 T: 08-898-17363

Queensland

Beaudesert Branch, Genealogical Society of Queensland Inc PO Box 664, Beaudesert, Queensland 4285

Bundaberg Genealocical association Inc PO Box 103, Bundaberg, Queensland 4670

Burdekin Contact Group Family Hist Assn of N Qld Inc PO Box 393, Home Hill, Queensland 4806

Caboolture FH Research Group Inc PO Box 837, Caboolture, Queensland 4510

Cairns & District Family History Society Inc PO Box 5069, Cairns, Queensland 4870 T: 07-40537113 W: http://cwpp.slq.qld.gov.au/cdfhs

Central Queensland Family History Association PO Box 8423, Woolloongabba, Queensland 4102 E: secretary@qfhs.org.au W: www.qfhs.org.au

Charters Towers & Dalrymple Family History Association Inc PO Box 783, 54 Towers Street, Charters Towers, Queensland 4820 T: 07-4787-2124

Cooroy Noosa Genealogical & Historical Research Group Inc PO Box 792, Cooroy, Queensland 4563 E: info@genealogy-noosa.org.au W: www.genealogy-noosa.org.au

Dalby FHS inc PO Box 962, Dalby, Queensland 4405

Darling Downs Family History Society PO Box 2229, Toowoomba, Queensland 4350

Genealogical Society of Queensland Inc PO Box 8423, Woolloongabba, Queensland 4102 W: www.gsq.org.au

Gladstone Branch G.S.Q. PO Box 1778, Gladstone, Queensland 4680

Gold Coast FH Research Group PO Box 1126, Southport, Gold Coast, Queensland 4215

Gold Coast FHS Inc PO Box 2763, Southport, Queensland 4215 W: http://members.ozemail.com.au/~annmorse/nerang.html

Goondiwindi & District Family History Society PO Box 190, Goondiwindi, Queensland 4390 T: 746712156 F: 746713019 E: pez@bigpond.com

Gympie Ancestral Research Society Inc PO Box 767, Gympie, Queensland 4570

Ipswich Genealogical Society Inc. PO Box 323, 1st Floor, Ipswich Campus Tafe, cnr. Limestone & Ellenborough Streets, Ipswich, Queensland 4305 T: (07)-3201-8770

Kingaroy Family History Centre PO Box 629, James Street, Kingaroy, Queensland 4610

Mackay Branch Genealogical Society of Queensland Inc PO Box 882, Mackay, Queensland 4740 T: (07)-49426266

Maryborough District Family History Society PO Box 408, Maryborough, Queensland 4650 W: www.satcom.net.au/mdfhs

Mount Isa Family History Society Inc PO Box 1832, Mount Isa, Queensland 4825 E: krp8@+opend.com.au

North Brisbane Branch - Genealogical Society of Queensland Inc PO Box 353, Chermside South, Queensland 4032

Queensland FHS Inc PO Box 171, Indooroophilly, Queensland 4068

Rockhampton Genealogical Society of Queensland Inc PO Box 992, Rockhampton, Queensland 4700

Roma & District Local & Family History Society PO Box 877, Roma, Queensland 4455

South Burnett Genealogical & Family History Society PO Box 598, Kingaroy, Queensland 4610

Southern Suburbs Branch - G.S.Q. Inc PO Box 844, Mount Gravatt, Queensland 4122

Sunshine Coast Historical & Genealogical Resource Centre Inc PO Box 1051, Nambour, Queensland 4560

Toowoomba Family History Centre c/o South Town Post Office, South Street, Toowoomba, Queensland 4350 T: 0746-355895

Townsville - Family History Association of North Queensland Inc PO Box 6120, Townsville M.C., Queensland 4810

Whitsunday Branch - Genealogical Society Queensland Inc PO Box 15, Prosperpine, Queensland 4800

South Australia

Fleurieu Peninsula Family History Group Inc Noarlunga Library, PO Box 411, Noarlunga Centre, South Australia 5168 E: fleurpengroup@yahoo.co.uk W: www.rootsweb.com/~safpfhg

South Australian Genealogical & Heraldic Society GPO Box 592, Adelaide 5001, South Australia T: (08)-8272-4222 F: (08)-8272-4910 W: www.saghs.org.au

South East FHG Inc PO Box 758, Millicent, South Australia 5280

Southern Eyre Peninsula FHG 26 Cranston Street, Port Lincoln, South Australia 5606

Whyalla FHG PO Box 2190, Whyalla Norrie, South Australia 5608

Yorke Peninsula Family History Group - 1st Branch SAGHS PO Box 260, Kadina, South Australia 5554

Tasmania

Tasmanian FHS (Launceston Branch) PO Box 1290, Launceston, Tasmania 7250 E: secretary@tasfhs.org W: www.tasfhs.org

Tasmanian FHS Inc PO Box 191, Launceston, Tasmania 7250 W: www.tasfhs.org

Victoria

Benalla & District FH Group Inc PO Box 268, St Andrews Church Hall, Church Street, Benalla, Victoria 3672 T: (03)-57-644258

Cobram Genealogical Group PO Box 75, Cobram, Victoria 3643

East Gippsland Family History Group Inc PO Box 1104, Bairnsdale, Victoria 3875

Echuca/Moama Family History Group Inc PO Box 707, Echuca, Victoria 3564

Emerald Genealogy Group 62 Monbulk Road, Emerald, Victoria 3782

Euroa Genealogical Group 43 Anderson Street, Euroa, Victoria 3666

Geelong Family History Group Inc PO Box 1187, Geelong, Victoria 3220 E: flw@deakin.edu.au W: www.home.vicnet.net.au/wgfamhist/index.htm

Genealogical Society of Victoria Level B1, 257 Collins Street, Melbourne 3000, Victoria T: +61-03-9670-7033 F: +61-03-9670-4490 E: gsv@gsv.org.au W: www.gsv.org.au
Hamilton Family & Local History Group PO Box 816, Hamilton, Victoria 3300 T: 61-3-55-724933 F: 61-3-55-724933 E: ham19.@mail.vicnet.net.au W: www.freenet.com.au/hamilton
Kerang & District Family History Group PO Box 325, Kerang, Victoria 3579
Mid Gippsland Family History Society Inc PO Box 767, Morwell, Victoria 3840
Mildura & District Genealogical Society Inc PO Box 2895, Mildura, Victoria 3502
Mornington Peninsula Family History Society 16 Tavisstock Road, Frankston South, Victoria 3199 T: 61 3 9783 8773 E: marjoryknight@bigpond.com W: http://mpfhs.org
Narre Warren & District Family History Group PO Box 149, Narre Warren, Victoria 3805 W: www.ozemail.com.au/~narre/fam-hist.html
Nathalia Genealogical Group Inc R.M.B. 1003, Picola, Victoria 3639
Port Genealogical Society of Victoria Inc PO Box 1070, Warrambool, Victoria 3280 E: joyceaustin@start.co.au
Sale & District FH Group Inc PO Box 773, Sale, Victoria 3850
Stawell Biarri Group for Genealogy Inc PO Box 417, Stawell, Victoria 3380
Swam Hill Genealogical & Historical Society Inc PO Box 1232, Swan Hill, Victoria 3585
Toora & District FH Group Inc PO Box 41, Toora, Victoria 3962
Wangaratta Genealogical Soc Inc PO Box 683, Wangaratta, Victoria 3676
West Gippsland Genealogical Society Inc PO Box 225, Old Shire Hall, Queen Street, Warragul, Victoria 3820 T: 03-56252743 E: watts@dcsi.net.au W: www.vicnet.net.au/~wggs/
Wimmera Assoc for Genealogy PO Box 880, Horsham, Victoria 3402
Wodonga FHS Inc PO Box 289, Wodonga, Victoria 3689
Yarram Genealogical Group Inc PO Box 42, 161 Commercial Road, Yarram, Victoria 3971
Western Australia
Australasian Federation of Family History Organisations Inc PO Box 3012, Weston Creek, ACT 2611 W: www.affho.org
Australasian Federation of FH Orgs Inc 6/48 May Street, Bayswater, Western Australia 6053 W: www.affho.org
Geraldton FHS PO Box 2502, Geralton 6531, Western Australia W: www.com.au/gol/genealogy/gfhs/gfhsmain.htm
Goldfields Branch, West Australian Genealogical Society Inc PO Box 1462, Kalgoorlie, Western Australia 6430
Melville Family History Centre PO Box 108 (Rear of Church of Jesus Christ Latter Day Saints, 308 Preston Point Road, Attadale, Melville, Western Australia 6156
Western Australia Genealogical Society 6/48 May Street, Bayswater, Western Australia 6053
Western Australia Genealogical Society Inc 6/48 May Street, Bayswater, Western Australia 6053 T: 08-9271-4311 F: 08-9271-4311 E: wags@cleo.murdoch.edu.au W: www.cleo.murdoch.edu.au/~wags

New Zealand
Bishopdale Branch, NZ Society of Genealogists Inc. c/o 19a Resolution Place, Christchurch, 8005 T: 03 351 0625
Cromwell Family History Group 3 Porcell Court, Cromwell, 9191
Fairlie Genealogy Group c/o 38 Gray Street, Fairlie , 8771
General Research Institute of New Zealand PO Box 12531, Thorndon, Wellington, 6038
Hawkes Bay Branch, NZ Society of Genealogists Inc.
 P O Box 7375, Taradale, Hawkes Bay,
Kapiti Branch, NZ Society of Genealogists Inc. P O Box 6, Paraparaumu, Kapiti Coast, 6450
Mercury Bay Branch, NZ Society of Genealogists Inc. 31 Catherine Cres., Whitianga, 2856 T: 0 7 866 2355
Morrinsville Branch, NZ Society of Genealogists Inc. 1 David St., Morrinsville, 2251
N.Z. Fencible Society P O Box 8415, Symonds Street, Auckland, 1003
New Zealand Family History Society Inc PO Box 13301, Armagh, Christchurch, E: ranz@extra.co.nz
New Zealand Society of Genealogists P O Box 8795, Symonds Street, Auckland, 1035 T: 09-525--0625 F: 09-525-0620 E: nzsg-contact@genealogy.org.nz W: www.genealogy.org.nz
Northern Wairoa Branch, NZ Society of Genealogists Inc. 60 Gordon Street, Dargaville, 300
NZ Society of Genealogists Inc. - Alexandra Branch 21 Gregg Street, Alexandra, 9181
Palmerston North Genealogy Group P O Box 1992, Palmerston North, 5301
Panmure Branch, NZ Society of Genealogists Inc. 29 Mirrabooka Ave, Howick, Auckland, 1705
Papakura Branch, NZ Society of Genealogists Inc. P O Box 993, Papakura, Auckland,
Polish Genealogical Society of New Zealand Box 88, Urenui, Taranaki, T: 06 754 4551 E: pgs.newzealand@clear.net.nz
Rotorua Branch, NZ Society of Genealogists Inc. 17 Sophia Street, Rotorua, 3201 T: 0 7 347 9122

Scottish Interest Group, NZ Society of Genealogists Inc. P O Box 8164, Symonds Street, Auckland, 1003
South Canterbury Branch, NZ Society of Genealogists Inc. 9 Burnett Street, Timaru, 8601
Tairua Branch, NZ Society of Genealogists Inc. c/o 10 Pepe Road, Tairua, 2853
Te Awamutu Branch, NZ Society of Genealogists Inc. Hairini, RD1, Te Awamutu, 2400
Te Puke Branch, NZ Society of Genealogists Inc. 20 Valley Road, Te Puke, 3071
The New Zealand Family History Society "P O Box13,301", Armagh, Christchurch, T: 03 352 4506 E: ranz@xtra.co.nz
Waimate Branch, NZ Society of Genealogists Inc. 4 Saul Shrives Place, Waimate, 8791
Wairarapa Branch, NZ Society of Genealogists Inc. 34 Rugby Street, Masterton, 5901
Whakatane Branch, NZ Society of Genealogists Inc. P O Box 203, Whakatane, 3080
Whangamata Genealogy Group 116 Hetherington Road, Whangamata, 3062
Whangarei Branch, NZ Society of Genealogists Inc. P O Box 758, Whangarei, 115 T: 09 434 6508

South Africa
Genealogical Institute of South Africa 115 Banheok Road, Stellenbosch, Western Cape T: 021-887-5070 E: GISA@RENET.SUN.AC.ZA
Genological Society of South Africa Suite 143, Postnet X2600, Houghton, 2041
Human Sciences Research Council Genealogy Information, HSRC Library & Information Service, Private Bag X41, Pretoria 0001, T: (012)-302-2636 F: (012)-302-2933 E: ig@legii.hsrc.ac.za
West Rand Family History Society The Secretary, PO Box 760, Florida 1710, W: www.geocities.com/Heartland/8256/westrand.html

Zimbabwe
Heraldry & Genealogy Society of Zimbabwe Harare Branch, 8 Renfrew Road, Eastlea, Harare

North America - Canada
Alberta
Alberta Family Histories Society 712-16 Avenue NW, Station B, Calgary, Alberta T2M 0J8 E: chairman@afhs.ab.ca W: www.afhs.ab.ca
Alberta Genealogical Society # 116, 10440-108 Avenue, Edmonton, Alberta T5H 3Z9 T: (403)-424-4429 F: (403)-423-8980 E: agsedm@compusmart.ab.ca W: www.abgensoc.ca/
Alberta Genealogical Society Drayton Valley Branch PO Box 6358, Drayton Valley, Alberta T7A 1R8 T: 403-542-2787 F: 403-542-2787 E: c_or_c@telusplanet.net
Alberta Genealogical Society Fort McMurray Branch PO Box 6253, Fort McMurray, Alberta T9H 4W1
Alberta Genealogical Society Grande Prairie & District Branch PO Box 1257, Grande Prairie, Alberta T8V 4Z1
Alberta Genealogical Society Medicine Hat & District Branch PO Box 971, Medicine Hat, Alberta T1A 7G8
Alberta Genealogical Society Red Deer & District Branch PO Box 922, Red Deer, Alberta T4N 5H3 E: evwes@telusplanet.net
Brooks & District Branch, Alberta Genealogical Society PO Box 1538, Brooks, Alberta T1R 1C4
Ukrainian Genealogical & Historical Society of Canada R.R.2, Cochrane, Alberta T0L 0W0 T: (403) 932 6811 F: (403) 932 6811
British Columbia
British Colombia Gen Soc PO Box 88054, Lansdowne, Richmond, British Columbia V6X 3T6 W: www.bcgs.ca
Campbell River Genealogy Club PO Box 884, Campbell River, British Columbia V9W 6Y4 E: rcase@connected.bc.ca W: www.connected.bc.ca/~genealogy/
Comox Valley Family History Research Group c/o Courtenay & District Museum & Archives, 360 Cliffe Street, Courtenay, British Columbia V9N 2H9
Kamloops Family History Society Box 1162, Kamloops, British Columbia V2C 6H3 E: drforeman@shaw.ca W: www.kfhs.org
Kelowna & District Genealogical Society PO Box 501, Station A, Kelowna, British Columbia V1Y 7P1 T: 1-250-763-7159 F: 1-250-763-7159 E: doug.ablett@bc.sympatico.ca
Nanaimo FHS PO Box 1027, Nanaimo, British Columbia V9R 5Z2
Port Alberni Genealogy Club Site 322, Comp. 6, R.R.3, Port Alberni, British Columbia V9Y 7L7
Powell River Genealogy Club PO Box 446, Powell River, British Columbia V8A 5C2
Prince George Genealogical Society PO Box 1056, Prince George, British Columbia V2L 4V2
Revelstoke Genealogy Group PO Box 2613, Revelstoke, British Columbia V0E 2S0
Shuswap Lake Genealogical Society R.R.1, Site 4, Com 4, Sorrento, British Columbia V0E 2W0
South Okanagan Genealogical Society c/o Museum, 785 Main Street, Penticton, British Columbia V2A 5E3

Vernon & District FHS PO Box 1447, Vernon BC V1T 6N7
Victoria Genealogical Society PO Box 43021, RPO Victoria North, Victoria BC V8X 3G2 E: www.islandnet.com/~vgs/homepage.html
Manitoba
Canadian Federation of Genealogical & Family History Societies 227 Parkville Bay, Winnipeg, Manitoba R2M 2J6 W: www.geocities.com/athens/troy/2274/index.html
East European Genealogical Society PO Box 2536, Winnipeg, Manitoba R3C 4A7
La Societe Historique de Saint Boniface 220 Ave de la Cathedral, Saint Boniface, Manitoba R2H 0H7
Manitoba Genealogical Society Unit A, 1045 St James Street, Winnipeg, Manitoba R3H 1BI
South West Branch of Manitoba Genealogical Society 53 Almond Crescent, Brandon, Manitoba R7B 1A2 T: 204-728-2857 F: 204-725-1719 E: mla@access.tkm.mb.ca
Winnipeg Branch of Manitoba Genealogical Society PO Box 1244, Winnipeg, Manitoba R3C 2Y4
New Brunswick
Centre d'Etudes Acadiennes Universite de Moncton, Moncton, New Brunswick E1A 3E9
New Brunswick Genealogical Society PO Box 3235, Station B, Fredericton, New Brunswick E3A 5G9
Newfoundland
Newfoundland & Labrador Genealogical Society Colonial Building, Military Road, St John's, Newfoundland A1C 2C9 E: nlgs@nf.sympatico.ca W: www3.nf.sympatico.ca/nlgs
Nova Scotia
Archelaus Smith Historical Society PO Box 291, Clarks Harbour, Nova Scotia B0W 1P0 E: timkins@atcon.com
Cape Breton Genealogical Society PO Box 53, Sydney, Nova Scotia B1P 6G9
Genealogical Association of Nova Scotia PO Box 641, Station Central, Halifax, Nova Scotia B3J 2T3
Queens County Historical Society PO Box 1078, Liverpool, Nova Scotia B0T 1K0
Shelburne County Genealogical Society PO Box 248 Town Hall, 168 Water Street, Shelburne, Nova Scotia B0T 1W0
Ontario
British Isles FHS of Greater Ottawa Box 38026, Ottawa, Ontario K2C 3Y7 E: queries@bifhsgo.ca W: www.bifhsgo.ca
Bruce & Grey Branch - Ontario Genealogical Society PO Box 66, Owen Sound, Ontario N4K 5P1
Bruce County Genealogical Society PO Box 1083, Port Elgin, Ontario N0H 2C0
Elgin County Branch Ontario Genealogical Society PO Box 20060, St Thomas, Ontario N5P 4H4
Essex County Branch Ontario Genealogical Society PO Box 2, Station A, Windsor, Ontario N9A 6J5
Haliburton Highlands Genealogy Group Box 834, Minden, Ontario K0M 2K0 T: (705) 286-3154 E: hhgroup@hotmail.com
Halton-Peel Branch Ontario Genealogical Society PO Box 70030, 2441 Lakeshore Road West, Oakville, Ontario L6L 6M9 E: jwatt@ica.net W: www.hhpl.on.c9/sigs/ogshp/ogshp.htm
Hamilton Branch Ontario Genealogical Society PO Box 904, LCD 1, Hamilton, Ontario L8N 3P6
Huron County Branch Ontario Genealogical Society PO Box 469, Goderich, Ontario N7A 4C7
Jewish Genealogical Society of Canada PO Box 446, Station A, Willowdale, Ontario M2N 5T1 E: henry_wellisch@tvo.org
Jewish Genealogical Society of Canada (Toronto) PO Box 91006, 2901 Bayview Avenue, Toronto, Ontario M2K 2Y6 E: info@jgstoronto.ca W: www.jgstoronto.ca
Kawartha Branch Ontario Genealogical Society PO Box 861, Peterborough, Ontario K9J 7AZ
Kent County Branch Ontario Genealogical Society PO Box 964, Chatham, Ontario N7M 5L3
Kingston Branch, Ontario Genealogical Society PO Box 1394, Kingston, Ontario K7L 5C6
Lambton County Branch Ontario Genealogical Society PO Box 2857, Sarnia, Ontario N7T 7W1
Lanark County Genealogical Society PO Box 512, Perth, Ontario K7H 3K4 E: gjbyron@magma.ca W: www.globalgenealogy.com/LCGs
Marilyn Adams Genealogical Research Centre PO Box 35, Ameliasburgh, Ontario K0K 1A0 T: 613-967-6291
Niagara Peninsula Branch Ontario Genealogical Society PO Box 2224, St Catharines, Ontario L2R 7R8
Nipissing District Branch Ontario Genealogical Society PO Box 93, North Bay, Ontario P1B 8G8
Nor-West Genealogy & History Society PO Box 35, Vermilion Bay, Ontario P0V 2V0 T: 807-227-5293
Norfolk County Branch Ontario Genealogical Society PO Box 145, Delhi, Ontario N4B 2W9 E: oxford.net/~mihaley/ogsnb/main.htm
Norwich & District Historical Society c/o Archives, R.R. #3, Norwich, Ontario N0J 1P0 T: (519)-863-3638
Ontario Genealogical Society Suite 102, 40 Orchard View Boulevard, Toronto, Ontario M4R 1B9 E: provoffice@ogs.on.ca W: www.ogs.on.ca

Ontario Genealogical Society (Toronto Branch) Box 518, Station K, Toronto, Ontario M4P 2G9 W: www.torontofamilyhistory.org
Ottawa Branch Ontario Genealogical Society PO Box 8346, Ottawa, Ontario K1G 3H8
Perth County Branch Ontario Genealogical Society PO Box 9, Stratford, Ontario N5A 6S8 T: 519-273-0399
Simcoe County Branch Ontario Genealogical Society PO Box 892, Barrie, Ontario L4M 4Y6
Sioux Lookout Genealogical Club PO Box 1561, Sioux Lookout, Ontario P8T 1C3
Societe Franco-Ontarienne DÕHistoire et de Genealogie C.P.720, succursale B, Ottawa, Ontario K1P 5P8
Stormont, Dundas & Glengarry Genealogical Society PO Box 1522, Cornwall, Ontario K6H 5V5
Sudbury District Branch Ontario Genealogical Society c/o Sudbury Public Library, 74 MacKenzie Street, Sudbury, Ontario P3C 4X8 T: (705)-674-9991 F: (705)-670-6574 E: fredie@isys.ca
Thunder Bay District Branch Ontario Genealogical Society PO Box 10373, Thunder Bay, Ontario P7B 6T8
Upper Ottawa Genealogical Group PO Box 972, Pembroke, Ontario K8A 7M5
Waterdown East Flamborough Heritage Society PO Box 1044, Waterdown, Ontario L0R 2H0 T: 905-689-4074
Waterloo-Wellington Branch Ontario Genealogical Society 153 Frederick Street, Ste 102, Kitchener, Ontario N2H 2M2 E: lestrome@library.uwaterloo.ca W: www.dos.iwaterloo.ca/~marj/genealogy/ww.html
West Elgin Genealogical & Historical Society 22552 Talbot Line, R.R.#3, Rodney, Ontario N0L 2C0
Whitby - Oshawa Branch Ontario Genealogical Society PO Box 174, Whitby, Ontario L1N 5S1
Quebec
Brome County Historical Society PO Box 690, 130 Lakeside, Knowlton, Quebec J0E 1V0 T: 450-243-6782
Federation Quebecoise des Societies de Genealogie C.P. 9454, Sainte Foy, Quebec G1V 4B8
Les Patriotes Inc 105 Prince, Sorel, Quebec J3P 4J9
Missisquoi Historical Society PO Box 186, Stanbridge East, Quebec J0J 2H0 T: (450)-248-3153 F: (450)-248-0420 E: sochm@globetrotter.com
Quebec Family History Society PO Box 1026, Postal Station, Pointe Claire, Quebec H9S 4H9 E: genealogy W: www.cam.org/~qfhs
Societ de Genealogie de la Maurice et des Bois Francs C.P. 901, Trois Rivieres, Quebec G9A 5K2
Societe d'Histoire d'Amos 222 1ere Avenue Est, Amos, Quebec J9T 1H3
Societe d'Histoire et d'Archeologie des Monts C.P. 1192, 675 Chemin du Roy, Sainte Anne des Monts, Quebec G0E 2G0
Societe d'Histoire et de Genealogie de Matane 145 Soucy, Matane, Quebec G4W 2E1
Societe d'Histoire et de Genealogie de Riviere du Loup 300 rue St Pierre, Riviere du Loup, Quebec G5R 3V3 T: (418)-867-4245 E: shgrd@icrdl.net W: www.icrdl.net/shgrdl/index.html
Societe d'Histoire et de Genealogie de Verdun 198 chemin de lÕAnce, Vaudreuil, Quebec J7V 8P3
Societe d'histoire et de genealogie du Centre-du-Quebec 34-A, rue Laurier est, Victoriaville, Quebec G6P 6P7 T: (819)-357-4029 F: (819)-357-9668 E: geneatique@netscape.net W: www.geneatique.qc.ca
Societe d'Histoire et de Genealogie Maria Chapdeleine 1024 Place des Copains, C.P. 201, Dolbeau, Quebec G8L 3N5
Societe d'Histoire et Genealogie de Salaberry de Valley Field 75 rue St Jean Baptiste, Valleyfield, Quebec J6T 1Z6
Societe de Conservation du Patrimoine de St Fracois de la Riviere du Sud C P 306, 534 Boul St Francois Ouest, St Francois, Quebec G0R 3A0
Societe de Genealogie de Drummondville 545 des Ecoles, Drummondville, Quebec J2B 8P3
Societe de Genealogie de Quebec C.P. 9066, Sainte Foy, Quebec G1V 4A8
Societe de Genealogie des Laurentides C.P. 131, 185 Rue Du Palais, St Jerome, Quebec J7Z 5T7 T: (450)-438-8158 W: www.societe-genalogie-laurentides.gc.ca
Societe de Genealogie et d'Histoire de Chetford Mines 671 boul. Smith Sud, Thetford Mines, Quebec G6G 1N1
Societe Genealogie d'Argenteuil 378 Principale, Lachute, Quebec J8H 1Y2
Societe Genealogique Canadienne-Francaise Case Postale 335, Place de Armes, Montreal, Quebec H2Y 2H1
Socictie de Genealogie de L'Outaouaid Inc C.P. 2025, Succ. ÛBÕ, Hull, Quebec J8X 3Z2
Saskatchewan
Battleford's Branch Saskatchewan Genealogical Society 8925 Gregory Drive, North Battleford, Saskatchewan S9A 2W6
Central Butte Branch Saskatchewan Genealogical Society P.O. Box 224, Central Butte, Saskatchewan S0H 0T0
Grasslands Branch Saskatchewan Genealogical Society P.O. Box 272, Mankota, Saskatchewan S0H 2W0 T: 306-264-5149
Grenfell Branch Saskatchewan Genealogical Society P.O. Box 61, Grenfell, Saskatchewan S0G 2B0 T: (306)-697-3176

Moose Jaw Branch Saskatchewan Genealogical Society 1037 Henry Street, Moose Jaw, Saskatchewan S6H 3H3
Pangman Branch Saskatchewan Genealogical Society P.O. Box 23, Pangman, Saskatchewan S0C 2C0
Radville Branch Saskatchewan Genealogical Society P.O. Box 27, Radville, Saskatchewan S0C 2G0
Regina Branch Saskatchewan Genealogical Society 95 Hammond Road, Regina, Saskatchewan S4R 3C8
Saskatchewan Genealogical Society 1870 Lorne Street, Regina, Saskatchewan S4P 3E1
South East Branch Saskatchewan Genealogical Society P.O. Box 460, Carnduff, Saskatchewan S0C 0S0
West Central Branch Saskatchewan Genealogical Society P.O. Box 1147, Eston, Saskatchewan S0L 1A0
Yorkton Branch Saskatchewan Genealogical Society 28 Dalewood Crescent, Yorkton, Saskatchewan S3N 2P7
Yukon
Dawson City Museum & Historical Society P.O. Box 303, Dawson City, Yukon Y0B 1G0 T: 867-993-5291 F: 867-993-5839 E: dcmuseum@yknet.yk.ca

EUROPE
AUSTRIA
Heraldisch-Genealogische Gesellschaft 'Adler'
Universitatsstrasse 6, Wien, A-1096, Austria
BELGIUM
Cercle de Genealogie Juive de Belgique
74 Avenue Stalingrad, Bruxelles, B-1000, Belgium T: 32 0 2 512 19 63 Fax: 32 0 513 48 59 E: mjb<d.dratwa@mjb-jmb.org>
Federation des Associations de Famille
Bruyeres Marion 10, Biez, B-1390, Belgium
Federation Genealogique et Heraldique de Belgique
Avenue Parmentier 117, Bruxelles, B-1150, Belgium
Office Genealogique et Heraldique de Belgique
Avenue C Thielemans 93, Brussels, B-1150, Belgium
CROATIA
Croatian Genealogical Society
2527 San Carlos Ave, San Carlos, CA, 94070, USA
CZECHOSLOVAKIA
Czechoslovak Genealogical Society International
PO Box 16225, St Paul, MN, 55116-0225, USA
DENMARK
Danish Soc. for Local History
Colbjornsensvej 8, Naerum, DK-2850, Denmark
Sammenslutningen af Slaegtshistoriske Foreninger
Klostermarker 13, Aalborg, DK-9000, Denmark E: ulla@silkeborg.bib.dk
Society for Danish Genealogy & Biography
Grysgardsvej 2, Copenhagen NV, DK-2400, Denmark W: www.genealogi.dk
ESTONIA
Estonia Genealogical Society
Sopruse puiestec 214-88, Tallin, EE-0034, Estland
FINLAND
Genealogiska Samfundet i Finland
Fredsgatan 15 B, Helsingfors, SF-00170, Finland
Helsingfors Slaktforskare R.F.
Dragonvagen 10, Helsingfors, FIN-00330, Finland
FRANCE
Amicale des Familles d'alliance Canadiennne-Francaise
BP10, Les Ormes, 86220, France
Amities Genealogiques Bordelaises 2 rue Paul Bert, Bordeaux, Aquitaine, 33000, France T: 05 5644 8199 Fax: 05 5644 8199
Assoc. Genealogique et Historique des Yvelines Nord
Hotel de Ville, Meulan, 78250, France
Association Catalane de Genealogie
BP 1024, Perpignan Cedex, Languedoc Rousillon, 66101, **Association de la Bourgeoisie Ancienne Francaise**
74 Avenue Kleber, Paris, 75116, France
Association Genealogique de la Charente
Archives Departementales, 24 avenue Gambetta, Angouleme, Poitou Charentes, 16000, France
Association Genealogique de l'Anjou
75 rue Bressigny, Angers, Pays de la Loire, 49100, France
Association Genealogique de l'Oise
BP 626, Compiegne Cedex, Picardie, 60206, France
Association Genealogique des Bouches-du-Rhone
BP 22, Marseilles Cedex, Provence Alpes Cote d'Azur, 1, **Association Genealogique des Hautes Alpes**
Archives Departementales, route de Rambaud, Gap, Provence Alpes Cote d'Azur, 5000, France
Association Genealogique du Pas de Calais
BP 471, Arras Cedex, Nord-Pas de Calais, 62028
Association Genealogique du Pays de Bray
BP 62, Serqueux, Normandie, 76440 Fax: 02 3509 8756
Association Genealogique du Var
BP 1022, Toulon Cedex, Provence Alpes Cote d'Azur, 83051
Association Genealogique Flandre-Hainaut
BP493, Valenciennes Cedex, Nord-Pas de Calais, 59321

Association Recherches Genealogiques Historique d'Auvergne
Maison des Consuls, Place Poly, Clermont Ferrand, Auvergne, 63100
Bibliotheque Genealogique
3 Rue de Turbigo, Paris, 75001, France T: 01 4233 5821
Brive-Genealogie Maison des Associations, 11 place J M Dauaier, Brive, Limousin, 19100, France
Centre de Recherches Genealogiques Flandre-Artois
BP 76, Bailleul, Nord-Pas de Calais, 59270, France
Centre d'Entraide Genealogique de France 3 Rue de Turbigo, Paris, 75001, France T: 33 4041 9909 Fax: 33 4041 9963 E: cegf@usa.net W: www.mygale.org/04cabrigol/cegf/
Centre Departemental d'Histoire des Familles 5 place Saint Leger, Guebwiller, Alsace, 68500, France E: cdhf@telmat-net.fr W: web.telemat-net-fr~cdhf
Centre Entraide Genealogique Franche Comte
35 rue du Polygone, Besancon, Franche Comte, 25000
Centre Genealogique de la Marne
BP 20, Chalons-en-Champagne, Champagne Ardennes, 51005
Centre Genealogique de Savoie
BP1727, Chambery Cedex, Rhone Alpes, 73017, France
Centre Genealogique de Touraine
BP 5951, Tours Cedex, Centre, 37059, France
Centre Genealogique des Cotes d'Armor3bis rue Bel Orient, Saint Brieuc, Bretagne, 22000, France Fax: 02 9662 8900
Centre Genealogique des Landes
Societe de Borda, 27 rue de Cazarde, Dax, Aquitaine, 40100
Centre Genealogique des Pyrenees Atlantique
BP 1115, Pau Cedex, Aquitaine, 64011, France
Centre Genealogique du Perche 9 rue Ville Close, Bellame, Normandie, 61130, France T: 02 3383 3789
Centre Genealogique du Sud Ouest Hotel des Societes Savantes, 1 Place Bardineau, Bordeaux, Aquitaine, 33000, France
Centre Genealogique et Heraldique des Ardennes
Hotel de Ville, Charleville Mezieres, Champagne Ardennes, 8000
Centre Genealogique Protestant
54 rue des Saints-Peres, Paris, 75007, France
Cercle de Genealogie du Calvados Archives Departementales, 61 route de Lion-sur-Mer, Caen, Normandie, 14000, France
Cercle de Genealogie et d'Heraldique de Seine et Marne
BP 113, Melun Cedex, 77002, France
Cercle de Genealogie Juive (Jewish)
14 rue St Lazare, Paris, 75009, France T: 01 4023 0490 Fax: 01 4023 0490 E: cgjgeniefr@aol.com
Cercle d'Etudes Genealogiques et Heraldique d'Ile-de-France
46 Route de Croissy, Le Vesinet, 78110, France
Cercle d'Histoire et Genealogique du Perigord
2 rue Roletrou, Perigueux, Aquitaine, 24000, France
Cercle Genealogique Bull
rue Jean Jaures, BP 53, Les-Clayes-sous-Bois, 78340,
Cercle Genealogique d'Alsace
Archives du Bas-Rhin, 5 rue Fischart, Strasbourg, Alsace, 67000
Cercle Genealogique d'Aunis et Saintonge c/o Mr Provost, 10 ave de Metz, La Rochelle, Poitou Charentes, 17000, France
Cercle Genealogique de la Manche
BP 410, Cherbourg Cedex, Normandie, 50104, France
Cercle Genealogique de la Meurthe et Moselle
4 rue Emile Gentil, Briey, Lorraine, 54150, France
Cercle Genealogique de la Region de Belfort
c/o F Werlen, 4 ave Charles de Gaulle, Valdoie, Franche Comte, 90300
Cercle Genealogique de l'Eure Archives Departementales, 2 rue de Verdun, Evreux Cedex, Normandie, 27025, France
Cercle Genealogique de Saintonge
8 rue Mauny, Saintes, Poitou Charentes, 17100, France
Cercle Genealogique de Vaucluse
Ecole Sixte Isnard, 31 ter Avenue de la Trillade, Avignon, Provence Alpes Cote d'Azur, 84000, France
Cercle Genealogique des Deux-Sevres
26 rue de la Blauderie, Niort, Poitou Charentes, 79000, **Cercle Genealogique des P.T.T.** BP33, Paris Cedex 15, 75721, France
Cercle Genealogique d'Ille-et-Vilaine
6 rue Frederic Mistral, Rennes, Bretagne, 35200 T: 02 9953 6363
Cercle Genealogique du C.E. de la Caisse d'Epargne Ile de France-Paris 19 rue du Louvre, Paris, 75001, France
Cercle Genealogique du Finistere Salle Municipale, rue du Commandant Tissot, Brest, Bretagne, 29000 Fax: 02 9843 0176 E: cgf@eurobretagne.fr W: www.karolus.org/membres/cgf.htm
Cercle Genealogique du Haut-Berry place Martin Luther King, Bourges, Centre, 18000 F: 02 4821 0483 E: cgh-b@wanadoo.fr
Cercle Genealogique du Languedoc 18 rue de la Tannerie, Toulouse, Languedoc Rousillon, 31400, France T: 05 6226 1530
Cercle Genealogique du Loir-et-Cher
11 rue du Bourg Neuf, Blois, Centre, 41000 T: 02 5456 0711
Cercle Genealogique d'Yvetot et du Pays de Caux
Pavillion des Fetes, Yvetot, Normandie, 76190, France
Cercle Genealogique et Historique du Lot et Garonne
13 rue Etienne Marcel, Villeneuve sur Lot, Aquitaine, 47340
Cercle Genealogique Poitevin
22bis rue Arsene Orillard, Poitiiers, Poitou Charentes, 86000

Cercle Genealogique Rouen Seine-Maritime
Archives Departementales, Cours Clemenceau, Normandie, 76101
Cercle Genealogique Saone-et-Loire
115 rue des Cordiers, Macon, Bourgogne, 71000, France
Cercle Genelogique Vendeen Bat.H, 307bis, Cite de la Vigne aux
Roses, La Roche-sur-Yon, Pays de la Loire, 85000, France
Cercle Genealogique Versailles et Yvelines Archives Departementales,
1 avenue de Paris, Versailles, 78000, France T: 01 3952 7239 Fax: 01
3952 7239
Cercle Genelogique du Rouergue Archives Departementales, 25 av
Victor Hugo, Rodez, Midi-Pyrenees, 12000, France
Club Genealogique Air France CE Air France Roissy Exploitation, BP
10201, Roissy CDG Cedex, 95703, France Fax: 01 4864 3220
Club Genealogique Group IBM France CE IBM St Jean de Braye-Ste
Marie, 50-56 ave Pierre Curie, St Jean de Braye Cedex, 45807, France
Confederation Internationale de Genealogie et d'Heraldique
Maison de la Genealogie, 3 rue Turbigo, Paris, F - 75001
Etudes Genealogique Drome-Ardeche
14 rue de la Manutention, Valence, Rhone Alpes, 26000
Federation Francaise de Genealogie 3 Rue de Turbigo, Paris, 75001,
France T: 01 4013 0088 F: 01 4013 0089 W: www.karolus.org
France-Louisuane/Franco-Americanie Commission Retrouvailles,
Centre CommercialeGatie, 80 avenue du Maine, Paris 75014 Fax: 01
4047 8321 W: www.noconnet.com:80/forms/cajunews.htm
Genealogie Algerie Maroc Tunisie Maison Marechal Alphonse, Juin
28 Av. de Tubingen, Aix en Provence, 13090, France
Genealogie Entraide Recherche en Cote d'Or
97 rue d'Estienne d'Orves, Clarmart, Bourgogne, 92140
Genealogie et Histoire de la Caraibe Pavillion 23, 12 avenue Charles
de Gaulle, Le Pecq, Overseas, 78230, France E: ghcaraibe@aol.com
W: //members.aol.com/ghcaraibe
Groupement Genealogique de la Region dy Nord
BP 62, Wambrechies, Nord-Pas de Calais, 59118, France
Groupement Genealogique du Havre et de Seine Maritime
BP 80, Le Havre Cedex, Normandie, 76050 T: 02 3522 7633
Institut Francophone de Genealogie et d'Histoire 5 rue de l'Aimable
Nanette, le Gabut, La Rochelle, Overseas, 17000 T: 05 4641 9032
Fax: 05 4641 9032
Institut Genealogique de Bourgogne 237 rue Vendome, BP 7076,
Lyon, Bourgogne, 69301
Loiret Genealogique BP 9, Orleans Cedex, Centre, 45016, France
Salon Genealogique de Vichy et du Centr48 Boulevard de Sichon,
Vichy, Auvergne, 3200, France W: www.genea.com
Section Genealogique de l'Assoc. Artistique-Banque de France
2 rue Chabanais, Paris, 75002, France
Societe Genealogique du Bas-Berr Maison des Associations, 30 Espace
Mendez France, Chateauroux, Centre, 36000, France
Societe Genealogique du Lyonnais
7 rue Major Martin, Lyon, Rhone Alpes, 69001, France
GERMANY
Arbeirkreis fur Familienforschung e.V Muhlentorturm,
Muhlentortplatz 2, Lubeck, Schleswig-Holstein, D - 23552, Germany
Bayerischer Landesverein fur Familienkunde Ludwigstrasse 14/1,
Munchen, Bayern, D - 80539 E: blf@rusch.m.shuttle.de W:
www.genealogy.com/gene/reg/BAY/BLF-d.html
Deutsche Zentalstelle fur Genealogie
Schongaver str. 1, Leipzig, D - 04329, Germany
Dusseldorfer Verein fur Familienkunde e.V Krummenweger Strasse
26, Ratingen, Nordrhein Westfalen, D - 40885, Germany
Herold - Verein fur Genealogie Heraldik und Reiwandte
Wissen-Scahaften Archiv Str. 12-14, Berlin, D -14195, Germany
Niedersachsischer Gesellschaft fur Familienkunde e.V Stadtarchiv,
Am Bokemahle 14 - 16, Hannover, Niedersachsen, D - 30171
Oldenburgische Gesellschaft fur Familienkunde
Lerigauweg 14, Oldenurg, Niedersachsen, D - 26131, Germany
Verein fur Familien-U. Wappenkunde in Wurttemberg und Baden
Postfach 105441, Stuttgart, Baden-Wuerttemberg, D - 70047, Germany
Westdeutsche Gesellschaft fur Familienkunde e.V Sitz Koln Unter
Gottes Gnaden 34, Koln-Widdersdorf, Nordrhein Westfalen, D - 50859,
Germany T: 49 221 50 48 88
Zentralstelle fur Personnen und Familiengeschichte
Birkenweg 13, Friedrichsdorf, D - 61381, Germany

GREECE
Heraldic-Genealogical Society of Greece
56 3rd Septemvriou Str., Athens, GR - 10433, Greece
HUNGARY
Historical Society of Hungary University of Eoetveos Lorand, Pesti
Barnabas utca 1, Budapest, H - 1052, Hungary T: 267 0966
ICELAND
The Genealogical Society
P O Box 829, Reykjavick, 121, Iceland Fax: 354 1 679840
ITALY
Ancetres Italien 3 Rue de Turbigo, Paris, 75001, France T: 01 4664
2722 W: //members.aol.com/geneaita/
NETHERLANDS
Centraal Bureau voor Genealogie P O Box 11755, The Hague, NL -
2502 AT T: 070 315 0500 F: 070 347 8394 W: www.cbg.nl
Koninklijk Nederlandsch Genootschap voor Geslacht-en
Wapen-KundeP O Box 85630, Den Haag, 2508 CH, Netherlands
Nederlandse Genealogische Vereniging Postbus 976, Amsterdam, NL
- 1000 AZ, Netherlands E: info@ngu.nl W: www.ngu.nl
Stichting 'Genealogisch Centrum Zeeland'
Wijnaardstraat, Goes, 4416DA T: 0113 232 895
The Caledonian Society
Zuiderweg 50, Noordwolde, NL 8391 KH T: 0561 431580
NORWAY
Norsk Slektshistorik Forening Sentrum Postboks 59, Oslo, N - 0101,
Norway T: 2242 2204 Fax: 2242 2204
POLAND
Polish Genealogical Society of America
984 N. Milwaukee Ave, Chicago, IL, 60622, USA
Polish Genealogical Society of New Zealand Box 88, Urenui,
Taranaki, New Zealand T: 06 754 4551 E:
pgs.newzealand@clear.net.nz
SLOVAKIA
Slovak GHS At Matica Slovenska Novomeskeho, 32, 036 52 Martin
SPAIN
Asociacion de Diplomados en Genealogia y Nobilaria
Alcala 20, 2 Piso, Madrid, 28014 T: 34 522 3822 Fax: 34 532 6674
Asociacion de Hidalgos a Fuerto de Espana
Aniceto Marinas 114, Madrid, 28008, Spain
Cercle Genealogic del Valles
Roca 29, 5 2, Sabadell, Barcelona, 8208, Spain
Circulo de Estudios Genealogicos Familiares
Prado 21, Ateneo de Madrid, Madrid, 28014, Spain
Instituto Aragones de Investigaciones Historiograficas
Madre Sacremento 33, 1', Zaragoza, 50004, Spain
Instituto de Estudios Heraldicos y Genealogicos de Extremadura
Lucio Cornelio Balbo 6, Caceres, 1004, Spain
Real Academia Matritense de Heraldica y Genealogia
Quintana 28, Madrid, 28008, Spain

Sociedad Toledana de Estudios Heraldicos y Genealogicos
Apartado de Correos No. 373, Toledo, Spain
Societat Catalona de Genealogia Heraldica Sigillografia Vexillologia
P O Box 2830, Barcelona, 8080, Spain
Societat Valenciana de Genealogia Heraldica Sigillografia
Vexillologia Les Tendes 22, Oliva, 46780, Spain
SWEDEN
Sveriges Slaktforskarforbund Box 30222, Stockholm, 104 25,
Sweden T: 08 695 0890 Fax: 08 695 0824 E: genealog@genealogi.se
SWITZERLAND
Genealogical & Heraldry Association of Zurich
Dammbodenstrasse 1, Volketswil, CH-8604, Switzerland
Swiss Genealogical Society Eggstr 46, Oberengstringen, CH 8102,
Switzerland W: www.eye.ch/swissgen/SGFF.html
Swiss Society for Jewish Genealogy
P O Box 876, Zurich, CH-8021, Switzerland
Zentralstelle fur Genealogie Vogelaustrasse 34, CH-8953, Switzerland
Fax: 44 1 742 20 84 E: aicher@eyekon.ch

Email and Internet or Web Addresses

Email and Web addresses shown in this book have been notified to us by the Organisation or
advertiser. Unlike a normal postal address these addresses are subject to frequent change. In
the case of businesses Email forwarding and Website transfer are usually provided by links to
the original address. This does not always happen and the only solution is to use the various
search engines available on the internet.

Local and History Societies

Association of Local History Tutors 47 Ramsbury Drive, Earley, Reading, RG6 7RT T: 0118 926 4729 E: ray.dils@lineone.net

Battlefields Trust 33 High Green, Brooke, Norwich, NR15 1HR T: 01508 558145 E: BattlefieldTrust@aol.com W: www.battlefieldstrust.com

Black and Asian Studies Association 28 Russell Square, London, WC1B 5DS T: (020) 7862 8844 E: marikas@sas.ac.uk

Brewery History Society Manor Side East, Mill Lane, Byfleet, West Byfleet, KT14 7RS E: membership@breweryhistory.com W: www.breweryhistory.com

British Association for Local History PO Box 6549, Somersal Herbert, Ashbourne, DE6 5WH T: 01283 585947 E: mail@balh.co.uk W: www.balh.co.uk

British Brick Society 19 Woodcroft Avenue, Stanmore, HA7 3PT T: 020 8954 4976 E: micksheila67@hotmail.com W: www.britishbricksoc.free-online.co.uk

British Deaf History Society 288 Bedfont Lane, Feltham, TW14 9NU E: bdhs@iconic.demon.co.uk

British Records Association c/o Finsbury Library, 245 St Johns Street, London, EC1V 4NB T: (020) 7833 0428 E: britrecassoc@hotmail.com W: www.hmc.gov.uk/bra

British Records Society Stone Barn Farm, Sutherland Road, Longsdon, ST9 9QD T: 01782 385446 E: carolyn@cs.keele.ac.uk britishrecordssociety@hotmail.com W: www.britishrecordssociety.org.uk

British Society for Sports History Dept of Sports & Science, John Moore's University, Byrom Street, Liverpool, L3 3AF

Chapels Society 25 Park Chase, Wembley, HA9 8EQ T: 020 8903 2198 E: agworth296@hotmail.com

Society of Cirplanologists 26 Roe Cross Green, Mottram, Hyde, SK14 6LP T: 01457 763485

Coble & Keelboat Society 19 Selwyn Avenue, Whitley Bay, NE25 9DH T: 0191 251 4412

Costume Society St Paul's House, 8 Warwick Road, London, EC4P 4BN W: www.costumesociety.org.uk

Cross & Cockade International - The First World War Aviation Historical Society 5 Cave Drive, Downend, Bristol, BS16 2TL W: www.crossandcockade.com

Current Archaeology 9 Nassington Road, London, NW3 2TX T: (020) 7435-7517 E: editor@archaeology.co.uk W: www.archaeology.co.uk

Ecclesiastical History Society 6 Gallows Hill, Saffron Walden CB11 4DA

English Place Name Society c/o School of English Studies, University of Nottingham, Nottingham, NG7 2RD T: 0115 951 5919 E: janet.rudkin@nottingham.ac.uk W: www.nottingham.ac.uk/english/

Family & Community Historical Society Woburn Lane, Aspley Suise, Milton Keynes, MK17 8JR W: www.fachrs.com

Heraldry Society PO Box 32, Maidenhead, SL6 3FD T: 0118-932-0210 E: heraldry-society@cwcom.net

Historical Association (Local History) 59A Kennington Park Road, London, SE11 4JH T: (020) 7735-3901 E: enquiry@history.org.uk W: www..history.org.uk

Historical Medical Equipment Society 8 Albion Mews, Apsley, HP3 9QZ E: hmes@antiageing.freeserve.co.uk

Hugenot Society of Great Britain & Ireland Hugenot Library University College, Gower Street, London, WC1E 6BT T: 020 7679 5199 E: s.massil@ucl.ac.uk W: (Library) www.ucl.ac.uk/ucl-info/divisions/library/huguenot.htm (Society) www.hugenotsociety.org.uk

Labour Heritage 18 Ridge Road, Mitcham, CR4 2EY

Local Population Studies Society 63 Barncliffe Crescent, Lodge Moor, Sheffield, S10 4DB

Local Population Studies Society 63 Barncliffe Crescent, Lodge Moor, Sheffield, S10 4DB

Local Studies Group of CILIP - Formerly the Library Association 25 Bromford Gardens, Edgbaston, Birmingham, B15 3XD T: 0121 454 0935 E: prthomaspdt@aol.com

Mercia Cinema Society 5 Arcadia Avenue, Chester le Street, DH3 3UH

Museum of the Royal Pharmaceutical Society Museum of the Royal Pharmaceutical Society, 1 Lambeth High Street, London, SE1 7JN T: (020) 7572 2210 E: museum@rpsgb.org W: www.rpsgb.org/museum

Parish Register Transcription Society 50 Silvester Road, Waterlooville, PO8 5TL E: mail@prtsoc.org.uk W: www.prtsoc.org.uk

Postal History Society 60 Tachbrook Street, London, SW1V 2NA T: (020) 7821-6399

Pub History Society 13 Grovewood, Sandycombe Road, Kew, Richmond, TW9 3NF T: (020) 8296-8794 E: sfowler@sfowler.force9.co.uk W: www.pubhistorysociety.co.uk

Royal Geographical Society (with IBG) 1 Kensington Gore, London, SW7 2AR T: 020 7291 3001 W: www.rgs.org

Royal Photographic Society Historical Group 7A Cotswold Road, Belmont, Sutton, SM2 5NG T: (020) 8643 2743

Royal Society 6 - 9 Carlton House Terrace, London, SW1Y 5AG T: 020 7451 2606 E: library@royalsoc.ac.uk W: www.royalsoc.ac.uk

Royal Society of Chemistry Library & Information Centre Burlington House, Piccadilly, London, W1J 0BA T: (020) 7440 3373 E: library@rsc.org W: www.rsc.org

Society for Nautical Research Stowell House, New Pond Hill, Cross in Hand, Heathfield, TN21 0LX

Society of Antiquaries Burlington House, Piccadilly, London, W1J 0BE T: (020) 7479 7080 E: admin@sal.org.uk W: www.sal.org.uk

Society of Jewellery Historians Department of Scientific Research, The British Museum, Great Russell Street, London, WC1B 3DG E: jewelleryhistorians@yahoo.co.uk

Tennyson Society Central Library, Free School Lane, Lincoln, LN2 1EZ T: 01522-552862 E: linnet@lincolnshire.gov.uk W: www.tennysonsociety.org.uk

The Garden History Society 70 Cowcross Street, London, EC1M 6EJ T: (020) 7608 2409 E: enquiries@gardenhistorysociety.org W: www.gardenhistorysociety.org

United Kingdom Reminiscence Network Age Exchange Reminiscence Centre, 11 Blackheath Village, London, SE3 9LA T: 020 8318 9105 E: age-exchange@lewisham.gov.uk

United Reformed Church History Society Westminster College, Madingley Road, Cambridge, CB3 0AA T: 01223-741300 (NOT Wednesdays)

University of London Extra-Mural Society For Genealogy and History of The Family 136 Lennard Road, Beckenham, BR3 1QT

Vernacular Architecture Group Ashley, Willows Green, Chelmsford, CM3 1QD T: 01245 361408 E: www.vag.org.uk

Veterinary History Society 608 Warwick Road, Solihull, B91 1AA

Victorian Revival - Discontinued 2005 Sugar Hill Farm, Knayton, Thirsk, YO7 4BP T: 01845 537827 E: pamelagoult@hotmail.com

Victorian Society 1 Priory Gardens, Bedford Park, London, W4 1TT T: (020) 8994 1019 E: admin@victorian-society.org.uk W: www.victorian-society.org.uk

Voluntary Action History Society National Centre for Volunteering, Regent's Wharf, 8 All Saints Street, London, N1 9RL T: (020) 7520 8900 E: instvolres.aol.com W: www.ivr.org.uk/vahs.htm

War Memorials Trust 4 Lower Belgrave Street, London, SW1W 0LA T: (020) 7259 0403 E: info@warmemorials.com W: www.warmemorials.com

War Research Society 27 Courtway Avenue, Birmingham, B14 4PP T: 0121 430 5348 E: battletour@aol.com W: www.battlefieldtours.com

Wesley Historical Society 34 Spiceland Road, Northfield, Birmingham, B31 1NJ T: 0121 475 4914 E: edgraham@tesco.net W: www.wesleyhistoricalsociety.org.uk

Bedfordshire

Ampthill & District Archaeological and Local History 14 Glebe Avenue, Flitwick, Bedford, MK45 1HS T: 01525 712778 E: petwood@waitrose.com W: www.museums.bedfordshire.gov.uk/localgroups/ampthill2/html

Ampthill & District Preservation Society Seventh House, 43 Park Hill, Ampthill, MK45 2LP

Ampthill History Forum 10 Mendham Way, Clophill, Bedford, MK45 4AL E: forum@ampthillhistory.co.uk W: www.ampthillhistory.co.uk

Bedfordshire Archaeological and Local History Society 7 Lely Close, Bedford, MK41 7LS T: 01234 365095 W: www.museums.bedfordshire.gov.uk/localgroups

Bedfordshire Historical Record Society 48 St Augustine's Road, Bedford, MK40 2ND T: 01234 309548 E: rsmart@ntlworld.com W: www.bedfordshirehrs.org.uk

Bedfordshire Local History Association 29 George Street, Maulden, Bedford, MK45 2DF T: 01525633029

Biggleswade History Society 6 Pine Close, Biggleswade, SG18 QEF

Caddington Local History Group 98 Mancroft Road, Caddington, Nr. Luton, LUL 4EN W: www.caddhist.moonfruit.com

Carlton & Chellington Historical Society 3 High Street, Carlton, MK43 7JX

Dunstable & District Local History Society 7 Castle Close, Totternhoe, Dunstable, LU6 1QJ T: 01525 221963

Dunstable Historic and Heritage Studies 184 West Street, Dunstable, LU6 1 NX T: 01582 609018

Harlington Heritage Trust 2 Shepherds Close, Harlington, Near Dunstable, LU5 6NR

Leighton-Linslade Heritage Display Society 25 Rothschild Road, Linslade, Leighton Buzzard, LU7 7SY

Luton & District Historical Society 22 Homerton Road, Luton, LU3 2UL T: 01582 584367

Social History of Learning Disability Research Group School of Health & Social Welfare, Open University, Milton Keynes, MK7 6AA

Toddington Historical Society 21 Elm Grove, Toddington, Dunstable, LU5 6BJ W: www.museums.bedfordshire.gov.uk/local/toddington.htm

Wrestlingworth History Society 18 Braggs Lane, Church Lane, Wrestlingworth, SG19 2ER

Berkshire

Berkshire Archaeology Research Group Wayfield, 20 Rances Lane, Wokingham, RG40 2LH W: www.berkshire-archaeology.info

Berkshire Industrial Archaeological Group 20 Auclum Close, Burghfield Common, Reading, RG7 DY

Berkshire Local History Association Department of History, University of Reading, Whiteknights, Reading, RG6 6AA E: secretary@blha.org.uk W: www.blha.org.uk

Berkshire Record Society Berkshire Record Office, 9 Coley Avenue, Reading, RG1 6AF T: 0118-901-5130 E: peter.durrant@reading.gov.uk

Blewbury Local History Group Spring Cottage, Church Road, Blewbury, Didcot, OX11 9PY T: 01235 850427

Bracknell & District Historical Society 16 Harcourt Road, Bracknell, RG12 7JD T: 01344 640341

Brimpton Parish Research Association Shortacre, Brimpton Common, Reading, RG7 4RY T: 0118 981 3649

Chiltern Heraldry Group Magpie Cottage, Pondwood Lane, Shottesbrooke, SL6 3SS T: 0118 934 3698

Cox Green LH Group 29 Bissley Drive, Maidenhead, SL6 3UX

Datchet Village Society Garden Flat, 3A Salisbury Road, Hove, BN3 3AB T: 01273 204330 E: janet@datchet.com W: www.datchet.com

Eton Wick History Group 47 Colenorton Crescent, Eton Wick, Windsor, SL4 6WW T: 01753 861674

Finchampstead History & Heritage Group 134 Kiln Ride, California, Wokingham, RG40 3PB T: 0118 973 3005

Friends of Reading Museums 15 Benyon Court, Bath Road, Reading, RG1 6HR T: 0118 958 0642

Friends of Wantage Vale & Downland Museum 19 Church Street, Wantage, OX12 8BL T: 01235 771447 W:

Goring & Streatley Local History Society 45 Springhill Road, Goring On Thames, Reading, RG8 OBY T: 01491 872625

Hare Hatch & Kiln Green Local History Group Shingleberry, Tag Lane, Hare Hatch, Twyford, RG10 9ST T: 0118 940 2157 E: richard.lloyd@wargrave.net

History of Reading Society 5 Wilmington Close, Woodley, Reading, RG5 4LR T: 0118 961 8559 E: peterrussell7@hotmail.com

Hungerford Historical Association Westbrook Farmhouse, Smitham Bridge Road, Hungerford, RG17 0QP T: 01488 682976 E: jaykay01@tiscali.co.uk W: www.hungerfordhistorical.org.uk

Maidenhead Archaeological & Historical Society 70 Lambourne Drive, Maidenhead, SL6 3HG T: 01628 672196

Middle Thames Archaeological & Historical Society 1 Saffron Close, Datchet, Slough, SL3 9DU T: 01753 543636

Mortimer Local History Group 19 Victoria Road, Mortimer, RG7 3SH T: 0118 933 2819

Newbury & District Field Club 4 Coombe Cottages, Coombe Road, Crompton, Newbury, RG20 6RG T: 01635 579076

Project Purley 4 Allison Gardens, Purley on Thames, RG8 8DF T: 0118 942 2485

Sandhurst Historical Society Beech Tree Cottage, Hancombe Road, Little Sandhurst, GU47 8NP T: 01344 777476 W: www.sandhurst-town.com/societies

Shinfield & District Local History Societies Long Meadow, Part Lane, Swallowfield, RG7 1TB

Swallowfield Local History Society Kimberley, Swallowfield, Reading, RG7 1QX T: 0118 988 3650

Thatcham Historical Society 72 Northfield Road, Thatcham, RG18 3ES T: 01635 864820 W: www.thatchamhistoricalsociety.org.uk

Twyford & Ruscombe Local History Society 26 Highfield Court, Waltham Road, Twyford, RG10 0AA T: 0118 934 0109

Wargrave Local History Society 6 East View Close, Wargrave, RG10 8BJ T: 0118 940 3121 E: peter.delaney2@btinternet.com W: www.wargrave.net/history

Windsor Local History Publications Group 256 Dedworth Road, Windsor, SL4 4JR T: 01753 864835 E: windlesora@hotmail.com

Wokingham History Group 39 Howard Road, Wokingham, RG40 2BX T: 0118 978 8519

Birmingham

Alvechurch Historical Society Bearhill House, Alvechurch, Birmingham, B48 7JX T: 0121 445 2222

Birmingham & District Local History Association 112 Brandwood Road, Kings Heath, Birmingham, B14 6BX T: 0121-444-7470

Birmingham Canal Navigation Society 37 Chestnut Close, Handsacre, Rugeley, WS15 4TH

Birmingham War Research Society 43 Norfolk Place, Kings Norton, Birmingham, B30 3LB T: 0121 459 9008

Small Heath Local History Society 381 St Benedicts Road, Small Heath, Birmingham, B10 9ND

Wythall History Society 64 Meadow Road, Wythall, Birmingham, B47 6EQ E: val@wythallhistory.co.uk W: www.wythallhistory.co.uk

Bristol

Alveston Local History Society 6 Hazel Gardens, Alveston, BS35 3RD T: 01454 43881 E: jc1932@alveston51.fsnet.co.uk

Avon Local History Association 4 Dalkeith Avenue, Kingswood, Bristol, BS15 1HH T: 0117 967 1362

Bristol & Avon Archaeological Society 3 Priory Avenue, Westbury on Trym, Bristol, BS9 4DA T: 0117 9620161 (evenings) W: http://www-digitalbristol.org/members/baas/

Bristol and Gloucestershire Archaeological Society Stonehatch, Oakridge Lynch, Stroud, GL6 7NR T: 01285 670460 E: john@loosleyj.freeserve.co.uk W: www.bgas.org.uk

Bristol Records Society Regional History Centre, Faculty of Humanities, University of the West of England, St Maththias Campus, Oldbury Court Road, Fishponds, Bristol, BS16 2JP T: 0117 344 4395 E: http://humanities.uwe.ac.uk/brs/index.htm

Congresbury History Group Venusmead, 36 Venus Street, Congresbury, Bristol, BS49 5EZ T: 01934 834780 E: rogerhards-venusmead@breathemail.net

Downend Local History Society 141 Overndale Road, Downend, Bristol, B516 2RN

The West of England Costume Society 4 Church Lane, Long Aston, Nr. Bristol, BS41 9LU T: 01275-543564

Whitchurch Local History Society 62 Nailsea Park, Nailsea, Bristol, B519 1BB

Yatton Local History Society 27 Henley Park, Yatton, Bristol, BS49 4JH T: 01934 832575

Buckinghamshire

Buckinghamshire Archaeological Society County Museum, Church Street, Aylesbury, HP20 2QP T: 01269 678114

Buckinghamshire Record Society Centre for Buckinghamshire Studies, County Hall, Aylesbury, HP20 1UU T: 01296 383013 E: archives@buckscc.gov.uk W: www.buckscc.gov.uk/archives/publications/brs.stm

Chesham Bois One-Place Study 70 Chestnut Lane, Amersham, HP6 6EH T: 01494 726103 E: cdjmills@hotmail.com

Chesham Society 54 Church Street, Chesham, HP5 IHY

Chess Valley Archaelogical & Historical Society 16 Chapmans Crescent, Chesham, NP5 2QU T: 01494 772914

Hedgerley Historical Society Broad Oaks, Parish Lane, Farnham Common, Slough, SL2 3JW T: 01753 645682 E: brendakenw@tiscali.co.uk

Pitstone and Ivinghoe Museum Society Vicarage Road, Pitstone, Leighton Buzzard, LU7 9EY T: 01296 668123 W: http://website.lineone.net/~pitstonemus

Princes Risborough Area Heritage Society Martin's Close, 11 Wycombe Road, Princes Risborough, HP27 0EE T: 01844 343004 E: sandymac@risboro35.freeserve.co.uk

Cambridgeshire

Cambridge Antiquarian Society PO Box 376, 96 Mill Lane, Impington, Cambridge, CB4 9HS T: 01223 502974 E: liz-allan@hotmail.com

Cambridge Group for History of Population and Social History Sir William Hardy Building, Downing Place, Cambridge, CB2 3EN T: 01223 333181 W: http://www-hpss.geog.cam.ac.uk

Cambridgeshire Archaeology Castle Court, Shire Hall, Cambridge, CB3 0AP T: 01223 717312 E: quentin.carroll@cambridgeshire.gov.uk W: http://edweb.camcnty.gov.uk/archaeology www.archaeology.freewire.co.uk

Cambridgeshire Local History Society 1A Archers Close, Swaffham Bulbeck, Cambridge, CB5 0NG

Cambridgeshire Records Society County Record Office, Shire Hall, Cambridge, CB3 0AP W: www.cambridgeshirehistory.com/societies/crs/index.html

Hemingfords Local History Society Royal Oak Corner, Hemingford Abbots, Huntingdon, PE28 9AE T: 01480 463430 E: hemlocs@hotmail.com

Houghton & Wyton Local History Society Church View, Chapel Lane, Houghton, Huntingdon, PE28 2AY T: 01480 469376 E: gerry.feake@one-name.org

Huntingdonshire Local History Society 2 Croftfield Road, Godmanchester, PE29 2ED T: 01480 411202

Sawston Village History Society 21 Westmoor Avenue, Sawston, Cambridge, CB2 4BU T: 01223 833475

Upwood & Raveley History Group The Old Post Office, 71-73 High Street, Upwood, Huntingdon, PE17 1QE

Cheshire

Altrincham History Society 10 Willoughby Close, Sale, M33 6PJ T: 0161 962 7658

Ashton & Sale History Society Tralawney House, 78 School Road, Sale, M33 7XB T: 0161 9692795

Bowdon History Society 5 Pinewood, Bowdon, Altrincham, WA14 3JQ T: 0161 928 8975

Cheshire Heraldry Society 24 Malvern Close, Congleton, CW12 4PD

Cheshire Local History Association Cheshire Record Office, Duke Street, Chester, CH1 1RL T: 01224 602559 E: chairman@cheshirehistory.org.uk W: www.cheshirehistory.org.uk

Chester Archaeological Society Grosvenor Museum, 27 Grosvenor Street, Chester, CH1 2DD T: 01244 402028 E: p.carrington@chestercc.gov.uk W: www.chesterarchaeolsoc.org.uk

Christleton Local History Group 25 Croft Close, Rowton, CH3 7QQ T: 01244 332410

Congleton History Society 45 Harvey Road, Congleton, CWI2 2DH T: 01260 278757 E: awill0909@aol.com

Department of History & Archaeology - University of Chester University of Chester, Dept of History & Archaeology, Parkgate Road, Chester, CH1 4BJ T: 01244 512160 E: history@chester.ac.uk W: www.chester.ac.uk/history

Disley Local History Society 5 Hilton Road, Disley, SK12 2JU T: 01663 763346 E: chgris.makepeace@talk21.com

Historic Society of Lancashire & Cheshire East Wing Flat, Arley Hall, Northwich, CW9 6NA T: 01565 777231

Lancashire & Cheshire Antiquarian Society 59 Malmesbury Road, Cheadle Hulme, SK8 7QL T: 0161 439 7202 E: morris.garratt@lineone.net W: www.lancashirehistory.co.uk www.cheshirehistory.org.uk

Lawton History Group 17 Brattswood Drive, Church Lawton, Stoke on Trent, ST7 3EJ T: 01270 873427 E: arthur@aburton83.freeserve.co.uk

Macclesfield Historical Society 42 Tytherington Drive, Macclesfield, SK10 2HJ T: 01625 420250

Northwich & District Heritage Society 13 Woodlands Road, Hartford, Northwich, CW8 1NS

Poynton Local History Society 6 Easby Close, Poynton, SK12 1YG

South Cheshire Family History Society incorporating S E Cheshire Local Studies Group PO Box 1990, Crewe, CW2 6FF W: www.scfhs.org.uk

Stockport Historical Society 59 Malmesbury Road, Cheadle Hulme, Stockport, SK8 7QL T: 0161 439 7202

Weaverham History Society Ashdown, Sandy Lane, Weaverham, Northwich, CW8 3PX T: 01606 852252 E: jg-davies@lineone.net

Wilmslow Historical Society 4 Campden Way, Handforth, Wilmslow, SK9 3JA T: 01625 529381

Cleveland

Cleveland & Teesside Local History Society 150 Oxford Road, Linthorpe, Middlesbrough, TS5 5EL

North-East England History Institute (NEEHI) Dept of History University of Durham, 43 North Bailey, Durham, DH1 3EX T: 0191-374-2004 E: m.a.mcallister@durham.ac.uk W: www.durham.ac.uk/neehi.history/homepage.htm

Cornwall

Bodmin Local History Group 1 Lanhydrock View, Bodmin, PL31 1BG

Cornwall Association of Local Historians St Clement's Cottage, Coldrinnick Bac, Duloe, Liskeard, PL14 4QF T: 01503 220947 E: anne@coldrinnick.freeserve.co.uk

Cornwall Family History Society 5 Victoria Square, Truro, TR1 2RS T: 01872 264044 E: secretary@cornwallfhs.com W: www.cornwallfhs.com

Lighthouse Society of Great Britain - Closed 2005

Royal Institution of Cornwall, Courtney Library & Cornish History Research Centre Royal Cornwall Museum, River Street, Truro, TR1 2SJ T: 01872 272205 W: www.cornwall-online.co.uk/genealogy

The Devon & Cornwall Record Society 7 The Close, Exeter, EX1 1EZ T: 01392 274727 (Ansaphone) W: www.cs.ncl.ac.uk/genuki/DEV/DCRS

County Durham

Architectural & Archaeological Society of Durham & Northumberland Broom Cottage, 29 Foundry Fielkds, Crook, DL15 9SY T: 01388 762620 E: belindaburke@aol.com

Darlington Railway Preservation Society Station Rd, Hopetown, Darlington, DL3 6ST T: 01325 483606

Durham County Local History Society 21 St Mary's Grove, Tudhoe Village, Spennymoor, DL16 6LR T: 01388 816209 E: johnbanham@tiscali.co.uk W: www.durhamweb.org.uk/dclhs

Durham Victoria County History Trust Redesdale, The Oval, North Crescent, Durham, DH1 4NE T: 0191 384 8305 W: www.durhampast.net

Elvet Local & Family History Groups 37 Hallgarth Street, Durham, DH1 3AT T: 0191-386-4098

Lanchester Local History Society 11 St Margaret's Drive, Tanfield Village, Stanley, DH9 9QW T: 01207-236634 E: jstl@supanet.com

Monkwearmouth Local History Group 75 Escallond Drive, Dalton Heights, Seaham, SR7 8JZ

North-East England History Institute (NEEHI) Department of History University of Durham, 43 North Bailey, Durham, DH1 3EX T: 0191-374-2004 E: m.a.mcallister@durham.ac.uk W: www.durham.ac.uk/neehi.history/homepage.htm

Southwick History and Preservation Society 8 St Georges Terrace, Roker, Sunderland, SR6 9LX T: 0191 567 2438 E: pamela2@freedomnames.co.uk W: www.southwickhistory.org.uk

St John Ambulance History Group 3 The Bower, Meadowside, Jarrow, NE32 4RS T: 0191 537 4252

Teesdale Heritage Group Wesley Terrace, Middleton in Teesdale, Barnard Castle, DL12 0Q T: 01833 641104

The 68th (or Durham) Regiment of Light Infantry Display Team 40 The Rowans, Orgill, Egremont, CA22 2HW T: 01946 820110 E: PhilMackie@aol.com W: www.68dli.com

The Derwentdale Local History Society 36 Roger Street, Blackhill, Consett, DH8 5SX

Tow Law History Society 27 Attleee Estate, Tow Law, DL13 4LG T: 01388-730056 W: www.historysociety.org.uk

Wheatley Hill History Club Broadmeadows, Durham Road, Wheatley Hill, DH6 3LJ T: 01429 820813 E: history.club2@btinternet.com W: www.wheatley-hill.org.uk

Cumbria

Ambleside Oral History Group 1 High Busk, Ambleside, LA22 0AW T: 01539 431070 E: history@amblesideonline.co.uk W: www.aoghistory.f9.co.uk

Appleby Archaeology Group Pear Tree Cottage, Kirkland Road, Skirwith, Penrith, CA10 1RL T: 01768 388318 E: martin@fellside-eden.freeserve.co.uk

Appleby In Westmorland Record Society Kingstone House, Battlebarrow, Appleby-In-Westmorland, CA16 6XT T: 017683 52282 E: barry.mckay@britishlibrary.net

Caldbeck & District Local History Society Whelpo House, Caldbeck, Wigton, CA7 8HQ T: 01697 478270

Cartmel Peninsula Local History Society Fairfield, Cartmel, Grange Over Sands, LA11 6PY T: 015395 36503

Cartmel Peninsula Local History Society 1 Barton House, Kents Bank Road, Grange-Over-Sands, LA11 7HD T: 01539 534814

Crosby Ravensworth Local History Society Brookside, Crosby Ravensworth, Penrith, CA10 3JP T: 01931 715324 E: david@riskd.freeserve.co.uk

Cumberland and Westmorland Antiquarian & Archaeological Society County Offices, Kendal, LA9 4RQ T: 01539 773431 E: info@cwaas.org.uk W: www.cwaas.org.uk

Cumbria Amenity Trust Mining History Society The Rise, Alston, CA9 3DB T: 01434 381903 W: www.catmhs.co.uk

Cumbria Industrial History Society Coomara, Carleton, Carlisle, CA4 0BU T: 01228 537379 E: gbrooksvet@tiscali.co.uk W: www.cumbria-industries.org.uk

Cumbria Local History Federation Oakwood, The Stripes, Cumwhinton, Carlisle, CA4 0AP

Cumbrian Railways Association Whin Rigg, 33 St Andrews Drive, Perton, Wolverhampton, WV6 7YL T: 01902 745472 W: www.cumbrian-rail.org

Dalton Local History Society 15 Kirkstone Crescent, Barrow in Furness, LA14 4ND T: 01229 823558 E: davidhsd@aol.com

Dudden Valley Local History Group Seathwaite Lodge, Dudden Valley, Broughton in Furness, LA20 6ED

Duddon Valley Local History Group High Cross Bungalow, Broughton in Furness, LA20 6ES T: 01229 716196

Friends of Cumbria Archives 42 Fairfield, Flookburgh, Grange over Sands, LA11 7NB T: 01539 558343 E: jc@baytsaiq.fsnet.co.uk W: www.focasonline.org.uk

Friends of The Helena Thompson Museum 24 Calva Brow, Workington, CA14 1DD T: 01900 603312

Holme & District Local History Society The Croft, Tanpits Lane, Burton, Carnforth, LA6 1HZ T: 01524 782121

Keswick Historical Society Windrush, Rogersfield, Keswick, CA12 4BN T: 01768 772771

Lorton and Derwent Fells Local History Society Beech Cottage, High Lorton, Cockermouth, CA13 9UQ T: 01900 85551 E: derekdenman@dsl.pipes.com W: www.derwentfells.com

Matterdale Historical and Archaeological Society The Knotts, Matterdale, Penrith, CA11 0LD T: 01768 482358

North Pennines Heritage Trust Nenthead Mines Heritage Centre, Nenthead, Alston, CA9 3PD T: 01434 382037 E: administration.office@virgin.net W: www.npht.com

Sedbergh & District History Society c/o 72 Main Street, Sedbergh, LA10 5AD T: 01539 620504 E: history@sedbergh.org.uk W: www.sedberghhistory.org

Shap Local History Society The Hermitage, Shap, Penrith, CA10 3LY T: 01931 716671 E: liz@amosshap.demon.co.uk

Solway History Society 9 Longthwaite Crescent, Wigton, CA7 9JN T: 01697 344257 E: s.l.thornhill@talk21.com

Staveley and District History Society Heather Cottage, Staveley, Kendal, LA8 9JE T: 01539 821194 E: Jpatdball@aol.com

Upper Eden History Society Copthorne, Brough Sowerby, Kirkby Stephen, CA17 4EG T: 01768 341007

Whitehaven Local History Society Cumbria Record Office & local Studies Library, Scotch Street, Whitehaven, CA28 7BJ T: 01946 852920 E: anne.dick@cumbriacc.gov.uk

Derbyshire

Allestree Local Studies Group 30 Kingsley Road, Allestree, Derby, DE22 2JH

Arkwright Society Cromford Mill, Mill Lane, Cromford, DE4 3RQ T: 01629 823256 E: info@cromfordmill.co.uk W: www.cromfordmill.co.uk

Chesterfield & District Local History Society Melbourne House, 130 Station Road, Bimington, Chesterfield, S43 1LU T: 01246 620266

Derbyshire Archaeological Society 2 The Watermeadows, Swarkestone, Derby, DE73 7FX T: 01332 704148 E: barbarafoster@talk21.com W: www.DerbyshireAS.org.uk

Derbyshire Local History Societies Network Derbyshire Record Office, Libraries & Heritage Dept, County Hall, Matlock, DE4 3AG T: 01629-580000-ext-3520-1 E: recordoffice@derbyshire.gov.uk W: www.derbyshire.gov.uk

Derbyshire Record Society 57 New Road, Wingerworth, Chesterfield, S42 6UJ T: 01246 231024 E: neapen@aol.com W: www.merton.dircon.co.uk/drshome.htm

Holymoorside and District History Society 12 Brook Close, Holymoorside, Chesterfield, S42 7HB T: 01246 566799 W: www.holymoorsidehistsoc.org.uk

Ilkeston & District Local History Society 16 Rigley Avenue, Ilkeston, DE7 5LW

New Mills Local History Society High Point, Cote Lane, Hayfield, High Peak, SK23 T: 01663 742814

Old Dronfield Society 2 Gosforth Close, Dronfield, S18 1NT

Pentrich Historical Society c/o The Village Hall, Main Road, Pentrich, DE5 3RE E: mail@pentrich.org.uk W: www.pentrich.org.uk

Devon

Chagford Local History Society Footaway, Westcott, Chagford, Newton Abbott, TQ13 8JF E: cjbaker@jetdash.freeserve.co.uk

Dulverton & District Civic Soc 39 jury Road, Dulverton, TA22 9EJ

Holbeton Yealmpton Brixton Society 32 Cherry Tree Drive, Brixton, Plymouth, PL8 2DD W: http://beehive.thisisplymouth.co.uk/hyb

Lashbrook One-Place Study 70 Chestnut Lane, Amersham, HP6 6EH T: 01494 726103 E: cdjmills@hotmail.com

Moretonhampstead History Society School House, Moreton, Hampstead, TQ13 8NX

Newton Tracey & District Local History Society Home Park, Lovacott , Newton Tracey, Barnstaple, EX31 3PY T: 01271 858451

Tavistock & District Local History Society 18 Heather Close, Tavistock, PL19 9QS T: 01822 615211 E: linagelliott@aol.com

The Devon & Cornwall Record Society 7 The Close, Exeter, EX1 1EZ T: 01392 274727 (Ansaphone) W: www.cs.ncl.ac.uk/genuki/DEV/DCRS

The Devon History Society c/o 112 Topsham Road, Exeter, EX2 4RW T: 01803 613336

The Old Plymouth Society 625 Budshead Road, Whitleigh, Plymouth, PL5 4DW

Thorverton & District History Society Ferndale, Thorverton, Exeter, EX5 5NG T: 01392 860932

Wembury Amenity Society 5 Cross Park Road, Wembury, Plymouth, PL9 0EU

Yelverton & District Local History Society 4 The Coach House, Grenofen, Tavistock, PL19 9ES W: www.floyds.org.uk/ylhs

Dorset

Bournemouth Local Studies Group 6 Sunningdale, Fairway Drive, Christchurch, BH23 1JY T: 01202 485903 E: mbhall@onetel.net.uk

Bridport History Society 22 Fox Close, Bradpole, Bridport, DT6 3JF T: 01308 456876 (Home)

Dorchester Association For Research into Local History 7 Stokehouse Street, Poundbury, Dorchester, DT1 3GP

Dorset Natural History & Archaeological Society Dorset County Museum, High West Street, Dorchester, DT1 1XA T: 01305 262735

Dorset Record Society Dorset County Museum, High West Street, Dorchester, DT1 1XA T: 01305-262735

Notes and Queries for Somerset and Dorset Marston House, Marston Bigot, Frome, BA11 5DU

Verwood Historical Society 74 Lake Road, Verwood, BH31 6BX T: 01202 824175 E: trevorgilbert@hotmail.com W: www.geocities.com/verwood_historical

William Barnes Society Pippins, 58 Mellstock Avenue, Dorchester, DT1 2BQ T: 01305 265358

Essex

Barking & District Historical Society 449 Ripple Road, Barking, IG11 9RB T: 020 8594 7381 E: barkinghistorical@hotmail.com

Barking & District Historical Society c/o 16 North Road, Chadwell Heath, Romford, RM6 6XU E: barkinghistorical@hotmail.com

Billericay Archaeological and Historical Society 24 Belgrave Road, Billericay, CM12 1TX T: 01277 658989

Brentwood & District Historical Society 51 Hartswood Road, Brentwood, CM14 5AG T: 01277 221637

Burnham & District Local History & Archaeological Society The Museum, The Quay, Burnham on Crouch, CM0 8AS

Chadwell Heath Historical Society Wangley Road Chapel, Wangley Road, Chadwell Heath, Romford, RM6 4BW E: chadwellheathhs@hotmail.com

Colchester Archaeological Group 172 Lexden Road, Colchester, CO3 4BZ T: 01206 575081 W: www.camulos.com//cag/cag.htm

Dunmow & District Historical and Literary Society 18 The Poplars, Great Dunmow, CM6 2JA T: 01371 872496

Essex Archaeological & Historical Congress Roseleigh, Epping Road, Epping, CM16 5HW T: 01992 813725 E: pmd2@ukonline.co.uk

Essex Historic Buildings Group 12 Westfield Avenue, Chelmsford, CM1 1SF T: 01245 256102 E: cakemp@hotmail.com

Essex Society for Archeaology & History 2 Landview Gardens, Ongar, CM5 9EQ T: 01277363106 E: family@leachies.freeserve.co.uk

Friends of Historic Essex 11 Milligans Chase, Galleywood, Chelmsford, CM2 8QD T: 01245 436043 E: geraldine.willden2@essexcc.gov.uk

Friends of The Hospital Chapel - Ilford 174 Aldborough Road South, Seven Kings, Ilford, IG3 8HF T: (020) 8590 9972

Friends of Thomas Plume's Library The Old Vicarage, Great Totham, Maldon, CM9 8NP T: 01621 892261

Halstead & District Local History Society Magnolia, 3 Monklands Court, Halstead, CO9 1AB

(HEARS) Herts & Essex Architectural Research Society 4 Nelmes Way, Hornchurch, RM11 2QZ T: 01708 473646 E: kath@nelmes.eclipse.co.uk

High Country History Group Repentance Cottage, Drapers Corner, Greensted, Ongar, CM5 9LS T: 01277 364305 E: rob.brooks@virgin.net

Ingatestone and Fryerning Historical and Archaeological Society 36 Pine Close, Ingatestone, CM4 9EG T: 01277 354001

Loughton & District Historical Society 6 High Gables, Loughton, IG10 4EZ T: (020) 8508 4974

Maldon Society 15 Regency Court, Heybridge, Maldon, CM9 4EJ

Nazeing History Workshop 16 Shooters Drive, Nazeing, EN9 2QD T: 01992 893264 E: d_pracy@hotmail.com W: www.eppingforestmuseum.org.uk/soc_page.php?username=nazeing_history_workshop&page=2

Newham History Society 52 Eastbourne Road, East Ham, London, E6 6AT T: (020) 8471 1171 W: www.pewsey.net/newhamhistory.htm

Romford & District Historical Society 67 Gelsthorpe Road, Collier Row, Rainham, RM13 9HP T: 01708 520673 E: jackie@arctic.eclipse.co.uk W: www.romford.org/histsoc.htm

Saffron Walden Historical Society 9 High Street, Saffron Walden, CB10 1AT

The Colne Smack Preservation Society 76 New Street, Brightlingsea, CO7 0DD T: 01206 304768 W: www.colne-smack-preservation.rest.org.uk

Thurrock Heritage Forum c/o Thurrock Museum, Orsett Road, Grays, RM17 5DX T: 01375 673828 E: enquiries@thurrockheritageforum.co.uk W: www.thurrockheritageforum.co.uk

Thurrock Local History Society 13 Rosedale Road, Little Thurrock, Grays, RM17 6AD T: 01375 377746 E: tcvs.tc@gtnet.gov.uk

Waltham Abbey Historical Society 28 Hanover Court, Quaker Lane, Waltham Abbey, EN9 1HR T: 01992 716830

Walthamstow Historical Society 24 Nesta Road, Woodford Green, IG8 9RG T: (020) 8504 4156

Wanstead Historical Society 28 Howard Road, Ilford, IG1 2EX

Westcliff High School for Girls Society Kenilworth Gardens, Westcliff on Sea, SS0 0BS

Witham History Group 35 The Avenue, Witham, CM8 2DN T: 01376 512566

Woodford Historical Society 2 Glen Rise, Woodford Green, IG8 0AW

Gloucestershire

Alveston Local History Society 6 Hazel Gardens, Alveston, BS35 3RD T: 01454 43881 E: jc1932@alveston51.fsnet.co.uk

Bristol and Gloucestershire Archaeological Society Stonehatch, Oakridge Lynch, Stroud, GL6 7NR T: 01285 670460 E: john@loosleyj.freeserve.co.uk W: www.bgas.org.uk

Campden & District Historical & Archaeological Society (CADWAS) The Old Police Station, High Street, Chipping Campden, GL55 6HB T: 01386 848840 E: enquiries@chippingcampdenhistory.org.uk W: www.chippingcampdenhistory.org.uk

Charlton Kings Local History Society 28 Chase Avenue, Charlton Kings, Cheltenham, GL52 6YU T: 01242 520492

Cheltenham Local History Society 1 Turkdean Road, Cheltenham, GL51 6AP

Cirencester Archaeological and Historical Society 8 Tower Street, Cirencester, GL7 1EF E: dviner@waitrose.com

Forest of Dean Local History Society Patch Cottage, Oldcroft Green, Lydney, GL15 4NL T: 01594 563165 W: www.forestofdeanhistory.co.uk

Frenchay Tuckett Society and Local History Museum 247 Frenchay Park Road, Frenchay, BS16 ILG T: 0117 956 9324 E: raybulmer@compuserve.com W: www.frenchay.org/museum.html

Friends of Gloucestershire Archives 17 Estcourt Road, Gloucester, GL13LU T: 01452 528930 E: patricia.bath@talk21.com

Gloucestershire County Local History Committee Gloucestershire RCC, Community House, 15 College Green, Gloucester, GL1 2LZ T: 01452 528491 E: glosrcc@grcc.org.uk

Lechlade History Society The Gables, High Street, Lechlade, GL7 3AD T: 01367 252457 E: Gillkeithnewson.aol.com

Leckhampton Local History Society 202 Leckhampton Road, Leckhampton, Cheltenham, GL53 OHG W: www.geocities.com/llhsgl53

Marshfield & District Local History Society Weir Cottage, Weir Lane, Marshfield, Chippenham, SN14 8NB T: 01225 891229 E: weircott@luna.co.uk

Moreton-In-Marsh & District Local History Society Chapel Place, Longborough, Moreton in Marsh, GL56 OQR T: 01451 830531 W: www.moretonhistory.co.uk

Newent Local History Society Arron, Ross Road, Newent, GL18 1BE T: 01531 821398

Painswick Local History Society Canton House, New Street, Painswick, GL6 6XH T: 01452 812419

Stroud Civic Society Blakeford House, Broad Street, Kings Stanley, Stonehouse, GL10 3PN T: 01453 822498

Stroud Local History Society 16 Barrowfield Road, Farmhill, Stroud, GL5 4DF T: 01453 766764 E: john@loosleyj.freeserve.co.uk

Swindon Village Society 3 Swindon Hall, Swindon Village, Cheltenham, GL51 9QR T: 01242 521723

Tewkesbury Historical Society 20 Moulder Road, Tewkesbury, GL20 8ED T: 01684 297871

The Waterways Trust The National Waterways Museum, Llanthony Warehouse, Gloucester Docks, Gloucester, GL1 2EH T: 01452 318053 E: info@nwm.org.uk W: www.nwm.org.uk

Hampshire

Aldershot Historical and Archaeological Society 10 Brockenhurst Road, Aldershot, GU11 3HH T: 01252 26589

Andover History and Archaeology Society 140 Weyhill Road, Andover, SPlO 3BG T: 01264 324926 E: johnl.barrell@virgin.net

Basingstoke Archaeological and Historical Society 57 Belvedere Gardens, Chineham, Basingstoke, RG21 T: 01256 356012

Bitterne Local History Society Heritage Centre, 225 Peartree Avenue, Bitterne, Southampton, T: 023 8049 0948 W: www.bitterne.net

Botley & Curdridge Local History 3 Mayfair Court, Botley, SO30 2GT

Fareham Local History Group Wood End Lodge, Wood End, Wickham, Fareham, PO17 6JZ W: www.cix.co.uk/~catisfield/farehist.htm

Farnham and District Museum Society Tanyard House, 13a Bridge Square, Farnham, GU9 7QR

Fleet & Crookham Local History Group 33 Knoll Road, Fleet, GU51 4PT W: www.hants.gov.uk/fclhg

Fordingbridge Historical Society 26 Lyster Road,, Manor Park, Fordingbridge, SP6 IQY T: 01425 655417

Hampshire Archives Trust 3 Scott-Paine Drive, Hythe, S045 6JY

Hampshire Field Club & Archaelogical Society (Local History Section) c/o Hampshire Record Office, Sussex Street, Winchester, SO23 8TH

Hampshire Field Club and Archaeological Society 8 Lynch Hill Park, Whitchurch, RG28 7NF T: 01256 893241 E: jhamdeveson@compuserve.com W: www.fieldclub.hants.org.uk/

Lymington & District Historical Society Larks Lees, Coxhill Boldre, Near Lymington, S041 8PS T: 01590 623933 E: birchsj@clara.co.uk

Lyndhurst Historical Society - disbanded May 2003

Milford-on-Sea Historical Record Society New House, New Road, Keyhaven, Lymington, S041 0TN

Newbury & District Field Club 4 Coombe Cottages, Coombe Road, Crompton, Newbury, RG20 6RG T: 01635 579076

North East Hampshire Historical and Archaeological Society 36 High View Road, Farnborough, GU14 7PT T: 01252-543023 E: nehhas@netscape.net W: www.hants.org.uk/nehhas

Porchester Society Mount Cottage, Nelson Lane, Portchester, PO17 6AW

Somborne & District Society Forge House, Winchester Road, Kings Somborne, Stockbridge, S020 6NY T: 01794 388742 E: w.hartley@ntlworld.com W: www.communigate.co.uk/hants/somsoc

South of England Costume Society Bramley Cottage, 9 Vicarage Hill, Hartley Witney, Hook, RG27 8EH E: j.sanders@lineone.net

Southampton Local History Forum Special Collections Library, Civic Centre, Southampton, SO14 7LW T: 023 8083 2462 E: local.studies@southampton.gov.uk

Stubbington & Hillhead History Society 34 Anker Lane, Stubbington, Fareham, PO14 3HE T: 01329 664554

Tadley and District History Society (TADS) PO Box 7642, Tadley, RG26 3AF T: 0118 981 4006 W: www.tadhistorey.com

West End Local History Society 20 Orchards Way, West End, Southampton, S030 3FB T: 023 8057 5244 E: westendlhs@aol.com W: www.telbin.demon.co.uk/westendlhs

Herefordshire

Eardisland Oral History Group Eardisland, Leominster, HR

Ewyas Harold & District WEA c/o Hillside, Ewyas Harold, Hereford, HR2 0HA T: 01981 240529

Kington History Society Kington Library, 64 Bridge Street, Kington, HR5 3BD T: 01544 230427 E: vee.harrison@virgin.net

Leominster Historical Society Fircroft, Hereford Road, Leominster, HR6 8JU T: 01568 612874

Weobley & District Local History Society and Museum Weobley Museum, Back Lane, Weobley, HR4 8SG T: 01544 340292

Hertfordshire

Abbots Langley Local History Society 19 High Street, Abbots Langley, WD5 0AA E: info@allhs.org.uk W: www.allhs.org.uk

Abbots Langley LH Soc 159 Cottonmill Lane, St Albans, AL1 2EX

Baptist Historical Society 60 Strathmore Avenue, Hitchin, SG5 1ST T: 01462-431816 E: slcopson@dial.pipex.com W: www.baptisthistory.org.uk

Barnet & District Local History Society 31 Wood Street, Barnet, EN4 9PA

Black Sheep Research 4 Quills, Letchworth Garden City, SG6 2RJ T: 01462 483706 E: J-M-Chambers@compuserve.com W: http://ourworld.compuserve.com/homepages/Jill_M_Chambers

Braughing LH Society Pantiles, Braughing Friars, Ware, SG11 2NS

Codicote Local History Society 34 Harkness Way, Hitchin, SG4 0QL T: 01462 622953

East Herts Archaeological Society 1 Marsh Lane, Stanstead Abbots, Ware, SG12 8HH T: 01920 870664

Family History and Army Research 39 Chatterton, Letchworth, SG6 2JY T: 01462 670918 E: BJCham2809@aol.com W: http://members.aol.com/BJCham2909/homepage.html

(HEARS) Herts & Essex Architectural Research Society 4 Nelmes Way, Hornchurch, RM11 2QZ T: 01708 473646 E: kath@nelmes.eclipse.co.uk

Hertford & Ware Local History Society 10 Hawthorn Close, Hertford, SG14 2DT

Hertford Museum (Hertfordshire Regiment) 18 Bull Plain, Hertford, SG14 1DT T: 01992 582686 W: www.hertfordmuseum.org

Hertfordshire Archaeological Trust The Seed Warehouse, Maidenhead Yard, The Wash, Hertford, SG14 1PX T: 01992 558 170 E: herts.archtrust@virgin.net W: www.hertfordshire-archaeological-trust.co.uk

Hertfordshire Association for Local History 19 Cringle Court, Thornton Road, Little Heath, EN6 1JR T: 01727 856250 E: john@brookmans79.fsnet.co.uk

Hertfordshire Record Society 119 Winton Drive, Croxley Green, Rickmansworth, WD3 3QS T: 01923-248581 E: info@hrsociety.org.uk W: www.hrsociety.org.uk

Hitchin Historical Society c/o Hitchin Museum, Paynes Park, Hitchin, SG5 2EQ

Kings Langley Local History & Museum Society Kings Langley Library, The Nap, Kings Langley, WD4 8ET T: 01923 263205 W: www.kingslangley.org.uk

London Colney Local History Society 6 Telford Road, London Colney, St Albans, AL2 1PQ

North Mymms Local History Society 89 Peplins Way, Brookmans Park, Hatfield, AL9 7UT T: 01707 655970 W: www.brookmans.com

Potters Bar and District Historical Society 9 Hill Rise, Potters Bar, EN6 2RX T: 01707 657586 E: johnscrivyer@aol.com

Rickmansworth Historical Society 20 West Way, Rickmansworth, WD3 7EN T: 01923 774998 E: geoff@gmsaul.freeserve.co.uk

Royston & District Local History Society 8 Chilcourt, Royston, SG8 9DD T: 01763 242677 E: david.allard@ntlworld.com W: www.royston.clara.net/localhistory

South West Hertfordshire Archaeological and Historical Society 29 Horseshoe Lane, Garston, Watford, WD25 0LN T: 01923 672482

St. Albans & Herts Architectural & Archaeological Society 24 Rose Walk, St Albans, AL4 9AF T: 01727 853204

The Berkhamsted Local History and Museum Society Rhenigidale, Ivy House Lane, Berkhamsted, HP4 2PP T: 01442 865 158 W: www.rollitt.co.uk/index_files/Programme.htm

The Dacorum Heritage Trust Ltd The Museum Store, Clarence Road, Berkhamsted, HP4 3YL T: 01442 879525

The Harpenden & District Local History Society The History Centre, 19 Arden Grove, Harpenden, AL5 4SJ T: 01582 713539

Watford and District Industrial History Society 79 Kingswood Road, Garston, Watford, WD25 0EF T: 01923 673253

Welwyn & District Local History Society 40 Hawbush Rise, Welwyn, AL6 9PP T: 01438 716415 E: p.jiggens-keen@virgin.net W: www.welwynhistory.org

Welwyn Archaeological Society The Old Rectory, 23 Mill Lane, Welwyn, AL6 9EU T: 01438 715300 E: tony.rook@virgin.net

Yorkshire Quaker Heritage Project Brynmore Jones Library, University of Hull, Hull, HU6 7RX

Isle of Wight

Isle of Wight Natural History & Archaeological Society Salisbury Gardens, Dudley Road, Ventnor, PO38 1EJ T: 01983 855385

Newchurch Parish Register Society 1 Mount Pleasant, Newport Road, Sandown, PO36 OLS

St Helens Historical Society Gloddaeth, Westfield Road, St. Helens, Ryde , PO33 LUZ

St. Helens History Society c/o The Castle, Duver Road, St Helens, Ryde, PO33 1XY T: 01983 872164

Kent

Anglo-Zulu War Historical Society Woodbury House, Woodchurch Road, Tenterden, TN30 7AE T: 01580-764189 W: www.web-marketing.co.uk/anglozuluwar

Appledore Local History Society 72 The Street, Appledore, Ashford, TN26 2AE T: 01233 758500 E: trothfw@aol.com

Ashford Archaeological and Historical Society Gablehook Farm, Bethersden, Ashford, TN26 3BQ T: 01233 820679

Aylesford Society 30 The Avenue, Greenacres, Aylesford, Maidstone, ME20 7LE

Bearsted & District Local History Society 17 Mount Lane, Bearsted, Maidstone, ME14 4DD

Bexley Civic Society 58 Palmeira Road, Bexleyheath, DA7 4UX

Bexley Historical Society 36 Cowper Close, Welling, DAI6 2JT

Biddenden Local History Society Willow Cottage, Smarden Road, Biddenden, Ashford, TN27 8JT

Brenchley & Matfield Local History Society Ashendene, Tong Road, Brenchley, Tonbridge, TN12 7HT T: 01892 723476

Bridge & District History Society La Dacha, Patrixbourne Road, Bridge, Canterbury, CT4 5BL

Broadstairs Society Roof Tops, 58 High Street, Broadstairs, CT10 1JT T: 01843 863453

Bromley Borough Local History Society 62 Harvest Bank Road, West Wickham, BR4 9DJ T: 020 8462 5002

Canterbury Archaeology Society Dane Court, Adisham, Canterbury, CT3 3LA E: jeancrane@tiscali.co.uk

Charing & District Local History Society Old School House, Charing, Ashford, TN27 OLS

Chatham Historical Society 69 Ballens Road, Walderslade, Chatham, ME5 8NX T: 01634 865176

Council for Kentish Archaeology 14 Florence House, Royal Hebbert Pavilion, Gilbert Close, London, SE18 4PP E: information@the-cka.fsnet.co.uk W: www.the-cka.fsnet.co.uk

Cranbrook & District History Society 61 Wheatfield Way, Cranbrook, TN17 3NE

Crayford Manor House Historical and Archaeological Society 17 Swanton Road, Erith, DA8 1LP T: 01322 433480

Croydon Natural History & Scientific Society Ltd 96a Brighton Road, South Croydon, CR2 6AD T: (020) 8688 4539 W: www.grieg51.freeserve.co.uk/cnhss

Dartford History & Antiquarian Society 14 Devonshire Avenue, Dartford, DA1 3DW

Deal & Walmer Local History Society 7 Northcote Road, Deal, CT14 7BZ

Detling Society. 19 Hockers Lane, Detling, Maidstone, ME14 3JL T: 01622 737940 E: johnowne@springfield19.freeserve.co.uk

Dover History Society 2 Courtland Drive, Kearsney, Dover, CT16 3BX T: 01304 824764

East Peckham Historical Society 13 Fell Mead, East Peckham, Tonbridge, TNI2 5EG

Edenbridge & District History Society 17 Grange Close, Edenbridge, TN8 5LT

Erith & Belvedere Local History Society 67 Merewood Road, Barnehurst, DA7 6PF

Farningham & Eynsford Local History Society Lavender Hill, Beesfield Lane, Farningham, Dartford, DA4 ODA

Faversham Society 10-13 Preston St, Faversham, ME13 8NS T: 01795 534542 E: fleurmuseum@tiscali.co.uk W: www.faversham.org

Fawkham & District Historical Society The Old Rectory, Valley Road, Fawkham, Longfield, DA3 8LX

Folkestone & District Local History Society 7 Shorncliffe Crescent, Folkestone,

Friends of Lydd 106 Littlestone Road, New Romney, TN28 8NH

Frittenden History Society Bobbyns, The Street, Frittenden, Cranbrook, TN17 2DG T: 01580 852459

Gillingham & Rainham Local History Society 23 Sunningdale Road, Rainham, Gillingham, ME8 9EQ

Goudhurst & Kilndown Local History Society 2 Weavers Cottages, Church Road, Goudhurst, TN17 1BL

Gravesend Historical Society 58 Vicarage Lane, Chalk, Gravesend, DA12 4TE T: 01474 363998 W: www.ghs.org.uk

Great Chart Society Swan Lodge, The Street, Great Chart, Ashford, TN23 3AH

Hadlow Historical Society Spring House, Tonbridge Road, Hadlow, Tonbridge, TN11 0DZ T: 01732 850214 E: billanne@hadlow12.freeserve.co.uk

Halling Local History Society 58 Ladywood Road, Cuxton, Rochester, ME2 1EP T: 01634 716139

Hawkhurst Local History Society 17 Oakfield, Hawkhurst, Cranbrook, TN18 4JR T: 01580 752376

Headcorn Local History Society Cecil Way, 2 Forge Lane, Headcorn, TN27 9QQ T: 01622 890253 W: www.headcorn.org.uk

Herne Bay Historical Records Society c/o Herne Bay Museum, 12 William St, Herne Bay, CT6 5EJ

Higham Village History Group Forge House, 84 Forge Lane, Higham, Rochester, ME3 7AH

Horton Kirby & South Darenth Local History Society Appledore, Rays Hill, Horton Kirby, Dartford, DA4 9DB T: 01322 862056

Hythe Civic Society 25 Napier Gardens, Hythe, CT2l 6DD

Isle of Thanet Historical Society 58 Epple Bay Avenue, Birchington on Sea,

Kemsing Historical & Art Society 26 Dippers Close, Kemsing, Sevenoaks, TN15 6QD T: 01732 761774

Kent Archaeological Rescue Unit Roman Painted House, New Street, Dover, CTl7 9AJ T: 01304 203279 W: www.the-cka.fsnet.co.uk

Kent History Federation 14 Valliers Wood Road, Sidcup, DA15 8BG

Kent Mills Group Windmill Cottage, Mill Lane, Willesborough, TN27 0QG

Kent Postal History Group 27 Denbeigh Drive, Tonbridge, TN10 3PW

Lamberhurst Local History Society 1 Tanyard Cotts, The Broadway, Lamberhurst, Tunbridge Wells, TN3 8DD

Lamorbey & Sidcup Local History Society 14 Valliers Wood Road, Sidcup, DA15 8BG

Legion of Frontiersmen of Commonwealth 4 Edwards Road, Belvedere, DA17 5AL

Leigh and District History Society Elizabeths Cottage, The Green, Leigh, Tonbridge, TN11 8QW T: 01732 832459

Lewisham LH Soc 2 Bennett Pk, Blackheath Village, London SE3 9RB

Loose Area History Society 16 Bedgebury Close, Maidstone, ME14 5QY

Lyminge Historical Society Ash Grove, Canterbury Road, Etchinghill, Folkestone, CTl8 8DF

Maidstone Area Archaeological Group 40 Bell Meadow, Maidstone, ME15 9ND

Maidstone Historical Society 37 Bower Mount Road, Maidstone, ME16 8AX T: 01622 676472

Margate Civic Society 19 Lonsdale Avenue, Cliftonville, Margate, CT9 3BT

Meopham Historical Society Tamar, Wrotham Road, Meopham, DA13 0EX

Orpington History Soc 42 Crossway, Petts Wood, Orpington BR5 1PE

Otford & District History Society Thyme Bank, Coombe Road, Otford, Sevenoaks, TNI4 5RJ

Otham Society Tudor Cottage, Stoneacre Lawn, Otham, Maidstone, ME15 8RT

Paddock Wood History Society 19 The Greenways, Paddock Wood, Tonbridge, TNI2 6LS

Plaxtol Local History Group Tebolds, High Street, Plaxtol, Sevenoaks, TN15 0QJ

Rainham Historical Society 52 Northumberland Avenue, Rainham, Gillingham, ME8 7JY

Ramsgate Society Mayfold, Park Road, Ramsgate, CT11 7QH

Ringwould History Society Back Street, Ringwould, Deal, CT14 8HL T: 01304 361030 E: julie.m.rayner@talk21.com jeanwinn@beeb.net W: www.ringwould-village.org.uk

Romney Marsh Research Trust 11 Caledon Terrace, Canterbury, CT1 3JS T: 01227 472490 E: s.m.sweetinburgh@kent.ac.uk W: www.kent.ac.uk/mts/rmrt/

Rye Local History Group 107 Military Road, Rye, TN31 7NZ

Sandgate Society The Old Fire Station, 51 High Street, Sandgate, CT20 3AH

Sandwich Local History Society Clover Rise, 14 Stone Cross Lees, Sandwich, CT13 OBZ T: 01304 613476 E: frankandrews@FreeNet.co.uk

Sevenoaks Historical Society 10 Plymouth Park, Sevenoaks, TN13 3RR E: wilkospin@beeb.net

Sheppey Local History Society 34 St Helens Road, Sheerness,

Shoreham & District Historical Society The Coach House, Darenth Hulme, Shoreham, TNI4 7TU

Shorne Local History Group 2 Calderwood, Gravesend, DAl2 4Q11

Sittingbourne Society 4 Stanhope Avenue, Sittingbourne, ME10 4TU T: 01795 473807 E: malcolm@malcolm29.wanadoo.co.uk

Smarden Local History Society 7 Beult Meadow, Cage Lane, Smarden, TN27 8PZ T: 01233 770 856 E: franlester@fish.co.uk

Snodland Historical Society 214 Malling Road, Snodland, ME6 SEQ E: aa0060962@blueyonder.co.uk W: www.snodlandhistory.org.uk

St Margaret's Bay History Society Rock Mount, Salisbury Road, St Margarets Bay, Dover, CT15 6DL T: 01304 852236

Staplehurst Society Willow Cottage, Chapel Lane, Staplehurst, TN12 0AN T: 01580 891059 E: awcebd@mistral.co.uk

Tenterden & District Local History Society Little Brooms, Ox Lane, St Michaels, Tenterden, TN30 6NQ

Teston History Society Broad Halfpenny, MaIling Road, Teston, Maidstone, ME18 SAN

Thanet Retired Teachers Association 85 Percy Avenue, Kingsgate, Broadstairs, CT10 3LD

The Kent Archaeological Society Maidstone Museum, St Faith's Street, Maidstone, ME14 1LH T: 01474 822280 E: secretary@kentarchaeology.org.uk W: www.kentarchaeology.org.uk

The Marden Society 6 Bramley Court, Marden, Tonbridge, TN12 9QN T: 01622 831904 W: www.marden.org.uk

Three Suttons Society Henikers, Henikers Lane, Sutton Valence, ME17 3EE

Tonbridge Historical Society 8 Woodview Crescent, Hildenborough, Tonbridge, TN11 9HD T: 01732 838698 E: s.broomfield@dial.pipex.com

Wateringbury Local History Society Vine House , 234 Tonbridge Road, Wateringbury, ME18 5NY

Weald History Group Brook Farm, Long Barn Road, Weald, Sevenoaks,

Wealden Buildings Study Group 64 Pilgrims Way, East Otford, Sevenoaks, TN14 5QW

Whitstable History Society 83 Kingsdown Park, Tankerton, Whitstable,

Wingham Local History Society 67 High Street, Wingham, Canterbury, CT3 1AA

Woodchurch Local History Society Woodesden, 24 Front Road, Woodclnurch, Ashford, TN26 3QE

Wrotham Historical Society Hillside House, Wrotham, TN15 7JH

Wye Historical Society 1 Upper Bridge Street, Wye, Ashford, TN2 5 SAW

Lancashire

Aspull and Haigh Historical Society 1 Tanpit Cottages, Winstanley, Wigan, WN3 6JY T: 01942 222769

Birkdale & Ainsdale Historical Research Society 20 Blundell Drive, Birkdale, Southport, PR8 4RG W: www.harrop.co.uk/bandahrs

Blackburn Civic Society 20 Tower Road, Blackburn, BB2 5LE T: 01254 201399

Burnley Historical Society 66 Langdale Road, Blackburn, BB2 5DW T: 01254 201162

Chadderton Historical Society 18 Moreton Street, Chadderton, 0L9 OLP T: 0161 652 3930 E: enid@chadderton-hs.freeuk.com W: www.chadderton-hs.freeuk.com

Denton Local History Society 94 Edward Street, Denton, Manchester, M34 3BR

Ewecross History Society Gruskholme, Bentham, Lancaster, LA2 7AX T: 015242 61420

Fleetwood & District Historical Society 54 The Esplanade, Fleetwood, FY7 6QE

Friends of Smithills Hall Museum Smithills Hall, Smithills deane Road, Bolton, BL1 7NP

Garstang Historical & Archealogical Society 7 Rivermead Drive, Garstang, PR3 1JJ T: 01995 604913 E: marian.fish@btinternet.com

Historic Society of Lancashire & Cheshire East Wing Flat, Arley Hall, Northwich, CW9 6NA T: 01565 777231

Hyndburn Local History Society 20 Royds Avenue, Accrington, BB5 2LE T: 01254 235511

Lancashire & Cheshire Antiquarian Society 59 Malmesbury Road, Cheadle Hulme, SK8 7QL T: 0161 439 7202 E: morris.garratt@lineone.net W: www.lancashirehistory.co.uk www.cheshirehistory.org.uk

Lancashire Family History and Heraldry Society 21 Baytree Road, Clayton le Woods, PR6 7JW E: secretary@lfhhs.org.uk W: www.lfhhs.org.uk

Lancashire History 4 Cork Road, Lancaster, LA1 4AJ

Lancashire Local History Federation 25 Trinity Court, Cleminson Street, Salford, M3 6DX E: secretary@lancashirehistory.co.uk W: www.lancashirehistory.co.uk

Lancashire Parish Register Society 19 Churton Grove, Shevington Moor, Wigan, WN6 0SZ E: MikeHuddy@aol.com W: www.lprs.org.uk

Leyland Historical Society 172 Stanifield Lane, Farington, Leyland, Preston, PR5 2QT

Littleborough Historical and Archaeological Society 8 Springfield Avenue, Littleborough, LA15 9JR T: 01706 377685

Maghull and Lydiate Local History Society 15 Brendale Avenue, Maghull, Liverpool, L31 7AX

Mourholme Local History Society 14 Langdale Crescent, Storth, Milnthorpe, LA7 7JG T: 01539 564 514 E: nt.stobbs@virgin.net

Nelson Local History Society 5 Langholme Street, Nelson, BB9 ORW T: 01282 699475

North West Sound Archive Old Steward's Office, Clitheroe Castle, Clitheroe, BB7 1AZ T: 01200 427897 E: nwsa@ed.lancscc.gov.uk W: www.lancashire.gov.uk/education/d_lif/ro/content/sound/imdex.asp

Saddleworth Historical Society 7 Slackcote, Delph, Oldham, OL3 5TW T: 01457 874530

Society for Name Studies in Britain & Ireland 22 Peel Park Avenue, Clitheroe, BB7 1ET T: 01200-423771

Urmston District Local History Society 78 Mount Drive, Urmston, Manchester, M41 9QA

Leicestershire

Desford & District Local History Group Lindridge House, Lindridge Lane, Desford, LE9 9FD T: 01455 824514 E: jshepherd@freeuk.com

East Leake & District Local History Society 8 West Leake Road, East Leake, Loughborough, LE12 6LJ T: 01509 852390

Glenfield and Western Archaeological and Historical Group 50 Chadwell Road, Leicester, LE3 6LF T: 1162873220

Great Bowden Historical Society 14 Langdon Road, Market Harborough, LE16 7EZ

Leicestershire Archaeological and Historical Society The Guildhall, Leicester, LE1 5FQ E: alan@dovedale2.demon.co.uk W: www.le.ac.uk/archaeology/lahs/lahs.html

Sutton Bonington Local History Society 6 Charnwood Fields, Sutton Bonington, Loughborough, LE12 5NP T: 01509 673107

Vaughan Archaeological and Historical Society c/o Vaughan College, St Nicholas Circle, Leicester, LEl 4LB

Lincolnshire

Lincoln Record Society Lincoln Cathedral Library, Cathedral, Minster Yard, Lincoln, LN2 1PX T: 01522 544544 E: librarian@lincolncathedral.com W: www.lincolncathedral.com

Long Bennington Local History Society Kirton House, Kirton Lane, Long Bennington, Newark, NG23 5DX T: 01400 281726

Society for Lincolnshire History & Archaeology Jews' Court, Steep Hill, Lincoln, LN2 1LS T: 01522-521337 E: slha@lincolnshirepast.org.uk W: www.lincolnshirepast.org.uk

London

Acton History Group 30 Highlands Avenue, London, W3 6EU T: (020) 8992 8698

Barking & District Historical Society 449 Ripple Road, Barking, IG11 9RB T: 020 8594 7381 E: barkinghistorical@hotmail.com

Birkbeck College Birkbeck College, Malet Street, London, WC1E 7HU T: (020) 7631 6633 E: info@bbk.ac.uk W: www.bbl.ac.uk

Brentford & Chiswick Local History Society 25 Hartington Road, London, W4 3TL

British Records Association c/o Finsbury Library, 245 St Johns Street, London, EC1V 4NB T: (020) 7833 0428 E: britrecassoc@hotmail.com W: www.hmc.gov.uk/bra

Brixton Society 82 Mayall Road, London, SE24 0PJ T: (020) 7207 0347 E: apiperbrix@aol.com W: www.brixtonsociety.org.uk

Bromley Borough Local History Society 62 Harvest Bank Road, West Wickham, BR4 9DJ T: 020 8462 5002

Centre for Metropolitan History Institute of Historical Research, Senate House, Malet Street, London, WC1E 7HU T: (020) 7862 8790 E: olwen.myhill@sas.ac.uk W: www.history.ac.uk/cmh

Costume Society St Paul's House, 8 Warwick Road, London, EC4P 4BN W: www.costumesociety.org.uk

Croydon Local Studies Forum Flat 2, 30 Howard Road, South Norwood, London, SE25 5BY T: (020) 8654-6454

Croydon Local Studies Forum c/o Local Studies Library, Catherine Street, Croydon, CR9 1ET

Croydon Natural History & Scientific Society Ltd 96a Brighton Road, South Croydon, CR2 6AD T: (020) 8688 4539 W: www.grieg51.freeserve.co.uk/cnhss

East London History Society 42 Campbell Road, Bow, London, E3 4DT T: 020 8980 5672 E: elhs@mernicks.com W: www.eastlondon.org.uk

Edmonton Hundred Historical Society Local History Unit, Southgate Town Hall, Green Lanes, London, N13 4XD T: (020) 8379 2724

Friends of Historic Essex 11 Milligans Chase, Galleywood, Chelmsford, CM2 8QD T: 01245 436043 E: geraldine.willden2@essexcc.gov.uk

Friends of The Metropolitan Police Museum Bromley Police Station, High Street, Bromley, BR1 1ER W: www.met.police.uk/history/friends.htm

Fulham And Hammersmith Historical Soceity Flat 12, 43 Peterborough Road, Fulham, London, SW6 3BT T: (020) 7731 0363 E: mail@fhhs.org.uk W: www.fhhs.org.uk

Hendon & District Archaeological Society 13 Reynolds Close, London, NW11 7EA T: (020) 8458 1352 E: denis@netmatters.co.uk W: www.hadas.org.uk

Hornsey Historical Society The Old Schoolhouse, 136 Tottenham Lane, London, N8 7EL T: (020) 8348 8429 W: www.hornseyhistorical.org.uk

Hornsey Historical Society The Old Schoolhouse, 136 Tottenham Lane, London, N8 7EL T: (020) 8348 8429 W: www.hornseyhistorical.org.uk

Hornsey Historical Society The Old Schoolhouse, 136 Tottenham Lane, London, N8 7EL T: (020) 8348 8429 W: www.hornseyhistorical.org.uk

London & Middlesex Archaeological Society Placements Office, University of North London, 62-66 Highbury Grove, London, N5 2AD

London Archaeologist 8 Woodview Crescent, Hildenborough, Tonbridge, TN11 9HD T: 01732 838698 E: s.broomfield@dial.pipex.com W: www.londonarchaeologist.org.uk

London Record Society c/o Institute of Historical Research, Senate House, Malet Street, London, WC1E 7HU T: (020) 7862-8798 E: heathercreaton@sas.ac.uk W: www.ihrinfo.ac.uk/cmh

Mill Hill Historical Society 41 Victoria Road, Mill Hill, London, NW7 4SA T: (020) 8959 7126

Newham History Society 52 Eastbourne Road, East Ham, London, E6 6AT T: (020) 8471 1171 W: www.pewsey.net/newhamhistory.htm

Paddington Waterways and Maida Vale Society (Local History) 19a Randolph Road, Maida Vale, London, W9 1AN T: 020 7289 0950

Richmond Local History Society 9 Bridge Road, St Margarets, Twickenham, TWI IRE

Royal Arsenal Woolwich Historical Society Main Guard House, Royal Arsenal Woolwich, Woolwich, London, SE18 6ST E: enquiries@royalarsenalwoolwich.co.uk W: www.royalarsenalwoolwich.co.uk

The Peckham Society 6 Everthorpe Road, Peckham, London, SE15 4DA T: (020) 8693 9412

The Vauxhall Society 20 Albert Square, London, SW8 1BS

Walthamstow Historical Society 24 Nesta Road, Woodford Green, IG8 9RG T: (020) 8504 4156

Wandsworth Historical Society 31 Hill Court, Putney Hill, London, SW15 6BB

Willesden Local History Society (London Borough of Brent) 9 Benningfield Gardens, Berkhamstead, HP4 2GW T: 01442 878477

Manchester

Stretford Local History Society 26 Sandy Lane, Stretford, Manchester, M32 9DA T: 0161 283 9434 E: m.dawson53@ntlworld.com W: www.stretfordlhs.cwc.net http://homepage.ntlworld.com/m.dawson53/

Merseyside

Birkdale & Ainsdale Historical Research Society 20 Blundell Drive, Birkdale, Southport, PR8 4RG W: www.harrop.co.uk/bandahrs

British Society for Sports History Dept of Sports & Science, John Moore's University, Byrom Street, Liverpool, L3 3AF

Friends of Williamson's Tunnels 15-17 Chatham Place, Edge Hill, Liverpool, L7 3HD T: 0151 475 9833 E: info@williamsontunnels.com W: www.williamsontunnels.com

Historic Society of Lancashire & Cheshire East Wing Flat, Arley Hall, Northwich, CW9 6NA T: 01565 777231

Liverpool Historical Society 46 Stanley Avenue, Rainford, WA11 8HU E: liverpoolhistsoc@merseymail.com W: www.liverpoolhistorysociety.merseyside.org

Maghull and Lydiate Local History Society 15 Brendale Avenue, Maghull, Liverpool, L31 7AX

Maghull and Lydiate Local History Society 15 Brendale Avenue, Maghull, Liverpool, L31 7AX

Merseyside Archaeological Society 20 Osborne Road, Formby, Liverpool, L37 6AR T: 01704 871802

Merseyside Archaeological Society 20 Osborne Road, Formby, Liverpool, L37 6AR T: 01704 871802

The Guild of Merseyside Historians and Tourist Guides 49 Parkhill Road, Prenton, Birkenhead, L42 9JD T: 0151 608 3769

Middlesex

Borough of Twickenham Local History Society 258 Hanworth Road, Hounslow, TW3 3TY E: pbarnfield@post.com

Edmonton Hundred Historical Society Local History Unit, Southgate Town Hall, Green Lanes, London, N13 4XD T: (020) 8379 2724

Honeslow Chronicle 142 Guildford Avenue, Feltham, TW13 4E

Hounslow & District History Society 16 Orchard Avenue, Heston, TW5 0DU T: (020) 8570 4264

London & Middlesex Archaeological Society Placements Office, University of North London, 62-66 Highbury Grove, London, N5 2AD

Middlesex Heraldry Society 4 Croftwell, Harpeden, AL5 1JG T: 01582 766372

Northwood & Eastcote Local History Society 3 Elbridge Close, Ruislip, HA4 7XA T: 01895 637134 W: www.rnelhs.flyer.co.uk

Pinner Local History Society 8 The Dell, Pinner, HA5 3EW T: (020) 8866 1918 E: mwg@pinnerlhs.freeserve.co.uk W: www.pinnerlhs.freeserve.co.uk/index.html

Ruislip Northwood & Eastcote Local History Society 3 Elmbridge Close, Ruislip, HA4 7XA T: 01895 637134 E: www.rnelhs.flyer.co.uk

Sunbury and Shepperton Local 30 Lindsay Drive, Shepperton, TW17 88JU T: 01932 226776 E: H.L.Brooking@eggconnect.net W: http://users.eggconnect.net/h.l.brooking/sslhs

Military

Lancaster Military Heritage Group 19 Middleton Road, Overton, Morecambe, LA3 1HB

Military Historical Society Court Hill Farm, Potterne, Devizes, SN10 5PN T: 01980 615689 Daytime

The 68th (or Durham) Regiment of Light Infantry Display Team 40 The Rowans, Orgill, Egremont, CA22 2HW T: 01946 820110 E: PhilMackie@aol.com W: www.68dli.com

Victorian Military Society PO Box 5837, Newbury, RG14 7FJ T: 01635 48628 E: vmsdan@msn.com W: www.vms.org.uk

Norfolk

Blakeney Area Historical Society 2 Wiveton Road, Blakeney, NR25 7NJ T: 01263 741063

Federation of Norfolk Historical and Archaeological Organisations 14 Beck Lane, Horsham St Faith, Norwich, NR10 3LD

Feltwell (Historical & Archaeological) Soc 16 High Street, Feltwell, Thetford, IP26 4AF T: 01842 828448 E: peterfeltwell@tinyworld.co.uk

Holt History Group 6 Kelling Close, Holt, NR23 6RU

Narborough Local History Society 101 Westfields, Narborough, Kings Lynn, PE32 ISY W: www.narboroughaerodrome.org.uk

Norfolk and Norwich Archaeological Society 30 Brettingham Avenue, Cringleford, Norwich, NR4 6XG T: 01603 455913

Norfolk Archaeological and Historical Research Group 50 Cotman Road, Norwich, NR1 4AH T: 01603 435470

Norfolk Heraldry Society 26c Shotesham Road, Poringland, Norwich, NR14 7LG T: 01508 493832 W: www.norfolkheraldry.co.uk

Norfolk Record Society 17 Christchurch Road, Norwich, NR2 2AE

Richard III Society - Norfolk Group 20 Rowington Road, Norwich, NR1 3RR

Northamptonshire

Bozeat Historical and Archaeological Society 44 Mile Street, Bozeat, NN9 7NB T: 01933 663647

Brackley & District History Society 32 Church Lane, Evenley, Brackley, NN13 5SG T: 01280 703508

Higham Chichele Society 3 Bramley Close, Rushden, NN10 6RL

Houghtons & Brafield History 5 Lodge Road, Little Houghton, NN7 IAE

Irchester Parish Historical Society 80 Northampton Road, Wellingborough, NN8 3HT T: 01933 274880 W: www.irchester.org www.iphs.org.uk

Northamptonshire Association for Local History 6 Bakers Lane, Norton, Daventry, NN11 2EL E: js-sec@tandjassociates.co.uk W: www.northants-history.org.uk

Northamptonshire Record Society Wootton Park Hall, Northampton, NN4 8BQ T: 01604 762297

Oundle Historical Society 13 Lime Avenue, Oundle, Peterborough PE8 4PT

Rushden & District History Society 25 Byron Crescent, Rushden, NN10 6BL E: rdhs.rushden@virgin.net W: www.rdhs.org.uk

Weedon Bec History Society 35 Oak Street, Weedon, Northampton, NN7 4RR

West Haddon Local History Group Bramley House, 12 Guilsborough Road, West Haddon, NN6 7AD

Northumberland

Architectural & Archaeological Society of Durham & Northumberland Broom Cottage, 29 Foundry Fielkds, Crook, DL15 9SY T: 01388 762620 E: belindaburke@aol.com

Association of Northumberland Local History Societies c/o The Black Gate, Castle Garth, Newcastle upon Tyne, NE1 1RQ T: 0191 257 3254

Bell View (Belford) Ltd 33 West Street, Belford, NE70 7ND T: 01668 219220 E: bellview-belford@tiscali.co.uk

Felton & Swarland Local History Society 23 Benlaw Grove, Felton, Morpeth, NE65 9NG T: 01670 787476 E: petercook@felton111.freeserve.co.uk

Hexham Local History Society Dilstone, Burswell Villas, Hexham, NE46 3LD T: 01434 603216

Morpeth Antiquarian Society 9 Eden Grove, Morpeth, NE61 2UN T: 01670 514792 E: hudson.c@virgin.net W: www.morpethnet.co.uk

Morpeth Nothumbrian Gathering Westgate House, Dogger Bank, Morpeth, NE61 1RF

North-East England History Institute (NEEHI) Department of History University of Durham, 43 North Bailey, Durham, DH1 3EX T: 0191-374-2004 E: m.a.mcallister@durham.ac.uk W: www.durham.ac.uk/neehi.history/homepage.htm

Northumberland Local History Society 44 Alwington Terrace, Newcastle upon Tyne, NE3 1UD

Northumbrian Language Society Westgate House, Dogger Bank, Morpeth, NE61 1RE T: 01670 513308 E: kim@northumbriana.org.uk W: www.northumbriana.org.uk

Prudhoe & District Local History Society Prudhoe Community Enterprise Office, 82 Front Street, Prudhoe, NE42 5PU

Stannington Local History Society Glencar House, 1 Moor Lane, Stannington, Morpeth, NE61 6EA

The Ponteland Local History Society Woodlands, Prestwick Village, Ponteland, NE20 9TX T: 01661 824017 E: jmichaeltaylor@talk21.com W: www.ponthistsoc.freeuk.com

War Memorials Trust Bilsdale, Ulgham, Morpeth, NE61 3AR T: 01670 790465 E: gjb@bilsdale.freeserve.co.uk

Nottinghamshire

Basford & District Local History Society 44 Cherry Tree Close, Bucinsley, Nottingham, NG16 5BA T: 0115 927 2370

Beeston & District Local History Society 16 Cumberland Avenue, Beeston, NG9 4DH T: 0115 922 3008

Bingham & District Local History Society 56 Nottingham Road, Bingham, NG13 8AT T: 01949 875866

Bleasby Local History Society 5 Sycamore Lane, Bleasby, NG14 7GJ T: 01636 830094

Bulwell Historical Society 19 Woodland Avenue, Bulwell, Nottingham, NG6 9BY T: 0115 927 9519

Burton Joyce and Bulcote Local History Society 9 Carnarvon Drive, Burton Joyce, Nottingham, NG14 5ER T: 0115 931 3669

Caunton Local History Society Beech House, Caunton, Newark, NG23 6AF T: 01636 636564

Chinemarelian Society 3 Main Street, Kimberley, NG16 2NL T: 0115 945 9306

Cotgrave Local History Society 81 Owthorpe Road, Cotgrave, NG T: 0115 989 2115

East Leake & District Local History Society 8 West Leake Road, East Leake, Loughborough, LE12 6LJ T: 01509 852390

East Midlands Historian School of Continuing Education, Nottingham University, University Park, Nottingham, NG7 2RD T: 0115 951 4398 E: susan.clayton@nottingham.ac.uk

Eastwood Historical Society 18 Park Crescent, Eastwood , NG16 3DU T: 01773 712080

Edwalton Local History Society Camelot, 74 Wellin Lane, Edwalton, Nottingham, NG12 4AH T: 0115 923 3015 E: hallatcamelot@aol.com

Edwinstowe Historical Society 12 Church Street, Edwinstowe, NG21 9QA T: 01623 824455

Epperstone History Society Sunny Mead, Main Street, Epperstone, NG14 6AG

Farndon & District Local History Society 22 Brockton Avenue, Farndon, Newark, NG24 4TH T: 01636 610070

Flintham Society & Flintham Museum Flintham Museum, Inholms Road, Flintham, NG23 5LF T: 0163.6 525111 E: flintham.museum@lineone.net W: www.flintham-museum.org.uk

Gotham & District Local History Society 108A Leake Road, Gotham, NG11 0JN T: 0115 983 0494

Hucknall Heritage Society 68 Papplewick Lane, Hucknall, Nottingham, NG15 8EF E: marion.williamson@ntlworld.com

Keyworth & District Local History Society Keyworth Library, Church Drive, Keyworth, Nottingham, NG12 5FF E: info@keyworth-history.org.uk W: www.keyworth-history.org.uk

Lambley Historical Society 11 Steeles Way, Lambley, Nottingham, NG4 4QN T: 0115 931 2588

Lenton Local History Society 53 Arnesby Road, Lenton Gardens, Nottingham, NG7 2EA T: 0115 970 3891

Newark Archaeological & Local History Society 13 Main Street, Sutton on Trent, Newark, NG23 6PF T: 01636 821781 (Evenings) E: jill.campbell@ic24.net

North Muskham History Group Roseacre, Village Lane, North Muskham, NG23 6ES T: 01636 705566

Nottingham Civic Society 57 Woodhedge Drive, Nottingham, NG3 6LW T: 0115 958 8247 E: secretary@nottinghamcivicsociety.org.uk W: www.nottinghamcivicsociety.org.uk

Nottingham Historical and Archaeological Society 9 Churchill Drive, Stapleford, Nottingham, NG9 8PE T: 0115 939 7140

Nottinghamshire Industrial Archaeology Society 18 Queens Avenue, Ilkeston, DE7 4DL T: 0115 932 2228

Nottinghamshire Local History Association 128 Sandhill Street, Worksop, S80 1SY T: 01909 488878 E: drossellis@aol.com

Nuthall & District Local History Society 14 Temple Drive, Nuthall, Nottingham, NG16 1BE T: 0115 927 1118 E: tony.horton@ntlworld.com

Old Mansfield Society 7 Barn Close, Mansfield, NG18 3JX T: 01623 654815 E: dcrut@yahoo.com W: www.old-mansfield.org.uk

Old Mansfield Woodhouse Society Burrwells, Newboundmill Lane, Pleasley, Mansfield, NG19 7QA T: 01623 810396

Old Warsop Society 1 Bracken Close, Market Warsop, NG20 0QQ

Pentagon Society Dellary, Mill Road, Elston, Newark, NG23 5NR T: 01636 525278

Pleasley History Group 8 Cambria Road, Pleasley, Mansfield, NG19 7RL T: 01623 810201

Radford Memories Project 25 Manston Mews, Alfreton Road, Radford, Nottingham, NG7 3QY T: 0115 970 1256

Retford & District Historical & Archaeological Society Cambridge House, 36 Alma Road, Retford, DN22 6LW T: 07790212360 E: JOAN@grant.demon.co.uk

Ruddington Local History Society St Peter's Rooms, Church Street, Ruddington, Nottingham, NG11 6HA T: 0115 914 6645

Sherwood Archaeological Society 32 Mapperley Hall Drive, Nottingham, NG3 5EY T: 0115 960 3032 E: pjneale@aol.com

Shireoaks Local History Group 22 Shireoaks Row, Shireoaks, Worksop, S81 8LP

Sneinton Environmental Society 248 Greenwood Road, Nottingham, NG3 7FY T: 0115 987 5035

Southwell & District Local History Society Fern Cottage, 70 Kirklington Road, Southwell, NG25 0AX T: 01636 812220

Stapleford & District Local History Society 25 Westerlands, Stapleford, Nottingham, NG9 7JE T: 0115 939 2573

Sutton Heritage Society 8 Sheepbridge Lane, Mansfield, NG18 5EA T: 01623 451179 E: lildawes@yahoo.co.uk

Sutton on Trent Local History Society 14 Grassthorpe Road, Sutton on Trent, Newark, NG23 6QD T: 01636 821228

Thoroton Society of Nottinghamshire 59 Briar Gate, Long Eaton, Nottingham, NG10 4BQ T: 0115-972-6590 E: thoroton@keithgoodman.com W: www.thorotonsociety.org.uk

Tuxford Heritage Society 140 lincoln Road, Tuxford, Newark, NG22 0HS

West Bridgford & District Local History Society 30 Repton Road, West Bridgford, NG2 7EJ T: 0115 923 3901

Whitwell Local History Group 34 Shepherds Avenue, Worksop, S81 0JB E: jandpwalker34@aol.com W: www.wlhg.freeuk.com

Wilford History Society 10 St Austell Drive, Wilford, Nottingham, NG11 7BP T: 0115 981 7061

Woodborough Local History Group The Woodpatch, 19 Sunningdale Drive, Woodborough, NG14 6EQ T: 0115 965 3103 W: www.woodborough-heritage.org.uk

Worksop Archaeological & Local History Society 42 Dunstan Crescent, Worksop, S80 1AF T: 01909 477575

Oxfordshire

Abingdon Area Archaeological and Historical Society 4 Sutton Close, Abingdon, OX14 1ER T: 01235 529720 E: rainslie@hotmail.com W: www.aaahs.org.uk

Ashbury Local History Society Claremont , Asbury, Swindon, SN6 8LN E: marionlt@waitrose.com

Banbury Historical Society c/o Banbury Museum, Spiceball Park Road, Banbury, OX16 2PQ T: 01295 672626

Berkshire Local History Association Department of History, University of Reading, Whiteknights, Reading, RG6 6AA E: secretary@blha.org.uk W: www.blha.org.uk

Blewbury Local History Group Spring Cottage, Church Road, Blewbury, Didcot, OX11 9PY T: 01235 850427

Bloxham Village History Group 1 Hyde Grove, Bloxham, Banbury, OX15 4HZ T: 01295 720037

Chadlington Local History Society 5 Webbs Close, Chadlington, Chipping Nortro, OX7 3RA T: 01608 676116 E: kagewinter@aol.com

Charlbury Society 7 Park Street, Charlbury, OX7 3PS T: 01608 810390 E: charles.tyzack@btinternet.com

Chinnor Historical & Archealogical Society 4 Beech Road, Thame, OX9 2AL T: 01844 216538 E: kendmason@macunlimited.net

Chipping Norton History Society 9 Toy Lane, Chipping Norton, OX7 5FH T: 01608 642754

Cumnor and District History Society 4 Kenilworth Road, Cumnor, Nr Oxford, OX2 9QP T: 01865 862965

Dorchester Historical Society 14 Queen Street, Dorchester on Thames, Wallingford, OX10 7HR T: 01865 340054 E: margot.metcalfe@fritillary.demon.co.uk

Enstone Local History Circle The Sheiling, Sibford Ferris, Banbury, OX15 5RG

Eynsham History Group 11 Newland Street, Eynsham, OX29 4LB T: 01865 883141

Faringdon Archaeological & Historical Society 1 Orchard Hill, Faringdon, SN7 7EH T: 01367 240885 E: fdahs@bigfoot.com W: www.faringdon.org/hysoc

Finstock Local History Society 81 High Street, Finstock, OX7 3DA T: 01993 868965 E: jon@joncarpenter.co.uk

Goring & Streatley Local History Society 45 Springhill Road, Goring On Thames, Reading, RG8 OBY T: 01491 872625

Hanney History Group Willow Tree House, The Green, East Hanney, Wantage, OX12 0HQ T: 01238 68375

Henley on Thames Archaeological and Historical Group 52 Elizabeth Road, Henley on Thames, RG9 1RA T: 01491 578 530

Hook Norton Local History Group Littlenook, Chapel Street, Hook Norton, OX15 5JT T: 01608 730355 E: sheila@littlenook.ndo.co.uk

Iffley Local History Society 4 Abberbury Avenue, Oxford, OX4 4EU T: 01865 779257

Kidlington and District Historical Society 18 Oak Drive, Kidlington, OX5 2HL T: 01865 373517 W: www.communigate.co.uk/oxford

Lashbrook One-Place Study 70 Chestnut Lane, Amersham, HP6 6EH T: 01494 726103 E: cdjmills@hotmail.com

Launton Historical Society Salamanca, Launton, OX26 5DQ T: 01869 253281 E: p_tucker@tesco.net

Lechlade History Society The Gables, High Street, Lechlade, GL7 3AD T: 01367 252457 E: Gillkeithnewson.aol.com

Longworth Local History Society 7 Norwood Avenue, Southmoor, Abingdon, OX13 5AD T: 01865 820522 E: info@l-h-s.org.uk W: www.l-h-s.org.uk

Marcham Society Prior's Corner, 2 Priory Lane, Marcham, Abingdon, OX13 6NY T: 01865 391439 E: e.dunford@btinternet.com

Over Norton History Group Fountain Cottage, The Green, Over Norton, OX7 5PT T: 01608 641057

Oxfordshire Architectural and Historical Society 53 Radley Road, Abingdon, Oxford, OX14 3PN T: 01235 525960 E: tony@oahs.org.uk W: www.oahs.org.uk

Oxfordshire Local History Association 12 Meadow View, Witney, OX28 6TY T: 01993 778345

Oxfordshire Record Society Bodleian Library, Oxford, OX1 3BG T: 01865 277164 E: srt@bodley.ox.ac.uk

Shrivenham Local History Society Ridgeway, Kings Lane, Loncot, Faringdon, SN7 7SS T: 01793783083

Thame Historical Society 12 Park Terrace, Thame, OX9 3HZ T: 01844 212336 E: Csear58229@aol.com W: www.thamehistory.net

The Bartons History Group 18 North Street, Middle Barton, OX7 7BJ T: 01869 347013 E: edbury@midbar18.freeserve.co.uk

Volunteer Corps of Frontiersmen Archangels' Rest, 26 Dark Lane, Witney, OX8 5LE

Wallingford Historical and Archaeological Society Wallingford Museum, Flint House, 52a High Street, Wallingford, OX1O 0DB T: 01491 835065

Whitchurch: The Ancient Parish of Whitchurch Historical Society Ashdown, Duchess Close, Whitchurch on Thames, RG8 7EN

Witney & District Historical & Archaeological Society 16 Church Green, Witney, OX28 4AW T: 01993 703289

Wolvercote Local History Society 18 Dovehouse Close, Upper Wolvercote, OX2 8BG T: 01865 514033

Wootton, Dry Sandford & District History Society 46 Church Lane, Dry Sandford, Abingdon, OX13 6JP T: 01865 390441

Wychwoods Local History Society Littlecott, Honeydale Farm, Shipton Under Wychwood, Chipping Norton, OX7 6BJ T: 01993 831023

Yarnton with Begbroke History Society 6 Quarry End, Begbroke, OX5 1SF

Rutland

Rutland Local History & Record Society c/o Rutland County Museum, Catmos Street, Oakham, LE15 6HW T: 01572 758440 E: rutlandhistory@rutnet.co.uk W: www.rutnet.co.uk/rlhrs

Shropshire

Cleobury Mortimer Historical Society The Old Schoolhouse, Neen Savage, Cleobury Mortimer, Kidderminster, DY14 8JU T: 01299 270319 E: paddy@treves.freeserve.co.uk

Field Studies Council Head office, Preston Montford, Montford Bridge, Shrewsbury, SY4 1HW T: 01743 852100 E: fsc.headoffice@ukonline.co.uk W: www.field-studies-council.org

Shropshire Archaeological and Historical Society Lower Wallop Farm, Westbury, Shrewsbury, SY5 9RT T: 01743 891215 E: walloparch@farming.co.uk W: www.shropshireonline.gov.uk/archandhistsociety.nsf

Whitchurch History and Archaeology Group Smallhythe, 26 Rosemary Lane, Whitchurch, SY13 1EG T: 01948 662120

Somerset

Avon Local History Association 4 Dalkeith Avenue, Kingswood, Bristol, BS15 1HH T: 0117 967 1362

Axbridge Archaeological and Local History Society King John's Hunting Lodge, The Square, Axbridge, BS26 2AR T: 01934 732012

Bathford Society 36 Bathford Hill, Bathford, BA1 7SL

Bruton Museum Society The Dovecote Building, High Street, Bruton, T: 01749 812851 W: www.southsomersetmuseum.org.uk

Castle Cary & District Museum & Preservation Society Woodville House, Woodcock Street, Castle Cary, BA7 7BJ T: 01963 3511122 W: Chard History Group 17 Kinforde, Chard, TA20 1DT T: 01460 62722 E: carterw@globalnet.co.uk W: www.users.globalnet.co.uk/~carterw

Congresbury History Group Venusmead, 36 Venus Street, Congresbury, Bristol, BS49 5EZ T: 01934 834780 E: rogerhards-venusmead@breathemail.net

Freshford & District Local History Society Quince Tree House, Pipehouse Lane, Freshford, Bath, BA2 7UH T: 01225 722339

Nailsea & District Local History Society PO Box 1089, Nailsea, BS48 2YP

Notes and Queries for Somerset and Dorset Marston House, Marston Bigot, Frome, BA11 5DU

Oakhill & Ashwick Local History Society Bramley Farm, Bath Road, Oakhill, BA3 5AF T: 01749 840 241

Somerset Archaeological & Natural History Society Taunton Castle, Taunton, TA1 4AD T: 01823 272429 E: office@sanhs.org W: www.sanhs.org

Somerset Record Society Somerset Studies Library, Paul Street, Taunton, TA1 3XZ T: 01823-340300

South East Somerset Archaeological and Historical Society Silverlands, Combe Hill, Templecombe, BA8 OLL T: 01963 371307

South Petherton Local History Crossbow, Hele Lane, South Petherton, TA13 5DY

South Petherton Local History Group Cobbetts Droveway, South Petherton, TAl3 5DA T: 01460 240252

Staffordshire

Berkswich History Society 1 Greenfield Road, Stafford, ST17 OPU T: 01785 662401

Birmingham Canal Navigation Society 37 Chestnut Close, Handsacre, Rugeley, WS15 4TH

Landor Society 38 Fortescue Lane, Rugeley, WS15 2AE

Lawton History Group 17 Brattswood Drive, Church Lawton, Stoke on Trent, ST7 3EJ E: arthur@aburton83.freeserve.co.uk

Mid-Trent Historical Association 36 Heritage Court, Lichfield, WS14 9ST T: 01543 301097
North Staffordshire Historians' Guild 14 Berne Avenue, Newcastle under Lyme, ST5 2QJ
Ridware History Society 8 Waters Edge, Handsacre, Nr. Rugeley, WS15 7HP T: 01543 307456 E: davidandmonty@carefree.net
Stafford Historical & Civic Society 86 Bodmin Avenue, Weeping Cross, Stafford, ST17 OEQ T: 01785 612194 E: esj@supanet.com
Staffordshire Archaeological and Historical Society 6 Lawson Close, Aldridge, Walsall, WS9 0RX T: 01922 452230 E: sahs@britishlibrary.net W: www.sahs.uk.net

Suffolk
Framlingham & District Local History & Preservation Society 28 Pembroke Road, Framlingham, IP13 9HA T: 01728 723214
Lowestoft Archaeological and Local History Society 1 Cranfield Close, Pakefield, Lowestoft, NR33 7EL T: 01502 586143
Suffolk Institute of Archaeology and History Roots, Church Lane, Playford, Ipswich, IP6 9DS T: 01473-624556 E: brianseward@btinternet.com W: www.suffolkarch.org.uk
Suffolk Local History Council Resource Centre, 2 Wharfedale Road, Ipswich, IP1 4JP E: admin@suffolklocalhistorycouncil.org.uk W: www.suffolklocalhistorycouncil.org.uk

Surrey
Addlestone History Society 53 Liberty Lane, Addlestone, Weybridge, KT15 1NQ
Beddington & Carshalton Historical Society 57 Brambledown Road, Wallington, SM6 0TF
Beddington Carshalton & Wallington History Society 7 Mortlake Close, Beddington, Croydon, CR0 4JW T: (020) 8726 0255
Bourne Society 54 Whyteleafe Road, Caterham, CR3 5EF E: secretary@bourne-society.org.uk W: www.bourne-society.org.uk
Carshalton Society 43 Denmark Road, Carshalton, SM5 2JE
Centre for Local History Studies Faculty of Human Sciences, Kingston University, Penrhyn Road, Kingston, KT1 2EE T: (020) 8547 7359 E: localhistory@kingston.ac.uk W: http://localhistory.kingston.ac.uk
Croydon Natural History & Scientific Society Ltd 96a Brighton Road, South Croydon, CR2 6AD T: (020) 8688 4539 W: www.grieg51.freeserve.co.uk/cnhss
Domestic Buildings Research Group (Surrey) The Ridings, Lynx Hill, East Horsley, KT24 5AX T: 01483 283917
Dorking Local History Group Dorking & District Museum, The Old Foundry, 62a West St, Dorking, RH4 1BS T: 01306 876591
Esher District LH Society 45 Telegraph Lane, Claygate, KT10 0DT
Farnham and District Museum Society Tanyard House, 13a Bridge Square, Farnham, GU9 7QR
Friends of Public Record Office The Public Record Office, Ruskin Avenue, Kew, Richmond, TW9 4DU T: (020) 8876 3444 ext 2226 E: friends-pro@pro.gov.uk W: www.pro.gov.uk/yourpro/friends.htm
Guildford Archaeology and Local History Group 6 St Omer Road, Guildford, GU1 2DB T: 01483 532201 E: H.E.Davies@surrey.ac.uk
Hayward Memorial Local History Centre The Guest House, Vicarage Road, Lingfield, RH7 6HA T: 01342 832058
History of Thursley Society 50 Wyke Lane, Ash, Aldershot, GU12 6EA E: norman.ratcliffe@ntlworld.com W: http://home.clara.net/old.norm/Thursley
Leatherhead and District Local History Society Leatherhead Museum, 64 Church Street, Leatherhead, KT22 8DP T: 01372 386348
Nonsuch Antiquarian Society 17 Seymour Avenue, Ewell, KT17 2RP T: (020) 8393 0531 W: www.nonsuchas.org.uk
Puttenham & Wanborough History Society Brown Eaves, 116 The Street, Puttenham, Guildford, GU3 1AU
Richmond LH Soc 9 Bridge Rd, St Margarets, Twickenham, TWI IRE
Send and Ripley History Society St Georges Farm House, Ripley, GU23 6AF T: 01483 222107
Shere Gomshall & Peaslake Local History Society Twiga Lodge, Wonham Way, Gomshall, Guildford, GU5 9NZ T: 01483 202112 E: twiga@gomshall.freeserve.co.uk W: www.gomshall.freeserve.co.uk/sglshhp.htm
Surrey Archaeological Society Castle Arch, Guildford, GU1 3SX T: 01483 532454 E: surreyarch@compuserve.com W: www.ourworld.compuserve.com/homepages/surreyarch
Surrey Local History Council Guildford Institute, University of Surrey, Ward Street, Guildford, GU1 4LH
Surrey Record Society c/o Surrey History Centre, 130 Goldsworth Road, Woking, GU21 1ND T: 01483 594603

The RH7 History Group Bidbury House, Hollow Lane, East Grinstead, RH19 3PS
The Woldingham History Society Picardie, High Drive, Woldingham, CR3 7ED

Walton & Weybridge Local History Society 67 York Gardens, Walton on Thames, KT12 3EN
Walton On The Hill District Local History Society 5 Russell Close, Walton On The Hill, Tadworth, KT2O 7QH T: 01737 812013
Westcott Local History Group 6 Heath Rise, Westcott, Dorking, RH4 3NN T: 01306 882624 E: info@westcotthistory.org.uk W: www.westcotthistory.org.uk

Sussex
Beeding & Bramber Local History Society 19 Roman Road, Steyning, BN44 3FN T: 01903 814083
Billingshurst Local History Society 2 Cleve Way, Billingshurst, RH14 9RW T: 01403 782472 E: jane.lecluse@atkinsglobal.com
Blackboys & District Historical Society 18 Maple Leaf Cottages, School Lane, Blackboys, Uckfield, TN22 5LJ E: baturner.18maple@btinternet.com
Bolney Local History Society Leacroft, The Street, Bolney, Haywards, RH17 5PG T: 01444 881550
Brighton & Hove Archealogical Society 115 Braeside Avenue, Patcham, Brighton, BN1 8SQ
Chichester Local History Society 38 Ferndale Road, Chichester, PO19 6QS
Danehill Parish Historical Society Butchers Barn, Freshfield Lane, Danehill, RH17 7HQ T: 01825 790292
Eastbourne Local History Society 12 Steeple Grange, 5 Mill Road, Eastbourne, BN21 2LY
Eastbourne Natural History and Archaeological Society 11 Brown Jack Avenue, Polegate, BN26 5HN T: 01323 486014
Family & Community Historical Research Society 56 South Way, Lewes, BN7 1LY T: 01273 471897
Friends of East Sussex Record Office The Maltings, Castle Precincts, Lewes, BN7 1YT T: 01273-482349 W: www.esrole.fsnet.co.uk
Henfield History Group Maleth, Chestnut Way, Henfield, BN5 9PA
Lewes Archaeological Group Rosemary Cottage, High Street, Barcombe, near Lewes, BN8 5DM T: 01273 400878
Maresfield Historical Society Hockridge House, London Road, Maresfield, TN22 2EH T: 01825 765386
Mid Sussex Local History Group Saddlers, Stud Farm Stables, Gainsborough Lane, Polegate, BN26 5HQ T: 01323 482215
Midland Railway Society 4 Canal Road, Yapton, BN18 OHA T: 01243-553401 E: BeeFitch@aol.com W: www.derby.org/midland
Peacehaven & Telscombe Historical Society 2 The Compts, Peacehaven, BN1O 75Q T: 01273 588874 E: paths@openlink.org W: www.history-peacehaven-telscombe.org.uk
Steyning Society 30 St Cuthmans Road, Steyning, BN44 3RN
Sussex Archaeological Society & Sussex Past Barbican House, 169 High Street, Lewes, BN7 1YE T: 01273 405738 E: library@sussexpast.co.uk W: sussexpast.co.uk
Sussex History Forum Barbican House, 169 High Street, Lewes, BN7 1YE T: 01273-405736 E: research@sussexpast.co.uk W: www.sussexpast.co.uk
Sussex History Study Group Colstock, 43 High Street, Ditchling, BN5 8SY
Sussex Local History Forum Anne of Cleves House, 52 Southover, High Street, Lewes, BN7 1JA
Sussex Record Society West Sussex Record Office, County Hall, Chichester, PO19 1RN T: 01243 753600 E: peter.wilkinson@westsussex.gov.uk
The Angmering Society 45 Greenwood Drive, Angmering, BNI6 4JW T: 01903-775811 E: editor@angmeringsociety.org.uk W: www.angmeringsociety.org.uk
Uckfield & District Preservation Society 89 Lashbrooks Road, Uckfield, TN22 2AZ
Warbleton & District History Group Hillside Cottage, North Road, Bodle Street Green, Hailsham, BN27 4RG T: 01323 832339 E: junegeoff.hillside@tiscali.co.uk
West Sussex Archives Society c/o West Sussex Record Office County Hall, Chichester, PO19 IRN T: 01243 753600 E: records.office@westsussex.gov.uk W: www.westsussex.gov.uk/cs/ro/rohome.htm
Wivelsfield Historical Society Wychwood, Theobalds Road, Wivelsfield, Haywards Heath, RH15 0Sx T: 01444 236491

Tyne and Wear
Assoc of Northumberland LH Socs c/o The Black Gate, Castle Garth, Newcastle upon Tyne, NE1 1RQ T: 0191 257 3254
Cullercoats Local History Society 33 St Georges Road, Cullercoats, North Shields, NE30 3JZ T: 0191 252 7042
North East Labour History Society Department of Historical & Critical Studies, University of Northumbria, Newcastle upon Tyne, NE1 8ST T: 0191-227-3193 E: joan.hugman@unn.ac.uk

North Eastern Police History Society Brinkburn Cottage, 28 Brinkburn Street, High Barnes, Sunderland, SR4 7RG T: 0191-565-7215 E: harry.wynne@virgin.net W: http://nepolicehistory.homestead.com

North-East England History Institute (NEEHI) Department of History University of Durham, 43 North Bailey, Durham, DH1 3EX T: 0191-374-2004 E: m.a.mcallister@durham.ac.uk W: www.durham.ac.uk/neehi.history/homepage.htm

Society of Antiquaries of Newcastle upon Tyne The Black Gate, Castle Garth, Newcastle upon Tyne, NE1 1RQ T: 0191 261 5390 E: admin@newcastle-antiquaries.org.uk W: www.newcastle-antiquaries.org.uk

South Hylton Local History Society 6 North View, South Hylton, Sunderland, SR4 0LH T: 0191 534 4251 E: south.hylton@ntlworld.com W: www.shlhs.com

Southwick History and Preservation Society 8 St Georges Terrace, Roker, Sunderland, SR6 9LX T: 0191 567 2438 E: pamela2@freedomnames.co.uk W: www.southwickhistory.org.uk

Sunderland Antiquarian Society 22 Ferndale Avenue, East Boldon, NE36 0TN T: 0191 536 1692

War Memorials Trust Bilsdale, Ulgham, Morpeth, NE61 3AR T: 01670 790465 E: gjb@bilsdale.freeserve.co.uk

Warwickshire

Alcester & District Local History Society Applecross, Worcester Road, Inkberrow, Worcester, WR7 4ET E: cjjohnson@care4free.net

Kineton and District Local History Group The Glebe House, Lighthorne Road, Kineton, CV35 0JL T: 01926 690298 E: p.holdsworth@virgin.net

Warwickshire Local History Society 9 Willes Terrace, Leamington Spa, CV31 1DL T: 01926 429671

West Midlands

Aldridge Local History Soc 45 Erdington Road, Walsall, WS9 8UU

Barr & Aston Local History 17 Booths Farm Road, Great Barr, Birmingham, 642 2NJ

Birmingham Heritage Forum 95 Church Hill Road, Solihull, B91 3JH

Birmingham War Research Society 43 Norfolk Place, Kings Norton, Birmingham, B30 3LB T: 0121 459 9008

Black Country Local History Consortium Canal Street, Tipton Road, Dudley, DY1 4SQ T: 0121 522 9643 E: info@bclm.co.uk W: ww.bclm.co.uk

Black Country Society PO Box 71, Kingswinford, DY6 9YN E: editor@blackcountrysociety.co.uk W: www.blackcountrysociety.co.uk

Council for British Archaeology - West Midlands c/o Rowley's House Museum, Barker Street, Shrewsbury, SY1 1QH T: 01743 361196 E: mikestokes@shrewsbury-atcham.gov.uk W: www.shrewsburymuseums.com www.darwincountry.org

Local History Consortium The Black Country Living Museum, Tipton Road, Dudley, DY1 4SQ T: 0121 557 9643

Quinton Local History Society 15 Worlds End Avenue, Quinton, Birmingham, B32 1JF T: 0121-422-1792 E: qlhs@bjtaylor.fsnet.co.uk W: www.qlhs.org.uk

Romsley & Hunnington History Society Port Erin, Green Lane, Chapmans Hill, Romsley, Halesowen, B62 0HB T: 01562 710295 E: ejhumphreys@mail.com

Smethwick Local History Society 47 Talbot Road, Smethwick, Warley, B66 4DX W: www.smethwicklocalhistory.co.uk

Wythall History Society 64 Meadow Road, Wythall, Birmingham, B47 6EQ E: val@wythallhistory.co.uk W: www.wythallhistory.co.uk

Wiltshire

Amesbury Society 34 Countess Road, Amesbury, SP4 7AS T: 01980 623123

Atworth History Group 48d Post Office Lane, Atworth, Melksham, SN12 8JX T: 01225 702351 E: joan.cocozza@btinternet.com kath@harl1111.fsnet.co.uk W: www.atworth-village-online.org.uk/History-group.htm

Chiseldon Local History Group 3 Norris Close, Chiseldon, SN4 0LW T: 01793 740432 E: DavidBailey22@aol.com

Devizes Local History Group 9 Hartfield, Devizes, SN10 5JH T: 01380 727369

Highworth Historical Society 6 Copper Beeches, Highworth, Swindon, SN6 7BJ T: 01793 763863

Marshfield & District Local History Society Weir Cottage, Weir Lane, Marshfield, Chippenham, SN14 8NB T: 01225 891229 E: weircott@luna.co.uk

Melksham & District Historical Association 13 Sandridge Road, Melksham, SN12 7BE T: 01225 703644

Mere Historical Society Bristow House, Castle Street, Mere, BA12 6JF T: 01747 860643

Mid Thorngate Society Yewcroft, Stoney Batter, West Tytherley, Salisbury, SP5 ILD

Pewsey Vale Local History Society 10 Holly Tree Walk, Pewsey, SN9 5DE T: 01672 562417 E: westerberg@onetel.co.uk

Purton Historical Society 1 Church Street, Purton, SN5 4DS T: 01793 770331

Redlynch & District Local History Society Fieldfare Gate, Quavey Road, Redlynch, Salisbury, SP5 2HL E: kate.crouch@hotmail.co.uk

Salisbury Civic Soc 4 Chestnut Close, Laverstock, Salisbury, SP1 1SL

Salisbury Local History Group 67 St Edmunds Church Street, Salisbury, SP1 1EF T: 01722 338346

South Wiltshire Industrial Archaeology Society 2 Byways Close, Salisbury, SP1 2QS T: 01722 323732 E: jackson.douglas@btinternet.com W: www.southwilts.co.uk/site/south-wiltshire-industrial-archaeology-society

Swindon Society 4 Lakeside, Swindon, SN3 1QE T: 01793-521910

The Hatcher Society 11 Turner Close, Harnham, Salisbury, SP2 8NX

The Historical Association (West Wiltshire Branch) 24 Meadowfield, Bradford on Avon, BA15 1PL T: 01225 862722

Tisbury Local History Society Suzay House, Court Street, Tisbury, SP3 6NF

Trowbridge Civic Society 43 Victoria Road, Trowbridge, BA14 7LD

Warminster History Society 13 The Downlands, Warminster, BA12 0BD T: 01985 216022

Wilton Historical Society 3 Wiley Terrace, North Street, Wilton, SP2 0HN T: 01722 742856

Wiltshire Archaeological and Natural History Society Wiltshire Heritage Library, 41 Long Street, Devizes, SN10 1NS T: 01380 727369 E: wanhs@wiltshireheritage.org.uk W: www.wiltshireheritage.org.uk

Wiltshire Local History Forum Tanglewood, Laverstock Park, Salisbury, SP1 1QJ T: 01722 328922 E: sarumjeh@aol.com

Wiltshire Record Society County Record Office, County Libraries HQ, Trowbridge, BA14 8BS T: 01225 713136

Wootton Bassett Historical Society 20 The Broadway, Rodbourne Cheney, Swindon, SN25 3BT

Wroughton History Group 32 Kerrs Way, Wroughton, SN4 9EH T: 01793 635838

Worcestershire

Alvechurch Historical Society Bearhill House, Alvechurch, Birmingham, B48 7JX T: 0121 445 2222

Bewdley Historical Research 8 Ironside Close, Bewdley, DY12 2HX T: 01299 403582 E: angela.ironside@clara.co.uk

Dodderhill Parish History Project - Discovering Wychbol's Past 9 Laurelwood Close, Droitwich Spa, WR9 7SF

Droitwich History and Archaeology Society 45 Moreland Road, Droitwich Spa, WR9 8RN T: 01905-773420

Feckenham Forest History Society Lower Grinsty Farmhouse, Callow Hill, Redditch, B97 5PJ T: 01527-542063

Feckenham Parish, Worcestershire One Place Study 33c Castle Street, Astwood Park, Worcester, B96 6DP E: benwright3@hotmail.com

Kidderminster & District Archaeological & Historical Society 39 Cardinal Drive, Kidderminster, DY104RZ E: kidderhist.soc@virgin.net W: www.communigate.co.uk/worcs/kidderminsterhistorysoc/index.phtml

Kidderminster District Archaeological and Historical Society 178 Birmingham Road, Kidderminster, DYlO 2SJ T: 01562 823530 W: www.communigate.co.uk/worcs/kidderminsterhistorysoc/index.phtml

Kidderminster Field Club 7 Holmwood Avenue, Kidderminster, DYL 1 6DA

Open University History Society 111 Coleshill Drive, Chapel End, Nuneaton, CV10 0PG T: (024) 76397668

Pershore Heritage & History Society 6 Abbey Croft, Pershore, WR10 1JQ T: 01386 552482 E: kenmar.abcroft@virgin.net

Suckley Local History Society Knowle Cottage, Suckley, WR6 5DJ T: 01886 884357 E: sea.bird@virgin.net

Wolverley & Cookley Historical Society 18/20 Caunsall Road, Cookley, Kidderminster, DYL 1 5YB

Wolverley & Cookley History Society The Elms, Drakelow Lane, Wolverley, Kidderminster, DY11 5RU T: 01562 850215

Worcestershire Archaeological Service Woodbury Hall, University College of Worcester, Henwick Grove, Worcester, WR2 6AJ T: 01905 855455 E: archaeology@worcestershire.gov.uk W: http://worcestershire.gov.uk/archaeology

Worcestershire Archaeological Society 26 Albert Park Road, Malvern, WR14 1HN T: 01684 565190

Worcestershire Industrial Archealogy & Local History Society 99 Feckenham Road, Headless Cross, Redditch, B97 5AM

Worcestershire Local History Forum 45 Moreland Road, Droitwich, WR9 8RN T: 01905-773420

Wythall History Society 64 Meadow Road, Wythall, Birmingham, B47 6EQ E: val@wythallhistory.co.uk W: www.wythallhistory.co.uk

Yorkshire
Forest of Galtres Society c/o Crawford House, Long Street, Easingwold, York, YO61 3JB T: 01347 821685
The Yorkshire Buildings Preservation Trust c/o Elmhirst & Maxton Solicitors, 17-19 Regent Street, Barnsley, S70 2HP
The Yorkshire Heraldry Society 2 Woodhall Park Grove, Pudsey, Leeds, DN4 7HJ
Victorian Revival - Discontinued 2005 Sugar Hill Farm, Knayton, Thirsk, YO7 4BP T: 01845 537827 E: pamelagoult@hotmail.com
York Georgian Society King's Manor, York, YO1 7EW
Yorkshire Architectural & York Archaeological Society c/o York Archaeological Trust, Cromwell House, 13 Ogleforth, York, YO1 7FG E: www.homepages.tesco.net/~hugh.murray/yayas/
Yorkshire Philosophical Society The Lodge, Museum Gardens, Museum Street, York, YO1 7DR T: 01904 656713 E: yps@yorkphil.fsnet.co.uk W: www.yorec.org.uk
Yorkshire Quaker Heritage Project Brynmore Jones Library, University of Hull, Hull, HU6 7RXYorkshire Vernacular Buildings Study Group 18 Sycamore Terrace, Bootham, York, YO30 7DN T: 01904 652387 E: dave.crook@suleacy.freeserve.co.uk W: www.yvbsg.org.uk

Yorkshire - East
East Riding Archaeological Society 455 Chanterland Avenue, Hull, HU5 4AY T: 01482 445232
East Yorkshire Local History Society 13 Oaktree Drive, Molescroft, Beverley, HU17 7BB

Yorkshire - North
Northallerton and District Local History Society 17 Thistle Close, Romanby Park, Northallerton, DL7 8FF T: 01609 771878
Poppleton History Society Russett House, The Green, Upper Poppleton, York, YO26 6DR T: 01904 798868 W: www.poppleton.net/historysoc
Scarborough Archaeological and Historical Society 10 Westbourne Park, Scarborough, YO12 4AT T: 01723 354237 E: archaeology@scarborough.co.uk W: www.scarborough-heritage.org
Snape Local History Group Lammas Cottage, Snape, Bedale, DL8 2TW T: 01677 470727 W: www.communigate.co.uk/ne/slhg/index.phtml
Stokesley Local History Study Group 8a Westholme, Hutton Rudby, Yarm, TS15 0EA T: 01642 700397 E: christinemiller46@hotmail.com W: http://pride.webspace.co.uk/stokesley.htm
The Haxby Local History Group 14 Old Dikelands, Haxby, York, YO32 2WN T: 01904 763 937
The Steel Bonnets - Re-enactment Society 12 Marske Road, Saltburn by the Sea, TS12 1PZ T: 01287 625744
Upper Dales Family History Group - affiliated to Cleveland Family History Society Croft House, Newbiggin in Bishopdale, Nr Leyburn, DL8 3TD T: 01969 663738 E: glenys@bishopdale.demon.co.uk W: www.bishopdale.demon.co.uk
Upper Wharfedale Field Society (Local History Section) Brookfield, Hebden Hall Park, Grassington, Skipton, BD23 5DX T: 01756-752012
Upper Wharfedale Museum Society & Folk Museum The Square, Grassington, BD23 5AU
Wensleydale Railway Association WRA Membership Administration, PO Box 65, Northallerton, DL7 8YZ T: 01969 625182 (Railway Shop, Leyburn) W: www.wensleydalerailway.com
Yorkshire Dialect Society 51 Stepney Avenue, Scarborough, YO12 5BW

Yorkshire - South
Barnscan - The Barnsdale Local History Group 23 Rushymoor Lane, Askern, Doncaster, DN6 0NH T: 01302 700083 E: barnscan@btinternet.com W: www.barnscan.btinternet.co.uk
Bentley with Arksey Heritage Society 45 Finkle Street, Bentley, Doncaster, DN5 0RP
Chapeltown & High Green Archives The Grange, 4 Kirkstead Abbey Mews, Thorpe Hesley, Rotherham, S61 2UZ T: 0114 245 1235 E: bellamyted@aol.com W: www.chgarchives.co.uk
Doncaster Archaeological Society a Group of the Yorkshire Archaeological Society The Poplars, Long Plantation, Edenthorpe, Doncaster, DN3 2NL T: 01302 882840 E: d.j.croft@talk21.com
Friends of Barnsley Archives and Local Studies 30 Southgate, Barnsley, S752QL E: hazel@snowie48.freeserve.co.uk
Grenoside & District Local History Group 4 Stepping Lane, Grenoside, Sheffield, S35 8RA T: 0114 257 1929 E: info@grenosidelocalhistory.co.uk W: www.grenosidelocalhistory.co.uk
Wombwell Heritage Group 9 Queens Gardens, Wombwell, Barnsley, S73 0EE T: 01226 210648

Yorkshire - West
Beeston Local History Society 30 Sunnyview Avenue, Leeds, LS11 8QY T: 0113 271 7095
East Leeds Historical Society 10 Thornfield Drive, Cross Gates, Leeds, LS15 7LS
Halifax Antiquarian Society 66 Grubb Lane, Gomersal, Cleckheaton, BD19 4BU T: 01274 865418
Kippax & District History Society 8 Hall Park Croft, Kippax, Leeds, West Yorkshire T: 0113 286 4785 E: mdlbrumwell@tinyworld.co.uk W: www.kippaxhistoricalsoc.leedsnet.org
Lowertown Old Burial Ground Trust 16 South Close, Guisley, Leeds, LS20 8TD
Northern Society of Costume and Textiles 43 Gledhow Lane, Leeds, LS8 1RT
Olicana Historical Society 54 Kings Road, Ilkley, LS29 9AT T: 01943 609206
Ossett & District Historical Society 29 Prospect Road, Ossett, T: 01924 279449
Pudsey Civic Society PO Box 146, Leeds, LS28 8WY
Shipley Local History Society 68 Wycliffe Gardens, Shipley, BD18 3NH E: ian@slhs.abelgratis.co.uk
Thoresby Society 23 Clarendon Road, Leeds, LS2 9NZ T: 0113 245 7910 W: www.thoresby.org.uk
Wetherby & District Historical Society 73 Aire Road, Wetherby, LS22 7UE T: 01937 584875
Yorkshire Archaeological Society - Local History Study Section Claremont, 23 Clarendon Rd, Leeds, LS2 9NZ T: 0113-245-6342 E: yas@wyjs.org.uk (Library and Archives) W: www.yas.org.uk

Yorkshire - York
Holgate Windmill Preservation Society 2 Murray Street, York, YO24 4JA T: 01904 799295 E: lambert49@ntlworld.com W: www.holgatewindmill.org
York Archaeological Trust 13 Ogleforth, York, YO1 7FG T: 01904 663000 E: enquiries@yorkarchaeology.co.uk W: www.yorkarchaeology.co.uk

Isle of Man
Isle of Man Natural History & Antiquarian Society Ballacrye Stream Cottage, Ballaugh, Isle of Man IM7 5EB T: 01624-897306
Isle of Man Natural History & Local History Society Stream Cottage, Ballacrye, Ballaugh, Isle Of Man IM7 5EB

Wales
Chapels Heritage Society - CAPEL 2 Sandy Way, Wood Lane, Hawarden, Flintshire CH5 3JJ T: 01244 531255
South Wales Record Society 13 St Cybi Drive, Llangybi, Usk, Monmouthshire NP15 1TU T: 01633 450353
Anglesey
The Anglesey Antiquarian Society & Field Club 1 Fronheulog, Sling, Tregarth, Bangor, Gwynedd LL57 4RD T: 01248 600083 W: www.hanesmon.btinternet.co.uk
Caernarvonshire
Federation of History Societies in Caernarvonshire 19 Lon Dinas, Cricieth, Gwynedd LL52 0EH T: 01766 522238
Cardiff
Pentyrch & District Local History Society 34 Castell Coch View, Tongwynlais, Cardiff, CF15 7LA
Carmarthenshire
Carmarthenshire Antiquarian Society 24 Hoel Beca, Carmarthen, Carmarthenshire SA31 3LS E: arfon.rees@btinternet.com W: www.carmantiqs.org.uk
Gwendraeth Val History Society 19 Grugos Avenue, Pontyberem, Llanelli, Carmarthenshire SA15 5AF
Gwendraeth Valley Hist Society 19 Grugos Avenue, Pontyberem, Llanelli, Carmarthenshire SA14 5AF
Llanelli Historical Society Gwynfryn, Mountain Road, Trimsaran, Kidwelly, Carmarthenshire SA17 4EU T: 01554 810677
Ceredigion
Ceredigion Antiquarian Society Archives Department, Ceredigion County Council, Aberystwyth, Ceredigion SY23 T: 01970 633697 E: info@ceredigion.gov.uk
Clwyd
Friends of The Clwyd Archives Bryn Gwyn, 2 Rhodea Anwyl, Rhuddlan, LL18 2SQ T: 01745 591676 F: 01745 591676
Conwy
Abergele Field Club and Historical Society Rhyd y Felin, 47 Bryn Twr, Abergele, Conwy LL22 8DD T: 01745 832497
Llandudno & District Historical Society Springfield, 97 Queen's Road, Llandudno, Conwy LL30 1TY T: 01492 876337
Denbighshire
Denbighshire Historical Society 1 Green Park, Erddig, Wrexham, Wrexham LL13 7YE

Flintshire Historical Society 69 Pen y Maes Avenue, Rhyl, Denbighshire LL18 4ED T: 01745 332220
Ruthin Local History Group 27 Tan y Bryn, Llanbedr D.C., Ruthin, Denbighsire LL15 1AQ T: 01824 702632 F: 01824 702632 E: gwynnemorris@btinternet.com
Flintshire
Flintshire Historical Society 69 Pen y Maes Avenue, Rhyl, Denbighshire LL18 4ED T: 01745 332220
Glamorgan
Glamorgan History Society 7 Gifford Close, Two Locks, Cwmbran NP44 7NX T: 01633 489725 (Evenings Only) E: rosemary_hewlett@yahoo.co.uk
Kenfig Society 6 Locks Lane, Porthcawl, CF36 3HY T: 01656 782351 E: terry.robbins@virgin.net W: www.kenfigsociety.supanet.com
Llantrisant & District Local History Society Cerrig Llwyd, Lisvane Road, Lisvane, Cardiff, CF14 0SG T: 029 2075 6173 E: BDavies203@aol.com
Merthyr Tydfil Historical Society Ronamar, Ashlea Drive, Twynyrodyn, Merthyr Tydfil CF47 0NY T: 01685 385871
Gwent
Abertillery & District Museum 5 Harcourt Terrace, Glandwr Street, Abertillery, Gwent NP3 ITS
Abertillery & District Museum Society The Metropole, Market Street, Abertillery, Gwent NP13 1AH T: 01495 211140
Gwent Local History Council 8 Pentonville, Newport, Gwent NP9 5XH T: 01633 213229 F: 01633 221812 E: byron.grubb@gavowales.org.uk
Pontypool Local History Society 24 Longhouse Grove, Henllys, Cwmbran, Gwent NP44 6HQ T: 01633 865662
Newport Local History Society 72 Risca Road, Newport, South Wales NP20 4JA
Gwynedd
Abergele Field Club and Historical Society Rhyd y Felin, 47 Bryn Twr, Abergele, Conwy LL22 8DD T: 01745 832497
Caernarvonshire Historical Society Gwynedd Archives, County offices, Caernarfon, Gwynedd LL555 1SH T: 01286 679088 E: caernarvonshirehistoricalsociety@btinternet.com W: www.caernarvonshirehistoricalsociety.btinternet.co.uk
Cymdeithas Hanes a Chofnodion Sir Feirionnydd
Meirioneth Historical and Record Society Archifdy Meirion Cae Penarlag, Dolgellau, Gwynedd LL40 2YB T: 01341 424444 F: 01341 424505
Cymdeithas Hanes Beddgelert - Beddgelert History Society Creua, Llanfrothen, Penrhyndeudraeth, Gwynedd LL48 6SH T: 01766770534
Mid Glamorgan
Merthyr Tydfil Historical Society Ronamar, Ashlea Drive, Twynyrodyn, Merthyr Tydfil, Mid Glamorgan CF47 0NY T: 01685 385871
Pembrokeshire
The Pembrokeshire Historical Society Dolau Dwrbach, Fishguard, Pembrokeshire SA65 9RN T: 01348 873316 E: mike.eastham@btinternet.com
Pentyrch
Pentyrch & District Local History Society 34 Castell Coch View, Tongwynlais, Cardiff, CF15 7LA
Powys
Radnorshire Society Pool House, Discoed, Presteigne LD8 2NW
Wrexham
Denbighshire Historical Society 1 Green Park, Erddig, Wrexham, Wrexham LL13 7YE
Flintshire Historical Society 69 Pen y Maes Avenue, Rhyl, Denbighshire LL18 4ED T: 01745 332220
Wrexham Maelor Historical Society 37 Park Avenue, Wrexham, LL12 7AL

Scotland
Airdrie
Monklands Heritage Society 141 Cromarty Road, Cairnhill, Airdrie, ML6 9RZ T: 01236 764192
Angus
Abertay Historical Society c/o Museum Services, University of Dundee, Dundee, DD5 1HN T: 01382 344310 E: museum@dundee.ac.uk W: www.abertay.org.uk
Ayrshire
Ayrshire Federation of Historical Societies 11 Chalmers Road, Ayr, Ayrshire KA7 2RQ
SW Scotland Local / Family History Maybole Historical Society 18A Shawfarm Place, Prestwick, Ayrshire KA9 1JQ T: 07776 445033 E: maybole@scotsfamilies.co.uk W: www.maybole.org
Dundee
Abertay Historical Society c/o Museum Services, University of Dundee, Dundee, DD5 1HN T: 01382 344310 E: museum@dundee.ac.uk W: www.abertay.org.uk

Friends of Dundee City Archives 21 City Square, Dundee, DD1 3BY T: 01382 434494 F: 01382 434666 E: richard.cullen@dundeecity.gov.uk W: www.dundeecity.gov.uk/archives
East Ayrshire
Stewarton Library Cunningham Institute, Stewarton, East Ayrshire KA3 5AB T: 01560 484385
Edinburgh
Scottish Records Association National Archives of Scotland, H M General Register House, Edinburgh, EH1 3YY T: 0141 287 2914 F: 0141 226 8452
Society of Antiquaries of Scotland Royal Museum of Scotland, Chambers Street, Edinburgh, EH1 1JF T: 0131 247 4115 F: 0131 247 4163 E: r.lancaster@nms.ac.uk W: www.socantscot.org
Falkirk
Falkirk Local History Society 11 Neilson Street, Falkirk, FK1 5AQ
Fife
Abertay Historical Society c/o Museum Services, University of Dundee, Dundee, DD5 1HN T: 01382 344310 E: museum@dundee.ac.uk W: www.abertay.org.uk
Glasgow
Glasgow Hebrew Burial Society 222 Fenwick Road, Griffnock, Glasgow, G46 6UE T: 0141 577 8226
Perthshire
Abertay Historical Society c/o Museum Services, University of Dundee, Dundee, DD5 1HN T: 01382 344310 E: museum@dundee.ac.uk W: www.abertay.org.uk
Dunning Parish Historical Society The Old Schoolhouse, Newtown of Pitcairns, Dunning, Perth, Perthshire PH2 0SL T: 01764 684448 E: postman@dunning.uk.net W: www.dunning.uk.net
Renfrewshire
Bridge of Weir History Society 41 Houston Road, Bridge Of Weir, Renfrewshire PA11 3QR
Paisley Philosophical Institution 26 Thornly Park Drive, Paisley, Renfrewshire PA2 7RP T: 0141 884 4690
Renfrewshire Local History Forum 15 Victoria Crescent, Clarkston, Glasgow, G76 8BP T: 0141 644 2522 W: www.rlhf.info
Stirling
Drymen Library The Square, Drymen, Stirlingshire G63 0BL T: 01360 660751 E: drymenlibrary@stirling.gov.uk
West Lothian
Linlithgow Union Canal Society Manse Road Basin, Linlithgow, West Lothian EH49 6AJ T: 01506-671215 (Answering Machine) E: info@lucs.org.uk W: www.lucs.org.uk
Scottish Local History Forum 45 High Street, Linlithgow, West Lothian EH54 6EW T: 01506 844649 F: 0131 260 6610 E: chantal.hamill@dial.pipex.com
Northern Ireland
Federation for Ulster Local Studies 18 May Street, Belfast, BT1 4NL T: (028) 90235254 F: (028) 9043 4086 E: fulsltd@aol.com W: www.ulsterlocalhistory.org
Co Tyrone
Centre for Migration Studies Ulster American Folk Park, Mellon Road, Castletown, Omagh, Co Tyrone BT78 5QY T: 028 82 256315 F: 028 82 242241 E: uafp@iol.ie W: www.qub.ac.uk/cms/ www.folkpark.com
County Londonderry
Roe Valley Historical Society 36 Drumachose Park, Limavady, County Londonderry BT49 0NZ

Ireland
Hugenot Society of Great Britain & Ireland Hugenot Library University College, Gower Street, London, WC1E 6BT T: 020 7679 5199 E: s.massil@ucl.ac.uk W: (Library) www.ucl.ac.uk/ucl-info/divisions/library/huguenot.htm (Society) www.hugenotsociety.org.uk
Presbyterian Historical Society of Ireland Church House, Fisherwick Place, Belfast, BT1 6DW T: (028) 9032 2284
Federation of Local History Societies - Ireland Rothe House, Kilkenny,
Mayo North Family Heritage Centre Enniscoe, Castlehill, Ballina, County Mayo T: 00 44 096 31809 F: 00 44 096 31885 E: normayo@iol.ie W: www.mayo-ireland.ie/motm.htm
South Mayo Family Research Centre Main Street, Ballinrobe, County Mayo T: 353 92 41214 E: soumayo@iol.ie W: http://mayo.irish-roots.net/
Dublin
Raheny Heritage Society 68 Raheny Park, Raheny, Dublin 5, Dublin T: 01 831 4729 E: joan.sharkey@gmail.com

Libraries

National

British Film Institute - Library & Film Library 21 Stephen Street London W1T 1LN T: 020 7957 4824 W: www.bfi.org.uk

British Geological Survey Library Kingsley Dunham Centre, Keyworth, Nottingham NG12 5GG T:0115 939 3205 E: libuser@bgs.ac.uk W: www.bgs.ac.uk

British Library Boston Spa, Wetherby LS23 7BY

British Library British Library Building, 96 Euston Road London NW1 2DB T:(020) 7412 7000 E: Reader/admissions@bl.uk W: www.portico.bl.uk

British Library - Early Printed Collections 96 Euston Road London NW1 2DB T:(020) 7412 7673 E: rare-books@bl.uk W: www.bl.uk

British Library Newspaper Library Colindale Avenue London NW9 5HE T:020 7412 7353 E: newspaper@bl.uk W: www.bl.uk/collections/newspapes.html/

British Library of Political and Economic Science London School of Economics, 10 Portugal Street London WC2A 2HD T:020 7955 7223 W: www.lse.ac.uk

Cambridge University Library - Department of Manuscripts & University Archives West Road, Cambridge CB3 9DR T:01223 333000 ext 33143 (Manuscripts) E: mss@ula.cam.ac.uk W: www.lib.cam.ac.uk/MSS/

Catholic Central Library Lancing Street London NW1 1ND T:(020) 7383-4333 E: librarian@catholic-library.demon.co.uk W: www.catholic-library.demon.co.uk

Centre for South Asian Studies Cambridge University, Laundress Lane, Cambriodge CB2 1SD T:01223 338094 W: www.s-asian.cam.ac.uk

Dr Williams's Library 14 Gordon Square London WC1H 0AR T:(020) 7387-3727 E: enquiries@dwlib.co.uk

Evangelical Library 78a Chiltern Street London W1M 2HB

House of Commons Library House of Commons, 1 Derby Gate London SW1A 2DG T:(020) 7219-5545

Huguenot Library University College, Gower Street London WC1E 6BT T:(020) 7679 7094 E: s.massilk@ucl.ac.u W: www.ucl.ac.uk/ucl-info/divisions/library/hugenot.htm

Institute of Heraldic & Genealogical Studies 79 - 82 Northgate, Canterbury CT1 1BA T:01227 462618 E: ihgs@ihgs.ac.uk W: www.ihgs.ac.uk

Jewish Studies Library University College, Gower Street London WC1E 6BT T:(020) 7387 7050

Lambeth Palace Library Lambeth Palace Road London SE1 7JU T:(020) 7898 1400 W: www.lambethpalacelibrary.org

Library of Primitive Methodism Englesea Brook Chapel and Museum, Englesea Brook, Crewe CW2 5QW T: E: engleseabrook-methodist-museum@supanet.com W: www.engleseabrook-museum.org

Library of the Religious Society of Friends (Quakers) Friends House, 173 - 177 Euston Rd London NW1 2BJ T:0207 663 1135 E: library@quaker.org.uk W: www.quaker.org.uk/library

Library of the Royal College of Surgeons of England 35-43 Lincoln's Inn Fields London WC2A 3PE T:(020) 7869 6555 E: library@rcseng.ac.uk W: www.rcseng.ac.uk

Linnean Society of London Burlington House, Piccadilly London W1J 0BF T:020 7437 4479 E: librarian@linnean.org W: www.linnean.org

Methodist Archives and Research Centre John Rylands University Library 150 Deansgate, Manchester M3 3EH T:0161 834 5343

Modern Records Centre University of Warwick Library Coventry CV4 7AL T:(024) 76524219 E: archives@warwick.ac.uk W: www.modernrecords.warwick.ac.uk

Museum of the Order of St John St John's Gate, St John's Lane, Clerkenwell London EC1M 4DA T:(020) 7253-6644 W: www.sja.org.uk/history

National Gallery Library and Library Trafalgar Square London WC2N 5DN T:020 7747 2542 E: iad@ng-london.org.uk W: www.nationalgallery.org.uk

National Maritime Museum Romney Road, Greenwich London SE10 9NF T:(020) 8858-4422 W: www.nmm.ac.uk

National Maritime Museum - Caird Library Park RowLondon, Greenwich London SE10 9NF T:(020) 8312 6673 E: ABuchanan@nmm.ac.uk W: www.nmm.ac.uk

Royal Armouries H.M Tower Of London, Tower Hill London EC3N 4AB T:(020) 7480 6358 ext 30 E: Bridgett.Clifford@armouries.org.uk W: www.armouries.org.uk

Royal Commonwealth Society Library West Road, Cambridge CB3 9DR T:01223 333198 E: tab@ula.cam.ac.uk W: www.lib.cam.ac.uk/MSS/

Royal Institute of British Architects' Library Manuscripts & Archives 66 Portland Place London W1N 4AD T:020 7307 3615

Royal Society of Chemistry Library & Information Centre Burlington House, Piccadilly London W1J 0BA T:(020) 7440 3373 E: library@rsc.org W: www.rsc.org

School of Oriental and African Studies Library Thornhaugh Street, Russell Square London WC1H 0XG T:020 7323 6112 E: study@soas.ac.uk W: www.soas.ac.uk/library/

Society of Antiquaries of London Burlington House, Piccadilly London W1J 0BE T:020 7479 7084 E: library@sal.org.uk W: www.sal.org.uk

Society of Genealogists - Library 14 Charterhouse Buildings, Goswell Road London EC1M 7BA T:020-7251-8799 E: library@sog.org.uk W: www.sog.org.uk

The Kenneth Ritchie Wimbledon Library The All England Lawn Tennis & Croquet Club, Church Road, Wimbledon London SW19 5AE T:(020) 8946 6131 W: www.wimbledon.org

The Library & Museum of Freemasonry Freemasons' Hall, 60 Great Queen Street London WC2B 5AZ T:(020) 7395 9257 W: www.grandlodge-england.org

The National Coal Mining Museum for England Caphouse Colliery, New Road, Overton, Wakefield WF4 4RH T:01924 848806 E: info@ncm.org.uk W: www.ncm.org.uk

The Science Museum Library Imperial College Road, South Kensington London SW7 5NH T:020 7938 8234

The Women's Library Old Castle Street London E1 7NT T:(020) 7320-1189 E: fawcett@lgu.ac.uk W: www.lgu.ac.uk./fawcett

Trades Union Congress Library Collections - University of North London 236 - 250 Holloway Road London N7 6PP T: E: tuclib@unl.ac.uk W: www.unl.ac.uk/library/tuc

Trinity College Library Cambridge University, Trinity College, Cambridge CB1 1TQ T:01223 338488 E: trin-lib@lists.cam.ac.uk W: http://rabbit.trin.cam.ac.uk

United Reformed Church History Society, Westminster College, Madingley Road, Cambridge CB3 0AA T:01223-741300 (NOT Wednesdays)

Victoria & Albert Museum - National Art Library Cromwell Road, South Kensington London SW7 2RL T:(020) 7938 8315 W: www.nal.vam.ac.uk

Victoria & Albert Museum - National Art Library - Archive of Art and Design Blythe House, 23 Blythe Road London W14 0QF T:(020) 7603 1514 E: archive@vam.ac.uk W: www.nal.vam.ac.uk

Wellcome Library - Contemporary Medical Archives & Library 183 Euston Road London NW1 2BE T:(020) 7611 8722 E: library@wellcome.ac.uk W: http://library.wellcome.ac.uk

England
Bedfordshire

Bedford Central Library Harpur Street, Bedford MK40 1PG T:01234-350931 E: stephensonB@bedfordshire.gov.uk W: www.bedfordshire.gov.uk

Biggleswade Library Chestnut Avenue, Biggleswade SG18 0LL T:01767 312324

Dunstable Library Vernon Place, Dunstable LU5 4HA T:01582 608441

Leighton Buzzard Library Lake Street, Leighton Buzzard LU7 1RX T:01525 371788

Local Studies Library Luton Central Library St George's Square, Luton LU1 2NG T:01582-547420 E: local.studies@luton.gov.uk W: www.luton.gov.uk

Berkshire

Ascot Heath Library Fernbank Road, North Ascot SL5 8LA T:01344 884030

Berkshire Medical Heritage Centre Level 4, Main Entrance, Royal Berkshire Hospital, London Road, Reading RG1 5AN T:0118 987 7298 W: www.bmhc.org

Binfield Library Benetfeld Road, Binfield RG42 4HD T:01344 306663

Bracknell Library - Local Studies Town Square, Bracknell RG12 1BH T:01344 352515

Crowthorne Library Lower Broadmoor Road, Crowthorne RG45 7LA T:01344 776431

Eton College, College Library Windsor SL4 6DB T:01753 671269 E: archivist@etoncollege.org.uk W: www.etoncollege.com

Newbury Reference Library Newbury Central Library The Wharf, Newbury RG14 5AU T:01635 519900 E: newburylib@westberks.gov.uk W: www.westberks.gov.uk

Reading Local Studies Library 3rd Floor, Central Library Abbey Square, Reading RG1 3BQ T:0118 901 5965 E: info@readinglibraries.org.uk W: www.readinglibraries.org.uk

Reading University Library University of Reading, Whiteknights PO Box 223, Reading RG6 6AE T:0118-931-8776 W: www.reading.ac.uk/

Royal Borough of Windsor & Maidenhead Local Studies Collections Maidenhead Library St Ives Road, Maidenhead SL6 1QU E: maidenhead.ref@rbwm.gov.uk W: www.rbwm.gov.uk

Royal Borough of Windsor and Maidenhead Local Studies Collections Windsor Library Bachelors Acre, Windsor SL4 1ER T:01753 743941 E: windsor.library@rbwm.gov.uk W: www.rbwm.gov.uk

Sandhurst Library The Broadway, Sandhurst GU47 9BL T:01252 870161

Slough Local Studies Library Top Floor, Slough Library High Street, Slough SL1 1EA T:01753 787511 E: librarytop@sloughlibrary.org.uk W: www.sloughlibrary.org.uk

Whitegrove Library 5 County Lane, Warfield RG42 3JP T:01344 424211

Wokingham Library Local Studies The Library Denmark Street, Wokingham RG40 2BB T:0118 978 1368 E: libraries@wokingham.gov.uk W: www.wokingham.gov.uk/libraries

Bristol
Bristol Central Library Reference Section, College Green, Bristol BS1 5TL T:0117 903 7202

Bristol University Library - Special Collections , Tyndall Avenue, Bristol BS8 1TJ T:0117 928 8014 E: special-collections@bris.ac.uk W: www.bris.ac.uk/is/services/specialcollections/

Buckinghamshire
County Reference Library Walton Street, Aylesbury HP20 1UU T:01296-382250p

High Wycombe Reference Library Queen Victoria Road, High Wycombe HP11 1BD T:01494-510241 E: lib-hiwref@buckscc.gov.uk W: www.buckscc.gov.uk

Milton Keynes Reference Library 555 Silbury Boulevard, Milton Keynes MK9 3HL T:01908 254160 E: mklocal@milton-keynes.gov.uk W: www.mkheritage.co.uk/mkl

Cambridgeshire
Cambridge Library Lion Yard, Cambridge CB2 3QD T:p

Homerton College Library The New Library Hills Road, Cambridge CB2 2PH

Norris Library and Museum, The Broadway St Ives, PE27 5BX T:01480 497317 E: bob@norrismuseum.fsnet.co.uk

Peterborough Archives Service and Local Studies Collection Central Library Broadway, Peterborough PE1 1RX T:01733 742700 E: libraryenquiries@peterborough.gov.uk W: www.peterboroughheritage.org.uk

Cheshire
Alderley Edge Library Heys Lane, Alderley Edge SK9 7JT T:01625 584487 W: www.cheshire.gov.uk

Alsager Library Sandbach Road North, Alsager ST7 2QH T:01270 873552 E: alsager.infopoint@cheshire.gov.uk W: www.cheshire.gov.uk

Barnton Library Townfield Lane, Barnton CW8 4LJ T:01606 77343 W: www.cheshire.gov.uk

Bishops' High School Library Vaughans Lane, Chester CH3 5XF T:01244 313806 W: www.cheshire.gov.uk

Blacon Library Western Avenue, Blacon, Chester CH1 5XF T:01244 390628 W: www.cheshire.gov.uk

Bollington Library Palmerston Street, Bollington SK10 5JX T:01625 573058 W: www.cheshire.gov.uk

Chester Library Northgate Street, Chester CH1 2EF T:01244-312935 E: chester.infopoint@cheshire.gov.uk W: www.cheshire.gov.uk

Congleton Library Market Square, Congleton CW12 1ET E: congleton.infopoint@cheshire.gov.uk W: www.cheshire.gov.uk

Crewe Library Prince Albert Street, Crewe CW1 2DH T:01270 211123 E: crewe.infopoint@cheshire.gov.uk W: www.cheshire.gov.uk

Ellesmere Port Library Civic Way, Ellesmere Port, South Wirral L65 0BG E: eport.infopoint@cheshire.gov.uk W: www.cheshire.gov.uk

Frodsham Library Rock Chapel, Main Street, Frodsham WA6 7AN T:01928 732775p

Golborne Library Tanners Lane, Golborne, Warrington WA3 3AW T:01942 777800

Great Boughton Library Green Lane, Vicars Cross, Chester CH3 5LB T:01244 320709 W: www.cheshire.gov.uk

Halton Lea Library Halton Lea, Runcorn WA7 2PF T:01928-715351 W: www.cheshire.gov.uk

Handforth Library The Green, Wilmslow Road, Handforth SK9 3ES T:01625 528062 W: www.cheshire.gov.uk

Helsby Library Lower Robin Hood Lane, Helsby WA5 0BW T:01928 724659 W: www.cheshire.gov.uk

Holmes Chapel Library London Road, Holmes Chapel CW4 7AP T:01477 535126 E: homeschapel.infopoint@cheshire.gov.uk W: www.cheshire.gov.uk

Hoole Library 91 Hoole Road, Chester T:01244 347401 W: www.cheshire.gov.uk

Hope Farm Library Bridge Meadow, Great Sutton CH66 2LE T:0151 355 8923 W: www.cheshire.gov.uk

Hurdsfield Library 7 Hurdsfield Green, Macclesfield SK10 2RJ T:01625 423788 W: www.cheshire.gov.uk

Knutsford Library Brook Street, Knutsford WA16 8BP T:01565 632909 E: knutsford.infopoint@cheshire.gov.uk W: www.cheshire.gov.uk

Lache Library Lache Park Avenue, Chester CH4 8HR T:01244 683385 W: www.cheshire.gov.uk

Little Sutton Library Chester Road, Little Sutton CH66 1QQ T:0151 339 3373 W: www.cheshire.gov.uk

Local Heritage Library Central Library Wellington Road South, Stockport SK1 3RS T:0161-474-4530 E: localherirtage.library@stockport.gov.uk W: www.stockport.gov.uk

Macclesfield Library 2 Jordongate, Macclesfield SK10 1EE T:01625-422512 E: macclesfield.infopoint@cheshire.gov.uk W: www.cheshire.gov.uk

Macclesfield Silk Museums, Paradise Mill, Park Lane, Macclesfield SK11 6TJ T:01625 612045 W: www.silk-macclesfield.org

Malpas Library Bishop Herber High School, Malpas SY14 8JD T:01948 860571 W: www.cheshire.gov.uk

Middlewich Library Lewin Street, Middlewich CW10 9AS T:01606 832801 W: www.cheshire.gov.uk

Nantwich Library Beam Street, Nantwich CW5 5LY T:01270 624867 E: nantwich.infopoint@cheshire.gov.uk W: www.cheshire.gov.uk

Northwich Library Witton Street, Northwich CW9 5DR T:01606 44221 E: northwich.infopoint@cheshire.gov.uk W: www.cheshire.gov.uk

Poynton Library Park Lane, Poynton SK12 1RB T:01625 876257 E: poynton.infopoint@cheshire.gov.uk W: www.cheshire.gov.uk

Prestbury Library The Reading Room, Prestbury SK10 4AD T:01625 827501 W: www.cheshire.gov.uk

Sandbach Library The Common, Sandbach CW11 1FJ T:01270 762309 E: sandbach.infopoint@cheshire.gov.uk W: www.cheshire.gov.uk

Sandiway Library Mere Lane, Cuddington, Northwich CW8 2NS T:01606 888065 W: www.cheshire.gov.uk

Stockport MBC Bibliographical Services Unit, Phoenix House, Bird Hall Lane, Stockport SK3 0RA T:p

Tameside Local Studies Library Stalybridge Library Trinity Street, Stalybridge SK15 2BN T:0161-338-2708 W: www.tameside.gov.uk

Tarporley Library High School, Eaton Road, Tarporley CW6 0BJ T:01829 732558 W: www.cheshire.gov.uk

Upton Library Wealstone Lane, Upton by Chester CH2 1HB T:01244 380053 W: www.cheshire.gov.uk

Warrington Library & Local Studies Centre, Museum Street, Warrington WA1 1JB T:01925 442890 E: library@warrington.gov.uk W: www.warrington.gov.uk

Weaverham Library Russett Road, Weaverham, Northwich CW8 3HY T:01606 853359 W: www.cheshire.gov.uk

Weston Library Heyes Hall, Weston, Macclesfield SK11 8RL T:01625 614008 W: www.cheshire.gov.uk

Wharton Library Willow Square, Wharton, Winsford CW7 3HP T:01606 593883 W: www.cheshire.gov.uk

Wilmslow Library South Drive, Wilmslow SK9 1NW T:01625 528977 E: wilmslow.infopoint@cheshire.gov.uk W: www.cheshire.gov.uk

Winsford Library High Street, Winsford CW7 2AS T:01606 552065 E: winsford.infopoint@cheshire.gov.uk W: www.cheshire.gov.uk

Wirral Central Library Borough Road, Birkenhead CH41 2XB T:0151 652 6106 E: birkenhead.library@merseymail.com,

Cleveland
Hartlepool Central Library 124 York Road, Hartlepool TS26 9DE T:01429 263778p

Middlesbrough Libraries & Local Studies Centre, Central Library Victoria Square, Middlesbrough TS1 2AY T:01642 729001 E: reference_library@middlesbrough.gov.uk W: www.middlesbrough.gov.uk

Redcar Reference Library Coatham Road, Redcar TS10 1RP T:01642 489292 E: reference_library@redcar-cleveland.gov.uk

Stockton Reference Library Church Road, Stockton on Tees TS18 1TU T:01642-393994 E: reference.library@stockton.bc.gov.uk W: www.stockton.bc.gov.uk

Cornwall

Royal Institution of Cornwall, Courtney Library & Cornish History Research Centre Royal Cornwall Museum, River Street, Truro TR1 2SJ T:01872 272205 W: www.cornwall-online.co.uk/genealogy
The Cornwall Centre Alma Place, Redruth TR15 2AT T:01209-216760 E: cornishstudies@library.cornwall.gov.uk W: www.cornwall.gov.uk/index.cfm?articleid=6773

County Durham

Darlington Local Studies Centre The Library Crown Street, Darlington DL1 1ND T:01325-349630 E: local.studies@darlington.gov.uk W: www.darlington.gov.uk/library/localstudies
Durham City Reference & Local Studies Library Durham Clayport Library Millennium Place, Durham DH1 1WA T:0191-386-4003 E: durhamcityref.lib@durham.gov.uk W: www.durham.gov.uk
Durham University Library Archives and Special Collections Palace Green Section, Palace Green, Durham DH1 3RN T:0191 334 2932 E: pg.library@durham.ac.uk W: www.dur.ac.uk/library/asc
The Oriental Museum University of Durham Museums, Elvet Hill, Durham DH1 3TH T:0191 334 5694 E: oriental.museum@dur.ar.uk W: www.durham.ac.uk

Cumbria

Barrow in Furness - Cumbria Record Office & Local Studies Library 140 Duke St, Barrow in Furness LA14 1XW T:01229 894363 E: barrow.record.office@cumbriacc.gov.uk W: www.cumbria.gov.uk/archives
Carlisle Library 11 Globe Lane, Carlisle CA3 8NX T:01228-607310 E: carlisle.library@cumbriacc.gov.uk W: www.cumbriacc.gov.uk
Kendal Library Stricklandgate, Kendal LA9 4PY T:01539-773520 E: kendal.library@cumbriacc.gov.uk W: www.cumbriacc.gov.uk
Penrith Library St Andrews Churchyard, Penrith CA11 7YA T:01768-242100 E: penrith.library@dial.pipexcom W: www.cumbria.gov.uk
Whitehaven - Cumbria Record Office & Local Studies Library Scotch Street, Whitehaven CA28 7BJ T:01946-852920 E: whitehaven.record.office@cumbriacc.gov.uk W: www.cumbria.gov.uk/archives
Workington Library Vulcans Lane, Workington CA14 2ND T:01900-325170 E: workington.library@cumbriacc.gov.uk W: www.cumbriacc.gov.uk

Derbyshire

Chesterfield Local Studies Department Chesterfield Library New Beetwell Street, Chesterfield S40 1QN T:01246-209292 E: chesterfield.library@derbyshire.gov.uk
Derby Local Studies Library 25b Irongate, Derby DE1 3GL T:01332 255393 E: localstudies.library@derby.gov.uk W: www.derby.gov.uk/libraries/about/local_studies.htm
Local Studies Library - Matlock County Hall, Smedley Street, Matlock DE4 3AG T:01629-585579 E: ruth.gordon@derbyshire.gov.uk W: www.derbyshire.gov.uk/librar/locstu.htm

Devon

Devon & Exeter Institution Library 7 The Close, Exeter EX1 1EZ T:01392 251017 E: m.midgley@exeter.ac.uk W: www.ex.ac.uk/library/devonex.html
Exeter University Library Stocker Road, Exeter EX4 4PT T:01392 263870 E: library@exeter.ac.uk W: www.library.exeter.ac.uk
Plymouth Local Studies Library Plymouth Central Library Drake Circus, Plymouth PL4 8AL T:01752 305909 E: localstudies@plymouth.gov.uk W: www.plymouth.gov.uk/content-705
Torquay Library Lymington Road, Torquay TQ1 3DT T:01803 208305p
West Country Studies Library Exeter Central Library Castle Street, Exeter EX4 3PQ T:01392 384216 E: dlaw@devon-cc.gov.uk W: www.devon-cc.gov.uk/library/locstudy

Dorset

Dorchester Reference Library Colliton Park, Dorchester DT1 1XJ T:01305-224448p
Dorset County Museum, High West Street, Dorchester DT1 1XA T:01305 262735 E: dorsetcountymuseum@dor-mus.demon.co.uk W: www.dorsetcc.gov.uk
Poole Central Reference Library Dolphin Centre, Poole BH15 1QE T:01202 262424 E: centrallibrary@poole.gov.uk W: www.boroughofpoole.com/libraries
Weymouth Library The Local Studies Library Great George Street, Weymouth DT4 8NN T:01305 762410 E: weymouthlibrary@dorsetcc.gov.uk W: www.dorsetcc.gov.uk

Essex

Chelmsford Library PO Box 882, Market Rd, Chelmsford CM1 1LH T:01245 492758 W: www.essexcc.gov.uk
Clacton Library Station Road, Clacton on Sea CO15 1SF T:01255 421207p
Colchester Central Library Trinity Square, Colchester CO1 1JB T:01206-245917 E: jane.stanway@essexcc.gov.uk W: www.essexcc.gov.uk
Harlow Library The High, Harlow CM20 1HA T:01279 413772p
Ilford Local Studies and Archives Central Library Clements Road, Ilford IG1 1EA T:020 8708 2417p
Loughton Library Traps Hill, Loughton IG10 1HD T:020 8502 0181p
Redbridge Library Central Library Clements Road, Ilford IG1 1EA T:(020) 8708 2417 E: studies@redbridge.gov.uk W: www.redbridge.gov.uk
Saffron Walden Library 2 King Street, Saffron Walden CB10 1ES T:01799 523178
Southend Library Central Library Victoria Avenue, Southend on Sea SS2 6EX T:01702-612621 E: library@southend.gov.uk W: www.southend.gov.uk/libraries/
Thomas Plume Library Market Hill, Maldon CM9 4PZ

Gloucestershire

Cheltenham Local Studies Centre Cheltenham Library Clarence Street, Cheltenham GL50 3JT T:01242-532678
Gloucester Library, Arts & Museums County Library Quayside, Shire Hall Gloucester GL1 1HY T:01452-425037 E: clams@gloscc.gov.uk W: www.gloscc.gov.uk
Gloucestershire County Library Brunswick Road, Gloucester GL1 1HT T:01452-426979 E: clams@gloscc.gov.uk W: www.gloscc.gov.uk
Gloucestershire Family History Society, 37 Barrington Drive, Hucclecote, Gloucester GL3 3BT T:01452 524344 (Resource Centre) E: alexwood@blueyonder.co.uk W: www.gfhs.org.uk
Yate Library 44 West Walk, Yate BS37 4AX T:01454 865661 E: yate_library@southglos.gov.uk W: www.southglos.gov.uk
Gloucestershire - South Thornbury Library St Mary Street, Thornbury BS35 2AA T:01454-865655 E: thornbury.library@southglos.gov.uk W: www.southglos.gov.uk

Hampshire

Aldershot Library 109 High Street, Aldershot GU11 1DQ T:01252 322456p
Andover Library Chantry Centre, Andover SP10 1LT T:01264 352807 E: clceand@hants.gov.uk W: www.hants.gov.uk
Basingstoke Library North Division Headquarters, 19 - 20 Westminster House, Potters Walk, Basingstoke RG21 7LS T:01256-473901 W: www.hants.gov.uk
Bournemouth Library 22 The Triangle, Bournemouth BH2 5RQ T:01202 454817
Eastleigh Library The Swan Centre, Eastleigh SO50 5SF T:023 8061 2513 E: clweeas@hants.gov.uk W: www.hants.gov.uk
Fareham Library South Division Headquarters, Osborn Road, Fareham PO16 7EN T:01329-282715 E: clsoref@hants.gov.uk W: www.hants.gov.uk
Farnborough Library Pinehurst, Farnborough GU14 7JZ T:01252 513838 E: clnoref@hants.gov.uk W: www.brit-a-r.demon.co.uk
Fleet Library 236 Fleet Road, Fleet GU13 8BX T:01252 614213 E: clnofle@hants.gov.uk W: www.hants.gov.uk
Gosport Library High Street, Gosport PO12 1BT T:(023) 9252 3431 E: clsos@hants.gov.uk W: www.hants.gov.uk
Hampshire County Library West Division Headquarters, The Old School, Cannon Street, Lymington SO41 9BR T:01590-675767 E: clwedhq@hants.gov.uk W: www.hants.gov.uk
Hampshire Local Studies Library Winchester Library Jewry Street, Winchester SO23 8RX T:01962 841408 E: clceloc@hants.gov.uk W: www.hants.gov.uk/library
Lymington Library Cannon Street, Lymington SO41 9BR T:01590 673050 E: clwelym@hants.gov.uk W: www.hants.gov.uk
Portsmouth City Libraries Central Library Guildhall Square, Portsmouth PO1 2DX T:023 9268 8045 (Bookings) E: reference.library@portsmouthcc.gov.uk W: www.portsmouth.gov.uk/learning/1035.html
Southampton City Libraries - Special Collections Southampton Reference Library Civic Centre, Southampton SO14 7LW T:023 8083 2205 E: local.studies@southampton.gov.uk W: www.southampton.gov.uk
Southampton University Library Highfield, Southampton SO17 1BJ T:023 8059 3724
Waterlooville Library The Precinct, Waterlooville PO7 7DT T:(023) 9225 4626 E: clsowvl@hants.gov.uk W: www.hants.gov.uk
Winchester Reference Library 81 North Walls, Winchester SO23 8BY T:01962-846059 E: clceref@hants.gov.uk W: www.hants.gov.uk

Herefordshire
Bromyard Library 34 Church Street, Bromyard HR7 4DP T:01885 482657
Colwall Library Humphrey Walwyn Library Colwall, Malvern WR13 6QT T:01684 540642
Hereford Cathedral Archives & Library 5 College Cloisters, Cathedral Close, Hereford HR1 2NG T:01432 374225 E: library@herefordcathedral.org W: www.herefordcathedral.org
Hereford Library Broad Street, Hereford HR4 9AU T:01432-272456 E: herefordlibrary@herefordshire.gov.uk W: www.libraries.herefordshire.gov.uk
Ledbury Library The Homend, Ledbury HR8 1BT T:01531 632133
Leominster Library 8 Buttercross, Leominster HR6 8BN T:01568-612384
Ross Library Cantilupe Road, Ross on Wye HR9 7AN T:01989 567937

Hertfordshire
Bushey Museum, Art Gallery and Local Studies Centre Rudolph Road, Bushey WD23 3HW T:020 8420 4057 E: busmt@bushey.org.uk W: www.busheymuseum.org
Hertfordshire Archives and Local Studies County Hall, Pegs Lane, Hertford SG13 8EJ T:01438 737333 E: herts.direct@hertscc.gov.uk W: http://hertsdirect.org/hals
Welwyn Garden City Central Library Local Studies Section, Campus West, Welwyn Garden City AL8 6AJ T:01438 737333

Hull
Brynmor Jones Library - University of Hull Cottingham Road, Hull HU6 7RX T:01482 465265 E: W: www.hull.ac.uk/lib www.hull.ac.uk/lib/archives
Hull Central Library Family and Local History Unit Central Library Albion Street, Kingston upon Hull HU1 3TF T:01482 616828 E: gareth.watkins@hullcc.gov.uk W: www.hullcc.gov.uk/genealogy
Hull College - Local History Unit James Reckitt Library Holderness Road, Hull HU9 1EA T:01482 331551 E: historyunit@netscape.net W: www.historyofhull.co.uk
Hull Local Studies Library Central Library Albion Street, Kingston upon Hull HU1 3TF T:01482 210077 E: local.studies@hullcc.gov.uk W: www.hullcc.gov.uk/genealogy/

Isle of Wight
Isle of Wight County Library Lord Louis Library Orchard Street, Newport PO30 1LL T:01983-823800 E: reflib@postmaster.co.uk W: www.iwight.com/thelibrary

Kent
Ashford Library Church Road, Asford TN23 1QX T:01233 620649 E: W: www.kent.gov.uk
Broadstairs Library The Broadway, Broadstairs CT10 2BS T:01843-862994 E: W: www.kcnt.gov.uk
Canterbury Cathedral Library The Precincts, Canterbury CT1 2EH T:01227-865287 E: catlib@ukc.ac.uk W: www.canterbury-cathedral.org
Canterbury Library & Local Studies Collection 18 High Street, Canterbury CT1 2JF T:01227-463608 W: www.kent.gov.uk
Dartford Central Library - Reference Department Market Street, Dartford DA1 1EU T:01322-221133 W: www.kent.gov.uk
Deal Library Broad Street, Deal CT14 6ER T:01304 374726 W: www.kent.gov.uk
Dover Library Maison Dieu House, Biggin Street, Dover CT16 1DW T:01304 204241 W: www.kent.gov.uk
Faversham Library Newton Road, Faversham ME13 8DY T:01759-532448 W: www.kent.gov.uk
Folkestone Library & Local Heritage Studies 2 Grace Hill, Folkestone CT20 1HD T:01303-256710 E: janet.adamson@kent.gov.uk W: www.kent.gov.uk
Gillingham Library High Street, Gillingham ME7 1BG T:01634-281066 E: Gillingham.Library@medway.gov.uk W: www.medway.gov.uk
Gravesend Library Windmill Street, Gravesend DA12 1BE T:01474 352758 W: www.kent.gov.uk
Greenhill Library Greenhill Road, Herne Bay CT6 7PN T:01227 374288 W: www.kent.gov.uk
Herne Bay Library 124 High Street, Herne Bay CT6 5JY T:01227-374896 W: www.kent.gov.uk
Maidstone Reference Library St Faith's Street, Maidstone ME14 1LH T:01622 701943 W: www.kent.gov.uk
Margate Library Local History Collection Cecil Square, Margate CT9 1RE T:01843-223626 W: www.kent.gov.uk
Ramsgate Library and Museum Guildford Lawn, Ramsgate CT11 9QY T:01843-593532 E: W: www.kent.gov.uk

Ramsgate Library Local Strudies Collection & Thanet Branch Archives Ramsgate Library Guildford Lawn, Ramsgate CT11 9AY T:01843-593532 W: www.kent.gov.uk
Sevenoaks Library Buckhurst Lane, Sevenoaks TN13 1LQ T:01732-453118 W: www.kent.gov.uk
Sheerness Library Russell Street, Sheerness ME12 1PL T:01795-662618 W: www.kent.gov.uk
Sittingbourne Library Central Avenue, Sittingbourne ME10 4AH T:01795-476545 W: www.kent.gov.uk
Sturry Library Chafy Crescent, Sturry, Canterbury CT2 0BA T:01227 711479 W: www.kent.gov.uk
Swalecliffe Library 78 Herne Bay Road, Chestfield CT5 2LX T:01227 792645
Tonbridge Library Avenbury Avenue, Tonbridge TN9 1TG T:01732 352754 W: www.kent.gov.uk
Tunbridge Wells Library Mount Pleasant, Tunbridge Wells TN1 1NS T:01892-522352 W: www.kent.gov.uk
University of Kent at Canterbury Library Canterbury CT2 7NU T:01227 764000
Whitstable Library 31-33 Oxford Street, Whitstable CT5 1DB T:01227-273309
Kent - Medway Medway Archives and Local Studies Centre Civic Centre Strood, Rochester ME2 4AU T:01634-332714 E: archives@medway.gov.uk local.studies@medway.gov.uk W: http://cityark.medway.gov.uk

Lancashire
Bacup Library St James's Square, Bacu OL13 9AH T:01706 873324
Barnoldswick Library Fernlea Avenue, Barnoldswick, Colne BB8 5DW T:01282 812147
Blackburn Central Library Town Hall Street, Blackburn BB2 1AG T:01254 587919 E: community.history@blackburn.gov.uk W: www.blackburn.gov.uk/library www.cottontown.org
Burnley Central & Local Studies Library Grimshaw Street, Burnley BB11 2BD T:01282-437115 E: burnley.reference@lcl.lancscc.gov.uk W: www.lancscc.gov.uk
Bury Central Library - References and Information Services Bury Central Library Manchester Road, Bury BL9 0DG T:0161-253-5871 E: information@bury.gov.uk Bury.lib@bury.gov.uk W: www.bury.gov.uk/culture.htm
Central Library Civic Centre, Le Mans Crescent, Bolton BL1 1SE T:01204-333185
Chethams Library Long Millgate, Manchester M3 1SB T:0161 834 7961 W: www.chethams.org.uk
Chorley Central Library Union Street, Chorley PR7 1EB T:01257 277222
Clitheroe Library Church Street, Clitheroe BB7 2DG T:01200 428788
Colne Library Market Street, Colne BB8 0AP T:01282-871155 E: colne.reference@lcl.lancscc.gov.uk
Haslingden Library Higher Deardengate, Haslingden, Rossendale BB4 5QL T:01706 215690
Heywood Local Studies Library Heywood Library Church Street, Heywood OL10 1LL T:01706 360947
Hyndburn Central Library St James Street, Accrington BB5 1NQ T:01254-872385 E: accrington.localstudies@lcl.lancscc.gov.uk W: www.lancscc.gov.uk
John Rylands University Library Special Collections Division, 150 Deansgate, Manchester M3 3EH T:0161-834-5343 E: spcoll72@fs1.li.man.ac.uk W: http://rylibweb.man.ac.uk
Lancashire Record Office Bow Lane, Preston PR1 2RE T:01772 533039 E: record.office@ed.lancscc.gov.uk W: www.archives.lancashire.gov.uk
Leigh Library Turnpike Centre, Civic Centre, Leigh WN7 1EB T:01942-404559 E: heritage@wiganmbc.gov.uk W: www.wiganmbc.gov.uk
Leyland Library Lancastergate, Leyland PR25 2EX T:01772 432804 E: leyland.library@lcl.lancscc.gov.uk W: www.lancashire.gov.uk/libraries
Manchester Central Library - Archives & Local Studies Manchester Central Library St Peter's Square, Manchester M2 5PD T:0161-234-1979 E: lsuarchiveslocalstudies W: www.manchester.gov.uk/libraries/index.htm
Middleton Local Studies Library Middleton Library Long Street, Middleton M24 6DU T:0161-643-5228
Morecambe Library Central Drive, Morecambe LA4 5DL T:01524 402110
Nelson Library Market Square, Nelson BB9 7PU T:01282 692511 E: nelson.reference@lcl.lancscc.gov.uk W: www.lancashire.gov.uk/libraries/
Oldham Local Studies and Archives 84 Union Street, Oldham OL1 1DN T:0161-911-4654 E: archives@oldham.gov.uk W: www.oldham.gov.uk/archives www.oldham.gov.uk/local_studies
Ormskirk Library Burscough St, Ormskirk L39 2EN T:01695 573448

Orrell Library Orrell Post, Orrell, Wigan WN5 8LY T:01942 705060
Prestwich Library Longfield Centre, Prestwich M25 1AY T:0161 253 7214 E: Prestwich.lib@bury.gov.uk W: www.bury.gov.uk
Radcliffe Library Stand Lane, Radcliffe M26 9WR T:0161 253 7160 E: Radcliuffe.lib@bury.gov.uk W: www.bury.gov.uk
Ramsbottom Library Carr Street, Ramsbottom BL0 9AE T:01706 822484 E: Ramsbottom.lib@bury.gov.uk W: www.bury.gov.uk
Rawtenstall Library Haslingden Road, Rawtenstall, Rossendale BB4 6QU T:01706 227911 E: rawtenstall.reference@lcl.lancscc.gov.uk W: www.lancashire.gov.uk/libraries
Rochdale Local Studies Centre Touchstones Rochdale, The Esplanade, Rochdale OL16 1AQ T:01706 924915 E: localstudies@rochdale.gov.uk W: www.rochdale.gov.uk/Living/Libraries.asp?URL=local
Salford Local History Library Peel Park, Salford M5 4WU T:0161 736 2649 E: local.history@salford.gov.uk W: www.salford.gov.uk
Salford Museum & Art Gallery Peel Park, Salford M5 4WU T:0161 736 2649 E: info@lifetimes.org.uk W: www.lifetimes.org.uk
Skelmersdale Central Library Southway, Skelmersdale WN8 6NL T:01695 720312
St Anne's Library 254 Clifton Drive, St Anne's on Sea FY8 1NR T:01253 643900
The Harris Reference Library Market Square, Preston PR1 2PP T:01772 404010 E: harris@airtime.co.uk
Working Class Movement Library Jubilee House, 51 The Crescent, Salford M5 4WX T:0161 736 3601 E: enquiries@wcml.org.uk W: www.wcml.org.uk

Leicestershire
Hinckley Library Local Studies Collection Hinckley Library Lancaster Road, Hinckley LE10 0AT T:01455-635106 E: hinckleylibrary@leics.gov.uk W: www.leics.gov.uk
Leicester Reference and Information Library Bishop Street, Leicester LE1 6AA T:0116 299 5401
Leicestershire Libraries & Information Service 929 - 931 Loughborough Road, Rothley LE7 7NH T:0116 267 8023 E: skettle@leics.gov.uk W: www.leicestershire.gov.uk/libraries
Loughborough Library Local Studies Collection Granby Street, Loughborough LE11 3DZ T:01509-238466 E: Jslater@leices.gov.uk W: www.leices.gov.uk/libraries
Market Harborough Library and Local Studies Collection Pen Lloyd Library Adam and Eve Street, Market Harborough LE16 7LT T:01858-821272
Melton Mowbray Library Wilton Road, Melton Mowbray LE13 0UJ T:01664 560161 W: www.leics.gov.uk
Southfields Library Reader Development Services, Saffron Lane, Leicester LE2 6QS,

Lincolnshire
Boston Library County Hall, Boston PE21 6LX T:01205 310010 ext 2874
Gainsborough Library Cobden Street, Gainsborough DN21 2NG T:01427 614780 E: gainsborough.library@lincolnshire.gov.uk
Grantham Library Issac Newton Centre, Grantham NG1 9LD T:01476 591411
Lincoln Cathedral Library Lincoln Cathedral Library The Cathedral, Lincoln LN2 1PZ England T:01522-544544 E: librarian@lincolncathedral.com W: www.lincolncathedral.com
Lincolnshire County Library Local Studies Section, Lincoln Central Library Free School Lane, Lincoln LN2 1EZ T:01522 510800 E: lincoln.library@lincolnshire.gov.uk W: www.lincolnshire.gov.uk
Stamford Library High Street, Stamford PE9 2BB T:01780 763442
Lincolnshire - North
Scunthorpe Central Library Carlton Street, Scunthorpe DN15 6TX T:01724-860161 E: scunthorpe.ref@central-library.demon.co.uk W: www.nothlincs.gov.uk/library
Lincolnshire - North East
Grimsby Central Library Reference Department , Central Library Town Hall Square, Great Grimsby DN31 1HG T:01472-323635 E: jennie.mooney@nelincs.gov.uk W: www.nelincs.gov.uk

Liverpool
Liverpool Record Office & Local History Department Central Library William Brown Street, Liverpool L3 8EW T:0151 233 5817 E: recoffice.central.library@liverpool.gov.uk W: www.liverpool.gov.uk
Liverpool University Special Collections & Archives University of Liverpool Library PO Box 123, Liverpool L69 3DA T:0151-794-2696 W: www.sca.lib.liv.ac.uk/collections/index.html

London
Bancroft Library 277 Bancroft Rd London E1 4DQ T:020 8980 4366
Barking & Dagenham Local Studies Library - LB of, Valence House Museum, Beacontree Avenue, Dagenham RM8 3HT T:020 8270 6896 E: localstudies@lbbd.gov.uk W: www.barking-dagenham.gov.uk
Barnet - Local Studies & Archives Centre - London Borough of Local Studies & Archives Centre, 80 Daws Lane, Mill Hill London NW7 4SL T:(020) 8959 6657 E: library.archives@barnet.gov.uk W: www.barnet.gov.uk/index/leisure-culture/libraries/archives.htm
Bishopsgate Institute Reference Librarian, 230 Bishopsgate London EC2M 4QH T:(020) 7392 9270 E: library@bishopsgate.org.uk W: www.bishopsgate.org.uk
Brent Archive - London Borough of 152 Olive Road, Cricklewood London NW2 6UY T:(020) 8937 3541 E: archive@brent.gov.uk W: www.brent.gov.uk/archive
Bromley Local Studies Library - London Borough of Central Library High Street, Bromley BR1 1EX T:020 8461 7170 E: localstudies.library@bromley.gov.uk W: www.bromley.gov.uk/libraries
Camden Local Studies & Archive Centre - London Borough of Holborn Library 32 - 38 Theobalds Road London WC1X 8PA T:020 7974 6342 E: localstudies@camden.gov.uk W: www.camden.gov.uk/localstudies
Chelsea Public Library - London Borough of Old Town Hall, King's Road London SW3 5EZ T:(020) 7352-6056
Chiswick & Brentford Local Studies Collection - London Borough of Chiswick Public Library Dukes Avenue, Chiswick London W4 2AB T:(020) 8994-5295
Croydon Library and Archives Service - London Borough of Central Library Katharine Street, Croydon CR9 1ET T:(020) 8760 6900 ext 61112 E: libraries@croydon.gov.uk W: www.croydon.gov.uk/
Ealing Local History Centre Central Library 103 Broadway Centre, Ealing London W5 5JY T:(020) 8567-3656-ext-37 E: localhistory@hotmail.com W: www.ealing.gov.uk/libraries
Fawcett Library London Guildhall University, Old Castle Street London E1 7NT T:(020) 7320-1189 E: fawcett@lgu.ac.uk W: WW W: www.lgu.ac.uk /fawcett
Greenwich Heritage Centre - London Borough of Artillery Square, Royal Arsenal, Woolwich London SE18 4DX T:(020) 8854 2452 E: local.history@greenwich.gov.uk W: www.greenwich.gov.uk
Guildhall Library, Manuscripts Section Aldermanbury London EC2P 2EJ T:(020) 7332-1863 E: manuscripts.guildhall@cityoflondon.gov.uk W: http://ihr.sas.ac.uk/ihr/gh/
Hammersmith Central Library, London Borough of Shepherds Bush Road London W6 7AT T:020 8753 3816 W: www.lbhf.gov.uk
Havering Central Reference Library - London Borough of Reference Library St Edward's Way, Romford RM1 3AR T:01708 432393
Hounslow Library (Local Studies & Archives) - London Borough of Centrespace, Treaty Centre, High Street, Hounslow TW3 1ES T:0845 456 2800 W: www.cip.com
Imperial College Archives London University, Room 455 Sherfield Building, Imperial College London SW7 2AZ T:020 7594 8850 E: library@imperial.ac.uk W: www3.imperial.ac.uk
Institute of Commonwealth Studies , University of London 28 Russell Square London WC1B 5DS T:(020) 7862 8844 E: icommlib@sas.ac.uk W: http://sas.ac.uk/commonwealthstudies
Islington History Centre - London Borough of Finsbury Library 245 St John Street London EC1V 4NB T:(020) 7527 7988 E: local.history@islington.gov.uk W: www.islington.gov.uk
James Clavell Library Royal Arsenal (West), Warren Lane, Woolwich London SE18 6ST T:020 8312 7125 E: W: www.firepower.org.uk
Jewish Museum, The Sternberg Centre for Judaism, 80 East End Road, Finchley London N3 2SY T:020 8349 1143 E: enquiries@jewishmuseum.org.uk W: www.jewishmuseum.org.uk
Kensington and Chelsea Libraries & Arts Service - Royal Borough of Central Library Phillimore Walk, Kensington London W8 7RX T:(020) 7361 3010 E: information@rbkc.gov.uk W: www.rbkc.gov.uk/libraries
Lambeth Archives Department - London Borough of Minet Library 52 Knatchbull Road, Lambeth London SE5 9QY T:(020) 7926 6076 E: W: www.lambeth.gov.uk
Lewisham Local Studies & Archives - London Borough of Lewisham Library 199 - 201 Lewisham High Street, Lewisham London SE13 6LG T:(020) 8297-0682 E: local.studies@lewisham.gov.uk W: www.lewisham.gov.uk
London Borough of Enfield Libraries Southgate Town Hall, Green Lanes, Palmers Green London N13 4XD T:(020) 8379-2724
London Borough of Islington Finsbury Library 245 St John Street London EC1V 4NB T:(020) 7527 7994 W: www.islington.gov.uk/htm
London Borough of Waltham Forest Local Studies Library Vestry House Museum, Vestry Road, Walthamstow, E17 9NH T:(020) 8509 1917 E: Vestry.House@al.lbwf.gov.uk W:

www.lbwf.gov.uk/vestry/vestry.htm

London Hillingdon Borough Libraries Central Library High Street, Uxbridge UB8 1HD T:01895 250702 E: clib@hillingdon.gov.uk W: www. hillingdon.gov.uk

London Metropolitan Archives 40 Northampton Road London EC1R 0HB T:020 7332 3820 E: ask.lma@cityoflondon.gov.uk W: www.cityoflondon.gov.uk/lma

London University - Institute of Advanced Studies Charles Clore House, 17 Russell Square London WC1B 5DR T:(020) 7637 1731 E: ials.sas.ac.uk W: http://ials.sas.ac.uk

Manuscripts Room, Library Services, University College, Gower Street London WC1E 6BT T:(020) 7387 7050 E: mssrb@ucl.ac.uk W: www.ucl.ac.uk/library/special-coll/

Merton Local Studies Centre - London Borough of Merton Civic Centre, London Road, Morden SM4 5DX T:(020) 8545-3239 E: local.studies@merton.gov.uk W: www.merton.gov.uk/libraries

Minet Library 52 Knatchbull Road, Lambeth London SE5 9QY T:(020) 7926 6076 E: lambetharchives@lambeth.gov.uk W: www.lambeth.gov.uk

Museum in Docklands Library & Archives Library & Library No 1 Warehouse, West India Quay, Hertsmere Road London E14 4AL T:(020) 7001 9825 (Librarian) E: bobaspinall@museumindocklands.org.uk W: www.museumindocklands.org.uk

Museum of London Library 150 London Wall London EC2Y 5HN T:020 7814 5588 E: library@museumoflondon.org.uk W: www.museumoflondon.org.uk

Newham Archives & Local Studies Library - London Borough of Stratford Library 3 The Grove London E15 1EL T:(020) 8430 6881 W: www.newham.gov.uk

Richmond upon Thames Local Studies Library, London Borough of , Old Town Hall, Whittaker Avenue, Richmond upon Thames TW9 1TP T:(020) 8332 6820 E: localstudies@richmond.gov.uk W: www.richmond.gov.uk

Royal Botanic Gardens, Library & Archives Kew, Richmond TW9 3AE T:020 8332 5414

Southwark Local Studies Library - London Borough of 211 Borough High Street, Southwark London SE1 1JA T:0207-403-3507 E: local.studies.library@southwark.gov.uk W: www.southwark.gov.uk

Sutton Central Library St Nicholas Way, Sutton SM1 1EA T:(020) 8770 4745 E: sutton.information@sutton.gov.uk W: www.sutton.gov.uk

Tower Hamlets Local History Library & Archives - London Borough of Bancroft Library 277 Bancroft Road London E1 4DQ T:(020) 8980 4366 Ext 129 E: localhistory@towerhamlets.gov.uk W: www.towerhamlets.gov.uk

Twickenham Library - collection transferred to Richmond Local Studies Library Twickenham Library Garfield Road, Twickenham TW1 3JS T:(020) 8891-7271 E: W: www.richmond.gov.uk

University of London (Library - Senate House) Palaeography Room, Senate House, Malet Street London WC1E 7HU T:(020) 7862 8475 E: enquiries@shl.lon.ac.uk W: www.ull.ac.uk/library

Wandsworth Local Studies - London Borough of Local Studies Service, Battersea Library 265 Lavender Hill London SW11 1JB T:(020) 8871 7753 E: wandsworthmuseum@wandsworth.gov.uk W: www.wandsworth.gov.uk

Westminster Abbey Library & Muniment Room Westminster Abbey, London SW1P 3PA T:(020) 7222 5152 Ext 4830 E: library@westminster-abbey.org W: www.westminster-abbey.org

Westminster University Archives Information Systems & Library Services, 4-12 Little Titchfield Street London W1W 7UW T:020 7911 5000 ext 2524 E: archive@westminster.ac.uk W: www.wmin.ac.uk/archives

Merseyside
Crosby Library (South Sefton Local History Unit) Crosby Road North, Waterloo, Liverpool L22 0LQ T:0151 257 6401 E: local-history.south@leisure.sefton.gov.uk W: www.sefton.gov.uk

Huyton Central Library Huyton Library Civic Way, Huyton, Knowsley L36 9GD T:0151-443-3738 W: www.knowsley.gov.uk/leisure/libraries/huyton/index.html

Southport Library (North Sefton Local History Unit) Lord Street, Southport PR8 1DJ T:0151 934 2119 E: local-history.north@leisure.sefton.gov.uk W:

St Helen's Local History & Archives Library Central Library, Gamble Institute, Victoria Square, St Helens WA10 1DY T:01744-456952

Middlesex
Harrow Local History Collection - Civic Centre Library - London Borough of PO Box 4, Station Road, Harrow HA1 2UU T:0208 424 1055 E: localhistory.library@harrow.gov.uk W: www.harrow.gov.uk

Military
Catterick Garrison Library Gough Road, Catterick Garrison DL9 3EL T:01748 833543 W: www.northyorks.gov.uk

Royal Marines Museum Eastney, Southsea PO4 9PX T:(023) 9281 9385 Exts 224 W: www.royalmarinesmuseum.co.uk

Royal Naval Museum Buildings 1 - 7, College Road, HM Naval Base, Portsmouth PO1 3LJ T:(023) 9283 9766 W: www.royalnavalmuseum.org

Norfolk
Family History Shop & Library The Family History Sho 51 Horns Lane, Norwich NR1 3ER T:01603 621152 E: jenlibrary@aol.com W: www.jenlibrary.u-net.com

Great Yarmouth Central Library Tolhouse Street, Great Yarmouth NR30 2SH T:01493-844551 E: yarmouth.lib@norfolk.gov.uk W: www.library.norfolk.gov.uk

Heritage Centre, Norfolk and Norwich Millennium Library Millennium Plain, Norwich NR2 1AW T:01603 774740 E: norfolk.studies.lib@norfolk.gov.uk W: www.norfolk.gov.uk

Kings Lynn Library London Road, King's Lynn PE30 5EZ T:01553-772568 E: kings.lynn.lib@norfolk.gov.uk W: www.norfolk.gov.uk

Thetford Public Library Raymond Street, Thetford IP24 2EA T:01842-752048 E: thetford.lib@norfolk.gov.uk W: www.culture.norfolk.gov.uk

Northumberland
Alnwick Library Green Batt, Alnwick NE66 1TU T:01665-602689 W: www.northumberland.gov.uk

Berwick upon Tweed Library Church Street, Berwick upon Tweed TD15 1EE T:01289-307320 W: www.northumberland.gov.uk

Blyth Library Bridge Street, Blyth NE24 2DJ T:01670-361352 W: www.northumberland.gov.uk

Border History Museum and Library Moothall, Hallgate, Hexham NE46 3NH T:01434-652349 E: museum@tynedale.gov.uk W: www.tynedale.gov.uk

Hexham Library Queens Hall, Beaumont Street, Hexham NE46 3LS T:01434 652474 E: cheane@northumberland.gov.uk W: www.northumberland.gov.uk

Morpeth Library Gas House Lane, Morpeth NE61 1TA

Nottinghamshire
Arnold Library Front Street, Arnold NG5 7EE T:0115-920-2247 W: www.nottscc.gov.uk

Beeston Library Foster Avenue, Beeston NG9 1AE T:0115-925-5168 W: www.nottscc.gov.uk

Department of Manuscripts and Special Collections Nottingham University , King's Meadow Campus, Lenton Lane, Nottingham NG7 2NR T:0115 951 4565 E: mss-library@nottingham.ac.uk W: www.nottingham.ac.uk/mss/

Eastwood Library Wellington Place, Eastwood NG16 3GB T:01773-712209 W: www.nottscc.gov.uk

Mansfield Library Four Seasons Centre, Westgate, Mansfield NG18 1NH T:01623-627591 E: mansfield.library@nottscc.gov.uk W: www.nottscc.gov.uk

Newark Library Beaumont Gardens, Newark NG24 1UW T:01636-703966 W: www.nottscc.gov.uk

Nottingham Central Library : Local Studies Centre Angel Row, Nottingham NG1 6HP T:0115 915 2873 W: www.nottinghamcity.gov.uk/libraries

Retford Library Denman Library Churchgate, Retford DN22 6PE T:01777-708724 W: www.nottscc.gov.uk

Southwell Minster Library Minster Office, Trebeck Hall, Bishop's Drive, Southwell NG25 0JP T:01636-812649 E: mail@southwellminster.org.uk W: www.southwellminster.org.uk

Sutton in Ashfield Library Devonshire Mall, Sutton in Ashfield NG17 1BP T:01623-556296 W: www.nottscc.gov.uk

University of Nottingham, Hallward Library University Park, Nottingham NG7 2RD T:0115-951-4514 W: www.nottingham.ac.uk/library/

West Bridgford Library Bridgford Road, West Bridgford NG2 6AT T:0115-981-6506 W: www.nottscc.gov.uk

Oxfordshire
Abingdon Library The Charter, Abingdon OX14 3LY T:01235-520374 E: abingdon_library@yahoo.com W: www.oxfordshire.gov.uk

Angus Library Regent's Park College, Pusey Street, Oxford OX1 2LB T:01865 288142

Banbury Library Marlborough Road, Banbury OX16 8DF T:01295-262282

Centre for Oxfordshire Studies Central Library Westgate, Oxford OX1 1DJ T:01865-815749 E: cos@oxfordshire.gov.uk W: www.oxfordshire.gov.uk

Henley Library Ravenscroft Road, Henley on Thames RG9 2DH

T:01491-575278
Middle East Centre, St Anthony's College, Pusey Street, Oxford OX2 6JF T:01865 284706
Nuffield College Library , Oxford OX1 1NF T:01865 278550 E: library-archives@nuf.ox.ac.uk W: www.nuff.ox.ac.uk/library/archives-information.asp
Puysey House Library Pusey House, 61 St Giles, Oxford OX1 1LZ T:01865 278415 E: pusey.house@ic24.net
Rhodes House Library Bodleian Library South Parks Road, Oxford OX1 3RG T:01865 270909
River & Rowing Museum Rowing & River Museum, Mill Meadows, Henley on Thames RG9 1BF T:01491 415625 E: museum@rrm.co.uk W: www..rrm.co.uk
The Bodleian Library Broad Street, Oxford OX1 3BG T:01865 277000 W: www.bodley.ox.ac.uk
Wantage Library Stirlings Road, Wantage OX12 7BB T:01235 762291
Witney Library Welch Way, Witney OX8 7HH T:01993-703659

Rutland
Oakham Library Catmos Street, Oakham LE15 6HW T:01572 722918

Shropshire
Wrekin Local Studies Forum Madeley Library Russell Square, Telford TF7 5BB T:01952 586575 W: www.madeley.org.uk

Somerset
Bath Central Library 19 The Podium, Northgate Street, Bath BA1 5AN T:01225 787400 E: Bath_Library@bathnes.gov.uk W: www.bathnes.gov.uk
Bridgewater Reference Library Binford Place, Bridgewater TA6 3LF T:01278-450082 E: pcstoyle@somerset.gov.uk W: www.somerset.gov.uk
Frome Reference Library Justice Lane, Frome BA11 1BA T:01373-462215
Nailsea Library Somerset Square, Nailsea BS19 2EX T:01275-854583
Somerset Studies Library Paul Street, Taunton TA1 3XZ T:01823-340300 E: somstud@somerset.gov.uk W: www.somerset.gov.uk/libraries
Weston Library The Boulevard, Weston Super Mare BS23 1PL T:01934-636638 E: weston.library@n-somerset.gov.uk W: www.n-somerset.gov.uk
Yeovil Library King George Street, Yeovil BA20 1PY T:01935-421910 E: ransell@somerset.gov.uk W: www.somerset.gov.uk

Staffordshire
Barton Library Dunstall Road, Barton under Needwood DE13 8AX T:01283-713753 W: www.staffordshire.gov.uk
Biddulph Library Tunstall Road, Biddulph, Stoke on Trent ST8 6HH T:01782-512103 W: www.staffordshire.gov.uk
Brewood Library Newport Street, Brewood ST19 9DT T:01902-850087 W: www.staffordshire.gov.uk
Burton Library Burton Library Riverside, High Street, Burton on Trent DE14 1AH T:01283-239556 E: burton.library@staffordshire.gov.uk W: www.staffordshire.gov.uk
Cannock Library Manor Avenue, Cannock WS11 1AA T:01543-502019 E: cannock.library@staffordshire.gov.uk W: www.staffordshire.gov.uk
Cheslyn Hay Library Cheslyn Hay, Walsall WS56 7AE T:01922-413956 W: www.staffordshire.gov.uk
Codsall Library Histons Hill, Codsall WV8 1AA T:01902-842764 W: www.staffordshire.gov.uk
Great Wyrley Library John's Lane, Great Wyrley, Walsall WS6 6BY T:01922-414632 W: www.staffordshire.gov.uk
Keele University Library
Keele, ST5 5BG T:01782 583237 E: library@keele.ac.uk W: www.keele.ac.uk/library
Kinver Library Vicarage Drive, Kinver, Stourbridge DY7 6HJ T:01384-872348 W: www.staffordshire.gov.uk
Leek Library Nicholson Institute, Stockwell Street, Leek ST13 6DW T:01538-483210 E: leek.library@staffordshire.gov.uk W: www.staffordshire.gov.uk
Lichfield Library (Local Studies Section) Lichfield Library The Friary, Lichfield WS13 6QG T:01543 510720
Newcastle Library Ironmarket, Newcastle under Lyme ST5 1AT T:01782-297310 E: newcastle.library@staffordshire.gov.uk W: www.staffordshire.gov.uk
Penkridge Library Bellbrock, Penkridge ST19 9DL T:01785-712916 W: www.staffordshire.gov.uk
Perton Library Severn Drive, Perton WV6 7QU T:01902-755794 E: perton.library@staffordshire.gov.uk W: www.staffordshire.gov.uk

Rugeley Library Anson Street, Rugeley WS16 2BB T:01889-583237 W: www.staffordshire.gov.uk
Staffordshire & Stoke on Trent Archive Service - Stoke on Trent City Archives Hanley Library Bethesda Street, Hanley, Stoke on Trent ST1 3RS T:01782-238420 E: stoke.archives@stoke.gov.uk W: www.staffordshire.gov.uk/archives
Tamworth Library Corporation Street, Tamworth B79 7DN T:01827-475645 E: tamworth.library@staffordshire.gov.uk W: www.staffordshire.gov.uk/leisure/libraryfacilities/localstudiesandfamily history/
Uttoxeter Library High Street, Uttoxeter ST14 7JQ T:01889-256371 W: www.staffordshire.gov.uk
William Salt Library 19 Eastgate Street, Stafford ST16 2LZ T:01785 278372 E: william.salt.library@staffordshire.gov.uk W: www.staffordshire.gov.uk/salt
Wombourne Library Windmill Bank, Wombourne WV5 9JD T:01902-892032 W: www.staffordshire.gov.uk

Suffolk
Chantry Library Chantry Library Hawthorne Drive, Ipswich IP2 0QY T:01473 686117

Surrey
Bourne Hall Library Bourne Hall, Spring Street, Ewell, Epsom KT17 1UF T:020 8394 0372 W: www.surrey.gov.uk
Caterham Valley Library Caterham Valley Library Stafford Road, Caterham CR3 6JG T:01883 343580 W: www.surrey.gov.uk
Cranleigh Library and Local History Centre High Street, Cranleigh GU6 8AE T:01483 272413 W: www.surrey.gov.uk
Epsom and Ewell Local History Centre, Bourne Hall, Spring Street, Ewell, Epsom KT17 1UF T:020 8394 0372 W: www.surrey.gov.uk
Horley Library Horley Library Victoria Road, Horley RH6 7AG T:01293 784141 W: www.surrey.gov.uk
Lingfield Library The Guest House, Vicarage Road, Lingfield RH7 6HA T:01342 832058 W: www.surrey.gov.uk
Minet Library 52 Knatchbull Road, Lambeth London SE5 9QY T:(020) 7926 6076 E: lambetharchives@lambeth.gov.uk W: www.lambeth.gov.uk
Redhill Library Warwick Quadrant, Redhill RH1 1NN T:01737 763332 W: www.surrey.gov.uk
Surrey Heath Museum Knoll Road, Camberley GU15 3HD T:01276 707284 E: museum@surreyheath.gov.uk W: www.surreyheath.gov.uk/leisure
Surrey History Centre and Archives Surrey History Centre, 130 Goldsworth Road, Woking GU21 6ND T:01483 518737 E: shs@surreycc.gov.uk W: www.surreycc.gov.uk/surreyhistoryservice
Sutton Central Library St Nicholas Way, Sutton SM1 1EA T:(020) 8770 4745 E: sutton.information@sutton.gov.uk W: www.sutton.gov.uk

Sussex
Sussex University Library Manuscript Collections , Falmer, Brighton BN1 9QL T:01273 606755
Sussex - East, Brighton & Hove Council Library Service Bibliographic Services, 44 St Annes Crescent, Lewes BN17 1SQ T:01273-481813
Brighton History Centre Brighton Museum and Art Gallery, Royal Pavilion Gardens, Brighton BN1 1EE T:01273 296972 (Enquiries) E: localhistory@brighton-hove.gov.uk W: www.citylibraries.info/localhistoryt
Hove Reference Library 182 - 186 Church Road, Hove BN3 2EG T:01273-296942 E: hovelibrary@brighton-hove.gov.uk W: www.brighton-hove.gov.uk
Sussex - West
Worthing Reference Library Worthing Library Richmond Road, Worthing BN11 1HD T:01903 704824 E: worthing.reference.library@westsussex.gov.uk W: www.westsussex.gov.uk/libraries

Tyne and Wear
City Library & Arts Centre 28 - 30 Fawcett Street, Sunderland SR1 1RE T:0191 514 8413 E: janet.robinson@sunderland.gov.uk W: www.sunderland.gov.uk
Gateshead Central Library & Local Studies Department Prince Consort Road, Gateshead NE8 4LN T:0191 433 8400 E: anthealang@gateshead.gov.uk W: www.gateshead.gov.uk
N Tyneside Libraries & Museums Service - Central Library, North Shields Northumberland Square, North Shields NE3O 1QU T:0191 200 5424 E: local.studies@northtyneside.gov.uk W: www.northtyneside.gov.uk/libraries/index.htm
Newcastle Local Studies Centre City Library Princess Square, Newcastle upon Tyne NE99 1DX T:0191 277 4116 E: local.studies@newcastle.gov.uk W: www.newcastle.gov.uk

North Shields Local Studies Centre Central Library Northumberland Square, North Shields NE3O 1QU T:0191-200-5424 E: eric.hollerton@northtyneside.gov.uk W: www.northtyneside.gov.uk/libraries.html

Robinson Library University of Newcastle upon Tyne, Newcastle Upon Tyne NE2 4HQ T:0191 222 7671 E: library@ncl.ac.uk W: www.ncl.ac.uk/library/

South Tyneside Central Library - Local Studies Prince Georg Street, South Shields NE33 2PE T:0191 427 7860 E: localstudies.library@southtyneside.gov.uk W: www.southtyneside.gov.uk

Warwickshire

Atherstone Library Long Street, Atherstone CV9 1AX T:01827 712395 E: atherstonelibrary@warwickshire.gov.uk W: www.warwickshire.gov.uk

Bedworth Library 18 High Street, Bedworth, Nuneaton CV12 8NF T:024 7631 2267 E: bedworthlibrary@warwickshire.gov.uk W: www.warwickshire.gov.uk

Kenilworth Library Smalley Place, Kenilworth CV8 1QG T:01926 852595 E: kenilworthlibrary@warwickshire.gov.uk W: www.warwickshire.gov.uk

Local Studies Library Central Library Smithford Way, Coventry CV1 1FY T:012476 832336 E: archives@coventry.gov.uk W: www.coventry.gov.uk/accent.htm

Nuneaton Library Church Street, Nuneaton CV11 4DR T:024 7638 4027 E: nuneatonlibrary@warwickshire.gov.uk W: www.warwickshire.gov.uk

Rugby Library Little ElborowStreet, Rugby CV21 3BZ T:01788 533250 E: rugbylibrary@warwickshire.gov.uk W: www.warwickshire.gov.uk

Shakespeare Birthplace Trust - Library Shakespeare Centre Library Henley Street, Stratford upon Avon CV37 6QW T:01789-204016 E: library@shakespeare.org.uk W: www.shakespeare.org.uk

Stratford on Avon Library 12 Henley Street, Stratford on Avon CV37 6PZ T:01789 292209 E: stratfordlibrary@warwickshire.gov.uk W: www.warwickshire.gov.uk

Warwick Library - Warwickshire Local Collection (County Collection) Warwick Library Barrack Street, Warwick CV34 4TH T:01926 412189 E: warwicklibrary@warwickshire.gov.uk W: www.warwickshire.gov.uk

Warwickshire County Library Leamington Library Royal Pump Rooms, The Parade, Leamington Spa CV32 4AA T:01926 742721 E: leamingtonlibrary@warwickshire.gov.uk W: www.warwickshire.gov.uk

West Midlands

Birmingham Central Library - The Genealogist, Local Studies & History Service Floor 6, Central Library Chamberlain Square, Birmingham B3 3HQ T:0121 303 4549 E: local.studies.library@birmingham.gov.uk W: www.birmingham.gov.uk

Birmingham University Information Services - Special Collections Main Library University of Birmingham, Edgbaston, Birmingham B15 2TT T:0121 414 5838 E: special-collections@bham.ac.uk W: www.is.bham.ac.uk

Dudley Archives & Local History Service Mount Pleasant Street, Coseley, Dudley WV14 9JR T:01384-812770 W: www.dudley.gov.uk

Local Studies Library Central Library Smithford Way, Coventry CV1 1FY T:012476 832336 E: archives@coventry.gov.uk W: www.coventry.gov.uk/accent.htm

Sandwell Community History & Archives Service Smethwick Library High Street, Smethwick B66 1AB T:0121 558 2561 E: archives.service@sandwell.gov.uk W: www.lea.sandwell.gov.uk/index/leisure_and_culture/localhistorycentre

Solihull Heritage and Local Studies Service Solihull Central Library Homer Road, Solihull B91 3RG T:0121-704-6977 W: www.solihull.gov.uk/wwwlib/#local

Sutton Coldfield Reference Library - Local Studies Section 43 Lower Parade, Sutton Coldfield B72 1XX T:0121 464 0164 E: sutton.coldfield.reference.lib@birmingham.gov.uk W: www.birmingham.gov.uk

Walsall Local History Centre Essex Street, Walsall WS2 7AS T:01922-721305 E: localhistorycentre@walsall.gov.uk W: www.walsall.gov.uk/index/leisure_and_culture/localhistorycentre

Wolverhampton Archives & Local Studies 42 - 50 Snow Hill, Wolverhampton WV2 4AG T:01902 552480 E: wolverhamptonarchives@dial.pipes.com W: www.wolverhampton.gov.uk/archives

Wigan

Abram Library Vicarage Road, Abram Wigan WN2 5QX T:01942 866350

Ashton Library Wigan Road, Ashton in Makerfield, Wigan WN2 9BH T:01942 727119

Aspull Library Oakfield Crescent, Aspull, Wigan WN2 1XJ T:01942 831303

Atherton Library York Street, Atherton, Manchester M46 9JH T:01942 404817

Beech Hill Library Buckley St West, Beech Hill, Wigan WN6 7PQ

Hindley Library Market St, Hindley, Wigan WN2 3AN T:01942 255287

Ince Library Smithy Green, Ince, Wigan WN2 2AT T:01942 255287

Leigh Library Turnpike Centre, Civic Square, Leigh WN7 1EB T:01942 404557

Marsh Green Library Harrow Road, Marsh Green, Wigan T:01942 760041

Shevington Library Gathurst Lane, Shevington, Wigan WN6 8HA T:01257 252618

Standish Library Cross Street, Standish, Wigan WN6 0HQ T:01257 400496

Tyldesley Library Stanley Street, Tyldesley, Manchester M29 8AH T:01942 882504

Wigan Library College Avenue, Wigan WN1 1NN T:01942 827619

Wigan MBC - Leisure Services Department Information Unit, Station Road, Wigan WN1 1WA

Wiltshire

Salisbury Reference and Local Studies Library Market Place, Salisbury SP1 1BL T:01722 411098 W: www.wiltshire.gov.uk

Swindon Borough Library Reference Library Regent Circus, Swindon SN1 1QG T:01793 463240 E: reference.library@swindon.gov.uk W: www.swindon.gov.uk

Swindon Local Studies Library Swindon Central Library Regent Circus, Swindon SN11QG T:01793 463240 E: swindonref@swindon.gov.uk W: www.swindon.gov.uk

Wiltshire Archaeological and Natural History Society Wiltshire Heritage Library 41 Long Street, Devizes SN10 1NS T:01380 727369 E: wanhs@wiltshireheritage.org.uk W: www.wiltshireheritage.org.uk

Wiltshire Buildings Record Libraries and Heritage HQ, Bythesea Road, Trowbridge BA14 8BS T:01225 713740 E: dorothytreasure@wiltshire.gov.uk W: www.wiltshire.gov.uk

Wiltshire Heritage Museum Library Wiltshire Archaeological & Natural History Society, 41 Long Street, Devizes SN10 1NS T:01380 727369 E: wanhs@wiltshireheritage.org.uk W: www.wiltshireheritage.org.uk

Wiltshire Studies Library Library & heritage HQ, Bythesea Road, Trowbridge BA14 8BS T:01225-713732 E: librarystudies@wiltshire.gov.uk W: www.wiltshire.gov.uk/community/

Worcestershire

Bewdley Museum Research Library Load Street, Bewdley DY12 2AE T:01229-403573 E: museum@online.rednet.co.uk angela@bewdleyhistory.evesham.net W: www.bewdleymuseum.tripod.com

Bromsgrove Library Stratford Road, Bromsgrove B60 1AP T:01527-575855 W: www.worcestershire.gov.uk

Evesham Library Oat Street, Evesham WR11 4PJ T:01386-442291 E: eveshamlib@worcestershire.gov.uk W: www.worcestershire.gov.uk

Kidderminster Library Market Street, Kidderminster DY10 1AD T:01562-824500 E: kidderminster@worcestershire.gov.uk W: www.worcestershire.gov.uk

Malvern Library Graham Road, Malvern WR14 2HU T:01684-561223 W: www.worcestershire.gov.uk

Redditch Library 15 Market Place, Redditch B98 8AR T:01527-63291 E: redditchlibrary@worcestershire.gov.uk W: www.worcestershire.gov.uk

Worcester Library Foregate Street, Worcester WR1 1DT T:01905 765312 E: worcesterlib@worcestershire.gov.uk W: www.worcestershire.gov.uk/libraries

Worcesterhire Library & History Centre History Centre, Trinity Street, Worcester WR1 2PW T:01905 765922 E: wlhc@worcestershire.gov.uk W: www.worcestershire.gov.uk/records

Yorkshire - East

Beverley Local Studies Library Beverley Library Champney Road, Beverley HU17 9BG T:01482 392755 E: beverleyref.library@eastriding.gov.uk W: www.eastriding.gov.uk

Bridlington Local Studies Library Bridlington Library King Street, Bridlington YO15 2DF T:01262 672917 E: bridlingtonref.library@eastriding.gov.uk W: www.eastriding.gov.uk

East Riding Heritage Library & Museum Sewerby Hall, Church Lane, Sewerby Bridlington, YO15 1EA T:01262-677874 E: museum@pop3.poptel.org.uk W: www.bridlington.net/sew

Goole Local Studies Library Goole Library Carlisle Street, Goole DN14 5DS T:01405-762187 E: goolref.library@eastriding.gov.uk W: www.eastriding.gov.uk

Yorkshire - North
Catterick Garrison Library Gough Road, Catterick Garrison DL9
3EL T:01748 833543 W: www.northyorks.gov.uk
Harrogate Reference Library Victoria Avenue, Harrogate HG1 1EG
T:01423-502744 W: www.northyorks.gov.uk
Malton Library St Michael's Street, Malton YO17 7LJ T:01653
692714 W: www.northyorks.gov.uk
North Yorkshire County Libraries 21 Grammar School Lane,
Northallerton DL6 1DF T:01609-776271 E:
elizabeth.melrose@northyorks.gov.uk W: www.northyorks.gov.uk
Northallerton Reference Library 1 Thirsk Road, Northallerton DL6
1PT T:01609-776202 E: northallerton.libraryhq@northyorks.gov.uk W:
www.northyorks.gov.uk
Pickering Reference Library The Ropery, Pickering YO18 8DY
T:01751-472185 W: www.northyorks.gov.uk
Richmond Library Queen's Road, Richmond DL10 4AE T:01748
823120 W: www.northyorks.gov.uk
Ripon Library The Arcade, Ripon HG4 1AG T:01765 792926 W:
www.northyorks.gov.uk
Scarborough Reference Library Vernon Road, Scarborough YO11
2NN T:01723-364285 E: scarborough.library@northyorks.gov.uk W:
www.northyorks.gov.uk
Selby Reference Library 52 Micklegate, Selby YO8 4EQ T:01757-
702020 W: www.northyorks.gov.uk
Skipton Reference Library High Street, Skipton BD23 1JX T:01756-
794726 W: www.northyorks.gov.uk
Whitby Library Windsor Terrace, Whitby YO21 1ET T:01947-
602554

Yorkshire - South
Barnsley Archives and Local Studies Department Central Library
Shambles Street, Barnsley S70 2JF T:01226-773950 E:
Archives@barnsley.gov.uk W: www.barnsley.gov.uk
Doncaster Libraries - Local Studies Section Central Library
Waterdale, Doncaster DN1 3JE T:01302-734307 E:
reference.library@doncaster.gov.uk W: www.doncaster.gov.uk
Rotherham Archives & Local Studies Central Library Walker Place,
Rotherham S65 1JH T:01709 823616 E: archives@rotherham.gov.uk
W: www.rotherham.gov.uk
Sheffield Central Library Surrey Street, Sheffield S1 1XZ T:0114
273 4753 E: localstudies.library@sheffield.gov.uk
Sheffield University Library Special Collections & Library Archives
Western Bank, Sheffield S10 2TN T:0114 222 7230 E: lib-
special@sheffield.ac.uk

Yorkshire - West
Batley Library Market Place, Batley WF17 5DA T:01924 326021 E:
batley.library@kirklees.gov.uk W: www.kirklees.gov.uk
Bradford Local Studies Reference Library Central Library Prince's
Way, Bradford BD1 1NN T:01274 433661 E:
local.studies@bradford.gov.uk W: www.bradford.gov.uk
British Library The British Library Boston Spa, Wetherby LS23 7BQ
T:01937-546212
Brotherton Library Department of Special Collections Leeds
University, Leeds LS2 9JT T:0113 233 55188 E: special-
collections@library.leeds.ac.uk W: http://leeds.ac.uk/library/spcoll/
Calderdale Central Library Northgate House, Northgate, Halifax
HX11 1UN T:01422 392631 W: www.calderdale.gov.uk
Castleford Library & Local Studies Dept, Carlton Street, Castleford
WF10 1BB T:01977-722085
Cleckheaton Library Whitcliffe Road, Cleckheaton BD19 3DX
T:01274 335170
Dewsbury Library Dewsbury Retail Park, Railway Street, Dewsbury
WF12 8EQ T:01924 325080
Huddersfield Local History Library Huddersfield Library & Art
Gallery, Princess Alexandra Walk, Huddersfield HD1 2SU T:01484-
221965 E: ref-library@geo2.poptel.org.uk W: www.kirkleesmc.gov.uk
Keighley Reference Library North Street, Keighley BD21 3SX
T:01535-618215 E: keighleylibrary@bradford.gov.uk W:
www.bradford.gov.uk
Leeds Local Studies Library Central Library Calverley Street, Leeds
LS1 3AB T:0113 247 8290 E: localstudies@leedslearning.net W:
www.leeds.gov.uk/library
Mirfield Library East Thorpe Lodge, Mirfield WF14 8AN T:01924
326470
Olicana Historical Society 54 Kings Road, Ilkley LS29 9AT
Pontefract Library & Local Studies Centre Pontefract Library
Shoemarket, Pontefract WF8 1BD T:01977-727692
Wakefield Local Studies Department Balne Lane, Wakefield WF2
0DQ T:01924-302224 W: www.wakefield.gov.uk
Yorkshire Archaeological Society Claremont, 23 Clarendon Rd,
Leeds LS2 9NZ T:0113-245-6342 E: yas@wyjs.org.uk (Library and
Archives) W: www.yas.org.uk

Yorkshire - York
York Minster Library York Minster Library & Archives Dean's Park,
York YO1 2JQ T:01904-625308 Library E: library@yorkminster.org
archives@yorkminster.org W: www.yorkminster.org
Yorkshire Family History - Biographical Database York Minster
Library & Archives Dean's Park, York YO1 7JQ T:01904-625308
Library E: library@yorkminster.org archives@yorkminster.org
www.yorkminster.org
York Local History & Reference Collection Central Library Museum
Street, York YO1 7DS T:01904-655631 E:
reference.library@york.gov.uk W: www.york.gov.uk

Wales
National
National Library of Wales Penglais, Aberystwyth, SY23 3BU T:
01970 632800 E: holi@llgc.org.uk W: www.llgc.org.uk
South Wales Miners' Library - University of Wales, Swansea
Hendrefoelan House, Gower Road, Swansea, SA2 7NB T: 01792-
518603 E: miners@swansea.ac.uk W: www.swan.ac.uk/lis/swml
University of Walwes Swansea library Library & Information
Centre, Singleton Park, Swansea, SA2 8PP T: 01792 295021
Blaenau Gwent
Ebbw Vale Library Ebbw Vale Library, 21 Bethcar Street, Ebbw Vale,
NP23 6HH T: 01495-303069
Tredegar library The Circle, Tredegar, NP2 3PS T: 01495-722687
Brecon
Brecon Area Library Ship Street, Brecon, LD3 9AE T: 01874-
623346 E: breclib@mail.powys.gov.uk W: www.powys.gov.uk
Caerphilly
Bargoed Library The Square, Bargoed, CF81 8QQ T: 01443-875548
E: 9e465@dial.pipex.com
Caerphilly Library HQ Unit 7 Woodfieldside Business Park,
Penmaen Road, Pontllanfraith, Blackwood, NP12 2DG T: 01495
235584 E: cael.libs@dial.pipex.com
Cardiff
Cardiff Central Library (Local Studies Department) St Davids
Link, Frederick Street, Cardiff, CF1 4DT T: (029) 2038 2116 E:
p.sawyer@cardlib.gov.uk W: www.cardiff.gov.uk
Carmarthenshire
Carmarthen Library St Peters Street, Carmarthen, SA31 1LN T:
01267-224822
Llanelli Public Library Vaughan Street, Lanelli, SA15 3AS T:
01554-773538
Ceredigion
Aberystwyth Reference Library Corporation Street, Aberystwyth,
SY23 2BU T: 01970-617464 E: llyfrygell.library@ceredigion.gov.uk
W: www.ceredigion.gov.uk/libraries
Flintshire
Flintshire Reference Library Headquarters County Hall, Mold,
CH7 6NW T: 01352 704411 E: libraries@flintshire.gov.uk W:
www.flintshire.gov.uk
Glamorgan
Bridgend Library & Information Service Coed Parc, Park Street,
Bridgend, CF31 4BA T: 01656-767451 E: blis@bridgendlib.gov.uk
W: www.bridgendlib.gov.uk
Dowlais Library Church Street, Dowlais, Merthyr Tydfil, CF48 3HS
T: 01985-723051
Merthyr Tydfil Central Library (Local Studies Department)
Merthyr Library, High Street, Merthyr Tydfil, CF47 8AF T: 01685-
723057 E: library@merthyr.gov.uk W: www.merthyr.gov.uk
Pontypridd Library Library Road, Pontypridd, CF37 2DY T: 01443-
486850 E: hywel.w.matthews@rhondda-cynon-taff.gov.uk W:
www.rhondda-cynon-taff.gov.uk/libraries/pontypri.htm
Port Talbot Library 1st Floor Aberafan Shopping Centre, Port
Talbot, SA13 1PB T: 01639-763490 W: www.neath-porttalbot.gov.uk
Treorchy Library Station Road, Treorchy, CF42 6NN T: 01443-
773204
Glamorgan - West
Neath Central Library (Local Studies Department) 29 Victoria
Gardens, Neath, SA11 3BA T: 01639-620139 W: www.neath-
porttalbot.gov.uk
Swansea Reference Library Alexandra Road, Swansea, SA1 5DX T:
01792 516753 E: central.library@swansea.gov.uk W:
www.swansea.gov.uk/libraries
West Glamorgan Archive Service - Port Talbot Access Point Port
Talbot Library, 1st Floor, Aberavon Shopping Centre, Port Talbot,
SA13 1PB T: 01639 763430 W: www.swansea.gov.uk/archives
Gwent
Abertillery Library Station Hill, Abertillery, NP13 1TE T: 01495-
212332
Chepstow Library Manor Way, Chepstow, NP16 5HZ T: 01291-
635730 E: chepstowlibrary@monmouthshire.gov.uk W:
www.monmouthshire.gov.uk/leisure/libraries

Newport Community Learning and Libraries Newport Central Library, John Frost Square, Newport, NP20 1PA T: 01633 656656 E: reference.library@newport.gov.uk W: www.newport.gov.uk
Gwynedd
Canolfan Llyfrgell Dolgellau Library FforddBala, Dolgellau, LL40 2YF T: 01341-422771 W: www.gwynedd.gov.uk
Llyfrgell Caernarfon Lon Pafiliwn, Caernafon, LL55 1AS T: 01286-679465 E: library@gwynedd.gov.uk W: www.gwynedd.gov.uk
Merthyr Tydfil
Treharris Library Perrott Street, Treharris, Merthyr Tydfil, CF46 5ET T: 01443-410517
Monmoputhshire
Chepstow Library & Information Centre Manor Way, Chepstow, NP16 5HZ T: 01291-635730 E: chepstowlibrary@monmouthshire.gov.uk W: www.monmouthshire.gov.uk/leisure/libraries
Neath Port Talbot
Lifelong Learning Service Theodore Road, Port Talbot, SA13 1SP T: 01639-898581 E: lls@neath-porttalbot.gov.uk W: www.neath-porttalbot.gov.uk
Pembrokeshire
Pembrokeshire Libraries The County Library, Dew Street, Haverfordwest, SA61 1SU T: 01437 775248 E: sue.armour@pembrokeshire.gov.uk W: www.pembrokeshire.gov.uk
Powys
Brecon Area Library Ship Street, Brecon, LD3 9AE T: 01874-623346 E: breclib@mail.powys.gov.uk W: www.powys.gov.uk
Llandrindod Wells Library Cefnllys Lanc, Llandrindod Wells, LD1 5LD T: 01597-826870 E: llandod.library@powys.gov.uk W: www.powys.gov.uk
Newtown Area Library Park Lane, Newtown, SY16 1EJ T: 01686-626934 E: nlibrary@powys.gov.uk W: www.powys.gov.uk
Rhondda Cynon Taff
Aberdare Library Green Street, Aberdare, CF44 7AG T: 01685 880053 E: alun.r.prescott@rhondda-cynon-taff.gov.uk W: www.rhondda-cynon-taff.gov.uk/libraries/aberdare.htm
Pontypridd Library Library Road, Pontypridd, CF37 2DY T: 01443-486850 E: hywel.w.matthews@rhondda-cynon-taff.gov.uk W: www.rhondda-cynon-taff.gov.uk/libraries/pontypri.htm
Treorchy Library Station Road, Treorchy, CF42 6NN T: 01443-773204
Vale of Glamorgan
Barry Library King Square, Holton Road, Barry, CF63 4RW T: 01446-735722
Wrexham CBC
Wrexham Library and Arts Centre Rhosddu Road, Wrexham, LL11 1AU T: 01978-292622 E: joy.thomas@wrexham.gov.uk W: www.wrexham.gov.uk

Scotland
National
Edinburgh University Library, Special Collections Department George Square, Edinburgh, EH8 9LJ T: 0131 650 3412 E: special.collections@ed.ac.uk W: www.lib.ed.ac.uk
Edinburgh University New College Library Mound Place, Edinburgh, EH1 2UL T: 0131 650 8957 E: New.College.Library@ed.ac.uk W: www.lib.ed.ac.uk
National Library of Scotland George IV Bridge, Edinburgh, EH1 1EW T: 0131-226-4531 E: enquiries@nls.uk W: www.nls.uk
National Monuments Record of Scotland Royal Commission on the Ancient & Historical Monuments of Scotland, John Sinclair House, 16 Bernard Terrace, Edinburgh, EH8 9NX T: 0131 662 1456 E: nmrs@rcahms.gov.uk W: www.rcahms.gov.uk
National Museums of Scotland Library Royal Museum, Chambers Street, Edinburgh, EH1 1JF T: 0131 247 4137 E: library@nms.ac.uk W: www.nms.ac.uk
National War Museum of Scotland Library The Castle, Museum Square, Edinburgh, EH1 1 2NG T: 0131 225 7534 Ext 2O4 E: library@nms.ac.uk W: www.nms.ac.uk
Royal Botanic Garden The Library, 20a Inverleith Row, Edinburgh, EH3 5LR T: 0131 552 7171
Scottish Genealogy Society 15 Victoria Terrace, Edinburgh, EH1 2JL T: 0131-220-3677 E: sales@scotsgenealogy.com W: www.scotsgenealogy.com
Scottish Genealogy Society - Library 15 Victoria Terrace, Edinburgh, EH1 2JL T: 0131-220 3677 E: info@scotsgenealogy.com W: www.scotsgenealogy.com
St Andrews University Library - Special Collections Department North Street, St Andrews, KY16 9TR T: 01334 462339 E: speccoll@st-and.ac.uk W: http://specialcollections.st-and.ac.uk
Strathclyde University Archives McCance Building, 16 Richmond Street, Glasgow, G1 1XQ T: 0141 548 2397

Aberdeenshire
Aberdeen Central Library - Reference & Local Studies Rosemount Viaduct, Aberdeen, AB25 1GW T: 01224-652511 E: refloc@arts-rec.aberdeen.net.uk W: www.aberdeencity.gov.uk
Aberdeenshire Library & Information Service The Meadows Industrial Estate, Meldrum Meg Way, Oldmeldrum, AB51 0GN T: 01651-872707 E: ALIS@aberdeenshire.gov.uk W: www.aberdeenshire.gov.uk
University of Aberdeen DISS: Heritage Division Special Collections & Archives Kings College, Aberdeen, AB24 3SW T: 01224-272598 E: speclib@abdn.ac.uk W: www.abdn.ac.uk/diss/heritage
Angus
Montrose Library - Angus District Montrose Library, 214 High Street, Montrose, MO10 8PH T: 01674-673256
Argyll & Bute
Argyll & Bute Council Library Service - Local studies Highland Avenue, Sandbank, Dunoon, PA23 8PB T: 01369 703214 E: eleanor.harris@argyll-bute.gov.uk W: www.argyll-bute.gov.uk
Campbeltown Library and Museum Hall St, Campbeltown, PA28 6BU T: 01586 552366 E: mary.vanhelmond@argyll-bute.gov.uk W: www.argyle-bute.gov.uk/content/leisure/museums
Ayrshire
Auchinleck Library Community Centre, Well Road, Auchinleck, KA18 2LA T: 01290 422829 W: www.east-ayrshire.gov.uk
Bellfield Library 79 Whatriggs Road, Kilmarnock, KA1 3RB T: 01563 534266 E: libraries@east-ayrshire.gov.uk W: www.east-ayrshire.gov.uk
Bellsbank Library Primary School, Craiglea Crescent, Bellsbank, KA6 7UA T: 01292 551057 E: libraries@east-ayrshire.gov.uk W: www.east-ayrshire.gov.uk
Catrine Library A M Brown Institute, Catrine, KA5 6RT T: 01290 551717 E: libraries@east-ayrshire.gov.uk W: www.east-ayrshire.gov.uk
Crosshouse Library 11-13 Gatehead Road, Crosshouse, KA2 0HN T: 01563 573640 E: libraries@east-ayrshire.gov.uk W: www.east-ayrshire.gov.uk
Cumnock Library 25-27 Ayr Road, Cumnock, KA18 1EB T: 01290-422804 W: www.east-ayrshire.gov.uk
Dalmellington Library Townhead, Dalmellington, KA6 7QZ T: 01292 550159 E: libraries@east-ayrshire.gov.uk W: www.east-ayrshire.gov.uk
Dalrymple Library Barbieston Road, Dalrymple, KA6 6DZ E: libraries@east-ayrshire.gov.uk W: www.east-ayrshire.gov.uk
Darvel Library Town Hall, West Main Street, Darvel, KA17 0AQ T: 01560 322754 E: libraries@east-ayrshire.gov.uk W: www.east-ayrshire.gov.uk
Drongan Library Mill O'Shield Road, Drongan, KA6 7AY T: 01292 591718 E: libraries@east-ayrshire.gov.uk W: www.east-ayrshire.gov.uk
East Ayrshire Council District History Centre & Museum Baird Institute, 3 Lugar Street, Cumnock, KA18 1AD T: 01290 421701 E: Baird.institute@east-ayrshire.gov.uk W: www.east-ayrshire.gov.uk
East Ayrshire Libraries Dick Institute, Elmbank Avenue, Kilmarnock, KA1 3BU T: 01563 554310 E: baird.institute@east-ayrshire.gov.uk W: www.east-ayrshire.gov.uk
Galston Library Henrietta Street, Galston, KA4 8HQ T: 01563 821994 E: libraries@east-ayrshire.gov.uk W: www.east-ayrshire.gov.uk
Hurlford Library Blair Road, Hurlford, KA1 5BN T: 01563 539899 E: libraries@east-ayrshire.gov.uk W: www.east-ayrshire.gov.uk
Kilmaurs Library Irvine Road, Kilmaurs, KA3 2RJ E: libraries@east-ayrshire.gov.uk W: www.east-ayrshire.gov.uk
Mauchline Library 2 The Cross, Mauchline, T: 01290 550824 E: libraries@east-ayrshire.gov.uk W: www.east-ayrshire.gov.uk
Muirkirk Library Burns Avenue, Muirkirk, KA18 3RH T: 01290 661505 E: libraries@east-ayrshire.gov.uk W: www.east-ayrshire.gov.uk
Netherthird Library Ryderston Drive, Netherthird, KA18 3AR T: 01290 423806 E: libraries@east-ayrshire.gov.uk W: www.east-ayrshire.gov.uk
New Cumnock Library Community Centre, The Castle, New Cumnock, KA18 4AH T: 01290 338710 E: libraries@east-ayrshire.gov.uk W: www.east-ayrshire.gov.uk
Newmilns Library Craigview Road, Newmilns, KA16 9DQ T: 01560 322890 E: libraries@east-ayrshire.gov.uk W: www.east-ayrshire.gov.uk
North Ayrshire Libraries Library Headquarters, 39 - 41 Princes Street, Ardrossan, KA22 8BT T: 01294 469137 W: www.north-ayrshire.gov.uk
Ochiltree Library Main Street, Ochiltree, KA18 2PE T: 01290 700425 E: libraries@east-ayrshire.gov.uk W: www.east-ayrshire.gov.uk
Patna Library Doonside Avenue, Patna, KA6 7LX T: 01292 531538 E: libraries@east-ayrshire.gov.uk W: www.east-ayrshire.gov.uk
South Ayrshire Library Carnegie Library, 12 Main Street, Ayr, KA8 8ED T: 01292-286385 E: carnegie@south-ayrshire.gov.uk W: www.south-ayrshire.gov.uk

Clackmannanshire
Clackmannanshire Archives Alloa Library, 26/28 Drysdale Street, Alloa, FK10 1JL T: 01259 722262 E: libraries@clacks.gov.uk W: www.clacksweb.org.uk/dyna/archives
Clackmannanshire Libraries Alloa Library, 26/28 Drysdale Street, Alloa, FK10 1JL T: 01259-722262 E: clack.lib@mail.easynet.co.uk
Dumfries & Galloway
Ewart Library Ewart Library, Catherine Street, Dumfries, DG1 1JB T: 01387 260285 E: ericaj@dumgal.gov.uk
W: www.dgc.gov.uk/service/depts/comres/library/gresearch
Dunbartonshire
Dumbarton Public library Strathleven Place, Dumbarton, G82 1BD T: 01389-733273 E: wdlibs@hotmail.com W: www.wdcweb.info
Dundee
Dundee Central Library The Wellgate, Dundee, DD1 1DB T: 01382-434377 E: local.studies@dundeecity.gov.uk W: www.dundeecity.gov.uk/dcchtml/nrd/loc_stud.htm
Tay Valley Family History Society & Family History Research Centre Family History Research Centre, 179–181 Princes Street, Dundee, DD4 6DQ T: 01382 461845 E: tvfhs@tayvalleyfhs.org.uk W: www.tayvalleyfhs.org.uk
East Dunbarton
Bishopbriggs Library 170 Kirkintilloch Road, Bishopbriggs, G64 2LX T: 0141 772 4513 W: www.eastdunbarton.gov.uk
Brookwood Library 166 Drymen Road, Bearsden, Glasgow, G61 3RJ T: 0141-942 6811 W: www.eastdunbarton.gov.uk
Craighead Library Milton of Campsie, G66 8Dl T: 01360 311925 W: www.eastdunbarton.gov.uk
Lennoxtown Library Main Street, Lennoxtown, G66 7HA T: 01360 311436
Lenzie Library 13 - 15 Alexandra Avenue, Lenzie, G66 5BG T: 0141 776 3021 W: www.eastdunbarton.gov.uk
Milgarvie Library Allander Road, Milngarvie, G62 8PN T: 0141 956 2776 W: www.eastdunbarton.gov.uk
Westerton Library 82 Maxwell Avenue, Bearsden, G61 1NZ T: 0141 943 0780
East Dunbartonshire
Local Record Offices and Reference Libraries William Patrick Library, 2 West High Street, Kirkintilloch, G66 1AD T: 0141 776 8090 E: libraries@eastdunbarton.gov.uk W: www.eastdunbarton.gov.uk
East Renfrewshire
Giffnock Library Station Road, Giffnock, Glasgow, G46 6JF T: 0141-577-4976 E: devinem@eastrenfrewshire.co.uk W: www.eastrenfrewshire.co.uk
Edinburgh
Edinburgh Central Library Edinburgh Room, George IV Bridge, Edinburgh, EH1 1EG T: 0131-242 8030 E: eclis@edinburgh.gov.uk W: www.edinburgh.gov.uk
Falkirk
Falkirk Library Hope Street, Falkirk, FK1 5AU T: 01324 503605 W: www.falkirk.gov.uk
Falkirk Museum History Research Centre Callendar House, Callendar Park, Falkirk, FK1 1YR T: 01324 503778 E: ereid@falkirkmuseums.demon.co.ukcallandarhouse@falkirkmuseums.demon.co.uk W: www.falkirkmuseums.demon.co.uk
Fife
Dunfermline Library - Local History Department Abbot Street, Dunfermline, KY12 7NL T: 01383-312994 E: info@dunfermline.fifelib.net W: www.fife.gov.uk
Fife Council Central Area Libraries Central Library, War Memorial Grounds, Kirkcaldy, KY1 1YG T: 01592-412878 E: info@kirkcaldy.fifelib.net W: www.fife.gov.uk
St Andrews Library Church Square, St Andrews, KY16 9NN T: 01334-412685 E: info@standres.fiflib.net W: www.fife.gov.uk
St Andrews University Library North Street, St Andrews, KY16 9TR T: 01334-462281 W: www.library.st-and.ac.uk
Tay Valley Family History Society & Family History Research Centre Family History Research Centre, 179–181 Princes Street, Dundee, DD4 6DQ T: 01382 461845 E: tvfhs@tayvalleyfhs.org.uk W: www.tayvalleyfhs.org.uk
Glasgow
Brookwood Library 166 Drymen Road, Bearsden, Glasgow, G61 3RJ T: 0141-942 6811 W: www.eastdunbarton.gov.uk
Glasgow City Libraries & Archives Mitchell Library, North Street, Glasgow, G3 7DN T: 0141 287 2937 E: history_and_glasgow @gcl.glasgow.gov.uk W: www.glasgow.gov.uk/html/council/cindex.htm
Glasgow University Library & Special Collections Department Hillhead Street, Glasgow, G12 8QE T: 0141 330 6704 E: library@lib.gla.ac.uk W: www.gla.ac.uk/library
Social Sciences Department - History & Glasgow Room The Mitchell Library, North Street, Glasgow, G3 7DN T: 0141-227-2935 E: history-and-glasgow@cls.glasgow.gov.uk W: www.libarch.glasgow

Highland
North Highland Archive Wick Library, Sinclair Terrace, Wick, KW1 5AB T: 01955 606432
Isle of Barra
Castlebay Community Library Community School, Castlebay, HS95XD T: 01871-810471
Isle of Benbecula
Community Library Sgoil Lionacleit, Liniclate, HS7 5PJ T: 01870-602211
Isle of Lewis
Stornoway Library 19 Cromwell Street, Stornoway, HS1 2DA T: 01851 708631 E: dfowler@cne-siar.gov.uk.
Lanarkshire
Airdrie Library Wellwynd, Airdrie, ML6 0AG T: 01236-763221 W: www.northlan.gov.uk/
Cumbernauld Central Library 8 Allander Walk, Cumbernauld, G67 1EE T: 01236-735964 W: www.northlan.org.uk
Leadhills Miners' Library 15 Main Street, Leadhills, ML12 6XP T: 01659-74326 E: anne@leadshilllibrary.co.uk W: www.lowtherhills.fsnet.co.uk
Midlothian
Midlothian Libraries Local History Centre Midlothian Council Libraries Headquarters, 2 Clerk Street, Loanhead, EH20 9DR T: 0131-440-2210 E: local.studies@midlothian.gov.uk W: www.earl.org.uk.partners/midlothian/index.html
Morayshire
Forres Library Forres House, High Street, Forres, IV36 0BJ T: 01309-672834 W: www.moray.gov.uk
Buckie Library Clunu Place, Buckie, AB56 1HB T: 01542-832121 E: buckie.lib@techleis.moray.gov.uk W: www.moray.gov.uk
Keith Library Union Street, Keith, AB55 5DP T: 01542-882223 E: keithlibrary@techleis.moray.gov.uk W: www.moray.gov.uk
Moray Local Heritage Centre Grant Lodge, Cooper Park, Elgin, IV30 1HS T: 01343 562644 E: graeme.wilson@techleis.moray.gov.uk W: www.morray.org/heritage/roots.html
North Lanarkshire
Kilsyth Library Burngreen, Kilsyth, G65 0HT T: 01236-823147 W: www.northlan.org.uk
Motherwell Heritage Centre High Road, Motherwell, ML1 3HU T: 01698-251000 E: heritage@mhc158.freeserve.co.uk W: www.northlan.org.uk
Shotts Library Benhar Road, Shotts, ML7 5EN T: 01501-821556 W: www.northlan.org.uk
Orkney
Orkney Library The Orkney Library, Laing Street, Kirkwall, KW15 1NW T: 01856-873166 W: www.orkney.gov.uk
Perthshire
Perth & Kinross Libraries A K Bell Library, 2 - 8 York Place, Perth, PH2 8EP T: 01738-477062 E: jaduncan@pkc.gov.uk W: www.pkc.gov.uk
Tay Valley Family History Society & Family History Research Centre Family History Research Centre, 179–181 Princes Street, Dundee, DD4 6DQ T: 01382 461845 E: tvfhs@tayvalleyfhs.org.uk W: www.tayvalleyfhs.org.uk
Renfrewshire
Renfrewshire Council Library & Museum Services Central Library & Museum Complex, High Street, Paisley, PA1 2BB T: 0141-889-2350 E: local_studies.library@renfrewshire.gov.uk W: www.renfrewshire.gov.uk
Watt Library 9 Union Street, Greenock, PA16 8JH T: 01475 715628 E: library.watt@inverclyde.gov.uk W: www.inverclyde-libraries.info
Scottish Borders
Scottish Borders Archive & Local History Centre Library Headquarters, St Mary's Mill, Selkirk, TD7 5EW T: 01750 20842 E: archives@scotborders.gov.uk W: www.scotborders.gov.uk/libraries
Shetland
Shetland Library Lower Hillhead, Lerwick, ZE1 0EL T: 01595-693868 E: info@shetland-library.gov.uk W: www.shetland-library.gov.uk
Stirling
Bridge of Allan Library Fountain Road, Bridge of Allan, FK9 4AT T: 01786 833680 W: www.stirling.gov.uk
Dunblane Library High Street, Dunbland, FK15 0ER T: 01786 823125 E: dunblanelibrary@stirling.gov.uk W: www.stirling.gov.uk
St Ninians Library Mayfield Centre, St Ninians, FK7 0DB T: 01786 472069 E: stninlibrary@stirling.gov.uk W: www.stirling.gov.uk
Stirling Central Library Central Library, Corn Exchange Road, Stirling, FK8 2HX T: 01786 432106 E: centrallibrary@stirling.gov.uk W: www.stirling.gov.uk
Tayside
Dundee University Archives Tower Building, University of Dundee, Dundee, DD1 4HN T: 01382-344095 E: archives@dundee.ac.uk W: www.dundee.ac.uk/archives/

West Lothian
West Lothian Council Libraries Connolly House, Hopefield Road, Blackburn, EH47 7HZ T: 01506-776331 E: localhistory@westlothian.org.uk W: www.wlonline.org

Northern Ireland
Centre for Migration Studies Ulster American Folk Park, Mellon Road, Castletown, Omagh, BT78 5QY T: 028 82 256315 E: uafp@iol.ie W: www.qub.ac.uk/cms/ www.folkpark.com
Antrim
North Eastern Library Board & Local Studies Area Reference Library, Demesne Avenue, Ballymena, BT43 7BG T: (028) 25 6641212 E: yvonne_hirt@hotmail.com W: www.neelb.org.uk
Belfast
Belfast Central Library Irish & Local Studies Dept, Royal Avenue, Belfast, BT1 1EA T: (028) 9024 3233 E: info@belb.co.uk W: www.belb.org.uk
Belfast Linen Hall Library 17 Donegall Square North, Belfast, BT1 5GD T: (028) 90321707
Co Antrim
Local Studies Service Area Library HQ, Demesne Avenue, Ballymena, BT43 7BG T: (028) 25 664121 E: yvonne_hirst@hotmail.com W: www.neelb.org.uk
South Eastern Library Board & Local Studies Library HQ, Windmill Hill, Ballynahinch, BT24 8DH T: (028) 9756 6400 E: ref@bhinchlibhq.demon.co.uk
Co Down
South Eastern Library Board & Local Studies Library HQ, Windmill Hill, Ballynahinch, BT24 8DH T: (028) 9756 6400 E: ref@bhinchlibhq.demon.co.uk
Co Fermanagh
Enniskillen Library Halls Lane, Enniskillen, BT1 3HP T: (028) 66322886 E: librarian@eknlib.demon.co.uk
Co Londonderry
Central and Reference Library 35 Foyle Street, Londonderry, BT24 6AL T: (028) 71272300 E: trishaw@online.rednet.co.uk
Irish Room Coleraine County Hall, Castlerock Road, Ballymena, BT1 3HP T: (028) 705 1026 W: www.neelb.org.uk
Co Tyrone
Omagh Library 1 Spillars Place, Omagh, BT78 1HL T: (028) 82244821 E: librarian@omahlib.demon.co.uk

Ireland
National Library of Ireland Kildare Street, Dublin, 2 T: 661-8811 E: coflaherty@nli.ie
Society of Friends (Quakers) - Historical Library Swanbrook House, Bloomfield Avenue, Dublin, 4 T: (01) 668-7157
Co Clare
Clare County Library The Manse, Harmony Row, Ennis, T: 065-6821616 E: clarelib@iol.ie W: www.iol.ic/-clarclib
Co Cork
Cork City Library Grand Parade, Cork, T: 021-277110 E: cork.city.library@indigo.ie W: www.corkcity.ie/
Mallow Heritage Centre 27/28 Bank Place, Mallow, T: 022-50302 W: www.corkcoco.com/
Co Dublin
Ballyfermot Public Library Ballyfermot, Dublin, 10 W: www.dublincity.ie
Dun Laoghaire Library Lower George's Street, Dun Laoghaire, T: 2801147 E: eprout@dlrcoco.ie W: www.dlrcoco.ie/library/lhistory.htm
County Donegal
Donegal Local Studies Centre Central Library & Arts Centre, Oliver Plunkett Road, Letterkenny, T: 00353 74 24950 W: www.donegal.ie/library
Co Kerry
Kerry County Library Genealogical Centre Cathedral Walk, Killarney, T: 353-0-64-359946
Co Kildare
Kildare County Library Newbridge, T: 045-431109 W: www.kildare.ie/countycouncil/
Kildare Hertiage & Genealogy Kildare County Library, Newbridge, T: 045 433602 E: capinfo@iol.ie W: www.kildare.ie
County Limerick
Limerick City Library The Granary, Michael Street, Limerick, T: 061-314668 E: doyledolores@hotmail.com W: www.limerickcoco.ie/
Co Mayo
Central Library Castlebar, T: 094-24444 E: cbarlib@iol.ie W: www.mayococo.ie
Co Sligo
Sligo County Library Westward Town Centre, Bridge Street, Sligo, T: 00-353-71-47190 E: sligolib@iol.ie W: www.sligococo.ie/
Co Tipperary

Tipperary County Libary Local Studies Department Castle Avenue, Thurles, T: 0504-21555 E: studies@tipplibs.iol.ie W: www.iol.ie/~TIPPLIBS
Co Waterford
Waterford County Library Central Library, Davitt's Quay, Dungarvan, T: 058 41231 W: www.waterfordcoco.ie/
Co Wexford
Enniscorthy Branch Library Lymington Road, Enniscorthy, T: 054-36055 W: www.wexford.ie/
New Ross Branch Library Barrack Lane, New Ross, T: 051-21877 W: www.wexford.ie/
Wexford Branch Library Teach Shionoid, Abbey Street, Wexford, T: 053-42211 W: www.wexford.ie/
Dublin
Dublin Public Libraries Gilbert Library - Dublin & Irish Collections, 138 - 142 Pearse Street, Dublin, 2 T: 353 1 674 4800 E: dublinpubliclibraries@dublincity.ie W: www.dublincity.ie

Isle of Man
Isle of Man
Manx National Heritage Library Manx Museum, Douglas, IM1 3LY T: 01624 648000 E: enquiries@mnh.gov.im W: www.gov.im/mnh

Channel Islands
Guernsey
Priaulx Library Candie Road, St Peter Port, GY1 1UG T: 01481 721998 W: www.priaulx.gov.gg
Jersey
Lord Coutanche Library Societe Jersiaise, 7 Pier Road, St Helier, JE2 4XW T: 01534-30538 E: library@societe-jersiaise.org W: www.societe-jersiaise.org

Australia
ACT
National Library of Australia Canberra, 2600 T: 02-6262-1111 W: www.nla.gov.au
New South Wales
Mitchell Library, The Macquarie Street, Sydney, 2000 T: 02-9230-1693 E: slinfo@slsw.gov.au W: www.slsw.gov.au
State Library of New South Wales Macquarie Street, Sydney, 2000 T: 02-9230-1414 W: www.slsw.gov.au
Queensland
State Library of Queensland, The PO Box 3488, Cnr Peel and Stanley Streets, South Brisbane, Brisbane, 4101 T: 07-3840-7775 E: genie@slq.qld.gov.au W: www.slq.qld.gov.au/subgenie/htm
South Australia
South Australia State Library PO Box 419, Adelaide, 5001 T: (08)-8207-7235 E: famhist@slsa.sa.gov.au W: www.slsa.sa.gov.au/library/collres/famhist/
Victoria
State Library of Victoria 328 Swanston Street Walk, Melbourne, 3000 T: 03-9669-9080 E: granth@newvenus.slv.vic.gov.au W: www.slv.vic.gov.au/slv/genealogy/index
Western Australia
State Library Alexander Library, Perth Cultural Centre, Perth, 6000 T: 09-427-3111 W: www.wa.gov.au/
New Zealand
Alexander Turnbull Library PO Box 12-349, Wellington, 6038 T: 04-474-3050
Auckland Research Centre, Auckland City Libraries PO Box 4138, 44-46 Lorne Street, Auckland, T: 64-9-377-0209 E: heritage@auckland-library.govt.nz W: www.auckland-library.govt.nz
Canterbury Public Library PO Box 1466, Christchurch, T: 03-379-6914
Dunedin Public Libraries PO Box 5542, Moray Place, Dunedin, T: 03-474-3651 E: library@dcc.govt.nz W: www.dcc.govt.nz
Fielding Public Library PO Box 264, Fielding, 5600 T: 06-323-5373
Hamilton Public Library PO Box 933, Garden Place, Hamilton, 2015 T: 07-838-6827
Hocken Library PO Box 56, Dunedin, T: 03-479-8873
National Library of New Zealand PO Box 1467, Thorndon, Wellington, T: (0064)4-474-3030 W: www.natlib.govt.nz
Porirua Public Library PO Box 50218, Porirua, 6215 T: 04-237-1541
Takapuna Public Library Private Bag 93508, Takapuna, 1309 T: 09-486-8466
Wanganui District Library Private Bag 3005, Alexander Building, Queens Park, Wanganui, 5001 T: 06-345-8195 E: wap@wdl.govt.nz W: www.wdl.govt.nz

South Africa
South African Library PO Box 496, Cape Town, 8000 T: 021-246320

Canada
Alberta
Calgary Public Library 616 MacLeod Tr SE, Calgary, T2G 2M2 T: 260-2785
Glenbow Library & Archives 130-9th Avenue SE, Calgary, T2G 0P3 T: 403-268-4197
British Columbia
British Columbia Archives 865 Yates Street, Victoria, V8V 1X4 T: 604-387-1952 E: rfrogner@maynard.bcars.gs.gov.bc.ca
Cloverdale Library 5642 - 176a Street, Surrey, V3S 4G9 T: 604-576-1384 E: GenealogyResearch@city.surrey.bc.ca W: www.city.surrey.bc.ca/spl/
New Brunswick
Harriet Irving Library PO Box 7500, Fredericton, E3B 5H5 T: 506-453-4748
Loyalist Collection & Reference Library PO Box 7500, Fredericton, E3B 5H5 T: 506-453-4749

Newfoundland Provincial Resource Library Arts and Cultural Centre, Allandale Road, St Johns, A1B 3A3 T: 709-737-3955 E: genealog@publib.nf.ca W: www.publib.nf.ca
Ontario
James Gibson Reference Library 500 Glenridge Avenue, St Catherines, L2S 3A1 T: 905-688-5550
National Library 395 Wellington Street, Ottawa, K1A 0N4 T: 613-995-9481 E: http://www.nlc-bnc.ca reference@nlc-bnc.ca
Public Library PO Box 2700, Station LCD 1, Hamilton, L8N 4E4 T: 546-3408 E: speccol@hpl.hamilton.on.ca

Public Library, The 85 Queen Street North, Kitchener, N2H 2H1 T: 519-743-0271
Public Library, The 305 Queens Avenue, London, N6B 3L7 T: 519-661-4600
Public Library, The 301 Burnhamthorpe Road West, Mississauga, L5B 3Y3 T: 905-615-3500 E: library.info@city.mississauga.on.ca W: www.city.mississauga.on.ca/library
Public Library, The 74 Mackenzie Street, Sudbury, P3C 4X8 T: 673-1155
St Catharines Public Library 54 Church Street, St Catharines, L2R 7K2 T: 905-688-6103 E: scpublib@stcatharines.library.on.ca W: www.stcatharines.library.on.ca
Toronto Public Library North York (Entral Library) Canadiana Department, 5120 Yonge Street, North York, M2N 5N9 T: 416-395-5623 W: www.tpl.tor.on.ca
Toronto Reference Library 789 Yonge Street, Toronto, M4W 2G8 T: 416-393-7155
Quebec
Bibliotheque De Montreal 1210, Rue Sherbrooke East Street, Montreal, H2L 1L9 T: 514-872-1616 E: daniel_olivier@ville.montreal.qc.ca W: www.ville.montreal.qc.ca/biblio/pageacc.htm
Saskatchewan
Public Library, The PO Box 2311, Regina, S4P 3Z5 T: 306-777-6011 E: kaitken@rpl.sk.ca
Public Library, The 311 - 23rd Street East, Saskatoon, S7K 0J6 T: 306-975-7555

Record Offices and Archives

Archives of the Independent Methodist Churches Independent Methodist Resource Centre, Fleet Street, Pemberton, Wigan, WN5 0DS T: 01942 223526 E: archives@imcgb.org.uk W: www.imcgb.org.uk
Archives of The Institution of Civil Engineers Great George Street, London, SW1P 3AA T: (020) 7222 7722 W: www.ice.org.uk
Bank of England Archive Archive Section HO-SV, The Bank of England, Threadneedle Street, London, EC2R 8AH T: (020) 7601-5096 E: archive@bankofengland.co.uk W: www.bankofengland.co.uk/archive
Barnardo's Film & Photographic Archive Aftercare Section - Barnardo's, Tanner Lane, Barkingside, Ilford, IG6 1QG T: (020) 8550-8822
Bass Museum Horninglow Street, Burton on Trent, DE14 1YQ T: 0845 6000598 W: www.bass-museum.com
BBC Written Archives Centre Caversham Park, Reading , RG4 8TZ T: 0118 948 6281 E: heritage@bbc.co.uk W: www.bbc.co.uk/heritage
Black Cultural Archives 378 Coldharbour Lane, London, SW9 8LF T: (020) 7738 4591 E: info@99mbh.org.uk W: www.99mbh.org.uk
Brassworkers Index 29 Gilda Court, Watford Way, Mill Hill, London, NW7 2QN
British Airways Archives Trident House - Block E S583, London heathrow airport, Hounslow, TW6 2JA
British Brick Society 19 Woodcroft Avenue, Stanmore, HA7 3PT T: 020 8954 4976 E: micksheila67@hotmail.com W: www.britishbricksoc.free-online.co.uk
British Deaf History Society 288 Bedfont Lane, Feltham, TW14 9NU E: bdhs@iconic.demon.co.uk
British Empire & Commonwealth Museum Clock Tower Yard, Temple Meads, Bristol, BS1 6QH T: 0117 925 4980 E: admin@empiremuseum.co.uk W: www.empiremuseum.co.uk
British Film Institute - Library & Film Archive 21 Stephen Street, London, W1T 1LN T: 020 7957 4824 W: www.bfi.org.uk
British Library Newspaper Library Colindale Avenue, London, NW9 5HE T: 020 7412 7353 E: newspaper@bl.uk W: www.bl.uk/collections/newspapes.html
British Library of Political and Economic Science London School of Economics, 10 Portugal Street, London, WC2A 2HD T: 020 7955 7223 W: www.lse.ac.uk
British Library Oriental and India Collections 96 Euston Road, London, NW1 2DB T: (020) 7412 7873 E: oioc-enquiries@bl.uk W: www.bl.uk/collections/oriental
British Library Sound Archive British Library Sound Archive, 96 Euston Road, London, NW1 2DB T: (020) 7412-7405 E: rob.perks@bl.uk W: www.bl.uk/collections/sound-archive/history.html www.ohs.org.uk
British Library Western Manuscripts Collections 96 Euston Road, London, NW1 2DB T: (020) 7412 7513 E: mss@bl.uk W: www.bl.uk/

British Pathe Plc c/o ITN Archive, 200 Gray's Inn Road, London, WC1X 8XZ T: 0207 430 4480 E: pathe@itnarchive.com W: www.britishpathe.com
British Red Cross Museum and Archives UK Office, 44 Moorfields, London, EC2Y 9AL T: 0870 170 7000 F: enquiry@redcross.org.uk W: www.redcross.org.uk/museum&archives
British Universities Film and Video Council 77 Wells Street, London, W1T 3QJ T: 020 7393 1500 W: www.bufvc.ac.uk
British Waterways Archives & The Waterways Trust Llanthony Warehouse, Gloucester Docks, Gloucester, GL1 2EJ T: 01452 318041 W: www.britishwaterways.org.uk
Cambridge University Library - Department of Manuscripts & University Archives West Road, Cambridge, CB3 9DR T: 01223 333000 ext 33143 (Manuscripts) E: mss@ula.cam.ac.uk W: www.lib.cam.ac.uk/MSS/
Canonbury Masonic Research Centre Canonbury Tower, London, N1 2NQ W: www.canonbury.ac.uk
Catholic Record Society 12 Melbourne Place, Wolsingham, DL13 3EH W: www.catholic-history.org/crs
Centre for South Asian Studies Cambridge University, Laundress Lane, Cambriodge, CB2 1SD T: 01223 338094 W: www.s-asian.cam.ac.uk
Churchill Archives Centre Churchill College, Cambridge, CB3 0DS T: 01223 336087 E: archives@chu.cam.ac.uk W: www.chu.cam.ac.uk/archives/home.htm
Church of England Record Centre 15 Galleywall Road, South Bermondsey, London, SE16 3PB T: 020 7898 1030 W: www.church-of-england.org
Coal Miners Records Cannock Record Centre, Old Mid-Cannock Colliery Site, Rumer Hill Road, Cannock, WS11 3EX T: 01543-570666
College of Arms 130 Queen Victoria Street, London, EC4V 4BT T: (020) 7248-2762 E: enquiries@college-of-arms.gov.uk W: www.college-of-arms.gov.uk
Commonwealth War Graves Commission 2 Marlow Road, Maidenhead, SL6 7DX T: 01628-634221 W: www.cwgc.org
Commonwealth War Graves Commission 2 Marlow Road, Maidenhead, SL6 7DX T: 01628-634221 W: www.cwgc.org
Connexional Archives for the Methodist Church 33 Harrow View, Harrow, HA1 1RE
Council for British Archaeology Bowes Morrell House, 111 Walmgate, York, YO1 9WA T: 01904 671417 E: info@britarch.ac.uk W: http:www.britarch.ac.uk/cba
Customs Officers Index 174a Wendover Road, Weston Turville, Aylesbury, HP22 5TG
Deed Poll Records Section Room E 15 Royal Courts of Justice, Strand, London, WC2A 2LL T: (020) 7947 6528
Dr Williams's Library 14 Gordon Square, London, WC1H 0AR T: (020) 7387-3727 E: enquiries@dwlib.co.uk

Entertainers Index 2 Summer Lane, Sheffield, S17 4AJ

Evangelical Library 78a Chiltern Street, London, W1M 2HB

Family Records Centre 1 Myddleton Street, London, EC1R 1UW T: (020) 8392-5300 W: www.familyrecords.gov.uk

Gas Industry Genealogical Index (GIGI) Old Barnshaw Cottage, Pepper Street, Mobberley, WA16 6JH E: tmm@tinyworld.co.uk

Guinness Archive Park Royal Brewery, London, NW10 7RR

Gunmakers and Allied Trades Index 20 Cautley Close, Quainton, Aylesbury, HP22 4BN

HM Land Registry HM Land Registry, Lincoln's Inn Fields, London, WC2A 3PH W: www.landreg.gov.uk

House of Lords Record Office - The Parliamentary Archives House of Lords Record office, London, SW1A 0PW T: (020) 7219 3074 E: hlro@parliament.uk W: www.parliament.uk/archives www.portcullis.parliament.uk

Huguenot Library University College, Gower Street, London, WC1E 6BT T: (020) 7679 7094 E: s.massilk@ucl.ac.u W: www.ucl.ac.uk/ucl-info/divisions/library/hugenot.htm

Images of England Project National Monuments Records Centre, Kemble Drive, Swindon, SN2 2GZ T: 01793 414779 W: www.imagesofengland.org.uk

Imperial War Museum - Department of Documents Department of Documents, Lambeth Road, London, SE1 6HZ T: (020) 7416-5221/2/3/6 E: docs@iwm.org.uk W: www.iwm.org.uk

Imperial War Museum Film and Video Archive Lambeth Road, London, SE1 6HZ T: 020 7416 5289 W: www.iwm.org.uk/collections/film.htm

Institute of Heraldic & Genealogical Studies 79 - 82 Northgate, Canterbury, CT1 1BA T: 01227 462618 E: ihgs@ihgs.ac.uk W: www.ihgs.ac.uk

Institution of Electrical Engineers Savoy Place, London, WC2R 0BL T: (020) 7240 1871 W: www.iee.org.uk

Institution of Mechanical Engineers 1 Birdcage Walk, London, SW1H 9JJ T: (020) 7222 7899 E: ils@imeche.org.uk W: www.imeche.org.uk

Institution of Mining & Metallurgy Hallam Court, 77 Hallam Street, London, England

Labour History Archive & Study Centre People's History Museum 103 Princess Street, Manchester, M1 6DD E: archives@phm.org.uk W: www.phm.org.uk

Lambeth Palace Library Lambeth Palace Road, London, SE1 7JU T: (020) 7898 1400 W: www.lambethpalacelibrary.org

Library of the Religious Society of Friends (Quakers) Friends House, 173 - 177 Euston Rd, London, NW1 2BJ T: 0207 663 1135 E: library@quaker.org.uk W: www.quaker.org.uk/library

Library of the Royal College of Surgeons of England 35-43 Lincoln's Inn Fields, London, WC2A 3PE T: (020) 7869 6555 E: library@rcseng.ac.uk W: www.rcseng.ac.uk

Liddell Hart Centre for Military Archives King's College London, Strand, London, WC2R 2LS T: 020 7848 2015 E: archives@kcl.ac.uk W: www.kcl.ac.uk/lhcma/top.htm

Linnean Society of London Burlington House, Piccadilly, London, W1J 0BF T: 020 7437 4479 E: librarian@linnean.org W: www.linnean.org

Lloyds Register of Shipping Information Services, 71 Fenchurch Street, London, EC3M 4BS T: (020) 7423 2531 W: www.lr.org

Manorial Documents Register Quality House, Quality Court, Chancery Lane, London, WC2A 1HP T: (020) 7242-1198 E: nra@hmc.gov.uk W: www.hmc.gov.uk

Maritime History Archive Memorial University of Newfoundland, St Johns, A1C 5S7 T: ++709-737-8428 W: www.mun.ca/mha/

Methodist Archives and Research Centre John Rylands University Library, 150 Deansgate, Manchester, M3 3EH T: 0161 834 5343

Ministry of Defence - Army Records Centre CS(R)2b, Bourne Avenue, Hayes, UB3 1RF

Ministry of Defence - Fleet Air Arm Records Service CS(R)2, Bourne Avenue, Hayes, UB3 1RF

Modern Archive Centre (King's College Library, Cambridge University) King's College, Cambridge, CB2 1ST T: 01223 331444 E: archivist@kings.cam.ac.uk W: www.kings.cam.ac.uk/library/archives

Modern Records Centre University of Warwick Library, Coventry, CV4 7AL T: (024) 76524219 E: archives@warwick.ac.uk W: www.modernrecords.warwick.ac.uk

Museum of the Order of St John St John's Gate, St John's Lane, Clerkenwell, London, EC1M 4DA T: (020) 7253-6644 W: www.sja.org.uk/history

Museum of the Royal Pharmaceutical Society Museum of the Royal Pharmaceutical Society, 1 Lambeth High Street, London, SE1 7JN T: (020) 7572 2210 E: museum@rpsgb.org W: www.rpsgb.org/museum

National Army Museum Department of Archives (Photographs, Film & Sound) Royal Hospital Road, London, SW3 4HT T: (020) 7730-0717 E: info@national-army-museum.ac.uk W: www.national-army-museum.ac.uk

National Gallery Library and Archive Trafalgar Square, London, WC2N 5DN T: 020 7747 2542 E: iad@ng-london.org.uk W: www.nationalgallery.org.uk

National Monuments Record Enquiry and Research Services 55 Blandford Street, London, W1H 3AF T: 020 7208 8200 W: www.english-heritage.org.uk/knowledge/nmr

National Museum of Photography, Film and Television Bradford, BD1 1NQ T: 01274-202030 W: www.nmpft.org.uk

National Police Officers' Roll of Honour Roll of Honour Project, Lancashire Contabulary Headquarters, Hutton, Preston, PR4 5SB

National Portrait Gallery Heinz Archive & library, 2 St. Martins Place, London, WC2H 0HE T: (020) 7306 0055 W: www.npg.org.uk

National Railway Museum Leeman Road, York, YO26 4XJ T: 01904 621261 E: nrm@nmsi.ac.uk W: www.nrm.org.uk

National Register of Archives Quality House, Quality Court, Chancery Lane, London, WC2A 1HP T: (020) 7242 1198 E: nra@hmc.gov.uk W: www.hmc.gov.uk

National Sound Archive British Library Building, 96 Euston Road, London, NW1 2DB T: (020) 7412-7440 W: www.bl.uk

Pilkington Group - Archives & Record Service Unit 2b Delphwood, Sherdley Industrial Estate, St Helens, WA9 5JE T: 01744 453 555

Probate Principal Registry of the Family Division First Avenue House, 42 - 49 High Holborn, London, WC1V 6NP T: (020) 7947 6939 W: www.courtservice.gov.uk

Probate Service Probate Sub Registry, 1st Floor, Castle Chambers, Clifford Street, York, YO1 9RG T: 01904 666777 W: www.courtservice.gov.uk

Royal College of Obstetricians and Gynaecologists College Archives, 27 Sussex Place, Regents Park, London, NW1 4RG T: 020 7772 6277 E: archives@rcog.org.uk W: www.rcog.org.uk

Royal Commission on Historical Manuscripts Quality House, Quality Court, Chancery Lane, London, WC2A 1HP T: (020) 7242-1198 E: nra@hmc.gov.uk W: www.hmc.gov.uk

Royal Commonwealth Society Library West Road, Cambridge, CB3 9DR T: 01223 333198 E: tab@ula.cam.ac.uk W: www.lib.cam.ac.uk/MSS

Royal Greenwich Observatory Archives West Road, Cambridge, CB3 9DR T: 01223 333056 W: www.lib.cam.ac.uk/MSS/

Royal Institution of Great Britain 21 Albemarle Street, London, W1X 4BS T: 020 7409 2992

Royal Society 6 - 9 Carlton House Terrace, London, SW1Y 5AG T: 020 7451 2606 E: library@royalsoc.ac.uk W: www.royalsoc.ac.uk

School of Oriental and African Studies library Thornhaugh Street, Russell Square, London, WC1H 0XG T: 020 7323 6112 E: study@soas.ac.uk W: www.soas.ac.uk/library/

Shakespeare Birthplace Trust - Records Office Shakespeare Centre, Henley Street, Stratford Upon Avon, CV37 6QW T: 01789 201816 E: records@shakespeare.org.uk W: www.shakespeare.org.uk

Society of Antiquaries of London Burlington House, Piccadilly, London, W1J 0BE T: 020 7479 7084 E: library@sal.org.uk W: www.sal.org.uk

Society of Genealogists - Library 14 Charterhouse Buildings, Goswell Road, London, EC1M 7BA T: 020-7251-8799 E: library@sog.org.uk - Sales at sales@sog.org.uk W: www.sog.org.uk

Society of Indexers Genealogical Group (SIGG) 35 Bank Crest, Baildon, Shipley, BD17 5HB E: craig@heath9869.freeserve.co.uk W: www.sigg.org.uk

Southern Courage Archives Southern Accounting Centre, PO Box 85, Counterslip, Bristol, BS99 7BT

Tate Archive Collection Tate Britain, Millbank, London, SW1P 4RG T: 020 7887 8831

Tennyson Research Centre Central Library, Free School Lane, Lincoln, LN2 1EZ T: 01522-552862 E: k W: www.lincolnshire.co.uk

The Archives of Worshipful Company of Brewers Brewers' Hall, Aldermanbury Square, London, EC2V 7HR T: (020) 7606 1301 E: archivist@brewershall.co.uk W: www.brewershall.co.uk

The Boat Museum & David Owen Waterways Archive South Pier Road, Ellesmere Port, CH65 4FW T: 0151-355-5017 W: www.boatmuseum.org.uk

The British Postal Museum & Archive Freeling House, Phoenix Place, London, WC1X 0DL T: (020) 7239 2570 E: info@postalheritage.org.uk W: www.postalheritage.org.uk

The Gypsy Collections University of Liverpool, PO Box 229, Liverpool, L69 3DA T: 0151 794 2696 W: www.sca.lib.liv.ac.uk/collections/index.html

The Historical Diving Society Little Gatton Lodge, 25 Gatton Road, Reigate, RH2 0HB W: www.thehds.com

The Institute of Brewing & Distilling 33 Clarges Street, London, W1J 7EE T: 020 7499 8144 E: enquiries@ibd.org.uk W: www.ibd.org.uk

The Library & Museum of Freemasonry Freemasons' Hall, 60 Great Queen Street, London, WC2B 5AZ T: (020) 7395 9257 W: www.grandlodge-england.org

The Mills Archive Trust Watlington House, 44 Watlington Street, Reading , RG1 4RJ T: 0118 947 8284 E: info@millarchive.com W: www.millarchive.org

The National Archive of Memorial Inscriptions (NAOMI) E: info@memorialinscriptions.org.uk W: www.memorialinscriptions.org.uk

The National Football Museum Sir Tom Finney Way, Deepdale, Preston, PR1 6RU T: 01772 908 400 E: enquiries@nationalfootballmuseum.com W: www.nationalfootballmuseum.com

The Piano Archive Walnut Cottage, 255 Raglan Street, Lowestoft, NR32 2LA T: 01502 531178 W: www.uk-piano.org/piano-gen

The Robert Dawson Romany Collection Rural History Centre, University of Reading, Whiteknights PO Box 229, Reading, RG6 6AG T: 0118-931-8664 E: j.s.creasey@reading.ac.uk W: www.ruralhistory.org/index.html

The Romany Collections Brotherton Library, Leeds University, Leeds, LS2 9JT T: 0113 343 55188 E: special-collections@library.leeds.ac.uk W: http://leeds.ac.uk/library/spcoll

The Royal College of Physicians 11 St Andrews Place, London, NW1 4LE T: (020) 7935 1174 ext 312 E: heritage@rcplondon.ac.uk W: www.rcplondon.ac.uk/heritage

The United Grand Lodge of England Freemasons' Hall, 60 Great Queen Street, London, WC2B 5AZ T: (020) 7831 9811 W: www.grandlodge.org

Traceline PO Box 106, Southport, PR8 2HH T: 0151 471 4811 E: traceline@ons.gov.uk W: www.ons.gov.uk

TRAP - Tracking Railway Archives Project Al Mafrak, George Hill Road, Broadstairs, CT10 3JT E: d.kelso@btinternet.com W: www.trap.org.uk

Trinity College Library Cambridge University, Trinity College, Cambridge, CB1 1TQ T: 01223 338488 E: trin-lib@lists.cam.ac.uk W: http://rabbit.trin.cam.ac.uk

United Reformed Church History Society Westminster College, Madingley Road, Cambridge, CB3 0AA T: 01223-741300 (NOT Wednesdays)

Victoria & Albert Museum - National Art Library - Archive of Art and Design Blythe House, 23 Blythe Road, London, W14 0QF T: (020) 7603 1514 E: archive@vam.ac.uk W: www.nal.vam.ac.uk

Wellcome Library 183 Euston Road, London, NW1 2BE T: (020) 7611 8722 E: library@wellcome.ac.uk W: http://library.wellcome.ac.uk

Whitbread Archives - Closed

Young's & Co's Brewery Archives Ram Brewery, High Street, Wandsworth, London, SW18 4JD

Brewing

Bass Museum Horninglow Street, Burton on Trent, DE14 1YQ T: 0845 6000598 W: www.bass-museum.com

Brewery History Society Manor Side East, Mill Lane, Byfleet, West Byfleet, KT14 7RS E: membership@breweryhistory.com W: www.breweryhistory.com

Guinness Archive Park Royal Brewery, London, NW10 7RR

Pub History Society 13 Grovewood, Sandycombe Road, Kew, Richmond, TW9 3NF T: (020) 8296-8794 E: sfowler@sfowler.force9.co.uk W: www.pubhistorysociety.co.uk

The Archives of Worshipful Company of Brewers Brewers' Hall, Aldermanbury Square, London, EC2V 7HR T: (020) 7606 1301 E: archivist@brewershall.co.uk W: www.brewershall.co.uk

The Institute of Brewing & Distilling 33 Clarges Street, London, W1J 7EE T: 020 7499 8144 E: enquiries@ibd.org.uk W: www.ibd.org.uk

Young's & Co's Brewery Archives Ram Brewery, High Street, Wandsworth, London, SW18 4JD

Film Archives

British Film Institute 21 Steven Street, London, W19 2LN T: 020 7255 1444 E: library@bfi.org.uk W: www.bfi.org.uk

Barnardo's Film & Photographic Archive Aftercare Section - Barnardo's, Tanner Lane, Barkingside, Ilford, IG6 1QG T: (020) 8550-8822

BBC Sound and Film Archives BBC Research Central, T: 020 7557 2452 E: research-central@bbc.co.uk W: www.bbcresearchcentral.com

Bill Douglas Centre for the History of Cinema and Popular Culture University of Exeter, Queen's Building, Queen's Drive, Exeter, EX4 4QH T: 01392 264321 W: www.ex.ac.uk/bill.douglas

British Film Institute - Library & Film Archive 21 Stephen Street, London, W1T 1LN T: 020 7957 4824 W: www.bfi.org.uk

British Pathe Plc c/o ITN Archive, 200 Gray's Inn Road, London, WC1X 8XZ T: 0207 430 4480 E: pathe@itnarchive.com W: www.britishpathe.com

British Universities Film and Video Council 77 Wells Street, London, W1T 3QJ T: 020 7393 1500 W: www.bufvc.ac.uk

East Anglian Film Archive The Archive Centre, Martineau Lane, Norwich, NR1 2DQ T: 01603 592664 W: www.uea.ac.uk/eafa

Imperial War Museum Film and Video Archive Lambeth Road, London, SE1 6HZ T: 020 7416 5289 W: www.iwm.org.uk/collections/film.htm

Media Archive for Central England Institute of Film Studies, University of Nottingham, Nottingham, NG7 2RD T: 0115 846 6448 W: www.nottingham.ac.uk/film/mace

National Army Museum Department of Archives (Photographs, Film & Sound) Royal Hospital Road, London, SW3 4HT T: (020) 7730-0717 E: info@national-army-museum.ac.uk W: www.national-army-museum.ac.uk

National Museum of Photography, Film and Television Bradford, BD1 1NQ T: 01274-202030 W: www.nmpft.org.uk

North West Film Archive Manchester Metropolitan University, Minshull House, 47-49 Chorlton Street, Manchester, M1 3EU T: 0161 247 3097 W: www.nwfa.mmu.ac.uk

Northern Region Film and Television Archive School of Law, Arts and Humanities, Room M616 Middlesbrough Tower, University of Teeside, Middlesbrough, TS1 3BA T: 01642 384022 W: www.tees.ac.uk

South East Film and Video Archive University of Brighton, Grand Parade, Brighton, BN2 2JY T: 01273 643213 W: www.bton.ac.uk/sefva

South West Film and Television Archive Melville Building, Royal William Yard, Stonehouse, Plymouth, PL1 3RP T: 01752 202650 W: www.tswfta.co.uk

Wessex Film and Sound Archive Hampshire Record Office, Sussex Street, Winchester, SO23 8TH T: 01962 847742 W: www.hants.gov.uk/record-office/film.htm

Yorkshire Film Archive York St John College, Lord Mayor's Walk, York, YO31 7EX T: 01904 716550 E: yfa@yorksj.ac.uk

Gypsy

Gordon Boswell Romany Museum Hawthorns Clay Lake, Spalding, PE12 6BL T: 01775 710599 W:

Romany & Traveller Family History Society 6 St James Walk, South Chailey, BN8 4BU W: http://website.lineone.net/~rtfhs

The Gypsy Collections University of Liverpool, PO Box 229, Liverpool, L69 3DA T: 0151 794 2696 W: www.sca.lib.liv.ac.uk/collections/index.html

The Robert Dawson Romany Collection Rural History Centre, University of Reading, Whiteknights PO Box 229, Reading, RG6 6AG T: 0118-931-8664 E: j.s.creasey@reading.ac.uk W: www.ruralhistory.org/index.html

The Romany Collections Brotherton Library, Leeds University, Leeds, LS2 9JT T: 0113 343 55188 E: special-collections@library.leeds.ac.uk W: http://leeds.ac.uk/library/spcoll/

Land Registries

Birkenhead District Land Registry Old Market House, Hamilton Street, Birkenhead, L41 5FL T: 0151 473 1110

Coventry District Land Registry Leigh Court, Torrington Avenue, Tile Hill, Coventry, CV4 9XZ T: (024) 76860860

Croydon District Land Registry Sunley House, Bedford Park, Croydon, CR9 3LE T: (020) 8781 9100

Durham (Boldon House) District Land Registry Boldon House, Wheatlands Way, Pity Me, Durham, DH1 5GJ T: 0191 301 2345

Durham (Southfield House) District Land Registry Southfield House, Southfield Way, Durham, England T: 0191 301 3500

Gloucester District Land Registry Twyver House, Bruton Way, Gloucester, GL1 1DQ T: 01452 511111

Harrow District Land Registry Lyon House, Lyon Road, Harrow, HA1 2EU T: (020) 8235 1181

Kingston Upon Hull District Land Registry Earle House, Portland Street, Hull, HU2 8JN T: 01482 223244

Leicester District Land Registry Westbridge Place, Leicester, LE3 5DR T: 0116 265 4000

Lytham District Land Registry Birkenhead House, East Beach, Lytham St Annes, FY8 5AB T: 01253 849 849

Nottingham District Land Registry Chalfont Drive, Nottingham, NG8 3RN T: 0115 935 1166

Peterborough District Land Registry Touthill Close, City Road, Peterborough, PE1 1XN T: 01733 288288

Plymouth District Land Registry Plumer House, Tailyour Road, Crownhill, Plymouth, PL6 5HY T: 01752 636000

Portsmouth District Land Registry St Andrews Court, St Michael's Road, Portsmouth, PO1 2JH T: (023) 92768888

Stevenage District Land Registry Brickdale House, Swingate, Stevenage, SG1 1XG T: 01438 788888

Swansea District Land Registry T^y Bryn Glas, High Street, Swansea, SA1 1PW T: 01792 458877

Telford District Land Registry Parkside Court, Hall Park Way, Telford, TF3 4LR T: 01952 290355

Tunbridge Wells District Land Registry Curtis House, Forest Road, Tunbridge Wells, TN2 5AQ T: 01892 510015
Weymouth District Land Registry Melcombe Court, 1 Cumberland Drive, Weymouth, DT4 9TT T: 01305 363636
York District Land Registry James House, James Street, York, YO1 3YZ T: 01904 450000

Military
Royal Dragoon Guards Military Museum (4th/7th Royal Dragoon Guards & 5th Royal Inniskilling Dragoon Guards) 3A Tower Street, York, YO1 9SB T: 01904-662790 W: www.rdg.co.uk
Royal Marines Museum Eastney, Southsea, PO4 9PX T: (023) 9281 9385 Exts 224 W: www.royalmarinesmuseum.co.uk

England
Bedfordshire
Bedfordshire & Luton Archives & Record Service Riverside Building, County Hall, Cauldwell Street, Bedford, MK42 9AP T: 01234-228833 E: archive@bedscc.gov.uk W: www.bedfordshire.gov.uk/archive

Berkshire
Berkshire Medical Heritage Centre Level 4, Main Entrance, Royal Berkshire Hospital, London Road, Reading, RG1 5AN T: 0118 987 7298 W: www.bmhc.org
Berkshire Record Office 9 Coley Avenue, Reading, RG1 6AF T: 0118-901-5132 E: arch@reading.gov.uk W: www.berkshirerecordoffice.org.uk
Eton College College Library, Windsor, SL4 6DB T: 01753 671269 E: archivist@etoncollege.org.uk W: www.etoncollege.com
Museum of English Rural Life University of Reading, Redlands Road, Reading, RG1 5EX T: 0118 378 8660 E: merl@reading.ac.uk W: www.merl.org.uk
The Museum of Berkshire Aviation Trust Mohawk Way, off Bader Way, Woodley, Reading, RG5 4UE T: 0118 944 8089 E: museumofberkshireaviation@fly.to W: http://fly.to/museumofberkshireaviation
West Berkshire Heritage Service - Newbury West Berkshire Museum, The Wharf, Newbury, RG14 5AS T: 01635 519532 E: jburrell@westberks.gov.uk W: www.westberkshiremuseum.org.uk

Bristol
Bristol Record Office B Bond Warehouse, Smeaton Road, Bristol, BS1 6XN T: 0117 922 4224 E: bro@bristol-city.gov.uk W: www.bristol-city.gov.uk/recordoffice
Bristol University Library - Special Collections Tyndall Avenue, Bristol, BS8 1TJ T: 0117 928 8014 E: special-collections@bris.ac.uk W: www.bris.ac.uk/is/services/specialcollections/

Buckinghamshire
Centre for Buckinghamshire Studies County Offices, Walton Street, Aylesbury, HP20 1UU T: 01296 382587 (Archives) E: archives@buckscc.gov.uk W: www.buckscc.gov.uk/archives

Cambridgeshire
Cambridgeshire Archive Service (Huntingdon) County Record Office Huntingdon, Grammar School Walk, Huntingdon, PE29 3LF T: 01480-375842 E: county.records.hunts@cambridgeshire.gov.uk W: www.cambridgeshire.gov.uk
Cambridgeshire Archives Service County Record Office Shire Hall, Castle Hill, Cambridge, CB3 0AP T: 01223 717281 E: County.Records.Cambridge@cambridgeshire.gov.uk W: www.cambridgeshire.gov.uk/
Centre for Regional Studies Anglia Polytechnic University, East Road, Cambridge, CB1 1PT T: 01223-363271 ext 2030 E: t.kirby@anglia.ac.uk W: www.anglia.ac.uk
Peterborough Archives Service and Local Studies Collection Central Library, Broadway, Peterborough, PE1 1RX T: 01733 742700 E: libraryenquiries@peterborough.gov.uk W: www.peterboroughheritage.org.uk

Cheshire
Cheshire & Chester Archives & Local Studies Duke Street, Chester, CH1 1RL T: 01244-602574 E: recordoffice@cheshire.gov.uk W: www.cheshire.gov.uk/recoff/home.htm
Chester History & Heritage St Michaels Church, Bridge Street Row, Chester, CH1 1NW T: 01244 402110 E: s.oswald.gov.uk W: www.chestercc.gov.uk/chestercc/htmls/heritage.htm
Macclesfield Silk Museums Paradise Mill, Park Lane, Macclesfield, SK11 6TJ T: 01625 612045 W: www.silk-macclesfield.org
Stockport Local Heritage library Central Library, Wellington Road South, Stockport, SK1 3RS T: 0161-474-4530 E: localheritage.library@stockport.gov.uk W: www.stockport.gov.uk

Tameside Local Studies Library Stalybridge Library, Trinity Street, Stalybridge, SK15 2BN T: 0161-338-2708 W: www.tameside.gov.uk
Trafford Local Studies Centre Public Library, Tatton Road, Sale, M33 1YH T: 0161-912-3013
Warrington Library & Local Studies Centre Museum Street, Warrington, WA1 1JB T: 01925 442890 E: library@warrington.gov.uk W: www.warrington.gov.uk

Cleveland
Friends of Teesside Archives 9 Killing Close, Billingham, TS23 3UJ
Tees Archaeology - The Archaeological Service for Teeside Sir William Gray, Clarence Road, Hartlepool, TS24 8BT T: 01429 523455 E: tees-archaeology@hartlepool.gov.uk W: www.hartlepool.gov.uk
Teesside Archives Exchange House, 6 Marton Road, Middlesbrough, TS1 1DB T: 01642 248321 E: teesside_archives@middlesbrough.gov.uk W: www.middlesbrough.gov.uk

Cornwall
Cornish-American Connection Murdoch House, Cross Street, Redruth, TR15 2BU T: 01209 216333 W: www.ex.ac.uk/~cnfrench/ics/welcome.htm
Cornwall Record Office County Hall, Truro, TRI 3AY T: 01872 323127 E: cro@cornwall.gov.uk W: www.cornwall.gov.uk
Porthcurno Telegraph Museum and Archive Eastern House,, Porthcurno, Penzance, TR19 6JX T: 01736 810478 E: info@porthcurno.org.uk W: www.porthcurno.org.uk
Royal Institution of Cornwall, Courtney Library & Cornish History Research Centre Royal Cornwall Museum, River Street, Truro, TR1 2SJ T: 01872 272205 W: www.cornwall-online.co.uk/genealogy
The Cornwall Centre Alma Place, Redruth, TR15 2AT T: 01209-216760 E: cornishstudies@library.cornwall.gov.uk W: www.cornwall.gov.uk/index.cfm?articleid=6773

County Durham
Darlington Local Studies Centre The Library, Crown Street, Darlington, DL1 1ND T: 01325-349630 E: local.studies@darlington.gov.uk W: www.darlington.gov.uk/library/localstudies
Durham County Record Office County Hall, Durham, DH1 5UL T: 0191 383 3253 E: record@durham.gov.uk W: www.durham.gov.uk/recordoffice
Durham University Library Archives and Special Collections Palace Green Section, Palace Green, Durham, DH1 3RN T: 0191 334 2932 E: pg.library@durham.ac.uk W: www.dur.ac.uk/library/asc
North East War Memorials Project Bilsdale, Ulgham, Morpeth, NE61 3AR T: 01670 790465 E: janet@newmp.org.uk W: www.newmp.org.uk
The Oriental Museum University of Durham Museums, Elvet Hill, Durham, DH1 3TH T: 0191 334 5694 E: oriental.museum@dur.ar.uk W: www.durham.ac.uk

Cumbria
Barrow in Furness Record Office & Local Studies Library 140 Duke St, Barrow in Furness, LA14 1XW T: 01229 894363 E: barrow.record.office@cumbriacc.gov.uk W: www.cumbria.gov.uk/archives
Carlisle - Cumbria Archive Service Cumbria Record Office, The Castle, Carlisle, CA3 8UR T: 01228-607285 E: carlisle.record.office@cumbriacc.gov.uk W: www.cumbriacc.gov.uk/archives
Heritage First - formerly Ulverston Heritage Centre Lower Brook St, Ulverston, LA12 7EE T: 01229 580820 W: www.rootsweb.com/~ukuhc/
Kendal Record Office County Offices, Stricklandgate, Kendal, LA9 4RQ T: 01539 773540 E: kendal.record.office@cumbriacc.gov.uk W: www.cumbria.gov.uk/archives
Whitehaven Record Office & Local Studies Library Scotch Street, Whitehaven, CA28 7BJ T: 01946-852920 E: whitehaven.record.office@cumbriacc.gov.uk W: www.cumbria.gov.uk/archives

Derbyshire
Derby Local Studies Library 25b Irongate, Derby, DE1 3GL T: 01332 255393 E: localstudies.library@derby.gov.uk W: www.derby.gov.uk/libraries/about/local_studies.htm
Derbyshire Record Office County Hall, Matlock, DE4 3AG T: 01629-580000-ext-35207
Erewash Museum The Museum, High Street, Ilkeston, DE7 5JA T: 0115 907 1141 E: museum@erewash.gov.uk W: www.erewash.gov.uk

Devon
Beaford Photograph Archive Barnstaple, EX32 7EJ T: 01271 288611
Devon Record Office Great Moor House, Bittern Road, Sowton, Exeter, EX2 7NL T: 01392 384253 E: devrec@devon.gov.uk W: www.devon gov.uk/record_office.htm
North Devon Record Office Tuly Street, Barnstaple, EX31 1EL T: 01271 388607 E: ndevrec@devon.gov.uk W: www.devon.gov.uk/dro/homepage
The Devonshire and Dorset Regiment (Archives) RHQ, Devonshire and Dorset Regiment, Wyvern Barracks, Barrack Road, Exeter, EX2 6AR T: 01392 492436

Dorset
Bridport Museum Trust - Local History Centre The Coach House, Gundy Lane, Bridport, DT6 3RJ T: 01308 458703 E: office@bridportmuseum.co.uk W: www.bridportmuseum.co.uk
Dorset Archives Service 9 Bridport Road, Dorchester, DT1 1RP T: 01305-250550 W: www.dorset-cc.gov.uk/archives
Poole Central Reference Library Dolphin Centre, Poole, BH15 1QE T: 01202 262424 E: centrallibrary@poole.gov.uk W: www.boroughofpoole.com/libraries
Waterfront Musuem and Local Studies Centre 4 High St, Poole, BH15 1BW T: 01202 683138 E: museums@poole.gov.uk mldavidw@poole.gov.uk W: www.poole.gov.uk

Essex
Chelmsford Library PO Box 882, Market Road, Chelmsford, CM1 1LH T: 01245 492758 E: answers.direct@essexcc.gov.uk W: www.essexcc.gov.uk
Essex Record Office Wharf Road, Chelmsford, CM2 6YT T: 01245 244644 E: ero.enquiry@essexcc.gov.uk (General Enquiries) ero.search@essexcc.gov.uk (Search Service) W: www.essexcc.gov.uk/ero
Essex Record Office, Colchester & NE Essex Branch Stanwell House, Stanwell Street, Colchester, CO2 7DL T: 01206-572099 W: www.essexcc.gov.uk/ero
Essex Record Office, Southend Branch Central Library, Victoria Avenue, Southend on Sea, SS2 6EX T: 01702-464278 W: www.essexcc.gov.uk/ero
Havering Central Reference Library - London Borough of Reference Library, St Edward's Way, Romford, RM1 3AR T: 01708 432393
Redbridge Library Central Library, Clements Road, Ilford, IG1 1EA T: (020) 8708 2417 E: studies@redbridge.gov.uk W: www.redbridge.gov.uk
Valence House Museum Valence House Museum, Becontree Avenue, Dagenham, RM8 3HT T: 020 8270 6866 W: www.barking-dagenham.gov.uk

Gloucestershire
Gloucestershire Record Office Clarence Row, Alvin Street, Gloucester, GL1 3DW T: 01452-425295 W: www.gloscc.gov.uk

Greater Manchester
Greater Manchester County Record Office 56 Marshall St, New Cross, Manchester, M4 5FU T: 0161-832-5284 E: archives@gmcro.co.uk W: www.gmcro.co.uk

Hampshire
Hampshire Local Studies Library Winchester Library, Jewry Street, Winchester, SO23 8RX T: 01962 841408 E: clceloc@hants.gov.uk W: www.hants.gov.uk/library
Hampshire Record Office Sussex St, Winchester, SO23 8TH T: 01962-846154 E: enquiries.archives@hants.gov.uk W: www.hants.gov.uk/record-office
Portsmouth City Libraries Central Library, Guildhall Square, Portsmouth, PO1 2DX T: 023 9268 8045 (Bookings) E: reference.library@portsmouthcc.gov.uk W: www.portsmouth.gov.uk/learning/1035.html
Portsmouth City Museum and Record Office Museum Road, Portsmouth, PO1 2LJ T: (023) 92827261
Portsmouth Roman Catholic Diocesan Archives St Edmund House, Edinburgh Road, Portsmouth, PO1 3QA T: 023 9282 5430
Southampton Archive Service Civic Centre, Southampton, Hants, SO14 7LY T: (023) 80832251 E: city.archives@southampton.gov.uk W: www.southampton.gov.uk
Southampton City Libraries - Special Collections Southampton Reference Library, Civic Centre, Southampton, SO14 7LW T: 023 8083 2205 E: local.studies@southampton.gov.uk W: www.southampton.gov.uk

Herefordshire
Hereford Cathedral Archives & Library 5 College Cloisters, Cathedral Close, Hereford, HR1 2NG T: 01432 374225 E: library@herefordcathedral.org W: www.herefordcathedral.org
Herefordshire Archive Service Herefordshire Record Office, Harold Street, Hereford, HR1 2QX T: 01432 260750 E: archives@herefordshire.gov.uk W: www.herefordshire.gov.uk/archives

Hertfordshire
Ashwell Education Services 59 High Street, Ashwell, SG7 5NP T: 01462 742385 E: aes@ashwell-education-services.co.uk W: www.ashwell-education-services.co.uk
Bushey Museum, Art Gallery and Local Studies Centre Rudolph Road, Bushey, WD23 3HW T: 020 8420 4057 E: busmt@bushey.org.uk W: www.busheymuseum.org
Hertfordshire Archives and Local Studies County Hall, Pegs Lane, Hertford, SG13 8EJ T: 01438 737333 E: herts.direct@hertscc.gov.uk W: http://hertsdirect.org/hals

Hull
Brynmor Jones Library - University of Hull Cottingham Road, Hull, HU6 7RX T: 01482 465265 W: www.hull.ac.uk/lib www.hull.ac.uk/lib/archives
Hull Central Library Family and Local History Unit Central Library, Albion Street, Kingston upon Hull, HU1 3TF T: 01482 616828 E: gareth.watkins@hullcc.gov.uk W: www.hullcc.gov.uk/genealogy
Hull City Archives 79 Lowgate, Kingston upon Hull, HU1 1HN T: 01482-615102 W: www.hullcc.gov.uk
Local History Unit Hull College, James Reckitt Library, Holderness Road, Hull, HU9 1EA T: 01482 308065 E: historyunit@netscape.net W: www.historyofhull.co.uk

Isle of Wight
Isle of Wight Record Office 26 Hillside, Newport, PO30 2EB T: 01983-823820/1 E: record.office@iow.gov.uk W: www.iwight.com/library/record_office/default.asp

Kent
Bexley Local Studies and Archive Centre - London Borough of Central Library, Townley Road, Bexleyheath, DA6 7HJ T: (020) 8836 7369 E: archives@bexley.gov.uk W: www.bexley.gov.uk
Canterbury Cathedral Archives The Precincts, Canterbury, CT1 2EH T: 01227 865330 E: archives@canterbury-cathedral.org W: www.canterbury-cathedral.org
Canterbury Library & Local Studies Collection 18 High Street, Canterbury, CT1 2JF T: 01227-463608 W: www.kent.gov.uk
Centre for Kentish Studies / Kent Archives Service Sessions House, County Hall, Maidstone, Kent, ME141XQ T: 01622-694363 E: archives@kent.gov.uk W: www.kent.gov.uk/archives
East Kent Archives Centre East Kent Archives Centre, Enterprise Zone, Honeywood Road, Whitfield, Dover, CT16 3EH T: 01304 829306 E: eastkentarchives@kent.gov.uk W: www.kent.gov.uk/kcc/arts/archives/kentish.html
Margate Library Local History Collection Cecil Square, Margate, CT9 1RE T: 01843-223626 W: www.kent.gov.uk
Ramsgate Library Local Strudies Collection & Thanet Branch Archives Ramsgate Library, Guildford Lawn, Ramsgate, CT11 9AY T: 01843-593532 W: www.kent.gov.uk
Sevenoaks Archives Office Central Library, Buckhurst Lane, Sevenoaks, TN13 1LQ T: 01732-453118

Lancashire
Blackburn Cathedral & Archives Cathedral Close, Blackburn, BB1 5AA T: 01254 51491 E: cathedral@blackburn.anglican.org W: www.blackburn.anglican.org
Blackburn Central Library Town Hall Street, Blackburn, BB2 1AG T: 01254 587919 E: community.history@blackburn.gov.uk W: www.blackburn.gov.uk/library www.cottontown.org
Bolton Archive & Local Studies Service Central Library, Civic Centre, Le Mans Crescent, Bolton, BL1 1SE T: 01204-332185 E: archives.library@bolton.gov.uk W: www.bolton.gov.uk
Bury Archive Service 1st Floor, Derby Hall Annexe, Edwin Street off Crompton Street, Bury, BL9 0AS T: 0161-797-6697 E: archives@bury.gov.uk W: www.bury.gov.uk/culture.htm
Centre for North West Regional Studies Fylde College, Lancaster University, Lancaster, LA1 4YF T: 01524 593770 E: christine.wilkinson@lancaster.ac.uk W: www.lancs.ac.uk/users/cnwrs
Lancashire Record Office Bow Lane, Preston, PR1 2RE T: 01772 533039 E: record.office@ed.lancscc.gov.uk W: www.archives.lancashire.gov.uk
North West Sound Archive Old Steward's Office, Clitheroe Castle, Clitheroe, BB7 1AZ T: 01200 427897 E: nwsa@ed.lancscc.gov.uk W: www.lancashire.gov.uk/education/d_lif/ro/content/sound/imdex.asp

Oldham Local Studies and Archives 84 Union Street, Oldham, OL1 1DN T: 0161-911-4654 E: archives@oldham.gov.uk W: www.oldham.gov.uk/archives www.oldham.gov.uk/local_studies

Rochdale Local Studies Centre Touchstones Rochdale, The Esplanade, Rochdale, OL16 1AQ T: 01706 924915 E: localstudies@rochdale.gov.uk W: www.rochdale.gov.uk/Living/Libraries.asp?URL=local

Salford City Archives Salford Archives Centre, 658/662 Liverpool Rd, Irlam, Manchester, M44 5AD T: 0161 775-5643

Salford Local History Library Peel Park, Salford, M5 4WU T: 0161 736 2649 E: local.history@salford.gov.uk W: www.salford.gov.uk

The Documentary Photography Archive - Manchester c/o 7 Towncroft Lane, Bolton, BL1 5EW T: 0161 832 5284

Wigan Heritage Service Town Hall, Leigh, Wigan, WN7 2DY T: 01942-404430 E: heritage@wiganmbc.gov.uk W: www.wiganmbc.gov.uk

Wigan Heritage Service Museum History Shop, Library Street, Wigan, WN1 1NU T: 01942 828128 E: heritage@wict.org W: www.wict.org/culture/heritage

Leicestershire
East Midlands Oral History Archive Centre for Urban History, University of Leicester, Leicester, LE1 7RH T: 0116 252 5065 E: emoha@le.ac.uk W: www.le.ac.uk/emoha

Melton Mowbray Library Wilton Road, Melton Mowbray, LE13 0UJ T: 01664 560161 W: www.leics.gov.uk

Record Office for Leicestershire, Leicester and Rutland Long Street, Wigston Magna, LE18 2AH T: 0116-257-1080 E: recordoffice@leics.gov.uk W: www.leics.gov.uk

Lincolnshire
Lincolnshire Archives St Rumbold Street, Lincoln, LN2 5AB T: 01522-526204 W: www.lincolnshire.gov.uk/archives

Lincolnshire County Library Local Studies Section, Lincoln Central Library, Free School Lane, Lincoln, LN2 1EZ T: 01522 510800 E: lincoln.library@lincolnshire.gov.uk W: www.lincolnshire.gov.uk

North East Lincolnshire Archives Town Hall, Town Hall Square, Grimsby, DN31 1HX T: 01472-323585 E: john.wilson@nelincs.gov.uk W: www.nelincs.gov.uk

Liverpool
Liverpool Record Office & Local History Department Central Library, William Brown Street, Liverpool, L3 8EW T: 0151 233 5817 E: recoffice.central.library@liverpool.gov.uk W: www.liverpool.gov.uk

Liverpool University Special Collections & Archives University of Liverpool Library, PO Box 123, Liverpool, L69 3DA T: 0151-794-2696 W: www.sca.lib.liv.ac.uk/collections/index.html

London
Alexander Fleming Laboratory Museum / St Mary's NHS Trust Archives St Mary's Hospital, Praed Street, Paddington, London, W2 1NY T: (020) 7886 6528 E: kevin.brown@st-marys.nhs.uk W: www.st-marys.nhs.uk

Barking & Dagenham Local Studies Library Valence House Museum, Beacontree Avenue, Dagenham, RM8 3HT T: 020 8270 6896 E: localstudies@lbbd.gov.uk W: www.barking-dagenham.gov.uk

Barnet - Local Studies & Archives Centre Local Studies & Archives Centre, 80 Daws Lane, Mill Hill, London, NW7 4SL T: (020) 8959 6657 E: library.archives@barnet.gov.uk W: www.barnet.gov.uk/index/leisure-culture/libraries/archives.htm

Bethlem Royal Hospital Archives and Museum, Monks Orchard Road, Beckenham, BR3 3BX T: (020) 8776 4307 E: museum@bethlem.freeserve.co.uk

Bexley Local Studies and Archive Centre Central Library, Townley Road, Bexleyheath, DA6 7HJ T: (020) 8836 7369 E: archives@bexley.gov.uk W: www.bexley.gov.uk

Brent Archive 152 Olive Road, Cricklewood, London, NW2 6UY T: (020) 8937 3541 E: archive@brent.gov.uk W: www.brent.gov.uk/archive

Bromley Local Studies Library Central Library, High Street, Bromley, BR1 1EX T: 020 8461 7170 E: localstudies.library@bromley.gov.uk W: www.bromley.gov.uk/libraries

Camden Local Studies & Archive Centre Holborn Library, 32 - 38 Theobalds Road, London, WC1X 8PA T: 020 7974 6342 E: localstudies@camden.gov.uk W: www.camden.gov.uk/localstudies

Chelsea Public Library Old Town Hall, King's Road, London, SW3 5EZ T: (020) 7352-6056

Chiswick & Brentford Local Studies Collection Chiswick Public Library, Dukes Avenue, Chiswick, London, W4 2AB T: (020) 8994-5295

City of Westminster Archives Centre 10 St Ann's Street, London, SW1P 2DE T: (020) 7641-5180 W: www.westminster.gov.uk

Corporation of London Records Office transferred to London Metropolitan Archives 40 Northampton Road, London, EC1R 0HB T: 020 7332 3820 E: ask.lma@corpoflondon.gov.uk W: www.cityoflondon.gov.uk/archives/clro

Croydon Library and Archives Service Central Library, Katharine Street, Croydon, CR9 1ET T: (020) 8760 6900 ext 61112 E: libraries@croydon.gov.uk W: www.croydon.gov.uk

Ealing Local History Centre Central Library, 103 Broadway Centre, Ealing, London, W5 5JY T: (020) 8567-3656-ext-37 E: localhistory@hotmail.com W: www.ealing.gov.uk/libraries

Enfield Archives & Local History Unit Southgate Town Hall, Green Lanes, Palmers Green, London, N13 4XD T: (020) 8379-2724

Greenwich Heritage Centre Artillery Square, Royal Arsenal, Woolwich, London, SE18 4DX T: (020) 8854 2452 E: local.history@greenwich.gov.uk W: www.greenwich.gov.uk

Grenadier Guards Record Office Wellington Barracks, Birdcage Walk, London, SW1E 6HQ E: rhqgrengds@yahoo.co.uk

Guildhall Library, Manuscripts Section Aldermanbury, London, EC2P 2EJ T: (020) 7332-1863 E: manuscripts.guildhall@cityoflondon.gov.uk W: http://ihr.sas.ac.uk/ihr/gh/

Hackney Archives Department London Borough of Hackney, 43 De Beauvoir Road, London, N1 5SQ T: (020) 7241 2886 E: archives@hackney.gov.uk W: www.hackney.gov.uk/index.htm/ca-history.htm

Hammersmith & Fulham Archives & Local History Centre The Lilla Huset, 191 Talgarth Road, London, W6 8BJ T: 0208 741 5159 W: www.lbhf.gov.uk

Haringey Local History Library and Archives Bruce Castle Museum, Lordship Lane, Tottenham, London, N17 8NU T: (020) 8808-8772 E: museum.services@haringey.gov.uk W: www.haringey.gov.uk

Hillingdon Local Studies & Archives Central Library, High Street, Uxbridge, London, UB8 1HD T: 01895 250702 W: www.hillingdon.gov.uk/goto/libraries

Hounslow Library (Local Studies & Archives) Centrespace, Treaty Centre, High Street, Hounslow, TW3 1ES T: 0845 456 2800 W: www.cip.com

Imperial College Archives London University, Room 455 Sherfield Building, Imperial College, London, SW7 2AZ T: 020 7594 8850 E: library@imperial.ac.uk W: www3.imperial.ac.uk

Institute of Commonwealth Studies , University of London 28 Russell Square, London, WC1B 5DS T: (020) 7862 8844 E: icommlib@sas.ac.uk W: http://sas.ac.uk/commonwealthstudies

Institute of Historical Research University of London , Senate House, Malet Street, London, WC1E 7HU T: 020 7862 8740 E: ihr@sas.ac.uk W: http://ihr.sas.ac.uk

Islington History Centre Finsbury library, 245 St John Street, London, EC1V 4NB T: (020) 7527 7988 E: local.history@islington.gov.uk W: www.islington.gov.uk

Kensington and Chelsea Libraries & Arts Service - Royal Borough of Central Library, Phillimore Walk, Kensington, London, W8 7RX T: (020) 7361 3010 E: information@rbkc.gov.uk W: www.rbkc.gov.uk/libraries

King's College London Archives Kins College, Strand, London, WC2R 2LS T: 020 7848 2015 E: archives@kcl.ac.uk W: www.kcl.ac.uk/depsta/iss/archives/top.htm

Kingston Museum & Heritage Service North Kingston Centre, Richmond Road, Kingston upon Thames, KT2 5PE T: (020) 8547-6738 E: local.history@rbk.kingston.gov.uk W: www.kingston.gov.uk/museum/

Lambeth Archives Department Minet Library, 52 Knatchbull Road, Lambeth, London, SE5 9QY T: (020) 7926 6076 W: www.lambeth.gov.uk

Lewisham Local Studies & Archives Lewisham Library, 199 - 201 Lewisham High Street, Lewisham, London, SE13 6LG T: (020) 8297-0682 E: local.studies@lewisham.gov.uk W: www.lewisham.gov.uk

London Metropolitan Archives 40 Northampton Road, London, EC1R 0HB T: 020 7332 3820 E: ask.lma@cityoflondon.gov.uk W: www.cityoflondon.gov.uk/lma

London University - Institute of Advanced Studies Charles Clore House, 17 Russell Square, London, WC1B 5DR T: (020) 7637 1731 E: ials@sas.ac.uk W: http://ials.sas.ac.uk

London University - Institute of Education 20 Bedford Way, London, WC1H 0AL T: 020 7612 6063 E: info@ioe.ac.uk W: www.ioe.ac.uk/library/

Manuscripts Room Library Services, University College, Gower Street, London, WC1E 6BT T: (020) 7387 7050 E: mssrb@ucl.ac.uk W: www.ucl.ac.uk/library/special-coll/

Merton Local Studies Centre Merton Civic Centre, London Road, Morden, SM4 5DX T: (020) 8545-3239 E: local.studies@merton.gov.uk W: www.merton.gov.uk/libraries

Museum of London Library 150 London Wall, London, EC2Y 5HN T: 020 7814 5588 E: library@museumoflondon.org.uk W: www.museumoflondon.org.uk

Newham Archives & Local Studies Library Stratford Library, 3 The Grove, London, E15 1EL T: (020) 8430 6881 W: www.newham.gov.uk

Royal Air Force Museum - Department of Research & Information Services Grahame Park Way, Hendon, London, NW9 5LL T: (020) 83584873 E: research@rafmuseum.org W: www.rafmuseum.org

Royal Botanic Gardens Library & Archives, Kew, Richmond, TW9 3AE T: 020 8332 5414

Royal London Hospital Archives and Museum Royal London Hospital Archives, 9 Prescot Street, Aldgate, London, E1 8PR T: (020) 7377 7608 E: jonathan.evans@bartsandthelondon.nhs.uk W: www.bartsandthelondon.org.uk

Southwark Local Studies Library 211 Borough High Street, Southwark, London, SE1 1JA T: 0207-403-3507 E: local.studies.library@southwark.gov.uk W: www.southwark.gov.uk

St Bartholomew's Hospital Archives & Museum Archives and Museum, North Wing, St Bartholomew's Hospital , West Smithfield, London, EC1A 7BE T: (020) 7601 8152 E: barts.archives@bartsandthelondon.nhs.uk W: www.bartsandthelondon.nhs.uk/aboutus/museums_and_archives.asp

Sutton Archives Central Library, St Nicholas Way, Sutton, SM1 1EA T: (020) 8770-4747 E: local.studies@sutton.gov.uk W: www.sutton.gov.uk

The Galton Institute 19 Northfields Prospect, London, SW18 1PE

Tower Hamlets Local History Library & Archives Bancroft Library, 277 Bancroft Road, London, E1 4DQ T: (020) 8980 4366 Ext 129 E: localhistory@towerhamlets.gov.uk W: www.towerhamlets.gov.uk

Twickenham Library - collection transferred to Richmond Local Studies Library Twickenham Library, Garfield Road, Twickenham, TW1 3JS T: (020) 8891-7271 W: www.richmond.gov.uk

University of London (Library - Senate House) Palaeography Room, Senate House, Malet Street, London, WC1E 7HU T: (020) 7862 8475 E: enquiries@shl.lon.ac.uk W: www.ull.ac.uk/library

Waltham Forest Archives Vestry House Museum, Vestry Road, Walthamstow, London, E17 9NH T: (020) 8509 1917 E: vestry.house@walthamforest.gov.uk W: www.walthamforest.gov.uk/index/leisure/local-history.htm

Wandsworth Local Studies Local Studies Service, Battersea Library, 265 Lavender Hill, London, SW11 1JB T: (020) 8871 7753 E: wandsworthmuseum@wandsworth.gov.uk W: www.wandsworth.gov.uk

Westminster Abbey Library & Muniment Room Westminster Abbey, London, SW1P 3PA T: (020) 7222 5152 Ext 4830 E: library@westminster-abbey.org W: www.westminster-abbey.org

Westminster Diocesan Archives 16a Abingdon Road, Kensington, London, W8 6AF T: (020) 7938-3580

Westminster University Archives Information Systems & Library Services, 4-12 Little Titchfield Street, London, W1W 7UW T: 020 7911 5000 ext 2524 E: archive@westminster.ac.uk W: www.wmin.ac.uk/archives

Manchester

John Rylands University Library Special Collections Division, 150 Deansgate, Manchester, M3 3EH T: 0161-834-5343 E: spcoll72@fs1.li.man.ac.uk W: http://rylibweb.man.ac.uk

Manchester Central Library - Archives & Local Studies Manchester Central Library, St Peter's Square, Manchester, M2 5PD T: 0161-234-1979 E: lsurchiveslocalstudies W: www.manchester.gov.uk/libraries/index.htm

Medway

Medway Archives and Local Studies Centre Civic Centre, Strood, Rochester, ME2 4AU T: 01634-332714 E: archives@medway.gov.uk local.studies@medway.gov.uk W: http://cityark.medway.gov.uk

Merseyside

Crosby Library (South Sefton Local History Unit) Crosby Road North, Waterloo, Liverpool, L22 0LQ T: 0151 257 6401 E: local-history.south@leisure.sefton.gov.uk W: www.sefton.gov.uk

Huyton Central Library Huyton Library, Civic Way, Huyton, Knowsley, L36 9GD T: 0151-443-3738 W: www.knowsley.gov.uk/leisure/libraries/huyton/index.html

Merseyside Maritime Museum Maritime Archives and Library, Albert Dock, Liverpool, L3 4AQ T: 0151-478-4418 E: archives@nmgmarchives.demon.co.uk W: www.nmgm.org.uk

Southport Library (North Sefton Local History Unit) Lord Street, Southport, PR8 1DJ T: 0151 934 2119 E: local-history.north@leisure.sefton.gov.uk

St Helen's Local History & Archives Library Central Library, Gamble Institute, Victoria Square, St Helens, WA10 1DY T: 01744-456952

Wirral Archives Service Wirral Museum, Birkenhead Town Hall, Hamilton Street, Birkenhead, CH41 5BR T: 0151-666 3903 E: archives@wirral-libraries.net W: www.wirral-libraries.net/archives

Methodist

Archives of the Independent Methodist Churches Independent Methodist Resource Centre, Fleet Street, Pemberton, Wigan, WN5 0DS T: 01942 223526 E: archives@imcgb.org.uk W: www.imcgb.org.uk

Connexional Archives for the Methodist Church 33 Harrow View, Harrow, HA1 1RE

Methodist - Central Hall Westminster Archives Central Hall Westminster, Storey's Gate, Westminster, London, SW1H 9NH T: 020 7654 3870 W: www.c-h-w.co.uk

Methodist Archives and Research Centre John Rylands University Library, 150 Deansgate, Manchester, M3 3EH T: 0161 834 5343

Middlesex

Harrow Local History Collection - Civic Centre Library PO Box 4, Station Road, Harrow, HA1 2UU T: 0208 424 1055 E: localhistory.library@harrow.gov.uk W: www.harrow.gov.uk

Norfolk

Kings Lynn Borough Archives The Old Gaol House, Saturday Market Place, Kings Lynn, PE30 5DQ T: 01553-774297 E: norfrec.nro@norfolk.gov.uk W: http://archives.norfolk.gov.uk

Norfolk Record Office The Archive Centre, Martineau Lane, Norwich, NR1 2DQ T: 01603222599 E: norfrec@norfolk.gov.uk W: http://archives.norfolk.gov.uk

Northamptonshire

Northamptonshire Central Library Abington Street, Northampton, NN1 2BA T: 01604-462040 E: ns-centlib@northamptonshire.gov.uk W: www.northamptonshire.gov.uk

Northamptonshire Record Office Wootton Hall Park, Northampton, NN4 8BQ T: 01604-762129 W: www.northamptonshire.gov.uk

Northumberland

Berwick upon Tweed Record Office Council Offices, Wallace Green, Berwick-Upon-Tweed, TD15 1ED T: 01289 301865 E: lh@berwick-upon-tweed.gov.uk W: www.bpears.org.uk/NR[index.html#Berwick

Friends of Northumberland Archives 6 Brecon Close, Ashington, NE63 0HT T: 01670 520350

Northumberland County Archive Service - closed September 2005 Morpeth Records Centre, The Kylins, Loansdean, Morpeth, NE61 2EQ T: 01670 504084 E: archives@northumberland.gov.uk W: www.swinnhopc.myby.co.uk/nro

Northumberland County Record Office - closed September 2005 Melton Park, North Gosforth, Newcastle upon Tyne, NE3 5QX T: 0191-236-2680 E: archives@northumberland.gov.uk W: www.swinnhopc.myby.co.uk/nro

The Stained Glass Museum South Triforium, Ely Cathedral, Ely, CB7 4DL T: 01353 660347 E: info@stainedglassmuseum.com W: www.stainedglassmuseum.com

Nottinghamshire

Department of Manuscripts and Special Collections Nottingham University , King's Meadow Campus, Lenton Lane, Nottingham, NG7 2NR T: 0115 951 4565 E: mss-library@nottingham.ac.uk W: www.nottingham.ac.uk/mss/

Nottingham Catholic Diocesan Archives Willson House, Derby Road, Nottingham, NG1 5AW T: 0115 953 9803 E: archives@nottinghamdiocese.org.uk W: www.nottinghamdiocese.org.uk

Nottingham Central Library : Local Studies Centre Angel Row, Nottingham, NG1 6HP T: 0115 915 2873 W: www.nottinghamcity.gov.uk/libraries

Nottinghamshire Archives Castle Meadow Road, Nottingham, NG2 1AG T: 0115-950-4524 Admin E: archives@nottscc.gov.uk W: www.nottinghamshire.gov.uk/archives

Sherwood Foresters Archives RHQ WFR, Foresters House, Chetwynd Barracks, Chilwell, Nottingham, NG9 5HA T: 0115 946 5415 E: curator@wfrmuseum.org.uk W: www.wfrmuseum.org.uk

Southwell Minster Library Minster Office, Trebeck Hall, Bishop's Drive, Southwell, NG25 0JP T: 01636-812649 E: mail@southwellminster.org.uk W: www.southwellminster.org.uk

Oxfordshire

Oxfordshire Archives St Luke's Church, Temple Road, Cowley, Oxford, OX4 2HT T: 01865 398200 E: archives@oxfordshire.gov.uk W: www.oxfordshire.gov.uk

Plymouth
Plymouth & West Devon Record Office Unit 3, Clare Place, Coxside, Plymouth, PL4 0JW T: 01752-305940 E: pwdro@plymouth.gov.uk W: www.plymouth.gov.uk/star/archives.htm

Shropshire
Ironbridge Gorge Museum, Library & Archives The Wharfage, Ironbridge, Telford, TF8 7AW T: 01952 432141 E: library@ironbridge.org.uk W: www.ironbridge.org.uk
Shropshire Archives Castle Gates, Shrewsbury, SY1 2AQ T: 01743 255350 E: research@shropshire-cc.gov.uk W: www.shropshire-cc.gov.uk/research.nsf
Wrekin Local Studies Forum Madeley Library, Russell Square, Telford, TF7 5BB T: 01952 586575 W: www.madeley.org.uk

Somerset
Bath & North East Somerset Record Office Guildhall, High Street, Bath, BA1 5AW T: 01225 477421 E: archives@bathnes.gov.uk W: www.batharchives.co.uk
Somerset Archive & Record Service Somerset Record Office, Obridge Road, Taunton, TA2 7PU T: 01823-337600 Appointments E: archives@somerset.gov.uk W: www.somerset.gov.uk/archives

Staffordshire
Burton Archives Burton Library, Riverside, High Street, Burton on Trent, DE14 1AH T: 01283 239556 E: burton.library@staffordshire.gov.uk W: www.staffordshire.gov.uk/leisure/libraries/branchlibraries/BurtonLibrary.htm
Keele University Special Collections & Archives Keele, ST5 5BG T: 01782 583237 E: h.burton@keele.ac.uk W: www.keele.ac.uk/depts/li/specarc
Lichfield Record Office Lichfield Library, The Friary, Lichfield, WS13 6QG T: 01543 510720 E: lichfield.record.office@staffordshire.gov.uk W: www.staffordshire.gov.uk/archives/
Staffordshire & Stoke on Trent Archive Service - Stoke on Trent City Archives Hanley Library, Bethesda Street, Hanley, Stoke on Trent, ST1 3RS T: 01782-238420 E: stoke.archives@stoke.gov.uk W: www.staffordshire.gov.uk/archives
Staffordshire Record Office Eastgate Street, Stafford, ST16 2LZ T: 01785 278373 (Bookings) W: www.staffordshire.gov.uk/archives
Tamworth Library Corporation Street, Tamworth, B79 7DN T: 01827-475645 E: tamworth.library@staffordshire.gov.uk W: www.staffordshire.gov.uk/leisure/libraryfacilities/localstudiesandfamilyhistory/
William Salt Library 19 Eastgate Street, Stafford, ST16 2LZ T: 01785 278372 E: william.salt.library@staffordshire.gov.uk W: www.staffordshire.gov.uk/salt

Suffolk
Suffolk Record Office - Ipswich Gatacre Road, Ipswich, IP1 2LQ T: 01473 584541 E: ipswich.ro@libher.suffolkcc.gov.uk W: www.suffolk.gov.uk/LeisureAndCulture/LocalHistoryAndHeritage/SuffolkRecordOffice
Suffolk Record Office - Lowestoft The Library, Clapham Road, Lowestoft, NR32 1DR T: 01502 405357 E: lowestoft.ro@libher.suffolkcc.gov.uk. W: www.suffolk.gov.uk/LeisureAndCulture/LocalHistoryAndHeritage/SuffolkRecordOffice

Suffolk Record Office - Bury St Edmunds 77 Raingate Street, Bury St Edmunds, IP33 2AR T: 01284 352352 E: bury.ro@libher.suffolkcc.gov.uk W: www.suffolk.gov.uk/LeisureAndCulture/LocalHistoryAndHeritage/SuffolkRecordOffice
Suffolk Regiment Archive - closed to the public Suffolk Record Office, 77 Raingate Street, Bury St Edmunds, IP33 2AR T: 01284-352352 E: bury.ro@libher.suffolkcc.gov.uk W: www.suffolkcc.gov.uk/sro/

Surrey
Cranleigh Library and Local History Centre High Street, Cranleigh, GU6 8AE T: 01483 272413 W: www.surrey.gov.uk
Domestic Buildings Research Group (Surrey) The Ridings, Lynx Hill, East Horsley, KT24 5AX T: 01483 283917
Epsom and Ewell Local History Centre Bourne Hall, Spring Street, Ewell, Epsom, KT17 1UF T: 020 8394 0372 W: www.surrey.gov.uk
Horley Local History Centre Horley Library, Victoria Road, Horley, RH6 7AG T: 01293 784141 W: www.surrey.gov.uk
North Tandridge Local History Centre Caterham Valley Library, Stafford Road, Caterham, CR3 6JG T: 01883 343580 W: www.surrey.gov.uk

Redhill Centre for Local and Family History Redhill Library, Warwick Quadrant, Redhill, RH1 1NN T: 01737 763332 W: www.surrey.gov.uk
Surrey History Centre and Archives Surrey History Centre, 130 Goldsworth Road, Woking, GU21 6ND T: 01483 518737 E: shs@surreycc.gov.uk W: www.surreycc.gov.uk/surreyhistoryservice

Sussex
Brighton History Centre Brighton Museum and Art Gallery, Royal Pavilion Gardens, Brighton, BN1 1EE T: 01273 296972 (Enquiries) E: localhistory@brighton-hove.gov.uk W: www.citylibraries.info/localhistoryt
East Sussex Record Office The Maltings, Castle Precincts, Lewes, BN7 1YT T: 01273 482349 E: archives@eastsussex.gov.uk W: www.eastsussex.gov.uk/archives/main.htm
West Sussex Record Office County Hall, Chichester, PO19 1RN T: 01243-753600 E: records.office@westsussex.gov.uk W: www.westsussex.gov.uk/ro/
Worthing Reference Library Worthing Library, Richmond Road, Worthing, BN11 1HD T: 01903 704824 E: worthing.reference.library@westsussex.gov.uk W: www.westsussex.gov.uk/libraries

Tyne & Wear
Gateshead Central Library & Local Studies Department Prince Consort Road, Gateshead, NE8 4LN T: 0191 433 8400 E: anthealang@gateshead.gov.uk W: www.gateshead.gov.uk
North Shields Local Studies Centre Central Library, Northumberland Square, North Shields, NE30 1QU T: 0191-200-5424 E: eric.hollerton@northtyneside.gov.uk W: www.northtyneside.gov.uk/libraries.html
South Tyneside Central Library - Local Studies Prince Georg Street, South Shields, NE33 2PE T: 0191 427 7860 E: localstudies.library@southtyneside.gov.uk W: www.southtyneside.gov.uk
Newcastle Local Studies Centre City Library, Princess Square, Newcastle upon Tyne, NE99 1DX T: 0191 277 4116 E: local.studies@newcastle.gov.uk W: www.newcastle.gov.uk
Tyne & Wear Archives Service Blandford House, Blandford Square, Newcastle upon Tyne, NE1 4JA T: 0191-232-6789 W: www.thenortheast.com/archives/

Warwickshire
Rugby School Archives Temple Reading Room, Rugby School, Barby Road, Rugby, CV22 5DW T: 01788 556227 W: www.rugby-school.warwks.sch.uk
Warwickshire County Record Office Priory Park, Cape Road, Warwick, CV34 4JS T: 01926 738959 E: recordoffice@warwickshire.gov.uk W: www.warwickshire.gov.uk

West Midlands
Birmingham City Archives Floor 7, Central Library, Chamberlain Square, Birmingham, B3 3HQ T: 0121 303 4217 E: archives@birmingham.gov.uk W: www.birmingham.gov.uk/archives
Birmingham Roman Catholic Archdiocesan Archives Cathedral House, St Chad's Queensway, Birmingham, B4 6EU T: 0121-236-2251 E: archives@rc-birmingham.org W: www.rc-birmingham.org
Birmingham University Information Services - Special Collections Main Library, University of Birmingham, Edgbaston, Birmingham, B15 2TT T: 0121 414 5838 E: special-collections@bham.ac.uk W: www.is.bham.ac.uk
Coventry City Archives Mandela House, Bayley Lane, Coventry, CV1 5RG T: (024) 7683 2418 E: coventryarchives@coventry.gov.uk W: www.coventry.gov.uk
Dudley Archives & Local History Service Mount Pleasant Street, Coseley, Dudley, WV14 9JR T: 01384-812770 W: www.dudley.gov.uk
MLA West Midlands: the Regional Council for Museums, Libraries and archives 2nd Floor, Grosvenor House, 14 Bennetts Hill, B2 5RS T: 01527 872258
Sandwell Community History & Archives Service Smethwick Library, High Street, Smethwick, B66 1AB T: 0121 558 2561 E: archives.service@sandwell.gov.uk W: www.lea.sandwell.gov.uk/libraries/chas.htm
Solihull Heritage and Local Studies service Solihull Central Library, Homer Road, Solihull, B91 3RG T: 0121-704-6977 W: www.solihull.gov.uk/wwwlib/#local
Sutton Coldfield Reference Library - Local Studies Section 43 Lower Parade, Sutton Coldfield, B72 1XX T: 0121 464 0164 E: sutton.coldfield.reference.lib@birmingham.gov.uk W: www.birmingham.gov.uk
Walsall Local History Centre Essex Street, Walsall, WS2 7AS T: 01922-721305 E: localhistorycentre@walsall.gov.uk W: www.walsall.gov.uk/index/leisure_and_culture/localhistorycentre

Wolverhampton Archives & Local Studies 42 - 50 Snow Hill, Wolverhampton, WV2 4AG T: 01902 552480 E: wolverhamptonarchives@dial.pipes.com W: www.wolverhampton.gov.uk/archives

Wiltshire
Salisbury Reference and Local Studies Library Market Place, Salisbury, SP1 1BL T: 01722 411098 W: www.wiltshire.gov.uk
Wiltshire and Swindon Record Office Libraries HQ, Bythesea Road, Trowbridge, BA14 8BS T: 01225 713709 E: wrso@wiltshire.gov.uk W: www.wiltshire.gov.uk
Wiltshire Buildings Record Libraries and Heritage HQ, Bythesea Road, Trowbridge, BA14 8BS T: 01225 713740 E: dorothytreasure@wiltshire.gov.uk W: www.wiltshire.gov.uk
Wiltshire Studies Library Library & heritage HQ, Bythesea Road, Trowbridge, BA14 8BS T: 01225-713732 E: librarystudies@wiltshire.gov.uk W: www.wiltshire.gov.uk/community/

Worcestershire
Worcesterhire Library & History Centre History Centre, Trinity Street, Worcester, WR1 2PW T: 01905 765922 E: wlhc@worcestershire.gov.uk W: www.worcestershire.gov.uk/records
Worcestershire Regimental Archives RHQ The Worcestershire & Sherwood Foresters Regiment, Norton Barracks, Worcester, WR5 2PA T: 01905-354359 W: www.wfrmuseum.org.uk

Yorkshire - East
East Yorkshire Archives Service County Hall, Champney Road, Beverley, HU17 9BA T: 01482 392790 E: archives.service@eastriding.gov.uk W: www.eastriding.gov.uk/learning

Yorkshire - North
Catterick Garrison Library Gough Road, Catterick Garrison, DL9 3EL T: 01748 833543 W: www.northyorks.gov.uk
North Yorkshire County Record Office N Malpas Road, Northallerton, DL7 8TB T: 01609 777585 E: archives@northyorks.gov.uk W: www.northyorks.gov.uk/archives
Ripon Local Studies Centre 42 Market Place, Ripon, HG4 1BZ T: 01765 692200 E: riponlocalstudy@btconnect.com W: www.riponlocalstudies.org
Whitby Pictorial Archives Trust Whitby Archives & Heritage Centre, Flowergate, Whitby, YO21 3BA T: 01947 821364 W: www.whitbyarchives.org.uk

Yorkshire - South
Barnsley Archives and Local Studies Department Central Library, Shambles Street, Barnsley, S70 2JF T: 01226-773950 E: Archives@barnsley.gov.uk W: www.barnsley.gov.uk
Doncaster Archives King Edward Road, Balby, Doncaster, DN4 0NA T: 01302-859811 W: www.doncaster.gov.uk
Northern General Hospital Project Clock Tower Reception, Herries Road, Sheffield, S5 7AU E: ngh.archives@blueyonder.co.uk
Rotherham Archives & Local Studies Central Library, Walker Place, Rotherham, S65 1JH T: 01709 823616 E: archives@rotherham.gov.uk W: www.rotherham.gov.uk
Sheffield Archives 52 Shoreham Street, Sheffield, S1 4SP T: 0114 203 9395 E: archives@sheffield.gov.uk W: www.sheffield.gov.uk/in-your-area/libraries/archives
Sheffield Central Library Surrey Street, Sheffield, S1 1XZ T: 0114 273 4753 E: localstudies.library@sheffield.gov.uk

Yorkshire - West
John Goodchild Collection Local History Study Centre Below Central Library, Drury Lane, Wakefield, WF1 2DT T: 01924-298929
Local Studies Library Leeds Central Library, Calverley Street, Leeds, LS1 3AB T: 0113 247 8290 E: localstudies@leedslearning.net W: www.leeds.gov.uk/library
Wakefield Library Headquarters - Local Studies Department Balne Lane, Wakefield, WF2 0DQ T: 01924-302224 W: www.wakefield.gov.uk
Kirklees - West Yorks Archive Service Central Library, Princess Alexandra Walk, Huddersfield, HD1 2SU T: 01484 221966 E: kirklees@wyjs.org.uk W: www.archives.wyjs.org.uk
Leeds - West Yorkshire Archive Service 2 Chapeltown Road, Sheepscar, Leeds, LS7 3AP T: 0113-214-5814 E: leeds@wyjs.org.uk W: www.archives.wyjs.org.uk
West Yorkshire Archive Service, Bradford West Yorkshire Archive Service, 15 Canal Road, Bradford, BD1 4AT T: 01274 731931 E: tberry@wyjs.org.uk W: www.wyjs.org.uk
West Yorkshire Archive Service, Calderdale Central Library, Northgate, Halifax, HX1 1UN T: 01422-392636 E: calderdale@wyjs.org.uk W: www.archives.wyjs.org.uk

West Yorkshire Archive Service, Wakefield Registry of Deeds, Newstead Road, Wakefield, WF1 2DE T: 01924-305980 E: tberry@wyjs.org.uk W: www.wyjs.org.uk
Yorkshire Archaeological Society Claremont, 23 Clarendon Rd, Leeds, LS2 9NZ T: 0113-245-6342 E:yas@wyjs.org.uk (Library and Archives) W: www.yas.org.uk

Yorkshire - York
Borthwick Institute of Historical Research University of York, Heslington, York, YO10 5DD T: 01904 321166 - archives W: www.york.ac.uk/inst/bihr www.york.ac.uk/borthwick
York Central Library - Local History & Reference Collection York Central Library, Library Square, Museum Street, York, YO1 7DS T: 01904-655631 E: reference.library@york.gov.uk W: www.york.gov.uk
York City Archives Exhibition Square, Bootham, York, YO1 7EW T: 01904-551878/9 E: archives@york.gov.uk W: www.york.gov.uk
Yorkshire Family History - Biographical Database York Minster Library & Archives, Dean's Park, York, YO1 7JQ T: 01904-625308 Library E: library@yorkminster.org archives@yorkminster.org W: www.yorkminster.org

Wales
Department of Manuscripts Main Library, University of Wales, College Road, Bangor, LL57 2DG T: 01248-382966
National Library of Wales Penglais, Aberystwyth, SY23 3BU T: 01970 632800 E: holi@llgc.org.uk W: www.llgc.org.uk
National Monuments Record of Wales Royal Commission on the Ancient & Historical Monuments of Wales, Crown Building, Plas Crug, Aberystwyth, Wales T: 01970-621200 E: nmr.wales@rcahmw.org.uk W: www.rcahmw.org.uk
National Monuments Record of Wales Royal Commission - Ancient & Historical Monuments Wales, Crown Building, Plas Crug, Aberystwyth, SY23 1NJ T: 01970 621200 E: nmr.wales@rcahmw.org.uk W: www.rcahmw.org.uk
Film Archives
National Screen and Sound Archive of Wales Unit 1, Science Park, Aberystwyth, SY23 3AH T: 01970 626007 E: http://screenandsound.llgc.org.uk
Land Registries
District Land Registry for Wales T^y Cwm Tawe, Phoenix Way, Llansamlet, Swansea, SA7 9FQ T: 01792 355000
Anglesey
Anglesey County Archives Service Shirehall, Glanhwfa Road, Llangefni, LL77 7TW T: 01248-752080 W: www.anglesey.gov.uk
Carmarthenshire
Carmarthenshire Archive Service Parc Myrddin, Richmond Terrace, Carmarthen, SA31 1DS T: 01267 228232 E: archives@carmarthenshire.gov.uk W: www.carmarthenshire.gov.uk
Ceredigion
Archifdy Ceredigion, Ceredigion Archives Swyddfa'r Sir, County Offices, Glan y Mor, Marine Terrace, Aberystwyth, SY23 2DE T: 01970-633697 E: archives@ceredigion.gov.uk W: www.archifdy-ceredigion.gov.uk
Conwy
Conwy Archive Service Old Board school, Lloyd Street, Llandudno, LL30 2YG T: 01492 860882 E: archifau.archives@conwy.gov.uk W: www.conwy.gov.uk/archives
Denbighshire
Denbighshire Record Office 46 Clwyd Street, Ruthin, LL15 1HP T: 01824-708250 E: archives@denbighshire.go.uk W: www.denbighshire.gov.uk
Flintshire
Flintshire Record Office The Old Rectory, Rectory Lane, Hawarden, CH5 3NR T: 01244-532364 E: archives@flintshire.gov.uk W: www.flintshire.gov.uk
Glamorgan
Aberkenfig Family Research Resource Centre Pensioners Hall, Heol Persondy Road, Aberkenfig, T: 01656 728 531 E: arc@glamfhs.info W: www.rootsweb.com/~wlsglfhs/direct.htm
Glamorgan Record Office Glamorgan Building, King Edward VII Avenue, Cathays Park, Cardiff, CF10 3NE T: (029) 2078 0282 E: GlamRO@cardiff.ac.uk W: www.glamro.gov.uk
Neath Central Library (Local Studies Department) 29 Victoria Gardens, Neath, SA11 3BA T: 01639-620139 W: www.neath-porttalbot.gov.uk
Swansea Reference Library Alexandra Road, Swansea, SA1 5DX T: 01792 516753 E: central.library@swansea.gov.uk W: www.swansea.gov.uk/libraries
West Glamorgan Archive Service County Hall, Oystermouth Road, Swansea, SA1 3SN T: 01792-636589 E: westglam.archives@swansea.gov.uk W: www.swansea.gov.uk/westglamorganarchives
West Glamorgan Archive Service - Neath Archives Access Point Neath Mechanics Institute, Church Place, Neath, SA11 3BA T: 01639-620139 W: www.swansea.gov.uk/archives

West Glamorgan Archive Service - Port Talbot Access Point Port Talbot Library, 1st Floor, Aberavon Shopping Centre, Port Talbot, SA13 1PB T: 01639 763430 W: www.swansea.gov.uk/archives

Gwent

Blaenavon Ironworks Blaenavon Tourist Information Office, North Street, Blaenavon, NP4 9RQ T: 01495 792615 W: www.btinternet.com~blaenavon.ironworks/pages/genealogy.htm

Gwent Record Office County Hall, Croesyceiliog, Cwmbran, NP44 2XH T: 01633-644886 E: gwent.records@torfaen.gov.uk W: www.llgc.org.uk/cac

Newport Community Learning and Libraries Newport Central Library, John Frost Square, Newport, NP20 1PA T: 01633 656656 E: reference.library@newport.gov.uk W: www.newport.gov.uk

Gwynedd

Archifdy Meirion Archives Swyddfeydd y Cyngor, Cae Penarlag, Dolgellau, LL40 2YB T: 01341-424444 W: www.gwynedd.gov.uk/archives/

Caernarfon Area Record Office, Gwynedd Archives Caernarfon Area Record Office, Victoria Dock, Caernarfon, LL55 1SH T: 01286 679095 E: archifau@gwynedd.gov.uk W: www.gwynedd.gov.uk/adrannau/addysg/archifau

Pembrokeshire

Pembrokeshire Libraries The County Library, Dew Street, Haverfordwest, SA61 1SU T: 01437 775248 E: sue.armour@pembrokeshire.gov.uk W: www.pembrokeshire.gov.uk

Pembrokeshire Record Office The Castle, Haverfordwest, SA61 2EF T: 01437 763707 E: record.office@pembrokeshire.gov.uk W: www.pembrokeshire.gov.uk

Tenby Museum Tenby Museum & Art Gallery, Castle Hill, Tenby, SA70 7BP T: 01834-842809 E: tenbymuseum@hotmail.com W: www.tenbymuseum.free-online.co.uk

Powys

Powys County Archives Office County Hall, Llandrindod Wells, LD1 5LG T: 01597 826088 E: archives@powys.gov.uk W: http://archives.powys.gov.uk

Wrexham

Wrexham Local Studies and Archives Service A N Palmer Centre, County Buildings, Regent Street, Wrexham, LL11 1RB T: 01978 317976 E: archives@wrexham.gov.uk localstudies@wrexham.gov.uk W: www.wrexham.gov.uk/heritage

Channel Islands

Guernsey Island Archives 29 Victoria Road, St Peter Port, GY1 1HU T: 01481 724512

Guernsey Island Archives Service 29 Victoria Rd, St Peter Port, GYI 1HU T: 01481-724512

Jersey Archives Service - Jersey Heritage Trust Clarence Road, St Helier, JE2 4JY T: 01534 833303

Judicial Greffe Morier House, Halkett Place, St Helier, JE1 1DD T: 01534-502300 E: jgreffe@super.net.uk W: www.jersey.gov.uk

Isle of Man

Civil Registry Registries Building, Deemster's Walk, Bucks Road, Douglas, IM1 3AR T: 01624 687039 E: civil@registry.gov.im

Isle of Man Public Record Office Unit 3 Spring Valley Industrial Estate, Braddan, Douglas, IM2 2QR T: 01624 613383

Manx National Heritage Library Manx Museum, Douglas, IM1 3LY T: 01624 648000 E: enquiries@mnh.gov.im W: www.gov.im/mnh

Scotland

General Register Office for Scotland New Register House, Edinburgh, EH1 3YT T: 0131 334 0380 E: records@gro-scotland.gsi.gov.uk W: www.gro-scotland.gov.uk www.scotlandpeople.gov.uk

Grand Lodge of Scotland Freemasons' Hall, 96 George Street, Edinburgh, EH2 3DH T: 0131 225 5304 E: gladmin@grandlodgescotland.com W: www.grandlodgescotland.com

Heriot-Watt University Archives Coporate Communications, Heriot-Watt university, Edinburgh, EH14 4AS T: 0131 451 3218 E: a.e.jones@hw.ac.uk W: www.hw.ac.uk/archive

National Archives of Scotland HM General Register House, 2 Princes Street, Edinburgh, EH1 3YY T: 0131 535 1314 E: enquiries@nas.gov.uk W: www.nas.gov.uk

National Archives of Scotland - West Search Room West Register House, Charlotte Square, Edinburgh, EH2 4DJ T: 0131-535-1413 E: wsr@nas.gov.uk W: www.nas.gov.uk

National Library of Scotland - Manuscript Collections National Library of Scotland, George IV Bridge, Edinburgh, EH1 1EW T: 0131 623 3876 E: manuscripts@nls.uk W: www.nls.uk

National Monuments Record of Scotland Royal Commission on the Ancient & Historical Monuments of Scotland, John Sinclair House, 16 Bernard Terrace, Edinburgh, EH8 9NX T: 0131 662 1456 E: nmrs@rcahms.gov.uk W: www.rcahms.gov.uk

National Register of Archives (Scotland) H M General Register House, 2 Princes Street, Edinburgh, EH1 3YY T: 0131 535 1405/1428 E: nra@nas.gov.uk W: www.nas.gov.uk/nras/default.asp

Scottish Archive Network The National archives of scotland, HM General register House, 2 princes Street, Edinburgh, EH1 3YY T: 0131 535 1314 E: enquiries@scan.org.uk W: www.scan.org.uk www.scottishhandwriting.com

Scottish Brewing Archive Glasgow University Archive Services, 13 Thurso Street, Glasgow, G11 6PE T: 0141 330 2640 E: sba@archives.gla.ac.uk W: www.archives.gla.ac.uk/sba/

Scottish Catholic Archives Columba House, 16 Drummond Place, Edinburgh, EH3 6PL T: 0131-5563661 W: www.scottishcatholicarchives.org

Scottish Genealogy Society 15 Victoria Terrace, Edinburgh, EH1 2JL T: 0131-220-3677 E: sales@scotsgenealogy.com W: www.scotsgenealogy.com

Scottish Genealogy Society - Library 15 Victoria Terrace, Edinburgh, EH1 2JL T: 0131-220 3677 E: info@scotsgenealogy.com W: www.scotsgenealogy.com

Scottish Jewish Archives Centre Garnethill Synagogue, 129 Hill Street, Garnethill, Glasgow, G3 6UB T: 0141 332 4911 E: archives@sjac.fsbusiness.co.uk W: www.sjac.org.uk

St Andrews University Library - Special Collections Department North Street, St Andrews, KY16 9TR T: 01334 462339 E: speccoll@st-and.ac.uk W: http://specialcollections.st-and.ac.uk

Strathclyde University Archives McCance Building, 16 Richmond Street, Glasgow, G1 1XQ T: 0141 548 2397

Brewing

Scottish Brewing Archive Glasgow University Archive Services, 13 Thurso Street, Glasgow, G11 6PE T: 0141 330 2640 E: sba@archives.gla.ac.uk W: www.archives.gla.ac.uk/sba/

Film Archives

Scottish Screen Archive Scottish Screen, 1 Bowmont Gardens, Glasgow, G12 9LR T: 0141 337 7400 W: www.scottishscreen.com

Military

Dunkeld Cathedral Chapter House Museum Dunkeld, PH8 0AW T: 01350 728732 W: www.dunkeldcathedral.org.uk

Regimental Museum and Archives of Black Watch Balhousie Castle, Hay Street, Perth, PH1 5HR T: 0131 310 8530 E: archives@theblackwatch.co.uk W: www.theblackwatch.co.uk

Scottish Horse Regimental Archives - Dunkeld Cathedral Dunkeld, PH8 0AW T: 01350 727614

Aberdeenshire

Aberdeen City Archives Aberdeen City Council, Town House, Broad Street, Aberdeen, AB10 1AQ T: 01224 522513 E: archives@aberdeencity.gov.uk W: www.aberdeencity.gov.uk

Aberdeen City Archives - Old Aberdeen House Branch Old Aberdeen House, Dunbar Street, Aberdeen, AB24 1UE T: 01224-481775 E: archives@legal.aberdeen.net.uk W: www.aberdeencity.gov.uk

Aberdeen Synagogue 74 Dee Street, Aberdeen, AB11 6DS T: 01224 582135

Angus

Angus Archives Hunter Library, Restenneth Priory, By Forfar, DD8 2SZ T: 01307 468644 E: angus.archives@angus.gov.uk W: www.angus gov.uk/history/default.htm

Dundee City Council - Genealogy Unit 89 Commercial Street, Dundee, DD1 2AF T: 01382-435222 E: grant.law@dundeecity.gov.uk W: www.dundeecity.gov.uk/registrars

Argyll

Argyll & Bute District Archives Manse Brae, Lochgilphead, PA31 8QU T: 01546 604120

Ayrshire

Ayrshire Archives Ayrshire Archives Centre, Craigie Estate, Ayr, KA8 0SS T: 01292 287584 E: archives@south-ayrshire.gov.uk W: www.ayrshirearchives.org.uk

East Ayrshire Council District History Centre & Museum Baird Institute, 3 Lugar Street, Cumnock, KA18 1AD T: 01290 421701 E: Baird.institute@east-ayrshire.gov.uk W: www.east-ayrshire.gov.uk

North Ayrshire Libraries Library Headquarters, 39 - 41 Princes Street, Ardrossan, KA22 8BT T: 01294 469137 W: www.north-ayrshire.gov.uk

Clackmannanshire Archives Alloa Library, 26/28 Drysdale Street, Alloa, FK10 1JL T: 01259 722262 E: libraries@clacks.gov.uk W: www.clacksweb.org.uk/dyna/archives

Ewart Library Ewart Library, Catherine Street, Dumfries, DG1 1JB T: 01387 260285 E: ericaj@dumgal.gov.uk W: www.dgc.gov.uk/service/depts/comres/library/grcsearch

Dumfries & Galloway Library and Archives Archive Centre, 33 Burns Street, Dumfries, DG1 1PS T: 01387 269254 W: www.dumgal.gov.uk

Dundee City Archives 21 City Square, (callers use 1 Shore Terrace), Dundee, DD1 3BY T: 01382 434494 E: archives@dundeecity.gov.uk W: www.fdca.org.uk www.dundeecity.gov.uk/roots

Dundee Synagogue St Mary Place, Dundee, DD1 5RB

East Dunbartonshire Local Record Offices and Reference Libraries William Patrick Library, 2 West High Street, Kirkintilloch, G66 1AD T: 0141 776 8090 E: libraries@eastdunbarton.gov.uk W: www.eastdunbarton.gov.uk

East Renfrewshire Record Offices East Renfrewshire District Council, Rouken Glen Road, Glasgow, G46 6JF T: 0141 577 4976
Edinburgh City Archives City Chambers, High St, Edinburgh, EH1 1YJ T: 0131 529 4616
Edinburgh Synagogue 4 Salisbury Road, Edinburgh, Scotland
Falkirk Library Hope Street, Falkirk, FK1 5AU T: 01324 503605 W: www.falkirk.gov.uk
Falkirk Museum History Research Centre Callendar House, Callendar Park, Falkirk, FK1 1YR T: 01324 503778 E: ereid@falkirkmuseums.demon.co.ukcallandarhouse@falkirkmuseums.demon.co.uk W: www.falkirkmuseums.demon.co.uk
Fife Council Archive Centre Carleton House, Haig Business Park, Balgonie Road, Markinch, Glenrothes, KY7 6AQ T: 01592 416504 E: archive.enquiries@fife.gov.uk W: www.fifedirect.org.uk
Glasgow
Glasgow City Archives Mitchell Library, North Street, Glasgow, G3 7DN T: 0141-287-2913 E: archives@cls.glasgow.gov.uk W: www.glasgow.gov.uk/en/Residents/Leisure_Culture/Libraries/Collections/ArchivesandSpecialCollections
Glasgow Jewish Representative Council 222 Fenwick Road, Giffnock, Glasgow, G46 6UE T: 0141 577 8200 E: jrepcouncil@aol.com W: www.j-scot.org/glasgow
Glasgow University Archive Services 13 Thurso Street, Glasgow, G11 6PE T: 0141 330 4159 E: enquiries@archives.gla.ac.uk W: www.archives.gla.ac.uk
Glasgow University Library & Special Collections Department Hillhead Street, Glasgow, G12 8QE T: 0141 330 6704 E: library@lib.gla.ac.uk W: www.gla.ac.uk/library
Royal College of Physicians and Surgeons of Glasgow 232 - 242 St Vincent Street, Glasgow, G2 5RJ T: 0141 221 6072 E: library@rcpsglasg.ac.uk W: www.rcpsglasg.ac.uk
Highland - North Highland Archive Wick Library, Sinclair Terrace, Wick, KW1 5AB T: 01955 606432
Invernesshire
Highland Council Genealogy Centre Inverness Public Library, Farraline Park, Inverness, IV1 1NH T: 01463-236463 : E: genealogy@highland.gov.uk W: www.highland.gov.uk/publicservices/genealogy.htm
Isle of Lewis
Stornoway Record Office Town Hall, 2 CromwellStreet, Stornoway, HS1 2BD T: 01851-709438 E: emacdonald@cne-siar.gov.uk
Lanarkshire
North Lanarkshire - Lenziemill Archives 10 Kelvin Road, Cumbernauld, G67 2BA T: 01236 737114 W: www.northlan.gov.uk
South Lanarkshire Council Archives 30 Hawbank Road, College Milton, East Kilbride, G74 5EX T: 01355 239193
Midlothian Archives and Local Studies Centre 2 Clerk Street, Loanhead, EH20 9DR T: 0131 271 3976 E: local.studies@midlothian.gov.uk W: www.midlothian.gov.uk
Moray Local Heritage Centre Grant Lodge, Cooper Park, Elgin, IV30 1HS T: 01343 562644 E: graeme.wilson@techleis.moray.gov.uk W: www.morray.org/heritage/roots.html
Orkney
Orkney Archives The Orkney Library, Laing Street, Kirkwall, KWI5 1NW T: 01856-873166 W: www.orkney.gov.uk
Orkney Library The Orkney Library, Laing Street, Kirkwall, KWI5 1NW T: 01856-873166 W: www.orkney.gov.uk
Perthshire
Perth and Kinross Council Archives A K Bell Library, 2 - 8 York Place, Perth, PH2 8EP T: 01738 477012 E: archives@pkc.gov.uk W: www.pkc.gov.uk/archives
Renfrewshire Archives Central Library & Museum Complex, High Street, Paisley, PA1 2BB T: 0141-889-2350 W: www.renfrewshire.gov.uk
Scottish Borders Archive & Local History Centre Library Headquarters, St Mary's Mill, Selkirk, TD7 5EW T: 01750 20842 E: archives@scotborders.gov.uk W: www.scotborders.gov.uk/libraries
Shetland Archives 44 King Harald St, Lerwick, ZE1 0EQ T: 01595-696247
Unst Heritage Centre Haroldswick, Unst, ZE2 9ED T: 01957 711504
Stirlingshire
Stirling Council Archives 5 Borrowmeadow Road, Stirling, FK7 7UW T: 01786 450745 E: archive@stirling.gov.uk W: www.stirling.gov.uk
West Lothian
West Lothian Council Archives - Archives & Records Management 9 Dunlop Square, Deans Industrial Esatte, Livingston, EH54 8SB T: 01506 4773770 E: archive@westlothian.gov.uk W: www.westlothian.gov.uk/content/leisure/libraries/Liblocal/archives

Northern Ireland
General Register Office of Northern Ireland Oxford House, 49 - 55 Chichester Street, Belfast, BT1 4HL T: (028) 90 252000 E: gro.nisra@dfpni.gov.uk W: www.groni.gov.uk
Northern Ireland Film Commission 21 Ormeau Avenue, Belfast, BT2 8HD W: www.nifc.co.uk

Presbyterian Historical Society of Ireland Church House, Fisherwick Place, Belfast, BT1 6DW T: (028) 9032 2284
Public Record Office of Northern Ireland 66 Balmoral Avenue, Belfast, BT9 6NY T: (028) 9025 5905 E: proni@dcalni.gov.uk valerie.adams@dcalni.gov.uk W: www.proni@dcalni.gov.uk
Belfast
Belfast Central Library Irish & Local Studies Dept, Royal Avenue, Belfast, BT1 1EA T: (028) 9024 3233 E: info@belb.co.uk W: www.belb.org.uk
Belfast Family History & Cultural Heritage Centre 64 Wellington Place, Belfast, BT1 6GE T: (028) 9023 5392
County Down
Banbridge Genealogy Services Gateway Tourist Information Centre, 200 Newry Road, Banbridge, BT32 3NB T: 028 4062 6369
County Londonderry
Derry City Council Heritage & Museum Service Harbour Museum, Harbour Square, Derry, BT48 6AF T: (028) 7137 7331

Ireland
Church of Ireland Archives Representative Church Body Library, Braemor Park, Churchtown, Dublin 14, T: 01-492-3979 E: library@ireland.anglican.org W: www.ireland.anglican.org/
Film Institute of Ireland 6 Eustace Street, Dublin, 2 T: 01 679 5744 W: www.fli.ie
Garda Siochana Museum & Archives The Records Tower, Dublin, 2 T: +353 1 6719 597 W: www.esatclear.ie/~garda/museum.html
Genealogical Office / Office of The Chief Herald Kildare Street, Dublin 2, T: +353 1 6030 311 E: herald@nli.ie W: www.nli.ie
Grand Lodge of Ireland Freemasons' Hall, 17 Molesworth Street, Dublin 2, T: 00 353 01 6760 1337
National Archives Bishop Street, Dublin 8, T: 01-407-2300 E: mail@nationalarchives.ie W: www..nationalarchives.ie
Registrar General for Ireland Joyce House, 8 - 11 Lombard Street East, Dublin 2, T: Dublin-711000
County Clare
Clare County Archives Clare County Council, New Road, Ennis, T: 065-28525 W: www.clare.ie
County Cork
Cork Archives Institute Christ Church, South Main Street, Cork, T: + 353 (021) 427 7809 E: archivist@corkcity.ie
County Donegal
Donegal Ancestry The Quay, Ramleton, T: 00353 74 51266 E: info@donegalancestry.com W: www.donegalancestry.com
Donegal County Archives Cultural Services, 3 Rivers Centre, Lifford, T: + 00353 74 72490 E: archivist@donegalcoco.ie W: www.donegal.ie
Donegal Local Studies Centre Central Library & Arts Centre, Oliver Plunkett Road, Letterkenny, T: 00353 74 24950 W: www.donegal.ie/library
County Dublin
Dublin Heritage Group Ballyfermot Library, Ballyfermot Road, Ballyfermot, Dublin, 10 T: 6269324
County Limerick
Limerick City Library Local History Collection The Granary, Michael Street, Limerick, T: +353 (0)61-314668 W: www.limerickcorp.ie/librarymain.htm
Limerick Regional Archives Limerick Ancestry, The Granary, Michael Street, Limerick, T: 061-415125 W: www.mayo-ireland.ie
County Louth
Louth County Archive Service Old Gaol, Ardee Road, Dundalk, T: + 353 (0)42 933 9387 E: archive@louthcoco.ie W: www.louthcoco.ie/
County Mayo
Local Record Offices The Registration Office, New Antrim Street, Castlebar, T: 094-23249
County Waterford
Waterford Archives and Local Records St Joseph's Hospital, Dungarvan, T: 058-42199

Dublin
Dublin City Archives City Assembly House, 58 South William Street, Dublin, 2 T: (01)-677-5877

Australia
ACT
National Archives of Australia PO Box 7425, Canberra Business Centre, Canberra, ACT 2610 T: 61 2 6212 3900 F: 61 2 6212 3699 E: ref@naa.gov.au W: www.naa.gov.au
New South Wales
National Archives of Australia - Sydney Office 120 Miller Road, Chester Hill, Sydney, New South Wales 2162 W: www.naa.gov.uk
State Archives Office 2 Globe Street, Sydney, New South Wales 2000 T: 02-9237-0254 F: 02-9237-0142
State Library of New South Wales Macquarie Street, Sydney, New South Wales 2000 T: 02-9230-1414 W: www.slsw.gov.au
Northern Territories
Australian Archives - Northern Territories Kelsey Crescent, Nightcliffe, Northern Territories 810 T: 08-8948-4577 F: 08-8948-0276
Queensland
National Archives of Australia - Queensland 996 Wynnum Road,

Cannon Hill, Queensland 4170 W: www.naa.gov.au
Queensland State Archives PO Box 1397, Sunnybanks Hills, Brisbane, Queensland 4109 W: www.archives.qld.gov.au
South Australia
Australian Archives - South Australia 11 Derlanger Avenue, Collingwood, South Australia 5081 T: 08-269-0100 F: 08-269-3234
South Australia State Archives PO Box 1056, Blair Athol West, South Australia 5084 T: 08-8226-8000 F: 08-8226-8002
Tasmania
National Archives of Australia - Hobart Office 4 Rosny Hill Road, Rosny Park, Tasmania 7018 T: 03-62-440101 F: 03-62-446834 E: reftas@naa.gov.au W: www.naa.gov.au
State Archives, The Archives Office of Tasmania, 77 Murray Street, Hobart, Tasmania 7000 T: (03)-6233-7488 F: (03)-6233-7471 W: www.tased.edu.au/archives
Victoria
Bendigo Regional Genealogical Society Inc PO Box 1049, Bendigo, Victoria 3552
National Archives of Australia - Victoria PO Box 8005, Burwood Heights, Victoria 3151 T: 03-9285-7900 F: 03-9285-7979
Victoria State Archives 57 Cherry Lane, Laverton North, Victoria 3028 T: 03-9360-9665 F: 03-9360-9685
Victoria State Archives Level 2 Casselden Place, 2 Lonsdale Street, Melbourne, Victoria 3000 T: 03-9285-7999 F: 03-9285-7953
Victoria State Archives State Offices, Corner of Mair & Doveton Streets, Ballarat, Victoria 3350 T: 03-5333-6611 F: 03-5333-6609
Western Australia
Australian Archives - Western Australia 384 Berwick Street East, Victoria Park, Western Australia 6101 T: 09-470-7500 F: 09-470-2787
State Archives and Public Record Office Alexander Library, Perth Cultural Centre, Perth, Western Australia 6000 T: 09-427-3360 F: 09-427-3256 E:

New Zealand
National Archives of New Zealand, The PO Box 10-050, 10 Mulgrave Street, Thorndon, Wellington, T: 04-499-5595 F: 04-495-6210 E: reference@archives.govt.nz W: www.archives.govt.nz
South Africa
Cape Town Archives Repository Private Bag X9025, Cape Town, 8000 T: 021-462-4050 F: 021-465-2960
Dutch Reformed Church Archive PO Box 398, Bloemfontein, 9301 T: 051-448-9546
Dutch Reformed Church Records Office PO Box 649, Pietermaritzburg, 3200 T: 0331-452279 F: 0331-452279
Free State Archives Repository Private Bag X20504, Bloemfontein, 9300 T: 051 522 6762 F: 051 522 6765
National Archives Private Bag X236, Pretoria, 1
National Archives - Pretoria Private Bag X236, Pretoria, 1 T: 323 5300 F: 323 5287
South African Library-National Reference & Preservation P O Box 496, Cape Town, 8000 T: 021 246320 F: 021 244848
Free State
Free State Archives Private Bag X20504, Bloemfontein, Free State 9300 T: 051-522-6762 F: 051-522-6765
Namibia
National Archives of Namibia Private Bag, Windhoek, 13250 T: 061 293 4386 F: 061 239042 E: Renate@natarch.mec.gov.na W: www.witbooi.natarch.mec.gov.na
Zimbabwe
National Archives of Zimbabwe Hiller Road, off Borrowdale Road, Gunhill, Harare, T: 792741/3 F: 792398
Europe
Belgium
Archives de l'Etat a Liege 79 rue du Chera, Liege, B-4000 T: 04 252 0393 F: 04 229 3350 E: archives.liege@skynet.be
De Kerk van Jezus Christus van den Heiligen Der Laaste Dagen, Kortrijkse Steenweg 1060, Sint-Deniss-Westrem, B-9051 T: 09 220 4316
In Flanders Fields Museum Lakenhallen, Grote Markt 34, Ieper, B-8900 T: 00-32-(0)-57-22-85-84 F: 00-32-(0)-57-22-85-89 W: www.inflandersfields.be
Provinciebestuur Limburg Universitilslaan 1, Afdeling 623 Archief, Hasselt, B-3500
Rijks Archief te Brugge Academiestraat 14, Brugge, 8000 T: 050 33 7288 F: 050 33 7288 E: rijksarchief.brugge@skynet.be
Rijksarchief Kruibekesteenweg 39/1, Beveren, B-9210 T: 03 775 3839
Staatsarchiv in Eupen Kaperberg 2-4, Eupen, B-4700 T: 087 55 4377
Stadsarchief te Veurne Grote Markt 29, Veurne, B-8630 T: 058 31 4115 F: 058 31 4554
The Passchendaele Archives Jan Van der Fraenen, leperstraat 5, Zonnebeke, B - 8980 E: archives@passchendaele.be W: www.passchendaele.be
Cyprus
Cyprus Center of Medievalism & Heraldry P O Box 80711, Piraeus, 185 10
Denmark
Association of Local History Archives P O Box 235, Enghavevej 2, Vejle, DK-7100 F: 45 7583 1801 W: www.lokalarkiver.dk

Cadastral Archives Rentemestervej 8, Copenhagen NV, DK-2400 F: 45 3587 5064 W: www.kms.min.dk
Danish Data Archive Islandsgade 10, Odense C, DK-5000 F: 45 6611 3060 W: www.dda.dk
Danish Emigration Archives P O Box 1731, Arkivstraede 1, Aalborg, DK-9100 T: 045 9931 4221 F: 45 9810 2248 E: bfl-kultur@aalbkom.dk W: www.cybercity.dk/users/ccc13656
Danish National Archives Rigsdagsgaarden 9, Copenhagen, DK-1218 T: 45 3392 3310 F: 45 3315 3239 W: www.sa.dk/ra/uk/uk.htm
Danish Society for Local History Colbjornsensvej 8, Naerum, DK-2850
Det Kongelige Bibliotek POB 2149, Copenhagen K, DK-1016 T: 045 3393 0111 F: 045 3393 2218
Frederiksberg Municipal Libraries Solbjergvej 21-25, Frederiksberg, DK-2000 F: 45 3833 3677 W: www.fkb.dk
Kobenshavns Stadsarkiv Kobenhavns Radhus, Kobenhavn, DK01599 T: 3366 2374 F: 3366 7039
National Business Archives Vester Alle 12, Aarhus C, DK-8000 T: 45 8612 8533 F: 45 8612 8560 E: mailbox@ea.sa.dk W: www.sa.dk/ea/engelsk.htm
Provincial Archives for Funen Jernbanegade 36, Odense C, DK-5000 T: 6612 5885 F: 45 6614 7071 W: www.sa.dk/lao/default.htm
Provincial Archives for Nth Jutland Lille Sct. Hansgade 5, Viborg, DK-8800 T: 45 8662 1788 F: 45 8660 1006 W: www.sa.dk/lav/default.htm
Provincial Archives for Southern Jutland Haderslevvej 45, Aabenraa, DK-6200 T: 45 7462 5858 F: 45 7462 3288 W: www.sa.dk/laa/default.htm
Provincial Archives for Zealand etc Jagtvej 10, Copenhagen, DK-2200 F: 45 3539 0535 W: www.sa.dk/lak.htm
Royal Library Christains Brygge 8, Copenhagen K, DK-1219 F: 45 3393 2219 W: www.kb.dk
State Library Universitetsparken, Aarhus C, DK-8000 T: 45 8946 2022 F: 45 8946 2130 W: www.sb.aau.dk/english
Finland
Institute of Migration Piispankatu 3, Turku, 20500 T: 2 231 7536 F: 2 233 3460 E: jouni.kurkiasaaz@utu.fi W: www.utu.fi/erill/instmigr/
France
Centre d'Accueil et de Recherche des Archives Nationales 60 rue des Francs Bourgeois, Paris Cedex 75141 T: 1 40 27 6000
Centre des Archives d'Outre-Mer 29 Chemin du Moulin de Testas, Aix-en-Provence, 13090
Service Historique de l'Armee de l'Air Chateau de Vincennes, Vincennes Cedex, 94304
Service Historique de l'Armee de Terre BP 107, Armees, 481
Service Historique de la Marine Chateau de Vincennes, Vincennes Cedex, 94304
Military (Army) Service Historique De L'Armee De Terre Fort de Vincennes, Boite Postale 107, 00481 ARMEES T: 01 4193 34 44 F: 01 41 93 38 90
Military (Navy) Service Historique De La Marine Chateau de Vincennes, Boite Postale 2, 00300 ARMEES T: 01 43 28 81 50 F: 01 43 28 31 60
Germany
Herold - Verein fur Genealogie Heraldik und Rciwandtc Wissen-Scahaften Archiv Str. 12-14, Berlin, D -14195
Historic Emigration Office Steinstr. 7, Hamburg, (D) 20095 T: 4940 300 51 282 F: 4940 300 51 220 W: users.cybercity.dk/gccc13652/addr/ger_heo.htm
Research Centre Lower Saxons in the USA Postfach 2503, Oldenburg, D-2900 T: 0441 798 2614 F: 0441 970 6180 E: holtmann@hrzl.uni-oldenburg.de W: www.uni-oldenburg.de/nausa
The German Emigration Museum Inselstrasse 6, Bremerhaven, D-2850 T: 0471 49096
Zentralstelle fur Personen und Familiengeschichte Birkenweg 13, Friedrichsdorf, D-61381 T: 06172 78263 W: www.genealogy.com/gene/genealogy.html
Zentralstelle fur Personnen und Familiengeschichte Birkenweg 13, Friedrichsdorf, D - 6138
Greece
Cyprus Center of Medievalism & Heraldry P O Box 80711, Piraeus, 185 10 T: 42 26 356
Liechtenstein
Major Archives, Record Offices & Libraries W: www.genealogy.com/gene/reg/CH/lichts.html
Netherlands
Amsterdam Municipal Archives P O 51140, Amsterdam, 1007 EC
Brabant-Collectie Tilburg University Library, P O Box 90153, Warandelaan, Tilburg, NL-5000 LE T: 0031 134 662127
Gemeentelijke Archiefdienst Amersfoort P O Box 4000, Amersfoort, 3800 EA T: 033 4695017 F: 033 4695451
Het Utrechts Archief Alexander Numankade 199/201, Utrecht, 3572 KW T: 030 286 6611 F: 030 286 6600
Rijksarchief in Drenthe P O Box 595, Assen, 9400 AN T: 0031 592 313523 F: 0031 592 314697 W: obd-server.obd.nl/instel/enderarch/radz.htm
Rijksarchief in Overijssel Eikenstraat 20, Zwolle, 8021 WX T: 038 454 0722 F: 038 454 4506 W: www.obd.nl/instel/arch/rkarch.htm
Zealand Documentation CTR P O Box 8004, Middelburg, 4330 EA

Norway
Norwegian Emigration Centre Strandkaien 31, Stavanger, 4005 T: 47 51 53 88 63 W: www.emigrationcenter.com
Poland
Head Office, State Archives Ul Dluga6 Skr, Poczt, Warsaw, 1005 00-950 F: 0-22 831 9222
Russia
Moscow Russian State Military Historical Archive 2 Baumanskaya 3, 107864, Moscow, T: 7 (095) 261-20-70
St Petersburg Russian State Historical Archive (RGIA) Naberejnaya 4 (English Embankment), 1900000 St Petersburg, F: 7 (812) 311-22-52
Spain
Archivo Historico National Serrano 115, Madrid, Spain 28006
Instituucion Fernando el Catolico Plaza de Espagna 2, Zaragoza, Spain 50071 T: 09 7628 8878 F: 09 7628 8869 E: ifc@isendanet.es.mail
Sweden
City & Provincial Archives Box 22063, Stockholm, S-104 22 T: 8 508 283 00 F: 8 508 283 01
House of Emigrants Box 201, Vaxjo, S-351 04 T: 470 201 20 E: info@svenskaemigrantinstitulet.g.se
Kinship Centre Box 331, Karlstad, S-651 08 T: 54 107720
Military Archives
Banergatan 64, Stockholm, S-115 88 T: 8 782 41 00
National Archives Box 12541, Stockholm, S-102 29 T: 8 737 63 50
Orebro Stadsarkiv Box 300, Orebro, S-701 35 T: 19 21 10 75
Provincial Archive Arkivvagen 1, Ostersund, S-831 31 T: 63 10 84 85 E: landsarkivet@landsarkivet-ostersund.ra.se W: www.ra.se/ola/
Provincial Archive Visborgsgatan 1, Visby, 621 57 T: 498 2129 55
Provincial Archive Box 126, Vadstena, S-592 23 T: 143 130 30
Provincial Archive Box 135, Uppsala, SE-751 04 T: 18 65 21 00
Provincial Archive Box 2016, Lund, S-220 02 T: 046 197000 F: 046 197070 E: landsarkivet@landsarkivet-lund.ra.se
Provincial Archive Box 161, Harnosand, S-871 24 T: 611 835 00 E: landsarkivet@landsarkivet-harnosand.ra.se W: www.ra.se/hla
Provincial Archive Box 19035, Goteborg, S-400 12 T: 31 778 6800
Switzerland
Archives Canonales Vaudoises Rue de la Mouline 32, Chavannes-pres-Renens, CH 1022 T: 021 316 37 11 F: 021 316 37 55
Staatsarchiv Appenzell Ausserhoden Obstmarkt 1, Regierungsgebaede, Herisau, CH-9100 T: 071 353 6111 F: 071 352 1277 E: staatsarchiv@ar.ch W: www.ar.ch/staatsarchiv
Staatsarchiv des Kantons Basel-Landschaft Wiedenhubstrasse 35, Liestal, 4410 T: 061 921 44 40 F: 061 921 32 W: www.baselland.ch
Staatsarchiv des Kantons Solothurn Bielstrasse 41, Solothurn, CH-4509 T: 032 627 08 21 F: 032 622 34 87
Staatsarchiv Luzern Postfach 7853, Luzern, 6000 T: 41 41 2285365 F: 41 41 2286663 W: www.staluzern.ch
Geneva
Archives d'Etat 1 Rue de l'Hotel de Ville, Case Postale 164, Geneve 3, T: 41 21 319 33 95 F: 41 21 319 33 65

Lausanne
Archives De La Ville De Lausanne Rue de Maupas 47, Case Postale CH-1000, Lausanne 9, T: 41 21 624 43 55 F: 41 21 624 06 01
Ukraine
Odessa State Archive 18 Shukovskovo Street, Odessa, 27000
North America - Canada
Manitoba
Hudson's Bay Company Archives 200 Vaughan Street, Winnipeg, Manitoba R3C 1T5 T: 204-945-4949 F: 204-948-3236 W: www.gov.mb.ca/chc/archives/hbca/index.html
Manitoba Provincial Archives 200 Vaughan Street, Winnepeg, Manitoba R3C 1T5 T: 204-945-4949 F: 204-948-3236
New Brunswick
Archives & Special Collections PO Box 7500, Fredericton, New Brunswick E3B 5H5 T: 506-453-4748 F: 506-453-4595
Loyalist Collection & Reference Department PO Box 7500, Fredericton, New Brunswick E3B 5H5 T: 506-453-4749
New Brunswick Provincial Archives PO Box 6000, Fredericton, New Brunswick E3B 5H1 W: www.gov.nb.ca/supply/archives
Newfoundland
Newfoundland & Labrador Archives Colonial Building, Military Road, St Johns, Newfoundland A1C 2C9 F: 709-729-0578
Nova Scotia
Nova Scotia State Archives 6016 University Avenue, Halifax, Nova Scotia B3H 1W4 T: 902-424-6060
Yarmouth County Museums & Archives 22 Collins St, Yarmouth, Nova Scotia B5A 3C8 W: www.ycn.library.ns.ca/museum/yarcomus.htm
Ontario
Archives of Ontario Unit 300, 77 Grenville Street, Toronto, Ontario M5S 1B3 T: 416-327-1582 F: 416-327-1999 E: reference@archives.gov.on.ca W: www.gov.on.ca/MCZCR/archives
National Archives of Canada 395 Wellington Street, Ottawa, Ontario K1A 0N3 T: 613-996-7458 F: 613-995-6274 E: http://www.archives.ca
Prince Edward Island
Public Archives & Record Office PO Box 1000, Charlottetown, Prince Edward Island C1A 7M4 E: archives@gov.pe.ca W: www.gov.pe.ca/educ/
Quebec
Archives Nationales PO Box 10450, Sainte Foy, Quebec G1V 4N1 T: 418-643-8904 F: 418-646-0868
Saskatchewan
Saskatchewan Archives Board - Regina 3303 Hillsdale Street, Regina, Saskatchewan S4S 0A2 W: www.gov.sk.ca/govt/archives
Saskatchewan Archives Board - Saskatoon Room 91, Murray Building, University of Saskatchewan, 3 Campus Drive, Saskatoon, Saskatchewan S7N 5A4 W: www.gov.sk.ca/govt/archives
Specialist Subjects
Maritime History Archive Memorial University of Newfoundland, St Johns, Newfoundland A1C 5S7 W: www.mun.ca/mha/

Family History Centres ~ *The Church of Jesus Christ of The Latter Day Saints*

Church of Jesus Christ of Latter Day Saints - North America Distribution Centre 1999 West 1700 South, Salt Lake City, Utah, 84104 United States of America
Church of Jesus Christ of Latter Day Saints - UK Distribution Centre 399 Garretts Green Lane, Birmingham, West Midlands, B33 0HU Tel: 0870-010-2051
Bedfordshire - St Albans Family History Centre London Road/Cutenhoe Road, Luton LU1 3NQ Tel: 01582-482234
Berkshire -Reading Family History Centre 280 The Meadway, Tilehurst, Reading RG3 4PF Tel: 0118-941 0211
Bristol - Bristol Family History Centre 721 Wells Road, Whitchurch, Bristol BS14 9HU Tel: 01275-838326
Cambridgeshire Family History Centre 670 Cherry Hinton Road, Cambridge CB1 4DR Tel: 01223-247010
Peterborough Family History Centre Cottesmore Close off Atherstone Av, Netherton Estate Peterborough PE3 9TP Tel: 01733-263374
Cleveland - Billingham Family History Centre The Linkway, Billingham TS23 3HG T: 01642-563162
Cornwall - Helston Family History Centre Clodgey Lane, Helston T: 01326-564503
Cumbria - Carlisle Family History Centre Langrigg Road, Morton Park, Carlisle CA2 5HT T: 01228-26767
Devon - Exeter Family History Centre Wonford Road Exeter T: 01392 250723
Devon - Plymouth Family History Centre Mannamead Road Plymouth PL3 5QJ T: 01752-668666
Dorset - Chickerell Family History Centre 396 Chickerell Road Chickerell Weymouth DT4 9TP T: 01305 787240
Dorset -Poole Family History Centre 8 Mount Road Parkstone Poole BH14 0QW T: 01202-730646
Essex - Romford Family History Centre 64 Butts Green Road Hornchurch RM11 2JJ T: 01708-620727
Gloucestershire - Cheltenham Family History Centre Thirlestaine

Road Cheltenham GL53 7AS T: 01242-523433
Gloucestershire - Forest of Dean Family History Centre Wynol's Hill Queensway Coleford T: 01594-542480
Gloucestershire - Yate Family History Centre Wellington Road Yate BS37 5UY T: 01454-323004
Hampshire - Portsmouth Family History Centre 82 Kingston Crescent Portsmouth PO2 8AQ T: (023) 92696243
Isle of Wight - Newport Family History Centre Chestnut Close Shide Road Newport PO30 1YE T: 01983-529643
Kent - Maidstone Family History Centre 76b London Road Maidstone ME16 0DR T: 01622-757811
Lancashire - Ashton Family History Centre Patterdale Road Ashton-under-Lyne OL7 T: 0161-330-1270
Lancashire - Blackpool Family History Centre Warren Drive Cleveleys Blackpool FY5 3TG T: 01253-858218
Lancashire - Chorley Family History Centre Preston Temple Chorley PR6 7EQ T: 01257 226147
Lancashire - Lancaster Family History Centre Ovangle Road Lancaster LA1 5HZ T: 01254-33571
Manchester Family History Centre Altrincham Road Wythenshawe Road Manchester M22 4BJ T: 0161-902-9279
Rawtenstall Family History Centre Haslingden Rawtenstall Rossendale BB4 6PU T: 01706 213460
Leicestershire Family History Centre Wakerley Road Leicester LE5 4WD T: 0116-233-5544
Lincoln Family History Centre Skellingthorpe Road Lincoln LN6 0PB T: 01522-680117 Email: dann.family@diamond.co.uk
Lincolnshire - Grimsby Family History Centre Linwood Avenue (NO LETTER BOX) Scartho Grimsby DN33 2NL T: 01472-828876
London - Hyde Park Family History Centre 64 - 68 Exhibition Road South Kensington London SW7 2PA T: (020) 789-8561
London - Wandsworth Family History Centre 149 Nightingale Lane Balham London SW12 T: (020) 8673-6741
Merseyside - Liverpool Family History Centre 4 Mill Bank

Liverpool L13 0BW T: 0151-228-0433
Middlesex - Staines Family History Centre 41 Kingston Road Staines TW14 0ND T: 01784-462627
Norfolk - Kings Lynn Family History Centre Reffley Lane Kings Lynn PE30 3EQ T: 01553-67000
Norfolk - Norwich Family History Centre 19 Greenways Eaton Norwich NR4 6PA T: 01603-452440
Northampton Family History Centre 137 Harlestone Road Duston Northampton NN5 6AA T: 01604-587630
Nottinghamshire - Mansfield Family History Centre Southridge Drive Mansfield NG18 4RJ T: 01623-26729
Nottingham Family History Centre Stanhome Square, West Bridgford, Nottingham NG2 7GF T: 0115 914 4255
Shropshire - Telford Family History Centre 72 Glebe Street Wellington
Somerset - Yeovil Family History Centre Forest Hill Yeovil BA20 2PH T: 01935 426817
South Yorkshire - Sheffield Family History Centre Wheel Lane Grenoside Sheffield S30 3RL T: 0114-245-3124
Staffordshire - Lichfield Family History Centre Purcell Avenue Lichfield WS14 9XA T: 01543-414843
Staffordshire - Newcastle under Lyme Family History Centre PO Box 457 Newcastle under Lyme ST5 0TD T: 01782-620653
Suffolk - Ipswich Family History Centre 42 Sidegate Lane West Ipswich IP4 3DB T: 01473-723182
Suffolk - Lowestoft Family History Centre 165 Yarmouth Road Lowestoft T: 01502-573851
Tyne and Wear - Sunderland Family History Centre Linden Road off Queen Alexandra Road Sunderland SR2 9BT T: 0191-528-5787
West Midlands - Coventry Family History Centre Riverside Close Whitley Coventry T: (024) 76301420
West Midlands - Harborne Family History Centre 38 Lordswood Road Harborne Birmingham B17 9QS T: 0121-427-9291
West Midlands - Sutton Coldfield Family History Centre 185 Penns Lane Sutton Coldfield Birmingham B76 1JU T: 0121-386-1690
West Midlands - Wednesfield Family History Centre Linthouse Lane Wednesfield Wolverhampton T: 01902-724097
Sussex - Crawley Family History Centre Old Horsham Road Crawley RH11 8PD T: 01293-516151
Sussex – Worthing Family History Centre Goring Street Worthing BN12 5AR
Wirral - Birkenhead Family History Centre Reservoir Road off Prenton Lane Prenton Birkenhead CH42 8LJ T: 0151 608 0157
Worcestershire - Redditch Family History Centre 321 Evesham Road Crabbs Cross Redditch B97 5JA T: 01527-550657
Yorkshire - East - -Hull Family History Centre 725 Holderness Road Kingston upon Hull HU4 7RT T: 01482-701439
Yorkshire – North - -Scarborough Family History Centre Stepney Drive/Whitby Road Scarborough
Yorkshire – West - Huddersfield Family History Centre 12 Halifax Road Birchencliffe Huddersfield HD3 3BS T: 01484-454573
Yorkshire – West - Leeds Family History Centre Vesper Road Leeds LS5 3QT T: 0113-258-5297
York Family History Centre West Bank Acomb York T: 01904-785128

Wales
Denbighshire - Rhyl Family History Centre Rhuddlan Road Rhyl
Glamorgan - Cardiff Family History Centre Heol y Deri Rhiwbina Cardiff CF4 6UH T: (029) 20620205
Glamorgan - Merthyr Tydfil Family History Centre Swansea Road Merthyr Tydfil CF 48 1NR T: 01685-722455
Glamorgan - Swansea Family History Centre Cockett Road Swansea SA2 0FH T: 01792-419520
Isle of Man - Douglas Family History Centre Woodbourne Road Douglas IM2 3AP T: 01624-675834
Jersey - St Helier Family History Centre La Rue de la Vallee St Mary JE3 3DL T: 01534-82171
Scotland
Aberdeen Family History Centre North Anderson Drive Aberdeen AB2 6DD T: 01224-692206
Ayrshire - Kilmarnock Family History Centre Wahtriggs Road Kilmarnock KA1 3QY T: 01563-26560
Dumfries Family History Centre 36 Edinburgh Road Albanybank Dumfries DG1 1JQ T: 01387-254865
Edinburgh Family History Centre 30a Colinton Road Edinburgh EH4 3SN T: 0130-337-3049
Fife - Kirkcaldy Family History Centre Winifred Crescent Forth Park Kirkcaldy KY2 5SX T: 01592-640041
Glasgow Family History Centre 35 Julian Avenue Glasgow G12 0RB T: 0141-357-1024
Highlands - Inverness Family History Centre 13 Ness Walk Inverness IV3 5SQ T: 01463-231220
Paisley Family History Centre Campbell Street Paisley PA5 8LD T: 01505-20886
Shetland - Lerwick Family History Centre Baila Croft Lerwick ZE1 0EY T: 01595-695732 Fax: 01950-431469
Tayside - Dundee Family History Centre 22 - 26 Bingham Terrace Dundee DD4 7HH T: 01382-451247
Northern Ireland
Belfast Family History Centre 401 Holywood Road Belfast BT4 2GU T: (028) 90768250
Londonderry Family History Centre Racecourse Road Belmont Estate Londonderry T: Sun-only-(028) 71350179
Ireland - Dublin Family History Centre The Willows Finglas Dublin 11 T: -4625962

Registrars of Births Marriages and Deaths

England
The General Register Office Room E201, Trafalgar Road, Birkdale, Southport, PR8 2HH T: 0870 243 7788 F: 01704 550013 E.
W: www.gro.gov.uk

Bath & North East Somerset - The Register Office, The Guildhall, High Street, Bath, BA1 5AW T: 01225 477234
Bedfordshire
Ampthill Court House, Woburn Street, Ampthill, Bedfordshire MK45 2HX T: 01525-403430 F: 01525-841984 E: denmanm@csd.bedfordshire.gov.uk
Bedfordshire The Register Office, Pilgrim House, 20 Brickhill Drive, Bedford, Bedfordshire MK41 7PZ T: 01234 290450 F: 01234 290454
Biggleswade The Register Office, 142 London Road, Biggleswade, Bedfordshire SG18 8EL T: 01767-312511 F: 01767-315033
Dunstable Grove House, 76 High Street North, Dunstable, Bedfordshire LU6 1NF T: 01582-660191 F: 01582-471004 E:
Leighton Buzzard Bossard House, West Street, Leighton Buzzard, Bedfordshire LU7 7DA T: 01525-851486 F: 01525-381483
Berkshire
Wokingham The Old School, Reading Road, Wokingham, Berkshire RG41 1RJ T: 0118 978 2514 F: 0118 978 2813
Bracknell Forest Easthampstead House, Town Square, Bracknell, Berkshire RG12 1AQ T: 01344 352027 F: 01344 352010
Reading The Register Office, Yeomanry House, 131 Castle Hill, Reading, Berkshire RG1 7TA T: 0118 901 5120 F: 0118 951 0212
Slough Slough Register Office, The Centre, Farnham Road, Slough, Berkshire SL1 4UT T: 01753 787600 F: 01753 787605
West Berkshire Peake House, 112 Newtown Road, Newbury, Berkshire RG14 7EB T: 01635 48133 F: 01635 524694
Windsor & Maidenhead Town Hall, St Ives Road, Maidenhead, Berkshire SL6 1RF T: 01628 796422 F: 01628 796625
Bexley London Borough
Bexley Manor House, The Green, Sidcup, Kent DA14 6BW T: (020) 8300 4537 F: (020) 8308 4967
Birmingham MD The Register Office, 300 Broad Street, Birmingham, B1 2DE T: 0121 212 3421 F: 0121 303 1396
Bolton MD The Register Office, Mere Hall, Merehall Street, Bolton, Lancashire BL1 2QT T: 01204 331185
Bournemouth The Register Office, The Town Hall, Bourne Avenue, Bournemouth, BH2 6DY T: 01202 454945
Bradford MD
Bradford The Register Office, 22 Manor Row, Bradford, West Yorkshire BD1 4QR T: 01274 432151
Keighley Town Hall, Bow Street, Keighley, West Yorkshire BD21 3PA T: 01535 618060 F: 01535 618208
Brent London Borough
Brent Brent Town Hall, Forty Lane, Wembley, Middlesex HA9 9EZ T: (020) 8937 1010 F: (020) 8937 1021
Brighton & Hove
Brighton & Hove Brighton Town Hall, Bartholomews, Brighton, BN1 1JA T: 01273 292016 F: 01273 292019
Bromley LB
Bromley Room S101, Bromley Civic Centre, Stockwell Close, Bromley, BR1 3UH T: (020) 8313 4666 F: (020) 8313 4699
Buckinghamshire
Aylesbury Vale County Offices, Walton Street, Aylesbury, Buckinghamshire HP20 1XF T: 01296 382581 F: 01296 382675
Chiltern and South Bucks
Chiltern Hills Wycombe Area Offices, Easton Street, High Wycombe, Buckinghamshire HP11 1NH T: 01494 475200 F: 01494 475040
Bury MD
Bury Town Hall, Manchester Road, Bury, Lancashire BL9 0SW T: 0161 253 6026 F: 0161 253 6028
Calderdale MD
Calderdale The Register Office, 4 Carlton Street, Halifax, West Yorkshire HX1 2AH T: 01422 353993 F: 01422 253370
Todmorden Municipal Offices, Rise Lane, Todmorden, Lancashire OL14 7AB T: 01706 814811 Ext 208 F: 01706 814811 Ext 208
Cambridgeshire
Cambridge Castle Lodge, Shire Hall, Castle Hill, Cambridge, Cambridgeshire CB3 0AP T: 01223 717401 F: 01223 717888

Ely Old School House, 74 Market Street, Ely, Cambridgeshire CB7 4LS T: 01353 663824

Fenland Audmoor House, High Street, March, Cambridgeshire PE15 9LH T: 01354 653053

Huntingdon Register Office, Ferrars Road, Huntingdon, Cambridgeshire PE29 3DH T: 01480 375821 F: 01480 375725

Peterborough The Lawns, 33 Thorpe Road, Peterborough, Cambridgeshire PE3 6AB T: 01733 566323 F: 01733 566049

Camden LB

Camden Camden Register Office, Camden Town Hall, Judd Street, London, WC1H 9JE T: (020) 7974 1900 F: (020) 7974 5792

Cheshire

Cheshire Central The Register Office, Delamere House, Chester Street, Crewe CW1 2LL T: 01270 505106 F: 01270 505107

Cheshire East The Register Office, Park Green, Macclesfield, Cheshire SK11 6TW T: 01625 423463 F: 01625 619225

Chester West Goldsmith House, Goss Street, Chester, Cheshire CH1 2BG T: 01244 602668 F: 01244 602934

Halton The Register Office, Heath Road, Runcorn, Cheshire WA7 5TN T: 0151 471 7636

Vale Royal

Warrington The Register Office, Museum Street, Warrington, Cheshire WA1 1JX T: 01925 442762 F: 01925 442739

City of Bristol
The Register Office, Quakers Friars, Bristol, BS1 3AR T: 0117 903 8888 F: 0117 903 8877

City of London
The Register Office, Islington Town Hall, Upper Street, Islington, London, N1 2UD T: (020) 7527 6347 F: (020) 7527 6308

Cornwall

Bodmin Lyndhurst, 66 St Nicholas Street, Bodmin, Cornwall PL31 1AG T: 01208 73677 F: 01208 73677

Camborne-Redruth The Register Office, Roskear, Camborne, Cornwall TR14 8DN T: 01209 612924 F: 01209 719956

Falmouth Berkeley House, 12-14 Berkeley Vale, Falmouth, Cornwall TR11 3PH T: 01326 312606 F: 01326 312606

Kerrier The Willows, Church Street, Helston, Cornwall TR13 8NU T: 01326 562848 F: 01326 562848

Launceston Hendra, Dunheved Road, Launceston, Cornwall PL15 9JG T: 01566 772464 F: 01566 775980

Liskeard Graylands, Dean Street, Liskeard, Cornwall PL14 4AH T: 01579 343442 F: 01872 327554

Penzance The Register Office, Alphington House, Alverton Place, Penzance, Cornwall TR18 4JJ T: 01736 330093 F: 01736 369666

St. Austell The Register Office, 12 Carlyon Road, St Austell, Cornwall PL25 4LD T: 01726 68974 F: 01726 67048 E:

St. Germans The Register Office, Plougastel Drive, St Germans, Saltash, Cornwall PL12 6DL T: 01752 842624 F: 01752 848556 W:

Stratton The Parkhouse Centre, Ergue Gaberic Way, Bude, Cornwall EX23 8LF T: 01288 353209 F: 01288 359968

Truro Dalvenie House, New County Hall, Truro, Cornwall TR1 3AY T: 01872 322241 F: 01872 323891

Coventry MD

Coventry The Register Office, Cheylesmore Manor House, Manor House Drive, Coventry CV1 2ND T: (024) 7683 3141 F: (024) 7683 3110

Croydon London Borough

Croydon The Register Office, Mint Walk, Croydon, CR10 1EA T: (020) 8760 5617 F: (020) 8760 5633

Cumbria

Barrow-in-Furness Nan Tait Centre, Abbey Road, Barrow-in-Furness, Cumbria LA14 1LG T: 01229 894510 F: 01229 894513

Carlisle The Register Office, 23 Portland Square, Carlisle, Cumbria CA1 1PE T: 01228 607432 F: 01228 607434

Cockermouth The Register Office, Fairfield, Station Road, Cockermouth, Cumbria CA13 9PT T: 01900 325960 F: 01900 325962

Kendal The Register Office, County Offices, Kendal, Cumbria LA9 4RQ T: 01539 773567 F: 01539 773565

Millom The Millom Council Centre, St Georges Road, Millom, Cumbria LA18 4DD T: 01229 772357 F: 01229 773412

Penrith The Register Office, Friargate, Penrith, Cumbria CA11 7XR T: 01768 242120 F: 01768 242122

Ulverston Town Hall, Queen Street, Ulverston, Cumbria LA12 7AR T: 01229 894170 F: 01229 894172

Whitehaven College House, Flatt Walks, Whitehaven, Cumbria CA28 7RW T: 01946 852690 F: 01946 852673

Wigton Wigton Registry Office, Station Road, Wigton, Cumbria CA7 9AH T: 016973 66117 F: 016973 66118

Darlington

Darlington The Register Office, Central House, Gladstone Street, Darlington, County Durham DL3 6JX T: 01325 346600

Derby

Derby The Register Office, Royal Oak House, Market Place, Derby, Derbyshire DE1 3AR T: 01332 256526

Derbyshire

South Derbyshire The Register Office, Royal Oak House, Market Place, Derby, DE1 3AR T: 01332 256526

Amber Valley The Register Office, Market Place, Ripley, Derbyshire DE5 3BT T: 01773 841380 F: 01773 841382

Ashbourne Town Hall, Market Place, Ashbourne, Derbyshire DE6 1ES T: 01335 300575 F: 01335 345252

Bakewell The Register Office, Town Hall, Bakewell, Derbyshire DE45 1BW T: 01629 812261

Chesterfield The Register Office, New Beetwell Street, Chesterfield, Derbyshire S40 1QJ T: 01246 234754 F: 01246 274493

Erewash The Register Office, 87 Lord Haddon Road, Ilkeston, Derbyshire DE7 8AX T: 0115 932 1014 F: 0115 932 6450

High Peak Council Offices, Hayfield Road, Chapel-en-le-Frith, Cheshire SK23 0QJ T: 01663 750473

Devon

East Devon The Register Office, Dowell Street, Honiton, Devon EX14 1LX T: 01404 42531 F: 01404 41475 E:

Exeter 1 Lower Summerlands, Heavitree Road, Exeter, Devon EX1 2LL T: 01392 686260 F: 01392 686262

Holsworthy The Register Office, 8 Fore Street, Holsworthy, Devon EX22 6ED T: 01409-253262

Mid Devon The Great House, 1 St Peter Street, Tiverton, Devon EX16 6NE T: 01884 255255 F: 01884 258852

North Devon The Register Office, Civic Centre, Barnstaple, Devon EX31 1ED T: 01271 388456

Okehampton

Plymouth The Register Office, Lockyer Street, Plymouth, Devon PL1 2QD T: 01752 268331 F: 01752 256046

South Hams Follaton House, Plymouth Road, Totnes, Devon TQ9 5NE T: 01803 861234 F: 01803 868965

Teignbridge The Register Office, 15 Devon Square, Newton Abbot, Devon TQ12 2HN T: 01626 206340 F: 01626 206346 E:

Torbay The Register Office, Oldway Mansion, Paignton, Devon TQ3 2TU T: 01803 207130 F: 01803 525388

Torridge Council Offices, Windmill Lane, Northam, Bideford, Devon EX39 1BY T: 01237 474977 F: 01237 473385

West Devon Town Council Offices, Drake Road, Tavistock, Devon PL19 0AU T: 01822 612137 F: 01822 618935

Doncaster MD

Doncaster The Register Office, Elmfield Park, Doncaster, South Yorkshire DN1 2EB T: 01302 364922

Dorset

East Dorset King George V Pavilion, Peter Grant Way, Ferndown, Dorset BH22 9EN T: 01202 892325

North Dorset The Register Office, Salisbury Road, Blandford Forum, Dorset DT11 7LN T: 01258 484096 F: 01258 484090

South and West Dorset The Guildhall, St Edmund Street, Weymouth, Dorset DT4 8AS T: 01305 760899 F: 01305 771269

West Dorset The Register Office, Mountfield Offices, Rax Lane, Bridport, Dorset DT6 3JL T: 01308 456047

Dudley MD

Dudley Priory Hall, Priory Park, Dudley DY1 4EU T: 01384 815373

Stourbridge Crown Centre, Crown Lane, Stourbridge, West Midlands DY8 1YA T: 01384 815384 F: 01384 815397

Durham

Durham Central The Register Office, 7 Thorneyholme Terrace, Stanley, Durham DH9 0BJ T: 01207 235849

Durham Eastern Register Office, York Road, Acre Rigg, Peterlee, Durham SR8 2DP T: 0191 586 6147 F: 0191 518 4607

Durham Northern The Register Office, 7 Thorneyholme Terrace, Stanley DH9 0BJ T: 01207 235849 F: 01207 235334

Durham Western Cockton House, 35 Cockton Hill Road, Bishop Auckland, Durham DL14 6HS T: 01388 607277 F: 01388 664388

Ealing LB

Ealing Ealing Town Hall, New Broadway, Ealing, London W5 2BY T: (020) 8825 7272

East Riding of Yorkshire
The Register Office, Walkergate House, Walkergate, Beverley, East Yorkshire HU17 9EJ T: 01482 393600 F: 01482 873414

East Sussex

Hastings & Rother The Register Office, Summerfields, Bohemia Road, Hastings TN34 1EX T: 01424 721722 F: 01424 465296

Lewes Southover Grange, Southover Road, Lewes, East Sussex BN7 1TP T: 01273 475589 F: 01273 488073

Enfield LB

Enfield Public Offices, Gentlemen's Row, Enfield, Middlesex EN2 6PS T: (020) 8367 5757 F: (020) 8379 8562

Essex

Castle Point and Rochford Civic Centre, Victoria Avenue, Southend-on-Sea, Essex SS2 6ER T: 01702 534351

Braintree John Ray House, Bocking End, Braintree, Essex CM7 9RW T: 01376 320762

Brentwood The Register Office, 1 Seven Arches Road, Brentwood, Essex CM14 4JG T: 01277 233565 F: 01277 262712

Chelmsford The Register Office, 17 Market Road, Chelmsford, Essex CM1 1GF T: 01245 430700 F: 01245 430707

Colchester Stanwell House, Stanwell Street, Colchester, Essex CO2 7DL T: 01206 572926 F: 01206 540626

Epping Forest The Register Office, St Johns Road, Epping, Essex CM16 5DN T: 01992 572788 F: 01992 571236

Harlow Watergarden Offices, College Square, The High, Harlow, Essex CM20 1AG T: 01279 421295

Southend-on-Sea Civic Centre, Victoria Avenue, Southend-on-Sea, Essex SS2 6ER T: 01702 534351 F: 01702 612610

Thurrock The Register Office, 2 Quarry Hill, Grays, Essex RM17 5BT T: 01375 375245 F: 01375 392649

Uttlesford Council Offices, London Road, Saffron Walden, Essex CB11 4ER T: 01799 510319 F: 01799 510332

Gateshead MD

Gateshead Civic Centre, Regent Street, Gateshead, Tyne and Wear NE8 1HH T: 0191 433 3000 F: 0191 477 9978

Gloucestershire

Cheltenham The Register Office, St Georges Road, Cheltenham, Gloucestershire GL50 3EW T: 01242 532455 F: 01242 254600

Cirencester Old Memorial Hospital, Sheep Street, Cirencester, Gloucestershire GL7 1QW T: 01285 650455 F: 01285 640253

Gloucester Maitland House, Spa Road, Gloucester, Gloucestershire GL1 1UY T: 01452 425275 F: 01452 385385

North Cotswold North Cotswold Register Office, High Street, Moreton-in-Marsh, Gloucestershire GL56 0AZ T: 01608 651199

Stroud The Register Office, Parliament Street, Stroud, Gloucestershire GL5 1DY T: 01453 766049 F: 01453 752961

Gloucestshire

Forest of Dean Belle Vue Centre, 6 Belle Vue Road, Cinderford, Gloucestershire GL14 2AB T: 01594 822113 F: 01594 826352

Greenwich LB

Greenwich The Register Office, Town Hall, Wellington Street, Greenwich, London, SE18 6PW T: (020) 8854 8888 F: (020) 8317 5754

Hackney LB

Hackney The Register Office, Town Hall, Mare Street, London, E8 1EA T: (020) 8356 3365 F: (020) 8356 3552

Hammersmith & Fulham LB

Hammersmith The Register Office, Nigel Playfair Avenue, London, W6 9JY T: (020) 8748-3020 F: (020) 8748-6619

Hammersmith and Fulham Hammersmith & Fulham Register Office, Fulham Town Hall, Harwood Road, Fulham, London, SW6 1ET T: (020) 8753 2140 F: (020) 8753 2146

Hampshire

Alton The Register Office, 4 Queens Road, Alton, Hampshire GU34 1HU T: 01420 85410

Andover Wessex Chambers, South Street, Andover, Hampshire SP10 2BN T: 01264 352943 F: 01264 366849

Droxford Bank House, Bank Street, Bishop's Waltham, Southampton SO32 1GP T: 01489 894044

Hampshire North Hampshire North Register Office, Goldings, London Road, Basingstoke, Hampshire RG21 4AN T: 01256 322188 F: 01256 350745

Kingsclere & Whitchurch Council Offices, Swan Street, Kingsclere,, Nr Newbury, Berkshire RG15 8PM T: 01635-298714

New Forest Public Offices, 65 Christchurch Road, Ringwood, Hampshire BH24 1DH T: 01425 470150 F: 01425 471732

North-East Hampshire The Register Office, 30 Grosvenor Road, Aldershot, Hampshire GU11 3EB T: 01252 322066 F: 01252 338004

Petersfield The Old College, College Street, Petersfield, Hampshire GU31 4AG T: 01730 265372 F: 01730 261050

Romsey Hayter House, Hayter Gardens, Romsey, Hampshire SO51 7QU T: 01794 513846 F: 01794 830491

South-East Hampshire The Register Office, 4-8 Osborn Road South, Fareham, Hampshire PO16 7DG T: 01329 280493 F: 01329 823184

Winchester The Register Office, Station Hill, Winchester, Hampshire SO23 8TJ T: 01962 869608 F: 01962 851912

Haringey London Borough The Register Office, Civic Centre, High Road, Wood Green, London, N22 4LE T: (020) 8489 2605

Harrow London Borough The Civic Centre, Station Road, Harrow, Middlesex HA1 2UX T: (020) 8424 1618 F: (020) 8424 1414

Hartlepool - The Register Office, Raby Road, Hartlepool, TS24 8AF T: 01429 236369 F: 01429 236373 E: registrar@hartlepool.gov.uk

Havering LB

Havering Langtons, Billet Lane, Hornchurch, Essex RM11 1XL T: 01708 433481 F: 01708 433413

Hendon see Barnet

Hereford & Worcester

Droitwich Council Offices, Ombersley Street East, Droitwich, Worcestershire WR9 8QX T: 01905 772280

Kidderminster Council Offices, Bewdley Road, Kidderminster, Worcestershire DY11 6RL T: 01562 820840

Ledbury Town Council Offices, Church Street, Ledbury, Herefordshire HR8 1DH T: 01531 632306

Hereford and Worcester

Bromsgrove The Register Office, School Drive, Bromsgrove, Worcestershire B60 1AY T: 01527 578759 F: 01527 578750

Bromyard Council Offices, 1 Rowberry Street, Bromyard, Hereford, Herefordshire HR7 4DU T: 01432 260258 F: 01432 260259

Redditch The Register Office, 29 Easmore Road, Redditch, Worcestershire B98 8ER T: 01527 60647 F: 01527 584561

Worcester The Register Office, 29-30 Foregate Street, Worcester, Worcestershire WR1 1DS T: 01905 765350 F: 01905 765355

Herefordshire

Hereford County Offices, Bath Street, Hereford, Herefordshire HR1 2HQ T: 01432 260565 F: 01432 261720 E:

Kington The Register Office, Old Court House, Market Hall Street,

Kington, Herefordshire HR5 3DP T: 01544 230156 F: 01544 231385

Leominster The Register Office, The Old Priory, Church Street, Leominster, Herefordshire HR6 8EQ T: 01568 610131 F: 01568 614954

Ross The Old Chapel, Cantilupe Road, Ross on Wye, Herefordshire HR9 7AN T: 01989 562795 F: 01989 564869

Hertfordshire

Bishops Stortford The Register Office, 2 Hockerill Street, Bishops Stortford, Hertfordshire CM23 2DL T: 01279 651318 F: 01279 461492

Broxbourne Borough Offices, Churchgate, Cheshunt, Hertfordshire EN8 9XH T: 01992 623107 F: 01992 627605

Dacorum The Bury, Queensway, Hemel Hemstead, Hertfordshire HP1 1HR T: 01442 228600 F: 01442 243974

Hatfield The Register Office, 19b St Albans Road East, Hatfield, Hertfordshire AL10 0NG T: 01707 283920 F: 01707 283924

Hertford & Ware County Hall, Pegs Lane, Hertford, Hertfordshire SG13 8DE T: 01992 555590 F: 01992 555493

Hitchen & Stevenage The Register Office, Danesgate, Stevenage, Hertfordshire SG1 1WW T: 01438 316579 F: 01438 357197

St Albans The Gatehouse, 1 Victoria Square, Victoria Street, St Albans, Hertfordshire AL1 3TF T: 01727 774030 F: 01727 774032

Watford The Register Office, 36 Clarendon Road, Watford, Hertfordshire WD17 1JQ T: 01923 231302 F: 01923 246852

Hillingdon London Borough The Register Office, Hillingdon Civic Centre, Uxbridge, Middlesex UB8 1UW T: 01895 250418 F: 01895 250678

Hounslow London Borough The Register Office, 88 Lampton Road, Hounslow, Middlesex TW3 4DW T: (020) 8583 2090 F: (020) 8577 8798

Isle of Wight The Register Office, County Hall, High Street, Newport, Isle of Wight PO30 1UD T: 01983 823233 F: 01983 823227

Isles of Scilly The Register Office, Porthcressa Bank, St Marys, Isles of Scilly TR21 0JL T: 01720 423751

Islington London Borough The Register Office, Islington Town Hall, Upper Street, London, N1 2UD T: (020) 7527 6347 F: (020) 7527 6308 E:

Kensington & Chelsea London Borough The Register Office, Chelsea Old Town Hall, Kings Road, London, SW3 5EE T: (020) 7361 4100 F: (020) 7361 4054

Kent

Kent The Archbishop's Palace, Palace Gardens, Mill Street, Maidstone, Kent ME15 6YE T: 0845 678 5000 F: 01622 663690

Kent - Medway

Medway Medway Register Office, Ingleside, 114 Maidstone Road, Chatham, Medway ME4 6DJ T: 01634 338899

Kingston-upon-Hull

Hull Municipal Offices, 181-191 George Street, Kingston Upon Hull, HU1 3BY T: 01482 615401 F: 01482 615411

Kingston-upon-Thames RB

Kingston upon Thames The Register Office, 35 Coombe Road, Kingston upon Thames, Surrey KT2 7BA T: (020) 8547 4600 F: (020) 8547 6188

Kirklees MD

Dewsbury The Register Office, Wellington Street, Dewsbury, West Yorkshire WF13 1LY T: 01924 324880

Huddersfield Civic Centre, 11 High Street, Huddersfield, West Yorkshire HD1 2PL T: 01484 221030 F: 01484 221315

Knowsley MD

Knowsley District Council Offices, High Street, Prescot, Merseyside L34 3LH T: 0151 443 5210 F: 0151 443 5216 E:

Lambeth MB

Lambeth The Register Office, Lambeth Town Hall, Brixton Hill, Lambeth, London, SW2 1RW T: (020) 7926 9859

Lancashire

Fleetwood and Fylde The Register Office, South King Street, Blackpool, Lancashire FY1 4AX T: 01253 477177 F: 01253 477176

Blackburn with Darwen The Register Office, Jubilee Street, Blackburn, Lancashire BB1 1EP T: 01254 587524 F: 01254 587538

Blackpool The Register Office, South King Street, Blackpool, Lancashire FY1 4AX T: 01253 477177 F: 01253 477176

Burnley and Pendle The Register Office, 12 Nicholas Street, Burnley, Lancashire BB11 2AQ T: 01282 436116 F: 01282 412221

Chorley The Register Office, 16 St George's Street, Chorley, Lancashire PR7 2AA T: 01257 263143 F: 01257 263808

Garstang Hyndburn & Rossendale The Mechanics Institute, Willow Street, Accrington, Lancashire BB5 1LP T: 01254 871360

Lancaster The Register Office, 4 Queen Street, Lancaster, Lancashire LA1 1RS T: 01524 65673 F: 01524 842285

Preston and South Ribble The Register Office, PO Box 24, Bow Lane, Preston, Lancashire PR1 8SE T: 01772 533800 F: 01772 531012

Ribble Valley The Register Office, Off Pimlico Road, Clitheroe, Lancashire BB7 2BW T: 01200 420492 F: 01200 420491

West Lancashire Greetby Buildings, Derby Street, Ormskirk, Lancashire L39 2BS T: 01695 585779 F: 01695 585819

Barking & Dagenham London Borough Arden House, 198 Longbridge Road, Barking, Essex IG11 8SY T: (020) 8270 4743

Barnet London Borough The Register Office, 182 Burnt Oak, Broadway, Edgware, Middlesex HA8 0AU T: (020) 8731 1100 F: (020) 8731 1111

Leeds MD - Belgrave House, Belgrave Street, Leeds, LS2 8DQ T: 0113

224 3604 F: 0113 247 6708
Leicester - The Register Office, 5 Pocklington's Walk, Leicester, Leicestershire LE1 6BQ T: 0116 253 6326 F: 0116 253 3008
Leicestershire - Register Office, County Hall, Glenfield, Leicester, Leicestershire LE3 8RN T: 0116 265 6565
Lewisham London Borough The Register Office, 368 Lewisham High Street, London, SE13 6LQ T: (020) 8690 2128
Lincolnshire The Register Office, 4 Lindum Road, Lincoln, Lincolnshire LN2 1NN T: 0845 330 1400 F: 01522 589524
Liverpool MD - Liverpool Register Office, The Cotton Exchange, Old Hall Street, Liverpool, L3 9UF T: 0151 233 3004
Luton The Register Office, 6 George Street West, Luton, LU1 2BJ T: 01582 722603 F: 01582 429522
Manchester MD - Heron House, 47 Lloyd Street, Manchester, M2 5LE T: 0161 234 5502 F: 0161 234 7888 E: register-office@manchester.gov.uk
Medway - Medway Register Office, Ingleside, 114 Maidstone Road, Chatham, Medway ME4 6DJ T: 01634 338899
Merton London Borough Morden Park House, Morden Hall, London Road, Morden, Surrey SM4 5QU T: (020) 8648 0414
Middlesbrough The Register Office, Corporation Road, Middlesbrough, TS1 2DA T: 01642 262078 F: 01642 262091
Milton Keynes - Bracknell House, Aylesbury Street, Bletchley, Milton Keynes MK2 2BE T: 01908 372101 F: 01908 645103
Newcastle-upon-Tyne MD - Civic Centre, Barras Bridge, Newcastle-upon-Tyne, Tyne and Wear NE1 8PS T: 0191 232 8520
Newham London Borough The Register Office, Passmore Edwards Building, 207 Plashet Grove, East Ham, London, E6 1BT T: (020) 8430 2000 F: (020) 8430 3127
Norfolk
Depwade Council Offices, 11-12 Market Hill, Diss, Norfolk IP22 3JX T: 01379 643915
Downham The Register Office, 15 Paradise Road, Downham Market, Norfolk PE38 9HS T: 01366 387104
East Dereham The Breckland Business Centre, St Withburga Lane, Dereham, Norfolk NR19 1FD T: 01362 698021
Fakenham The Register Office, Fakenham Connect, Oak Street, Fakenham, Norfolk NR21 9SR T: 01328 850111 F: 01328 850150
Great Yarmouth Ferryside, High Road, Southtown, Great Yarmouth, Norfolk NR31 0PH T: 01493 662313 F: 01493 602107
King's Lynn St Margaret's House, St Margaret's Place, King's Lynn, Norfolk PE30 5DW T: 01553 669251 F: 01553 769942
North Walsham The Register Office, 18 Kings Arms Street, North Walsham, Norfolk NR28 9JX T: 01692 406220 F: 01692 406220
Norwich Churchman House, 71 Bethel Street, Norwich, NR2 1NR T: 01603 767600 F: 01603 632677
Wayland Kings House, Kings Street, Thetford, Norfolk IP24 2AP T: 01842 766848 F: 01842 765996
North East Lincolnshire - The Register Office, Town Hall Square, Grimsby, North East Lincolnshire DN31 1HX T: 01472 324860
North Lincolnshire - Register Office, 92 Oswald Road, Scunthorpe, North Lincolnshire DN15 7PA T: 01724 843915 F: 01724 872668
North Somerset - The Register Office, 41 The Boulevard, Weston-super-Mare, North Somerset BS23 1PG T: 01934 627552 F: 01934 412014
North Tyneside MD - Maritime Chambers, 1 Howard Street, North Shields, Tyne and Wear NE30 1LZ T: 0191 200 6164
North Yorkshire
North Yorkshire Registration Service (Headquarters) Bilton House, 31 Park Parade, Harrogate HG1 5AG T: 01423 506949
Northamptonshire
Brackley Brackley Lodge, High Street, Brackley, Northamptonshire NN13 5BD T: 01280-702949
Corby The Old Stables, Cottingham Road, Corby, Nothamptonshire NN17 1TD T: 01536 203141
Daventry Council Offices, Lodge Road, Daventry, Northamptonshire NN11 5AF T: 01327 302209 F: 01327 300011 E:
Kettering The Register Office, 10 London Road, Kettering, Northamptonshire NN15 7QU T: 01536 514792 F: 01536 526948
Northampton The Guildhall, St Giles Square, Northampton, Northamptonshire NN1 1DE T: 01604 745390 F: 01604 745399 E:
Oundle and Thrapston The Old Courthouse, 17 Mill Road, Oundle, Peterborough, Cambridgeshire PE8 4BW T: 01832 273413
Towcester & Brackley Sunnybanks, 55 Brackley Road, Towcester, Northamptonshire NN12 6DH T: 01327 350774
Wellingborough Council Offices, Swanspool House, Wellingborough, Northamptonshire NN8 1BP T: 01933 231549
Northumberland
Northumberland Central The Register Office, 94 Newgate Street, Morpeth, Northumberland NE61 1BU T: 01670 513232 F: 01670 519260

Northumberland North First The Register Office, 5 Palace Street East, Berwick upon Tweed, Northumberland TD15 1HT T: 01289 307373
Northumberland North Second The Register Office, 6 Market Place, Alnwick, Northumberland NE66 1HP T: 01665 602363 F: 01665 510079
Northumberland West Abbey Gate House, Market Street, Hexham,

Northumberland NE46 3LX T: 01434 602355 F: 01434 604957
Nottinghamshire
Basford The Register Office, Highbury Road, Bulwell, Nottinghamshire NG6 9DA T: 0115 927 1294 F: 0115 977 1845
East Retford Notts County Council Offices, Chancery Lane, Retford, Nottinghamshire DN22 6DG T: 01777 708631 F: 01777 860667
Mansfield Registry Office, Dale Close, 100 Chesterfield Road South, Mansfield, Nottinghamshire NG19 7DN T: 01623 476564 F: 01623 636284
Newark County Offices, Balderton Gate, Newark, Nottinghamshire NG24 1UW T: 01636 705455 F: 01636 679259
Nottingham The Register Office, 50 Shakespeare Street, Nottingham, Nottinghamshire NG1 4FP T: 0115 947 5665 F: 0115 941 5773
Rushcliffe The Hall, Bridgford Road, West Bridgford, Nottinghamshire NG2 6AQ T: 0115 981 5307 F: 0115 969 6189
Worksop Queens Buildings, Potter Street, Worksop, Nottinghamshire S80 2AH T: 01909 535534 F: 01909 501067
Oldham MD - Metropolitan House, Hobson Street, Oldham, Lancashire OL1 1PY T: 0161 678 0137 F: 0161 911 3729
Oxfordshire
Oxford The Register Office, Tidmarsh Lane, Oxford, Oxfordshire OX1 1NS T: 01865 816246 F: 01865 815632
Poole - The Register Office, Civic Centre Annexe, Park Road, Poole, Dorset BH15 2RN T: 01202 633744 F: 01202 633725
Portsmouth - The Register Office, Milldam House, Burnaby Road, Portsmouth, Hampshire PO1 3AF T: (023) 9282 9041 F: (023) 9283 1996
Redbridge London Borough - Queen Victoria House, 794 Cranbrook Road, Barkingside, Ilford, Essex IG6 1JS T: (020) 8708 7160 F: (020) 8708 7161
Redcar and Cleveland - The Register Office, Westgate, Guisborough, Cleveland TS14 6AP T: 01287 632564 F: 01287 630768
Richmond Upon Thames London Borough - The Register Office, 1 Spring Terrace, Richmond, Surrey TW9 1LW T: (020) 8940 2853 F: (020) 8940 8226
Rochdale MD - Town Hall, The Esplanade, Rochdale, Lancashire OL16 1AB T: 01706 864783 F: 01706 864786
Rotherham MD - Bailey House, Rawmarsh Road, Rotherham, South Yorkshire S60 1TX T: 01709 382121 F: 01709 375530
Rutland - Catmose, Oakham, Rutland LE15 6JU T: 01572 758370 F: 01572 758371
Salford MD - Kingslea, Barton Road, Swinton, Manchester M27 5WH T: 0161 909 6501 F: 0161 794 4797
Sandwell MD - Highfields, High Street, West Bromwich, Sandwell, West Midlands B70 8RJ T: 0121 569 2480 F: 0121 569 2473
Sefton MD
Sefton North Town Hall, Corporation Street, Southport, Merseyside PR8 1DA T: 01704 533133 F: 0151 934 2014
Sefton South Crosby Town Hall, Great Georges Road, Waterloo, Liverpool, L22 1RB T: 0151 934 3045 F: 0151 934 3056
Sheffield MD - **Register Office** The Town Hall, Pinstone Street, Sheffield, South Yorkshire S1 2HH T: 0114 273 9423 E: registeroffice@sheffield.gov.uk
Shropshire
Bridgnorth The Register Office, 12 West Castle Street, Bridgnorth, Shropshire WV16 4AB T: 01746 762589 F: 01746 764270
Clun The Pines, Colebatch Road, Bishop's Castle, Shropshire SY9 5JY T: 01588 638588 F:
Ludlow The Register Office, Stone House, Corve Street, Ludlow, Shropshire SY8 1DG T: 01584 813208 F: 01584 813122
North Shropshire Edinburgh House, New Street, Wem, Shrewsbury, Shropshire SY4 5DB T: 01939 238418
Oswestry The Register Office, Holbache Road, Oswestry, Shropshire SY11 1AH T: 01691 652086
Shrewsbury The Register Office, Column Lodge, Preston Street, Shrewsbury, Shropshire SY2 5NY T: 01743 252925 F: 01743 252939
Telford and Wrekin The Beeches, 29 Vineyard Road, Wellinton, Telford, Shropshire TF1 1HB T: 01952 248292 F: 01952 240976
Solihull MD
Solihull The Register Office, Homer Road, Solihull, West Midlands B91 3QZ T: 0121 704 6099 F: 0121 704 6123
Solihull North The Library, Stephenson Drive, Chelmsley Wood, Birmingham, B37 5TA T: 0121-788-4376 F: 0121 788 4379
Somerset
Mendip The Register Office, 19b Commercial Road, Shepton Mallet, Somerset BA4 5BU T: 01749 343928 F: 01749 342324
Sedgemoor Morgan House, Mount Street, Bridgewater, Somerset TA6 3ER T: 01278 422527 F: 01278 452670
South Somerset South Somerset Register Office, Maltravers House, Petters Way, Yeovil, Somerset BA20 1SP T: 01935 411230 F: 01935 413993
Taunton Flook House, Belvedere Road, Taunton, Somerset TA1 1BT T: 01823 282251 F: 01823 351173
West Somerset 2 Long Street, Williton, Taunton, Somerset TA4 4QN T: 01984 633116
South Gloucestershire - Poole Court, Poole Court Drive, Yate, South Gloucestershire BS37 5PT T: 01454 863140 F: 01454 863145
South Tyneside
Jarrow The Register Office, Suffolk Street, Jarrow, Tyne and Wear

In association with The National Family History Fair

NE32 5BJ T: 0191-489 7595 F: 0191 428 0931 E:
South Tyneside MD
South Tyneside The Register Office, 18 Barrington Street, South Shields NE33 1AH T: 0191 455 3915 F: 0191 427 7564
Southampton
Southampton The Register Office, 6A Bugle Street, Southampton, SO14 2LX T: (023) 8063 1422 F: (023) 8063 3431
Southwark LB
Southwark The Register Office, 34 Peckham Road, Southwark, London, SE5 8QA T: (020) 7525 7651 F: (020) 7525 7652
St Helens MD
St Helens The Register Office, Central Street, St Helens, Merseyside WA10 1UJ T: 01744 23524 F: 01744 23524
Staffordshire
Registrar of Births, Deaths & Marriages - South Staffordshire Civic Centre, Gravel Hill, Wombourne, Wolverhampton, Staffordshire WV5 9HA T: 01902 895829 F: 01902 326779
Cannock Chase The Register Office, 5 Victoria Street, Cannock, Staffordshire WS11 1AG T: 01543 512345 F: 01543 512347 E:
East Staffordshire Rangemore House, 22 Rangemore Street, Burton-upon-Trent, Staffordshire DE14 2ED T: 01283 538701 F: 01283 547338
Lichfield The Old Library Building, Bird Street, Lichfield, Staffordshire WS13 6PN T: 01543 510770 F: 01543 510773
Newcastle-under-Lyme The Register Office, 20 Sidmouth Avenue, The Brampton, Newcastle-under-Lyme, Staffordshire ST5 0QN T: 01782 297581 F: 01782 297582
Stafford Eastgate House, 79 Eastgate Street, Stafford, Staffordshire ST16 2NG T: 01785 277880 F: 01785 277884
Staffordshire Moorlands The Register Office, High Street, Leek, Staffordshire ST13 5EA T: 01538 373166 F: 01538 386985
Stockport MD - Town Hall - John Street Entrance, Stockport, Cheshire SK1 3XE T: 0161 474 3399 F: 0161 474 3390
Stockton-on-Tees - Nightingale House, Balaclava Street, Stockton-on-Tees, TS18 2AL T: 01642 527720 F: 01642 393159
Stoke-on-Trent - Town Hall, Albion Street, Hanley, Stoke on Trent, Staffordshire ST1 1QQ T: 01782 235260 F: 01782 235258
Suffolk
Bury St. Edmunds St Margarets, Shire Hall, Bury St Edmunds, Suffolk IP33 1RX T: 01284 352373 F: 01284 352376
Deben Council Offices, Melton Hill, Woodbridge, Suffolk IP12 1AU T: 01394 444331
Gipping & Hartismere Milton House, 3 Milton Road, Stowmarket, Suffolk IP14 1EZ T: 01449 612054
Ipswich St Peter House, County Hall, 16 Grimwade Street, Ipswich, Suffolk IP4 1LP T: 01473 583050 F: 01473 584331
Sudbury The Register Office, 14 Cornard Road, Sudbury, Suffolk CO10 2XA T: 01787 372904
Waveney St Margarets House, Gordon Road, Lowestoft, Suffolk NR32 1JQ T: 01502 405096 F: 01502 508170
Sunderland MD - Town Hall & Civic Centre, PO Box 108, Sunderland, SR2 7DN T: 0191 553 1768 F: 0191 553 1762
Surrey
East Surrey East Surrey Register Office, The Mansion, 70 Church Street, Leatherhead, Surrey KT22 8DP T: 01372 832800
North Surrey Rylston, 81 Oatlands Drive, Weybridge, Surrey KT13 9LN T: 01932 794700 F: 01932 794701
West Surrey Artington House, Portsmouth Road, Guildford, Surrey GU2 4DZ T: 01483 562841 F: 01483 573232
Sussex - East
Crowborough Beaconwood, Beacon Road, Crowborough, East Sussex TN6 1AR T: 01892 653803 F: 01892 669884
Eastbourne Town Hall, Grove Road, Eastbourne, East Sussex BN21 4UG T: 01323 415051 F: 01323 431386
Sutton LB
Sutton Russettings, 25 Worcester Road, Sutton, Surrey SM2 6PR T: (020) 8770 6790 F: (020) 8770 6772
Swindon - 1st Floor, Aspen House, Temple Street, Swindon, SN1 1SQ T: 01793 521734 F: 01793 433887
Tameside MD - Tameside Register Office, Town Hall, King Street, Dukinfield, Cheshire SK16 4LA T: 0161 342 5032
Tower Hamlets London Borough - The Register Office, Bromley Public Hall, Bow Road, London E3 3AA T: (020) 7364 7883 F: (020) 7364 7885
Trafford MD - Sale Town Hall, School Road, Sale, Cheshire M33 7ZF T: 0161 912 3025 F: 0161 912 3031
Wakefield MD
Pontefract The Register Office, Town Hall, Pontefract, West Yorkshire WF8 1PG T: 01977 722670 F: 01977 722676

Wakefield The Register Office, 71 Northgate, Wakefield, West Yorkshire WF1 3BS T: 01924 302185 F: 01924 302186
Walsall M D - The Register Office, Civic Centre, Hatherton Road, Walsall, West Midlands WS1 1TN T: 01922 652260 F: 01922 652262
Waltham Forest London Borough - The Register Office, 106 Grove Road, Walthamstow, London E17 9BY T: (020) 8496 2716
Wandsworth London Borough - The Register Office, The Town Hall, Wandsworth High Street, London, SW18 2PU T: (020) 8871 6120 F: (020) 8871 8100

Warwickshire
Mid Warwickshire Pageant House, 2 Jury Street, Warwick, Warwickshire CV34 4EW T: 01926 494269 F: 01926 496287
North Warwickshire Warwick House, Ratcliffe Street, Atherstone, Warwickshire CV9 1JP T: 01827 713241 F: 01827 720467
Nuneaton and Bedworth Riversley Park, Coton Road, Nuneaton, Warwickshire CV11 5HA T: (024) 7634 8944 F: (024) 7635 0988
Rugby The Register Office, 5 Bloxam Place, Rugby, Warwickshire CV21 3DS T: 01788 571233 F: 01788 542024
South Warwickshire The Register Office, 7 Rother Street, Stratford-on-Avon, Warwickshire CV37 6LU T: 01789 293711 F: 01789 261423
West Sussex
Chichester Greyfriars, 61 North Street, Chichester, West Suusex PO19 1NB T: 01243 782307 F: 01243 773671
Crawley Town Hall, The Boulevard, Crawley, West Sussex RH10 1UZ T: 01293 438000 F: 01293 526454
Haywards Heath West Sussex County Council Offices, Oaklands Road, Haywards Heath, West Sussex RH16 1SU T: 01444 452157 F: 01444 410128
Horsham Town Hall, Market Square, Horsham, West Sussex RH12 1EU T: 01403 265368 F: 01403 217078
Worthing Centenary House, Durrington Lane, Worthing, West Sussex BN13 2QB T: 01903 839350 F: 01903 839356
Westminster London Borough - The Register Office, Westminster Council House, Marylebone Road, London, NW1 5PT T: (020) 7641 1161 F: (020) 7641 1246
Wigan MD - New Town Hall, Library Street, Wigan, Lancashire WN1 1NN T: 01942 705000 F: 01942 705013
Wiltshire
Chippenham The Register Office, 4 Timber Street, Chippenham, Wiltshire SN15 3BZ T: 01249 654361 F: 01249 658850
Devizes & Marlborough Browfort, Bath Road, Devizes, Wiltshire SN10 2AT T: 01380 722162
Marlborough The Register Office, 1 The Green, Marlborough, Wiltshire SN8 1AL T: 01672-512483
Salisbury The Laburnums, 50 Bedwin Street, Salisbury, Wiltshire SP1 3UW T: 01722 335340 F: 01722 326806
Swindon 1st Floor, Aspen House, Temple Street, Swindon, SN1 1SQ T: 01793 521734 F: 01793 433887
Trowbridge East Wing Block, County Hall, Trowbridge, Wiltshire BA14 8EZ T: 01225 713000 F: 01225 713096
Warminster The Register Office, 3 The Avenue, Warminster, Wiltshire BA12 9AB T: 01985 213435 F: 01985 217688
Wirral MD
Wallasey The Register Office, Town Hall, Wallasey, Merseyside L44 8ED T: 0151-691-8505
Wirral Town Hall, Mortimer Street, Birkenhead, Merseyside L41 5EU T: 0151 666 4096 F: 0151 666 3685
Wolverhampton
Wolverhampton Civic Centre, St Peters Square, Wolverhampton, WV1 1RU T: 01902 554989 F: 01902 554987
Worcestershire
Evesham County Offices, Swan Lane, Evesham, Worcestershire WR11 4TZ T: 01386 443945 F: 01386 448745
Malvern Hatherton Lodge, Avenue Road, Malvern, Worcestershire WR14 3AG T: 01684 573000 F: 01684 892378
Pershore Civic Centre, Queen Elizabeth Drive, Station Road, Pershore, Worcestershire WR10 1PT T: 01386 565610 F: 01386 553656
Tenbury Tenbury Wells Register Office, Tenbury Wells Pump Rooms, Tenbury Wells, Worcestershire WR15 8BA T: 01584 810588 F: 01584 819733
York
York The Register Office, 56 Bootham, York, YO30 7DA T: 01904 654477 F: 01904 638090
Yorkshire - South
Barnsley Town Hall, Church Street, Barnsley, South Yorkshire S70 2TA T: 01226 773085
Sheffield Register Office The Town Hall, Pinstone Street, Sheffield, South Yorkshire S1 2HH T: 0114 273 9423 E: registeroffice@sheffield.gov.uk

Wales
The General Register Office Room E201, Trafalgar Road, Birkdale, Southport, PR8 2HH T: 0870 243 7788 W: www.gro.gov.uk
Anglesey
Ynys Môn Shire Hall, Glanhwfa Road, Llangefni, Anglesey LL77 7TW T: 01248 752564
Blaenau Gwent
Blaenau Gwent (Abertillery) Council Offices, Mitre Street, Abertillery, Gwent NP3 1AE T: 01495 216082
Blaenau Gwent (Ebbw Vale & Tredegar) The Grove, Church Street, Tredegar, Gwent NP2 3DS T: 01495 722769
Bridgend - County Borough Offices, Sunnyside, Bridgend, Glamorgan CF31 4AR T: 01656 642391 F: 01656 667529
Caerphilly - The Council Offices, Ystrad Fawr, Caerphilly Road, Ystrad Mynach, Hengoed, CF82 7SF T: 01443 863478 F: 01443 863385
Cardiff - The Register Office, 48 Park Place, Cardiff, CF10 3LU T: (029) 2087 1690 F: (029) 2087 1691

Carmarthenshire
Carmarthen Carmarthen Register Office, Parc Myrddin, Richmond Terrace, Carmarthen, Carmarthenshire SA31 1DS T: 01267 228210 F: 01267 228215
Llanelli Llanelli Register office, 2 Coleshill Terrace, Llanelli, Carmarthenshire SA15 3DB T: 01554 744202 F: 01554 749424
Ceredigion
Cardiganshire Central The Register Office, 21 High Street, Lampeter, Ceredigion SA48 7BG T: 01570 422558 F: 01570 422558
Cardiganshire North Swyddfar Sir, Marine Terrace, Aberystwyth, Ceredigion SY23 2DE T: 01970 633580
Cardiganshire South Glyncoed Chambers, Priory Street, Cardigan, Ceredigion SA43 1BX T: 01239 612684 F: 01239 612684
Conwy
Aberconwy The Town Hall, Lloyd Street, Llandudno, Gwynedd LL30 2UP T: 01492 574045
Colwyn New Clinic and Offices, 67 Market Street, Abergele, Conwy LL22 7BP T: 01745 823976
Conwy CB
Public Protection Department - Conwy County Borough Council Civic Offices, Colwyn Bay, Conwy LL29 8AR T: 01492 575183 F: 01492 575204
Denbighshire
Denbighshire North Morfa Clwyd, Marsh Road, Rhyl, Denbighshire LL18 2AF T: 01745 366610 F: 01745 361424
Denbighshire South The Town Hall, Wynnstay Road, Ruthin, Denbighshire LL15 1YN T: 01824 706187
Flintshire
Flintshire East The Old Rectory, Rectory Lane, Hawarden, Flintshire CH5 3NN T: 01244 531512 F: 01244 534628
Flintshire West The Register Office, Park Lane, Holywell, Flintshire CH8 7UR T: 01352 711813 F: 01352 713292
Glamorgan
Merthyr Tydfil The Register Office, Ground Floor, Castle House, Glebeland Street, Merthyr Tydfil, Glamorgan CF47 8AT T: 01685 723318 F: 01685 721849
Neath Port Talbot The Register Office, 119 London Road, Neath, Port Talbot, SA11 1HL T: 01639 760020 F: 01639 760023
Gwent
Blaenau Gwent The Grove, Church Street, Tredegar, Gwent NP2 3DS T: 01495 722305
Gwynedd
Public Protection Department - Conwy County Borough Council Civic Offices, Colwyn Bay, Conwy LL29 8AR T: 01492 575183 F: 01492 575204
Aberconwy The Town Hall, Lloyd Street, Llandudno, Gwynedd LL30 2UP T: 01492 574045
Ardudwy Bryn Marian, Church Street, Blaenau Ffestiniog, Gwynedd LL41 3HD T: 01766 830217 F:
Bangor The Register Office, Town Hall, Bangor, Gwynedd LL57 2RE T: 01248 362418
Caernarfon Swyddfa Arfon, Pennrallt, Caernarfon, Gwynedd LL55 1BN T: 01286 682661
De Meirionndd Meirionnydd Area Office, Cae Penarlag, Dolgellau, Gwynedd LL40 2YB T: 01341 424341
Dwyfor The Register Office, Embankment Road, Pwllheli, Gwynedd LL53 5AA T: 01758 612546 F: 01758 701373
Penllyn Penllyn Register Office, Fron Faire, High Street, Bala, Gwynedd LL23 7AD T: 01678 521220 F: 01678 521243
Merthyr Tydfil - The Register Office, Ground Floor, Castle House, Glebeland Street, Merthyr Tydfil, Glamorgan CF47 8AT T: 01685 723318 F: 01685 721849
Monmouthshire
Monmouth The Register Office, Coed Glas, Firs Road, Abergavenny, Monmouthshire NP7 5LE T: 01873 735435 F: 01837 735429
Neath Port Talbot - The Register Office, 119 London Road, Neath, Port Talbot, SA11 1HL T: 01639 760020 F: 01639 760023
Newport
Newport The Register Office, 8 Gold Tops, Newport, Gwent NP20 4PH T: 01633 265547 F: 01633 220913
Pembrokeshire
Pembrokeshire The Register Office, Tower Hill, Haverfordwest, Pembrokeshire SA61 1SS T: 01437 775176 F: 01437 779357
South Pembroke The Register Office, East Back, Pembroke, Pembrokeshire SA71 4HL T: 01646 682432 F: 01646 621433
Powys
Welshpool & Llanfyllin (Llanfyllin Sub-district) Room 8 First Floor, Powys County Council Area Offices, Youth & Community Centre, Llanfyllin, Powys SY22 5DB T: 01691 649027
Brecknock Neuadd Brycheiniog, Cambrian Way, Brecon, Powys LD3 7HR T: 01874 624334 F: 01874 625781
Hay The Borough Council Offices, Broad Street, Hay-on-Wye, Powys HR3 5BX T: 01497 821371 F: 01497 821540
Machynlleth The Register Office, 11 Penrallt Street, Machynlleth, Powys SY20 8AG T: 01654 702335 F: 01654 703742
Mid Powys Powys County Hall, Llandrindod Wells, Powys LD1 5LG T: 01597 826020
Newtown Council Offices, The Park, Newtown, Powys SY16 2NZ T: 01686 627862

Radnorshire East The Register Office, 2 Station Road, Knighton, Powys LD7 1DU T: 01547 520758
Welshpool & Llanfyllin Neuadd Maldwyn, Severn Road, Welshpool, Powys SY21 7AS T: 01938 552828 Ext 228 F: 01938 551233
Ystradgynlais County Council Offices, Trawsffordd, Ystradgynlais, Powys SA9 1BS T: 01639 843104
Rhonda Cynon Taff - The Register Office, Courthouse Street, Pontypridd, CF37 1LJ T: 01443 486869 F: 01443 406587
Swansea - The Swansea Register Office, County Hall, Swansea, SA1 3SN T: 01792 636188 F: 01792 636909
Torfaen - The Register Office, Hanbury Road, Pontypool, Torfaen NP4 6YG T: 01495 762937 F: 01495 769049
Vale of Glamorgan - The Register Office, 2-6 Holton Road, Barry, Glamorgan CF63 4RU T: 01446 709490 F: 01446 709502
Wrexham
Wrexham Ty Dewi Sant, Rhosddu Road, Wrexham, LL11 1NF T: 01978 292027 F: 01978 292676

Guernsey
HM Greffier Royal Court House, St Peter Port, Guernsey GY1 2PB T: 01481 725277 F: 01481 715097

Isle of Man
Civil Registry Registries Building, Deemster's Walk, Bucks Road, Douglas, Isle of Man IM1 3AR T: 01624 687039 F: 01624 685237 E: civil@registry.gov.im

Northern Ireland
General Register Office of Northern Ireland Oxford House, 49 - 55 Chichester Street, Belfast, BT1 4HL T: (028) 90 252000 F: (028) 90 252120 E: gro.nisra@dfpni.gov.uk W: www.groni.gov.uk

Scotland
Aberdeen
Aberdeen St Nicholas House, Upperkirkgate, Aberdeen, AB10 1EY T: 01224 522616 F: 01224 522616 E: regsitrars@legal.aberdeen.net.uk
Aberdeen City Council
Peterculter Lilydale, 102 North Deeside Road, Peterculter, AB14 0QB T: 01224 732648 F: 01224 734637
Aberdeenshire
Skere and Echt Operating from Inverurie, Inverurie, AB32 6XX T: 01467 628011 (Direct) E: dianc.minty@aberdeenshire.gov.uk
Aberdeen St Nicholas House, Upperkirkgate, Aberdeen, AB10 1EY T: 01224 522616 F: 01224 522616 E: regsitrars@legal.aberdeen.net.uk
Braemar The Braemar Royal Highland So, Hillside Road, Braemar, AB35 5YU T: 01339 741349
Inverurie, Oldmeldrum, Skere and Echt Gordon House, Blackhall Road, Inverurie, AB51 3WA T: 01467 620981 F: 01467 628012 E: diane.minty@aberdeenshire.gov.uk
Maud County Offices, Nethermuir Road, Maud, Aberdeenshire AB42 4ND T: 01771 613667 F: 01771 613204 E: maureen.stephen@aberdeenshire.gov.uk
Peterhead Arbuthnot House, Broad Street, Peterhead, AB42 1DA T: 01779 483244 E: shirley.dickie@aberdeenshire.gov.uk
Stonehaven, East Kinkardine & Inverbervie Viewmount, Arduthie Road, Stonehaven, AB39 2DQ T: 01569 768360 F: 01569 765455 E: cressida.coates@aberdeenshire.gov.uk
Strathdon Area Office, School Road, Alford, AB33 8PY T: 01975 564811
Tarves Area Office, Schoolhill Road, Ellon, Aberdeenshire AB41 7PQ T: 01358 720295 E: kathleen.stopani@aberdeenshire.gov.uk
Turriff Towie House, Manse Road, Turriff, AB53 4AY T: 01888 562427 F: 01888 568559 E: sheila.donald@aberdeenshire.gov.uk
Aberfoyle + Mentheith - Aberfoyle Local Office, Main Street, Aberfoyle, FK8 3UQ T: 01877 382986
Aboyne and Torphin - District Council Offices, Bellwood Road, Aboyne, AB34 5HQ T: 01339 886109 F: 01339 86798 E: esther.halkett@aberdeenshire.gov.uk
Alford, Sauchen and Strathdo Council Office, School Road, Alford, AB33 8PY T: 01975 562421 F: 01975 563286 E: anne.shaw@aberdeenshire.gov.uk
Arbroath - The Register Office, 69/71 High Street, Arbroath, DD11 1AN T: 01241 873752 F: 01241 874805 E: macpherson@angus.gov.uk
Ardgour - The Register Office, 9 Clovullin, Ardgour, by Fort William, PH33 7AB T: 01855 841261

Argyle & Bute
Dunoon Council Offices, Hill Street, Dunoon, PA23 7AP T: 01369 704374 F: 01369 705948 E: ann.saidler@argyll-bute.gov.uk
Lismore Baleveolan, Isle of Lismore, Oban PA34 5UG T: 01631 760274
Rosneath Registration Office, Easter Garth, Rosneath, by Helensburgh, G84 0RF T: 01436 831679 E: elsa.rossetter@eastergarth.co.uk W: www.eastergarth.co.uk
Strontian Easgadail, Longrigg Road, Strontian Acharacle, Argyll PH36 4HY T: 01967 402037 E:
Campbeltown Council Office, Dell Road, Campbeltown, Argyll PA28 6JG T: 01586 552366 F: 01586 552366 E: isabella.soudan@argyll-bute.gov.uk W: www.argyll-bute.gov.uk

Kilbrandon and Kilchattan Dalanasaig, Clachan Seil, By Oban, Argyll PA34 4TJ T: 01852 300380

South Cowal Copeswood, Auchenlochan High Road, Tighnabruaich, PA21 2BE T: 01700 811601

Strachur Crosshaig, Strachur, Argyll PA27 8BY T: 01369 860203

Tobermory County Buildings, Breadalbane Street, Tobermory, PA75 6PX T: 01688 302051 E: iainmackinnon03@argyll.bute.gov.uk

Arrochar - The Register Office, 1 Cobbler View, Arrochar, G83 7AD T: 01301 702289

Assynt - Post Office House, Lochinver, Lochinver by Lairg, IV27 4JY T: 01571 844201

Auchinleck - The Register Office, 28 Well Road, Auchlinleck, Cummock, KA18 2LA T: 01290 420582

Auchterarder - The Ayton Hall, 91 High Street, Auchterarder, PH3 1BJ T: 01764 662155 F: 01764 662120 E: mmellis@pkc.gov.uk

Aviemore - Tremayne, Dalfaber Road, Aviemore, PH22 1PU T: 01479 810694

Ayr - Sandgate House, 43 Sandgate, Ayr, KA7 1DA T: 01292 284988 E: ayr.registrars@south-ayrshire.gov.uk

Ballater - An Creagan, 5 Queens Road., Ballater, AB35 5NJ T: 01339 755535

Banchory - Aberdeenshire Council, The Square, High Street, Banchory, AB31 5RW T: 01330 822878 F: 01330 822243 E: christine.handsley@aberdeenshire.gov.uk

Banff - Seafield House, 37 Castle Street, Banff, AB45 1DQ T: 01261 813439 E: kate.samuel@aderdeenshire.gov.uk

Barra - Council Offices, Castlebay, Barra, HS9 5XD T: 01871 810431

Barrhead - Council Office, 13 Lowndes Street, Barrhead, G78 2QX T: 0141 577 35551 F: 0141 577 35553 E: mcquadem@eastrenfrewshire.gov.uk

Beauly - Operating from Inverness, E: kathleen.chisholm@highland.gov.uk

Bellshill - The Register Office, 20/22 Motherwelt Road, Bellshill, ML4 1RB T: 01698 346780 F: 016989 346789 E: registrars-bellshill@nothlan.gov.uk

Benbecula - Council Offices, Balivanich, Benbecula, South Uist, HS7 5LA T: 01870 602425

Biggar - he Register Office, 4 Ross Square, Biggar, ML12 6DH T: 01899 220997

Bishopbriggs - Council Offices, The Triangle, Kirkintilloch Road, Bishopbriggs, G64 2TR T: 0141 578 8557 E: mary.neill@eastdunbarton.gov.uk

Black Isle - Black Isle Leisure Centre, Deans Road, Fortrose, IV10 8TJ T: 01381 620797 F: 01381 621085 E: marion.phimister@highland.gov.uk

Black Isle Black Isles Leisure Centre, Deans Road, Fortrose, IV10 8TJ T: 01381 620797 F: 01381 621085 E: marion.phimister@highland.gov.uk

Blairgowrie - Council Buildings, 46 Leslie Street, Blairgowrie, PH10 6AW T: 01250 872051 F: 01250 876029

Bo'ness and Carriden - Registration Office, 15a Seaview Place, Bo'ness, EH51 0AJ T: 01506 778992

Boisdale - Post Office House, Daliburgh, South Uist, HS8 5SS T: 01878 700300

Bonar and Kincardine - Post Office, Bonar Bridge, Ardgay, IV24 3EA T: 01863 766219

Bonnybridge - Operating from Denny, T: 01324-504280

Brechin - Contact Arbroath,

Bressay - The Register Office, No 2 Roadside Bressay, Lerwick, Shetland ZE2 9EL T: 01595 820356

Broardford - The Register Office, Fairwinds, Broadford, Skye IV49 9AB T: 01471 822270

Buckie - Town House West, Cluny Place, Buckie, AB56 1HB T: 01542 832691 F: 01542 833384 E: Jill.addison@chief.moray.gov.uk

Bucksburn - Area Office, 23 Inverurie Road, Bucksburn, AB21 9LJ T: 01224 712866 F: 01224 716997

Carnoch - Operating from, Dingwall, IV15 9QR T: 01349 863113

Carnoustie - Council Chambers, 26 High Street, Carnoustie, DD7 6AP T: 01241 853335/6 F: 01241 857554

Castle Douglas - District Council, 5 St Andrew Street, Castle Douglas, DG7 1DE T: 01557 330291 E: ruthpe@dumgal.gov.uk

Castleton - 10 Douglas Square, Newcastleton, TD9 0QD T: 01387 375606 E: maaitchison@scotborders.gsx.gov.uk

Chryston - The Register Office, Lindsaybeg Road, Muirhead, Glasgow, G69 9DW T: 0141 779 1714

Clackmannanshire - Marshill House, Marshill, Alloa, FK10 1AB T: 01259 723850 F: 01259 723850 E: registration@clacks.gov.uk W: www.clacksweb.org.uk

Clyne - Brora Service Point, Gower Street, Brora, KW9 6PD T: 01408 622644 E: margaret.mackintosh@highland.gov.uk

Coalburn - Pretoria, 200 Coalburn Road, Coalburn, ML11 0LT T: 01555 820664

Coigach - 29 Market Street, Ullapool, IV26 2XE T: 01854 612426

Coldstream - 73 High Street, Coldstream, TD12 4AE T: 01890 883156 E: sbrodie@scotborders.gsx.gov.uk

Coll - The Register Office, 9 Carnan Road, Isle of Coll, Argyll and Bute PA78 6TA T: 01879 230329

Colonsay & Oronsay - Colonsay Service Point, Village Hall, Colonsay, Argyll PA61 7YW T: 01951 200263

Comhaire Nan Eilean Siar

Stornoway and South Lochs Town Hall, 2 Cromwell Street, Stornoway, HS1 2DB T: 01851 709438 F: 01851 709438 E: emacdonald@cne-siar.gov.uk W: www.cne-siar.gov.uk/w-isles/registrars

Coupar-Angus - Union Bank Buildings, Coupar Angus, PH13 9AJ T: 01828 628395 F: 01828 627147 E: legalservices@wandlb.co.uk

Crawford - Raggengill, 45 Carlisle Road, Crawford, Biggar, ML12 6TP T: 01864 502633

Crieff - Crieff Area Office, 32 James Square, Crieff, PH7 3EY T: 01764 657550 F: 01764 657559

Cumbernauld - Council Offices, Bron Way, Cumbernauld, G67 1DZ T: 01236 616390 F: 01236 616386

Dalbeattie - Town Hall Buildings, Water Street, Dalbeattie, DG5 4JX T: 01557 330291 Ext 323

Dalmellington - Dalmellington Area Centre, 33 Main Street, Dalmellington, KA6 7QL T: 01292 552 880 F: 01292 552 884

Dalry - 42 Main Street, Dalry, Castle Douglas, DG7 3UW T: 01644 430310

Delting - Soibakkan, Mossbank, Shetland ZE2 9RB T: 01806 242209

Denny - Carronbank House, Carronbank Crescent, Denny, FK4 6GA T: 01324 504280 E: fiona.mitchell@falkirk.gov.uk

Dornoch - Service Point Office, The Meadows, Dornoch, IV25 3SG T: 01862 812008 E: lesley.conner@highland.gov.uk

Douglas - Post Office, Ayr Road, Douglas, ML11 0PU T: 01555 851227

Dumbarton - 18 College Street, Dumbarton, G82 1NR T: 01389 738350 F: 01389 738352 E: tony.gallagher@west-dunbarton.gov.uk

Dumfries - Municipal Chambers, Buccleuch Street, Dumfries, DG1 2AD T: 01387 245906 F: 01387 269605 E: isabeld@dumgal.gov.uk

Dumfries & Galloway

Wigtown Area Council Sub-office, County Buildings, Wigtown, Dumfriesshire DG8 9JH T: 01988 402624 F: 01988 403201 E: marm@dumgal.gov.uk

Dumfries & Galloway Council

Whithorn Area The Register Office, 75 George Street, Whithorn, Dumfries DG8 8NU T: 01988 500458 E: archietaylor@supanet.com

Dumfries and Galloway

Annan Council Offices, 15 Ednay Street, Annan, DG12 6EF T: 01461 204914 F: 01461 206896 E: shirleymo@dungal.gov.uk

Gretna Registration Office, Central Avenue, Gretna, DG16 5AQ T: 01461 337648 F: 01461 338459 E: gretnaonline@dumgal.gov.uk W: www.gretnaonline.net

Kirkcudbright District Council Offices, Daar Road, Kirkcudbrigbt, DG6 4JG T: 01557 332534 W: www.dumgal.gov.uk

Lockerbie Town Hall, High Street, Lockerbie, DG11 2ES T: 01576 204267 E: janeta@dumgal.gov.uk

Moffat Town Hall, High Street, Moffat, DG10 9HF T: 01683 220536 F: 01683 221489

Stranraer Area The Register Office, Council Offices, Sun Street, Stranraer, DG9 7JJ T: 01776 888439 E: murielc@dumgal.gov.uk

Thornhill One Stop Shop, Manse Road, Thornhill, Dumfriesshire DG3 5DR T: 01848 330303 E: margaretbr@dumgal.gov.uk

Dundee

Dundee City Council - Genealogy Unit 89 Commercial Street, Dundee, DD1 2AF T: 01382-435222 F: 01382-435224 E: grant.law@dundeecity.gov.uk W: www.dundeecity.gov.uk/registrars

Dundee The Register Office, 89 Commercial Street, Dundee, DD1 2AF T: 01382 435222/3 F: 01382 435224 E: grant.law@dundeecity.gov.uk W: www.dundeecity.gov.uk/registrars

Dunrossness - Baptist Manse, Dunrossness, Shetland ZE2 9JB T: 01950 460792

Duns - The Register Office, 8 Newtown Street, Duns, TD11 3DT T: 01361 882600

Durness - Service Point, Highlands of Scotland Tourist Board, Sangomore, Durness, IV27 4PZ T: 01971 511368 E: sheila.mather@highland.gov.uk

East Ayrshire

Catrine The Register Office, 9 Co-operative Avenue, Catrine, KA5 6SG T: 01290 551638

Darvel, Galston, Newmilns The Register Office, 11 Cross Street, Galston, KA4 8AA T: 01563 820218

Kilmarnock Civic Centre, John Dickie Street, Kilmarnock, Ayrshire KA1 1HW T: 01563 576695/6 E: cathy.dunlop@east-ayrshire.gov.uk

East Kilbride - Civic Centre, Cornwall Street, East Kilbride, Glasgow, G74 1AF T: 01355 806474 E: aileen.shiells@southlanarkshire.gov.uk

East Lothian

Dunbar Town House, 48 High Street, Dunbar, EH42 1JH T: 01368 863434 F: 01368 865728 E: fwhite@eastlothian.gov.uk

Haddington The Register Office, John Muir House, Brewery Park, Haddington, EH41 3HA T: 01620 827308 F: 01620 827438 E: sforsyth@eastlothian.gov.uk

Eastwood and Mearns - Council Offices, Eastwood Park, Roukenglen Road, Giffnock, G46 6UG T: 0141 577 3100 E: jim.clarke@eastrefrewshire.gov.uk

Eday and Pharay - Redbanks, Eday, Orkney, KW17 2AA T: 01857 622219

Edinburgh

Edinburgh (India Buildings) 2 India Buildings, Victoria Street, Edinburgh, EH1 2EX T: 0131 220 0349 F: 0131 220 0351 E:

registrars.indiabuildings@edinburgh.gov.uk
Edinburgh (Ratho) Operating from 2 India Buildings, Victoria Street, Edinburgh, Ratho, T: 0131 220 0349 F: 0131 220 0351 E: registrars.indiabuildings@edinburgh.gov.uk
Edinburgh (Currie) - The Register Office, 138 Lanark Road West, Currie, EH14 5NY T: 0131 449 5318
Edinburgh (Kirkliston) - 19 Station Road, Kirkliston, EH29 9BB T: 0131 333 3210
Edinburgh (Leith) - The Register Office, 30 Ferry Road, Edinburgh, EH6 4AE T: 0131 554 8452 E: registrars.leith@edinburgh.gov.uk
Edinburgh (Queensferry) - Council Office, 53 High Street, South Queensferry, EH30 9HP T: 0131 331 1590 W: margaret.kenny@edinburgh.gov.uk
Ellon - Area Office, Neil Ross Square, 29 Bridge Street, Ellon, AB41 9AA T: 01358 720295 F: 01358 726410 E: kathleen.stopani@aberdeenshire.gov.uk
Eyemouth - Community Centre, Albert Road, Eyemouth, TD14 5DE T: 01890 750690 E: pjohnston@scotborders.gsx.gov.uk
Falkirk - Old Burgh Buildings, Newmarket Street, Falkirk, FK1 lJE T: 01324 506580 F: 01324 506581 E: elinor.laing@falkirk.gov.uk
Fife (Auchterderran) - The Register Office, 145 Station Road, Cardenden, KY5 0BN T: 01592 414800 F: 01592 414848
Fife (Auchtermuchty) - Local Office, 15 High Street, Auchtermuchty, KY14 7AP T: 01337 828329 F: 01337 827166
Fife (Benarty) - Benarty Local Office, 6 Benarty Square, Ballingry, Fife KY5 8NR T: 01592 414343 F: 01592 414363 E: dorothy.thomson@fife.gov.uk
Fife (Bucknaven) - Local Office, Municipal Buildings, College Street, Buckhaven, KY8 1AB T: 01592 414446 F: 01592 414490 E: martha.shields@fife.gov.uk
Fife (Cowdenbeath) - The Register Office, 123 High Street, Cowdenbeath, KY4 9QB T: 01383 313190
Fife (Cupar) - County Buildings, St Catherine Street, Cupar, KY15 4TA T: 01334 412885
Fife (Dunfermline) - The Register Office, 34 Viewfield Terrace, Dunfermline, KY12 7HZ T: 01383 312121 F: 01383 312123 E: anne.williamson@fife.gov.uk
Fife (East Neuk) - Anstruther Local Office, Ladywalk, Anstruther, KY10 3EX T: 01333 592110 F: 01333 592117 E: helen.moist@fife.gov.uk
Fife (Glenrothes) - Albany House, Albany Gate Kingdom Centre, Glenrothes, KY7 5NX T: 01592 416570 F: 01592 416565 E: sophia.semple@fife.gov.uk
Fife (Inverkeithing) - Civic Centre, Queen Street, Inverkeithing, Fife KY11 1PA T: 01383 313570 F: 01383 313585 E: alexandra.birrell@fife.gov.uk
Fife (Kennoway) - 6/7 Bishops Court, Kennoway, Fife, KY8 5LA T: 01333 352635
Fife (Kirkcaldy) - District Office, Town House, Kirkcaldy, KY1 1XW T: 01592 412121 F: 01592 412123 E: jennifer.brymer@fife.gov.uk
Fife (Leven) - Carberry House, Scoonie Road, Leven, KY8 4JS T: 01333 592412 E: irene.ballantyne@fife.gov.uk
Fife (Lochgelly) - Lochgelly Local Office, Town House, Hall Street, Lochgelly, KY5 9JN T: 01592 418180 F: 01592 418190 E: jacqueline.redpath@fife.gov.uk
Fife (Newburgh) - Tayside Institute, 90-92 High Street, Newburgh, Fife KY14 6DA T: 01337 883000 E: sophia.semple@fife.gov.uk
Fife (Newport on Tay) - Blyth Hall, Scott Street, Newport On Tay, Fife DD6 8DD T: 01382 543345 E: carol.traill@fife.gov.uk
Fife (St Andrews) - Area Office, St Mary's Place, St Andrews, Fife KY16 9UY T: 01334 412525 F: 01334 412650 E: jennifer.millar@fife.gov.uk
Fife (Tayport) - Burgh Chambers, Tayport, Fife DD6 9JY T: 01382 552544
Fife (West Fife) - The Health Centre , Chapel Street, High Valleyfield, Dunfermline, Fife KY12 8SJ T: 01383 880682
(Fife) Kelty - Kelty Local Services, Sanjana Court, 51 Main Street, Kelty, KY4 0AA T: 01383 839999 E: karen.henderson@fife.gov.uk
Forfar - The Register Office, 9 West High Street, Forfar, DD8 1BD T: 01307 464973 E: regforfar@angus.gov.uk
Forres - 53 High Street, Forres, Moray IV36 1DX T: 01309 694070 E: forres.registrar@chief.moray.gov.uk
Fort Augustus - Highland Council Service Point, Memorial Hall, Oich Road, Fort Augustus, PH32 4DJ T: 01320 366733 E: heather.smart@highland.gov.uk
Forth - The Register Office, 4 Cloglands, Forth, Lanarkshire ML11 8ED T: 01555 811631
Fraserburgh - The Register Office, 14 Saltoun Square, Fraserburgh, AB43 9DA T: 01346 513281 E: eyoung.la@aberdeenshire.gov.uk
Gairloch - The Service Point, Achtercairn, Gairloch, IV22 2BP T: 01445 712572 E: trudy.mackenzie@highland.gov.uk
Gairloch (South) - The Service Point, Achtercairn, Gairloch, Ross-shire IV21 2BP T: 01445 712572 F: 01445 712911 E: trudy.mackenzie@highland.gov.uk
Gigha - 10 Ardminish, Gigha, PA41 7AB T: 01583 505249
Girthon and Anwoth - 63 High Street, Gatehouse of Fleet, DG7 2HS T: 01557 814646 E: mhairiw@dumgal.gov.uk
Glasgow - The Register Office, 22 Park Circus, Glasgow, G3 6BE T: 0141 287 8350 F: 0141 287 8357 E: bill.craig@pas.glasgow.gov.uk

Glasgow (Martha Street) The Register Office, 1 Martha Street, Glasgow, G1 1JJ T: 0141 287 7677 F: 0141 287 7666 E: robert.sneddon@pas.glasgow.gov.uk
Glasgow (Park Circus) The Register Office, 22 Park Circus, Glasgow, G3 6BE T: 0141 287 8350 F: 0141 287 8357 E: bill.craig@pas.glasgow.gov.uk
Golspie - Council Offices, Main Street, Golspie, KW10 6RB T: 01408 635200 F: 01408 633120 E: moira.macdonald@highland.gov.uk
Grangemouth - Municipal Chambers, Bo'ness Road, Grangemouth, FK3 8AY T: 01324 504499
Hamilton (Blantyre) - Local Office, 45 John Street, Blantyre, Lanarkshire G72 0JG T: 01698 527901 F: 01698 527923 E: carole.cartwright@southlanarkshire.gov.uk
Harris - Council Offices, Tarbert, Harris HS3 3DJ T: 01859 502367 F: 01859 502283 E: marionmorrison@cne-siar.gov.uk
Hawick - Council Offices, Town Hall, Hawick, TD9 9EF T: 01450 364710 E: 01450 364720 E: mfhope@scotborders.gsx.gov.uk
Helensburgh - Scotcourt House, 45 West Princes Street, Helensburgh, G84 8BP T: 01436 658822 F: 01436 658821
Helmsdale - Operating from, Gower Street, Brora, KW8 6LD T: 01408 622644 F: 01408 622645
Highland
Applecross Coire-ringeal, Applecross, Kyle, Ross-shire IV54 8LU T: 01520 744248
Area Repository Ross and Cromarty Council Offices, Ferry Road, Dingwall, IV15 9QR T: 01349 863113 F: 01349 866164 E: alison.matheson@highland.gov.uk anna.gallie@highland.gov.uk
Dingwall and Carnoch Council Offices, Ferry Road, Dingwall, IV15 9QR T: 01349 863113 F: 01349 866164 E: alison.matheson@highland.gov.uk anna.gallie@highland.gov.uk
Dunvegan Tigh-na-Bruaich, Dunvegan, Isle Of Skye IV55 8WA T: 01470 521296 F: 01470 521519
Fort William and Ballachulish Tweeddale Buildings, High Street, Fort William, PH33 6EU T: 01397 704583 F: 01397 702757 E: isobel.mackellaig@highland.gov.uk W: www.highland.gov.uk
Glenelg Taobh na Mara, Na Mara, Glenelg Kyle, Ross-shire IV40 8JT T: 01599 522310
Grantown-on-Spey and Nethyridge Council Offices, The Square, Grantown On Spey, PH26 3HF T: 01479 872539 F: 01479 872942 E: diane.brazier@highland.gov.uk
Inverness Moray House, 16/18 Bank Street, Inverness, IV1 1QY T: 01463 239792 F: 01463 712412 E: margaret.straube@highland.gov.uk W: www.highland.gov.uk
Kirkton and Tongue The Service Point, Naver Teleservice Centre, Bettyhill, By Thurso, KW14 7SS T: 01641 521242 F: 01641 521242 E: mary.cook@highland.gov.uk
Mallaig and Knoydart Sandholm, Morar, Mallaig, Inverness-shire PH40 4PA T: 01687 462592 F: 01687 462592
Rosskeen Invergordon Service Point, 62 High St, Invergordon, IV18 0DH T: 01349 852472 F: 01349 853803 E: alison.mathieson@highland.gov.uk
Tain 24 High Street, Tain, IV19 1AE T: 01862 892122
Tarradale Service Point Office, Seaforth Road, Muir Of Ord, IV6 7TA T: 01463 870201 F: 01463 871047 E: lorraine.ross@highland.gov.uk
Thurso, Strathy and Mey Library Buildings, Davidsons Lane, Thurso, Caithness KW14 7AF T: 01847 892786 F: 01847894611 E: pauline.edmunds@highland.gov.uk
Wick Town Hall, Bridge Street, Wick, KW1 4AN T: 01955 605713 E: margaret.wood@highland.gov.uk
Highlands Council
Thurso, Strathy and Mey District Office, Library Buildings, Davidson's Lane, Thurso, KW14 7AF T: 01847 892786 F: 01847 894611 E: pauline.edmunds@highland.gov.uk
Huntly - The Register Office, 25 Gordon Street, Huntly, AB54 8AN T: 01466 794488
Insch - Marbert, George Street, Insch, AB52 6JL T: 01464 820964
Inveraray - Operating from Lochgilphead
Inverclyde - The Register Office, 40 West Stewart Street, Greenock, PA15 1YA T: 01475 714250E: maureen.bradley@inverclyde.gov.uk
Inveresk - Brunton Hall, Ladywell Way, Musselburgh, EH21 6AF T: 0131 653 4224 E: acurrie@eastlothian.gov.uk
Irvine - The Register Office, 106-108 Bridgegate House, Irvine, KA12 8BD T: 01294 324988 F: 01294 324984 E: jmcdowall@north-ayrshire.gov.uk
Islay - Council Office, Jamieson Street, Bowmore, Islay PA43 7HL T: 01496 301301 E: sharon.mcharrie@argyll-bute.gov.uk
Isle of Bute - Council Office, Mount Pleasant Road, Rothesay, Isle of Bute PA20 9HH T: 01700 5033l-551
Isle of Eigg
Small Isles Kildonan House, Isle Of Eigg, Isle Of Eigg PH42 4RL T: 01687 482446
Isle of Lewis
Carloway The Registry, Knock, Carloway, Isle Of Lewis HS2 9AU T: 01851 643264
Isle Of Tyree
Tyree The Register Office, Crossapol, Isle Of Tyree PA77 6UP T: 01879 220349

Jedburgh - Library Building, Castlegate, Jedburgh, TD8 6AS T: 01835 863670 F: 01835 863670 E: aveitch@scotborders.gov.uk W: www.scotborders.gov.uk

Johnstone - The Register Office, 16-18 McDowall Street, Johnstone, Renfrewshire PA5 8QL T: 01505 320012 F: 01505 382130 W: www.renfrewshire.gov.uk

Jura - Forestry Cottage, Craighouse, Jura, PA60 7XG T: 01496 820326

Kelso - Town House, Kelso, TD5 7HF T: 01573 225659 E: dgittus@scotborders.gsx.gov.uk

Kenmore - Operating from Aberfeldy, Acharn by Aberfeldy

Kilbirnie, Beith & Dalry - 19 School Wynd, Kilbirnie, KA25 7AY T: 01505 682416 F: 01505 684334 E: amcgurran@north-ayrshire.gov.uk

Kilfinichen & Kilvickeon - The Anchorage, Fionnphort, Isle Of Mull PA66 6BL T: 01681 700241

Kilwinning - The Regsitrar's Office, 32 Howgate, Kilwinning, Ayrshire KA13 6EJ T: 01294 552261/2 F: 01294 557787 E: mmccorquindale@north-ayrshire.gov.uk

Kingussie - Council Offices, Ruthven Road, Kingussie, Inverness-shire PH21 1EJ T: 01540 664529 F: 01540 661004 E: lorna.mcgregor@highland.gov.uk

Kinlochbervie - Operating from Service Point Durness, IV27 4RH T: 01971 511259 E: sheila.mather@highland.gov.uk

Kinlochluichart - The Old Manse, Garve, Ross-shire IV23 2PX T: 01997 414201

Kirkconnell - Nith Buildings, Greystone Avenue, Kelloholm, Kirkconnel, DG4 6RX T: 01659 67206 F: 01659 66052

Kirkintilloch and Lennoxtown - Council Office, 21 Southbank Road, Kirkintilloch, G66 1NH T: 0141 776 2109 E: rab.macaulay@eastdunbarton.gov.uk

Kirkmabreck - The Bogue, Creetowm, Newton Stewart, DG8 7JW T: 01671 820266

Kirriemuir - Contact Arbroath,

Lairg - The Service Point, Main Street, Lairg, Sutherland IV27 4DB T: 01549 402588

Langholm - Town Hall, Langholm, DG13 0JQ T: 01387 380255 F: 01387 81142

Larbert - The Register Office, 318 Main Street, Stenhousemuir, FK5 3BE T: 01324 503580 F: 01324 503581

Larkhall - Council Office, 55 Victoria Street, Larkhall, ML9 2BN T: 01698 882864

Latherton - Post Office, Latheron, KW5 6DG T: 01593 741201

Laurencekirk - Royal Bank Buildings, Laurencekirk, AB30 1AF T: 01561 377245 F: 01561 378020

Leadhills - Operating from Lanark

Lerwick - County Buildings, Lerwick, Shetland ZE1 0HD T: 01595 744562 E: registrar@sic.shetland.gov.uk

Lesmahagow - The Register Office, 40/42 Abbeygreen, Lesmahagow, ML11 0EQ T: 01555 893812

Loch Duich - Operating from Lochalsh

Lochalsh - Hamilton House, Plock Road, Kyle, IV40 8BL E: joyce.smith@highland.gov.uk

Lochbroom and Coigach - Locality Office, North Road, Ullapool, IV26 2XL T: 01854 613900 E: doreen.macleod@highland.gov.uk

Lochcarron and Shieldaig - Lochcarron Service Point, Main Street, Lochcarron, IV54 8YB T: 01520 722241 E: fiona.sproule@highland.gov.uk

Lochgilphead - Dairiada House, Lochnell Street, Lochgilphead, PA31 8ST T: 01546 604511 E: isabella.soudan@argyll-bute.gov.uk

Lochgoilhead - Dervaig, Lettermay, Lochgoilhead, PA24 8AE T: 01301 703306

Lonforgan - The Register Office, 8 Norval Place, Longforgan, Dundee, DD2 5ER T: 01382 360283

Mauchline - The Register Office, 2 The Cross, Mauchline, Ayrshire KA5 5DA T: 01290 550231 F: 01290 551991

Melrose - Ormiston Institute, Market Square, Melrose, TD6 9PN T: 01896 823114 E: jnorman@scotborders.gsx.gov.uk

Mid and South Yell - Schoolhouse, Ulsta, Yell, ZE2 9BD T: 01957 722260

Midlothian Dalkeith Register Office, 2-4 Buccleuch Street, Dalkeith EH22 1HA T: 0131 271 3281 E: dkregistrars@midlothian.gov.uk

Milnathort - Rowallan, 21 Church Street, Milnathort, KY13 9XH T: 01577 862536

Mochrum - 13 South Street, 85 Main Street, Port William, Newton Stewart, Dumfries DG8 9SH T: 01988 700741 E: francess@dumgal.gov.uk

Montrose - The Register Office, 51 John Street, Montrose, Angus DD10 8LZ T: 01674 672351 E: regmontrose@angus.gov.uk

Moray Council

Elgin inc Tomintoul The Register Office, 240 High Street, Elgin, IV30 1BA T: 01343 554600 F: 01343 554644 E: heather.grieg@moray.gov.uk

Morayshire

Keith and Upper Speyside Area Office, Mid Street, Keith, AB55 5BJ T: 01542 885525 F: 01542 885522 E: keith.registrar@chief.moray.gov.uk

Morvern - The Register Office, Dungrianach, Lochaline, Morvern, PA34 5XT T: 01961 421662

Motherwell and Wishaw - Civic Centre, Windmillhill Street, Motherwell, ML1 1TW T: 01698 302206 E: muiris@northlan.gov.uk

Muckhart and Glendevon - Operating from Alloa, T: 01259 723850

Muirkirk - 44 Main Street, Muirkirk, KA18 3RD T: 01290 661227 E: muirkirk@east-ayrshire.gov.uk

Nairn - The Court House, Nairn, IV12 4AU T: 01667 458500 E: anthea.lindsay@highland.gov.uk

New Cumnock - Town Hall, The Castle, New Cumnock, KA18 4AN T: 01290 338214

New Kilpatrick - Council Office, 38 Roman Road, Bearsden, G61 2SH T: 0141 942 2352/3

Newton Stewart Area - McMillan Hall, Dashwood Square, Newton Stewart, DG8 6EQ T: 01671 404187 E: marm@dumgal.gov.uk

North Ayrshire

Isle of Arran District Council Office, Lamlash, Isle Of Arran KA27 8LB T: 01770 600338 F: 01770 600028 E: ladamson@north-ayrshire.gov.uk

Largs Moorburn, 24 Greenock Road, Largs, KA30 8NE T: 01475 676552 E: gmcginty@north-ayrshire.gov.uk W: www.north-ayrshire.gov.uk

Saltcoats The Register Office, 45 Ardrossan Road, Saltcoats, KA21 5BS T: 01294 463312 F: 01294 604868 E: jkimmett@north-ayrshire.gov.uk W: www.north-ayrshire.gov.uk

West Kilbride Kirktonhall, 1 Glen Road, West Kilbride, KA23 9BL T: 01294 823569 F: 01294 823569 E: jkimmett@north-ayrshire.gov.uk W: www.north-ayrshire.gov.uk

North Ayrshire

Cumbrae Operating from Largs, Largs, T: 01475 674521 F: 01475 687304 E: gmcginty@north-ayrshire.gov.uk W: www.north-ayrshire.gov.uk

North Berwick - The Register Office, 2 Quality Street, North Berwick, EH39 4HW T: 01620 893957 E: ddoman@eastlothian.gov.uk

North Lanarkshire

Airdrie Area Registration Office, 37 Alexander Street, Airdrie, ML6 0BA T: 01236 758080 F: 01236 758088 E: registrars-airdrie@northlan.gov.uk

Coatbridge The Register Office, 183 Main Street, Coatbridge, ML5 3HH T: 01236 812647 F: 01236 812643 E: registrars-coatbridge@northlan.gov.uk W: www.northlan.gov.uk

Kilsyth Health Centre, Burngreen Park, Kilsyth, G65 0HU T: 01236 826813

Shotts Council Offices, 106 Station Road, Shotts, ML7 4BH T: 01501 824740

North Ronaldsay - Hooking, North Ronaldsay, Orkney KW17 2BE T: 01857 633257

North Uist - Fairview, Lochmaddy, North Uist, HS6 5AW T: 01876 500239

Oban - Lorn House, Albany Street, Oban, PA34 4AW T: 01631 567930 F: 01631 570379 E: gemma.cummins@argyll-bute.gov.uk

Old Cumnock - Council Office Millbank, 14 Lugar Street, Cummock, KA18 1AB T: 01290 420666 F: 01290 426164

Old Kilpatrick - Council Offices, Rosebery Place, Clydebank, G81 1TG T: 01389 738770 F: 01389 738775

Oldmeldrum - operating from Inverurie

Orkney

Birsay Sandveien, Dounby, Orkney, KW17 2HS T: 01856 771226

Orphir The Bu, Orphir, Kirkwall, KW17 2RD T: 01856 811319

Orkney Island

Sanday The Register Office, Hyndhover, Sanday, Orkney KW17 2BA T: 01856 600441

Firth & Stenness The Register Office, Langbigging, Stenness, Orkney KW16 3LB T: 01856 850320

Flotta Post Office, Flotta , Stromness, Orkney KW16 3NP T: 01856 701252

Harray New Breckan, Harray, Orkney KW17 2JR T: 01856 771233

Holm and Paplay The Register Office, Netherbreck , Holm, Orkney KW17 2RX T: 01856 781231

Hoy Laundry House, Melsetter, Longhope, Orkney KW16 3NZ T: 01856 791337

Kirkwall Council Offices, School Place, Kirkwall, Orkney KW15 1NY T: 01856 873535 F: 01856 873319 E: chief.registrar@orkney.gov.uk W: www.orkney.gov.uk

Shapinsay The Register Office, Girnigoe, Shapinsay, Orkney KW17 2EB T: 01856 711256 E: jean@girnigoe.f9.co.uk W: www.visitorkney.com/accommodation/girnigoe

Stromness The Register Office, Ferry Terminal Building, Ferry Road, Stromness, Orkney KW16 3AE T: 01856 850854

Westray Myrtle Cottage, Pierowall, Westray, Orkney KW17 2DH T: 01857 677278

Papa Westray - Bewan, Papa Westray, Orkney KW17 2BU T: 01857 644245

Penicuik and Glencorse - The Registry Office, 33 High Street, Penicuik, EH26 8HS T: 01968 672281 F: 01968 679547

Perth & Kinross

Blair Athol Operating from Pitlochry,

Dunkeld Operating from Perth, Perth, PH8 0AH T: 01738 475121 F: 01738 444133 E: ringham@pkc.gov.uk

Kinross Kinross Area Office, 21/25 High Street, Kinross, KY13 8AP T: 01577 867602

Logierait Operating from Pitlochry,

Perth The Register Office, 3 High Street, Perth, PH1 5JS T: 01738 475122 F: 01738 444133 E: ringham@pkc.gov.uk

Perth & Kinross - Aberfeldy Duntaggart, Crieff Road, Aberfeldy, PH15 2BJ T: 01887 829218

Pitlochry District Area Office, 26 Atholl Road, Pitlochry, PH16 5BX T: 01796 472323 F: 01796 474226

Polmont and Muiravonside - Council Offices, Redding Road, Brightons, Falkirk, FK2 0HG T: 01324 503990

Portree and Raasay - Registrars Office, King's House, The Green, Portree, IV51 9BS T: 01478 613277 F: 01478 613277 E: meg.gillies@highland.gov.uk

Portsoy - The Register Office, 2 Main Street, Portsoy, Banffshire AB45 2RT T: 01261 842510 F: 01261 842510

Prestonpans - Aldhammer House, High Street, Prestonpans, EH32 9SH T: 01875 810232 F: 01875 814921 E: sross@eastlothian.gov.uk

Prestwick - The Register Office, 2 The Cross, Prestwick, KA9 1AJ T: 01292 671666

Rannoch and Foss - Altdruidhe Cottage, Kinloch-rannoch, Pitlochry, PH17 2QJ T: 01882 632208

Renfrew - Town Hall, Renfrew, PA4 8PF T: 0141 886 3589

Renfrewshire

Paisley Registration Office, 1 Cotton Street, Paisley, PA1 1BU T: 0141 840 3388 F: 0141 840 3377 E: marion.mcglynn@refrewshire.gov.uk W: www.renfrewshire.gov.uk

Rousay, Egilsay and Wyre - Braehead , Rousay, Kirkwall, Orkney KW17 2PT T: 01856 821222

Sanquhar - Council Offices, 100 High Street, Sanquhar, DG4 6DZ T: 01659 50697

Scottish Borders

Chirnside Operating from , 8 Newton Street, Duns, TD11 3XL T: 01361 882600 E: mdick@scotborders.gsx.gov.uk

Galashiels Library Buildings, Lawyers Brae, Galashiels, TD1 3JQ T: 01896 752822 E: eczajka2@scotborders.gsx.gov.uk

Lauder The Old Jail, Mid Row, Lauder, TD2 6SZ T: 01578 722795 E: bgoldie@scotborders.gsx.gov.uk

Peebles Chambers Institute, High Street, Peebles, EH45 8AG T: 01721 723817 F: 01721 723817 E: showitt@scotborders.gsx.gov.uk

Selkirk Municipal Buildings, High Street, Selkirk, TD7 4JX T: 01750 23104 E: jstock@scotborders.gsx.gov.uk

West Linton Council Office, West Linton, Borders EH46 7ED T: 01968 660267 E: ptodd@scotborders.gsx.gov.uk

Scourie Operating from, Assynt, Lochinver, Lairg IV27 4TD T: 01571 844201

Shetland

Burra Isles Roadside, Hannavoe, Lerwick, Shetland ZE2 9LA T: 01595 859201

Sandness The Register Office, 13 Melby, Sandness, Shetland ZE2 9PL T: 01595 870257

Tingwall Vindas, Laxfirth, Tingwall, Shetland ZE2 9SG T: 01595 840450

Whiteness and Weisdale Vista, Whiteness, Shetland ZE2 9LJ T: 01595 830332

Fair Isle Field, Fair Isle, Shetland ZE2 9JU T: 01595 760224

Sandsting and Aithsting The Register Office, Modesty, West Burrafirth, Aithsting, Shetland ZE2 9NT T: 01595 809428

Fetlar Lower Toft Funzie, Fetlar, Shetland ZE2 9DJ T: 01957 733273

Foula Magdala, Foula, Shetland ZE2 9PN T: 01595 753236

Lunnasting Vidlin Farm, Vidlin, Shetland ZE2 9QB T: 01806 577204

Nesting Laxfirth Brettabister, North Nesting, Shetland ZE2 9PR T: 01595 890260

North Yell Breckon, Cullivoe, Yell, ZE2 9DD T: 01957 744244 F: 01957 744352

Northmaven Uradell, Eshaness, Shetland ZE2 9RS T: 01806 503362

Papa Stour North House, Papa Stour, Shetland ZE2 9PW T: 01595 873238

Sandwick The Register Office, Lee Cottage, Sandwick, Stromness, Shetland KW16 3JF T: 01856 841518

Sandwick and Cunningsbur The Register Office, Pytaslee Leebitton, Sandwick, Shetland ZE2 9HP T: 01950 431367

Walls Victoria Cottage, Walls, Lerwick, Shetland ZE2 9PD T: 01595 809478

Whalsay Conamore, Brough, Whalsay, Shetland ZE2 9AL T: 01806 566544

Whalsay-Skerries Fairview, East Isle, Skerries, Lerwick ZE2 9AR T: 01806 515255

Slamannan - Operating from Falkirk

South Ayrshire

Girvan, Barrhill, Barr, Dailly, Colmonell, Ballantrae Registration Office, 22 Dalrymple Street, Girvan, KA26 9AE T: 01465 712894 F: 01465 715576 E: girvan.registrars@south-ayrshire.gov.uk

Maybole, Crosshill, Dunure, Kirkmichael, Kirkoswald, Straiton Council Office, 64 High Street, Maybole, KA19 7BZ T: 01655 882124 E: maybole.registrars@south-ayrshire.gov.uk

South Lanarkshire

Cambuslang Council Office, 6 Glasgow Road, Cambuslang, G72 7BW T: 0141 641 9605 F: 0141 641 8542 E: registration@southlanarkshire.gov.uk W: www.southlanarkshire.gov.uk

Carluke The Register Office, 9 Kirkton Street, Carluke, ML8 4AB T: 01555 777844 F: 01555 773721 E: catherine.watson@southlanarkshire.gov.uk

Hamilton The Register Office, 21 Beckford Street, Hamilton,

Lanarkshire ML3 0BT T: 01698 454213 F: 01698 455746 E: jean.lavelle@southlanarkshire.gov.uk

Lanark The Register Office, South Vennel, Lanark, ML11 7JT T: 01555 673261

Rutherglen 1st Floor, 169 Main Street, Rutherglen, G73 2HJ T: 0141 613 5332 F: 0141 613 5335 E: wndy.cranston@southlanarkshire.gov.uk

South Ronaldsay - The Register Office, West Cara, Grimness, South Ronaldsay, KW17 2TH T: 01856 831509

Stirling

Callander The Register Office, 1 South Church Street, Callander, FK17 8BN T: 01877 330166

Dunblane Municipal Buildings, Dunblane, FK15 0AG T: 01786 823300 E: muirm@stirling.gov.uk

Killin 8 Lyon Villas, Killin, FK21 8TF T: 01567 820655

Stirling Municipal Buildings, 8 - 10 Corn Exchange Road, Stirling, FK8 2HU T: 01786 432343 F: 01786 432056 E: registrar@stirling.gov.uk

Strathendrick Balfron Local Office, 32 Buchanan Street, Balfron, G63 0TR T: 01360 440315

Strathaven - Royal Bank of Scotland Buildings, 34 Common Green, Strathaven, ML10 6AQ T: 01357 520316

Stronsay - The Register Office, Strynie, Stronsay, Kirkwall, Orkney KW17 2AR T: 01857 616239

Tarbat - The Bungalow, Chaplehill, Portmahomack, Portmahom Tain, IV20 1XJ T: 01862 871328

Tarbert - Argyll House, School Road, Tarbert, PA29 6UJ T: 01880 820374

Tayinloan - Bridge House, Tayinloan, Tarbert, PA29 6XG T: 01583 441239

Tranent - The Register Office, 8 Civic Square, Tranent, EH33 1LH T: 01875 610278 F: 01875 615420 E: bmcnaught@eastlothian.gov.uk

Troon - Municipal Buildings, 8 South Beach, Troon, KA10 6EF T: 01292 313555 F: 01292 318009

Uig (Lewis) - The Register Office, 10 Valtos, Uig, Lewis, HS2 9HR T: 01851 672213

Uig(Skye) (Inverness) - The Register Office, 3 Ellishadder, Staffin, Portree, IV51 9JE T: 01470 562303

Unst - New Hoose, Baltasound, Unst, ZE2 9DX T: 01957 711348

Wanlockhead - Operating from Sanquhar, T: 01659 74287

West Dunbartonshire

Vale of Leven The Register Office, 77 Bank Street, Alexandria, West Dunbartonshire G83 0LE T: 01389 608980 F: 01389 608982 E: brenda.wilson@west-dunbarton.gov.uk

West Lothian - (Bathgate) The Register Office, 76 Mid Street, Bathgate, West Lothian EH48 1QD T: 01506 776192 F: 01506 776194 E: agnesmcconnell@westlothian.gov.uk

West Lothian (Linlithgow) The Register Office, High Street, Linlithgow, EH49 7EZ T: 01506 775373 F: 01506 775374 E: joyce.duncan@westlothian.gov.uk

West Lothian (East Calder) - East Calder Library, 200 Main Street, East Calder, EH53 0EJ T: 01506 884680 F: 01506 883944 E: gillian.downie@wled.org.uk

West Lothian (Livingston) - Lammermuir House, Owen Square, Avondale, Livingston, West Lothian EH54 6PW T: 01506 773754 E: frances.kane@westlothian.gov.uk

West Lothian (Uphall) - Strathbrock Partnership, 189a West Main Street, Broxburn, West Lothian EH52 5LH T: 01506 775509 E: laura.clarke@westlothian.gov.uk

West Lothian (West Calder) - The Register Office, 24 - 26 Main Street, West Calder, West Lothian EH55 8DR T: 01506 874704 E: gary.bandoo@westlothian.gov.uk

West Lothian (Whitburn) - The Register Office, 5 East Main Street, Whitburn, West Lothian EH47 0RA T: 01501 678005 F: 01506 678085 E: agnes.mcconnell@westlothian.gov.uk

Western Ardnamurchan - Operating from Strontian, Acharacle, PH36 4HY T: 01967 402037

Ireland

Registration Records in The Republic of Ireland Oifig An Ard-Chlaraitheora (General Register Office) Joyce House, 8/11 Lombard Street East, Dublin, 2. Postal address: General Register Office, Government Offices,, Convent Road, Roscommon, Ireland T: +353 (0) 90 6632900 F: +353 (0) 90 6632999 W: www.groireland.ie/research

Information from Probate records can provide vital pieces of the genealogical puzzle. Although often not as useful as records of births, marriages and deaths, which can evidence crucial links to previous generations, they can provide evidence of relatedness within generations, and often contain fascinating insights into the financial affairs of people in times past.

Probate is a process whereby some person or persons, usually the executor(s) of a Will if there was one, or one or more of the next-of-kin if there was no Will, are appointed in law to administer the estate of someone who has died. This is usually only necessary if the deceased person left fairly substantial assets, so don't expect to find any Probate record relating to the estate of a person who had little or no estate of their own. The Probate concept of 'estate' refers just to assets held in the sole name of the person who has died, and so Probate isn't necessary for the release of assets held jointly with another person. When an application for Probate is made, any Will that the deceased person left must be submitted to the Probate Registry. The Will, if judged to be valid, is thereafter kept on file, and it is normally possible for anyone to obtain a copy of it. There are exceptions, however, such as the Wills of members of the Royal family. The important point is that Wills are available from the Probate Registries only as a by-product of the Probate process: if Probate wasn't needed, then the Probate Registries have no record of the estate at all.

You should bear in mind that the Probate record, if any, will be dated some time after the date of death of the person concerned, so start searching from the year of death, or the year in which you think the person died. You should normally expect to find the Probate record within the first year or two after the date of death, and, if you have not found it within three, you can usually assume that Probate wasn't necessary. However, in a very small number of cases, Probate is granted many years after the person in question died. Take a tip from the professionals: if you don't find a probate record within the first few years, the next most likely time to search is the year in which their heir(s) died. This is because unadministered estate is most likely to come to light at that time. How far you want to go with the search will probably depend on how crucial the person in question is to your research, but there is as yet no shortcut: you will have to search the index for each year separately.

Control of Probate record-keeping passed from the Church to the state in 1858, at which point the records were unified into one Calendar index. These indexes, which summarise all Probate grants for England and Wales during a given year, act as a table of contents for the vast store of records held by the Probate Registries. If the subject of your research died before 1858, it will be more difficult to trace their Will. However, if they were very wealthy or owned a lot of land, consult the indexes of the Prerogative Court of Canterbury (PCC) first, and then those of the lesser ecclesiastical courts of the region in which they lived. PCC records are held by the Family Records Centre in London (Tel: (020) 8392 5300), but records of the lesser ecclesiastical Probate courts are highly dispersed. Try the local authority archives, such as public libraries and County Record Offices of the appropriate region, and also any local historical research institutes. Major ecclesiastical centres are also likely to have their own archives.

The table below lists the Calendar indexes held by the various Probate Registries in England and Wales. You can usually call in to consult the indexes, but check with the Registry concerned first, especially if you intend to travel any distance. Probate grants for each year are listed alphabetically by surname. The crucial parts of the Probate record are the Grant type, which is usually 'Probate', 'Administration' or 'Administration with Will', the issuing Registry, and the grant issue date. They are normally written in sequence towards the end of the index entry, but the older books give the grant date first and highlight the issuing Registry in

the text of the entry. The grant type can be inferred from the text, but note that the indexes prior to 1871 listed the 'Administration' grants in a separate part of the book from the 'Probate' and 'Administration with Will' grants, so be sure to search in both places for years prior to this. In addition, there may be a handwritten number next to entries for Wills proved in the Principal Probate Registry (London) between 1858 and 1930. This is the Folio number, which is used by the Probate Registries when obtaining copies of the Will. Always make a note of this if applicable.

If the grant type is 'Administration', this tells you that the person in question did not leave a valid Will. However, the Probate Registries can still supply a copy of the grant, which is the document naming the person appointed in law as the administrator of the estate. This can provide genealogical information, especially in older grants where the relationship of the applicant to the deceased was stated. It also gives the value of the estate, although in most cases this is stated as 'not exceeding' a certain figure rather than quoting an exact amount. In fact, the Probate record contains very little information about the estate at all, and no information about its composition. Don't expect to find inventories on file for records after 1858, although they sometimes form part of the Probate record prior to this.

In many cases you can save a lot of time and money by making the search yourself, but there is a postal service by which a search is made on your behalf for a period of four years. There is a fee of £5 for this, but this includes copies of the Will and/or grant if a record is found. It also gives you the benefit of the experience of Probate staff, for instance in knowing when to search and judging under which name the record is likely to be listed. If you want the Probate Registry to conduct a search for a period longer than the standard four years, there is an additional fee of £3 for each 4-year period after the first four. Thus, an 8-year search will cost £8, a 12-year search £11, and so on.

If you want to make a postal search, contact
The Postal Searches and Copies Department, York Probate Sub-Registry, 1st Floor, Castle Chambers, Clifford Street, York YO1 9RG UK Tel: +44 (1904) 666777 Fax: +44 (1904) 666776

Applications for searches must be made in writing, and give the full name, last known address and date of death of the person concerned. A search can normally be made using less detail, but if the date of death is not known, you must state the year from which you want the search to be made, or give some other evidence that might indicate when the person died. If

you have information about legal actions related to Probate or the disposition of assets, include that on your application. Many people find it convenient to order copies in this way even if they have already made a search of the Probate indexes and located a record relating to the subject of their research, but if this is the case, please include the grant type, issuing Registry and grant issue date on your application, as well as the Folio number if applicable (see above) as this can speed up the supply of copies considerably. The fee should be payable to "HMCS", and if it is paid from abroad, must be made by International Money Order or bank draft, payable through a United Kingdom bank and

made out in £ sterling. If you are applying for a search as well, you can request a search of any length, and fees for this are outlined above.

The records referred to here relate only to estates in England and Wales.

Most Registries will have had indexes dating back to 1858, but are not required to keep them for more than fifty years. Usually, the older indexes will have been donated to local authority archives. Contact your local public library or County/City Record Office to see what Probate records they have. If you know of any historical research institute in your area, find out if they have any Probate records.

Please note that, since the York Probate Registry serves as a national centre for postal requests for searches and copies, it is not possible to inspect the Probate indexes in person there. The Service has undergone a process of computerisation, but as yet this covers only recently-issued grants, which will be of limited interest to genealogists. However, anyone who is interested in checking up on grants since 1996 can search the Probate Service database themselves. To date, workstations for public use have been installed at the Principal Probate Registry and Manchester District Probate Registry. The Postal Searches and Copies Department at York is also completing a long period of computerisation, which should see a much-improved service to family history researchers, with clearer and more comprehensive information and quicker supply of documents.
This information is based on details supplied by the Probate Service. The details are liable to change without notice. Always telephone the Registry before visiting, to check opening times and the availability of records. While every effort is made to ensure the accuracy of these details, the Probate Service cannot be held responsible for any consequence of errors.

Please check our website at www.courtservice.gov.uk before applying for searches or copy documents by post.

Probate Registries & Sub-Registries

Principal Probate Registry (020) 7947 6939 First Avenue House, 42-49 High Holborn, London WC1
Probate Registry of Wales - Cardiff (029) 2037 6479 PO Box 474, 2 Park Street, Cardiff CF1 1ET
Bangor Probate Sub-Registry (01248) 362410 Council Offices, FFord, Bangor LL57 1DT
Birmingham District Probate Registry (0121) 681 3400 The Priory Courts, 33 Bull Street, Birmingham B4 6DU
Bodmin Probate Sub-Registry (01208) 72279 Market Street, Bodmin PL31 2JW
Brighton District Probate Registry (01273) 573510 William Street, Brighton BN2 2LG
Bristol District Probate Registry (0117) 927 3915 Ground Floor, The Crescent Centre, Temple Back, Bristol BS1 6EP
Carlisle Probate Sub- Registry (01228) 521751 Courts of Justice, Earl Street, Carlisle CA1 1DJ
Carmarthen Probate Sub-Registry (01267) 242560 14 King Street, Carmarthen SA31 1BL
Chester Probate Sub-Registry (01244) 345082 5th Floor, Hamilton House, Hamilton Place, Chester CH1 2DA
Exeter Probate Sub-Registry (01392) 415370 2nd Floor, Exeter Crown & County Courts, Southernhay Gardens, Exeter EX1 1UH
Gloucester Probate Sub-Registry (01452) 834966 2nd Floor, Combined Court Building, Kimbrose Way, Gloucester GL1 2DG
Ipswich District Probate Registry (01473) 284260 Ground Floor, 8 Arcade Street, Ipswich IP1 1EJ
Lancaster Probate Sub-Registry (01524) 36625 Mitre House, Church St, Lancaster LA1 1HE
Leeds District Probate Registry (0113) 386 3540 3rd Floor, Coronet House, Queen Street, Leeds LS1 2BA
Leicester Probate Sub-Registry (0116) 285 3380 Crown Court Building, 90 Wellington St, Leicester LE1 6HG

Lincoln Probate Sub-Registry (01522) 523648 360 High Street, Lincoln LN5 7PS
Liverpool District Probate Registry (0151) 236 8264 Queen Elizabeth II Law Courts, Derby Square, Liverpool L2 1XA
Maidstone Probate Sub-Registry (01622) 202048 The Law Courts, Barker Road, Maidstone ME16 8EQ
Manchester District Probate Registry (0161) 837 6070 9th Floor, Astley House, 23 Quay St, Manchester M3 4AT
Middlesbrough Probate Sub-Registry (01642) 340001 Teesside Combined Court Centre, Russell Street, Middlesbrough TS1 2AE
Newcastle-upon-Tyne District Probate Registry (0191) 261 8383 2nd Floor, Plummer House, Croft Street, Newcastle-upon-Tyne NE1 6NP
Norwich Probate Sub-Regsitry (01603) 728267 Combined Court Building, The Law Courts, Bishopgate, Norwich NR3 1UR
Nottingham Probate Sub-Registry (0115) 941 4288 Butt Dyke House, Park Row, Nottingham NG1 6GR
Oxford District Probate Registry (01865) 793055 Combined Court Building, St.Aldates, Oxford OX1 1LY
Peterborough Probate Sub-Registry (01733) 562802 1st Floor, Crown Building, Rivergate, Peterborough PE1 1EJ
Sheffield Probate Sub-Registry (0114) 281 2596 PO Box 832, The Law Courts, 50 West Bar Sheffield S3 8YR
Stoke-on-Trent Probate Sub-Registry (01782) 854065 Combined Court Centre, Bethesda Street, Hanley, Stoke-on-Trent ST1 3BP
Winchester District Probate Registry (01962) 897029 4th Floor, Cromwell House, Andover Road, Winchester SO23 7EW
York Probate Sub-Registry, 1st Floor, Castle Chambers, Clifford Street, York YO1 9RG UK Tel: +44 (1904) 666777 Fax: +44 (1904) 666776

Avon
Bristol General Cemetery Co East Lodge, Bath Rd, Arnos Vale, Bristol, Avon BS4 3EW T: 0117 971 3294
Canford Crematorium & Cemetery Canford Lane, Westbury On Trym, Bristol, Avon BS9 3PQ T: 0117 903 8280 F: 0117 903 8287
Cemetery of Holy Souls Bath Rd, Bristol, Avon BS4 3EW T: 0117 977 2386
Haycombe Crematorium & Cemetery Whiteway Rd, Bath, Avon BA2 2RQ T: 01225 423682
South Bristol Crematorium & Cemetery Bridgwater Rd, Bristol, Avon BS13 7AS T: 0117 963 4141
Westerleigh Crematorium Westerleigh Rd, Westerleigh, Bristol, Avon BS37 8QP T: 0117 937 4619
Weston Super Mare Crematorium Ebdon Rd, Worle, Weston-Super-Mare, Avon BS22 9NY T: 01934 511717
Bedfordshire
Church Burial Ground 26 Crawley Green Rd, Luton, Bedfordshire LU2 0QX T: 01582 722874 W: www.stmarysluton.org
Dunstable Cemetery West St, Dunstable, Bedfordshire LU6 1PB T: 01582 662772
Luton Crematorium The Vale, Butterfield Green Road, Stopsley, Luton, Bedfordshire LU2 8DD T: 01582 723700 F: 01582 723700
Luton General Cemetery Rothesay Rd, Luton, Bedfordshire LU1 1QX T: 01582 727480
Norse Rd Crematorium 104 Norse Rd, Bedford, Bedfordshire MK41 0RL T: 01234 353701
Bedfordshire
Kempston Cemetery Cemetery Lodge, 2 Green End Rd, Kempston, Bedford, Bedfordshire MK43 8RJ T: 01234 851823
Berkshire
Easthampstead Park Cemetry & Crematorium Nine Mile Ride, Wokingham, Berkshire RG40 3DW T: 01344 420314
Henley Road Cemetery & Reading Crematorium All Hallows Road, Henley Road, Caversham, Reading RG4 5LP T: 0118 947 2433
Larges Lane Cemetery Larges Lane, Bracknell, Berkshire RG12 9AL T: 01344 450665
Newbury Cemetery Shaw Hill, Shaw Fields, Shaw, Newbury, Berkshire RG14 2EQ T: 01635 40096
Slough Cemetery & Crematorium Stoke Rd, Slough, Berkshire SL2 5AX T: 01753 523127 (Cemetery) F: 01753 520702 (Crematorium) E: sloughcrem@hotmail.com W: www.slough.gov.uk
Bristol
South Bristol Crematorium & Cemetery Bridgwater Rd, Bedminster Down, Bristol, BS13 7AS T: 0117 903 8330 F: 0117 903 8337
Buckinghamshire
Chilterns Crematorium Whielden Lane, Winchmore Hill, Amersham, Buckinghamshire HP7 0ND T: 01494 724263
Crownhill Crematorium Dansteed Way, Crownhill, Milton Keynes, Buckinghamshire T: 01908 568112
Cambridgeshire
American Military Cemetery Madingley Rd, Coton, Cambridge, Cambridgeshire CB3 7PH T: 01954 210350 F: 01954 211130 E: Cambridge.Cemetery@ambc-er.org W: www.ambc.gov
Cambridge City Crematorium Huntingdon Rd, Girton, Cambridge, Cambridgeshire CB3 0LT T: 01954 780681
City of Ely Council Ely Cemetery, Beech Lane, Ely, Cambridgeshire CB7 4QZ T: 01353 669659
Marholm Crematorium Mowbray Rd, Peterborough, Cambridgeshire PE6 7JE T: 01733 262639
Cheshire
Altrincham Cemetery Hale Rd, Altrincham, Cheshire WA14 2EW T: 0161 980 4441
Altrincham Crematorium White House Lane, Dunham Massey, Altrincham, Cheshire WA14 5RH T: 0161 928 7771
Chester Cemeteries & Crematorium Blacon Avenue, Blacon, Chester, Cheshire CH1 5BB T: 01244 372428
Dukinfield Crematorium Hall Green Rd, Dukinfield, Cheshire SK16 4EP T: 0161 330 1901
Macclesfield Cemetery Cemetery Lodge, 87 Prestbury Rd, Macclesfield, Cheshire SK10 3BU T: 01625 422330
Middlewich Cemetery 12 Chester Rd, Middlewich, Cheshire CW10 9ET T: 01606 737101
Overleigh Rd Cemetery The Lodge, Overleigh Rd, Chester, Cheshire CH4 7HW T: 01244 682529
Walton Lea Crematorium Chester Rd, Higher Walton, Warrington, Cheshire WA4 6TB T: 01925 267731
Widnes Cemetery & Crematorium Birchfield Rd, Widnes, Cheshire WA8 9EE T: 0151 471 7332
Cleveland
Teesside Crematorium Acklam Rd, Middlesbrough, Cleveland TS5 7HE T: 01642 817725 F: 01642 852424 E: peter_gitsham@middlesbrough.gov.uk W: www.middlesbrough.gov.uk

Cornwall
Glynn Valley Crematorium Turfdown Rd, Fletchers Bridge, Bodmin, Cornwall PL30 4AU T: 01208 73858
Penmount Crematorium Penmount, Truro, Cornwall TR4 9AA T: 01872 272871 E: mail@penmount-crematorium.org.uk W: www.penmount-crematorium.org.uk

County Durham
Birtley Cemetery & Crematorium Windsor Rd, Birtley, Chester Le Street, County Durham DH3 1PQ T: 0191 4102381
Chester Le Street Cemetery Chester Le Street District Council Civic Centre, Newcastle Rd, Chester Le Street DH3 3UT T: 0191 3872117
Horden Parish Council Horden Cemetery Lodge, Thorpe Rd, Horden, Peterlee, County Durham SR8 4TP T: 0191 5863870
Mountsett Crematorium Ewehurst Rd, Dipton, Stanley, County Durham DH9 0HN T: 01207 570255
Murton Parish Council Cemetery Lodge, Church Lane, Murton, Seaham, County Durham SR7 9RD T: 0191 5263973
Newton Aycliffe Cemetery Stephenson Way, Newton Aycliffe, County Durham DL5 7DF T: 01325 312861
Princess Road Cemetery Princess Rd, Seaham, County Durham SR7 7TD T: 0191 5812943
Trimdon Foundry Parish Council Cemetary Lodge, Thornley Rd, Trimdon Station, County Durham TS29 6NX T: 01429 880592
Trimdon Parish Council Cemetery Lodge, Northside, Trimdon Grange, Trimdon Station TS29 6HN T: 01429 880538
Wear Valley District Council Cemetery Lodge, South Church Rd, Bishop Auckland, County Durham DL14 7NA T: 01388 603396
Cumbria
Carlisle Cemetery Richardson St, Carlisle, Cumbria CA2 6AL T: 01228 625310 F: 01228 625313 E: junec@carlisle-city.gov.uk
Penrith Cemetery Beacon Edge, Penrith, Cumbria CA11 7RZ T: 01768 862152
Wigton Burial Joint Committee Cemetery House, Station Hill, Wigton, Cumbria CA7 9BN T: 016973 42442
Derbyshire
Castle Donington Parish Council Cemetery House, The Barroon, Castle Donington, Derby, Derbyshire DE74 2PF T: 01332 810202
Chesterfield & District Council Crematorium Chesterfield Rd, Brimington, Chesterfield S43 1AU T: 01246 345888 F: 01246 345889
Clay Cross Cemetery Cemetery Rd, Danesmoor, Chesterfield, Derbyshire S45 9RL T: 01246 863225
Dronfield Cemetery Cemetery Lodge, 42 Cemetery Rd, Dronfield, Derbyshire S18 1XY T: 01246 412373
Glossop Cemetery Arundel House, Cemetery Rd, Glossop, Derbyshire SK13 7QG T: 01457 852269
Markeaton Crematorium Markeaton Lane, Derby, Derbyshire DE22 4NH T: 01332 341012 F: 01332 331273
Melbourne Cemetery Pack Horse Rd, Melbourne, Derby, Derbyshire DE73 1BZ T: 01332 863369
Shirebrook Town Council Common Lane, Shirebrook, Mansfield, Nottinghamshire NG20 8PA T: 01623 742509
Devon
Drake Memorial Park Ltd The Haye Rd, Plympton, Plymouth, Devon PL7 1UQ T: 01752 337937
Exeter & Devon Crematorium Topsham Rd, Exeter, Devon EX2 6EU T: 01392 496333
Ford Park Cemetery Trust Ford Park Rd, Plymouth PL4 6NT T: 01752 665442 E: trustees@ford-park-cemetery.org W: www.ford-park-cemetery.org
Littleham Church Yard Littleham Village, Littleham, Exmouth, Devon EX8 2RQ T: 01395 223379
Mole Valley Green Burial Ground Woodhouse Farm, Queens Nympton, South Molton, Devon EX36 4JH T: 01769 574512 F: 01769 574512 E: woodhouse.org.farm@farming.co.uk
North Devon Crematorium Old Torrington Rd, Barnstaple, Devon EX31 3NW T: 01271 345431
Tavistock Cemetery Cemetery Office, Plymouth Rd, Tavistock, Devon PL19 8BY T: 01822 612799 F: 01822 618300 E: tavistocktc@aol.com W: www.tavistock.gov.uk
Torquay Crematorium & Cemetery Hele Rd, Torquay, Devon TQ2 7QG T: 01803 327768
Dorset
Dorchester Cemetery Office 31a Weymouth Avenue, Dorchester, Dorset DT1 2EN T: 01305 263900
Parkstone Cemetery 134 Pottery Rd, Parkstone, Poole, Dorset BH14 8RD T: 01202 741104
Poole Cemetery Dorchester Rd, Oakdale, Poole BH15 3RZ T: 01202 741106
Poole Crematorium Gravel Hill, Poole BH17 9BQ T: 01202 602582
Sherborne Cemetery Lenthay Rd, Sherborne, Dorset DT9 6AA T: 01935 812909
Weymouth Crematorium Quibo Lane, Weymouth, Dorset DT4 0RR T: 01305 786984
East Sussex
Brighton Borough Mortuary Lewes Rd, Brighton, East Sussex BN2 3QB T: 01273 602345
Downs Crematorium Bear Rd, Brighton, East Sussex BN2 3PL T: 01273 601601
Eastbourne Cemeteries & Crematorium Hide Hollow, Langney, Eastbourne, East Sussex BN23 8AE T: 01323 766536
Woodvale Crematorium Lewes Rd, Brighton, East Sussex BN2 3QB T: 01273 604020
Essex
Basildon & District Crematorium Church Rd, Bowers Gifford, Basildon, Essex SS13 2HG T: 01268 584411

Chadwell Heath Cemetery Whalebone Lane, North Chadwell Heath, Romford, Essex RM6 5QX T: 0208 590 3280

Chelmsford Crematorium Writtle Rd, Chelmsford, Essex CM1 3BL T: 01245 256946

Chigwell Cemetery Frog Hall LaneChapman, Manor Rd, Chigwell, Essex IG7 4JX T: 020 8501 4275 E: chigwell@tesco.net

Colchester Cemetery & Crematorium Mersea Rd, Colchester, Essex CO2 8RU T: 01206 282950

Eastbrookend Cemetery Dagenham Rd, Dagenham, Essex RM10 7DR T: 01708 447451

Federation of Synagogues Burial Society 416 Upminster Rd North, Rainham, Essex RM13 9SB T: 01708 552825

Great Burstead Cemetery Church St, Great Burstead, Billericay, Essex CM11 2TR T: 01277 654334

Parndon Wood Crematorium and Cemetery Parndon Wood Rd, Essex CM19 4SF T: 01279 446199 E: chris.brown@harlow.gov.uk

Pitsea Cemetery Church Rd, Pitsea, Basildon, Essex SS13 2EZ T: 01268 552132

Romford Cemetery Crow Lane, Romford RM7 0EP T: 01708 740791

Sewardstone Road Cemetery Sewardstone Rd, Waltham Abbey, Essex EN9 1NX T: 01992 712525

South Essex Crematorium Ockendon Rd, Corbets Tey, Upminster, Essex RM14 2UY T: 01708 222188

Sutton Road Cemetery The Lodge, Sutton Rd, Southend-On-Sea, Essex SS2 5PX T: 01702 603907 F: 01702 603906

Weeley Crematorium Colchester Rd, Weeley, Clacton-On-Sea, Essex CO16 9JP T: 01255 831108 F: 01255 831440

Wickford Cemetery Park Dr, Wickford SS12 9DH T: 01268 733335

Gloucestershire

Cheltenham Cemetery & Crematorium Bouncers Lane, Cheltenham, Gloucestershire GL52 5JT T: 01242 244245 F: 01242 263123 E: cemetery.admin@cheltenham.gov.uk W: www.cheltenham.gov.uk

Coney Hill Crematorium Coney Hill Rd, Gloucester, Gloucestershire GL4 4PA T: 01452 523902

Forest of Dean Crematorium Yew Tree Brake, Speech House Rd, Cinderford, Gloucestershire GL14 3HU T: 01594 826624

Mile End Cemetery Mile End, Coleford, GL16 7DB T: 01594 832848

Hampshire

Aldershot Crematorium 48 Guildford Rd, Aldershot, Hampshire GU12 4BP T: 01252 321653

Anns Hill Rd Cemetery Anns Hill Rd, Gosport, Hampshire PO12 3JX T: 023 9258 0181 F: 023 9251 3191 W: www.gosport.gov.uk

Basingstoke Crematorium Manor Farm, Stockbridge Rd, North Waltham, Basingstoke, Hampshire RG25 2BA T: 01256 398784

Magdalen Hill Cemetery Magdalen Hill, Arlesesford Rd, Winchester, Hampshire SO21 1HE T: 01962 854135

Portchester Crematorium Upper Cornaway Lane, Portchester, Fareham, Hampshire PO16 8NE T: 01329 822533

Portsmouth Cemeteries Office Milton Rd, Southsea, Hampshire PO4 8 T: 023 9273 2559

Southampton City Council 6 Bugle St, Southampton, Hampshire SO14 2AJ T: 023 8022 8609

Warblington Cemetery Church Lane, Warblington, Havant PO9 2TU

Worting Rd Cemetery 105 Worting Rd, Basingstoke, Hampshire RG21 8YZ T: 01256 321737

Herefordshire

Hereford Cemetery & Crematorium Bereavement Services office, Westfaling Street, Hereford, Herefordshire HR4 0JE T: 01432 383200

Hertfordshire

Almonds Lane Cemetery Almonds Lane, Stevenage, Hertfordshire SG1 3RR T: 01438 350902

Bushey Jewish Cemetery Little Bushey Lane, Bushey, Watford, Hertfordshire WD2 3TP T: 0208 950 6299

Chorleywood Road Cemetery Chorleywood Rd, Rickmansworth, Hertfordshire WD3 4EH T: 01923 772646

Dacorum Borough Council Woodwells Cemetery, Buncefield Lane, Hemel Hempstead, Hertfordshire HP2 7HY T: 01442 252856

Harwood Park Crematorium Ltd Watton Rd, Stevenage, Hertfordshire SG2 8XT T: 01438 815555

Hatfield Road Cemetery Hatfield Rd, St. Albans AL1 4LU T: 01727 819362 F: 01727 819362 E: stalbans@cemeteries.freeserve.co.uk

North Watford Cemetery North Western Avenue, Watford, Hertfordshire WD25 0AW T: 01923 672157 F: 01923 672157

Tring Cemetery Aylesbury Rd, Aylesbury, Tring, Hertfordshire HP23 4DH T: 01442 822248

Vicarage Road Cemetery Vicarage Road, Watford, Hertfordshire WD18 0EJ T: 01923 672157 F: 01923 672157

Vicarage Road Cemetery Vicarage Rd, Watford WD1 8EJ T: 01923 225147

Watton Rd Cemetery Watton Rd, Ware, Hertfordshire SG12 0AX T: 01920 463261

West Herts Crematorium High Elms Lane, Watford WD25 0JS T: 01923 673285 E: postmaster@weshertscrem.org W: www.westhertscrem.org

Western Synagogue Cemetery Cheshunt Cemetery, Bulls Cross Ride, Waltham Cross, Hertfordshire EN7 5HT T: 01992 717820

Weston Road Cemetery Weston Rd, Stevenage, Hertfordshire SG1 4DE T: 01438 367109

Woodcock Hill Cemetery Lodge, Woodcock Hill, Harefield Rd, Rickmansworth, Hertfordshire WD3 1PT T: 01923 775188

Isle Of Wight

Shanklin Cemetery 1 Cemetery Rd, Lake Sandown, Sandown, Isle Of Wight PO36 9NN T: 01983 403743

Kent

Barham Crematorium Canterbury Rd, Barham, Canterbury, Kent CT4 6QU T: 01227 831351 F: 01227 830258

Beckenham Crematorium & Cemetery Elmers End Rd, Beckenham, Kent BR3 4TD T: 0208 650 0322

Chartham Cemetery Lodge Ashford Rd, Chartham, Canterbury, Kent CT4 7NY T: 01227 738211 F: 01227 738211

Gravesham Borough Council Old Rd West, Gravesend, Kent DA11 0LS T: 01474 337491

Hawkinge Cemetery & Crematorium Aerodrome Rd, Hawkinge, Folkestone, Kent CT18 7AG T: 01303 892215

Kent & Sussex Crematorium Benhall Mill Rd., Tunbridge Wells, Kent TN2 5JH T: 01892 523894

Kent County Crematorium plc Newcourt Wood, Charing, Ashford, Kent TN27 0EB T: 01233 712443 F: 01233 713501

Medway Crematorium Robin Hood Lane, Blue Bell Hill, Chatham, ME5 9QU T: 01634 861639 E: paul.edwards@medway.gov.uk

Northfleet Cemetery Springhead Rd, Northfleet, Gravesend, Kent DA11 8HW T: 01474 533260

Snodland Cemetery Cemetery Cottage, Cemetery Rd, Snodland, Kent ME6 5DN T: 01634 240764

Thanet Crematorium Manston Rd, Margate, Kent CT9 4LY T: 01843 224492 F: 01843 292218

The Cremation Society 2nd Floor Brecon House, 16/16a Albion Place, Maidstone, Kent ME14 5DZ T: 01622 688292/3 F: 01622 686698 E: cremsoc@aol.com W: www.cremation.org.uk

Vinters Park Crematorium Bearstead Rd, Weavering, Maidstone, Kent ME14 5LG T: 01622 738172 F: 01622 630560

Lancashire

Accrington Cemetery & Crematorium Burnley Rd, Accrington, Lancashire BB5 6HA T: 01254 232933 F: 01254 232933

Atherton Cemetery Leigh Road, Atherton, Lancashire

Audenshaw Cemetery Cemetery Rd, Audenshaw, Manchester, Lancashire M34 5AH T: 0161 336 2675

Blackley Cemetery & Crematorium Victoria Avenue, Manchester, Lancashire M9 8 T: 0161 740 5359

Burnley Cemetery Rossendale Rd, Burnley, Lancashire BB11 5DD T: 01282 435411 F: 01282 458904 W: www.burnley.gov.uk

Carleton Crematorium Stocks Lane, Carleton, Poulton-Le-Fylde, Lancashire FY6 7QS T: 01253 882541

Central & North Manchester Synagogue Jewish Cemetery Rainsough Brow, Prestwich, Manchester, Lancashire M25 9XW T: 0161 773 2641

Central & North Manchester Synagogue Jewish Cemetery Rochdale Rd, Manchester, Lancashire M9 6FQ T: 0161 740 2317

Chadderton Cemetery Cemetery Lodge, Middleton Rd, Chadderton, Oldham, Lancashire OL9 0JZ T: 0161 624 2301

Gidlow Cemetery Gidlow Lane, Standish, Wigan, Lancashire WN6 8RT T: 01257 424127

Greenacres Cemetery Greenacres Rd, Oldham, Lancashire OL4 3HT T: 0161 624 2294

Hindley Cemetery Castle Hill Road Road, Ince, Wigan WN3

Hollinwood Cemetery (inc Oldham Crematorium) Central Cemeteries Office, Roman Rd, Hollinwood, Oldham, Lancashire OL8 3LU T: 0161 681 1312 E: oper.cemeteries@oldham.gov.uk W: www.oldham.gov.uk

Howe Bridge Crematorium Crematorium Management Ltd, Lovers Lane, Atherton, Manchester, Lancashire M46 0PZ T: 01942 870811

Howebridge Cemetery Lovers Lane, Atherton, Lancashire

Ince in Makerfield Cemetery Warrington Road, Lower Ince, Wigan,

Leigh Cemetery Manchester Rd, Leigh, Lancashire WN7 2 T: 01942 671560 F: 01942 828877 W: www.wiganbc.gov.uk

Lower Ince Cemetery and Crematorium Cemetery Road, Lower Ince, Wigan WN3 4NH T: 01942 866455 E: t.bassett@wiganmbc.gov.uk

Lytham Park Cemetery & Crematorium Regent Avenue, Lytham St. Annes, Lancashire FY8 4AB T: 01253 735429 F: 01253 731903

Manchester Crematorium Ltd Barlow Moor Rd, Manchester, Lancashire M21 7GZ T: 0161 881 5269

Middleton New Cemetery Boarshaw Rd, Middleton, Manchester, Lancashire M24 6 T: 0161 655 3765

New Manchester Woodland Cemetery City Rd, Ellenbrook, Worsley, Manchester, Lancashire M28 1BD T: 0161 790 1300

Overdale Crematorium Overdale Drive, Chorley New Rd, Heaton, Bolton, Lancashire BL1 5BU T: 01204 840214

Padiham Public Cemetery St. Johns Rd, Padiham, Burnley, Lancashire BB12 7BN T: 01282 778139

Preston Cemetery New Hall Lane, Preston PR1 4SY T: 01772 794585 F: 01772 703857 E: m.birch@preston.gov.uk W: www.preston.gov.uk

Preston Crematorium Longridge Rd, Ribbleton, Preston PR2 6RL T: 01772 792391 E: m.birch@preston.gov.uk W: www.preston.gov.uk

Rochdale Cemetery Bury Rd, Rochdale OL11 4DG T: 01706 645219

Southern Cemetery Barlow Moor Rd, Manchester, Lancashire M21 7GL T: 0161 881 2208

St Joseph's Cemetery Moston Lane, Manchester, Lancashire M40 9QL T: 0161 681 1582 E: cemeteries@salforddiocese.org

St. Mary's Catholic Cemetery Manchester Rd, Wardley, Manchester, M28 2QT T: 0161 794 2194 E: cemeteries@salforddiocese.org

Tyldesley Cemetery Hough Lane, Tyldesley, Lancashire

United Synagogue Burial Ground Worsley Hill Farm, Phillips Park Rd, Whitefield, Manchester, Lancashire M45 7ED T: 0161 766 2065
Westwood Cemetery Westwood Lane, Lower Ince, Wigan, Lancashire
Whitworth Cemetery Edward St, Whitworth, Rochdale, Lancashire OL16 2EJ T: 01706 217777
Wigan Council Cemeteries and Crematorium Section 1 - 3 Worsley Terrace, Standishgate, Wigan, Lancashire WN1 1XW T: 01942 828993 F: 01942 828877 E: t.boussele@wiganmbc.gov.uk
Leicestershire
Cemetery Lodge Thorpe Rd, Melton Mowbray, Leicestershire LE13 1SH T: 01664 562223
Loughborough Crematorium Leicester Rd, Loughborough, Leicestershire LE11 2AF T: 01743 353046
Saffron Hill Cemetery Stonesby Ave, Leicester LE2 6TY T: 0116 222 1049
Lincolnshire
Boston Crematorium Cemeteries and Crematorium Office, Marian Rd, Boston PE21 9HA T: 01205 364612 E: martin.potts@boston.gov.uk W: www.boston.gov.uk
Bourne Town Cemetery South Rd, Bourne PE10 9JB T: 01778 422796
Grantham Cemetery & Crematorium Harrowby Rd, Grantham, Lincolnshire NG31 9DT T: 01476 563083 F: 01476 576228
Horncastle Cemetery Boston Rd, Horncastle, Lincolnshire LN9 6NF T: 01507 527118
Stamford Cemetery Wichendom, Little Casterton Rd, Stamford, Lincolnshire PE9 1BB T: 01780 762316
Tyler Landscapes Newport Cemetery, Manor Rd, Newport, Lincoln, Lincolnshire LN4 1RT T: 01522 525195
London
Abney Park Cemetery Trust The South Lodge, Abney Park Cemetery, High Street, Stoke Newington, London, N16 0LN T: 020 7278 7557 E: abneypark@geo2.poptel.org.uk W: www.abney-park.org.uk
Brockley Ladywell Hithergreen & Grove Park Cemeteries Verdant Lane, Catford, London , SE6 1TP T: 0208 697 2555
Brompton Cemetery Fulham Rd, London, SW10 9UG T: 0207 352 1201
Cemetery Management Ltd The City of Westminster Office, 38 Uxbridge Rd, London, W7 3PP T: 0208 567 0913
Charlton Cemetery Cemetery Lane, London, SE7 8DZ T: 0208 854 0235
City of London Cemetery & Crematorium Aldersbrook Rd, London, E12 5DQ T: 0208 530 2151
Coroners Court 8 Ladywell Rd, Lewisham, London, SE13 7UW T: 0208 690 5138
East London Cemetery Co.Ltd Grange Rd, London, E13 0HB T: 020 7476 5109 F: 020 7476 8338 E: enquiries@eastlondoncemetery.co.uk W: www.eastlondoncemetery.co.uk
Edmonton Cemetery Church St, Edmonton, London, N9 9HP T: 0208 360 2157
Eltham Cemetery & Crematorium Crown Woods Way, Eltham, London, SE9 2RF T: 0208 850 2921 (Cemetery)
Gap Road Cemetery Gap Rd, London, SW19 8JF T: 0208 879 0701
Golders Green Crematorium 62 Hoop Lane, London, NW11 7NL T: 0208 455 2374
Greenwich Cemetery Well Hall Rd, London, SE9 6TZ T: 0208 856 8666
Hendon Cemetery & Crematorium Holders Hill Rd, London, NW7 1NB T: 0208 346 0657
Highgate Cemetery Swains Lane, London, N6 6PJ T: 0208 340 1834
Honor Oak Crematorium Brenchley Gardens, London, SE23 3RB T: 020 7639 3121 F: 020 7732 3557 E: terry.connor@southwark.gov.uk
Islington Cemetery & Crematorium High Rd, East Finchley, London, N2 9AG T: 0208 883 1230
Kensal Green Cemetery Harrow Road, London, W10 4RA T: 020 8969 0152 F: 020 8960 9744
L B S Cemeteries Brenchley Gardens, London, SE23 3RD T: 020 7639 3121 F: 020 7732 3557 E: terry.connor@southwark.gov.uk
Lambeth Cemetery and Crematorium Cemetary Lodge, Blackshaw Rd, Tooting, London, SW17 0BY T: 0208 672 1390
Lewisham Crematorium Verdant Lane, London, SE6 1TP T: 0208 698 4955
Liberal Jewish Cemetery The Lodge, Pound Lane, London, NW10 2HG T: 0208 459 1635
London Borough of Hackney Mortuary Lower Clapton Rd, London, E5 8EQ T: 0208 985 2808
Manor Park Cemetery Co Ltd Sebert Rd, Forest Gate, London, E7 0NP T: 020 8534 1486 E: supt@manorpark15.fsbusiness.co.uk W: www.mpark.co.uk
New Southgate Cemetery & Crematorium Ltd 98 Brunswick Park Rd, London, N11 1JJ T: 0208 361 1713
Newham London Borough, High St South, London, E6 6ET T: 0208 472 9111
Plumstead Cemetery Wickham Lane, London, SE2 0NS T: 0208 854 0785
Putney Vale Cemetery & Crematorium Kingston Rd, London, SW15 3SB T: 0208 788 2113
South London Crematorium & Streatham Park Cemetery Rowan Rd, London, SW16 5JG T: 0208 764 2255
St. Marylebone Crematorium East End Rd, Finchley, London, N2 0RZ T: 0208 343 2233

St. Pancras Cemetery (London Borough Of Camden) High Rd, East Finchley, London, N2 9AG T: 0208 883 1231
St. Patrick's Catholic Cemetery Langthorne Rd, London, E11 4HL T: 020 8539 2451
St.Mary's Catholic Cemetery Harrow Rd, London, NW10 5NU T: 0208 969 1145
Tottenham Park Cemetery Montagu Rd, Edmonton, London N18 2NF T: 0208 807 1617
United Synagogue Beaconsfield Rd, Willesden, London, NW10 2JE T: 0208 459 0394
West End Chesed V'Ameth Burial Society 3 Rowan Rd, London, SW16 5JF T: 0208 764 1566
West Ham Cemetery Cemetery Rd, London, E7 9DG T: 0208 534 1566
West London Synagogue Hoop Lane, London, NW11 7NJ T: 0208 455 2569
West Norwood Cemetery & Crematorium Norwood Rd, London, SE27 9AJ T: 0207926 7900
Woodgrange Park Cemetery Romford Rd, London, E7 8AF T: 0208 472 3433
Woolwich Cemetery Kings Highway, London, SE18 2BJ T: 0208 854 0740
London B Waltham Forest - Chingford Mount Cemetery London Borough of Waltham Forest, Old Church Rd, London, E4 6ST T: 020 8524 5030
London Borough Hackney -see also **Abney Park Cemetery**
Merseyside
Anfield Crematorium Priory Rd, Anfield, Liverpool, Merseyside L4 2SL T: 0151 263 3267
Southport Cemeteries & Crematoria Southport Rd, Scarisbrick, Southport, Merseyside PR8 5JQ T: 01704 533443
St. Helens Cemetery & Crematorium Rainford Rd, Windle, St. Helens, Merseyside WA10 6DF T: 01744 677406 F: 01744 677411
Thornton Garden Of Rest Lydiate Lane, Thornton, Liverpool, Merseyside L23 1TP T: 0151 924 5143
Middlesex
Adath Yisroel Synagogue & Burial Society Carterhatch Lane, Enfield, Middlesex EN1 4BG T: 0208 363 3384
Breakspear Crematorium Breakspear Road, Ruislip, Middlesex HA4 7SJ T: 01895 632843 F: 01895 624209
Enfield Crematorium Great Cambridge Rd, Enfield, Middlesex EN1 4DS T: 0208 363 8324
Heston & Isleworth Borough Cemetry 190 Powder Mill Lane, Twickenham, Middlesex TW2 6EJ T: 0208 894 3830
Richmond Cemeteries London Borough of Richmond upon Thames, Sheen Rd, Richmond, Surrey TW10 5BJ T: 020 8876 4511 F: 020 8878 8118 E: cemeteries@richmond.gov.uk
South West Middlesex Crematorium Hounslow Rd, Hanworth, Feltham, Middlesex TW13 5JH T: 0208 894 9001
Spelthorne Borough Council Green Way, Sunbury-On-Thames, Middlesex TW16 6NW T: 01932 780244
Norfolk
Colney Wood Memorial Park Colney Hall, Watton Rd, Norwich, Norfolk NR4 7TY T: 01603 811556
Mintlyn Crematorium Lynn Rd, Bawsey, King's Lynn, Norfolk PE32 1HB T: 01553 630533 F: 01553 630998 E: colin.houseman@west norfolk.gov.uk W: www.west-norfolk.gov.uk
Norwich & Norfolk Crematoria - St. Faiths & Earlham 75 Manor Rd, Horsham St. Faith, Norwich, Norfolk NR10 3LF T: 01603 898264
Sprowston Cemetery Church Lane, Sprowston, Norwich, Norfolk NR7 8AU T: 01603 425354
North East Lincolnshire
North East Lincolnshire Council - Cleethorpes Cemetery Beacon Avenue, Cleethorpes DN35 8EQ T: 01472 324869 F: 01472 324870
North East Lincolnshire Council Crematorium & Cemeteries Dept Weelsby Avenue, Grimsby, North East Lincolnshire DN32 0BA T: 01472 324869 F: 01472 324870
North Lincolnshire
Woodlands Crematorium Brumby Wood Lane, Scunthorpe, South Humberside DN17 1SP T: 01724 280289 F: 01724 871235 E: crematorium@northlincs.gov.uk W: www.northlincs.gov.uk/environmentalhealth/cemetery.htm
North Tyneside
Whitley Bay Cemetery, Blyth Road, Whitley Bay NE26 4NH T: 0191 200 5861 F: 0191 200 5860
Earsdon Cemetery, Earsdon, Whitley Bay NE25 9LR T: 0191 200 5861 F: 0191 200 5860
North Yorkshire
Fulford New Cemetery Cemetery Lodge, Fordlands Rd, Fulford, York, North Yorkshire YO19 4QG T: 01904 633151
Mowthorpe Garden of Rest Southwood Farm, Terrington, York, North Yorkshire YO60 6QB T: 01653 648459 F: 01653 648225 E: robert@robertgoodwill.co.uk
Stonefall Cemetery & Cremetoria Wetherby Rd, Harrogate, North Yorkshire HG3 1DE T: 01423 883523
Waltonwrays Cemetery The Gatehouse, Carlton Rd, Skipton, North Yorkshire BD23 3BT T: 01756 793168
York Cemetery Gate House, Cemetery Rd, York, North Yorkshire YO10 5AF T: 01904 610578

Northamptonshire
Counties Crematorium Towcester Rd, Milton Malsor, Northampton, Northamptonshire NN4 9RN T: 01604 858280
Dallington Cemetery Harlstone Rd, Dallington, Northampton, Northamptonshire NN5 7 T: 01604 751589
Northumberland
Alnwick Cemetary Lodge Office, South Rd, Alnwick NE66 2PH T: 01665 602598 F: 01665 579272 W: www.alnwicktown.com
Blyth Cemetery Links Rd, Blyth NE24 3PJ T: 01670 369623
Cowpen Cemetery Cowpen Rd, Blyth NE24 5SZ T: 01670 352107
Embleton Joint Burial Committee Spitalford, Embleton, Alnwick, Northumberland NE66 3DW T: 01665 576632
Haltwhistle & District Joint Burial Committee Cemetery Lodge, Haltwhistle NE49 0LF T: 01434 320266 F: 01434 320266
Rothbury Cemetery Cemetery Lodge, Whitton Rd , Rothbury, Morpeth, Northumberland NE65 7RX T: 01669 620451
Nottinghamshire
Bramcote Crematorium Coventry Lane, Beeston, Nottingham, Nottinghamshire NG9 3GJ T: 0115 922 1837
Mansfield & District Crematorium Derby Rd, Mansfield, Nottinghamshire NG18 5BJ T: 01623 621811
Northern Cemetery Hempshill Lane, Bulwell, Nottingham, NG6 8PF T: 0115 915 3245 E: alec.thomson@nottinghamcity.gov.uk W: www.nottinghamcity.gov.uk/bereavement
Southern Cemetery & Crematoria Wilford Hill, West Bridgford, Nottingham, Nottinghamshire NG2 7FE T: 0115 915 2340
Tithe Green Woodland Burial Ground Salterford Lane, Calverton, Nottingham, Nottinghamshire NG14 6NZ T: 01623 882210
Oxfordshire
Oxford Crematorium Ltd Bayswater Rd, Headington, Oxford, Oxfordshire OX3 9RZ T: 01865 351255
Sheffield
Sheffield Central Cemetery The Cemetery Gatehouse, Cemetery Avenue, Sheffield S11 8NT T: 0114 268 3486 W: www.gencem.org
Shropshire
Bridgnorth Cemetery Mill St, Bridgnorth WV15 5NG T: 01746 762386
Emstrey Crematorium London Rd, Shrewsbury, Shropshire SY2 6PS T: 01743 359883
Hadley Cemetery 85 Hadley Park Rd, Hadley, Telford, Shropshire TF1 4PY T: 01952 223418
Longden Road Cemetery Longden Road, Shrewsbury, Shropshire SY3 7HS T: 01743 353046
Market Drayton Burial Committee Cemetery Lodge, Cemetery Rd, Market Drayton, Shropshire TF9 3BD T: 01630 652833
Oswestry Cemetery Cemetery Lodge, Victoria Rd, Oswestry, SY11 2HU T: 01691 652013 F: 01691 652013 E: graham.lee2@btinternet.com
Whitchurch Joint Cemetery Board The Cemetery Lodge, Mile Bank Rd, Whitchurch, Shropshire SY13 4JY T: 01948 665477
Somerset
Burnham Area Burial Board The Old Courthouse, Jaycroft Rd, Burnham-On-Sea, Somerset TA8 1LE T: 01278 795111
Chard Town Council Holyrood Lace Mill, Hoilyrood Street, Chard, Somerset TA20 12YA T: 01460 260370 F: 01460 260372
Minehead Cemetery Porlock Rd, Woodcombe, Minehead, Somerset TA24 8RY T: 01643 705243
Sedgemoor District Council The Cemetery, Quantock Rd, Bridgwater, Somerset TA6 7EJ T: 01278 423993
Taunton Deane Cemeteries & Crematorium Wellington New Rd, Taunton TA1 5NE T: 01823 284811 F: 01823 323152 W: www.tauntondeane.gov.uk/TDBCsites/crem
Wells Burial Joint Committee 127 Portway, Wells, Somerset BA5 1LY T: 01749 672049
Yeovil Cemetery Preston Rd, Yeovil, Somerset BA21 3AG T: 01935 423742
Yeovil Crematorium Bunford Ln, Yeovil BA20 2EJ T: 01935 476718
South Yorkshire
Barnsley Crematorium & Cemetery Doncaster Rd, Ardsley, Barnsley, South Yorkshire S71 5EH T: 01226 206053
City Road Cemetery City Rd, Sheffield S2 1GD T: 0114 239 6068
Ecclesfield Cemetery Priory Lane, Ecclesfield, Sheffield, South Yorkshire S35 9XZ T: 0114 239 6068 F: 0114 239 3757
Eckington Cemetery Sheffield Rd, Eckington, Sheffield, South Yorkshire S21 9FP T: 01246 432197
Grenoside Crematorium 5 Skew Hill Lane, Grenoside, Sheffield, South Yorkshire S35 8RZ T: 0114 245 3999
Handsworth Cemetery 51 Orgreave Lane, Handsworth, Sheffield, South Yorkshire S13 9NE T: 0114 254 0832
Hatfield Cemetery Cemetery Rd, Hatfield, Doncaster, South Yorkshire DN7 6LX T: 01302 840242
Mexborough Cemetery Cemetery Rd, Mexborough, South Yorkshire S64 9PN T: 01709 585184
Rose Hill Crematorium Cantley Lane, Doncaster DN4 6NE T: 01302 535191
Rotherham Cemeteries & Crematorium Ridgeway East, Herringthorpe, Rotherham, South Yorkshire S65 3NN T: 01709 850344
Sheffield Cemeteries City Rd, Sheffield, South Yorkshire S2 1GD T: 0114 253 0614
Stainforth Town Council Cemetery Office, Church Rd, Stainforth, Doncaster, South Yorkshire DN7 5AA T: 01302 845158

Staffordshire
Bretby Crematorium Geary Lane, Bretby, Burton-On-Trent, Staffordshire DE15 0QE T: 01283 221505 F: 01283 224846 E: bretby.crematorium@eaststaffsbc.gov.uk W: www.eaststaffsbc.gov.uk
Cannock Cemetery Cemetery Lodge, 160 Pye Green Rd, Cannock, Staffordshire WS11 2SJ T: 01543 503176
Carmountside Cemetery and Crematorium Bereavement Care Services, Leek Rd, Milton, Stoke-On-Trent, Staffordshire ST2 7AB T: 01782 235050 F: 01782 235050 E: karendeaville@civic2.stoke.gov.uk
Leek Cemetery Condlyffe Rd, Leek, Staffordshire ST13 5PP T: 01538 382616
Newcastle Cemetery Lymewood Grove, Newcastle, Staffordshire ST5 2EH T: 01782 616379 F: 01782 630498 E: jeanette.hollins@newcastle-staffs.gov.uk
Newcastle Crematorium Chatterley Close, Bradwell, Newcastle, Staffordshire ST5 8LE T: 01782 635498 F: 01782 710859
Stafford Crematorium Tixall Rd, Stafford ST18 0XZ T: 01785 242594
Stapenhill Cemetery 38 Stapenhill Rd, Burton-On-Trent, Staffordshire DE15 9AE T: 01283 508572 F: 01283 566586 E: cemetery@eaststaffsbc.gov.uk W: www.eaststaffsbc.gov.uk
Stilecop Cematary Stilecop Rd, Rugeley WS15 1ND T: 01889 577739
Uttoxeter Town Council Cemetery Lodge, Stafford Rd, Uttoxeter , Staffordshire ST14 8DS T: 01889 563374
Stockton on Tees
Tees Cemetery Records , Nightingale House, Balaclava Street, Stockton-on-Tees, TS18 2AL T: 01642 527720 W: www.stockton.gov.uk
Suffolk
Brinkley Woodland Cemetery 147 All Saints Rd, Newmarket, Suffolk CB8 8HH T: 01638 600693
Bury St. Edmunds Cemetery 91 Kings Rd, Bury St. Edmunds, Suffolk IP33 3DT T: 01284 754447
Hadleigh Town Council Friars Rd, Hadleigh, Ipswich, Suffolk IP7 6DF T: 01473 822034
Haverhill Cemetery Withersfield Rd, Haverhill, Suffolk CB9 9HF T: 01440 703810
Ipswich Cemetery & Crematorium Cemetery Lane, Ipswich, Suffolk IP4 2TQ T: 01473 433580 E: carol.egerton@ipswich.gov.uk
Leiston Cemetery Waterloo Avenue, Leiston, Suffolk IP16 4EH T: 01728 831043
West Suffolk Crematorium Risby, Bury St. Edmunds, Suffolk IP28 6RR T: 01284 755118 F: 01284 755135
Surrey
American Cemetery Cemetery Pales, Brookwood, Woking, Surrey GU24 0BL T: 01483 473237
Bandon Hill Cemetery Joint Committee Plough Lane, Wallington, Surrey SM6 8JQ T: 0208 647 1024
Brookwood Cemetery Cemetery Pales, Brookwood, Woking, Surrey GU24 0BL T: 01483 472222
Confederation of Burial Authorities The Gate House, Kew Meadow Path, Richmond, Surrey TW9 4EN T: 0208 392 9487
Dorking Cemetery Reigate Rd, Dorking, Surrey RH4 1QF T: 01306 879299 F: 01306 876821W: www.mole-valley.gov.uk
Guildford Crematorium & Cemetaries Broadwater, New Pond Rd, Goldaming, Surrey GU7 3DB T: 01483 444711
Kingston Cematary & Crematorium Bonner Hill Rd, Kingston Upon Thames, Surrey KT1 3EZ T: 020 8546 4462 F: 020 8546 4463
London Road Cemetery Figs Marsh, London Rd, Mitcham, Surrey CR4 3 T: 0208 648 4115
Merton & Sutton Joint Cemetery Garth Rd, Morden, Surrey SM4 4LL T: (020) 8337 4420 F: (020) 8337 4420
Mortlake Crematorium Board Kew Meadow Path, Town Mead Rd, Richmond, Surrey TW9 4EN T: 0208 876 8056
Mount Cemetery Weyside Rd, Guildford GU1 1HZ T: 01483 561927
North East Surrey Crematorium Board Lower Morden Lane, Morden, SM4 4NU T: 020 8337 4835 E: nescb.crematorium@talk21.com W: www.nes-crematorium.org.uk
Randalls Park Crematorium Randalls Rd, Leatherhead, Surrey KT22 0AG T: 01372 373813
Redstone Cemetery Philanthropic Rd, Redhill, Surrey RH1 4DN T: 01737 761592
Richmond Cemeteries L B of Richmond upon Thames, Sheen Rd, Richmond TW10 5BJ T: 020 8876 4511 E: cemeteries@richmond.gov.uk
Surbiton Cemetery Lower Marsh Lane, Kingston Upon Thames, Surrey KT1 3BN T: 0208 546 4463
Sutton & Cuddington Cemeteries Alcorn Close, off Oldfields Road, Sutton, Surrey SM3 9PX T: 020 8644 9437 F: 020 8644 1373
The Godalming Joint Burial Committee New Cemetery Lodge, Ockford Ridge, Godalming, Surrey GU7 2NP T: 01483 421559
Woking Crematorium Hermitage Rd, Woking, Surrey GU21 8TJ T: 01483 472197
Tyne And Wear
Byker & Heaton Cemetery 18 Benton Rd, Heaton, Newcastle Upon Tyne NE7 7DS T: 0191 2662017
Gateshead East Cemetery Cemetery Rd, Gateshead NE8 4HJ T: 0191 4771819
Heworth Cemetery Sunderland Rd, Felling, Gateshead, Tyne And Wear NE10 0NT T: 0191 4697851
Longbenton Cemetery, Longbenton, Newcastle Upon Tyne, Tyne And Wear NE12 8EY T: 0191 2661261

Preston Cemetery & Tynemouth Crematorium Walton Avenue, North Shields, Tyne And Wear NE29 9NJ T: 0191 2005861

Saltwell Crematorium Saltwell Road South, Gateshead, Tyne And Wear NE8 4TQ T: 0191 4910553

St. Andrews Cemetery Lodges 1-2, Great North Rd, Jesmond, Newcastle Upon Tyne, Tyne And Wear NE2 3BU T: 0191 2810953

St. Johns & Elswick Cemetery Elswick Rd, Newcastle Upon Tyne, Tyne And Wear NE4 8DL T: 0191 2734127

St. Nicholas Cemetery Wingrove Avenue Back, Newcastle Upon Tyne, Tyne And Wear NE4 9AP T: 0191 2735112

Union Hall Cemetery Union Hall Rd, Newcastle Upon Tyne, Tyne And Wear NE15 7JS T: 0191 2674398

West Road Cemetery West Rd, Newcastle Upon Tyne, Tyne And Wear NE5 2JL T: 0191 2744737

Warwickshire

Mid-Warwickshire Crematorium & Cemeteries Oakley Wood, Bishops Tachbrook, Leamington Spa CV33 9QP T: 01926 651418

Nuneaton Cemetery Oaston Rd, Nuneaton, Warwickshire CV11 6JZ T: 024 7637 6357 F: 024 7637 6485

Stratford-on-Avon Cemetery Evesham Rd, Stratford-Upon-Avon, Warwickshire CV37 9AA T: 01789 292676

West Midlands

Birmingham Crematorium 1973 389 Walsall Rd, Perry Barr, Birmingham, West Midlands B42 2LR T: 0121 356 9476

Birmingham Hebrew Congregation Cemetery The Ridgeway, Erdington, Birmingham B23 7TD T: 0121 356 4615

Brandwood End Cemetery Woodthorpe Rd, Kings Heath, Birmingham, West Midlands B14 6EQ T: 0121 444 1328

Coventry Bereavement Services The Cemeteries & Crematorium Office, Cannon Hill Rd, Canley, Coventry CV4 7DF T: 024 7641 8055

Handsworth Cemetery Oxhill Rd, Birmingham, West Midlands B21 8JT T: 0121 554 0096

Lodge Hill Cemetery & Cremetorium Weoley Park Rd, Birmingham, West Midlands B29 5AA T: 0121 472 1575

Quinton Cemetery Halesowen Rd, Halesowen, West Midlands B62 9AF T: 0121 422 2023

Robin Hood Cemetery and Crematorium Sheetsbrook Road, Shirley, Solihull, West midlands B90 3NL T: 0121 744 1121 F: 0121 733 8674

Stourbridge Cemetry & Crematorium South Rd, Stourbridge, West Midlands DY8 3RQ T: 01384 813985

Streetly Cemetery & Crematorium Walsall MBC - Bereavement Services Division, Little Hardwick Road, Aldridge, Walsall, WS9 0SG T: 0121 353 7228 F: 0121 353 6557 E: billingss@walsall.gov.uk

Sutton Coldfield Cemetery Rectory Rd, Sutton Coldfield, West Midlands B75 7RP T: 0121 378 0224

Sutton Coldfield Cremetorium Tamworth Rd, Four Oaks, Sutton Coldfield, West Midlands B75 6LG T: 0121 308 3812

West Bromwich Crematorium Forge Lane, West Bromwich, West Midlands B71 3SX T: 0121 588 2160

Widney Manor Cemetery Widney Manor Road, Bentley Heath, Solihull, West Midlands B93 3LX

Willenhall Lawn Cemetery Bentley Lane, Willenhall, West Midlands WV12 4AE T: 01902 368621

Witton Cemetery Moor Lane Witton, Birmingham, West Midlands B6 7AE T: 0121 356 4363 F: 0121 331 1283 E: wittoncem@birmingham.gov.uk

Woodlands Cemetery and Crematorium Birmingham Rd, Coleshill, Birmingham, West Midlands B46 2ET T: 01675 464835

West Sussex

Chichester Crematorium Westhampnett Rd, Chichester, West Sussex PO19 4UH T: 01243 787755

Midhurst Burial Authority Cemetery Lodge, Carron Lane, Midhurst, West Sussex GU29 9LF T: 01730 812758

Surrey & Sussex Crematorium Balcombe Rd, Crawley, West Sussex RH10 3NQ T: 01293 888930

Worthing Crematorium & Cemeteries Horsham Rd, Findon, Worthing, West Sussex BN14 0RG T: 01903 872678 F: 01903 872051 E: crematorium@worthing.gov.uk

West Yorkshire

Brighouse Cemetery Cemetery Lodge, 132 Lightcliffe Rd, Brighouse, West Yorkshire HD6 2HY T: 01484 715183

Cottingly Hall Elland Rd, Leeds, West Yorkshire LS11 0 T: 0113 271 6101

Dewsbury Moor Crematorium Heckmondwike Rd, Dewsbury, West Yorkshire WF13 3PL T: 01924 325180

Exley Lane Cemetery Exley Lane, Elland, West Yorkshire HX5 0SW T: 01422 372444

Killingbeck Cemetery York Rd, Killingbeck, Leeds, West Yorkshire LS14 6AB T: 0113 264 5247

Lawnswood Cemetery & Crematorium Otley Rd, Adel, Leeds, West Yorkshire LS16 6AH T: 0113 267 3188

Leeds Jewish Workers Co-Op Society 717 Whitehall Rd, New Farnley, Leeds, West Yorkshire LS12 6JL T: 0113 285 2521

Moorthorpe Cemetery Barnsley Rd, Moorthorpe, Pontefract, West Yorkshire WF9 2BP T: 01977 642433

Nab Wood Crematorium Bingley Rd, Shipley, West Yorkshire BD18 4BG T: 01274 584109 F: 01274 530419

Oakworth Crematorium Wide Lane, Oakworth, Keighley, West Yorkshire BD22 0RJ T: 01535 603162

Park Wood Crematorium Park Rd, Elland, West Yorkshire HX5 9HZ T: 01422 372293

Pontefract Crematorium Wakefield Rd, Pontefract, West Yorkshire WF8 4HA T: 01977 723455

Rawdon Crematorium Leeds Rd, Rawdon, Leeds, West Yorkshire LS19 6JP T: 0113 250 2904

Scholemoor Cemetery & Crematorium Necropolis Road, Bradford, West Yorkshire BD7 2PS T: 01274 571313

Sowerby Bridge Cemetery Sowerby New Rd, Sowerby Bridge, West Yorkshire HX6 1LQ T: 01422 831193

Undercliffe Cemetery 127 Undercliffe Lane, Bradford BD3 0QD T: 01274 631445

United Hebrew Congregation Leeds Jewish Cemetery, Gelderd Rd, Leeds, West Yorkshire LS7 4BU T: 0113 263 8684

Wakefield Crematorium Standbridge Lane, Crigglestone, Wakefield, West Yorkshire WF4 3JA T: 01924 303380

Wetherby Cemetery Sexton House, Hallfield Lane, Wetherby, West Yorkshire LS22 6JQ T: 01937 582451

Wiltshire

Box Cemetery Bath Road, Box, Corsham SN13 8AA T: 01225 742476

Devizes & Roundway Joint Burial Committee Cemetry Lodge, Rotherstone, Devizes, Wiltshire SN10 2DE T: 01380 722821

Salisbury Crematorium Barrington Road, Salisbury, Wiltshire SP1 3JB T: 01722 333632

Swindon Crematorium Kingsdown, Swindon, Wiltshire SN25 6SG T: 01793 822259

The Cemetery Chippenham London Road, Chippenham, Wiltshire SN15 3RD T: 01249 652728

West Wiltshire Crematorium Devizes Road, Semington, Trowbridge, Wiltshire BA14 7QH T: 01380 871101

Wirral

Landican Cemetery Arrowe Park Rd, Birkenhead, Wirral CH49 5LW T: 0151 677 2361

Worcestershire

Pershore Cemetery Defford Rd, Pershore, Worcestershire WR10 3BX T: 01386 552043

Redith Crematorium & Abbey Cemetary Bordesley Lane, Redditch, Worcestershire B97 6RR T: 01527 62174

Westall Park Woodland Burial Holberrow Green, Redditch, Worcestershire B96 6JY T: 01386 792806

Worcester Crematorium Astwood Rd, Tintern Avenue, Worcester, Worcestershire WR3 8HA T: 01905 22633

Yorkshire - East

East Riding Crematorium Ltd Octon Cross Rd, Langtoft, Driffield, YO25 3BL T: 01377 267604

East Riding of Yorkshire Council Cemetery Lodge, Sewerby Rd, Bridlington YO16 7DS T: 01262 672142

Goole Cemetery Hook Rd, Goole DN14 5LU T: 01405 762725

Yorkshire - South

Sheffield Central Cemetery The Cemetery Gatehouse, Cemetery Avenue, Sheffield, South Yorkshire S11 8NT T: 0114 268 3486 W: www.gencem.org

WALES

Bridgend

Bridgend County Borough Council Cemeteries Civic Offices, Angel Street, Bridgend, Glamorgan CF31 1LX T: 01656 643422

Caerphilly

Caerphilly County Borough Council Cemeteries Council Offices, Pontllanfraith, Blackwood, NP2 2YW

Clwyd

Golden Memorial Care 5 Golden Grove, Rhyl, Clwyd LL18 2RR T: 0800 9178281

Mold Town Cemetery Cemetery Lodge, Alexandra Rd, Mold, Clwyd CH7 1HJ T: 01352 753820

Wrexham Cemeteries & Crematorium Pentre Bychan, Wrexham, Clwyd LL14 4EP T: 01978 840068

Wrexham Cemetery Lodge Ruabon Rd, Wrexham, Clwyd LL13 7NY T: 01978 263159

Conwy County

Colwyn Bay Crematorium Bron y Nant, Dinerth Rd, Colwyn Bay, Conwy County LL28 4YN T: 01492 544677

Dyfed

Aberystwyth Crematorium Clarach Rd, Aberystwyth, Dyfed SY23 3DG T: 01970 626942

Carmarthen Cemetery Elim Rd, Carmarthen, Dyfed SA31 1TX T: 01267 234134

Llanelli District Cemetery Swansea Rd, Llanelli, Dyfed SA15 3EX T: 01554 773710

Milford Haven Cemetery The Cemetery, Milford Haven, Dyfed SA73 2RP T: 01646 693324

Glamorgan

Barry Town Council Cemetery Barry Town Council, 7 Gladstone Road, Barry, Glamorgan CF62 8NA T: 01446 738663

Cowbridge (The Limes Cemetery (1925) Cemetery Cowbridge Town Council, Town Hall, Cowbridge, Glamorgan CF71 7AD T: 01446 772901

Llantwit Major Cemetery Llantwit Major Town Council, Llantwit Major, Glamorgan CF61 1SD T: 01446 793707

Merthyr Tydfil County Borough Council Cemeteries Civic Centre, Merthyr Tydfil, Glamorgan CF47 8AN T: 01685 725146

Penarth Cemetery Penarth Town Council, West House, Stanwell Road, Penarth, Glamorgan CF64 2YG T: 029 2070 0721
Penryhs Cemetery Cemetery Offices, PenryhsRoad, Tylorstown, Glamorgan CF43 3BA T: 01443 730465
Rhondda Cynon Taff CBC Cemeteries Crematorium and Cemeteries Section, Cemetery Rd, Glyntaff, Pontypridd CF37 4BE T: 01443 402810
Trealaw Cemetery Cemetery Offices, Brithweunydd Road, Trealaw, Glamorgan CF40 2UQ T: 01443 682829
Gwent
Christchurch Cemetery Christchurch, Newport, Gwent NP18 1JJ T: 01633 277566
Ebbw Vale Cemetery Waun-y-Pound Rd, Ebbw Vale, Gwent NP23 6LE T: 01495 302187
Gwent Crematorium Treherbert Rd, Croesyceiliog, Cwmbran, Gwent NP44 2BZ T: 01633 482784
Gwynedd
Bangor Crematorium Llandygai Rd, Bangor, Gwynedd LL57 4HP T: 01248 370500
Mid Glamorgan
Cemetery Section - Rhondda Cynon Taff County Borough Council Monks St, Aberdare, Mid Glamorgan CF44 7PA T: 01685 885345
Ferndale Cemetery Cemetery Lodge, Highfield, Ferndale, Mid Glamorgan CF43 4TD T: 01443 730321
Llwydcoed Crematorium Llwydcoed, AberdareCF44 0DJ T: 01685 874115 E: enquiries@crematorium.org.uk W: www.crematorium.org.uk
Maesteg Cemetery Cemetery Rd, Maesteg, Mid Glamorgan CF34 0DN T: 01656 735485
Penrhys Cemetery Cemetery Lodge, Penrhys Rd, Tylorstown, Ferndale, Mid Glamorgan CF43 3PN T: 01443 730465
Trane Cemetery Gilfach Rd, Tonyrefail, Porth, Mid Glamorgan CF39 8HL T: 01443 670280 F: 01443 676916
Treorchy Cemetery The Lodge, Cemetery Rd, Treorchy, Mid Glamorgan CF42 6TB T: 01443 772336
Ynysybwl Cemetery 37 Heol Y Plwyf, Ynysybwl, Pontypridd, Mid Glamorgan CF37 3HU T: 01443 790159
South Glamorgan
Cardiff Crematorium and Thornhill Cemetery Bereavement Services, Thornhill Road, Cardiff, South Glamorgan CF14 9UA T: 029 2062 3294 F: 029 20692904 W: www.cardiff.gov.uk
Cathays Cemetery Fairoak Rd, Cathays, Cardiff, South Glamorgan CF24 4PY T: 029 2062 3294 W: www.cardiff.gov.uk
Western Cemetery Cowbridge Road West, Ely, Cardiff, South Glamorgan CF5 5TF T: 029 2059 3231 W: www.cardiff.gop.uk
West Glamorgan
Goytre Cemetery Neath Port Talbot CBC, Abrafan House, Port Talbot, West Glamorgan SA13 1PJ T: 01639 763415
Margam Crematorium Longland Lane, Margam, Port Talbot, West Glamorgan SA13 2PP T: 01639 883570
Oystermouth Cemetery Newton Road, Oystermouth, Swansea, West Glamorgan SA3 4GW T: 07980 721 559
Wrexham
Coedpoeth Cemetery The Lodge, Cemetery Rd, Coedpoeth, Wrexham LL11 3SP T: 01978 755617
SCOTLAND
Aberdeenshire
Aberdeen Cemeteries St Nicholas House, Broad Street, Aberdeen, AB10 1BX T: 01224 523 155
Aberdeenshire (except Aberdeen City) Cemeteries (North) 1 Church Street, Macduff AB44 1UR T: 01261 813387
Springbank Cemetery Countesswells Rd, Springbank, Aberdeen, Aberdeenshire AB15 7YH T: 01224 317323
St. Peter's Cemetery King St, Aberdeen, Aberdeenshire AB24 3BX T: 01224 638490
Trinity Cemetery Erroll St, Aberdeen, Aberdeenshire AB24 5PP T: 01224 633747
Angus
Angus (except Dundee City) Cemeteries County Buildings, Market Street, Forfar, ANGUS DD8 3WA T: 01307 461 460 F: 01307 466 220
Barnhill Cemetery 27 Strathmore St, Broughty Ferry, Dundee, Angus DD5 2NY T: 01382 477139
Dundee City Cemeteries Tayside House, Dundee, ANGUS DD1 3RA T: 01382 434 000 E: parks.burials@dundeecity.gov.uk
Dundee Crematorium Ltd Crematorium, Macalpine Rd, Dundee, Angus DD3 8 T: 01382 825601
Park Grove Crematorium Douglasmuir, Friocheim, Arbroath, Angus DD11 4UN T: 01241 828959
Argyll
Argyll & Bute Council Cemeteries Amenity Services, Kilmory, Lochgilphead, Argyll PA31 8RT T: 01546 604 360 E: alison.mcilroy@argyll-bute.gov.uk W: www.argyll-bute.gov.uk/couninfo/dev.htm
Ayrshire
Ardrossan Cemetery Sorbie Rd, Ardrossan, Ayrshire KA22 8AQ T: 01294 463133
Dreghorn Cemetery Station Rd, Dreghorn, Irvine, Ayrshire KA11 4AJ T: 01294 211101
Hawkhill Cemetery Kilwinning Rd, Saltcoats, Stevenston, Ayrshire KA20 3DE T: 01294 465241
Holmsford Bridge Crematorium Dreghorn, Irvine, Ayrshire KA11 4EF T: 01294 214720

Kilwinning Cemetery Bridgend, Kilwinning, Ayrshire KA13 7LY T: 01294 552102
Largs Cemetery Greenock Rd, Largs KA30 8NG T: 01475 673149
Maybole Cemetery Crosshill Rd, Maybole, Ayrshire KA19 7BN T: 01655 884852 E: maybole.registrars@south-ayrshire.gov.uk
Newmilns Cemetery Dalwhatswood Rd, Newmilns, Ayrshire KA16 9LT T: 01560 320191
North Ayrshire Cemeteries 43 Ardrossan Road, Saltcoats KA21 5BS T: 01294 605 436 E: CemeteriesOffice@north-ayrshire.gov.uk
Prestwick Cemetery Shaw Rd, Prestwick, KA9 2LP T: 01292 477759
South Ayrshire Cemeteries Masonhill Crematorium, By Ayr, KA6 6EN T: 01292 266 051 F: 01292 610 096
Stewarton Cemetery Dalry Rd, Stewarton, Kilmarnock, Ayrshire KA3 3DY T: 01560 482888
West Kilbride Cemetery Hunterston Rd, West Kilbride, Ayrshire KA23 9EX T: 01294 822818
Banffshire
Moray Crematorium Clochan, Buckie AB56 5HQ T: 01542 850488
Berwickshire
Scottish Borders Council Cemeteries Council Offices, 8 Newtown Street, Duns TD11 3DT T: 01361 882 600
Bute
Arran and Cumbrae Cemeteries 43 Ardrossan Road, Saltcoats, Bute KA21 5BS T: 01294 605 436 F: 01294 606 416 E: CemeteriesOffice@north-ayrshire.gov.uk
Caithness
Caithness Cemeteries Wick, Caithness, CAITHNESS KW1 4AB T: 01955 607 737 F: 01955 606 376
Clackmannanshire
Alva Cemetery The Glebe, Alva, Clackmannanshire FK12 5HR T: 01259 760354
Sunnyside Cemetery Sunnyside Rd, Alloa, Clackmannanshire FK10 2AP T: 01259 723575
Tillicoultry Cemetery Dollar Rd, Tillicoultry, Clackmannanshire FK13 6PF T: 01259 750216
Dumfries-shire
Annan & Eskdale Cemeteries Dumfries and Galloway Council, Dryfe Road, Lockerbie DG11 2AP T: 01576 205 000
Dumfrieshire Cemeteries Kirkbank, English Street, Dumfries, DG1 2HS T: 01387 260042 F: 01387 260188
Dunbartonshire
Cardross Crematorium Main Rd, Cardross, Dumbarton, Dunbartonshire G82 5HD T: 01389 841313
Dumbarton Cemetery Stirling Rd, Dumbarton, Dunbartonshire G82 2PF T: 01389 762033
East Dunbartonshire Cemeteries Broomhill Industrial Estate, Kilsyth Road, Kirkintilloch G66 1TF T: 0141 574 5549 F: 0141 574 5555 E: Alan-Copeland@EastDunbarton.gov.uk
Vale Of Leven Cemetery Overton Rd, Alexandria G83 0LJ T: 01389 752266
West Dumbartonshire Crematorium North Dalnottar, Clydebank, Dunbartonshire G81 4SL T: 01389 874318
West Dunbartonshire Cemeteries Roseberry Place, Clydebank, G81 1TG T: 01389 738 709 F: 01389 733 493
West Dunbartonshire Crematorium Richmond Street, Clydebank, Dunbartonshire G81 1RF T: 01389 738709 F: 01389 738690 E: helen.murray@westdunbarton.gov.uk
East Dunbartonshire
Cadder Cemetery Kirkintilloch Road, Bishopbriggs, Glasgow, Lanarkshire G64 2QG T: 0141 772 1977 F: 0141 775 0696
Edinburgh
Edinburgh Crematorium Ltd 3 Walker St, Edinburgh, Midlothian, EH3 7JY T: 0131 225 7227
Fife
Central Fife Cemeteries Rosemount Avenue, Dunnikier, Kirkcaldy, KY1 3PL T: 01592 260 277 F: 01592 203 438
Dunfermline Cemetery Halbeath Rd, Dunfermline, Fife KY12 7RA T: 01383 724899
Dunfermline Crematorium Masterton Rd, Dunfermline, Fife KY11 8QR T: 01383 724653
East Fife Cemeteries St Catherine Street, Cupar, FIFE KY15 4TA T: 01334 412 818 F: 01334 412 896
East Fife Cemeteries Masterton Road, Dunfermline, FIFE KY11 8QR T: 01383 724 653 F: 01383 738 636
Kirkcaldy Crematorium Rosemount Avenue, Dunnikier, Kirkcaldy, Fife KY1 3PL T: 01592 260277 F: 01592 203438
Glasgow
Glasgow Cemeteries 20 Trongate, Glasgow G1 5ES T: 0141 287 3961
Inverness-shire
Badenoch & Strathspey Cemeteries Ruthven Road, Kingussie, PH21 1EJ T: 01540 664 500 F: 01540 661 004
Highland Council Cemeteries T.E.C. Services, Broom Place, Portree, Isle of Skye, IV51 9HF T: 01478 612717 F: 01478 612255
Inverness Cemeteries Administration Office, Kilvean Cemetery, Kilvean Road, Inverness, IV3 8JN T: 01463 717849 F: 01463 717850 E: derek.allan@highland.gov.uk
fiona.morrison@highland.gov.uk W: www.highland.gov.uk
Inverness Crematorium Kilvean Rd, Kilvean, Inverness, Inverness-Shire IV3 8JN T: 01463 717849 F: 01463 717850

Invernessshire Cemeteries Fulton House, Gordon Square, Fort William, PH33 6XY T: 01397 707 008 F: 01397 707 009
Isle Of Cumbrae
Millport Cemetery Golf Rd, Millport, Isle Of Cumbrae KA28 0HB T: 01475 530442
Kirkcudbright
Cemeteries Daar Road, Kirkcudbright DG6 4JG T: 01557 330 291
Lanarkshire
Airbles Cemetery Airbles Rd, Motherwell ML1 3AW T: 01698 263986
Bedlay Cemetery Bedlay Walk, Moodiesburn, Glasgow, Lanarkshire G69 0QG T: 01236 872446
Bothwellpark Cemetery New Edinburgh Rd, Bellshill, Lanarkshire ML4 3HH T: 01698 748146
Cambusnethan Cemetery Kirk Road, Wishaw ML2 8NP T: 01698 384481
Campsie Cemetery High Church of Scotland, Main Street, Lennoxtown, Glasgow, Lanarkshire G66 7DA T: 01360 311127
Cardonald Cemetery 547 Mosspark Boulevard, Glasgow, Lanarkshire G52 1SB T: 0141 882 1059
Daldowie Crematorium Daldowie Estate, Uddingston, Glasgow, Lanarkshire G71 7RU T: 0141 771 1004
Glasgow Crematorium Western Necropolis, Tresta Rd, Glasgow, Lanarkshire G23 5AA T: 0141 946 2895
Glebe Cemetery Vicars Rd, Stonehouse, Larkhall, Lanarkshire ML9 3EB T: 01698 793674
Glenduffhill Cemetery 278 Hallhill Rd, Glasgow, Lanarkshire G33 4RU T: 0141 771 2446
Kilsyth Parish Cemetery Howe Rd, Kirklands, Glasgow, Lanarkshire G65 0LA T: 01236 822144
Larkhall Cemetery The Cemetery Lodge, Duke St, Larkhall, Lanarkshire ML9 2AL T: 01698 883049
North Lanarkshire Cemeteries Old Edinburgh Road, Bellshill, Lanarkshire ML4 3JS T: 01698 506 301 F: 01698 506 309
Old Aisle Cemetery Old Aisle Rd, Kirkintilloch, Glasgow, Lanarkshire G66 3HH T: 0141 776 2330
St. Conval's Cemetery Glasgow Rd, Barrhead, Glasgow, Lanarkshire G78 1TH T: 0141 881 1058
St. Patrick's Cemetery Kings Drive, New Stevenston, Motherwell, Lanarkshire ML1 4HY T: 01698 732938
St. Peters Cemetery 1900 London Rd, Glasgow, Lanarkshire G32 8RD T: 0141 778 1183
The Necropolis 50 Cathedral Square, Glasgow, Lanarkshire G4 0UZ T: 0141 552 3145
Midlothian
City of Edinburgh Council Cemeteries Howdenhall Road, Edinburgh, Midlothian EH16 6TX T: 0131 664 4314 F: 0131 664 2031 E: env.svs@edinburgh.gov.uk
Dean Cemetery Dean Path, Edinburgh, Midlothian EH4 3AT T: 0131 332 1496
Midlothian Council Cemeteries Dundas Buildings, 62A Polton Street, Bonnybrigg, Midlothian EH22 3YD T: 0131 561 5280 F: 0131 654 2797 E: nancy.newton@midlothian.gov.uk
Seafield Cemetery & Crematorium Seafield Rd, Edinburgh, Midlothian EH6 7LQ T: 0131 554 3496
Warriston Crematorium 36 Warriston Rd, Edinburgh, Midlothian EH7 4HW T: 0131 552 3020
Morayshire
Morayshire Cemeteries Cooper Park, Elgin, Morayshire IV30 1HS T: 01343 544 475 F: 01343 549 050 E: graeme.wilson@moray.gov.uk W: www.moray.org/heritage/roots.html
Peebles-shire
Scottish Borders Council Burial Grounds Department Council Offices, Rosetta Road, Peebles, Peebles-shire EH45 8HG T: 01721 726306 F: 01721 726304 E: p.allan@scot.borders.gov.uk
Perthshire
Perth Crematorium Crieff Rd, Perth, Perthshire PH1 2PE T: 01738 625068 F: 01738 445977 E: dpmartin@pkc.gov.uk
Renfrewshire
Cemeteries Division - Renfrewshire Council Environmental Services Department, Cotton Street, South Building, Paisley, Renfrewshire PA1 1BR T: 0141 840 3504 F: 0141 842 1179
East Renfrewshire - including Neilston, Newton Mearns and Eaglesham Cemeteries Rhuallan House, 1 Montgomery Drive, Giffnock, Renfrewshire G46 6PY T: 0141 577 3913 F: 0141 577 3919 E: sandra.donnelly@eastrenfrewshire.gov.uk
Hawkhead Cemetery 133 Hawkhead Rd, Paisley, Renfrewshire PA2 7BE T: 0141 889 3472
Paisley Cemetery Co.Ltd 46 Broomlands St, Paisley, Renfrewshire PA1 2NP T: 0141 889 2260
Renfrew Cemeteries 3 Longcroft Drive, Renfrew, Renfrewshire PA4 8NF T: 0141 848 1450 F: 0141 886 2807

Renfrewshire Cemeteries Tweedie Halls, Ardlamont Square, Linwood, Renfrewshire PA3 3DE T: 01505 322 135 F: 01505 322135
Roxburghshire
Roxburghshire Environmental Health - Burials High Street, Hawick, Roxburghshire TD9 9EF T: 01450 375 991
Scottish Borders
Scottish Borders Council - Burials Paton Street, Galashiels, Selkirkshire TD1 3AS T: 01896 662739 F: 01896 750329

Shetland
Shetland Burial Ground Management Grantfield, Lerwick, Shetland ZE1 0NT T: 01595 744 871 E: jim.grant@sic.shetland.gov.uk W: www.users.zetnet.co.uk/eats-operations
South Lanarkshire
South Lanarkshire Cemeteries Atholl House, East Kilbride, Lanarkshire G74 1LU T: 01355 806 980 F: 01355 806 983
Stirlingshire
Falkirk Cemeteries and Crematorium Dorrator Road, Camelon, Falkirk, Stirlingshire FK2 7YJ T: 01324 503 654 F: 01324 503 651 E: billbauchope@falkirk.gov.uk
Larbert Cemetery 25 Muirhead Rd, Larbert, Stirlingshire FK5 4HZ T: 01324 557867
Stirlingshire Cemeteries Viewforth, Stirling, Stirlingshire FK8 2ET T: 01786 442 559 E: mcbrier@stirling.gov.uk W: www.stirling.gov.uk
West Lothian
West Lothian Cemeteries County Buildings, High Street, Linlithgow, West Lothian EH49 7EZ T: 01506 775 300 F: 01506 775 412
Wigtown
Wigtown Cemeteries Dunbae House, Church Street, Stranraer, Wigtown DG9 7JG T: 01776 888 405

IRELAND

County Antrim
Ballymena Cemetery Cushendall Rd, Ballymena, County Antrim BT43 6QE T: 01266 656026
Ballymoney Cemetery 44 Knock Rd, Ballymoney, County Antrim BT53 6LX T: 012656 66364
Blaris New Cemetery 25 Blaris Rd, Lisburn, County Antrim BT27 5RA T: 01846 607143
Carnmoney Cemetery 10 Prince Charles Way, Newtownabbey, County Antrim BT36 7LG T: 01232 832428
City Cemetery 511 Falls Rd, Belfast, County Antrim BT12 6DE T: 028 90323112
Greenland Cemetery Upper Cairncastle Rd, Larne, County Antrim BT40 2EG T: 01574 272543
Milltown Cemetery Office 546 Falls Rd, Belfast BT12 6EQ T: 01232 613972
County Armagh
Kernan Cemetery Kernan Hill Rd, Portadown, Craigavon, County Armagh BT63 5YB T: 028 38339059
Lurgan Cemetery 57 Tandragee Rd, Lurgan, Craigavon, County Armagh BT66 8TL T: 028 38342853
County Down
Ballyvestry Cemetery 6 Edgewater Millisle, Newtownards, County Down BT23 5 T: 01247 882657
Banbridge Public Cemetery Newry Rd, Banbridge, County Down BT32 3NB T: 018206 62623
Bangor Cemetery 62 Newtownards Rd, Bangor, County Down BT20 4DN T: 028 91271909
City of Belfast Crematorium 129 Ballgowan Road, Crossacreevy, Belfas BT5 7TZ T: 028 9044 8342 E: crematorium@belfastcity.gov.uk W: www.belfastcrematorium.co.uk
Clandeboye Cemetery 300 Old Belfast Rd, Bangor, County Down BT19 1RH T: 028 91853246
Comber Cemetery 31 Newtownards Rd, Comber, Newtownards, County Down BT23 5AZ T: 01247 872529
Down District Council Struell Cemetery, Old Course Rd, Downpatrick, County Down BT30 8AQ T: 01396 613946
Down District Council - Lough Inch Cemetery Lough Inch Cemetery, Riverside Rd, Ballynahinch, County Down BT24 8JB T: 01238 562987
Kirkistown Cemetary Main Rd, Portavogie, Newtownards, County Down BT22 1EL T: 012477 71773
Movilla Cemetary Movilla Rd, Newtownards, County Down BT23 8EY T: 01247 812276
Redburn Cemetery Old Holywood Rd, Holywood, County Down BT18 9QH T: 01232 425547
Roselawn Cemetery 127 Ballygowan Rd, Crossnacreevy, Belfast, County Down BT5 7TZ T: 01232 448288
Whitechurch Cemetary 19 Dunover Rd, Newtownards, County Down BT22 2LE T: 01247 58659
County Londonderry
Altnagelvin Cemetery Church Brae, Altnagelvin, Londonderry, County Londonderry BT47 3QG T: 01504 343351
City Cemetery Lone Moor Rd, Londonderry, County Londonderry BT48 9LA T: 02871 362615 F: 02871 362085
County Tyrone
Greenhill Cemetery Mountjoy Rd, Omagh, County Tyrone BT79 7BL T: 028 8224 4918
Westland Road Cemetery Westland Rd, Cookstown, County Tyrone BT80 8BX T: 016487 66087

FRANCE

Russian Cemetery
Cimetiere Russe de Sainte Genevierve des Bois (Russian Cemetery) 8 Rue Léo Lagrange, 91700, Sainte Genevierve des Bois,

Museums

National

Bass Museum Horninglow Street, Burton on Trent, DE14 1YQ T: 0845 6000598 W: www.bass-museum.com

Battlefields Trust 33 High Green, Brooke, Norwich, NR15 1HR T: 01508 558145 E: BattlefieldTrust@aol.com W: www.battlefieldstrust.com

Black Cultural Archives 378 Coldharbour Lane, London, SW9 8LF T: (020) 7738 4591 E: info@99mbh.org.uk W: www.99mbh.org.uk

British Empire & Commonwealth Museum Clock Tower Yard, Temple Meads, Bristol, BS1 6QH T: 0117 925 4980 E: admin@empiremuseum.co.uk W: www.empiremuseum.co.uk

British Museum The Secretariat, Great Russell St, London, WC1B 3DG T: (020) 7323 8768 E: jwallace@thebritishmuseum.ac.uk W: www.thebritishmuseum.ac.uk

British Red Cross Museum and Archives UK Office, 44 Moorfields, London, EC2Y 9AL T: 0870 170 7000 E: enquiry@redcross.org.uk W: www.redcross.org.uk/museum&archives

Commonwealth War Graves Commission 2 Marlow Road, Maidenhead, SL6 7DX T: 01628-634221 W: www.cwgc.org

Imperial War Museum Lambeth Road, London, SE1 6HZ T: (020) 7416-5000 E: books@iwm.org.uk W: www.iwm.org.uk

Imperial War Museum - Duxford Imperial War Museum, Airfield, Duxford, Cambridge, CB2 4QR T: 01223 835 000 E: duxford@iwm.org.uk

Kensington Palace State Apartments Kensington Palace, London, W8 4PX T: (020) 7937 9561

Labour History Archive and Study Centre People's History Museum & study Centre, 103 Princess Street, Manchester, M1 6DD T: 0161 228 7212 E: archives@phm.org.uk W: www.phm.org.uk

Library of Primitive Methodism Englesea Brook Chapel and Museum, Englesea Brook, Crewe, CW2 5QW E: engleseabrook-methodist-museum@supanet.com W: www.engleseabrook-museum.org

Library of the Royal College of Surgeons of England 35-43 Lincoln's Inn Fields, London, WC2A 3PE T: (020) 7869 6555 E: library@rcseng.ac.uk W: www.rcseng.ac.uk

Locomotion - The National Railway Museum @ Shildon Shildon, DL4 1PQ T: 01388 777 999 E: gmuirhead@locomotion.uk.com W: www.locomotion.uk.com

Ministry of Defence - Army Records Centre CS(R)2b, Bourne Avenue, Hayes, UB3 1RF

Museum of the Order of St John St John's Gate, St John's Lane, Clerkenwell, London, EC1M 4DA T: (020) 7253-6644 W: www.sja.org.uk/history

Museum of the Royal Pharmaceutical Society Museum of the Royal Pharmaceutical Society, 1 Lambeth High Street, London, SE1 7JN T: (020) 7572 2210 E: museum@rpsgb.org W: www.rpsgb.org

Museums Association 42 Clerkenwell Close, London, EC1R 0PA T: (020) 7250 1789

National Army Museum Department of Archives (Photographs, Film & Sound) Royal Hospital Road, London, SW3 4HT T: (020) 7730-0717 E: info@national-army-museum.ac.uk W: www.national-army-museum.ac.uk

National Army Museum Royal Hospital Road, London, SW3 4HT T: (020) 7730 0717 E: info@national-army-museum.ac.uk W: www.national-army-museum.ac.uk

National Motorboat Museum Wattyler Country Park, Pitsea Hall Lane, Pitsea, Basildon, SS16 4UH T: 01268 550077

National Museum of Photography, Film and Television Bradford, BD1 1NQ T: 01274-202030 W: www.nmpft.org.uk

National Portrait Gallery 2 St. Martins Place, London, WC2H 0HE T: (020) 7306 0055 W: www.npg.org.uk

National Railway Museum Leeman Road, York, YO26 4XJ T: 01904 621261 E: nrm@nmsi.ac.uk W: www.nrm.org.uk

National Tramway Museum Crich Tramway Village, Crich, Matlock, DE4 5DP T: 01773 852565 E: info@tramway.co.uk W: www.tramway.co.uk

National Waterways Museum, Llanthony Warehouse, Gloucester Docks, Gloucester, GL1 2EH T: 01452 318054 E: curatorial1@nwm.demon.co.uk W: www.nwm.demon.co.uk

Natural History Museum Cromwell Rd, London, SW7 5BD T: (020) 7938 9238 W: www.nhm.ac.uk

River & Rowing Museum Rowing & River Museum, Mill Meadows, Henley on Thames, RG9 1BF T: 01491 415625 E: museum@rrm.co.uk W: www..rrm.co.uk

Royal Air Force Museum Grahame Park Way, Hendon, London, NW9 5LL T: (020) 8200 1763 W: www.rafmuseum.org.uk

Royal Armouries H.M Tower Of London, Tower Hill, London, EC3N 4AB T: (020) 7480 6358 ext 30 E: Bridgett.Clifford@armouries.org.uk W: www.armouries.org.uk

Royal Observatory Greenwich Romney Road, Greenwich, London, SE10 9NF T: (020) 8858-4422 W: www.nmm.ac.uk

Science Museum Exhibition Road, South Kensington, London, SW7 2DD T: 0870 870 4771 W: www.sciencemuseum.org.uk

Sherlock Holmes Museum 221b Baker St, London, NW1 6XE T: (020) 7935 8866 E: sherlock@easynet.co.uk W: www.sherlock-holmes.co.uk

The Boat Museum & David Owen Waterways Archive South Pier Road, Ellesmere Port, CH65 4FW T: 0151-355-5017 W: www.boatmuseum.org.uk

The Library & Museum of Freemasonry Freemasons' Hall, 60 Great Queen Street, London, WC2B 5AZ T: (020) 7395 9257 W: www.grandlodge-england.org

The National Coal Mining Museum for England Caphouse Colliery, New Road, Overton, Wakefield, WF4 4RH T: 01924 848806 E: info@ncm.org.uk W: www.ncm.org.uk

The National Football Museum Sir Tom Finney Way, Deepdale, Preston, PR1 6RU T: 01772 908 400 E: enquiries@nationalfootballmuseum.com W: www.nationalfootballmuseum.com

The Natural History Museum Cromwell Road, London, SW7 5BD T: (020) 7942 5000 W: www.nhm.ac.uk

The Science Museum Exhibition Rd, London, SW7 2DD T: 0870 8704868 E: sciencemuseum@nmsp.ac.uk

Theatre Museum Russell Street, Convent Garden, London, WC2 T: 020 7943 4700 E: info@theatremuseum.org W: www.theatremuseum.org

Victoria & Albert Museum Cromwell Rd, South Kensington, London, SW7 2RL T: (020) 7942 2164

Victoria & Albert Museum South Kensington, London, SW7 2RL T: (020) 7638 8500 W: www.nal.vam.ac.uk

Bath

Roman Baths Museum Abbey Churchyard, Bath, BA1 1LZ T: 01225 477773

Bedfordshire

Bedford Museum & Befordshire Yeomanry Museum Castle Lane, Bedford, MK40 3XD T: 01234 353323 E: bmuseum@bedford.gov.uk W: www.bedfordmuseum.org

Bedfordshire and Hertfordshire Regt Museum Luton Museum, Wardown Park, Luton, LU2 7HA T: 01582 546722 W: www.luton.gov.uk/enjoying/museums

Buckinghamshire Military Museum Trust Collection Old Gaol Museum, Market Hill, Buckingham, MK18 13X T: 01280 823020

Cecil Higgins Art Gallery Castle Close, Castle Lane, Bedford, MK40 3RP T: 01234 211222 E: W:

Elstow Moot Hall Elstow, Bedford, MK42 9XT T: 01234 266889 E: wilemans@deed.bedfordshire.gov.uk W: www.bedfordshire.gov.uk

John Dony Field Centre Hancock Drive, Bushmead, Luton, LU2 7SF T: 01582 486983

Luton Museum Service & Art Gallery Wardown Park, Luton, LU2 7HA T: 01582 546725 E: adeye@luton.gov.uk

Museum of Defence Intelligence Chicksands, Shefford, SG17 5PR T: 01462 752340

Shuttleworth Collection Old Warden Aerodrome, Biggleswade, SG18 9ER T: 01767 627288 E: collection@shuttleworth.org W: www.shuttlewaorth.org

Shuttleworth Veteran Aeroplane Society PO Box 42, Old Warden Aerodrome, Biggleswade, SG18 9UZ T: 01767 627398 E: svas@oldwarden.fsnet.co.uk

Station X - Bletchley Park Bletchley Park Trust, The Mansion, Bletchley, Milton Keynes, MK3 6EB T: 01908 640404 W: www.bletchelypark.org.uk

Berkshire

Blake's Lock Museum Gasworks Rd, Reading, RG1 3DS T: 0118 939 0918

Maidenhead Heritage Centre 41 Nicholsons Centre, Maidenhead, SL6 1LL T: 01628 780555

Museum of English Rural Life University of Reading, Redlands Road, Reading, RG1 5EX T: 0118 378 8660 E: merl@reading.ac.uk W: www.merl.org.uk

R.E.M.E. Museum of Technology Isaac Newton Road, Arborfield, Reading, RG2 9NJ T: 0118 976 3375 W: www.rememuseum.org.uk

Royal Berkshire Yeomanry Cavalry Museum T A Centre, Bolton Road, Windsor, SL4 3JG T: 01753 860600

Royal Borough Collection - Windsor, Friends of 14 Park Avenue, Wraysbury, TW19 5ET T: 01784 482771

Royal Borough Museum (Windsor & Maidenhead) Tinkers Lane, Windsor, SL4 4LR T: 01628 796829 E: olivia.gooden@rbwm.gov.uk

Slough Museum 278-286 High St, Slough, SL1 1NB T: 01753 526422

The Household Cavalry Museum Combermere Barracks, Windsor, SL4 3DN T: 01753 755112

The Museum of Berkshire Aviation Trust Mohawk Way, off Bader Way, Woodley, Reading, RG5 4UE T: 0118 944 8089 E: museumofberkshireaviation@fly.to W: http://fly.to/museumofberkshireaviation

The Museum of Reading Town Hall, Blagrave Street, Reading, RG1 1QH T: 0118-939-9800 W: ww.readingmuseum.org.uk

Wantage Vale & Downland Museum Church Street, Wantage, OX12 8BL T: 01235 771447

Wellington Exhibition Stratfield Saye House, Reading, RG7 2BT T: 01256 882882 W: www.stratfield-saye.co.uk

West Berkshire Heritage Service - Newbury West Berkshire Museum, The Wharf, Newbury, RG14 5AS T: 01635 519532 E: jburrell@westberks.gov.uk W: www.westberkshiremuseum.org.uk

West Berkshire Museum The Wharf, Newbury, RG14 5AS T: 01635 30511 E: heritage@westberks.gov.uk W: www.westberks.gov.uk

Bristol

Ashton Court Visitor Centre Ashton Court, Long Ashton, Bristol, BS41 8JN T: 0117 963 9174

Blaise Castle House Museum Henbury, Bristol, BS10 7QS T: 0117 903 9818 E: general_museum@bristol-city.gov.uk W: www.bristol-city.gov.uk/museums

Bristol Industrial Museum Princes Wharf, Wapping Road, Bristol, BS1 4RN T: 0117 925 1470

City Museum & Art Gallery Queens Road, Bristol, BS8 1RL T: 0117 921 3571 E: general_museum@bristol-city.gov.uk W: www.bristol-city.gov.uk/museums

Clevedon Story Heritage Centre Waterloo House, 4 The Beach, Clevedon, BS21 7QU T: 01275 341196

Clifton Suspension Bridge Visitor Centre Bridge House, Sion Place, Bristol, BS8 4AP T: 0117 974 4664 E: visitinfo@clifton-suspension-bridge.org.uk W: www.clifton-suspension-bridge.org.uk

Georgian House 7 Great George Street, Bristol, BS1 5RR T: 0117 921 1362

Harveys Wine Museum 12 Denmark St, Bristol, BS1 5DQ T: 0117 927 5036 E: alun.cox@adwev.com W: www.j-harvey.co.uk

Red Lodge Park Row, Bristol, BS1 5LJ T: 0117 921 1360 W: www.bristol-city.gov.uk/museums

SS Great Britain and Maritime Heritage Centre Wapping Wharf, Gasferry Road, Bristol, BS1 6TY T: 0117 926 0680

Buckinghamshire

Amersham Local History Museum 49 High Street, Amersham, HP7 0DP T: 01494 725754

Bletchley Park Trust The Mansion, Bletchley Park, Bletchley, Milton Keynes, MK3 6EB T: 01908 640404 E: info@bletchleypark.org.uk W: ww.bletchleypark.org.uk

Blue Max Wycombe Air Park, Booker, Marlow, SL7 3DP T. 01494 449810

Buckinghamshire County Museum Church Street, Aylesbury, HP20 2QP T: 01296 331441 E: museum@buckscc.gov.uk

Chesham Town Museum Project Chesham Library, Elgiva Lane, Chesham, HP5 2JD T: 01494 783183

Chiltern Open Air Museum Ltd Newland Park, Gorelands Lane, Chalfont St. Giles, HP8 4AB T: 01494 871117

Milton Keynes Museum Stacey Hill Farm, Southern Way, Wolverton, Milton Keynes, MK12 5EJ T: 01908 316222

Pitstone and Ivinghoe Museum Society Vicarage Road, Pitstone, Leighton Buzzard, LU7 9EY T: 01296 668123 W: http://website.lineone.net/~pitstonemus

Wycombe Museum Priory Avenue, High Wycombe, HP13 6PX T: 01494 421895 E: enquiries@wycombemuseum.demon.co.uk W: www.wycombe.gov.uk/museum

Cambridgeshire

Cambridge Brass Rubbing The Round Church, Bridge St, Cambridge, CB2 1UB T: 01223 871621

Cambridge Museum of Technology Old Pumping Station, Cheddars Lane, Cambridge, CB5 8LD T: 01223 368650

Cromwell Museum The Cromwell Museum, Huntingdon, T: 01480 375830 E: cromwellmuseum@cambridgeshire.gov.uk W: http://edweb.camcnty.gov.uk/cromwell

Cromwell Museum Grammar School Walk, Huntingdon, PE18 6LF T: 01480 375830

Duxford Displays Ltd Duxford Airfield, Duxford, Cambridge, CB2 4QR T: 01223 836593

Ely Museum The Old Goal, Market Street, Ely, CB7 4LS T: 01353-666655 E: info@elymuseum.org.uk W: www.elymuseum.org.uk

Farmland Museum Denny Abbey, Ely Rd, Waterbeach, Cambridge, CB5 9PQ T: 01223 860988 E: f.m.denny@tesco.net W: www.dennyfarmlandmuseum.org.uk

Fenland & West Norfolk Aviation Museum Lynn Rd, West Walton, Wisbech, PE14 7 T: 01945 584440

Folk Museum 2 - 3 Castle St, Cambridge, CB3 0AQ T: 01223 355159 E: info@folkmuseum.org.uk W: www.folkmuseum.org.uk

March & District Museum Society Museum, High St, March, PE15 9JJ T: 01354 655300

Museum of Classical Archaeology Sidgwick Avenue, Cambridge, CB3 9DA T: 01223 335153 W: www.classics.cam.ac.uk/ark.html/

Nene Valley Railway Wansford Station, Peterborough, PE8 6LR T: 01780 782833

Norris Library and Museum The Broadway, St Ives, PE27 5BX T: 01480 497317 E: bob@norrismuseum.fsnet.co.uk

Octavia Hill Birthplace Museum Trust 1 South Brink Place, Wisbech, PE13 1JE T: 01945 476358

Peterborough Museum & Art Gallery Priestgate, Peterborough, PE1 1LF T: 01733 343329 E: museum@peterborough.gov.uk

Prickwillow Drainage Engine Museum Main St, Prickwillow, Ely, CB7 4UN T: 01353 688360

RAF Witchford Display of Memorabilia Grovemere Building, Lancaster Way Business Park, Ely, T: 01353 666666

Railworld Museum - Nene Valley Railway Oundle Road, Peterborough, PE2 9NR T: 01733 344240 W: www.railworld.net

Ramsey Rural Museum The Woodyard, Wood Lane, Ramsey, Huntingdon, PE17 1XD T: 01487 815715

Sedgwick Museum University of Cambridge, Downing St, Cambridge, CB2 3EQ T: 01223 333456 E: mgd2@esc.cam.ac.uk

Soham Community History Museum PO Box 21, The Pavilion, Fountain Lane, Soham, CB7 5PL

Wisbech and Fenland Museum Museum Square, Wisbech, PE13 1ES T: 01945-583817 E: wisbechmuseum@beeb.net

Cheshire

Catalyst Gossage Building, Mersey Road, Widnes, WA8 0DF T: 0151 420 1121

Cheshire Military Museum The Castle, Chester, CH1 2DN T: 01244 327617 W: www.chester.cc.uk/militarymuseum

Chester Heritage Centre - closed August 2000 St. Michaels Church, Bridge St, Chester, CH1 1NQ T: 01244 317948

Deva Roman Experience Pierpoint Lane , off Bridge Street, Chester, CH1 2BJ T: 01244 343407

Griffin Trust The Hangars, West Road, Hutton Park airfield, Ellesmere Port, CH65 1BQ T: 0151 350 2598

Grosvenor Museum 27 Grosvenor St, Chester, CH1 2DD T: 01244 402008 E: s.rogers@chestercc.gov.uk W: www.chestercc.gov.uk/heritage/museums

Hack Green Secret Nuclear Bunker PO Box 127, Nantwich, CW5 8AQ T: 01270 623353 E: coldwar@dial.pipex.com W: www.hackgreen.co.uk

Historic Warships at Birkenhead East Float Dock, Dock Road, Birkenhead, L41 1DJ T: 0151 6501573 W: www.warships.freeserve.co.uk

Lion Salt Works Trust Ollershaw Lane, Marston, Northwich, CW9 6ES T: 01606 41823 E: afielding@lionsalt.demon.co.uk W: www.lionsaltworkstrust.org.uk

Macclesfield Museums Heritage Centre, Roe St, Macclesfield, SK11 6UT T: 01625 613210 E: postmaster@silk-macc.u-net.com W:

Macclesfield Silk Museums Paradise Mill, Park Lane, Macclesfield, SK11 6TJ T: 01625 612045 W: www.silk-macclesfield.org

Miniature AFV Association (MAFVA) 45 Balmoral Drive, Holmes Chapel, CW4 7JQ T: 01477 535373 E: MAFVAHQ@aol.com W: www.mafva.org.uk

Nantwich Museum Pillory St, Nantwich, CW5 5BQ T: 01270 627104

Norton Priory Museum Trust Ltd Tudor Road, Manor Park, Runcorn, WA7 1SX T: 01928 569895 E: info@nortonpriory.org W: www.nortonpriory.org

Stockport Air Raid Shelters 61 Chestergate, Stockport, SK1 1NG T: 0161 474 1942

Warrington Library, Museum & Archives Service 3 Museums Street, Warrington, WA1 1JB T: 01925 442733 E: museum@warrington.gov.uk W: www.warrington.gov.uk/museum

West Park Museum Prestbury Rd, Macclesfield, SK10 3BJ T: 01625 619831

Cleveland

Captain Cook & Staithes Heritage Centre High St, Staithes, Saltburn-By-The-Sea, TS13 5BQ T: 01947 841454

Captain Cook Birthplace Museum Stewart Park, Marton, Middlesbrough, TS7 6AS T: 01642 311211 W: www.aboutbritain.com/CaptainCookBirthplaceMuseum

Dorman Musuem Linthorpe Rd, Middlesbrough, TS5 6LA T: 01642 813781 E: dormanmuseum@middlesbrough.gov.uk W: www.dormanmuseum.co.uk

Green Dragon Museum Theatre Yard, High Street, Stockton-On-Tees, TS18 1AT T: 01642 393938

Hartlepool Historic Quay Maritime Avenue, Hartlepool Marina, Hartlepool, TS24 0XZ T: 01429 860077 E: arts-museum@hartlepool.gov.uk W: www.thisishartlepool.com

HMS Trincomalee Maritime Avenue, Hartlepool Marina, Hartlepool, TS24 0XZ T: 01429 223193 W: www.thisishartlepool.com

Margrove Heritage Centre Margrove Park, Boosbeck, Saltburn-By-The-Sea, TS12 3BZ T: 01287 610368

Preston Hall Museum Yarm Road, Stockton-On-Tees, TS18 3RH T: 01642 781184

Stockton Museums Service Education, Leisure & Cultural Services, PO Box 228, Municipal Buildings, Church Road, Stockton on Tees, TS18 1XE T: 01642 415382 E: rachel.mason@stockton.gov.uk W: www.stockton.gov.uk

The Tom Leonard Mining Experience Deepdale, Skinningrove, Saltburn, TS13 4AA T: 01287 642877

Cornwall

Automobilia The Old Mill, Terras Rd, St. Austell, PL26 7RX T: 01726 823092

Bodmin Museum Mount Folly, Bodmin, PL31 2DB T: 01208 77067

Charlestown Shipwreck & Heritage Centre Quay Rd, Charlestown, St. Austell, PL25 3NX T: 01726 69897

Duke of Cornwall's Light Infantry Museum The Keep, Bodmin, PL31 1EG T: 01208 72810 W: www.britrishlightinfantry.org.ca

Flambards Village and Cornwall Aircraft Park Flambards Village Theme Park, Culdrose Manor, Helston, TR12 0GA T: 01326 573404 E: info@flambards.co.uk W: www.flambards.co.uk

Helston Folk Museum Market Place, Helston, TR13 8TH T: 01326 564027 E: enquiries@helstonmuseum.org.uk W: www.helstonmuseum.org.uk

John Betjeman Centre Southern Way, Wadebridge, PL27 7BX T: 01208 812392

Lanreath Farm & Folk Museum Lanreath Farm, Near Looe, PL13 2NX T: 01503 220321

Lawrence House Museum 9 Castle St, Launceston, PL15 8BA T: 01566 773277

Maritime Museum 19 Chapel Street, Penzance, TR18 4AF T: 01736 68890

Merlin's Cave Crystal Mineral & Fossil Museum & Shop Molesworth St, Tintagel, PL34 0BZ T: 01840 770023

Mevagissey Museum Society Frazier House, The Quay, Mevagissey, St. Austell, PL26 6QU T: 01726 843568 E: haycas02@yahoo.co.uk W: www.geocities.com/mevamus

National Maritime Museum (Falmouth, Cornwall) 48 Arwenack St, Falmouth, TR11 3SA T: 01326 313388

National Maritime Museum (Saltash, Cornwall) Cotehele Quay, Cotehele, Saltash, PL12 6TA T: 01579 350830

Penryn Museum Town Hall, Higher Market St, Penryn, TR10 8LT T: 01326 372158

Penzance Maritime Museum 19 Chapel St, Penzance, TR18 4AW T: 01736 368890 E:

Porthcurno Telegraph Museum and Archive Eastern House,, Porthcurno, Penzance, TR19 6JX T: 01736 810478 E: info@porthcurno.org.uk W: www.porthcurno.org.uk

Potter's Museum of Curiosity Jamaica Inn Courtyard, Bolventor, Launceston, PL15 7TS T: 01566 86838

Royal Cornwall Museum River St, Truro, TR1 2SJ T: 01872 272205

Trinity House National Lighthouse Centre Wharf Road, Penzance, TR18 4BN T: 01736 60077

County Durham

Darlington Railway Centre & Museum North Road Station , Station Rd, Darlington, DL3 6ST T: 01325 460532

Darlington Railway Preservation Society Station Rd, Hopetown, Darlington, DL3 6ST T: 01325 483606

Discovery Centre Grosvenor House, 29 Market Place, Bishop Auckland, DL14 7NP T: 01388-662666 E: west.durham@groundwork.org.uk

Durham Heritage Centre St Mary le Bow, North Bailey, Durham, DH1 5ET T: 0191-384-5589

Durham Light Infantry Museum Aykley Heads, Durham, DH1 5TU T: 0191-384-2214 E: dli@durham.gov.uk W: www.durham.gov.uk/dli

Durham Mining Museum 43 Primrose Crescent, Fulwell, Sunderland, SR6 9RJ T: 07931 421709 E: webmaster@dmm.org.uk W: www.dmm.org.uk

Durham University Library Archives and Special Collections Palace Green Section, Palace Green, Durham, DH1 3RN T: 0191 334 2932 E: pg.library@durham.ac.uk W: www.dur.ac.uk/library/asc

Fulling Mill Museum of Archaeology The Banks, Durham, T: 0191 374 3623

Killhope Lead Mining Centre Cowshill, Weardale, DL13 1AR T: 01388-537505 E: killhope@durham.gov.uk W: www.durham.gov.uk/killhope/index.htm

The Bowes Museum Newgate, Barnard Castle, DL12 8NP T: 01833 690606 E: info@bowesmuseum.org.uk W: www.bowesmuseum.org.uk

The Oriental Museum University of Durham Museums, Elvet Hill, Durham, DH1 3TH T: 0191 334 5694 E: oriental.museum@dur.ar.uk W: www.durham.ac.uk

Weardale Museum South View, 2 Front Street, Ireshopeburn, DL13 1EY T: 01388-537417

Cumbria

Aspects of Motoring Western Lakes Motor Museum The Maltings, The Maltings, Brewery Lane, Cockermouth, CA13 9ND T: 01900 824448

Birdoswald Roman Fort Gilsland, Brampton, CA6 7DD T: 01697 747602

Border Regiment & Kings Own Royal Border Regiment Museum Queen Mary's Tower, The Castle, Carlisle, CA3 8UR T: 01228 532774 E: borderregiment@aol.com W: www.armymuseums.org

Dove Cottage & The Wordsworth Museum Town End, Grasmere, Ambleside, LA22 9SH T: 015394 35544

Friends of The Helena Thompson Museum 24 Calva Brow, Workington, CA14 1DD T: 01900 603312

Haig Colliery Mining Museum Solway Road, Kells, Whitehaven, CA28 9BG T: 01946 599949 W: www.haigpit.com

Heritage First - formerly Ulverston Heritage Centre Lower Brook St, Ulverston, LA12 7EE T: 01229 580820 W: www.rootsweb.com/~ukuhc/

Keswick Museum & Art Gallery Station Rd, Keswick, CA12 4NF T: 017687 73263 E: hazel.davison@allerdale.gov.uk

Lakeland Motor Museum Holker Hall, Cark In Cartmel, Grange-Over-Sands, LA11 7PL T: 015395 58509

Lakeside & Haverthwaite Railway Haverthwaite Station, Ulverston, LA12 8AL T: 01539 531594

Laurel & Hardy Museum 4c Upper Brook St, Ulverston, LA12 7BH T: 01229 582292

Maritime Museum 1 Senhouse Street, Maryport, CA15 6AB T: 01900 813738

Maryport Steamship Museum Elizabeth Dock South Quay, Maryport, CA15 8AB T: 01900 815954

North Pennines Heritage Trust Nenthead Mines Heritage Centre, Nenthead, Alston, CA9 3PD T: 01434 382037 E: administration.office@virgin.net W: www.npht.com

Penrith Museum Middlegate, Penrith, CA11 7PT T: 01768 212228 E: museum@eden.gov.uk

Roman Army Museum Carvoran House, Greenhead, Carlisle, CA6 7JB T: 016977 47485

Ruskin Museum Yewdale Rd, Coniston, LA21 8DU T: 015394 41164 W: www.coniston.org.uk

Senhouse Roman Museum The Battery, Sea Brows, Maryport, CA15 6JD T: 01900 816168 E: romans@senhouse.freeserve.co.uk W: www.senhousemuseum.co.uk

Solway Aviation Museum Carlisle Airport, Carlisle, CA6 4NW T: 01228 573823

Solway Aviation Museum Aviation House, Carlisle Airport, Carlisle , CA6 4NW T: 01227 573823 W: www.solway-aviation-museum.org.uk

The Dock Museum North Rd, Barrow-In-Furness, LA14 2PW T: 01229 894444 E: docmuseum@barrowbc.gov.uk W: www.barrowtourism.co.uk

The Guildhall Museum Green Market, Carlisle, CA3 8JE T: 01228 819925

Tullie House Museum and Art Gallery Castle Street, Carlisle, CA3 8TP T: 01228-534781

William Creighton Mineral Museum & Gallery 2 Crown St, Cockermouth, CA13 0EJ T: 01900 828301

Windermere Steamboat Museum Rayrigg Rd, Windermere, LA23 1BN T: 015394 45565 W: www.steamboat.co.uk

Derbyshire

Chesterfield Museum & Art Gallery St Mary's Gate, Chesterfield, S41 7TY T: 01246 345727

Derby Industrial Museum Silk Mill Lane, Off Full Street, Derby, DE1 3AF T: 01332 255308 W: www.derby.gov.uk/museums

Derby Museum & Art Gallery The Strand, Derby, DE1 1BS T: 01332-716659 W: www.derby.gov.uk/museums

Derwent Valley Visitor Centre Belper North Mill, Bridge Foot, Belper, DE56 1YD T: 01773 880474

Donington Grandprix Collection Donington Park, Castle Donington, Derby, DE74 2RP T: 01332 811027

Elvaston Castle Estate Museum Elvaston Castle Country Park, Borrowash Road, Elvaston, Derby, DE72 3EP T: 01332 573799
Erewash Museum The Museum, High Street, Ilkeston, DE7 5JA T: 0115 907 1141 E: museum@erewash.gov.uk W: www.erewash.gov.uk
Eyam Museum Eyam, S32 5QP T: 01433 631371 E: johnbeck@classicfm.net W: www.eyam.org.uk
Glossop Heritage Centre Bank House, Henry St, Glossop, SK13 8BW T: 01457 869176
High Peak Junction Workshop High Peak Junction, Cromford, Matlock, DE4 5HN T: 01629 822831
High Peak Trail Middleton Top, Rise End, Middleton, Matlock, DE4 4LS T: 01629 823204
Midland Railway Centre Butterley Station, Ripley, DE5 3QZ T: 01773 570140
National Stone Centre Porter Lane, Wirksworth, Matlock, DE4 4LS T: 01629 824833
Peak District Mining Museum The Pavilion, South Parade, Matlock Bath, DE4 3NR T: 01629 583834 E: mail@peakmines.co.uk W: www.peakmines.co.uk
Pickford's House Museum 41 Friar Gate, Derby, DE1 1DA T: 01332 255363 W: www.derby.gov.uk/museums
Regimental Museum of the 9th/12th Royal Lancers Derby City Museum and Art Gallery, The Strand, Derby, DE1 1BS T: 01332 716656 W: www.derby.gov.uk/museums

Devon

Allhallows Museum of Lace & Antiquities High St, Honiton, EX14 1PG T: 01404 44966 E: dyateshoniton@msn.com W: www.honitonlace.com
Brixham Heritage Museum Bolton Cross, Brixham, TQ5 8LZ T: 01803 856267 E: mail@brixhamheritage.org.uk W: www.brixhamheritage.org.uk
Century of Playtime 30 Winner St, Paignton, TQ3 3BJ T: 01803 553850 E:
Crownhill Fort Crownhill Fort Road, Plymouth, PL6 5BX T: 01752 793754
Devon & Cornwall Constabulary Museum Middlemoor, Exeter, EX2 7HQ T: 01392 203025
Dunkeswell Memorial Museum Dunkeswell Airfield, Dunkeswell Ind Est, Dunkeswell, Honiton, EX14 0RA T: 01404 891943
Fairlynch Art Centre & Museum 27 Fore St, Budleigh Salterton, EX9 6NP T: 01395 442666
Finch Foundary Museum of Rural Industry Sticklepath, Okehampton, EX20 2NW T: 01837 840046
Ilfracombe Museum Wilder Rd, Ilfracombe, EX34 8AF T: 01271 863541 E: ilfracombe@devonmuseums.net W: www.devonmuseums.net
Museum of Barnstaple & North Devon incorporating Royal Devon Yeomanry Museum Peter A Boyd, The Square, Barnstaple, EX32 8LN T: 01271 346 747
Newton Abbot Town & Great Western Railway Museum 2A St. Pauls Rd, Newton Abbot, TQ12 2HP T: 01626 201121
Newhall Visitor & Equestrian Centre Newhall, Budlake, Exeter, EX5 3LW T: 01392 462453
North Devon Maritime Museum Odun House, Odun Rd, Appledore, Bideford, EX39 1PT T: 01237 422064 W: www.devonmuseums.net/appledore
North Devon Museum Service St.Anne's Chapel, Paternoster Row, Barnstaple, EX32 8LN T: 01271 378709
Otterton Mill Otterton, Budleigh Salterton, EX9 7HG T: 01395 568521 E: escape@ottertonmill.com W: www.ottertonmill.com
Park Pharmacy Trust Thorn Park Lodge, Thorn Park , Mannamead, Plymouth, PL3 4TF T: 01752 263501
Plymouth City Museum Drake Circus, Plymouth, PL4 8AJ T: 01752 304774 E: plymouth.museum@plymouth.gov.uk W: www.plymouthmuseum.gov.uk www.cottoniancollection.org.uk
Royal Albert Memorial Museum Queen Street, Exeter, EX4 3RX T: 01392 265858
Seaton Tramway Harbour Road, Seaton , EX12 2NQ T: 01297 20375 E: info@tram.co.uk W: www.tram.co.uk
Sidmouth Museum Hope Cottage, Church St, Sidmouth, EX10 8LY T: 01395 516139
Teignmouth Museum 29 French St, Teignmouth, TQ14 8ST T: 01626 777041
The Dartmouth Museum The Butterwalk, Dartmouth, TQ6 9PZ T: 01803 832923
The Devonshire and Dorset Regiment (Archives) RHQ, Devonshire and Dorset Regiment, Wyvern Barracks, Barrack Road, Exeter, EX2 6AR T: 01392 492436
The Museum of Dartmoor Life West Street, Okehampton, EX20 1HQ T: 01837 52295 E: dartmoormuseum@eclipse.co.uk W: www.museumofdartmoorlife.eclipse.co.uk

Tiverton Museum of Mid Devon Life Beck's Square, Tiverton, EX16 6PJ T: 01884 256295 E: tiverton@eclipse.co.uk W: www.tivertonmuseum.org.uk

Dorset

Bournemouth Aviation Museum Hanger 600, Bournemouth International Airport, Christchurch, BH23 6SE T: 01202 580858 E: admin@aviation-museum.co.uk W: www.aviation-museum.co.uk
Bridport Harbour Museum West Bay, Bridport, DT6 4SA T: 01308 420997
Bridport Museum Trust - Local History Centre The Coach House, Gundy Lane, Bridport, DT6 3RJ T: 01308 458703 E: office@bridportmuseum.co.uk W: www.bridportmuseum.co.uk
Cavalcade of Costume Museum Lime Tree House, The Plocks, Blandford Forum, DT11 7AA T: 01258 453006 W: www.cavalcadeofcostume.com
Christchurch Motor Museum Matchams Lane, Hurn, Christchurch, BH23 6AW T: 01202 488100
Dinosaur Land Coombe St, Lyme Regis, DT7 3PY T: 01297 443541
Dinosaur Museum, Icen Way, Dorchester, DT1 1EW T: 01305 269880
Dorset County Museum High West Street, Dorchester, DT1 1XA T: 01305 262735 E: dorsetcountymuseum@dor-mus.demon.co.uk W: www.dorsetcc.gov.uk
Dorset Volunteers, Dorset Yeomanry Museum Gillingham Museum, Chantry Fields, Gillingham, SP8 4UA T: 01747 821119 W: www.brWebsites.com/gillingham.museum
Lyme Regis Philpot Museum Bridge St, Lyme Regis, DT7 3QA T: 01297 443370 E: info@lymeregismuseum.co.uk W: www.lymeregismuseum.co.uk
Nothe Fort Barrack Rd, Weymouth, DT4 8UF T: 01305 766626 E: fortressweymouth@btconnect.com W: www.fortressweymouth.co.uk
Portland Museum Wakeham, Portland, DT5 1HS T: 01305 821804
Priest's House Museum 23-27 High St, Wimborne, BH21 1HR T: 01202 882533
Red House Museum & Gardens Quay Rd, Christchurch, BH23 1BU T: 01202 482860
Royal Signals Museum Blandford Camp, Nr Blandford Forum, DT11 8RH T: 01258-482248 W: www.royalsignalsarmy.org.uk/museum/
Russell-Cotes Art Gallery & Museum East Cliff, Bournemouth, BH1 3AA T: 01202 451858 E: diane.edge@bournemouth.gov.uk W: www.russell-cotes.bournemouth.gov.uk
Shaftesbury Abbey Museum & Garden Park Walk, Shaftesbury, SP7 8JR T: 01747 852910
Shaftesbury Town Museum Gold Hill, Shaftesbury, SP7 8JW T: 01747 852157
Sherborne Museum Association Abbey Gate House, Church Avenue, Sherborne, DT9 3BP T: 01935 812252
Tank Museum Bovington, BH20 6JG T: 01929 405096 E: librarian@tankmuseum.co.uk davidw@tankmuseum.co.uk W: www.tankmuseum.co.uk
The Keep Military Museum The Keep, Bridport Road, Dorchester, DT1 1RN T: 01305 264066 E: info@keepmilitarymuseum.org W: www.keepmilitarymuseum.org
The Nothe Fort Museum of Coastal Defence Barrack Road, Weymouth , DT4 5UF T: 01305 787243
Tolpuddle Museum TUC Memorial Cottages, Tolpuddle, DT2 7EH T: 01305 848237 W: www.tolpuddlemartyrs.org.uk
Wareham Town Museum 5 East St, Wareham, BH20 4NS T: 01929 553448
Waterfront Musuem and Local Studies Centre 4 High St, Poole, BH15 1BW T: 01202 683138 E: museums@poole.gov.uk mldavid@poole.gov.uk W: www.poole.gov.uk
Weymouth & Portland Museum Service The Esplanade, Weymouth, DT4 8ED T: 01305 765206
Weymouth Museum Brewers Quay, Hope Square, Weymouth, DT4 8TR T: 01305 777622 E: admin@brewers-quay.co.uk W: www.brewers-quay.co.uk

Essex

Barleylands Farm Museum & Visitors Centre Barleylands Farm, Billericay, CM11 2UD T: 01268 282090
Battlesbridge Motorcycle Museum Muggeridge Farm, Maltings Road, Battlesbridge, Wickford, SS11 7RF T: 01268 560866
Castle Point Transport Museum Society 105 Point Rd, Canvey Island, SS8 7TJ T: 01268 684272
Chelmsford Museum Oaklands Park, Moulsham Street, Chelmsford, CM2 9AQ T: 01245 615100 E: oaklands@chelmsfordbc.gov.uk
East England Tank Museum Oak Business Park, Wix Rd, Beaumont, Clacton-On-Sea, CO16 0AT T: 01255 871119
East Essex Aviation Society & Museum Martello Tower, Point Clear, Clacton on Sea, T: 01255 428020

Epping Forest District Museum 39-41 Sun St, Waltham Abbey, EN9 1EL T: 01992 716882

Essex Police Museum Police Headquarters, PO Box 2, Springfield, Chelmsford, CM2 6DA T: 01245 491491-ext-50771

Essex Regiment Museum Oaklands Park, Moulsham Street, Chelmsford, CM2 9AQ T: 01245 615101 W: www.essexregimentmuseum.co.uk

Essex Secret Bunker Crown Building, Shrublands Road, Mistley, CO11 1HS T: 01206 392271 (24 hour information line)

Essex Volunteer Units Colchester Museums, 14 Ryegate Road, Colchester, CO1 1YG T: 01206 282935

Essex Yeomanry Collection Springfield Lyons TA Centre, Colchester Road, Chelmsford , CM2 5TA T: 01245 462298

Great Dunmow Maltings Museum The Maltings, Mill Lane, Great Dunmow, CM6 1BG T: 01371 878979

Harwich Maritime Museum Low Lightouse, Harbour Crescent, Harwich, T: 01255 503429 W: www.harwich-society.com

Harwich Redoubt Fort Behind 29 Main Road, Harwich, T: 01255 503429 W: www.harwich-society.com

Hollytrees Museum High St, Colchester, CO1 1DN T: 01206 282940

Kelvedon Hatch Secret Nuclear Bunker Kelvedon Hall Lane, Kelvedon Common, Kelvedon Hatch, Brentwood, CM15 0LB T: 01277 364883 E: bunker@japar.demon.co.uk W: www.japar.demon.co.uk

Leigh Heritage Centre & Museum 13a High St, Leigh-On-Sea, SS9 2EN T: 01702 470834 E: palmtree@nothdell.demon.co.uk

Maldon District Museum 47 Mill Rd, Maldon, CM9 5HX T: 01621 842688

Royal Gunpowder Mills administrative Office, Beaulieu drive, Powdermill Lane, Waltham Abbey, EN9 1JY T: 01992 767022 W: www.royalgunpowder.co.uk

Saffron Walden Museum Museum Street, Saffron Walden, CB10 1JL T: 01799 510333 E: museum@uttlesford.gov.uk

Southend Central Museum Museum Victoria Avenue, Southend-On-Sea, SS2 6EW T: 01702 434449

The Cater Museum 74 High St, Billericay, CM12 9BS T: 01277 622023

The Museum of Harlow Muskham Rd, Harlow, CM20 2LF T: 01279 4549569 W: www.tmoh.com

Thurrock Museum Ossett Road, Grays, RM17 5DX

Valence House Museum Valence House Museum, Becontree Avenue, Dagenham, RM8 3HT T: 020 8270 6866 W: www.barking-dagenham.gov.uk

Gloucestershire

Campden & District Historical & Archaeological Society The Old Police Station, High Street, Chipping Campden, GL55 6HB T: 01386 848840 E: enquiries@chippingcampdenhistory.org.uk W: www.chippingcampdenhistory.org.uk

Dean Heritage Centre Soudley, Cinderford, Forest of dean, GL14 2UB T: 01594 822170 E: deanmuse@btinternet.com

Frenchay Tuckett Society and Local History Museum 247 Frenchay Park Road, Frenchay, BS16 ILG T: 0117 956 9324 E: raybulmer@compuserve.com W: www.frenchay.org/museum.html

Gloucester City Museum & Art Gallery Brunswick Rd, Gloucester, GL1 1HP T: 01452 524131

Gloucester Folk Museum 99-103 Westgate St, Gloucester, GL1 2PG T: 01452 526467 E: christopherm@glos-city.gov.uk W: WWW:

Holst Birthplace Museum 4 Clarence Rd, Cheltenham, GL52 2AY T: 01242 524846

Jet Age Museum Hangar 7 Meteor Business Park, Gloucestershire Airport, Cheltenham Road East, Gloucester, GL2 9QY T: 01452 715100 w: www.aboutbritain.com/JetAgeMuseum.htm

John Moore Countryside Museum 42 Church St, Tewkesbury, GL20 5SN T: 01684 297174

Nature In Art Wallsworth Hall, Tewkesbury Rd, Twigworth, Gloucester, GL2 9PG T: 01452 731422 E: rinart@globalnet.co.uk W: www.nature-in-art.org.uk

Regiments Of Gloucestershire Museum Gloucester Docks, Gloucester, GL1 2HE T: 01452 522682

Shambles Museum Church Street, Newent, GL18 1PP T: 01531 822144

Soldiers of Gloucestershire Museum Custom House, Gloucester Docks, Gloucester, GL1 2HE T: 01452 522682 W: www.glosters.org.uk

The Great Western Railway Museum (Coleford) The Old Railway Station, Railway Drive, Coleford, GL16 8RH T: 01594 833569

The Guild Of Handicraft Trust Silk Mill, Sheep Street, Chipping Campden, GL55 6DS T: 01386 841417

The Jenner Museum Church Lane, Berkeley, GL13 9BH T: 01453 810631 E: manager@jennermuseum.com W: www.jennermuseum.com

Wellington Aviation Museum Broadway Road, Moreton in the Marsh, GL56 0BG T: 01608 650323 W: www.wellingtonaviation.org

Hampshire

Action Stations Boathouse No 6, HM Naval Base, Portsmouth, PO1 3LR T: 023 9286 1512

Airbourne Forces Museum Browning Barracks, Aldershot, GU11 2BU T: 01252 349619

Aldershot Military Historical Trust Evelyn Woods Rd, Aldershot, GU11 2LG T: 01252 314598

Andover Museum & Iron Age Museum 6 Church Close, Andover, SP10 1DP T: 01264 366283 E: andover.museum@virgin.nbet musmda@hants.gov.uk musmad@hants.gov.uk W: www.hants.gov.uk/andoverm

Army Medical Services Museum Keogh Barracks, Ash Vale, Aldershot, GU12 5RQ T: 01252 868612 E: armymedicalmuseum@btinternet.com W: www.ams-museum.org.uk

Army Physical Training Corps Museum ASPT, Fox Line, Queen's Avenue, Aldershot, GU11 2LB T: 01252 347168 W: www.aptc.org.uk

Balfour Museum of Hampshire Red Cross History Red Cross House, Weeke, Winchester, SO22 5JD T: 01962 865174

Bishops Waltham Museum Brookstreet, Bishop's Waltham, Southampton, S032 1EB

Broadlands Romsey, SO51 9ZD T: 01794 505010 E: admin@broadlands.net W: www.broadlands.net

D-Day Museum and Overlord Museum Clarence Esplanade, Southsea, PO5 3NT T: 023 9282 7261

Dockyard Apprentice Exhibition Portsmouth Royal Dockyard Historical trust, 19 College Road, HM Naval Base, Portsmouth, PO1 3LJ

Eastleigh Museum 25 High St, Eastleigh, SO50 5LF T: (023) 8064 3026 E: musmst@hants.gov.uk W: www.hants.gov.uk/museum/eastlmus/index.html

Eling Tide Mill Trust Ltd The Tollbridge, Eling Hill, Totton, Southampton, SO40 9HF T: (023) 80869575

Explosion! The Museum of Naval Firepower Priddy's Hard, Gosport, PO12 4LE T: 023 9258 6505 E: info@explosion.org.uk W: www.explosion.org.uk

Gosport Museum Walpole Rd, Gosport, PO12 1NS T: (023) 9258 8035 E: musmie@hunts.gov.uk

Hampshire County Museums Service Chilcomb House, Chilcomb Lane, Winchester, SO23 8RD T: 01962 846304

Havant Museum Havant Museum, 56 East Street, Havant, P09 1BS T: 023 9245 1155 E: musmop@hants.gov.uk W: www.hants.gov.uk/museum

Historic Ships and The Naval Dockyard HM Naval Base, Portsmouth, PO1 3LR T: 023 9286 1512 W: www.flagship.org.uk

HMS Victory Victory Gate, HM Naval Base, Portsmouth, PO1 3LR T: (023) 9277 8600 E: info@hmswarrior.org W: www.hmswarrior.org

HMS Warrior (1860) Victory Gate, HM Naval Base, Portsmouth, PO1 3LR T: (023) 9277 8600 E: info@hmswarrior.org W: www.hmswarrior.org

Hollycombe Steam Collection Iron Hill, Midhurst Rd, Liphook, GU30 7LP T: 01428 724900

Museum of Army Chaplaincy Amport House, Nr Andover , Andover, SP11 8BG T: 01264 773144 x 4248 E: rachdcurator@tiscali.co.uk W: www.army.mod.uk/chaps/museum/index.htm

Museum of Army Flying Middle Wallop, Stockbridge, SO20 8DY T: 01980 674421 W: www.flying-museum.org.uk

New Forest Museum & Visitor Centre High St, Lyndhurst, SO43 7NY T: (023) 8028 3914 E: nfmuseum@lineone.net

Portsmouth City Museum and Record Office Museum Road, Portsmouth, PO1 2LJ T: (023) 92827261

Priddy's Hard Armament Museum Priory Rd, Gosport, PO12 4LE T: (023) 92502490

Rockbourne Roman Villa Rockbourne, Fordingbridge, SP6 3PG T: 01725 518541

Royal Armouries - Fort Nelson Fort Nelson , Down End Roadd, Fareham , PO17 6AN T: 01329 233734 E: enquiries@armouries.org.uk W: www.armouries.org.uk

Royal Marines Museum Eastney, Southsea, PO4 9PX T: (023) 9281 9385 Exts 224 W: www.royalmarinesmuseum.co.uk

Royal Naval Museum Buildings 1 - 7, College Road, HM Naval Base, Portsmouth, PO1 3LJ T: (023) 9283 9766 W: www.royalnavalmuseum.org

Royal Navy Submarine Museum Haslar Jetty Road, Gosport, PO12 2AS T: (023) 92510354 E: admin@rnsubmus.co.uk W: www.rnsubmus.co.uk

Sammy Miller Motor Cycle Museum Bashley Manor Farm, Bashley Cross Rd, New Milton, BH25 5SZ T: 01425 620777

Search 50 Clarence Rd, Gosport, PO12 1BU T: (023) 92501957

Southampton Hall of Aviation Albert Road South, Southampton, SO1 1FR T: 01703 635830

Southampton Maritime Museum Bugle St, Southampton , SO14 2AJ T: (023) 80223941

The Bear Museum 38 Dragon St, Petersfield, GU31 4JJ T: 01730 265108 E: judy@bearmuseum.freeserve.co.uk W: www.bearmuseum.co.uk

The Gurkha Museum Peninsula Barracks, Romsey Road, Winchester, SO23 8TS T: 01962 842832 E: curator@thegurkhamuseum.co.uk W: www.thegurkhamuseum.co.uk

The King's Royal Hussars Museum (10th Royal Hussars PWO 11th Hussars PAO and The Royal Hussars PWO) Peninsula Barracks, Romsey Road, Winchester, SO23 8TS T: 01962 828540 E: beresford@krhmuseum.freeserve.co.uk W: www.hants.gov.uk/leisure/museum/royalhus/index.html

The Light Infantry Museum Peninsula Barracks, Romsey Road, Winchester, SO23 8TS T: 01962 868550

The Mary Rose Trust 1-10 College Road, HM Naval Base, Portsmouth, PO1 3LX T: (023) 92750521

The Museum of The Adjutant General's Corps RHQ Adjutant General's Corps, Worthy Down, Winchester, SO21 2RG T: 01962 887435

The Royal Green Jackets Museum (Oxford and Bucks Light Infantry King's Royal Rifle Corps and The Rifle Brigade) Peninsula Barracks, Romsey Road, Winchester, SO23 8TS T: 01962 828549 E: museum@royalgreenjackets.co.uk W: www.royalgreenjackets.co.uk

The Willis Museum Of Basingstoke Town & Country Life Old Town Hall, Market Place, Basingstoke, RG21 7QD T: 01256 465902 E: willismuseum@hotmail.com W: www.hants.gov.uk/leisure/museums/willis/index.html

West End Local History Society 20 Orchards Way, West End, Southampton, SO30 3FB T: 023 8057 5244 E: westendlhs@aol.com W: www.telbin.demon.co.uk/westendlhs

Westbury Manor Museum West St, Fareham, PO16 0JJ T: 01329 824895 W: www.hants.gov.uk/museum/westbury/

Whitchurch Silk Mill 28 Winchester St, Whitchurch, RG28 7AL T: 01256 892065

Winchester Museums Service 75 Hyde St, Winchester, SO23 7DW T: 01962 848269 E: museums@winchester.gov.uk W: www.winchester.gov.uk/heritage/home.htm

Herefordshire

Churchill House Museum Venns Lane, Hereford, HR1 1DE T: 01432 260693

Cider Museum & King Offa Distillery 21 Ryelands St, Hereford, HR4 0LW T: 01432 354207 E: thompson@cidermuseum.co.uk W: www.cidermuseum.co.uk

Leominster Museum Etnam St, Leominster, HR6 8 T: 01568 615186

Teddy Bears of Bromyard 12 The Square, Bromyard, HR7 4BP T: 01885 488329

Waterworks Museum 86 Park Street, Broomy Hill, Hereford, HR1 2RE T: 01432-356653

Weobley & District Local History Society and Museum Weobley Museum, Back Lane, Weobley, HR4 8SG T: 01544 340292

Hertfordshire

Bushey Museum, Art Gallery and Local Studies Centre Rudolph Road, Bushey, WD23 3HW T: 020 8420 4057 E: busmt@bushey.org.uk W: www.busheymuseum.org

De Havilland Heritage Centre inc The Mosquito Aircraft Museum PO Box 107, Salisbury Hall, London Colney, AL10 1EX T: 01727 822051 W: www.hertsmuseums.org

First Garden City Heritage Museum 296 Norton Way South, Letchworth Garden City, SG6 1SU T: 01462 482710 E: fgchm@letchworth.com

Hertford Museum (Hertfordshire Regiment) 18 Bull Plain, Hertford, SG14 1DT T: 01992 582686 W: www.hertfordmuseum.org

Hitchin British Schools 41-42 Queen St, Hitchin, SG4 9TS T: 01462 420144 E: brsch@britishschools.freeserve.co.uk W: www.hitchinbritishschools.org.uk

Hitchin Museum Paynes Park, Hitchin, SG5 1EQ T: 01462 434476 W: www.nndc.gov.uk

Kingsbury Water Mill Museum St. Michaels Street, St. Albans, AL3 4SJ T: 01727 853502

Letchworth Museum & Art Gallery Broadway, Letchworth Garden City, SG6 3PF T: 01462 685647 E: l.museum@north-herts.gov.uk W: www.north-herts.gov.uk

Mill Green Museum & Mill Mill Green, Hatfield, AL9 5PD T: 01707 271362

Rhodes Memorial Museum & Commonwealth Centre South Rd, Bishop's Stortford, CM23 3JG T: 01279 651746 E: rhodesmuseum@freeuk.com W: www.hertsmuseums.org.uk

Royston & District Museum 5 Lower King St, Royston, SG8 5AL T: 01763 242587

Stondon Transport Museum Station Road, Lower Stondon, SG16 6JN T: 01462 850339 E: info@transportmuseum.co.uk W: www.transportmuseum.co.uk

The De Havilland Aircraft Museum Trust P.O Box 107, Salisbury Hall, London Colney, St. Albans, AL2 1EX T: 01727 822051

The Environmental Awareness Trust 23 High St, Wheathampstead, St. Albans, AL4 8BB T: 01582 834580

The Forge Museum High St, Much Hadham, SG10 6BS T: 01279 843301

Verulamium Museum St. Michaels St, St. Albans, AL3 4SW T: 01727 751810 E: d.thorold.stalbans.gov.uk W: WWW:

Walter Rothschild Zoological Museum Akeman St, Tring, HP23 6AP T: (020) 7942 6156 E: ornlib@nhm.ac.uk W: www.nhm.ac.uk

Ware Museum Priory Lodge, 89 High St, Ware, SG12 9AD T: 01920 487848

Watford Museum 194 High St, Watford, WD1 2DT T: 01923 232297

Welwyn Hatfield Museum Service Welwyn Roman Baths, By-Pass-Road, Welwyn, AL6 0 T: 01438 716096

Hull

Ferens Art Gallery Kingston upon Hull City Museums, Queen Victoria Square, Kingston upon Hull, HU1 3RA T: 01482 613902

Wilberforce House Kingston upon Hull City Museums, 23-25 High Street, Kingston upon Hull, HU1 T: 01482 613902

Isle Of Wight

Bembridge Maritime Museum & Shipwreck Centre Providence House, Sherborne St, Bembridge, PO35 5SB T: 01983 872223

Calbourne Water Mill Calbourne Mill, Newport, PO30 4JN T: 01983 531227

Carisbroke Castle Newport, PO30 1XL W: www.english-heritage.org.uk

Carisbrooke Castle Museum Carisbrooke Castle, Newport, PO30 1XY T: 01983 523112 E: carismus@lineone.net

East Cowes Heritage Centre 8 Clarence Rd, East Cowes, PO32 6EP T: 01983 280310

Guildhall Museum Newport High St, Newport, PO30 1TY T: 01983 823366 E: rachel.silverson@iow.gov.uk W: www.iwight.com

Natural History Centre High St, Godshill, Ventnor, PO38 3HZ T: 01983 840333

Needles Old Battery West High Down, Totland Bay, PO39 0JH T: 01983 754772

The Classic Boat Museum Seaclose Wharf, Town Quay, Newport, PO30 2EF T: 01983 533493 E: ebmiow@fsmail.net

The Island Aeroplane Company Ltd Embassy Way, Sandown Airport, Sandown, PO36 9PJ T: 01983 404448

The Lilliput Museum of Antique Dolls & Toys High St Brading, Sandown, PO36 0DJ T: 01983 407231 E: lilliput.museum@btconnect.com W: lilliputmuseum.co.uk

Ventnor Heritage Museum 11 Spring Hill, Ventnor, PO38 1PF T: 01983 855407

Kent

Brenzett Aeronautical Museum Ivychurch Road, Brenzett, Romney Marsh, TN29 0EE T: 01233 627911 W: www.aboutbritain.com/renzettAeronauticalMuseum

Buffs Regt Museum The Royal Museum & Art Gallery, 18 High Street, Canterbury, CT1 2RA T: 01227-452747 W: www.canterbury-museums.co.uk

Canterbury Roman Museum Butchery Lane, Canterbury, CT1 2JR T: 01227 785575

Chartwell House Chartwell, Westerham, TN16 1PS T: 01732 866368 E: chartwell@nationaltrust.org.uk W: www.nationaltrust.org.uk

Chatham Dockyard Historical Society Museum Cottage Row, Barrack Rd, Chatham Dockyard, Chatham, ME4 4TZ T: 01634 844897(museum)

Cobham Hall Cobham, DA12 3BL T: 01474 823371

Dickens House Museum 2 Victoria Parade, Broadstairs, CT10 1QS T: 01843 861232

Dolphin Sailing Barge Museum Crown Quay Lane, Sittingbourne, ME10 3SN T: 01795 423215

Dover Castle Dover, CT16 1HU T: 01304 201628 W: www.english-heritage.org.uk

Dover Museum Market Square, Dover, CT16 1PB T: 01304 201066 E: museum@dover.gov.uk W: www.dovermuseum.co.uk

Dover Transport Museum Old Park Barracks, Whitfield, Dover, CT16 2HQ T: 01304 822409

Fleur De Lis Heritage Centre 13 Preston Street, Faversham, ME13 8NS T: 01795 534542 E: faversham@btinternet.com W: www.faversham.org

Fort Armherst Dock Road, Chatham , ME4 4UB T: 01634 847747 W: www.fortamhurst.org.uk

Fort Luton Museum Magpie Hall Road, Chatham, ME4 5XJ T: 01634 813969

Guildhall Museum Guildhall Museum, High Street, Rochester, ME1 1PY T: 01634 848717 E: guildhall@medway.gov.uk W: www.medway.gov.uk

Gunpowder Chart Mills Off Stonebridge Way, Faversham, ME13 7SE T: 01795 534542 E: faversham@btinternet.com W: www.faversham.org

Herne Bay Museum Centre 12 William St, Herne Bay, CT6 5EJ T: 01227 367368 E: museum@canterbury.gov.uk W: www.hernebay-museum.co.uk

Kent and Sharpshooters Yeomanry Museum Hever Castle, Edenbridge, TN8 7DB T: 020 8688 2138

Kent Battle of Britain Museum Aerodrome Rd, Hawkinge, Folkestone, CT18 7AG T: 01303 893140

Kent Battle of Britain Museum Aerodrome Road, Hawkinge, Folkestone, CT18 7AG T: 01303 893140

Lashenden Air Warfare Museum Headcorn Aerodrome, Headcorn, Nr Ashford, TN27 9HX T: 01622 890226

Maidstone Museum & Art Gallery St. Faith St, Maidstone, ME14 1LH T: 01622 754497

Margate Old Town Hall Museum Old Town Hall, Market Place, Margate, CT9 1ER T: 01843 231213

Masonic Library & Museum St. Peters Place, Canterbury, CT1 2DA T: 01227 785625

Minster Abbey Gatehouse Museum Union Rd, Minster On Sea, Sheerness, ME12 2HW T: 01795 872303

Minster Museum Craft & Animal Centre Bedlam Court Lane, Minster, Ramsgate, CT12 4HQ T: 01843 822312

Museum of Kent Life Cobtree, Lock Lane, Sandling, Maidstone, ME14 3AU T: 01622 763936 E: enquiries@museum-kentlife.co.uk W: www.museum-kentlife.co.uk

Penshurst Place & Gardens Penshurts, Tonbridge, TN11 8DG T: 01892 870307 E: enuiries@penshurstplace.com W: www.penshurstplace.com

Powell-Cotton Museum, Quex House and Gardens Quex Park, Birchington, CT7 0 T: 01843 842168 E: powell-cotton.museum@virgin.net W: www.powell-cottonmuseum.co.uk

Princess of Wales's Royal Regt & Queen's Regt Museum Howe Barracks, Canterbury, CT1 1JY T: 01227-818056

Quebec House Quebec Square, Westerham, TN16 1TD T: 01892 890651

RAF Manston History Museum The Airfield, Manston Road, Ramsgate, CT11 5DF T: 01843 825224 W: www.rafmuseum.fsnet.co.uk

Ramsgate Maritime Museum The Clock House, Pier Yard, Royal Harbour, Ramsgate, CT11 8LS T: 01843 570622 E: museum@ekmt.fsnet.co.uk curator@greatstorm.fsnet.co.uk W: www.ekmt.fsnet.co.uk

Rochester Cathedral Militia Museum Guildhall Museum, High Street, Rochester, ME1 1PY T: 01634 848717

Roman Dover Tourist Centre Painted House, New street, Dover, CT17 9AJ T: 01304 203279

Roman Museum Butchery Lane, Canterbury, CT1 2JR T: 01227 785575 W: www.aboutbritain.com/CanterburyRomanMuseum

Romney Toy & Model Museum New Romney Station, Romney, TN28 8PL T: 01797 362353

Royal Engineers Library Brompton Barracks, Chatham, ME4 4UX T: 01634 822416

Royal Engineers Museum of Military Engineering Prince Arthur Road, Gillingham, ME4 4UG T: 01634 822839 W: www.army.mod.uk/armymuseums

Royal Museum & Art Gallery 18 High St, Canterbury, CT1 2RA T: 01227 452747

Sheerness Heritage Centre 10 Rose St, Sheerness, ME12 1AJ T: 01795 663317

Shoreham Aircraft Museum High Street, Shoreham, Sevenoaks, TN14 7TB T: 01959 524416 W: www.s-a-m.freeserve.co.uk

Spitfire and Hurricane Memorial Building The Airfield, Manston Road, Ramsgate, CT11 5DF T: 01843 821940 W: www.spitfire-museum.com

St Margaret's Museum Beach Road, St Margaret's Bay, Dover, CT15 6DZ T: 01304 852764

Tenterden Museum Station Rd, Tenterden, TN30 6HN T: 01580 764310

The Buffs Regt Museum The Royal Museum, 18 High Street, Canterbury, CT1 2JE T: 01227 452747

The C.M Booth Collection Of Historic Vehicles 63-67 High St, Rolvenden, Cranbrook, TN17 4LP T: 01580 241234

The Charles Dickens Centre Eastgate House, High St, Rochester, ME1 1EW T: 01634 844176

The Grand Shaft Snargate Street, Dover, CT16 T: 01304 201066

The Historic Dockyard Chatham, ME4 4TZ T: 01634 823800 E: info@chdt.org.uk W: www.thedockyard.co.uk

The Queen's Own Royal West Kent Regiment Museum Maidstone Museum and Art Gallery, St. Faith's Street, Maidstone, ME14 1LH T: 01622 602842 E: simonlace@maidstone.gov.uk

The Romney, Hythe & Dymchurch Railway New Romney Station, Romney, TN28 8PL T: 01797 362353

The West Gate St Peters Street, Canterbury, T: 01227 452747

Timeball Tower Victoria Parade, Deal, CT14 7BP T: 01304 360897

Victoriana Museum Deal Town Hall, High St, Deal, CT14 6BB T: 01304 380546

Walmer Castle and Gardens Kingsdown Road, Walmer, Deal, CT14 7LJ T: 01304 364288 W: www.english-heritage.org.uk

Watts Charity Poor Travellers House, 97 High St, Rochester, ME1 1LX T: 01634 845609

Whitstable Museum & Gallery 5a Oxford St, Whitstable, CT5 1DB T: 01227 276998 W: www.whitstable-museum.co.uk

Lancashire
Blackburn Museum and Art Gallery Museum Street, Blackburn, BB1 7AJ T: 01254 667130 E: paul.flintoff@blackburn.gov.uk W: www.blackburnworld.com

Bolton Museum & Art Gallery Le Mans Crescent, Bolton, BL1 1SE T: 01204 332190 E: bolwg@gn.apc.org

British in India Museum Newton Street, Colne, BB8 0JJ T: 01282 870215

Duke of Lancaster's Own Yeomanry Stanley St, Preston, PR1 4AT T: 01772 264074

East Lancashire Railway Bolton Street Station, Bolton Street, Bury, BL9 0EY T: 0161 764 7790 E: admin@east-lancs-rly.co.uk W: www.east-lancs-rly.co.uk

East Lancashire Regiment Towneley Hall, Burnley, BB11 3RQ T: 01282424213 E: towneleyhall@burnley.gov.uk W: www.towneleyhall.org.uk

Ellenroad Trust Ltd Ellenroad Engine House, Elizabethan Way, Milnrow, Rochdale, OL16 4LG T: 01706 881952 E: ellenroad@aol.com W: http:\\ellenroad.homepage.com

Fleetwood Museum Queens Terrace, Fleetwood, FY7 6BT T: 01253 876621 E: fleetwood.museum@mus.lancscc.gov.uk W: www.nettingthebay.org.uk

Gawthorpe Hall Habergham Drive, Padiham, Burnley, BB12 8UA T: 01282 771004 E: gawthorpehall@museumsoflancs.org.uk W: www.museumsoflancs.org.uk

Hall I'Th' Wood Museum Hall I Th Wood, Tonge Moor, Bolton, BL1 8UA T: 01204 301159

Heaton Park Tramway (Transport Museum) Tram Depot, Heaton Park, Prestwich, Manchester, M25 2SW T: 0161 740 1919

Helmshore Textile Museums Holcombe Road, Helmshore, Rossendale, BB4 4NP T: 01706 226459

Heritage Trust for the North West within Pendle Heritage Centre, Colne Rd, Barrowford, Nelson, BB9 6JQ T: 01282 661704

Judge's Lodgings Museum Church St, Lancaster, LA1 1LP T: 01524 32808

King's Own Royal Regt Museum The City Museum, Market Square, Lancaster, LA1 1HT T: 01524 64637 E: kingsownmuseum@iname.com W: www.kingsownmuseum.plus.com

Kippers Cats 51 Bridge St, Ramsbottom, Bury, BL0 9AD T: 01706 822133

Lancaster City Museum Market Square, Lancaster, LA1 1HT T: 01524 64637 E: awhite@lancaster.gov.uk W:

Lancaster Maritime Museum Custom House, St George's Quay, Lancaster, LA1 1RB T: 01524 64637

Lytham Heritage Group 2 Henry St, Lytham St. Annes, FY8 5LE T: 01253 730767

Manchester Museum University of Manchester, Oxford Rd, Manchester, M13 9PL T: 0161 275 2630 E: education@man.ac.uk W: http://museum.man.ac.uk

Museum of Lancashire Stanley Street, Preston, Lancashire, PR1 4YP T: 01772 264079 E: museum@lancs.co.uk

Museum of Lancashire (Queen's Lancashire Regiment Duke of Lancaster's Own Yeomanry Lancashire Hussars 14th/20th King's Hussars) Stanley Street, Preston, PR1 4YP T: 01772 534075

Museum of the Manchester Regiment Ashton Town Hall, Market Place, Ashton-u-Lyne, OL6 6DL T: 0161 342 3078 W: www.tameside.gov.uk

Museum of the Queen's Lancashire Regiment (East South and Loyal (North Lancashire) Regiments, Lancashire Regiment (PWV) and The Queen's Lancashire Regiment Fulwood Barracks, Preston, PR2 8AA T: 01772 260362 E: rhq.qlr@talk21.com

North West Sound Archive Old Steward's Office, Clitheroe Castle, Clitheroe, BB7 1AZ T: 01200 427897 E: nwsa@ed.lancscc.gov.uk W: www.lancashire.gov.uk/education/d_lif/ro/content/sound/imdex.asp

Oldham Museum Greaves St, Oldham, OL1 1 T: 0161 911 4657

Ordsall Hall Museum Taylorson St, Salford, M5 3HT T: 0161 872 0251

Pendle Heritage Centre Park Hill, Colne Rd, Barrowford, Nelson, BB9 6JQ T: 01282 661702

Portland Basin Museum Portland Place, Ashton-Under-Lyne, OL7 0QA T: 0161 343 2878

Queen St Mill Harle Syke, Queen St, Briercliffe, Burnley, BB10 2HX T: 01282 459996

Rawtenstall Museum Whitaker Park, Haslingden Road, Rawtenstall, T: 01706 244682

Ribchester Museum of Roman Antiquities Riverside, Ribchester, Preston, PR3 3XS T: 01254 878261 W: www.aboutbritain.com/Ribchester Roman Museum.htm

Rochdale Museum Service The Arts & Heritage Centre, Esplanade, Rochdale, OL16 1AQ T: 01706 641085

Rochdale Pioneers Museum Toad Lane, Rochdale, OL12 0NU T: 01706 524920

Saddleworth Museum & Art Gallery High St, Uppermill, Oldham, OL3 6HS T: 01457 874093

Salford Museum & Art Gallery Peel Park, Salford, M5 4WU T: 0161 736 2649 E: info@lifetimes.org.uk W: www.lifetimes.org.uk

Slaidburn Heritage Centre 25 Church St, Slaidburn, Clitheroe, BB7 3ER T: 01200 446161 E: slaidburn.heritage@htnw.co.uk W: www.slaidburn.org.uk

Smithills Hall Museum Smithills Hall, Dean Road, Bolton, BL1 7NP T: 01204 841265

South Lancashire Regiment Prince of Wales Volunteers Museum Peninsula Barracks, Warrington,

The Fusiliers Museum (Lancashire) Wellington Barracks, Bolton Road, Bury, BL8 2PL T: 0161 764 2208

The Greater Manchester Police Museum 57 Newton St, Manchester, M1 1ES T: 0161 856 3287

The Museum of Science and Industry In Manchester Liverpool Rd, Castlefield, Manchester, M3 4JP T: 0161 832 2244 E: marketing@msim.org.uk W: www.msim.org.uk

The Rochdale Pioneers' Museum 31 Toad Lane, Rochdale, T: 01706-524920

Weaver's Cottage Heritage Centre Weavers Cottage, Bacup Rd, Rawtenstall, Rossendale, BB4 7NW T: 01706 229828

Whitworth Museum North Street, Whitworth, T: 01706 343231 E: rossendale_leisure@compuserve.com

Wigan Heritage Service Museum History Shop, Library Street, Wigan, WN1 1NU T: 01942 828128 E: heritage@wict.org W: www.wict.org/culture/heritage

Leicestershire

Abbey Pumping Station Corporation Rd, Abbey Lane, Leicester, LE4 5PX T: 0116 299 5111 W: www.leicestermuseums.ac.uk

Ashby De La Zouch Museum North St, Ashby-De-La-Zouch, LE65 1HU T: 01530 560090

Belgrave Hall & Gardens Church Rd, Belgrave, Leicester, LE4 5PE T: 0116 266 6590 E: marte001@leicester.gov.uk W: www.leicestermuseums.org.uk

Bellfoundry Museum Freehold St, Loughborough, LE11 1AR T: 01509 233414

Bosworth Battlefield Visitor Centre Sutton Cheney, Market Bosworth, Nuneaton, CV13 0AD T: 01455 290429 E: bosworth@leics.gov.uk W: www.leics.gov.uk

British Aviation Heritage Bruntingthorpe Aerodrome, Bruntingthorpe, Lutterworth, LE17 5QH T: 0116 221 8426 W: www.jetman.dircon.co.uk/brunty

Charnwood Museum Granby St, Loughborough, LE11 3DU T: 01509 233754 W: www.leics.gov.uk/museums/musinliecs.htm#charnwood

Foxton Canal Museum Middle Lock, Gumley Rd, Foxton, Market Harborough, LE16 7RA T: 0116 279 2657

Harborough Museum Council Offices, Adam and Eve Street, Market Harborough, LE16 7AG T: 01858 821085 E: museums@leics.gov.uk W: www.leics.gov.uk/museums/musinliecs.htm#harborough

Hinckley & District Museum Ltd Framework Knitters Cottage, Lower Bond St, Hinckley, LE10 1QU T: 01455 251218

Jewry Wall Museum St. Nicholas Circle, Leicester, LE1 4LB T: 0116 247 3021

Leicester City Museum & Art Gallery 53 New Walk, Leicester, LE1 7EA T: 0116 255 4100

Leicester Gas Museum - Closed Aylestone Rd, Leicester, LE2 7LF T: 0116 250 3190

Leicestershire Ecology Centre Holly Hayes Environmental Resources Centre, 216 Birstall Rd, Birstall, Leicester, LE4 4DG T: 0116 267 1950 E: dlott@leics.gov.uk

Leicestershire Yeomanry, Leicestershire Tigers Museum Loughborough War Memorial, Queen's Park, Loughborough, T: 01509 263370

Melton Carnegie Museum Thorpe End, Melton Mowbray, LE13 1RB T: 01664 569946 E: museums@leics.gov.uk W: www.liecs.gov.uk/museums/#melton

New Walk Museum New Walk Museum, 53 New Walk, Leicester, LE1 7AE T: 0116 247 3220 E: hide001@leicester.gov.uk W: www.leicestermuseums.co.uk

Royal Leicestershire Regiment Gallery New Walk Museum, 53 New Walk, Leicester, LE1 7AE T: 0116 247 3220 W: www.leicestermuseums.co.uk

Snibston Discovery Park Ashby Rd, Coalville, LE67 3LN T: 01530 510851 E: museums@lcics.gov.uk W: www.leics.gov.uk/museums/musinliecs.htm#snibston

The Guildhall Guildhall Lane, Leicester, LE1 5FQ T: 0116 253 2569

The Manor House Manor Rd, Donington Le Heath, Coalville, LE67 2FW T: 01530 831259 E: museums@leics.gov.uk W: www.leics.gov.uk/museums/musinliecs.htm#manor

Lincolnshire

50 and 61 Squadrons Museum The Lawn, Union Road, Lincoln,

Alford Civic Trust Manor House Museum, West Street, Alford, LN13 9DJ T: 01507 463073

Ayscoughfee Hall Museum & Gardens Churchgate, Spalding, PE11 2RA T: 01775 725468

Battle of Britain Memorial Flight Visitor Centre R.A.F Coningsby, Coningsby, Lincoln, LN4 4SY T: 01526 344041 E: bbmf@lincolnshire.gov.uk W: www.lincolnshire.gov.uk/bbmt

Baysgarth House Museum Caistor Rd, Barton-Upon-Humber, DN18 6AH T: 01652 632318

Bomber County Aviation Museum Ex RAF Hemswell, Hemswell Cliff, Gainsborough, T: 01724 855410

Boston Guildhall Museum South Street, Boston, PE21 6HT T: 01205 365954 E: heritage@originalboston.freeserve.co.uk

Church Farm Museum Church Rd South, Skegness, PE25 2HF T: 01754 766658 E: wifff@lincolnshire.gov.uk W:

Cranwell Avation Heritage Centre Heath Farm, North Raunceby, Near Cranwell, Sleaford, NG34 8QR T: 01529 488490

Gainsborough Old Hall Parnell St, Gainsborough, DN21 2NB T: 01427 612669

Gordon Boswell Romany Museum Hawthorns Clay Lake, Spalding, PE12 6BL T: 01775 710599

Grantham Museum St. Peters Hill, Grantham, NG31 6PY T: 01476 568783

Immingham Museum Immingham Resorce Centre, Margaret St, Immingham, DN40 1LE T: 01469 577066

Lincolnshire Aviation Heritage Centre East Kirkby Airfield, East Kirkby, Spilsby, PE23 4DE T: 01790 763207 E: enquiries@lincsaviation.co.uk W: www.lincsaviation.co.uk

Lincs Vintage Vehicle Society Whisby Rd, North Hykeham, Lincoln, LN6 3QT T: 01522 500566

Louth Naturalists Antiquarian & Literary Society 4 Broadbank, Louth, LN11 0EQ T: 01507 601211

Metheringham Airfield Visitor Centre Westmoor Farm, Martin Moor, Metheringham, LN4 3BO T: 01526 378270

Museum of Lincolnshire Life Old Barracks, Burton Road, Lincoln, LN1 3LY T: 01522-528448 E: lincolnshirelife_museum@lincolnshire.gov.uk W: www.lincolnshire.gov.uk/museumoflincolnshirelife

National Fishing Heritage Centre Alexander Dock, Great Grimsby, DN31 1UZ T: 01472-323345 W: www.nelincs.gov.uk

North Lincolnshire Museum Oswald Rd, Scunthorpe, DN15 7BD T: 01724 843533 E: David.Williams@northlincs.gov.uk W: www.northlincs.gov.uk/museums

RAF Digby Ops Room Museum RAF Digby, Scopwick, Lincoln, LN4 3LH T: 01526 327503 W: www.airops.freeserve.co.uk

Royal Lincolnshire Regiment Lincolnshire Yeomanry Museum Old Barracks, Burton Road, Lincoln, LN1 3LY T: 01522-528448

The Incredibly Fantastic Old Toy Show 26 Westgate, Lincoln, LN1 3BD T: 01522 520534

The Queen's Royal Lancers Regt Museum (16th/5th and 17th/21st Lancers) Belvoir Castle, nr Grantham , NG32 1PD T: 0115 957 3295

Thorpe Camp Visitor Centre Tattersall Thorpe, Lincoln, LN4 4PE T: 01526 342249 E: mjhodgson@lancfile.demon.co.uk W: www.thorpecamp.org.uk

Liverpool

King's Regiment Collection Museum of Liverpool Life, Pier Head, Liverpool, L3 1PZ T: 0151-478-4062

Liverpool Maritime Museum William Brown Street, Liverpool, L3 8EN T: 0151-2070001

London

Alexander Fleming Laboratory Museum / St Mary's NHS Trust Archives St Mary's Hospital, Praed Street, Paddington, London, W2 1NY T: (020) 7886 6528 E: kevin.brown@st-marys.nhs.uk W: www.st-marys.nhs.uk

Berkshire and Westminster Dragoons Museum Cavalry House, Duke of York's Headquarters, Kings Road, Chelsea, London, SW3 4SC T: 020 7414 5233

Bethlem Royal Hospital Archives and Museum, Monks Orchard Road, Beckenham, BR3 3BX T: (020) 8776 4307 E: museum@bethlem.freeserve.co.uk

Bethnal Green Museum of Childhood Cambridge Heath Rd, London, E2 9PA T: (020) 8980 2415 E: k.bines@vam.ac.uk

Britain at War Experience Winston Churchill, 64-66 Tooley Street, London Bridge, London, SE1 2TF T: 020 7403 3171 E: britainatwar@dial.pipex.com W: www.britainatwar.co.uk

British Dental Association Museum - Closed 64 Wimpole Street, London, W1M 8AL T: (020) 7935-0875-ext-209

Cabinet War Rooms Clive Steps, King Charles Street, SW1A 2AQ T: (020) 7930 6961 E: cwr@iwm.org.uk W: www.iwm.org.uk

Church Farmhouse Museum Greyhound Hill, Hendon, NW4 4JR T: (020) 8203 0130 W: www.earl.org.uk/partners/barnet/churchf.htm

Coldstream Guards Record Office Wellington Barracks, Birdcage Walk, London, SW1E 6HQ

Crystal Palace Museum Anerley Hill, London, SE19 T: 020 8676 0700

Cutty Sark King William Walk, London, SE10 9HT T: (020) 8858 2698 E: info@cuttysark.org.uk W: www.cuttysark.org.uk

Design Museum Butlers Wharf 28, Shad Thames, London, SE1 2YD T: (020) 7940 8791 E: enquiries@designmuseum.org.uk W: www.designmuseum.org.uk

Dickens House Museum 48 Doughty St, London, WC1N 2LF T: (020) 7405 2127 E: DHmuseum@rmplc.co.uk W: www.dickensmuseum.com

Doctor Johnson's House 17 Gough Square, London, EC4A 3DE T: (020) 7353 3745

Firepower - The Royal Artillery Museum Royal Arsenal, Woolwich, London, SE18 6ST T: (020) 8855 7755 E: info@firepower.org.uk W: www.firepower.org.uk

Florence Nightingale Museum 2 Lambeth Palace Road, London, SE1 7EW T: (020) 7620-0374 E: curator@florence-nightingale.co.uk W: www.florence-nightingale.co.uk

Freud Museum 20 Maresfield Gardens, London, NW3 5SX T: (020) 735-2002 E: freud@gn.apc.org W: www.freud.org.uk

Fusiliers' London Volunteer Museum 213 Balham High Road, London, SW17 7BQ T: 020 8672 1168

Geffrye Museum Kingsland Rd, London, E2 8EA T: (020) 7739 9893 E; info@geffrye-museum.org.uk W: www.geffrye-museum.org.uk

Golden Hinde Living History Museum St. Mary Overie Dock, Cathedral St, SE1 9DE T: 08700 118700 E: info@goldenhinde.co.uk W: www.goldenhinde.co.uk

Grange Museum of Community History The Grange, Neasden Lane, Neasden, London, NW10 1QB T: (020) 8452 8311

Greenwich Heritage Centre Artillery Square, Royal Arsenal, Woolwich, London, SE18 4DX T: 020 8854 2452 E: heritage.centre@greenwich.gov.uk W: www.greenwich.gov.uk

Grenadier Guards Record Office Wellington Barracks, Birdcage Walk, London, SW1E 6HQ E: rhqgrengds@yahoo.co.uk

Guards Museum Wellington Barracks, Birdcage Walk, London, SW1E 6HQ T: (020) 7414 3271/3428

Gunnersbury Park Museum Gunnersbury Park, Popes Lane, W3 8LQ T: (020) 8992 1612 E: gp-museum@cip.org.uk

H.M.S. Belfast Morgans Lane, Tooley Street, London, SE1 2JH T: (020) 7940 6300 W: www.iwm.org.uk

Hackney Museum Service, London Borough of Parkside Library, Victoria Park Rd, London, E9 7JL T: (020) 8986 6914 E: hmuseum@hackney.gov.uk W: www.hackney.gov.uk/hackneymuseum

Handel House Museum 25 Brook Street, London, W1K 4HB T: (020) 7495 1685 E: mail@handelhouse.org W: www.handelhouse.org

Hogarth's House Hogarth Lane, Chiswick, London, W4 2QN T: (020) 8994 6757

Honourable Artillery Company Armoury House, City Road, London, EC1Y 2BQ T: 020 7382 1537 E: hac@hac.org.uk W: www.hac.org.uk

Horniman Museum 100 London Rd, Forest Hill, London, SE23 3PQ T: (020) 8699 1872 E: enquiries@horniman.co.uk W: www.horniman.co.uk

House Mill River Lea Tidal Mill Trust , Three Mills Island, Three Mill Lane, Bromley by Bow, London, E3 3DU T: (020) 8980-4626

Inns of Court and City Yeomanry Museum 10 Stone buildings, Lincoln's Inn, London, WC2A 3TG T: 020 7405 8112

Irish Guards Record Office Wellington Barracks, Birdcage Walk, London, SW1E 6HQ W: www.army.mod.uk/ig~assoc

Island History Trust St. Matthias Old Church, Woodstock Terrace, Poplar High St, London, E14 0AE T: (020) 7987 6041

Islington Museum Foyer Gallery, Town Hall, Upper St, N1 2UD T: (020) 7354 9442

James Clavell Library Royal Arsenal (West), Warren Lane, Woolwich, London, SE18 6ST T: 020 8312 7125 W: www.firepower.org.uk

Jewish Museum The Sternberg Centre for Judaism, 80 East End Road, Finchley, London, N3 2SY T: 020 8349 1143 E: enquiries@jewishmuseum.org.uk W: www.jewishmuseum.org.uk

Keats House Museum Wentworth Place, Keats Grove, NW3 2RR T: (020) 7435 2062

Kingston Museum & Heritage Service - London Borough of North Kingston Centre, Richmond Road, Kingston upon Thames, KT2 5PE T: (020) 8547-6738 E: local.history@rbk.kingston.gov.uk W: www.kingston.gov.uk/museum/

Leighton House Museum 12 Holland Park Rd, London, W14 8LZ T: 020 7602 3316 E: museums@rbkc.gov.uk W: www.rbkc.gov.uk/leightonhousemuseum

Livesey Museum for Children 682 Old Kent Rd, London, SE15 1JF T: (020) 7639 5604 E: livesley.museum@southwark.gov.uk

Lloyds Nelson Collection Lloyds of London, Lime Street, London, EC3M 7HA T: 020 7327 6260

London Canal Museum 12-13 New Wharf Rd, London, N1 9RT T: (020) 7713 0836 W: www.charitynet.org/~LCanalMus/

London Fire Brigade Museum 94a Southwark Bridge Rd, London, SE1 0EG T: (020) 7587 2894 E: esther.mann@london-fire.gov.uk

London Gas Museum Twelvetrees Crescent, London, E3 3JH T: (020) 7538 4982

London Irish Rifles Regt Museum Duke of York's Headquarters, Kings Road, Chelsea, London, SW3 4SA

London Toy & Model Museum 21-23 Craven Hill, London, W2 3EN T: (020) 7706 8000

London Transport Museum Covent Garden Piazza, London, WC2E 7BB T: (020) 7379 6344 E: contact@ltmuseum.co.uk W: www.ltmuseum.co.uk

Mander & Mitchenson Theatre Collection c/o Salvation Army Headquarters, PO BOx 249, 101 Queen Victoria Street, London, EC49 4EP T: (020) 7236 0182

Markfield Beam Engine & Museum Markfield Rd, London, N15 4RB T: (020) 8800 7061 E: alan@mbeam.org W: www.mbeam.org

Museum in Docklands Library & Archives Library & Archive, No 1 Warehouse, West India Quay, Hertsmere Road, London, E14 4AL T: (020) 7001 9825 (Librarian) E: bobaspinall@museumindocklands.org.uk W: www.museumindocklands.org.uk

Museum of London London Wall, London, EC2Y 5HN E: info@museumoflondon.org.uk

National Gallery St. Vincent House, 30 Orange St, London, WC2H 7HH T: (020) 7747 5950

Newham Museum Service The Old Town Hall, 29 The Broadway, Stratford, E15 4BQ T: (020) 8534 2274

North Woolwich Old Station Musuem Pier Rd, North Woolwich, London, E16 2JJ T: (020) 7474 7244

Percival David Foundation of Chinese Art 53 Gordon Square, London, WC1H 0PD T: (020) 7387 3909

Petrie Museum of Egyptian Archaeology University College London, Gower St, WC1E 6BT T: (020) 7504 2884 E: petrie.museum@ucl.ac.uk

Pitshanger Manor & Gallery Mattock Lane, London, W5 5EQ T: (020) 8567 1227 E: pitshanger@ealing.gov.uk

Polish Institute & Sikorski Museum 20 Princes Gate, London, SW7 1PT T: (020) 7589 9249

Pollock's Toy Museum 1 Scala St, London, W1P 1LT T: (020) 7636 3452

Princess Louise's Kensington Regiment Museum Duke of York's Headquarters, Kings Road, Chelsea, London, SW3 4RX

Pump House Educational Museum Lavender Pond & Nature Park, Lavender Rd, Rotherhithe, SE16 1DZ T: (020) 7231 2976

Ragged School Museum Trust 46-50 Copperfield Rd, London, E3 4RR T: (020) 8980 6405 W: www.ics-london.co.uk/rsm

RHQ Scots Guards Archives Wellington Barracks, Birdcage Walk, London, SW1E 6HQ E: sgarchives@dial.pipex.com

Royal London Hospital Archives and Museum Royal London Hospital Archives, 9 Prescot Street, Aldgate, London, E1 8PR T: (020) 7377 7608 E: jonathan.evans@bartsandthelondon.nhs.uk W: www.bartsandthelondon.org.uk

Royal London Hospital Museum Royal London Hospital , St Philip's Church, Newark Street, London, E1 2AA T: (020) 7377 7608 E: jonathan.evans@bartsandthelondon.nhs.uk W: www.bartsandthelondon.org.uk

Sam Uriah Morris Society 136a Lower Clapton Rd, London, E5 0QJ T: (020) 8985 6449

Sir John Soane's Museum 13 Lincolns Inn Fields, London, WC2A 3BP T: (020) 7430 0175 W: www.soane.org

St Bartholomew's Hospital Archives & Museum Archives and Museum, North Wing, St Bartholomew's Hospital , West Smithfield, London, EC1A 7BE T: (020) 7601 8152 E: barts.archives@bartsandthelondon.nhs.uk W: www.bartsandthelondon.nhs.uk/aboutus/museums_and_archives.asp

The Association of Jewish Ex-Service Men and Women Military Museum AJEX House, East Bank, Stamford, London, N16 5RT T: 020 8800 2844 W: www.ajex.org.uk

The Clink Prison Museum 1 Clink St, London, SE1 9DG T: (020) 7403 6515

The Fan Museum 12 Crooms Hill, London, SE10 8ER T: (020) 8858 7879 E: admin@fan-museum.org W: www.fan-museum.org

The Iveagh Bequest Kenwood House, Hampstead Lane, London, NW3 7JR T: (020) 8348 1286

The Museum of Women's Art 3rd Floor, 11 Northburgh St, London, EC1V 0AN T: (020) 7251 4881

The Old Operating Theatre Museum & Herb Garret 9a St. Thomas's St, London, SE1 9RY T: (020) 7955 4791 E: curator@thegarret.org.uk W: www.the garret.org.uk

The Polish Institute and Sikorski Museum 20 Princes Gate, London, SW7 1QA T: 020 7589 9249

The Regt Museum RHQ The London Scottish Regiment, 95 Horseferry Road, Westminster, London, SW1P 2DX T: 020 7630 1639 E: archiveslsregt@aol.com W: www.londonscottishregt.org

The Royal Regiment of Fusiliers H M Tower of London, London, EC3N 4AB T: (020) 7488 5610

The Wellcome Trust 183 Euston Rd, London, NW1 2BE T: (020) 7611 8888 E: infoserv@wellcome.ac.uk W: www.wellcome.ac.uk

Vestry House Museum Vestry Road, Walthamstow, London, E17 9NH T: (020) 8509-1917 E: vestry.house@al.lbwf.gov.uk W: WWW: www.lbwf.gov.uk/vestry/vestry.htm

Veterinary Museum Royal Vetinerary College, Royal College Street, London, NW1 0TU T: (020) 768-5165 E: fhouston@rvc.ac.uk W: www.rvc.uk

Wallace Collection Hertford House, Manchester Square, London, W1V 3BN T: 020 7563 9500 E: enquiries@wallacecollection.org W: www.wallacecollection.org

Wellington Museum - Apsley House Apsley House, 149 Piccadilly, Hyde Park Corner, London, W1J 7NT T: 020 7499 5676 W: www.apsleyhouse.org.uk

Welsh Guards Record Office Wellington Barracks, Birdcage Walk, London, SW1E 6HQ T: 020 7414 3291

Westminster Abbey Museum Westminster Abbey, Deans Yard, SW1P 3PA T: (020) 7233 0019

Wimbledon Lawn Tennis Museum The All England Lawn Tennis & Croquet Club, Church Road, Wimbledon, London, SW19 5AE T: (020) 8946 6131 E: museum@aeltc.com W: www.wimbledon.org/museum

Wimbledon Museum of Local History 22 Ridgeway, London, SW19 4QN T: (020) 8296 9914

Manchester
Manchester Museum of Science and Industry Liverpool Road, Castlefield, Manchester, M3 4FP T: 0161 832 2244 E: n.forder@msim.org.uk W: www.msim.org.uk

Manchester Jewish Museum 190 Cheetham Hill Road, Manchester, M8 8LW T: 0161 834 9879 E: info@machesterjewishmuseum.com W: www.machesterjewishmuseum.com

Merseyside
Beatle Story Ltd Britannia Vaults, Albert Dock, Liverpool, L3 4AA T: 0151 709 1963

Botanic Gardens Museum Churchtown, Southport, PR9 7NB T: 01704 227547

Liverpool Scottish Regt Museum 15 Rydal Bank, Lower Bebington, Wirral, L23 2SH T: 0151 645 5717 E: ilriley@liverpoolscottish.org.uk W: www.liverpoolscottish.org.uk

Merseyside Maritime Museum Maritime Archives and Library, Albert Dock, Liverpool, L3 4AQ T: 0151-478-4418 E: archives@nmgmarchives.demon.co.uk W: www.nmgm.org.uk

National Museums & Galleries on Merseyside 127 Dale St, Liverpool, L2 2JH T: 0151 207 0001

Prescot Museum 34 Church St, Prescot, L34 3LA T: 0151 430 7787

Shore Road Pumping Station Shore Rd, Birkenhead, CH41 1AG T: 0151 650 1182

The World of Glass Charlton Way East, St Helens, WA10 1BX T: 08700 114 466 E: info@worldofglass.com W: www.worldofglass.com

Western Approaches 1 Rumford St, Liverpool, L2 8SZ T: 0151 227 2008

Middlesex
Forty Hall Museum Forty Hill, Enfield, EN2 9HA T: (020) 8363 8196

Harrow Museum & Heritage Centre Headstone Manor, Pinner View, Harrow, HA2 6PX T: 020 8861 2626

HQ No 11 (Fighter) Group Battle of Britain Operations Room RAF Uxbridge, Uxbridge, UB10 0RZ T: 01895 815400

Kew Bridge Steam Museum Green Dragon Lane, Brentford, TW8 0EN T: (020) 8568 4757 E: info@kbsm.org W: www.kbsm.org

Royal Military School of Music Museum Kneller Hall, Twickenham, TW2 7DU T: 020 8744 8652

The Musical Museum 368 High St, Brentford, TW8 0BD T: (020) 8560 8108

Norfolk
100 Bomb Group Memorial Museum Common Road, Dickleburgh, Diss, IP21 4PH T: 01379 740708

Air Defence Radar Museum RAF Neatishead, Norwich, NR12 8YB T: 01692 631485 E: curator@radarmuseum.co.uk W: www.radarmuseum.co.uk

Bressingham Steam & Gardens Bressingham, Diss, IP22 2AB T: 01379 687386

Bure Valley Railway Norwich Road, Aylsham, NR11 6BW T: 01263 733858

Castle Museum Castle Hill, Norwich, NR1 3JU T: 01603 493624

Cholmondeley Collection of Model Soldiers Houghton Hall, Houghton, Kings Lynn, PE31 6UE T: 01485 528569 E: administrator@houghtonhall.com W: www.houghtonhall.com

City of Norwich Aviation Museum Ltd Old Norwich Rd, Horsham St. Faith, Norwich, NR10 3JF T: 01603 893080

Diss Museum The Market Place, Diss, IP22 3JT T: 01379 650618

EcoTech Swaffham, PE37 7HT T: 01760 726100 E: info@ecotech.rmplc.co.uk W: www.ecotech.org.uk

Elizabethan House Museum 4 South Quay, Great Yarmouth, NR30 2QH T: 01493 855746

Feltwell (Historical and Archaeological) Society 16 High Street, Feltwell, Thetford, IP26 4AF T: 01842 828448 E: peterfeltwell@tinyworld.co.uk

Glandford Shell Museum Church House, Glandford, Holt, NR25 7JR T: 01263 740081

Iceni Village & Museums Cockley Cley, Swaffham, PE37 8AG T: 01760 721339

Inspire Hands On Science Centre Coslany St, Norwich, NR3 3DJ T: 01603 612612

Lynn Museum Old Market St, King's Lynn, PE30 1NL T: 01553 775001 W: www.norfolk.gov.uk/tourism/museums

Maritime Museum for East Anglia 25 Marine Parade, Great Yarmouth, NR30 2EN T: 01493 842267

Norfolk Motorcycle Museum Station Yard, Norwich Rd, North Walsham, NR28 0DS T: 01692 406266

Norfolk Rural Life Museum & Union Farm Beach House, Gressenhall, East Dereham, NR20 4DR T: 01362 860563 E: frances.collinson.mus@norfolk.gov.uk W: www.norfolk.gov.uk

Royal Norfolk Regt Museum Shirehall, Market Avenue, Norwich, NR1 3JQ T: 01603 493649 W: www..norfolk.gov.uk

Sheringham Museum Station Rd, Sheringham, NR26 8RE T: 01263 821871

Shirehall Museum Common Place, Walsingham, NR22 6BP T: 01328 820510 E: walsinghammuseum@farmline.com

The Air Defence Battle Command & Control Museum Neatishead, Norwich, NR12 8YB T: 01692 633309

The Muckleburgh Collection Weybourne, Holt, NR25 7EG T: 01263 588210 W: www.muckleburgh.co.uk

The North Norfolk Railway The Station, Sheringham, NR26 8RA T: 01263 822045 W: www.nnrailway.co.uk

Northamptonshire
Abington Museum and Museum of The Northamptonshire Regiment Abington Park Museum, Abington, NN1 5LW T: 01604 635412 W: www.northampton.co.uk/museums

Canal Museum Stoke Bruerne, Towcester, NN12 7SE T: 01604 862229

Naseby Battle Museum Purlieu Farm, Naseby, Northampton, NN6 7DD T: 01604 740241

National Dragonfly Museum Ashton Mill, Ashton, Peterborough, PE8 5LB T: 01832 272427 E: ndmashton@aol.com W: natdragonflymuseum.org.uk

Northampton & Lamport Railway Preservation Society Pitsford & Brampton Station, Pitsford Road, Chapel Brampton, Northampton, NN6 8BA T: 01604 820327

Northampton Iron Stone Railway Trust Hunsbury Hill Country Park, Hunsbury Hill Rd, West Hunsbury, Northampton, NN4 9UW T: 01604 702031 E: bnile98131@aol.com raf968y@aol.com

Rushden Historical Transport Society The Station, Station Approach, Rushden, NN10 0AW T: 01933 318988

Wellingborough Heritage Centre Croyland Hall, Burystead Place, Wellingborough, NN8 1AH T: 01933 276838

Northumberland

A Soldier's Life 15th/19th The King's Royal Hussars Northumberland Hussars and Light Dragoons Discovery Museum, Blandford Square, Newcastle-upon-Tyne, NE1 4JA T: 0191 232 6789 E: ralph.thompson@twmuseums.org.uk

Berwick Borough Museum The Barracks, Parade, Berwick-Upon-Tweed, TD15 1DG T: 01289 330933

Bewick Studios Mickley Square, Mickley, Stocksfield, NE43 7BL T: 01661 844055

Border History Museum and Library Moothall, Hallgate, Hexham, NE46 3NH T: 01434-652349 E: museum@tynedale.gov.uk W: www.tynedale.gov.uk

Chesterholm Museum Vindolanda Trust, Bardon Mill, Hexham, NE47 7JN T: 01434 344 277 E: info@vindolanda.com W: www.vindolanda.com

Chesters Roman Fort and Clayton Collection Museum Vindolanda Trust, Chollerford, Humshaugh, Hexham, NE46 4EP T: 01434 681 379 E: info@vindolanda.com W: www.vindolanda.com

Corbridge Roman Site Corbridge, NE45 5NT T: 01434 632349 W: www.english-heritage.org.uk

Fusiliers Museum of Northumberland The Abbot's Tower, Alnwick Castle, Alnwick, NE66 1NG T: 01665-602151

Housteads Roman Fort Museum Haydon Bridge, Hexham, NE47 6NN T: 01434 344363

King's Own Scottish Borderers Museum The Barracks, Parade, Berwick upon Tweed, TD15 1DG T: 01289 307426 W: www.kosh.co.uk

Marine Life Centre & Fishing Museum 8 Main St, Seahouses, NE68 7RG T: 01665 721257

Roman Army Museum Carvoran, Greenhead, CA6 7JB T: 01697 747485 E: info@vindolanda.com W: www.vindolanda.com

The Heritage Centre Station Yard, Woodburn Road, Bellingham, Hexham, NE48 2DF T: 01434 220050 E: bell.heritage@btopenworld.com W: www.bellingham-heritage.org.uk

The Vindolanda Trust Chesterholm Museum, Bardon Mill, Hexham, NE47 7JN T: 01434 344277 E: info@vindolanda.com W: www.vindolanda.com

Tynedale Council Museums Department of Leisure & Tourism, Prospect House, Hexham, NE46 3NH T: 01461 652351 E: museum@tynedale.gov.uk W: www.tynedale.gov.uk

Nottinghamshire

D.H Lawrence Heritage Durban House Heritage Centre, Mansfield Rd, Eastwood, Nottingham, NG16 3DZ T: 01773 717353 E:

Flintham Society & Flintham Museum Flintham Museum, Inholms Road, Flintham, NG23 5LF T: 0163.6 525111 E: flintham.museum@lineone.net W: www.flintham-museum.org.uk

Greens Mill & Science Musuem Windmill Lane, Sneinton, Nottingham, NG2 4QB T: 0115 915 6878

Harley Gallery Welbeck, Worksop, S80 3LW T: 01909 501700

Mansfield Museum & Art Gallery Leeming Street, Mansfield, NG18 1NG T: 01623-463088

Millgate Museum of Folk Life 48 Millgate, Newark, NG24 4TS T: 01636 655730 E: museums@newark-sherwood.gov.uk W: www.newark-sherwood.gov.uk

Natural History and Industrial Musuem Wollaton Hall, Wollaton Park, Nottingham, NG8 2AE T: 0115 915 3910

Newark (Notts & Lincs) Air Museum The Airfield, Winthorpe, Newark, NG24 2NY T: 01636 707170 W: www.newarkairmuseum.co.uk

Newark Museum - Closed in 2005

Newark Town Treasures and Art Gallery The Town Hall, Market Place, Newark, NG24 1DU T: 01636 680333 E: post@newark.gov.uk W: www.newarktowntreasures.co.uk

Newstead Abbey Museum Newstead Abbey Park, Ravenshead, Nottingham, NG15 8NA T: 01623 455900 E: sally@newsteadabbey.org.uk W: www.newsteadabbey.org.uk

Nottingham Castle Museum & Art Gallery Castle Rd, Nottingham, NG1 6EL T: 0115 915 3700

Ruddington Framework Knitters' Museum Chapel St, Ruddington, Nottingham, NG11 6HE T: 0115 984 6914 W: www.rfkm.org

Ruddington Village Museum St. Peters Rooms, Church St, Ruddington, Nottingham, NG11 6HD T: 0115 914 6645

Sherwood Foresters (Notts and Derby Regiment) Museum The Castle, Nottingham, NG1 6EL T: 0115 946 5415 E: rhqwfr-nottm@lineone.net W: www.wfrmuseum.org.uk

The Galleries of Justice Shire Hall, High Pavement, Lace Market, Nottingham, NG1 1HN T: 0115-952-0555 E: info@galleriesofjustice.org.uk W: www.galleriesofjustice.org.uk

The Museum of Nottingham Lace 3-5 High Pavement, Lace Market, Nottingham, NG1 1HF T: 0115 989 7365 E: info@nottinghamlace.org W: www.nottinghamlace.org

The Vina Cooke Museum Dolls & Bygone Childhood The Old Rectory, Cromwell, Newark, NG23 6JE T: 01636 821364

Whaley Thorn Heritage & Environment Centre Portland Terrace, Langwith, Mansfield, NG20 9HA T: 01623 742525

Oxfordshire

Abingdon Museum County Hall, Market Place, Abingdon, OX14 3HG T: 01235 523703

Ashmolean Museum University of Oxford, Beaumont Street, Oxford, OX1 2PH T: 01865 278000

Chipping Norton Museum 4 High Street, Chipping Norton, OX7 5AD E: museum@cn2001.fsnet.co.uk

Edgehill Battle Museum The Estate Yard, Farnborough Hall, Farnborough, Banbury, OX17 1DU T: 01926 332213

Great Western Society Ltd Didcot Railway Centre, Station Rd, Didcot, OX11 7NJ T: 01235 817200

Oxfordshire and Buckinghamshire Light Infantry Regt Museum Slade Park, Headington, Oxford, OX3 7JL T: 01865 780128

Pitt Rivers Museum University Of Oxford, South Parks Rd, Oxford, OX1 3PP T: 01865 270927 E: prm@prm.ox.ac.uk W: www.prm.ox.ac.uk

The Oxfordshire Museum Fletchers House, Park St, Woodstock, OX20 1SN T: 01993 811456 E: oxon.museum@oxfordshire.gov.uk

Vale & Downland Museum 19 Church St, Wantage, OX12 8BL T: 01235 771447 E: museum@wantage.com W: WWW:

Wallingford Museum Flint House, High St, Wallingford, OX10 0DB T: 01491 835065

Witney & District Museum Gloucester Court Mews, High St, Witney, OX8 6LX T: 01993 775915 E: janecavell@aol.com W:

Rutland

Rutland County Museum Catmose Street, Oakham, LE15 6HW T: 01572-723654 W: www.rutnet.co.uk

Rutland Railway Museum Iron Ore Mine Sidings, Ashwell Rd, Cottesmore, Oakham, LE15 7BX T: 01572 813203

Shropshire

Acton Scott Historic Working Farm Wenlock Lodge, Acton Scott, Church Stretton, SY6 6QN T: 01694 781306

Blists Hill Open Air Museum Ironbridge Gorge Museum Trust Ltd, Legges Way, Madeley, Telford, TF7 5DU T: 01952 586063

Coalport China Museum Ironbridge Gorge Museum Trust Ltd, High St, Coalport, Telford, TF8 7AW T: 01952 580650

Cosford Royal Air Force Museum Cosford , Shifnal, TF11 8UP T: 01902 376200 E: cosford@rafmuseum.org W: www.rafmuseum.org

Ironbridge Gorge Museum, Library & Archives The Wharfage, Ironbridge, Telford, TF8 7AW T: 01952 432141 E: library@ironbridge.org.uk W: www.ironbridge.org.uk

Jackfield Tile Museum Ironbridge Gorge Museum Trust Ltd, Jackfield, Telford, TF8 7AW T: 01952 882030

Ludlow Museum Castle St, Ludlow, SY8 1AS T: 01584 875384

Midland Motor Museum Stanmore Hall, Stourbridge Rd, Stanmore, Bridgnorth, WV15 6DT T: 01746 762992

Museum of Iron Ironbridge Gorge Museum Trust Ltd, Coach Rd, Coalbrookdale, Telford, TF8 7EZ T: 01952 433418

Museum Of The River Visitor Centre Ironbridge Gorge Museum Trust Ltd, Wharfage, Ironbridge, TF8 7AW T: 01952 432405

Oswestry Transport Museum Oswald Rd, Oswestry, SY11 1RE T: 01691 671749 E: lignetts@enterprise.net W: www.cambrian-railways-soc.co.uk

Queen's Own Mercian Yeomanry Museum Bridgeman House, Cavan Drive, Cemetery Road, Dawley, Telford, TF4 2BQ T: 01952 632930

Rosehill House Ironbridge Gorge Museum Trust Ltd, Telford, TF8 7AW T: 01952 432141

Rowley's House Museum Barker Street, Shrewsbury, SY1 1QH T: 01743 361196

Shropshire Regt Museum (King's Shropshire Light Infantry, Shropshire Yeomanry) Shropshire Militia, Volunteers and TA The Castle, Shrewsbury, SY1 2AT T: 01743 358516 W: www.shropshireregimental.co.uk

Somerset

Abbey Barn - Somerset Rural Life Museum Abbey Barn, Chilkwell St, Glastonbury, BA6 8DB T: 01458 831197 E: county-museum@somerset.gov.uk W: www.somerset.gov.uk/museums

Admiral Blake Museum Bridgwater House, King Square, Bridgwater, TA6 3AR T: 01278 435399 E: museums@sedgemoor.gov.uk

American Museum Claverton Manor, Bath, BA2 7BD T: 01225 460503

Bakelite Museum Orchard Mill, Bridge St Williton, Taunton, TA4 4NS T: 01984 632133

Bath Postal Museum 8 Broad St, Bath, BA1 5LJ T: 01225 460333 E: a.swindells@virgin.net W: www.bathpostalmuseum.org

Bath Royal Literary & Scientific Institution 16-18 Queen Square, Bath, BA1 2HN T: 01225 312084

Blake Museum Blake Street, Bridgwater, TA6 3NB T: 01278 456127 E: museums@sedgemoor.gov.uk W: www.sedgemoor.gov.uk

Blazes Fire Museum Sandhill Park, Bishops Lydeard, Taunton, TA4 3DE T: 01823 433964

Bruton Museum Society The Dovecote Building, High Street, Bruton, T: 01749 812851 W: www.southsomersetmuseum.org.uk

Chard & District Museum Godworthy House, High St, Chard, TA20 1QB T: 01460 65091

Fleet Air Arm Museum R.N.A.S Yeovilton, Yeovil, BA22 8HT T: 01935 840565

Fleet Air Arm Museum Records Research Centre Box D61, RNAS Yeovilton, Nr Ilchester, BA22 8HT T: 01935-840565

Glastonbury Lake Village Museum The Tribunal, 9 High St, Glastonbury, BA6 9DP T: 01458 832949

Holburne Museum of Art Great Pulteney St, Bath, BA2 4DB T: 01225 466669 W: www.bath.ac.uk/holbourne

Lambretta Scooter Museum 77 Alfred St, Weston-Super-Mare, BS23 1PP T: 01934 614614 E: lambretta@wsparts.force.net

Museum of Bath at Work Camden Works, Julian Road, Bath, BA1 2RH T: 01225 318348 E: mobaw@hotmail.com W: www.bath-at-work.org.uk

Museum of Costume Bennett Street, Bath, BA1 2QH T: 01225 477 173 E: costume_enquiries@bathnes.gov.uk W: www.museumofcostume.co.uk

Museum of South Somerset Henford, Yeovil, T: 01935 424774 E: heritage.services@southsomerset.gov.uk W: southsomersetmuseums.org

No.1 Royal Crescent 1 Royal Crescent, Bath, BA1 2LR T: 01225 428126 E: no1Qbptrust.demon.co.uk W: www.bath-preservation-trust.org.uk

North Somerset Museum Service Burlington St, Weston-Super-Mare, BS23 1PR T: 01934 621028 E: museum.service@n-somerset.gov.uk W: www.n-somerset.gov.uk

Radstock, Midsomer Norton & District Museum Waterloo Road, Radstock, Bath, BA3 3ER T: 01761 437722 E: radstockmuseum@ukonline.co.uk W: www.radstockmuseum.co.uk

Somerset & Dorset Railway Trust Washford Station, Washford, Watchet, TA23 0PP T: 01984 640869 E: info@sdrt.org W: www.sdrt.org

Somerset County Museum Service Taunton Castle, Taunton, TA1 4AA T: 01823 320200

Somerset Military Museum (Somerset Light Infantry, YeomanryMilitia and Volunteers) County Museum The County Museum, Taunton Castle, Taunton, TA1 4AA T: 01823 333434 E: info@sommilmuseum.org.uk W: www.sommilmuseum.org.uk

The Building of Bath Museum The Countess of Huntingdon's Chapel, Vineyards, Bath, BA1 5NA T: 01225 333 895 E: admin@bobm.freeserve.co.uk W: www.bath-preservation-trust.org.uk

The Haynes Motor Museum Castle Cary Rd, Sparkford, Yeovil, BA22 7LH T: 01963 440804 E: mike@gmpwin.demon.co.uk W: www.haynesmotormuseum.co.uk

The Helicopter Museum The Heliport, Locking Moor Road, Weston-Super-Mare, BS24 8PP T: 01934 635227 E: office@helimuseum.fsnet.co.uk W: www.helicoptermuseum.co.uk

The Jane Austen Centre 40 Gay Street, Bath, BA1 2NT T: 01225 443000 E: info@janeausten.co.uk

The John Judkyn Memorial Garden Thorpe, Freshford, Bath, BA3 6BX T: 01225 723312

The Museum Of East Asian Art 12 Bennett St, Bath, BA1 2QL T: 01225 464640 E: museum@east-asian-art.freeserve.co.uk W: www.east-asian-art.co.uk

The South West Museums Council Hestercombe House, Cheddon Fitzpaine, Taunton, TA2 8LQ T: 01823 259696 E: robinbourne@swmuseums.co.uk

Wells Museum 8 Cathedral Green, Wells, BA5 2UE T: 01749 673477

West Somerset Museum The Old School, Allerford, Minehead, TA24 8HN T: 01643 862529

William Herschel Museum 19 New King St, Bath, BA1 2BL T: 01225 311342

Staffordshire
Borough Museum & Art Gallery Brampton Park, Newcastle, ST5 0QP T: 01782 619705

Clay Mills Pumping Engines Trust Ltd Sewage Treatment Works, Meadow Lane, Stretton, Burton-On-Trent, DE13 0DB T: 01283 509929

Etruria Industrial Museum Lower Bedford St, Etruria, Stoke-On-Trent, ST4 7AF T: 01782 233144 E: etruria@swift.co.uk W: www.stoke.gov.uk/museums

Gladstone Pottery Museum Uttoxeter Rd, Longton, Stoke-On-Trent, ST3 1PQ T: 01782 319232

Hanley Museum & Art Gallery Bethesda St, Hanley, Stoke-On-Trent, ST1 3DW T: 01782 232323

Museum of The Staffordshire Regiment Whittington Barracks, Lichfield, WS14 9PY T: 0121 311 3240 E: museum@rhqstaffords.fsnet.co.uk

Museum of the Staffordshire Yeomanry The Ancient High House, Greengate Street, Stafford, ST16 2HS T: 01785 619130

Samuel Johnson Birthplace Museum Breadmarket St, Lichfield, WS13 6LG T: 01543 264972 W: www.lichfield.gov.uk

The Potteries Museum & Art Gallery Bethesda Street, Hanley, Stoke-On-Trent, ST1 3DE T: 01782 232323 E: museums@stoke.gov.uk W: www.stoke.gov.uk/museums

Uttoxeter Heritage Centre 34-36 Carter St, Uttoxeter, ST14 8EU T: 01889 567176

Suffolk
390th Bomb Group Memorial Air Museum Parham Airfield, Parham, Framlington, T: 01743 711275

British Resistance Organisation Museum Parham Airfield, Parham, Framlingham, T: 01743 711275 W: www.auxunit.org.uk

Christchurch Mansion & Wolsey Art Gallery Christchurch Park, Soane St, Ipswich, IP4 2BE T: 01473 253246

Dunwich Museum St. James's Street, Dunwich, Saxmundham, IP17 3DT T: 01728 648796

East Anglia Transport Museum Chapel Rd, Carlton Colville, Lowestoft, NR33 8BL T: 01502 518459

Felixstowe Museum Landguards Fort, Felixstowe, IP11 8TW T: 01394 674355

Gainsborough House Society Gainsborough St, Sudbury, CO10 2EU T: 01787 372958 E: mail@gainsborough.org W: www.gainsborough.org

HMS Ganges Museum Victory House, Shotley Point Marina, Ipswich, IP9 1QJ T: 01473 684749

International Sailing Craft Association Maritime Museum Caldecott Rd, Oulton Broad, Lowestoft, NR32 3PH T: 01502 585606 E: admin@isca-maritimemuseum.org

Ipswich Museum & Exhibition Gallery High St, Ipswich, IP1 3QH T: 01473 213761

Ipswich Transport Museum Ltd Old Trolley Bus Depot, Cobham Rd, Ipswich, IP3 9JD T: 01473 715666

Long Shop Steam Museum Main St, Leiston, IP16 4ES T: 01728 832189 W: www.suffolkcc.gov.uk/libraries_and_heritage/sro/garrett/index.html

Lowestoft Museum Broad House, Nicholas Everitt Park, Oulton Broad, Lowestoft, NR33 9JR T: 01502 511457

Maritime Museum Sparrows Nest The Museum, Whapload Rd, Lowestoft, NR32 1XG T: 01502 561963

Mid Suffolk Light Railway Brockford Station, Wetheringsett, Stowmarket, IP14 5PW T: 01449 766899

Mildenhall and District Museum 6 King Street, Mildenhall, Bury St Edmunds, IP28 7EX T: 01638 716970

Norfolk and Suffolk Aviation Museum - East Anglia's Aviation Heritage Centre Buckeroo Way, Street, Flixton, Bungay, NR35 1NZ T: 01986 896644 E: nsam.flixton@virgin.net W: www.aviationmuseum.net

R.A.F. Regiment Museum Home of The RAF Regiment, R A F Honington, Bury St Edmonds, IP31 1EE T: 01359 269561 ext 7824

Rougham Tower Association Rougham Estate Office, Rougham, Bury St. Edmunds, IP30 9LZ T: 01359 271471 E: bplsto@aol.com

Royal Naval Patrol Association Museum Sparrows Nest, Lowestoft, NR32 1XG T: 01502 586250

Suffolk Regiment Museum The Keep, Gibraltar Barracks, Out Risbygate Street, Bury St Edmonds, IP33 3RN

Suffolk Regiment Archive - closed to the public Suffolk Record Office, 77 Raingate Street, Bury St Edmunds, IP33 2AR T: 01284-352352 E: bury.ro@libher.suffolkcc.gov.uk W: www.suffolkcc.gov.uk/sro/

The National Horseracing Museum & Tours 99 High St, Newmarket, CB8 8JH T: 01638 667333

West Stow Country Park & Anglo-Saxon Village The Visitor Centre, Icklingham Road, West Stow, Buet ST edmunds, IP28 6HG T: 01284 728718

Surrey

Bourne Hall Museum Bourne Hall, Spring St, Ewell, Epsom, KT17 1UF T: (020) 8394 1734 W: www.epsom.townpage.co.uk

Chertsey Museum The Cedars, 33 Windsor St, Chertsey, KT16 8AT T: 01932 565764 E: enquiries@chertseymuseum.org.uk W:

Dorking & District Museum Dorking & District Museum, Old Foundry, 62a West St, Dorking, RH4 1BS T: 01306 876591

East Surrey Museum 1 Stafford Rd, Caterham, CR3 6JG T: 01883 340275

Elmbridge Museum Church St, Weybridge, KT13 8DE T: 01932 843573 E: info@elm-mus.datanet.co.uk W: www.surrey-online.co.uk/elm-mus

Godalming Museum 109a High St, Godalming, GU7 1AQ T: 01483 426510 E: musaeum@goldaming.ndo.co.uk W:

Guildford Museum Castle Arch, Quarry St, Guildford, GU1 3SX T: 01483 444750 E: museum@remote.guildford.gov.uk W:

Haslemere Educational Museum 78 High St, Haslemere, GU27 2LA T: 01428 642112 E: haslemere_museum@compuserve.com W:

Kingston Upon Thames Museum North Kingston Centre, Richmond Road, New Malden, KT3 3UQ T: 020 8547 6738

Merton Heritage Centre The Cannons, Madeira Rd, Mitcham, CR4 4HD T: (020) 8640 9387

Queen's Royal Surrey Regiment Museum (Queen's Royal, East Surrey & Queen's Royal Surrey Regiments) Clandon Park, West Clandon, Guildford, GU4 7RQ T: 01483 223419 W: www.surrey-online.co.uk/queenssurreys www.queensroyalsurreys.org.uk

Regimental Museum Royal Logistic Corps Princess Royal Barracks, Deepcut, Camberley, GU16 6RW T: 01252 833371 W: www.army-rlc.co.uk/museum

Reigate Priory Museum Reigate Priory, Bell St, Reigate, RH2 7RL T: 01737 222550

Rural Life Centre Old Kiln Museum, Reeds, Tilford, Farnham, GU10 2DL T: 01252 795571 E: rural.life@argonet.co.uk W:

Sandhurst Collection Royal Military Academy Sandhurst, Camberley, GU15 4PQ T: 01276 412489

Staff College Museum Old Staff College Building, Camberley, GU15 4NP T: 01276 412719

Surrey Heath Museum Knoll Road, Camberley, GU15 3HD T: 01276 707284 E: museum@surreyheath.gov.uk W: www.surreyheath.gov.uk/leisure

Wandle Industrial Museum Vestry Hall Annex, London Rd, Mitcham, CR4 3UD T: (020) 8648 0127 W: www.wandle.org

Woking Museum & Arts & Craft Centre The Galleries, Chobham Rd, Woking , GU21 1JF T: 01483 725517 E: the.galleries@dial.pipex.com

Sussex

Amberley Working Museum Station Rd, Amberley, Arundel, BN18 9LT T: 01798 831370 E: office@amberleymuseum.co.uk W: www.amberleymuseum.co.uk

Anne of Cleves House Museum 52 Southover, High St, Lewes, BN7 1JA T: 01273 474610

Battle Museum Langton Memorial Hall, High St, Battle, TN33 0AQ T: 01424 775955

Bexhill Museum Egerton Rd, Bexhill-On-Sea, TN39 3HL T: 01424 787950 E: museum@rother.gov.uk W: www.1066country.com

Bexhill Museum of Costume & Social History Association Manor Gardens, Upper Sea Rd, Bexhill-On-Sea, TN40 1RL T: 01424 210045

BN1 Visual Arts Project Brighton Media Centre, 9-12 Middle St, Brighton, BN1 1AL T: 01273 384242

Booth Musuem 194 Dyke Rd, Brighton, BN1 5AA T: 01273 292777 E: boothmus@pavilion.co.uk

Brighton Fishing Museum 201 Kings Road, Arches, Brighton, BN1 1NB T: 01273-723064

Chichester District Museum 29 Little London, Chichester, PO19 1PB T: 01243 784683 E: chichmus@breathemail.net

Dave Clarke Prop Shop Long Barn, Cross In Hand, Heathfield,

Fishbourne Roman Palace Roman Way, Salthill Rd, Fishbourne, Chichester, PO19 3QR T: 01243 785859 E: adminfish@sussexpast.co.uk W: www.sussexpast.co.uk

Filching Manor Motor Museum Filching Manor, Jevington Rd, Polegate, BN26 5QA T: 01323 487838

Fishermans Museum Rock A Nore Rd, Hastings, TN34 3DW T: 01424 461446

Hastings Museum & Art Gallery Johns Place, Bohemia Rd, Hastings, TN34 1ET T: 01424 781155 E: museum@hastings.gov.uk W: www.hmag.org.uk

Horsham Museum 9 The Causeway, Horsham, RH12 1HE T: 01403-254959 E: museum@horsham.gov.uk

Hove Musuem & Art Gallery 19 New Church Rd, Hove, BN3 4AB T: 01273 290200 E: abigail.thomas@brighton-hove.gov.uk W: www.brighton-hove.gov.uk

How We Lived Then Museum of Shops 20 Cornfield Terrace, Eastbourne, BN21 4NS T: 01323 737143

Marlipins Museum High St, Shoreham-By-Sea, BN43 5DA T: 01273 462994 E: smermich@sussexpast.co.uk W: www.sussexpast.co.uk

Michelham Priory Upper Dicker, Hailsham, BN27 3QS

Museum of The Royal National Lifeboat Institution King Edward Parade, Eastbourne, BN T: 01323 730717

Newhaven Fort Fort Road, Newhaven, BN9 9DL T: 01273 517622 W: www.newhavenfort.org.uk

Newhaven Local & Maritime Museum Garden Paradise, Avis Way, Newhaven, BN9 0DH T: 01273 612530

Petworth Cottage Museum 346 High St, Petworth, GU28 0AU T: 01798 342100 W: www.sussexlive.co.uk

Preston Manor Musuem Preston Drove, Brighton, BN1 6SD T: 01273 292770

Royal Military Police Museum Roussillon Barracks, Chichester, PO19 6BL T: 01243 534225 E: museum@rhqrmp.freeserve.co.uk W: www.rhqrmp.freeserve.co.uk

Rye Castle Museum East St, Rye, TN31 7JY T: 01797 226728

Seaford Museum of Local History Martello Tower, Esplanade, Seaford, BN25 1NP T: 01323 898222 E: museumseaford@tinyonline.co.uk W: www.seaforedmuseum.org

Sussex Combined Services Museum (Royal Sussex Regiment and Queen's Royal Irish Hussars) Redoubt Fortress, Royal Parade, Eastbourne, BN22 7AQ T: 01323 410300

Sussex Yeomanry Museum 198 Dyke Road, Brighton, BN1 5AS

The Engineerium The Droveway, Nevill Rd, Hove, BN3 7QA T: 01273 554070 E: info@britishengineerium.com W:

Tangmere Military Aviation Museum Tangmere, Chichester, PO20 2ES T: 01243 775223 W: www.tangmere-museum.org.uk

The Mechanical Music & Doll Collection Church Rd, Portfield, Chichester, PO19 4HN T: 01243 372646

Weald & Downland Open Air Museum Singleton, Chichester, PO18 0EU T: 01243-811363 E: wealddown@mistral.co.uk W: www.wealddown.co.uk

Wish Tower Puppet Museum Tower 73, King Edwards Parade, Eastbourne, BN21 4BY T: 01323 411620 E: puppet.workshop@virgin.net W: www.puppets.co.uk

Tyne And Wear

101 (Northumbrian) Regiment Royal Artillery (Volunteers) Museum Napier Armoury, Gateshead, NE8 4HX T: 0191 239 6130

Arbeia Roman Fort and Museum Baring Street, South Shields, NE33 2BB T: 0191 456 1369 W: www.aboutbritain.com/ArbeiaRomanFort.htm

Bede's World Museum Church Bank, Jarrow, NE32 3DY T: 0191 4892106

Castle Keep Castle Garth, St. Nicholas St, Newcastle Upon Tyne, NE1 1RE T: 0191 2327938

Fulwell Windmill Newcastle Road, Sunderland, SR5 1EX T: 0191 516 9790 M: 07989 409 296 E: fulwell.windmill@sunderland.gov.uk W: www.fulwell-windmill.com

Hancock Museum Barras Bridge, Newcastle Upon Tyne, NE2 4PT T: 0191 2227418 E: hancock.museum@ncl.ac.uk

Military Vehicles Museum Exhibition Park Pavilion, Newcastle Upon Tyne, NE2 4PZ T: 0191 2817222 E: miltmuseum@aol.com W: www.military-museum.org.uk

Newburn Motor Museum Townfield Gardens, Newburn, Newcastle Upon Tyne, NE15 8PY T: 0191 2642977

North East Aircraft Museum Old Washington Road, Sunderland, SR5 3HZ T: 0191 519 0662

North East Mills Group Blackfriars, Monk Street, Newcastle upon Tyne, NE1 4XN T: 0191 232 9279 E: nect@lineone.net W: WWW://welcome.to/North.East.Mill.Group

Ryhope Engines Trust Pumping Station, Stockton Rd, Ryhope, Sunderland, SR2 0ND T: 0191 5210235 W: www.g3wte.demon.co.uk

Segedunum Roman Fort, Baths and Museum Wallsend, NE T: 0191 236 9347 W: www.twmuseums.org.uk

South Shields Museum & Art Gallery Ocean Road, South Shields, NE33 2JA T: 0191-456-8740

Stephenson Railway Museum Middle Engine Lane, North Shields, NE29 8DX T: 0191 200 7146

Sunderland Maritime Heritage 1st Floor Office, North East Side, South Dock, Port of Sunderland, Sunderland, SR1 2EE T: 0191 510 2055 E: info@sunderlandMH.fsnet.co.uk W: www.sunderlandmaritimeheritage.com

Sunderland Museum & Art Gallery and Monkwearmouth Station Museum Borough Road, Sunderland, SR1 1PP T: 0191 565 0723 E: martin.routledge@tyne-wear-museums.org.uk

The Bowes Railway Co Ltd Springwell Rd, Springwell Village, Gateshead, NE9 7QJ T: 0191 4161847 E: alison_gibson77@hotmail.com W: www.bowesrailway.co.uk

The National Glass Centre Liberty Way, Sunderland, SR6 0GL T: 0191 515 5555 E: info@nationalglasscentre.com W: www.nationalglasscentre.com

Warwickshire

Heritage Motor Museum Banbury Road, Gaydon, CV35 0BJ T: 01926 641188 E: enquiries@heritage-motor-centre.co.uk W: www.heritage-motor-centre.co.uk

Leamington Spa Art Gallery & Musuem Royal Pump Rooms, Parade, Leamington Spa, CV32 4AA T: 01926 742700 E: prooms@warcickdc.gov.uk W: www.royal-pump-rooms.co.uk

Lunt Roman Fort Coventry Road, Baginton, Coventry, T: 024 7683 2381

Midland Air Museum Coventry airport, Baginton, CV8 3AZ T: 024 7630 1033 W: www.discover.co.uk/~mam/

Nuneaton Museum & Art Gallery Riversley Park, Nuneaton, CV11 5TU T: (024) 76376473

Regimental Museum of The Queen's Own Hussars (The 3rd King's Own Hussars and 7th Queen's Own Hussars) The Lord Leycester Hospital, High Street, Warwick, CV34 4EW T: 01926 492035 E: trooper@qohm.fsnet.co.uk W: www.qohmuseum.org.uk

Shakespeare Birthplace Trust - Museum Henley Street, Stratford upon Avon, CV37 6QW T: 01789-204016 E: museums@shakespeare.org.uk W: www.shakespeare.org.uk

The Royal Regiment of Fusiliers Museum (Royal Warwickshire) St. John's House, Warwick , CV34 4NF T: 01926 491653

Warwick Castle Warwick, CV34 4QU T: 01926 406600 E: media.enquiries@warwick-castle.com W: www.warwick-castle.co.uk

Warwick Doll Museum Okens House, Castle St, Warwick, CV34 4BP T: 01926 495546

Warwickshire Market Hall Museum Market Place, Warwick, CV34 4SA T: 01926 412500 E: museum@warwickshire.gov.uk W: www.warwickshire.gov.uk/museum

Warwickshire Yeomanry Museum The Court House, Jury Street, Warwick, CV34 4EW T: 01926 492212 E: wtc.admin@btclick.com W: www.armymuseums.org.uk

Wellesborough Aviation Museum Control Tower Entrance, Wellesborough, Warwick, CV34 4EW

West Midlands

Aston Manor-Road Transport Museum Ltd 208-216 Witton Lane, Birmingham, B6 6QE T: 0121 322 2298

Bantock House & Park Bantock Park,, Finchfield Rd, Wolverhampton, WV3 9LQ T: 01902 552195

Birmingham & Midland Museum Of Transport Chapel Lane, Wythall, B47 6JX T: 01564 826471 E: enquiries@bammot.org.uk W: www.bammot.org.uk

Birmingham Museum & Art Gallery Chamberlain Square, Birmingham, B3 3DH T: 0121 235 2834 W: www.birmingham.gov.uk/bmag

Birmingham Railway Museum 670 Warwick Rd, Tyseley, Birmingham, B11 2HL T: 0121 707 4696

Black Country Living Museum Canal St, Tipton Rd, Dudley, DY1 4SQ T: 0121 522 9643 E: info@bclm.co.uk W: ww.bclm.co.uk

Blakesley Hall Blakesley Rd, Yardley, Birmingham, B25 8RN T: 0121 783 2193

Coventry Transport Museum Milennium Place, Hales Street, Coventry, CV1 1PN T: 024 7623 4270 E: museum@transport-museum.com W: www.transport-museum.com

Dudley Museum & Art Gallerey St James's Road, Dudley, DY1

Haden Hall & Haden Hill House Haden Hill Park, Barrs Road, Cradley Heath, B64 7JX T: 01384 569444 Haden Hill House

Herbert Art Gallery & Museum Jordan Well, Coventry, CV1 5QP T: 024 76832381

Midland Air Museum Coventry Airport, Coventry Rd, Baginton, Coventry, CV8 3AZ T: (024) 76301033

Museum of the Jewellery Quarter 75-79 Vyse St, Hockley, Birmingham, B18 6HA T: 0121 554 3598 E: bmag_enquiries@birmingham.gov.uk W: www.bmag.org.uk

Oak House Museum Oak Rd, West Bromwich, B70 8HJ T: 0121 553 0759

Selly Manor Museum Maple Rd, Birmingham, B30 2AE T: 0121 472 0199

Soho House Museum Soho Avenue, Handsworth, Birmingham, B18 5LB T: 0121 554 9122 E: bmag_enquiries@birmingham.gov.uk W: www.birminghamheritage.org.uk/soho_hous

The Broadfield House Glass Museum Compton Drive, Kingswinford, DY6 9NS T: 01384 812 745 E: glassmuseum@dudley.gov.uk W: www.glassmuseum.org.uk

The Lock Museum 55 New Rd, Willenhall, WV13 2DA T: 01902 634542 W: http://members.tripod.co.uk/lock_museum/

Walsall Leather Museum Littleton St West, Walsall, WS2 8EN T: 01922 721153 E: leather.museum@walsall.gov.uk W:

West Midlands Police Museum Sparkhill Police Station, Stratford Rd, Sparkhill, Birmingham, B11 4EA T: 0121 626 7181

Whitlocks End Farm Bills Lane, Shirley, Solihull, B90 2PL T: 0121 745 4891

Wiltshire

Alexander Keiller Museum High St, Avebury, Marlborough, SN8 1RF T: 01672 539250 E: avebury@nationaltrust.org.uk

Atwell-Wilson Motor Museum Trust Stockley Lane, Calne, SN11 0 T: 01249 813119

Lydiard House Lydiard Park, Lydiard Tregoze, Swindon, SN5 9PA T: 01793 770401

RGBW (Salisbury) Museum The Wardrobe, 58 The Close, Salisbury, SP1 2EX T: 01722 419419 W: www.thewardrobe.org.uk

Royal Wiltshire Yeomanry Museum A (RWY) Sqn Royal Yeomanry, Church Place, Swindon, SN1 5EH T: 01793 523865

Salisbury & South Wiltshire Museum The King's House, 65 The Close, Salisbury, SP1 2EN T: 01722 332151 E: museum@salisburymuseum.freeserve.co.uk

Sevington Victorian School Sevington, Grittleton, Chippenham, SN14 7LD T: 01249 783070

Steam: Museum of the Great Western Railway Kemble Drive, Swindon, SN2 2TA T: 01793 466646 E: tbryan@swindon.gov.uk

The Infantry and Small Arms School Corps Weapons Collection HQ SASC, HQ infantry, Warminster Training Centre, Warminster, BA12 0DJ T: 01985 222487

The Science Museum Wroughton, Wroughton, Swindon, SN4 9NS T: 01793 814466 E: enquiries.wroughton@nmsi.ac.uk W: www.sciencemuseum.org.uk/wroughton

Wiltshire Heritage Museum Library Wiltshire Archaeological & Natural History Society, 41 Long Street, Devizes, SN10 1NS T: 01380 727369 E: wanhs@wiltshireheritage.org.uk W: www.wiltshireheritage.org.uk

Yelde Hall Museum Market Place, Chippenham , SN15 3HL T: 01249 651488

Worcestershire

Avoncroft Museum of Historic Buildings Redditch Rd, Stoke Heath, Bromsgrove, B60 4JR T: 01527 831363 E: Avoncroft1@compuserve.com W: www.avoncroft.org.uk

Bewdley Museum Research Library Load Street, Bewdley, DY12 2AE T: 01229-403573 E: museum@online.rednet.co.uk angela@bewdleyhistory.evesham.net W: www.bewdleymuseum.tripod.com

Kidderminster Railway Museum Station Drive, Kidderminster, DY10 1QX T: 01562 825316

Malvern Museum Priory Gatehouse, Abbey Road, Malvern, WR14 3ES T: 01684 567811

Museum of Worcester Porcelain The Royal Porcelain Works, Severn Street, Worcester, WR1 2NE E: rwgeneral@royal-worcester.co.uk

The Almonry Heritage Centre Abbey Gate, Evesham, WR11 4BG T: 01385 446944 E: tic@almonry W: www.almonry.ndo.co.uk

The Commandery Civil War Museum Sidbury, Worcester, WR1 2HU T: 01905 361821 E: thecommandery@cityofworcester.gov.uk W: www.worcestercitymuseums.org.uk

The Elgar Birthplace Museum Crown East Lane, Lower Broadheath, Worcester, WR2 6RH T: 01905 333224 W: www.elgarfoundation.org

The Mueseum of Local Life Tudor House, Friar Street, Worcester, WR1 2NA T: 01905 722349 W: www.worcestercitymuseums.org.uk

The Worcestershire Regiment Museum Worcester City Museum & Art Gallery, Foregate Street, Worcester, WR1 1DT T: 01905-25371E: tbridges@cityofworcester.gov.uk W: www.worcestercitymuseums.org.uk

Worcestershire City Museum and Art Gallery Foregate Street, Worcester, WR1 1DT T: 01905 25371 E: artgalleryandmuseum@cityofworcester.gov.uk W: www.worcestercitymuseums.org.uk

Worcestershire County Museum Hartlebury Castle, Hartlebury, DY11 7XZ T: 01229-250416 E: museum@worcestershire.gov.uk W: www.worcestershire.gov.uk/museum

Worcestershire Regiment Archives (Worcestershire and Sherwood Forester's Regiment) RHQ WFR Norton Barracks, Worcester, WR5 2PA T: 01905 354359 E: rhg_wfr@lineone.net

Yorkshire - East

4th Battalion East Yorkshire Regiment Collection Kingston upon Hull City Museums, Wilberforce House, 23-25 High Street, Kingston upon Hull, HU1 T: 01482 613902

East Riding Heritage Library & Museum Sewerby Hall, Church Lane, Sewerby, Bridlington, YO15 1EA T: 01262-677874 E: museum@pop3.poptel.org.uk W: www.bridlington.net/sew

Museum of Army Transport Flemingate, Beverley, HU17 0NG T: 01482 860445

The Hornsea Museum Burns Farm, 11 Newbegin, Hornsea, HU18 1AB T: 01964 533 443 W: www.hornseamuseum.com

Withernsea Lighthouse Museum Hull Rd, Withernsea, HU19 2DY T: 01964 614834

Yorkshire - North

Aysgarth Falls Carriage Museum Yore Mill , Asgarth Falls, Leyburn, DL8 3SR T: 01969 663399

Beck Isle Museum of Rural Life Pickering, YO18 8DU T: 01751 473653

Captain Cook Memorial Museum Grape Lane, Whitby, YO22 4BA T: 01947 601900 E: captcookmuseumwhitby@ukgateway.net W: www.cookmuseumwhitby.co.uk

Captain Cook Schoolroom Museum 10 High Street, Great Ayton, TS9 7HB T: 01642 723358

Dales Countryside Museum Station Yard, Burtersett Rd, Hawes, DL8 3NT T: 01969 667494 E: dcm@yorkshiredales.org.uk

Eden Camp Museum Malton, YO17 6RT T: 01653 697777 E: admin@edencamp.co.uk W: www.edencamp.co.uk

Green Howards Regt Museum Trinity Church Square, Richmond, DL10 4QN T: 01748 822133

Life In Miniature 8 Sandgate, Whitby, YO22 4DB T: 01947 601478

Malton Museum The Old Town Hall, Market Place, Malton, YO17 7LP T: 01653 695136

Micklegate Bar Museum Micklegate, York, YO1 6JX T: 01904 634436

Nidderdale Museum Council Offices, King Street, Pateley Bridge, HG3 5LE T: 01423-711225

Old Courthouse Museum Castle Yard, Knaresborough, T: 01423 556188 W: www.harrogate.gov.uk/museums

Richard III Museum Monk Bar, York, YO1 2LH T: 01904 634191 W: www.richardiiimuseum.co.uk

Richmondshire Museum Ryder's Wynd, Richmond, DL10 4JA T: 01748 825611

Ripon Museum Trust Ripon Prison & Police Museum, St Marygate, Ripon, HG4 1LX T: 01765-690799 E: ralph.lindley@which.net

Ripon Workhouse - Museum of Poor Law Allhallowgate, Ripon, HG4 1LE T: 01765 690799

Rotunda Museum Vernon Rd, Scarborough, YO11 2NN T: 01723 374839

Royal Dragoon Guards Military Museum (4th/7th Royal Dragoon Guards & 5th Royal Inniskilling Dragoon Guards) 3A Tower Street, York, YO1 9SB T: 01904-662790 W: www.rdg.co.uk

Royal Pump Room Museum Crown Place, Harrogate, T: 01423-556188 E: lg12@harrogate.gov.uk W: www.harrogate.gov.uk

Ryedale Folk Museum Hutton le Hole, YO62 6UA T: 01751 417367 E: library@dbc-lib.demon.co.uk

The Forbidden Corner Tupgill Park Estate, Coverham, Middleham, Leyburn, DL8 4TJ T: 01969 640638

The North Yorkshire Moors Railway Pickering Station, Pickering, YO18 7AJ T: 01751 472508 E: info@northyorkshiremoorsrailway.com W: www.northyorkshiremoorsrailway.com

The Real Aeroplane Museum The Aerodrome, Breighton, Selby, YO8 7DH T: 01757 289065

The World of James Herriott 23 Kirkgate, Thirsk, YO7 1PL T: 01845 524234 E: anne.keville@hambleton.gov.uk W: www.hambleton.gov.uk

Upper Wharfedale Museum Society & Folk Museum The Square, Grassington, BD23 5AU

War Room and Motor House Collection 30 Park Parade, Harrogate, HG1 5AG T: 01423 500704

Whitby Lifeboat Museum Pier Rd, Whitby, YO21 3PU T: 01947 602001

Whitby Museum Pannett Park, Whitby, YO21 1RE T: 01947 602908 E: graham@durain.demon.co.uk W: www.durain.demon.co.uk

Yorkshire Air Museum Halifax Way, Elvington, York, YO41 4AU T: 01904 608595 E: museum@yorkshireairmuseum.co.uk W: www.yorkshireairmuseum.co.uk

Yorkshire Museum of Farming Murton Park, Murton Lane, York, YO19 5UF T: 01904 489966

Yorkshire - South

Abbeydale Industrial Hamlet Abbeydale Road South, Sheffield, S7 2 T: 0114 236 7731

Bishops' House Norton Lees Lane, Sheffield, S8 9BE T: 0114 278 2600 W: www.sheffieldgalleries.org.uk

Cannon Hall Museum Cannon Hall, Cawthorne, Barnsley, S75 4AT T: 01226 790270

Clifton Park Museum Clifton Lane, Rotherham, S65 2AA T: 01709 823635 E: guy.kilminster@rotherham.gov.uk W: www.rotherham.gov.uk

Doncaster AeroVenture - The South Yorkshire Air Museum Aero Venture, Lakeside, Doncaster, T: 01302 761616

Fire Museum (Sheffield) Peter House, 101-109 West Bar, Sheffield, S3 8PT T: 0114 249 1999 W: www.hedgepig.freeserve.co.uk

Kelham Island Museum Alma St, Kelham Island, Sheffield, S3 8RY T: 0114 272 2106

King's Own Yorkshire Light Infantry Regt Gallery Doncaster Museum and Art Gallery, Chequer Road, Doncaster, DN1 2AE T: 01302 734293 E: museum@doncaster.gov.uk W: www.doncaster.gov.uk/museums

Magna Sheffield Road, Templeborough, Rotherham, S60 1DX T: 01709 720002 E: info@magnatrust.co.uk W: www.magnatrust.org.uk

Regimental Museum 13th/18th Royal Hussars and The Light Dragoons Cannon Hall, Cawthorne, Barnsley, S75 4AT T: 01226 790270

Sandtoft Transport Centre Ltd Belton Rd, Sandtoft, Doncaster, DN8 5SX T: 01724 711391

Sheffield City Museum Weston Park, Sheffield, S10 2TP T: 0114 278 2600 W: www.sheffieldgalleries.org.uk

Sheffield Industrial Museums Trust Alma Street, off Corporation Road, Sheffield, S3 8RY T: 0114 272 2106 W: www.simt.co.uk

Sheffield Police and Fire Museum 101-109 West Bar, Sheffield, S3 8TP T: 0114 249 1999 W: www.hedgepig.freeserve.co.uk

York and Lancaster Regt Museum Library and Arts Centre, Walker Place, Rotherham, S65 1JH T: 01709 336633 E: karl.noble@rotherham.gov.uk W: www.rotherham.gov.uk

Yorkshire - West

Armley Mills Canal Rd, Leeds, LS12 2QF T: 0113 263 7861

Bankfield Museum & Gallery Boothtown Rd, Halifax, HX3 6HG T: 01422 354823 E: bankfield-museum@calderdale.gov.uk W: www.calderdale.gov.uk

Bolling Hall Museum Bowling Hall Rd, Bradford, BD4 7 T: 01274 723057

Bracken Hall Countryside Centre Glen Rd, Baildon, Shipley, BD17 5ED T: 01274 584140

Bradford Industrial Museum & Horses at Work Moorside Rd, Eccleshill, Bradford, BD2 3HP T: 01274 631756

Calderdale Museums & Arts Piece Hall, Halifax, HX1 1RE T: 01422 358087

Castleford Museum Room Carlton St, Castleford, WF10 1BB T: 01977 722085

Cliffe Castle Museum Spring Gardens Lane, Keighley, BD20 6LH T: 01535 618231

Duke of Wellington's Regt Museum Bankfield Museum, Akroyd Park, Boothtown Road, Halifax, HX3 6HG T: 01422 354823

Eureka The Museum For Children Discovery Road, Halifax, HX1 2NE T: 01422 330069

Keighley Bus Museum Trust 47 Brantfell Drive, Burnley, BB12 8AW T: 01282 413179 W: www.kbmt.freeuk.com

Kirkstall Abbey and Abbey House Museum Abbey Walk, Kirkstall, Leeds, LS5 3EH T: 0113 230 5492 E: abbeyhouse.museum@virgin.net W: www.leeds.gov.uk

Leeds Museums Resource Centre Moorfield Industrial Estate, Moorfield Road, Yeadon, Leeds, LS19 7BN T: 0113 214 6526 W: www.leeds.gov.uk

Leeds Rifles Museum c/o 7 Wentworth Court, Raistrick, Brighouse, HD6 3XD

Lotherton Hall Lotherton Lane, Aberford, Leeds, LS25 3EB T: 0113 281 3259

Manor House Art Gallery & Museum Castle Yard, Castle Hill, Ilkley, LS29 9D T: 01943 600066

Middleton Railway The Station, Moor Road, Hunslet, Leeds, LS10 2JQ T: 0113 271 0320 E: howhill@globalnet.co.uk W: wwww.personal.leeds.ac.uk/mph6mip/mrt/mrt.htm

Royal Armouries Armouries Drive, Leeds, LS10 1LT T: 0990 106666

Shibden Hall Lister Rd, Shibden, Halifax, HX3 6AG T: 01422 352246 E: shibden.hall@calderdale.gov.uk W: www.calderdale.gov.uk

Skopos Motor Museum Alexandra Mills, Alexandra Rd, Batley, WF17 6JA T: 01924 444423

Temple Newsham House Temple Newsham Road, off Selby Road, Leeds, LS15 0AE T: 0113 264 7321

Thackray Medical Museum Beckett Street, Leeds, LS9 7LN T: 0113-244-4343 E: info@thackraymuseum.org W: www.thackraymuseum.org

The Colour Museum 1 Providence Street, Bradford, BD1 2PW T: 01274 390955 E: museums@sdc.org.uk W: www.sdc.org.uk

The Launds Inn Museum 23 Launds, Rochdale Road, Golcar, Huddersfiled, HD7 4NN T: 01484 645961 E: robert@laundsinnmuseum.co.uk W: www.laundsinnmuseum.co.uk

Thwaite Mills Watermill Thwaite Lane, Stourton, Leeds, LS10 1RP T: 0113 249 6453

Vintage Carriages Trust Station Yard, Ingrow, Keighley, BD21 1DB T: 01535 680425 E: admin@vintagecarriagestrust.org W: www.vintagecarriagestrust.org

Wakefield Museum Wood St, Wakefield, WF1 2EW T: 01924 305351 E: cjohnstone@wakefield.gov.uk W: www.wakefield.gov.uk/culture
Yorkshire & Humberside Museums Council Farnley Hall Hall Lane, Leeds, LS12 5HA T: 0113 263 8909

Yorkshire - York
Archaeoligical Resource Centre St Saviourgate, York, YO1 8NN T: 01904 654324 E: enquiries.ar.yat@yorkarch.demon.co.uk W: www.jorvik-viking-centre.co.uk
Bar Convent 17 Blossom Street, York, YO24 1AQ T: 01904 643238 E: info@bar-convent.org.uk W: www.bar-convent.org.uk
Kohima Museum Imphal Barracks, Fulford Road, York, YO10 4AD T: 01904 665806 E: thekohimamuseum@hotmail.com
York Archaeological Trust 13 Ogleforth, York, YO1 7FG T: 01904 663000 E: enquiries@yorkarchaeology.co.uk W: www.yorkarchaeology.co.uk
York Castle Museum The Eye of York, York, YO1 9RY T: 01904 687687 W: www.yorkcastlemuseum.org.uk/
Yorkshire Museum Museum Gardens, York, YO1 7FR T: 01904 629745 W: www.york.gov.uk

Wales
Anglesey
Beaumaris Gaol Museum Bunkers Hill, Beaumaris, LL58 8EP T: 01248 810921 E: beaumariscourtand gaol@anglesey.gov.uk
The Maritime Museum Beach Rd, Newry Beach, Holyhead, LL65 1YD T: 01407 769745 E: cave@holyhead85.freeserve.co.uk
Caernarfon
National Slate Museum Padarn Country Park, Llanberis, Gwynedd LL55 4TY T: 01286 870630 E: wsmpost@btconnect.com W: www.nmgw.ac.uk/en/slate
Cardiff
1st The Queen's Dragoon Guards Regimental Museum Cardiff Castle, Cardiff, CF10 2RB T: (029) 2078 1271 E: curator@qdg.org.uk W: www.qdg.org.uk
Cardiff Castle Castle Street, Cardiff, CF1 2RB T: (029) 20822083 E: cardiffcastle@cardiff.gov.uk
Techniquest Stuart St, Cardiff, CF10 5BW T: (029) 20475475
Carmarthenshire
Kidwelly Industrial Museum Broadford, Kidwelly, SA17 4UF T: 01554 891078
National Museum & Galleries of Wales Cathays Park, Cardiff, CF10 3NP T: (029) 20397951
Parc Howard Museum & Art Gallery Mansion House, Parc Howard, Llanelli, SA15 3LJ T: 01554 772029 E: W:
Welch Regiment Museum of Royal Regiment of Wales The Black & Barbican Towers, Cardiff Castle And Grounds, Cardiff, CF10 3RB T: 029 2022 9367 E: welch@rrw.org.uk john.dart@rrw.org.uk W: www.rrw.org.uk
Ceredigion
Cardigan Heritage Centre Teifi Wharf, Castle St, Cardigan, SA43 3AA T: 01239 614404 E: W:
Ceredigion Museum Coliseum, Terrace Rd, Aberystwyth, SY23 2AQ T: 01970 633088 E: museum@ceredigion.gov.uk W: www.ceridigion.gov.uk
Mid-Wales Mining Museum- Silver River Mines Ltd Llywernog Mine, Ponterwyd, Aberystwyth, SY23 3AB T: 01970 890620 E: silverrivermine@aol.com W: www.silverminetours.co.uk
Museum of Welsh Life St Fagans, Cardiff, CF5 6XB T: (029) 2057 3500 E: post@nmgw.ac.uk W: www.nmgw.ac.uk/mwl/
Conwy
Great Orme Tramway Tramffordd Y Gogarth Goprsaf Victoria, Church Walks, Llandudno, LL30 1AZ T: 01492 575350 E: enq@greatormetramway.com W: www.greatormetramway.com
Sir Henry Jones Museum Y Cwm, Llangernyw, Abergele, LL22 8PR T: 01492 575371 E: info@sirhenryjones-museums.org W: www.sirhenryjones-museums.org
Denbighshire
Cae Dai Trust Cae Dai Lawnt, Denbigh, LL16 4SU T: 01745 812107
Llangollen Motor Museum Pentrefelin, Llangollen, LL20 8EE T: 01978 860324 E: W:
Dyfed
Wilson Museum of Narberth Market Square, Narberth, SA67 7AX T: 01834 861719 E: W:
Dyfed
Pembrokeshire Motor Museum Keeston Hill, Haverfordwest, SA62 6EH T: 01437 710950 E: W:
Glamorgan
Brecon Mountain Railway Pant Station, Merthyr Tydfil, CF48 2UP T: 01685 722988 E: enquiries@breconmountainrailway.co.uk W: www.breconmountainrailway.co.uk

Gwent
Abergavenny Museum The Castle, Castle St, Abergavenny, NP7 5EE T: 01873 854282
Big Pit Mining Museum Blaenavon, Torfaen, NP4 9XP T: 01495-790311
Castle & Regimental Museum Monmouth Castle, Monmouth, NP25 3BS T: 01600 772175 E: curator@monmouthshirecastlemuseum.org.uk W: www.monmouthshirecastlemuseum.org.uk
Drenewydd Museum 26-27 Lower Row, Bute Town, Tredegar, NP22 5QH T: 01685 843039 E: morgac1@caerphilly.gov.uk W:
Newport Museum & Art Gallery John Frost Square, Newport, NP20 1PA T: 01633-840064 E: museum@newport.gov.uk
Pillgwenlly Heritage Community Project within Baptist Chapel, Alexandra Rd, Newport, NP20 2JE T: 01633 244893 E: W:
Roman Legionary Museum High Street, Caerleon, NP6 1AE T: 01633 423134 W: www.nmgw.ac.uk
Valley Inheritance Park Buildings, Pontypool, Torfaen, NP4 6JH T: 01495-752036
Gwynedd
Bala Lake Railway Rheilfford Llyn Tegid The Station Yr Orsaf, Llanuwchllyn, LL23 7DD T: 01678 540666 W: www.bala-lake-railway.co.uk
Betws-y-Coed Motor Museum Museum Cottage, Betws-Y-Coed, LL24 0AH T: 01690 710760
Caernarfon Air World Caernarfon Airport, Dinas Dinlle, Caernarfon, LL54 5TP
Gwynedd Museums Service Victoria Dock, Caernarvon, LL55 1SH T: 01286 679098 E: amgueddflydd-museums@gwynedd.gov.uk
Llanberis Lake Railway Rheilffordd Llyn Padarn LLanberis, LL55 4TY T: 01286 870549 E: info@lake-railway.co.uk W: www.lake-railway.co.uk
Llandudno & Conwy Valley Railway Society Welsh Slate Museum, Llanberis, T: 01492 874590
Llandudno Royal Artillery Llandudno Museum, 17-19 Gloddaeth Street, Llandudno, LL30 2DD T: 01492 876517
Lloyd George Museum Llanstumdwy, Criccieth, LL52 0SH T: 01766 522071 W: www.gwynedd.gov.uk/adrannau/addysg/amgueddfeydd/english/lg_1.htm
Porthmadog Maritime Museum Oakley Wharf 1, The Harbour, Porthmadog, LL49 9LU T: 01766 513736 E: W:
Segontium Roman Museum Beddgelert Road, Caernarfon, LL55 2LN T: 01286 675625 W: www.nmgw.ac.uk
Snowdon Mountain Railway Llanberis, LL55 4TY T: 0870 4580033 E: info@snowdonrailway.co.uk W: www.snowdonrailway.co.uk
Teapot Museum 25 Castle St, Conwy, LL32 8AY T: 01492 596533
The Royal Welch Fusiliers Regimental Museum The Queen's Tower, The Castle, Caernarfon, LL55 2AY T: 01286 673362 E: rwfusiliers@callnetuk.com W: www.rwfmuseum.org.uk
Welsh Highland Railway Tremadog Road, Porthmadog, LL49 9DY T: 01766 513402 W: www.whr.co.uk
Welsh Slate Museum Llanberis, LL55 4TY T: 01286 870630 E: slate@nmgw.ac.uk W: www.nmgw.ac.uk
Gwyness
Home Front Experience New Street, Llandudno, LL30 2YF T: 01492 871032 W: www.homefront-enterprises.co.uk
Mid Glamorgan
Cyfartha Castle Museum Cyfartha Park, Brecon Road, Merthyr Tydfil, CF47 8RE T: 01685 723112
Joseph Parrys Cottage 4 Chapel Row, Merthyr Tydfil, CF48 1BN T: 01685 383704
Pontypridd Historical & Cultural Centre Bridge St, Pontypridd, CF37 4PE T: 01443 409512
Ynysfach Iron Heritage Centre Merthyr Tydfil Heritage Trust, Ynysfach Rd, Merthyr Tydfil, CF48 1AG T: 01685 721858
Monmouthshire
Nelson Museum & Local History Centre Priory St, Monmouth, NP5 3XA T: 01600 710630 E: nelsonmuseum@monmouthshire.gov.uk
Chepstow Museum Bridge St, Chepstow, NP16 5EZ T: 01291 625981 E: chepstowmuseum@monmouthshire.gov.uk
The Royal Monmouthshire Royal Engineers (Militia) Castle and Regimental Museum, The Castle, Monmouth, NP25 3BS T: 01600-712935 E: curator@monmouthcastlemuseum.org.uk W: www.monmouthcastlemuseum.org.uk
Usk Rural Life Museum The Malt Barn, New Market Street, Usk, NP15 1AU T: 01291-673777 E: uskrurallife.museum@virgin.net W: www.uskmuseum.members.easyspace.com
Pembrokeshire
Haverfordwest Town Museum Castle St, Haverfordwest, SA61 2EF T: 01437 763087 W: www.haverfordwest-town-museum.org.uk
Milford Haven Museum Old Customs House, The Docks, Milford Haven, SA73 3AF T: 01646 694496 E: W:

Pembroke Yeomanry, Royal Pembroke Militia, Pembrokeshire Volunteers Museum Scolton Manor Museum, Spittal, Haverfordwest, SA62 5QL T: 01437 731328

Pembrokeshire Museum Service Castle Gallery, Castle St, Haverfordwest, SA61 2EF T: 01437 775246 E: W:

Tenby Museum Tenby Museum & Art Gallery, Castle Hill, Tenby, SA70 7BP T: 01834-842809 E: tenbymuseum@hotmail.com W: www.tenbymuseum.free-online.co.uk

Powys

Brecknock Militia Howell Harris Museum, Coleg Trefeca, Brecon, LD3 0PP T: 01874 711423 E: post@trefeca.org.uk W: www.trefeca.org.uk

Llanidloes Museum The Town Hall, Great Oak Street, Llanidloes, SY18 6BN T: 01686 413777 W: http://powysmuseums.powys.gov.uk

Powysland Museum & Montgomery Canal Centre Canal Yard, Welshpool, SY21 7AQ T: 01938 554656 W: http://powysmuseums.powys.gov.uk

Radnorshire Museum Temple St, Llandrindod Wells, LD1 5DL T: 01597 824513 E: radnorshire.museum@powys.gov.uk

South Wales Borderers & Monmouthshire Regimental Museum of the Royal Regt of Wales (24th/41st Foot) The Barracks, Brecon, LD3 7EB T: 01874 613310 E: swb@rrw.org.uk W: www.rrw.org.uk

The Judge's Lodging Broad St, Presteigne, LD8 2AD T: 01544 260650 W: www.judgeslodging.org.uk

Water Folk Canal Centre Old Store House, Llanfrynach, Brecon, LD3 7LJ T: 01874 665382

West Glamorgan

Cefn Coed Colliery Museum Blaenant Colliery, Crynant, Neath, SA10 8SE T: 01639 750556

Glynn Vivian Art Gallery Alexandra Rd, Swansea, SA1 5DZ T: 01792 655006 E: glynn.vivian.gallery@business.ntl.com W: www.sawnsea.gov.uk

Neath Museum The Gwyn Hall, Orchard Street, Neath, SA11 1DT T: 01639 645726

Wrexham

Wrexham County Borough Museum County Buildings, Regent Street, Wrexham, LL11 1RB T: 01978-317970 E: museum@wrexham.gov.uk W: www.wrexham.gov.uk/heritage

Scotland

Aberdeenshire

Aberdeen Maritime Museum 52-56 Shiprow, Aberdeen, AB11 5BY T: 01224 337700 E: johne@arts-recreation.aberdeen.net.uk W: www.aagm.co.uk

Alford Heritage Centre Alford & Donside Heritage Association, Mart Road, Alford, AB33 8BZ T: 019755 62906

Arbuthnot Museum St. Peter St, Peterhead, AB42 1DA T: 01779 477778

Fraserburgh Heritage Society Heritage Centre, Quarry Rd, Fraserburgh, AB43 9DT T: 01346 512888 E: W: www.fraserburghheritage.com

Grampian Transport Museum Alford, AB33 8AE T: 019755-62292

Hamilton T.B Northfield Farm, New Pitsligo, Fraserburgh, AB43 6PX T: 01771 653504

Provost Skene's House Guestrow, Aberdeen, AB10 1AS T: 01224 641086

Satrosphere The Tramsheds, 179 Constitution Street, Aberdeen, AB11 6LU T: 01224 640340 E: info@satrosphere.net W: www.satrosphere.net

The Gordon Highlanders Museum St Luke's, Viewfield Road, Aberdeen, AB15 7XH T: 01224 311200 E: museum@gordonhighlanders.com W: www.gordonhighlanders.com

The Museum of Scottish Lighthouses Kinnaird Head, Fraserburgh, AB43 9DU T: 01346-511022 E: enquiries@lighthousemuseum.demon.co.uk

Angus

Arbroath Museum Signal Tower, Ladyloan, Arbroath, DD11 1PY T: 01241 875598 E: signal.tower@angsu.gov.uk W: www.angus.gov.uk/history

Glenesk Folk Museum The Retreat, Glenesk, Brechin, DD9 7YT T: 01356 670254 E: retreat@angusglens.co.uk W: www.angusglens.co.uk

Montrose Air Station Museum Waldron Road, Montrose, DD10 9BB T: 01674 673107 E: info@RAFmontrose.org.uk W: www.RAFmontrose.org.uk

The Meffan Institute 20 High St., West, Forfar, DD8 1BB T: 01307 464123 E: the.meffan@angus.gov.uk W:

Argyll

Campbeltown Heritage Centre Big Kiln, Witchburn Rd, Campbeltown, PA28 6JU T: 01586 551400

Campbeltown Library and Museum Hall St, Campbeltown, PA28 6BU T: 01586 552366 E: mary.vanhelmond@argyll-bute.gov.uk W: www.argyle-bute.gov.uk/content/leisure/museums

Castle House Museum Castle Gardens, Argyll St, Dunoon, PA23 7HH T: 01369 701422 E: info@castlehousemuseum.org.uk W: www.castlehousemuseum.org.uk

Kilmartin House Trust Kilmartin House, Kilmartin, Lochgilphead, PA31 8RQ T: 01546 510278 E: museum@kilmartin.org W: www.kilmartin.org

Ayrshire

Ayrshire Yeomanry Museum Rozelle House, Monument Road, Alloway by Ayr, KA7 4NQ T: 01292 445400 (Museum)

Dalgarven Mill Dalry Rd, Dalgarven, Kilwinning, KA13 6PL T: 01294 552448

East Ayrshire Council District History Centre & Museum Baird Institute, 3 Lugar Street, Cumnock, KA18 1AD T: 01290 421701 E: Baird.institute@east-ayrshire.gov.uk W: www.east-ayrshire.gov.uk

Glasgow Vennel Museum 10 Glasgow, Vennel, Irvine, KA12 0BD T: 01294 275059

Irvine Burns Club & Burgh Museum 28 Eglinton St, Irvine, KA12 8AS T: 01294 274511

McKechnie Institute Dalrymple St, Girvan, KA26 9AE T: 01465 713643 E: mkigir@ukgateway.net

North Ayrshire Museum Manse St, Saltcoats, KA21 5AA T: 01294 464174 E: namuseum@globalnet.co.uk

Rozelle House Rozelle Park, Ayr, KA7 4NQ T: 01292 445447

The Largs Museum Kirkgate House, Manse Court, Largs, KA30 8AW T: 01475 687081

The Scottish Maritime Museum Gottries Road, Irvine, KA12 3QE T: 01294 278283 E: jgrant5313@aol.com W: WWW:

West Lowland Fencibles Culzean Castle, Maybole, KA19 8LE T: 01655 884455 E: culzean@nts.org.uk W: www.culzeancastle.net

Banffshire

The Buckie Drifter Maritime Heritage Centre Freuchny Rd, Buckie, AB56 1TT T: 01542 834646

Berwickshire

Coldstream Guards Coldstream Museum, 13 Market Square, Coldstream, TD12 4BD T: 01890 882630

The Jim Clark Room 44 Newtown St, Duns, TD11 3DT T: 01361 883960

Caithness

Clangunn Heritage Centre & Museum Old Parish Kirk, Lathcron, KW5 6DL T: 01593 741700

Dunbeath Preservation Trust Old School, Dunbeath, KW6 6EG T: 01593 731233 E: info@dunbeath-heritage.org.uk W: www.dunbeath-heritage.org.uk

The Last House John O'Groats, Wick, KW1 4YR T: 01955 611250

Dumfriesshire

Dumfries Museum & Camera Obscura The Observatory, Dumfries, DG2 7SW T: 01387 253374 E: info@dumgal.gov.uk W: www.dumfriesmuseum.demon.co.uk

Ellisland Trust Ellisland Farm, Dumfries, DG2 0RP T: 01387 740426

Gretna Museum & Tourist Services Headless Cross, Gretna Green, DG16 5EA T: 01461 338441 E: info@gretnagreen.com W: www.gretnagreen.com

John Paul Jones Birthplace Museum Arbigland, Kirkbean, Dumfries, DG2 8BQ T: 01387 880613 W: www.jpj.demon.co.uk

Old Bridge House Museum Old Bridge, Mill Rd, Dumfries, DG2 7BE T: 01387 256904 W: www.dumfriesmuseum.demon.co.uk

Robert Burns Centre Mill Road, Dumfries, DG2 7BE T: 01387 264808 E: dumfreis.museum@dumgal.gov.uk W: www.dumgal.gov.uk/museums

Robert Burns House Burns Street, Dumfries, DG1 2PS T: 01387 255297

Sanquhar Tolbooth Museum High St, Sanquhar, DG4 6BL T: 01659 50186

Savings Banks Museum Ruthwell, Dumfries, DG1 4NN T: 01387 870640 E: tsbmuseum@btinternet.com

Shambellie House Museum of Costume New Abbey, Dumfries, DG2 8HQ T: 01387 850375 E: info@nms.ac.uk W: www.nms.ac.uk

Dundee

Dundee Heritage Trust Verdant Works, West Henderson's Wynd, Dundee, DD1 5BT T: 01382-225282 E: info@dundeeheritage.sol.co.uk W: www.verdant-works.co.uk

HM Frigate Unicorn Victoria Dock, South Victoria Dock Road, Dundee, DD1 3BP T: 01382 200893 E: frigateunicorn@hotmail.com W: www.frigateunicorn.org

Royal Research Ship Discovery Discovery point, Discovery Quay, Dundee, DD1 4XA T: 01382 201245 E: info@dundeeheritage.sol.co.uk W: www.rrs-discovery.co.uk

East Lothian

Dunbar Museum High St, Dunbar, EH42 1ER T: 01368 863734

John Muir House Museum 126-128 High St, Dunbar, EH42 1JJ T: 01368 862585

Myreton Motor Museum Aberlady, EH32 0PZ T: 01875 870288

North Berwick Museum School Rd, North Berwick, EH39 4JU T: 01620 895457

Edinburgh

Heritage Projects (Edinburgh) Ltd Castlehill, Royal Mile, Midlothian EH1 2NE T: 0131 225 7575

Museum of Edinburgh Huntly House, 142 Canongate, Edinburgh, EH8 8DD T: 0131 529 4143 W: www.cac.org.uk

Royal Scots Regimental Museum The Castle, Edinburgh, EH1 2YT T: 0131-310-5014 E: rhqroyalscots@edinburghcastle.fsnet.co.uk W: www.theroyalscots.co.uk

Royal Yatch Britannia & Visitor Centre Ocean Drive, Leith, edinburgh, EH6 6JJ T: 0131 555 5566 W: www.royalyatchbritannia.co.uk

Scottish Museum Council County House, 20-22 Torphichen Street, Edinburgh, EH3 8JB T: 0131 229 7465 E: inform@scottish.museums.org.uk W: www.scottish.museums.org.uk

The Real Mary King's Close 2 Warriston's Close, Writers' Court, Edinburgh, EH1 1PG T: 08702 430160 W: www.realmarykingsclose.com

Falkirk

Falkirk Museum History Research Centre Callendar House, Callendar Park, Falkirk, FK1 1YR T: 01324 503778 E: ereid@falkirkmuseums.demon.co.ukcallandarhouse@falkirkmuseums.demon.co.uk W: www.falkirkmuseums.demon.co.uk

Fife

Andrew Carnegie Birthplace Museum Moodie St, Dunfermline, KY12 7PL T: 01383 724302

Dunfermline Museum Viewfield, Dunfermline, KY12 7HY T: 01383 313838

Fife and Forfar Yeomanry Museum Yeomanry House, Castlebrook Road, Cupar, KY15 4BL T: 01334 656155

Inverkeithing Museum The Friary, Queen St, Inverkeithing, KY11 1 T: 01383 313595

John McDouall Stuart Museum Rectory Lane, Dysart, Kirkcaldy, KY1 2TP T: 01592 653118

Kirkcaldy Museum and Art Gallery War Memorial Gardens, Kirkcaldy, KY1 1YG T: 01592 412860

Methil Heritage Centre 272 High St, Methil, Leven, KY8 3EQ T: 01333 422100

Pittencrieff House Museum Pittencrieff Park, Dunfermline, KY12 8QH T: 01383 722935

Scotland's Secret Bunker Underground Nuclear Command Centre, Crown Buildings (Near St Andrews), KY16 8QH T: 01333-310301

Scottish Fisheries Museum St. Ayles, Harbourhead, Anstruther, KY10 3AB T: 01333 310628 E: andrew@scottish-fisheries-museum.org W: www.scottish-fisheries-museum.org

The Fife Folk Museum High St, Ceres, Cupar, KY15 5NF T: 01334 828180

Verdant Works - A Working Jute mill West Henderson's Wynd, Dundee, DD1 5BT T: 01382-225282 E: info@dundeeheritage.sol.co.uk W: www.verdantworks.co.uk

Glasgow

Fossil Grove Victoria Park, Glasgow, G14 1BN T: 0141 287 2000 W: www.glasgowmuseums.com

Glasgow Museum of Transport 1 Burnhouse Road, Glasgow, G3 8DP T: 0141 287 2720 W: www.glasgowmuseums.com

Glasgow Police Museum 68 St Andrews Square, Glasgow, G2 4JS T: 07788 532691 E: curator@policemuseum.org.uk W: www.policemusaeum.org.uk

Heatherbank Museum Glasgow Caledonian University, Cowcaddens Road, Glasgow, G4 0BA T: 0141 331 8637 E: A.Ramage@gcla.ac.uk W: www.lib.gcal.ac.uk/heatherbank

Kelvingrove Art Gallery and Museum Kelvingrove, Glasgow, G3 8AG T: 0141 287 2699 W: www.cis.glasgow.gov.uk

Martyrs School Parson street, Glasgow, G4 0PX T: 0141 552 2356 W: www.glasgowmuseums.com

McLellan Galleries 270 Sauchiehall Street, Glasgow, G2 3EH T: 0141 565 4100 W: www.glasgowmuseums.com

Museum of Piping The Piping Centre, 30-34 McPhater Street, Cowcaddens, Glasgow, T: 0141-353-0220

Open Museum 161 Woodhead Road, South Nitshill Industrial Estate, Glasgow, G53 7NN T: 0141 552 2356 W: www.glasgowmuseums.com

Pollok House Pollok Country Park, 2060 Pollokshaws Road, Glasgow, G43 1AT T: 0141 616 6410 W: www.cis.glasgow.gov.uk

Provand's Lordship 3 Castle Street, Glasgow, G4 0RB T: 0141 552 8819 W: www.glasgowmuseums.com

Scotland Street School Museum 225 Scotland St, Glasgow, G5 8QB T: 0141 287 0500 W: www.glasgowmuseums.com

St Mungo Museum of Religious Life and Art 2 Castle Street, Glasgow, G4 0RH T: 0141 553 2557 W: www.glasgowmuseums.com

The Burrell Collection Pollok Country Park, 2060 Pollokshaws Road, Glasgow, G43 1AT T: 0141 287 2550 W: www.glasgowmuseums.com

The Hunterian Museum Glasgow University, Glasgow, G12 8QQ T: 0141 330 3711 E: e.smith@admin.gla.ac.uk

The Lighthouse 11 Mitchell Lane, Glasgow, G1 3NU T: 0141 221 6362 E: enquiries@thelighthouse.co.uk W: www.thelighthouse.co.uk

Highland

Regimental Museum of The Highlanders (The Queen's Own Highlanders Collection) Fort George, IV2 7TD T: 01463 224380 E: rhqthehighlanders@btopenworld.com

Inverness-shire

Clan Cameron Museum Achnacarry , Spean Bridge, PH34 4EJ T: 01397 712090 E: museum@achnarcarry.fsnet.co.uk W: www.clan-cameron.org

Culloden Visitor Centre Culloden Moor, Inverness, IV2 5EU T: 01463 790607 E: dsmyth@nts.org.uk W: www.nts.org.uk

Highland Folk Museum Duke St, Kingussie, PH21 1JG T: 01540 661307 E: rachel.chisholm@highland.gov.uk W:

Highland Folk Museum Aultlarie Croft, Kingussie Rd, Newtonmore, PH20 1AY T: 01540 673551 E: highland.folk@highland.gov.uk W: www.highlandfolf.com

Highland Railway Museum 5 Druimlon, Drumnadrochit, Inverness, IV63 6TY T: 01456 450527

Inverness Museum & Art Gallery Castle Wynd, Inverness, IV2 3ED T: 01463 237114

Mallaig Heritage Centre Station Rd, Mallaig, PH41 4PY T: 01687 462085 E: curator@mallaigheritage.org.uk W: www.mallaigheritage.org.uk

Queen's Own Cameron Highlanders Fort George, Arderseir, Inverness, IV1 2TD T: 01667 462777

Queen's Own Highlanders (Seaforth & Camerons) Regimental Museum Archives Fort George, Ardersier, Inverness, IV1 7TD T: 01463-224380**The Clansman Centre** Canalside, Fort Augustus, PH32 4AU T: 01320 366444

West Highland Museum Cameron Square, Fort William, PH33 6AJ T: 01397 702169 E: info@westhighlandmuseum.org.uk W: www.westhighlandmuseum.org.uk

Isle Of Arran

Arran Heritage Museum Rosaburn House, Brodick, KA27 8DP T: 01770 302636

Isle Of Islay

Finlaggan Trust The Cottage, Ballygrant, PA45 7QL T: 01496 840644 E: lynmags@aol.com W: www.islay.com

Isle Of Mull

The Columba Centre Fionnphort, Isle Of Mull, PA66 6BN T: 01681 700660

Isle Of North Uist

Taigh Chearsabhagh Trust Taigh Chearsabhagh, Lochmaddy, HS6 5AE T: 01876 500293 E: taighchearsabhagh@zetnet.co.uk W: www.taighchearsabhagh.org.uk

Isle Of South Uist

Kildonan Museum Kildonan, Lochboisdale, HS8 5RZ T: 01878 710343

Kinross-shire

Perth Museum & Art Gallery Perth Museum & Art Gallery, George Street, Perth, PH1 5LB T: 01738-632488 E: museum@pkc.gov.uk W: www.pkc.gov.uk/ah

Kirkcudbrightshire

The Stewartry Museum St Mary Street, Kirkcudbright, DG6 4AQ T: 01557 331643 E: david@dumgal.gov.uk W: www.dumgal.gov.uk/museums

Lanarkshire

Auld Kirk Musuem The Cross, Kirkintilloch, Glasgow, G66 1 T: 0141 578 014

Biggar Museum Trust Moat Park Kirkstyle, Biggar, ML12 6DT T: 01899 221050

Discover Carmichael Visitors Centre Warrenhill Farm, Warrenhill Road, Thankerton, Biggar, ML12 6PF T: 01899 308169

Greenhill Covenanters House Museum Kirkstyle, Biggar, ML12 6DT T: 01899 221572

Heritage Engineering 22 Carmyle Avenue, Glasgow, G32 8HJ T: 0141 763 0007

Hunter House Maxwellton Rd, East Kilbride, Glasgow, G74 3LW T: 01355 261261

John Hastie Museum Threestanes Road, Strathaven, ML10 6EB T: 01357 521257

Lanark Museum 7West Port, Lanark, ML11 9HD T: 01555 666680 E: paularchibald@hotmail.com W: www.biggar-net.co.uk/lanarkmuseum

Low Parks Museum 129 Muir St, Hamilton, ML3 6BJ T: 01698 283981

New Lanark Conservation Trust Visitors Centre Mill No 3, New Lanark Mills, Lanark, ML11 9DB T: 01555 661345 E: visit@newlanark.org W: www.newlanark.org

The Cameronians (Scottish Rifles) Museum & Low Parks Museum c/o Low Parks Museum, 129 Muir Street, Hamilton, ML3 6BJ T: 01698 452163

The People's Palace Glasgow Green, Glasgow, G40 1AT T: 0141 554 0223 W: www.glasgowmuseums.com

Weavers' Cottages Museum 23-25 Wellwynd, Airdrie, ML6 0BN T: 01236 747712

Midlothian

History of Education Centre East London St, Edinburgh, EH7 4BW T: 0131 556 4224

Lauriston Castle 2a Cramond Rd South, Edinburgh, EH4 5QD T: 0131 336 2060

Newhaven Heritage Museum 24 Pier Place, Edinburgh, EH6 4LP T: 0131 551 4165 E: W: www.cac.org.uk

Scots Dragoon Guards Museum Shop The Castle, Edinburgh, EH1 2YT T: 0131 220 4387

Scottish Mining Museum Trust Lady Victoria Colliery, Newtongrange, Dalkeith, EH22 4QN T: 0131 663 7519 E: enwuiries@scottishminingmuseum.com W: www.scottishminingmuseum.com

Morayshire

Elgin Museum 1 High St, Elgin, IV30 1EQ T: 01343 543675 E: curator@elginmuseum.demon.co.uk W: www.elginmuseum.demon.co.uk

Falconer Museum Tolbooth St, Forres, IV36 1PH T: 01309 673701 E: alasdair.joyce@techleis.moray.gov.uk W: www.moray.gov.uk

Grantown Museum & Heritage Trust Burnfield House, Burnfield Avenue, Grantown-On-Spey, PH26 3HH T: 01479 872478 E: Molly.Duckett@btinternet.com W: www.grantown-on-spey.co.uk

Lossiemouth Fisheries Museum Pitgaveny St, Lossiemouth, IV31 6TW T: 01343 813772

Nairnshire

Nairn Museum Viewfield House, King St, Nairn, IV12 4EE T: 01667 456791

Orkney

Orkney Farm & Folk Museum Corrigall Farm Museum, Harray, KW17 2LQ T: 01856 771411

Orkney Farm & Folk Museum Kirbister Farm, Birsay, KW17 2LR T: 01856 771268

Orkney Fossil & Vintage Centre Viewforth Burray, KW17 2SY T: 01856 731255

Orkney Museum Tankerness House, Broad Street, Kirkwall, KW15 1DH T: 01856-873191

Orkney Wireless Museum Kiln Corner, Kirkwall, KW15 1LB T: 01856-871400

Scapa Flow Visitor Centre Lyness, Stromness, KW16 3NT T: 01856 791300 W: www.scapaflow.co.uk

Stromness Museum 52 Alfred Street, Stromness, T: 01856 850025

Perthshire

Atholl Country Collection The Old School, Blair Atholl, PH18 5SP T: 01796-481232 E: r.cam@virgin.net

Atholl Highlanders Blair Castle, Blair Atholl, PH18 5TL T: 01796 481207 E: office@blair-castle.co.uk W: www.blair-castle.co.uk

Clan Donnachaidh (Robertson) Museum Clan Donnachaidh Centre, Bruar, Pitlochry, PH18 5TW T: 01796-483338 E: clandonnachaidh@compuserve.com donkey3@freenetname.co.uk

Clan Menzies Museum Castle Menzies, Weem, by Aberfeldy, PH15 2JD T: 01887-820982

Dunkeld Cathedral Chapter House Museum Dunkeld, PH8 0AW T: 01350 728732 W: www.dunkeldcathedral.org.uk

Meigle Museum Dundee Rd, Meigle, Blairgowrie, PH12 8SB T: 01828 640612

Scottish Horse Regimental Archives - Dunkeld Cathedral Dunkeld, PH8 0AW T: 01350 727614

The Hamilton Toy Collection 111 Main St, Callander, FK17 8BQ T: 01877 330004

Renfrewshire

Mclean Museum & Art Gallery 15 Kelly St, Greenock, PA16 8JX T: 01475 715624

Old Paisley Society George Place, Paisley, PA1 2HZ T: 0141 889 1708

Paisley Museum Paisley Museum & Art Galleries, High Street, Paisley, PA1 2BA T: 0141-889-3151

Ross-Shire

Dingwall Museum Trust Town Hall, High St, Dingwall, IV15 9RY T: 01349 865366

Highland Museum of Childhood The Old Station, Strathpeffer, IV14 9DH T: 01997 421031 E: info@hmoc.freeserve.co.uk W: www.hmoc.freeserve.co.uk

Tain Through Time Tain & District Museum Tower St, Tain, IV19 1DY T: 01862 894089

The Groam House Museum High St, Rosemarkie, Fortrose, IV10 8UF T: 01381 620961

Ullapool Museum & Visitor Centre 7 & 8 West Argyle St, Ullapool, IV26 2TY T: 01854 612987 E: ulmuseum@waverider.co.uk

Roxburghshire

Borders Museum of Arms Henderson's Knowe, Teviot, Hawick, TD9 0LF T: 01450 850237

Hawick Museum & Scott Gallery Wilton Lodge Park, Hawick, TD9 7JL T: 01450 373457 E: hawickmuseum@hotmail.com

Jedburgh Castle Jail Museum Castlegate, Jedburgh, TD8 6BD T: 01835 863254

Mary Queen of Scots House and Visitor Centre Queens St, Jedburgh, TD8 6EN T: 01835 863331

Selkirkshire

Halliwells House Museum Halliwells Close, Market Place, Selkirk, TD7 4BL T: 01750 20096 E: museums@scotborders.gov.uk W: WWW:

Shetland

Fetlar Interpretive Centre Beach Of Houbie, Fetlar, ZE2 9DJ T: 01957 733206 E: fic@zetnet.co.uk W: www.zetnet.co.uk/sigs/centre/

Shetland Islands

Old Haa Museum Burravoe Yell, Shetland, ZE2 9AY T: 01957 722339

Shetland Museum Lower Hillhead, Lerwick, ZE1 0EL T: 01595 695057 E: shetland.museum@zetnet.co.uk W: www.shetland-museum.org.uk

Tangwick Haa Museum Tangwick, Eshaness, Shetland, ZE2 9RS T: 01806 503389

The Shetland Textile Working Museum Weisdale Mill, Weisdale, Shetland, ZE2 9LW T: 01595 830419

Stirlingshire

Stirling Smith Art Gallery & Museum Dumbarton Road, Stirling, FK8 2RQ T: 01786 471917 E: museum@smithartgallery.demon.co.uk

Regimental Museum Argyll and Sutherland Highlanders Stirling Castle, Stirling, FK8 1EH T: 01786 475165

Stranraer

Stranraer Museum 55 George Street, Stranraer, DG9 7JP T: 01776 705088 E: JohnPic@dumgal.gov.uk W: www.dumgal.gov.uk

Strathclyde

Museum of The Royal Highland Fusiliers (Royal Scots Fusiliers and Highland Light Infantry) 518 Sauchiehall Street, Glasgow, G2 3LW T: 0141 332 0961 W: www.rhf.org.uk

Sutherland

Strathnaver Museum Bettyhill, KW14 7SS T: 01641 521 418 E: strathnavermuseum@ukonline.co.uk www.strathnaver.org

Tayside

Perth Museum & Art Gallery Perth Museum & Art Gallery, George Street, Perth, PH1 5LB T: 01738-632488 E: museum@pkc.gov.uk W: www.pkc.gov.uk/ah

West Lothian

Almond Valley Heritage Trust Livingston Mill Farm, Millfield, Livingston, EH54 7AR T: 01506 414957

Bennie Museum Mansefield St, Bathgate, EH48 4HU T: 01506 634944 W: www.benniemuseum.homestead.co.uk

Kinneil Museum Kinneil Estate, Bo'Ness, EH51 0AY T: 01506 778530

Queensferry Museum 53 High St, South Queensferry, EH30 9HP T: 0131 331 5545 W: www.cac.org.uk

The Linlithgow Story Annet House, 143 High St, Linlithgow, EH49 7EJ T: 01506 670677 E: enquiries@linlithgowstory.fsnet.co.uk W: www.linlithgowstory.org.uk

Wigtownshire

Taylor's Farm Tradition Barraer, Newton Stewart, DG8 6QQ T: 01671 404890 E: jtaylor@bosinternet.com

Northern Ireland

Ulster Aviation Heritage Centre Langford Lodge Airfield, Belfast, T: 028 9267 7030 W: www.d-n-a.net/users/dnetrAzQ

Belfast

Royal Ulster Rifles Regimental Museum RHQ Royal Irish Regiment, 5 Waring Street, Belfast, BT1 2EW T: (028) 90232086 E: rurmuseum@yahoo.co.uk W: www.rurmuseum.tripod.com

Ulster Museum Botanic Gardens Botanic Gardens, Stranmillis Road, Belfast, BT9 5AB T: (028) 90381251

Co Down

Ulster Folk and Transport Museum Cultra, Holywood, BT18 0EU T: (028) 9042 8728

County Antrim

Ballymoney Museum & Heritage Centre 33 Charlotte St, Ballymoney, BT53 6AY T: (028) 2762280

Friends of the Ulster Museum 12 Malone Road, Belfast, BT9 5BN T: (028) 90681606

NI Museums Council 66 Donegall Pass, Belfast, BT7 1BU T: (028) 90550215 W: www.nimc.co.uk

Odyssey Science Centre Project Office Project Office NMGNI, Botanic Gardens, Belfast, BT9 5AB T: (028) 90682100

The Museum Of The Royal Irish Regiment St. Patricks Barracks, Demesne Avenue, Ballymena, BT43 7BH T: (028) 2566 1386 E: hqrirish@royalirishregiment.co.uk W: www.royalirishregiment.co.uk

Ulster American Folk Park Project Team Belfast 4 The Mount Albert Bridge Rd, Belfast, BT5 4NA T: (028) 90452250

Ulster Aviation Society Langford Lodge Airfield 97, Largy Rd, Crumlin, BT29 4RT T: (028) 9445 4444 E. ernie@airni.freeserve.co.uk W: www.d-n-a.net/users/dnetsAzQ/

County Armagh

Armagh County Museum The Mall East, Armagh, BT61 9BE T: (028) 37523070 E: acm.um@nics.gov.uk W: www.magni.org.uk

Royal Irish Fusilers Museum Sovereign's House, Mall East, Armagh, BT61 9DL T: (028) 3752 2911 W: www.rirfus-museum.freeserve.co.uk

County Down

Down County Museum The Mall, Downpatrick, BT30 6AH T: (028) 44615218

Downpatrick Railway Museum Railway Station, Market St, Downpatrick, BT30 6LZ T: (028) 44615779

The Somme Heritage Centre 233 Bangor Road, Newtownards, BT23 7PH T: 028 9182 3202 E: sommeassociation@dnet.co.uk W: www.irishsoldier.org

County Fermanagh

Fermanagh County Museum Enniskillen Castle Castle Barracks, Enniskillen, BT74 7HL T: 028 66 32 5000 E: castle@fermanagh.gov.uk

Roslea Heritage Centre Church St, Roslea, Enniskillen, BT74 7DW T: (028) 67751750

Royal Inniskilling Fusiliers Regimental Museum The Castle, Enniskillen, BT74 7BB T: (028) 66323142

County Londonderry

Garvagh Museum 142 Main St, Garvagh, Coleraine, BT51 5AE T: (028) 295 58216 E: jclyde@garvaghhigh.garvagh.ni.sch.uk

County Tyrone

The Ulster History Park Cullion, Lislap, BT79 7SU T: (028) 8164 8188 E: uhp@omagh.gov.uk W: www.omagh.gov.uk/historypark.htm

Ulster American Folk Park Centre for Migration Studies, Mellon Rd, Castletown, Omagh, BT78 5QY T: (028) 8225 6315 E: uafp@iol.ie W: www.folkpark,com www.qub.ac.uk/cms/

Londonderry

Foyle Valley Railway Museum Foyle Rd, Londonderry, BT48 6SQ T: (028) 71265234

Londonderry Harbour Museum Harbour Square, Londonderry, BT48 6AF T: 01504 377331

Ireland

Dublin Civic Museum 58 South William Street, Dublin, 2 T: 679-4260

Irish Jewish Museum 3 - 4 Walworth Road, South Circular Road, Dublin, 8 T: 453-1797

Channel Islands

Alderney

The Alderney Society Museum Alderney, GY9 3TG T: 01481 823222

German Occupation Museum Les Houards, Forest, Guernsey GY8 0BG T: 01481 328205 W: www.aboutbritain.com/OccupationMuseum.htm

Guernsey

18th Century Loopholed Tower PO Box 23, St Peter Port, Guernsey GY1 3AN

Clarence Battery Fort George, St Peter Port, Guernsey

Fort Grey Rocquaine Bay, St Saviours, Guernsey

German Direction Finding Tower PO Box 23, St Peter Port, Guernsey GY1 3AN

German Military Underground Hospital La Vassalerie Road, St Andrew's, Guernsey T: 01481 239100

German Naval Signals Headquarters St Jacques, Guernsey

La Hougue Bie Grouville, GuernseyT: 01534 633300

La Valette Underground Military Museum St Peter Port, Guernsey T: 01481 722300

Royal Guernsey Militia and Royal Geurnsey Light Infantry Castle Comet, St Peter Port, Guernsey T: 01481 726518 W: www.museum.guernsey.net/castle.htm

Jersey

Elizabeth Castle - Jersey Militia St Aubin's Bay, St Helier, Jersey T: 01534 633300

German Underground Hospital Meadowbank, St Lawrence, Jersey T: 01534 863442

Island Fortress Occupation Museum 9 Esplanade, St Helier, Jersey T: 01534 633300

Maritime Museum and Occupation Tapestry Gallery New North Quay, St Helier Jersey T: 01534 811043 E: marketing@jerseyheritagetrust.org W: www.jerseyheritagetrust.org

Mont Orgueil Castle Gorey, St Martin, Jersey T: 01534 633300

Noirmont Command Bunker Noirmont Point, St Brelade, Jersey T: 01534 482089

St Peter's Bunker Museum of Wartime German Equipment and Occupation Relics La Petite Rue De L'eglise, St Peter, Jersey JE3 7AF T: 01534 722316

The Channel Islands Military Museum The Five Mile Road, St Ouen, Jersey T: 01534 23136

Sark

German Occupation Museum Rue Lucas, Sark, T: 01481 832564

Military Museums

100 Bomb Group Memorial Museum Common Road, Dickleburgh, Diss, IP21 4PH T: 01379 740708

101 (Northumbrian) Regt Royal Artillery (Volunteers) Museum Napier Armoury, Gateshead, NE8 4HX T: 0191 239 6130

4th Battalion East Yorkshire Regt Collection Kingston upon Hull City Museums, Wilberforce House, 23-25 High Street, Kingston upon Hull, HU1 T: 01482 613902

50 and 61 Sduadrons Museum The Lawn, Union Road, Lincoln,

A Soldier's Life 15th/19th The King's Royal Hussars Northumberland Hussars and Light Dragoons Discovery Museum, Blandford Square, Newcastle-upon-Tyne, NE1 4JA T: 0191 232 6789 E: ralph.thompson@twmuseums.org.uk

Abington Museum and Museum of The Northamptonshire Regt Abington Park Museum, Abington, NN1 5LW T: 01604 635412 W: www.northampton.gov.uk/museums

Airbourne Forces Museum Browning Barracks, Aldershot, GU11 2BU T: 01252 349619

Army Medical Services Museum Keogh Barracks, Ash Vale, Aldershot, GU12 5RQ T: 01252 868612 E: armymedicalmuseum@btinternet.com W: www.ams-museum.org.uk

Army Medical Services Museum Keogh Barracks, Ash Vale, Aldershot, GU12 5RQ T: 01252 868612 E: museum@keogh72.freeserve.co.uk

Bankfield Museum & Gallery Boothtown Rd, Halifax, HX3 6HG T: 01422 354823 E: bankfield-museum@calderdale.gov.uk W: www.calderdale.gov.uk

Battle of Britain Memorial Flight R A F Coningsby, Coningsby, LN4 4SY

Battlefields Trust 33 High Green, Brooke, Norwich, NR15 1HR T: 01508 558145 E: BattlefieldTrust@aol.com W: www.battlefieldstrust.com

Bedford Museum Bedfordshire Yeomanry Castle Lane, Bedford, MK40 3XD T: 01234 353323 E: bmuseum@bedford.gov.uk W: www.bedfordmuseum.org

Bedfordshire and Hertfordshire Regimental Museum Luton Museum, Wardown Park, Luton, LU2 7HA T: 01582 546722 W: www.luton.gov.uk/enjoying/museums

Berkshire and Westminster Dragoons Museum Cavalry House, Duke of York's Headquarters, Kings Road, Chelsea, London, SW3 4SC T: 020 7414 5233

Blake Museum Blake Street, Bridgwater, TA6 3NB T: 01278 456127 E: museums@sedgemoor.gov.uk W: www.sedgemoor.gov.uk

Bomber County Aviation Museum Ex RAF Hemswell, Hemswell Cliff, Gainsborough, T: 01724 855410

Border Regt & Kings Own Royal Border Regt Museum Queen Mary's Tower, The Castle, Carlisle, CA3 8UR T: 01228 532774 E: borderregiment@aol.com W: www.armymuseums.org

Bournemouth Aviation Museum Hanger 600, Bournemouth International Airport, Christchurch, BH23 6SE T: 01202 580858 E: admin@aviation-museum.co.uk phil@philbc.freeserve.co.uk W: www.aviation-museum.co.uk

Brecknock Militia Howell Harris Museum, Coleg Trefeca, Brecon, LD3 0PP T: 01874 711423 E: post@trefeca.org.uk W: www.trefeca.org.uk

Brenzett Aeronautical Museum Ivychurch Road, Brenzett, Romney Marsh, TN29 0EE T: 01233 627911 W: www.aboutbritain.com/renzettAeronauticalMuseum

Britain at War Experience Winston Churchill, 64-66 Tooley Street, London Bridge, London, SE1 2TF T: 020 7403 3171 E: britainatwar@dial.pipex.com W: www.britainatwar.co.uk

Brixham Heritage Museum Bolton Cross, Brixham, TQ5 8LZ T: 01803 856267 E: mail@brixhamheritage.org.uk W: www.brixhamheritage.org.uk

Buckinghamshire Military Museum Trust Collection Old Gaol Museum, Market Hill, Buckingham, MK18 13X T: 01280 823020

Buffs Regimental Museum The Royal Museum & Art Gallery, 18 High Street, Canterbury, CT1 2RA T: 01227-452747 W: www.canterbury-museums.co.uk

Cheshire Military Museum The Castle, Chester, CH1 2DN T: 01244 327617

Cheshire Military Museum The Castle, Chester, CH1 2DN T: 01244 327617 W: www.chester.cc.uk/militarymuseum

Cholmondeley Collection of Model Soldiers Houghton Hall, Houghton, Kings Lynn, PE31 6UE T: 01485 528569 E: administrator@houghtonhall.com W: www.houghtonhall.com

Coldstream Guards Record Office Wellington Barracks, Birdcage Walk, London, SW1E 6HQ

Commonwealth War Graves Commission 2 Marlow Road, Maidenhead, SL6 7DX T: 01628-634221 W: www.cwgc.org

Cosford Royal Air Force Museum Cosford , Shifnal, TF11 8UP T: 01902 376200 E: cosford@rafmuseum.org W: www.rafmuseum.org

Cranwell Avation Heritage Centre Heath Farm, North Raunceby, Near Cranwell, Sleaford, NG34 8QR T: 01529 488490

D-Day Museum and Overlord Museum Clarence Esplanade, Southsea, PO5 3NT T: 023 9282 7261

De Havilland Heritage Centre inc The Mosquito Aircraft Museum PO Box 107, Salisbury Hall, London Colney, AL10 1EX T: 01727 822051 W: www.hertsmuseums.org

Dover Castle Dover, CT16 1HU T: 01304 211067

Duke of Cornwall's Light Infantry Museum The Keep, Bodmin, PL31 1EG T: 01208 72810 W: www.britrishlightinfantry.org.ca

Duke of Wellington's Regimental Museum Bankfield Museum, Akroyd Park, Boothtown Road, Halifax, HX3 6HG T: 01422 354823

Durham Light Infantry Museum Aykley Heads, Durham, DH1 5TU T: 0191-384-2214 E: dli@durham.gov.uk W: www.durham.gov.uk/dli

East Essex Aviation Society & Museum Martello Tower, Point Clear, Clacton on Sea, T: 01255 428020

East Lancashire Regt Towneley Hall, Burnley, BB11 3RQ T: 01282424213 E: towneleyhall@burnley.gov.uk W: www.towneleyhall.org.uk

Eden Camp Museum Malton, YO17 6RT T: 01653 697777 E: admin@edencamp.co.uk W: www.edencamp.co.uk

Essex Regt Museum Oaklands Park, Moulsham Street, Chelmsford, CM2 9AQ T: 01245 615101 W: www.essexregimentmuseum.co.uk

Essex Secret Bunker Crown Building, Shrublands Road, Mistley, CO11 1HS T: 01206 392271 (24 hour information line)

Essex Volunteer Units Colchester Museums, 14 Ryegate Road, Colchester, CO1 1YG T: 01206 282935

Essex Yeomanry Collection Springfield Lyons TA Centre, Colchester Road, Chelmsford , CM2 5TA T: 01245 462298

Explosion! The Museum of Naval Firepower Priddy's Hard, Gosport, PO12 4LE T: 023 9258 6505 E: info@explosion.org.uk W: www.explosion.org.uk

Firepower - The Royal Artillery Museum Royal Arsenal, Woolwich, London, SE18 6ST T: (020) 8855 7755 E: info@firepower.org.uk W: www.firepower.org.uk

Flambards Village and Cornwall Aircraft Park Flambards Village Theme Park, Culdrose Manor, Helston, TR13 0GA T: 01326 573404 E: info@flambards.co.uk W: www.flambards.co.uk

Fort Armherst Dock Road, Chatham , ME4 4UB T: 01634 847747 W: www.fortamhurst.org.uk

Fort Luton Museum Magpie Hall Road, Chatham, ME4 5XJ T: 01634 813969

Fusiliers Museum of Northumberland The Abbot's Tower, Alnwick Castle, Alnwick, NE66 1NG T: 01665-602151

Fusiliers' London Volunteer Museum 213 Balham High Road, London, SW17 7BQ T: 020 8672 1168

Green Howards Regimental Museum Trinity Church Square, Richmond, DL10 4QN T: 01748 822133

Grenadier Guards Record Office Wellington Barracks, Birdcage Walk, London, SW1E 6HQ E: rhqgrengds@yahoo.co.uk

Hertford Museum (Hertfordshire Regiment) 18 Bull Plain, Hertford, SG14 1DT T: 01992 582686 W: www.hertfordmuseum.org

Historic Ships and The Naval Dockyard HM Naval Base, Portsmouth, PO1 3LR T: 023 9286 1512 W: www.flagship.org.uk

Historic Warships at Birkenhead East Float Dock, Dock Road, Birkenhead, L41 1DJ T: 0151 6501573 W: www.warships.freeserve.co.uk

HMS Ganges Museum Victory House, Shotley Point Marina, Ipswich, IP9 1QJ T: 01473 684749

HMS Victory Victory Gate, HM Naval Base, Portsmouth, PO1 3LR T: (023) 9277 8600 E: info@hmswarrior.org W: www.hmswarrior.org

Honourable Artillery Company Armoury House, City Road, London, EC1Y 2BQ T: 020 7382 1537 E: hac@hac.org.uk W: www.hac.org.uk

HQ No 11 (Fighter) Group Battle of Britain Operations Room RAF Uxbridge, Uxbridge, UB10 0RZ T: 01895 815400

Imperial War Museum Lambeth Road, London, SE1 6HZ T: (020) 7416-5000 E: books@iwm.org.uk W: www.iwm.org.uk

Inns of Court and City Yeomanry Museum 10 Stone buildings, Lincoln's Inn, London, WC2A 3TG T: 020 7405 8112

Irish Guards Record Office Wellington Barracks, Birdcage Walk, London, SW1E 6HQ W: www.army.mod/ig~assoc

James Clavell Library Royal Arsenal (West), Warren Lane, Woolwich, London, SE18 6ST T: 020 8312 7125 W: www.firepower.org.uk

Kelvedon Hatch Secret Nuclear Bunker Kelvedon Hall Lane, Kelvedon Common, Kelvedon Hatch, Brentwood, CM15 0LB T: 01277 364883 E: bunker@japar.demon.co.uk W: www.japar.demon.co.uk

Kent Battle of Britain Museum Aerodrome Road, Hawkinge, Folkestone, CT18 7AG T: 01303 893140

King's Own Royal Regimental Museum The City Museum, Market Square, Lancaster, LA1 1HT T: 01524 64637 E: kingsownmuseum@iname.com W: www.kingsownmuseum.plus.com

King's Own Scottish Borderers Museum The Barracks, The Parade, Berwick upon Tweed, TD15 1DG T: 01289 307426 W: www.kosh.co.uk

King's Own Yorkshire Light Infantry Regimental Gallery Doncaster Museum and Art Gallery, Chequer Road, Doncaster, DN1 2AE T: 01302 734293 E: museum@doncaster.gov.uk W: www.doncaster.gov.uk/museums

King's Regt Collection Museum of Liverpool Life, Pier Head, Liverpool, L3 1PZ T: 0151-478-4062

Kohima Museum Imphal Barracks, Fulford Road, York, YO10 4AD T: 01904 665806 E: thekohimamuseum@hotmail.com

Lashenden Air Warfare Museum Headcorn Aerodrome, Headcorn, Nr Ashford, TN27 9HX T: 01622 890226

Leeds Rifles Museum c/o 7 Wentworth Court, Raistrick, Brighouse, HD6 3XD

Leicestershire Yeomanry, Leicestershire Tigers Museum Loughborough War Memorial, Queen's Park, Loughborough, T: 01509 263370

London Irish Rifles Regimental Museum Duke of York's Headquarters, Kings Road, Chelsea, London, SW3 4SA

Midland Air Museum Coventry airport, Baginton, CV8 3AZ T: 024 7630 1033 W: www.discover.co.uk/~mam/

Ministry of Defence - Royal Naval Personnel Records Centre CS(RM)2 Navy Search, Bourne Avenue, Hayes, UB3 1RF

Museum of Army Chaplaincy Amport House, Nr Andover , Andover, SP11 8BG T: 01264 773144 x 4248 E: rachdcurator@tiscali.co.uk W: www.army.mod.uk/chaps/museum/index.htm

Museum of Army Flying Middle Wallop, Stockbridge, SO20 8DY T: 01980 674421 W: www.flying-museum.org.uk

Museum of Army Transport Flemingate, Beverley, HU17 0NG T: 01482 860445

Museum of Barnstaple & North Devon incorporating Royal Devon Yeomanry Museum Peter A Boyd, The Square, Barnstaple, EX32 8LN T: 01271 346 747

Museum of Defence Intelligence Chicksands, Shefford, SG17 5PR T: 01462 752340

Museum of Lancashire (Queen's Lancashire Regt Duke of Lancaster's Own Yeomanry Lancashire Hussars 14th/20th King's Hussars) Stanley Street, Preston, PR1 4YP T: 01772 534075

Museum of the Manchester Regt Ashton Town Hall, Market Place, Ashton-u-Lyne, OL6 6DL T: 0161 342 3078 W: www.tameside.gov.uk

Museum of the Queen's Lancashire Regt (East South and Loyal (North Lancashire) Regiments, Lancashire Regt (PWV) and The Queen's Lancashire Regt Fulwood Barracks, Preston, PR2 8AA T: 01772 260362 E: rhq.qlr@talk21.com

Museum of The Staffordshire Regt Whittington Barracks, Lichfield, WS14 9PY T: 0121 311 3240 E: museum@rhqstaffords.fsnet.co.uk

Museum of the Staffordshire Yeomanry The Ancient High House, Greengate Street, Stafford, ST16 2HS T: 01785 619130

National Army Museum Department of Archives (Photographs, Film & Sound) Royal Hospital Road, London, SW3 4HT T: (020) 7730-0717 E: info@national-army-museum.ac.uk W: www.national-army-museum.ac.uk

National Maritime Museum Romney Road, Greenwich, London, SE10 9NF T: (020) 8858-4422 W: www.nmm.ac.uk

Norfolk and Suffolk Aviation Museum - East Anglia's Aviation Heritage Centre Buckeroo Way, The Street, Flixton, Bungay, NR35 1NZ T: 01986 896644 E: nsam.flixton@virgin.net W: www.aviationmuseum.net

North East War Memorials Project Bilsdale, Ulgham, Morpeth, NE61 3AR T: 01670 790465 E: janet@newmp.org.uk W: www.newmp.org.uk

Oxfordshire and Buckinghamshire Light Infantry Regimental Museum Slade Park, Headington, Oxford, OX3 7JL T: 01865 780128

Princess Louise's Kensington Regt Museum Duke of York's Headquarters, Kings Road, Chelsea, London, SW3 4RX

Princess of Wales's Royal Regt & Queen's Regt Museum Howe Barracks, Canterbury, CT1 1JY T: 01227-818056

Queen's Own Mercian Yeomanry Museum Bridgeman House, Cavan Drive, Cemetery Road, Dawley, Telford, TF4 2BQ T: 01952 632930

Queen's Royal Surrey Regt Museum (Queen's Royal, East Surrey & Queen's Royal Surrey Regiments) Clandon Park, West Clandon, Guildford, GU4 7RQ T: 01483 223419 W: www.surrey-online.co.uk/queenssurreys www.queensroyalsurreys.org.uk

R.A.F. Regt Museum Home of The RAF Regiment, R A F Honington, Bury St Edmonds, IP31 1EE T: 01359 269561 ext 7824

R.E.M.E. Museum of Technology Isaac Newton Road, Arborfield, Reading, RG2 9NJ T: 0118 976 3375 W: www.rememuseum.org.uk

RAF Digby Ops Room Museum RAF Digby, Scopwick, Lincoln, LN4 3LH T: 01526 327503 W: www.airops.freeserve.co.uk

RAF Manston History Museum The Airfield, Manston Road, Ramsgate, CT11 5DF T: 01843 825224 W: www.rafmuseum.fsnet.co.uk

RAF Witchford Display of Memorabilia Grovemere Building, Lancaster Way Business Park, Ely, T: 01353 666666

Regimental Museum 13th/18th Royal Hussars and The Light Dragoons Cannon Hall, Cawthorne, Barnsley, S75 4AT T: 01226 790270

Regimental Museum of the 9th/12th Royal Lancers Derby City Museum and Art Gallery, The Strand, Derby, DE1 1BS T: 01332 716656 W: www.derby.gov.uk/museums

Regimental Museum of The Queen's Own Hussars (The 3rd King's Own Hussars and 7th Queen's Own Hussars) The Lord Leycester Hospital, High Street, Warwick, CV34 4EW T: 01926 492035 E: trooper@qohm.fsnet.co.uk W: www.qohmuseum.org.uk

Regimental Museum Royal Logistic Corps Princess Royal Barracks, Deepcut, Camberley, GU16 6RW T: 01252 833371 W: www.army-rlc.co.uk/museum

RGBW (Salisbury) Museum The Wardrobe, 58 The Close, Salisbury, SP1 2EX T: 01722 419419 W: www.thewardrobe.org.uk

RHQ Scots Guards Archives Wellington Barracks, Birdcage Walk, London, SW1E 6HQ E: sgarchives@dial.pipex.com

Royal Air Force Museum Grahame Park Way, Hendon, London, NW9 5LL T: (020) 8200 1763 W: www.rafmuseum.org.uk

Royal Berkshire Yeomanry Cavalry Museum T A Centre, Bolton Road, Windsor, SL4 3JG T: 01753 860600

Royal Dragoon Guards Military Museum (4th/7th Royal Dragoon Guards & 5th Royal Inniskilling Dragoon Guards) 3A Tower Street, York, YO1 9SB T: 01904-662790 W: www.rdg.co.uk

Royal Engineers Library Brompton Barracks, Chatham, ME4 4UX T: 01634 822416

Royal Gunpowder Mills administrative Office, Beaulieu drive, Powdermill Lane, Waltham Abbey, EN9 1JY T: 01992 767022 W: www.royalgunpowder.co.uk

Royal Hampshire Regimental Museum Serle's House, Southgate Street, Winchester, SO23 9EG T: 01962 863658

Royal Leicestershire Regt Museum Gallery New Walk Museum, New Walk, Leicester, LE1 7FA T: 0116 2470403

Royal Leicestershire Regimental Gallery New Walk Museum, 53 New Walk, Leicester, LE1 7AE T: 0116 247 3220 W: www.leicestermuseums.co.uk

Royal Lincolnshire Regt Lincolnshire Yeomanry Museum Old Barracks, Burton Road, Lincoln, LN1 3LY T: 01522-528448

Royal Marines Museum Eastney, Southsea, PO4 9PX T: (023) 9281 9385 Exts 224 W: www.royalmarinesmuseum.co.uk

Royal Military Police Museum Roussillon Barracks, Chichester, PO19 6BL T: 01243 534225 E: museum@rhqrmp.freeserve.co.uk W: www.rhqrmp.freeserve.co.uk

Royal Military School of Music Museum Kneller Hall, Twickenham, TW2 7DU T: 020 8744 8652

Royal Naval Museum Buildings 1 - 7, College Road, HM Naval Base, Portsmouth, PO1 3LJ T: (023) 9283 9766 W: www.royalnavalmuseum.org

Royal Naval Patrol Association Museum Sparrows Nest, Lowestoft, NR32 1XG T: 01502 586250

Royal Navy Submarine Museum Haslar Jetty Road, Gosport, PO12 2AS T: (023) 92510354 E: admin@rnsubmus.co.uk W: www.rnsubmus.co.uk

Royal Norfolk Regimental Museum Shirehall, Market Avenue, Norwich, NR1 3JQ T: 01603 493649 W: www..norfolk.gov.uk

Royal Wiltshire Yeomanry Museum A (RWY) Sqn Royal Yeomanry, Church Place, Swindon, SN1 5EH T: 01793 523865

Sandhurst Collection Royal Military Academy Sandhurst, Camberley, GU15 4PQ T: 01276 412489

Sherwood Foresters (Notts and Derby Regiment) Museum The Castle, Nottingham, NG1 6EL T: 0115 946 5415 E: rhqwfr-nottm@lineone.net W: www.wfrmuseum.org.uk

Shropshire Regimental Museum (King's Shropshire Light Infantry, Shropshire Yeomanry) Shropshire Militia, Volunteers and TA The Castle, Shrewsbury, SY1 2AT T: 01743 358516 W: www.shropshireregimental.co.uk

Soldiers of Gloucestershire Museum Gloucester Docks, Commercial Road, Gloucester, GL1 2EH T: 01452 522682

Solway Aviation Museum Carlisle Airport, Carlisle, CA6 4NW T: 01228 573823

Solway Aviation Museum Aviation House, Carlisle Airport, Carlisle , CA6 4NW T: 01227 573823 W: www.solway-aviation-museum.org.uk

Somerset Military Museum (Somerset Light Infantry, YeomanryMilitia and Volunteers) County Museum The County Museum, Taunton Castle, Taunton, TA1 4AA T: 01823 333434 E: info@sommilmuseum.org.uk W: www.sommilmuseum.org.uk

South Lancashire Regt Prince of Wales Volunteers Museum Peninsula Barracks, Warrington,

Spitfire and Hurricane Memorial Building The Airfield, Manston Road, Ramsgate, CT11 5DF T: 01843 821940 W: www.spitfire-museum.com

Staff College Museum Old Staff College Building, Camberley, GU15 4NP T: 01276 412719

Suffolk Regt Museum The Keep, Gibraltar Barracks, Out Risbygate Street, Bury St Edmonds, IP33 3RN

Sussex Combined Services Museum (Royal Sussex Regt and Queen's Royal Irish Hussars) Redoubt Fortress, Royal Parade, Eastbourne, BN22 7AQ T: 01323 410300

Sussex Yeomanry Museum 198 Dyke Road, Brighton, BN1 5AS

Tangmere Military Aviation Museum Tangmere, Chichester, PO20 2ES T: 01243 775223 W: www.tangmere-museum.org.uk

Tank Museum Bovington, BH20 6JG T: 01929 405096 E: librarian@tankmuseum.co.uk davidw@tankmuseum.co.uk W: www.tankmuseum.co.uk

The Association of Jewish Ex-Service Men and Women Military Museum AJEX House, East Bank, Stamford, London, N16 5RT T: 020 8800 2844 W: www.ajex.org.uk

The Buffs Regimental Museum The Royal Museum, 18 High Street, Canterbury, CT1 2JE T: 01227 452747

The Commandery Civil War Museum Sidbury, Worcester, WR1 2HU T: 01905 361821 E: thecommandery@cityofworcester.gov.uk W: www.worcestercitymuseums.org.uk

The Devonshire and Dorset Regt (Archives) RHQ, Devonshire and Dorset Regiment, Wyvern Barracks, Barrack Road, Exeter, EX2 6AR T: 01392 492436

The Fusiliers Museum (Lancashire) Wellington Barracks, Bolton Road, Bury, BL8 2PL T: 0161 764 2208

The Gurkha Museum Peninsula Barracks, Romsey Road, Winchester, SO23 8TS T: 01962 842832 E: curator@thegurkhamuseum.co.uk W: www.thegurkhamuseum.co.uk

The Household Cavalry Museum Combermere Barracks, Windsor, SL4 3DN T: 01753 755112

The Infantry and Small Arms School Corps Weapons Collection HQ SASC, HQ infantry, Warminster Training Centre, Warminster, BA12 0DJ T: 01985 222487

The Keep Military Museum The Keep, Bridport Road, Dorchester, DT1 1RN T: 01305 264066 E: info@keepmilitarymuseum.org W: www.keepmilitarymuseum.org

The King's Royal Hussars Museum (10th Royal Hussars PWO 11th Hussars PAO and The Royal Hussars PWO) Peninsula Barracks, Romsey Road, Winchester, SO23 8TS T: 01962 828540 E: beresford@krhmuseum.freeserve.co.uk W: www.hants.gov.uk/leisure/museum/royalhus/index.html

The Light Infantry Museum Peninsula Barracks, Romsey Road, Winchester, SO23 8TS T: 01962 868550

The Muckleburgh Collection Weybourne, Holt, NR25 7EG T: 01263 588210 W: www.muckleburgh.co.uk

The Museum of The Adjutant General's Corps RHQ Adjutant General's Corps, Worthy Down, Winchester, SO21 2RG T: 01962 887435

The Museum of Berkshire Aviation Trust Mohawk Way, off Bader Way, Woodley, Reading, RG5 4UE T: 0118 944 8089 E: museumofberkshireaviation@fly.to W: http://fly.to/museumofberkshireaviation

The Museum of the Worcestershire Yeomanry Cavalry Worcester City Museum & Art Gallery, Foregate St, Worcester, WR1 1DT T: 01905 25371 E: tbridges@cityofworcester.gov.uk W: www.worcestercitymuseums.org.uk

The Nothe Fort Museum of Coastal Defence Barrack Road, Weymouth , DT4 5UF T: 01305 787243

The Polish Institute and Sikorski Museum 20 Princes Gate, London, SW7 1QA T: 020 7589 9249

The Potteries Museum & Art Gallery Bethesda Street, Hanley, Stoke-On-Trent, ST1 3DE T: 01782 232323 E: museums@stoke.gov.uk W: www.stoke.gov.uk/museums

The Queen's Own Royal West Kent Regt Museum Maidstone Museum and Art Gallery, St. Faith's Street, Maidstone, ME14 1LH T: 01622 602842 E: simonlace@maidstone.gov.uk

The Queen's Royal Lancers Regimental Museum (16th/5th and 17th/21st Lancers) Belvoir Castle, nr Grantham , NG32 1PD T: 0115 957 3295

The Regimental Museum RHQ The London Scottish Regiment, 95 Horseferry Road, Westminster, London, SW1P 2DX T: 020 7630 1639 E: archiveslsregt@aol.com W: www.londonscottishregt.org

The Royal Green Jackets Museum (Oxford and Bucks Light Infantry King's Royal Rifle Corps and The Rifle Brigade) Peninsula Barracks, Romsey Road, Winchester, SO23 8TS T: 01962 828549 E: museum@royalgreenjackets.co.uk W: www.royalgreenjackets.co.uk

The Royal Regt of Fusiliers H M Tower of London, London, EC3N 4AB T: (020) 7488 5610

The Royal Regt of Fusiliers Museum (Royal Warwickshire) St. John's House, Warwick , CV34 4NF T: 01926 491653

The Shuttleworth Collection Old Warden Aerodrome, Old Warden Park, Biggleswade, SG18 9EA T: 01767 627288 E: enquire@shuttleworth.org W: www.shuttleworth.org

The Worcestershire Regt Museum Worcester City Museum & Art Gallery, Foregate Street, Worcester, WR1 1DT T: 01905-25371 Museum

Warwickshire Yeomanry Museum The Court House, Jury Street, Warwick, CV34 4EW T: 01926 492212 E: wtc.admin@btclick.com W: www.armymuseums.co.uk

Wellesborough Aviation Museum Control Tower Entrance, Wellesborough, Warwick, CV34 4EW

Wellington Aviation Museum Broadway Road, Moreton in the Marsh, GL56 0BG T: 01608 650323 W: www.wellingtonaviation.org

Welsh Guards Record Office Wellington Barracks, Birdcage Walk, London, SW1E 6HQ T: 020 7414 3291

Worcestershire Regt Archives (Worcestershire and Sherwood Forester's Regiment) RHQ WFR Norton Barracks, Worcester, WR5 2PA T: 01905 354359 E: rhg_wfr@lineone.net

York and Lancaster Regimental Museum Library and Arts Centre, Walker Place, Rotherham, S65 1JH T: 01709 336633 E: karl.noble@rotherham.gov.uk W: www.rotherham.gov.uk

Yorkshire Air Museum Halifax Way, Elvington, York, YO41 4AU T: 01904 608595 E: museum@yorkshireairmuseum.co.uk W: www.yorkshireairmuseum.co.uk

Wales

1st The Queen's Dragoon Guards Regimental Museum Cardiff Castle, Cardiff, Cardiff CF10 2RB T: (029) 2078 1271 E: curator@qdg.org.uk W: www.qdg.org.uk

Llandudno Royal Artillery Llandudno Museum, 17-19 Gloddaeth Street, Llandudno, Gwynedd LL30 2DD T: 01492 876517

Nelson Museum & Local History Centre Priory St, Monmouth, Monmouthshire NP5 3XA T: 01600 710630 E: nelsonmuseum@monmouthshire.gov.uk

Pembroke Yeomanry, Royal Pembroke Militia, Pembrokeshire Volunteers Museum Scolton Manor Museum, Spittal, Haverfordwest, Pembrokeshire SA62 5QL T: 01437 731328

Powysland Museum The Canal Wharf, Welshpool, Powys SY21 7AQ T: 01938 554656 W: http://powysmuseums.powys.gov.uk

South Wales Borderers & Monmouthshire Regimental Museum of the Royal Regt of Wales (24th/41st Foot) The Barracks, Brecon, Powys LD3 7EB T: 01874 613310 E: swb@rrw.org.uk W: www.rrw.org.uk

The Royal Monmouthshire Royal Engineers (Militia) Castle and Regimental Museum, The Castle, Monmouth, Monmouthshire NP25 3BS T: 01600-712935 E: curator@monmouthcastlemuseum.org.uk W: www.monmouthcastlemuseum.org.uk

The Royal Welch Fusiliers Regimental Museum The Queen's Tower, The Castle, Caernarfon, Gwynedd LL55 2AY T: 01286 673362 E: rwfusiliers@callnetuk.com W: www.rwfmuseum.org.uk

Scotland

Atholl Highlanders Blair Castle, Blair Atholl, Perthshire PH18 5TL T: 01796 481207 E: office@blair-castle.co.uk W: www.blair-castle.co.uk

Ayrshire Yeomanry Museum Rozelle House, Monument Road, Alloway by Ayr, Ayrshire KA7 4NQ T: 01292 445400 (Museum)

Culloden Visitor Centre Culloden Moor, Inverness, inverness-shire IV2 5EU T: 01463 790607 E: dsmyth@nts.org.uk W: www.nts.org.uk

Fife and Forfar Yeomanry Museum Yeomanry House, Castlebrook Road, Cupar, Fife KY15 4BL T: 01334 656155

HM Frigate Unicorn Victoria Dock, South Victoria Dock Road, Dundee, DD1 3BP T: 01382 200893 E: frigateunicorn@hotmail.com W: www.frigateunicorn.org

Montrose Air Station Museum Waldron Road, Montrose, Angus DD10 9BB T: 01674 673107 E: info@RAFmontrose.org.uk W: www.RAFmontrose.org.uk

Museum of The Royal Highland Fusilers (Royal Scots Fusiliers and Highland Light Infantry) 518 Sauchiehall Street, Glasgow, G2 3LW T: 0141 332 0961 W: www.rhf.org.uk

Queen's Own Cameron Highlanders Fort George, Arderseir, Inverness, Inverness-shire IV1 2TD T: 01667 462777

Queen's Own Highlanders (Seaforth & Camerons) Regimental Museum Archives Fort George, Ardersier, Inverness, Invernesshire IV1 7TD T: 01463-224380

Regimental Museum Argyll and Sutherland Highlanders Stirling Castle, Stirling, Stirlingshire FK8 1EH T: 01786 475165

Regimental Museum of The Highlanders (The Queen's Own Highlanders Collection) Fort George, Inverness-shire IV2 7TD T: 01463 224380 E: rhqthehighlanders@btopenworld.com

Royal Scots Regimental Museum The Castle, Edinburgh, EH1 2YT T: 0131-310-5014 E: rhqroyalscots@edinburghcastle.fsnet.co.uk W: www.theroyalscots.co.uk

Scottish Horse Regimental Archives - Dunkeld Cathedral Dunkeld, PH8 0AW T: 01350 727614

Stromness Museum 52 Alfred Street, Stromness, Orkney T: 01856 850025

The Cameronians (Scottish Rifles) Museum & Low Parks Museum c/o Low Parks Museum, 129 Muir Street, Hamilton, Lanarkshire ML3 6BJ T: 01698 452163

West Lowland Fencibles Culzean Castle, Maybole, Ayrshire KA19 8LE T: 01655 884455 E: culzean@nts.org.uk W: www.culzeancastle.net

Northern Ireland

Royal Inniskilling Fusiliers Regimental Museum The Castle, Enniskillen, Co Fermanagh BT74 7BB T: (028) 66323142

Royal Irish Fusiliers Museum Sovereign's House, Mall East, Armagh, BT61 9DL T: (028) 3752 2911 W: www.rirfus-museum.freeserve.co.uk

Royal Ulster Rifles Regimental Museum RHQ Royal Irish Regiment, 5 Waring Street, Belfast, BT1 2EW T: (028) 90232086 E: rurmuseum@yahoo.co.uk W: www.rurmuseum.tripod.com

The Museum Of The Royal Irish Regt St. Patricks Barracks, Demesne Avenue, Ballymena, County Antrim BT43 7BH T: (028) 2566 1386 E: hqrirish@royalirishregiment.co.uk W: www.royalirishregiment.co.uk

The Somme Heritage Centre 233 Bangor Road, Newtownards, County Down BT23 7PH T: 028 9182 3202 E: sommeassociation@dnet.co.uk W: www.irishsoldier.org

Ulster Aviation Heritage Centre Langford Lodge Airfield, Belfast, T: 028 9267 7030 W: www.d-n-a.net/users/dnetrAzQ

Channel Islands

18th Century Loopholed Tower PO Box 23, St Peter Port, Guernsey GY1 3AN

Clarence Battery Fort George, St Peter Port, Guernsey

Elizabeth Castle - Jersey Militia St Aubin's Bay, St Helier, Jersey T: 01534 633300

Fort Grey Rocquaine Bay, St Saviours, Guernsey

German Direction Finding Tower PO Box 23, St Peter Port, Guernsey GY1 3AN

German Military Underground Hospital La Vassalerie Road, St Andrew's, Guernsey T: 01481 239100

German Naval Signals Headquarters St Jacques, Guernsey

German Occupation Museum Les Houards, Forest, Guernsey GY8 0BG T: 01481 328205 W: www.aboutbritain.com/OccupationMuseum.htm

German Occupation Museum Rue Lucas, Sark, Sark T: 01481 832564

German Underground Hospital Meadowbank, St Lawrence, Jersey T: 01534 863442

Island Fortress Occupation Museum 9 Esplanade, St Helier, Jersey T: 01534 633300

La Hougue Bie Grouville, Jersey T: 01534 633300

La Valette Underground Military Museum St Peter Port, Guernsey T: 01481 722300

Maritime Museum and Occupation Tapestry Gallery New North Quay, St Helier, Jersey T: 01534 811043 E:

marketing@jerseyheritagetrust.org W: www.jerseyheritagetrust.org
Noirmont Command Bunker Noirmont Point, St Brelade, Jersey T: 01534 482089
Royal Guernsey Militia and Royal Geurnsey Light Infantry Castle Comet, St Peter Port, Guernsey T: 01481 726518 W: www.museum.guernsey.net/castle.htm
St Peter's Bunker Museum of Wartime German Equipment and Occupation Relics La Petite Rue De L'eglise, St Peter, Jersey JE3

7AF T: 01534 723136
The Channel Islands Military Museum The Five Mile Road, St Ouen, Jersey T: 01534 23136

Belgium
In Flanders Fields Museum Lakenhallen, Grote Markt 34, Ieper, B-8900 T: 00-32-(0)-57-22-85-84 W: www.inflandersfields.be

Police Records & Museums

Essex Police Museum Police Headquarters, PO Box 2, Springfield, Chelmsford, CM2 6DA T: 01245 491491-ext-50771
Friends of The Metropolitan Police Museum Bromley Police Station, High Street, Bromley, BR1 1ER W: www.met.police.uk/history/friends.htm
Garda Siochana Museum & Archives The Records Tower, Dublin, 2 T: +353 1 6719 597 W: www.esatclear.ie/~garda/museum.html
Garda Siochana Museum & Archives The Records Tower, Dublin, 2 T: +353 1 6719 597 W: www.esatclear.ie/~garda/museum.html
Glasgow Police Heritage Society 68 St Andrews Square, Glasgow, G2 4JS T: 07788 532691 E: curator@policemuseum.org.uk W: www.policemusaeum.org.uk
Glasgow Police Museum 68 St Andrews Square, Glasgow, G2 4JS T: 07788 532691 E: curator@policemuseum.org.uk W: www.policemusaeum.org.uk
International Police Association - British Section - Genealogy Group Thornholm, Church Lane, South Muskham, Newark, NG23 6EQ T: 01636 676997 E: ipagenuk@thornholm.freeserve.co.uk
Kent Police Museum The Historic Dockyard, Chatham, ME4 4TZ T: 01634 403260 E: info@kent-police-museum.co.uk W: www.kent-police-museum.co.uk
Metropolitan Police Archives Room 517, Wellington House, 67-73 Buckingham Gate, London, SW1E 6BE T: 020 7230 7186
Metropolitan Police Historical Museum c/o T.P.H.Q. Fin & Res, 4th Floor, Victoria Embankment, London, SW1A 2JL T: (020) 8305-2824
National Police Officers' Roll of Honour Roll of Honour Project, Lancashire Contabulary Headquarters, Hutton, Preston, PR4 5SB
North Eastern Police History Society Brinkburn Cottage, 28 Brinkburn Street, High Barnes, Sunderland, SR4 7RG T: 0191-565-7215 E: harry.wynne@virgin.net W: http://nepolicehistory.homestead.com
Police History Society 37 Greenhill Road, Timperley, Altrincham, WA15 7BG T: 0161-980-2188 E: info@policehistorysociety.co.uk steve.bridge@ukgateway.net W: www.policehistorysociety.co.uk
Research into Family and Police History 52 Symons Avenue, Eastwood, Leigh on Sea, SS9 5QE T: 01702 522992 E: fred@feather1.demon.co.uk
Ripon Prison & Police Museum Ripon Museum Trust, St Marygate, Ripon, IIG4 1LX T: 01765-690799 E: ralph.lindley@which.net
Royal Military Police Museum Roussillon Barracks, Chichester, PO19 6BL T: 01243 534225 E: museum@rhqrmp.freeserve.co.uk W: www.rhqrmp.freeserve.co.uk
Sheffield Police and Fire Museum 101-109 West Bar, Sheffield, S3 8TP T: 0114 249 1999 W: www.hedgepig.freeserve.co.uk
Surrey Police Museum Mount Browne, Sandy Lane, Guildford, GU3 1HG T: 01483 482155 W: www.surreymuseums.org.uk/museums/Police.htm

Thames Valley Police Museum Sulhamstead, Nr Reading, RG7 4DX T: 0118 932 5748 E: ken.wells@thamesvalley.police.uk W: www.thamesvalley.police.uk
The Greater Manchester Police Museum 57 Newton St, Manchester, M1 1ES T: 0161 856 3287
West Midlands Police Museum Sparkhill Police Station, Stratford Rd, Sparkhill, Birmingham, B11 4EA T: 0121 626 7181

List of Current Police Forces
England and Wales - Avon and Somerset Constabulary, Bedfordshire Police, Cambridgeshire Constabulary, Cheshire Constabulary, City of London Police, Cleveland Constabulary, Cumbria Constabulary, Derbyshire Constabulary, Devon and Cornwall Constabulary, Dorset Police, Durham Constabulary, Dyfed-Powys Police, Essex Police, Gloucestershire Constabulary, Greater Manchester Police, Gwent Constabulary, Hampshire Constabulary, Hertfordshire Constabulary, Humberside Police, Kent County Constabulary, Lancashire Constabulary, Leicestershire Constabulary, Lincolnshire Police, Merseyside Police, Metropolitan Police, Norfolk Constabulary, North Wales Police - Heddlu Gogledd Cymru , North Yorkshire Police, Northamptonshire Police, Northumbria Police, Nottinghamshire Constabulary, South Wales Police - Heddlu de Cymru, South Yorkshire Police, Staffordshire Police, Suffolk Constabulary, Surrey Constabulary, Sussex Police, Thames Valley Police, Warwickshire Constabulary, West Mercia Police, West Midlands Police, West Yorkshire Police, Wiltshire Constabulary
Non Geographic Police Forces
British Transport Police, Ministry of Defence Police, UK Atomic Energy Constabulary, Port of Dover Police, The National Crime Squad

Scotland - Central Scotland Police, Dumfries and Galloway Constabulary, Fife Constabulary, Grampian Police, Lothian and Borders Police, Northern Constabulary, Strathclyde Police, Tayside Police

Ireland
Northern Ireland - Police Service of Northern Ireland (Royal Ulster Constabulary)
Southern Ireland - Garda Síochána

Channel Islands - Guernsey Police, States of Jersey Police

Isle of Man - Isle of Man Constabulary

Other Forces - Royal Military Police, Belfast Harbour Police, Mersey Tunnels Police, Port of Bristol Police, Port of Tilbury London Police, Royal Parks Constabulary, Port of Liverpool Police

The National Family History Fair

Gateshead International Stadium
Saturday 8th September 2007

10.00a.m. - 4.30.p.m.

Admission £3.00
Accompanied Children under 15 Free

Meet the national experts!

The largest family history event in the British Isles.

**Free help & advice. Internet Demonstrations.
Family History Talks.**

**Easy Access by Road, Rail, Metro & Air.
Free Parking. Café**

www.nationalfamilyhistoryfair.com

2008 - Saturday 13th September 2008

Index to Advertisers

In association with The National Family History Fair

Index

In association with The National Family History Fair

Published by
Robert Blatchford Publishing Ltd
33 Nursery Road, Nether Poppleton YORK, YO26 6NN England
E: sales@genealogical.co.uk W: www.genealogical.co.uk

The Genealogical Services Directory
1st Edition Published March 1997 ISBN 0 9530297 0 0 ISSN 1368-9150
2nd Edition Published January 1998 ISBN 0 9530297 1 9 ISSN 1368-9150
3rd Edition Published January 1999 ISBN 0 9530297 2 7 ISSN 1368-9150
4th Edition Published January 2000 ISBN 0 9530297 3 5 ISSN 1368-9150

The Family & Local History Handbook

5th Edition Published January 2001 ISBN 0 9530297 4 3
6th Edition Published February 2002 ISBN 0 9530297 5 1
7th Edition Published February 2003 ISBN 0 9530297 6 X
8th Edition Published March 2004 ISBN 0 9530297 7 8
9th Edition Published March 2005 ISBN 0 9530297 8 6
10th Edition Published September 2006 ISBN 0 9530297 9 4 (2006)
                        ISBN 978 0 9530297 9 2 (2007)

ISSN 1745-3887 ISBN 0 9530297 9 4 (2006)
ISBN 978 0 9530297 9 2 (2007)

Printed by
Warwick Printing
Caswell Road, Leamington Spa, Warwickshire CV31 1QD
T: 01926 883355 E: sales@warwickprinting.co.uk W: www.warwickprinting.co.uk

Robert Blatchford LL.B (Hons)

is a law graduate of The University of Hull, England. He is a member of The Society of Genealogists as well as Cleveland, The City of York, Devon, Dyfed, Glamorgan, Somerset & Dorset & Gwent Family History Societies. He is also a member of The British Association for Local History and Poppleton History Society. He is a former Chairman of The City of York Family History Society and former Vice Chairman of the North East Group of Family History Societies. He has undertaken research in England, Wales, Scotland, Belgium and France as well as in Ireland, Australia and the United States. He has edited and published each edition of *The Family and Local History Handbook*.

Elizabeth Blatchford

has been involved in genealogy and family history for over 20 years. She is a member of several family and local history societies. Elizabeth has been involved with this publication since its inception and has assisted with the editing of several editions. Since taking early retirement from Local Governement Elizabeth is taking a greater part in the editing of *The Family and Local History Handbook*. She has an NVQ consultancy business and is fully involved with our four grandchildren.

Technical Information

For the technically minded, all design, layout and preparation is done in house on Apple Macintosh computers, a G4 Desktop, a G4 Power Book, and a Mac Mini using Quark Xpress 6.5, Adobe Photoshop CS and Adobe Acrobat CS. The *Handbook* is produced electronically and is transferred to paper only when it is printed. The first time it is appears in book form is when it is delivered from the printers.

© Apple Computer